OAKEY'S SPECIALITIES.

WELLINGTON KNIFE POLISH.

Prepared for Oakey's Patent Rubber Knife Boards and all Patent Knife-Cleaning Machines. In Canisters, 3d., 6d., 1s., 2s. 6d., and 4s. each.

"POLYBRILLIANT" ROUGE POMADE.

For Cleaning all Metals. In Tins, 1d., 2d., 3d., and 6d. each.

WELLINGTON BLACK LEAD.

The Best for Polishing Stoves, Grates, and Iron Work without waste, dirt or dust. In 1d., 2d., and 4d. Blocks; and 1s. Boxes.

FURNITURE CREAM.

For Cleaning and Polishing Furniture, Patent Leather, Oilcloth, &c. Glass and Stone Bottles, 6d. and 1s.

BRUNSWICK BLACK.

For Beautifying and Preserving Stoves and all kinds of Iron Work. Bottles, 6d., 1s., and 2s.

SILVERSMITHS' SOAP.

(Non-Mercurial) for Cleaning and Polishing Silver, Electro-Plate, Plate Glass, Marble, &c. Tablets, 6d.

Sold Everywhere by Ironmongers, Grocers, Druggists, Oilmen, &c.

JOHN OAKEY & SONS, LONDON, S.E.

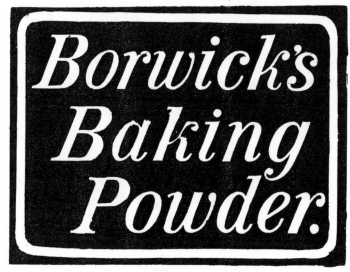

Guaranteed Pure and Free from Alum.

Borwick's Baking Powder.

THE BEST THAT MONEY CAN BUY

Awarded Five Gold Medals for Superiority.

MRS BEETON'S EVERY DAY COOKERY AND HOUSEKEEPING BOOK

MRS BEETON'S
EVERY DAY
COOKERY
AND HOUSEKEEPING BOOK

A facsimile of the original 1865 edition

GALLERY BOOKS
An Imprint of W. H. Smith Publishers Inc.
112 Madison Avenue
New York, New York 10016

This edition published 1984 for USA, Canada
and the Philippines by Gallery Books,
an imprint of W. H. Smith Publishers Inc.
112 Madison Avenue, New York, NY 10016.

Mrs Beeton' is a registered trade mark
and copyright property of Ward Lock Ltd.
This edition published under license.

ISBN 0-8317-6176-8

Manufactured in Yugoslavia

BEETON'S
EVERY-DAY COOKERY

AND

HOUSEKEEPING BOOK:

COMPRISING

INSTRUCTIONS FOR MISTRESS AND SERVANTS,

AND A COLLECTION OF

OVER SIXTEEN HUNDRED AND FIFTY

PRACTICAL RECEIPTS.

With Numerous Wood Engravings

AND

ONE HUNDRED AND FORTY-TWO COLOURED FIGURES,

SHOWING THE PROPER MODE OF SENDING DISHES
TO TABLE.

WARD, LOCK AND CO.,
LONDON, NEW YORK, AND MELBOURNE.

PREFACE.

——o——

The reasons for the publication of this Volume—the First of a Series of Practical Manuals which were to be called the "All About It" Books— were thus explained in a Prospectus issued a few months ago, and approved by the late Mrs. S. O. BEETON :—

MANY wishes have been expressed to the Authoress of the "Book of Household Management" that a volume of Recipes in Cookery should be written which could be sold at a price somewhere between the seven-and-sixpenny "Household Management" and the Shilling Cookery Book. Accordingly Mrs. BEETON has prepared a Collection of Recipes, and of other Practical Information concerning the Dressing and Serving of Family Fare, which, when completed, will be published, in serviceable binding, at the price of Three Shillings and Sixpence.

As Mistress, Cook, and Critic have declared that the details in Mrs. BEETON's larger work are *so easy to understand*, the Authoress has followed, in every Recipe printed in the present Dictionary, the same simple plan she originally used. Regarding, however, the *arrangement* of the Recipes, the Authoress has chosen the Dictionary form, believing an alphabetical arrangement to be the best for a book that is being constantly referred to. By the adoption of a very intelligible system, all *cross* reference, and that very disagreeable parenthesis (*See* So-and-so) is avoided, except in a very few instances. Where any warning as to what should *not* be done is likely to be needed, it is given, as well as advice as to what ought to be done. No pains have been thought too great to make *little things* clearly understood. Trifles constitute perfection. It is just the knowledge or ignorance of little things that usually makes the difference between the success of the careful and experienced housewife or servant, and the failure of her who is careless and inexperienced. Mrs. BEETON has brought to her new offering to the Public a most anxious care to describe plainly and fully all the more difficult and recondite portions of Cookery, whilst the smallest items have not been "unconsidered trifles," but each Recipe and preparation have claimed minute attention.

CONTENTS.

—·—

PHILOSOPHY OF HOUSEKEEPING.

ROUTINE OF HOUSEHOLD WORKS AND WAYS.

1. If the MISTRESS of a household considers that she is steward of her husband's property, and that upon her diligence, knowledge, and capability depends the entire happiness of her household, she will understand how important is her post, and how any negligence on her part must necessarily repeat itself in the conduct of her domestics. It is seldom requisite that a mistress should perform other work than that of supervising her household, choosing and paying for household requisites; but it is imperative that she should clearly understand the "Philosophy of Housekeeping," and that she should not be the dupe of designing servants or the ignorant director of an equally ignorant maid. Every household arrangement must differ in detail—in way and modes of living as well as in numbers. No book can give exact laws and regulations which will be found suitable to every house; but common-sense rules apply to every household in all stations of life, and the results of years of experience must be of service to young beginners.

2. The difficulties which beset young mistresses of households are great, but an intelligent arrangement soon makes these difficulties disappear; and once the routine duties of households are arranged, it is easy to go on with regularity and comfort.

3. No amount of love, of beauty, or of intelligence will make home happy without a "right judgment" on the part of the housewife. A woman must rule her household, or be ruled by it; she must either hold the reins with a tight, firm hand, never parting with, but seldom using, the whip; or the reins fall from the idle, careless hand, and are seized by subordinates, and the hard-working husband is placed, by his wife's indolence, under the control of his domestics, and has to depend upon their honesty and zeal alone.

4. EARLY RISING on the part of the mistress is even more essential than for the servants to be early risers; for if the maids see that the mistress does not stir at an early hour, they think that they may indulge a little too: but if the mistress be regular in making her appearance, the maids do not like a good, kind lady to have cheerless, undusted rooms to go into, and take care to be in good time.

5. A MISTRESS should rise at *latest* at seven o'clock. This will appear dreadfully late to some notables, but will be found to be a good hour *all the year round.* The mistress should take her cold bath, and perform a neat, careful, and pretty morning toilet. Having performed this careful toilet, she will be ready to descend at eight o'clock, but before leaving her room will place two chairs at the end of the bed, and turn the whole of the bedclothes over them, and, except on very rainy mornings, will throw open the windows of her room. She should then fold her own and husband's night-dress, which have been airing during her toilet, and place them in their ornamented cover; she will put brushes, combs, hair-pins, &c., in their proper places, and leave her toilet-table clear and tidy, and make the whole room as neat as possible. Key-basket in hand, she should descend to the breakfast-room, at once ring for the kettle or tea-urn, according to the season, and make the tea, coffee, cocoa, or chocolate, as the case may be. Her eye should now glance over the table to see that everything required for the table is in its place, and that all is neatly arranged and ready for the family —flowers on the table, preserve or marmalade in cut-glass dishes.

6. IF A MOTHER, with a young infant, she should don a dressing-gown in place of a dress, and wash her baby before coming down; indeed, if children of any age take morning baths, we advocate that no one but *mamma* should *dry* them. As soon as these duties are over, the mistress should proceed to the breakfast-room and make the tea, coffee, or chocolate, and ring the bell for the breakfast, as above stated. When it is possible to get the master to enjoy an eight o'clock breakfast, household matters go on charmingly. He is usually out of the house by nine, and by that hour the windows are wide open, every door set open (weather permitting), and a thorough draught of "delicious air" is passed through the whole dwelling.

7. As soon as THE MISTRESS hears her husband's step, the bell should be rung for the hot dish; and should he be, as business men usually are, rather pressed for time, she should herself wait upon him, cutting his bread, buttering his toast, &c. Also give standing orders that coat, hat, and umbrella shall be brushed and ready; and see that they are, by helping on the coat, handing the hat, and glancing at the umbrella.

8. THE WORK OF THE HOUSEHOLD will proceed with a far greater regularity and despatch when the mistress is able and willing to assist in the lighter duties.

9. As soon as the husband has gone off to his work, have the breakfast cleared, and go into the kitchen to give orders for the day; but in some old families, before the breakfast is cleared a spotlessly clean wood-bowl is brought in upon

a tray, accompanied by tea-cloths; the mistress then proceeds to wash up the cups, saucers, &c., dries and places them upon a tray, the servant carrying them to their places. This custom is a relic of the old Puritan system of orderly work, and is not as general as could be desired; but some mistresses still wash up the breakfast things in order to leave the maid time to get on with her upstairs duties.

10. THE FIRST DUTY of the mistress after breakfast is to give her orders for the day, and she naturally begins with the cook.

11. ON ENTERING THE KITCHEN, invariably say, "Good morning, cook" (a courtesy much appreciated below stairs), go into the larder—do not give a mere glance, careless or nervous, as the case may be, but examine every article there ; never let anything that displeases your neat eye pass : it is much easier to correct as you go along, than to overburden a maid with directions or reprimands. Do not allow any shy fear of strangers, as new servants of course are, to interfere with the careful discharge of your duty as a wife and mistress o. the household. Look in the bread-pan and see that there is no waste. After all joints a good basin of dripping *ought* to be in the larder.

12. IN ORDERING DINNER it is best to write down what you intend having; for instance, one o'clock dinner, " Cold beef, potatoes, greens, apple pudding ;" six (seven or eight) o'clock dinner, " Julienne soup, fish, roast fowl, gravy, bread sauce, boiled bacon, browned potatoes, spinach, plum tart, custard pudding."

13. Another good result from writing down the dinner ; it keeps both mistress and cook up to the mark in seeing that every proper accompaniment to a dish is served with it.

14. The COOK then knows exactly what she has to prepare, and the order-book is a useful check on butcher, grocer, and greengrocer.

15. IF A LADY is content to order daily what is wanted, she will not have the excellent dinners obtained by a little forethought. Few butchers can be relied on to send meat in prime condition for roasting ; there are but few weeks in England when it is not safe to hang meat ; in autumn mutton will often hang for eight days, in winter fourteen or twenty-one will not be too long. A good housekeeper will always arrange so as to have a joint or two hanging in the winter, and one joint hanging *nearly* always. The day decided on for cooking a leg of mutton, order another in for hanging.

16. WELL-HUNG MEAT " goes further " than hard fresh meat ; and does credit to buyer and cook.

17. IF A MISTRESS devote careful thought to her dinners for servants and husband she is doing her best to keep the health of her household.

18. Cooks will frequently suggest dishes : this is a great help to a young wife ; but a mistress should possess courage to say, " I cannot afford this."

19. If a Servant find that her mistress is determined to see for herself that her orders involve no extravagance and no waste, she will do one of two things— either enter fully into her mistress's views, or leave her place. Both courses are good for the mistress, but naturally the first is the pleasanter to all parties.

20. We once told a good-hearted but extravagant cook, that we should much like to give her *carte blanche* in cooking details, but that if we did so and spent all the housekeeping money on eating and drinking, we should be unable to do what we have always done—give the maids good medical advice when they were ill, pay for their medicine, and give them wine if ordered by the doctor. Her only reply was, " Lor, mum !" but a speedy change took place, and she remained a careful, faithful woman, until her marriage.

21. Invariably speak the exact truth to servants, be firm, but mind and *never address an unnecessary word to a new servant ;* old tried servants are privileged, but new ones must be kept " in place," and all temptation to gossip checked at once. This is not easy to do kindly, but tact and dignity will make it easy.

22. Young Wives are often lonely and talk to their maids for a change ; it is a bad plan, depend upon it, and often causes disagreeable liberties to be taken.

23. Before leaving the Lower Regions, the mistress should look into scullery, washhouse (larder she has been in), and kitchen proper ; see that all is neat and tidy ; remembering that she is steward of her husband's property, and accountable for any misuse of it. All things in the house belong to you and to him, and if you do not care to see every article clean, bright, and tidy, you cannot expect your maids to care about it.

24. On leaving the Kitchen, it is the duty of the mistress to go into every room of the house to see if all is cleanly and in order ; she should first go into her own room, which ought by this time to be arranged, unless it is the regular day for cleaning it thoroughly, when the housemaid should be busily engaged on it. The mistress should carefully inspect every portion of the room, as it is her careful and observant eye alone that will detect careless or unhealthy habits in her maids.

25. Windows should look bright and clean ; no dust should deface the furniture, or thread or speck the carpet ; all water-vessels should be clean, and filled with pure water: a small quantity of hot water should be placed in the chamber utensils. The towels should be taken out to air in the garden, weather permitting or dried in the kitchen.

26. The bed should look neat, the counterpane being smoothly drawn over it

and curtains arranged in seemly folds. The blinds should hang evenly, and the window curtains be neatly looped back.

27. In the MASTER'S ROOM the bath should be dry and spotless, the water-cans filled, and standing on a Kamptulicon mat, the sponge drying in its basket, the toilet-table neat, brushes put by, and all things in order: boots arranged in pairs, and slippers (if worked) brushed and put ready for use.

28. The SPARE ROOM should next be inspected, whether in or out of use, the window opened, and well aired.

29. Then the SERVANTS' ROOM. There is no need for a mistress to do more than take a glance in to see if the window be open, the room aired, the bed made, the slops emptied, and the floor neat and clean. A lady should tell her maids that she looks in once a day to see that all is right and comfortable in their room or rooms; this puts everything on a straightforward open footing, and prevents unhealthy, untidy habits, and gives the mistress a chance of making all within the house comfortable.

30. The CLOSEST INSPECTION should be made of every room in the house, not excepting the very smallest; and nothing should be omitted to be placed where required. Bedroom, clothes, and other closets should be kept scrupulously clean, and everything wanted should be put ready to hand. Water supplies and drains should be carefully and regularly supervised, and newspaper, it should be remembered, is apt to stop up the drain and cause much expense, which curling-paper does not. The mistress should ascertain that the water supply is plentiful, for it is on these apparent trifles that the health of households depends.

31. Nor let any one feel surprised at the details of a mistress's work being clearly set down; it is to ignorance of these facts that we owe the minor miseries of life. A few hours' neglect of a drain may breed pestilence, and the *cause* of such a disaster is the mistress's neglect of sanitary precautions.

32. The GARDEN should now be inspected, and orders given to the gardener, and the plants in the house attended to by the lady.

33. As it is good for the maids to have a settled plan of their work, so it is good for the mistress to arrange her day, by rule, as far as possible. Interruptions will occur from time to time, but a resolute woman will generally carry out her plans for the week satisfactorily.

34. It is impossible to arrange the time of any individual. The following work a mistress should do. Two hours devoted to the house and morning duties brings one to eleven o'clock; on Monday the mending must be carefully executed up lunch time. A daily walk should be taken, weather permitting, and the lady

should first go and order anything required for the house, then return visits, or take a good constitutional until four o'clock. From four to five write letters, or read for an hour (serious reading, leaving light reading for evening). At five, when necessary, go downstairs to speak to cook, glance round to see all preparations are getting forward for the six o'clock dinner; then go upstairs, inspect the housemaid's performance of needlework, always laid in your room for that purpose, and dress for dinner. Go into the dining-room, and see all is ready, put out the wine, arrange dessert and flowers. Then be ready at a quarter to six to receive *le mari*, and see that he has his hot water, slippers, &c. At six, dinner, after which coffee and amusements of music, reading, cards, or needle-work of a light nature.

35. TUESDAY, Thursday, and Friday mornings may be devoted to the garden and plants, the afternoon to walking or driving as before, or any particular hobby or study.

36. MINOR DETAILS OF HOUSEWORK should be attended to by the mistress, who should see that her servants attend to the little things that give a neat and cared-for appearance to the house. For example, the doorsteps must be cleaned and whitened daily ; the blinds drawn down and shutters closed regularly as soon as it is dark ; all windows closed at sunset, and opened as soon as possible in the morning. The mistress must look at the outside of her house as well as see that the inside is all right. She should survey her house on all sides from a little distance, and note if it is as nice as she could wish in respect to repairs, arrangement of curtains, blinds, &c. The forecourt and garden also must be trim and neat, if not gay with flowers. Periodically the roof and gutters should be examined, and all refuse matter removed, and free passage given for the rain-water. Even in London soft water may be enjoyed by the careful housewife who will take the trouble and go to the expense of *starting* a proper system of catching and preserving it.

37. First, she must purchase an ordinary water-butt, provided with a tap near the bottom, and with a removable lid ; the water from the roof passes naturally through an ordinary pipe into this butt. A tank, about ten feet deep and four feet in diameter, bricked and cemented, must be provided as near as possible to this, and from the water-butt to the tank a pipe is carried, one end of it being cemented in the tank, the other carried up to within six inches of the *top* of the water-butt, and fitted with a rose. As soon as the water-butt is filled, the water flows down the pipe into the tank ; a common pump in the house brings it in fresh and clean, ready for use. "But how clean?" asks an anxious matron. "How can London roof-washings be clean?" For ten minutes after rain "sets in," turn the tap of your water-butt, and allow the water to run. In less than this time a smart shower will have thoroughly cleansed your roof. Then stop the flow, and allow the water-butt to fill; all the deposits in the water will be

left at the bottom of your butt, while the clean, pure, bright water will fill the tank; and this simple plan is all that is required to obtain the great luxury of clean *soft* water.

HOW TO KEEP A LINEN-PRESS.

38. As Mrs. Glasse said, first catch your hare, so I say, first fill your linen-press. Good linen, though expensive, is far more economical than is cheap linen.

39. SHEETS should be wider and longer than the bed they are used on, and should be marked in pairs, as, "E. J. Brown, Pair 5," with date of the year. The hems should be sewn, not hemmed, with linen thread. They should be folded in pairs, and a ring of wide cotton elastic passed round each pair; on this ring a card should be sewn, with the mark repeated on it, the size of the sheet added, or, in a small set of linen, the name of the bedroom, as "E. J. Brown, Pair 6, 1871— spare room." This enables a new servant, or entire stranger, to select sheets required in a hurry; for it should be the chief aim of the mistress so to arrange her house that even in her absence all should go on with regularity and order, and that in case of illness everything may be found without her assistance.

40. PILLOW-CASES.—These should be of fine linen, the cases to fit easily the pillows, and made with a double hem, in which button-holes are placed. Finely-frilled pillow-cases look very nice, but unless expense is of little object, should be kept for the use of the spare room. Pillow-cases should be arranged in half-dozens, and an elastic band and card placed round each parcel, with the mark, number, and room to which they belong clearly written on the card.

41. TABLE-CLOTHS.—These should be folded carefully, and each table-cloth should have the band and card, with the mark, date, &c., and, in addition, the size of the table-cloth. By this plan the size is known at a glance, and all trouble and loss of time in unfolding and refolding avoided.

42. TABLE NAPKINS should not be marked in ink, but the monogram worked in raised embroidery. These are usually kept in a silk case, but may be tied by tapes, on which a card describing them is sewn; as, for instance, "Dinner" or "Breakfast," "Dinner, best," "Dinner, daily."

43. TOWELS should be arranged in the same way as the other parcels of linen; the elastic band and card are convenient for these; they should be arranged in half-dozens, whether rough, bath, fine, or of medium quality.

44. BATH SHEETS are far pleasanter to use than ordinary towels. They should be of fine huckaback, and measure three yards each way; better still if the length is allowed another half-yard. They should be dried daily, and brought in hot at the hour for rising. On leaving the bath, one is entirely enveloped in the warm sheet, and the process of drying is conducted with rapidity and comfort.

45. SERVANTS' SHEETS, PILLOW-CASES, TOWELS, &c., should be all arranged in the same manner, and attended to with equal care; they should be given out when required by the mistress, who should have all changes of bed-linen made with exact regularity. The old-fashioned plan was to change the upper-sheet every fortnight, giving a clean upper-sheet, and taking the upper-sheet in place of the lower. This plan insures regularity of wear in the sheets.

46. GLASS CLOTHS should be of good linen; that sold for white roller blinds answers admirably, as it is soft, without fluff, and is not expensive.

47. TEA CLOTHS are of coarser linen, but very coarse cloths are not economical, as they are clumsy, and often cause breakages.

48. KITCHEN CLOTHS.—Round towels are made of coarse linen, and what is called "Crash," respectively. A good supply of these is required in every house.

49. DUSTERS are sold at prices varying from sixpence to a shilling each, but are far more effective when made of old chintz, old linings, &c., being softer, and taking up the dust far better than the dressed stiff linen. Ugly, old-fashioned chintz is often sold at threepence and fourpence a yard, and when washed, makes admirable dusters at this low price.

50. Every mistress who wishes to preserve her kitchen cloths from holes and ourns will provide a kettle-holder for the kitchen, and a pot and saucepan-holder; these may be bought at the door for threepence, or, made out of old pieces, will save many a good cloth and duster from being burnt, made dirty, or destroyed.

51. The following list of HOUSEHOLD LINEN is intended for the guidance of those whose income is moderate. Fewer articles of each kind may comfortably answer where strict economy is an object in starting; but the numbers here given have been found by experience to suit a household of medium income, keeping two servants:—BEST SHEETS, six pairs; spare room, two pairs; servants, six pairs PILLOW-CASES, six best, twelve good, six common; TOWELS, twelve rough, twelve coarse, twenty-four fine, twelve servants'; BATH SHEETS, four; TABLE-CLOTHS, six breakfast, six dinner, two best, six servants'; TABLE NAPKINS, twelve dinner, twelve best, six breakfast; GLASS-CLOTHS, twelve; TEA-CLOTHS, eighteen; DUSTERS, twelve; ROUND TOWELS, six. KITCHEN-CLOTHS, twenty-four; CHAMBER-CLOTHS, six; PUDDING-CLOTHS, six. A list of all the contents of the linen-press should be neatly entered in a book, with the marks carefully copied, and a space left for remarks in time to come. Example: Six pairs

sheets; mark, E. J. B., 6, 1871.   1 pair turned, 1877 ; 1 pair cut up into glass-cloths, 1880.

52. At the periodical counting of the linen, the mistress should carefully examine each article, opening sheets, darning thin places with *flax*, not cotton, and should endeavour each year to add some article to her stock.

53. After the first six years, a pair of sheets and a table-cloth should be bought each year, at least, as these are very expensive articles to purchase in quantity.

54. BLANKETS are usually kept in the linen-press when out of use. They should be tied in pairs, and sewn up in an old linen pillow-case, with a lump of camphor in each parcel, the name of the room or bed to which they belong should be added to the card sewn to the case.

55. COLOURED TABLE-CLOTHS, when out of use, should be kept in the linen-press.

56. We prefer the good old-fashioned plan of the mistress herself counting over the clean linen, examining it for repairs, and replacing it in the linen-press. By these means she sees exactly what is wanted to be repaired or renewed, and is able, by taking things in time, to get a great deal of needlework done at home with perfect ease to herself and maids ; and by looking over the linen herself, she knows exactly what mending is to be done each week, and neither allows an idle girl to impose upon her, nor, on the other hand, makes unreasonable demands on her housemaiden's industry. At certain seasons a week's rest from all needle-work should be given to servants ; this is to enable them to make a dress, or turn or alter their clothes to advantage, as they can do more in a week's steady work than in a hundred odds and ends of stolen time.

HOUSE-LINEN.

57. Of course, the HOUSE and BODY LINEN is regularly mended every week, but every housewife knows that there are times when linen should undergo a more "thorough repair"-ing than it receives weekly.   The linen list should be examined, the linen counted, the list corrected, and any new linen carefully made and marked.   Sheets should be turned sides and middle and re-hemmed, or rather re-sewn, for the hems of all house-linen should be sewn, not hemmed. Old tablecloths may be cut up into tray or lunch cloths, old finger-napkins be darned and fringed out into d'oyleys for vegetables or for placing under pie-dishes.

58. Faded CHINTZ HANGINGS make excellent dusters, neatly hemmed round, and very pretty fringed d'oyleys may be made out of small squares of holland, either bleached or unbleached.   New tablecloths or dinner-napkins may be marked in

satin stitch embroidery in white or in ingrain colours. Do not forget to re-mark any linen that has had the hems cut off and the marks turned in.

59. For MARKING with ink, use a quill pen and Bond's marking-ink. The writing should be neat, and the word ironed as soon as written. For ironing after marking, a small board about a foot square should be used, and kept for the purpose. It should be covered with a thick flannel, nailed on, and with a clean linen cover *tacked* on. The iron-rest must never be placed on the table, in case of the heat drawing the polish into blisters. To ascertain if an iron is hot, scatter a drop of water on it ; the water should fizz and roll off in haste to escape. Always try the iron on a coarse cloth first before placing it over the name, and do not keep it on more than a second if the iron is hot, as it should be. Never mark clothes or linen when it is returned from the wash, unless *perfectly dry*, which is not often the case. The ink runs on a damp surface, and an untidy mark appears in place of a neatly-written name.

60. As the HOUSE-LINEN requires inspection and mending, so the body-linen of the household should undergo revision during leisurely winter days, and every article should be re-taped, re-buttoned, darned, and mended. New sets of clothes should be cut out and made. It is best, in cutting out, to tear the skirts of chemises off from the piece, and use the remainder for the smaller parts, as sleeves, gores, bands, &c. Gores are usually cut from the upper part and added to the lower. In making under-clothing, whether by hand or by machine, care and exactness of detail should prevail. The machine-worker should take her place at the window, with the machine well cleaned, oiled, and worked for a few seconds without being threaded up. The seams should be prepared and handed to her. Let us take six chemises for an example. The gores must first be stitched, then felled, so the twelve gores must be handed to her lightly tacked in position. While she is stitching these, the fells must be turned down and tacked ; she then fells these ; while felling, the finished gores are being tacked in their proper places, and the chemise length closed on each side ; the twelve sides and the other side of the gore are then stitched and felled in due succession. The sleeves follow in the same order, and the band, if plain ; if made with much tucking and stitching, much adornment with insertion, it is best to complete the bands before beginning the skirts ; get sufficient tucking done in strips from three to five tucks in a strip ; arrange and baste them with the embroidery or lace at night, as the work is light and easy, and can be taken up or left at will. Then the stitching can be com-pleted altogether. The difficulties met with by some ladies in working their sewing-machines are, we regret to say, very much their own fault ; of course, we do not mean to say that if a lady buys a common imitation of a good machine at about a quarter of the real cost, she must not expect to have some trouble with her "bargain" ; but a lady possessing a Willcox & Gibbs, a Wheeler & Wilson, a Silencieuse, or a Little Wanzer, should not have anything but praise to give her iron seamstress. But no machine will work well without oil, and they all require clean and kind treatment, to be kept under cover, to be well oiled and

wiped with a soft cloth, to have the needle set properly, the stitch and tension in unison, and the cotton or silk suitable to both the needle and the fabric. In working upon dressed longcloth, it is well to soap the seams, as one would do in hand-sewing, to avoid breaking our hand-sewing needles, but the easiest mode is to ask the housemaid to wash out the longcloth, when torn into lengths, with plenty of soap and water, and to iron it out smoothly for cutting out; this will give a very pleasant softness to the work, and allow its being stitched very nicely. In working in thin *sleezy* fabrics, some machines draw the work in with the teeth of the feed-box; this is remedied by placing strips of paper below the work and stitching through all; the paper tears away very easily afterwards. Another fault common to machine-workers is the over-quick pace at which they drive the machine, a pace at which they can scarcely guide the work or see the stitches. It is the nature of women when riding and driving to go very fast; and so we drive on our machines, and are surprised that we cannot keep our stitching as even as we should like to see it. To cure this rapid driving we must practise working the machine slowly; braiding is good practice for this, and teaches one *to manage* a machine better than any other kind of work.

61. HAND-MACHINES are exceedingly convenient when really good, as the Little Wanzer, &c. The work can be done easily and far more quickly than by hand, and it is very pleasant to sit at the table at work as in hand-sewing.

62. Attention to HOUSE-LINEN should comprise the careful inspection and repair of the muslin curtains, which should be "roughed" in October. These should be darned, and lace sewn on where accidentally removed. Long curtains half worn-out will make capital short muslin blinds; be sure to choose small designs in buying your curtains, if you destine them to this use in the future. Make wide hems if you wish brass rods to pass through them for window screens, and use patent Valenciennes lace for trimming them; it washes admirably and wears well. Stair-covers and holland druggets, too, must be mended by prudent housewives.

HOUSEKEEPING ACCOUNTS.

63. One of the greatest trials of the young wife is the ACCOUNT-BOOK. This book becomes a perfect bugbear to some ladies, who are yet perfectly capable of keeping a neat and regular debtor and creditor account if they could be once started with a regular system of account-keeping.

64. Girls, whose monetary responsibilities have begun and ended with their quarterly allowance, find housekeeping accounts very difficult to manage properly; and although experienced matrons may smile at these words, a lesson in easy account-keeping is not without value.

65. We must state at the beginning that although we know of many other methods of keeping accounts, yet we believe our method to be so easy, that we can conscientiously recommend it to housewives.

66. A neatly-bound ACCOUNT-BOOK of oblong shape, an ivory slate and pencil, and a card and pencil in the purse is the whole stock-in-trade as account-keeper. The account-book is kept in the mistress's Davenport, the slate hangs up in the kitchen, and the card and purse are naturally in the pocket.

67. Every time any money is spent enter the item at once on the card, which is kept in place in the purse by an elastic passed over it. Every Saturday remove the card and insert a fresh one, copying the list on the card into the account-book.

68. Every Saturday morning receive the HOUSEHOLD BOOKS from the cook, who hands the slate, on which she has marked the sums paid at the kitchen door for parcels and sundries not put down in the weekly books; this statement includes all extras. To this add the housekeeping expenses: butcher, baker, milkman, grocer, greengrocer, washing, &c., and add this up.

69. Then copy the sums written on the slate into the weekly account-book, of which we subjoin a specimen page. It will be observed that we "enter," or write down the sums paid out on the right-hand page only, reserving the left-hand page for sums received.

70. WEEKLY PAGE OF HOUSEKEEPING BOOK.

RECEIVED.				PAID.			
1872.	January.			1872. Week ending 29th.	January.		
	£	s.	d.		£	s.	d.
23rd, Cheque	6	10	0	Washing	0	11	10
				Butcher	1	10	2½
				Baker	0	7	1
				Grocer	0	12	6
				Milk	0	7	6
				Greengrocer	0	9	2
				Parcels	0	2	9
				Ale	0	17	0
				Fish	0	5	3
					5	3	3½
				Balance	1	6	8½
	£6	10	0		£6	10	0

71. EXTRAS.

	£	s.	d.	Wages:—	£	s.	d.
23rd, Cheque	8	10	0	Cook	4	10	0
25th, Cheque	2	12	9	Housemaid	4	0	0
				Taxes	1	5	7
				Parish rates	1	7	2
	£11	2	9		£11	2	9

72. QUARTERLY ACCOUNT.
HOUSE EXPENSES.

	RECEIVED. £ s. d.	PAID. £ s. d.
1st week, ending 1st January	6 10 0	6 8 2
2nd ,, ,, 8th ,,	6 10 0	6 4 0
3rd ,, ,, 15th ,,	6 10 0	6 10 0
4th ,, ,, 22nd ,,	6 10 0	6 3 1
5th ,, ,, 29th ,,	6 10 0	5 3 3
6th ,, ,, 5th February	6 10 0	6 5 8
7th ,, ,, 12th ,,	6 10 0	6 7 3
8th ,, ,, 19th ,,	6 10 0	6 12 1
9th ,, ,, 26th ,,	6 10 0	5 13 8
10th ,, ,, 5th March	6 10 0	7 5 0
11th ,, ,, 12th ,,	6 10 0	6 2 1
12th ,, ,, 19th ,,	6 10 0	4 18 7
13th ,, ,, 26th ,,	6 10 0	6 7 2
		80 0 0
Balance		4 10 0
	£84 10 0	£84 10 0

73. EXTRAS.

	£ s. d.		£ s. d.
8rd January, Cheque	12 10 0	Rent	12 10 0
23rd ,, ,,	2 12 9	Taxes	1 5 7
25th ,, ,,	8 10 0	Rates	1 7 2
6th February ,,	7 6 6	Wages	8 10 0
20th March ,,	4 18 0	Coals	7 6 6
		Wine	4 18 0
	£35 17 3		£35 17 3

74. Each double page is complete in itself. At the end of every quarter or thirteen weeks enter the totals of sums received and paid, giving the dates of each week, as above shown. It will be seen that the balance of each week is shown on the week's account, and the quarterly balance is struck on the page which shows the quarter's total expenses. Every week you put down extra expenses, as taxes, or wages (for which a cheque or money is received), on the right-hand page, entering in the same line on the *left*-hand page the cheque for taxes, wages, &c., or whatever the item is; thus the actual expense is shown each week, independently of all sums given and paid for extras other than housekeeping.

75. Besides which, you should take out a "schedule" of expenses; that is, write a list every thirteen weeks of the sums paid to each tradesman, so that you can tell at a glance what the quarterly cost of every article consumed is.

76. But ACCOUNT-KEEPING does not begin and end with the account-book. Every

tradesman's book should be compared with the cook's slate or tally, or tickets brought with the meat, as in the butcher's case, for instance ; then the books must be added up, or the statements verified by the ready-reckoner, as few ladies are clever enough to keep reckoning tables in their heads as one does the multiplication tables.

77. The MEAT TICKETS should be kept on a hook in the kitchen, and verified by the mistress when comparing the weight charged with that sent in. The cook must of course weigh the meat before allowing the butcher to leave the door ; she will then be able to see if the weight is correct, and make the butcher alter the ticket or take back the joint if the weight is not correct. Groceries must also be weighed, as well as bread, and, indeed, all goods sold by weight. Washing should be counted over by the housemaid on Monday morning in presence of the mistress, who should enter the items in the washing-book, and, on the return of the linen, the housemaid should compare the quantities returned with the book before airing and putting the linen away.

PURCHASING.

78. A few REMARKS as to the best MODES and PLACES of BUYING articles of DOMESTIC CONSUMPTION may be useful here.

79. It is not enough to have plenty of money ; one must try to become a really clever buyer. A "clever" buyer is not one who beats down the price of every article until she is well known, and prices are put up to come down to their smallest value only. She must know the real value of every article at each season of the year, and either give that exact value or know how to go without gracefully, or to make up by purchasing an equivalent at less cost. American women are wonderfully clever buyers: they know exactly what they want, and *will have it*. Before purchasing, they inquire at many shops various prices, or, as they quaintly say, go "pricing, not shopping."

80. The Civil Service Co-operative Association is invaluable to the members and the friends of members possessing tickets. These tickets cost 5s. annually, and are renewed at the end of February in each year. It is now considered a great favour to obtain one of these tickets, as the number is restricted. At the stores every article of grocery, housekeeping, and drapery requirements is sold at little more than cost price, while the shops in connection with the stores allow members 15, 20, 25, and 30 per cent. discount off the sums spent with them. Of course, all this is the advantage of the ready-money system of cash payments ; but the saving is undoubted, and one has the great satisfaction of feeling that every article one has is paid for. In short, whether for making or for mending, the stores, and shops in connection with the stores, are invaluable.

81. When the weather allows of meat hanging, and the larder is commodious,

it is well to purchase a week's consumption at once, and hang the articles until in prime condition.

DAILY HOUSE-WORK.

82. The DAILY DUTIES of the HOUSE SERVANTS are as follow:—

83. The beds are stripped, and slops emptied in all the rooms. Then bed-making follows ; then the sitting-room not used for breakfast must be swept, dusted, and arranged ; and then the routine cleaning of the day must follow. Every household has good reasons for each day's work. The following regulation has been thought to be a good guide :—

Monday—One bedroom ; washing.
Tuesday—Spare room and library.
Wednesday—Dining-room ; ironing.
Thursday—Mistress's bed and dressing rooms.
Friday—Drawing-room and one bedroom.
Saturday—Plate, stairs, and sundries.

84. The NURSE cleans her own nursery, night nursery, and her own bedroom. The COOK undertakes steps and hall, passages, kitchen, larder, scullery, and wash-house, and downstairs closets, and, *by arrangement* with the mistress at time of hiring, cleans the dining-room and helps to make the beds.

85. WINDOW-CLEANING is also a matter of special arrangement. The cook "answers the door" until twelve o'clock, after which hour the housemaid is supposed to be dressed, and should be, if she is quick and clever at her work. The cook should clean her own bedroom, even if shared by the housemaid ; and the housemaid is bound, by kitchen etiquette, the unspoken tradition of the spit, to make the tea at breakfast, to arrange and make tea at the afternoon meal, and to lay the cloth for the kitchen supper. This rule has originated, no doubt, in the kindly feeling which prompts those who have no cooking to do to prepare the meals for those whose work is almost entirely cooking, and who are, therefore, little disposed to do so for themselves.

86. It is well, WHEN ENGAGING SERVANTS, to mention all the rules that a mistress considers best for the happiness of her household, and these details cannot be too much studied by those who hold the reins. A holiday every six weeks should be given to each servant, and by turns they should be allowed to go out on Sunday evenings. Some families can manage to allow one maid the Sunday morning, the other the Sunday evening, but this cannot always be done. The wages should be paid regularly upon quarter-day—the 25th March, 21st June, 29th September, and 25th December,—upon which last day a nice Christmas-box should be added to encourage good service and promote kindly feelings. It is best to provide tea, sugar, beer, and washing, unless washing is done at home, when, of course, it is done by the maids and laundress. If servants work hard they require some ale, and by providing a cask of good ale, and putting it in the cook's charge, they have sufficient, and there is no objectionable calling of public-house boys for orders or beer-cans. The ale should be computed to last a certain time, and the brewer be ordered to call at regular intervals. Women servants are allowed a pint and men servants a quart per diem, and a gallon over should be allowed in small households for waste in constant drawing. The family, if ale-drinkers, should have a separate cask, as it is impossible to ascertain the right quantity to be used when friends drop in.

87. The USUAL ALLOWANCE for SERVANTS is :—

Vegetables chiefly potatoes and greens.
Ale or stout: men, 1 quart ; maids, 1 pint per diem.
Washing, from 1s. to 1s. 6d.
Tea, ¼ lb. per week.
Sugar, ½ lb. per week.
Butter, ½ lb. per week.
Meat, 3½ lb. per week.
Bread, 1 lb. per diem ; ¼ lb. cheese per week.
Soap, 1 lb. per week for house-cleaning, and 1 cake for personal use.

88. Tea and bread and butter, or bread and preserve, are the servants' ordinary breakfast.

89. DINNER, hot meat and vegetables, alternately with cold meat and pudding; but a considerate mistress will consult her servants' health and her own interest, by giving them an agreeable change of food.

90. TEA and bread and butter for tea.

91. SUPPER, bread and meat or bread and cheese.

92. Coffee makes an agreeable change with tea, and should be occasionally allowed in the proportion of ½ lb. per head per week.

93. Care and economy without meanness, on the part of a mistress, will do more to correct the extravagance of servants than any precept. If a maid sees her mistress carefully throw up the ashes, put out unnecessary candles, or gaslights, and economize properly, she will try also to save her mistress's property.

94. We think that by laying aside all pretence, and being open and honest with servants, we make them careful and exact too. Where the mistress is given to changing her servants, complaining of them, &c., the fault is *usually* her own. The fault is with the driver, not with the horses, who, in light but firm hands, would run well together, and do their work well and quickly.

95. SERVANTS should never be reproved before each other or before anyone. If there is occasion for more than a word of direction, a lady should ring for her servant and speak kindly and seriously to her, showing a willingness to help her, though by no means slighting over the subject in question, or allowing any timidity of demeanour to appear.

96. DOMESTIC QUARRELS often embitter the peace of households and cause dismissals ; these can be quelled by a gentle firmness and the following rules :—Never listen to what one servant says of another ; never ask a question about a new comer of the old trusted servant; if angry voices and loud talk reach your ear, ring for the delinquents, and before *both* say, "I have no wish to interfere with your quarrels; say and do what you please; but *I* must never hear a sound of dispute or anger in this house." The utter absurdity of being *allowed* to quarrel will, in most cases, prevent a repetition of the offence ; and as this is a *tried* recipe for domestic *broils*, we give it verbatim.

97. But it is only a gentlewoman who *can* say this—one who never is betrayed into an angry word or cross retort; example and precept must go hand in hand. Our experience is, that in life what we believe people to be, *we make them.* "I believe you to be honest," has kept many a poor tempted soul from evil, and it is the duty of mistresses to guard their *household* as they would their children from opportunities of doing wrong. Young girls should not be sent out late at night to post letters or to fetch beer; should be advised to put by a little of each quarter's money in the post-office savings-bank; should be counselled as to what is nice to buy in the way of dress; should never be given old finery; should be lent nice books, not only religious but amusing works; should be led to take an interest in the garden, or in the growing flowers, the birds or animals of the house; and in the children, for if the children are not utterly spoiled, and the maids not utterly bad, they cannot help taking an interest in the nursery.

98. If "suspicion haunts" the mistress's mind (we are supposing her to be a sensible, kind-hearted person), her best plan is to change her servants; she cannot be comfortable with them, and there is usually more or less ground to these doubts. A mistress cannot follow her stores into the kitchen and *see* that every ounce is carefully used, but she can resist the continual petty larceny, which destroys all her attempts at economy and heavily burdens her purse.

99. ENGAGING SERVANTS.—This important business is usually thought a pleasing excitement by one class of mistresses, who are constantly changing, and who do not know how to appreciate a good servant ; or a dreadful trouble and worry by those who are idle or careless.

100. If a lady will reflect upon the importance of engaging a good servant, she will hesitate before taking a written character, unless under very exceptional circumstances. There are four ways of obtaining servants : inquiring of trades-

b

persons; advertising for servants; answering advertisements: and applying at servants' offices.

101. When servants are obtained through TRADESMEN, which is one of the easiest modes, there are some disadvantages. The servant is placed under favour to her patron, and in case of a dishonest butcher, for example, would be expected to shut her eyes to short weights, inferior meat, &c. Then she frequently has acquaintances in the neighbourhood, or has been servant of some of one's friends : two objections to begin with, and many others will suggest themselves. ADVER-TISING for servants costs from three to five shillings, according to the length of advertisement, and entails remaining at home during the hours stated.

102. This, where practicable, is an excellent plan, for when the lady sees a servant whose appearance pleases her whose recommendations are apparently good, and whose "character" is not "short," she can enter into details of the work, show the servant the house, the rooms, and ascertain whether the arrangements, if carried out, are likely to be permanent. The servant, on her side, can judge of the kind of place and mistress, and decide for or against it at once, instead of in a "month's time."

103. *But,* as every plan has its drawbacks, if evilly disposed, the servant about to leave can prejudice the new comer against the place.

104. Answering advertisements is by no means a certain way of obtaining servants, and should not be resorted to when time is an object.

105. Applying at servants' offices and homes is one of the best plans; and at some of these, ladies can comfortably see and engage servants. The characters are all inspected by the managers; but as, with so large a number, the minute points which so particularly affect the comfort of a household cannot be determined, a mistress should never think any trouble too great which allows a personal interview with the late mistress of the proposed maid.

OBSERVATIONS ON SERVANTS, WITH REGARD TO THEIR COMING AND GOING.

106. WARNINGS on either side are usually for that day month on which the warning was given, and it is well for a mistress to begin at once to look out for a good maid to replace the going-out servant.

107. An excellent place to meet with respectable servants is the Soho Bazaar, where one can see them quietly ; and the terms are only five shillings, paid when one is suited with a servant. It is well at the time of hiring to state distinctly the exact nature of the service required. For example, if a cook is wanted to undertake the dining-room, hall, and passages, it should be distinctly stated

xix

Observations on Servants, with regard to their Coming and Going.

that such is her work. If the housemaid is to wait on the lady, it should be named, and so on through all the duties of each place.

108. And at the time of hiring, it is important to specify the holidays, time allowed on Sundays, and the following particulars, so that a servant clearly understands what she is to expect, and enters upon her duties clearly under.standing the kind of situation she accepts. The wages should be increased yearly, and every encouragement given to good servants.

109. After warning has been given on either side, the mistress, even if annoyed with her maid, should behave with quiet courtesy towards her ; not, as we have remarked some mistresses do, treat her as if she had committed a crime. A change may be desirable for many reasons, although it is not possible to over-estimate a quiet, well-conducted servant, who is attached to her mistress, and who will not leave her even for fairer prospects and a more luxurious home.

110. In ENGAGING SERVANTS state—

111. The wages given now, and what rise may be expected.

112. The time on Sunday allowed for church or chapel, &c.

113. Inquiries to be made of the lady who gives the character as to " honesty, sobriety, cleanliness, also if she is industrious, neat, tidy in person, and in work, regular and systematic."

114. If a COOK, ask particulars of soups, roasting and boiling, pastry-making, and general care and economy.

115. If a NURSE, temper, kindness and watchful care, and experience.

116. If a HOUSEMAID, care of stoves, ornaments, careful, and neat.

117. If a LADY'S-MAID, clever hairdresser and dressmaker, discreet and quiet ; and so on through the various classes of servants required.

118. Number of years in place.

119. From whom taken.

120. Reason for leaving.

121. Any particular fault or peculiarity.

122. When the servant is engaged, the mistress should enter these particulars, together with the date of entry of service, amount of wages, &c., in a book kept for that purpose.

123. By the STYLE of HOUSE, and the class of lady, one can judge of the servant's character, whether the lady gives a true character or not. High praise is often accorded by a mistress who does not know what a good servant is, and this applies particularly to cooks, for here taste and style of serving differ essentially. As a rule, a lady is safe in taking a servant who has lived over two years in a family in the same position as her own, neither above nor below it, of whom the mistress distinctly and clearly states that she is honest, sober, clean, and industrious ; the mistress's appearance being quiet, ladylike, and tidy ; the house well-cared for and neat. It is a great advantage to know something of the past history of one's servants, and inquiries should be made respecting the other places held by the servant.

124. A MISTRESS is often shy about telling a new servant her ways and wishes, allows herself to be as indulgent at first as she is strict and fault-finding when used to her new maid. Now, if this plan were reversed, and a lady had the courage to be strict and particular when the maid is at her best, and in her most pains-taking humour, a servant would naturally fall into the right way of pleasing by being useful to her mistress.

125. Gentleness, kindness, and firmness are the qualities required in a mistress, with a thorough practical knowledge of what are her servants' duties. We may here remark that those households are best conducted where the mistress never converses with her servants ; never speaks but to gently give an order, ask a question, or say good morning and evening to her maids. Of course, this does not apply in times of sorrow for the servants, or with a general servant, who is depending on her mistress for all occasions of speaking, or to old, well-tried servants, but it is a safe rule for the MISTRESS.

126. When two SERVANTS are kept, the mistress has more time at her disposal, but should nevertheless take a close and watchful interest in the work of the house, inspecting the work when finished, and remarking on badly-cleaned rooms, neglected corners, and seeing that the fault is repaired at the moment. By never passing over a fault during the first twelve months, but kindly and gently pointing it out, there will be no need for a word of correction afterwards.

127. When SERVANTS first enter a service they naturally try their best to please, and require only teaching the "ways" of the family. They soon see if "missus" is "particular" or no, and whether they are ruled by a careful, clever hand, or by a careless, idle, anyhow mistress, and will act accordingly.

128. What has passed into a proverb respecting the master's eye equally applies to the mistress of a household. Her observant glance ought to take in, and the mind note, every detail of housewifery. She should in herself be an example to her maids of neatness, cleanliness, and order. "So particular," should be the verdict of her handmaidens. A woman who does her duty to her husband and household MUST be particular, must be strict and watchful. At the same time, this care and strictness does not preclude her being gentle in manner and word, kind and sympathizing with her servants in illness or trouble, tending them and helping them when such assistance is needed.

129. And this kindness, this help, can be given only by a careful, watchful mistress,—a woman whose life is regulated by strong principles, and by love of order.

130. If WASTE is allowed to run riot in a household,—if articles of daily food are wasted, badly *bought*, badly cooked, badly carved, and made the *least* of,—there will be no funds left in the mistress's hands with which to pay for the doctor her kindness would call in to her sick servant. Care and thrift mean *power to help others;* economy in daily life permits good actions in life's trials. Good house. wifery comprises the duty of woman. Pages might be written upon this subject, but a few hints will suffice to prove this to a thoughtful woman.

131. The WASHING of a family should be put out where one servant alone is kept, as we have stated ; but many clever managers find time to do all the family washing at home, and yet are not "in a muddle," as it is expressively termed, upon washing-day ; the damping, folding, and ironing being done by the mis-tress, the hard labour by the maid. With the help of one of Bradford's washing-machines this labour is much reduced, and the wringer and mangle are equally handy.

132. But unless it is *absolutely* necessary, no lady should attempt to have the whole of the washing done at home when one servant alone is kept.

133. In the EVENING the mistress should only make the tea and attend to her husband ; the last thing at night she should inspect the doors and the whole of the basement, noting every want of cleanliness in the scullery or wash-house, and ascertaining that all be secure, and the plate in her room before she retires to rest, which should be not later than eleven o'clock ; for, unless she is allowed a certain season of rest, it is impossible for a woman, however willing, to rise at seven, and fulfil the innumerable duties of a mistress. Many of the duties of a mistress, as occasional cooking, washing-up, &c., may be omitted when there is an experienced general servant, or where two maids are kept. We may mention that, as it is desirable that a lady's hands should always look white and nice, gloves should be worn during dusting operations and household work, whenever possible. Household gloves should be a quarter size larger than those ordinarily worn, and have a loose cuff sewn to them, with an elastic at top to protect the sleeves.

134. In FAMILIES where there are children and no nurse of any kind is kept, the *mother is the nurse,* and should not attempt to pay and receive formal visits, but

content herself with domestic duties until she is in a position to have her after-noons, at least, free. Nothing is more trying to the health and temper than being constantly called away from domestic duties by frivolous and inconsiderate visitors.

135. With the CARE of her CHILDREN, their daily walks, and the superintendence of their clothing, the mistress will find but little time for assisting the general servant, who will have, in addition to the work we have mentioned, the prepara-tion of the nursery dinner, and the carrying of water, both hot and cold, to the nurseries, with the cleaning and care of the rooms used by the children.

THE CHILDREN.

136. The first point to be considered is their HEALTH. Where it is possible, large airy rooms at the top of the house should be given up to the babies. A day and night nursery are required, and the night nursery should be the larger of the two. It should contain single iron beds or cots, placed upon well-scrubbed boards ; a strip of carpet or long rug should be placed at each bedside to enable the little feet to alight from bed safely. Slippers should be kept under each little bed, and the children taught never to go a step without them. The bed should consist of a hard mattress covered with two folds of blanket and a pillow, the ordinary bolster being dispensed with ; of course a pair of sheets and one, two, or three blankets, according to the season. A chair for each child, a washstand, and a hip-bath should constitute the rest of the furniture, though in large rooms a wardrobe and chest of drawers may be placed. Every room occupied by children should have a fireplace and chimney to allow of ventilation during the night. A large window is also requisite. In winter it is well to carpet the bed-room, but this should be removed at the spring cleaning. Once a week at least the bedroom fire should be lighted during the winter. If bedrooms, whether for children or adults, are scrubbed in the winter time, it should be done early in the morning, a good fire lit in the room, and be perfectly dry before being slept in. No flowers of any kind or growing plants should be placed in the bedrooms of children at night.

137. The CHILDREN'S DAY NURSERY should also be airy, well-ventilated, and kept perfectly clean. It is well to have as little furniture as possible ; a round table and chairs are all that is really wanted if there are good deep cupboards in the room ; if not, an *armoire* of some kind must be provided for children's toys and nurse's tea and breakfast service, and sundries that should always stand in order under a good nurse's care. On a high shelf, or, better still, locked up, but handy, should be a few simple medicines for children—castor-oil, rhubarb, and magnesia, and a pot of jam to help these down. Then a box should contain lint, strapping-plaster, and court-plaster ; " Jones's Epsom " is the best, as it neither inflames a wound nor does it easily wash off. A pair of scissors should be kept in this box, and never used for other purposes : a neat roll of old linen, a roll of

new flannel, and some bandage strips should also be placed close at hand. Nurse should be provided with two enamelled saucepans, with a block-tin kettle with neat jars, containing sugar, pearl barley, Embden grits, mustard, linseed, and linseed-meal. She should keep a bottle of camphorated spirits, and of ipecacuanha wine ; also among her medicines she should have a store of night-lights a food-warmer, and some candles ; a tin of plain biscuits may also be placed in her charge.

138. Both NURSE and MOTHER should inspect the stores once a week, and see that nothing is wanting at any time that would be required at night in a hurry. An old worn knife or a palette-knife and some spoons are required for plasters and poultices, and should be at hand.

139. CHILDREN require to run and skip, dance and jump, and to take good walks. Children's nursery hours should be as follows :—All out of bed at seven, all dressed and sitting down to breakfast at eight, nine o'clock should see the little troop out of doors in garden, in park, or on country roads. Two hours' walk in the morning and two in the afternoon is necessary in fine weather. After the 20th of October all children under six should be indoors after three o'clock : this rule should be continued until spring days again come round.

140. Dinner at 1, tea at 4.30, bed at 6 or 7, according to the ages of the children.

141. A glass of cold water morning and night is the best medicine they can take.

142. The MORNING BATH for healthy children of four or five years of age should be of cold water in summer and tepid in winter. It is an excellent plan to fill a large brown pickle-jar with bay salt and Tidman's sea-salt in equal parts, and to fill up with soft water, and tie a muslin cap over the jar; pour off the water every morning into the bath, adding fresh until all the salt is melted, when we must begin again. A hip-bath should be used for the morning bath, and the child rapidly sluiced all over, and then enveloped in a large well-aired sheet of fine huckaback, not less than two yards square ; rub quickly but not roughly, and see that the little limbs glow before you part with them. Then quickly dress the child in well-aired clothes, and brush the hair, clean the teeth, and hear the morning prayer before setting him to table.

143. BREAKFAST should be *ready*, for many children are so constituted as to be cross, because they feel ill, before breakfast : such children cannot bear the sinking feeling caused by want of food. If such there be in a family, and the number of little ones prevents the breakfast being ready for all directly, give the child a crust of bread or a biscuit, and it will play happily until summoned to its breakfast.

CHILBLAINS.

144. Between three and four of a cold winter's night, the CHILBLAINS begin their torture, and the poor little things to cry with pain. The circulation is in fault, and the vital energy must be increased in order to cope with the depressing influence of the cold. The child should take strengthening medicine, as quinine or steel (under advice, of course), or stout or port wine at eleven o'clock in the day, and the feet must be kept unchilled by plenty of exercise. If chilled after a walk, getting wet unavoidably, or after a long journey, the little feet must be judiciously unchilled by placing them in lukewarm water and bay salt, and gradually adding warmer water until quite hot, over blood heat; let the feet remain in this until the water cools perceptibly (it is easy to amuse the child with pretty stories), then carefully dry and wipe with a soft towel, and then gently rub the feet with the hands until they are " bone dry ;" this must be done the very day the chill appears, or it will be more difficult to **cure,** and must be repeated every other night if the chills do not disappear.

145. For the chilblains, when they have been allowed to get to the irritating stage, there are several remedies—one to be had of Keating, chemist, St. Paul's Churchyard, called Eidolon, and the other, which instantly stops the itching, is as follows :—For *unbroken* chilblains only : ¼ oz. hydrochloric acid, diluted, 6 oz. camphor water, 30 drops hydrochloric acid, diluted. This recipe contains a deadly poison, and must never be used except by experienced and responsible hands—indeed, none but a mother should apply it. Any one may use the Eidolon, which is equally effective. These remedies are for *unbroken* chilblains only. When chilblains do manifest themselves, the best remedy, not only for preventing them ulcerating, but overcoming the tingling, itching pain, and stimulating the circulation of the part to healthy action, is the *liniment of belladonna (two drachms), the liniment of aconite (one drachm), carbolic acid (ten drops), to collodion flexile (one ounce)*, painted with a camel's-hair pencil over the surface. But for broken chilblains, alas ! what can we do? The only course is perfect rest, perfect warmth, and the application of a new skin. New skin can be formed of the inner skin of an unboiled egg, or of gold-beater's skin. When friction is to be avoided, these thin skins should be covered by court plaster cut longer than the wound, which should be entirely covered with the thin skin. Children should wear lamb's-wool stockings and thick boots (or cork soles), laced up the centre, or buttoned; elastic sides should never be worn by anyone suffering from chilblains. When the chilblains vesicate, ulcerate, or slough, it is better to omit the aconite, and apply the other components of the liniment without it. The collodion flexile forms a coating or protecting film, which excludes the air, whilst the sedative liniments allay the irritation, generally of no trivial nature. For chapped hands we advise the free use of glycerine and good olive-oil in the proportion of two parts of the former to four of the latter; after this has been well rubbed into the hands, and allowed to remain for a little time, and the hands subsequently washed with Castile soap and tepid water, we recommend the belladonna and collodion flexile to be painted, and the protective film allowed to permanently remain. Obstinate cases are occasionally met with which no local application will remedy, until some disordered state of the system is removed, or the general condition of the health improved.

SPRING CLEANING.

146. In spring and autumn more extended cleaning operations go on, and the time for these periodical cleanings is usually May and October. All white-washing, painting, and general repairs should be done in the spring, and during the cleaning carpets should be taken up, well beaten, mended, and turned so as to bring the worn pieces out of sight. Care must be taken to match the design of the carpet. All ornaments should be carefully washed, cleaned, or relacquered. Curtain-poles taken down, washed with vinegar, and rubbed bright with furniture-polish, page lxiii. Looking-glasses cleaned, see page lxiv. Chairs and sofas re-covered or invested with loose chintz covers. Paper rubbed down with the clean crumb of stale quartern loaves. Ornaments placed in fire-stoves, and white curtains hung up in place of the damask or chintz, which should be well shaken, folded in large folds, with a couple of handfuls of dry bran laid between each fold, and a piece of camphor placed in the drawer or box in which they are kept.

147. All woollen antimacassars should be replaced by lace or cotton couvrettes.

148. When carpets are re-laid, the colours are greatly revived by adding a small quantity of ox-gall to warm water and washing them over with the mixture: plenty of air must be admitted after this, as the smell is very strong.

149. Locks should now be taken off, cleaned, and oiled, bell-wires adjusted, and bell-handles tightened, if necessary.

150. The chimney of each room should be swept, and care taken to see that the brush is sent up through the top of the chimney.

151. In olden days, all fires save the kitchen were left off on the twenty-fifth March, and the house-cleaning began as soon after as possible. Now, in these degenerate days, it is not until May that many among us begin to turn the house out of windows. The first fine week after May 1st is a good rule, but a fine hot April will sometimes tempt us to begin before the sun gains much power. At the end of March all the blankets that can be spared should be washed and hung out in the brisk wind to dry, then thoroughly aired by a good fire for twelve hours, and stored in a dry place.

152. The first thing to be done when beginning a " spring clean," whether in March, April, or May, is to ascertain what pieces of furniture want renovating,

and if any require to be taken from home, they should be sent off at once. Then the sweep must be consulted, and ordered to come on the most convenient days. If the family are away, all the rooms can be swept in one day, but if not, the arrangements must be altered by circumstances. To "begin with the top floor and go down" is not a bad rule. Before the sweep's arrival all carpets must come up, and go away or out to be beaten ; all ornaments must be removed, pictures taken down, and looking-glasses covered. All furniture should be covered with sheets or with dusting-sheets.

153. After the sweep's necessary but grimy labours, all traces of his presence must be got rid of, and the room swept *towards* the fireplace, and all dirt taken up, and the stove cleaned. The walls, if panelled, are washed down ; if papered, either rubbed down with stale bread or cleaned by passing a clean cloth down them, taking care to remove all cobwebs from corners. In cleaning with bread act as follows :—

154. First blow off the dust with the bellows. Divide a stale loaf of white bread into eight pieces. Take the crust into your hand, and, beginning at the top of the paper, wipe it *downwards* in the lightest manner with the crumb ; do not cross or go upwards ; wipe about half a yard at a stroke, and when all the upper part is done, go round again, beginning a little above where you left off. It must be done with great lightness, or the dirt will adhere to the paper, but if properly done the paper looks like new. Then the floor is scrubbed with sand and hot water—*no soap, no soda*—and allowed to dry. The furniture is thoroughly cleansed while the floor is drying.

155. Those articles which are French-polished should be washed with weak vinegar and water, and the following polish used to them :—3 oz. of common beeswax, 1 oz. of white wax, 1 oz. of curd soap, 1 pint of turpentine, 1 pint of *boiled* soft water ; mix these, adding the water when cold, shake well, and keep for 48 hours. Apply with a flannel, and polish first with a duster, and then with a silk handkerchief.

156. The furniture should be replaced in position, or changed to suit the altered room, which looks differently with white curtains and dressed-up fireplace. The fireplace may be concealed by a card-table, with a handsome cover of cloth embroidered with some pretty design. Firegrate adornments are to be avoided by chilly persons, whose health demands that every wet evening, every cold evening, shall see a cheerful fire in the *salon*.

157. Very pretty modes there are, however, of ornamenting grates and fireplaces. We all know the eternal crinoline, fringed out and adorned with ivy and real or artificial flowers. The blank space filled by looking-glass, with fender of ferns and pot plants in front, is nice but expensive ; but the trellis basket-work screen and fender is within the reach of all. The price, to begin with, is moderate, and

the trellis is soon covered with creepers, nasturtium, jasmine, clematis. The front or fender may be filled with green moss and cut flowers, or by pots containing growing plants.

158. WINTER CURTAINS must be put away carefully, after hanging out in the air for three or four days if in fine weather, bringing them in at night. On the day you intend to pack them away, beat them lightly with a thin stick, and fold them carefully in as large folds as your store-place will allow, scatter a handful of bran (bone-dry) between each fold, and if placed in a large drawer or chest, add a big lump of camphor.

159. LINED CHINTZ CURTAINS should be treated in a similar way, but do not require the camphor. The bran cleans both chintz and damask curtains in a wonderful manner, and there is but one thing to remember, that you must carefully shake out the bran when you draw them out again. The nicely washed and mended muslin curtains should hang in their due place, the pictures be replaced in position. And now we turn to the blinds, a vexed subject in many households. I venetian blinds are in question, they want simply washing, perhaps repainting, the tapes renovating, not a long business in willing hands; but if the blinds be white holland, on rollers, it is sad work. First, to get the blinds from the rollers, then to wash them and iron them straight, then to replace them, and then to find that no one in the house can pull them up straight. Roller-blinds that go up with a gentle spring, and come down with a gentle click-click are best; but if they are not quite clean and new, they should be taken down and made into nice glass-cloths, for which they are well adapted, and new ones placed upon the rollers.

160. The OUTSIDE of a HOUSE, both back and front, is an index to the character of its mistress. Every room should have a window neatly dressed with curtains and blinds clean, neat, and hanging straight.

161. The STEPS should rival the snow in whiteness, and be fresh whitened *daily.*

162. The BEDROOMS require a few words. The bedding should be taken out o doors, if possible, and well beaten and brushed, the bedstead taken to pieces, whether of wood or of iron, and well washed with hot water and soap. When quite dry the bedding should be replaced, and the summer bed-curtains be arranged with the bed-furniture. An opportunity should be taken of sending all japanned goods to be repaired, as cans, baths, hot-water cans, &c. All the glass and extra china should be washed or dusted in the china closet, the list gone over, and all missing articles accounted for and replaced as soon as possible.

163. A few items of housewifery may be jotted down here. Have the pianos tuned as soon as the house-cleaning is over; oil all the door locks, keys, and bolts once every month. Oil all door and window hinges. Have every trifling repair

mended at once, and paid for at once; this saves much trouble, and is consider-ably cheaper than having carpenter's and glazing jobs booked.

164. Turn out every box, cupboard, and corner in the house-cleaning. Separate all stores required for or likely to be useful in needlework, and keep these in tiny rolls or parcels in a drawer known as the work-drawer. Wash out and fill up inkstands once a week. Few writers like much ink in the inkstand; half an inch deep is quite enough for ordinary writing for a week, and more than enough to spill if there is an accident with the inkstand.

165. Warm skirts and cloth jackets should be hung out in the air, and well beaten with a light cane, and stored with plenty of camphor in presses or boxes. Muslin dresses and petticoats should take the place of the heavier garments, and notable housewives prepare in May their summer costumes for the children and for themselves. The little ones look best and are happiest in holland frocks and blouses, or knickerbocker suits of brown holland. Boys of five and six will require four suits a week of these. Little girls are more reasonable, and can be kept in nice order with three suits weekly. We are, of course, speaking for children who are allowed to play about a garden and enjoy themselves. White piqué, nicely braided, makes good best summer clothing for both boys and girls. Straw hats for both, but while girls want pretty little wreaths of flowers, a plain ribbon does for Master Jack; but that ribbon should match the little bow tied beneath his clean linen collar.

166. Muslin, holland, or print costumes are nice for morning wear, for ladies' costumes should always be made in accordance with the time they are to be worn. Many ladies in the country do not change their dress until late in the day; the morning costume should then be made in dressy style; but if it is discarded before the children's early dinner, it should be as plain as possible, although *always* neat and pretty.

167. All cloth, merino, and stuff dresses which are worn daily should be hung out for one day in each week in the open air, beaten lightly with a cane, and well brushed, folded, and put away. This cleansing and rest keeps the dress fresh and pleasant, and makes it look better and wear longer than if this little care is neglected.

168. A fresh ribbon, a new collar, some variety in one's ornament, makes a refreshing change to the eyes of our family. Variety should be studied for the sake of pleasing and cheering those who work for us and with us.

169. In the evening various amusements should be allowed in a family—music, cards, reading, games, such as chess, draughts, jacquet, backgammon, &c. A good romp with the little ones is a healthy amusement for every one who will

join in, and most beneficial to the little darlings, who go merrily to "Bedfordshire."

170. If guests are expected at any time, rooms should be well aired, and everything placed in readiness; chimneys aired by good fires, so as to have no smoke to dishearten the arriving guests, or to blacken the dainty toilet arrangements.

171. Mutton and beef should hang for ten days if the weather be cold, and for a week under any conditions.

172. In order to allure guests to our table we must give them a good dinner nay, more, we must have and enjoy the reputation of a good cook, a good cellar, a carefully-appointed table, and quiet, clever waiting. The damask tablecloth must be spotless, the napkins folded in the last mode, flowers arranged on the table with or without the dessert. The glasses should be brilliant, the silver well polished, and plenty of light, either gas, lamp, or, best of all, wax lights. The waiting should be performed noiselessly. Unless men-servants are thoroughly well drilled, it is better to dispense with their services; at any rate, do not employ anyone from the stable to assist the footman. The aroma arising from the ordinary duties of coachman, groom, or stable-boy is too plainly perceptible in a dining-room, and is very trying to delicate persons. A neat nice-looking housemaid is far pleasanter than such "grooms in waiting."

173. That the dinner may be perfect, we must study what is seasonable as well as what is nice. Good housewives will replace all glass and china in fitting order the day following any little party. Fruit should be removed from delicately-painted dessert services as soon as the *convives* assemble in the drawing-room. If there is not time to wash them up at once (by far the best plan), the first opportunity should be taken of doing so, and before going to bed this should be done.

174. In extinguishing wax candles in chandeliers, candelabra, and piano candle-sticks, care should be taken to avoid disturbing the wax; if blown out, the hand should be placed behind the light to guard the "spirt" of wax from the carpet, &c., but the neatest plan is to have an extinguisher mounted on a long stick, and the lights extinguished one by one by this.

THE GENERAL SERVANT.

175. WHETHER the entire WORK of a HOUSEHOLD can be efficiently performed with one servant, is a question very frequently discussed, and one that often gives rise to a very considerable diversity of opinion. Our own judgment—deduced from long experience—is, that it can be done. That a methodical, considerate mistress,

thoroughly acquainted herself with household affairs, can, with one active, intelligent, and obliging servant, manage her establishment both comfortably and creditably ; that she can have a clean and neat house, and well-cooked meals punctually served at regular hours, without being herself a " household drudge.' We believe that uncleanliness, untidiness, and waste, with unwholesome food at uncertain intervals—than which there is nothing more trying to the temper and digestion of man—and all the other discomforts and annoyances of an ill-organized household, are no more necessities in a family where only one servant can be afforded, than in one that is served by a whole retinue of domestics.

176. The following account of the daily work of a general servant, which we make as accurate and minute as possible, shows how a household can be managed with one servant ; we trust that it may prove useful to mistress and maid ; more particularly in those cases where, from want of an early training, or from having but recently entered on those duties and responsibilities, the mistress does not possess the knowledge required for ordering her household.

THE DIVISION OF LABOUR

177. Is a most important part of household economy. A mistress can assist her servant in her work, and lighten it for her, without having to perform offices uncongenial and distasteful to a woman of education and refinement. In order to explain these relative duties in the most clear and comprehensive manner possible, we give an outline of the servant's work in the order in which it is necessary and most convenient that she should perform it, followed by an outline of the share of the domestic duty which falls most pleasantly and naturally to the mistress, concluding with tried methods of " the best mode of doing things."

THE SERVANT.

178. Early rising is a most essential point ; therefore, as a rule, six, summer and winter, is the hour at which to rise. The morning work, with fires and extra boot-cleaning, is heavier in winter than in summer ; therefore at that season the maid can less afford to lie late in bed.

179. On coming downstairs she should open all the shutters, and, if the weather be fine, the windows of all the lower rooms.

180. She should then go to the kitchen, and having cleared out the remains or the fire of the night before, and brushed up, blacked, and brightened the range, she should proceed—

TO LIGHT THE KITCHEN FIRE.

181. She will then go on—

TO SWEEP THE BREAKFAST-ROOM.

To Sweep the Breakfast-Room.

182. Having laid down a coarse cloth over the carpet in front of the fireplace, she will first clear away all the cinders and ashes from the grate, putting them in the cinder-pail. This is a japanned tin pail, with a wire sifter inside and a closely fitting top. In this the cinders are sifted, and reserved for use in the kitchen or for the copper-fire, the ashes alone being thrown away. She will then blacklead the grate, first laying on the blacklead with a soft brush, then brushing it vigorously with a hard one, finishing it off with a polishing brush. No blacklead is to be put upon any portions of the grate that may be of polished steel ; these should be rubbed with a clean dry leather and putty powder. If any spots of rust appear, a paste made of fresh lime and oil should be at once applied, and renewed until it has disappeared ; the fire-irons are to be cleaned in the same way if bright, and then rubbed with the leather ; all the bright-steel portions of the fender should be rubbed with the leather ; emery-paper must on no account be used to bright steel.

183. She will then light the fire. Fire-lighting, however simple, is an operation requiring some skill. A fire is readily made by laying a few cinders at the bottom in open order ; over this a few pieces of paper, and over that again eight or ten pieces of dry wood ; over the wood, a course of moderate-sized pieces of coal, taking care to leave hollow spaces between for air at the centre, and taking care to lay the whole well back in the grate, so that the smoke may go up the chimney and not into the room. This done, fire the paper with a match from below, and, if properly laid, it will soon burn up ; the stream of flame from the wood and paper soon communicating to the coals and cinders, provided there is plenty of air at the centre.

184. A new method of lighting a fire is sometimes practised with advantage, the fire lighting from the top and burning down, in place of being lighted and burning up from below. This is arranged by laying the coals at the bottom, mixed with a few good-sized cinders, and the wood at the top, with another layer of coals and some paper over it ; the paper is lighted in the usual way, and soon burns down to a good fire, with some economy of fuel, it is said.

185. That being done, she will clean the hearthstone, bringing up for the purpose a small pail of hot water, a house-flannel, and piece of hearthstone. Having well washed the hearthstone, she will whiten it by rubbing it while wet with the hearthstone ; but in doing this she must be very careful to let none of the water touch the grate, fender, or fire-irons. Then, having removed all her brushes and boxes, the dust-pan, pail, house-flannel, and stone, and having shut the parlour-door, she will sweep the hall, using for it the house-sweeping brush, and not the carpet-broom. She will also sweep the halldoor-steps, and, taking out the door-mats, beat and shake them well.

186. Then she will return to the breakfast-room, where the dust will be by this time settled, and dust it all carefully.

187. In doing this, she will be particular not to omit dusting the legs of the various pieces of furniture, and lifting and dusting under as well as round all the small articles on chimneypiece, sideboard, side-table, and bookshelves, also the window-ledges and sills.

188. She will then arrange the various articles of furniture in their places, replace the rug and fender, and leave the room, shutting the door after her again.

189. BRUNSWICK BLACK.

INGREDIENTS.—1 lb. of common asphaltum, ½ pint of linseed oil, 1 quart of oil of turpentine.

Mode.—Melt the asphaltum, and add gradually to it the other two ingredients. Apply this with a painter's brush, and leave it to become perfectly dry. The grate will need no other cleaning, but will merely require dusting every day, and occasionally brushing with a dry blacklead brush. This is, of course, when no fires are used. When they are required, the bars, cheeks, and back of the grate will need blackleading in the usual manner.

190. POLISH FOR BRIGHT STOVES AND STEEL ARTICLES.

INGREDIENTS.—1 tablespoonful of turpentine, 1 ditto of sweet oil, emery powder.

Mode.—Mix the turpentine and sweet oil together, stirring in sufficient emery powder to make the mixture of the thickness of cream. Put it on the article with a piece of soft flannel, rub off quickly with another piece, then polish with a little emery powder and clean leather.

TO CLEAN BOOTS.

191. She should then clean any boots unavoidably left since the night before; after which, the last of the morning's "dirty work" being done, the servant goes upstairs and knocks at the different bedroom doors to "call" the family, supplying those who require it with warm water, which—not to empty her kettle—she should draw from the boiler, where, by this time, it will be quite warm enough, except for shaving-water, which must be boiling and taken from the kettle. She should then go to her own room, wash her face and hands, brush her hair, and put on a clean cap and apron.

192. Her next work is—

TO LAY THE BREAKFAST-TABLE.

193. The requisites for this for a family of four, will be found on page xlvii. These she should collect on her tray, placing them carefully, the large plates one over another, and the small plates on them; the four saucers one over another, and

two of the cups one within the other on them, the two other cups one within the other in the slop-basin; the tablecloth and napkins are usually kept in the side-board drawer.

194. Having spread the cloth carefully, she should lay at each person's place a large and small knife, a fork, and a large and small plate; the knives are to be at the right hand side of the large plates and close to them, the forks at the left and close too, the small egg-plates next to the forks; the cups and saucers should be ranged together before the mistress's place, the teapot, or coffee-urn, stand behind them, and the slop-basin next to it, the milk-jug and sugar-basin on the other side; the small carving-knife and fork should be put with his own knife and fork at the master's place, and a mat before it for the hot dish, the tablespoon, placed lengthways, in front of that; the teaspoons should be put each in one of the saucers, the egg-spoons each on one of the small plates, and the napkins each on one of the large plates; the cruet-stand in the centre of the table, one of the salt cellars at the right hand top corner, the other at the right hand bottom corner of the table; the dessert-spoon placed on the plate with the marmalade, which will be taken from the cellaret; the butter-knife laid close to the butter-dish, the bread-knife in the bread-platter, the large carving-knife and fork on the side-board.

195. This being done, she will bring up the cold meat, having first put it on a clean dish, and place it on the sideboard; bring up the bread in the bread-basket or on the bread-platter, which should be clean and white, and place it at the side of the table and the butter in the butter-dish, where the mistress will put the sugar-basin when she takes it from the cellaret. Should there be a portion of a loaf of bread cut the day before, that should be brought up; but unless it be more than half a loaf, an entire one should be brought up also. About a quarter of a pound of butter will be sufficient, and half a pint of milk.

196. She will then go to the kitchen to—

GET THE BREAKFAST READY.

197. The kettle being boiling, she will move it a little to the side—still keeping it boiling—to make room for the pan or gridiron. Having put down the rashers of bacon, or whatever other/meat is to be cooked for breakfast, and put a dish and four plates into the oven to warm, she may, while attending to the meat, make, if any of the family require it, two or three rounds of thin toast, which, as soon as each one is finished, should be placed in the toast-rack. The meat being cooked, it should be put on the hot dish, and covered close to keep warm.

198. The mistress will then be down to take out the tea and sugar from the cellaret, and the servant having brought down the tea, will make it, first rinsing the teapot with boiling water.

199. Most mistresses prefer to make both tea and coffee; for this purpose an urn is used in summer, and the bright copper kettle in winter.

200. While the tea is drawing, she will boil the eggs. These being done and placed in the egg-cups, she will put them on a dish and the dish on her tray; she will put on it also the teapot, the dish of hot meat, and the hot plates, and take all to the breakfast-room; she will place the teapot on the stand before her mistress, the dish on the mat before her master, the plates also before him, the eggs at the side; she will then wait a few moments in the room to hand the plates. All this, if done in the above order and quickly, without *dawdling*, can be accomplished by eight o'clock, winter or summer. While the family are at their breakfast, she should take her own; and then, immediately she is done, she should go upstairs and open all the bedroom windows, and turn down the beds to air.

201. When the family have finished breakfast, she should first clear away the breakfast things, then take up the crumbs in the dustpan, arrange the chairs in their places, and sweep up the hearth. Where but one servant is kept, and in a town house, it is better immediately after breakfast to attend to *downstair* work, rather than go to make up the bedrooms. For, as between nine and ten o'clock is the usual hour for the tradespeople to call, the continued running up and down stairs to attend to them, if she be engaged in the upper part of the house, besides being a severe tax upon her strength, greatly retards a servant in work. The unavoidable delays, too, which it occasions in attending to them, is a considerable trial to the patience of the butcher and greengrocer, who are also trying to get through *their* morning's work as quickly as possible. After breakfast, therefore, the first thing for the general servant to do is to—

WASH UP THE BREAKFAST THINGS.
(See page l.)

202. When all the things are done they should be put instantly by, the plates and dishes in their appointed places on the dresser, the china cups and saucers in the cupboard, the knives in the knife-basket, the silver in the plate-basket, and at once taken up to the dining-room, and placed in the cellaret, and locked in.

203. The servant should then wash down the kitchen-table, empty, wipe out, and put aside the pail, hang up the towels to dry, clean and put aside the egg-saucepan and frying-pan; arrange the kitchen fire, sweep up the hearth, and generally tidy up the kitchen for her mistress's inspection.

204. Then, having washed her hands, she will go upstairs, and proceed—

TO ARRANGE THE BEDROOMS.
(See Housemaid.)

265. The first thing to be done in the rooms is to empty the slops, and for this she should take with her the slop-pail, a jug of boiling water, and two slop-cloths.

266. She should then lightly sweep up into her dustpan any fluff, scraps of paper, &c., that may be about the floor ; straighten the carpet, if only side strips are used, and arrange any of the furniture that may be out of its proper place. Then dust the room thoroughly, lifting all the things from the dressing-table and chimney-piece and wiping each, dusting the looking-glass back and front, and removing, by rubbing, any spots that may appear on the plate. She should also dust the top and front of the chest of drawers, the front of the wardrobe, the sills and ledges of the windows and the door. She should then fill the water-jugs with soft and the bottles with clean cold water. Having completely finished one room, she should proceed to the next, and so through them all ; and when all are done, she should take downstairs all the candlesticks and hot-water jugs. Besides this ordinary cleaning, each bedroom in the house should get a thorough cleaning once a week ; and they should be taken in regular rotation with the other work. Thus the following is a good division :—

207. THE WEEK'S WORK OF AN EIGHT-ROOMED HOUSE.

Monday—Large bed- and dressing-room.
Tuesday—Second large bedroom, or two small.
Wednesday—Dining-room and breakfast-room.
Thursday—Two smaller bedrooms.
Friday—Drawing-room.
Saturday—Hall, kitchen, basement.

208. Also, if not carpeted all over, each bedroom should be scoured out once a fortnight.

209. Supposing, then, that it is Monday, and that one of the large bedrooms is to be scoured, she will, after having arranged the three others in the ordinary way, proceed to—

THOROUGHLY CLEAN A BEDROOM.

210. For this she will first require a sweeping-brush, dustpan, and some moist tea-leaves, a furniture-brush, and duster.

211. Her first work will be to remove all the mattresses from the beds and brush them with the furniture-brush, and to dust thoroughly all the joints and crevices of the bedstead.

212. She will then make the bed, proceeding as before directed, except that she

will put on clean sheets, bolster and pillow cases; will fold up the counterpane over the side of the bed, and pin up the curtains as high as she can ; also pin up the valance of the bed, and spread over all a large dusting-sheet.

213. She will then remove from the room all the dressing-table apparatus, all small ornamental articles, the towels and sponges, and any clothes that may be hanging on pegs ; she will put the soiled sheets, bolster and pillow cases, window-blind and toilet-cover into the clothes-basket, remove the fender and fire-irons, and roll up and remove the strips of carpets and the hearth-rug.

214. She will then sprinkle the tea-leaves over the floor, and sweep the room, beginning at the door, going into all the corners, and bringing the dust to the hearthstone, where she will collect it in the dustpan.

215. She will then brush down the walls, for this purpose using the cornice-brush, or tying a clean duster over the sweeping-brush, and being careful to remove any cobwebs from the cornice and ceiling.

216. She will then take the sweeping-brush and dustpan downstairs and bring up the housemaid's box with the blacklead-brushes, &c., for cleaning the grate ; also a small pail and bowl, a can of hot water, a house-flannel and hearthstone, a piece of soap, a clean small flannel, and a clean glass-cloth.

217. She will then clean the grate, fender, fire-irons, and hearthstone, in the same manner and rotation as she did those of the breakfast-parlour.

218. She will then dust the room, doing it very thoroughly, not flapping and slapping the duster about, but wiping carefully with it the dust off the furniture, window-sills and ledges, the door, and wainscot.

219. Then she will wash with warm water and soap all the china on the wash-stand, rinsing it afterwards with cold water and wiping it dry with the cloth for that purpose ; then wash the water-carafe and tumbler with warm water and soap, or a bit of soda, rinsing them very thoroughly afterwards with cold water, and rubbing them dry with the glass-cloth ; then, also with warm water and soap, she will wash the top of the stand if it be of marble, using for this purpose the small flannel.

220. She will then wash, also with soap and warm water and flannel, the china handles and plates of the door. If any part of the paint is dirty, it should be washed, too, but very carefully, and with cold water, or the paint will be injured.

221. To do this properly she will require pieces of stiff cardboard cut to fit

To Scour the Bedroom.

closely round the handle and door-plate; these are held in place while the washing and drying is done, and prevent the paint from being worn away.

222. TO CLEAN MARBLE.

Mix with ¼ pint of soap-lees, ½ gill of turpentine, sufficient pipe-clay and bullocks' gall to make the whole into a rather thick paste. Apply it to the marble with a soft brush, and after a day or two, when quite dry, rub it off with a soft rag. Apply this a second or third time, till the marble is quite clean.

223. *Another Method.*—Take two parts of soda, one of pumice-stone, and one of finely-powdered chalk. Sift these through a fine sieve, and mix them into a paste with water. Rub this well over the marble, and the stains will be removed: then wash it with soap and water, and a beautiful bright polish will be produced.

224. She will then wash with soap and *warm* water if it be summer, but *cold* water if it be frosty winter weather, the window-panes, as much as she can get at without going outside. The warm soap and water should be applied first briskly with the flannel; the glass should then be rinsed down with cold water, and dried and polished off afterwards with clean, dry cloths. For the rinsing, a sponge will be found very useful. The window-sills, if dirty, should also be washed, but, like the door, gently, for fear of injuring the paint.

225. For all these purposes she will use the small bowl, which she can empty into the pail, and refill from the can as often as required.

226. TO CLEAN WINDOWS.

(*French Mode.*)

With a clean washleather, kept for the purpose alone, wash down the window with clean cold water, moving the leather one way only (downwards); rinse in clean water, and repeat with the wrung-out leather. Wash all the windows in this way both inside and out, and leave them to dry. *Note.*—This plan should not be used in a dusty thoroughfare, or when the sun shines hotly on the window

227. All this work being finished, and having taken downstairs her pail, bowl, can, housemaid's box, stone, soap, cloths, flannels, &c., she will next proceed to—

SCOUR THE BEDROOM.

228. For this, if the room be scoured regularly once a fortnight, she will require nothing more than plenty of clean cold soft water, a good scrubbing-brush, and a house-flannel. Having scrubbed well with the brush, and plenty of water, a portion as far as her arm will reach, she should dry it off with the flannel before

moving to do another portion, and she must be careful not to omit scrubbing equally all the floor, else it will have a patchy appearance afterwards, some portions being whiter than others. She should also empty her pail and refill it with clean water very frequently.

229. But if the boards have not been washed for a long time, and are really dirty, soap and sand must be used and the water must be changed very frequently.

230. The following is a very good recipe—

TO WHITEN BOARDS THAT HAVE BEEN NEGLECTED.

231. ¼ lb. lime, ½ lb. washing soda, 1 quart boiling water. Mix all together, and leave until cold. Then drain off the water, and use the sediment instead of soap.

232. In scrubbing a room, the servant should begin with the part most remote from the door, and scrub regularly to the door. It should be done as quickly as possible, and when finished the windows and door should be set wide open, so as to allow a good current of air to pass through the room and dry the boards. In winter a fire ought to be lighted. A bedroom should never be scoured in wet, or even damp, weather. When the room is thoroughly dry, she will replace the carpets, after well shaking or beating them, bring back the towels, sponges, clothes, ornaments, &c., which she had removed, and arrange them all in their places ; rub and polish the furniture, remove the dusting-sheet from the bed, let down the valance, counterpane, and curtains, and put on a clean toilet-cover, and put up clean muslin blinds.

233. We have thus given a description of the thorough cleaning of a bedroom, so that, when necessary, the general servant will know how to do everything that is requisite to be done : but in many houses the bedrooms are carpeted all over, and are, therefore, only scoured once or twice a year, when the carpets are taken up. Also, in very few families where but one servant is kept, are the bed-linen, blinds, and toilet-covers changed so often as once a week.

234. The bedrooms being all finished, the servant will dust down the banisters, rubbing the handrail well. She will also dust the closet and the lobby windows, the sills, and ledges.

235. But, on a day when a bedroom is being thoroughly cleaned out, these duties need not be deferred until the bedroom is quite completed. While the dust is settling in the room after the sweeping, and before the dusting, is a good time to do the stairs, &c.

236. At twelve o'clock the maid must peel and put in the potatoes for her own dinner, and for the children's dinner or mistress's lunch.

To Get the Dinner Ready.

237. The morning housework being completed with the drawing-room, the servant will now

TAKE UP THE LUNCHEON.

238. The things required for this will depend upon the nature of the meal. If tea or coffee is used, cups and saucers must be taken up. Cold meat must be placed on a clean dish, and plates, besides the small breakfast-plates, supplied for it. Also large knives and forks, and a carving knife and fork, tumblers and wine-glasses, and a sufficient number of articles, whatever be the kind used, must be provided for the number of people as at breakfast : if four people, four of everything. The table will be laid the same as at breakfast, only that, if there are but one or two ladies for luncheon, it will be sufficient to lay the cloth over half the table only.

239. While the family are at luncheon she should take her own dinner, then remove and wash up the things.

240. After this she should take out a sufficient supply of coals for the rest of the day ; when, all dirty work being over, she should go up and dress herself for the afternoon. From this time (about two o'clock) until four she may occupy herself with starching, sprinkling, and folding, or ironing, any things of her own or her mistress's that go in the week's home wash, which she can do, and keep herself clean and tidy at the same time to attend the hall-door during this the usual visiting hour. We may here remark that no washing should be done by a general servant when it is possible to put it out. The afternoons in the week that she has not got this to do she should give to needlework, making, mending, and keeping her own clothes in order. If six be the dinner-hour, at four she will begin to—

GET THE DINNER READY.

241. However, if a large joint has to be roasted, she would have to begin her preparations earlier. For example, an 8-lb. leg of mutton would take from a quarter before four ; but if the dinner were to consist of cold meat, fried fish, and soup, perhaps made the day before, if she set to work at half-past four she would have ample time for all preparations. This part of a servant's business, however, varies so much with each day's dinner, that it is impossible to lay down any exact rule to be precisely followed each day; but when a servant knows from experience the length of time it will take her to prepare a number of dishes of certain kinds, she should always commence sufficiently early to allow herself that length of time, and not try and cheat herself into the belief that she can do it equally well in half. If a shoulder of mutton weighing 7 lb., gravy soup, an apple-tart, mashed turnips and potatoes are ordered for dinner at four o'clock, she should put down the joint, then she should make the tart (putting it in a cool place afterwards), then lay the cloth for dinner, then put

in the turnips, then the potatoes, then put the tart in the oven. While the turnips and potatoes are boiling she should clear the soup, and add the vegetables thereto. At a quarter to six she should take up the turnips, and, if quite tender, mash them, adding the butter and pepper and salt; put them back in the saucepan, and place it at the side of the fire to keep warm. The gravy for the mutton should then be prepared. At six precisely the soup should be served, and, having handed round the potatoes, the servant should return to the kitchen and dish the mutton and vegetables, which she will get done just by the time the family are ready for them. By following this course she will be able to serve all her dinner punctually and satisfactorily.

242. TO LAY THE DINNER-TABLE.

(See page lviii.)

243. Everything should be as clean as possible. The bread-plates free from crumbs, the butter-dish unsmeared with butter, the salt-cellars bright and filled with fine salt, the cruet-stand quite bright and clean, the mustard-pot half filled with fresh mustard, the vinegar-bottle filled with vinegar, and the other bottles with whatever sauces may be used. If dessert and wine be taken, the dessert will be placed down the middle of the table, in which case the cruet-stand will be put on the sideboard, and a vase of flowers substituted for it on the table. The wine will be placed at the corners of the table, inside the salt-cellars and table-spoons; if there are but two decanters one will be placed at the right hand top corner and one at the right hand bottom corner.

244. When dessert and wine are used, four dessert plates and four dessert knives will have to be brought up and placed on the sideboard. Four additional table-spoons will also have to be put on the table at the other corners. Each person must have as many glasses as there are different kinds of wines. If only sherry and claret, a sherry and claret glass to each person; if sherry, claret, and port, a sherry glass, claret glass, and port glass to each person.

245. If nuts in the shells form part of the dessert, a pair of nut-crackers should be placed on each dish of nuts.

246. If the servant adopts a particular system in bringing up and laying all these various things, and adheres to it regularly each day, she will find that it may all be accomplished in a very short space of time, and nothing be forgotten.

247. The table laid and the cooking completed, her next work will be to—

DISH UP THE DINNER.

248. Five minutes before beginning this she should put four soup-plates in the oven, or in the plate-warmer if there be one, to warm.

To Dish up the Dinner.

249. She should first rinse out the soup-tureen with hot water to warm it, then place it on the table. Then take the digester from the fire, remove the cover carefully, and pour the soup *quickly* from it into the tureen. It should be done at once, not allowing the soup to dribble at all over the side of the digester. She should then put aside the digester, and examine the soup carefully; if there be the slightest sign of grease floating on it or any black that may have got accidentally from the side or cover of the digester, it should be instantly removed with a spoon or piece of clean blotting-paper.

250. She should then put the cover on the tureen, place the tureen on its dish, carry it upstairs, and put it on the table, at the head.

251. She should then take up the plates, and having announced to the family that dinner is served, should wait in the room to hand round the soups, then return to the kitchen.

252. She should then put four plates, a large dish, and two vegetable dishes to warm.

253. The dish being hot she should wipe it, take the mutton from the spit and place it on it, carefully examining the meat and removing any small cinder that might happen to have flown from the fire on it. She should pour the gravy round the meat—not over it—then cover it.

254. She should then dish the potatoes, taking them carefully one by one with a spoon from saucepan or steamer, not shaking them all out together.

255. Then dish the mashed turnips; these *should* be turned out altogether from the saucepan, as taking them up in spoonfuls would cool them.

256. She should then take up the meat and plates (having first wiped them), and place them on the tray outside the door. Then when the bell rings she should remove the soup, soup-plates, under-plates, and spoons, and put on the meat and plates for that both before her master, she should then return to the kitchen, bring up the potatoes and turnips, and place them on the table, one dish on each side.

257. She should, having waited in the room to hand the plates and vegetables, return to the kitchen, taking with her the soup-tureen. While the family are partaking of the meal she should put four plates to warm, for the tart. She may also bring down the soup-plates and spoons, and wash up them and the tureen while waiting.

258. When she removes the tart from the oven, she should place it on a clean dish. Before taking up this and the plates for it, she should remove the meat, plates, and vegetables.

259. Having placed it on the table, and also the sifted sugar, she should wait in the room to hand about the plates ; then return to the kitchen, taking some of the things from the tray with her, and continue her washing up.

260. Having removed the tart she should take that and the meat to the pantry : the latter should be placed on a clean, cold dish, and the gravy put aside in a basin. She should then also remove all the rest of the things, taking the bread, butter, and cheese to the pantry, and all the used plates, dishes, knives, forks, spoons, and glasses to the kitchen.

261. She should perform this work of removing as quietly and noiselessly as possible, following, as in the laying, a regular system.

262. She should first remove the dish, then the plates, and collecting the knives, forks, and spoons, in a basket, or putting them all together on the tray, the plates piled one upon another on the tray ; but she should never attempt to pile the plates with the knives, forks, and spoons on them. She should remove the glasses carefully, not clashing them together. Dinner being removed, she should then remove the crumbs with the brush for that purpose, fold the cloth neatly, and proceed—

TO WASH UP THE DINNER THINGS.

263. But this, as we have shown, she may have commenced beforehand.

264. She should have a large tub of hot water and a couple of good dry rubbers for the greasy plates and dishes. She should wash them first very thoroughly, and wipe them well dry. Then the knives : she should hold the blades in the water, not letting it touch the handle, and should wipe them quite dry. Then the silver spoons, for which she should take some fresh hot water ; after being washed and wiped they should be rubbed well with a very dry soft cloth.

265. The glasses must not be washed in the same pail used for the greasy things ; she should have another pail for them, with some warm, not hot, water. They should be washed first and left to drain, then dried quickly with a fine dry linen glass-cloth.

266. When all the things are washed, they should be put by in their proper places, and the towels used hung up to dry.

267. Then having put the kettle on to boil, she should go to the scullery and clean up all the pots, pans, and saucepans, the roaster, and whatever else was used in cooking the dinner, and clean the knives. This last will be but little trouble if a knife-cleaner is used. She should then clean any boots and shoes dry enough to be done ; take out a sufficient supply of coals for next morning's fires. She should

To Wash up the Dinner Things.

then tidy up her kitchen, and having resumed her white apron, which she will have exchanged for a common coarse one while doing the dirty work, she will take up the tray for tea, or coffee, or whatever else the family may be in the habit of taking in the evening. She should also take up the chamber candlesticks and leave them in the hall.

268. It will now be about half-past eight, and occasionally she may ask leave to go out for an hour, or possibly her master or mistress may send her out on some errand; if the evening be fine, a short walk in the fresh air will refresh and invigorate her.

269. Having removed the tea-tray and washed up the things used, she should go up to the bedrooms, taking with her the slop-pail and a large can of clean cold water. Having emptied the slops and refilled any jugs and bottles that may require it, she should turn down the beds. In doing this she should first fold back the small portion of the sheet that is in excess of length of the other clothes, then turn back all together, but not bringing them down farther than to expose the bolster and pillows. She should then let down the curtains at each side of the bed.

270. She should also close any windows that may be open and hasp them, draw down the blinds, and shut the shutters, or draw the window curtains, according as the people to occupy the room desire.

271. Having come downstairs again, she should empty the slop-pail, rinse it, wipe it dry, and set it aside.

272. She should then lock all the lower doors and turn off the kitchen gas, and having taken up the keys and the plate to her mistress, she should go to bed.

273. This, except on rare occasions of late company, she ought not to delay, if she can help, later than ten o'clock. If her master and mistress do not require her to sit up, she should never loiter about. Plenty of sleep is absolutely necessary for any one who daily undergoes hard bodily labour; and this a general servant who rises at six cannot have unless she goes to bed at ten o'clock.

274. The daily routine of a general servant's work, of course, to a certain extent, must vary, no one day being exactly the same as the one before or the one to come after.

275. For instance, in the day described, we have given for afternoon work starching or ironing; but another afternoon it would be rubbing plate, cleaning brass candlesticks, cleaning lamps, gaselier shades, &c.

276. Washing should be done in the forenoon ; but supposing that one bedroom is scoured every week, the servant should never attempt washing on the same day.

277. Sweeping the stairs should be done on one of the bedroom cleaning days, but *not* on the bedroom *scouring* day.

278. Cleaning the doorsteps should be daily work. They should be done in the morning before breakfast, if possible ; if not, immediately after the bedrooms are done up, and before putting on the luncheon.

279. In all washing up, scouring, &c., the servant should never grudge herself plenty of clean water and clean cloths ; it saves trouble in the end, for it is impossible to make things look clean with dirty cloths and water.

280. ROUTINE OF HOUSE-WORK FOR TWO SERVANTS.

Where two servants, housemaid and cook, are kept,

281. To get through the work in a regular and orderly manner, such as will give satisfaction to the mistress, it is necessary that the cook and housemaid should divide it judiciously between them, certain duties being taken entirely by the one, and certain other duties by the other ; so that when anything is to be done, it may always be definitely understood who is to do it.

282. To show how it may best be divided, the following outline of one day's work in a house assigns to each servant the share of the duties that it is usually most convenient she should take.

283. They should both rise at six o'clock. On coming downstairs the cook should go to the kitchen and lower offices ; the housemaid to the sitting-rooms, to open all the shutters, and if the weather be fine, the windows of the various apartments.

284. She then—

ARRANGES THE BREAKFAST-ROOM,

And gets it ready for the family ; for this she brings upstairs a carpet-broom dustpan, and some damp tea-leaves.

285. She should then first remove the fender and fire-irons, and roll up and remove the rug ; take off the tablecloth, shake and fold it ; also shake and fold any antimacassars that may be in the room, and place all together on the table, which she should cover with a dusting-sheet. She should also cover the sofa, if there be one in the room, and the easy chair, and place the other chairs one

seat upon the other, and get all the furniture as much together and into the middle of the room as possible. She should then, having sprinkled the carpet all over with the tea-leaves—

SWEEP THE ROOM,

Beginning at the door, going into all the corners; when it is swept all round, moving the furniture and sweeping where that stood, and bringing all the dust to the hearthstone, where she should collect it in the dustpan and remove it.

286. She should then shut the door, and while the dust is settling sweep out the hall and down the doorsteps, using for this not the carpet-broom, but the common house-sweeping brush. She should also take out the hall mats and shake them.

287. She should then return to the breakfast-room, bringing with her the housemaid's box, well supplied with brushes, blacklead, emery paper, and leathers. The cinder-pail, a small pail of hot water, a house flannel, a piece of hearthstone, a large coarse cloth, and paper, firewood, coals and matches to light the fire. She should then first lay down the cloth before the fireplace to save the carpet—

CLEAN THE GRATE, FENDER, AND FIRE-IRONS.

288. She should first clear out of the grate all the remains of the fire of the day before, placing the cinders and ashes in the cinder-box.

289. Then blacklead the grate, laying on the black lead with a soft brush, rubbing it off vigorously with a harder one, and finishing it off with a polishing brush. Then rub with a leather all the polished steel portion of the grate, which should not be touched at all with the blacklead or brushes; where any spots appear, rubbing first with the emery paper, and afterwards with the leather. The fender the same way; any portion that is of polished steel being cleaned with emery paper and leather. The fire-irons always with emery paper and leather only.

290. She will then—

LIGHT THE FIRE,

Proceeding in exactly the same manner as the cook does with the kitchen fire. (See page xlviii.) Then—

WASH THE HEARTHSTONE,

Washing it very thoroughly, rinsing it quite free from all dirt and black;

then, while wet, she should rub it well all over with the hearthstone, but in doing this she must be very careful to let none of the water or stone touch the grate, fender, or fire-irons.

291. She should then remove to the scullery all the tools and utensils she used for the grate and fire, and, bringing up a clean duster, she should thoroughly—

DUST THE BREAKFAST PARLOUR.

292. In doing this, she should go over every article carefully, not flapping the duster about, but *wiping* the dust off with it. She should go over the backs and legs of the various pieces of furniture, and should lift every small article from chimney-piece and sideboard, and dust under them. She should also dust round the cornice of the room, dust the door and the window-panes, sills, and ledges.

293. She should then rearrange the furniture all in its proper place, and everything being in order, she should leave the room, shutting the door after her.

294. She should then—

CLEAN THE LADIES' BOOTS AND SHOES.

295. Except in the case of very stout common leather boots, which some ladies use in the country in bad weather, or very old kid boots, ladies' boots must not be touched with blacking. If the soles are very muddy, they must be scraped round with an old knife, great care being taken not to touch the uppers, nor to do more to the soles than take the mud off, the leather itself must not be scraped. The mud off the uppers should be removed with a sponge dipped in milk. When boots are not actually muddy, it will be sufficient to go round the edges of the soles with a very soft brush, and to wipe the uppers gently with a flannel. When boots become old and discoloured, the "Kid Reviver" that most bootmakers sell is better to use than common blacking. It is laid on with a sponge, and left to dry, no brushing or polishing is necessary. Their morning's "dirty work" being then concluded, the servants should go to their own room, wash their faces and hands, arrange their hair, and put on clean caps and aprons. Having washed her hands, the housemaid will then go upstairs and knock at the different chamber-doors to arouse the family, supplying each room with warm water, and leaving the boots and shoes outside the doors of their wearers. Then—

THE HOUSEMAID LAYS THE BREAKFAST-TABLE.

296. The laying of the breakfast-table will vary according to the number of the

---

family. In the present instance we will suppose it to be four, therefore she will first collect on her tray and take upstairs—

The tablecloth.	4 Forks.
4 Napkins.	1 Large carving knife and fork.
4 Breakfast cups and saucers.	1 Smaller carving knife and fork.
4 Large plates.	4 Teaspoons.
4 Smaller plates.	1 Dessert-spoon.
The teapot-stand.	The cruet-stand.
4 Large knives.	2 Salt-cellars.
4 Small knives.	2 Pairs of knife-rests.
The bread-knife.	The slop-basin.
The butter-knife.	

In placing these on the tray, she should be careful to let the tablecloth and napkins intervene between the china and the other things. She should place the tray on the stand outside the parlour-door, putting it in a convenient position so that she can easily pass in and out. She should first spread the cloth, doing it very carefully so as to avoid creasing it, keeping it quite straight, and an equal length hanging down at each end and at the sides.

297. She should then place at the head of the table—the mistress's place—the teapot-stand. In front of that the cups and saucers, arranged in a double row, room being left between them and the edge of the table for the mistress's plate. Then the slop-basin at the left-hand side of the cups and saucers. The smaller plates should then be put round the table, one at each person's place, a napkin on each; they should be near the edge, but not near enough to be in danger of falling off. One large and one small knife should be put at the right hand side of each plate, a fork at the left hand side. The small carving knife and fork should be put at the foot of the table—the master's place; next his own knife and fork; one pair of rests in front of them. The large carving knife and fork should be put on the sideboard with the other rests, the four large plates should be put there also. The cruet-stand should be placed in the centre of the table; the bread-knife at one side, the butter-knife at the other; one salt-cellar at the right-hand top corner, the other at the right-hand bottom corner; the dessert-spoon should be placed on the plate with the marmalade or honey when it is taken from the cellaret. A table-mat should be placed before the master's place.

298. All these things should be scrupulously clean and free from dust; the mustard-pot should be half-filled with fresh mustard, and the salt-cellars supplied with fine table-salt.

299. Having put all these things on, she should fetch up from the pantry—

The cold meat—on a clean dish,
The bread on the bread-plate or in the bread-basket,
The butter in the butter-dish,
The milk in the milk-jug,
The cream in the cream-ewer.

300. The bread-basket should be free from crusts and crumbs, and there should not be less than a loaf; 3 oz. of butter, nicely rolled in pats, will be sufficient, and half a pint of milk.

301. The milk and cream should be placed at the right-hand side of the breakfast-cups, where the sugar-basin will be placed also when it is taken from the cellaret. The bread should be at the side of the table where the bread-knife was placed, the butter where the butter-knife. The cold meat should be put on the sideboard.

302. Whilst the housemaid is thus engaged—

THE COOK LIGHTS THE KITCHEN FIRE.

303. She should first clean out of the fireplace the remains of the fire of the night before, then thoroughly brush all the range. For lighting the fire she will require some paper, a dozen sticks of firewood, a few lumps of round coal, some good cinders, and a few matches. She should first place the paper at the bottom of the grate, but to the front near the bars; then most of the firewood, the sticks placed lengthways, one end resting on the second bar, the other at the back of the bottom of the grate, leaving a little space between each. She should then strike a match and set fire to the paper, and as it blazes up, and the wood catches, she should put on the coals and cinders lightly, and the rest of the sticks among them. If the paper burns away before the sticks have caught, she should replace it with some more paper; but when the sticks have caught with a few of the coals and cinders, then as the fire lights up it will not sink.

304. The fire being lighted, the cook should clear away all the ashes and cinders, rub up with a leather the bright parts of the range, and wash the hearth; when washed quite clean, but while it is still wet, she should rub it with a piece of hearthstone to whiten it, and place the kettle, filled with water, on the fire to boil. She should then thoroughly dust the kitchen, and put everything straight and in order; and having removed to the scullery the brushes, the leather, the blacklead, the pail, flannel, brick, and whatever else she may have used with the fireplace, she should—

CLEAN THE GENTLEMEN'S BOOTS AND SHOES.

305. For this she will require some blacking and three brushes—one hard, one soft, and one medium. She should first, with the hard brush, brush off the mud—but if the boots be very muddy she must scrape it off with an old knife round the edges of the soles, being very careful, however, not to touch the upper leather—then with the soft brush lay on the blacking, and when that has dried on the boot polish it off with the medium brush. Each of the brushes should be used for its own particular purpose only. The cook then washes her hands, and proceeds to

xlix

the hall, where she fastens the front door open, removes all coats, hats, umbrellas, and sweeps down the hall, collecting all the dust and dirt into her pan with the banister broom. If the hall be dirty, she removes all marks with a piece of flannel wrung out in warm water and polishes with another piece dipped in milk. Twice a week the hall is washed down as follows :—

TO CLEAN A HALL.

306. Thoroughly wash off the dirt with flannel and warm, not hot, water; re dry with a cloth as you go ; and when all is finished, rub lightly with the oilcloth restorer (page lxiv), or with new milk, and brighten it. By using the simple restorer, an oilcloth may be preserved for a dozen years " as good as new."

307. Having cleaned the hall, she will dust the chairs and hat-stand and pegs, and return the coats and hats to their places, receiving them from the housemaid, who will have brushed them carefully downstairs. The cook beats the mat in the garden or street, and returns it to its place. She will next—

CLEAN THE STEPS.

308. Scrubbing-brush, clean warm water, flannel, and hearthstone. She should first scrub the steps down, then dry off with the flannel, and while wet rub in the hearthstone. Some steps are whitened by a composition of pipeclay and water made into a thin paste, and laid on with a brush. This is an admirable white, but has the disadvantages of marking dresses, &c.

309. The scraper in country houses is taken indoors and cleaned, but when a fixture, as in London houses, the dirt must be removed daily, and the scraper washed and kept bright. After the steps, hall-door, &c., are cleaned—

THE COOK GETS THE BREAKFAST READY.

310. When the kettle boils, she should move it aside, to make room for the pan or gridiron, still keeping it boiling, however. If she have an omelette to make, or fish, or cutlets to be prepared with eggs and breadcrumbs, they will have her first attention. If both fried fish and fried meat are wanted for breakfast, the fish should be done first, then covered close and kept warm while the meat is being cooked, not using the same pan. However, if the meat were only for one—such as a chop or a rasher of bacon—it might be done in a gridiron in front of the fire, while the fish or omelette was being fried on the top.

311. While the cooking is going on, she should put four plates to warm. She should also make some pieces of nice thin toast, and place them in the toast-rack.

312. When the pan is removed from the fire, she should boil the eggs, first

d

putting four egg-cups to warm ; she should also make the tea—if that be done in the kitchen; if an urn is used, she should fill that and send it up to the breakfast-parlour by the housemaid, when the mistress will make it herself.

313. She will then place on a tray the hot dish, the eggs in the egg-cups on a dish with four egg-spoons, the toast and the teapot, and give it to the housemaid, who will take it to the breakfast-parlour.

314. The housemaid will wait a few moments in the parlour to hand the plates, &c. ; after that—

THE COOK ATTENDS THE BREAKFAST-PARLOUR,

while—

THE HOUSEMAID GOES TO THE BEDROOMS,

to open all the windows and turn down the beds.

315. She should open out and separate all the bedclothes, placing them over the ends of the bedsteads and the backs of the chairs to air. Then, while the family are finishing breakfast, the servants should take theirs ; and both parlour and kitchen breakfasts being concluded—

THE COOK WILL REMOVE THE BREAKFAST THINGS.

After which, she should bring up a hand-brush and dustpan, and sweep up the crumbs. She should also arrange the fire, sweep up the hearth, and put the chairs in their places. She will then—

WASH UP THE BREAKFAST THINGS.

316. For this she will require a pail of hot water, two tea-towels, and a coarse dish-cloth. These latter should be all quite clean and dry. She should first remove the tea-leaves from the teapot, and put them aside carefully for sweeping. She should then rinse out the teapot, if it be of metal, and put it aside to be rubbed up with the rest of the plate ; if it be china, it should be rinsed both outside and inside, and left to drain.

317. Then wash the cups and saucers and all the rest of the ware, except the greasy plates and dishes, and leave them to drain.

318. Then wash the greasy plates and dishes, adding some fresh hot water to the pail.

319. Then the knives. These should not be dipped entirely into the water. The blades should be held down in it for a short time ; the handles should not

touch it at all. They should be immediately wiped in the coarse cloth, and laid aside to be cleaned.

320. She should then wipe thoroughly dry all the china and ware, using for the cups and saucers the tea-towels only; but the dishes and plates must be wiped first with the coarse towel, and finished off afterwards with the finer one.

321. The silver should be washed in a separate bowl. It should be wiped thoroughly dry, and afterwards be rubbed up with a clean leather. The teapot, if of silver or Britannia metal, should be rubbed up also.

322. All the things being clean, they should be immediately put by—the china and ware in their appointed places on the dresser or in the cupboard, the knives in the knife-box, the silver in the silver-basket, the salt-cellars and cruet-stand wherever they are usually kept, but the sideboard cellaret is the best place. It is a good thing, also, to take the silver up and put it in the sideboard immediately. Then the pails should be emptied and wiped out, and the cloths rinsed and hung up to dry.

323. The cook should then tidy up her kitchen and scullery in readiness for her mistress when she comes down to inspect and give her orders for the day.

324. THE BEDROOMS.

Whilst the cook has been removing the breakfast things and washing them up—

THE HOUSEMAID EMPTIES THE SLOPS.

325. For this she should take upstairs a slop-pail, a can of boiling water, and two slop-cloths.

326. As she empties each vessel she should scald it out, then wipe it perfectly dry. She should empty the tin baths, wipe them very dry, and turn them up on end against the wall. Empty any water that may remain in the water-jugs, bottles, and tumblers, and rinse them out—the bottles and tumblers with tepid water. Rinse out and wipe the soap-dish and the brush-dish; wipe down the tops of the stands, and replace all the things in their proper position. In doing this she must be very particular to use one of the cloths with the washing apparatus only. Having finished this work in one room, she should go to another, and so through them all. She should then take downstairs her slop-pail, water-can, cloths, and hot-water jugs and chamber candlesticks, and then, being joined by the cook, who will have washed her hands and put on a large clean apron for the purpose, they will—

BOTH MAKE THE BEDS

327. Feather-beds and mattresses should be turned every day, the former, also, will require to be well beaten and shaken. They should first seize it firmly by the top corners, and shake the feathers to the bottom. Then take it by the bottom corners and shake the feathers to the top. Then shake them down equally through it all, taking care to break up any lumps. Then, when the feathers are evenly distributed throughout the whole, it should be smoothed down, and the mattress, if it be used, placed on gently and quite evenly.

328. The under blanket comes next. It should come quite down to the bottom of the bed, and be spread smoothly without wrinkles.

329. Then the under sheet. It should be spread quite equally and evenly over the bed, no wrinkle, and should be tucked firmly in all round.

330. Then the bolster. They should first hold it, one at each end, and shake it well; then beat the feathers out equally through the whole, and if the strings or buttons of the case have become undone, re-fasten them.

331. Then the pillows. They should be well shaken and smoothed, and the buttons or strings fastened.

332. Then the upper sheet. This should be drawn up quite to the top of the bed. It should be put on quite evenly, and should be firmly tucked in at the bottom.

333. Then the blankets, one by one. They should be put on—first, at the top, not coming up quite as high as the sheet. They should be spread gently down, taking care not to draw the sheet, and should be tucked in at the bottom of the bed.

334. Then the counterpane should be spread over all very evenly and smoothly. It should not be tucked in, but allowed to hang down on either side.

335. The bed-curtain should then be drawn up to the top, folded, and laid across over the bolster.

336. When one bed is done they should go to the next, and so through them all. When finished, the cook should retire to her downstairs work, while—

THE HOUSEMAID SWEEPS AND DUSTS THE BEDROOMS.

337. It is not necessary to give a thorough sweeping to a bedroom every day. It is enough to lightly brush over the carpets with a hand-broom, collecting the dust as she goes in the dustpan; but she should particularly do so under the

lili

To Thoroughly Clean and Scour a Bedroom.

---

beds, **where** fluff collects the most. Having swept one bedroom, she should **now** dust **it** and finish it off before going to another. She should dust every article in the room carefully. She should remove the looking-glass, bottles, boxes, &c., from the dressing-table, and dust it thoroughly ; and she should carefully dust the looking-glass and other things before replacing them. She should dust each of the chairs, the wardrobe, and chest of drawers, removing any article that may be on the top of the latter, and dusting under them ; the same with the chimney-piece. She must also dust the door and the sills and ledges of the windows. She should then fill all the jugs and bottles with clean cold water, and, having **shut all** the bedroom doors, she should—

SWEEP DOWN THE STAIRS.

338. Which should be done with a hand-broom and dustpan, collecting the dust **as** she goes. When the stairs and closet are swept down she should dust down the banisters, rubbing the handrail well ; also the lobby windows, frames, sills, and ledges ; and the outsides of all the doors, going thoroughly over all the panels.

339. Besides this daily " doing up," every bedroom in a house should get a thorough cleaning once a week ; and, if not carpeted all over, should be scoured once every three weeks.

340. This in a house with four bedrooms—two large and two small—would give one large bedroom to be done on Tuesday, one on Wednesday, and the two small on Thursday. The housemaid would then have Friday for the drawing-room, **and** Saturday for plate-cleaning, lamp-cleaning, &c. If any washing be done at home, Monday is the best day for it, and no other extra work should be done on that day.

341. TO THOROUGHLY CLEAN AND SCOUR A BEDROOM.

The slops **will have** been emptied, of course, but **no other work** done in it previously.

342. Having brought up a furniture dusting brush and a duster, she will begin by removing the bed, mattress, and palliasse from the bedstead. She will then dust the bedstead thoroughly, going into all the joints and crevices ; then brush the mattress. She will then remove the sheets and pillows and bolster-cases, and place them in the soiled-clothes basket, and having replaced the bed, mattresses, bolster, pillows, blankets, and counterpane on the bedstead, but without making the bed, she will cover all with a large dusting-sheet. She will then fold and pin up as high as she can the bed and window curtains, and remove the soiled muslin blinds and toilet cover, and place them in the soiled-clothes basket. She will then remove from the bedroom the towel-stand, all clothes that may be hanging on pegs, the looking-glass and all small ornamental articles from the dressing-

table and chimneypiece. She will also roll up and remove the strips of carpeting and hearth-rug, the fender and fire-irons, and any small portable articles of furniture.

343. Then, having brought up a sweeping-brush, dustpan, and some damp tea-leaves, she will sweep the room, beginning at the door, going into all the corners, and bringing the dust to the hearthstone, from which she will collect and remove it. She should also remove the dustpan and sweeping-brush, and shut the room door.

344. Although on ordinary days the staircase is not swept down until all the bed-rooms are done, on these "thorough cleaning" days it is best to do it immediately after this sweeping, because while the dust is settling there, nothing else can be done in the room.

345. The dust having settled, she should return, bringing with her the housemaid's box, a small pail of hot water, a house-flannel, and piece of Bath brick.

346. She should then clean the grate, proceeding in the same manner as with the breakfast-parlour grate, and wash and whiten the hearthstone.

347. She should then thoroughly dust the room, wiping every article of furniture carefully, wiping down the walls with a clean duster tied over a sweeping-brush, going all round the cornice and over the door. She should also dust the window-panes, sills, and ledges.

348. The dusting being done, she should take downstairs the housemaid's box, the sweeping-brush and dusters, the house-flannel and Bath brick, and bring up a large clean bowl, a can of hot water, a piece of soap, some washing soda, a piece of clean flannel, a sponge, a clean basin-cloth, and a clean linen glass-cloth.

349. She should then thoroughly wash, with soap, soda, and warm water, all the washing-table apparatus, and wipe them thoroughly dry; the water-bottle and tumbler should be wiped with the glass-cloth. She should also wash down the marble top of the washstand with warm soap and water and the flannel.

350. She should then clean the windows.

351. Two leathers, two pails of cold water. Rub the windows up and down with a leather dipped in cold water, until all dirt, dust, and stains have disappeared, then, with a clean leather and fresh water, rub down one way only, and leave the glass to dry.

852. The window-panes being washed, she should wash the sills and ledges.

353. She should also wash the china plates and handles of the door, and any part of the paint that may be dirty; but this, as also the paint of the window-sills and ledges, should be done with *cold* water and soap, and very carefully, or the paint will be injured.

354. In doing all this work, she should frequently empty her bowl into the pail, and refill it with clean water.

355. Her next work, having removed the bowl, cloths, &c., will be to—

SCOUR THE ROOM.

356. Boards that are scoured regularly once every three weeks require nothing more than plenty of clean cold soft water and hard scrubbing with a good scrubbing-brush, to make and keep them a good colour; but if they have been allowed to get very dirty, hot water, soda, and a little soap will be necessary. The house-maid should bring up a good large pail of water, a scrubbing-brush, and a clean house-flannel. She should begin to scour at the end of the room farthest from the door and work towards it. She should first scrub well a portion as far as she can reach kneeling, using plenty of water; then wipe it off dry with the flannel, move a little, and do the next portion; but she should take care to leave not the smallest bit of board unscrubbed or less scrubbed than the rest. If she use soap she must be careful to wash it off well again with the flannel, else the boards will blacken. She should empty her pail and refill it with fresh water very frequently, it will save trouble in the end, for it is impossible to wash anything clean with dirty water.

357. As soon as the room is all scoured out she should open the windows and the door to allow a thorough draught to pass through the room and dry it. In winter a fire should be lighted. But a bedroom should never be scoured in wet or even damp weather.

358. As soon as the room is dry, the cook will come up and assist her to make the bed, on which she will put clean sheets, bolster, and pillow-cases.

359. She will then bring back and lay down the carpets; if possible they should first be shaken. Bring back the fender and fire-irons and all the furniture orna-ments and clothes which she had removed, and rearrange them in their proper places. She should put up clean blinds, put on a clean toilet-cover, and polish the looking-glass; then, having filled the jug and bottle with fresh cold water, the room will be quite finished.

360. TO THOROUGHLY CLEAN THE DRAWING-ROOM.

First remove all furniture to the centre of the room, packing it up carefully and placing all ornaments, pictures, &c., upon the centre table. Cover all with the dusting-sheets. Strew the carpet with well-washed tea-leaves, and sweep as directed on page liv ; dust walls and cornices with the brushes for that purpose ; then clean the grate, hearth, &c., mantelpiece, looking-glasses, and windows ; dust and replace the pictures, washing the frames with *gin*, and rubbing the cords well with a duster. Replace the furniture after well dusting and rubbing it with furniture-polish (page lxiii). Carefully wash or rub the ornaments, and replace them. A large room with much furniture can be cleaned in this manner in from three to four hours by two persons.

361. The cook also, in her department, should have particular days for " thorough cleanings."

362. Thus, Mondays she too gives to the washing. Tuesday she washes the hall. Wednesday, thoroughly cleans the dining-room. Thursday, cleans the front kitchen and scours all the tins. Friday, the back kitchen and pantries ; and Saturday, the hall, the kitchen stairs, and basement passage. Steps every day.

363. Therefore, on Tuesday, while the housemaid is engaged with the bed-rooms,

THE COOK CLEANS THE HALL AND STEPS.

(*See page* xlix.)

364. TO THOROUGHLY CLEAN THE DINING-ROOM,

She should first roll up the rug and remove the fender and fire-irons. Then gather together the furniture in the middle of the room, the chairs turned one upon another, and cover them all with dusting-sheets. She should remove all the plate, &c., from the top of the sideboard, and either put it into the sideboard or remove it from the room. She should then, having first sprinkled the carpet with damp tea-leaves, sweep the room, beginning at the door, going into all the corners, and bringing the dust to the hearthstone, where she should collect it in the dustpan and remove it.

365. She should then clean the grate and hearthstone, bringing up for the purpose the housemaid's box, a pail of hot water, a house-flannel, and hearthstone. She should first lay down a coarse cloth over the carpet in front of the fireplace, and place her utensils upon it. If there are the remains of a fire in the grate, that must be first cleared away and placed in the cinder-box. She should then black-lead the grate, laying it on with a soft brush, rubbing it off with a harder, and

finishing it with a polishing-brush. All the bright polished steel part should be rubbed with emery paper, and afterwards with a leather, as should also be the fire-irons and the steel portion of the fender. In washing the hearthstone she should be very careful not to let any of the water touch the grate; if a fire is to be lighted, that should be done before the washing of the hearthstone.

366. She should then remove all these utensils, and having provided herself with a clean duster and a cornice-broom, she should dust all the room carefully, wiping down the walls, going over all the cornices, and the doors, the window-panes, sills, and ledges. If there are any pictures in the rooms they should be dusted with a light feather-brush, as should the frame of the chimney-glass; the plate should be polished with a clean dry linen cloth. She should then dust all the furniture, and replace the several articles in their proper positions.

367. Her morning's occupation of washing or house-cleaning being over, the cook will probably have to occupy herself with some work in the culinary department, the making of soup, or preparing sweet dishes for the late dinner; or, if there be children in the family who dine early, she will have to get their dinner. At one o'clock, or half-past—

THE HOUSEMAID TAKES UP THE LUNCHEON-TRAY.

368. The children's dinner will be served at the same time. The things to be taken up will depend entirely on the nature of the meal, but for whatever is served there must be a sufficient supply of knives, forks, spoons, plates, glasses, &c., for the number of persons who are to partake of it. While the family are at luncheon the servants will take their dinner. The tray being removed—

THE COOK WASHES UP THE THINGS,

proceeding the same as she did with the breakfast things, while the housemaid goes to her room, changes her morning print dress for a neat stuff, and puts on a clean white apron, cap, collar, and cuffs. She is then ready to open the door for visitors.

369. The afternoon the housemaid will employ, on some days, in starching, wrinkling, or ironing the fine things; on others she may have some house needlework, such as hemming dusters and glass-cloths, or mending stockings, sheets, &c., to do.

370. Before or at four o'clock, the cook will have to set about getting the dinner ready. If the dinner-hour be half-past six or seven, five will be time enough for the housemaid to begin her preparations.

371. She should first clean the knives; this, if done in the patent knife-cleaner,

will be very little trouble, but they should be carefully dusted afterwards. She will then take up the stand, and place it in the hall in a convenient position, then collect on her tray all the things she will require for laying the table.

372. This will, of course, depend upon the nature of the meal and the number of persons to partake of it. Supposing, then, the dinner to consist of soup, fish, a roast joint, potatoes, vegetables, and a sweet dish, and, as at breakfast, four persons to sit down to table, she will require—

4 Knives.	4 Dessert-spoons.
4 Small knives.	4 Tablespoons.
4 Fish knives.	1 Gravy-spoon.
4 Forks.	1 Soup-ladle.
4 Small forks.	4 Plates.
4 Fish forks.	4 Napkins.
1 Carving knife and fork.	2 Salt-cellars.
1 Small knife and fork for cutting the tart.	The cruet-stand.
	The tablecloth.
1 Fish slice.	4 Tumblers.
1 Pair of knife rests.	4 Sherry glasses.
4 Soup-spoons.	4 Claret glasses.

373. She should place the tray on the stand in the hall, or, if the dining-room be large, the stand and tray may be put in a convenient position there, and then proceed to—

LAY THE DINNER-TABLE.

374. She should first spread the cloth, doing it very carefully so as not to crumple or wrinkle it; it should be quite even, an equal length hanging down at the top and bottom of the table and at the sides.

375. She should then put round to each person's place one large, one small, and one fish knife; then one large, one small, and one fish fork; leaving a space between the knives and the forks for the plates, and the knives being at the right hand and the forks at the left of the space. Then the carving knives and forks at the master's place at the head of the table; next his own knives and forks, the rests in front of them. Then a soup-spoon to each person next the knives; the soup-ladle and gravy-spoon at the master's place, lengthways in front of where the dishes will stand; the fish-slice next to the carving-knives, and the four tablespoons crossways at the right-hand corners.

376. Then to each person's place a plate in the space between the knives and the forks—these are to rest the soup-plates upon—and on each plate a napkin neatly folded or else rolled in a ring.

377. Then to each person a tumbler, a sherry glass, and a claret glass. These at the right-hand side, close to the knives, but not too close.

378. Then the cruet-stand in the middle of the table, and the two salt-cellars at the corners between the spoons.

379. Thin table-mats at each place where a dish is to stand.

380. She should then bring up and place on the sideboard the bread on the bread-plate or in the bread-basket. She should cut some up, and place a small piece in the folds of each napkin or beside it.

381. She should also place on the sideboard the bottled ale or stout, if any member of the family is in the habit of partaking of it ; and the corkscrew next. Also a jug of cold water, an empty jug for the table beer, if that be used, and a basin of sifted sugar.

382. If cheese be used, that should be placed on the sideboard, and butter on the butter-dish. For this four additional plates will be required, and four knives, which should be also placed on the sideboard.

383. If dessert is taken, that should be placed on the table down the centre, in which case the cruet-stand will be put on the sideboard. For dessert four dessert plates will be required, and four dessert knives and forks, which should be kept on the sideboard till wanted. The wine should be put on—the sherry at the right-hand top corner, the claret at the right-hand bottom corner, not near the edge of the table, but inside the spoons and salt-cellars.

384. All these things should be scrupulously clean and bright. Before bringing them up the housemaid ought to go over all the glass with a clean linen cloth.

385. While the housemaid lays the table—

THE COOK GETS THE DINNER READY.

386. To send a dinner to table all in nice order and thoroughly well cooked, depends not only on the cook's skill in preparing each particular dish nicely itself, but on her knowledge of how to prepare them all with regard to each other ; many people quite capable of frying a dish of fish, or roasting a joint very well, *by themselves,* would yet make a complete muddle of a dinner of four courses.

387. The first and most important thing is to set about it in time; nothing can be properly done unless sufficient time is taken to do it in. The next is to understand what things in the dinner will bear to be cooked some little time before they are to be eaten without spoiling, and to get them ready first.

388. And as the difficulty of cooking a dinner consists, not so much in the number of dishes as in the way they are to be cooked, if the cook be at all con-sulted by her mistress in the ordering of the dinner, she should take care, above all things, not to have several things to be cooked in the same manner, as, for instance, with soup and boiled fish not to have a boiled joint, and a boiled pudding ; or with fried fish, not to have fried cutlets and a fried omelette. With a small open range it is impossible to boil many things at once, and boiled things—particularly fish and puddings—spoil completely by being cooked sooner than required, if left in the water they get sodden, if dished they get flabby.

389. Supposing a dinner to consist of soup, boiled fish requiring 20 minutes to cook, a piece of roast beef, a baked plum-pudding, potatoes and brocoli. The plum-pudding should be made in the morning ; the soup, except the thickening and adding of wine, sauce, &c., should also be made in the morning.

390. The beef should be put down in time to allow a quarter of an hour to every pound, and a quarter of an hour over; if the dinner-time be half-past six she may calculate to have it done at a quarter to seven ; the fish she should calculate to have done at twenty-five minutes to seven ; the potatoes and brocoli should not be ready until the beef is to be served ; the soup may be drawn aside on the range to let the fish-kettle go on, but the potatoes and brocoli, when once they are put down and have begun to simmer, must be kept so or else they will be spoiled.

391. The soup should be served punctually at half-past six. The cook should previously have warmed four plates, she should also warm the soup-tureen by rinsing it out with boiling water ; and some toasted bread cut up into dice should be served with it if it be brown soup. In dishing it she should be very careful to pour it boldly from the digester into the tureen so that none may drip over the side of the tureen and carry blacks into it.

392. As soon as the soup is served, she should prepare the melted butter for the fish, taking care to have four hot plates and a hot dish ready for it also.

393. The fish being served, she should dish the beef and vegetables, having ready hot plates and dishes for them also.

394. This course will be the longest of any, and while the family are partaking for it, the cook can employ herself washing up the soup and fish plates.

395. The plum-pudding should then be served, turned out, and sifted sugar strewn over ; it will also require a hot dish and four hot plates.

396. If the housemaid's attendance is required continually in the dining-

room, the cook will have to carry up all the dishes and plates to the hall for her.

397. The cook should also carry down the plates and dishes as each course is ended.

398. Dinner being concluded—

THE HOUSEMAID REMOVES THE DINNER THINGS.

399. She should do all as quickly as possible, but at the same time gently and carefully, not crashing the glasses together, placing the knives and forks together in the knife-box, piling the plates one over another, but never with the knives, forks, or spoons left between. When the things are all removed, she should sweep the crumbs from the tablecloth with a crumb-brush, and, as soon as the cloth is removed, she should rub the table quickly all over with a soft cloth.

400. When the things are taken down, the table-cloth should be immediately shaken and folded, and placed in the linen-press.

401. The next work is to—

WASH UP THE DINNER THINGS.

402. In this the housemaid should assist the cook ; she should do the glass and the plate, leaving the plates and dishes and knives to the cook.

403. The plates and dishes should be washed in the dish-tub, in very hot water, to get off the grease; they should be allowed to drain, and then wiped very dry with a clean cloth.

404. The water should not be so hot for the knives. The blades should be held down in the water for a little time, the handles should not touch at all. They should be wiped very dry and perfectly free from grease, and then laid aside to be cleaned.

405. For the glasses the water should be only tepid. They should be rinsed very thoroughly and left to drain ; then wiped dry, and well rubbed, to brighten them, with a clean fine linen cloth.

406. The silver will require hotter water. They should not be mixed with the glasses at all in the washing, as many of them will be greasy. They should be first wiped dry with a linen cloth, and then rubbed with a leather.

407. When all the things are washed, they should be put by in their proper places.

408. The cook should then clean up all her cooking-utensils, and the housemaid should clean the knives.

409. The cook now takes out a sufficient supply of coals to last until the next forenoon. This concludes her work for the day.

410. About eight o'clock—

THE HOUSEMAID TAKES UP THE TRAY

For tea, coffee, or whatever else the family may be in the habit of taking in the evening. When removed, she will wash them up and put them all by in their places; and then

THE HOUSEMAID SHOULD GO UP TO THE BEDROOMS,

Taking the slop-pail with her. She should empty all slops, close the bedroom windows (in winter these must be shut by three o'clock), and, when desired, the shutters, and draw the curtain. She should also let down the curtains of the beds, and neatly fold back the bedclothes from the bolster. In doing this, she should first draw up and fold back the portion of sheet that comes up higher than the rest of the clothes, then fold them all down together. She should also refill with clean cold water any of the water-bottles and jugs that may have been emptied during the day.

411. Before going to bed, the housemaid should bring up all the plate to her mistress, having counted to see if it be all right. If anything is short, an instant search should be made; and, if not found, the mistress should be at once told of the missing article.

412. The cook will lock all the doors, turn off the kitchen gas, and take up the keys.

413. We have thus given the whole day's work, dividing it as we went; but, to make it still clearer, we will now make a division of the different departments of work.

414. *The Kitchens*—and all the cleaning appertaining to them, and *all* cooking, except making toast for afternoon or evening tea, belong to the cook.

415. *The Bedrooms*—and all work appertaining to them, with the exception of assistance in bedmaking, belong to the housemaid.

Furniture Polish.

416. *The Dining-room*—that is, the weekly cleaning of it, falls to the cook's share.

417. *The Drawing-room*—to the housemaid.

418. *The Breakfast Parlour*—to the housemaid.

419. All attendance, except the waiting at breakfast, which the cook does while the housemaid is engaged with the bedrooms, falls to the housemaid. Answering door before twelve, the cook ; afterwards the housemaid.

420. The Glass and the Plate are exclusively the housemaid's care.

421. The Knives are washed by the cook when she washes the other things, but cleaned by the housemaid.

422. The Table-linen is also the housemaid's care, as is the mending of linen going and returning from the wash.

423. The Boots and Shoes.—The cook does the gentlemen's, the housemaid the ladies' boots and shoes.

424. The Washing.—This is divided ; generally the housemaid does all the finer things, the cook the coarser and heavier, the housemaid having all the starching and ironing. But if the cook were a very good ironer, it would be better for her to take that, and the housemaid to do more at the washtub. But it is almost impossible to lay down any definite rules for this department of work, as it must depend entirely on the extent of the washing done at home and the abilities of the servants. One general rule for all the work—Both the cook and housemaid should be obliging to each other, and endeavour always to facilitate each other in their several duties. And though it is desirable that they adhere as much as possible each to her own department of work, yet neither should object, in case of her fellow servant being ill, or getting leave to go out, to perform her duties for her.

425. FURNITURE POLISH.

INGREDIENTS.—1 oz. white wax, 1 oz. Naples soap, 1 pint of turpentine, 1 pint of boiled soft water.

Mode.—Boil the water, let it get cold, shred the wax and soap into it, stand it in the oven until all is melted ; add the turpentine, drop by drop stirring until cold. Bottle and cork closely.

426. OILCLOTH RESTORER.

Melt ½ oz. of beeswax in a saucer of turpentine, rub the surface of the oil-cloth all over with it, then rub with a dry cloth.

427. TO CLEAN LOOKING-GLASSES.

Sponge the surface with equal parts of gin-and-water; then dust with powder blue, and rub off with an old silk handkerchief.

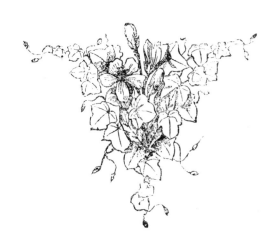

THE
DICTIONARY OF COOKERY.

ALMOND CAKE.

Ingredients.—½ lb. of sweet almonds, 1 oz. of bitter almonds, 6 eggs, 8 tablespoonfuls of sifted sugar, 5 tablespoonfuls of fine flour, the grated rind of 1 lemon, 3 oz. of butter. *Mode.*—Blanch and pound the almonds to a paste; separate the whites from the yolks of the eggs; beat the latter, and add them to the almonds. Stir in the sugar, flour, and lemon-rind; add the butter, which should be beaten to a cream; and, when all these ingredients are well mixed, put in the whites of the eggs, which should be whisked to a stiff froth. Butter a cake-mould, put in the mixture, and bake in a good oven from 1¼ to 1¾ hour. *Time.*—1¼ to 1¾ hour. *Average cost, 2s. 6d.* Seasonable at any time.

ALMOND CHEESECAKES.

Ingredients.—¼ lb. of sweet almonds, 4 bitter ones, 3 eggs, 2 oz. of butter, the rind of ¼ lemon, 1 tablespoonful of lemon-juice, 3 oz. of sugar. *Mode.*—Blanch and pound the almonds smoothly in a mortar, with a little rose or spring water; stir in the eggs, which should be well beaten, and the butter, which should be warmed; add the grated lemon-peel and juice, sweeten, and stir well until the whole is thoroughly mixed. Line some patty-pans with puff-paste, put in the mixture, and bake for 20 minutes, or rather less, in a quick oven. *Time.*—20 minutes, or rather less. *Average cost, 10d.* Sufficient for about 12 cheesecakes.

ALMOND PASTE, for Second-Course Dishes.

Ingredients.—1 lb. of sweet almonds, ¼ bitter ones, 1 lb. of very finely-sifted sugar, the whites of 2 eggs. *Mode.*—Blanch the almonds, and dry them thoroughly; put them into a mortar, and pound them well, wetting them gradually with the whites of 2 eggs. When well pounded, put them into a small preserving-pan, add the sugar, and place the pan on a small but clear fire (a hot plate is better); keep stirring until the paste is dry, then take it out of the pan, put it between two dishes, and, when cold, make it into any shape that fancy may dictate. *Time.*—½ hour. *Average cost, 2s. 8d.* for the above quantity. Sufficient for 3 small dishes of pastry. Seasonable at any time.

ALMOND PUDDING, Baked (very rich).

Ingredients.—¼ lb. of almonds, 4 bitter ditto, 1 glass of sherry, 4 eggs, the rind and juice of ½ lemon, 3 oz. of butter, 1 pint of cream, 2 tablespoonfuls of sugar. *Mode.*—Blanch and pound the almonds to a smooth paste with the water; mix these with the butter, which should be melted; beat up the eggs, grate the lemon-rind, and strain the juice; add these, with the cream, sugar, and wine, to the other ingredients, and stir them well together. When well mixed, put it into a pie-dish lined with puff-paste, and bake for ½ hour. To make this pudding more economically, substitute milk for the cream; but then add rather more than 1 oz. of finely-grated bread. *Time.*—½ to ¾ hour. *Average cost, 3s.,* with cream at 1s. 6d. per pint. *Sufficient* for 4 or 5 persons. Seasonable at any time.

ALMOND PUDDINGS, Small.

Ingredients.—½ lb. of sweet almonds, 6 bitter ones, ¼ lb. of butter, 4 eggs, 2 tablespoonfuls of sifted sugar, 2 tablespoonfuls of cream, 1 tablespoonful of brandy. *Mode.*—Blanch and pound the almonds to a smooth paste with a spoonful of water; warm the butter, mix the

Almond Puffs

almonds with this, and add the other ingredients, leaving out the whites of 2 eggs, and be particular that these are well beaten.

SMALL ALMOND PUDDINGS.

Mix well, but ter some cups, half fill them, and bake the puddings from 20 minutes to ½ hour. Turn them out on a dish, and serve with sweet sauce, or with sifted sugar only. *Time.*—20 minutes to ½ hour. *Average cost, 2s. Sufficient* for 4 or 5 persons. *Seasonable* at any time.

ALMOND PUFFS.

Ingredients.—2 tablespoonfuls of flour, 2 oz. of butter, 2 oz. of pounded sugar, 2 oz. of sweet almonds, 4 bitter almonds. *Mode.*—Blanch and pound the almonds in a mortar to a smooth paste ; melt the butter, dredge in the flour, and add the sugar and pounded almonds. Beat the mixture well, and put it into cups or very tiny jelly-pots, which should be well buttered, and bake in a moderate oven for about 20 minutes, or longer, should the puffs be large. Turn them out on a dish, the bottom of the puff uppermost, and serve. *Time.*—20 minutes. *Average cost, 8d. Sufficient* for 2 or 3 persons. *Seasonable* at any time.

ALMOND SOUP.

Ingredients.—4 lbs. of lean beef or veal, a few vegetables as for Stock (*see* STOCK), 1 oz. of vermicelli, 4 blades of mace, 6 cloves, ½ lb. of sweet almonds, the yolks of 6 eggs, 1 gill of thick cream, rather more than 3 quarts of water. *Mode.*—Boil the beef or veal, vegetables, and spices gently in water that will cover them, till the gravy is very strong, and the meat very tender ; then strain off the gravy, and set it on the fire with the specified quantity of vermicelli to 2 quarts. Let it boil till sufficiently cooked. Have ready the almonds, blanched and pounded very fine ; the yolks of the eggs boiled hard ; mixing the almonds, whilst pounding, with a little of the soup, lest the latter should grow oily. Pound them to a pulp, and keep adding to them, by degrees, a little soup, until they are thoroughly mixed together. Let the soup be cool when mixing, and do it perfectly smooth. Strain it through a sieve, set it on the

Anchovies, Fried

fire, stir frequently, and serve hot. Just before taking it up, add the cream. *Time.*—From 4 to 5 hours to simmer meat and vegetables ; 20 minutes to cook the vermicelli. *Average cost* per quart, 2s. 3d. *Seasonable* all the year. *Sufficient* for 8 persons.

ANCHOVY BUTTER.

Ingredients.—To every lb. of butter allow 6 anchovies, 1 small bunch of parsley. *Mode.*—Wash, bone, and pound the anchovies well in a mortar ; scald the parsley, chop it, and rub through a sieve ; then pound all the ingredients together, mix well, and make the butter into pats immediately. This makes a pretty dish, if fancifully moulded, for breakfast or supper, and should be garnished with parsley. *Average cost, 1s. 8d. Sufficient* to make 2 dishes, with 4 small pats each. *Seasonable* at any time.

ANCHOVY SAUCE, for Fish.

Ingredients.—4 anchovies, 1 oz. of butter, ½ pint of melted butter, cayenne to taste. *Mode.*—Bone the anchovies, and pound them in a mortar to a paste, with 1 oz. of butter. Make the melted butter hot, stir in the pounded anchovies and cayenne ; simmer for 3 or 4 minutes ; and, if liked, add a squeeze of lemon-juice. A more general and expeditious way of making this sauce is to stir in 1½ tablespoonfuls of anchovy essence to ½ pint of melted butter, and to add seasoning to taste. Boil the whole up for 1 minute, and serve hot. *Time.*—5 minutes. *Average cost, 6d.* for ½ pint. *Sufficient,* this quantity, for a brill, small turbot, 2 soles, &c.

ANCHOVY TOAST.

Ingredients.—Toast 2 or 3 slices of bread, or, if wanted very savoury, fry them in clarified butter, and spread on them the paste made by recipe for potted anchovies. Made mustard, or a few grains of cayenne, may be added to the paste before laying it on the toast.

ANCHOVIES, Fried.

Ingredients.—1 tablespoonful of oil, ½ a glass of white wine, sufficient flour to thicken ; 12 anchovies. *Mode.*—Mix the oil and wine together, with sufficient flour to make them into a thickish paste ; cleanse the anchovies, wipe them, dip

Anchovies, Potted

them in the paste, and fry of a nice brown colour. *Time.*—½ hour. *Average cost,* for this quantity, 9d. *Sufficient* for 2 persons. *Seasonable* all the year.

ANCHOVIES, Potted, or Anchovy Butter.

Ingredients.—2 dozen anchovies, ½ lb. of fresh butter. *Mode.*—Wash the anchovies thoroughly; bone and dry them, and pound them in a mortar to a paste. Mix the butter gradually with them, and rub the whole through a sieve. Put it by in small pots for use, and carefully exclude the air with a bladder, as it soon changes the colour of anchovies, besides spoiling them. To potted anchovies may be added pounded mace, cayenne, and nutmeg to taste.

APPLE CHARLOTTE, a very simple.

Ingredients.—9 slices of bread and butter, about 6 good-sized apples, 1 tablespoonful of minced lemon-peel, 2 tablespoonfuls of juice, moist sugar to taste. *Mode.*—Butter a pie-dish; place a layer of bread and butter, without the crust, at the bottom; then a layer of apples, pared, cored, and cut into thin slices; sprinkle over these a portion of the lemon-peel and juice, and sweeten with moist sugar. Place another layer of bread and butter, and then one of apples, proceeding in this manner until the dish is full; then cover it up with the peel of the apples, to preserve the top from browning or burning; bake in a brisk oven for rather more than ¾ hour; turn the charlotte on a dish, sprinkle sifted sugar over, and serve. *Time.*—¾ hour, or a few minutes longer. *Average cost,* 1s. *Sufficient* for 5 or 6 persons. *Seasonable* from August to March.

APPLE CHEESECAKES.

Ingredients.—½ lb. of apple pulp, ¼ lb. of sifted sugar, ¼ lb. of butter, 4 eggs, the rind and juice of 1 lemon. *Mode.*—Pare, core, and boil sufficient apples to make ½ lb. when cooked; add to these the sugar, the butter, which should be melted, the eggs, leaving out 2 of the whites, and the grated rind and juice of 1 lemon; stir the mixture well; line some patty-pans with puff-paste; put in the mixture, and bake about 20 minutes.— *Time.*—About 20 minutes. *Average cost,*

Apple Dumplings, Boiled

for the above quantity, with the paste, 1s. 6d. *Sufficient* for about 18 or 20 cheesecakes. *Seasonable* from August to March.

APPLE CUSTARD, Baked.

Ingredients.—1 dozen large apples, moist sugar to taste, 1 small teacupful of cold water, the grated rind of 1 lemon, 1 pint of milk, 4 eggs, 2 oz. of loaf sugar. *Mode.*—Peel, cut, and core the apples; put them into a lined saucepan with the cold water, and, as they heat, bruise them to a pulp; sweeten with moist sugar, and add the grated lemon-rind. When cold, put the fruit at the bottom of a pie-dish, and pour over it a custard, made with the above proportion of milk, eggs, and sugar; grate a little nutmeg over the top, place the dish in a moderate oven, and bake from 25 to 35 minutes. The above proportions will make rather a large dish. *Time.*—25 to 35 minutes. *Average cost,* 1s. 6d., if fruit has to be bought. *Sufficient* for 6 or 7 persons. *Seasonable* from August to March.

APPLE DUMPLINGS, Baked Plain Family Dish).

Ingredients.—6 apples, suet-crust, sugar to taste. *Mode.*—Pare and take out the cores of the apples with a scoop, and make a suet-crust with ¾ lb. of flour to 6 oz. of suet; roll the apples in the crust, previously sweetening them with moist sugar, and taking care to join the paste nicely. When they are formed into round balls, put them on a tin, and bake them for about ½ hour, or longer, should the apples be very large; arrange them pyramidically on a dish, and sift over them some pounded white sugar. These may be made richer by using puff-paste instead of suet-crust. *Time.*—From ½ to ¾ hour, or longer. *Average cost,* 1½d. each. *Sufficient* for 4 persons. *Seasonable* from August to March, but flavourless after the end of January.

APPLE DUMPLINGS, Boiled.

Ingredients.—6 apples, suet-crust, sugar to taste. *Mode.*—Pare and take out the cores of the apples with a scoop; sweeten, and roll each apple in a piece of crust, made with ¾ lb. of flour to 6 oz. of suet, and be particular that the paste is nicely joined. Put the dumplings into floured cloths, tie them securely,

1*

Apple Fritters

and place them in boiling water. Keep them boiling from ¾ to 1 hour ; remove the cloths, and send them hot and quickly to table. Dumplings boiled in knitted cloths have a very pretty appearance when they come to table. The cloths should be made square, just large enough to hold one dumpling, and should be knitted in plain knitting, with *very coarse* cotton. *Time.*—¾ to 1 hour, or longer should the dumplings be very large. *Average cost,* 1½*d.* each. *Sufficient* for 4 persons. *Seasonable* from August to March, but flavourless after the end of January.

APPLE FRITTERS.

Ingredients.—For the batter, 2 table-spoonfuls of flour, ½ oz. of butter, ¼ saltspoonful of salt, 2 eggs, milk, 4 medium-sized apples, hot lard or clarified beef-dripping. *Mode.*—Break the eggs, dividing the whites from the yolks, and beat them separately. Put the flour into a basin, stir in the butter, which should be melted to a cream ; add the salt, and moisten with sufficient warm milk to make it of a proper consistency, that is to say, a batter that will drop from the spoon. Stir this well, rub down any lumps that may be seen, add the yolks and then the whites of the eggs, which have been previously well whisked ; beat up the batter for a few minutes, and it is ready for use. Now peel and cut the apples into rather thick whole slices, without dividing them, and stamp out the middle of each slice, where the core is, with a cutter. Throw the slices into the batter ; have ready a pan of boiling lard or clarified dripping ; take out the pieces of apple one by one, put them into the hot lard, and fry a nice brown, turning them when required. When done, lay them on a piece of blotting-paper before the fire, to absorb the greasy moisture ; then dish on a white d'oyley, piling the fritters one above the other ; strew over them some pounded sugar, and serve very hot. The flavour of the fritters would be very much improved by soaking the pieces of apple in a little wine, mixed with sugar and lemon-juice, for 3 or 4 hours before wanted for table ; the batter, also, is better for being mixed some hours before the fritters are made. *Time.*—From 7 to 10 minutes to fry the fritters ; 5 minutes to strain them. *Average cost,* 9*d.* *Sufficient*

Apple Jelly

for 4 or 5 persons. *Seasonable* from August to March.

APPLE JAM.

Ingredients.—To every lb. of fruit weighed after being pared, cored, and sliced, allow ¾ lb. of preserving-sugar, the grated rind of 1 lemon, the juice of ¼ lemon. *Mode.*—Peel the apples, cor and slice them very thin, and be particular that they are all the same sort. Put them into a jar, stand this in a saucepan of boiling water, and let the apples stew until quite tender. Previously to putting the fruit into the jar, weigh it, to ascertain the proportion of sugar that may be required. Put the apples into a preserving-pan, crush the sugar to small lumps, and add it, with the grated lemon-rind and juice, to the apples. Simmer these over the fire for ½ hour, reckoning from the time the jam begins to simmer properly ; remove the scum as it rises, and, when the jam is done, put it into pots for use. Place a piece of oiled paper over the jam, and, to exclude the air, cover the pots with tissue paper dipped in the white of an egg, and stretched over the top. This jam will keep good for a long time. *Time.*—From 3 to 4 hours to stew in the jar ; ½ hour to boil after the jam begins to simmer. *Average cost,* for this quantity, 5*s.* *Sufficient.*—7 or 8 lbs. of apples for 6 pots of jam. *Seasonable.*—Make this in September, October, or November, when apples can be bought at a reasonable price.

APPLE JELLY.

Ingredients.—To 6 lbs. of apples allow 3 pints of water ; to every quart of juice allow 2 lbs. of loaf sugar ;—the juice of ½ lemon. *Mode.*—Pare, core, and cut the apples into slices, and put them into a jar, with water in the above proportion. Place them in a cool oven, with the jar well covered, and, when the juice is thoroughly drawn and the apples are quite soft, strain them through a jelly-bag. To every quart of juice allow 2 lbs. of loaf sugar, which should be crushed to small lumps, and put into a preserving-pan with the juice. Boil these together for rather more than ½ hour, remove the scum as it rises, add the lemon-juice just before it is done, and put the jelly into pots for use. This preparation is useful for garnishing sweet dishes, and may be turned out for dessert. *Time.*—The

Apple Jelly	Apple Pudding

apples to be put in the oven over-night, and left till morning ; rather more than ½ hour to boil the jelly. *Average cost*, for this quantity, 3s. *Sufficient* for 6 small pots of jelly. *Seasonable.*—This should be made in September, October, or November.

APPLE JELLY.

Ingredients.—Apples, water ; to every pint of syrup allow ¾ lb. of loaf sugar. *Mode.*—Pare and cut the apples into pieces, remove the cores, and put them in a preserving-pan with sufficient cold water to cover them. Let them boil for an hour ; then drain the syrup from them through a hair sieve or jelly-bag, and measure the juice ; to every pint allow ¼ lb. of loaf sugar, and boil these together for ¾ hour, removing every particle of scum as it rises, and keeping the jelly well stirred, that it may not burn. A little lemon-rind may be boiled with the apples, and a small quantity of strained lemon-juice may be put in the jelly just before it is done, when the flavour is liked. This jelly may be ornamented with preserved greengages, or any other preserved fruit, and will turn out very prettily for dessert. It should be stored away in small pots. *Time.*—1 hour to boil the fruit and water ; ¾ hour to boil the juice with the sugar. *Average cost*, for 6 lbs. of apples, with the other ingredients in proportion, 3s. *Sufficient* for 6 small pots of jelly. *Seasonable.*—Make this in September, October, or November.

APPLE JELLY, Clear, for immediate Eating.

Ingredients.—2 dozen small apples, 1½ pint of spring-water ; to every pint of juice allow ½ lb. of loaf sugar, ½ oz. of isinglass, the rind of ½ lemon. *Mode.*—Pare, core, and cut the apples into quarters, and boil them, with the lemon-peel, until tender ; then strain off the apples, and run the juice through a jelly-bag ; put the strained juice, with the sugar and isinglass, which has been previously boiled in ⅓ pint of water, into a lined saucepan or preserving-pan ; boil all together for about ½ hour, and put the jelly into moulds. When this jelly is clear, and turned out well, it makes a pretty addition to the supper-table, with a little custard or whipped cream round

it : a little lemon-juice improves the flavour, but it is apt to render the jelly muddy and thick. If required to be kept any length of time, rather a larger proportion of sugar must be used. *Time.*—About 1 hour to boil the apples ; ½ hour the jelly. *Average cost*, 2s. *Sufficient* for 1½-pint mould. *Seasonable* from August to March.

APPLE JELLY, Thick, or Marmalade, for Entremets or Dessert Dishes.

Ingredients.—Apples ; to every lb. of pulp allow ¾ lb. of sugar, ½ teaspoonful of minced lemon-peel. *Mode.*—Peel, core, and boil the apples with only sufficient water to prevent them from burning ; beat them to a pulp, and to every lb. of pulp allow the above proportion of sugar in lumps. Dip the lumps into

APPLE JELLY, STUCK WITH ALMONDS.

water ; put these into a saucepan, and boil till the syrup is thick and can be well skimmed ; then add this syrup to the apple pulp, with the minced lemon-peel, and stir it over a quick fire for about 20 minutes, or till the apples cease to stick to the bottom of the pan. The jelly is then done, and may be poured into moulds which have been previously dipped in water, when it will turn out nicely for dessert or a side dish ; for the latter, a little custard should be poured round, and it should be garnished with strips of citron or stuck with blanched almonds. *Time.*—From ½ to ¾ hour to reduce the apples to a pulp ; 20 minutes to boil after the sugar is added. *Sufficient.*—1½ lb. of apple pulp sufficient for a small mould. *Seasonable* from August to March ; but is best and cheapest in September, October, or November.

APPLE PUDDING, Rich Baked.

Ingredients.—½ lb. apple pulp, ½ lb. of loaf sugar, 6 oz. of butter, the rind of 1

Apple Pudding

lemon, 6 eggs, puff-paste. *Mode.*—Peel, core, and cut the apples, as for sauce; put them into a stewpan, with only just sufficient water to prevent them from burning, and let them stew until reduced to a pulp. Weigh the pulp, and to every ½ lb. add the sifted sugar, grated lemon-rind, and 6 well-beaten eggs. Beat these ingredients well together; then melt the butter, stir it to the other things, put a border of puff-paste round the dish, and bake for rather more than ½ hour. The butter should not be added until the pudding is ready for the oven. *Time.*—½ to ¾ hour. *Average cost,* 1s. 10d. *Sufficient* for 5 or 6 persons. *Seasonable* from August to March.

APPLE PUDDING, Baked.

Ingredients.—12 large apples, 6 oz. of moist sugar, ¼ lb. of butter, 4 eggs, 1 pint of bread crumbs. *Mode.*—Pare, core, and cut the apples, as for sauce, and boil them until reduced to a pulp; then add the butter, melted, and the eggs, which should be well whisked. Beat up the pudding for 2 or 3 minutes; butter a pie-dish; put in a layer of bread crumbs, then the apple, and then another layer of bread crumbs; flake over these a few tiny pieces of butter, and bake for about ½ hour. A very good economical pudding made be made merely with apples, boiled and sweetened, with the addition of a few strips of lemon-peel. A layer of bread crumbs should be placed above and below the apples, and the pudding baked for ½ hour. *Time.*—About ½ hour. *Average cost,* 1s. 6d. *Sufficient* for 5 or 6 persons. *Seasonable* from August to March.

APPLE PUDDING, Baked (Very Good).

Ingredients.—5 moderate-sized apples, 2 tablespoonfuls of finely-chopped suet, 3 eggs, 3 tablespoonfuls of flour, 1 pint of milk, a little grated nutmeg. *Mode.*—Mix the flour to a smooth batter with the milk; add the eggs, which should be well whisked, and put the latter into a well-buttered pie-dish. Wipe the apples clean, but do not pare them; cut them in halves, and take out the cores; lay them in the batter, rind uppermost; shake the suet on the top, over which also grate a little nutmeg; bake in a moderate oven for an hour, and cover,

Apple Sauce

when served, with sifted loaf sugar. This pudding is also very good with the apples pared, sliced, and mixed with the batter. *Time.*—1 hour. *Average cost,* 9d. *Sufficient* for 5 or 6 persons.

APPLE PUDDING, Boiled.

Ingredients.—Suet crust, apples, sugar to taste, 1 small teaspoonful of finely-minced lemon-peel, 2 tablespoonfuls of lemon-juice. *Mode.*—Make a butter or suet crust by either of the given recipes, using for a moderate-sized pudding from ¾ to 1 lb. of flour, with the other ingredients in proportion. Butter a basin, line it with some paste; pare, core, and cut the apples into slices, and fill the basin with these; add the sugar, the lemon-peel and juice, and cover with crust; pinch the edges together, flour the cloth, place it over the pudding, tie it securely, and put it into plenty of fast-boiling water; let it boil from 2½ to 3 hours; then turn it out of the basin and send to table quickly. Apple puddings may also be boiled in a cloth without a basin; but, when made in this way, must be served without the least delay, as the crust soon becomes heavy. Apple pudding is a very convenient dish to have when the dinner-hour is rather uncertain, as it does not spoil by being boiled an extra hour; care, however must be taken to keep it well covered with water all the time, and not to allow it to stop boiling. *Time.*—From 2½ to 5 hours, according to the quality of the apples. *Average cost,* 10d. *Sufficient,* made with 1 lb. of flour, for 7 or 8 persons. *Seasonable* from August to March; but the apples become flavourless and scarce after February.

APPLE SAUCE, for Geese, Pork, &c.

Ingredients. — 6 good-sized apples, sifted sugar to taste, a piece of butter the size of a walnut; water. *Mode.*—Pare, core, and quarter the apples, and throw them into cold water to preserve their whiteness. Put them in a saucepan, with sufficient water to moisten them, and boil till soft enough to pulp. Beat them up, adding sugar to taste, and a small piece of butter. This quantity is sufficient for a good-sized tureen. *Time.*—According to the apples, about ½ hour. *Average cost,* 4d. *Sufficient,* this quantity, for a goose or couple of ducks.

APPLE SNOW (a pretty Supper Dish).

Ingredients. — 10 good-sized apples, the whites of 10 eggs, the rind of 1 lemon, ½ lb. of pounded sugar. *Mode.* —Peel, core, and cut the apples into quarters, and put them into a saucepan with the lemon-peel, and sufficient water to prevent them from burning,—rather less than ½ pint. When they are tender, take out the peel, beat them into a pulp, let them cool, and stir them to the whites of the eggs, which should be previously beaten to a strong froth. Add the sifted sugar, and continue the whisking until the mixture becomes quite stiff, and either heap it on a glass dish or serve it in small glasses. The dish may be garnished with preserved barberries or strips of bright-coloured jelly, and a dish of custards should be served with it, or a jug of cream. *Time.*—From 30 to 40 minutes to stew the apples. *Average cost,* 1s. 6d. *Sufficient* to fill a moderate-sized glass dish. *Seasonable* from August to March.

APPLE SNOWBALLS.

Ingredients. — 2 teacupfuls of rice, apples, moist sugar, cloves. *Mode.*— Boil the rice and milk until three-parts done ; then strain it off, and pare and core the apples without dividing them. Put a small quantity of sugar and a clove into each apple, put the rice round them, and tie each ball separately in a cloth. Boil until the apples are tender ; then take them up, remove the cloths, and serve. *Time.*—½ hour to boil the rice separately ; ½ to 1 hour with the apple. *Seasonable* from August to March.

APPLE SOUFFLE.

Ingredients.—6 oz. of rice, 1 quart of milk, the rind of ½ lemon, sugar to taste, the yolks of 4 eggs, the whites of 6, 1½ oz. of butter, 4 tablespoonfuls of apple marmalade. *Mode.*—Boil the milk with the lemon-peel until the former is well flavoured ; then strain it, put in the rice, and let it gradually swell over a slow fire, adding sufficient sugar to sweeten it nicely. Then crush the rice to a smooth pulp with the back of a wooden spoon ; line the bottom and sides of a round cake-tin with it, and put it into the oven to set ; turn it out of the tin dexterously,

and be careful that the border of rice is firm in every part. Mix with the marmalade the beaten yolks of eggs and the butter, and stir these over the fire until the mixture thickens. Take it off the fire ; to this add the whites of the eggs, which should be previously beaten to a strong froth ; stir all together, and put it into the rice border. Bake in a moderate oven for about an hour, or until the soufflé rises very light. It should be watched, and served instantly, or it will immediately fall after it is taken from the oven. *Time.* — ½ hour. *Average cost,* 1s. 8d. *Sufficient* for 4 or 5 persons. *Seasonable* from August to March.

APPLE TART or PIE.

Ingredients. — Puff-paste, apples ; to every lb. of unpared apples allow 2 oz. of moist sugar, ½ teaspoonful of finely-minced lemon-peel, 1 tablespoonful of lemon-juice. *Mode.*—Make puff-paste by either of the given recipes, with ½ lb. of flour ; place a border of it round the edge of a pie-dish, and fill the dish with apples pared, cored, and cut into slices ; sweeten with moist sugar, add the lemon-peel and juice, and 2 or 3 tablespoonfuls of water ; cover with crust, cut it evenly round close to the edge of the pie-dish, and bake in a hot oven from ½ to ¾ hour, or rather longer, should the pie be very large. When it is three-parts done, take it out of the oven, put the white of an egg on a plate, and, with the blade of a knife, whisk it to a froth ; brush the pie over with this, then sprinkle upon it some sifted sugar, and then a few drops of water. Put the pie back into the oven, and finish baking, and be particularly careful that it does not catch or burn, *which it is very liable to do after the crust is iced.* If made with a plain crust, the icing may be omitted. Many things are suggested for the flavouring of apple pie ; some say 2 or 3 tablespoonfuls of beer, others the same quantity of sherry, which very much improve the taste ; whilst the old-fashioned addition of a few cloves is, by many persons, preferred to anything else, as also a few slices of quince. *Time.*—½ hour before the crust is iced ; 10 to 15 minutes afterwards. *Average cost,* 9d. *Sufficient.*—Allow 2 lbs. of apples to a tart for 6 persons. *Seasonable* from August to March ; but the apples become flavourless after February.

APPLE TART (Creamed).

Mode.—Make an apple tart by the preceding recipe, with the exception of omitting the icing. When the tart is baked, cut out the middle of the lid or crust, leaving a border all round the dish. Fill up with a nicely-made boiled custard, grate a little nutmeg over the top, and the pie is ready for table. This tart is usually eaten cold; is rather an old-fashioned dish, but, at the same time, extremely nice. *Time.*—½ to ¾ hour. *Average cost*, 1s. 3d. *Sufficient* for 5 or 6 persons. *Seasonable* from August to March.

APPLE TRIFLE (a Supper Dish).

Ingredients.—10 good-sized apples, the rind of ½ lemon, 6 oz. of pounded sugar, ½ pint of milk, ½ pint of cream, 2 eggs, whipped cream. *Mode.*—Peel, core, and cut the apples into thin slices, and put them into a saucepan with 2 tablespoonfuls of water, the sugar, and minced lemon-rind. Boil all together until quite tender, and pulp the apples through a sieve; if they should not be quite sweet enough, add a little more sugar, and put them at the bottom of the dish to form a thick layer. Stir together the milk, cream, and eggs, with a little sugar, over the fire, and let the mixture thicken, but do not allow it to reach the boiling-point. When thick, take it off the fire; let it cool a little, then pour it over the apples. Whip some cream with sugar, lemon-peel, &c., the same as for other trifles; heap it high over the custard, and the dish is ready for table. It may be garnished as fancy dictates, with strips of bright apple jelly, slices of citron, &c. *Time.*—From 30 to 40 minutes to stew the apples; 10 minutes to stir the custard over the fire. *Average cost*, 2s., with cream at 1s. 6d. per pint. *Sufficient* for a moderate-sized trifle. *Seasonable* from August to March.

APPLES à la Portugaise.

Ingredients.—8 good boiling apples, ¾ pint of water, 6 oz. of sugar, a layer of apple marmalade, 8 preserved cherries, garnishing of apricot jam. *Mode.*—Peel the apples, and, with a scoop, take out the cores; boil the fruit in the above proportion of sugar and water, without being too much done, and take care the apples do not break. Have ready

some apple marmalade; cover the bottom of a glass dish with this, level it, and lay the apples in a sieve to drain; pile them neatly on the marmalade, raising them in the centre, and place a preserved cherry in the middle of each. Garnish with strips of candied citron or apricot jam, and the dish is ready for table. *Time.*—From 20 to 30 minutes to stew the apples. *Average cost*, 1s. 3d. *Sufficient* for 1 entremets. *Seasonable* from August to March.

APPLES, Buttered (Sweet Entremets).

Ingredients.—Apple marmalade or 7 good boiling apples, ½ pint of water, 6 oz. of sugar, 2 oz. of butter, a little apricot jam. *Mode.*—Pare the apples, and take out the cores with a scoop; boil up the sugar and water for a few minutes; then lay in the apples and simmer them very gently until tender, taking care not to let them break. Have ready sufficient marmalade made by the recipe for APPLE MARMALADE, flavoured with lemon, to cover the bottom of the dish; arrange the apples on this with a piece of butter placed in each, and in between them a few spoonfuls of apricot jam or marmalade; put the dish in the oven for 10 minutes, then sprinkle over the top sifted sugar, and either brown it before the fire or with a salamander, and serve hot. The syrup that the apples were boiled in should be saved for another time. *Time.*—From 20 to 30 minutes to stew the apples very gently, 10 minutes in the oven. *Average cost*, 1s. 6d. *Sufficient* for 1 entremets.

APPLES and RICE (a Plain Dish).

Ingredients.—8 good-sized apples, 3 oz. of butter, the rind of ½ lemon minced very fine, 6 oz. of rice, 1½ pints of milk, sugar to taste, ½ teaspoonful of grated nutmeg, 6 tablespoonfuls of apricot jam. *Mode.*—Peel the apples, halve them, and take out the cores; put them into a stewpan with the butter, and strew sufficient sifted sugar over to sweeten them nicely, and add the minced lemon-peel. Stew the apples very gently until tender, taking care they do not break. Boil the rice, with the milk, sugar, and nutmeg, until soft, and, when thoroughly done, dish it, piled high in the centre; arrange the apples on it, warm the apricot jam,

Apples and Rice

pour it over the whole, and serve hot. *Time.*—About 30 minutes to stew the apples very gently; about ¾ hour to cook the rice. *Average cost, 1s. 6d. Sufficient* for 5 or 6 persons. *Seasonable* from August to March.

APPLES AND RICE (a pretty Dish of).

Ingredients.—6 oz. of rice, 1 quart of milk, the rind of ½ lemon, sugar to taste, ½ saltspoonful of salt, 8 apples, ¼ lb. of sugar, ¼ pint of water, ½ pint of boiled custard. *Mode.*—Flavour the milk with lemon-rind, by boiling them together for a few minutes; then take out the peel, and put in the rice, with sufficient sugar to sweeten it nicely, and boil gently until the rice is quite soft; then let it cool. In the meantime pare, quarter, and core the apples, and boil them until tender in a syrup made with sugar and water in the above proportion; and, when soft, lift them out on a sieve to drain. Now put a middling-sized gallipot in the centre of a dish; lay the rice all round till the top of the gallipot is reached; smooth the rice with the back of a spoon, and stick the apples into it in rows, one row sloping to the right, and the next to the left. Set it in the oven to colour the apples; then, when required for table, remove the gallipot, garnish the rice with preserved fruits, and pour in the middle sufficient custard, made by the recipe for boiled custard, to be level with the top of the rice, and serve hot. *Time.*—From 20 to 30 minutes to stew the apples; ¾ hour to simmer the rice; ¼ hour to bake. *Average cost, 1s. 6d. Sufficient* for 5 or 6 persons. *Seasonable* from August to March.

APPLES, Compote of (Soyer's Recipe,—a Dessert Dish).

Ingredients.—6 ripe apples, 1 lemon, ¼ lb. of lump sugar, ½ pint of water. *Mode.*—Select the apples of a moderate size, peel them, cut them in halves, remove the cores, and rub each piece over with a little lemon. Put the sugar and water together into a lined saucepan, and let them boil until forming a thickish syrup, when lay in the apples with the rind of the lemon cut thin, and the juice of the same. Let the apples simmer till tender; then take them out very carefully, drain them on a sieve, and

Apples, Flanc of

reduce the syrup by boiling it quickly for a few minutes. When both are cold, arrange the apples neatly on a glass dish,

COMPOTE OF APPLES.

pour over the syrup, and garnish with strips of green angelica or candied citron. Smaller apples may be dressed in the same manner: they should not be divided in half, but peeled, and the cores pushed out with a vegetable-cutter. *Time.*—10 minutes to boil the sugar and water together; from 20 to 30 minutes to simmer the apples. *Average cost, 6d. Sufficient* for 4 or 5 persons. *Seasonable* from August to March.

APPLES, Flanc of; or Apples in a raised Crust. (Sweet Entremets.)

Ingredients.—¾ lb. of short crust, 9 moderate-sized apples, the rind and juice of ½ lemon, ¼ lb. of white sugar, ¾ pint of water, a few strips of candied citron. *Mode.*—Make a plain stiff short crust, roll it out to the thickness of ½ inch, and butter an oval mould; line it with the crust, and press it carefully all round the sides, to obtain the form of the mould, but be particular not to break the paste. Pinch the part that just rises above the mould with the paste-pincers, and fill the case with flour; bake it for about ¾ hour; then take it out of the oven, remove the flour, put the case back in the oven for another ¼ hour, and do not allow it to get scorched. It is now ready for the apples, which should be prepared in the following manner: peel, and take out the cores with a small knife, or a scoop for the purpose, without dividing the apples; put them into a small lined saucepan, just capable of holding them, with sugar, water, lemon-juice and rind, in the above proportion. Simmer them very gently until tender; then take out the apples, let them cool, arrange them in the flanc or case, and boil down the syrup until reduced to a thick jelly; pour it over the apples, and garnish with a few slices of candied citron.

A more simple flanc may be made by rolling out the paste, cutting the bottom of a round or oval shape, and then a narrow strip for the sides: these should be stuck on with the white of an egg to the bottom piece, and the flanc then filled with raw fruit, with sufficient sugar to sweeten it nicely. It will not require so long baking as in a mould; but the crust must be made everywhere of an equal thickness, and so perfectly joined that the juice does not escape. This dish may also be served hot, and should be garnished in the same manner, or a little melted apricot jam may be poured over the apples, which very much improves their flavour. *Time.*—Altogether, 1 hour to bake the flanc; from 30 to 40 minutes to stew the apples very gently. *Average cost,* 1s. 6d. *Sufficient* for 1 entremets or side-dish. *Seasonable* from August to March.

APPLES, Ginger (a pretty Supper or Dessert Dish).

Ingredients.—1½ oz. of whole ginger, ¼ pint of whiskey, 3 lbs. of apples, 2 lbs. of white sugar, the juice of 2 lemons. *Mode.*—Bruise the ginger, put it into a small jar, pour over sufficient whiskey to cover it, and let it remain for 3 days; then cut the apples into thin slices, after paring and coring them; add the sugar and the lemon-juice, which should be strained; and simmer all together *very gently* until the apples are transparent, but not broken. Serve cold, and garnish the dish with slices of candied lemon-peel or preserved ginger. *Time.*—3 days to soak the ginger; about ¼ hour to simmer the apples very gently. *Average cost,* 2s. 6d. *Sufficient* for 3 dishes. *Seasonable* from August to March.

APPLES Iced, or Apple Hedge-hog.

Ingredients. — About 3 dozen good boiling apples, 1 lb. of sugar, ½ pint of water, the rind of ½ lemon minced very fine, the whites of 2 eggs, 3 tablespoonfuls of pounded sugar, a few sweet almonds. *Mode.*—Peel and core a dozen of the apples without dividing them, and stew them very gently in a lined saucepan with ½ lb. of the sugar and ½ pint of water, and when tender lift them carefully on to a dish. Have ready the remainder of the apples, pared, cored, and cut into thin slices; put them into the same syrup with the other ½ lb. of sugar, the lemon-peel, and boil gently until they are reduced to a marmalade; keeping them stirred, to prevent them from burning. Cover the bottom of the dish

with some of the marmalade, and over that a layer of the stewed apples, in the insides of which, and between each, place some of the marmalade; then place another layer of apples, and fill up the cavities with marmalade as before, forming the whole into a raised oval shape. Whip the whites of the eggs to a stiff froth, mix with them the pounded sugar, and cover the apples very smoothly all over with the icing; blanch and cut each almond into 4 or 5 strips; place these strips at equal distances over the icing, sticking up; strew over a little rough pounded sugar, and put the dish in a very slow oven, to colour the almonds, and so allow the apples to get warm through. This entremets may also be served cold, and makes a pretty supper-dish. *Time.*—From 20 to 30 minutes to stew the apples. *Average cost,* 2s. to 2s. 6d. *Sufficient* for 5 or 6 persons. *Seasonable* from August to March.

APPLES in Red Jelly (a pretty Supper Dish).

Ingredients.—6 good-sized apples, 12 cloves, 6 oz. of pounded sugar, 1 lemon, 2 teacupfuls of water, 1 tablespoonful of gelatine, a few drops of prepared cochineal. *Mode.* —Choose rather large apples; peel them and take out the cores, either with a scoop or a small silver knife, and put into each apple 2 cloves and as much sifted sugar as they will hold. Place them, without touching each other, in a large pie-dish; add more white sugar, the juice of 1 lemon, and 2 teacupfuls of water. Bake in the oven, with a dish over them, until they are done. Look at them frequently, and, as each apple is cooked, place it in a glass dish. They must not be left in the oven after they are done, or they will break, and so would spoil the appearance of the dish. When the apples are neatly arranged in the dish without touching each other, strain the liquor in which they have been stewing into a lined saucepan; add to it the rind of the lemon, and a tablespoonful of gelatine which has been previously dissolved in cold water, and, if not sweet, a little more sugar, and 6 cloves. Boil till quite clear; colour with a few drops of prepared cochineal, and strain the jelly through a double muslin into a jug; let it cool *a little;* then pour it into the dish round the apples. When quite cold,

Apples, to preserve

garnish the tops of the apples with a bright-coloured marmalade, jelly, or the white of an egg beaten to a strong froth, with a little sifted sugar. *Time.*—From 30 to 50 minutes to bake the apples. *Average cost,* 1s., with the garnishing. *Sufficient* for 4 or 5 persons. *Seasonable* from August to March.

APPLES, to preserve, in Quarters (in imitation of Ginger).

Ingredients.—To every lb. of apples allow ¾ lb. of sugar, 1½ oz. of the best white ginger ; 1 oz. of ginger to every ½ pint of water. *Mode.*—Peel, core, and quarter the apples, and put the fruit, sugar, and ginger in layers into a wide-mouthed jar, and let them remain for 2 days ; then infuse 1 oz. of ginger in ½ pint of boiling water, and cover it closely, and let it remain for 1 day : this quantity of ginger and water is for 3 lbs. of apples, with the other ingredients in proportion. Put the apples, &c., into a preserving-pan with the water strained from the ginger, and boil till the apples look clear and the syrup is rich, which will be in about an hour. The rind of a lemon may be added just before the apples have finished boiling ; and great care must be taken not to break the pieces of apple in putting them into the jars. Serve on glass dishes for dessert. *Time.*— 2 days for the apples to remain in the jar with sugar, &c. ; 1 day to infuse the ginger ; about 1 hour to boil the apples. *Average cost,* for 3 lbs. of apples, with the other ingredients in proportion, 2s. 3d. *Sufficient.*—3 lbs. should fill 3 moderate-sized jars. *Seasonable.*—This should be made in September, October, or November.

APPLES, Stewed, and Custard (a pretty Dish for a Juvenile Supper).

Ingredients.—7 good-sized apples, the rind of ½ lemon or 4 cloves, ½ lb. of sugar, ¾ pint of water, ½ pint of custard. *Mode.* —Pare and take out the cores of the apples, without dividing them, and, if possible, leave the stalks on ; boil the sugar and water together for 10 minutes ; then put in the apples with the lemon-rind or cloves, whichever flavour may be preferred, and simmer gently until they are tender, taking care not to let them break. Dish them neatly on a glass dish, reduce the syrup by boiling it

Apricot Jam

quickly for a few minutes, let it cool a little ; then pour it over the apples Have ready quite ½ pint of custard made by the recipe for Boiled Custard ; pour it round, but not over, the apples when they are quite cold, and the dish is ready for table. A few almonds blanched and cut into strips, and stuck in the apples, would improve their appearance. *Time.* —From 20 to 30 minutes to stew the apples. *Average cost,* 1s. *Sufficient* to fill a large glass dish. *Seasonable* from August to March.

APRICOT CREAM.

Ingredients.—12 to 16 ripe apricots, ½ lb. of sugar, 1½ pint of milk, the yolks of 8 eggs, 1 oz. of isinglass. *Mode.*—Divide the apricots, take out the stones, and boil them in a syrup made with ¼ lb. of sugar and ¼ pint of water, until they form a thin marmalade, which rub through a sieve. Boil the milk with the other ¼ lb. of sugar, let it cool a little, then mix with it the yolks of eggs which have been previously well beaten ; put this mixture into a jug, place this jug in boiling water, and stir it one way over the fire until it thickens ; but on no account let it boil. Strain through a sieve, add the isinglass, previously boiled with a small quantity of water, and keep stirring it till nearly cold ; then mix the cream with the apricots ; stir well, put it into an oiled mould, and, if convenient, set it on ice ; at any rate, in a very cool place. It should turn out on the dish without any difficulty. In winter-time, when fresh apricots are not obtainable, a little jam may be substituted for them. *Time.*— From 20 to 30 minutes to boil the apricots. *Average cost,* 3s. 6d. *Sufficient* to fill a quart mould. *Seasonable* in August, September, and October.

APRICOT JAM, or Marmalade.

Ingredients.—To every lb. of ripe apricots, weighed after being skinned and stoned, allow 1 lb. of sugar. *Mode.* —Pare the apricots, which should be ripe, as thinly as possible, break them in half, and remove the stones. Weigh the fruit and to every lb. allow the same propa tion of loaf sugar. Pound the sugar very finely in a mortar, strew it over the apricots, which should be placed on dishes, and let them remain for 12 hours. Break the stones, blanch the kernels, and put them with the sugar and fruit into a

Apricot Pudding

preserving-pan. Let these simmer very gently until clear ; take out the pieces of apricot singly as they become so, and, as fast as the scum rises, carefully remove it. Put the apricots into small jars, pour over them the syrup and kernels, cover the jam with pieces of paper dipped in the purest salad-oil, and stretch over the top of the jars tissue paper, cut about 2 inches larger and brushed over with the white of an egg : when dry, it will be perfectly hard and air-tight. *Time.*—12 hours, sprinkled with sugar ; about ¾ hour to boil the jam. *Average cost.*—When cheap, apricots may be purchased for preserving at about 1s. 6d. per gallon. *Sufficient.*— 10 lbs. of fruit for 12 pots of jam. *Seasonable.*—Make this in August or September.

APRICOT PUDDING, Baked.

Ingredients.—12 large apricots, ¾ pint of bread crumbs, 1 pint of milk, 3 oz. of pounded sugar, the yolks of 4 eggs, 1 glass of sherry. *Mode.*—Make the milk boiling hot, and pour it on to the bread crumbs ; when half cold, add the sugar, the well-whisked yolks of the eggs, and the sherry. Divide the apricots in half, scald them until they are soft, and break them up with a spoon, adding a few of the kernels, which should be well pounded in a mortar ; then mix the fruit and other ingredients together, put a border of paste round the dish, fill with the mixture, and bake the pudding from ½ to ¾ hour. *Time.*—½ to ¾ hour. *Average cost*, in full season, 1s. 6d. *Sufficient* for 4 or 5 persons. *Seasonable* in August, September, and October.

APRICOT TART.

Ingredients.—12 or 14 apricots, sugar to taste, puff-paste or short crust. *Mode.*—Break the apricots in half, take out the stones, and put them into a pie-dish, in the centre of which place a very small cup or jar, bottom uppermost ; sweeten with good moist sugar, but add no water. Line the edge of the dish with paste, put on the cover, and ornament the pie in any of the usual modes. Bake from ½ to ¾ hour, according to size ; and if puff-paste is used, glaze it about 10 minutes before the pie is done, and put it into the oven again to set the glaze. Short crust merely requires a little sifted sugar sprinkled over it before being sent

Apricots, Flanc of

to table. Green apricots make very good tarts, but they should be boiled with a little sugar and water before they are covered with the crust. *Time.*—⅓ to ¾ hour. *Average cost*, in full season, 1s. *Sufficient* for 4 or 5 persons. *Seasonable* in August, September, and October ; green ones rather earlier.

APRICOTS, Compote of (an elegant Dish).

Ingredients.— ½ pint of syrup (see SYRUP), 12 green apricots. *Mode.*— Make the syrup by the given recipe, and, when it is ready, put in the apricots whilst the syrup is boiling. Simmer them very gently until tender, taking care not to let them break ; take them out carefully, arrange them on a glass dish, let the syrup cool a little, pour it over the apricots, and, when cold, serve. *Time.*—From 15 to 20 minutes to simmer the apricots. *Average cost*, 9d. *Sufficient* for 4 or 5 persons. *Seasonable* in June and July, with green apricots.

APRICOTS, Flanc of, or Compote of Apricots in a Raised Crust (Sweet Entremets).

Ingredients.—¾ lb. of short crust (see CRUST), from 9 to 12 good-sized apricots, ¾ pint of water, ½ lb. of sugar. *Mode.*— Make a short crust by the given recipe, and line a mould with it. Boil the sugar and water together for 10 minutes; halve the apricots, take out the stones, and simmer them in the syrup until tender; watch them carefully, and take them up, for fear they should break. Arrange them neatly in the flanc or case ; boil the syrup until reduced to a jelly; pour it over the fruit, and serve either hot or cold. Greengages, plums of all kinds, peaches, &c., may be done in the same manner, as also currants, raspberries, gooseberries, strawberries, &c. ; but with the last-named fruits, a little currant-juice added to them will be found an improvement. *Time.*—Altogether, 1 hour to bake the flanc, from 15 to 20 minutes to simmer the apricots. *Average cost*, 1s. 6d. *Sufficient* for 1 entremets or side-dish. *Seasonable* in July, August, and September.

The pretty appearance of this dish depends on the fruit being whole ; as each apricot is done, it should be taken out of the syrup immediately.

April—Bills of Fare	April—Dinners for 6 persons

APRIL—BILLS OF FARE.
Dinner for 18 persons.
First Course.

Fillets of Mackerel.	Spring Soup, removed by Salmon and Lobster Sauce.	Fried Smelts.
	Vase of Flowers.	
	Soles à la Crème.	

Second Course.

Stewed Beef à la Jardinière.	Roast Ribs of Lamb.	Boiled Ham.
	Larded Capon.	
	Vase of Flowers.	
	Spring Chickens.	
	Braised Turkey.	

Entrées.

Curried Lobster.	Lamb Cutlets, Asparagus and Peas.	Oyster Patties.
	Vase of Flowers.	
	Grenadines de Veau.	

Third Course.

Raspberry-Jam Tartlets.	Clear Jelly.	Ducklings, removed by Cabinet Pudding.	Orange Jelly.	Rhubarb Tart.
Victoria Sandwiches.		Charlotte à la Parisienne.		Cheese-cakes.
		Vase of Flowers.		
		Raspberry Cream.		
		Nesselrode Pudding.		

Dessert and Ices.

Dinner for 12 persons.
First Course.—Soup à la reine; julienne soup; turbot and lobster sauce; slices of salmon à la genévése. *Entrées.*—Croquettes of leveret; fricandeau de veau; vol-au-vent; stewed mushrooms. *Second Course.*—Fore-quarter of lamb; saddle of mutton; boiled chickens, asparagus and peas; boiled tongue garnished with tufts of broccoli; vegetables. *Third Course.*—Ducklings; larded guinea-fowls; charlotte à la parisienne; orange jelly; meringues; ratafia ice pudding; lobster salad; sea-kale; dessert and ices.

Dinner for 10 persons.
First Course.—Gravy soup; salmon and dressed cucumber; shrimp sauce; fillets of whitings. *Entrées.*—Lobster cutlets; chicken patties. *Second Course.*—Roast fillet of veal; boiled leg of lamb; ham, garnished with broccoli; vegetables. *Third Course.*—Ducklings; compôte of rhubarb; custards; vanilla cream; orange jelly; cabinet pudding; ice pudding; dessert.

Dinner for 8 persons.
First Course.—Spring soup; slices of salmon and caper sauce; fried filleted soles. *Entrées.* — Chicken vol-au-vent; mutton cutlets and tomato sauce. *Second Course.*—Roast loin of veal; boiled fowls à la béchamel; tongue; vegetables. *Third Course.*—Guinea-fowls; sea-kale; artichoke bottoms; cabinet pudding; blancmange; apricot tartlets; rice fritters; macaroni and Parmesan cheese; dessert.

Dinners for 6 persons.
First Course. — Tapioca soup; boiled salmon and lobster sauce. *Entrées.*—Sweetbreads; oyster patties. *Second Course.* — Haunch of mutton; boiled capon and white sauce; tongue; vegetables. *Third Course.*—Soufflé of rice; lemon cream; charlotte à la parisienne; rhubarb tart; dessert.

First Course. — Julienne soup; fried whitings; red mullet. *Entrées.*—Lamb cutlets and cucumbers; rissoles. *Second Course.*—Roast ribs of beef; neck of veal à la béchamel; vegetables. *Third Course.* — Ducklings; lemon pudding; rhubarb tart; custards; cheesecakes; dessert.

First Course.—Vermicelli soup; brill and shrimp sauce. *Entrées.* — Fricandeau of veal; lobster cutlets. *Second Course.*—Roast fore-quarter of lamb; boiled chickens; tongue; vegetables. *Third Course.*—Goslings; sea-kale; plum pudding; whipped cream; compôte of rhubarb; cheesecakes; dessert.

First Course.—Ox-tail soup; crimped salmon. *Entrées.*—Croquettes of chicken; mutton cutlets and soubise sauce. *Second Course.* — Roast fillet of veal; boiled bacon-cheek, garnished with sprouts; boiled capon; vegetables. *Third Course.*—Sea-kale; lobster salad; cabinet pudding, ginger cream; raspberry-jam tartlets; rhubarb tart; macaroni; dessert.

APRIL, Plain Family Dinners for.

Sunday.— 1. Clear gravy soup. 2. Roast haunch of mutton, sea-kale, potatoes. 3. Rhubarb tart, custards in glasses.

Monday.—1. Crimped skate and caper sauce. 2. Boiled knuckle of veal and rice, cold mutton, mashed potatoes. 3. Baked plum-pudding.

Tuesday.—1. Vegetable soup. 2. Toad-in-the-hole, made from remains of cold mutton. 3. Stewed rhubarb and baked custard puddings.

Wednesday.—1. Fried soles, anchovy sauce. 2. Boiled beef and carrots, suet dumplings. 3. Lemon pudding.

Thursday.—1. Pea-soup, made with liquor that beef was boiled in. 2. Cold beef, mashed potatoes, mutton cutlets and tomato sauce. 3. Macaroni.

Friday.—1. Bubble-and-squeak made with remains of cold beef, roast shoulder of veal stuffed, spinach and potatoes. 2. Boiled batter pudding and sweet sauce.

Saturday.—1. Stewed veal with vegetables, made of remains of cold shoulder, broiled rump-steak and oyster sauce. 2. Yeast dumplings.

Sunday.—Boiled salmon and dressed cucumber, anchovy sauce. 2. Roast fore-quarter of lamb, spinach, potatoes, and mint sauce. 3. Rhubarb tart and cheesecakes.

Monday.—Curried salmon, made with remains of salmon, dish of boiled rice. 2. Cold lamb, rump-steak and kidney pudding, potatoes. 3. Spinach and poached eggs.

Tuesday.—1. Scotch mutton broth with

pearl barley. 2. Boiled neck of mutton, caper sauce, suet dumplings, carrots. 3. Baked rice puddings.

Wednesday.—1. Boiled mackerel and melted butter and fennel sauce, potatoes. 2. Roast fillet of veal, bacon and greens. 3. Fig pudding.

Thursday.—1. Flemish soup. 2. Roast loin of mutton, broccoli, potatoes, veal rolls made from remains of cold veal. 3. Boiled rhubarb pudding.

Friday.—1. Irish stew or haricot for cold mutton, minced veal. 2. Half-pay pudding.

Saturday.—1. Rump-steak pie, broiled mutton chops. 2. Baked arrowroot pudding.

APRIL, Things in Season.

Fish.—Brill, carp, cockles, crabs, dory, flounders, ling, lobsters, red and grey mullet, mussels, oysters, perch, prawns, salmon (but rather scarce and expensive), shad, shrimps, skate, smelts, soles, tench, turbot, whitings.

Meat.—Beef, lamb, mutton, veal.

Poultry.—Chickens, ducklings, fowls, pigeons, pullets, rabbits.

Game.—Leverets.

Vegetables.—Broccoli, celery, lettuces, young onions, parsnips, radishes, small salad, sea-kale, spinach, sprouts, various herbs.

Fruit.—Apples, nuts, pears, forced cherries, &c. for tarts, rhubarb, dried fruits, crystallized preserves.

ARROWROOT BISCUITS, or Drops.

Ingredients.—½ lb. of butter, 6 eggs, ½ lb. of flour, 6 oz. of arrowroot, ½ lb. of pounded loaf sugar. *Mode.*—Beat the butter to a cream : whisk the eggs to a strong froth, add them to the butter, stir in the flour a little at a time, and beat the mixture well. Break down all the lumps from the arrowroot, and add that with the sugar to the other ingredients. Mix all well together, drop the dough on a buttered tin, in pieces the size of a shilling, and bake the biscuits about ¼ hour in a slow oven. If the whites of the eggs are separated from the yolks, and both are beaten separately before being added to the other ingredients, the biscuits will be much lighter. *Time.*— ¼ hour. *Average cost*, 2s. 6d. *Sufficient* to make from 3 to 4 dozen biscuits. *Seasonable* at any time.

Arrowroot Blancmange	Artichokes, Boiled

ARROWROOT BLANCMANGE (an inexpensive Supper Dish).

Ingredients.—4 heaped tablespoonfuls of arrowroot, 1½ pint of milk, 3 laurel-leaves or the rind of ½ lemon, sugar to taste. *Mode.*—Mix to a smooth batter the arrowroot with ½ pint of the milk; put the other pint on the fire, with laurel-leaves or lemon-peel, whichever may be preferred, and let the milk steep until it is well flavoured; then strain the milk, and add it, boiling, to the mixed arrowroot; sweeten it with sifted sugar, and let it boil, stirring it all the time, till it thickens sufficiently to come from the saucepan. Grease a mould with pure salad-oil, pour in the blancmange, and, when quite set, turn it out on a dish, and pour round it a compôte of any kind of fruit, or garnish it with jam. A tablespoonful of brandy, stirred in just before the blancmange is moulded, very much improves the flavour of this sweet dish. *Time.*—Altogether, ½ hour. *Average cost, 6d.* without the garnishing. *Sufficient* for 4 or 5 persons. *Seasonable* at any time.

ARROWROOT PUDDING, Baked or Boiled.

Ingredients.—2 tablespoonfuls of arrowroot, 1½ pint of milk, 1 oz. of butter, the rind of ½ lemon, 2 heaped tablespoonfuls of moist sugar, a little grated nutmeg. *Mode.*—Mix the arrowroot with as much cold milk as will make it into a smooth batter, moderately thick; put the remainder of the milk into a stewpan with the lemon-peel, and let it infuse for about ½ hour; when it boils, strain it gently to the batter, stirring it all the time to keep it smooth; then add the butter; beat this well in until thoroughly mixed, and sweeten with moist sugar. Put the mixture into a pie-dish, round which has been placed a border of paste; grate a little nutmeg over the top, and bake the pudding from 1 to 1¼ hour, in a moderate oven, or boil it the same length of time in a well-buttered basin. To enrich this pudding, stir to the other ingredients, just before it is put in the oven, 3 well-whisked eggs, and add a tablespoonful of brandy. For a nursery pudding, the addition of the latter ingredients will be found quite superfluous, as also the paste round the edge of the dish. *Time.*—1 to 1¼ hour, baked or boiled.

Average cost, 7d. Sufficient for 5 or 6 persons. *Seasonable* at any time.

ARROWROOT SAUCE, for Puddings.

Ingredients.—2 small teaspoonfuls of arrowroot, 4 dessertspoonfuls of pounded sugar, the juice of 1 lemon, ¼ teaspoonful of grated nutmeg, ½ pint of water. *Mode.*—Mix the arrowroot smoothly with the water; put this into a stewpan; add the sugar, strained lemon-juice, and grated nutmeg. Stir these ingredients over the fire until they boil, when the sauce is ready for use. A small quantity of wine, or any liqueur, would very much improve the flavour of this sauce: it is usually served with bread, rice, custard, or any dry pudding that is not very rich. *Time.*—Altogether, 15 minutes. *Average cost, 4d. Sufficient* for 6 or 7 persons.

ARROWROOT, to make.

Ingredients.—Two teaspoonfuls of arrowroot, 3 tablespoonfuls of cold water, ½ pint of boiling water. *Mode.*—Mix the arrowroot smoothly in a basin with the cold water, then pour on it the *boiling* water, *stirring* all the time. The water must be *boiling* at the time it is poured on the mixture, or it will not thicken; if mixed with hot water only, it must be put into a clean saucepan, and boiled until it thickens; but this occasions more trouble, and is quite unnecessary, if the water is boiling at first. Put the arrowroot into a tumbler, sweeten it with lump sugar, and flavour it with grated nutmeg or cinnamon, or a piece of lemon-peel, or, when allowed, 3 tablespoonfuls of port or sherry. As arrowroot is in itself flavourless and insipid, it is almost necessary to add the wine to make it palatable. Arrowroot made with milk instead of water is far nicer, but is not so easily digested. It should be mixed in the same manner, with 3 tablespoonfuls of cold water, the boiling milk then poured on it, and well stirred. When made in this manner, no wine should be added, but merely sugar, and a little grated nutmeg or lemon-peel. *Time.*—If obliged to be boiled, 2 minutes. *Average cost, 2d.* per pint. *Sufficient* to make ½ pint of arrowroot.

ARTICHOKES, Boiled.

Ingredients.—To each ½ gallon of water,

Artichokes, a French Mode

allow 1 heaped tablespoonful of salt, a piece of soda the size of a shilling; artichokes. *Mode.*—Wash the artichokes well in several waters; see that no insects remain about them, and trim away

ARTICHOKES.

the leaves at the bottom. Cut off the stems and put them into *boiling* water, to which has been added salt and soda in the above proportion. Keep the saucepan uncovered, and let them boil quickly until tender; ascertain when they are done by thrusting a fork in them, or by trying if the leaves can

JERUSALEM ARTICHOKES.

be easily removed. Take them out, let them drain for a minute or two, and serve in a napkin, or with a little white sauce poured over. A tureen of melted butter should accompany them. This vegetable, unlike any other, is considered better for being gathered two or three days; but they must be well soaked and washed previous to dressing. *Time.*—20 to 25 minutes, after the water boils. *Sufficient,*—a dish of 5 or 6 for 4 persons. *Seasonable* from July to the beginning of September.

ARTICHOKES, a French Mode of Cooking.

Ingredients.—5 or 6 artichokes; to each ¼ gallon of water allow 1 heaped tablespoonful of salt, ½ teaspoonful of pepper, 1 bunch of savoury herbs, 2 oz. of butter. *Mode.*—Cut the ends of the leaves, as also the stems; put the artichokes into boiling water, with the above proportion of salt, pepper, herbs, and butter; let them boil quickly until tender, keeping the lid of the saucepan off, and when the leaves come out easily, they are cooked enough. To keep them a beautiful green, put a large piece of cinder into a muslin bag, and let it boil with them. Serve with plain melted butter. *Time.*—20 to 25

Artichokes, Boiled Jerusalem

minutes. *Sufficient,*—5 or 6 sufficient for 4 or 5 persons. *Seasonable* from July to the beginning of September.

ARTICHOKES, Fried (Entremets, or small dish to be served with the Second Course).

Ingredients.—5 or 6 artichokes, salt and water: for the batter, — ¼ lb. of flour, a little salt, the yolk of 1 egg, milk. *Mode.*—Trim and boil the artichokes, and rub them over with lemon-juice, to keep them white. When they are quite tender, take them up, remove the chokes, and divide the bottoms; dip each piece into batter, fry them into hot lard or dripping, and garnish the dish with crisped parsley. Serve with plain melted butter. *Time.*—20 minutes to boil the artichokes, 5 to 7 minutes to fry them. *Sufficient,*—5 or 6 for 4 or 5 persons. *Seasonable* from July to the beginning of September.

ARTICHOKES à l'Italienne.

Ingredients.—4 or 5 artichokes, salt and butter, about ½ pint of good gravy. *Mode.*—Trim and cut the artichokes into quarters, and boil them until tender in water mixed with a little salt and butter. When done, drain them well, and lay them all round the dish, with the leaves outside. Have ready some good gravy, highly flavoured with mushrooms; reduce it until quite thick, and pour it round the artichokes, and serve. *Time.*—20 to 25 minutes to boil the artichokes. *Sufficient* for one side-dish. *Seasonable* from July to the beginning of September.

ARTICHOKES, Boiled Jerusalem.

Ingredients.—To each ½ gallon of water allow 1 heaped tablespoonful of salt; artichokes. *Mode.*—Wash, peel, and shape the artichokes in a round or oval form, and put them into a saucepan with sufficient *cold* water to cover them salted in the above proportion. Let them boil gently until tender; take them up, drain them, and serve them in a napkin, or plain, whichever mode is preferred; send to table with them a tureen of melted butter or cream sauce, a little of which may be poured over the artichokes when they are *not* served in a napkin. *Time.*—About twenty minutes after the water boils. *Average cost, 2d. per lb.*

Artichokes, Mashed Jerusalem

Sufficient,—10 for a dish for 6 persons. *Seasonable.*—from September to June.

ARTICHOKES, Mashed Jerusalem.

Ingredients.—To each ½ gallon of water allow 1 oz. of salt, 15 or 16 artichokes, 1 oz. butter, pepper and salt to taste. *Mode.*—Boil the artichokes as in the preceding recipe until tender; drain and press the water from them, and beat them up with a fork. When thoroughly mashed and free from lumps, put them into a saucepan with the butter and a seasoning of *white* pepper and salt; keep stirring over the fire until the artichokes are quite hot, and serve. A pretty way of serving Jerusalem artichokes as an entremets, or second course dish, is to shape the artichokes in the form of a pear, and to serve them covered with white sauce, garnished with Brussels sprouts. *Time.*—About 20 minutes. *Average cost,* 2d. per lb. *Sufficient* for 6 or 7 persons. *Seasonable* from September to June.

ARTICHOKE (Jerusalem) SOUP, sometimes called Palestine Soup (a White Soup).

Ingredients.—3 slices of lean bacon or ham, ½ a head of celery, 1 turnip, 1 onion, 3 oz. of butter, 4 lbs. of artichokes, 1 pint of boiling milk, or ½ pint of boiling cream, salt and cayenne to taste, 2 lumps of sugar, 2½ quarts of white stock. *Mode.*—Put the bacon and vegetables, which should be cut into thin slices, into the stewpan with the butter. Braise these for ¼ of an hour, keeping them well stirred. Wash and pare the artichokes, and after cutting them into thin slices, add them, with a pint of stock, to the other ingredients. When these have gently stewed down to a smooth pulp, put in the remainder of the stock. Stir it well, adding the seasoning, and when it has simmered for five minutes, pass it through a strainer. Now pour it back into the stewpan, let it again simmer five minutes, taking care to skim it well, and stir it to the boiling milk or cream. Serve with small sippets of bread fried in butter. *Time.*—1 hour. *Average cost* per quart, 1s. 2d. *Seasonable* from June to October. *Sufficient* for 8 persons.

ASPARAGUS, Boiled.

Ingredients.—To each ½ gallon of water

Asparagus-Peas

allow 1 heaped tablespoonful of salt: asparagus. *Mode.*—Asparagus should be dressed as soon as possible after it is cut, although it may be kept for a day or two by putting the stalks into cold water, yet to be good, like every other vegetable, it cannot be cooked too fresh. Scrape

BOILED ASPARAGUS.

the white part of the stems, *beginning* from the *head*, and throw them into cold water; then tie them into bundles of about 20 each, keeping the heads all one way, and cut the stalks evenly, that they may all be the same length; put them into *boiling* water, with salt in the above

ASPARAGUS TONGS.

proportion; keep them boiling quickly until tender, with the saucepan uncovered. When the asparagus is done, dish it upon toast, which should be dipped in the water it was cooked in, and leave the white ends outward each way, with the points meeting in the middle. Serve with a tureen of melted butter. *Time.*— 15 to 18 minutes after the water boils. *Average cost,* in full season, 2s. 6d. the 100 heads. *Sufficient.*—Allow about 50 heads for 4 or 5 persons. *Seasonable.*— May be had forced from January, but cheapest in May, June and July.

ASPARAGUS-PEAS (Entremets, or to be served as a Side Dish with the Second Course).

Ingredients.—100 heads of asparagus, 2 oz. of butter, a small bunch of parsley, 2 or 3 green onions, flour, 1 lump of sugar, the yolks of 2 eggs, 4 tablespoonfuls of cream, salt. *Mode.*—Carefully scrape the asparagus, cut it into pieces of an equal size, avoiding that which is in the least hard or tough, and throw them into cold water. Then boil the asparagus in salt and water until three-parts done; take it out, drain, and place it on a cloth to dry the moisture away from it. Put it into a stewpan with the butter, parsley, and onions, and shake over a brisk fire for 10 minutes. Dredge in a little flour, add the sugar

2

Asparagus Pudding	August—Bills of Fare

and moisten with boiling water. When boiled a short time and reduced, take out the parsley and onions, thicken with the yolks of 2 eggs beaten with the cream ; add a seasoning of salt, and when the whole is on the point of simmering, serve. Make the sauce sufficiently thick to adhere to the vegetable. *Time.*—Altogether, ½ hour. *Average cost,* 1s. 6d. a pint. *Seasonable* in May, June, and July.

ASPARAGUS PUDDING (a delicious Dish, to be served with the Second Course).

Ingredients.—½ pint of asparagus peas, 4 eggs, 2 tablespoonfuls of flour, 1 tablespoonful of *very finely* minced ham, 1 oz. of butter, pepper and salt to taste, milk. *Mode.*—Cut up the nice green tender parts of asparagus, about the size of peas ; put them into a basin with the eggs, which should be well beaten, and the flour, ham, butter, pepper, and salt. Mix all these ingredients well together, and moisten with sufficient milk to make the pudding of the consistency of thick batter ; put it into a pint buttered mould, tie it down tightly with a floured cloth, place it in *boiling water*, and let it boil for 2 hours ; turn it out of the mould on to a hot dish, and pour plain melted butter *round*, but not over, the pudding. Green peas pudding may be made in exactly the same manner, substituting peas for the asparagus. *Time.*—2 hours. *Average cost,* 1s. 6d. per pint. *Seasonable* in May, June, and July.

ASPARAGUS SOUP.

Ingredients.—100 heads of asparagus, 2 quarts of medium stock (see STOCK), 1 pint of water, salt. *Mode.*—Scrape the asparagus, but do not cut off any of the stems, and boil it in a pint of water salted, *until the heads are nearly done.* Then drain the asparagus, cut off the green heads very neatly, and put them on one side until the soup is ready. If the stock is not made, add the stems of asparagus to the rest of the vegetables ; if, however, the stock is ready, boil the stems a little longer in the same water that they were first cooked in. Then strain them off, add the asparagus water to the stock, and when all is boiling drop in the green heads (or peas as they are called), and simmer for 2 or 3 minutes.

If the soup boils long after the asparagus is put in, the appearance of the vegetable would be quite spoiled: A small quantity of sherry, added after the soup is put into the tureen, would improve this soup very much. Sometimes a French roll is cut up and served in it. *Time.*—Nearly cook the asparagus, 12 minutes. *Average cost,* 1s. 9d. per quart. *Sufficient* for 6 or 8 persons. *Seasonable* from May to August.

ASPIC, or Ornamental Savoury Jelly.

Ingredients.—4 lbs. of knuckle of veal, 1 cow-heel, 3 or 4 slices of ham, and poultry trimmings, 2 carrots, 1 onion, 1 faggot of savoury herbs, 1 glass of sherry, 3 quarts of water ; seasoning to taste of salt and whole white pepper ; 3 eggs. *Mode.*—Lay the ham on the bottom of a stewpan, cut up the veal and cow-heel into small pieces and lay them on the ham ; add the poultry trimmings, vegetables, herbs, sherry, and water, and let the whole simmer very gently for 4 hours, carefully taking away all scum that may rise to the surface ; strain through a fine sieve, and pour into an earthen pan to get cold. Have ready a clean stewpan, put in the jelly, and be particular to leave the sediment behind, or it will not be clear. Add the whites of 3 eggs, with salt and pepper, to clarify ; keep stirring over the fire till the whole becomes very white ; then draw it to the side, and let it stand till clear. When this is the case, strain it through a cloth or jelly-bag, and use it for moulding poultry, &c. Tarragon vinegar may be added to give an additional flavour. *Time.*—Altogether 4 hours. *Average cost* for this quantity 4s.

AUGUST—BILLS OF FARE.
Dinner for 18 persons.
First Course.

Red Mullet.

Mock-Turtle Soup,
removed by
Broiled Salmon and
Caper Sauce.

Vase of
Flowers.

Soup à la Julienne,
removed by
Brill and Shrimp Sauce.

Perch.

August—Bills of Fare

Second Course.

Capon à la Financière.

Haunch of Venison.

Ham, garnished.

Vase of Flowers.

Leveret Pie.

Saddle of Mutton.

Roast Fowls.

Entrées.

Curried Lobster.

Fricandeau de Veau à la Jardinière.

Vase of Flowers.

Fillets of Ducks and Peas.

Lamb Cutlets à la Purée de Pommes de Terre.

Third Course.

Lobster Salad. Charlotte à la Vanille. Raspberry Tartlets.

Grouse removed by Cabinet Pudding.

Fruit Jelly.

Vase of Flowers.

Vol-au-Vent of Pears.

Larded Peahen, removed by Iced Pudding.

Custards. Cheesecakes. Prawns.

Dessert and Ices.

Dinner for 12 persons.

First Course.—Vermicelli soup; soup à la reine; boiled salmon; fried flounders; trout en matelot. *Entrées.* — Stewed pigeons; sweetbreads; ragoût of ducks; fillets of chickens and mushrooms. *Second Course.* — Quarter of lamb; cotellette de bœuf à la jardinière; roast fowls and boiled tongue; bacon and beans. *Third Course.*—Grouse; wheatears; greengage tart; whipped

August, Plain Family Dinners for

cream; vol-au-vent of plums; fruit jelly; iced pudding; cabinet pudding; dessert and ices.

Dinner for 8 persons.

First Course.—Julienne soup; fillets of turbot and Dutch sauce; red mullet. *Entrées.* — Riz de veau aux tomates; fillets of ducks and peas. *Second Course.* —Haunch of venison ; boiled capon and oysters ; ham, garnished; vegetables. *Third Course.* — Leveret; fruit jelly; compôte of greengages; plum tart; custards, in glasses; omelette soufflé; dessert and ices.

Dinner for 6 persons.

First Course.—Macaroni soup; crimped salmon and sauce Hollandaise; fried fillets of trout. *Entrées.* —Tendrons de veau and stewed peas; salmi of grouse. *Second Course.*—Roast loin of veal ; boiled bacon, garnished with French beans ; stewed beef à la jardinière; vegetables. *Third Course.*— Turkey poult ; plum tart ; custard pudding; vol-au-vent of pears; strawberry cream ; ratafia soufflé ; dessert.

First Course.—Vegetable-marrow soup; stewed mullet ; fillets of salmon and ravigotto sauce. *Entrées.*—Curried lobster ; fricandeau de veau à la jardinière. *Second Course.*—Roast saddle of mutton ; stewed shoulder of veal, garnished with forcemeat balls ; vegetables. *Third Course.*—Roast grouse and bread sauce; vol-au-vent of greengages ; fruit jelly; raspberry cream ; custards; fig pudding; dessert.

AUGUST, Plain Family Dinners for.

Sunday.—1. Vegetable-marrow soup. 2. Roast quarter of lamb, mint sauce; French beans and potatoes. 3. Raspberry-and-currant tart, custard pudding.
Monday.—1. Cold lamb and salad, small meat-pie, vegetable marrow, and white sauce. 2. Lemon dumplings.
Tuesday.—1. Boiled mackerel. 2. Stewed loin of veal, French beans and potatoes. 3. Baked raspberry pudding.
Wednesday.—1. Vegetable soup. 2. Lamb cutlets and French beans ; the remains of stewed shoulder of veal, mashed vegetable marrow. 3. Black-currant pudding.

August, Things in Season

Thursday.—1. Roast ribs of beef, Yorkshire pudding, French beans and potatoes. 2. Bread-and-butter pudding. *Friday.*—1. Fried soles and melted butter. 2. Cold beef and salad, lamb cutlets and mashed potatoes. 3. Cauliflowers and white sauce instead of pudding. *Saturday.*—1. Stewed beef and vegetables, with remains of cold beef ; mutton pudding. 2. Macaroni and cheese.

Sunday.—1. Salmon pudding. 2. Roast fillet of veal, boiled bacon-cheek garnished with tufts of cauliflowers, French beans and potatoes. 3. Plum tart, boiled custard pudding. *Monday.*—1. Baked soles. 2. Cold veal and bacon, salad, mutton cutlets and tomato sauce. 3. Boiled currant pudding. *Tuesday.*—1. Rice soup. 2. Roast fowls and water-cresses, boiled knuckle of ham, minced veal garnished with croûtons ; vegetables. 3. College pudding. *Wednesday.*—1. Curried fowl with remains of cold fowl ; dish of rice, stewed rump-steak and vegetables. 2. Plum tart. *Thursday.*—1. Boiled brisket of beef, carrots, turnips, suet dumplings, and potatoes. 2. Baked bread pudding. *Friday.*—1. Vegetable soup, made from liquor that beef was boiled in. 2. Cold beef and dressed cucumber, veal cutlets and tomato sauce. 3. Fondue. *Saturday.* — 1. Bubble-and-squeak, made from remains of cold beef ; cold veal-and-ham pie, salad. 2. Baked raspberry pudding.

AUGUST, Things in Season.

Fish.—Brill, carp, chub, crayfish, crabs, dory, eels, flounders, grigs, herrings, lobsters, mullet, pike, prawns, salmon, shrimps, skate, soles, sturgeon, thornback, trout, turbot. *Meat.*—Beef, lamb, mutton, veal, buck venison. *Poultry.*—Chickens, ducklings, fowls, green geese, pigeons, plovers, pullets, rabbits, turkey poults, wheatears, wild ducks. *Game.*—Leverets, grouse, blackcock. *Vegetables.* — Artichokes, asparagus, beans, carrots, cabbages, cauliflowers, celery, cresses, endive, lettuces, mush-

Bacon, Broiled Rashers of

rooms, onions, peas, potatoes, radishes, sea-kale, small salading, sprouts, turnips, various kitchen herbs, vegetable marrows. *Fruit.*—Currants, figs, filberts, gooseberries, grapes, melons, mulberries, nectarines, peaches, pears, pineapples, plums, raspberries, walnuts.

BACON, Boiled.

Ingredients.—Bacon ; water. *Mode.*— As bacon is frequently excessively salt, let it be soaked in warm water for an hour or two previous to dressing it ; then pare off the rusty parts, and scrape the under-side and rind as clean as possible. Put it into a saucepan of cold water ; let it

BOILED BACON.

come gradually to a boil, and as fast as the scum rises to the surface of the water, remove it. Let it simmer very gently until it is *thoroughly* done ; then take it up, strip off the skin, and sprinkle over the bacon a few bread raspings, and garnish with tufts of cauliflower or Brussels sprouts. When served alone, young and tender broad beans or green peas are the usual accompaniments. *Time.*—1 lb. of bacon, ¾ hour ; 2 lbs., 1½ hour. *Average cost,* 10d. to 1s. per lb. for the primest parts. *Sufficient.*—2 lbs., when served with poultry or veal, sufficient for 10 persons. *Seasonable* at any time.

BACON, Broiled Rashers of.

Before purchasing bacon, ascertain that it is perfectly free from rust, which may easily be detected by its yellow colour ; and for broiling, the streaked part of the thick flank is generally the most esteemed. Cut it into *thin* slices, take off the rind, and broil over a nice clear fire ; turn it two or three times, and serve very hot. Should there be any cold bacon left from the previous day, it answers very well for breakfast, cut into slices, and broiled or fried. *Time.*—3 or 4 minutes. *Average cost,* 10d. to 1s. per lb. for the primest parts. *Seasonable* at any time. *Note.*—When the bacon is cut very thin, the slices may be curled round and fastened by means of small skewers, and fried or toasted before the fire.

BACON and HAMS, Curing of.

The carcass of the hog, after hanging over-night to cool, is laid on a strong bench or stool, and the head is separated from the body at the neck close behind the ears; the feet and also the internal fat are removed. The carcass is next divided into two sides in the following manner:—The ribs are divided about an inch from the spine on each side, and the spine, with the ends of the ribs attached, together with the internal flesh between it and the kidneys, and also the flesh above it, throughout the whole length of the sides, are removed. The portion of the carcass thus cut out is in the form of a wedge—the breadth of the interior consisting of the breadth of the spine, and about an inch of the ribs on each side, being diminished to about half an inch at the exterior or skin along the back. The breast-bone, and also the first anterior rib, are also dissected from the side. Sometimes the whole of the ribs are removed; but this, for reasons afterwards to be noticed, is a very bad practice. When the hams are cured separately from the sides, which is generally the case, they are cut out so as to include the hock-bone, in a similar manner to the London mode of cutting a haunch of mutton. The carcass of the hog thus cut up is ready for being salted, which process, in large curing establishments, is generally as follows:— The skin side of the pork is rubbed over with a mixture of fifty parts by weight of salt, and one part of saltpetre in powder, and the incised parts of the ham or flitch, and the inside of the flitch, covered with the same. The salted bacon, in pairs of flitches with the insides to each other, is piled one pair of flitches above another on benches slightly inclined, and furnished with spouts or troughs to convey the brine to receivers in the floor of the salting-house, to be afterwards used for pickling pork for navy purposes. In this state the bacon remains a fortnight, which is sufficient for flitches cut from hogs of a carcass weight less than 15 stone (14 lbs. to the stone). Flitches of a larger size, at the expiration of that time, are wiped dry and reversed in their place in the pile, having, at the same time, about half the

first quantity of fresh, dry, common salt sprinkled over the inside and incised parts; after which they remain on the benches for another week. Hams being thicker than flitches, will require, when less than 20 lbs. weight, 3 weeks; and when above that weight, 4 weeks to remain under the above described process. The next and last process in the preparation of bacon and hams, previous to being sent to market, is drying. This is effected by hanging the flitches and hams for 2 or 3 weeks in a room heated by stoves, or in a smoke-house, in which they are exposed for the same length of time to the smoke arising from the slow combustion of the sawdust of oak or other hard wood. The latter mode of completing the curing process has some advantages over the other, as by it the meat is subject to the action of *creosote*, a volatile oil produced by the combustion of the sawdust, which is powerfully antiseptic. The process also furnishing a thin covering of a resinous varnish, excludes the air not only from the muscle, but also from the fat—thus effectually preventing the meat from becoming rusted; and the principal reasons for condemning the practice of removing the ribs from the flitches of pork are, that by so doing the meat becomes unpleasantly hard and pungent in the process of salting, and, by being more exposed to the action of the air, becomes sooner and more extensively rusted. Notwithstanding its superior efficacy in completing the process of curing, the flavour which smoke-drying imparts to meat is disliked by many persons, and it is therefore by no means the most general mode of drying adopted by mercantile curers. A very impure variety of *pyroligneous* acid, or vinegar made from the destructive distillation of wood, is sometimes used, on account of the highly preservative power of the creosote which it contains, and also to impart the smoke-flavour; in which latter object, however, the coarse flavour of tar is given, rather than that derived from the smoke from combustion of wood. A considerable portion of the bacon and hams salted in Ireland is exported from that country packed amongst salt, in bales, immediately from the salting process, without having been in any degree dried. In the process of salting above described, pork loses from 8 to 10 per cent. of its weight, according to the size and quality of the

Bacon, to Cure and Keep

meat ; and a further diminution of weight, to the extent of 5 to 6 per cent. takes place in drying during the first fortnight after being taken out of salt; so that the total loss in weight occasioned by the preparation of bacon and hams in a proper state for market, is not less on an average than 15 per cent. on the weight of the fresh pork.

BACON, to Cure and Keep it free from Rust (Cobbett's Recipe).

The two sides that remain, and which are called flitches, are to be cured for bacon. They are first rubbed with salt on their insides, or flesh sides, then placed one on the other, the flesh sides uppermost, in a salting-trough which has a gutter round its edges to drain away the brine ; for, to have sweet and fine bacon, the flitches must not be sopping in brine, which gives it the sort of vile taste that barrel and sea pork have. Every one knows how different is the taste of fresh dry salt from that of salt in a dissolved state ; therefore change the salt often,— once in 4 or 5 days ; let it melt and sink in, but not lie too long ; twice change the flitches, put that at bottom which was first on the top : this mode will cost you a great deal more in salt than the sopping mode, but without it your bacon will not be so sweet and fine, nor keep so well. As for the time required in making your flitches sufficiently salt, it depends on circumstances. It takes a longer time for a thick than a thin flitch, and longer in dry than in damp weather, or in a dry than in a damp place ; but for the flitches of a hog of five score, in weather not very dry or damp, about 6 weeks may do ; and as yours is to be fat, which receives little injury from over-salting, give time enough, for you are to have bacon until Christmas comes again. The place for salting should, like a dairy, always be cool, but well ventilated ; confined air, though cool, will taint meat sooner than the midday sun accompanied by a breeze. With regard to smoking the bacon, two precautions are necessary : first, to hang the flitches where no rain comes down upon them ; and next, that the smoke must proceed from wood, not peat, turf, or coal. As to the time required to smoke a flitch, it depends a good deal upon whether there be a constant fire beneath, and whether the fire be large or small ; a month will do, if the fire be pretty

Bacon or Hams, to Cure

constant and rich, as a farm-house fir usually is ; but over-smoking, or rathe too long hanging in the air, makes th bacon rust ; great attention should ther fore be paid to this matter. The flitc ought not to be dried up to the hardnes of a board, and yet it ought to be pe fectly dry. Before you hang it up, lay on the floor, scatter the flesh side prett thickly over with bran, or with son fine sawdust, not of deal or fir ; rub it c the flesh, or pat it well down upon i this keeps the smoke from getting int the little openings, and makes a sort crust to be dried on. To keep the bace sweet and good, and free from hopper sift fine some clean and dry wood ashe Put some at the bottom of a box or che long enough to hold a flitch of bacon ; la in one flitch, then put in more ashes, the another flitch, and cover this with six c eight inches of the ashes. The place whe the box or chest is kept ought to be dr and, should the ashes become damp, the should be put in the fireplace to dry, an when cold, put back again. With the precautions, the bacon will be as good the end of the year as on the first day. F simple general rules, these may be safe taken as a guide ; and those who impl citly follow the directions given, w possess at the expiration of from 6 weel to 2 months well-flavoured and well-cure bacon.

BACON or HAMS, to Cure in th Devonshire way.

Ingredients.—To every 14 lbs. of mea allow 2 oz. of saltpetre, 2 oz. of salt pr nella, 1 lb. of common salt. For th pickle, 3 gallons of water, 5 lbs. of comme salt, 7 lbs. of coarse sugar, 3 lbs. of ba salt. *Mode.*—Weigh the sides, ham and cheeks, and to every 14 lbs. allow th above proportion of saltpetre, salt pr nella, and common salt. Pound and m these together, and rub well into th meat ; lay it in a stone trough or tu rubbing it thoroughly, and turning daily for two successive days. At th end of the second day, pour on it a pick made as follows :—Put the above ingr dients into a saucepan, set it on the fir and stir frequently ; remove all the scu allow it to boil for ¼ hour, and pour hot over the meat. Let the hams, &c be well rubbed and turned daily ; if th meat is small, a fortnight will be suf cient for the sides and shoulders to r

Bacon, to Cure

main in the pickle, and the hams 3 weeks; it from 30 lbs. and upwards, 3 weeks will be required for the sides, &c., and from 4 to 5 weeks for the hams. On taking the pieces out, let them drain for an hour, cover with dry sawdust, and smoke from a fortnight to three weeks. Boil and carefully skim the pickle after using, and it will keep good, closely corked, for 2 years. When boiling it for use, add about 2 lbs. of common salt, and the same of treacle, to allow for waste. Tongues are excellent put into this pickle cold, having been first rubbed well with saltpetre and salt, and allowed to remain 24 hours, not forgetting to make a deep incision under the thick part of the tongue, so as to allow the pickle to penetrate more readily. A fortnight or three weeks, according to the size of the tongue, will be sufficient. *Time.*—Small meat to remain in the pickle a fortnight, hams 3 weeks; to be smoked from a fortnight to 3 weeks.

BACON, to Cure in the Wiltshire way.

Ingredients.—1½ lb. of coarse sugar ½ lb. of bay salt, 6 oz. of saltpetre, 1 lb. of common salt. *Mode.*—Sprinkle each flitch with salt, and let the blood drain off for 24 hours; then pound and mix the above ingredients well together and rub it well into the meat, which should be turned every day for a month; then hang it to dry, and afterwards smoke it for 10 days. *Time.*—To remain in the pickle from three to four weeks, to be smoked 10 days, or rather longer.

BACON, Fried Rashers of, and Poached Eggs.

Ingredients. — Bacon; eggs. *Mode.*— Cut the bacon into thin slices, trim away the rusty parts, and cut off the rind. Put it into a *cold* frying-pan, that is to say, do not place the pan on the fire before the bacon is in it. Turn it 2 or 3 times, and dish it on a very hot dish. Poach the eggs and slip them on to the bacon without breaking the yolks, and serve quickly. *Time.*—3 or 4 minutes. *Average cost,* 10d. to 1s. per lb. for the primest parts. *Sufficient.*—Allow 6 eggs for 3 persons. *Seasonable* at any time. *Note.* — Fried rashers of bacon, curled, serve as a pretty garnish to many dishes; and, for small families, answer very well as a

Barberries

substitute for boiled bacon, to serve with a small dish of poultry, &c.

The Bain Marie. — It is an open kind of vessel, as shown in the engraving, and is a utensil much used in modern

THE BAIN MARIE.

cookery, both in English and French kitchens. It is filled with boiling or nearly boiling water; and into this water should be put all the stewpans containing those ingredients which it is desired to keep hot. The quantity and quality of the contents of these vessels are not at all affected; and if the hour of dinner is uncertain in any establishment, by reason of the nature of the master's business, nothing is so sure a means of preserving the flavour of all dishes as the employment of the bain marie.

BARBEL.

Ingredients.—½ pint of port wine, a saltspoonful of salt, 2 tablespoonfuls of vinegar, 2 sliced onions, a faggot of sweet herbs, nutmeg and mace to taste, the juice of a lemon, 2 anchovies; 1 or 2 barbels, according to size. *Mode.* —Boil the barbels in salt and water till done; pour off some of the water, and to the remainder put the ingredients mentioned above. Simmer gently for ½ hour or rather more, and strain. Put in the fish, heat it gradually, but do not let it boil, or it will be broken. *Time.*—Altogether 1 hour. *Sufficient* for 4 persons. *Seasonable* from September to November.

BARBERRIES (Berberris vulgaris).

A fruit of such great acidity, that even birds refuse to eat it. In this respect, it nearly approaches the tamarind. When boiled with sugar, it makes a very agreeable preserve or jelly, according to the different modes of preparing it. Barberries are also used as a dry sweetmeat, and in sugarplums or comfits; are pickled with vinegar, and are used for various culinary purposes. They are well calculated to allay heat and thirst in persons afflicted with fevers. The berries, arranged on

Barberries, to preserve

bunches of nicely curled parsley, make an exceedingly pretty garnish for supper dishes, particularly for white meats, like boiled fowl à la Béchamel, the three colours, scarlet, green, and white, contrasting well, and producing a very good effect.

BARBERRIES, to preserve in Bunches.

Ingredients.—1 pint of syrup, barberries. *Mode.*—Prepare some small pieces of clean white wood, 3 inches long and ¼ inch wide, and tie the fruit on to these in nice bunches. Have ready some clear syrup (*see* SYRUP) ; put in the barberries, and simmer them in it for 2 successive days, boiling them for nearly ½ hour each day, and covering them each time with the syrup when cold. When the fruit looks perfectly clear it is sufficiently done, and should be stowed away in pots, with the syrup poured over, or the fruit may be candied. *Time.*—½ hour to simmer each day. *Seasonable* in autumn.

BARLEY SOUP.

Ingredients.—2 lbs. of shin of beef, ¼ lb. of pearl barley, a large bunch of parsley, 4 onions, 6 potatoes, salt and pepper, 4 quarts of water. *Mode.*—Put in all the ingredients, and simmer gently for 3 hours. *Time.*—3 hours. *Average cost*, 2½d. per quart. *Seasonable* all the year, but more suitable for winter.

BARLEY-SUGAR, to make.

Ingredients.—To every lb. of sugar allow ½ pint of water, ½ the white of an egg. *Mode.*—Put the sugar into a well-tinned saucepan, with the water, and, when the former is dissolved, set it over a moderate fire, adding the well-beaten egg before the mixture gets warm, and stir it well together. When it boils, remove the scum as it rises, and keep it boiling until no more appears, and the syrup looks perfectly clear ; then strain it through a fine sieve or muslin bag, and put it back into the saucepan. Boil it again like caramel, until it is brittle, when a little is dropped in a basin of cold water : it is then sufficiently boiled. Add a little lemon-juice and a few drops of essence of lemon, and let it stand for a minute or two. Have ready a marble slab or large dish, rubbed over with salad-oil ; pour on it the sugar, and cut

Batter Pudding

it into strips with a pair of scissors : these strips should then be twisted, and the barley-sugar stored away in a very dry place. It may be formed into lozenges or drops, by dropping the sugar in a very small quantity at a time on to the oiled slab or dish. *Time.*—¼ hour. *Average cost, 7d. Sufficient* for 5 or 6 sticks.

BARLEY-WATER, to make.

Ingredients.—2 oz. of pearl barley, 2 quarts of boiling water, 1 pint of cold water. *Mode.*—Wash the barley in cold water ; put it into a saucepan with the above proportion of cold water, and when it has boiled for about ¼ hour, strain off the water, and add the 2 quarts of fresh boiling water. Boil it until the liquid is reduced one half ; strain it, and it will be ready for use. It may be flavoured with lemon-peel, after being sweetened, or a small piece may be simmered with the barley. When the invalid may take it, a little lemon-juice gives this pleasant drink in illness a very nice flavour ; as does also a small quantity of port wine. *Time.*—To boil until the liquid is reduced one half. *Sufficient* to make 1 quart of barley-water.

BATTER PUDDING, Baked.

Ingredients.—1½ pint of milk, 4 tablespoonfuls of flour, 2 oz. of butter, 4 eggs, a little salt. *Mode.*—Mix the flour with a small quantity of cold milk ; make the remainder hot, and pour it on to the flour, keeping the mixture well stirred ; add the butter, eggs, and salt ; beat the whole well, and put the pudding into a buttered pie-dish ; bake for ¾ hour, and serve with sweet sauce, wine sauce, or stewed fruit. Baked in small cups, very pretty little puddings may be made ; they should be eaten with the same accompaniments as above. *Time.*—¾ hour. *Average cost, 9d. Sufficient* for 5 or 6 persons. *Seasonable* at any time.

BATTER PUDDING, Baked, with Dried or Fresh Fruit.

Ingredients.—1½ pint of milk, 4 tablespoonfuls of flour, 3 eggs, 2 oz. of finely-shredded suet, ¼ lb. of currants, a pinch of salt. *Mode.*—Mix the milk, flour, and eggs to a smooth batter ; add a little salt, the suet, and the currants, which should be well washed, picked, and dried ;

Batter Pudding, Boiled

put the mixture into a buttered pie-dish, and bake in a moderate oven for 1¼ hour. When fresh fruits are in season, this pudding is exceedingly nice, with damsons, plums, red currants, gooseberries, or apples; when made with these, the pudding must be thickly sprinkled over with sifted sugar. Boiled batter pudding, with fruit, is made in the same manner, by putting the fruit into a buttered basin, and filling it up with batter made in the above proportion, but omitting the suet. It must be sent quickly to table, and covered plentifully with sifted sugar. *Time.*—Baked batter pudding, with fruit, 1¼ to 1½ hour; boiled ditto, 1½ to 1¾ hour, allowing that both are made with the above proportion of batter. Smaller puddings will be done enough in ¾ or 1 hour. *Average cost,* 10d. *Sufficient* for 7 or 8 persons. *Seasonable* at any time, with dried fruits.

BATTER PUDDING, Boiled.

Ingredients.—3 eggs, 1 oz. of butter, 1 pint of milk, 3 tablespoonfuls of flour, a little salt. *Mode.*—Put the flour into a basin, and add sufficient milk to moisten it; carefully rub down all the lumps with a spoon, then pour in the remainder of the milk, and stir in the butter, which should be previously melted; keep beating the mixture, add the eggs and a pinch of salt, and, when the batter is quite smooth, put it into a well-buttered basin, tie it down very tightly, and put it into boiling water; move the basin about for a few minutes after it is put into the water, to prevent the flour settling in any part, and boil for 1¼ hour. This pudding may also be boiled in a floured cloth that has been wetted in hot water: it will then take a few minutes less than when boiled in a basin. Send batter puddings very quickly to table, and serve with sweet sauce, wine sauce, stewed fruit, or jam of any kind: when the latter is used, a little of it may be placed round the dish in small quantities, as a garnish. *Time.* 1¼ hour in a basin, 1 hour in a cloth. *Average cost,* 7d. *Sufficient* for 5 or 6 persons. *Seasonable* at any time.

BATTER PUDDING, with Orange Marmalade.

Ingredients.—4 eggs, 1 pint of milk, 1½ oz. of loaf sugar, 3 tablespoonfuls of flour. *Mode.*—Make the batter with the

Beans, Broad, à la Poulette

above ingredients, put it into a well-buttered basin, tie it down with a cloth, and boil for 1 hour. As soon as it is turned out of the basin, put a small jar of orange marmalade all over the top, and send the pudding very quickly to table. It is advisable to warm the marmalade to make it liquid. *Time.*—1 hour. *Average cost,* with the marmalade, 1s. 3d. *Sufficient* for 5 or 6 persons. *Seasonable* at any time; but more suitable for a winter pudding.

BEANS, Boiled Broad or Windsor.

Ingredients. — To each ½ gallon of water, allow 1 heaped tablespoonful of salt; beans. *Mode.*—This is a favourite vegetable with many persons, but, to be nice, should be 'young and freshly gathered. After shelling the beans, put them into *boiling* water, salted in the above proportion, and let them boil rapidly until tender. Drain them well in a colander; dish, and serve with them separately a tureen of parsley and butter. Boiled bacon should always accompany this vegetable, but  the beans should be cooked separately.

BROAD BEANS.

It is usually served with the beans laid round, and the parsley and butter in a tureen. Beans also make an excellent garnish to a ham, and when used for this purpose, if very old, should have their skins removed. *Time.* — Very young beans, 15 minutes; when a moderate size, 20 to 25 minutes, or longer. *Average cost,* unshelled, 6d. per peck. *Sufficient.*—Allow one peck for 6 or 7 persons. *Seasonable* in July and August.

BEANS, Broad, à la Poulette.

Ingredients.—2 pints of broad beans, ½ pint of stock or broth, a small bunch of savoury herbs, including parsley, a small lump of sugar, the yolk of 1 egg, ½ pint of cream, pepper and salt to taste. *Mode.*—Procure some young and freshly-gathered beans, and shell sufficient to make 2 pints; boil them, as in the

Beans, Boiled French

preceding recipe, until nearly done; then drain them and put them into a stewpan with the stock, finely-minced herbs, and sugar. Stew the beans until perfectly tender, and the liquor has dried away a little; then beat up the yolk of an egg with the cream, add this to the beans, let the whole get thoroughly hot, and when on the point of simmering, serve. Should the beans be very large, the skin should be removed previously to boiling them. *Time.*—10 minutes to boil the beans, 15 minutes to stew them in the stock. *Average cost,* unshelled, 6*d.* per peck. *Seasonable* in July and August.

BEANS, Boiled French.

Ingredients.—To each ½ gallon of water allow 1 heaped tablespoonful of salt, a *very small* piece of soda. *Mode.*—This vegetable should always be eaten young, as when allowed to grow too long it tastes stringy and tough when cooked. Cut off the heads and tails, and a thin strip on each side of the beans to remove the strings; then divide each bean into 4 or 6 pieces, according to size, cutting them lengthways in a slanting direction, and as they are cut put them into cold water, with a small quantity of salt dissolved in it. Have ready a saucepan of boiling water, with salt and soda in the above proportion; put in the beans, keep them boiling quickly, with the lid uncovered, and be careful that they do not get smoked. When tender, which may be ascertained by their sinking to the bottom of the saucepan, take them up, pour them into a colander, and when drained, dish and serve with plain melted butter. When very young, beans are sometimes served whole: thus dressed, their colour and flavour are much better preserved, but the more general way of sending them to table is to cut them into thin strips. *Time.*—Very young beans, 10 to 12 minutes; moderate size, 15 to 20 minutes, after the water boils. *Average cost,* in full season, 1*s.* 4*d.* per peck, but when forced very expensive. *Sufficient.* —Allow ½ peck for 6 or 7 persons. *Seasonable* from the middle of July to the end of September, but may be had forced from February to the beginning of June.

BEANS, French Mode of Cooking French.

Ingredients.—A quart of French beans, 3 oz. of fresh butter, pepper and salt to

Beans, Haricots Blancs, &c.

taste, the juice of ½ lemon. *Mode.*—Cut and boil the beans by the preceding recipe, and when tender, put them into a stewpan, and shake over the fire, to dry away the moisture from the beans. When quite dry and hot, add the butter, pepper, salt, and lemon-juice; keep moving the stewpan, without using a spoon, as that would break the beans; and when the butter is melted, and all is thoroughly hot, serve. If the butter should not mix well, add a tablespoonful of gravy, and serve very quickly. *Time.*— About ¼ hour to boil the beans; 10 minutes to shake them over the fire. *Average cost,* in full season, about 1*s.* 4*d.* per peck. *Sufficient* for 3 or 4 persons. *Seasonable* from the middle of July to the end of September.

BEANS, to Boil Haricots Blancs, or White Haricot.

Ingredients.—1 quart of white haricot beans, 2 quarts of soft water, 1 oz. of butter, 1 heaped tablespoonful of salt. *Mode.*—Put the beans into cold water, let them soak from 2 to 4 hours, according to their age; then put them into cold water salted in the above proportion, bring them to boil, and let them simmer very slowly until tender; pour the water away from them, let them stand by the side of the fire, with the lid of the saucepan partially off, to allow the beans to dry; then add 1 oz. of butter and a seasoning of pepper and salt. Shake the beans about for a minute or two, and serve: do not stir them with a spoon, for fear of breaking them to pieces. *Time.*—After the water boils, from 2 to 2½ hours. *Average cost,* 4*d.* per quart. *Sufficient* for 4 or 5 persons. *Seasonable* in winter, when other vegetables are scarce.

Note.—Haricots blancs, when new and fresh, should be put into boiling water, and do not require any soaking previous to dressing.

BEANS, Haricots Blancs & Minced Onions.

Ingredients.—1 quart of white haricot beans, 4 middling-sized onions, ¼ pint of good brown gravy, pepper and salt to taste, a little flour. *Mode.*—Peel and mince the onions not too finely, and fry them in butter of a light brown colour; dredge over them a little flour, and add

Beans, Haricots Blancs, &c.

the gravy and a seasoning of pepper and salt. Have ready a pint of haricot beans well boiled and drained ; put them with the onions and gravy, mix all well together, and serve very hot. *Time.*—From 2 to 2½ hours to boil the beans ; 5 minutes to fry the onions. *Average cost, 4d.* per tart. *Sufficient* for 4 or 5 persons. *Seasonable* in winter.

BEANS, Haricots Blancs à la Maître d'Hôtel.

Ingredients.—1 quart of white haricot beans, ¼ lb. of fresh butter, 1 tablespoonful of minced parsley, pepper and salt to taste, the juice of ½ lemon. *Mode.* — Should the beans be very dry, soak them for an hour or two in cold water, and boil them until perfectly tender, as in the preceding recipe. If the water should boil

away, replenish it with a little more cold, which makes the skin of the beans tender. Let them be very thoroughly done; drain them well ; then add to them the butter, minced parsley, and a seasoning of pepper and salt. Keep moving the stewpan over the fire without using a spoon, as this would break

HARICOT BEANS.

the beans ; and, when the various ingredients are well mixed with them, squeeze in the lemon-juice, and serve very hot. *Time.*—From 2 to 2½ hours to boil the beans. *Average cost, 4d.* per quart. *Sufficient* for 4 or 5 persons. *Seasonable* in winter.

BECHAMEL, or French White Sauce.

Ingredients.—1 small bunch of parsley, 2 cloves, ½ bay-leaf, 1 small bunch of savoury herbs, salt to taste ; 3 or 4 mushrooms, when obtainable ; 2 pints of white stock, 1 pint of milk or cream, 1 tablespoonful of arrowroot. *Mode.*—Put the stock into a stewpan, with the parsley, cloves, bay-leaf, herbs, and mushrooms ; add a seasoning of salt, but no pepper, as that would give the sauce a dusty appearance, and should be avoided. When it has boiled long enough to extract the flavour

Beef, Aitchbone of, Boiled

of the herbs, &c., strain it, and boil it up quickly again, until it is nearly half reduced. Now mix the arrowroot smoothly with the milk or cream, and let it simmer very gently for 5 minutes over a slow fire ; pour to it the stock, and continue to simmer slowly for 10 minutes, if the sauce be thick. If, on the contrary, it be too thin, it must be stirred over a sharp fire till it thickens. Always make it thick, as it can easily be thinned with cream, milk, or white stock. This sauce is excellent for pouring over boiled fowls. *Time.*—Altogether, 2 hours. *Average cost, 3s.* per quart, with cream at 1s. 6d. per pint.

BECHAMEL MAIGRE, or Without Meat.

Ingredients.—2 onions, 1 blade of mace, mushroom trimmings, a small bunch of parsley, 1 oz. of butter, flour, ½ pint of water, 1 pint of milk, salt, the juice of ½ lemon, 2 eggs. *Mode.*—Put in a stewpan the milk and ½ pint of water, with the onions, mace, mushrooms, parsley, and salt. Let these simmer gently for 20 minutes. In the meantime, rub on a plate 1 oz. of flour and butter ; put it to the liquor, and stir it well till it boils up ; then place it by the side of the fire, and continue stirring until it is perfectly smooth. Now strain it through a sieve into a basin, after which put it back in the stewpan, and add the lemon-juice. Beat up the yolks of the eggs with about 4 dessertspoonfuls of milk ; strain this to the sauce, keep stirring it over the fire, *but do not let it boil, or it will curdle.* *Time.*—Altogether, ¾ hour. *Average cost,* 5d. per pint.

This is a good sauce to pour over boiled fowls when they are a bad colour.

BEEF, Aitchbone of, Boiled.

Ingredients. — Beef, water. *Mode.*—After this joint has been in salt 5 or 6 days, it will be ready for use, and will not take so long boiling as a round, for it is not so solid. Wash the meat, and, if too salt, soak it for a few hours, changing the water once or twice, till the required freshness is obtained. Put into a saucepan, or boiling-pot, sufficient water to cover the meat ; set it over the fire, and when it boils, plunge in the joint, and let it boil up quickly. Now draw the pot to the side of the fire, and let the

Beef à la Mode

process be very gradual, as the water must only simmer, or the meat will be hard and tough. Carefully remove the scum from the surface of the water, and

AITCH-BONE OF BEEF.

continue doing this for a few minutes after it first boils. Carrots and turnips are served with this dish, and sometimes suet dumplings, which may be boiled with the beef. Garnish with a few of the carrots and turnips, and serve the remainder in a vegetable-dish. *Time.*— An aitch-bone of 10 lbs., 2½ hours after the water boils; one of 20 lbs., 4 hours. *Average cost*, 6d. per lb. *Sufficient.*— 10 lbs. for 7 or 8 persons. *Seasonable* all the year, but best from September to March.

Note.—The liquor in which the meat has been boiled may be easily converted into a very excellent pea-soup. It will require very few vegetables, as it will be impregnated with the flavour of those boiled with the meat.

BEEF A LA MODE.

Ingredients.—6 or 7 lbs. of the thick flank of beef, a few slices of fat bacon, 1 teacupful of vinegar, black pepper, allspice, 2 cloves well mixed and finely pounded, making altogether 1 heaped teaspoonful; salt to taste, 1 bunch of savoury herbs, including parsley, all finely minced and well mixed; 3 onions, 1 large carrots, 1 turnip, 1 head of celery, 1½ pint of water, 1 glass of port wine. *Mode.*—Slice and fry the onions of a pale brown, and cut up the other vegetables in small pieces, and prepare the beef for stewing in the following manner:—Choose a fine piece of beef, cut the bacon into long slices, about an inch in thickness, dip them into vinegar, and then into a little of the above seasoning of spice, &c., mixed with the same quantity of minced herbs. With a sharp knife make holes deep enough to let in the bacon; then rub the beef over with the remainder of the

Beef, Baked

seasoning and herbs, and bind it up in a nice shape with tape. Have ready a well-tinned stew-pan (it should not be much larger than the piece of meat you are cooking), into which put the beef, with the vegetables, vinegar, and water. Let it simmer *very gently* for 5 hours, or rather longer, should the meat not be extremely tender, and turn it once or twice. When ready to serve, take out the beef, remove the tape, and put it on a hot dish. Skim off every particle of fat from the gravy, add the port wine, just let it boil, pour it over the beef, and it is ready to serve. Great care must be taken that this does not boil fast, or the meat will be tough and tasteless; it should only just bubble. When convenient, all kinds of stews, &c. should be cooked on a hot plate, as the process is so much more gradual than on an open fire. *Time.*—5 hours, or rather more. *Average cost*, 7d. per lb. *Sufficient* for 7 or 8 persons. *Seasonable* all the year, but more suitable for a winter dish.

BEEF A LA MODE (Economical).

Ingredients.—About 3 lbs. of clod or sticking of beef, 2 oz. of clarified dripping, 1 large onion, flour, 2 quarts of water, 12 berries of allspice, 2 bay-leaves, ½ teaspoonful of whole black pepper, salt to taste. *Mode.*—Cut the beef into small pieces, and roll them in flour; put the dripping into a stewpan with the onion, which should be sliced thin. Let it get quite hot; lay in the pieces of beef, and stir them well about. When nicely browned all over, add *by degrees* boiling water in the above proportion, and, as the water is added, keep the whole well stirred. Put in the spice, bay-leaves, and seasoning, cover the stewpan closely, and set it by the side of the fire to stew very *gently*, till the meat becomes quite tender, which will be in about 3 hours, when it will be ready to serve. Remove the bay-leaves before it is sent to table. *Time.*—3 hours. *Average cost*, 1s. 3d. *Sufficient* for 6 persons. *Seasonable* at any time.

BEEF, Baked.

[COLD MEAT COOKERY. 1.] *Ingredients.* About 2 lbs. of cold roast beef, 2 small onions, 1 large carrot or 2 small ones, 1 turnip, a small bunch of savoury herbs, salt and pepper to taste, quite

Beef-Bones, Broiled

½ pint of gravy, 3 tablespoonfuls of ale, crust or mashed potatoes. *Mode.*—Cut the beef in slices, allowing a small amount of fat to each slice; place a layer of this in the bottom of a pie-dish, with a portion of the onions, carrots, and turnips, which must be sliced; mince the herbs, strew them over the meat, and season with pepper and salt. Then put another layer of meat, vegetables, and seasoning; and proceed in this manner until all the ingredients are used. Pour in the gravy and ale (water may be substituted for the former, but it is not so nice), cover with a crust or mashed potatoes, and bake for ½ hour, or rather longer. *Time.*—Rather more than ½ hour. *Average cost,* exclusive of the meat, 6d. *Sufficient* for 5 or 6 persons. *Seasonable* at any time.

Note. — It is as well to parboil the carrots and turnips before adding them to the meat, and to use some of the liquor in which they were boiled as a substitute for gravy; that is to say, when there is no gravy at hand. Be particular to cut the onions in very *thin* slices.

[COLD MEAT COOKERY. 2.] *Ingredients.*—Slices of cold roast beef, salt and pepper to taste, 1 sliced onion, 1 teaspoonful of minced savoury herbs. 12 tablespoonfuls of gravy or sauce of any kind, mashed potatoes. *Mode.*—Butter the sides of a deep dish, and spread mashed potatoes over the bottom of it; on this place layers of beef in thin slices (this may be minced, if there is not sufficient beef to cut into slices), well seasoned with pepper and salt, and a very little onion and herbs, which should be previously fried of a nice brown; then put another layer of mashed potatoes, and beef, and other ingredients, as before; pour in the gravy or sauce, cover the whole with another layer of potatoes, and bake for ½ hour. This may be served in the dish, or turned out. *Time.*—½ hour. *Average cost,* exclusive of the cold beef, 6d. *Sufficient.*—A large pie-dish full for 5 or 6 persons. *Seasonable* at any time.

BEEF-BONES, Broiled.

COLD MEAT COOKERY.] *Ingredients.*—The bones of ribs or sirloin; salt, pepper and cayenne. *Mode.*—Separate the bones, taking care that the meat on them is not too thick in any part; sprinkle

Beef, Brisket of, Stewed

them well with the above seasoning, and broil over a very clear fire. When nicely browned, they are done; but do not allow them to blacken.

BEEF, Brisket of, à la Flamande.

Ingredients.—About 6 or 8 lbs. of the brisket of beef, 4 or 5 slices of bacon, 2 carrots, 1 onion, a bunch of savoury herbs, salt and pepper to taste, 4 cloves, 4 whole allspice, 2 blades of mace. *Mode.*—Choose that portion of the brisket which contains the gristle, trim it, and put it into a stewpan with the slices of bacon, which should be placed under and over the meat. Add the vegetables, herbs, spices, and seasoning, and cover with a little weak stock or water; shut the stewpan-lid as closely as possible, and simmer very gently for 4 hours. Strain the liquor, reserve a portion of it for sauce, and the remainder boil quickly over a sharp fire until reduced to a glaze, with which glaze the meat. Garnish the dish with scooped carrots and turnips, and, when liked, a little cabbage; all of which must be cooked separately. Thicken and flavour the liquor that was saved for sauce, pour it round the meat, and serve. The beef may also be garnished with glazed onions, artichoke-bottoms, &c. *Time.*—4 hours. *Average cost,* 7d. per lb. *Sufficient* for 6 or 8 persons. *Seasonable* at any time.

BEEF, Brisket of, Stewed.

Ingredients.—7 lbs. of the brisket of beef, vinegar and salt, 6 carrots, 6 turnips, 6 small onions, 1 blade of pounded mace, 2 whole allspice pounded, thickening of butter and flour, 2 tablespoonfuls of ketchup; stock, or water. *Mode.*—About an hour before dressing it, rub the meat over with vinegar and salt; put it into a stewpan, with sufficient stock to cover it (when this is not at hand, water may be substituted for it), and be particular that the stewpan is not much larger than the meat. Skim well, and when it has simmered very gently for 1 hour, put in the vegetables, and continue simmering till the meat is perfectly tender. Draw out the bones, dish the meat, and garnish either with tufts of cauliflower or braised cabbage cut in quarters. Thicken as much gravy as required, with a little butter and flour; add spices and ketchup in the above proportion, give one boil, pour some of it

Beef, Broiled, and Mushroom Sauce

over the meat, and the remainder send in a tureen. *Time.*—Rather more than 3 hours. *Average cost,* 7d. per lb. *Sufficient* for 7 or 8 persons. *Seasonable* at any time.

Note.—The remainder of the liquor in which the beef was boiled may be served as a soup, or it may be sent to table with the meat in a tureen.

BEEF, Broiled, and Mushroom Sauce.

[COLD MEAT COOKERY.] *Ingredients.* —2 or 3 dozen small button mushrooms, 1 oz. of butter, salt and cayenne to taste, 1 tablespoonful of mushroom ketchup, mashed potatoes, slices of cold roast beef. *Mode*—Wipe the mushrooms free from grit with a piece of flannel, and salt ; put them in a stewpan with the butter, seasoning, and ketchup ; stir over the fire until the mushrooms are quite done, when pour it in the middle of mashed potatoes browned. Then place round the potatoes slices of cold roast beef, nicely broiled over a clear fire. In making the mushroom sauce the ketchup may be dispensed with, if there is sufficient gravy. *Time.*—½ hour. *Average cost,* exclusive of the meat, 8s. *Seasonable* from August to October.

BEEF, Broiled, and Oyster Sauce.

[COLD MEAT COOKERY.] *Ingredients.* —2 dozen oysters, 3 cloves, 1 blade of mace, 2 oz. of butter, ½ teaspoonful of flour, cayenne and salt to taste, mashed potatoes, a few slices of cold roast beef. *Mode.*—Put the oysters in a stewpan, with their liquor strained ; add the cloves, mace, butter, flour, and seasoning, and let them simmer gently for 5 minutes. Have ready in the centre of a dish round walls of mashed potatoes, browned ; into the middle pour the oyster sauce quite hot, and round the potatoes place, in layers, slices of the beef, which should be previously broiled over a nice clear fire. *Time.*— 5 minutes. *Average cost,* 1s. 6d., exclusive of the cold meat. *Sufficient* for 4 or 5 persons. *Seasonable* from September to April.

BEEF BUBBLE-AND-SQUEAK.

[COLD MEAT COOKERY.] *Ingredients.* —A few thin slices of cold boiled beef ;

Beef, Collared

butter, cabbage, 1 sliced onion, pepper and salt to taste. *Mode.*—Fry the slices of beef gently in a little butter, taking care not to dry them up. Lay them on a flat dish, and cover with fried greens. The greens may be prepared from cabbage sprouts or green savoys. They should be boiled till tender, well drained, minced, and placed till quite hot in a frying-pan, with butter, a sliced onion, and seasoning of pepper and salt. When the onion is done it is ready to serve. *Time.*—Altogether, ½ hour. *Average cost,* exclusive of the cold beef, 3d. *Seasonable* at any time.

BEEF CAKE.

[COLD MEAT COOKERY.] *Ingredients.* —The remains of cold roast beef ; to each pound of cold meat allow ¼ lb. of bacon or ham ; seasoning to taste of pepper and salt, 1 small bunch of minced savoury herbs, 1 or 2 eggs. *Mode.*—Mince the beef very finely (if underdone it will be better), add to it the bacon, which must also be chopped very small, and mix well together. Season, stir in the herbs, and bind with an egg, or 2 should 1 not be sufficient. Make it into small square cakes, about ½ inch thick, fry them in hot dripping, drain them, and serve in a dish with good gravy poured round. *Time.*—10 minutes. *Average cost,* exclusive of the cold meat, 6d. *Seasonable* at any time.

BEEF, Collared.

Ingredients.—7 lbs. of the thin end of the flank of beef, 2 oz. of coarse sugar, 6 oz. of salt, 1 oz. of saltpetre, 1 large handful of parsley, minced, 1

COLLARED BEEF.

dessert-spoonful of minced sage, a bunch of savoury herbs, ½ teaspoonful of pounded allspice ; salt and pepper to taste. *Mode.*—Choose fine tender beef, but not too fat ; lay it in a dish, rub in

Beef Collops

the sugar, salt, and saltpetre, and let it remain in the pickle for a week or ten days, turning and rubbing it every day. Then bone it, remove all the gristle and the coarse skin of the inside part, and sprinkle it thickly with parsley, herbs, spice, and seasoning in the above proportion, taking care that the former are finely minced, and the latter well pounded. Roll the meat up in a cloth as tightly as possible; bind it firmly with broad tape, and boil it gently for 6 hours. Immediately on taking it out of the pot put it under a good weight, without undoing it, and let it remain until cold. This dish is a very nice addition to the breakfast-table. *Time.*—6 hours. *Average cost*, for this quantity, 4s. *Seasonable* at any time.

Note.—During the time the beef is in pickle it should be kept cool, and regularly rubbed and turned every day.

BEEF COLLOPS.

Ingredients. — 2 lbs. of rump-steak, ½ lb. of butter, 1 pint of gravy (water may be substituted for this), salt and pepper to taste, 1 shalot, finely minced, pickled walnut, 1 teaspoonful of capers. *Mode.*—Have the steak cut thin, and divide it in pieces about 3 inches long; beat these with the blade of a knife, and dredge with flour. Put them in a frying-pan with the butter, and let them fry for about 3 minutes; then lay them in a small stewpan, and pour over them the gravy. Add a piece of butter kneaded with a little flour, put in the seasoning and all the other ingredients, and let the whole simmer, but not boil, for 10 minutes. Serve in a hot covered dish. *Time.*—10 minutes. *Average cost*, 1s. per lb. *Sufficient* for 4 or 5 persons. *Seasonable* at any time.

BEEF CARVING.

Beef, Aitchbone of. — A boiled aitchbone of beef is not a difficult joint

to carve, as will be seen on reference to the accompanying engraving. By following with the knife the direction of the

Beef Carving

line from 1 to 2, nice slices will be easily cut. It may be necessary, as in a round of beef, to cut a thick slice off the outside before commencing to serve.

Beef, Brisket of. — There is but little description necessary to add to show the carving of a boiled brisket of beef beyond the engraving here inserted.

The only point to be observed is, that the joint should be cut evenly and firmly quite across the bones, so that on its reappearance at table it should not have a jagged and untidy look.

Beef, Ribs of.—This dish resembles the sirloin, except that it has no fillet or undercut. As explained in the recipes, the end piece is often cut off, salted and boiled. The mode of carving is similar to

that of the sirloin, viz., in the direction of the dotted line from 1 to 2. This joint will be the more easily cut if the plan be pursued which is suggested in carving the sirloin; namely, the inserting of the knife immediately between the bone and the meat, before commencing to cut it into slices. All joints of roast beef should be cut in even and thin slices. Horseradish, finely scraped, may be served as a garnish; but horseradish sauce is preferable for eating with the beef.

Beef, a Round of. — A round of beef is more easily carved than any other

joint of beef, but, to manage it properly, a thin-bladed and very sharp knife is

Beef Carving

necessary. Off the outside of the joint, at its top, a thick slice should first be cut, so as to leave the surface smooth : then thin and even slices should be cleverly carved in the direction of the line 1 to 2 ; and with each slice of the lean a delicate morsel of the fat should be served.

Beef, Sirloin of. — This dish is served differently at various tables, some preferring it to come to table with the fillet, or, as it is usually called, the undercut, uppermost. The reverse way, as shown in the cut, is that most usually adopted. Still the undercut is best eaten

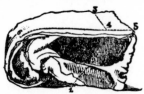

when hot; consequently, the carver himself may raise the joint, and cut some slices from the under side, in the direction of from 1 to 2, as the fillet is very much preferred by some eaters. The upper part of the sirloin should be cut in the direction of the line from 5 to 6, and care should be taken to carve it evenly and in thin slices. It will be found a great assistance, in carving this joint well, if the knife be first inserted just above the bone at the bottom, and run sharply along between the bone and meat, and also to divide the meat from the bone in the same way at the side of the joint; the slices will then come away more readily. Some carvers cut the upper side of the sirloin across, as shown by the line from 3 to 4 ; but this is a wasteful plan, and one not to be recommended. With the sirloin, very finely-scraped horseradish is usually served, and a little given, when liked, to each guest. Horseradish sauce is preferable, however, for serving on the plate, although the scraped horseradish may still be used as a garnish.

Beef Tongue.—Passing the knife

own in the direction of from 1 to 2, a

Beef, Fricandeau of

not too thin slice should be helped ; and the carving of a tongue may be continued in this way until the best portions of the upper side are served. The fat which lies about the root can be served by turning the tongue, and cutting in the direction of from 3 to 4.

BEEF, Curried.

[COLD MEAT COOKERY.] *Ingredients.*—A few slices of tolerably lean cold roast or boiled beef, 3 oz. of butter, 2 onions, 1 wineglassful of beer, a dessert-spoonful of curry powder. *Mode.*—Cut up the beef into pieces about 1 inch square, put the butter into a stewpan with the onions sliced, and fry them of a light-brown colour. Add all the other ingredients, and stir gently over a brisk fire for about 10 minutes. Should this be thought too dry, more beer, or a spoonful or two of gravy or water, may be added ; but a good curry should not be very thin. Place it in a deep dish, with an edging of dry boiled rice, in the same manner as for other curries. *Time.*—10 minutes. *Average cost,* exclusive of the meat, 4d. *Seasonable* in winter.

BEEF, Roast Fillet of (Larded).

Ingredients.—About 4 lbs. of the inside fillet of the sirloin, 1 onion, a small bunch of parsley, salt and pepper to taste, sufficient vinegar to cover the meat, glaze, Spanish sauce (*see* SAUCE). *Mode.*—Lard the beef with bacon, and put it into a pan with sufficient vinegar to cover it, with an onion sliced, parsley, and seasoning, and let it remain in this pickle for 12 hours. Roast it before a nice clear fire for about 1¼ hour, and, when done, glaze it. Pour some Spanish sauce round the beef, and the remainder serve in a tureen. It may be garnished with Spanish onions boiled and glazed. *Time.*—1¼ hour. *Average cost,* exclusive of the sauce, 4s. *Sufficient* for 6 or 8 persons. *Seasonable* at any time.

BEEF, Fricandeau of.

Ingredients.—About 3 lbs. of the inside fillet of the sirloin (a piece of the rump may be substituted for this), pepper and salt to taste, 3 cloves, 2 blades of mace, 4 whole allspice, 1 pint of stock (*see* STOCK), or water, 1 glass of sherry, 1 bunch of savoury herbs, 2 shalots, bacon. *Mode.*—Cut some bacon into thin strips, and

Beef, Fried Salt

sprinkle over them a seasoning of pepper and salt, mixed with cloves, mace, and allspice, well pounded. Lard the beef with these, put it into a stewpan with the stock or water, sherry, herbs, shalots, 2 cloves, and more pepper and salt. Stew the meat gently until tender, when take it out, cover it closely, skim off all the fat from the gravy, and strain it. Set it on the fire, and boil, till it becomes a glaze. Glaze the larded side of the beef with this, and serve on sorrel sauce, which is made as follows :—Wash and pick some sorrel, and put it into a stewpan with only the water that hangs about it. Keep stirring, to prevent its burning, and when done, lay it in a sieve to drain. Chop it, and stew it with a small piece of butter and 4 or 5 tablespoonfuls of good gravy, for an hour, and rub it through a sieve. If too acid, add sugar ; a little cabbage-lettuce boiled with the sorrel will be found an improvement. *Time.*—2 hours to gently stew the meat. *Average cost,* for this quantity, 4s. *Sufficient* for 6 persons. *Seasonable* at any time.

BEEF, Fried Salt.

[COLD MEAT COOKERY.] *Ingredients.* —A few slices of cold salt beef, pepper to taste, ½ lb. of butter, mashed potatoes. *Mode.* — Cut any part of cold salt beef into thin slices, fry them gently in butter, and season with a little pepper. Have ready some very hot mashed potatoes, lay the slices of beef on them, and garnish with 3 or 4 pickled gherkins. Cold salt beef, warmed in a little liquor from mixed pickle, drained, and served as above, will be found good. *Time.*—About 5 minutes. *Average cost,* exclusive of the meat, 4d. *Seasonable* at any time.

BEEF FRITTERS.

[COLD MEAT COOKERY.] *Ingredients.* —The remains of cold roast beef, pepper and salt to taste, ¾ lb. of flour, ½ pint of water, 2 oz. of butter, the whites of 2 eggs. *Mode.*—Mix very smoothly, and, by degrees, the flour with the above proportion of water ; stir in 2 oz. of butter, which must be melted but not oiled, and, just before it is to be used, add the whites of two well-whisked eggs. Should the batter be too thick, more water must be added. Pare down the cold beef into thin shreds, season with pepper and salt, and mix it with the batter. Drop a small quantity at a time into a pan of

Beef, Hashed

boiling lard, and fry from 7 to 10 minutes, according to the size. When done on one side, turn and brown them on the other. Let them dry for a minute or two before the fire, and serve on a folded napkin. A small quantity of finely-minced onions, mixed with the batter, is an improvement. *Time.* — From 7 to 10 minutes. *Average cost,* exclusive of the meat, 6d. *Seasonable* at any time.

BEEF, Hashed.

[COLD MEAT COOKERY. 1.] *Ingredients.* —Gravy saved from the meat, 1 teaspoonful of tomato sauce, one teaspoonful of Harvey's sauce, one teaspoonful of good mushroom ketchup, ½ glass of port wine or strong ale, pepper and salt to taste, a little flour to thicken, 1 onion finely minced, a few slices of cold roast beef. *Mode.* — Put all the ingredients but the beef into a stewpan with whatever gravy may have been saved from the meat the day it was roasted ; simmer these gently for 10 minutes, then take the stewpan off the fire ; let the gravy cool and skim off the fat. Cut the beef into thin slices, dredge them with flour, and lay them in the gravy ; let the whole simmer gently for 5 minutes, but not boil, or the meat will be tough and hard. Serve very hot, and garnish with sippets of toasted bread. *Time.* — 20 minutes. *Average cost,* exclusive of the cold meat, 4d. *Seasonable* at any time.

[COLD MEAT COOKERY. 2.] *Ingredients.* —The remains of ribs or sirloin of beef, 2 onions, 1 carrot, 1 bunch of savoury herbs, pepper and salt to taste, ½ blade of pounded mace, thickening of flour, rather more than 1 pint of water. *Mode.*—Take off all the meat from the bones of ribs or sirloin of beef ; remove the outside brown and gristle ; place the meat on one side, and well stew the bones and pieces, with the above ingredients, for about 2 hours, till it becomes a strong gravy, and is reduced to rather more than ½ pint ; strain this, thicken with a teaspoonful of flour, and let the gravy cool ; skim off all the fat ; lay in the meat, let it get hot through, but do not allow it to boil ; and garnish with sippets of toasted bread. The gravy should be flavoured as in the preceding recipe. *Time.* — Rather more than 2 hours. *Average cost,* exclusive of the cold meat, 6d. *Seasonable* at any time.

Beef, Hunter's

Note.—Either of the above recipes may be served in walls of mashed potatoes browned; in which case the sippets should be omitted. *Be careful that hashed meat does not boil, or it will become tough.*

BEEF, Hunter's.

Ingredients. — For a round of beef weighing 25 lbs. allow 3 oz. of saltpetre, 8 oz. of coarse sugar, 1 oz. of cloves, 1 grated nutmeg, ½ oz. of allspice, 1 lb. of salt, ¼ lb. bay-salt. *Mode.*—Hang the beef for 2 or 3 days, and remove the bone. Pound spices, salt, &c. in the above proportion, and let them be reduced to the finest powder. Put the beef into a pan, rub all the ingredients well into it, and turn and rub it every day for rather more than a fortnight. When it has been sufficiently long in pickle, wash the meat, bind it up securely with tape, and put it into a pan with ½ pint of water at the bottom; mince some suet, cover the top of the meat with it, and over the pan put a common crust of flour and water; bake for 6 hours, and when cold remove the paste. Save the gravy that flows from it, as it adds greatly to the flavour of hashes, stews, &c. The beef may be glazed and garnished with meat jelly. *Time.* — 6 hours. *Seasonable* all the year.

Note.—In salting or pickling beef or pork for family consumption, it not being generally required to be kept for a great length of time, a less quantity of salt and a larger quantity of other matters more adapted to retain mellowness in meat, may be employed, which could not be adopted by the curer of the immense quantities of meat required to be preserved for victualling the shipping of this maritime country. Sugar, which is well known to possess the preserving principle in a very great degree, without the pungency and astringency of salt, may be, and is, very generally used in the preserving of meat for family consumption. Although it acts without corrugating or contracting the fibres of meat, as is the case in the action of salt, and, therefore, does not impair its mellowness, yet its use in sufficient quantities for preservative effect, without the addition of other antiseptics, would impart a flavour not agreeable to the taste of many persons. It may be used, however, together with salt, with the greatest advantage in imparting mildness and mellowness to

Beef Kidney, to Dress

cured meat, in a proportion of about one part by weight to four of the mixture; and, perhaps, now that sugar is so much lower in price than it was in former years, one of the obstructions to its more frequent use is removed.

BEEF KIDNEY, to Dress.

Ingredients.—1 kidney, clarified butter, pepper and salt to taste, a small quantity of highly-seasoned gravy, 1 tablespoonful of lemon-juice, ¼ teaspoonful of powdered sugar. *Mode.*—Cut the kidneys into neat slices, put them into warm water to soak for two hours, and change the water 2 or 3 times; then lay them on a clean cloth to dry the water from them, place them in a frying-pan with some clarified butter, and fry them of a nice brown; season each side with pepper and salt, put them round the dish, with the gravy in the middle. Before pouring the gravy in the dish, add the lemon-juice and sugar. *Time.*—From 5 to 10 minutes. *Average cost, 9d.* each. *Seasonable* at any time.

BEEF KIDNEY, to Dress.

Ingredients.—1 kidney, 1 dessertspoonful of minced parsley, 1 teaspoonful of minced shalot, salt and pepper to taste, ¼ pint of gravy (follow one of the gravy recipes), 3 tablespoonfuls of sherry. *Mode.*—Take off a little of the kidney fat, mince it very fine, and put it in a frying-pan; slice the kidney, sprinkle over it parsley and shalots in the above proportion, add a seasoning of pepper and salt, and fry it of a nice brown. When it is done enough, dredge over a little flour, and pour in the gravy and sherry. Let it just simmer, but not boil any more, or the kidney would harden; serve very hot, and garnish with croûtons. Where the flavour of the shalot is disliked it may be omitted, and a small quantity of savoury herbs substituted for it. *Time.*—From 5 to 10 minutes, according to the thickness of the slices. *Average cost, 9d.* each. *Sufficient* for 3 persons. *Seasonable* at any time.

BEEF KIDNEY, to Dress (a more simple method).

Cut the kidneys into thin slices, flour them, and fry of a nice brown. When done, make a gravy in the pan by pouring away the fat, putting in a small piece

Beef Marrowbones, Boiled	Beef Olives

of butter, ¼ pint of boiling water, pepper and salt, a dessertspoonful of lemon-juice, and a tablespoonful of mushroom ketchup. Let the gravy just boil up, pour over the kidney, and serve.

BEEF MARROWBONES, Boiled.

Ingredients.—Bones, a small piece of common paste, a floured cloth. *Mode.*—Have the bones neatly sawed into convenient sizes, and cover the ends with a small piece of common crust, made with flour and water. Over this tie a floured cloth, and place them

MARROW-BONES.

upright in a saucepan of boiling water, taking care there is sufficient to cover the bones. Boil the bones for 2 hours, remove the cloth and paste, and serve them upright on a napkin with dry toast. Many persons clear the marrow from the bones after they are cooked, spread it over a slice of toast, and add a seasoning of pepper; when served in this manner, it must be very expeditiously sent to table, as it so soon gets cold. *Time.*—2 hours. *Seasonable* at any time.

Note.—Marrow-bones may be baked after preparing them as in the preceding recipe; they should be laid in a deep dish, and baked for 2 hours.

BEEF, Minced.

[COLD MEAT COOKERY.] *Ingredients.*—1 oz. of butter, 1 small onion, 12 tablespoonfuls of gravy left from the meat, 1 tablespoonful of strong ale, 1 teaspoonful of flour, salt and pepper to taste, a few slices of lean roast beef. *Mode.*—Put into a stewpan the butter with an onion chopped fine; add the gravy, ale, and a teaspoonful of flour to thicken; season with pepper and salt, and stir these ingredients over the fire until the onion is a rich brown. Cut (but do not chop) the meat *very fine*, add it to the gravy, stir till quite hot, and serve. Garnish with sippets of toasted bread. Be careful in not allowing the gravy to boil after the meat is added, as it would render it hard and tough. *Time.*—About ½ hour. *Average cost*, exclusive of the meat, 3d. *Seasonable* at any time.

BEEF, Minced Collops of (an Entrée).

Ingredients.—1 lb. of rump-steak, salt and pepper to taste, 2 oz. of butter, 1 onion minced, ¼ pint of water, 1 tablespoonful of Harvey's sauce, or lemon-juice, or mushroom ketchup; 1 small bunch of savoury herbs. *Mode.*—Mince the beef and onion very small, and fry the latter in butter until of a pale brown. Put all the ingredients together in a stewpan, and boil gently for about 10 minutes; garnish with sippets of toasted bread, and serve very hot. *Time.*—10 minutes. *Average cost*, 1s. per lb. *Sufficient* for 2 or 3 persons. *Seasonable* at any time.

BEEF, Miroton of.

[COLD MEAT COOKERY.] *Ingredients.*—A few slices of cold roast beef, 3 oz. of butter, salt and pepper to taste, 3 onions, ½ pint of gravy. *Mode.*—Slice the onions and put them into the frying-pan with the cold beef and butter; place it over the fire, and keep turning and stirring the ingredients to prevent them burning. When a pale brown, add the gravy and seasoning; let it simmer for a few minutes, and serve very hot. The dish is excellent and economical. *Time.*—5 minutes. *Average cost*, exclusive of the meat, 6d. *Seasonable* at any time.

BEEF OLIVES.

Ingredients.—2 lbs. of rump-steak, 1 egg, 1 tablespoonful of minced savoury herbs, pepper and salt to taste, 1 pint of stock, 2 or 3 slices of bacon, 2 tablespoonfuls of any kind of store sauce, a slight thickening of butter and flour. *Mode.*—Have the steaks cut rather thin, beat them to make them level, cut them into 6 or 7 pieces, brush over with egg, and sprinkle with herbs, which should be very finely minced; season with pepper and salt, roll up the pieces tightly, and fasten with a small skewer. Put the stock in a stewpan that will exactly hold the ingredients, for, by being pressed together, they will keep their shape better; lay in the rolls of meat, cover them with the bacon, cut in thin slices, and over that put a piece of paper. Stew them very *gently* for full 2 hours; for the slower they are done the better. Take them out, remove the skewers, thicken the gravy with butter and flour, and flavour

Beef Olives

with any store sauce that may be preferred. Give one boil, pour over the meat, and serve. *Time.*—2 hours. *Average cost*, 1*s*. per pound. *Sufficient* for 4 or 5 persons. *Seasonable* at any time.

BEEF OLIVES (Economical).

[COLD MEAT COOKERY.] *Ingredients.*—The remains of underdone cold roast beef, bread crumbs, 1 shalot finely minced, pepper and salt to taste, gravy made from the beef bones, thickening of butter and flour, 1 tablespoonful of mushroom ketchup. *Mode.*— Cut some slices of underdone roast beef about half an inch thick; sprinkle over them some bread crumbs, minced shalot, and a little of the fat and seasoning; roll them, and fasten with a small skewer. Have ready some gravy made from the beef bones; put in the pieces of meat, and stew them till tender, which will be in about 1¼ hour, or rather longer. Arrange the meat in a dish, thicken and flavour the gravy, and pour it over the meat, when it is ready to serve. *Time.*— 1½ hour. *Average cost*, exclusive of the beef, 2*d*. *Seasonable* at any time.

BEEF PALATES, to Dress (an Entrée).

Ingredients. — 4 palates, sufficient gravy to cover them, cayenne to taste, 1 tablespoonful of mushroom ketchup, 1 tablespoonful of pickled-onion liquor, thickening of butter and flour. *Mode.* — Wash the palates, and put them into a stewpan, with sufficient water to cover them, and let them boil until perfectly tender, or until the upper skin may be easily peeled off. Have ready sufficient gravy to cover them; add a good seasoning of cayenne, and thicken with a little butter kneaded with flour; let it boil up, and skim. Cut the palates into square pieces, put them in the gravy, and let them simmer gently for ½ hour; add ketchup and onion-liquor, give one boil, and serve. *Time.*— From 3 to 5 hours to boil the palates. *Sufficient* for 4 persons. *Seasonable* at any time.

Note.—Palates may be dressed in various ways with good onion sauce, tomato sauce, &c., &c., and may also be served in a *vol-au-vent;* but the above will be found a more simple method of dressing them.

Beef, Potted

BEEF PICKLE. (This may also be used for any kind of Meat, Tongues, or Hams.)

Ingredients.— 6 lbs. of salt, 2 lbs. of fine sugar, 3 oz. of powdered saltpetre, 3 gallons of spring water. *Mode.*—Boil all the ingredients gently together, so long as any scum or impurity arises, which carefully remove; when quite cold, pour it over the meat, every part of which must be covered with the brine. This may be used for pickling any kind of meat, and may be kept for some time, if boiled up occasionally with an addition of the ingredients. *Time.*—A ham should be kept in pickle for a fortnight; a piece of beef weighing 14lbs., 12 or 15 days; a tongue, 10 days or a fortnight.

Note.—For salting and pickling meat, it is a good plan to rub in only half the quantity of salt directed, and to let it remain for a day or two to disgorge and effectually to get rid of the blood and slime; then rub in the remainder of the salt and other ingredients, and proceed as above. This rule may be applied to all recipes for salting and pickling meat

BEEF, POTTED.

[COLD MEAT COOKERY. 1.] *Ingredients.*—2 lbs. of lean beef, 1 tablespoonful of water, ¼ lb. of butter, a seasoning to taste of salt, cayenne, pounded mace, and black pepper. *Mode.*—Procure a nice piece of lean beef, as free as possible from gristle, skin, &c., and put it into a jar (if at hand, one with a lid) with 1 tablespoonful of water.

JAR FOR POTTED MEATS.

Cover it *closely*, and put the jar into a saucepan of boiling water, letting the water come within 2 inches of the top of the jar. Boil gently for 3½ hours, then take the beef, chop it very small with a chopping-knife, and pound it thoroughly in a mortar. Mix with it by degrees all, or a portion, of the gravy that will have run from it, and a little clarified butter; add the seasoning, put it in small pots for use, and cover with a little butter just warmed and poured over. If much gravy is added to it, it will keep but a short time; on the contrary, if a large

Beef, Potted	Beef, Roast Ribs of

proportion of butter is used, it may be preserved for some time. *Time.*—3½ hours. *Average cost*, for this quantity, 1s. 10d. *Seasonable* at any time.

[COLD MEAT COOKERY. 2.] *Ingredients.* —The remains of cold roast or boiled beef, ¼ lb. of butter, cayenne to taste, 2 blades of pounded mace. *Mode.*—The outside slices of boiled beef may, with a little trouble, be converted into a very nice addition to the breakfast-table. Cut up the meat into small pieces and pound it well, with a little butter, in a mortar; add a seasoning of cayenne and mace, and be very particular that the latter spice is reduced to the finest powder. When all the ingredients are thoroughly mixed, put them into glass or earthen potting-pots, and pour on the top a coating of clarified butter. *Seasonable* at any time.

Note.—If cold *roast* beef is used, remove all pieces of gristle and dry outside pieces, as these do not pound well.

BEEF RAGOUT.

[COLD MEAT COOKERY.] *Ingredients.*— About 2 lbs. of cold roast beef, 6 onions, pepper, salt, and mixed spices to taste; ½ pint of boiling water, 3 tablespoonfuls of gravy. *Mode.*—Cut the beef into rather large pieces, and put them into a stewpan with the onions, which must be sliced. Season well with pepper, salt, and mixed spices, and pour over about ½ pint of boiling water, and gravy in the above proportion (gravy saved from the meat answers the purpose); let the whole stew very gently for about 2 hours, and serve with pickled walnuts, gherkins, or capers, just warmed in the gravy. *Time.* 2 hours. *Average cost*, exclusive of the meat, 4d. *Seasonable* at any time.

BEEF, Rib-bones of (a pretty Dish).

[COLD MEAT COOKERY.] *Ingredients.* —Ribs of beef bones, 1 onion chopped fine, a few slices of carrot and turnip, ¼ pint of gravy. *Mode.* — The bones for this dish should have left on them a slight covering of meat; saw them into pieces 3 inches long; season them with pepper and salt, and put them into a stewpan with the remaining ingredients. Stew gently, until the vegetables are tender, and serve on a flat dish within walls of mashed potatoes. *Time.*—¾ hour.

Average cost, exclusive of the bones, 2d. *Seasonable* at any time.

BEEF, Roast Ribs of.

Ingredients.—Beef, a little salt. *Mode.* —The fore-rib is considered the primest roasting piece, but the middle-rib is considered the most economical. Let the meat be well hung (should the weather permit), having previously cut off the ends of the bones, which should be salted for a few days, and then boiled. Put the meat down to a nice clear fire, with some clean dripping in the pan, dredge the joint with a little flour, and keep continually basting it all the time it is cooking. Sprinkle some fine salt over it (this must never be done until the joint is dished, as it draws the juices from the meat); pour the dripping from the pan, put in a little boiling water, and *strain* the gravy over the meat. Garnish with tufts of scraped horseradish, and send horseradish sauce to table with it. A Yorkshire pudding (*see* PUDDINGS) sometimes accompanies this dish, and, if lightly made and well cooked, will be found a very agreeable addition. *Time.*—10 lbs. of beef, 2½ hours; 14 to 16 lbs., from 3½ to 4 hours. *Average cost*, 9d. per lb. *Sufficient.*—A joint of 10 lbs. sufficient for 8 or 9 persons. *Seasonable* at any time.

BEEF, Roast Ribs of, Boned and Rolled (a very convenient Joint for a small Family).

Ingredients. — 1 or 2 ribs of beef. *Mode.*—Choose a fine rib of beef, and have it cut according to the weight you require, either wide or narrow. Bone and roll the meat round, secure it with wooden skewers, and, if necessary, bind it round with a piece of tape. Spit the beef firmly, or, if a bottle-jack is used, put the joint on the hook, and place it *near* a nice clear fire. Let it remain so till the outside of the meat is set, when draw it to a distance, and keep continually basting until the meat is done, which can be ascertained by the steam from it drawing towards the fire. As this joint is solid, rather more than ¼ hour must be allowed for each lb. Remove the skewers, put in a plated or silver one, and send the joint to table with gravy in the dish, and garnish with tufts of horseradish. Horseradish sauce is a great improvement to roast beef.

Beef Rissoles

Time.—For 10lbs. of the rolled ribs, 3 hours (as the joint is very solid, we have allowed an extra ½ hour); for 6 lbs., 1½ hour. *Average cost, 9d.* per lb. *Sufficient.*—A joint of 10 lbs. for 6 or 8 persons. *Seasonable* all the year.

Note.—When the weight exceeds 10 lbs., we would not advise the above method of boning or rolling; only in the case of 1 or 2 ribs, when the joint cannot stand upright in the dish, and would look awkwardly. The bones should be put on with a few vegetables and herbs, and made into stock.

BEEF RISSOLES.

[COLD MEAT COOKERY.] *Ingredients.* —The remains of cold roast beef; to each pound of meat allow ¾ lb. of bread crumbs, salt and pepper to taste, a few chopped savoury herbs, ½ a teaspoonful of minced lemon-peel, 1 or 2 eggs, according to the quantity of meat. *Mode.* —Mince the beef very fine, which should be rather lean, and mix with this bread crumbs, herbs, seasoning, and lemon-peel, in the above proportion, to each pound of meat. Make all into a thick paste with 1 or 2 eggs; divide into balls or cones, and fry a rich brown. Garnish the dish with fried parsley, and send to table some good brown gravy in a tureen. Instead of garnishing with fried parsley, gravy may be poured in the dish round the rissoles; in this case, it will not be necessary to send any in a tureen. *Time.*—From 5 to 10 minutes, according to size. *Average cost,* exclusive of the meat, *5d.* *Seasonable* at any time.

BEEF, Rolled, to eat like Hare.

Ingredients.—About 5 lbs. of the inside of the sirloin, 2 glasses of port wine, 2 glasses of vinegar, a small quantity of forcemeat, 1 teaspoonful of pounded allspice. *Mode.*—Take the inside of a large sirloin, soak it in 1 glass of port wine and 1 glass of vinegar, mixed, and let it remain for 2 days. Make a forcemeat (*see* FORCEMEAT), lay it on the meat, and bind it up securely. Roast it before a nice clear fire, and baste it with 1 glass each of port wine and vinegar, with which mix a teaspoonful of pounded allspice. Serve, with a good gravy in the dish, and send redcurrant jelly to table with it. *Time.*— A piece of 5 lbs about 1½ hour before a

Beef, Boiled Round of

brisk fire. *Average cost,* for this quantit 5s. 4d. *Sufficient* for 4 persons. *Seasonable* at any time.

BEEF ROLLS.

[COLD MEAT COOKERY.] *Ingredien* —The remains of cold roast or boil beef, seasoning to taste of salt, peppe and minced herbs; puff paste. *Mode.* Mince the beef tolerably fine with *small* amount of its own fat; add a se soning of pepper, salt, and chopp herbs; put the whole into a roll of p paste, and bake for ½ hour, or rath longer, should the roll be very larg Beef patties may be made of cold mea by mincing and seasoning beef as rected above, and baking in a rich p paste in patty-tins. *Time.*—½ hou *Seasonable* at any time.

BEEF, Boiled Round of.

Ingredients.—Beef, water. *Mode.*— a whole round of beef, generally speakin is too large for small families, and ve seldom required, we here give the reci for dressing a portion of the silver si of the round. Take from 12 to 16 lbs after it has been in salt about 10 day just wash off the salt, skewer it up in nice round-looking form, and bind it wi tape to keep the skewers in their place Put it in a saucepan of boiling wate set it upon a good fire, and when begins to boil, carefully remove all scu from the surface, as, if this is not a tended to, it sinks on to the meat, an when brought to table, presents a ve unsightly appearance. After it is we skimmed, draw the pot to the corner the fire, allow the liquor to cool, the let the beef simmer very gently un done. Remove the tape and skewer which should be replaced by a silv one; pour over a little of the po liquor, and garnish with carrots. Ca rots, turnips, parsnips, and sometim suet dumplings, accompany this dis and these may all be boiled with t beef. The pot-liquor should be save and converted into pea-soup; and t outside slices, which are generally har and of an uninviting appearance, may cut off before being sent to table, a potted. These make an excellent reli for the breakfast or luncheon tabl *Time.*—Part of a round of beef weighi 12 lbs., about 3 hours after the wat boils. *Average cost, 8d.* per lb. *Sufficie*

Beef, Miniature Round of

for 10 persons. *Seasonable* all the year, but more suitable for winter.

Soyer's Recipe for Preserving the Gravy in Salt Meat, when it is to be served Cold.—Fill two tubs with cold water, into which throw a few pounds of rough ice; and when the meat is done, put it into one of the tubs of ice-water; let it remain 1 minute, when take out, and put it into the other tub. Fill the first tub again with water, and continue this process for about 20 minutes; then set it upon a dish, and let it remain until quite cold. When cut, the fat will be as white as possible, besides having saved the whole of the gravy. If there is no ice, spring water will answer the same purpose, but will require to be more frequently changed.

Note.—The brisket and rump may be boiled by the above recipe; of course allowing more or less time, according to the size of the joint.

BEEF, Miniature Round of (an excellent Dish for a small Family).

Ingredients.—From 5 to 10 lbs. of ribs of beef, sufficient brine to cover the meat. *Mode.*—Choose a fine rib, have the bone removed, rub some salt over the inside, and skewer the meat up into a nice round form, and bind it with tape. Put it into sufficient brine to cover it (*see* BEEF PICKLE), and let it remain for 6 days, turning the meat every day. When required to be dressed, drain from the pickle, and put the meat into very hot water; boil it rapidly for a few minutes, then draw the pot to the side of the fire, and simmer the beef very gently until done. Remove the skewer, and replace it by a plated or silver one. Carrots and turnips should be served with this dish, and may be boiled with the meat. *Time.*—A small round of 8 lbs., about 2 hours after the water boils; one of 12 lbs., about 3 hours. *Average cost,* 9d. per lb. *Sufficient* for 6 persons. *Seasonable* at any time.

Note.—Should the joint be very small, 4 or 5 days will be sufficient time to salt it.

BEEF, to Pickle part of a Round, for Hanging.

Ingredients.—For 14 lbs. of a round of beef allow 1½ lb. of salt, ½ oz. of powdered saltpetre; or, 1 lb. of salt, ¼ lb. of sugar,

Beef, Roast Sirloin of

¼ oz. of powdered saltpetre. *Mode.*—Rub in, and sprinkle either of the above mixtures on 14 lbs. of meat. Keep it in an earthenware pan, or a deep wooden tray, and turn twice a week during 3 weeks; then bind up the beef tightly with coarse linen tape, and hang it in a kitchen in which a fire is constantly kept, for 3 weeks. Pork, hams, and bacon may be cured in a similar way, but will require double the quantity of the salting mixture; and, if not smoke-dried, they should be taken down from hanging after 3 or 4 weeks, and afterwards kept in boxes or tubs, amongst dry oat-husks. *Time.*—2 or 3 weeks to remain in the brine; to be hung 3 weeks. *Seasonable* at any time.

Note.—The meat may be boiled fresh from this pickle, instead of smoking it.

BEEF SAUSAGES.

Ingredients.—To every lb. of suet allow 2 lbs. of lean beef; seasoning to taste of salt, pepper, and mixed spices. *Mode.*—Clear the suet from skin, and chop that and the beef as finely as possible; season with pepper, salt, and spices, and mix the whole well together. Make it into flat cakes, and fry of a nice brown. Many persons pound the meat in a mortar after it is chopped, but this is not necessary when the meat is minced finely. *Time.*—10 minutes. *Average cost,* for this quantity, 1s. 6d. *Seasonable* at any time.

BEEF, Roast Sirloin of.

Ingredients.—Beef, a little salt. *Mode.*—As a joint cannot be well roasted without a good fire, see that it is well made up about ¾ hour before it is required, so

ROAST SIRLOIN OF BEEF.

that when the joint is put down, it is clear and bright. Choose a nice sirloin, the weight of which should not exceed 16 lbs., as the outside would be too much done, whilst the inside would not be done enough. Spit it or hook it on to the

Beef, Sliced and Broiled	Beef, Stewed Rump of

jack firmly, dredge it slightly with flour, and place it near the fire at first. Then draw it to a distance, and keep continually basting until the meat is done. Dish the meat, sprinkle a small quantity of salt over it, empty the dripping-pan of all the dripping, pour in some boiling water, stir it about, and *strain* over the meat. Garnish with tufts of horseradish, and send horseradish sauce and Yorkshire pudding to table with it. *Time.*—A sirloin of 10 lbs., 2½ hours; 14 to 16 lbs., about 4 or 4½ hours. *Average cost*, 8½d. per lb. *Sufficient.*—A joint of 10 lbs. for 8 or 9 persons. *Seasonable* at any time. The rump, round, and other pieces of beef are roasted in the same manner, allowing for solid joints ¼ hour to every lb.

Note.—The above is the usual method of roasting meat; but to have it in perfection and the juices kept in, the meat should at first be laid *close* to the fire, and when the outside is set and firm, drawn away to a good distance, and then left to roast very slowly. Where economy is studied, this plan would not answer, as the meat requires to be at the fire double the time of the ordinary way of cooking; consequently, double the quantity of fuel would be consumed.

BEEF, Sliced and Broiled (a pretty Dish).

[COLD MEAT COOKERY.] *Ingredients.*—A few slices of cold roast beef, 4 or 5 potatoes, a thin batter, pepper and salt to taste. *Mode.*—Pare the potatoes as you would peel an apple; fry the parings in a thin batter seasoned with salt and pepper, until they are of a light brown colour, and place them on a dish over some slices of beef, which should be nicely seasoned and broiled. *Time.*—5 minutes to broil the meat. *Seasonable* at any time.

BEEF, Spiced (to serve Cold).

Ingredients.—14 lbs. of the thick flank or rump of beef, ½ lb. of coarse sugar, 1 oz. of saltpetre, ¼ lb. of pounded allspice, 1 lb. of common salt. *Mode.*—Rub the sugar well into the beef, and let it lie for 12 hours; then rub the saltpetre and allspice, both of which should be pounded, over the meat, and let it remain for another 12 hours; then rub in the salt. Turn daily in the liquor for a fortnight, soak it for a few hours in water, dry with a cloth, cover with a coarse paste,

put a little water at the bottom of the pan, and bake in a moderate oven for 4 hours. If it is not covered with a paste, be careful to put the beef into a deep vessel, and cover with a plate, or it will be too crisp. During the time the meat is in the oven it should be turned once or twice. *Time.*--4 hours. *Average cost, 7d.* per lb. *Seasonable* at any time.

BEEF, Stewed. (A Polish Dish.)

Ingredients.— A thick beef or rump-steak of about 2 lbs., an onion, some bread crumbs, pepper and salt, ¼ lb. of butter. *Mode.*—Mince the onion fine, mix it with the bread, pepper, and salt; make deep incisions in the beef, but do not cut it through; fill the spaces with the bread, &c. Roll up the steak and put it in a stewpan with the butter; let it stew very gently for more than two hours; serve it with its own gravy, thickened with a little flour, and flavoured, as may be required, either with tomato sauce, ketchup, or Harvey's sauce. *Time.*—About 2 hours, or rather more. *Average cost, 2s. 6d. Sufficient* for 4 persons. *Seasonable* at any time.

BEEF, Stewed Rump of.

Ingredients.—½ rump of beef, sufficient stock to cover it, 4 tablespoonfuls of vinegar, 2 tablespoonfuls of ketchup, 1 bunch of savoury herbs, 2 onions, 12 cloves, pepper and salt to taste, thickening of butter and flour, 1 glass of port wine. *Mode.*—Cut out the bone, sprinkle the meat with a little cayenne (this must be sparingly used), and bind and tie it firmly up with tape; put it into a stewpan with sufficient stock to cover it, add vinegar, ketchup, herbs, onions, cloves, and seasonings in the above proportions, and simmer very gently for 4 or 5 hours, or until the meat is perfectly tender, which may be ascertained by piercing it with a thin skewer. When done, remove the tape, lay it into a deep dish, which keep hot; strain and skim the gravy, thicken it with butter and flour, add a glass of port wine and any flavouring to make the gravy rich and palatable; let it boil up, pour over the meat, and serve. This dish may be very much enriched by garnishing with forcemeat balls, or filling up the space whence the bone is taken with a good forcemeat; sliced carrots, turnips, and

Beef, Stewed Shin of

onions boiled with the meat are also a great improvement, and, where expense is not objected to, it may be glazed. This, however, is not necessary where a good gravy is poured round and over the meat. *Time.*—½ rump stewed gently from 4 to 5 hours. *Average cost,* 10d. per lb. *Sufficient* for 8 or 10 persons. *Seasonable* at any time.

Note.—A stock or gravy in which to boil the meat may be made of the bone and trimmings, by boiling them with water, and adding carrots, onions, turnips, and a bunch of sweet herbs. To make this dish richer and more savoury, half-roast the rump, and afterwards stew it in strong stock and a little Madeira. This is an expensive method, and is not, after all, much better than a plainer-dressed joint.

BEEF, Stewed Shin of.

Ingredients.—A shin of beef, 1 head of celery, 1 onion, a faggot of savoury herbs, ¼ teaspoonful of allspice, ½ teaspoonful of whole black pepper, 4 carrots, 12 button onions, 2 turnips, thickening of butter and flour, 3 tablespoonfuls of mushroom ketchup, 2 tablespoonfuls of port wine; pepper and salt to taste. *Mode.*—Have the bone sawn into 4 or 5 pieces, cover with hot water, bring it to a boil, and remove any scum that may rise to the surface. Put in the celery, onion, herbs, spice, and seasoning, and simmer very gently until the meat is tender. Peel the vegetables, cut them into any shape fancy may dictate, and boil them with the onions until tender; lift out the beef, put it on a dish, which keep hot, and thicken with butter and flour as much of the liquor as will be wanted for gravy; keep stirring till it boils, then strain and skim. Put the gravy back in the stewpan, add the seasoning, port wine, and ketchup, give one boil, and pour it over the beef; garnish with the boiled carrots, turnips and onions. *Time.*— The meat to be stewed about 4 hours. *Average cost,* 5d. per lb. with bone. *Sufficient* for 7 or 8 persons. *Seasonable* at any time.

BEEF-TEA.

Ingredients.—1 lb. of lean gravy-beef, 1½ pint of water, 1 saltspoonful of salt. *Mode.*—Have the meat cut without fat and bone, and choose a nice fleshy piece. Cut it into small pieces about the size of

Beef-Tea, Baked

dice, and put it into a clean saucepan. Add the water *cold* to it; put it on the fire, and bring it to the boiling-point; then skim well. Put in the salt when the water boils, and *simmer* the beef-tea *gently* from ½ to ¾ hour, removing any more scum should it appear on the surface. Strain the tea through a hair sieve, and set it by in a cool place. When wanted for use, remove every particle of fat from the top ; warm up as much as may be required, adding, if necessary, a little more salt. This preparation is simple beef-tea, and is to be administered to those invalids to whom flavourings and seasonings are not allowed. When the patient is very weak, use double the quantity of meat to the same proportion of water. Should the invalid be able to take the tea prepared in a more palatable manner, it is easy to make it so by following the directions in Soyer's recipe, which is an admirable one for making savoury beef-tea. Beef-tea is always better when made the day before it is wanted, and then warmed up. It is a good plan to put the tea into a small cup or basin, and to place this basin in a saucepan of boiling water. When the tea is hot, it is ready to serve. *Time.* —½ to ¾ hour. *Average cost,* 6d. per pint. *Sufficient.*—Allow 1 lb. of meat for a pint of *good* beef-tea.

BEEF-TEA, Baked.

Ingredients.—1 lb. of fleshy beef, 1 pint of water, ½ saltspoonful of salt. *Mode.*—Cut the beef into small square pieces, after trimming off all the fat, and put it into a baking-jar (these jars are sold expressly for the purpose of making soups, gravies, &c., in the oven, and are arranged with tightly-fitting lids), with the above proportion of water and salt ; close the jar well, place it in a warm but not hot oven, and bake for 3 or 4 hours. When the oven is very fierce in the daytime, it is a good plan to put the jar in at night, and let it remain till next morning, when the tea will be done. It should be strained, and put by in a cool place until wanted. It may also be flavoured with an onion, a clove, and a few sweet herbs, &c., when the stomach is sufficiently strong to take these. *Time.*—3 or 4 hours, or to be left in the oven all night. *Average cost,* 6d. per pint. *Sufficient.*— Allow 1 lb. of meat for 1 pint of good beef-tea.

BEEF-TEA, Savoury (Soyer's Recipe).

Ingredients.—1 lb. of solid beef, 1 oz. of butter, 1 clove, 2 button onions or ½ a large one, 1 saltspoonful of salt, 1 quart of water. *Mode.*—Cut the beef into very small dice; put it into a stewpan with the butter, clove, onion, and salt; stir the meat round over the fire for a few minutes until it produces a thin gravy, then add the water, and let it simmer gently from ½ to ¾ of an hour, skimming off every particle of fat. When done, strain it through a sieve, and put it by in a cool place until required. The same, if wanted quite plain, is done by merely omitting the vegetables, salt, and clove; the butter cannot be objectionable, as it is taken out in skimming. *Time.*—½ to ¾ hour. *Average cost*, 8*d.* per pint. *Sufficient.*—Allow 1 lb. of beef to make 1 pint of good beef-tea.

Note.—The meat left from beef-tea may be boiled a little longer, and pounded with spices, &c., for potting. It makes a very nice breakfast dish.

BEETROOT, Boiled.

Ingredients.—Beetroot; boiling water. *Mode.*—When large, young, and juicy, this vegetable makes a very excellent addition to winter salads, and may easily be converted into an economical and quickly-made pickle. (*See* BEETROOT, PICKLED.) Beetroot is more frequently served cold than hot: when the latter mode is preferred, melted butter should be sent to table with it. It may also be stewed with button onions, or boiled and served with roasted onions. Wash the beets thoroughly; but do not prick or break the skin before they are cooked, as they would lose their beautiful colour in boiling. Put them into boiling water, and let them boil until tender, keeping them well covered. If to be served hot, remove the peel quickly, cut the beetroot into thick slices, and send to table melted butter. For salads, pickle, &c., let the root cool, then peel, and cut it into slices. *Time.*—Small beetroot, 1½ to 2 hours; large, 2½ to 3 hours. *Average cost*, in full season, 2*d.* each. *Seasonable.*—May be had at any time.

BEETROOT, Pickled.

Ingredients.—Sufficient vinegar to cover the beets, 2 oz. of whole pepper, 2 oz. of allspice to each gallon of vinegar. *Mode.* —Wash the beets free from dirt, and be very careful not to prick the outside skin, or they would lose their beautiful colour. Put them into boiling water, let them simmer gently, and when about three parts done, which will be in 1½ hour, take them out and let them cool. Boil the vinegar with pepper and allspice, in the above proportion, for 10 minutes, and when cold, pour it on the beets, which must be peeled and cut into slices about ⅓ inch thick. Cover with bladder to exclude the air, and in a week they will be fit for use.

BISCUITS, Crisp.

Ingredients.—1 lb. of flour, the yolk of 1 egg, milk. *Mode.*—Mix the flour and the yolk of the egg with sufficient milk to make the whole into a very stiff paste; beat it well, and knead it until it is perfectly smooth. Roll the paste out *very thin;* with a round cutter shape it into small biscuits, and bake them a nice brown in a slow oven from 12 to 18 minutes. *Time.*—12 to 18 minutes. *Average cost*, 4*d.* *Seasonable* at any time.

BISCUITS, Dessert, which may be flavoured with Ground Ginger, Cinnamon, &c.

Ingredients.—1 lb. of flour, ½ lb. of butter, ¼ lb. of sifted sugar, the yolks of 6 eggs, flavouring to taste. *Mode.*—Put the butter into a basin; warm it, but do not allow it to oil; then with the hand beat it to a cream. Add the flour by degrees, then the sugar and flavouring, and moisten the whole with the yolks of the eggs, which should previously be well beaten. When all the ingredients are thoroughly incorporated, drop the mixture from a spoon on to a buttered paper, leaving a distance between each cake, for they spread as soon as they begin to get warm. Bake in rather a slow oven from 12 to 18 minutes, and do not let the biscuits acquire too much colour. In making the above quantity, half may be flavoured with ground ginger and the other half with essence of lemon or currants, to make a variety. With whatever the preparation is flavoured, so are the biscuits called, and an endless variety may be made in this manner. *Time.*—12 to 18 minutes, or rather longer, in a very slow oven. *Average cost*, 1*s.* 6*d.*

| Biscuits, Simple Hard | Blanc-mange |

Sufficient to make from 3 to 4 dozen cakes. *Seasonable* at any time.

BISCUITS, Simple Hard.

Ingredients.—To every lb. of flour allow 2 oz. of butter, about ½ pint of skimmed milk. *Mode.*—Warm the butter in milk until the former is dissolved, and then mix it with the flour into a very stiff paste ; beat it with a rolling-pin until the dough looks perfectly smooth. Roll it out thin ; cut it with the top of a glass into round biscuits ; prick them well, and bake them from 6 to 10 minutes. The above is the proportion of milk which we think would convert the flour into a stiff paste ; but should it be found too much, an extra spoonful or two of flour must be put in. These biscuits are very nice for the cheese course. *Time.*— 6 to 10 minutes. *Seasonable* at any time.

BLACK-COCK, to Roast.

Ingredients.—Black-cock, butter, toast. *Mode.*—Let these birds hang for a few days, or they will be tough and tasteless, if not well kept. Pluck and draw them, and wipe the insides and outsides with a damp cloth, as washing spoils the flavour. Cut off the heads, and truss them, the same as a roast fowl, cutting off the toes, and scalding and peeling the feet. Trussing them with the head on, as shown in the engraving, is still practised by many cooks, but the former method

ROAST BLACK-COCK.

is now considered the best. Put them down to a brisk fire, well baste them with butter, and serve with a piece of toast under, and a good gravy and bread sauce. After trussing, some cooks cover the breast with vine-leaves and slices of bacon, and then roast them. They should be served in the same manner and with the same accompaniments as with the plainly-roasted birds. *Time.*— 45 to 50 minutes. *Average cost,* from 5s. to 6s. the brace ; but seldom bought. *Sufficient,*—2 or 3 for a dish. *Seasonable* from the middle of August to the end of December.

BLACK-COCK, to Carve.

Skilful carving of game undoubtedly adds to the pleasure of the guests at a dinner-table ; for game seems pre-eminently to be composed of such delicate limbs and tender flesh that an inapt practitioner appears to more disadvantage when mauling these pretty and favourite dishes, than larger and more robust *pièces de résistance.* This bird is variously served with or without the head on ; and, although we do not personally object to the appearance of the head as shown in the woodcut, yet it seems to be more in vogue to serve it without. The carving is not difficult, but should be elegantly and deftly done. Slices from the

BLACK-COCK.

breast, cut in the direction of the dotted line from 2 to 1, should be taken off, the merrythought displaced, and the leg and wing removed by running the knife along from 3 to 4, reserving the thigh, which is considered a great delicacy, for the most honoured guests, some of whom may also esteem the brains of this bird.

BLANC-MANGE (a Supper Dish)

Ingredients. — 1 pint of new milk, 1¼ oz. of isinglass, the rind of ½ lemon, ¼ lb. of loaf sugar, 10 bitter almonds, ½ oz. of sweet almonds, 1 pint of cream. *Mode.* — Put the milk into a saucepan, with the isinglass, lemon-rind, and sugar, and let these ingredients stand by the side of the fire until the milk is well flavoured ; add the almonds, which should be blanched and pounded in a mortar to a paste, and let the milk just boil up ; strain it through a fine sieve or muslin into a jug, add the cream, and stir the mixture occasionally until nearly cold. Let it stand for a few minutes, then pour it into the mould, which should be previously oiled with the purest salad-oil, or dipped in cold water. There will be a sediment at the bottom of the jug, which must not be poured into the mould, as, when turned out, it would very much disfigure the appearance of the blanc-mange. This blanc-mange may be made very much richer by using 1½ pint of cream, and melting the isinglass in ½ pint of boiling water. The flavour may also be very much

Blanc-mange, Cheap

varied by adding bay-leaves, laurel-leaves, or essence of vanilla, instead of the lemon-rind and almonds. Noyeau, Maraschino, Curaçoa, or any favourite liqueur, added in small proportions, very much enhances

BLANC-MANGE MOULD.

the flavour of this always favourite dish. In turning it out, just loosen the edges of the blanc-mange from the mould, place a dish on it, and turn it quickly over: it should come out easily, and the blanc-mange have a smooth glossy appearance when the mould is oiled, which it frequently has not when it is only dipped in water. It may be garnished as fancy dictates. *Time.*—About 1½ hour to steep the lemon-rind and almonds in the milk. *Average cost*, with cream at 1s. per pint, 3s. 6d. *Sufficient* to fill a quart mould. *Seasonable* at any time.

BLANC-MANGE, Cheap.

Ingredients.—¼ lb. of sugar, 1 quart of milk, 1½ oz. of isinglass, the rind of ½ lemon, 4 laurel-leaves. *Mode.*—Put all the ingredients into a lined saucepan, and boil gently until the isinglass is dissolved; taste it occasionally to ascertain when it is sufficiently flavoured with the laurel-leaves; then take them out, and

BLANC-MANGE.

keep stirring the mixture over the fire for about 10 minutes. Strain it through a fine sieve into a jug, and, when nearly cold, pour it into a well-oiled mould, omitting the sediment at the bottom. Turn it out carefully on a dish, and garnish with preserves, bright jelly, or a compôte of fruit. *Time.*—Altogether, ¾

Brawn, to make

hour. *Average cost,* 8d. *Sufficient* to fill a quart mould. *Seasonable* at any time.

BOUDIN à la REINE (an Entrée; M. Ude's Recipe).

Ingredients.—The remains of cold roast fowls, 1 pint of Béchamel, salt and cayenne to taste, egg and bread crumbs. *Mode.*—Take the breasts and nice white meat from the fowls; cut it into small dice of an equal size, and throw them into some good Béchamel (*see* BECHAMEL); season with salt and cayenne, and put the mixture into a dish to cool. When this preparation is quite cold, cut it into 2 equal parts, which should be made into boudins of a long shape, the size of the dish they are intended to be served on; roll them in flour, egg and bread-crumb them, and be careful that the ends are well covered with the crumbs, otherwise they will break in the frying-pan; fry them a nice colour, put them before the fire to drain the greasy moisture from them, and serve with the remainder of the Béchamel poured round: this should be thinned with a little stock. *Time.*—10 minutes to fry the boudins. *Average cost,* exclusive of the fowl, 1s. 3d. *Sufficient* for 1 entrée.

BRAWN, to make.

Ingredients.—To a pig's head weighing 6 lbs. allow 1½ lb. lean beef, 2 tablespoonfuls of salt, 2 teaspoonfuls of pepper, a little cayenne, 6 pounded cloves. *Mode.*—Cut off the cheeks and salt them, unless the head be small, when all may be used. After carefully cleaning the head, put it on in sufficient cold water to cover it, with the beef, and skim it just before it boils. A head weighing 6 lbs. will require boiling from 2 to 3 hours. When sufficiently boiled to come off the bones easily, put it into a hot pan, remove the bones, and chop the meat with a sharp knife before the fire, together with the beef. *It is necessary to do this as quickly as possible to prevent the fat settling in it.* Sprinkle in the seasoning, which should have been previously mixed. Stir it well and put it quickly into a brawn-tin if you have one; if not, a cake-tin or mould will answer the purpose, if the meat is well pressed with weights, which must not be removed for several hours. When quite cold, dip the tin into boiling water for a minute or two, and the preparation will turn out

Bread-making

and be fit for use. *Time.*—From 2 to 3 hours. *Average cost*, for a pig's head, 4½d. per lb. *Seasonable* from September to March.

Note.—The liquor in which the head was boiled will make good pea soup, and the fat, if skimmed off and boiled in water, and afterwards poured into cold water, answers the purpose of lard.

BREAD-MAKING.

PANIFICATION, or bread-making, consists of the following processes, in the case of Wheaten Flour. Fifty or sixty per cent. of water is added to the flour, with the addition of some leavening matter, and preferably, of yeast from malt and hops. All kinds of leavening matter have, however, been, and are still used in different parts of the world: in the East Indies, "toddy," which is a liquor that flows from the wounded cocoa-nut tree; and in the West Indies, "dunder," or the refuse of the distillation of rum. The dough then undergoes the well-known process called *kneading.* The yeast produces fermentation, a process which may be thus described :—The dough reacting upon the leavening matter introduced, the starch of the flour is transformed into saccharine matter, the saccharine matter being afterwards changed into alcohol and carbonic acid. The dough must be well "bound," and yet allow the escape of the little bubbles of carbonic acid which accompany the fermentation, and which, in their passage, cause the numerous little holes which are seen in light bread.

The yeast must be good and fresh, if the bread is to be digestible and nice. Stale yeast produces, instead of vinous fermentation, an acetous fermentation, which flavours the bread and makes it disagreeable. A poor thin yeast produces an imperfect fermentation, the result being a heavy, unwholesome loaf.

When the dough is well kneaded, it is left to stand for some time, and then, as soon as it begins to swell, it is divided into loaves ; after which it is again left to stand, when it once more swells up, and manifests for the last time the symptoms of fermentation. It is then put into the oven, where the water contained in the dough is partly evaporated, and the loaves swell up again, while a yellow crust begins to form upon the surface. When the bread is sufficiently baked, the

Bread-making

bottom crust is hard and resonant if struck with the finger, while the crumb is elastic, and rises again after being pressed down with the finger. The bread is, in all probability, baked sufficiently if, on opening the door of the oven, you are met by a cloud of steam, which quickly passes away.

One word as to the unwholesomeness of new bread and hot rolls. When bread is taken out of the oven, it is full of moisture ; the starch is held together in masses, and the bread, instead of being crusted so as to expose each grain of starch to the saliva, actually prevents their digestion by being formed by the teeth into leathery poreless masses, which lie on the stomach like so many bullets. Bread should always be at least a day old before it is eaten ; and, if properly made, and kept in a *cool dry* place, ought to be perfectly soft and palatable at the end of three or four days. Hot rolls, swimming in melted butter, and new bread, ought to be carefully shunned by everybody who has the slightest respect for that much-injured individual—the Stomach.

AERATED BREAD.—It is not unknown to some of our readers that Dr. Dauglish, of Malvern, has recently patented a process for making bread "light," without the use of leaven. The ordinary process of bread-making by fermentation is tedious, and much labour of human hands is requisite in the kneading, in order that the dough may be thoroughly interpenetrated with the leaven. The new process impregnates the bread, by the application of machinery, with carbonic acid gas, or fixed air. Different opinions are expressed about the bread ; but it is curious to note, that, as corn is now reaped by machinery, and dough is baked by machinery, the whole process of bread-making is probably in course of undergoing changes which will emancipate both the housewife and the professional baker from a large amount of labour.

In the production of Aërated Bread, wheaten flour, water, salt, and carbonic acid gas (generated by proper machinery), are the only materials employed. We need not inform our readers that carbonic acid gas is the source of the effervescence, whether in common water coming from a depth, or in lemonade, or any aërated drink. Its action, in the new bread, takes the place of fermentation in the old.

Bread-making

In the patent process, the dough is mixed in a great iron ball, inside which is a system of paddles, perpetually turning, and doing the kneading part of the business. Into this globe the flour is dropped till it is full, and then the common atmospheric air is pumped out, and the pure gas turned on. The gas is followed by the water, which has been aërated for the purpose, and then begins the churning or kneading part of the business.

Of course, it is not long before we have the dough, and very "light" and nice it looks. This is caught in tins, and passed on to the floor of the oven, which is an endless floor, moving slowly through the fire. Done to a turn, the loaves emerge at the other end of the apartment,—and the Aërated Bread is made.

It may be added, that it is a good plan to change one's baker from time to time, and so secure a change in the quality of the bread that is eaten.

MIXED BREADS.—Rye bread is hard of digestion, and requires longer and slower baking than wheaten bread. It is better when made with leaven of wheaten flour rather than yeast, and turns out lighter. It should not be eaten till two days old. It will keep a long time.

A good bread may be made by mixing rye-flour, wheat-flour, and rice-paste, in equal proportions; also by mixing rye, wheat, and barley. In Norway, it is said that they only bake their barley bread once a year, such is its "keeping" quality.

Indian-corn flour mixed with wheat-flour (half with half) makes a nice bread, but it is not considered very digestible, though it keeps well.

Rice cannot be made into bread, nor can potatoes; but one-third potato-flour to three-fourths wheaten flour makes a tolerably good loaf.

A very good bread, better than the ordinary sort, and of a delicious flavour, is said to be produced by adopting the following recipe : — Take ten parts of wheat-flour, five parts of potato-flour, one part of rice-paste ; knead together, add the yeast, and bake as usual. This is, of course, cheaper than wheaten bread.

Flour, when freshly ground, is too glutinous to make good bread, and should therefore not be used immediately, but should be kept dry for a few weeks, and stirred occasionally until it becomes

Bread-making

dry, and crumbles easily between fingers.

Flour should be perfectly dry be being used for bread or cakes; if at damp, the preparation is sure to heavy. Before mixing it with the ot ingredients, it is a good plan to plac for an hour or two before the fire, u it feels warm and dry.

Yeast from home-brewed beer is g rally preferred to any other : it is v bitter, and on that account should well washed, and put away until thick mass settles. If it still contin bitter, the process should be repeat and, before being used, all the w floating at the top must be poured German yeast is now very much u and should be moistened, and thorou mixed with the milk or water with wl the bread is to be made.

The following observations are tracted from a valuable work on Bre making, and will be found very us to our readers :—

The first thing required for mak wholesome bread is the utmost clea ness ; the next is the soundness sweetness of all the ingredients used it ; and, in addition to these, th must be attention and care through whole process.

An almost certain way of spoi dough is to leave it half-made, an allow it to become cold before it finished. The other most comr causes of failure are using yeast whic no longer sweet, or which has b frozen, or has had hot liquid poured c it.

Too small a proportion of yeast, or sufficient time allowed for the doug rise, will cause the bread to be heavy.

Heavy bread will also most likely the result of making the dough v hard, and letting it become quite c particularly in winter.

If either the sponge or the doug permitted to overwork itself, that i say, if the mixing and kneading be glected when it has reached the pro point for either, sour bread will proba be the consequence in warm weat and bad bread in any. The good will also be endangered by placing i near the fire as to make any part o hot, instead of maintaining the ge and equal degree of heat required for due fermentation.

MILK OR BUTTER.—Milk which is

Bread-making

perfectly sweet will not only injure the flavour of the bread, but, in sultry weather, will often cause it to be quite uneatable; yet either of them, if *fresh and good*, will materially improve its quality.

To keep bread sweet and fresh, as soon as it is cold it should be put into a clean earthen pan, with a cover to it: this pan should be placed at a little distance from the ground, to allow a current of air to pass underneath. Some persons prefer keeping bread on clean wooden shelves without being covered, that the crust may not soften. Stale bread may be freshened by warming it through in a gentle oven. Stale pastry, cakes, &c., may also be improved by this method.

The utensils required for making bread on a moderate scale, are a kneading-trough or pan, sufficiently large that the dough may be kneaded freely without throwing the flour over the edges, and also to allow for its rising; a hair sieve for straining yeast, and one or two strong spoons.

Yeast must always be good of its kind, and in a fitting state to produce ready and proper fermentation. Yeast of strong beer or ale produces more effect than that of milder kinds; and the fresher the yeast, the smaller the quantity will be required to raise the dough.

As a general rule, the oven for baking bread should be rather quick, and the heat so regulated as to penetrate the dough without hardening the outside. The oven door should not be opened after the bread is put in until the dough is set, or has become firm, as the cool air admitted, will have an unfavourable effect on it.

Brick ovens are generally considered the best adapted for baking bread: these should be heated with wood faggots, and then swept and mopped out, to cleanse them for the reception of the bread. Iron ovens are more difficult to manage, being apt to burn the surface of the bread before the middle is baked. To remedy this, a few clean bricks should be set at the bottom of the oven, close together, to receive the tins of bread. In many modern stoves the ovens are so much improved that they bake admirably, and they can always be brought to the required temperature, when it is higher than is needed, by leaving the door open for a time.

Bread, to make good Home-made

BREAD, to make good Home-made (Miss Acton's Recipe).

Ingredients.—1 quartern of flour, 1 large tablespoonful of solid brewer's yeast, or nearly 1 oz. of fresh German yeast, 1¼ to 1½ pint of warm milk-and-water. *Mode.*—Put the flour into a large earthenware bowl or deep pan; then, with a strong metal or wooden spoon, hollow out the middle; but do not clear it entirely away from the bottom of the pan, as, in that case, the sponge, or leaven (as it was formerly termed) would stick to it, which it ought not to do.

COTTAGE LOAF.

Next take either a large table-spoonful of brewer's yeast which has been rendered solid by mixing it with plenty of cold water, and letting it afterwards stand to settle for a day and night; or nearly an ounce of German yeast; put it into a large basin, and proceed to mix it, so that it shall be as smooth as cream, with ¾ pint of warm milk-and-water, or with water only; though even a very little milk will much improve the bread. Pour the yeast into the hole made in the flour, and stir into it as much of that which lies round it as will make a thick batter, in which there must be no lumps. Strew plenty of flour on the top, throw a thick clean cloth over, and set it where the air is warm; but do not place it upon

TIN BREAD.

the kitchen fender, for it will become too much heated there. Look at it from time to time: when it has been laid for nearly an hour, and when the yeast has risen and broken through the flour, so that bubbles appear in it, you will know that it is ready to be made up into dough. Then place the pan on a strong chair, or dresser, or table, of convenient height; pour into the sponge the remainder of the warm milk-and-water;

Bread, to make a Peck of good

stir into it as much of the flour as you can with the spoon ; then wipe it out clean with your fingers, and lay it aside. Next take plenty of the remaining flour, throw it on the top of the leaven, and begin, with the knuckles of both hands, to knead 'it well. When the flour is nearly all kneaded in, begin to draw the edges of the dough towards the middle, in order to mix the whole thoroughly ; and when it is free from flour and lumps and crumbs, and does not stick to the hands when touched, it will be done, and may be covered with the cloth, and left to rise a second time. In ¾ hour look at it, and should it have swollen very much and begin to crack, it will be light enough to bake. Turn it then on to a paste-board or very clean dresser, and with a large sharp knife divide it in two; make it up quickly into loaves, and despatch it to the oven: make one or two incisions across the tops of the loaves, as they will rise more easily if this be done. If baked in tins or pans, rub them with a tiny piece of butter laid on a piece of clean paper, to prevent the dough from sticking to them. All bread should be turned upside down, or on its side, as soon as it is drawn from the oven: if this be neglected, the under part of the loaves will become wet and blistered from the steam, which cannot then escape from them. *To make the dough without setting a sponge,* merely mix the yeast with the greater part of the warm milk-and-water, and wet up the whole of the flour at once after a little salt has been stirred in, proceeding exactly, in every other respect, as in the directions just given. As the dough will *soften* in the rising, it should be made quite firm at first, or it will be too lithe by the time it is ready for the oven. *Time.*—To be left to rise an hour the first time, ¾ hour the second time ; to be baked from 1 to 1¼ hour, or baked in one loaf from 1½ to 2 hours.

BREAD, to make a Peck of good.

Ingredients.—3 lbs. of potatoes, 6 pints of cold water, ½ pint of good yeast, a peck of flour, 2 oz. of salt. *Mode.*—Peel and boil the potatoes ; beat them to a cream while warm ; then add 1 pint of cold water, strain through a colander, and add to it ½ pint of good yeast, which should have been put in water over-night to take off its bitterness. Stir all well

together with a wooden spoon, and pour the mixture into the centre of the flour ; mix it to the substance of cream, cover it over closely, and let it remain near the fire for an hour ; then add the 5 pints of water, milk-warm, with 2 oz. of salt; pour this in, and mix the whole to a nice light dough. Let it remain for about 2 hours ; then make it into 7 loaves, and bake for about 1½ hour in a good oven. When baked, the bread should weigh nearly 20 lbs. *Time.*—About 1½ hour.

BREAD - AND - BUTTER FRITTERS.

Ingredients.—Batter, 8 slices of bread and butter, 3 or 4 tablespoonfuls of jam. *Mode.*—Make a batter, the same as for apple fritters ; cut some slices of bread and butter, not very thick ; spread half of them with any jam that may be preferred, and cover with the other slices ; slightly press them together, and cut them out in square, long, or round pieces. Dip them in the batter, and fry in boiling lard for about 10 minutes ; drain them before the fire on a piece of blotting-paper or cloth. Dish them, sprinkle over sifted sugar, and serve. *Time.*—About 10 minutes. *Average cost,* 1s. *Sufficient* for 4 or 5 persons. *Seasonable* at any time.

BREAD - AND - BUTTER PUDDING, Baked.

Ingredients.—9 thin slices of bread and butter, 1½ pint of milk, 4 eggs, sugar to taste, ¼ lb. of currants, flavouring of vanilla, grated lemon-peel, or nutmeg. *Mode.*—Cut 9 slices of bread and butter, not very thick, and put them into a pie-dish, with currants between each layer, and on the top. Sweeten and flavour the milk, either by infusing a little lemon-peel in it, or by adding a few drops of essence of vanilla ; well whisk the eggs, and stir these to the milk. *Strain* this over the bread and butter, and bake in a moderate oven for 1 hour, or rather longer. This pudding may be very much enriched by adding cream, candied peel, or more eggs than stated above. It should not be turned out, but sent to table in the pie-dish, and is better for being made about two hours before it is baked. *Time.*—1 hour, or rather longer. *Average cost,* 9d. *Sufficient* for 6 or 7 persons. *Seasonable* at any time.

Bread Crumbs, Fried	Brill

BREAD CRUMBS, Fried.

Cut the bread into thin slices, place them in a cool oven overnight, and when thoroughly dry and crisp, roll them down into fine crumbs. Put some lard, or clarified dripping, into a frying-pan; bring it to the boiling-point, throw in the crumbs, and fry them very quickly. Directly they are done, lift them out with a slice, and drain them before the fire from all greasy moisture. When quite crisp, they are ready for use. The fat they are fried in should be clear, and the crumbs should not have the slightest appearance or taste of having been, in the least degree, burnt.

BREAD, Fried, for Borders.

Proceed by frying some slices of bread, cut in any fanciful shape, in boiling lard. When quite crisp, dip one side of the sippet into the beaten white of an egg mixed with a little flour, and place it on the edge of the dish. Continue in this manner till the border is completed, arranging the sippets a pale and a dark one alternately.

BREAD, Fried Sippets of, for Garnishing many Dishes.

Cut the bread into thin slices, and stamp them out in whatever shape you like,—rings, crosses, diamonds, &c. &c. Fry them in the same manner as the bread crumbs, in clear boiling lard or clarified dripping, and drain them until thoroughly crisp before the fire. When variety is desired, try some of a pale colour, and others of a darker hue.

BREAKFASTS.

It will not be necessary to give here a long bill of fare of cold joints, &c., which may be placed on the sideboard, and do duty at the breakfast-table. Suffice it to say, that any cold meat the larder may furnish should be nicely garnished and be placed on the buffet. Collared and potted meats or fish, cold game or poultry, veal-and-ham pies, game-and-rumpsteak pies, are all suitable dishes for the breakfast-table; as also cold ham, tongue, &c. &c.

The following list of hot dishes may perhaps assist our readers in knowing what to provide for the comfortable meal called breakfast. Broiled fish, such as mackerel, whiting, herrings, dried haddocks, &c.; mutton chops and rump-steaks, broiled sheep's kidneys, kidneys à la maître d'hôtel, sausages, plain rashers of bacon, bacon and poached eggs, haɪɪ and poached eggs, omelets, plain boiled eggs, œufs-au-plat, poached eggs on toast, muffins, toast, marmalade, butter, &c. &c.

In the summer, and when they are obtainable, always have a vase of freshly-gathered flowers on the breakfast-table, and, when convenient, a nicely-arranged dish of fruit: when strawberries are in season, these are particularly refreshing; as also grapes, or even currants.

BRILL.

Ingredients.—¼ lb. of salt to each gallon of water; a little vinegar. *Mode.*—Clean the brill, cut off the fins, and rub it over with a little lemon-juice, to preserve its whiteness. Set the fish in sufficient cold water to cover it; throw in salt, in the above proportions, and a little vinegar, and bring it gradually to boil: simmer very gently till the fish is done, which will be in about 10 minutes for a small brill, reckoning from the time the water begins to simmer. It is difficult to give the *exact* number of minutes required for cooking a brill, as the fish varies somewhat in thickness, but the cook can always bear in mind that fish of every description should be *very thoroughly dressed,* and never come to table in the *least degree underdone.* The time for boiling of course depends entirely on the size of the fish. Serve it on a hot napkin, and garnish with cut lemon, parsley, horseradish, and a little lobster coral sprinkled over the fish. Send lobster or shrimp sauce and plain melted butter to table with it. *Time.*—After the water boils, a small brill, 10 minutes; a medium sized brill, 15 to 20 minutes; a large brill, ½ hour. *Average cost,* from 4s. to 8s.; but when the market is plentifully supplied, may be had from 2s. each. *Seasonable* from August to April.

To choose Brill.—The flesh of this fish, like that of turbot, should be of a yellowish tint, and should be chosen on account of its thickness. If the flesh has a bluish tint, it is not good.

A Brill and John Dory are carved in the same manner as a Turbot.

| Browning, for Stock | Bubble-and-Squeak |

Note.—The thick parts of the middle of the back are the best slices in a tur-

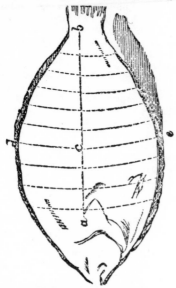

HOW TO CARVE A BRILL.

bot; and the rich gelatinous skin covering the fish, as well as a little of the thick part of the fins, are dainty morsels, and should be placed on each plate.

BROWNING, for Stock.

Ingredients.—2 oz. of powdered sugar, and ½ a pint of water. *Mode.*—Place the sugar in a stewpan over a slow fire until it begins to melt, keeping it stirred with a wooden spoon until it becomes black, when add the water, and let it dissolve. Cork closely, and use a few drops when required.

Note.—In France, burnt onions are made use of for the purpose of browning. As a general rule, the process of browning is to be discouraged, as apt to impart a slightly unpleasant flavour to the stock, and consequently all soups made from it.

BROWNING for Gravies and Sauces.

The browning for stock answers equally well for sauces and gravies, when it is absolutely necessary to colour them in this manner; but where they can be made to look brown by using ketchup, wine, browned flour, tomatoes, or any coloured sauce, it is far preferable. As, however,

in cooking so much depends on appearance, perhaps it would be as well for the inexperienced cook to use the artificial means. When no browning is at hand, and you wish to heighten the colour of your gravy, dissolve a lump of sugar in an iron spoon close to a sharp fire; when it is in a liquid state, drop it into the sauce or gravy quite hot. Care, however, must be taken not to put in too much, as it would impart a very disagreeable flavour to the preparation.

BRUSSELS-SPROUTS, Boiled.

Ingredients.—To each ½ gallon of water allow 1 heaped tablespoonful of salt; a *very small* piece of soda. *Mode.*—Clean the sprouts from insects, nicely wash them, and pick off any dead or discoloured leaves from the outsides; put them into a saucepan of *boiling* water, with salt and soda in the above proportion; keep the pan uncovered, and let them boil quickly over a brisk fire until tender; drain, dish, and serve with a tureen of melted butter, or with a maître d'hôtel sauce poured over them. Another mode of serving them is, when they are dished, to stir in about 1½ oz. of butter and a seasoning of pepper and salt. They must, however, be sent to table very quickly, as, being so very small, this vegetable soon cools. Where the cook is very expeditious, this vegetable may be cooked may be arranged on the dish in the form of a pineapple, and so served has a very pretty appearance. *Time.*—from 9 to 12 minutes after the water boils. *Average cost,* 1s. 4d. per peck. *Sufficient.*—Allow between 40 and 50 for 5 or 6 persons. *Seasonable* from November to March.

BUBBLE-AND-SQUEAK.

[COLD MEAT COOKERY.] *Ingredients.* —A few thin slices of cold boiled beef, butter, cabbage, 1 sliced onion, pepper and salt to taste. *Mode.* — Fry the slices of beef gently in a little butter, taking care not to dry them up. Lay them on a flat dish, and cover with fried greens. The greens may be prepared from cabbage sprouts or green savoys. They should be boiled till tender, well drained, minced, and placed, till quite hot, in a frying-pan, with butter, a sliced onion, and seasoning of pepper and salt. When the onion is done, it is ready to serve. *Time.*--Alto-

Bullock's Heart, to Dress a

gether, ½ hour. *Average cost*, exclusive of the cold beef, 3d. *Seasonable* at any time.

BULLOCK S HEART, to Dress a.

Ingredients.—1 heart, stuffing of veal forcemeat. *Mode.*—Put the heart into warm water to soak for 2 hours; then wipe it well with a cloth, and, after cutting off the lobes, stuff the inside with a highly-seasoned forcemeat. Fasten it in, by means of a needle and coarse thread; tie the heart up in paper, and set it before a good fire, being very particular to keep it well basted, or it will eat dry, there being very little of its own fat. Two or three minutes before dishing remove the paper, baste well, and serve with good gravy and red-currant jelly or melted butter. If the heart is very large, it will require 2 hours, and, covered with a caul, may be baked as well as roasted. *Time.*—Large heart, 2 hours. *Average cost*, 2s. 6d. *Sufficient* for 6 or 8 persons. *Seasonable* all the year.

Note.—This is an excellent family dish, is very savoury, and, though not seen at many good tables, may be recommended for its cheapness and economy.

BUNS, Light.

Ingredients.—½ teaspoonful of tartaric acid, ½ teaspoonful of bicarbonate of soda, 1 lb. of flour, 2 oz. of butter, 2 oz. of loaf sugar, ¼ lb. of currants or raisins,—when liked, a few caraway seeds, ½ pint of cold new milk, 1 egg. *Mode.*—Rub the tartaric acid, soda, and flour all together through a hair sieve; work the butter into the flour; add the sugar, currants,

BUNS.

and caraway seeds, when the flavour of the latter is liked. Mix all these ingredients well together; make a hole in the middle of the flour, and pour in the milk, mixed with the egg, which should be well beaten; mix quickly, and set the dough, with a fork, on baking-tins, and bake the buns for about 20 minutes. This mixture makes a very good cake, and if put into a tin, should be baked 1½ hour. The same quantity of flour, soda, and tartaric acid, with ½ pint of milk and a little salt, will make either bread or

Butter, Clarified

teacakes, if wanted quickly. *Time.*—20 minutes for the buns; if made into a cake, 1½ hour. *Sufficient* to make about 12 buns.

BUNS, Plain.

Ingredients.—1 lb. of flour, 6 oz. of good butter, ¼ lb. of sugar, 1 egg, nearly ¼ pint of milk, 2 small teaspoonfuls of baking-powder, a few drops of essence of lemon. *Mode.*—Warm the butter, without oiling it; beat it with a wooden spoon; stir the flour in gradually with the sugar, and mix these ingredients well together. Make the milk lukewarm, beat up with it the yolk of the egg and the essence of lemon, and stir these to the flour, &c. Add the baking-powder, beat the dough well for about 10 minutes, divide it into 24 pieces, put them into buttered tins or cups, and bake in a brisk oven from 20 to 30 minutes. *Time.*—20 to 30 minutes. *Average cost*, 1s. *Sufficient* to make 12 buns. *Seasonable* at any time.

BUNS, Victoria.

Ingredients. — 2 oz. of pounded loaf sugar, 1 egg, 1½ oz. of ground rice, 2 oz. of butter, 1½ oz. of currants, a few thin slices of candied-peel, flour. *Mode.* — Whisk the egg, stir in the sugar, and beat these ingredients both together; beat the butter to a cream, stir in the ground rice, currants, and candied-peel, and as much flour as will make it of such a consistency that it may be rolled into 7 or 8 balls. Place these on a buttered tin, and bake them for ½ to ¾ hour. They should be put into the oven immediately or they will become heavy, and the oven should be tolerably brisk. *Time.*—½ to ¾ hour. *Average cost*, 6d. *Sufficient* to make 7 or 8 buns. *Seasonable* at any time.

BUTTER, Browned.

Ingredients.—¼ lb. of butter, 1 tablespoonful of minced parsley, 3 tablespoonfuls of vinegar, salt and pepper to taste. *Mode.*—Put the butter into a fryingpan over a nice clear fire, and when it smokes, throw in the parsley, and add the vinegar and seasoning. Let the whole simmer for a minute or two, when it is ready to serve. This is a very good sauce for skate. *Time.*—¼ hour.

BUTTER, Clarified.

Put the butter in a basin before the

Butter, Curled	Butter, Rancid

fire, and when it melts, stir it round once or twice, and let it settle. Do not strain it, unless absolutely necessary, as it causes so much waste. Pour it gently off into a clean dry jar, carefully leaving all sediment behind. Let it cool, and carefully exclude the air by means of a bladder, or piece of wash-leather, tied over. If the butter is salt, it may be washed before melting, when it is to be used for sweet dishes.

BUTTER, Curled.

Tie a strong cloth by two of the corners to an iron hook in the wall; make a knot with the other two ends, so that a stick might pass through. Put the butter into the cloth; twist it tightly over a dish, into which the butter will fall through the knot, so forming small and pretty little strings. The butter may then be garnished with parsley, if to serve with a cheese course; or it may be sent to table plain for breakfast, in an ornamental dish. Squirted butter for garnishing hams, salads, eggs, &c., is made by forming a piece of stiff paper in the shape of a cornet, and squeezing the butter in fine strings from the hole at the bottom. Scooped butter is made by dipping a teaspoon or scooper in warm water, and then scooping the butter quickly and thin. In warm weather, it would not be necessary to heat the spoon.

BUTTER, Fairy.

Ingredients. — The yolks of 2 hard-boiled eggs, 1 tablespoonful of orange-flower water, 2 tablespoonfuls of pounded sugar, ¼ lb. of good fresh butter. *Mode.* —Beat the yolks of the eggs smoothly in a mortar, with the orange-flower water and the sugar, until the whole is reduced to a fine paste; add the butter, and force all through an old but clean cloth by wringing the cloth and squeezing the butter very hard. The butter will then drop on the plate in large and small pieces, according to the holes in the cloth. Plain butter may be done in the same manner, and is very quickly prepared, besides having a very good effect.

BUTTER, to keep Fresh.

Butter may be kept fresh for ten or twelve days by a very simple process. Knead it well in cold water till the buttermilk is extracted; then put it in a glazed

jar, which invert in another, putting into the latter a sufficient quantity of water to exclude the air. Renew the water every day.

BUTTER, Maître d'Hôtel, for putting into Broiled Fish just before it is sent to Table.

Ingredients. —¼ lb. of butter, 2 dessert spoonfuls of minced parsley, salt and pepper to taste, the juice of 1 large lemon. *Mode.* —Work the above ingredients well together, and let them be thoroughly mixed with a wooden spoon. If this is used as a sauce, it may be poured either under or over the meat or fish it is intended to be served with. *Average cost,* for this quantity, 5d.

Note. —4 tablespoonfuls of Béchamel, 2 do. of white stock, with 2 oz. of the above maître d'hôtel butter stirred into it, and just allowed to simmer for 1 minute, will be found an excellent hot maître d'hôtel sauce.

BUTTER, Melted.

Ingredients. —¼lb. of butter, a dessertspoonful of flour, 1 wineglassful of water, salt to taste. *Mode.* —Cut the butter up into small pieces, put it into a saucepan, dredge over the flour, and add the water and a seasoning of salt; stir it *one way* constantly till the whole of the ingredients are melted and thoroughly blended. Let it just boil, when it is ready to serve. If the butter is to be melted with cream, use the same quantity as of water, but omit the flour; keep stirring it, but do not allow it to boil. *Time.* —1 minute to simmer. *Average cost* for this quantity, 4d.

BUTTER, Melted (more Economical).

Ingredients. —2 oz. of butter, 1 dessertspoonful of flour, salt to taste, ½ pint of water. *Mode.* —Mix the flour and water to a smooth batter, which put into a saucepan. Add the butter and a seasoning of salt, keep stirring *one way* till all the ingredients are melted and perfectly smooth; let the whole boil for a minute or two, and serve. *Time.* —2 minutes to simmer. *Average cost* for this quantity, 2d.

BUTTER, Rancid, What to do with.

When butter has become very rancid,

Butter, Melted

it should be melted several times **by a** moderate heat, with or without the addition of water, and as soon as it has been well kneaded, after the cooling, in order to extract any water it may have retained, it should be put into brown freestone pots, sheltered from the contact of the air. The French often add to it, after it has been melted, a piece of toasted bread, which helps to destroy the tendency of the butter to rancidity.

BUTTER, Melted (the French Sauce Blanche).

Ingredients.—¼ lb. of fresh butter, 1 tablespoonful of flour, salt to taste, ⅓ gill of water, ⅓ spoonful of white vinegar, a very little grated nutmeg. *Mode.*—Mix the flour and water to a smooth batter, carefully rubbing down with the back of a spoon any lumps that may appear. Put it in a saucepan with all the other ingredients, and let it thicken on the fire, but do not allow it to boil, lest it should taste of the flour. *Time.*—1 minute to simmer. *Average cost, 5d.* for this quantity.

BUTTER, Melted, made with Milk.

Ingredients.—1 teaspoonful of flour, 2 oz. of butter, ⅓ pint of milk, a few grains of salt. *Mode.*—Mix the butter and flour smoothly together on a plate, put it into a lined saucepan, and pour in the milk. Keep stirring it *one way* over a sharp fire; let it boil quickly for a minute or two, and it is ready to serve. This is a very good foundation for onion, lobster, or oyster sauce : using milk instead of water makes it look much whiter and more delicate. *Time.*—Altogether, 10 minutes. *Average cost for this quantity, 3d.*

CABBAGE, Boiled.

Ingredients.—To each ⅓ gallon of water allow 1 heaped tablespoonful of salt; a *very small* piece of soda. *Mode.*—Pick off all the dead outside leaves, cut off as much of the stalk as possible, and cut the cabbages across twice, at the stalk end ; if they should be very large, quarter them. Wash them well in cold water, place them in a colander, and drain ; then put them into *plenty* of *fast-boiling* water, to which have been added salt and soda in the above proportions. Stir them down once or twice in the

Cabbage, Red, Stewed

water, keep the pan uncovered, and let them boil quickly until tender. The instant they are done, take them up into a colander, place a plate over them, let them thoroughly drain, dish, and serve. *Time.*—Large cabbages, or savoys, ½ to ¾ hour, young summer cabbage, 10 to 15 minutes, after the water boils. *Average cost, 2d.* each in full season. *Sufficient.*—2 large ones for 4 or 5 persons. *Seasonable.*—Cabbages and sprouts of various kinds at any time.

CABBAGE, Red, Pickled.

Ingredients.—Red cabbages, salt and water ; to each quart of vinegar, ½ oz. of ginger well bruised, 1 oz. of whole black pepper, and, when liked, a little cayenne. *Mode.*—Take off the outside decayed leaves of a nice red cabbage, cut it in quarters, remove the stalks, and cut it across in very thin slices. Lay these on a dish, and strew them plentifully with salt, covering them with another dish. Let them remain for 24 hours, turn into a colander to drain, and, if necessary, wipe lightly with a clean soft cloth. Put them in a jar ; boil up the vinegar with spices in the above proportion, and, when cold, pour it over the cabbage. It will be fit for use in a week or two, and, if kept for a very long time, the cabbage is liable to get soft and to discolour. To be really nice and crisp, and of a good red colour, it should be eaten almost immediately after it is made. A little bruised cochineal boiled with the vinegar adds much to the appearance of this pickle. Tie down with bladder, and keep in a dry place. *Seasonable* in July and August, but the pickle will be much more crisp if the frost has just touched the leaves.

CABBAGE, Red, Stewed.

Ingredients.—1 red cabbage, a small slice of ham, ½ oz. of fresh butter, 1 pint of weak stock or broth, 1 gill of vinegar, salt and pepper to taste, 1 tablespoonful of pounded sugar. *Mode.*—Cut the cabbage into very thin slices, put it into a stewpan, with the ham cut in dice, the butter, ⅓ pint of stock, and the vinegar ; cover the pan closely, and let it stew for 1 hour. When it is very tender, add the remainder of the stock, a seasoning of salt and pepper, and the pounded sugar ; mix all well together, stir over the fire until nearly all the liquor is dried away, and serve. Fried sausages are usually sent to table with this dish : they should be laid round and on the cabbage, as a garnish. *Time.*—Rather more than 1 hour. *Average cost*, 4*d*. each. *Sufficient* for 4 persons. *Seasonable* from September to January.

CABBAGE SOUP.

Ingredients.—1 large cabbage, 3 carrots, 2 onions, 4 or 5 slices of lean bacon, salt and pepper to taste, 2 quarts of medium stock. *Mode.*—Scald the cabbage, cut it up and drain it. Line the stewpan with the bacon, put in the cabbage, carrots, and onions; moisten with skimmings from the stock, and simmer very gently, till the cabbage is tender ; add the stock, stew softly for half an hour, and carefully skim off every particle of fat. Season and serve. *Time.* 1½ hour. *Average cost*, 1*s*. per quart. *Seasonable* in winter. *Sufficient* for 8 persons.

CABINET or CHANCELLOR'S PUDDING.

Ingredients.—1½ oz. of candied peel, 4 oz. of currants, 4 dozen sultanas, a few slices of Savoy cake, sponge cake, a French roll, 4 eggs, 1 pint of milk, grated lemon-rind, ¼ nutmeg, 3 tablespoonfuls of sugar. *Mode.*—Melt some butter to a paste, and with it, well grease the mould or basin in which the pudding is to be boiled, taking care that it is buttered in every part. Cut the peel into thin slices, and place these in a fanciful device at the bottom of the mould, and fill in the spaces between with currants and sultanas; then add a few slices of sponge cake or French roll; drop a few drops of melted butter on these, and between

CABINET PUDDING.

each layer sprinkle a few currants. Proceed in this manner until the mould is nearly full; then flavour the milk with nutmeg and grated lemon-rind ; add the sugar, and stir to this the eggs, which should be well beaten. Beat this mixture for a few minutes ; then strain it into the mould, which should be quite full; tie a piece of buttered paper over it, and let it stand for two hours ; then tie it down with a cloth, put it into

boiling water, and let it boil slowly for 1 hour. In taking it up, let it stand for a minute or two before the cloth is removed ; then quickly turn it out of the mould or basin, and serve with sweet sauce separately. The flavouring of this pudding may be varied by substituting for the lemond-rind essence of vanilla or bitter almonds ; and it may be made much richer by using cream ; but this is not at all necessary. *Time.*—1 hour. *Average cost*, 1*s*. 3*d*. *Sufficient* for 5 or 6 persons. *Seasonable* at any time.

CABINET or BOILED BREAD-AND-BUTTER PUDDING, Plain.

Ingredients.—2 oz. of raisins, a few thin slices of bread and butter, 3 eggs, 1 pint of milk, sugar to taste, ¼ nutmeg. *Mode.*—Butter a pudding-basin, and line the inside with a layer of raisins that have been previously stoned; then nearly fill the basin with slices of bread and butter with the crust cut off, and, in another basin, beat the eggs; add to them the milk, sugar, and grated nutmeg ; mix all well together, and pour the whole on to the bread and butter ; let it stand ½ hour, then tie a floured cloth over it ; boil for 1 hour, and serve with sweet sauce. Care must be taken that the basin is quite full before the cloth is tied over. *Time.*—1 hour. *Average cost*, 9*d*. *Sufficient* for 5 or 6 persons. *Seasonable* at any time.

CAFE AU LAIT.

This is merely very strong coffee added to a large proportion of good hot milk ; about 6 tablespoonfuls of strong coffee being quite sufficient for a breakfast-cupful of milk. Of the essence which answers admirably for *café au lait*, so much would not be required. This preparation is infinitely superior to the weak watery coffee so often served at English tables. A little cream mixed with the milk, if the latter cannot be depended on for richness, improves the taste of the coffee, as also the richness of the beverage. *Sufficient.*—6 tablespoonfuls of strong coffee, or 2 tablespoonfuls of the essence, to a breakfast-cupful of milk.

CAFE NOIR.

This is usually handed round after dinner, and should be drunk well

Cakes, Making and Baking of

sweetened, with the addition of a little brandy or liqueurs, which may be added or not at pleasure. The coffee should be made very strong, and served in very small cups, but never mixed with milk or cream. *Café noir* may be made of the essence of coffee by pouring a tablespoonful into each cup, and filling it up with boiling water. This is a very simple and expeditious manner of preparing coffee for a large party, but the essence for it must be made very good, and kept well corked until required for use.

CAKES, Making and Baking of.

Eggs should always be broken into a cup, the whites and yolks separated, and they should always be strained. Breaking the eggs thus, the bad ones may be easily rejected without spoiling the others, and so cause no waste. As eggs are used instead of yeast, they should be very thoroughly whisked; they are generally sufficiently beaten when thick enough to carry the drop that falls from the whisk.

Loaf Sugar should be well pounded, and then sifted through a fine sieve.

Currants should be nicely washed, picked, dried in a cloth, and then carefully examined, that no pieces of grit or stone may be left amongst them. They should then be laid on a dish before the fire, to become thoroughly dry; as, if added damp to the other ingredients, cakes will be liable to be heavy.

Good Butter should always be used in the manufacture of cakes; and, if beaten to a cream, it saves much time and labour to warm, but not melt, it before beating.

Less butter and eggs are required for cakes when yeast is mixed with the other ingredients.

The heat of the oven is of great importance, especially for large cakes. If the heat be not tolerably fierce, the batter will not rise. If the oven is too quick, and there is any danger of the cake burning or catching, put a sheet of clean paper over the top: newspaper, or paper that has been printed on, should never be used for this purpose.

To know when a cake is sufficiently baked, plunge a clean knife into the middle of it; draw it quickly out, and if it looks in the least sticky put the cake back, and close the oven door until the cake is done.

Cake, Common

Cakes should be kept in closed tin canisters or jars, and in a dry place. Those made with yeast do not keep so long as those made without it.

CAKES, nice Breakfast.

Ingredients.—1 lb. of flour, ½ teaspoonful of tartaric acid, ½ teaspoonful of salt, ¼ teaspoonful of carbonate of soda, 1½ breakfast-cupful of milk, 1 oz. of sifted loaf sugar, 2 eggs. *Mode.*—These cakes are made in the same manner as the soda bread, with the addition of eggs and sugar. Mix the flour, tartaric acid, and salt well together, taking care that the two latter ingredients are reduced to the finest powder, and stir in the sifted sugar which should also be very fine. Dissolve the soda in the milk, add the eggs, which should be well whisked, and with this liquid work the flour, &c. into a light dough. Divide it into small cakes, put them into the oven immediately, and bake for about 20 minutes. *Time.*—20 minutes.

CAKE, Christmas.

Ingredients.—5 teacupfuls of flour, 1 teacupful of melted butter, 1 teacupful of cream, 1 teacupful of treacle, 1 teacupful of moist sugar, 2 eggs, ½ oz. of powdered ginger, ½ lb. of raisins, 1 teaspoonful of carbonate of soda, 1 tablespoonful of vinegar. *Mode.*— Make the butter sufficiently warm to melt it, but do not allow it to oil; put the flour into a basin, add to it the sugar, ginger, and raisins, which should be stoned and cut into small pieces. When these dry ingredients are thoroughly mixed, stir in the butter, cream, treacle, and well-whisked eggs, and beat the mixture for a few minutes. Dissolve the soda in the vinegar, add it to the dough, and be particular that these latter ingredients are well incorporated with the others; put the cake into a buttered mould or tin, place it in a moderate oven immediately, and bake it from 1¾ to 2¼ hours. *Time.* —1¾ to 2¼ hours. *Average cost, 1s. 6d.*

CAKE, Common (suitable for sending to Children at School).

Ingredients.—2 lbs. of flour, 4 oz. of butter or clarified dripping, ½ oz. of caraway seeds, ¼ oz. of allspice, ½ lb. of pounded sugar, 1 lb. of currants, 1 pint of milk, 3 tablespoonfuls of fresh yeast.

Cake, Economical

Mode.—Rub the butter lightly into the flour; add all the dry ingredients, and mix these well together. Make the milk warm, but not hot; stir in the yeast, and with this liquid mix the whole into a light dough; knead it well, and line the cake-tins with strips of buttered paper: this paper should be about 6 inches higher than the top of the tin. Put in the dough; stand it in a warm place to rise for more than an hour, then bake the cakes in a well-heated oven. If this quantity be divided into two, they will take from 1½ to 2 hours' baking, *Time.* —1½ to 2 hours. *Average cost*, 1s. 9d. *Sufficient* to make 2 moderate-sized cakes.

CAKE, Economical.

Ingredients.—1 lb. of flour, ¼ lb. of sugar, ¼ lb. of butter or lard, ½ lb. of currants, 1 teaspoonful of carbonate of soda, the whites of 4 eggs, ½ pint of milk. *Mode.*—In making many sweet dishes, the whites of eggs are not required, and if well beaten and added to the above ingredients, make an excellent cake with

CAKE-MOULD.

or without currants. Beat the butter to a cream, well whisk the whites of the eggs, and stir all the ingredients together but the soda, which must not be added until all is well mixed, and the cake is ready to be put into the oven. When the mixture has been well beaten, stir in the soda, put the cake into a buttered mould, and bake it in a moderate oven for 1½ hour. *Time.*—1½ hour. *Average cost*, 1s. 3d.

CAKE, Good Holiday.

Ingredients.—1½d. worth of Borwick's German baking-powder, 2 lbs. of flour, 6 oz. of butter, ¼ lb. of lard, 1 lb. of currants, ½ lb. of stoned and cut raisins, ¼ lb. of mixed candied peel, ½ lb. of moist sugar, 3 eggs, ¾ pint of cold milk. *Mode.* —Mix the baking-powder with the flour; then rub in the butter and lard; have ready the currants, washed, picked, and dried, the raisins stoned and cut into small pieces (not chopped), and the peel cut into neat slices. Add these with the sugar to the flour, &c., and mix all the dry ingredients well together. Whisk the eggs, stir to them the milk, and with this liquid moisten the cake; beat it up

Cake, a nice useful

well, that all may be very thoroughly mixed; line a cake-tin with buttered paper, put in the cake, and bake it from 2¼ to 2¾ hours in a good oven. To ascertain when it is done, plunge a clean knife into the middle of it, and if, on withdrawing it, the knife looks clean, and not sticky, the cake is done. To prevent it burning at the top, a piece of clean paper may be put over whilst the cake is soaking, or being thoroughly cooked in the middle. A steamer, such as is used for steaming potatoes, makes a very good cake-tin, if it be lined at the bottom and sides with buttered paper. *Time.*—2¼ to 2¾ hours. *Average cost*, 2s. 6d. *Seasonable* at any time.

CAKE, Luncheon.

Ingredients.—½ lb. of butter, 1 lb. of flour, ½ oz. of caraway seeds, ¼ lb. of currants, 6 oz. of moist sugar, 1 oz. of candied peel, 3 eggs, ½ pint of milk, 1 small teaspoonful of carbonate of soda. *Mode.*—Rub the butter into the flour until it is quite fine; add the caraway seeds, currants (which should be nicely washed, picked, and dried), sugar, and candied peel cut into thin slices; mix these well together, and moisten with the eggs, which should be well whisked. Boil the milk, and add to it, whilst boiling, the carbonate of soda, which must be well stirred into it, and, with the milk, mix the other ingredients. Butter a tin, pour the cake into it, and bake it in a moderate oven from 1 to 1½ hour. *Time.*—1 to 1½ hour. *Average cost*, 1s. 8d. *Seasonable* at any time.

CAKE, a nice useful.

Ingredients.—¼ lb. of butter, 6 oz. of currants, ¼ lb. of sugar, 1 lb. of dried flour, 2 teaspoonfuls of baking-powder, 3 eggs, 1 teacupful of milk, 2 oz. of sweet almonds, 1 oz. of candied peel. *Mode.*— Beat the butter to a cream; wash, pick, and dry the currants; whisk the eggs; blanch and chop the almonds, and cut the peel into neat slices. When all these are ready, mix the dry ingredients together; then add the butter, milk, and eggs, and beat the mixture well for a few minutes. Put the cake into a buttered mould or tin, and bake it for rather more than 1½ hour. The currants and candied peel may be omitted, and a little lemon or almond flavouring substituted for them; made in this manner, the cake will be found very good. *Time.*—Rather more than 1½ hour. *Average cost,* 1*s.* 9*d.*

CAKE, a Pavini.

Ingredients.—½ lb. of flour, ½ lb. of ground rice, ½ lb. of raisins stoned and cut into small pieces, ¼ lb. of currants, ¼ lb. of butter, 2 oz. of sweet almonds, ¼ lb. of sifted loaf sugar, ½ nutmeg grated, 1 pint of milk, 1 teaspoonful of carbonate of soda. *Mode.*—Stone and cut the raisins into small pieces; wash, pick, and dry the currants; melt the butter to a cream, but without oiling it; blanch and chop the almonds, and grate the nutmeg. When all these ingredients are thus prepared, mix them well together; make the milk warm, stir in the soda, and with this liquid make the whole into a paste. Butter a mould, rather more than half fill it with the dough, and bake the cake in a moderate oven from 1½ to 2 hours, or less time should it be made into 2 cakes. *Time.*—1½ to 2 hours. *Average cost,* 1*s.* 8*d.* *Seasonable* at any time.

CAKE, a nice Plain.

Ingredients.—1 lb. of flour, 1 teaspoonful of Borwick's baking-powder, ¼ lb. of good dripping, 1 teacupful of moist sugar, 3 eggs, 1 breakfast-cupful of milk, 1 oz. of caraway seeds, ½ lb. of currants. *Mode.* Put the flour and the baking-powder into a basin; stir these together; then rub in the dripping, add the sugar, caraway seeds, and currants; whisk the eggs with the milk, and beat all together very thoroughly until the ingredients are well mixed. Butter a tin, put in the cake, and bake it from 1½ to 2 hours. Let the dripping be quite clean before using: to insure this, it is a good plan to clarify it. Beef dripping is better than any other for cakes, &c., as mutton dripping frequently has a very unpleasant flavour, which would be imparted to the preparation. *Time.*—1½ to 2 hours. *Average cost,* 1*s.* *Seasonable* at any time.

CAKE, a nice Plain, for Children.

Ingredients.—1 quartern of dough, ¼ lb. of moist sugar, ¼ lb. of butter or good beef dripping, ¼ pint of warm milk, ½ grated nutmeg or ½ oz. of caraway seeds. *Mode.*—If you are not in the habit of making bread at home, procure the dough from the baker's, and as soon as it comes in put it into a basin near the fire; cover the basin with a thick cloth, and let the dough remain a little while to rise. In the mean time, beat the butter to a cream, and make the milk warm; and when the dough has risen, mix with it thoroughly all the above ingredients, and knead the cake well for a few minutes. Butter some cake-tins, half fill them, and stand them in a warm place, to allow the dough to rise again. When the tins are three parts full, put the cakes into a good oven, and bake them from 1¾ to 2 hours. A few currants might be substituted for the caraway seeds when the flavour of the latter is disliked. *Time.*—1¾ to 2 hours. *Average cost,* 1*s.* 2*d.* *Seasonable* at any time.

CAKE, Queen.

Ingredients.—1 lb. of flour, ½ lb. of butter, ½ lb. of pounded loaf sugar, 3 eggs, 1 teacupful of cream, ½ lb. of currants, 1 teaspoonful of carbonate of soda, essence of lemon, or almonds to taste. *Mode.*—Work the butter to a cream; dredge in the flour, add the sugar and currants, and mix the ingredients well together. Whisk the eggs, mix them with the cream and flavouring, and stir these to the flour; add the carbonate of soda, beat the paste well for 10 minutes, put it into small buttered pans, and bake the cake from ¼ to ½ hour. Grated lemon-rind may be substituted for the lemon and almond flavouring, which will make the cakes equally nice. *Time.*—¼ to ½ hour. *Average cost,* 1*s.* 9*d.* *Seasonable* at any time.

CAKE, Saucer, for Tea.

Ingredients.—¼ lb. of flour, ¼ lb. of *tous-les-mois*, ¼ lb. of pounded white sugar, ¼ lb. of butter, 2 eggs, 1 oz. of candied orange or lemon-peel. *Mode.*—Mix the flour and *tous-les-mois* together; add the sugar, the candied peel cut into thin slices, the butter beaten to a cream, and the eggs well whisked. Beat the mixture for 10 minutes, put it into a buttered cake-tin or mould, or, if this is not obtainable, a soup-plate answers the purpose, lined with a piece of buttered paper. Bake the cake in a moderate oven from 1 to 1¼ hour, and when cold, put it away in a covered canister. It will remain good some weeks, even if it be

Cakes, Scrap

cut into slices.   *Time.*—1 to 1¼ hour
Average cost, 1s.   *Seasonable* at any time.

CAKES, Scrap.

Ingredients.—2 lbs. of leaf, or the inside
fat of a pig; 1½ lb. of flour, ¼ lb. of
moist sugar, ¼ lb. of currants, 1 oz. of
candied lemon-peel, ground allspice to
taste. *Mode.*—Cut the leaf, or head, as
it is sometimes called, into small pieces;
put it into a large dish, which place in a
quick oven; be careful that it does not
burn, and in a short time it will be reduced to oil, with the small pieces of
leaf floating on the surface; and it is of
these that the cakes should be made.
Gather all the scraps together, put them
into a basin with the flour, and rub them
well together. Add the currants, sugar,
candied peel, cut into thin slices, and
the ground allspice. When all these
ingredients are well mixed, moisten with
sufficient cold water to make the whole
into a nice paste; roll it out thin, cut it
into shapes, and bake the cakes in a
quick oven from 15 to 20 minutes. These
are very economical and wholesome cakes
for children, and the lard, melted at
home, produced from the flead, is generally better than that you purchase. To
prevent the lard from burning, and to
insure its being a good colour, it is better
to melt it in a jar placed in a saucepan
of boiling water; by doing it in this
manner, there will be no chance of its
discolouring. *Time.*—15 to 20 minutes.
Sufficient to make 3 or 4 dozen cakes.
Seasonable from September to March.

CALF.

The manner of cutting up a calf for
the English market is to divide the
carcase into four quarters, with eleven
ribs to each fore quarter; which are
again subdivided into joints, as exem-
plified on the cut.

Hind quarter :—
1. The loin.
2. The chump, consisting of the
rump and hock-bone.
3. The fillet.
4. The hock, or hind knuckle.

Fore quarter :—
5. The shoulder.
6. The neck.
7. The breast.
8. The fore knuckle.

Calf's Feet, Baked or Stewed

The several parts of a moderately-sized
well-fed calf, about eight weeks old, are
nearly of the following weights:—loin

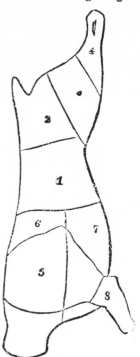

SIDE OF A CALF, SHOWING
THE SEVERAL JOINTS.

and chump 13 lbs., fillet 12½ lbs., hind
knuckle 5½ lbs., shoulder 11 lbs., neck
11 lbs., breast 9 lbs., and fore knuckle
5 lbs.; making a total of 144 lbs. weight.
The London mode of cutting the carcase is considered better than that pursued in Edinburgh, as giving three
roasting joints and one boiling in each
quarter; besides the pieces being more
equally divided, as regards flesh, and
from the handsomer appearance they
make on the table.

CALF'S FEET, Baked or Stewed.

Ingredients.—1 calf's foot, 1 pint of milk,
1 pint of water, 1 blade of mace, the rind of
¼ lemon, pepper and salt to taste. *Mode.*
Well clean the foot, and either stew
or bake it in the milk-and-water with
the other ingredients from 3 to 4 hours.
To enhance the flavour, an onion and a
small quantity of celery may be added, if

Calf's Feet, Boiled

approved ; ½ a teacupful of cream, stirred in just before serving, is also a great improvement to this dish. *Time.*—3 to 4 hours. *Average cost,* in full season, 9d. each. *Sufficient* for 1 person. *Seasonable* from March to October.

CALF'S FEET, Boiled, and Parsley and Butter.

Ingredients.—2 calf's feet, 2 slices of bacon, 2 oz. of butter, two tablespoonfuls of lemon-juice, salt and whole pepper to taste, 1 onion, a bunch of savoury herbs, 4 cloves, 1 blade of mace, water, parsley, and butter. *Mode.*— Procure 2 white calf's feet ; bone them as far as the first joint, and put them into warm water to soak for 2 hours. Then put the bacon, butter, lemon-juice, onion, herbs, spices, and seasoning into a stewpan ; lay in the feet, and pour in just sufficient water to cover the whole. Stew gently for about three hours ; take out the feet, dish them, and cover with parsley and butter. The liquor they were boiled in should be strained and put by in a clean basin for use : it will be found very good as an addition to gravies, &c. *Time.*—Rather more than 3 hours. *Average cost,* in full season, 9d. each. *Sufficient* for 4 persons. *Seasonable* from March to October.

CALF'S-FOOT BROTH.

Ingredients.—1 calf's foot, 3 pints of water, 1 small lump of sugar, nutmeg to taste, the yolk of 1 egg, a piece of butter the size of a nut. *Mode.*—Stew the foot in the water with the lemon-peel *very gently,* until the liquid is half wasted, removing any scum, should it rise to the surface. Set it by in a basin until quite cold, then take off every particle of fat. Warm up about ½ pint of the broth, adding the butter, sugar, and a very small quantity of grated nutmeg ; take it off the fire for a minute or two, then add the beaten yolk of the egg ; keep stirring over the fire until the mixture thickens, but do not allow it to boil again after the egg is added, or it will curdle, and the broth will be spoiled. *Time.*—To be boiled until the liquid is reduced one half. *Average cost,* in full season, 9d. each. *Sufficient* to make 1½ pint of broth. *Seasonable* from March to October.

Calf's-Feet Jelly

CALF'S FEET, Fricasseed.

Ingredients.—A set of calf's feet ; for the batter, allow for each egg 1 tablespoonful of flour, 1 tablespoonful of bread-crumbs, hot lard, or clarified dripping, pepper and salt to taste. *Mode.*—If the feet are purchased uncleaned, dip them into warm water repeatedly, and scrape off the hair, first one foot and then the other, until the skin looks perfectly clean, a saucepan of water being kept by the fire until they are finished. After washing and soaking in cold water, boil them in just sufficient water to cover them, until the bones come easily away. Then pick them out, and after straining the liquor into a clean vessel, put the meat into a pie-dish until the next day. Now cut it down in slices about ½ inch thick, lay on them a stiff batter made of egg, flour, and bread-crumbs in the above proportion ; season with pepper and salt, and plunge them into a pan of boiling lard. Fry the slices a nice brown, dry them before the fire for a minute or two, dish them on a napkin, and garnish with tufts of parsley. This should be eaten with melted butter, mustard, and vinegar. Be careful to have the lard boiling to *set* the batter, or the pieces of feet will run about the pan. The liquor they were boiled in should be saved, and will be found useful for enriching gravies, making jellies, &c. *Time.*—About 3 hours to stew the feet, 10 or 15 minutes to fry them. *Average cost,* in full season, 9d. each. *Sufficient* for 8 persons. *Seasonable* from March to October.

Note.—This dish can be highly recommended to delicate persons.

CALF'S-FEET JELLY.

Ingredients.—1 quart of calf's-feet stock, ½ lb. sugar, ½ pint of sherry, 1 glass of brandy, the shells and whites of 5 eggs, the rind and juice of 2 lemons, ½ oz. of isinglass. *Mode.*—Prepare the stock as directed in recipe for stock, taking care to leave out the sediment, and to remove all the fat from the surface. Put it into a saucepan cold, without clarifying it ; add the remaining ingredients, and stir them well together before the saucepan is placed on the fire. Then simmer the mixture gently for ½ hour, *but do not stir it after it begins to warm.* Throw in a teacupful of cold water, boil for another 5 minutes, and keep the saucepan covered by the side of the fire for about ½ hour,

Calf's-Feet Jelly

but do not let it boil again. In simmering, the head or scum may be carefully removed as it rises; but particular attention must be given to the jelly, that it be not stirred in the slightest degree after it is heated. The isinglass should be added when the jelly begins to boil : this assists to clear it, and makes it firmer for turning out. Wring out a jelly-bag in hot water; fasten it on to a stand, or the back of a chair ; place it near the fire with a basin underneath it, and run the jelly through it. Should it not be perfectly clear the first time, repeat the process until the desired brilliancy is obtained. Soak the moulds

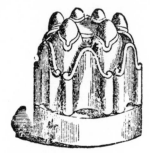

JELLY-MOULD.

in water, drain them for half a second, pour in the jelly, and put it in a cool place to set. If ice is at hand, surround the moulds with it, and the jelly will set sooner, and be firmer when turned out. In summer it is necessary to have ice in which to put the moulds, or the cook will be, very likely, disappointed, by her jellies being in too liquid a state to turn out properly, unless a great deal of isinglass is used. When wanted for table, dip the moulds in hot water for a minute, wipe the outside with a cloth, lay a dish on the top of the mould, turn it quickly over, and the jelly should slip out easily. It is sometimes served broken into square lumps, and piled high in glasses. Earthenware moulds are preferable to those of pewter or tin for red jellies, the colour and transparency of the composition being often spoiled by using the latter. To make this jelly more economically, raisin wine may be substituted for the sherry and brandy, and the stock made from cow-heels, instead of calf's feet. *Time.*—20 minutes to simmer the jelly, hour to stand covered. *Average cost,*

Calf's Head, Boiled

reckoning the feet at 6*d.* each, 5*s.* 6*d.* *Sufficient* to fill two 1½-pint moulds. *Seasonable* at any time.

Note.—As lemon-juice, unless carefully strained, is liable to make the jelly muddy, see that it is clear before it is added to the other ingredients. Omit the brandy when the flavour is objected to.

CALF'S HEAD à la Maître d'Hotel.

[COLD MEAT COOKERY.] *Ingredients.* —The remains of a cold calf's head, rather more than ½ pint of maître d'hôtel sauce. *Mode.*—Make the sauce by the given recipe, and have it sufficiently thick that it may nicely cover the meat; remove the bones from the head, and cut the meat into neat slices. When the sauce is ready, lay in the meat; *gradually* warm it through, and, after it boils up, let it simmer very gently for 5 minutes, and serve. *Time.* —Rather more than 1½ hour. *Average cost,* exclusive of the meat, 1*s.* 2*d.* *Seasonable* from March to October.

CALF'S HEAD, Boiled (with the Skin on).

Ingredients. — Calf's head, boiling water, bread crumbs, 1 large bunch of parsley, butter, white pepper and salt to taste, 4 tablespoonfuls of melted butter, 1 tablespoonful of lemon juice, 2 or 3 grains of cayenne. *Mode.*—Put the head into boiling water, and let it remain by the side of the fire for 3 or 4 minutes ; take it out, hold it by the ear, and with the back of a knife, scrape off the hair (should it not come off easily, dip the head again into boiling water). When perfectly clean, take the eyes out, cut off the ears, and remove the brain, which soak for an hour in warm water. Put the head into hot water to soak for a few minutes, to make it look white, and then have ready a stewpan, into which lay the head ; cover it with cold water, and bring it gradually to boil. Remove the scum, and add a little salt, which assists to throw it up. Simmer it very gently from 2½ to 3 hours, and when nearly done, boil the brains for ¼ hour; skin and chop them, not too finely, and add a tablespoonful of minced parsley which has been previously scalded. Season with pepper and salt, and stir the brains, parsley, &c., into about 4 tablespoonfuls of melted butter; add the lemon-juice and cayenne, and

Calf's Head, Boiled

keep these hot by the side of the fire. Take up the head, cut out the tongue, skin it, put it on a small dish with the brains round it; sprinkle over the head a few bread crumbs mixed with a little minced parsley; brown these before the fire, and serve with a tureen of parsley and butter, and either boiled bacon, ham, or pickled pork as an accompaniment. *Time.*—2½ to 3 hours. *Average cost,* according to the season, from 3s. to 7s. 6d. *Sufficient* for 8 or 9 persons. *Seasonable* from March to October.

CALF'S HEAD, Boiled (without the Skin).

Ingredients.—Calf's head, water, a little salt, 4 tablespoonfuls of melted butter, 1 tablespoonful of minced parsley, pepper and salt to taste, 1 tablespoonful of lemon-juice. *Mode.*—After the head has been thoroughly cleaned, and the brains removed, soak it in warm water to blanch it. Lay the brains also into warm water to soak, and let them remain

CALF'S HEAD.

for about an hour. Put the head into a stewpan, with sufficient cold water to cover it, and, when it boils, add a little salt; take off every particle of scum as it rises, and boil the head until perfectly tender. Boil the brains, chop them, and mix with them melted butter, minced parsley, pepper, salt, and lemon-juice in the above proportion. Take up the head,

HALF A CALF'S HEAD.

skin the tongue, and put it on a small dish with the brains round it. Have ready some parsley and butter, smother the head with it, and the remainder send to table in a tureen. Bacon, ham, pickled pork, or a pig's cheek, are indispensable with calf's head. The brains are sometimes chopped with hard-boiled eggs, and

Calf's Head, Fricasseed

mixed with a little Bechamel or white sauce. *Time.*—From 1½ to 2¼ hours. *Average cost,* according to the season, from 3s. to 5s. *Sufficient* for 6 or 7 persons. *Seasonable* from March to October.

Note.—The liquor in which the head was boiled should be saved: it makes excellent soup, and will be found a nice addition to gravies, &c. Half a calf's head is as frequently served as a whole one, it being a more convenient-sized joint for a small family. It is cooked in the same manner, and served with the same sauces, as in the preceding recipe.

CALF'S HEAD, Collared.

Ingredients.—A calf's head, 4 tablespoonfuls of minced parsley, 4 blades of pounded mace, ½ teaspoonful of grated nutmeg, white pepper to taste, a few thick slices of ham, the yolks of 6 eggs boiled hard. *Mode.*—Scald the head for a few minutes; take it out of the water, and with a blunt knife scrape off all the hair. Clean it nicely, divide the head and remove the brains. Boil it tender enough to take out the bones, which will be in about 2 hours. When the head is boned, flatten it on the table, sprinkle over it a thick layer of parsley, then a layer of ham, and then the yolks of the eggs cut into thin rings and put a seasoning of pounded mace, nutmeg, and white pepper between each layer; roll the head up in a cloth, and tie it up as tightly as possible. Boil it for 4 hours, and when it is taken out of the pot, place a heavy weight on the top, the same as for other collared meats. Let it remain till cold; then remove the cloth and binding, and it will be ready to serve. *Time.*—Altogether, 6 hours. *Average cost,* 5s. to 7s. each. *Seasonable* from March to October.

CALF'S HEAD, Fricasseed (an Entrée).

['OLD MEAT COOKERY.] *Ingredients.*— The remains of a boiled calf's head, 1½ pint of the liquor in which the head was boiled, 1 blade of pounded mace, 1 onion minced, a bunch of savoury herbs, salt and white pepper to taste, thickening of butter and flour, the yolks of 2 eggs, 1 tablespoonful of lemon-juice, forcemeat balls. *Mode.*—Remove all the bones from the head, and cut the meat into nice square pieces. Put 1½ pint of the liquor it was boiled in into a saucepan, with mace, onions, herbs, and seasoning

Calf's Head, Hashed	Calf's Liver

m the above proportion : let this simmer gently for ¾ hour, then strain it and put in the meat. When quite hot through, thicken the gravy with a little butter rolled in flour, and, just before dishing the fricassee, put in the beaten yolks of eggs, and lemon-juice; but be particular, after these two latter ingredients are added, that the sauce does not boil, or it will curdle. Garnish with forcemeat balls and curled slices of broiled bacon. To insure the sauce being smooth, it is a good plan to dish the meat first, and then to add the eggs to the gravy : when these are set, the sauce may be poured over the meat. *Time.*—Altogether, 1¼ hour. *Average cost*, exclusive of the meat, 6d.

CALF'S HEAD, Hashed.

[COLD MEAT COOKERY.] *Ingredients.*— The remains of a cold boiled calf's head, 1 quart of the liquor in which it was boiled, a faggot of savoury herbs, 1 onion, 1 carrot, a strip of lemon-peel, 2 blades of pounded mace, salt and white pepper to taste, a very little cayenne, rather more than 2 tablespoonfuls of sherry, 1 tablespoonful of lemon-juice, 1 table-spoonful of mushroom ketchup, forcemeat balls. *Mode.*—Cut the meat into neat slices, and put the bones and trimmings into a stewpan with the above proportion of liquor that the head was boiled in. Add a bunch of savoury herbs, 1 onion, 1 carrot, a strip of lemon-peel, and 2 blades of pounded mace, and let these boil for 1 hour, or until the gravy is reduced nearly half. Strain it into a clean stewpan, thicken it with a little butter and flour, and add a flavouring of sherry, lemon-juice, and ketchup, in the above proportion ; season with pepper, salt, and a little cayenne ; put in the meat, let it *gradually* warm through, but not boil more than *two* or *three* minutes. Garnish the dish with forcemeat balls and pieces of bacon rolled and toasted, placed alternately, and send it to table very hot. *Time.*—Altogether 1½ hour. *Average cost*, exclusive of the remains of the head, 6d. *Seasonable* from March to October.

CALF'S HEAD, Moulded.

[COLD MEAT COOKERY.] *Ingredients.*— The remains of a calf's head, some thin slices of ham or bacon, 6 or 8 eggs boiled hard, 1 dessertspoonful of salt, pepper,

mixed spice, and parsley, ½ pint of g white gravy. *Mode.*—Cut the head i thin slices. Butter a tin mould, cut yolks of eggs in half, and put som them round the tin ; sprinkle some the parsley, spice, &c., over it ; then in the head and the bacon in lay adding occasionally more eggs and s till the whole of the head is used. P in the gravy, cover the top with a t paste of flour and water, and bake an hour. Take off the paste, and, w cold, turn it out. *Time.*—From ¾ 1 hour to bake the preparation. *Sea able* from March to October.

CALF'S HEAD, to Carve.

This is not altogether the most ea looking dish to cut when it is put bef a carver for the first time ; there is much real difficulty in the operation, h ever, when the head has been attentiv examined, and, after the manner c phrenologist, you get to know its bum good and bad. In the first place, serting the knife quite down to the bone, cut slices in the di-rection of the line 1 to 2 ; with each of these should be helped

CALF'S HEAD.

a piece of what is called the thr sweetbread, cut in the direction of fr 3 to 4. The eye, and the flesh rou are favourite morsels with many, should be given to those at the table w are known to be the greatest connoisseu The jawbone being removed, there then be found some nice lean ; and palate, which is reckoned by some a bit, lies under the head. On a separ dish there is always served the ton and brains, and each guest should asked to take some of these.

CALF'S LIVER aux Fines Herl and Sauce Piquante.

Ingredients.—A calf's liver, flour, bunch of savoury herbs, including p sley ; when liked, 2 minced shalots teaspoonful of flour, 1 tablespoonful vinegar, 1 tablespoonful of lemon-jui pepper and salt to taste, ¼ pint wat *Mode.*—Procure a calf a liver as white possible, and cut it into slices of a g and equal shape. Dip them in flour, a fry them of a good colour in a lit

Calf's Liver and Bacon

butter. When they are done, put them on a dish, which keep hot before the fire. Mince the herbs very fine, put them in the frying-pan with a little more butter ; add the remaining ingredients, simmer gently until the herbs are done, and pour over the liver. *Time.*—According to the thickness of the slices, from 5 to 10 minutes. *Average cost*, 10d. per lb. *Sufficient* for 7 or 8 persons. *Seasonable* from March to October.

CALF'S LIVER and BACON

Ingredients.—2 or 3 lbs. of liver, bacon, pepper and salt to taste, a small piece of butter, flour, 2 tablespoonfuls of lemon-juice, ¼ pint of water. *Mode.*—Cut the liver in thin slices, and cut as many slices of bacon as there are of liver ; fry the bacon first, and put that on a hot dish before the fire. Fry the liver in the fat which comes from the bacon, after seasoning it with pepper and salt and dredging over it a very little flour. Turn the liver occasionally to prevent its burning, and when done, lay it round the dish with a piece of bacon between each. Pour away the bacon fat, put in a small piece of butter, dredge in a little flour, add the lemon-juice and water, give one boil, and pour it in the *middle* of the dish. It may be garnished with slices of cut lemon, or forcemeat balls. *Time.*—According to the thickness of the slices, from 5 to 10 minutes. *Average cost*, 10d. per lb. *Sufficient* for 6 or 7 persons. *Seasonable* from March to October.

CALF'S LIVER, Larded and Roasted (an Entrée).

Ingredients.—A calf's liver, vinegar, 1 onion, 3 or 4 sprigs of parsley and thyme, salt and pepper to taste, 1 bay-leaf, lardoons, brown gravy. *Mode.*—Take a fine white liver, and lard it the same as a fricandeau ; put it into vinegar with an onion cut in slices, parsley, thyme, bay-leaf, and seasoning in the above proportion. Let it remain in this pickle for 24 hours, then roast and baste it frequently with the vinegar, &c. ; glaze it, serve under it a good brown gravy, or sauce piquante, and send it to table very hot. *Time.*—Rather more than 1 hour. *Average cost*, 10d. per lb. *Sufficient* for 7 or 8 persons. *Seasonable* from March to October.

Note.—Calf's liver stuffed with forcemeat (*see* FORCEMEAT), to which has

Cannelons, or Fried Puffs

been added a little fat bacon, will be found a very savoury dish. It should be larded or wrapped in buttered paper, and roasted before a clear fire. Brown gravy and currant jelly should be served with it.

CAMP VINEGAR.

Ingredients.—1 head of garlic, ½ oz. cayenne, 2 teaspoonfuls of soy, 2 ditto walnut ketchup, 1 pint of vinegar, cochineal to colour. *Mode.*—Slice the garlic, and put it, with all the above ingredients, into a clean bottle. Let it stand to infuse for a month, when strain it off quite clear, and it will be fit for use. Keep it in small bottles well sealed, to exclude the air. *Average cost* for this quantity, 8d.

CANARY PUDDING (very good).

Ingredients.—The weight of 3 eggs in sugar and butter, the weight of 2 eggs in flour, the rind of 1 small lemon, 3 eggs. *Mode.*—Melt the butter to a liquid state, but do not allow it to oil ; stir to this the sugar and finely-minced lemon-peel, and gradually dredge in the flour, keeping the mixture well stirred ; whisk the eggs ; add these to the pudding ; beat all the ingredients until thoroughly blended, and put them into a buttered mould or basin ; boil for 2 hours, and serve with sweet sauce. *Time.*—2 hours. *Average cost*, 9d. *Sufficient* for 4 or 5 persons. *Seasonable* at any time.

CANNELONS, or Fried Puffs (Sweet Entremets).

Ingredients.—½ lb. of puff-paste ; apricot, or any kind of preserve that may be preferred ; hot lard. *Mode.*—Cannelons, which are made of puff-paste rolled very thin, with jam inclosed, and cut out in long narrow rolls or puffs, make a very pretty and elegant dish. Make some good puff-paste by the recipe given ; roll it out very thin, and cut it into pieces of an equal size, about 2 inches wide and 8 inches long ; place upon each piece a spoonful of jam, wet the edges with the white of egg, and fold the paste over *twice* ; slightly press the edges together, that the jam may not escape in the frying ; and when all are prepared, **fry** them in boiling lard until of a nice brown, letting them remain by the side of the fire after they are coloured, that the paste may be thoroughly done. Drain

Caper Sauce, for Fish

them before the fire, dish on a d'oyley, sprinkle over them sifted sugar, and serve. These cannelons are very delicious made with fresh instead of preserved fruit, such as strawberries, raspberries, or currants: it should be laid in the paste, plenty of pounded sugar sprinkled over, and folded and fried in the same manner as stated above. *Time.*—About 10 minutes. *Average cost*, 1s. *Sufficient.* —½ lb. of paste for a moderate-sized dish of cannelons. *Seasonable,* with jam, at any time.

CAPER SAUCE, for Fish.

Ingredients.—½ pint of melted butter, 3 dessertspoonfuls of capers, 1 dessert-spoonful of their liquor, a small piece of glaze, if at hand (this may be dispensed with), ¼ teaspoonful of salt, ditto of pepper, 1 tablespoonful of anchovy essence. *Mode.*—Cut the capers across once or twice, but do not chop them fine ; put them in a saucepan with ½ pint of good melted butter, and add all the other ingredients. Keep stirring the whole until it just simmers, when it is ready to serve. *Time.*—1 minute to simmer. *Average cost* for this quantity, 5d. *Sufficient* to serve with a skate, or 2 or 3 slices of salmon.

CAPER SAUCE, for Boiled Mutton.

Ingredients.—½ pint of melted butter, 3 tablespoonfuls of capers or nasturtiums, 1 tablespoonful of their liquor. *Mode.*— Chop the capers twice or thrice, and add them, with their liquor, to ½ pint of melted butter, made very smoothly with milk ; keep stirring well; let the sauce just simmer, and serve in a tureen. Pickled nasturtium-pods are fine-flavoured, and by many are eaten in preference to capers. They make an excellent sauce. *Time.*—2 minutes to simmer. *Average cost* for this quantity, 8d. *Sufficient* to serve with a leg of mutton.

CAPER SAUCE, a Substitute for.

Ingredients. ½ pint of melted butter, 2 tablespoonfuls of cut parsley, ½ teaspoonful of salt, 1 tablespoonful of vinegar. *Mode.*—Boil the parsley slowly to let it become a bad colour ; cut, but do not chop it fine. Add it to ½ pint of smoothly-made melted butter, with salt and vinegar in the above proportions.

Carp, Stewed

Boil up and serve. *Time.*—2 minutes to simmer. *Average cost* for this quantity, 3d.

CAPSICUMS, Pickled.

Ingredients.—Vinegar, ¼ oz. of pounded mace, and ¼ oz. of grated nutmeg, to each quart ; brine. *Mode.*—Gather the pods with the stalks on, before they turn red ; slit them down the side with a small-pointed knife, and remove the seeds only ; put them in a strong brine for 3 days, changing it every morning ; then take them out, lay them on a cloth, with another one over them, until they are perfectly free from moisture. Boil sufficient vinegar to cover them, with mace and nutmeg in the above proportions; put the pods in a jar, pour over the vinegar when cold, and exclude them from the air by means of a wet bladder tied over.

CARP, Baked.

Ingredients.—1 carp, forcemeat, bread crumbs, 1 oz. butter, ½ pint of stock (*see* STOCK), ½ pint of port wine, 6 anchovies, 2 onions sliced, 1 bay-leaf, a faggot of sweet herbs, flour to thicken, the juice of 1 lemon ; cayenne and salt to taste ; ½ teaspoonful of powdered sugar. *Mode.* —Stuff the carp with a delicate forcemeat, after thoroughly cleansing it, and sew it up, to prevent the stuffing from falling out. Rub it over with an egg, and sprinkle it with bread crumbs, lay it a deep earthen dish, and drop the butter, oiled, over the bread crumbs. Add the stock, onions, bay-leaf, herbs, wine, and anchovies, and bake for 1 hour. Put 1 oz. of butter into a stewpan, melt it, and dredge in sufficient flour to dry it up ; put in the strained liquor from the carp, stir frequently, and when it has boiled, add the lemon-juice and seasoning. Serve the carp on a dish garnished with parsley and cut lemon, and the sauce in a boat. *Time.*—1¼ hour. *Average cost.* Seldom bought. *Seasonable* from March to October. *Sufficient* for 1 or 2 persons.

CARP, Stewed.

Ingredients. — 1 carp, salt, stock, 2 onions, 6 cloves, 12 peppercorns, 1 blade of mace, ¼ pint of port wine, the juice of ½ lemon, cayenne and salt to taste, a faggot of savoury herbs. *Mode.*—Scale

Carrot Jam

the fish, clean it nicely, and, if very large, divide it; lay it in the stewpan, after having rubbed a little salt on it, and put in sufficient stock to cover it; add the herbs, onions and spices, and stew gently for 1 hour, or rather more, should it be very large. Dish up the fish with great care, strain the liquor, and add to it the port wine, lemon-juice, and cayenne; give one boil, pour it over the fish, and serve. *Time.* 1¼ hour. *Average cost.* Seldom bought. *Seasonable* from March to October. *Sufficient* for 1 or 2 persons.

Note.—This fish can be boiled plain, and served with parsley and butter. Chub and Char may be cooked in the same manner as the above, as also Dace and Roach.

CARROT JAM, to Imitate Apricot Preserve.

Ingredients.—Carrots; to every lb. of carrot pulp allow 1 lb. of pounded sugar, the grated rind of 1 lemon, the strained juice of 2, 6 chopped bitter almonds, 2 tablespoonfuls of brandy. *Mode.*—Select young carrots; wash and scrape them clean, cut them into round pieces, put them into a saucepan with sufficient water to cover them, and let them simmer, until perfectly soft; then beat them through a sieve. Weigh the pulp, and to every lb. allow the above ingredients. Put the pulp into a preserving-pan with the sugar, and let this boil for 5 minutes, stirring and skimming all the time. When cold, add the lemon-rind and juice, almonds and brandy; mix these well with the jam; then put it into pots, which must be well covered and kept in a dry place. The brandy may be omitted, but the preserve will then not keep: with the brandy it will remain good for months. *Time.*—About ¾ hour to boil the carrots; 5 minutes to simmer the pulp. *Average cost,* 1s. 2d. for 1 lb. of pulp, with the other ingredients in proportion. *Sufficient* to fill 3 pots. *Seasonable* from July to December.

CARROT PUDDING, Baked or Boiled.

Ingredients.—½ lb. of bread crumbs, 4 oz. suet, ¼ lb. of stoned raisins, ¾ lb. of carrot, ¼ lb. of currants, 3 oz. of sugar, 3 eggs, milk, ¼ nutmeg. *Mode.*—Boil the carrots, until tender enough to mash to a pulp; add the remaining ingre-

Carrots, Boiled

dients, and moisten with sufficient milk to make the pudding of the consistency of thick batter. If to be boiled, put the mixture into a buttered basin, tie it down with a cloth, and boil for 2½ hours: if to be baked, put it into a pie-dish, and bake for nearly an hour; turn it out of the dish, strew sifted sugar over it, and serve. *Time.*—2½ hours to boil; 1 hour to bake. *Average cost,* 1s. 2d. *Sufficient* for 5 or 6 persons. *Seasonable* from September to March.

CARROT SOUP.

Ingredients.—4 quarts of liquor in which a leg of mutton or beef has been boiled, a few beef-bones, 6 large carrots, 2 large onions, 1 turnip; seasoning of salt and pepper to taste; cayenne. *Mode.*—Put the liquor, bones, onions, turnip, pepper, and salt, into a stewpan, and simmer for 3 hours. Scrape and cut the carrots thin, strain the soup on them, and stew them till soft enough to pulp through a hair sieve or coarse cloth; then boil the pulp with the soup, which should be of the consistency of pea-soup. Add cayenne. Pulp only the red part of the carrot, and make this soup the day before it is wanted. *Time.*—4½ hours. *Average cost,* per quart, 1½d. *Seasonable* from October to March. *Sufficient* for 8 persons.

CARROT SOUP.

Ingredients.—2 lbs. of carrots, 3 oz. of butter, seasoning to taste of salt and cayenne, 2 quarts of stock or gravy soup. *Mode.*—Scrape and cut out all specks from the carrots, wash, and wipe them dry, and then reduce them into quarter-inch slices. Put the butter into a large stewpan, and when it is melted, add 2 lbs. of the sliced carrots, and let them stew gently for an hour without browning. Add to them the soup, and allow them to simmer till tender,—say for nearly an hour. Press them through a strainer with the soup, and add salt and cayenne if required. Boil the whole gently for 5 minutes, skim well, and serve as hot as possible. *Time* 1¼ hour. *Average cost,* per quart, 1s. 1d.

CARROTS, Boiled.

Ingredients.—To each ½ gallon of water, allow one heaped tablespoonful of salt; carrots. *Mode.*—Cut off the green tops

5

Carrots, to Dress

Wash and scrape the carrots, and should there be any black specks, remove them. If very large, cut them in halves, divide them lengthwise into four pieces, and put them into boiling water, salted in the above proportion; let them boil until tender, which may be ascertained by thrusting a fork into them: dish, and serve very hot. This vegetable is an indispensable accompaniment to boiled beef. When thus served, it is usually boiled with the beef; a few carrots are placed round the dish as a garnish, and the remainder sent to table in a vegetable-dish. Young carrots do not require nearly so much boiling, nor should they be divided: these make a nice addition to stewed veal, &c. *Time.*—Large carrots, 1¾ to 2¼ hours; young ones, about ½ hour. *Average cost*, 6*d.* to 8*d.* per bunch of 18. *Sufficient.*—4 large carrots for 5 or 6 persons. *Seasonable.* — Young carrots from April to July, old ones at any time.

CARROTS, to dress, in the German way.

Ingredients.—8 large carrots, 3 oz. of butter, salt to taste, a very little grated nutmeg, 1 tablespoonful of finely-minced parsley, 1 dessertspoonful of minced onion, rather more than 1 pint of weak stock or broth, 1 tablespoonful of flour. *Mode.*—Wash and scrape the carrots, and cut them into rings of about ¼ inch in thickness. Put the butter into a stewpan; when it is melted, lay in the carrots, with salt, nutmeg, parsley, and onion in the above proportions. Toss the stewpan over the fire for a few minutes, and when the carrots are well saturated with the butter, pour in the stock, and simmer gently until they are nearly tender. Then put into another stewpan a small piece of butter; dredge in about a tablespoonful of flour; stir this over the fire, and when of a nice brown colour, add the liquor that the carrots have been boiling in; let this just boil up, pour it over the carrots in the other stewpan, and let them finish simmering until quite tender. Serve very hot. This vegetable, dressed as above, is a favourite accompaniment to roast pork, sausages, &c., &c. *Time.*—About ¾ hour. *Average cost*, 6*d.* to 8*d.* per bunch of 18. *Sufficient* for 6 or 7 persons. *Seasonable.* — Young carrots from April to July, old ones at any time.

Cauliflowers à la Sauce Blanche

CARROTS, Sliced (Entremets, or to be served with the Second Course, as a Side-Dish).

Ingredients.—5 or 6 large carrots, a large lump of sugar, 1 pint of weak stock, 3 oz. of fresh butter, salt to taste. *Mode.*—Scrape and wash the carrots, cut them into slices of an equal size, and boil them in salt and water until half done; drain them well, put them into a stewpan with the sugar and stock, and let them boil over a brisk fire. When reduced to a glaze, add the fresh butter and a seasoning of salt; shake the stewpan about well, and when the butter is well mixed with the carrots, serve. There should be no sauce in the dish when it comes to table, but it should all adhere to the carrots. *Time.* — Altogether, ¾ hour. *Average cost*, 6*d.* to 8*d.* per bunch of 18. *Sufficient* for 1 dish. *Seasonable.*—Young carrots from April to July, old ones at any time.

CARROTS, Stewed.

Ingredients.—7 or 8 large carrots, 1 teacupful of broth, pepper and salt to taste, ½ teacupful of cream, thickening of butter and flour. *Mode.*—Scrape the carrots nicely; half-boil, and slice them into a stewpan; add the broth, pepper and salt, and cream; simmer till tender, and be careful the carrots are not broken. A few minutes before serving, mix a little flour with about 1 oz. of butter; thicken the gravy with this; let it just boil up, and serve. *Time.*—About ¾ hour to boil the carrots, about 20 minutes to cook them after they are sliced. *Average cost*, 6*d.* to 8*d.* per bunch of 18. *Sufficient* for 5 or 6 persons. *Seasonable.* —Young carrots from April to July, old ones at any time.

CAULIFLOWERS à la SAUCE BLANCHE (Entremets, or Side-dish, to be served with the Second Course).

Ingredients.—3 cauliflowers, ½ pint of sauce blanche, or French melted butter, 3 oz. of butter, salt and water. *Mode.*—Cleanse the cauliflowers as in the succeeding recipe, and cut the stalks off flat at the bottom; boil them until tender in salt and water, to which the above proportion of butter has been added, and be careful to take them up the moment they are done, or they will break, and

Cauliflowers, Boiled

the appearance of the dish will be spoiled. Drain them well, and dish them in the shape of a large cauliflower. Have ready ⅔ pint of sauce made by recipe, pour it over the flowers, and serve hot and quickly. *Time.*—Small cauliflowers, 12 to 15 minutes ; large ones, 20 to 25 minutes, after the water boils. *Average cost,* large cauliflowers, in full season, 6*d.* each. *Sufficient,* 1 large cauliflower for 3 or 4 persons. *Seasonable* from the beginning of June to the end of September.

CAULIFLOWERS, Boiled.

Ingredients.—To each ½ gallon of water allow 1 heaped tablespoonful of salt. *Mode.*—Choose cauliflowers that are close and white ; trim off the decayed outside leaves, and cut the stalk off flat at the bottom. Open the flower a little in places to remove the insects, which are generally found about the stalk, and let the cauliflowers lie in salt and water for an hour previous to dressing them, with their heads downwards :

BOILED CAULIFLOWER.

this will effectually draw out all the vermin. Then put them into fast-boiling water, with the addition of salt in the above proportion, and let them boil briskly over a good fire, keeping the saucepan uncovered, and the water well skimmed. When the cauliflowers are tender, take them up with a slice ; let them drain. and, if large enough, place them upright in the dish. Serve with plain melted butter, a little of which may be poured over the flower. *Time.* —Small cauliflower 12 to 15 minutes, large one 20 to 25 minutes, after the water boils. *Average cost,* for large cauliflowers, 6*d.* each. *Sufficient.* — Allow 1 large cauliflower for 3 persons. *Seasonable* from the beginning of June to the end of September.

CAULIFLOWERS, with Parmesan Cheese (Entremets, or Side-dish, to be served with the Second Course).

Ingredients.—2 or 3 cauliflowers, rather more than ½ pint of white sauce, 2 tablespoonfuls of grated Parmesan cheese, 2 oz. of fresh butter, 3 tablespoonfuls of bread

Celery

crumbs. *Mode.*—Cleanse and boil the cauliflowers by the preceding recipe, drain them, and dish them with the flowers standing upright. Have ready the above proportion of white sauce ; pour sufficient of it over the cauliflowers just to cover the top ; sprinkle over this some rasped Parmesan cheese and bread crumbs, and drop on these the butter, which should be melted, but not oiled. Brown with a salamander, or before the fire, and pour round, but not over, the flowers the remainder of the sauce, with which should be mixed a small quantity of grated Parmesan cheese. *Time.*—Altogether, ½ hour. *Average cost,* for large cauliflowers, 6*d.* each. *Sufficient.*—3 small cauliflowers for 1 dish. *Seasonable* from the beginning of June to the end of September.

CAYENNE CHEESES.

Ingredients.—½ lb. of butter, ½ lb. of flour, ½ lb. of grated cheese, ¼ teaspoonful of cayenne, ¼ teaspoonful of salt ; water. *Mode.*—Rub the butter in the flour ; add the grated cheese, cayenne, and salt, and mix these ingredients well together. Moisten with sufficient water to make the whole into a paste ; roll out, and cut into fingers about 4 inches in length. Bake them in a moderate oven a very light colour, and serve very hot. *Time.*—15 to 20 minutes. *Average cost,* 1*s.* 4*d. Sufficient* for 6 or 7 persons. *Seasonable* at any time.

CAYENNE VINEGAR, or Essence of Cayenne.

Ingredients.—½ oz. of cayenne pepper, ½ pint of strong spirit, or 1 pint of vinegar. *Mode.*—Put the vinegar, or spirit, into a bottle, with the above proportion of cayenne, and let it steep for a month, when strain off and bottle for use. This is excellent seasoning for soups or sauces, but must be used very sparingly.

CELERY.

With a good heart, and nicely blanched, this vegetable is generally eaten raw, and is usually served with the cheese. Let the roots be washed free from dirt, all the decayed and outside leaves being cut off, preserving as much of the stalk as possible, and all specks or blemishes being carefully removed. Should the celery be large, divide it lengthwise

Celery Sauce

into quarters, and place it, root downwards, in a celery-glass, which should be rather more than half filled with water. The top leaves may be curled, by shredding them in narrow strips with the point of a clean skewer, at a distance of about 4 inches from the top. *Average cost, 2d.* per head. *Sufficient.* — Allow 2 heads for 4 or 5 persons. *Seasonable* from October to April.

CELERY, IN GLASS.

Note.—This vegetable is exceedingly useful for flavouring soups, sauces, &c., and makes a very nice addition to winter salad.

CELERY SAUCE, for Boiled Turkey, Poultry, &c.

Ingredients. — 9 heads of celery, 1 pint of white stock, 2 blades of mace, 1 small bunch of savoury herbs; thickening of butter and flour, or arrowroot, ½ pint of cream, lemon-juice. *Mode.* — Boil the celery in salt and water until tender, and cut it into pieces 2 inches long. Put the stock into a stewpan with the mace and herbs, and let it simmer for ½ hour to extract their flavour. Then strain the liquor, add the celery, and a thickening of butter kneaded with flour, or, what is still better, with arrowroot; just before serving, put in the cream, boil it up, and squeeze in a little lemon-juice. If necessary, add a seasoning of salt and white pepper. *Time.*—25 minutes to boil the celery. *Average cost, 1s. 3d. Sufficient,* this quantity for a boiled turkey.

Note.—This sauce may be made brown by using gravy instead of white stock, and flavouring it with mushroom ketchup or Harvey's sauce.

CELERY SAUCE (a more simple Recipe).

Ingredients —4 heads of celery, ½ pint of melted butter made with milk, 1 blade of pounded mace; salt and white pepper to taste. *Mode.*—Wash the celery, boil it in salt and water till tender, and cut

Celery, Stewed

it into pieces 2 inches long; make ½ melted butter by recipe; put in celery, pounded mace, and season, simmer for 3 minutes, when the s will be ready to serve. *Time.*—25 nutes to boil the celery. *Average* 6d. *Sufficient,* this quantity for a bo fowl.

CELERY SOUP.

Ingredients.—9 heads of celery, 1 spoonful of salt, nutmeg to taste, 1 l of sugar, ½ pint of strong stock, a pi cream, and 2 quarts of boiling wa *Mode.*—Cut the celery into small pie throw it into the water, seasoned with nutmeg, salt, and sugar. Boil it till ficiently tender; pass it through a si add the stock, and simmer it for ha hour. Now put in the cream, bring the boiling-point, and serve immediat *Time.*—1 hour. *Average cost, 1s.* quart. *Seasonable* from Septembe March. *Sufficient* for 8 persons.

Note.—This soup can be made br instead of white, by omitting the cre and colouring it a little. When ce cannot be procured, half a drachm of seed, finely pounded, will give a fla to the soup, if put in a quarter of an l before it is done. A little of the ess of celery will answer the same purpo

CELERY, Stewed, à la Crême.

Ingredients.—6 heads of celery; to ½ gallon of water allow 1 heaped ta spoonful of salt, 1 blade of pounded m ½ pint of cream. *Mode.* — Wash celery thoroughly; trim, and boil salt and water until tender. Put cream and pounded mace into a stew shake it over the fire until the cr thickens, dish the celery, pour over sauce, and serve. *Time.*—Large h of celery, 25 minutes; small ones, 20 minutes. *Average cost, 2d.* per h *Sufficient* for 5 or 6 persons. *Season* from October to April.

CELERY, Stewed (with W. Sauce).

Ingredients.—6 heads of celery, of butter; to each half gallon of w allow 1 heaped teaspoonful of salt, ½ of white sauce (*see* WHITE SAUCE). *M* —Have ready sufficient boiling water to cover the celery, with salt and b in the above proportion. Wash

Celery, Stewed	Charlotte-aux-Pommes

celery well, cut off the decayed outside leaves, trim away the green tops, and shape the root into a point; put it into the boiling water, let it boil rapidly until tender, then take it out, drain well, place it upon a dish, and pour over it about ½ pint of white sauce, made by recipe. It may also be plainly boiled as above, placed on toast, and melted butter poured over, the same as asparagus is dished. *Time.*—Large heads of celery 25 minutes, small ones 15 to 20 minutes, after the water boils. *Average cost, 2d.* per head. *Sufficient* for 5 or 6 persons. *Seasonable* from October to April.

CELERY, Stewed (with White Sauce).

Ingredients.—6 heads of celery, ½ pint of white stock or weak broth, 4 tablespoonfuls of cream, thickening of butter and flour, 1 blade of pounded mace, a *very little* grated nutmeg; pepper and salt to taste. *Mode.*—Wash the celery, strip off the outer leaves, and cut it into lengths of about 4 inches. Put these into a saucepan, with the broth, and stew till tender, which will be in from 20 to 25 minutes; then add the remaining ingredients, simmer altogether for 4 or 5 minutes, pour into a dish, and serve. It may be garnished with sippets of toasted bread. *Time.*—Altogether, ½ hour. *Average cost, 2d.* per head. *Sufficient* for 5 or 6 persons. *Seasonable* from October to April.

Note. — By cutting the celery into smaller pieces, by stewing it a little longer, and, when done, by pressing it through a sieve, the above stew may be converted into a Purée of Celery.

CELERY VINEGAR.

Ingredients.—¼ oz. of celery-seed, 1 pint of vinegar. *Mode.*—Crush the seed by pounding it in a mortar; boil the vinegar, and when cold, pour it to the seed; let it infuse for a fortnight, when strain and bottle off for use. This is frequently used in salads.

CHAMPAGNE-CUP.

Ingredients.—1 quart bottle of champagne, 2 bottles of soda-water, 1 liqueur-glass of brandy or Curaçoa, 2 tablespoonfuls of powdered sugar, 1 lb. of pounded ice, a sprig of green borage. *Mode.*—Put all the ingredients into a silver cup;

stir them together, and serve the same as claret-cup. Should the above proportion of sugar not be found sufficient to suit some tastes, increase the quantity. When borage is not easily obtainable, substitute for it a few slices of cucumber-rind. *Seasonable.*—Suitable for pic-nics, balls, weddings, and other festive occasions.

CHARLOTTE-AUX-POMMES.

Ingredients.— A few slices of rather stale bread ½ inch thick, clarified butter, apple marmalade, with about 2 dozen apples, ½ glass of sherry. *Mode.*—Cut a slice of bread the same shape as the bottom of a plain round mould, which has been well buttered, and a few strips the height of the mould, and about 1½ inch wide; dip the bread in clarified butter (or spread it with cold butter, if not wanted quite so rich); place the round piece at the bottom of the mould, and

CHARLOTTE-AUX-POMMES.

set the narrow strips up the sides of it, overlapping each other a little, that no juice from the apples may escape, and that they may hold firmly to the mould. Brush the *interior* over with the white of egg (this will assist to make the case firmer); fill it with the apple marmalade, with the addition of a little sherry, and cover them with a round piece of bread, also brushed over with egg, the same as the bottom; slightly press the bread down to make it adhere to the other pieces; put a plate on the top, and bake the *charlotte* in a brisk oven, of a light colour. Turn it out on the dish, strew sifted sugar over the top, and pour round it a little melted apricot jam. *Time.*—40 to 50 minutes. *Average cost, 1s. 9d. Sufficient* for 5 or 6 persons. *Seasonable* from July to March.

CHARLOTTE - AUX - POMMES, an easy method of making.

Ingredients.—½ lb. of flour, ¼ lb. of butter, ¼ lb. of powdered sugar, ½ teaspoonful of baking-powder, 1 egg, milk. 1 glass of raisin-wine, apple marmalade, ¼ pint of cream, 2 dessert spoonfuls of pounded sugar, 2 tablespoonfuls of lemon-

Charlotte, Russe

juice. *Mode.*—Make a cake with the flour, butter, sugar, and baking-powder; moisten with the egg and sufficient milk to make it the proper consistency, and bake it in a round tin. When cold, scoop out the middle, leaving a good thickness all round the sides, to prevent them breaking ; take some of the scooped-out pieces, which should be trimmed into neat slices ; lay them in the cake, and pour over sufficient raisin-wine, with the addition of a little brandy, if approved, to soak them well. Have ready some apple marmalade, made by recipe ; place a layer of this over the soaked cake, then a layer of cake and a layer of apples ; whip the cream to a froth, mixing with it the sugar and lemon-juice ; pile it on the top of the *charlotte,* and garnish it with pieces of clear apple jelly. This dish is served cold, but may be eaten hot by omitting the cream, and merely garnishing the top with bright jelly just before it is sent to table. *Time.*—1 hour to bake the cake. *Average cost,* 2s. *Sufficient* for 5 or 6 persons. *Seasonable* from July to March.

CHARLOTTE, Russe (an elegant Sweet Entremet).

Ingredients.—About 18 Savoy biscuits, ⅜ pint of cream, flavouring of vanilla, liqueurs, or wine, 1 tablespoonful of pounded sugar, ½ oz. of isinglass. *Mode.* Procure about 18 Savoy biscuits, or ladies'-fingers, as they are sometimes called ; brush the edges of them with the white of an egg, and line the bottom of a plain round mould, placing them like a star or rosette. Stand them upright all round the edge, carefully put them so closely together that the white of egg connects them firmly, and place this case in the oven for about 5 minutes, just to dry the egg. Whisk the cream to a stiff froth, with the sugar, flavouring, and melted isinglass ; fill the charlotte with it, cover with a slice of sponge-cake cut in the shape of the mould ; place it in ice, where let it remain till ready for table ; then turn it on a dish, remove the mould, and serve. 1 tablespoonful of liqueur of any kind, or 4 tablespoonfuls of wine, would nicely flavour the above proportion of cream. For arranging the biscuits in the mould, cut them to the shape required, so that they fit in nicely, and level them with the mould at the top, that, when turned out, there may be

Cheese

something firm to rest upon. Great care and attention is required in the turning out of this dish, that the cream does not burst the case ; and the edges of the biscuits must have the smallest quantity of egg brushed over them, or it would stick to the mould, and so prevent the charlotte from coming away properly. *Time.* —5 minutes in the oven. *Average cost,* with cream at 1s. per pint, 2s. 6d. *Sufficient* for 1 charlotte. *Seasonable* at any time.

CHEESE.

Cheese is the curd formed from milk by artificial coagulation, pressed and dried for use. Curd, called also casein and caseous matter, or the basis of cheese, exists in the milk, and not in the cream, and requires only to be separated by coagulation: the coagulation, however, supposes some alteration of the curd. By means of the substance employed to coagulate it, it is rendered insoluble in water. When the curd is freed from the whey, kneaded and pressed to expel it entirely, it becomes cheese ; this assumes a degree of transparency, and possesses many of the properties of coagulated albumen. If it be well dried, it does not change by exposure to the air ; but if it contain moisture, it soon putrefies ; it therefore requires some salt to preserve it, and this acts likewise as a kind of seasoning. All our cheese is coloured more or less, except that made from skim milk. The colouring substances employed are arnatto, turmeric, or marigold, all perfectly harmless unless they are adulterated ; and it is said that arnatto sometimes contains red lead.

Cheese varies in quality and richness according to the materials of which it is composed. It is made—1. Of entire milk, as in Cheshire ; 2. of milk and cream, as at Stilton ; 3. of new milk mixed with skim milk, as in Gloucestershire ; 4. of skimmed milk only, as in Suffolk, Holland, and Italy.

The principal varieties of cheese used in England are the following : *Cheshire cheese,* famed all over Europe for its rich quality and fine piquante flavour. It is made of entire new milk, the cream not being taken off. *Gloucester cheese* is much milder in its taste than the Cheshire. There are two kinds of Gloucester cheese, single and double :—*Single Gloucester* is made of skimmed milk, or of the milk deprived of half the cream; *Double Gloucester* is a cheese that pleases almost every palate: it is made of the whole milk and cream. *Stilton cheese* is made by adding the cream of one day to the entire milk of the next: it was first made at Stilton, in Leicestershire. *Sage cheese* is so called from the practice of colouring some curd with bruised sage, marigold-leaves, and parsley, and mixing this with some uncoloured curd. With the Romans, and during the middle ages, this practice was extensively adopted. *Cheddar cheese* much resembles Parmesan. It has a very agreeable taste and flavour, and has a spongy appearance. *Brickbat cheese* has nothing remarkable except its form. It is made by turning with rennet a mixture of cream and new milk; the curd is put into a wooden vessel the shape of a brick, and is then pressed and dried in the usual way. *Dunlop cheese* has a peculiarly mild and rich taste: the best is made entirely from new milk. *New cheese* (as it is called in London) is made chiefly in Lincolnshire, and is either made of all cream, or, like Stilton, by adding the cream of one day's milking to the milk that comes immediately from the cow: they are extremely thin, and are compressed gently two or three times, turned for a few days, and then eaten new with radishes, salad, &c. *Skimmed Milk cheese* is made for sea voyages principally. *Parmesan cheese* is made in Parma and Piacenza. It is the most celebrated of all cheese: it is made entirely of skimmed cows' milk; the high flavour which it has is supposed to be owing to the rich herbage of the meadows of the Po, where the cows are pastured. The best Parmesan is kept for three or four years, and none is carried to market till it is at least six months old. *Dutch cheese* derives its peculiar pungent taste from the practice adopted in Holland of coagulating the milk with muriatic acid instead of rennet. *Swiss cheeses*, in their several varieties, are all remarkable for their fine flavour; that from *Gruyère*, a bailiwick in the canton of Fribourg, is best known in England; it is flavoured by the dried herb of *Melilotos officinalis* in powder. Cheese from milk and potatoes is manufactured in Thuringia and Saxony. *Cream cheese*, although so called, is not properly cheese, but is nothing more than cream dried sufficiently to be cut with a knife.

CHEESE.

In families where much cheese is consumed, and it is bought in large quantities, a piece from the whole cheese should be cut, the larger quantity spread with a thickly-buttered sheet of white paper, and the outside occasionally wiped. To keep cheeses moist that are in daily use, when they come from table a damp cloth should be wrapped round them, and the cheese put into a pan with a cover to it, in a cool but not very dry place. To ripen cheeses, and bring them forward, put them into a damp cellar; and to check too large a production of mites, spirits may be poured into the parts affected. Pieces of cheese which are too near the rind, or too dry to put on table, may be made into Welsh rarebits, or grated down and mixed with macaroni. Cheeses may be preserved in a perfect state for years, by covering them with parchment made pliable by soaking in water, or by rubbing them over with a coating of melted fat. The cheeses selected should be free from cracks or bruises of any kind.

CHEESE, Mode of Serving.

The usual mode of serving cheese at good tables is to cut a small quantity of it into neat square pieces, and to put them into a glass cheese-dish, this dish being handed round. Should the cheese crumble much, of course this method is rather wasteful, and it

CHEESE-GLASS.

may then be put on the table in the piece, and the host may cut from it. When served thus, the cheese must always be carefully scraped, and laid on a white d'oyley or napkin, neatly folded. Cream cheese is often served in a cheese course, and, sometimes, grated Parmesan: the latter should be put into a covered glass dish. Rusks, cheese-biscuits, pats or slices of butter, and salad, cucumber, or water-cresses, should always form part of a cheese-course.

CHEESE, Pounded.

Ingredients.—To every lb. of cheese allow 3 oz. of fresh butter. *Mode.*—To pound cheese is an economical way of using it if it has become dry; it is ex-

| Cheese, Toasted | Cheesecakes |

ceedingly good spread on bread, and is the best way of eating it for those whose digestion is weak. Cut up the cheese into small pieces, and pound it smoothly in a mortar, adding butter in the above proportion. Press it down into a jar, cover with clarified butter, and it will keep for several days. The flavour may be very much increased by adding mixed mustard (about a teaspoonful to every lb.), or cayenne, or pounded mace. Curry-powder is also not unfrequently mixed with it.

CHEESE, Toasted, or Scotch Rarebit.

Ingredients. — A few slices of rich cheese, toast, mustard, and pepper. *Mode.*—Cut some nice rich sound cheese into rather thin slices ; melt it in a cheese-toaster on a hot plate or over steam, and, when melted, add a small quantity of mixed mustard and a seasoning of pepper ; stir the cheese until it is completely dissolved, then brown it before the fire, or with a salamander. Fill the bottom of the cheese-toaster with hot water, and serve with dry or buttered toasts, whichever may be preferred. Our

 engraving illustrates a cheese-toaster with hot-water reservoir : the cheese is melted

HOT-WATER CHEESE-DISH.

in the upper tin, which is placed in another vessel of boiling water, so keeping the preparation beautifully hot. A small quantity of porter, or port wine, is sometimes mixed with the cheese ; and, if it be not very rich, a few pieces of butter may be mixed with it to great advantage. Sometimes the melted cheese is spread on the toasts, and then laid in the cheese-dish at the top of the hot water. Whichever way it is served, it is highly necessary that the mixture be very hot, and very quickly sent to table, or it will be worthless. *Time.*—About 5 minutes to melt the cheese. *Average cost*, 1½d. per slice. *Sufficient.*—Allow a slice to each person. *Seasonable* at any time.

CHEESE, Toasted, or Welsh Rarebit.

Ingredients.—Slices of bread, butter, Cheshire or Gloucester cheese, mustard, and pepper. *Mode.*—Cut the bread into

slices about ½ inch in thickness ; par the crust, toast the bread slightly w out hardening or burning it, and sp it with butter. Cut some slices, quite so large as the bread, from a g rich fat cheese ; lay them on the toa bread in a cheese-toaster ; be careful the cheese does not burn, and let i equally melted. Spread over the t little made mustard and a seasonin pepper, and serve very hot, with hot plates. To facilitate the meltin the cheese, it may be cut into thin fla or toasted on one side before it is on the bread. As it is so essentia send this dish hot to table, it is a g plan to melt the cheese in small r silver or metal pans, and to send t pans to table, allowing one for guest. Slices of dry or buttered t should always accompany them, mustard, pepper, and salt. *Tim* About 5 minutes to melt the che *Average cost*, 1½d. per slice. *Sufficien* Allow a slice to each person. *Seasona* at any time. *Note.*—Should the cheese be dr little butter mixed with it will b improvement.

CHEESE SANDWICHES.

Ingredients. — Slices of brown br and-butter, thin slices of cheese. *M* —Cut from a nice fat Cheshire, or good rich cheese, some slices about ½ thick, and place them between s slices of brown bread-and-butter, sandwiches. Place them on a plat the oven, and, when the bread is toas serve on a napkin very hot and quickly. *Time.*—10 minutes in a b oven. *Average cost*, 1½d. each sandw *Sufficient.*—Allow a sandwich for person. *Seasonable* at any time.

CHEESECAKES.

Ingredients.—8 oz. of pressed cu 2 oz. of ratafias, 6 oz. of sugar, 2 o butter, the yolks of 6 eggs, nutm salt, rind of 2 oranges or lemons. *M* —Rub the sugar on the orange or le rind, and scrape it off. Press the in a napkin, to get rid of moisture ; po it thoroughly in a mortar with the o ingredients till the whole becomes a paste. Line 2 dozen, or more, tar pans with good puff-paste, garnish t with the cheese-custard, place a stri

Cherokee

candied-peel on the top of each, and bake in a moderate oven a light colour ; when done, shake a little sifted sugar over them. Currants, dried cherries, sultanas, and citron may be used instead of candied-peel. *Time.*—20 minutes to bake. *Average cost*, 6d. per dozen. *Seasonable* at any time.

CHEROKEE, or Store Sauce.

Ingredients.—½ oz. of cayenne pepper, 5 cloves of garlic, 2 tablespoonfuls of soy, 1 tablespoonful of walnut ketchup, 1 pint of vinegar. *Mode.*— Boil all the ingredients *gently* for about ½ hour; strain the liquor, and bottle off for use. *Time.* —½ hour. *Seasonable.*—This sauce can be made at any time.

CHERRIES, Dried.

Cherries may be put into a slow oven and thoroughly dried before they begin to change colour ; they should then be taken out of the oven, tied in bunches, and stored away in a dry place. In the winter, they may be cooked with sugar for dessert, the same as Normandy pippins. Particular care must be taken that the oven be not too hot. Another method of drying cherries is to stone them, and to put them into a preserving-pan, with plenty of loaf sugar strewed amongst them. They should be simmered till the fruit shrivels, when they should be strained from the juice. The cherries should then be placed in an oven cool enough to dry without baking them. About 5 oz. of sugar would be required for 1 lb. of cherries, and the same syrup may be used again to do another quantity of fruit.

CHERRIES, Morello, to Preserve.

Ingredients.—To every lb. of cherries allow 1¼ lb. of sugar, 1 gill of water. *Mode.*—Select ripe cherries, pick off the stalks, and reject all that have any blemishes. Boil the sugar and water together for 5 minutes ; put in the cherries, and boil them for 10 minutes, removing the scum as it rises. Then turn the fruit, &c., into a pan, and let it remain until the next day, when boil it all again for another 10 minutes, and, if necessary, skim well. Put the cherries into small dots, pour over them the syrup, and, when cold, cover down with oiled papers, and the tops of the jars with tissue-paper

Cherry Brandy, to make

brushed over on both sides with the white of an egg, and keep in a dry place. *Time.* —Altogether, 25 minutes to boil. *Average cost*, from 8d. to 10d. per lb. pot. *Seasonable.*—Make this in July or August.

CHERRIES, to Preserve in Syrup (very delicious).

Ingredients.—4 lbs. of cherries, 3 lbs. of sugar, 1 pint of white-currant juice. *Mode.*—Let the cherries be as clear and as transparent as possible, and perfectly ripe ; pick off the stalks, and remove the stones, damaging the fruit as little as you can. Make a syrup with the above proportion of sugar, mix the cherries with it, and boil them for about 15 minutes, carefully skimming them ; turn them gently into a pan, and let them remain till the next day, then drain the cherries on a sieve, and put the syrup and white-currant juice into the preserving-pan again. Boil these together until the syrup is somewhat reduced and rather thick, then put in the cherries, and let them boil for about 5 minutes ; take them off the fire, skim the syrup, put the cherries into small pots or wide-mouthed bottles ; pour the syrup over, and, when quite cold, tie them down carefully, so that the air is quite excluded. *Time.*—15 minutes to boil the cherries in the syrup ; 10 minutes to boil the syrup and currant-juice ; 5 minutes to boil the cherries the second time. *Average cost* for this quantity, 3s. 6d. *Seasonable.*—Make this in July or August.

CHERRY BRANDY, to make.

Ingredients. — Morello cherries, good brandy ; to every lb. of cherries allow 3 oz. of pounded sugar. *Mode.*—Have ready some glass bottles, which must be perfectly dry. Ascertain that the cherries are not too ripe and are freshly gathered, and cut off about half of the stalks. Put them into the bottles, with the above proportion of sugar to every lb. of fruit; strew this in between the cherries, and, when the bottles are nearly full, pour in sufficient brandy to reach just below the cork. A few peach or apricot kernels will add much to their flavour, or a few blanched bitter almonds. Put corks or bungs into the bottles, tie over them a piece of bladder, and store away in a dry place. The cherries will be fit to eat in 2 or 3 months, and will remain good for years. They are liable

Cherry Jam

to shrivel and become tough if too much sugar be added to them. *Average cost*, 1*s.* to 1*s.* 6*d.* per lb. *Sufficient.*—1 lb. of cherries and about a ¼ pint of brandy for a quart bottle. *Seasonable* in August and September.

CHERRY JAM.

Ingredients. — To every lb. of fruit, weighed before stoning, allow ½ lb. of sugar; to every 6 lbs. of fruit allow 1 pint of red-currant juice, and to every pint of juice 1 lb. of sugar. *Mode.*— Weigh the fruit before stoning, and allow half the weight of sugar; stone the cherries, and boil them in a preserving-pan until nearly all the juice is dried up, then add the sugar, which should be crushed to powder, and the currant-juice, allowing 1 pint to every 6 lbs. of cherries (original weight), and 1 lb. of sugar to every pint of juice. Boil all together until it jellies, which will be in from 20 minutes to ½ hour; skim the jam well, keep it well stirred, and, a few minutes before it is done, crack some of the stones, and add the kernels: these impart a very delicious flavour to the jam. *Time.*— According to the quality of the cherries, from ¾ to 1 hour to boil them; 20 minutes to ½ hour with the sugar. *Average sost*, from 7*d.* to 8*d.* per lb. pot. *Sufficient.* —1 pint of fruit for a lb. pot of jam. *Seasonable.*—Make this in July or August.

CHERRY SAUCE, for Sweet Puddings (German Recipe).

Ingredients.—1 lb. of cherries, 1 tablespoonful of flour, 1 oz. of butter, ½ pint of water, 1 wineglassful of port wine, a little grated lemon-rind, 4 pounded cloves, 2 tablespoonfuls of lemon-juice, sugar to taste. *Mode.*—Stone the cherries, and pound the kernels in a mortar to a smooth paste; put the butter and flour into a saucepan, stir them over the fire until of a pale brown, then add the cherries, the pounded kernels, the wine, and the water. Simmer these gently for ¼ hour, or until the cherries are quite cooked, and rub the whole through a hair sieve; add the remaining ingredients, let the sauce boil for another 5 minutes, and serve. This is a delicious sauce to serve with boiled batter pudding, and when thus used, should be sent to table poured over the pudding. *Time.*—20 minutes to ½ hour.

Chestnut Sauce

Average cost, 1*s.* 2*d.* *Sufficient* for 4 or 5 persons. *Seasonable* in June, July, and August.

CHERRY TART.

Ingredients.—1½ lb. of cherries, 2 small tablespoonfuls of moist sugar, ½ lb. of short crust. *Mode.* — Pick the stalks from the cherries, put them, with the sugar, into a *deep* pie-dish just capable of holding them, with a small cup placed upside down in the midst of them. Make a short crust with ½ lb. of flour, by either of the recipes for short crust, lay a border round the edge of the dish, put on the cover, and ornament the edges ; bake in a brisk oven from ½ hour to 40 minutes ; strew finely-sifted sugar over, and serve hot or cold, although the latter is the more usual mode. It is more economical to make two or three tarts at one time, as the trimmings from one tart answer for lining the edges of the dish for another, and so much paste is not required as when they are made singly. Unless for family use, never make fruit pies in very *large* dishes ; select them, however, as *deep* as possible. *Time.* — ½ hour to 40 minutes. *Average cost*, in full season, 8*d.* *Sufficient* for 5 or 6 persons. *Seasonable* in June, July, and August.

Note.—A few currants added to the cherries will be found to impart a nice piquante taste to them.

CHESTNUT SAUCE, Brown.

Ingredients.—½ lb. of chestnuts, ½ pint of stock, 2 lumps of sugar, 4 tablespoonfuls of Spanish sauce (*see* SAUCES). *Mode.* —Prepare the chestnuts as in the succeeding recipe, by scalding and peeling them ; put them in a stewpan with the stock and sugar, and simmer them till tender. When done, add Spanish sauce in the above proportion, and rub the whole through a tammy. Keep this sauce rather liquid, as it is liable to thicken. *Time.*—1½ hour to simmer the chestnuts. *Average cost*, 8*d.*

CHESTNUT SAUCE, for Fowls or Turkey.

Ingredients.—½ lb. of chestnuts, ½ pint of white stock, 2 strips of lemon-peel, cayenne to taste, ¼ pint of cream or milk. *Mode.*—Peel off the outside skin of the chestnuts, and put them into boiling

| Chestnut Soup | Chicken Broth |

water for a few minutes; take off the thin inside peel, and put them into a saucepan with the white stock and lemon-peel, and let them simmer for 1½ hour, or until the chestnuts are quite tender. Rub the whole through a hair-sieve with a wooden spoon; add seasoning and the cream; let it just simmer, but not boil, and keep stirring all the time. Serve very hot, and quickly. If milk is used instead of cream, a very small quantity of thickening may be required: that, of course, the cook will determine. *Time.*—Altogether, nearly 2 hours. *Average cost,* 8d. *Sufficient,* this quantity for a turkey.

CHESTNUT (Spanish) SOUP.

Ingredients.—¾ lb. of Spanish chest-nuts, ¼ pint of cream; seasoning to taste of salt, cayenne, and mace; 1 quart of stock. *Mode.*—Take the outer rind from the chestnuts, and put them into a large pan of warm water. As soon as this becomes too hot for the fingers to remain in it, take out the chestnuts, peel them quickly, and immerse them in cold water, and wipe and weigh them. Now cover them with good stock, and stew them gently for rather more than ¾ of an hour, or until they break when touched with a fork; then drain, pound, and rub them through a fine sieve reversed; add suffi-cient stock, mace, cayenne, and salt, and stir it often until it boils, and put in the cream. The stock in which the chest-nuts are boiled can be used for the soup, when its sweetness is not objected to, or it may, in part, be added to it; and the rule is, that ¾ lb. of chestnuts should be given to each quart of soup. *Time.*—Rather more than 1 hour. *Average cost,* per quart, 1s. 6d. *Sufficient* for 4 persons. *Seasonable* from October to February.

CHICKENS, Boiled.

Ingredients.—A pair of chickens, wa-ter. *Choosing and Trussing.*—In choos-ing fowls for boiling, it should be borne in mind that those which are not black-legged are generally much whiter when dressed. Pick, draw, singe, wash, and truss them in the following manner, without the livers in the wings; and, in drawing, be careful not to break the gall-bladder:—Cut off the neck, leaving sufficient skin to skewer back. Cut the feet off to the first joint, tuck the stumps into a slit made on each side of the belly,

twist the wings over the back of the fowl, and secure the top of the leg and the bottom of the wing together by running a skewer through them and the body. The other side must be done in the same manner. Should the fowl be very large and old, draw the sinews of the legs before tucking them in. Make a slit in the apron of the fowl, large enough to admit the parson's nose, and tie a string on the tops of the legs to keep them in their proper place. *Mode.*—When they are firmly trussed, put them into a stew-pan with plenty of hot water, bring it to boil, and carefully remove all the scum as it rises. *Simmer very gently* until the fowl is tender, and bear in mind that the slower it boils the plumper and whiter

BOILED FOWL.

will the fowl be. Many cooks wrap them in a floured cloth to preserve the colour, and to prevent the scum from clinging to them; in this case, a few slices of lemon should be placed on the breasts, over these a sheet of buttered paper, and then the cloth; cooking them in this manner renders the flesh very white. Boiled ham, bacon, boiled tongue, or pickled pork, are the usual accompani-ments to boiled fowls, and they may be served with Béchamel, white sauce, par-sley and butter, oyster, lemon, liver, celery, or mushroom sauce. A little should be poured over the fowls after the skewers are removed, and the remainder sent in a tureen to table. *Time.*—Large fowl, 1 hour; moderate-sized one, ¾ hour; chicken, from 20 minutes to ½ hour. *Average cost,* in full season, 5s. the pair. *Sufficient* for 7 or 8 persons. *Seasonable* all the year, but scarce in early spring.

CHICKEN BROTH.

Ingredients.—½ fowl, or the inferior joints of a whole one; 1 quart of water, 1 blade of mace, ¼ onion, a small bunch of sweet herbs, salt to taste, 10 pepper-corns. *Mode.*—An old fowl not suitable for eating may be converted into very good broth; or, if a young one be used, the inferior joints may be put in the broth, and the best pieces reserved for

Chicken, Curried

dressing in some other manner. Put the fowl into a saucepan, stew all the ingredients, and simmer gently for 1½ hour, carefully skimming the broth well. When done, strain, and put by in a cool place until wanted ; then take all the fat off the top, warm up as much as may be required, and serve. This broth is, of course, only for those invalids whose stomachs are strong enough to digest it, with a flavouring of herbs, &c. It may be made in the same manner as beef tea, with water and salt only, but the preparation will be but tasteless and insipid. When the invalid cannot digest this chicken broth with the flavouring, we would recommend plain beef tea in preference to plain chicken tea, which it would be without the addition of herbs, onions, &c. *Time.*—1½ hour. *Sufficient* to make rather more than 1 pint of broth.

CHICKEN, Curried.

[COLD MEAT COOKERY.] *Ingredients.* —The remains of cold roast fowls, 2 large onions, 1 apple, 2 oz. of butter, 1 dessert-spoonful of curry-powder, 1 teaspoonful of flour, ½ pint of gravy, 1 tablespoonful of lemon-juice. *Mode.*—Slice the onions, peel, core, and chop the apple, and cut the fowl into neat joints ; try these in the butter of a nice brown, then add the curry-powder, flour, and gravy, and stew for about 20 minutes. Put in the lemon-juice, and serve with boiled rice, either placed in a ridge round the dish or separately. Two or three shalots or a little garlic may be added, if approved. *Time.* —Altogether, ½ hour. *Average cost*, exclusive of the cold fowl, 6d. *Seasonable* in the winter.

CHICKEN CUTLETS (an Entrée).

Ingredients.—2 chickens ; seasoning to taste of salt, white pepper, and cayenne ; 2 blades of pounded mace, egg and bread crumbs, clarified butter, 1 strip of lemon-rind, 2 carrots, 1 onion, 2 tablespoonfuls of mushroom ketchup, thickening of butter and flour, 1 egg. *Mode.*—Remove the breast and leg-bones of the chickens ; cut the meat into neat pieces after having skinned it, and season the cutlets with pepper, salt, pounded mace, and cayenne. Put the bones, trimmings, &c., into a stewpan with 1 pint of water, adding carrots, onions, and lemon-peel in the above proportion ; stew gently for 1½ hour, and strain the gravy. Thicken it

Chicken, Fricasseed

with butter and flour, add the ketchup and 1 egg well beaten ; stir it over the fire, and bring it to the simmering-point, but do not allow it to boil. In the mean time, egg and bread crumb the cutlets, and give them a few drops of clarified butter ; fry them a delicate brown, occasionally turning them ; arrange them pyramidically on the dish, and pour over them the sauce. *Time.*—10 minutes to fry the cutlets. *Average cost*, 2s. each. *Sufficient* for an entrée. *Seasonable* from April to July.

CHICKEN CUTLETS, French.

[COLD MEAT COOKERY.] *Ingredients.* —The remains of cold roast or boiled fowl, fried bread, clarified butter, the yolk of 1 egg, bread crumbs, ½ teaspoonful of finely-minced lemon-peel ; salt, cayenne, and mace to taste. For sauce,— 1 oz. of butter, 2 minced shalots, a few slices of carrot, a small bunch of savoury herbs, including parsley, 1 blade of pounded mace, 6 peppercorns, ½ pint of gravy. *Mode.* — Cut the fowls into as many nice cutlets as possible ; take a corresponding number of sippets about the same size, all cut one shape ; fry them a pale brown, put them before the fire, then dip the cutlets into clarified butter mixed with the yolk of an egg, cover with bread crumbs seasoned in the above proportion, with lemon-peel, mace, salt, and cayenne ; fry them for about 5 minutes, put each piece on one of the sippets, pile them high in the dish, and serve with the following sauce, which should be made ready for the cutlets. Put the butter into a stewpan, add the shalots, carrot, herbs, mace, and peppercorns ; fry for 10 minutes, or rather longer ; pour in ½ pint of good gravy, made of the chicken-bones ; stew gently for 20 minutes, strain it, and serve. *Time.* —5 minutes to fry the cutlets ; 35 minutes to make the gravy. *Average cost*, exclusive of the chicken, 9d. *Seasonable* from April to July.

CHICKEN, Fricasseed (an Entrée).

Ingredients.—2 small fowls or 1 large one, 3 oz. of butter, a bunch of parsley and green onions, 1 clove, 2 blades of mace, 1 shalot, 1 bay-leaf, salt and white pepper to taste, ½ pint of cream, the yolks of 3 eggs. *Mode.* —Choose a couple of fat plump chickens, and, after drawing, singeing, and washing them, skin and

Chicken Patties

carve them into joints; blanch these in boiling water for 2 or 3 minutes, take them out, and immerse them in cold water to render them white. Put the trimmings, with the necks and legs, into a stewpan; add the parsley, onions, clove, mace, shalot, bay-leaf, and a seasoning of pepper and salt; pour to these the water that the chickens were blanched in, and simmer gently for rather more than 1 hour. Have ready another stewpan; put in the joints of fowl, with the above proportion of butter; dredge them with flour, let them get hot, but do not brown them much; then moisten the fricassee with the gravy made from the trimmings, &c., and stew very gently for ½ hour. Lift the fowl into another stewpan, skim the sauce, reduce it quickly over the fire by letting it boil fast, and strain it over them. Add the cream, and a seasoning of pounded mace and cayenne; let it boil up, and when ready to serve, stir to it the well-beaten yolks of 3 eggs; these should not be put in till the last moment, and the sauce should be made *hot*, but must *not boil*, or it will instantly curdle. A few button-mushrooms stewed with the fowl are by many persons considered an improvement. *Time.*—1 hour to make the gravy, ½ hour to simmer the fowl. *Average cost,* 5s. the pair. *Sufficient.*—1 large fowl for 1 entrée. *Seasonable* at any time.

CHICKEN (or Fowl) PATTIES.

[Cold Meat Cookery.] *Ingredients.* —The remains of cold roast chicken or fowl; to every ¼ lb. of meat allow 2 oz. of ham, 3 tablespoonfuls of cream, 2 tablespoonfuls of veal gravy, ½ teaspoonful of minced lemon-peel; cayenne, salt, and pepper to taste; 1 tablespoonful of lemon-juice, 1 oz. of butter rolled in flour, puff paste. *Mode.*—Mince very small the white meat from a cold roast fowl, after removing all the skin; weigh it, and to every ¼ lb. of meat allow the above proportion of minced ham. Put these into a stewpan with the remaining ingredients, stir over the fire for 10 minutes or ¼ hour, taking care that the mixture does not burn. Roll out some puff paste about ¼ inch in thickness, line the patty-pans with this, put upon each a small piece of bread, and cover with another layer of paste; brush over with the yolk of an egg, and bake in a brisk oven for about ¼ hour. When done, cut a round

Chicken, Potted

piece out of the top, and, with a small spoon, take out the bread (be particular in not breaking the outside border of the crust), and fill the patties with the mixture. *Time.*—¼ hour to prepare the meat; not quite ¼ hour to bake the crust. *Seasonable* at any time.

CHICKEN (or Fowl) PIE.

Ingredients.—2 small fowls or 1 large one, white pepper and salt to taste, ½ teaspoonful of grated nutmeg, ½ teaspoonful of pounded mace, a few slices of ham, 3 hard-boiled eggs, ½ pint of water, puff crust. *Mode.*— Skin and cut up the fowls into joints, and put the neck, leg, and backbones in a stewpan, with a little water, an onion, a bunch of savoury herbs, and a blade of mace; let these stew for about an hour, and, when done, strain off the liquor: this is for gravy. Put a layer of fowl at the bottom of a pie-dish, then a layer of ham, then one of forcemeat and hard-boiled eggs cut in rings; between the layers put a seasoning of pounded mace, nutmeg, pepper, and salt. Proceed in this manner until the dish is full, and pour in about ½ pint of water; border the edge of the dish with puff crust, put on the cover, ornament the top, and glaze it by brushing over it the yolk of an egg. Bake from 1¼ to 1½ hour, should the pie be very large, and, when done, pour in at the top the gravy made from the bones. If to be eaten cold, and wished particularly nice, the joints of the fowls should be boned, and placed in the dish with alternate layers of forcemeat; sausage-meat may also be substituted for the forcemeat, and is now very much used. When the chickens are boned, and mixed with sausage-meat, the pie will take about 2 hours to bake. It should be covered with a piece of paper when about half-done, to prevent the paste being dried up or scorched. *Time.*—For a pie with unboned meat, 1¼ to 1½ hour; with boned meat and sausage or forcemeat, 1½ to 2 hours. *Average cost,* with 2 fowls, 6s. 6d. *Sufficient* for 6 or 7 persons. *Seasonable* at any time.

CHICKEN, Potted (a Luncheon or Breakfast Dish).

Ingredients.—The remains of cold roast chicken; to every lb. of meat allow ¼ lb. of fresh butter, salt and cayenne to taste,

Chicken Salad

1 teaspoonful of pounded mace, ¼ small nutmeg. *Mode.*—Strip the meat from the bones of cold roast fowl ; when it is treed from gristle and skin, weigh it, and to every lb. of meat allow the above proportion of butter, seasoning, and spices. Cut the meat into small pieces, pound it well with the fresh butter, sprinkle in the spices gradually, and keep pounding until reduced to a perfectly smooth paste. Put it into potting-pots for use, and cover it with clarified butter, about ¼ inch in thickness, and, if to be kept for some time, tie over a bladder : 2 or 3 slices of ham, minced and pounded with the above ingredients, will be found an improvement. It should be kept in a dry place. *Seasonable* at any time.

CHICKEN (or Fowl) SALAD.

Ingredients.—The remains of cold roast or boiled chicken, 2 lettuces, a little endive, 1 cucumber, a few slices of boiled beetroot, salad-dressing. *Mode.*—Trim neatly the remains of the chicken ; wash, dry, and slice the lettuces, and place in the middle of a dish ; put the pieces of fowl on the top, and pour the salad-dressing over them. Garnish the edge of the salad with hard-boiled eggs cut in rings, sliced cucumber, and boiled beetroot cut in slices. Instead of cutting the eggs in rings, the yolks may be rubbed through a hair sieve, and the whites chopped very finely, and arranged on the salad in small bunches, yellow and white alternately. This should not be made long before it is wanted for table. *Average cost*, exclusive of the cold chicken, 8d. *Sufficient* for 4 or 5 persons. *Seasonable* at any time.

CHILI VINEGAR.

Ingredients.—50 fresh red English chilies, 1 pint of vinegar. *Mode.*—Pound or cut the chilies in half, and infuse them in the vinegar for a fortnight, when it will be fit for use. This will be found an agreeable relish to fish, as many people cannot eat it without the addition of an acid and cayenne pepper.

CHINA CHILO.

Ingredients.—1½ lb. of leg, loin, or neck of mutton, 2 onions, 2 lettuces, 1 pint of green peas, 1 teaspoonful of salt, 1 teaspoonful of pepper, ¼ pint of water, ¼ lb. of clarified butter · when liked, a little

Chocolate Cream

cayenne. *Mode.*—Mince the above quantity of undressed leg, loin, or neck of mutton, adding a little of the fat, also minced ; put it into a stewpan with the remaining ingredients, previously shredding the lettuce and onion rather fine ; closely cover the stewpan, after the ingredients have been well stirred, and simmer gently for rather more than two hours. Serve in a dish, with a border of rice round, the same as for curry. *Time.*—Rather more than two hours. *Average cost*, 1s. 6d. *Sufficient* for 3 or 4 persons. *Seasonable* from June to August.

CHOCOLATE, to Make.

Ingredients.—Allow ½ oz. of chocolate to each person ; to every oz. allow ¼ pint of water, ½ pint of milk. *Mode.*—Make the milk-and-water hot ; scrape the chocolate into it, and stir the mixture constantly and quickly until the chocolate is dissolved ; bring it to the boiling-point, stir it well, and serve directly with white sugar. Chocolate prepared within a mill, as shown in the engraving, is made by putting in the scraped chocolate, pouring over it the boiling milk-and-water, and milling it over the fire until hot and frothy. *Sufficient.*—Allow ½ oz. of cake chocolate to each person.

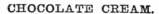

MILL.

CHOCOLATE CREAM.

Ingredients.—3 oz. of grated chocolate, ¼ lb. of sugar, 1½ pint of cream, 1½ oz. of clarified isinglass, the yolks of 6 eggs. *Mode.*—Beat the yolks of the eggs well, put them into a basin with the grated

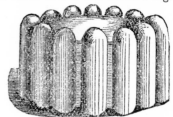

CREAM-MOULD.

chocolate, the sugar, and 1 pint of the cream ; stir these ingredients well together, pour them into a jug, and set this jug in a saucepan of boiling water ; stir it one way until the mixture thickens, but *do not allow it to boil*, or it will

Chocolate Soufflé

curdle. Strain the cream through a sieve into a basin; stir in the isinglass and the other ½ pint of cream, which should be well whipped; mix all well together, and pour it into a mould which has been previously oiled with the purest salad-oil, and, if at hand, set it in ice until wanted for table. *Time.*—About 10 minutes to stir the mixture over the fire. *Average cost, 4s. 6d.,* with cream at 1s. per pint. *Sufficient* to fill a quart mould. *Seasonable* at any time.

CHOCOLATE SOUFFLE.

Ingredients.—4 eggs, 3 teaspoonfuls of pounded sugar, 1 teaspoonful of flour, 3 oz. of the best chocolate. *Mode.* — Break the eggs, separating the whites from the yolks, and put them into different basins; add to the yolks the sugar, flour, and chocolate, which should be very finely grated, and stir these ingredients for 5 minutes. Then well whisk the whites of the eggs in the other basin until they are stiff, and, when firm, mix lightly with the yolks till the whole forms a smooth and light substance; butter a round cake-tin, put in the mixture, and bake in a moderate oven from 15 to 20 minutes. Pin a white napkin round the tin, strew sifted sugar over the top of the soufflé, and send it immediately to table. The proper appearance of this dish depends entirely on the expedition with which it is served; and some cooks, to preserve its lightness, hold a salamander over the soufflé until it is placed on the table. If allowed to stand after it comes from the oven it will be entirely spoiled, as it falls almost immediately. *Time.*— 15 to 20 minutes. *Average cost,* 1s. *Sufficient* for a moderate-sized soufflé. *Seasonable* at any time.

CLARET-CUP.

Ingredients.—1 bottle of claret, 1 bottle of soda-water, about ½ lb. of pounded ice, 4 tablespoonfuls of powdered sugar, ¼ teaspoonful of grated nutmeg, 1 liqueur - glass of Maraschino, a sprig of green borage. *Mode.*—Put all the ingredients into a silver cup, regulating the proportion of ice by

CLARET-CUP.

Cocoa, to make

the state of the weather; if very warm, a larger quantity would be necessary. Hand the cup round with a clean napkin passed through one of the handles, that the edge of the cup may be wiped after each guest has partaken of the contents thereof. *Seasonable* in summer.

COCK-A-LEEKIE.

Ingredients.—A capon or large fowl (sometimes an old cock, from which the recipe takes its name, is used), which should be trussed as for boiling, 2 or 3 bunches of fine leeks, 5 quarts of stock (*see* STOCK), pepper and salt to taste. *Mode.*—Well wash the leeks (and, if old, scald them in boiling water for a few minutes), taking off the roots and part of the heads, and cut them into lengths of about an inch. Put the fowl into the stock, with, at first, one half of the leeks, and allow it to simmer gently. In half an hour add the remaining leeks, and then it may simmer for 3 or 4 hours longer. It should be carefully skimmed, and can be seasoned to taste. In serving, take out the fowl and carve it neatly, placing the pieces in a tureen, and pouring over them the soup, which should be very thick of leeks (a *purée* of leeks, the French would call it). *Time.*—4 hours. *Average cost,* 1s. 6d. per quart; or with stock, 1s. *Sufficient* for 10 persons. *Seasonable* in winter.

Note.—Without the fowl, the above, which would then be merely called leek soup, is very good, and also economical. Cock-a-leekie was largely consumed at the Burns Centenary Festival at the Crystal Palace, Sydenham, in 1859.

COCOA to Make.

Ingredients.—Allow 2 teaspoonfuls of the prepared cocoa, or 1 teaspoonful of cocoa essence, to 1 breakfast-cup; boiling milk and boiling water. *Mode.*—Put the cocoa into a breakfast-cup, pour over it sufficient cold milk to make it into a smooth paste; then add equal quantities of boiling milk and boiling water, and stir all well together, boiling for one or two minutes. Care must be taken not to allow the milk to get burnt, as it will entirely spoil the flavour of the preparation. The rock cocoa, or that bought in a solid piece, should be scraped, and made in the same manner, taking care to rub down all the lumps before the boiling liquid is added. *Suffi-*

Cod

cient.—2 teaspoonfuls of prepared cocoa, or 1 of cocoa essence, for 1 breakfast-cup, or ¼ oz. of the rock cocoa for the same quantity.

COD.

Cod should be chosen for the table when it is plump and round near the tail, when the hollow behind the head is deep, and when the sides are undulated as if they were ribbed. The glutinous parts about the head lose their delicate flavour after the fish has been twenty-four hours out of the water. The great point by which the cod should be judged is the firmness of its flesh ; and, although the cod is not firm when it is alive, its quality may be arrived at by pressing the finger into the flesh : if this rises immediately, the flesh is good ; if not, it is stale. Another sign of its goodness is, if the fish, when it is cut, exhibits a bronze appearance, like the silver side of a round of beef ; when this is the case the flesh will be firm when cooked. Stiffness in a cod, or in any other fish, is a sure sign of freshness, though not always of quality. Sometimes codfish, though exhibiting signs of rough usage, will eat much better than those with red gills, so strongly recommended by many cookery-books. This appearance is generally caused by the fish having been knocked about at sea, in the well-boats, in which they are conveyed from the fishing-grounds to market.

COD à la BECHAMEL.

[COLD MEAT COOKERY.] *Ingredients.*— Any remains of cold cod, 4 tablespoonfuls of béchamel (*see* BECHAMEL SAUCE), 2 oz. of butter ; seasoning to taste of pepper and salt ; fried bread, a few bread crumbs. *Mode.*—Flake the cod carefully, leaving out all skin and bone ; put the béchamel in a stewpan with the butter, and stir it over the fire till the latter is melted : add seasoning, put in the fish, and mix it well with the sauce. Make a border of fried bread round the dish, lay in the fish, sprinkle over with bread crumbs, and baste with butter. Brown either before the fire or with a salamander, and garnish with toasted bread cut in fanciful shapes. *Time.*—¼ hour. *Average cost,* exclusive of the fish, 6d.

COD à la CREME.

[COLD MEAT COOKERY.] *Ingredients.*

Cod à la Maître d'Hôtel

—1 large slice of cod, 1 oz. of butter, 1 chopped shalot, a little minced parsley, ¼ teacupful of white stock, ¼ pint of milk or cream, flour to thicken, cayenne and lemon-juice to taste, ¼ teaspoonful of powdered sugar. *Mode.*—Boil the cod, and while hot, break it into flakes ; put the butter, shalot, parsley, and stock into a stewpan, and let them boil for 5 minutes. Stir in sufficient flour to thicken, and pour to it the milk or cream. Simmer for 10 minutes, add the cayenne and sugar, and, when liked, a little lemon-juice. Put the fish in the sauce to warm gradually, but do not let it boil. Serve in a dish garnished with croûtons. *Time.*—Rather more than ¼ hour. *Average cost,* with cream, 2s. *Sufficient* for 3 persons. *Seasonable* from November to March.

Note.—The remains of fish from the preceding day answer very well for this dish.

COD à l'ITALIENNE.

Ingredients.—2 slices of crimped cod, 1 shalot, 1 slice of ham minced very fine, ½ pint of white stock, when liked, ½ teacupful of cream ; salt to taste ; a few drops of garlic vinegar, a little lemon-juice, ½ teaspoonful of powdered sugar. *Mode.*—Chop the shalots, mince the ham very fine, pour on the stock, and simmer for 15 minutes. If the colour should not be good, add cream in the above proportion, and strain it through a fine sieve ; season it, and put in the vinegar, lemon-juice, and sugar. Now boil the cod, take out the middle bone, and skin it ; put it on the dish without breaking, and pour the sauce over it. *Time.*—¾ hour. *Average cost,* 3s. 6d., with fresh fish. *Sufficient* for 4 persons. *Seasonable* from November to March.

COD à la MAITRE D'HOTEL.

[COLD MEAT COOKERY.] *Ingredients.*—2 slices of cod, ¼ lb. of butter, a little chopped shalot and parsley ; pepper to taste ; ¼ teaspoonful of grated nutmeg, or rather less when the flavour is not liked ; the juice of ¼ lemon. *Mode.*—Boil the cod, and either leave it whole, or, what is still better, flake it from the bone, and take off the skin. Put it into a stewpan with the butter, parsley, shalot, pepper, and nutmeg. Melt the butter gradually, and be very careful that it does not become like oil. When all is

Cod, Curried

well mixed and thoroughly hot, add the lemon-juice, and serve. *Time.*—½ hour. *Average cost*, 2s. 6d. ; with remains of cold fish, 5d. *Sufficient* for 4 persons. *Seasonable* from November to March.

Note.—Cod that has been left will do for this.

COD, Curried.

[COLD MEAT COOKERY.] *Ingredients.* —2 slices of large cod, or the remains of any cold fish ; 3 oz. of butter, 1 onion sliced, a teacupful of white stock, thickening of butter and flour, 1 *small* teaspoonful of curry-powder, ¼ pint of cream, salt and cayenne to taste. *Mode.*—Flake the fish, and fry it of a nice brown colour with the butter and onions ; put this in a stewpan, add the stock and thickening, and simmer for 10 minutes. Stir the curry-powder into the cream ; put it, with the seasoning, to the other ingredients ; give one boil, and serve. *Time.*—¾ hour. *Average cost*, with fresh fish, 3s. *Sufficient* for 4 persons. *Seasonable* from November to March.

COD PIE.

Ingredients.—2 slices of cod ; pepper and salt to taste ; ½ a teaspoonful of grated nutmeg, 1 large blade of pounded mace, 2 oz. of butter, ½ pint of stock, a paste crust (*see* PASTRY). For sauce,— 1 tablespoonful of stock, ¼ pint of cream or milk, thickening of flour or butter, lemon-peel chopped very fine to taste, 12 oysters. *Mode.*—Lay the cod in salt for 4 hours, then wash it and place it in a dish ; season, and add the butter and stock ; cover with the crust, and bake for 1 hour, or rather more. Now make the sauce, by mixing the ingredients named above ; give it one boil, and pour it into the pie by a hole made at the top of the crust, which can easily be covered by a small piece of pastry cut and baked in any fanciful shape,—such as a leaf, or otherwise. *Time.*—1½ hour. *Average cost*, with fresh fish, 2s. 6d. *Sufficient* for 6 persons. *Seasonable* from November to March.

Note.—The remains of cold fish may be used for this pie.

COD PIE. (Economical.)

[COLD MEAT COOKERY.] *Ingredients.* Any remains of cold cod, 12 oysters, sufficient melted butter to moisten it ;

Cod Sounds, en Poule

mashed potatoes enough to fill up the dish. *Mode.*—Flake the fish from the bone, and carefully take away all the skin. Lay it in a pie-dish, pour over the melted butter and oysters (or oyster sauce, if there is any left), and cover with mashed potatoes. Bake for ½ an hour, and send to table of a nice brown colour. *Time.*—½ hour. *Seasonable* from November to March.

COD, Salt, commonly called "Salt-fish."

Ingredients.—Sufficient water to cover the fish. *Mode.* — Wash the fish, and lay it all night in water, with a ¼ pint of vinegar. When thoroughly soaked, take it out, see that it is perfectly clean, and put it in the fish-kettle with sufficient cold water to cover it. Heat it gradually, but do not let it boil much, or the fish will be hard. Skim well, and when done, drain the fish, and put it on a napkin garnished with hard-boiled eggs cut in rings. *Time.* — About 1 hour. *Average cost*, 6d. per lb. *Sufficient* for each person, ¼ lb. *Seasonable* in the spring.

Note.—Serve with egg sauce and parsnips. This is an especial dish on Ash Wednesday.

COD SOUNDS

Should be well soaked in salt and water, and thoroughly washed before dressing them. They are considered a great delicacy, and may either be broiled, fried, or boiled ; if they are boiled, mix a little milk with the water.

COD SOUNDS, en Poule.

Ingredients.—For forcemeat, 12 chopped oysters, 3 chopped anchovies, ¼ lb. of bread crumbs, 1 oz. of butter, 2 eggs, seasoning of salt, pepper, nutmeg, and mace to taste ; 4 cod sounds. *Mode.*— Make the forcemeat by mixing the ingredients well together. Wash the sounds, and boil them in milk and water for ½ an hour ; take them out, and let them cool. Cover each with a layer of forcemeat, roll them up in a nice form, and skewer them. Rub over with lard, dredge with flour, and cook them gently before the fire in a Dutch oven. *Time.*—1 hour. *Average cost*, 6d. per lb.

6

COD'S HEAD & SHOULDERS.

Ingredients.—Sufficient water to cover the fish; 5 oz. of salt to each gallon of water. *Mode.* — Cleanse the fish thoroughly, and rub a little salt over the thick part and inside of the fish 1 or 2 hours before dressing it, as this very much improves the flavour. Lay it in the fish-kettle, with sufficient cold water to cover it. Be very particular not to pour the water on the fish, as it is liable to break it, and only keep it just simmering. If the water should boil away, add a little by pouring it in at the side of the kettle, and not on the fish. Add salt in the above proportion, and bring it gradually to a boil. Skim very carefully, draw it to the side of the fire, and let it gently simmer till done. Take it out and drain it; serve on a hot napkin, and garnish with cut lemon and horseradish. *Time.*—According to size, ½ an hour, more or less. *Average cost,* from 3s. to 6s. *Sufficient* for 6 or 8 persons. *Seasonable* from November to March.

Note.—Oyster sauce and plain melted butter should be served with this.

COD'S HEAD & SHOULDERS, to Carve.

First run the knife along the centre of the side of the fish, namely, from *d* to *b*, down to the bone; then carve it in un-

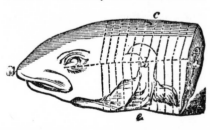

broken slices downwards from *d* to *e*, or upwards from *d* to *c*, as shown in the engraving. The carver should ask the guests if they would like a portion of the roe and liver.

Note.—Of this fish, the parts about the backbone and shoulders are the firmest and most esteemed by connoisseurs. The sound, which lines the fish beneath the backbone, is considered a delicacy, as are also the gelatinous parts about the head and neck.

COFFEE, Essence of.

Ingredients.—To every ¼ lb. of ground coffee allow 1 small teaspoonful of powdered chicory, 3 small teacupfuls, or 1 pint, of water. *Mode.*—Let the coffee be freshly ground, and, if possible, freshly roasted; put it into a percolater, or filter, with the chicory, and pour *slowly* over it the above proportion of boiling water. When it has all filtered through, warm the coffee sufficiently to bring it to the simmering-point, but do not allow it to boil; then filter it a second time, put it into a clean and dry bottle, cork it well, and it will remain good for several days. Two tablespoonfuls of this essence are quite sufficient for a breakfast-cupful of hot milk. This essence will be found particularly useful to those persons who have to rise extremely early; and having only the milk to make boiling, is very easily and quickly prepared. When the essence is bottled, pour another 3 teacupfuls of *boiling* water slowly on the grounds, which, when filtered through, will be a very weak coffee. The next time there is essence to be prepared, make this weak coffee boiling, and pour it on the ground coffee instead of water. *Time.*—To be filtered once, then brought to the boiling point, and filtered again. *Average cost,* with coffee at 1s. 8d. per lb., 6d. *Sufficient.*—Allow 2 tablespoonfuls for a breakfastcupful of hot milk.

Coffee Essence can now be obtained ready for use, thus saving time and trouble. That prepared by Messrs. Thos. Symington, containing only sugar in addition to the soluble constituents of fresh coffee, forms an excellent substitute

COFFEE, Nutritious.

Ingredients.—½ oz. of ground coffee, 1 pint of milk. *Mode.*—Let the coffee be freshly ground; put it into a saucepan with the milk, which should be made nearly boiling before the coffee is put in, and boil together for 3 minutes; clear it by pouring some of it into a cup, and then back again, and leave it on the hob for a few minutes to settle thoroughly. This coffee may be made still more nutritious by the addition of an egg well beaten, and put into the coffee-cup. *Time.*—5 minutes to boil, 5 minutes to settle. *Sufficient* to make 1 large breakfast-cupful of coffee.

COFFEE, Simple Method of Making.

Ingredients.—Allow ½ oz., or 1 tablespoonful, of coffee to each person ; to every oz. allow ½ pint of water. *Mode.* —Have a small iron ring made to fit the top of the coffee-pot inside, and to this ring sew a small muslin bag (the muslin for the purpose must not be too thin). Fit the bag into the pot, warm the pot with some boiling water; throw this away, and put the ground coffee into the bag ; pour over as much boiling water as is required, close the lid, and, when all the water has filtered through, remove the bag, and send the coffee to table. Making it in this manner prevents the necessity of pouring the coffee from one vessel to another, which cools and spoils it. The water should be poured on the coffee gradually, so that the infusion may be stronger ; and the bag must be well made, that none of the grounds may escape through the seams, and so make the coffee thick and muddy. *Sufficient.* —Allow 1 tablespoonful, or ½ oz., to each person.

COFFEE, to Make.

Ingredients.—Allow ½ oz., or 1 tablespoonful, of ground coffee to each person ; to every oz. of coffee allow ½ pint of water. *Mode.*—To make coffee good, *it should never be boiled*, but the boiling water merely poured on it, the same as for tea. The coffee should always be purchased in the berry,— if possible, freshly roasted ; and it should never be ground long before it is wanted for use.

LOYSEL'S HYDROSTATIC URN.

There are very many new kinds of coffee-pots, but the method of making the coffee is nearly always the same, namely,

pouring the boiling water on the powder, and allowing it to filter through. Our illustration shows one of Loysel's Hydrostatic Urns, which are admirably adapted for making good and clear coffee, which should be made in the following manner :—Warm the urn with boiling water, remove the lid and movable filter, and place the ground coffee at the bottom of the urn. Put the movable filter over this, and screw the lid, inverted, tightly on the end of the centre pipe. Pour into the inverted lid the above proportion of boiling water, and when all the water so poured has disappeared from the funnel, and made its way down the centre pipe and up again through the ground coffee by *hydrostatic pressure*, unscrew the lid and cover the urn. Pour back direct into the urn, *not through the funnel*, one, two, or three cups, according to the size of the percolater, in order to make the infusion of uniform strength ; the contents will then be ready for use, and should run from the tap strong, hot, and clear. The coffee made in these urns generally turns out very good, and there is but one objection to them,—the coffee runs rather slowly from the tap ; this is of no consequence where there is a small party, but tedious where there are many persons to provide for. A remedy for this objection may be suggested, namely, to make the coffee very strong, so that not more than ½ cup would be required, as the rest would be filled up with milk. Making coffee in filters or percolaters does away with the necessity of using isinglass, white of egg, and various other preparations, to clear it. Coffee should always be served very hot, and, if possible, in the same vessel in which it is made, as pouring it from one pot to another cools, and consequently spoils it. Many persons may think that the proportion of water we have given for each oz. of coffee is rather small ; it is so, and the coffee produced from it will be very strong ; ½ of a cup will be found quite sufficient, which should be filled with nice hot milk, or milk and cream mixed. This is the *café au lait* for which our neighbours over the Channel are so justly celebrated. Should the ordinary method of making coffee be preferred, use double the quantity of water, and, in pouring it into the cups, put in more coffee and less milk. *Sufficient.*— For very good coffee, allow ½ oz., or 1 tablespoonful, to each person.

COFFEE, to Roast. (A French Recipe.)

It being an acknowledged fact that French coffee is decidedly superior to that made in England, and as the roasting of the berry is of great importance to the flavour of the preparation, it will be useful and interesting to know how they manage these things in France. In Paris, there are two houses justly celebrated for the flavour of their coffee,— *La Maison Corcellet* and *La Maison Royer de Chartres;* and to obtain this flavour, before roasting, they add to every 3 lbs. of coffee a piece of butter the size of a nut, and a dessertspoonful of powdered sugar: it is then roasted in the usual manner. The addition of the butter and sugar develops the flavour and aroma of the berry; but it must be borne in mind, that the quality of the butter must be of the very best description.

COLLOPS, Scotch.

[COLD MEAT COOKERY.] *Ingredients.* —The remains of cold roast veal, a little butter, flour, ½ pint of water, 1 onion, 1 blade of pounded mace, 1 tablespoonful of lemon-juice, ½ teaspoonful of finely-minced lemon-peel, 2 tablespoonfuls of sherry, 1 tablespoonful of mushroom ketchup. *Mode.*—Cut the veal the same thickness as for cutlets, rather larger than a crown piece; flour the meat well, and fry a light brown in butter; dredge again with flour, and add ½ pint of water, pouring it in by degrees; set it on the fire, and when it boils, add the onion and mace, and let it simmer very gently about ¾ hour; flavour the gravy with lemon-juice, peel, wine, and ketchup, in the above proportion; give one boil, and serve. *Time.*—¾ hour. *Seasonable* from March to October.

COLLOPS, Scotch, White.

[COLD MEAT COOKERY.] *Ingredients.* The remains of cold roast veal, ½ teaspoonful of grated nutmeg, 2 blades of pounded mace, cayenne and salt to taste, a little butter, 1 dessertspoonful of flour, ¼ pint of water, 1 teaspoonful of anchovy sauce, 1 tablespoonful of lemon-juice, ¼ teaspoonful of lemon-peel, 1 tablespoonful of mushroom ketchup, 3 tablespoonfuls of cream, 1 tablespoonful of sherry. *Mode.*—Cut the veal into thin slices about 3 inches in width; hack them

with a knife, and grate on them the nutmeg, mace, cayenne, and salt, and fry them in a little butter. Dish them, and make a gravy in the pan by putting in the remaining ingredients. Give one boil, and pour it over the collops; garnish with lemon and slices of toasted bacon, rolled. Forcemeat balls may be added to this dish. If cream is not at hand, substitute the yolk of an egg beaten up well with a little milk. *Time.*—About 5 or 7 minutes. *Seasonable* from May to October.

COMPOTE,

A confiture made at the moment of need, and with much less sugar than would be ordinarily put to preserves. They are very wholesome things, suitable to most stomachs which cannot accommodate themselves to raw fruit or a large portion of sugar: they are the happy medium, and far better than ordinary stewed fruit. For Fruit Compôtes refer to the recipes relating to the various Fruits.

CONFECTIONARY.

In speaking of confectionary, it should be remarked that many preparations come under that head; for the various fruits, flowers, herbs, roots, and juices, which, when boiled with sugar, were formerly employed in pharmacy as well as for sweetmeats, were called *confections,* from the Latin word *conficere,* 'to make up;' but the term confectionary embraces a very large class indeed of sweet food, many kinds of which should not be attempted in the ordinary cuisine. The thousand and one ornamental dishes that adorn the tables of the wealthy should be purchased from the confectioner: they cannot profitably be made at home. Apart from these, cakes, biscuits, and tarts, &c., the class of sweetmeats called confections may be thus classified:— 1. Liquid confects, or fruits either whole or in pieces, preserved by being immersed in a fluid transparent syrup; as the liquid confects of apricots, green citrons, and many foreign fruits. 2. Dry confects are those which, after having been boiled in the syrup, are taken out and put to dry in an oven, as citron and orange-peel, &c. 3. Marmalade, jams, and pastes, a kind of soft compounds made of the pulp of fruits or other vegetable substances, beat up with sugar or

Cow-Heel, Fried

honey; such as oranges, apricots, pears, &c. **4.** Jellies are the juices of fruits boiled with sugar to a pretty thick consistency, so as, upon cooling, to form a trembling jelly; as currant, gooseberry, apple jelly, &c. **5.** Conserves are a kind of dry confects, made by beating up flowers, fruits, &c., with sugar, not dissolved. **6.** Candies are fruits candied over with sugar after having been boiled in the syrup.

COW-HEEL, Fried.

Ingredients. — Ox-feet, the yolk of 1 egg, bread crumbs, parsley, salt and cayenne to taste, boiling butter. *Mode.* —Wash, scald, and thoroughly clean the feet, and cut them into pieces about 2 inches long; have ready some fine bread crumbs mixed with a little minced parsley, cayenne, and salt; dip the pieces of heel into the yolk of egg, sprinkle them with the bread crumbs, and fry them until of a nice brown in boiling butter. *Time.*—¼ hour. *Average cost, 6d.* each. *Seasonable* at any time.

Note.—Ox-feet may be dressed in various ways, stewed in gravy or plainly boiled and served with melted butter. When plainly boiled, the liquor will answer for making sweet or relishing jellies, and also to give richness to soups or gravies.

COW-HEEL STOCK, for Jellies (More Economical than Calf's-Feet).

Ingredients.—2 cow-heels, 3 quarts of water. *Mode.* — Procure 2 heels that have only been scalded, and not boiled; split them in two, and remove the fat between the claws; wash them well in warm water, and put them into a saucepan with the above proportion of cold water; bring it gradually to boil, remove all the scum as it rises, and simmer the heels gently from 7 to 8 hours, or until the liquor is reduced one-half; then strain it into a basin, measuring the quantity, and put it in a cool place. Clarify it in the same manner as calf's-feet stock, using, with the other ingredients, about ½ oz. of isinglass to each quart. This stock should be made the day before it is required for use. Two dozen shank-bones of mutton, boiled for 6 or 7 hours, yield a quart of strong firm stock. They should be put on in 2 quarts of water, which should be reduced one-half. Make

Crab, Hot

this also the day before it is required. *Time.*—7 to 8 hours to boil the cow-heels, 6 to 7 hours to boil the shank-bones. *Average cost,* from 4d. to 6d. each. *Sufficient.*—2 cow-heels should make 3 pints of stock. *Seasonable* at any time.

COWSLIP WINE.

Ingredients.—To every gallon of water allow 3 lbs. of lump sugar, the rind of 2 lemons, the juice of 1, the rind and juice of 1 Seville orange, 1 gallon of cowslip pips. To every 4½ gallons of wine allow 1 bottle of brandy. *Mode.*—Boil the sugar and water together for ½ hour, carefully removing all the scum as it rises. Pour this boiling liquor on the orange and lemon-rinds and the juice, which should be strained; when milk-warm, add the cowslip pips or flowers, picked from the stalks and seeds; and to 9 gallons of wine 3 tablespoonfuls of good fresh brewers' yeast. Let it ferment 3 or 4 days, then put all together in a cask with the brandy, and let it remain for 2 months, when bottle it off for use. *Time.*—To be boiled ½ hour; to ferment 3 or 4 days; to remain in the cask 2 months. *Average cost,* exclusive of the cowslips, which may be picked in the fields, 2s. 9d. per gallon. *Seasonable.* Make this in April or May.

CRAB, to Choose.

The middle-sized crab is the best; and the crab, like the lobster, should be judged by its weight; for if light, it is watery.

CRAB, to Dress.

Ingredients.—1 crab, 2 tablespoonfuls of vinegar, 1 ditto of oil; salt, white pepper, and cayenne, to taste. *Mode.*—Empty the shells, and thoroughly mix the meat with the above ingredients, and put it in the large shell. Garnish with slices of cut lemon and parsley. The quantity of oil may be increased when it is much liked. *Average cost,* from 10d. to 2s. *Seasonable* all the year; but not so good in May, June, and July. *Sufficient* for 3 persons.

CRAB, Hot.

Ingredients.—1 crab, nutmeg, salt and pepper to taste, 3 oz. of butter, ¼ lb. of bread crumbs, 3 tablespoonfuls of vinegar. *Mode.* — After having boiled the

Crab Sauce

crab, pick the meat out from the shells, and mix with it the nutmeg and seasoning. Cut up the butter in small pieces, and add the bread crumbs and vinegar. Mix altogether, put the whole in the large shell, and brown before the fire or with a salamander. *Time.*—1 hour. *Average cost,* from 10*d.* to 2*s.* *Sufficient* for 3 persons. *Seasonable* all the year; but not so good in May, June, and July.

CRAB SAUCE, for Fish (equal to Lobster Sauce).

Ingredients.—1 crab; salt, pounded mace, and cayenne to taste; ½ pint of melted butter made with milk. *Mode.*—Choose a nice fresh crab, pick all the meat away from the shell, and cut it into small square pieces. Make ½ pint of melted butter, put in the fish and seasoning; let it gradually warm through, and simmer for 2 minutes: it should not boil. *Average cost,* 1*s.* 2*d.*

CRAYFISH.

Crayfish should be thrown into boiling water, to which has been added a good seasoning of salt and a little vinegar. When done, which will be in ¼ hour, take them out and drain them. Let them cool, arrange them on a napkin, and garnish with plenty of double parsley.

Note.—This fish is frequently used for garnishing boiled turkey, boiled fowl, calf's head, turbot, and all kinds of boiled fish.

CRAYFISH, Potted.

Ingredients.—100 crayfish; pounded mace, pepper, and salt to taste; 2 oz. butter. *Mode.*—Boil the fish in salt and water. pick out all the meat, and pound it in a mortar to a paste. Whilst pounding, add the butter gradually, and mix in the spice and seasoning. Put it in small pots, and pour over it clarified butter, carefully excluding the air. *Time.*—15 minutes to boil the crayfish. *Average cost,* 2*s.* 9*d.* *Seasonable* all the year.

CRAYFISH SOUP.

Ingredients.—50 crayfish, ¼ lb. of butter, 6 anchovies, the crumb of 1 French roll, a little lobster-spawn, seasoning to taste, 2 quarts of medium stock, or fish stock. *Mode.* —Shell the crayfish, and put the fish between two plates until they

Cream, Devonshire

are wanted; pound the shells in a mortar with the butter and anchovies; when well beaten, add a pint of stock, and simmer for ¾ of an hour. Strain it through a hair sieve, put the remainder of the stock to it, with the crumb of the roll; give it one boil, and rub it through a tammy, with the lobster-spawn. Put in the fish, but do not let the soup boil after it has been rubbed through the tammy. If necessary, add seasoning. *Time.*—1½ hour. *Average cost,* 2*s.* 3*d.* or 1*s.* 9*d.* per quart. *Sufficient* for 8 persons. *Seasonable* from January to July.

CREAM à la VALOIS.

Ingredients. — 4 sponge cakes, jam, ¾ pint of cream, sugar to taste, the juice of ½ lemon, ¼ glass of sherry, 1¼ oz. of isinglass. *Mode.*—Cut the sponge-cakes into thin slices, place two together with preserve between them, and pour over them a small quantity of sherry mixed with a little brandy. Sweeten and flavour the cream with the lemon-juice and sherry; add the isinglass, which should be dissolved in a little water, and beat up the cream well. Place a little in an oiled mould; arrange the pieces of cake in the cream, then fill the mould with the remainder, let it cool, and turn it out on a dish. By oiling the mould the cream will have a much smoother appearance, and will turn out more easily than when merely dipped in cold water. *Average cost,* 3*s.* 6*d.* *Sufficient* to fill a 1½ pint mould. *Seasonable* at any time.

CREAM CHEESE.

Cream cheese should be served on a d'oyley, and garnished either with water-cresses or parsley; of the former, a plentiful supply should be given, as they add greatly to the appearance of the dish, besides improving the flavour of the cheese.

CREAM, Devonshire.

The milk should stand 24 hours in the winter, half that time when the weather is very warm. The milkpan is then set on a stove, and should there remain until the milk is quite hot; but it must not boil, or there will be a thick skin on the surface. When it is sufficiently done the undulations on the surface look thick, and small rings appear. The time required for scalding cream depends on

Cream, Italian

the size of the pan and the heat of the fire, but the slower it is done the better. The pan should be placed in the dairy when the cream is sufficiently scalded, and skimmed the following day. This cream is so much esteemed that it is sent to the London markets in small square tins, and is exceedingly delicious eaten with fresh fruit. In Devonshire, butter is made from this cream, and is usually very firm.

CREAM, Italian.

Ingredients.—½ pint of milk, ½ pint of cream, sugar to taste, 1 oz. of isinglass, 1 lemon, the yolks of 4 eggs. *Mode.*— Put the cream and milk into a saucepan, with sugar to sweeten, and the lemon-rind. Boil until the milk is well flavoured, then strain it into a basin and add the beaten yolks of eggs. Put this mixture into a jug, place the jug in a saucepan of boiling water over the fire, and stir the contents until they thicken, but do not allow them to boil. Take the cream off the fire, stir in the lemon-juice and isinglass, which should be melted, and whip well; fill a mould, place it in ice if at hand, and, when set, turn it out on a dish, and garnish as taste may dictate. The mixture may be whipped and drained, and then put into small glasses, when this mode of serving is preferred. *Time.*—From 5 to 8 minutes to stir the mixture in the jug. *Average cost,* with the best isinglass, 2*s.* 6*d.* *Sufficient* to fill 1½ pint mould. *Seasonable* at any time.

CREAM SAUCE, for Fish or White Dishes.

Ingredients.—⅓ pint of cream, 2 oz. of butter, 1 teaspoonful of flour, salt and cayenne to taste; when liked, a small quantity of pounded mace or lemon-juice. *Mode.*—Put the butter in a very clean saucepan, dredge in the flour, and keep shaking round till the butter is melted. Add the seasoning and cream, and stir the whole till it boils; let it just simmer for 5 minutes, when add either pounded mace or lemon-juice to taste to give it a flavour. *Time.*—5 minutes to simmer. *Average cost* for this quantity, 7*d.* *Note.*—This sauce may be flavoured with very finely-shredded shalot.

CREAM, Stone, of tous les Mois.

Ingredients.—½ lb. of preserve, 1 pint

Cream, Vanilla

of milk, 2 oz. of lump sugar, 1 heaped tablespoonful of tous les mois, 3 drops of essence of cloves, 3 drops of almond-flavouring. *Mode.*—Place the preserve at the bottom of a glass dish; put the milk into a lined saucepan, with the sugar, and make it boil. Mix to a smooth batter the tous les mois with a very little cold milk; stir it briskly into the boiling milk, add the flavouring, and simmer for 2 minutes. When rather cool, but before turning solid, pour the cream over the jam, and ornament it with strips of red-currant jelly or preserved fruit. *Time.* —2 minutes. *Average cost,* 10*d.* *Sufficient* for 4 or 5 persons. *Seasonable* at any time.

CREAM, Swiss.

Ingredients.—¼ lb. of macaroons or 6 small sponge-cakes, sherry, 1 pint of cream, 5 oz. of lump sugar, 2 large tablespoonfuls of arrowroot, the rind of 1 lemon, the juice of ½ lemon, 3 tablespoonfuls of milk. *Mode.*—Lay the macaroons or sponge-cakes in a glass dish, and pour over them as much sherry as will cover them, or sufficient to soak them well. Put the cream into a lined saucepan, with the sugar and lemon-rind, and let it remain by the side of the fire until the cream is well flavoured, when take out the lemon-rind. Mix the arrowroot smoothly with the cold milk; add this to the cream, and let it boil gently for about 3 minutes, keeping it well stirred. Take it off the fire, stir till nearly cold, when add the lemon-juice, and pour the whole over the cakes. Garnish the cream with strips of angelica, or candied citron cut thin, or bright-coloured jelly or preserve. This cream is exceedingly delicious, flavoured with vanilla instead of lemon: when this flavouring is used the sherry may be omitted, and the mixture poured over the dry cakes. *Time.*—About ½ hour to infuse the lemon-rind; 5 minutes to boil the cream. *Average cost,* with cream at 1*s.* per pint, 3*s.* *Sufficient* for 5 or 6 persons. *Seasonable* at any time.

CREAM, Vanilla.

Ingredients.—1 pint of milk, the yolks of 8 eggs, 6 oz. of sugar, 1 oz. of isinglass, flavouring to taste of essence of vanilla. *Mode.*—Put the milk and sugar into a saucepan, and let it get hot over a slow fire; beat up the yolks of the eggs, to which add gradually the sweetened milk;

Cream, Whipped

flavour the whole with essence of vanilla, put the mixture into a jug, and place this jug in a saucepan of boiling water. Stir the contents with a wooden spoon one way until the mixture thickens, but do

not allow it to boil, or it will be full of lumps. Take it off the fire; stir in the isinglass, which should be previously dissolved

VANILLA-CREAM MOULD.

in about ¼ pint of water, and boiled for 2 or 3 minutes; pour the cream into an oiled mould, put it in a cool place to set, and turn it out carefully on a dish. Instead of using the essence of vanilla, a pod may be boiled in the milk until the flavour is well extracted. A pod, or a pod and a half, will be found sufficient for the above proportion of ingredients. *Time.*—About 10 minutes to stir the mixture. *Average cost*, with the best isinglass, 2s. 6d. *Sufficient* to fill a quart mould. *Seasonable* at any time.

CREAM, Whipped, for putting on Trifles, serving in Glasses, &c.

Ingredients.—To every pint of cream allow 3 oz. of pounded sugar, 1 glass of sherry or any kind of sweet white wine, the rind of ½ lemon, the white of 1 egg. *Mode.*—Rub the sugar on the lemon-rind, and pound it in a mortar until quite fine, and beat up the white of the egg until quite stiff; put the cream into a large bowl, with the sugar, wine, and beaten egg, and whip it to a froth; as fast as the froth rises take it off with a

PASTRY-LEAF.

skimmer, and put it on a sieve to drain in a cool place. This should be made the day before it is wanted, as the whip is then so much firmer. The cream should be whipped in a cool place, and in sum-

Crust, Common

mer over ice, if it is obtainable. A plain whipped cream may be served on a glass dish, and garnished with strips of angelica, or pastry-leaves, or pieces of bright-coloured jelly: it makes a very pretty addition to the supper-table. *Time.*—About 1 hour to whip the cream. *Average cost*, with cream at 1s. per pint, 1s. 9d. *Sufficient* for 1 dish or 1 trifle. *Seasonable* at any time.

CRUMPETS.

These are made in the same manner as muffins, only, in making the mixture, let it be more like batter than dough. Let it rise for about ½ hour; pour it into iron rings, which should be ready on a hot-plate; bake them, and when one side appears done, turn them quickly on the other. *To toast them,* have ready a very *bright clear* fire; put the crumpet on a toasting-fork, and hold it before the fire, *not too close*, until it is nicely brown on one side, but do not allow it to blacken; turn it, and brown the other side; then spread it with good butter, cut it in half, and, when all are done, pile them on a hot dish, and send them quickly to table. Muffins and crumpets should always be served on separate dishes, and both toasted and served as expeditiously as possible. *Time.*—From 10 to 15 minutes to bake them. *Sufficient.*—Allow 2 crumpets to each person.

CRUST, Butter, for Boiled Puddings.

Ingredients.—To every lb. of flour allow 6 oz. of butter, ½ pint of water. *Mode.*—With a knife, work the flour to a smooth paste with ½ pint of water; roll the crust out rather thin; place the butter over it in small pieces, dredge lightly over it some flour, and fold the paste over; repeat the rolling once more, and the crust will be ready for use. It may be enriched by adding another 2 oz. of butter; but, for ordinary purposes, the above quantity will be found quite sufficient. *Average cost*, 6d. per lb.

CRUST, Common, for Raised Pies.

Ingredients.—To every lb. of flour allow ½ pint of water, 1½ oz. of butter, 1½ oz. of lard, ½ saltspoonful of salt. *Mode.*—Put into a saucepan the water, when it boils, add the butter and lard, and when these are melted, make a hole

Crust, Dripping

in the middle of the flour; pour in the water gradually, beat it well with a wooden spoon, and be particular in not making the paste too soft. When it is well mixed, knead it with the hands until quite stiff, dredging a little flour over the paste and board to prevent them from sticking. When it is well kneaded, place it before the fire, with a cloth covered over it, for a few minutes; it will then be more easily worked into shape. This paste does not taste so nicely as a richer one, but it is worked with greater facility, and answers just as well for raised pies, for the crust is seldom eaten. *Average cost, 5d. per lb.*

CRUST, Dripping, for Kitchen Puddings, Pies, &c.

Ingredients.—To every lb. of flour allow 6 oz. of clarified beef dripping, ½ pint of water. *Mode.*—After having clarified the dripping, weigh it, and to every lb. of flour allow the above proportion of dripping. With a knife, work the flour into a smooth paste with the water, rolling it out three times, each time placing on the crust 2 oz. of the dripping broken into small pieces. If this paste is lightly made, if good dripping is used, and *not too much of it*, it will be found good; and by the addition of two tablespoonfuls of fine moist sugar, it may be converted into a common short crust for fruit pies. *Average cost, 4d. per lb.*

CRUST, Lard or Flead.

Ingredients.—To every lb. of flour allow ½ lb. of lard or flead, ½ pint of water, ¼ saltspoonful of salt. *Mode.*—Clear the flead from skin, and slice it into thin flakes; rub it into the flour, add the salt, and work the whole into a smooth paste, with the above proportion of water; fold the paste over two or three times, beat it well with the rolling-pin, roll it out, and it will be ready for use. The crust made from this will be found extremely light, and may be made into cakes or tarts; it may also be very much enriched by adding more flead to the same proportion of flour. *Average cost, 8d. per lb.*

CRUST, Suet, for Pies or Puddings.

Ingredients.—To every lb. of flour allow 5 or 6 oz. of beef suet, ½ pint of water. *Mode.* —Free the suet from skin and

Crust, good Short

shreds, chop it extremely fine, and rub it well into the flour; work the whole to a smooth paste with the above proportion of water; roll it out, and it is ready for use. This crust is quite rich enough for ordinary purposes, but when a better one is desired, use from ½ to ¾ lb. of suet to every lb. of flour. Some cooks, for rich crusts, pound the suet in a mortar, with a small quantity of butter. It should then be laid on the paste in small pieces, the same as for puff-crust, and will be found exceedingly nice for hot tarts. 5 oz. of suet to every lb. of flour will make a very good crust; and even ¼ lb. will answer very well for children, or where the crust is wanted very plain. *Average cost, 5d. per lb.*

CRUST, Common Short.

Ingredients.—To every lb. of flour allow 2 oz. of sifted sugar, 3 oz. of butter, about ½ pint of boiling milk. *Mode.*— Crumble the butter into the flour as finely as possible, add the sugar, and work the whole up to a smooth paste with the boiling milk. Roll it out thin, and bake in a moderate oven. *Average cost, 6d. per lb.*

CRUST, Very good Short for Fruit Tarts.

Ingredients.—To every lb. of flour allow ½ or ¾ lb. of butter, 1 tablespoonful of sifted sugar, ½ pint of water. *Mode.*— Rub the butter into the flour, after having ascertained that the latter is perfectly dry; add the sugar, and mix the whole into a stiff paste with about ½ pint of water. Roll it out two or three times, folding the paste over each time, and it will be ready for use. *Average cost, 1s. 1d. per lb.*

CRUST, Another good Short.

Ingredients.—To every lb. of flour allow 8 oz. of butter, the yolks of 2 eggs, 2 oz. of sifted sugar, about ¼ pint of milk. *Mode.*—Rub the butter into the flour, add the sugar, and mix the whole as lightly as possible to a smooth paste, with the yolks of the eggs well beaten, and the milk. The proportion of the latter ingredient must be judged of by the size of the eggs; if these are large so much will not be required, and more if the eggs are smaller. *Average cost, 1s. per lb.*

Cucumber Sauce | Cucumbers, to Dress

CUCUMBER SAUCE.

Ingredients.—3 or 4 cucumbers, 2 oz. of butter, 6 tablespoonfuls of brown gravy. *Mode.* — Peel the cucumbers, quarter them, and take out the seeds; cut them into small pieces, put them in a cloth, and rub them well to take out the water that hangs about them. Put the butter in a saucepan, add the cucumbers, and shake them over a sharp fire until they are of a good colour; then pour over them the gravy, mixed with the cucumbers, and simmer gently for 10 minutes, when it will be ready to serve. *Time.*—Altogether, ½ hour.

CUCUMBER SAUCE, White.

Ingredients.—3 or 4 cucumbers, ½ pint of white stock, cayenne and salt to taste, the yolks of 3 eggs. *Mode.*—Cut the cucumbers into small pieces, after peeling them and taking out the seeds. Put them in the stewpan with the white stock and seasoning; simmer gently till the cucumbers are tender, which will be in about ¼ hour. Then add the yolks of the eggs, well beaten; stir them to the sauce, but do not allow it to boil, and serve very hot. *Time.*—Altogether, ½ hour.

CUCUMBER SOUP (French Recipe).

Ingredients.—1 large cucumber, a piece of butter the size of a walnut, a little chervil and sorrel cut in large pieces, salt and pepper to taste, the yolks of 2 eggs, 1 gill of cream, 1 quart of medium stock. *Mode.*—Pare the cucumber, quarter it, and take out the seeds; cut it in thin slices, put these on a plate with a little salt, to draw the water from them; drain, and put them in your stewpan with the butter. When they are warmed through, without being browned, pour the stock on them. Add the sorrel, chervil, and seasoning, and boil for 40 minutes. Mix the well-beaten yolks of the eggs with the cream, which add at the moment of serving. *Time.* — 1 hour. *Average cost*, 1s. 2d. per quart. *Sufficient* for 4 persons. *Seasonable* from June to September.

CUCUMBER VINEGAR (a very nice addition to Salads).

Ingredients.—10 large cucumbers, or 12 smaller ones. 1 quart of vinegar, 2

onions, 2 shalots, 1 tablespoonful of salt, 2 tablespoonfuls of pepper, ¼ teaspoonful of cayenne. *Mode.*—Pare and slice the cucumbers, put them in a stone jar or wide-mouthed bottle with the vinegar; slice the onions and shalots, and add them, with all the other ingredients, to the cucumbers. Let it stand 4 or 5 days, boil it all up, and, when cold, strain the liquor through a piece of muslin, and store it away in small bottles well sealed. This vinegar is a very nice addition to gravies, hashes, &c., as well as a great improvement to salads, or to eat with cold meat.

CUCUMBERS, to Dress.

Ingredients.—3 tablespoonfuls of salad-oil, 4 tablespoonfuls of vinegar, salt and pepper to taste. *Mode.*—Pare the cucumber, cut it equally into *very thin*

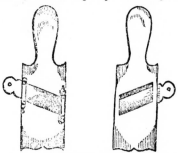

CUCUMBER-SLICES.

slices, and *commence* cutting from the *thick end;* if commenced at the stalk, the cucumber will most likely have an exceedingly bitter taste, far from agreeable. For the purpose of slicing cucumbers evenly and very thin, we recommend the slice in preference to an ordinary knife. Put the slices into a dish, sprinkle over salt and pepper, and pour over oil and vinegar in the above proportion; turn the cucumber about, and it is ready to serve. This is a favourite accompaniment to boiled salmon, is a nice addition to all descriptions of salads, and makes a pretty garnish to lobster salad. *Average cost*, when scarce, 1s. to 2s. 6d.; when cheapest, may be had for 1d. each. *Seasonable.*—Forced from the beginning of March to the end of June; in full season in July, August, and September.

SLICED CUCUMBERS.

CUCUMBERS, Fried.

Ingredients.—2 or 3 cucumbers, pepper and salt to taste, flour, oil or butter. *Mode.*—Pare the cucumbers, and cut them into slices of an equal thickness, commencing to slice from the thick and not the stalk end of the cucumber. Wipe the slices dry with a cloth, dredge them with flour, and put them into a pan of boiling oil or butter ; keep turning them about until brown ; lift them out of the pan, let them drain, and serve, piled lightly in a dish. These will be found a great improvement to rump-steak : they should be placed on a dish with the steak on the top. *Time.*—5 minutes. *Average cost*, when cheapest, 1*d.* each. *Sufficient* for 4 or 5 persons. *Seasonable.*—Forced from the beginning of March to the end of June ; in full season in July and August.

CUCUMBERS à la Poulette.

Ingredients.—2 or 3 cucumbers, salt and vinegar, 2 oz. of butter, flour, ½ pint of broth, 1 teaspoonful of minced parsley, a lump of sugar, the yolks of 2 eggs, salt and pepper to taste. *Mode.*—Pare and cut the cucumbers into slices of an equal thickness, and let them remain in a pickle of salt and vinegar for ½ hour, then drain them in a cloth, and put them into a stewpan with the butter. Fry them over a brisk fire, but do not brown them, and then dredge over them a little flour ; add the broth, skim off all the fat, which will rise to the surface, and boil gently until the gravy is somewhat reduced, but the cucumber should not be broken. Stir in the yolks of the eggs, add the parsley, sugar, and a seasoning of pepper and salt ; bring the whole to the *point of boiling*, and serve. *Time.*—Altogether, 1 hour. *Average cost*, when cheapest, 1*d.* each. *Sufficient* for 5 or 6 persons. *Seasonable* in July, August, or September ; but may be had, forced, from the beginning of March.

CUCUMBERS, Pickled.

Ingredients.—1 oz. of whole pepper, 1 oz. of bruised ginger, sufficient vinegar to cover the cucumbers. *Mode.*—Cut the cucumbers in thick slices, sprinkle salt over them, and let them remain for 24 hours. The next day, drain them well for 6 hours, put them into a jar, pour boiling vinegar over them, and keep them

in a warm place. In a short time, boil up the vinegar again, add pepper and ginger in the above proportion, and instantly cover them up. Tie them down with bladder, and in a few days they will be fit for use.

CUCUMBERS, an excellent way of Preserving.

Ingredients.—Salt and water, 1 lb. of lump sugar, the rind of 1 lemon, 1 oz. of ginger, cucumbers. *Mode.*—Choose the greenest cucumbers, and those that are most free from seeds ; put them in strong salt and water, with a cabbage-leaf to keep them down ; tie a paper over them, and put them in a warm place till they are yellow, then wash them and set them over the fire in fresh water with a very little salt, and another cabbage-leaf over them ; cover very closely, but take care they do not boil. If they are not a fine green, change the water again, cover them as before, and make them hot. When they are a good colour take them off the fire and let them cool ; cut them in quarters, take out the seeds and pulp, and put them into cold water ; let them remain for 2 days, changing the water twice each day, to draw out the salt. Put the sugar, with ½ pint of water, in a saucepan over the fire ; remove the scum as it rises, and add the lemon-peel and ginger with the outside scraped off ; when the syrup is tolerably thick, take it off the fire, and when *cold*, wipe the cucumbers *dry* and put them in. Boil the syrup once in 2 or 3 days for 3 weeks ; strengthen it if required, and let it be quite cold before the cucumbers are put in. Great attention must be paid to the directions in the commencement of this recipe, as, if these are not properly carried out, the result will be far from satisfactory. *Seasonable.*—This recipe should be used in June, July, or August.

CUCUMBERS, German Method of keeping for Winter use.

Ingredients.—Cucumbers, salt. *Mode.*—Pare and slice the cucumbers (as for the table), sprinkle well with salt, and let them remain for 24 hours ; strain off the liquor, pack in jars, a thick layer of cucumbers and salt alternately ; tie down closely, and, when wanted for use, take out the quantity required. Now wash them well in fresh water, and

Cucumbers, Stewed

dress as usual with pepper, vinegar, and oil.

CUCUMBERS, Stewed.

Ingredients.—3 large cucumbers, flour, butter, rather more than ½ pint of good brown gravy. *Mode.*—Cut the cucumbers lengthwise the size of the dish they are intended to be served in; empty them of the seeds, and put them into boiling water with a little salt, and let them simmer for 5 minutes; then take them out, place them in another stewpan, with the gravy, and let them boil over a brisk fire until the cucumbers are tender. Should these be bitter, add a lump of sugar; carefully dish them, skim the sauce, pour over the cucumbers, and serve. *Time.*—Altogether, 20 minutes. *Average cost*, when cheapest, 1*d.* each. *Sufficient* for 3 or 4 persons. *Seasonable* in June, July, and August; but may be had, forced, from the beginning of March.

CUCUMBERS, Stewed with Onions

Ingredients.—6 cucumbers, 3 moderate-sized onions, not quite 1 pint of white stock, cayenne and salt to taste, the yolks of 2 eggs, a very little grated nutmeg. *Mode.*—Pare and slice the cucumbers, take out the seeds, and cut the onions into thin slices; put these both into a stewpan, with the stock, and let them boil for ¼ hour or longer, should the cucumbers be very large. Beat up the yolks of 2 eggs; stir these into the sauce; add the cayenne, salt, and grated nutmeg; bring it to the point of boiling, and serve. Do not allow the sauce to boil, or it will curdle. This is a favourite dish with lamb or mutton chops, rump-steaks, &c. *Time.*—Altogether, 20 minutes. *Average cost*, when cheapest, 1*d.* each. *Sufficient* for 6 or 7 persons. *Seasonable* in July, August, and September; but may be had, forced, from the beginning of March.

CURRANT DUMPLINGS.

Ingredients.—1 lb. of flour, 6 oz. of suet, ½ lb. of currants, rather more than ½ pint of water. *Mode.*—Chop the suet finely, mix it with the flour, and add the currants, which should be nicely washed, picked, and dried; mix the whole to a limp paste with the water (if wanted very nice, use milk); divide it into 7 or 8 dumplings: tie them in cloths, and

Currant Jam, Black.

boil for 1¼ hour. They may be boiled without a cloth: they should then be made into round balls, and dropped into boiling water, and should be moved about at first, to prevent them from sticking to the bottom of the saucepan. Serve with a cut lemon, cold butter, and sifted sugar. *Time.*—In a cloth, 1¼ hour; without, ¾ hour. *Average cost*, 9*d.* *Sufficient* for 6 or 7 persons. *Seasonable* at any time.

CURRANT FRITTERS.

Ingredients.—½ pint of milk, 2 tablespoonfuls of flour, 4 eggs, 3 tablespoonfuls of boiled rice, 3 tablespoonfuls of currants, sugar to taste, a very little grated nutmeg, hot lard or clarified dripping. *Mode.*—Put the milk into a basin with the flour, which should previously be rubbed to a smooth batter with a little cold milk; stir these ingredients together; add the well-whisked eggs, the rice, currants, sugar, and nutmeg. Beat the mixture for a few minutes, and, if not sufficiently thick, add a little more boiled rice; drop it, in small quantities, into a pan of boiling lard or clarified dripping; fry the fritters a nice brown, and, when done, drain them on a piece of blotting-paper, before the fire. Pile them on a white d'oyley, strew over sifted sugar, and serve them very hot. Send a cut lemon to table with them. *Time.*—From 8 to 10 minutes to fry the fritters. *Average cost*, 9*d.* *Sufficient* for 3 or 4 persons. *Seasonable* at any time.

CURRANT JAM, Black.

Ingredients.—To every lb. of fruit, weighed before being stripped from the stalks, allow ¾ lb. of loaf sugar, 1 gill of water. *Mode.*—Let the fruit be very ripe, and gathered on a dry day. Strip it from the stalks, and put it into a preserving-pan, with a gill of water to each lb. of fruit; boil these together for 10 minutes; then add the sugar, and boil the jam again for 30 minutes, reckoning from the time when the jam simmers equally all over, or longer, should it not appear to set nicely when a little is poured on to a plate. Keep stirring it to prevent it from burning, carefully remove all the scum, and, when done, pour it into pots. Let it cool, cover the top of the jam with oiled paper, and the top of the jars with a piece of tissue paper brushed over on both sides with

Currant Jam, Red

the white of an egg : this, when cold, forms a hard stiff cover, and perfectly excludes the air. Great attention must be paid to the stirring of this jam, as it is very liable to burn, on account of the thickness of the juice. *Time.*—10 minutes to boil the fruit and water ; 30 minutes with the sugar, or longer. *Average cost*, from 6*d.* to 8*d.* for a pot capable of holding 1 lb. *Sufficient.*— Allow from 6 to 7 quarts of currants to make 1 dozen pots of jam, each pot to hold 1 lb. *Seasonable.*—Make this in July.

CURRANT JAM, Red.

Ingredients.—To every lb. of fruit allow ¾ lb. of loaf sugar. *Mode.*—Let the fruit be gathered on a fine day ; weigh it, and then strip the currants from the stalks ; put them into a preserving-pan with sugar in the above proportion ; stir them, and boil them for about ¾ hour. Carefully remove the scum as it rises. Put the jam into pots, and, when cold, cover with oiled papers ; over these put a piece of tissue-paper brushed over on

JAM-POT.

both sides with the white of an egg ; press the paper round the top of the pot, and, when dry, the covering will be quite hard and air-tight. *Time.*—½ to ¾ hour, reckoning from the time the jam boils all over. *Average cost*, for a lb. pot, from 6*d.* to 8*d.* *Sufficient.*—Allow from 6 to 7 quarts of currants to make 12 1-lb. pots of jam. *Seasonable.*—Make this in July.

CURRANT JELLY, Black.

Ingredients. — Black currants ; to every pint of juice allow ¼ pint of water, 1 lb of loaf sugar. *Mode.*—Strip the currants from the stalks, which may be done in an expeditious manner, by holding the bunch in one hand, and passing a small silver fork down the currants : they will then readily fall from the stalks. Put them into a jar, place this jar in a saucepan of boiling water, and simmer them until their juice is extracted; then strain them, and to every pint of juice allow the above proportion of sugar and water ; stir these ingredients together cold until the sugar is dissolved ; place the pre-

Currant Jelly, Red

serving-pan on the fire, and boil the jelly for about ½ hour, reckoning from the time it commences to boil all over, and carefully remove the scum as it rises. If the jelly becomes firm when a little is put on a plate, it is done ; it should then be put into *small* pots, and covered the same as the jam in the preceding recipe. If the jelly is wanted very clear, but, of course, so much juice will not be obtained. If the fruit is not much squeezed, it may be converted into a jam for immediate eating, by boiling it with a little common sugar : this answers very well for a nursery preserve. *Time.*— About ¾ hour to extract the juice ; ½ hour to boil the jelly. *Average cost*, from 8*d.* to 10*d.* per ½-lb. pot. *Sufficient.*—From 3 pints to 2 quarts of fruit should yield a pint of juice. *Seasonable.*—Make this in July.

CURRANT JELLY, Red.

Ingredients.—Red currants ; to every pint of juice allow ¾ lb. of loaf sugar. *Mode.*—Have the fruit gathered in fine weather ; pick it from the stalks, put it into a jar, and place this jar in a saucepan of boiling water over the fire, and let it simmer gently until the juice is well drawn from the currants ; then strain them through a jelly-bag or fine cloth, and if the jelly is wished very clear, do not squeeze them *too much*, as the skin and pulp from the fruit will be pressed through with the juice, and so make the jelly muddy. Measure the juice, and to each pint allow ¾ lb of loaf sugar ; put these into a preserving-pan, set it over the fire, and keep stirring the jelly until it is done, carefully removing every particle of scum as it rises, using a wooden or silver spoon for the purpose, as metal or iron ones would spoil the colour of the jelly. When it has boiled from 20 minutes to ½ hour, put a little of the jelly on a plate, and if firm when cool, it is done. Take it off the fire, pour it into small gallipots, cover each of the pots with an oiled paper, and then with a piece of tissue-paper brushed over on both sides with the white of an egg. Label the pots, adding the year when the jelly was made, and store it away in a dry place. A jam may be made with the currants, if they are not squeezed too dry, by adding a few fresh raspberries, and boiling all together, with sufficient sugar

Currant Jelly, White | Currant and Raspberry Tart

to sweeten it nicely. As this jam is not worth storing away, but is only for immediate eating, a smaller proportion of sugar than usual will be found enough: it answers very well for children's puddings, or for a nursery preserve. *Time.*—From ¾ to 1 hour to extract the juice; 20 minutes to ½ hour to boil the jelly. *Average cost,* from 8*d.* to 10*d.* per ½-lb. pot. *Sufficient.*—8 quarts of currants will make from 10 to 12 pots of jelly. *Seasonable.*—Make this in July.

Note.—Should the above proportion of sugar not be found sufficient for some tastes, add an extra ¼ lb. to every pint of juice, making altogether 1lb.

CURRANT JELLY, White.

Ingredients.—White currants; to every pint of juice allow ¾lb. of good loaf sugar. *Mode.*—Pick the currants from the stalks, and put them into a jar; place this jar in a saucepan of boiling water, and simmer until the juice is well drawn from the fruit, which will be in from ¾ to 1 hour. Then strain the currants through a fine cloth or jelly-bag; do not squeeze them too much, or the jelly will not be clear, and put the juice into a very clean preserving-pan, with the sugar. Let this simmer gently over a clear fire until it is firm, and keep stirring and skimming until it is done; then pour it into small pots, cover them, and store away in a dry place. *Time.*—¾ hour to draw the juice; ½ hour to boil the jelly. *Average cost,* from 8*d.* to 10*d.* per ½-lb. pot. *Sufficient.*—From 3 pints to 2 quarts of fruit should yield 1 pint of juice. *Seasonable* in July and August.

CURRANT PUDDING, Boiled (Plain and Economical).

Ingredients.—1 lb. of flour, ½ lb. of suet, ½ lb. of currants, milk. *Mode.*—Wash the currants, dry them thoroughly, and pick away any stalks or grit; chop the suet finely; mix all the ingredients together, and moisten with sufficient milk to make the pudding into a stiff batter; tie it up in a floured cloth, put it into boiling water, and boil for 3½ hours; serve with a cut lemon, cold butter, and sifted sugar. *Time.*—3½ hours. *Average cost,* 10*d.* *Sufficient* for 7 or 8 persons. *Seasonable* at any time.

CURRANT PUDDING, Black or Red.

Ingredients.—1 quart of red or black currants, measured with the stalks, ¼ lb. of moist sugar, suet crust or butter crust (*see* recipes for CRUSTS). *Mode.*—Make, with ¾ lb. of flour, either a suet crust or butter crust (the former is usually made); butter a basin, and line it with part of the crust; add the currants, which should be stripped from the stalks, and sprinkle the sugar over them; put the cover of the pudding on; make the edges very secure, that the juice does not escape; tie it down with a floured cloth, put it into boiling water, and boil from 2½ to 3 hours. Boiled without a basin, allow ½ hour less. We have given rather a large proportion of sugar; but we find fruit puddings are so much more juicy and palatable when *well sweetened* before they are boiled, besides being more economical. A few raspberries added to red-currant pudding are a very nice addition; about ½ pint would be sufficient for the above quantity of fruit. Fruit puddings are very delicious if, when they are turned out of the basin, the crust is browned with a salamander, or put into a very hot oven for a few minutes to colour it: this makes it crisp on the surface. *Time.*—2½ to 3 hours; without a basin, 2 to 2½ hours. *Average cost,* in full season, 8*d.* *Sufficient* for 6 or 7 persons. *Seasonable* in June, July, and August.

CURRANT AND RASPBERRY TART, Red.

Ingredients.—1½ pint of picked currants, ½ pint of raspberries, 3 heaped tablespoonfuls of moist sugar, ½ lb of short crust. *Mode.*—Strip the currants from the stalks, and put them into a deep pie-dish, with a small cup placed in the midst, bottom upwards; add the raspberries and sugar; place a border of paste round the edge of the dish, cover with crust, ornament the edges, and bake from ½ to ¾ hour; strew some sifted sugar over before being sent to table. This tart is more generally served cold than hot. *Time.*—½ to ¾ hour. *Average cost,* 1*s.* *Sufficient* for 5 or 6 persons. *Seasonable* in June, July, and August.

Note.—In tarts of this description carefully avoid washing the fruit.

Currants, Iced

CURRANTS, Iced, for Dessert.

Ingredients.—¼ pint of water, the whites of 2 eggs, currants, pounded sugar. *Mode.*—Select very fine bunches of red or white currants, and well beat the whites of the eggs. Mix these with the water; then take the currants, a bunch at a time, and dip them in; let them drain for a minute or two, and roll them in very fine-pounded sugar. Lay them to dry on paper, when the sugar will crystallize round each currant, and have a very pretty effect. All fresh fruit may be prepared in the same manner; and a mixture of various fruits iced in this manner, and arranged on one dish, looks very well for a summer dessert. *Time.*—¼ day to dry the fruit. *Average cost, 8d.* for a pint of iced currants. *Seasonable* in summer.

CURRY.

Ingredients.—Veal, mutton, fowl, or rabbit; a large onion, butter, brown gravy or stock, a tablespoonful of curry-powder. *Mode.*—Let the meat be half fried. Cut the onion into small pieces, and fry it in butter till quite brown; add the meat, with a small quantity of brown gravy or stock, also the curry-powder, and stew all for about 20 minutes. This is for a dry curry; more gravy and curry-powder can be used if preferred. *Time.* —20 minutes. *Seasonable* at any time.

CURRY ST. LEONARDS.

Ingredients.—Chicken, or any meat; 2 tablespoonfuls of butter, 2 tablespoonfuls of curry-powder, 4 or 5 leaves of mint, a teacup of good gravy, salt, a dessertspoonful of vinegar, 3 tablespoonfuls of cream. *Mode.*—Fry together for 10 minutes the butter, curry-powder, and mint; then add the meat *cut into dice,* also the gravy, salt, and vinegar. Let all these simmer for 20 minutes, and then pour over the cream, and serve quite hot. *Time.*—30 minutes. *Seasonable* at any time.

CURRY-POWDER (Founded on Dr. Kitchener's Recipe).

Ingredients.—¼ lb. of coriander-seed, ¼ lb. of turmeric, 2 oz. of cinnamon-seed, ½ oz. of cayenne, 1 oz. of mustard, 1 oz. of ground ginger, ½ ounce of all-spice, 2 oz. of fenugreek seed. *Mode.*— Put all the ingredients in a cool oven,

Custards, Boiled

where they should remain one night; then pound them in a mortar, rub them through a sieve, and mix thoroughly together; keep the powder in a bottle, from which the air should be completely excluded.

CURRY-POWDER (Capt. White's Recipe; most excellent).

Ingredients.—1 lb. of pale turmeric seed, 4 oz. of cumming seed, 8 oz. of coriander seed, 4 oz. of black pepper, 2 oz. of cayenne pepper, 4 oz. of Jamaica ginger, 10 oz. of caraway seed, ¼ oz. of cardamums. *Mode.* — Mix together all these ingredients, well pounded, and then place the mixture in the sun, or before the fire, stirring it frequently. *Average cost, 5s. 2d.*

Note.—This will be found a most excellent curry-powder, if care be taken to purchase the ingredients at a good druggist's.

CUSTARDS, Boiled.

Ingredients.—1 pint of milk, 5 eggs, 3 oz. of loaf sugar, 3 laurel-leaves, or the rind of ½ lemon, or a few drops of essence of vanilla, 1 tablespoonful of brandy. *Mode.*—Put the milk into a *lined* saucepan, with the sugar and whichever of the above flavourings may be preferred (the lemon-rind flavours custards most deliciously), and let the milk steep by the side of the fire until it is well flavoured. Bring it to the point of boiling, then strain it into a basin;

CUSTARDS IN GLASSES.

whisk the eggs well, and, when the milk has cooled a little, stir in the eggs, and *strain* this mixture into a jug. Place this jug in a saucepan of boiling water over the fire; keep stirring the custard *one way* until it thickens; but on no account allow it to reach the boiling point, as it will instantly curdle and be full of lumps. Take it off the fire, stir in the brandy, and when this is well mixed with the custard, pour it into glasses, which should be rather more than three-parts full; grate a little nutmeg over the top, and the dish is ready for table. To make custards look

Custard Pudding, Baked

and eat better, ducks' eggs should be used, when obtainable; they add very much to the flavour and richness, and so many are not required as of the ordinary eggs, 4 ducks' eggs to the pint of milk making a delicious custard. When desired extremely rich and good, cream should be substituted for the milk, and double the quantity of eggs used to those mentioned, omitting the whites. *Time.*—½ hour to infuse the lemon-rind, about 10 minutes to stir the custard. *Average cost*, 8*d. Sufficient* to fill 8 custard-glasses. *Seasonable* at any time.

CUSTARD PUDDING, Baked.

Ingredients.—1½ pint of milk, the rind of ¼ lemon, ¼ lb. of moist sugar, 4 eggs. *Mode.*—Put the milk into a saucepan with the sugar and lemon-rind, and let this infuse for about ½ hour, or until the milk is well flavoured; whisk the eggs, yolks and whites; pour the milk to them, stirring all the while; then have ready a pie-dish, lined at the edge with paste ready baked; strain the custard into the dish, grate a little nutmeg over the top, and bake in a *very slow* oven for about ½ hour, or rather longer. The flavour of this pudding may be varied by substituting bitter almonds for the lemon-rind; and it may be very much enriched by using half cream and half milk, and doubling the quantity of eggs. *Time.*—½ to ¾ hour. *Average cost, 9d. Sufficient* for 5 or 6 persons. *Seasonable* at any time.

Note.—This pudding is usually served cold with fruit tarts.

CUSTARD PUDDING, Boiled.

Ingredients.—1 pint of milk, 1 tablespoonful of flour, 4 eggs, flavouring to taste. *Mode.*—Flavour the milk by infusing in it a little lemon-rind or cinnamon; whisk the eggs, stir the flour gradually to these, and pour over them the milk, and stir the mixture well. Butter a basin that will exactly hold it; put in the custard, and tie a floured cloth over; plunge it into boiling water, and turn it about for a few minutes, to prevent the flour from settling in one part. Boil it slowly for ½ hour; turn it out of the basin, and serve. The pudding may be garnished with red-currant jelly, and sweet sauce may be sent to table with it. *Time.*—½ hour.

Custard Tartlets

Average cost, 7d. Sufficient for 5 or 6 persons. *Seasonable* at any time.

CUSTARD SAUCE, for Sweet Puddings or Tarts.

Ingredients.—½ pint of milk, 2 eggs 3 oz. of pounded sugar, 1 tablespoonful of brandy. *Mode.*—Put the milk in a very clean saucepan, and let it boil. Beat the eggs, stir to them the milk and pounded sugar, and put the mixture into a jug. Place the jug in a saucepan of boiling water; keep stirring well until it thickens, but do not allow it to boil, or it will curdle. Serve the sauce in a tureen, stir in the brandy, and grate a little nutmeg over the top. This sauce may be made very much nicer by using cream instead of milk; but the above recipe will be found quite good enough for ordinary purposes. *Average cost*, 6*d.* per pint. *Sufficient,* this quantity, for 2 fruit tarts, or 1 pudding.

CUSTARD TARTLETS, or Fanchonnettes.

Ingredients.—For the custard, 4 eggs, ¾ pint of milk, 2 oz. of butter, 2 oz. of pounded sugar, 3 dessertspoonfuls of flour, flavouring to taste; the whites of 2 eggs, 2 oz. of pounded sugar. *Mode.*—Well beat the eggs; stir to them the milk, the butter, which should be beaten to a cream, the sugar, and flour; mix these ingredients well together; put them into a very clean saucepan, and bring them to the simmering point, but do not allow them to boil. Flavour with essence of vanilla, bitter almonds, lemon, grated chocolate, or any flavouring ingredient that may be preferred. Line some round tartlet-pans with good puff-paste; fill them with the custard, and bake in a moderate oven for about 20 minutes; then take them out of the pans; let them cool, and in the meantime whisk the whites of the eggs to a stiff froth; stir into this the pounded sugar, and spread smoothly over the tartlets a little of this mixture. Put them in the oven again to set the icing, but be particular that they do not scorch; when the icing looks crisp, they are done. Arrange them, piled high in the centre, on a white napkin, and garnish the dish, and in between the tartlets, with strips of bright jelly, or very firmly-made preserve. *Time.*—20 minutes to bake the

Cutlet, the Invalid's

tartlets; 5 minutes after being iced. *Average cost*, exclusive of the paste, 1s. *Sufficient* to fill 10 or 12 tartlets. *Seasonable* at any time.

Note.—The icing may be omitted on the top of the tartlets, and a spoonful of any kind of preserve put at the bottom of the custard instead: this varies both the flavour and appearance of this dish.

UTLET, the Invalid's.

Ingredients.—1 nice cutlet from a loin or neck of mutton, 2 teacupfuls of water, 1 very small stick of celery, pepper and salt to taste. *Mode.*—Have the cutlet cut from a very nice loin or neck of mutton; take off all the fat; put it into a stewpan, with the other ingredients; stew *very gently* indeed for nearly 2 hours, and skim off every particle of fat that may rise to the surface from time to time. The celery should be cut into thin slices before it is added to the meat, and care must be taken not to put in too much of this ingredient, or the dish will not be good. If the water is allowed to boil fast, the cutlet will be hard. *Time.* —2 hours' very gentle stewing. *Average cost*, 6d. *Sufficient* for 1 person. *Seasonable* at any time.

CUTLETS, Mutton, Italian.

Ingredients.—About 3 lbs. of the neck of mutton, clarified butter, the yolk of 1 egg, 4 tablespoonfuls of bread crumbs, 1 tablespoonful of minced savoury herbs, 1 tablespoonful of minced parsley, 1 teaspoonful of minced shalot, 1 saltspoonful of finely-chopped lemonpeel; pepper, salt, and pounded mace to taste; flour, ½ pint of hot broth or water, 2 teaspoonfuls of Harvey's sauce, 1 teaspoonful of joy, 2 teaspoonfuls of tarragon vinegar, 1 tablespoonful of port wine. *Mode.*— Cut the mutton into nicely-shaped cutlets, flatten them, and trim off some of the fat, dip them in clarified butter, and then into the beaten yolk of an egg. Mix well together bread crumbs, herbs, parsley, shalot, lemon-peel, and seasoning in the above proportion, and cover the cutlets with these ingredients. Melt some butter in a frying-pan, lay in the cutlets, and fry them a nice brown; take them out, and keep them hot before the fire. Dredge some flour into the pan, and, if there is not sufficient butter, add a little more; stir till it looks brown,

Dampfnudeln

then put in the hot broth or water, and the remaining ingredients; give one boil, and pour round the cutlets. If the gravy should not be thick enough, add a little more flour. Mushrooms, when obtainable, are a great improvement to this dish, and when not in season, mushroom-powder may be substituted for them. *Time.*—10 minutes; rather longer, should the cutlets be very thick. *Average cost*, 2s. 9d. *Sufficient* for 5 or 6 persons. *Seasonable* at any time.

CUTLETS of Cold Mutton.

[COLD MEAT COOKERY.] *Ingredients.* —The remains of cold loin or neck of mutton, 1 egg, bread crumbs, brown gravy or tomato sauce. *Mode.*—Cut the remains of cold loin or neck of mutton into cutlets, trim them, and take away a portion of the fat, should there be too much; dip them in beaten egg, and sprinkle with bread crumbs, and fry them a nice brown in hot dripping. Arrange them on a dish, and pour round them either a good gravy or hot tomato sauce. *Time.*—About 7 minutes. *Seasonable.*— Tomatoes to be had most reasonably in September and October.

DAMPFNUDELN, or German Puddings.

Ingredients.—1 lb. of flour, ¼ lb. of butter, 5 eggs, 2 small tablespoonfuls of yeast, 2 tablespoonfuls of finely-pounded sugar, milk, a very little salt. *Mode.*— Put the flour into a basin, make a hole in the centre, into which put the yeast, and rather more than ¼ pint of warm milk; make this into a batter with the middle of the flour, and let the sponge rise in a warm temperature. When sufficiently risen, mix the eggs, butter, sugar, and salt, with a little more warm milk, and knead the whole well together with the hands, beating the dough until it is perfectly smooth, and it drops from the fingers. Then cover the basin with a cloth, put it in a warm place, and when the dough has nicely risen, knead it into small balls; butter the bottom of a deep sauté-pan, strew over some pounded sugar, and let the dampfnudeln be laid in, but do not let them touch one another; then pour over sufficient milk to cover them, put on the lid, and let them rise to twice their original size by the side of the fire. Now place them in the oven for a few minutes to acquire a nice

Damson Cheese

brown colour, and serve them on a napkin, with custard sauce flavoured with vanilla, or a compôte of any fruit that may be preferred. *Time.*—½ to ¾ hour for the sponge to rise; 10 to 15 minutes for the puddings to rise; 10 minutes to bake them in a brisk oven. *Sufficient* for 10 or 12 dampfnudeln. *Seasonable* at any time.

DAMSON CHEESE.

Ingredients.—Damsons; to every lb. of fruit pulp allow ½ lb. of loaf sugar. *Mode.* —Pick the stalks from the damsons, and put them into a preserving-pan; simmer them over the fire until they are soft, occasionally stirring them, then beat them through a coarse sieve, and put the pulp and juice into the preserving-pan, with sugar in the above proportion, having previously carefully weighed them. Stir the sugar well in, and simmer the damsons slowly for 2 hours. Skim well, then boil the preserve quickly for ½ hour, or until it looks firm and hard in the spoon; put it quickly into shallow pots, or very tiny earthenware moulds, and when cold, cover it, with oiled papers, and the jars with tissue-paper brushed over on both sides with the white of an egg. A few of the stones may be cracked, and the kernels boiled with the damsons, which very much improves the flavour of the cheese. *Time.*—1 hour to boil the damsons without the sugar; 2 hours to simmer them slowly, ½ hour quickly. *Average cost,* from 8d. to 10d. per ¼-lb. pot. *Sufficient.*—1 pint of damsons to make a *very small* pot of cheese. *Seasonable.*—Make this in September or October.

DAMSON JAM.

Ingredients.—Damsons; to every lb. of fruit allow ¾ lb. of loaf sugar. *Mode.*— Have the fruit gathered in dry weather, pick it over, and reject any that is at all blemished. Stone the damsons, weigh them, and to every lb. allow ¾ lb. of loaf sugar. Put the fruit and sugar into a preserving-pan; keep stirring them gently until the sugar is dissolved, and carefully remove the scum as it rises. Boil the jam for about an hour, reckoning from the time it commences to simmer all over alike: it must be well stirred all the time, or it will be liable to burn and stick to the pan, which will cause the jam to have a very disagreeable flavour. When

Damsons, Baked

the jam looks firm, and the juice appears to set, it is done; then take it off the fire, put it into pots, cover it down, when quite cold, with oiled and egged papers, and store it away in a dry place. *Time.* —1 hour after the jam simmers all over *Average cost,* from 6d. to 8d. per lb. pot. *Sufficient.*—1½ pint of damsons for a lb. pot. *Seasonable.*—Make this in September or October.

DAMSON PUDDING.

Ingredients.—1½ pint of damsons, ¾ lb. of moist sugar, ¾ lb. of suet or butter crust. *Mode.*—Make a suet crust with ¾ lb. of flour by recipe; line a buttered pudding-basin with a portion of it; fill the basin with the damsons, sweeten them, and put on the lid; pinch the edges of the crust together, that the juice does not escape; tie over a floured cloth, put the pudding into boiling water and boil from 2½ to 3 hours. *Time.*— 2½ to 3 hours. *Average cost,* 8d. *Sufficient* for 6 or 7 persons. *Seasonable* in September and October.

DAMSON TART

Ingredients.—1½ pint of damsons, ¼ lb of moist sugar, ½ lb. of short or puff crust *Mode.*—Put the damsons, with the sugar between them, into a deep pie-dish, in the midst of which place a small cup or jar turned upside down; pile the fruit high in the middle, line the edges of the dish with short or puff crust, whichever may be preferred; put on the cover, ornament the edges, and bake from ½ to ¾ hour in a good oven. If puff-crust is used, about 10 minutes before the pie is done, take it out of the oven, brush it over with the white of an egg beaten to a froth with the blade of a knife; strew some sifted sugar over, and a few drops of water, and put the tart back to finish baking: with short crust, a little plain sifted sugar, sprinkled over, is all that will be required. *Time.*—½ to ¾ hour. *Average cost,* 10d. *Sufficient* for 5 or 6 persons. *Seasonable* in September and October.

DAMSONS, Baked, for Winter use.

Ingredients.—To every lb. of fruit allow 6 oz. of pounded sugar; melted mutton suet. *Mode.*—Choose sound fruit, not too ripe; pick off the stalks, weigh it, and to every lb. allow the above pro-

Damsons, Compôte of.

portion of pounded sugar. Put the fruit into large dry stone jars, sprinkling the sugar amongst it; cover the jars with saucers, place them in a rather cool oven, and bake the fruit until it is quite tender. When cold, cover the top of the fruit with a piece of white paper cut to the size of the jar; pour over this melted mutton suet about an inch thick, and cover the tops of the jars with thick brown paper well tied down. Keep the jars in a cool dry place, and the fruit will remain good till the following Christmas, but not much longer. *Time.*—From 5 to 6 hours to bake the damsons in a very cool oven. *Seasonable* in September and October.

DAMSONS, Compôte of.

Ingredients.—1 quart of damsons, 1 pint of syrup (*see* SYRUP). *Mode.*—Procure sound ripe damsons, pick the stalks from them, and put them into boiling syrup made by the recipe. Simmer them gently until the fruit is tender, but not sufficiently soft to break; take them up, boil the syrup for 5 minutes, pour it over the damsons, and serve. This should be sent to table in a glass dish. *Time.*—About ¼ hour to simmer the damsons; 5 minutes to boil the syrup. *Average cost,* 9d. *Sufficient* for 4 or 5 persons. *Seasonable* in September and October.

DAMSONS, Preserved.

Ingredients.—To every quart of damsons allow ½ lb. of loaf sugar. *Mode.*—Put the damsons (which should be picked from the stalks and quite free from blemishes) into a jar, with pounded sugar sprinkled amongst them in the above proportion; tie the jar closely down, set it in a saucepan of cold water; bring it gradually to boil, and simmer gently until the damsons are soft, without being broken. Let them stand till cold; then strain the juice from them, boil it up well, strain it through a jelly-bag, and pour it over the fruit. Let it cool, cover with oiled papers, and the jars with tissue-paper brushed over on both sides with the white of an egg, and store away in a dry place. *Time.*—About ¾ hour to simmer the fruit after the water boils; ¼ hour to boil the juice. *Seasonable.*—Make this in September or October.

December—Bills of Fare

DAMSONS, or any kind of Plum, to Preserve. (Useful in Winter.)

Ingredients.—Damsons or plums; boiling water. *Mode.*—Pick the fruit into clean dry stone jars, taking care to leave out all that are broken or blemished. When full, pour boiling water on the plums, until it stands one inch above the fruit; cut a piece of paper to fit the inside of the jar, over which pour melted mutton-suet; cover down with brown paper, and keep the jars in a dry cool place. When used, the suet should be removed, the water poured off, and the jelly at the bottom of the jar used and mixed with the fruit. *Seasonable* in September and October.

DARIOLES A LA VANILLE. (Sweet Entremets.)

Ingredients.—½ pint of milk, ½ pint of cream, 2 oz. of flour, 3 oz. of pounded sugar, 6 eggs, 2 oz. of butter, puff-paste, flavouring of essence of vanilla. *Mode.*—Mix the flour to a smooth batter, with the milk; stir in the cream, sugar, the eggs, which should be well whisked, and the butter, which should be beaten to a cream. Put in some essence of vanilla, drop by drop, until the mixture is well flavoured; line some dariole-moulds with puff-paste, three-parts fill them with the batter, and bake in a good oven from 25 to 35 minutes. Turn them out of the moulds on a dish, without breaking them; strew over sifted sugar, and serve. The flavouring of the darioles may be varied by substituting lemon, cinnamon, or almonds, for the vanilla. *Time.*—25 to 35 minutes. *Average cost,* 1s. 8d. *Sufficient* to fill 6 or 7 dariole-moulds. *Seasonable* at any time.

DECEMBER—BILLS OF FARE.

Dinner for 18 persons.
First Course.

Mock-Turtle Soup,
removed by
Cod's Head & Shoulders
and Oyster Sauce.

Stewed Eels.

Vase of
Flowers.

Fried Whitings.

Julienne Soup,
removed by
Soles aux fines herbes.

December—Bills of Fare

Second Course.

Roast Goose.	Haunch of Mutton. Ham and Brussels Sprouts. Vase of Flowers. Game Pie. Boiled Turkey and Celery Sauce.	**Stewed Beef à la Jardinière.**

Entrées.

Curried Lobster.	Fillets of Grouse and Sauce Piquante. Vase of Flowers. Sweetbreads.	**Mutton Cutlets and Soubise Sauce.**

Third Course.

Apricot Tourte.	Pheasants, removed by Plum-Pudding. Vanilla Cream. Vase of Flowers. Blancmange. Wild Ducks, removed by Iced Pudding.	**Champagne Jelly.** **Lemon Jelly.** **Tipsy Cake.**	**Victoria Sandwiches.** **Mince Pies.**

Dessert and Ices.

Dinner for 12 persons.

First Course.—Game soup; clear vermicelli soup; codfish au gratin; fillets of whitings à la maître d'hôtel. *Entrées.* —Filet de bœuf and sauce piquante; fricasseed chicken; oyster patties; curried rabbit. *Second Course.*—Roast turkey and sausages; boiled leg of pork and vegetables; roast goose; stewed beef à la Jardinière. *Third Course.*—Widgeon; partridges; Charlotte aux pommes;

December—Dinners for 6 persons.

mince pies; orange jelly, lemon cream : apple tart; cabinet pudding. Dessert and ices.

Dinner for 10 persons.

First Course. — Mulligatawny soup; fried slices of codfish; soles à la crême. *Entrées.*—Croquettes of fowl; pork cutlets and tomato sauce. *Second Course.*— Roast ribs of beef; boiled turkey and celery sauce; tongue, garnished; lark pudding; vegetables. *Third Course.*— Roast hare; grouse; plum-pudding; mince pies; Charlotte à la Parisienne; cheesecakes; apple tart; Nesselrode pudding. Dessert and ices.

Dinner for 8 persons.

First Course.—Carrot soup; crimped cod and oyster sauce; baked soles. *Entrées.*—Mutton kidneys à la Française, oyster patties. *Second Course.*—Boiled beef and vegetables; marrow-bones; roast fowls and water-cresses; tongue, garnished; game pie. *Third Course.*— Partridges; blancmange; compôte of apples; vol-au-vent of pears; almond cheesecakes; lemon pudding. Dessert and ices.

Dinners for 6 persons.

First Course.—Rabbit soup; brill and shrimp sauce. *Entrées.*—Curried fowl; oyster patties. *Second Course.*—Roast turkey and sausages; boiled leg of pork; vegetables. *Third Course.* — Hunters' pudding; lemon cheesecakes; apple tart; custards, in glasses; raspberry cream. Dessert.

First Course.—Ox-tail soup; crimped cod and oyster sauce. *Entrées.*—Savoury rissoles; fowl scollops à la Béchamel. *Second Course.* — Haunch of mutton; boiled chickens and celery sauce; bacon-cheek, garnished with Brussels sprouts; vegetables. *Third Course.* — Snipes; orange jelly; cheesecakes; apples à la Portugaise; apricot-jam tartlets; souffl of rice. Dessert.

First Course.—Vermicelli soup; soles à la maître d'hôtel; fried eels. *Entrées.* —Pork cutlets and tomato sauce; ragout of mutton à la Jardinière. *Second Course.* —Roast goose; boiled leg of mutton and vegetables. *Third Course.* —Pheasants; whipped cream; meringues; compôte of

December, Plain Family Dinners

Normandy pippins; mince pies; plum-pudding. Dessert.

First Course. — Carrot soup ; baked **cod** ; fried smelts. *Entrées.* — Stewed rump-steak à la Jardinière ; fricasseed chicken. *Second Course.*—Roast leg of mutton, boned and stuffed ; boiled turkey and oyster sauce ; vegetables. *Third Course.* — Wild ducks ; fancy pastry ; lemon cream ; damson tart, with bottled fruit ; custards, in glasses ; cabinet pudding. Dessert.

DECEMBER, Plain Family Dinners for.

Sunday.—1. Carrot soup. 2. Roast beef, horseradish sauce, vegetables. 3. Plum-pudding, mince pies.

Monday.—1. Fried whitings, melted butter. 2. Rabbit pie, cold beef, mashed potatoes. 3. Plum-pudding cut in slices and warmed, apple tart.

Tuesday.—1. Hashed beef and broiled bones, pork cutlets and tomato sauce ; vegetables. 2. Baked lemon pudding.

Wednesday.—1. Boiled neck of mutton and vegetables,—the broth served first with a little pearl barley or rice boiled in it. 2. Bakewell pudding.

Thursday.—1. Roast leg of pork, apple sauce ; vegetables. 2. Rice snowballs.

Friday.—1. Soles à la crême. 2. Cold pork and mashed potatoes, broiled rump-steaks and oyster sauce. 3. Rolled jam pudding.

Saturday.—1. The remains of cold pork curried, dish of rice, mutton cutlets and mashed potatoes. 2. Baked apple dump-lings.

Sunday.—1. Roast turkey and sausages, boiled leg of pork, pease pudding ; vegetables. 2. Baked apple pudding, mince pies.

Monday. — 1. Hashed turkey, cold pork, mashed potatoes. 2. Mincemeat pudding.

Tuesday.—1. Pea-soup made from liquor in which pork was boiled. 2. Boiled fowls and celery sauce, vegetables. 3. Baked rice pudding.

Wednesday.—1. Roast leg of mutton, stewed Spanish onions, potatoes. 2. Baked rolled jam pudding.

Thursday.—1. Baked cod's head. 2. Cold mutton, roast hare, gravy and red-currant jelly. 3. Macaroni.

Friday.—1. Hare soup, made with stock and remains of roast hare. 2.

Dessert

Hashed mutton, pork cutlets, and mashed potatoes. 3. Open tarts, rice blancmange.

Saturday.—1. Rumpsteak-and-kidney pudding, vegetables. 2. Mince pies, baked apple dumplings.

DECEMBER, Things in Season.

Fish.—Barbel, brill, carp, cod, crabs, eels, dace, gudgeons, haddocks, herrings, lobsters, oysters, perch, pike, shrimps, skate, sprats, soles, tench, thornback, turbot, whiting.

Meat.—Beef, house lamb, mutton, pork, venison.

Poultry. — Capons, chickens, fowls, geese, pigeons, pullets, rabbits, teal, turkeys, widgeons, wild ducks.

Game.—Hares, partridges, pheasants, snipes, woodcocks.

Vegetables. — Broccoli, cabbages, carrots, celery, leeks, onions, potatoes, parsnips, Scotch kale, turnips, winter spinach.

Fruit. — Apples, chestnuts, filberts, grapes, medlars, oranges, pears, walnuts, dried fruits, such as almonds and raisins, figs, dates, &c.,—crystallized preserves.

DESSERT.

With moderns the dessert is not so profuse, nor does it hold the same relationship to the dinner that it held with the ancients,—the Romans more especially. On ivory tables they would spread hundreds of different kinds of raw, cooked, and preserved fruits, tarts, and cakes, as substitutes for the more substantial comestibles with which the guests were satiated. However, as late as the reigns of our two last Georges, fabulous sums were often expended upon fanciful desserts. The dessert certainly repays, in its general effect, the expenditure upon it of much pains ; and it may be said, that if there be any poetry at all in meals, or the process of feeding, there is poetry in the dessert, the materials for which should be selected with taste, and, of course, must depend, in a great measure, upon the season. Pines, melons, grapes, peaches, nectarines, plums, strawberries, apples, pears, oranges, almonds, raisins, figs, walnuts, filberts, medlars, cherries, &c. &c., all kinds of dried fruits, and choice and delicately-flavoured cakes and biscuits, make up the dessert, together with the most costly and *recherché* wines. The shape of the dishes varies at different periods, the prevailing fashion at present

Dessert

being oval and circular dishes on stems. The patterns and colours are also subject to changes of fashion; some persons selecting china, chaste in pattern and colour; others, elegantly-shaped glass dishes on stems, with gilt edges. The beauty of the dessert services at the tables of the wealthy tends to enhance the splendour of the plate. The general mode of putting a dessert on table, now the elegant tazzas are fashionable, is, to place them down the middle of the table, a tall and short dish alternately; the fresh fruits being arranged on the tall dishes, and dried fruits, bon-bons, &c., on small round or oval glass plates. The garnishing needs especial attention, as the contrast of the brilliant-coloured fruits with nicely-arranged foliage is very charming. The garnish *par excellence* for dessert is the ice-plant; its crystallized dewdrops producing a marvellous effect in the height of summer, giving a most inviting sense of coolness to the fruit it encircles. The double-edged mallow, strawberry, and vine leaves have a pleasing effect; and for winter desserts, the bay, cuba, and laurel are sometimes used. In town, the expense and difficulty of obtaining natural foliage is great, but paper and composite leaves are to be purchased at an almost nominal price. Mixed fruits of the larger sort are now frequently served on one dish. This mode admits of the display of much taste in the arrangement of the fruit: for instance, a pine in the centre of the dish, surrounded with large plums of various sorts and colours, mixed with pears, rosy-cheeked apples, all arranged with a due regard to colour, have a very good effect. Again, apples and pears look well mingled with plums and grapes, hanging from the border of the dish in a négligé sort of manner, with a large bunch of the same fruit lying on the top of the apples. A dessert would not now be considered complete without candied and preserved fruits and confections. The candied fruits may be purchased at a less cost than they can be manufactured at home. They are preserved abroad in most ornamental and elegant forms. And since, from the facilities of travel, we have become so familiar with the tables of the French, chocolate in different forms is indispensable to our desserts. Olives, too, should not be omitted; these should be served in a small, deep glass dish, with a little of the liquor, or brine poured over.

Dessert Dishes

DESSERT DISHES.

The tazza, or dish with stem, the same as that shown in our illustrations, is now the favourite shape for dessert-dishes. The fruit can be arranged and shown to better advantage on these tall high dishes than on the short flat ones. All the dishes are now usually placed down the centre of the table, dried and fresh fruit alternately, the former being arranged on small round or oval glass plates, and the latter on the dishes with stems. The fruit should always be gathered on the same day that it is required for table, and should be tastefully arranged on the dishes, with leaves between and round it. By purchasing fruits that *are in season*, a dessert can be supplied at a very moderate cost. These, with a few fancy biscuits, crystallized fruit, bon-bons, &c., are sufficient for an ordinary dessert. When fresh fruit cannot be obtained, dried and foreign fruits, compôtes, baked pears, stewed Normandy pippins, &c. &c., must supply its place, with the addition of preserves, bon-bons, cakes, biscuits, &c. At fashionable tables, forced fruit is served growing in pots, these pots being hidden in more ornamental ones, and arranged with the other dishes. A few vases of fresh flowers, tastefully arranged, add very much to the appearance of the dessert; and, when these are not obtainable, a few paper ones, mixed with green leaves, answer very well as a substitute. In decorating a table, whether for luncheon, dessert, or supper, a vase or two of flowers should never be forgotten, as they add so much to the elegance of the *tout ensemble*. In summer and autumn, ladies residing in the country can always manage to have a few freshly-gathered flowers on their tables, and should never be without this inexpensive luxury. On the Continent, vases or epergnes filled with flowers are invariably placed down the centre of the dinner-table at regular distances. Ices for dessert are usually moulded; when this is not the case, they are handed round in glasses, with wafers to accompany them. Preserved ginger is frequently handed round after ices, to prepare the palate for the delicious dessert wines. A basin or glass of finely-pounded lump sugar must never be omitted at a dessert, as also a glass jug of fresh cold water (iced, if possible), and two goblets by its side. Grape scissors,

Dessert Dishes

t. melon-knife and fork, and nutcrackers, should always be put on table, if there are dishes of fruit requiring them. Zests are sometimes served at the close of the dessert; such as anchovy toasts or biscuits. The French often serve plain or grated cheese with a dessert of fresh or dried fruits. At some tables, finger-glasses are placed at the right of each person, nearly half filled with cold spring water, and in winter with tepid water. These precede the dessert. At other tables, a glass or vase is simply handed round, filled with perfumed water, into which each guest dips the corner of his napkin, and, when needful, refreshes his lips and the tips of his fingers. After the dishes are placed, and every one is provided with plates, glasses, spoons, &c., the wine should be put at each end of the table, cooled or otherwise, according to the season. If the party be small, the wine may be placed only at the top of the table, near the host. The following dishes may be introduced at dessert, according to season :—

Dish of Nuts.—These are merely arranged piled high in the centre of the dish, as shown in the engraving, with or without leaves round the edge. Filberts should always be served with the outer skin or husk on them; and walnuts should be well wiped with a damp cloth, and then with a dry one,

DISH OF NUTS.

to remove the unpleasant sticky feeling the shells frequently have. *Seasonable.*—Filberts from September to March; walnuts from September to January.

Box of French Plums. — If the box which contains them is exceedingly ornamental, it may be placed on the table; if small, on a glass dish; if large, without one. French plums may also be arranged on a glass

BOX OF FRENCH PLUMS.

Dessert Dishes

plate, and garnished with bright-coloured sweetmeats, which make a very good effect. All fancy boxes of preserved and crystallized fruit may be put on the table or not, at pleasure. These little matters of detail must, of course, be left to individual taste. *Seasonable.*—May be purchased all the year ; but are in greater perfection in the winter.

Dish of Mixed Fruit. — For a centre dish, a mixture of various fresh fruits has a remarkably good effect, particularly if a pine be added to the list. A high raised appearance should be given to the fruit, which is done in the following manner. Place a tumbler in the centre of the dish, and, in this tumbler,

DISH OF MIXED FRUIT.

the pine, crown uppermost; round the tumbler put a thick layer of moss, and, over this, apples, pears, plums, peaches, and such fruit as is simultaneously in season. By putting a layer of moss underneath, so much fruit is not required, besides giving a better shape to the dish. Grapes should be placed on the top of the fruit, a portion of some of the bunches hanging over the sides of the dish in a négligé kind of manner, which takes off the formal look of the dish. In arranging the plums, apples, &c., let the colours contrast well. *Seasonable.*—Suitable for a dessert in September or October.

Dessert Dishes | Devonshire Junket

Box of Chocolate.—This is served in an ornamental box, placed on a glass plate or dish. *Seasonable.* — May

BOX OF CHOCOLATE.

be purchased at any time.

Dish of Apples.—The apples should be nicely wiped with a dry cloth, and arranged on a dish, piled high in the centre, with evergreen leaves between each layer. The inferior apples should form the bottom layer, with the bright-colour-ed large ones at the top. The leaves of the laurel, bay, holly, or any shrub green in win-

DISH OF APPLES.

ter, are suitable for garnishing dessert dishes. Oranges may be arranged in the same manner ; they should also be wiped with a dry cloth before being sent to table.

Dish of Mixed Summer Fruit.— This dish consists of cherries, raspberries, currants, and strawberries, piled in different layers, with plenty of leaves between each layer, so that each fruit is well separated. The fruit should be arranged with a due regard to colour, so that they contrast nicely one with the other. Our engraving shows

DISH OF MIXED SUMMER FRUIT.

a layer of white cherries at the bottom, then one of red raspberries, over that a layer of white currants, and at the top some fine scarlet strawberries. *Seasonable* in June, July, and August.

Almonds and Raisins.—These are usually served on glass dishes, the fruit

piled high in the centre, and the almonds blanched and strewn over. To blanch the almonds, put them into a small mug or teacup, pour over them boiling water, let them remain for 2 or 3 minutes, and

ALMONDS AND RAISINS.

the skins may then be easily removed Figs, dates, French plums, &c., are a served on small glass plates or oval dishes but without the almonds. *Seasonable a* any time, but more suitable in winter when fresh fruit is not obtainable.

Dish of Strawberries.—Fine strawberries, arranged in the manner shown in the engraving, look exceedingly well. The inferior ones should be placed at the bottom of the dish, and the others put in rows pyramidically, with the stalks downwards, so that when the whole is completed, nothing but the red part of the

DISH OF STRAWBERRIES.

fruit is visible. The fruit should be gathered with rather long stalks, as there is then something to support it, and it can be placed more upright in each layer. A few of the finest should be reserved to crown the top.

DEVONSHIRE JUNKET.

Ingredients.—To every pint of new milk allow 2 dessertspoonfuls of brandy, 1 dessertspoonful of sugar, and 1½ dessertspoonful of prepared rennet ; thick cream, pounded cinnamon, or grated nutmeg. *Mode.*—Make the milk blood-warm ; put it into a deep dish with the brandy, sugar, and rennet ; stir it altogether, and cover it over until it is set. Then spread some thick or clotted cream over the top, grate some nutmeg, and strew some sugar over, and the dish will be ready to serve. *Time.*—About 2 hours to set the milk. *Seasonable* at any time

Dinner

DINNER,

Being the grand solid meal of the day, is a matter of considerable importance; and a well-served table is a striking index of human ingenuity and resource.

The elegance with which a dinner is served depends, of course, partly upon the means, but still more upon the taste of the master and mistress of the house. It may be observed, in general, that there should always be flowers on the table, and, as they form no item of expense where a garden is, there is no reason why they should not be employed every day.

The variety of the dishes which furnish forth a modern dinner-table, does not necessarily imply anything unwholesome, or anything capricious. Food that is not well relished cannot be well digested; and the appetite of the over-worked man of business, or statesman, or of any dweller in towns, whose occupations are exciting and exhausting, is jaded, and requires stimulation. Men and women who are in rude health, and who have plenty of air and exercise, eat the simplest food with relish, and commonly digest it well; but those conditions are out of the reach of many men. They must suit their mode of dining to their mode of living, if they cannot choose the latter. It is in serving up food that is at once appetizing and wholesome that the skill of the modern housewife is severely tasked; and she has scarcely a more important duty to fulfil. It is, in fact, her particular vocation, in virtue of which she may be said to hold the health of the family, and of the friends of the family, in her hands from day to day.

The following aphorisms and short directions in relation to dinner-parties, are well deserving of notice:—" Let the number of your guests never exceed twelve, so that the conversation may be general. Let the temperature of the dining-room be about 68°. Let the dishes be few in number in the first course, but proportionally good. The order of food is from the most substantial to the lightest. The order of drinking wine is from the mildest to the most foamy and most perfumed. To invite a person to your house is to take charge of his happiness so long as he is beneath your roof. The mistress of the house should always be certain that the coffee is excellent; whilst the master should be

Dinner

answerable for the quality of his wines and liqueurs."

Dinners à la Russe differ from ordinary dinners in the mode of serving the various dishes. In a dinner à la Russe, the dishes are cut up on a sideboard, and handed round to the guests, and each dish may be considered a course. The table for a dinner à la Russe should be laid with flowers and plants in fancy flowerpots down the middle, together with some of the dessert dishes. A *menu* or bill of fare should be placed by the side of each guest.

The following are bills of fare for dinners à la Russe, and eatable from July to November: the dishes can easily be varied to suit other months.

SERVICE A LA RUSSE (July).

Julienne Soup, Vermicelli Soup. Boiled Salmon, Turbot and Lobster Sauce. Soles-Water Souchy, Perch-Water Souchy. Matelote d'Anguilles à la Toulouse, Filets de Soles à la Normandie. Red Mullet, Trout. Lobster Rissoles, Whitebait. Riz de Veau à la Banquière, Filets de Poulets aux Coucombres. Canards à la Rouennaise, Mutton Cutlets à la Jardinière. Braised Beef à la Flamande, Spring Chickens, Roast Quarter of Lamb, Roast Saddle of Mutton, Tongue, Ham and Peas. Quails, larded, Roast Ducks, Turkey Poult, larded. Mayonnaise of Chicken, Tomatos, Green Peas à la Française. Suédoise of Strawberries, Charlotte Russe, Compôte of Cherries. Neapolitan Cakes, Pastry, Madeira Wine Jelly. Iced Pudding à la Nesselrode. Dessert and Ices.

SERVICE A LA RUSSE (November).

Ox-tail Soup, Soup à la Jardinière. Turbot and Lobster Sauce, Crimped Cod and Oyster Sauce. Stewed Eels, Soles à la Normandie. Pike and Cream Sauce. Fried Fileted Soles. Filets de Bœuf à la Jardinière, Croquettes of Game aux Champignons. Chicken Cutlets, Mutton Cutlets and Tomato Sauce. Lobster Rissoles, Oyster Patties. Partridges aux fines Herbes, Larded Sweetbreads. Roast Beef, Poulets aux Cressons, Haunch of Mutton, Roast Turkey, Boiled Turkey and Celery Sauce, Ham. Grouse, Pheasants, Hare. Salad, Artichokes, Stewed Celery. Italian Cream.

Dormers | Ducks, Roast

Charlotte aux Pommes, Compôte of Pears. Croûtes madrées aux Fruits, Pastry, Punch Jelly. Iced Pudding. Dessert and Ices.

DORMERS.

[COLD MEAT COOKERY.] *Ingredients.* —½ lb. of cold mutton, 2 oz. of beef suet, pepper and salt to taste, 3 oz. of boiled rice, 1 egg, bread crumbs, made gravy. *Mode.*—Chop the meat, suet, and rice finely; mix well together, and add a high seasoning of pepper and salt, and roll into sausages; cover them with egg and bread crumbs, and fry in hot dripping of a nice brown. Serve in a dish with made gravy poured round them, and a little in a tureen. *Time.*—¼ hour to fry the sausages. *Average cost*, exclusive of the meat, 6d. *Seasonable* at any time.

DRAUGHT for Summer.

Ingredients.—The juice of 1 lemon, a tumblerful of cold water, pounded sugar to taste, ½ small teaspoonful of carbonate of soda. *Mode.*—Squeeze the juice from the lemon; strain, and add it to the water, with sufficient pounded sugar to sweeten the whole nicely. When well mixed, put in the soda, stir well, and drink while the mixture is in an effervescing state.

DRINK, Pleasant, for Warm Weather.

Ingredients.—To every ½ pint of good ale allow 1 bottle of ginger beer. *Mode.*—For this beverage the ginger beer must be in an effervescing state, and the beer not in the least turned or sour. Mix them together, and drink immediately. The draught is refreshing and wholesome, as the ginger corrects the action of the beer. It does not deteriorate by standing a little, but, of course, is better when taken fresh.

DRIPPING, to Clarify.

Good and fresh dripping answers very well for basting everything except game and poultry, and, when well clarified, serves for frying nearly as well as lard; it should be kept in a cool place, and will remain good some time. To clarify it put the dripping into a basin, pour over it boiling water, and keep stirring the whole to wash away the impurities. Let

it stand to cool, when the water and dirty sediment will settle at the bottom of the basin. Remove the dripping, and put it away in jars or basins for use.

Another Way.—Put the dripping into a clean saucepan, and let it boil for a few minutes over a slow fire, and be careful to skim it well. Let it stand to cool a little, then strain it through a piece of muslin into jars for use. Beef dripping is preferable to any other for cooking purposes, as, with mutton dripping, there is liable to be a tallowy taste and smell.

DUCK, Hashed.

[COLD MEAT COOKERY.] *Ingredients.* —The remains of cold roast duck, rather more than 1 pint of weak stock or water, 1 onion, 1 oz. of butter, thickening of butter and flour, salt and cayenne to taste, ½ teaspoonful of minced lemon peel, 1 dessertspoonful of lemon-juice, ½ glass of port wine. *Mode.*—Cut the duck into nice joints, and put the trimmings into a stewpan; slice and fry the onion in a little butter; add these to the trimmings, pour in the above proportion of weak stock or water, and stew gently for 1 hour. Strain the liquor, thicken it with butter and flour, season with salt and cayenne, and add the remaining ingredients; boil it up and skim well; lay in the pieces of duck, and let them get thoroughly hot through by the side of the fire, but do not allow them to boil: they should soak in the gravy for about ½ hour. Garnish with sippets of toasted bread. The hash may be made richer by using a stronger and more highly-flavoured gravy; a little spice or pounded mace may also be added, when their flavour is liked. *Time.*—1½ hour. *Average cost*, exclusive of cold duck, 4d. *Seasonable* from November to February; ducklings from May to August.

DUCKS, Roast.

Ingredients.—A couple of ducks; sage-and-onion stuffing; a little flour. *Choosing and Trussing.*—Choose ducks with plump bellies, and with thick and yellowish feet. They should be trussed with the feet on, which should be scalded, and the skin peeled off, and then turned up close to the legs. Run a skewer through the middle of each leg, after having drawn them as close as

Duck, Roast, to carve

possible to the body, to plump up the breast, passing the same quite through the body. Cut off the heads and necks, and the pinions at the first joint; bring these close to the sides, twist the feet

ROAST DUCK.

round, and truss them at the back of the bird. After the duck is stuffed, both ends should be secured with string, so as to keep in the seasoning. *Mode.*— To insure ducks being tender, never dress them the same day they are killed; and, if the weather permits, they should hang a day or two. Make a stuffing of sage and onion sufficient for one duck, and leave the other unseasoned, as the flavour is not liked by everybody. Put them down to a brisk clear fire, and keep them well basted the whole of the time they are cooking. A few minutes before serving, dredge them lightly with flour, to make them froth and look plump; and when the steam draws towards the fire, send them to table hot and quickly, with a good brown gravy poured *round*, but not *over* the ducks, and a little of the same in a tureen. When in season, green peas should invariably accompany this dish. *Time.* — Full-grown ducks from ¾ to 1 hour; ducklings from 25 to 35 minutes. *Average cost*, from 2s. 3d. to 2s. 6d. each. *Sufficient.*—A couple of ducks for 6 or 7 persons. *Seasonable.*— Ducklings from April to August; ducks from November to February.

DUCK, Roast, to carve.

No dishes require so much knowledge and skill in their carving as do game and poultry; for it is necessary to be well acquainted with the anatomy of the bird

ROAST DUCK.

order to place the knife at exactly the proper point. A tough fowl and an old goose are sad triers of a carver's powers and temper, and, indeed, sometimes of the good humour of those in the neighbourhood of the carver; for a sudden tilt

Duck, Roast, to carve.

of the dish may eventuate in the placing of a quantity of the gravy in the lap of the right or left-hand supporter of the host. We will endeavour to assist those who are unacquainted with the "gentle art of carving," and also those who are but slightly acquainted with it, by simply describing the rules to follow, and referring to the distinctly-marked illustrations of each dish, which will further help to bring light to the minds of the uninitiated. If the bird be a young duckling,

LEG, WING, AND NECKBONE OF DUCK.

it may be carved like a fowl, viz., by first taking off the leg and the wing on either side; but in cases where the duckling is very small, it will be as well not to separate the leg from the wing, as they will not then form too large a portion for a single serving. After the legs and wings are disposed of, the remainder of the duck will be also carved in the same manner as a fowl; and not much difficulty will be experienced, as ducklings are tender, and the joints are easily broken by a little gentle forcing, or penetrated by the knife. In cases where the duck is a large bird, the better plan to pursue is then to carve it like a goose, that is, by cutting pieces from the breast in the direction indicated by the lines marked from 1 to 2, commencing to carve the slices close to the wing, and then proceeding upwards from that to the breastbone. If more should be wanted than can be obtained from both sides of the breast, then the legs and wings must be attacked, in the same way as is described in connection with carving a fowl. It may be here remarked, that as the legs of a duck are placed far more backward than those of a fowl, their position causing the waddling motion of the bird, the thigh-bones will be found considerably nearer towards the backbone than in a chicken; this is the only difference worth mentioning. The carver should ask each guest if a portion of stuffing would be agreeable; and in order to get at this, a cut should be made below the breast, as shown by the line from 3 to 4, at the part called the "apron," and the spoon inserted.

Duck and Peas, Stewed

*As described in the recipe, it is an excellent plan, when a couple of ducks are served, to have one with, and the other without, stuffing.) As to the prime parts of a duck, it has been said that "the wing of a flier and the leg of a swimmer" are severally the best portions. Some persons are fond of the feet of the duck; and, in trussing, these should never be taken off. The leg, wing, and neckbone are here shown; so that it will be easy to see the shape they should be when cut off.

Note.—Ducklings are trussed and roasted in the same manner, and served with the same sauces and accompaniments. When in season, do not omit apple sauce.

DUCK AND PEAS, Stewed.

[COLD MEAT COOKERY.] *Ingredients.* —The remains of cold roast duck, 2 oz. of butter, 3 or 4 slices of lean ham or bacon, 1 tablespoonful of flour, 2 pints of thin gravy, 1, or a small bunch of green onions, 3 sprigs of parsley, 3 cloves, 1 pint of young green peas, cayenne and salt to taste, 1 teaspoonful of pounded sugar. *Mode.*—Put the butter into a stewpan; cut up the duck into joints, lay them in with the slices of lean ham or bacon; make it brown, then dredge in a tablespoonful of flour, and stir this well in before adding the gravy. Put in the onion, parsley, cloves, and gravy, and when it has simmered for ¼ hour, add a pint of young green peas, and stew gently for about ½ hour. Season with cayenne, salt, and sugar; take out the duck, place it round the dish, and the peas in the middle. *Time.*—¾ hour. *Average cost,* exclusive of the cold duck, 1s. *Seasonable* from June to August.

DUCK AND PEAS, Stewed.

[COLD MEAT COOKERY.] *Ingredients.* —The remains of cold roast duck, ½ pint of good gravy, cayenne and salt to taste, ½ teaspoonful of minced lemon-peel, 1 teaspoonful of pounded sugar, 2 oz. of butter rolled in flour, 1½ pint of green peas. *Mode.*—Cut up the duck into joints, lay it in the gravy, and add a seasoning of cayenne, salt, and minced lemon-peel; let this gradually warm through, but not boil. Throw the peas into boiling water slightly salted, and boil them rapidly until tender. Drain them, stir in the pounded sugar, and the

butter rolled in flour; shake them over the fire for two or three minutes, and serve in the centre of the dish, with the duck laid round. *Time.*—15 minutes to boil the peas, when they are full grown. *Average cost,* exclusive of the cold duck, 10d. *Seasonable* from June to August.

DUCK, Stewed, in Turnips.

[COLD MEAT COOKERY.] *Ingredients.* —The remains of cold duck, ½ pint of good gravy, 4 shalots, a few slices of carrot, a small bunch of savoury herbs, 1 blade of pounded mace, 1 lb. of turnips weighed after being peeled, 2 oz. of butter, pepper and salt to taste. *Mode.* —Cut up the duck into joints, fry the shalots, carrots, and herbs, and put them with the duck into the gravy. Cut about 1 lb. of turnips into ½ inch squares, put the butter into a stewpan, and stew them till quite tender, which will be in about ½ hour, or rather more; season with pepper and salt, and serve on the centre of the dish, with the duck, &c., laid round. *Time.*—Rather more than ½ hour to stew the turnips. *Average cost,* exclusive of cold duck, 1s. *Seasonable* from November to February.

DUCK, to Ragout a whole.

Ingredients.—1 large duck, pepper and salt to taste, good beef gravy, 2 onions sliced, 4 sage-leaves, a few leaves of lemon thyme, thickening of butter and flour. *Mode.*—After having emptied and singed the duck, season it inside with pepper and salt, and truss it. Roast it before a clear fire for about 20 minutes, and let it acquire a nice brown colour. Put it into a stewpan with sufficient well-seasoned beef gravy to cover it; slice and fry the onions, and add these, with the sage-leaves and lemon thyme, both of which should be finely minced, to the stock. Simmer gently until the duck is tender; strain, skim, and thicken the gravy with a little butter and flour; boil it up, pour over the duck, and serve. When in season, about 1½ pint of young green peas, boiled separately, and put in the ragoût, very much improve this dish. *Time.*— 20 minutes to roast the duck; 20 minutes to stew it. *Average cost,* from 2s. 3d. to 2s. 6d. each. *Sufficient* for 4 or 5 persons. *Seasonable* from November to February; ducklings from April to August.

Duck, Wild, Hashed	Dumplings, Sussex

DUCK, Wild, Hashed.

Ingredients.—The remains of cold roast wild duck, 1 pint of good brown gravy, 2 tablespoonfuls of bread crumbs, 1 glass of claret, salt, cayenne, and mixed spices to taste; 1 tablespoonful of lemon or Seville orange-juice. *Mode.*—Cut the remains of the duck into neat joints, put them into a stewpan, with all the above ingredients; let them get gradually hot by the side of the fire, and occasionally stir the contents; when on the point of boiling, serve, and garnish the dish with sippets of toasted bread. *Time.*—About ¼ hour. *Seasonable* from November to February.

DUCK, Wild, Ragout of.

Ingredients.—2 wild ducks, 4 shalots, 1 pint of stock (*see* STOCK), 1 glass of port wine, 1 oz. of butter, a little flour, the juice of ½ lemon, cayenne and salt to taste. *Mode.*—Ducks that have been dressed and left from the preceding day will answer for this dish. Cut them into joints, reserve the legs, wings, and breasts until wanted; put the trimmings into a stewpan with the shalots and stock, and let them simmer for about ½ hour, and strain the gravy. Put the butter into a stewpan; when melted, dredge in a little flour, and pour in the gravy made from the bones; give it one boil, and strain it again; add the wine, lemon-juice, and cayenne; lay in the pieces of duck, and let the whole gradually warm through, but do not allow it to boil, or the duck will be hard. The gravy should not be too thick, and should be very highly seasoned. The squeeze of a Seville orange is a great improvement to this dish. *Time.*—About ½ hour to make the gravy; ¼ hour for the duck gradually to warm through. *Seasonable* from November to February.

DUCK, Wild. Roast.

Ingredients.—Wild duck, flour, butter. *Mode.*—Carefully pluck and draw them; cut off the heads close to the necks, leaving sufficient skin to turn over, and do not cut off the feet; some twist each leg at the knuckle, and rest the claws on each side of the breast; others truss them as shown in our illustration. Roast the birds before a quick fire, and, when they are first put down, let them remain for 5 minutes without basting (this will keep the gravy in); afterwards baste plentifully with butter, and a few minutes

Dumplings, Sussex

before serving dredge them lightly with flour; baste well, and send them to table nicely frothed, and full of gravy. If

ROAST WILD DUCK.

overdone, the birds will lose their flavour, Serve with a good gravy in the dish, or orange gravy, and send to table with them a cut lemon. To take off the fishy taste which wild fowl sometimes have, baste them for a few minutes with hot water to which have been added an onion and a little salt; then take away the pan, and baste with butter. *Time.*—When liked underdressed, 20 to 25 minutes; well done, 25 to 35 minutes. *Average cost*, 4s. to 5s. the couple.

DUCK, Wild, to Carve.

As game is almost universally served as a dainty, and not as a dish to stand the assaults of an altogether fresh appetite, these dishes are not usually cut up entirely, but only those parts are served of each which are considered

WILD DUCK.

the best flavoured and the primest. Of wild fowl, the breast alone is considered by epicures worth eating, and slices are cut from this, in the direction indicated by the lines, from 1 to 2; if necessary, the leg and the wing can be taken off by passing the knife from 3 to 4, and by generally following the directions described for carving boiled fowl.

DUMPLINGS, Sussex, or Hard.

Ingredients.—1 lb. of flour, ½ pint of water, ½ saltspoonful of salt. *Mode.*— Mix the flour and water together to a smooth paste, previously adding a small quantity of salt. Form this into small round dumplings; drop them into boiling water, and boil from ½ to ¾ hour They may be served with roast or boiled meat; in the latter case, they may be cooked with the meat, but should be dropped into the water when it is quite boiling. *Time.*—½ to ¾ hour. *Sufficient*

Dutch Flummery

for 10 or 12 dumplings. *Seasonable* at any time.

DUTCH FLUMMERY.

Ingredients.—1½ oz. of isinglass, the rind and juice of 1 lemon, 1 pint of water, 4 eggs, 1 pint of sherry, Madeira, or raisin-wine; sifted sugar to taste. *Mode.* —Put the water, isinglass, and lemon-rind into a lined saucepan, and simmer gently until the isinglass is dissolved; strain this into a basin, stir in the eggs, which should be well beaten, the lemon-juice, which should be strained, and the wine; sweeten to taste with pounded sugar, mix all well together, pour it into a jug, set this jug in a saucepan of boiling water over the fire, and keep stirring it one way until it thickens; but *take care that it does not boil.* Strain it into a mould that has been oiled or laid in water for a short time, and put it in a cool place to set. A tablespoonful of brandy stirred in just before it is poured into the mould, improves the flavour of this dish: it is better if it is made the day before it is required for table. *Time.* —¼ hour to simmer the isinglass; about ¼ hour to stir the mixture over the fire. *Average cost, 4s. 0d.,* if made with sherry; less with raisin-wine. *Sufficient* to fill a quart mould. *Seasonable* at any time.

EEL BROTH.

Ingredients.—⅓ lb. of eel, a small bunch of sweet herbs, including parsley, ¼ onion, 10 peppercorns, 3 pints of water, 2 cloves, salt and pepper to taste. *Mode.* —After having cleaned and skinned the eel, cut it into small pieces, and put it into a stewpan with the other ingredients; simmer gently until the liquid is reduced to nearly half, carefully removing the scum as it rises. Strain it through a hair sieve: put it by in a cool place, and, when wanted, take off all the fat on the top; warm up as much as is required, and serve with sippets of toasted bread. This is a very nutritious broth, and easy of digestion. *Time.*—To be simmered until the liquor is reduced to half. *Average cost, 6d. Sufficient* to make 1½ pint of broth. *Seasonable* from June to March.

EEL PIE.

Ingredients.—1 lb. of eels, a little chopped parsley, 1 shalot, grated nutmeg, pepper and salt to taste, the juice

Eel, Collared

of ½ a lemon, small quantity of forcemeat, ¼ pint of Béchamel; puff paste. *Mode.*—Skin and wash the eels, cut them in pieces 2 inches long, and line the bottom of the pie-dish with forcemeat. Put in the eels, and sprinkle them with the parsley, shalots, nutmeg, seasoning, and lemon-juice, and cover with puff-paste. Bake for 1 hour, or rather more; make the Béchamel hot, and pour it into the pie. *Time.*—Rather more than 1 hour. *Seasonable* from August to March.

EEL SOUP.

Ingredients.— 3 lbs. of eels, 1 onion, 2 oz. of butter, 3 blades of mace, 1 bunch of sweet herbs, ¼ oz. of peppercorns, salt to taste, 2 tablespoonfuls of flour, ¼ pint of cream, 2 quarts of water. *Mode.*— Wash the eels, cut them into thin slices, and put them into the stewpan with the butter; let them simmer for a few minutes, then pour the water to them, and add the onion, cut in thin slices, the herbs, mace, and seasoning. Simmer till the eels are tender, but do not break the fish. Take them out carefully, mix the flour smoothly to a batter with the cream, bring it to a boil, pour over the eels, and serve. *Time.*—1 hour or rather more. *Average cost, 10d.* per quart. *Seasonable* from June to March. *Sufficient* for 8 persons.

Note. — This soup may be flavoured differently by omitting the cream, and adding a little ketchup or Harvey's sauce.

EELS, Boiled.

Ingredients. — 4 small eels, sufficient water to cover them; a large bunch of parsley. *Mode.*—Choose small eels for boiling; put them into a stewpan with the parsley, and just sufficient water to cover them; simmer till tender. Take them out, pour a little parsley and butter over them, and serve some in a tureen. *Time.* —½ hour. *Average cost, 6d.* per lb. *Seasonable* from June to March. *Sufficient* for 4 persons.

EEL, Collared.

Ingredients.—1 large eel; pepper and salt to taste; 2 blades of mace, 2 cloves, a little allspice very finely pounded, 3 leaves of sage, and a small bunch of herbs minced very small. *Mode.*—Bone the eel and skin it; split it, and sprinkle

Eels, Fried

i+ over with the ingredients, taking care that the spices are very finely pounded, and the herbs chopped very small. Roll t up and bind with a broad piece of tape, and boil it in water, mixed with a little salt and vinegar, till tender. It may either be served whole or cut in slices; and when cold, the eel should be kept in the liquor it was boiled in, but with a little more vinegar put to it. *Time.*—2 hours. *Average cost,* 6d. per lb. *Seasonable* from August to March.

EELS, Fried.

Ingredients.—1 lb. of eels, 1 egg, a few bread crumbs, hot lard. *Mode.*—Wash the eels, cut them into pieces 3 inches long, trim and wipe them very dry; dredge with flour, rub them over with egg, and cover with bread crumbs; fry a nice brown in hot lard. If the eels are small, curl them round, instead of cutting them up. Garnish with fried parsley. *Time.*—20 minutes or rather less. *Average cost,* 6d. per lb. *Seasonable* from June to March.

EELS, en Matelote.

Ingredients.—5 or 6 young onions, a few mushrooms, when obtainable; salt, pepper, and nutmeg to taste; 1 laurel leaf, ½ pint of port wine, ½ pint of medium stock, butter and flour to thicken; 2 lbs. of eels. *Mode.*—Rub the stewpan with butter, dredge in a little flour, add the onions cut very small, slightly brown them, and put in all the other ingredients. Wash, and cut up the eels into pieces 3 inches long; put them in the stewpan, and simmer for ½ hour. Make round the dish a border of croûtons, or pieces of toasted bread; arrange the eels in a pyramid in the centre, and pour over the sauce. Serve very hot. *Time.*—¾ hour. *Average cost,* 1s. 9d. for this quantity. *Seasonable* from August to March. *Sufficient* for 5 or 6 persons.

EELS, Stewed.

Ingredients. — 2 lbs. of eels, 1 pint of rich strong stock, 1 onion, 3 cloves, a piece of lemon-peel, 1 glass of port or Madeira, 3 tablespoonfuls of cream; thickening of flour; cayenne and lemon-juice to taste. *Mode.*—Wash and skin the eels, and cut them into pieces about 3 inches long; pepper and salt them, and put them in a stewpan; pour over the

Eggs

stock, add the onion stuck with cloves, the lemon-peel, and the wine. Stew gently for ½ hour, or rather more, and lift them carefully on a dish, which keep hot. Strain the gravy, stir the cream, sufficient flour to thicken; mix altogether, boil for 2 minutes, and add the cayenne and lemon-juice; pour over the eels and serve. *Time.*—¾ hour. *Average cost* for this quantity, 2s. 3d. *Seasonable* from June to March. *Sufficient* for 5 or 6 persons.

EELS, Stewed.

Ingredients. — 2 lbs. of middling-sized eels, 1 pint of medium stock, ¼ pint of port wine; salt, cayenne, and mace to taste; 1 teaspoonful of essence of anchovy, the juice of ½ a lemon. *Mode.*— Skin, wash, and clean the eels thoroughly; cut them into pieces 3 inches long, and put them into strong salt and water for 1 hour; dry them well with a cloth, and fry them brown. Put the stock on with the heads and tails of the eels, and simmer for ½ hour; strain it, and add all the other ingredients. Put in the eels, and stew gently for ½ hour, when serve. *Time.*—2 hours. *Average cost,* 1s. 9d. *Seasonable* from June to March. *Sufficient* for 5 or 6 persons.

EELS, à la Tartare.

Ingredients.—2 lbs. of eels, 1 carrot, 1 onion, a little flour, 1 glass of sherry; salt, pepper, and nutmeg to taste; bread-crumbs, 1 egg, 2 tablespoonfuls of vinegar. *Mode.* — Rub the butter on the bottom of the stewpan; cut up the carrot and onion, and stir them over the fire for 5 minutes; dredge in a little flour, add the wine and seasoning, and boil for ½ an hour. Skin and wash the eels, cut them into pieces, put them to the other ingredients, and simmer till tender. When they are done, take them out, let them get cold, cover them with egg and bread crumbs, and fry them of a nice brown. Put them on a dish, pour sauce piquante over, and serve them hot. *Time.*—1½ hour. *Average cost,* 1s. 8d., exclusive of the sauce piquante. *Seasonable* from August to March. *Sufficient* for 5 or 6 persons.

EGGS.

There is only one opinion as to the nutritive properties of eggs, though the qualities of those belonging to different birds vary somewhat. Those of the common hen are most esteemed as delicate food, particularly when "new-laid." The quality of eggs depends much upon the food given to the hen. Eggs in general are considered most easily digestible when little subjected to the art of cookery. The lightest way of dressing them is by poaching, which is effected by putting them for a minute or two into brisk boiling water: this coagulates the external white, without doing the inner part too much. Eggs are much better when new-laid than a day or two afterwards. The usual time allotted for boiling eggs in the shell is 3 to 3¾ minutes: less time than that in boiling water will not be sufficient to solidify the white, and more will make the yolk hard and less digestible: it is very difficult to *guess* accurately as to the time. Great care should be employed in putting them into the water, to prevent cracking the shell, which inevitably causes a portion of the white to exude, and lets water into the egg. For the purpose of placing eggs in water, always choose a *large* spoon in preference to a small one. Eggs are often beaten up raw in nutritive beverages.

The eggs of the *turkey* are almost as mild as those of the hen; the egg of the *goose* is large, but well-tasted. *Ducks' eggs* have a rich flavour; the albumen is slightly transparent, or bluish, when set or coagulated by boiling, which requires less time than hens' eggs. *Guinea-fowl eggs* are smaller and more delicate than those of the hen. Eggs of *wild fowl* are generally coloured, often spotted; and the taste generally partakes somewhat of the bird they belong to. Those of land birds that are eaten, as the *plover*, *lapwing*, *ruff*, &c., are in general much esteemed; but those of *sea-fowl* have, more or less, a strong fishy taste. The eggs of the *turtle* are very numerous: they consist of yolk only, without shell, and are delicious.

When fresh eggs are dropped into a vessel *full* of boiling water, they crack, because the eggs being well filled, the shells give way to the efforts of the interior fluids, dilated by heat. If the volume of hot water be small, the shells do not crack, because its temperature is reduced by the eggs before the interior dilation can take place. Stale eggs, again, do not crack, because the air inside is easily compressed.

EGG BALLS, for Soups and made Dishes.

Ingredients.—8 eggs, a little flour; seasoning to taste of salt. *Mode.*—Boil 6 eggs for 20 minutes, strip off the shells, take the yolks and pound them in a mortar. Beat the yolks of the 2 uncooked eggs; add them, with a little flour and salt, to those pounded; mix all well together, and roll into balls. Boil them before they are put into the soup or other dish they may be intended for.

EGG SAUCE, for Salt Fish.

Ingredients.—4 eggs, ½ pint of melted butter, when liked, a very little lemon-juice. *Mode.*—Boil the eggs until quite hard, which will be in about 20 minutes, and put them into cold water for ¼ hour. Strip off the shells, chop the eggs into small pieces, not, however, too fine. Make the melted butter very smooth, and, when boiling, stir in the eggs, and serve very hot. Lemon-juice may be added at pleasure. *Time.*—20 minutes to boil the eggs. *Average cost, 8d.* *Sufficient.*—This quantity for 3 or 4 lbs. of fish.

Note.—When a thicker sauce is required, use one or two more eggs to the same quantity of melted butter.

EGG SOUP.

Ingredients.—A tablespoonful of flour, 4 eggs, 2 small blades of finely-pounded mace, 2 quarts of stock. *Mode.*—Beat up the flour smoothly in a teaspoonful of cold stock, and put in the eggs; throw them into boiling stock, stirring all the time. Simmer for ¼ of an hour. Season and serve with a French roll in the tureen or fried sippets of bread. *Time.*—½ an hour. *Average cost,* 11d. per quart. *Seasonable* all the year. *Sufficient* for 8 persons.

EGG WINE.

Ingredients.—1 egg, 1 tablespoonful and ½ glass of cold water, 1 glass of sherry, sugar and grated nutmeg to taste. *Mode.*—Beat the egg, mixing with it a tablespoonful of cold water; make the wine-and-water hot, but not boiling; pour it on the egg, stirring all the time. Add sufficient lump sugar to sweeten the mixture, and a little grated nutmeg; put all into a very clean saucepan, set it on a gentle fire, and stir the

Eggs, to Boil

contents one way until they thicken, but *do not allow them to boil.* Serve in a glass with sippets of toasted bread or plain crisp biscuits. When the egg is not warmed, the mixture will be found easier of digestion, but it is not so pleasant a drink. *Sufficient* for 1 person.

EGGS, to Boil for Breakfast, Salads, &c.

Eggs for boiling cannot be too fresh, or boiled too soon after they are laid; but rather a longer time should be allowed for boiling a new-laid egg than for one that is three or four days old. Have ready a saucepan of boiling water; put the eggs into it gently with a spoon, letting the spoon touch the bottom of the saucepan before it is withdrawn, that the egg may not fall, and consequently crack. For those who like eggs lightly boiled, 3 minutes will be found sufficient; 3¾ to 4 minutes will be ample time to set the white nicely; and, if liked hard, 6 to 7 minutes will not be found too long. Should

EGG-STAND FOR THE BREAKFAST-TABLE.

the eggs be unusually large, as those of black Spanish fowls sometimes are, allow an extra ½ minute for them. Eggs for salads should be boiled from 10 minutes to ¼ hour, and should be placed in a basin of cold water for a few minutes; they should then be rolled on the table with the hand, and the shell will peel off easily. *Time.*—To boil eggs lightly, for invalids or children, 3 minutes; to boil eggs to suit the generality of tastes, 3¾ to 4 minutes; to boil eggs hard, 6 to 7 minutes; for salads, 10 to 15 minutes.

EGGS, Buttered.

Ingredients.—4 new-laid eggs, 2 oz. of butter. *Mode.*—Procure the eggs new-laid if possible; break them into a basin, and beat them well; put the butter into

Eggs, Fried

another basin, which place in boiling water, and stir till the butter is melted. Pour that and the eggs into a lined saucepan; hold it over a gentle fire, and, as the mixture begins to warm, pour it two or three times into the basin, and back again, that the two ingredients may be well incorporated. Keep stirring the eggs and butter one way until they are hot, *without boiling,* and serve on hot buttered toast. If the mixture is allowed to boil, it will curdle, and so be entirely spoiled. *Time.*—About 5 minutes to make the eggs hot. *Average cost, 7d. Sufficient.*—Allow a slice to each person. *Seasonable* at any time.

EGGS, to Choose.

In choosing eggs, apply the tongue to the large end of the egg, and, if it feels warm, it is new, and may be relied on as a fresh egg. Another mode of ascertaining their freshness is to hold them before a lighted candle or to the light, and, if the egg looks clear, it will be tolerably good; if thick, it is stale; and if there is a black spot attached to the shell, it is worthless. No egg should be used for culinary purposes with the slightest taint in it, as it will render perfectly useless those with which it has been mixed. Eggs that are purchased, and that cannot be relied on, should always be broken in a cup, and then put into a basin: by this means stale or bad eggs may be easily rejected, without wasting the others.

EGGS, Ducks'.

Ducks' eggs are usually so strongly flavoured that, plainly boiled, they are not good for eating; they answer, however, very well for various culinary preparations where eggs are required; such as custards, &c. &c. Being so large and highly-flavoured, 1 duck's egg will go as far as 2 small hen's eggs, besides making whatever they are mixed with exceedingly rich. They also are admirable when used in puddings.

EGGS, Fried.

Ingredients. — 4 eggs, ¼ lb. of lard, butter or clarified dripping. *Mode.*—Place a delicately-clean frying-pan over a gentle fire; put in the fat, and allow

8

Eggs à la Maître d'Hôtel

it to come to the boiling-point. Break the eggs into cups, slip them into the boiling fat, and let them remain until the whites are delicately

FRIED EGGS ON BACON.

set; and, whilst they are frying, ladle a little of the fat over them. Take them up with a slice, drain them for a minute from their greasy moisture, trim them neatly, and serve on slices of fried bacon or ham; or the eggs may be placed in the middle of the dish, with the bacon put round as a garnish. *Time.*—2 to 3 minutes. *Average cost,* 1d. each; 2d. when scarce. *Sufficient* for 2 persons. *Seasonable* at any time.

EGGS à la Maître d'Hôtel.

Ingredients.—¼ lb. of fresh butter, 1 tablespoonful of flour, ½ pint of milk, pepper and salt to taste, 1 tablespoonful of minced parsley, the juice of ½ lemon, 6 eggs. *Mode.*—Put the flour and half the butter into a stewpan; stir them over the fire until the mixture thickens; pour in the milk, which should be boiling; add a seasoning of pepper and salt, and simmer the whole for 5 minutes. Put the remainder of the butter into the sauce, and add the minced parsley; then boil the eggs hard, strip off the shell, cut the eggs into quarters, and put them on a dish. Bring the sauce to the boiling-point, add the lemon-juice, pour over the eggs and serve. *Time.*—5 minutes to boil the sauce; the eggs, 10 to 15 minutes. *Average cost,* 1s. *Sufficient* for 4 or 5 persons. *Seasonable* at any time.

EGGS, to Pickle.

Ingredients. — 16 eggs, 1 quart of vinegar, ½ oz. of black pepper, ½ oz. of Jamaica pepper, ½ oz. of ginger. *Mode.*— Boil the eggs for 12 minutes, then dip them into cold water, and take off the shells. Put the vinegar, with the pepper and ginger, into a stewpan, and let it simmer for 10 minutes. Now place the eggs in a jar, pour over them the vinegar, &c., boiling hot, and, when cold, tie them down with bladder to exclude the air. This pickle will be ready for use in a month. *Average cost,* for this quantity, 1s. 9d. *Seasonable.*—This should be made about Easter, as at this time eggs are plentiful and cheap. A store of pickled eggs will be found very useful

Eggs, Poached

and ornamental in serving with many first and second course dishes.

EGGS AU PLAT, or AU MIROIR, served on the Dish in which they are Cooked.

Ingredients.—4 eggs, 1 oz. of butter, pepper and salt to taste. *Mode.*—Butter a dish rather thickly with good fresh butter; melt it, break the eggs into it the same as for poaching, sprinkle them with white pepper and fine salt, and put the remainder of the butter, cut into very small pieces, on the top of them. Put the dish on a hot plate, or in the oven, or before the fire, and let it remain until the whites become set, but not hard, when serve immediately, placing the dish they were cooked in on another. To hasten the cooking of the eggs, a salamander may be held over them for a minute; but great care must be taken that they are not too much done. This is an exceedingly nice dish, and one very easily prepared for breakfast. *Time.*—3 minutes. *Average cost,* 5d. *Sufficient* for 2 persons. *Seasonable* at any time.

EGGS, Plovers'.

Plovers' eggs are usually served boiled hard, and sent to table in a napkin, either hot or cold; they may also be shelled, and served the same as eggs à la Tripe, with a good Béchamel sauce, or brown gravy, poured over them. They are also used for decorating salads, the beautiful colour of the white being generally so much admired.

EGGS, Poached.

Ingredients.—Eggs, water. To every pint of water allow 1 tablespoonful of vinegar. *Mode.* — Eggs for poaching should be perfectly fresh, but not quite new-laid; those that are about 36 hours old are the best for the purpose. If quite new-laid, the white is so milky it is almost impossible to set it; and, on the other hand, if the egg be at all stale, it is equally difficult to poach it nicely. Strain some boiling water into a deep clean frying-pan; break the egg into a cup without damaging the yolk, and, when the water boils, remove the pan to the side of the fire, and gently slip the egg into it. Place the pan over a gentle fire, and keep the water simmering until the white looks nicely set, when the egg is ready. Take it up gently with a slice

Eggs, Poached	Eggs, Snow

cut away the ragged edges of the white, and serve either on toasted bread or on

slices of ham or bacon, or on spinach, &c. A poached egg should not be overdone,

EGGS POACHED ON TOAST.

as its appearance and taste will be quite spoiled if the yolk be allowed to harden. When the egg is slipped into the water, the white should be gathered together, to keep it a little in form, or the cup should be turned over it for ½ minute. To poach an egg to perfection is rather a difficult operation; so, for inexperienced cooks, a tin egg-poacher may be purchased, which greatly facilitates this manner of dressing eggs. Our illustration clearly shows what it is: it consists

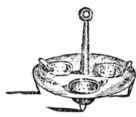

TIN EGG-POACHER.

of a tin plate with a handle, with a space for three perforated cups. An egg should be broken into each cup, and the machine then placed in a stewpan of boiling water, which has been previously strained. When the whites of the eggs appear set, they are done, and should then be carefully slipped on to the toast or spinach, or with whatever they are served. In poaching eggs in a frying-pan, never do more than four at a time; and, when a little vinegar is liked mixed with the water in which the eggs are done, use the above proportion. *Time.*— 2½ to 3½ minutes, according to the size of the egg. *Sufficient.*—Allow 2 eggs to each person. *Seasonable* at any time, but less plentiful in winter.

EGGS, Poached, with Cream.

Ingredients.—1 pint of water, 1 teaspoonful of salt, 4 teaspoonfuls of vinegar, 4 fresh eggs, ½ gill of cream, salt, pepper, and pounded sugar to taste, 1 oz. of butter. *Mode.*—Put the water, vinegar, and salt into a frying-pan, and break each egg into a separate cup; bring the water, &c., to boil, and slip the eggs

gently into it without breaking the yolks. Simmer them from 3 to 4 minutes, but not longer, and, with a slice, lift them out on to a hot dish, and trim the edges. Empty the pan of its contents, put in the cream, add a seasoning to taste of pepper, salt, and pounded sugar; bring the whole to the boiling-point; then add the butter, broken into small pieces; toss the pan round and round till the butter is melted; pour it over the eggs, and serve. To insure the eggs not being spoiled whilst the cream, &c. is preparing, it is a good plan to warm the cream with the butter, &c. before the eggs are poached, so that it may be poured over them immediately after they are dished. *Time.*—3 to 4 minutes to poach the eggs, 5 minutes to warm the cream. *Average cost* for the above quantity, 9d. *Sufficient* for 2 persons. *Seasonable* at any time.

EGGS, Scotch.

Ingredients.—6 eggs, 6 tablespoonfuls of forcemeat, hot lard, ½ pint of good brown gravy. *Mode.*—Boil the eggs for 10 minutes; strip them from the shells, and cover them with forcemeat, or substitute pounded anchovies for the ham. Fry the eggs a nice brown in boiling lard, drain them before the fire from their greasy moisture, dish them, and pour round from ¼ to ½ pint of good brown gravy. To enhance the appearance of the eggs, they may be rolled in beaten egg and sprinkled with breadcrumbs; but this is scarcely necessary if they are carefully fried. The flavour of the ham or the anchovy in the forcemeat must preponderate, as it should be very relishing. *Time.*—10 minutes to boil the eggs, 5 to 7 minutes to fry them. *Average cost*, 1s. 4d. *Sufficient* for 3 or 4 persons. *Seasonable* at any time.

EGGS, Snow, or Œufs à la Neige (a very pretty Supper Dish).

Ingredients.—4 eggs, ¾ pint of milk, pounded sugar to taste, flavouring of vanilla, lemon-rind, or orange-flower water. *Mode.*—Put the milk into a saucepan with sufficient sugar to sweeten it nicely, and the rind of ½ lemon. Let this steep by the side of the fire for ½ hour, when take out the peel; separate the whites from the yolks of the eggs, and whisk the former to a perfectly stiff froth, or until there is no liquid remain-

Eggs, to keep Fresh

ing; bring the milk to the boiling-point, drop in the snow a tablespoonful at a time, and keep turning the eggs until sufficiently cooked. Then place them on a glass dish, beat up the yolks of the eggs, stir to them the milk, add a little more sugar, and strain this mixture into a jug; place the jug in a saucepan of boiling water, and stir it one way until the mixture thickens, but do not allow it to boil, or it will curdle. Pour this custard over the eggs, when they should rise to the surface. They make an exceedingly pretty addition to a supper, and should be put in a cold place after being made. When they are flavoured with vanilla or orange-flowered water, it is not necessary to steep the milk. A few drops of the essence of either may be poured into the milk just before the whites are poached. In making the custard, a little more flavouring and sugar should always be added. *Time.*— About 2 minutes to poach the whites; 8 minutes to stir the custard. *Average cost,* 8d. *Sufficient for* 4 or 6 persons. *Seasonable* at any time.

EGGS, to keep Fresh for several Weeks.

Have ready a large saucepan, capable of holding 3 or 4 quarts, full of boiling water. Put the eggs into a cabbage-net, say 20 at a time, and hold them in the water (which must be kept boiling) *for* 20 *seconds.* Proceed in this manner till you have done as many eggs as you wish to preserve; then pack them away in sawdust. We have tried this method of preserving eggs, and can vouch for its excellence. They will be found, at the end of 2 or 3 months, quite good enough for culinary purposes; and although the white may be a little tougher than that of a new-laid egg, the yolk will be nearly the same. Many persons keep eggs for a long time by smearing the shells with butter or sweet oil: they should then be packed in plenty of bran or sawdust, and the eggs not allowed to touch each other. Eggs for storing should be collected in fine weather, and should not be more than 24 hours old when they are packed away, or their flavour, when used, cannot be relied on. Another simple way of preserving eggs is to immerse them in lime-water soon after they have been laid, and then to put the vessel containing the lime-water in a

Elder Wine

cellar or cool outhouse. *Seasonable.*— The best time for preserving eggs is from April to September.

EGGS, à la Tripe.

Ingredients.—8 eggs, ¾ pint of Béchamel sauce, dessertspoonful of finely-minced parsley. *Mode.* — Boil the eggs hard; put them into cold water, peel them, take out the yolks whole, and shred the whites. Make ¾ pint of Béchamel sauce; add the parsley, and, when the sauce is quite hot, put the yolks of the eggs into the middle of the dish, and the shred whites round them; pour over the sauce, and garnish with leaves of puff-paste or fried croûtons. There is no necessity for putting the eggs into the saucepan with the Béchamel; the sauce, being quite hot, will warm the eggs sufficiently. *Time.*—10 minutes to boil the eggs. *Average cost,* 1s. *Sufficient* for 5 or 6 persons. *Seasonable* at any time.

ELDER WINE.

Ingredients.—To every 3 gallons of water allow 1 peck of elderberries; to every gallon of juice allow 3 lbs. of sugar, ½ oz. of ground ginger, 6 cloves, 1 lb. of good Turkey raisins; ¼ pint of brandy to every gallon of wine. To every 9 gallons of wine, 3 or 4 tablespoonfuls of fresh brewer's yeast. *Mode.*—Pour the water, quite boiling, on the elderberries, which should be picked from the stalks, and let these stand covered for 24 hours; then strain the whole through a sieve or bag, breaking the fruit to express all the juice from it. Measure the liquor, and to every gallon allow the above proportion of sugar. Boil the juice and sugar with the ginger, cloves, and raisins for 1 hour, skimming the liquor the whole time; let it stand until milk-warm, then put it into a clean dry cask, with 3 or 4 tablespoonfuls of good fresh yeast to every 9 gallons of wine. Let it ferment for about a fortnight; then add the brandy, bung up the cask, and let it stand some months before it is bottled, when it will be found excellent. A bunch of hops suspended to a string from the bung, some persons say, will preserve the wine good for several years. Elder wine is usually mulled, and served with sippets of toasted bread and a little grated nutmeg. *Time.* —To stand covered for 24 hours; to be boiled 1 hour. *Average*

Endive | February—Bills of Fare

cost, when made at home, 3*s*. 6*d*. per gallon. *Seasonable.*—Make this in September.

ENDIVE.

This vegetable, so beautiful in appearance, makes an excellent addition to winter salad, when lettuces and other winter salads are not obtainable. It is usually placed in the centre of the dish, and looks remarkably pretty with slices of beetroot, hard-boiled eggs, and curled celery placed round it, so that the colours contrast nicely. In preparing it, carefully wash and cleanse it free from insects, which are generally found near the heart; remove any decayed or dead leaves, and dry it thoroughly by shaking in a cloth. This vegetable may also be served hot, stewed in cream, brown gravy, or butter; but when dressed thus, the sauce it is stewed in should not be very highly seasoned, as that would destroy and overpower the flavour of the vegetable. *Average cost*, 1*d*. per head. *Sufficient.*— 1 head for a salad for 4 persons. *Seasonable* from November to March.

ENDIVE, à la Française.

Ingredients.—6 heads of endive, 1 pint of broth, 3 oz. of fresh butter; salt, pepper, and grated nutmeg to taste. *Mode.*—Wash and boil the endive as in the preceding recipe; chop it rather fine, and put into a stewpan with the broth; boil over a brisk fire until the sauce is all reduced; then put in the butter, pepper, salt, and grated nutmeg (the latter must be very sparingly used); mix all well together, bring it to the boiling point, and serve very hot. *Time.* —10 minutes to boil, 5 minutes to simmer in the broth. *Average cost*, 1*d*. per head. *Sufficient* for 3 or 4 persons. *Seasonable* from November to March.

ENDIVE, Stewed.

Ingredients.—6 heads of endive, salt and water, 1 pint of broth, thickening of butter and flour, 1 tablespoonful of lemon-juice, a small lump of sugar. *Mode.*— Wash and free the endive thoroughly from insects, remove the green part of the leaves, and put it into boiling water, slightly salted. Let it remain for 10 minutes; then take it out, drain it till there is no water remaining, and chop it very fine. Put it into a stewpan with the broth; add a little salt and a lump

of sugar, and boil until the endive is perfectly tender. When done, which may be ascertained by squeezing a piece between the thumb and finger, add a thickening of butter and flour and the lemon-juice; let the sauce boil up, and serve. *Time.*—10 minutes to boil, 5 minutes to simmer in the broth. *Average cost*, 1*d*. per head. *Sufficient* for 3 or 4 persons. *Seasonable* from November to March.

ESPAGNOLE, or Brown Spanish Sauce.

Ingredients.—2 slices of lean ham, 1 lb. of veal, 1½ pint of white stock, 2 or 3 sprigs of parsley, ½ a bay-leaf, 2 or 3 sprigs of savoury herbs, 6 green onions, 3 shalots, 2 cloves, 1 blade of mace, 2 glasses of sherry or Madeira, thickening of butter and flour. *Mode.*—Cut up the ham and veal into small square pieces, and put them into a stewpan. Moisten these with ½ pint of the stock, and simmer till the bottom of the stewpan is covered with a nicely-coloured glaze, when put in a few more spoonfuls to detach it. Add the remainder of the stock, with the spices, herbs, shalots, and onions, and simmer very gently for 1 hour. Strain and skim off every particle of fat, and, when required for use, thicken with butter and flour, or with a little roux. Add the wine, and, if necessary, a seasoning of cayenne; when it will be ready to serve. *Time.*—1½ hour. *Average cost*, 2*s*. per pint.

Note.—The wine in this sauce may be omitted, and an onion sliced and fried of a nice brown substituted for it. This sauce or gravy is used for many dishes, and with most people is a general favourite.

FEBRUARY—BILLS OF FARE
Dinner for 18 persons.
First Course.

Hare Soup,
removed by
Turbot and Oyster Sauce.

Vase of
Flowers.

Oyster Soup,
removed by
Crimped Cod à la Maitre d'Hôtel.

Fried Eels.

Fried Whitings.

February—Bills of Fare

Second Course.

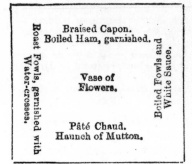

Roast Fowls, garnished with Water-cresses.

Braised Capon.
Boiled Ham, garnished.

Vase of Flowers.

Pâté Chaud.
Haunch of Mutton.

Boiled Fowls and White Sauce.

Entrées.

Lobster Patties.

Lark Pudding.

Vase of Flowers.

Fricasseed Chicken.

Filets de Perdrix.

Third Course.

Meringues.

Orange Jelly.

Victoria Sandwiches.

Ducklings, removed by Iced Pudding.

Coffee Cream.

Vase of Flowers.

Blancmange.

Partridges, removed by Cabinet Pudding.

Clear Jelly.

Cheese-cakes.

Gâteau de Pommes.

Dessert and Ices.

Dinner for 12 persons.

First Course.—Soup à la reine; clear gravy soup; brill and lobster sauce; fried smelts. *Entrées.*—Lobster rissoles; beef palates; pork cutlets à la soubise; grilled mushrooms. *Second Course.*—Braised turkey; haunch of mutton; boiled capon and **oysters**; tongue, garnished with tufts of broccoli; vegetables and salads. *Third Course.* — Wild ducks; plovers; orange jelly; clear jelly; Charlotte Russe; Nesselrode pudding; gâteau de riz; sea-kale; maids of honour; dessert and ices.

February—Bills of Fare

Dinner for 10 persons.

First Course.—Palestine soup; John Dory, with Dutch sauce; red mullet, with sauce Génoise. *Entrées.*—Sweetbread cutlets, with poivrade sauce; fowl au Béchamel. *Second Course.*—Roast saddle of mutton; boiled capon and oysters; boiled tongue, garnished with Brussels sprouts. *Third Course.*—Guinea-fowls; ducklings; pain de rhubarb; orange jelly; strawberry cream; cheesecakes; almond pudding; fig pudding; dessert and ices.

Dinner for 8 persons.

First Course.—Mock turtle soup; fillets of turbot à la crème; fried filleted soles and anchovy sauce. *Entrées.*—Larded fillets of rabbits; tendrons de veau with purée of tomatoes. *Second Course.*—Stewed rump of beef à la Jardinère; roast fowls; boiled ham. *Third Course.*—Roast pigeons or larks; rhubarb tartlets; meringues; clear jelly; cream; ice pudding; soufflé; dessert and ices.

Dinners for 6 persons.

First Course.—Rice soup; red mullet, with Génoise sauce; fried smelts. *Entrées.*—Fowl pudding; sweetbreads. *Second Course.*—Roast turkey and sausages; boiled leg of pork; pease pudding. *Third Course.*—Lemon jelly; Chariotte à la vanille; maids of honour; plum-pudding, removed by ice pudding; dessert.

First Course.—Spring soup; boiled turbot and lobster sauce. *Entrées.*—Fricasseed rabbit; oyster patties. *Second Course.*—Boiled round of beef and marrow-bones; roast fowls, garnished with water-cresses and rolled bacon; vegetables. *Third Course.*—Marrow pudding; cheesecakes; tartlets of greengage jam; lemon cream; rhubarb tart; dessert.

First Course.—Vermicelli soup; fried whitings; stewed eels. *Entrées.*—Poulet à la Marengo; breast of veal stuffed and rolled. *Second Course.*—Roast leg of pork and apple sauce; boiled capon and oysters; tongue, garnished with tufts of broccoli. *Third Course.*—Wild ducks; lobster salad; Charlotte aux pommes; pain de rhubarb; vanilla cream; orange jelly; dessert.

February, Plain Family Dinners

First Course.—Ox-tail soup; cod à la crème; fried soles. *Entrées.*—Lark pudding; fowl scollops. *Second Course.*—Roast leg of mutton; boiled turkey and celery sauce; pigeon pie; small ham, boiled and garnished; vegetables. *Third Course.*—Game, when liked; tartlets of raspberry jam; vol-au-vent of rhubarb; Swiss cream; cabinet pudding; broccoli and sea-kale; dessert.

FEBRUARY, Plain Family Dinners for.

Sunday.—1. Ox-tail soup. 2. Roast beef, Yorkshire pudding, broccoli, potatoes. 3. Plum-pudding, apple tart. Cheese.

Monday.—1. Fried soles, plain melted butter, and potatoes. Cold roast beef, mashed potatoes. 3. The remains of plum-pudding cut in slices, warmed, and served with sifted sugar sprinkled over it. Cheese.

Tuesday.—1. The remains of ox-tail soup from Sunday. 2. Pork cutlets with tomato sauce; hashed beef. 3. Rolled jam pudding. Cheese.

Wednesday.—1. Boiled haddock and plain melted butter. 2. Rump-steak pudding, potatoes, greens. 3. Arrowroot, blancmange, garnished with jam.

Thursday.—1. Boiled leg of pork, greens, potatoes, pease pudding. 2. Apple fritters, sweet macaroni.

Friday.—1. Pea-soup made with liquor that the pork was boiled in. 2. Cold pork, mashed potatoes. 3. Baked rice pudding.

Saturday.—1. Broiled herrings and mustard sauce. 2. Haricot mutton. 3. Macaroni, either served as a sweet pudding or with cheese.

Sunday.—1. Carrot soup. 2. Boiled leg of mutton and caper sauce, mashed turnips, roast fowls, and bacon. 3. Damson tart made with bottled fruit, ratafia pudding.

Monday.—1. The remainder of fowl curried and served with rice; rumpsteaks and oyster sauce, cold mutton. 2. Rolled jam pudding.

Tuesday.—1. Vegetable soup made with liquor the mutton was boiled in on Sunday. 2. Roast surloin of beef, Yorkshire pudding, broccoli, and potatoes. 3. Cheese.

Wednesday.—1. Fried soles, melted butter. Cold beef and mashed potatoes:

Fennel Sauce

if there is any cold mutton left, cut it into neat slices and warm it in a little caper sauce. 2. Apple tart.

Thursday.—1. Boiled rabbit and onion sauce, stewed beef and vegetables, made with the remains of cold beef and bones. 2. Macaroni.

Friday.—1. Roast leg of pork, sage and onions and apple sauce, greens and potatoes. 2. Spinach and poached eggs instead of pudding. Cheese and watercresses.

Saturday.—1. Rump-steak and kidney pudding, cold pork and mashed potatoes. 2. Baked rice pudding.

FEBRUARY, Things in Season.

Fish.—Barbel, brill, carp; cod may be bought, but is not so good as in January; crabs, crayfish, dace, eels, flounders, haddocks, herrings, lampreys, lobsters, mussels, oysters, perch, pike, place, prawns, shrimps, skate, smelts, soles, sprats, sturgeon, tench, thornback, turbot, whiting.

Meat.—Beef, house lamb, mutton, pork, veal.

Poultry.—Capons, chickens, ducklings, tame and wild pigeons, pullets with eggs, turkeys, wild-fowl, though now not in full season.

Game.—Grouse, hares, partridges, pheasants, snipes, woodcock.

Vegetables.—Beetroot, broccoli (purple and white), Brussels sprouts, cabbages, carrots, celery, chervil, cresses, cucumbers (forced), endive, kidney-beans, lettuces, parsnips, potatoes, savoys, spinach, turnips—various herbs.

Fruit.—Apples (golden and Dutch pippins), grapes, medlars, nuts, oranges, pears (Bon Chrétien), walnuts, dried fruits (foreign), such as almonds and raisins; French and Spanish plums; prunes, figs, dates, crystallized preserves.

FENNEL SAUCE, for Mackerel.

Ingredients.—½ pint of melted butter, rather more than 1 tablespoonful of chopped fennel. *Mode.*—Make the melted butter very smooth, chop the fennel rather small, carefully cleansing it from any grit or dirt, and put it to the butter when this is on the point of boiling. Simmer for a minute or two, and serve in a tureen. *Time.*—2 minutes. *Average cost, 4d. Sufficient* to serve with 5 or 6 mackerel.

FIG PUDDING.

Ingredients. — 2 lbs. of figs, ½ lb. of suet, ½ lb. of flour, ½ lb. of bread crumbs, 2 eggs, milk. *Mode.* — Cut the figs into small pieces, grate the bread finely, and chop the suet very small ; mix these well together, add the flour, the eggs, which should be well beaten, and sufficient milk to form the whole into a stiff paste ; butter a mould or basin, press the pudding into it very closely, tie it down with a cloth, and boil for 3 hours, or rather longer ; turn it out of the mould, and serve with melted butter, wine-sauce, or cream. *Time.* — 3 hours, or longer. *Average cost*, 2s. *Sufficient* for 7 or 8 persons. *Seasonable.* — Suitable for a winter pudding.

FIG PUDDING (Staffordshire Recipe).

Ingredients. — 1 lb. of figs, 6 oz. of suet, ¾ lb. of flour, milk. *Mode.* — Chop the suet finely, mix with it the flour, and make these into a smooth paste with milk ; roll it out to the thickness of about ¼ inch, cut the figs in small pieces, and strew them over the paste ; roll it up, make the ends secure, tie the pudding in a cloth, and boil it from 1½ to 2 hours. *Time.* — 1½ to 2 hours. *Average cost*, 1s. 1d. *Sufficient* for 5 or 6 persons. *Seasonable* at any time.

FIGS, Compôte of Green.

Ingredients. — 1 pint of syrup, 1½ pint of green figs, the rind of ½ lemon. *Mode.* — Make a syrup as directed, boiling with it the lemon-rind, and carefully remove all the scum as it rises. Put in the figs, and simmer them very slowly until tender ; dish them on a glass dish ; reduce the syrup by boiling it quickly for 5

COMPÔTE OF FIGS.

minutes ; take out the lemon-peel, pour the syrup over the figs, and the compôte, when cold, will be ready for table. A little port wine, or lemon-juice, added just before the figs are done, will be found an improvement. *Time.* — 2 to 3 hours to stew the figs. *Average cost*, figs, 2s. to 3s. per dozen. *Seasonable* in August and September.

FISH.

Fish shortly before they spawn are, in general, best in condition. When the spawning is just over, they are out of season, and unfit for human food.

When fish is out of season, it has a transparent, bluish tinge, however much it may be boiled ; whenever it is in season, its muscles are firm, and boil white and curdy.

As food for invalids, white fish, such as the ling, cod, haddock, coal-fish, and whiting, are the best ; flat fish, as soles, skate, turbot, and flounders, are also good.

Salmon, mackerel, herrings, and trout soon spoil or decompose after they are killed ; therefore, to be in perfection, they should be prepared for the table on the day they are caught. With flat fish, this is not of such consequence, as they will keep longer. The turbot, for example, is improved by being kept for a few hours

FISH, General Directions for Dressing

In dressing fish of any kind, the first point to be attended to, is to see that it is perfectly clean. It is a common error to wash it too much, as by doing so the flavour is diminished. If the fish is to be boiled, a little salt and vinegar should be put into the water, to give it firmness, after it is cleaned. Cod-fish, whiting, and haddock, are none the worse for being a little salted, and kept a day ; and, if the weather be not very hot, they will be good for two days.

When fish is cheap and plentiful, and a larger quantity is purchased than is immediately wanted, the overplus of such as will bear it should be potted, or pickled, or salted, and hung up ; or it may be fried, that it may serve for stewing the next day. Fresh-water fish, having frequently a muddy smell and taste, should be soaked in strong salt and water, after it has been well cleaned. If of a sufficient size, it may be scalded in salt and water, and afterwards dried and dressed.

Fish should be put into cold water and set on the fire to do very gently, or the outside will break before the inner part is done. Unless the fishes are small, they should never be put into warm water ; nor should water, either hot or cold, be poured on to the fish, as it is

Fish, General Directions

liable to break the skin; if it should be necessary to add a little water whilst the fish is cooking, it ought to be poured in gently at the side of the vessel. The fish-plate may be drawn up, to see if the fish be ready, which may be known by its easily separating from the bone. It should then be immediately taken out of the water, or it will become woolly. The fish-plate should be set crossways over the kettle, to keep hot for serving, and a cloth laid over the fish, to prevent its losing its colour.

In garnishing fish great attention is required, and plenty of parsley, horseradish, and lemon should be used. If fried parsley be used, it must be washed and picked, and thrown into fresh water. When the lard or dripping boils, throw the parsley into it immediately from the water, and instantly it will be green and crisp, and must be taken up with a slice. When well done, and with very good sauce, fish is more appreciated than almost any other dish. The liver and roe, in some instances, should be placed on the dish, in order that they may be distributed in the course of serving; but to each recipe will be appended the proper mode of serving and garnishing.

If fish is to be fried or broiled it must be dried in a nice soft cloth after it is well cleaned and washed. If for frying, brush it over with egg, and sprinkle it with some fine crumbs of bread. If done a second time with the egg and bread, the fish will look so much the better. If required to be very nice, a sheet of white blotting-paper must be placed to receive it, that it may be free from all grease; it must also be of a beautiful colour, and all the crumbs appear distinct. Butter gives a bad colour; lard and clarified dripping are most frequently used; but oil is the best, if the expense be no objection. The fish should be put into the lard when boiling, and there should be a sufficiency of this to cover it.

When fish is broiled, it must be seasoned, floured, and laid on a very clean gridiron, which, when hot, should be rubbed with a bit of suet, to prevent the fish from sticking. It must be broiled over a very clear fire, that it may not taste smoky; and not too near, that it may not be scorched.

In choosing fish, it is well to remember that it is possible it may be *fresh*, and yet not *good*. Under the head of each particular fish in this work, are appended

Fish and Oyster Pie

rules for its choice, and the months when it is in season. Nothing can be of greater consequence to a cook than to have the fish good; as, if this important course in a dinner does not give satisfaction, it is rarely that the repast goes off well.

FISH, General Directions for Carving.

In carving fish, care should be taken to help it in perfect flakes, as, if these are broken, the beauty of the fish is lost. The carver should be acquainted, too, with the choicest parts and morsels; and to give each guest an equal share of these *titbits* should be his maxim. Steel knives and forks should on no account be used in helping fish, as these are liable to impart to it a very disagreeable flavour. When silver fish-carvers are considered too dear to be bought, good electroplated ones answer very well, and are inexpensive.

FISH CAKE.

Ingredients.—The remains of any cold fish, 1 onion, 1 faggot of sweet herbs; salt and pepper to taste, 1 pint of water, equal quantities of bread-crumbs and cold potatoes, ½ teaspoonful of parsley, 1 egg, bread-crumbs. *Mode.*—Pick the meat from the bones of the fish, which latter put, with the head and fins, into a stewpan with the water; add pepper and salt, the onion and herbs, and stew slowly for gravy about 2 hours; chop the fish fine, and mix it well with breadcrumbs and cold potatoes, adding the parsley and seasoning; make the whole into a cake with the white of an egg, brush it over with egg, cover with breadcrumbs, fry of a light brown; strain the gravy, pour it over, and stew gently for ¾ of an hour, stirring it carefully once or twice. Serve hot, and garnish with thin slices of lemon and parsley. *Time.*—½ an hour after the gravy is made.

FISH AND OYSTER PIE.

[COLD MEAT COOKERY.] *Ingredients.*—Any remains of cold fish, such as cod or haddock; 2 dozen oysters, pepper and salt to taste, bread-crumbs sufficient for the quantity of fish; ½ teaspoonful of grated nutmeg, 1 teaspoonful of finely-chopped parsley. *Mode.*—Clear the fish from the bones, and put a layer of it in a pie-dish, which sprinkle with pepper and salt; then a layer of bread-crumbs,

Fish Pie

oysters, nutmeg, and chopped parsley. Repeat this till the dish is quite full. You may form a covering either of bread-crumbs, which should be browned, or puff-paste, which should be cut into long strips, and laid in cross-bars over the fish, with a line of the paste first laid round the edge. Before putting on the top, pour in some made melted butter, or a little thin white sauce, and the oyster-liquor, and bake. *Time.*—If made of cooked fish, ¼ hour; if made of fresh fish and puff-paste, ¾ hour. *Average cost,* 1s. 6d. *Seasonable* from September to April.

Note.—A nice little dish may be made by flaking any cold fish, adding a few oysters, seasoning with pepper and salt, and covering with mashed potatoes; ¼ hour will bake it.

FISH PIE, with Tench and Eels.

Ingredients.—2 tench, 2 eels, 2 onions, a faggot of herbs, 4 blades of mace, 3 anchovies, 1 pint of water, pepper and salt to taste, 1 teaspoonful of chopped parsley, the yokes of 6 hard-boiled eggs, puff-paste. *Mode.*—Clean and bone the tench, skin and bone the eels, and cut them into pieces 2 inches long, and leave the sides of the tench whole. Put the bones into a stewpan with the onions, herbs, mace, anchovies, water, and sea-soning, and let them simmer gently for 1 hour. Strain it off, put it to cool, and skim off all the fat. Lay the tench and eels in a pie-dish, and between each layer put seasoning, chopped parsley, and hard-boiled eggs; pour in part of the strained liquor, cover in with puff-paste, and bake for ½ hour or rather more. The oven should be rather quick, and when done, heat the remainder of the liquor, which pour into the pie. *Time.*—½ hour to bake, or rather more if the oven is slow.

FISH SAUCE.

Ingredients.—1½ oz. of cayenne, 2 ta-blespoonfuls of walnut ketchup, 2 table-spoonfuls of soy, a few shreds of garlic and shalot, 1 quart of vinegar. *Mode.*— Put all the ingredients into a large bottle, and shake well every day for a fortnight. Keep it in small bottles well sealed, and in a few days it will be fit for use. *Average cost,* for this quantity, 1s.

FISH, Scalloped.

[COLD MEAT COOKERY.] *Ingredients.*—

Flounders, Boiled

Remains of cold fish of any sort, ½ pint of cream, ¼ tablespoonful of anchovy sauce, ½ teaspoonful of made mustard, ditto of walnut ketchup, pepper and salt to taste (the above quantities are for ¼ lb. of fish when picked): bread-crumbs. *Mode.*—Put all the ingredients into a stewpan, carefully picking the fish from the bones; set it on the fire, let it re-main till nearly hot, occasionally stir the contents, but do not allow it to boil. When done, put the fish into a deep dish or scallop shell, with a good quantity of bread-crumbs; place small pieces of butter on the top, set in a Dutch oven before the fire to brown, or use a sala-mander. *Time.*—¼ hour. *Average cost,* exclusive of the cold fish, 10d.

FISH, Scalloped.

[COLD MEAT COOKERY.] *Ingredients.* —Any cold fish, 1 egg, milk, 1 large blade of pounded mace, 1 tablespoonful of flour, 1 teaspoonful of anchovy sauce, pepper and salt to taste, bread-crumbs, butter. *Mode.*—Pick the fish carefully from the bones, and moisten with milk and the egg; add the other ingredients, and place in a deep ditch or scallop shells; over with bread-crumbs, butter the top, and brown before the fire; when quite hot, serve. *Time.*—20 minutes. *Average cost,* exclusive of the cold fish, 4d.

FISH STOCK.

Ingredients.—2 lbs. of beef or veal (these can be omitted), any kind of white fish trimmings of fish which are to be dressed for table, 2 onions, the rind of ½ a lemon, a bunch of sweet herbs, 2 carrots, 2 quarts of water. *Mode.*—Cut up the fish, and put it, with the other ingredients, into the water. Simmer for 2 hours; skim the liquor carefully, and strain it. When a richer stock is wanted, fry the vegetables and fish before adding the water. *Time.*—2 hours. *Average cost,* with meat, 10d. per quart; without, 3d.

Note.—Do not make fish stock long before it is wanted, as it soon turns sour.

FLOUNDERS, Boiled.

Ingredients.—Sufficient water to cover the flounders, salt in the proportion of 6 oz. to each gallon, a little vinegar. *Mode.*—Put on a kettle with enough water to cover the flounders, lay in the

Flounders, Fried.

fish, add salt and vinegar in the above proportions, and when it boils, simmer very gently for 5 minutes. They must not boil fast, or they will break. Serve with plain melted butter, or parsley and butter. *Time*—After the water boils, 5 minutes. *Average cost*, 3d. each. *Seasonable* from August to November.

FLOUNDERS, Fried.

Ingredients.—Flounders, egg, and breadcrumbs; boiling lard. *Mode.*—Cleanse the fish, and, two hours before they are wanted, rub them inside and out with salt, to render them firm; wash and wipe them very dry, dip them into egg, and sprinkle over with bread-crumbs; fry them in boiling lard, dish on a hot napkin, and garnish with crisped parsley. *Time.*—From 5 to 10 minutes, according to size. *Average cost*, 3d. each. *Seasonable* from August to November. *Sufficient*, 1 for each person.

FLOWERS, Almond.

Ingredients —Puff-paste; to every ½ lb. of paste allow 3 oz. of almonds, sifted sugar, the white of an egg. *Mode.*—Roll the paste out to the thickness of ¼ inch, and, with a round fluted cutter, stamp out as many pieces as may be required. Work the paste up again, roll it out, and, with a smaller cutter, stamp out some pieces the size of a shilling. Brush the larger pieces over with the white of an egg, and place one of the smaller pieces on each. Blanch and cut the almonds into strips lengthwise; press them slanting into the paste closely round the rings; and when they are all completed, sift over some pounded sugar, and bake for about ¼ hour or twenty minutes. Garnish between the almonds with strips of apple jelly, and place in centre of the ring a small quantity of strawberry jam; pile them high on the dish, and serve. *Time.*—¼ hour or 20 minutes. *Sufficient.*—18 or 20 for a dish. *Seasonable* at any time.

FLOWERS, to Preserve Cut.

A bouquet of freshly-cut flowers may be preserved alive for a long time by placing them in a glass or vase with fresh water, in which a little charcoal has been steeped, or a small piece of camphor dissolved. The vase should be set upon a plate or dish, and covered with a bellglass, around the edges of which, when

Fondue, Brillat Savarin's.

it comes in contact with the plate, a little water should be poured to exclude the air.

FLOWERS, to Revive after Packing.

Plunge the stems into boiling water, and, by the time the water is cold, the flowers will have revived. Then cut afresh the ends of the stems, and keep them in fresh cold water.

FONDUE.

Ingredients.—4 eggs, the weight of 2 in Parmesan or good Cheshire cheese, the weight of 2 in butter; pepper and salt to taste. *Mode.*—Separate the yolks from the whites of the eggs; beat the former in a basin, and grate the cheese, or cut it into *very thin* flakes. Parmesan or Cheshire cheese may be used, whichever is the most convenient, although the former is considered more suitable for this dish; or an equal quantity of each may be used. Break the butter into small pieces, add to it the other ingredients, with sufficient pepper and salt to season nicely, and beat the mixture thoroughly. Well whisk the whites of the eggs, stir them lightly in, and either bake the fondue in a soufflé-dish or small round cake-tin. Fill the dish only half full, as the fondue should rise very much. Pin a napkin round the tin or dish, and serve very hot and very quickly. If allowed to stand after it is withdrawn from the oven, the beauty and lightness of this preparation will be entirely spoiled. *Time.*—From 15 to 20 minutes. *Average cost*, 10d. *Sufficient* for 4 or 5 persons. *Seasonable* at any time.

FONDUE, Brillat Savarin's (an excellent Recipe).

Ingredients. — Eggs, cheese, butter, pepper and salt. *Mode.*—Take the same number of eggs as there are guests; weigh the eggs in the shell, allow a third of their weight in Gruyère cheese, and a piece of butter one-sixth of the weight of the cheese. Break the eggs into a basin, beat them well; add the cheese, which should be grated, and the butter, which should be broken into small pieces. Stir these ingredients together with a wooden spoon; put the mixture into a lined saucepan, place it over the fire, and stir until the substance is thick and soft.

Food for Infants

Put in a little salt, according to the age of the cheese, and a good sprinkling of pepper, and serve the fondue on a very hot silver or metal plate. Do not allow the fondue to remain on the fire after the mixture is set, as, if it boils, it will be entirely spoiled. Brillat Savarin recommends that some choice Burgundy should be handed round with this dish. We have given this recipe exactly as he recommends it to be made ; but we have tried it with good Cheshire cheese, and found it answer remarkably well. *Time.* —About 4 minutes to set the mixture. *Average cost,* for 4 persons, 10*d. Sufficient.* —Allow 1 egg, with the other ingredients in proportion, for 1 person. *Seasonable* at any time.

FOOD FOR INFANTS, and its Preparation.

The articles generally employed as food for infants consist of arrowroot, bread, flour, baked flour, prepared groats, farinaceous food, biscuit-powder, biscuits, tops-and-bottoms, and semolina, or manna croup, as it is otherwise called, which, like tapioca, is the prepared pith of certain vegetable substances. Of this list the least efficacious, though, perhaps, the most believed in, is arrowroot, which only as a mere agent, for change, and then only for a very short time, should ever be employed as a means of diet to infancy or childhood. It is a thin, flatulent, and innutritious food, and incapable of supporting infantine life and energy. Bread, though the universal *régime* with the labouring poor, where the infant's stomach and digestive powers are a reflex, in miniature, of the father's, should never be given to an infant under three months, and, even then, however finely beaten up and smoothly made, is a very questionable diet. Flour, when well boiled, though infinitely better than arrowroot, is still only a kind of fermentative paste, that counteracts its own good by after-acidity and flatulence. Baked flour, when cooked into a pale brown mass, and finely powdered, makes a far superior food to the others, and may be considered as a very useful diet, especially for a change. Prepared groats may be classed with arrowroot and raw flour, as being innutritious. The articles that now follow on our list are all good, and such as we could, with conscience and safety, trust to the health and development of any child whatever.

Food for Infants

We may observe in this place, that an occasional change in the character of the food is highly desirable, both as regards the health and benefit of the child ; and, though the interruption should only last for a day, the change will be advantageous.

The packets sold as farinaceous food are unquestionably the best aliment that can be given from the first to a baby, and may be continued, with the exception of an occasional change, without alteration of the material, till the child is able to take its regular meals of animal and vegetable food. Some infants are so constituted as to require a frequent and a total change in their system of living, seeming to thrive for a certain time on any food given to them, but if persevered in too long, declining in bulk and appearance as rapidly as they had previously progressed. In such cases, the food should be immediately changed, and when that which appeared to agree best with the child is resumed, it should be altered in its quality, and perhaps in its consistency.

For the farinaceous food there are directions with each packet, containing instructions for the making ; but, whatever the food employed is, enough should be made at once to last the day and night ; at first, about a pint basinful, but, as the child advances, a quart will hardly be too much. In all cases, let the food boil a sufficient time, constantly stirring, and taking every precaution that it does not get burnt, in which case it is on no account to be used.

The food should always be made with water, the whole sweetened at once, and of such a consistency that, when poured out, and it has had time to cool, it will cut with the firmness of a pudding or custard. One or two spoonfuls are to be put into the pap saucepan and stood on the hob till the heat has softened it, when enough milk is to be added, and carefully mixed with the food, till the whole has the consistency of ordinary cream ; it is then to be poured into the nursing-bottle, and the food having been drawn through to warm the nipple, it is to be placed in the child's mouth. For the first month or more, half a bottleful will be quite enough to give the infant at one time ; but, as the child grows, it will be necessary not only to increase the quantity given at each time, but also gradually to make its food more con-

Forcemeats.

distent, and, after the third month, to add an egg to every pint basin of food made. At night, the mother puts the food into the covered pan of her lamp, instead of the saucepan—that is, enough for one supply, and, having lighted the rush, she will find, on the waking of her child, the food sufficiently hot to bear the cooling addition of the milk. But, whether night or day, the same food should never be heated twice, and what the child leaves should be thrown away.

The biscuit powder is used in the same manner as the farinaceous food, and both prepared much after the fashion of making starch. But when tops-and-bottoms, or the whole biscuit, are employed, they require soaking in cold water for some time previously to boiling. The biscuit or biscuits are then to be slowly boiled in as much water as will, when thoroughly soft, allow of their being beaten by a three-pronged fork into a fine, smooth, and even pulp, and which, when poured into a basin and become cold, will cut out like a custard. If two large biscuits have been so treated, and the child is six or seven months old, beat up two eggs, sufficient sugar to properly sweeten it, and about a pint of skim milk. Pour this on the beaten biscuit in the saucepan, stirring constantly; boil for about five minutes, pour into a basin, and use, when cold, in the same manner as the other.

This makes an admirable food, at once nutritious and strengthening. When tops-and-bottoms or rusks are used, the quantity of the egg may be reduced, or altogether omitted.

Semolina, or manna croup, being in little hard grains, like a fine millet-seed, must be boiled for some time, and the milk, sugar, and egg added to it on the fire, and boiled for a few minutes longer, and, when cold, used as the other preparations.

Many persons entertain a belief that cow's milk is hurtful to infants, and, consequently, refrain from giving it; but this is a very great mistake, for both sugar and milk should form a large portion of every meal an infant takes.

FORCEMEATS.

The points which cooks should, in this branch of cookery, more particularly observe, are the thorough chopping of the suet, the complete mincing of the

Forcemeat, French

herbs, the careful grating of the bread-crumbs, and the perfect mixing of the whole. These are the three principal ingredients of forcemeats, and they can scarcely be cut too small, as nothing like a lump or fibre should be anywhere perceptible. To conclude, the flavour of no one spice or herb should be permitted to predominate.

FORCEMEAT BALLS, for Fish Soups.

Ingredients.—1 middling-sized lobster, ½ an anchovy, 1 head of boiled celery, the yolk of a hard-boiled egg; salt, cayenne, and mace to taste; 4 table-spoonfuls of bread-crumbs, 2 oz. of butter, 2 eggs. *Mode.*—Pick the meat from the shell of the lobster, and pound it, with the soft parts, in a mortar; add the celery, the yolk of the hard-boiled egg, seasoning, and bread-crumbs. Continue pounding till the whole is nicely amalgamated. Warm the butter till it is in a liquid state; well whisk the eggs, and work these up with the pounded lobster-meat. Make the balls of about an inch in diameter, and fry of a nice pale brown. *Sufficient*, from 18 to 20 balls for 1 tureen of soup.

FORCEMEAT, French.

It will be well to state, in the beginning of this recipe, that French forcemeat, or quenelles, consist of the blending of three separate processes; namely, panada, udder, and whatever meat you intend using.

Panada. *Ingredients.*—The crumb of 2 penny rolls, 4 tablespoonfuls of white stock, 1 oz. of butter, 1 slice of ham, 1 bay-leaf, a little minced parsley, 2 shalots, 1 clove, 2 blades of mace, a few mushrooms, butter, the yolks of 2 eggs. *Mode.*—Soak the crumb of the rolls in milk for about ½ hour, then take it out, and squeeze so as to press the milk from it; put the soaked bread into a stewpan with the above quantity of white stock, and set it on one side; then put into a separate stewpan 1 oz. of butter, a slice of lean ham cut small, with a bay-leaf, herbs, mushrooms, spices, &c., in the above proportions, and fry them gently over a slow fire. When done, moisten with 2 teacupfuls of white stock, boil for 20 minutes, and strain the whole through a sieve over the panada

Forcemeat for Cold Savoury Pies.	Forcemeat Veal

in the other stewpan. Place it over the fire, keep constantly stirring, to prevent its burning, and, when quite dry, put in a small piece of butter. Let this again dry up by stirring over the fire; then add the yolks of 2 eggs, mix well, put the panada to cool on a clean plate, and use it when required. Panada should always be well flavoured, as the forcemeat receives no taste from any of the other ingredients used in its preparation.

Boiled Calf's Udder for French Forcemeat.—Put the udder into a stewpan with sufficient water to cover it; let it stew gently till quite done, when take it out to cool. Trim all the upper parts, cut it into small pieces, and pound well in a mortar, till it can be rubbed through a sieve. That portion which passes through the strainer is one of the three ingredients of which French forcemeats are generally composed; but many cooks substitute butter for this, being a less troublesome and more expeditious mode of preparation.

FORCEMEAT, for Cold Savoury Pies.

Ingredients.—1 lb. of veal, 1 lb. of fat bacon; salt, cayenne, pepper, and pounded mace to taste; a very little nutmeg, the same of chopped lemon-peel, ½ teaspoonful of chopped parsley, ½ teaspoonful of minced savoury herbs, 1 or 2 eggs. *Mode.*—Chop the veal and bacon together, and put them into a mortar with the other ingredients mentioned above. Pound well, and bind with 1 or 2 eggs which have been previously beaten and strained. Work the whole well together, and the forcemeat will be ready for use. If the pie is not to be eaten immediately, omit the herbs and parsley, as these will prevent it from keeping. Mushrooms or truffles may be added. *Sufficient* for 2 small pies.

FORCEMEAT, for Pike, Carp, Haddock, and various Kinds of Fish.

Ingredients.—1 oz. of fresh butter, 1 oz. of suet, 1 oz. of fat bacon, 1 small teaspoonful of minced savoury herbs, including parsley; a little onion, when liked, shredded very fine; salt, nutmeg, and cayenne to taste; 4 oz. of bread-crumbs, 1 egg. *Mode.*—Mix all the ingredients well together, carefully mincing them very finely; beat up the egg,

moisten with it, and work the whole very smoothly together. Oysters or anchovies may be added to this forcemeat, and will be found a great improvement. *Average cost,* 6d. *Sufficient* for a moderate-sized haddock or pie.

FORCEMEAT, for Baked Pike.

Ingredients.—3 oz. of bread-crumbs, 1 teaspoonful of minced savoury herbs, 8 oysters, 2 anchovies (these may be dispensed with), 2 oz. of suet; salt, pepper, and pounded mace to taste; 6 tablespoonfuls of cream or milk, the yolks of 2 eggs. *Mode.*—Beard and mince the oysters, prepare and mix the other ingredients, and blend the whole thoroughly together. Moisten with the cream and eggs, put all into a stewpan, and stir it over the fire till it thickens, when put it into the fish, which should have previously been cut open, and sew it up. *Time.*—4 or 5 minutes to thicken. *Average cost,* 10d. *Sufficient* for a moderate-sized pike.

FORCEMEAT, or QUENELLES, for Turtle Soup. (Soyer's Recipe.)

Take a pound and a half of lean veal from the fillet, and cut it in long thin slices; scrape with a knife till nothing but the fibre remains; put it into a mortar, pound it 10 minutes, or until in a purée; pass it through a wire sieve (use the remainder in stock); then take 1 pound of good fresh beef suet, which skin, shred, and chop very fine; put it into a mortar and pound it; then add 6 oz. of panada (that is, bread soaked in milk and boiled till nearly dry) with the suet; pound them well together, and add the veal; season with a teaspoonful of salt, a quarter one of pepper, half that of nutmeg; work all well together; then add four eggs by degrees, continually pounding the contents of the mortar. When well mixed, take a small piece in a spoon, and poach it in some boiling water; and if it is delicate, firm, and of a good flavour, it is ready for use.

FORCEMEAT VEAL, or VEAL QUENELLES.

Ingredients.—Equal quantities of veal, panada, and calf's udder, 2 eggs; seasoning to taste of pepper, salt, and pounded mace and grated nutmeg; a

Forcemeat for Veal

little flour. *Mode.*—Take the fleshy part of veal, scrape it with a knife, till all the meat is separated from the sinews, and allow about ½ lb. for an entrée. Chop the meat, and pound it in a mortar till reduced to a paste ; then roll it into a ball ; make another of panada the same size, and another of udder, taking care that these three balls be of the same *size.* (It is to be remembered, that equality of *size*, and not of weight, is here necessary.) When the three ingredients are properly prepared, pound them altogether in a mortar for some time ; for the more quenelles are pounded, the more delicate they are. Now moisten with the eggs, whites and yolks, and continue pounding, adding a seasoning of pepper, spices, &c. When the whole is well blended together, mould it into balls, or whatever shape is intended, roll them in flour, and poach in boiling water, to which a little salt should have been added. If the quenelles are not firm enough, add the yolk of another egg, but omit the white, which only makes them hollow and puffy inside. In the preparation of this recipe, it would be well to bear in mind that the ingredients are to be well pounded and seasoned, and must be made hard or soft according to the dishes they are intended for. For brown or white ragoûts they should be firm, and when the quenelles are used very small, extreme delicacy will be necessary in their preparation. Their flavour may be varied by using the flesh of rabbit, fowl, hare, pheasant, grouse, or an extra quantity of mushroom, parsley, &c.

FORCEMEAT for Veal, Turkeys, Fowls, Hare, &c.

Ingredients.—2 oz. of ham or lean bacon, ¼ lb. of suet, the rind of half a lemon, 1 teaspoonful of minced parsley, 1 teaspoonful of minced sweet herbs ; salt, cayenne, and pounded mace to taste ; 6 oz. of bread-crumbs, 2 eggs. *Mode.*— Shred the ham or bacon, chop the suet, lemon-peel, and herbs, taking particular care that all be very finely minced ; add a seasoning to taste of salt, cayenne, and mace, and blend all thoroughly together with the bread-crumbs, before wetting. Now beat and strain the eggs ; work these up with the other ingredients, and the forcemeat will be ready for use. When it is made into balls, fry of a nice

Fowls, Boiled, to Carve

brown, in boiling lard, or put them on a tin and bake for ½ hour in a moderate oven. As we have stated before, no one flavour should predominate greatly, and the forcemeat should be of sufficient body to cut with a knife, and yet not dry and heavy. For very delicate forcemeat, it is advisable to pound the ingredients together before binding with the eggs ; but for ordinary cooking, mincing very finely answers the purpose. *Average cost*, 8d. *Sufficient* for a turkey, a moderate-sized fillet of veal, or a hare. *Note.*—In the forcemeat for Hare, the liver of the animal is sometimes added. Boil for 5 minutes, mince it very small, and mix it with the other ingredients. If it should be in an unsound state, it must be on no account made use of.

FOWLS, Boiled, à la Béchamel.

Ingredients.—A pair of fowls, 1 pint of Béchamel, a few bunches of boiled broccoli or cauliflower. *Mode.*—Truss and boil the flowers ; make a pint of Béchamel sauce ; pour some of this over the fowls, and the remainder send to table in a tureen. Garnish the dish with bunches of boiled cauliflowers or broccoli, and serve very hot. The sauce should be made sufficiently thick to adhere to the fowls ; that for the tureen should be thinned by adding a spoonful or two of stock. *Time.*—From ½ to 1 hour, according to size. *Average cost*, in full season, 5s. a pair. *Sufficient* for 6 or 7 persons. *Seasonable* all the year, but scarce in early spring.

FOWLS, Boiled, to Carve.

This will not be found a very difficult member of the poultry family to carve, unless, as may happen, a very old farmyard occupant, useless for egg-laying purposes, has, by some unlucky mischance, been introduced into the kitchen as a " fine young chicken." Skill, however, and

BOILED FOWL.

the application of a small amount of strength, combined with a fine keeping of the temper, will even get over that difficulty. Fixing the fork firmly in the breast, let the knife be firmly passed along the line shown from 1 to 2 ; then cut downwards from that line to fig. 3 ;

Fowls, Boiled, to Carve

and the wing, it will be found, can be easily withdrawn. The shape of the wing should be like the accompanying engraving. Let the fork be placed inside the leg, which should be gently forced away from the body of the fowl; and the joint, being thus discovered, the carver can readily cut through it, and the leg can be served. When the leg is displaced, it should be of the same shape as that shown in the annexed woodcut.

LEG, WING, AND NECKBONE OF FOWL.

The legs and wings on either side having been taken off, the carver should draw his knife through the flesh in the direction of the line 4 to 5; by this means the knife can be slipped underneath the merrythought, which, being lifted up and pressed backward, will immediately come off. The collar- or neck-bones are the next to consider : these lie on each side of the merry-thought, close under the upper part of the wings ; and, in order to free these from the fowl, they must also be raised by the knife at their broad end, and turned from the body towards the breast-bone, until the shorter piece of the bone, as shown in the cut, breaks off. There will now be left only the breast, with the ribs. The breast can be, without difficulty, disengaged from the ribs by cutting through the latter, which will offer little impediment. The side bones are now to be taken off ; and to do this, the 'ower end of the back should be turned from the carver, who should press the point of the knife through the top of the backbone, near the centre, bringing it down towards the end of the back completely through the bone. If the knife be now turned in the opposite direction, the joint will be easily separated from the vertebræ. The backbone being now uppermost, the fork should be pressed firmly down on it, whilst at the same time the knife should be employed in raising up the lower small end of the fowl towards the fork, and thus the back will be dislocated about its middle. The wings, breast, and

Fowls, Boiled

merrythought are esteemed the prime parts of a fowl, and are usually served to the ladies of the company, to whom legs, except as a matter of paramount necessity, should not be given. Byron gave it as one reason why he did not like dining with ladies, that they always had the wings of the fowls, which he himself preferred. We heard a gentleman who, when he might have had a wing, declare his partiality for a leg, saying that he had been obliged to eat legs for so long a time that he had at last come to like them better than the other more prized parts. If the fowl is, capon-like, very large, slices may be carved from its breast in the same manner as from a turkey's.

FOWL, Boiled, with Oysters. (Excellent.)

Ingredients.—1 young fowl, 3 dozen oysters, the yolks of 2 eggs, ¼ pint of cream. *Mode.*—Truss a young fowl as for boiling ; fill the inside with oysters which have been bearded and washed in their own liquor ; secure the ends of the fowl, put it into a jar, and plunge the jar into a saucepan of boiling water. Keep it boiling for 1½ hour, or rather longer ; then take the gravy that has flowed from the oysters and fowl, of which there will be a good quantity ; stir in the cream and yolks of eggs, add a few oysters scalded in their liquor ; let the sauce get quite *hot*, but do not allow it to *boil ;* pour some of it over the fowl, and the remainder send to table in a tureen. A blade of pounded mace added to the sauce, with the cream and eggs, will be found an improvement. *Time.*—1½ hour. *Average cost*, 4s. 6d. *Sufficient* for 3 or 4 persons. *Seasonable* from September to April.

FOWLS, Broiled, and Mushroom Sauce.

Ingredients.—A large fowl ; seasoning, to taste, of pepper and salt, 2 handfuls of button mushrooms, 1 slice of lean ham, ¾ pint of thickened gravy, 1 teaspoonful of lemon juice, ¼ teaspoonful of pounded sugar. *Mode.*—Cut the fowl into quarters, roast it until three-parts done, and keep it well basted whilst at the fire. Take the fowl up, broil it for a few minutes over a clear fire, and season it with pepper and salt. Have ready some mushroom sauce made in the fol-

Fowl, Boiled, and Rice

lowing manner. Put the mushrooms into a stewpan with a small piece of butter, the ham, a seasoning of pepper and salt, and the gravy; simmer these gently for ½ hour, add the lemon-juice and sugar, dish the fowl, and pour the sauce round them. *Time.*—To roast the fowl, 35 minutes; to broil it, 10 to 15 minutes. *Average cost*, in full season, 2s. 6d. *Sufficient* for 4 or 5 persons. *Seasonable.*—In full season from May to January.

FOWL, Boiled, and Rice.

Ingredients.—1 fowl, mutton broth, 2 onions, 2 small blades of pounded mace, pepper and salt to taste, ¼ pint of rice, parsley and butter. *Mode.*—Truss the fowl as for boiling, and put it into a stewpan with sufficient clear well-skimmed mutton broth to cover it; add the onion, mace, and a seasoning of pepper and salt; stew very gently for about 1 hour, should the fowl be large, and about ½ hour before it is ready put in the rice, which should be well washed and soaked. When the latter is tender, strain it from the liquor, and put it on a sieve reversed to dry before the fire, and, in the mean time, keep the fowl hot. Dish it, put the rice round as a border, pour a little parsley and butter over the fowl, and the remainder send to table in a tureen. *Time.*—A large fowl, 1 hour. *Average cost*, 2s. 6d. *Sufficient* for 3 or 4 persons. *Seasonable* all the year.

FOWLS, to Bone, for Fricassees, Curries, and Pies.

First carve them entirely into joints, then remove the bones, beginning with the legs and wings, at the head of the largest bone; hold this with the fingers, and work the knife as directed in the recipe above. The remainder of the birds is too easily done to require any instructions.

FOWL, Croquettes of (an Entrée).

Ingredients.—3 or 4 shalots, 1 oz. of butter, 1 teaspoonful of flour, white sauce; pepper, salt, and pounded mace to taste; ½ teaspoonful of pounded sugar, the remains of cold roast fowls, the yolks of 2 eggs, egg, and bread-crumbs. *Mode.* —Mince the fowl, carefully removing all skin and bone, and fry the shalots in the butter; add the minced fowl, dredge in the flour, put in the pepper, salt, mace,

Fowl, Curried

pounded sugar, and sufficient white sauce to moisten it; stir to it the yolks of 2 well-beaten eggs, and set it by to cool. Then make the mixture up into balls, egg and bread-crumb them, and fry a nice brown. They may be served on a border of mashed potatoes, with gravy or sauce in the centre. *Time.*—10 minutes to fry the balls. *Seasonable* at any time.

FOWL AND RICE, Croquettes of (an Entrée).

Ingredients.—¼ lb. of rice, 1 quart of stock or broth, 3 oz. of butter, minced fowl, egg, and bread-crumbs. *Mode.*—Put the rice into the above proportion of cold stock or broth, and let it boil very gently for ½ hour; then add the butter, and simmer it till quite dry and soft. When cold, make it into balls, hollow out the inside, and fill with minced fowl made by recipe. The mince should be rather thick. Cover over with rice, dip the balls into egg, sprinkle them with bread-crumbs, and fry a nice brown. Dish them, and garnish with fried parsley. Oysters, white sauce, or a little cream, may be stirred into the rice before it cools. *Time.*—½ hour to boil the rice, 10 minutes to fry the croquettes. *Average cost*, exclusive of the fowl, 8d. *Seasonable* at any time.

FOWL, Curried.

Ingredients.—1 fowl, 2 oz. of butter, 3 onions sliced, 1 pint of white veal gravy, 1 tablespoonful of curry-powder, 1 table-spoonful of flour, 1 apple, 4 tablespoon-fuls of cream, 1 tablespoonful of lemon-juice. *Mode.*—Put the butter into a stewpan, with the onions sliced, the fowl cut into small joints, and the apple peeled, cored, and minced. Fry of a pale brown, add the stock, and stew gently for 20 minutes; rub down the curry-powder and flour with a little of the gravy, quite smoothly, and stir this to the other ingredients; simmer for rather more than ½ hour, and just before serving, add the above proportion of hot cream and lemon-juice. Serve with boiled rice, which may either be heaped lightly on a dish by itself, or put round the curry as a border. *Time.*—50 minutes. *Average cost*, 3s. 3d. *Sufficient* for 3 or 4 persons. *Seasonable* in the winter.

Note.—This curry may be made of cold

Q

Fowl, Fricasseed

chicken, but undressed meat will be found far superior.

FOWL, Fricasseed.

[COLD MEAT COOKERY.] *Ingredients.* —The remains of cold roast fowl, 1 strip of lemon-peel, 1 blade of pounded mace, a bunch of savoury herbs, 1 onion, pepper and salt to taste, 1 pint of water, 1 teaspoonful of flour, ¼ pint of cream, the yolks of 2 eggs. *Mode.*—Carve the fowls into nice joints; make gravy of the trimmings and legs, by stewing them with the lemon-peel, mace, herbs, onion, seasoning, and water, until reduced to ½ pint; then strain, and put in the fowl. Warm it through, and thicken with a teaspoonful of flour; stir the yolks of the eggs into the cream; add these to the sauce, let it get thoroughly hot, but do not allow it to boil, or it will curdle. *Time.*—1 hour to make the gravy, ¼ hour to warm the fowl. *Average cost,* exclusive of the cold chicken, 8d. *Seasonable* at any time.

FOWLS, Fried.

[COLD MEAT COOKERY.] *Ingredients.* —The remains of cold roast fowls, vinegar, salt and cayenne to taste, 3 or 4 minced shalots. For the batter,—½ lb. of flour, ½ pint of hot water, 2 oz. of butter, the whites of 2 eggs. *Mode.*— Cut the fowl into nice joints; steep them for an hour in a little vinegar, with salt, cayenne, and minced shalots. Make the batter by mixing the flour and water smoothly together; melt in it the butter, and add the whites of egg beaten to a froth; take out the pieces of fowl, dip them in the batter, and fry in boiling lard, a nice brown. Pile them high in the dish, and garnish with fried parsley or rolled bacon. When approved, a sauce or gravy may be served with them. *Time.*—10 minutes to fry the fowl. *Average cost,* exclusive of the cold fowl, 8d. *Seasonable* at any time.

FOWLS, Fried.

[COLD MEAT COOKERY.] *Ingredients.* —The remains of cold roast fowl, vinegar, salt and cayenne to taste, 4 minced shalots, yolk of egg; to every teacupful of bread-crumbs allow 1 blade of pounded mace, ½ teaspoonful of minced lemon-peel, 1 saltspoonful of salt, a few grains of cayenne. *Mode.*—Steep the pieces of fowl as in the preceding recipe, then dip

Fowl, Hashed

them into the yolk of an egg or clarified butter; sprinkle over bread-crumbs with which have been mixed salt, mace, cayenne, and lemon-peel in the above proportion. Fry a light brown, and serve with or without gravy, as may be preferred. *Time.*—10 minutes to fry the fowl. *Average cost,* exclusive of the cold fowl, 6d. *Seasonable* at any time.

FOWLS, Fried, and French Beans.

[COLD MEAT COOKERY.] *Ingredients.* —The remains of cold roast fowl; the yolk of 1 egg, 2 oz. of butter, 1 blade of pounded mace, ¼ saltspoonful of grated nutmeg, bread-crumbs and chopped parsley. *Mode.*—Cut the fowl into neat joints, brush them over with the yolk of egg, and sprinkle them with bread-crumbs, with which the *parsley, nutmeg,* and *mace* have been well mixed. Fry the fowl in the butter until of a nice brown, and dish the pieces on French beans boiled, and afterwards simmered for a minute or two in butter. The dish should be garnished with rolled bacon. *Time.*—10 minutes to fry the fowl. *Average cost,* exclusive of the cold fowl, 6d. *Seasonable* from July to September.

FOWL au Gratin.

[COLD MEAT COOKERY.] *Ingredients.* —The remains of either cold roast or boiled fowl, ½ pint of Béchamel sauce, a dessertspoonful of grated Parmesan cheese, pepper and salt to taste, ¼ saltspoonful of grated nutmeg, ¼ pint of cream, 2 tablespoonfuls of bread-crumbs, fried potatoes. *Mode.*—Mince the fowl not too finely, and make it hot in the Béchamel sauce, to which the nutmeg, pepper and salt, and cream, have been added. When well mixed, serve the fowl on to a dish, cover it with the bread-crumbs and Parmesan cheese, drop over a little clarified butter, and bake in the oven until of a pale brown. Garnish the dish with fried potatoes. *Time.*—10 minutes to warm the fowl, 10 minutes to bake. *Seasonable* at any time.

FOWL, Hashed. An Entree.

[COLD MEAT COOKERY.] *Ingredients.* —The remains of cold roast fowl, 1 pint of water, 1 onion, 2 or 3 small carrots, 1 blade of pounded mace, pepper and salt to taste, 1 small bunch of savoury

Fowl, Hashed

herbs, thickening of butter and flour, 1½ tablespoonful of mushroom ketchup. *Mode.*—Cut off the best joints from the fowl, and the remainder make into gravy, by adding to the bones and trimmings a pint of water, an onion sliced and fried cf a nice brown, the carrots, mace, seasoning, and herbs. Let these stew gently for 1½ hour, strain the liquor, and thicken with a little flour and butter. Lay in the fowl, thoroughly warm it through, add the ketchup, and garnish with sippets of toasted bread. *Time.*—Altogether 1¾ hour. *Average cost*, exclusive of the cold fowl, 4*d*. *Seasonable* at any time.

FOWL, Hashed, Indian Fashion (an Entree).

[COLD MEAT COOKERY.] *Ingredients.* — The remains of cold roast fowl, 3 or 4 sliced onions, 1 apple, 2 ob. of butter, pounded mace, pepper and salt to taste, 1 tablespoonful of curry-powder, 2 tablespoonfuls of vinegar, 1 tablespoonful of flour, 1 teaspoonful of pounded sugar, 1 pint of gravy. *Mode.* —Cut the onions into slices, mince the apple, and fry these in the butter; add pounded mace, pepper, salt, curry-powder, vinegar, flour, and sugar in the above proportions; when the onion is brown, put in the gravy, which should be previously made from the bones and trimmings of the fowls, and stew for ¾ hour; add the fowl cut into nice-sized joints, let it warm through, and when quite tender, serve. The dish should be garnished with an edging of boiled rice. *Time.*—1 hour. *Average cost*, exclusive of the fowl, 8*d*. *Seasonable* at any time.

FOWL, an Indian Dish of (an Entrée).

[COLD MEAT COOKERY.] *Ingredients.* -The remains of cold roast fowl, 3 or 4 sliced onions, 1 tablespoonful of curry-powder, salt to taste. *Mode.*—Divide the fowl into joints; slice and fry the onions in a little butter, taking care not to burn them; sprinkle over the fowl a little curry-powder and salt; fry these nicely, pile them high in the centre of the dish, cover with the onion, and serve with a cut lemon on a plate. Care must be taken that the onions are not greasy: they should be quite dry, but not burnt. *Time.*—5 minutes to fry the onions, 10 minutes to fry the fowl. *Average cost,*

Fowl, Minced

exclusive of the fowl, 4*d*. *Seasonable* during the winter months.

FOWL à la Mayonnaise.

Ingredients.—A cold roast fowl, Mayonnaise sauce, 4 or 5 young lettuces, 4 hard-boiled eggs, a few water-cresses, endive. *Mode.*—Cut the fowl into neat joints, lay them in a deep dish, piling them high in the centre, sauce the fowl with Mayonnaise, and garnish the dish with young lettuces cut in halves, water-cresses, endive, and hard-boiled eggs: these may be sliced in rings, or laid on the dish whole, cutting off at the bottom a piece of the white, to make the egg stand. All kinds of cold meat and solid fish may be dressed à la Mayonnaise, and make excellent luncheon or supper dishes. The sauce should not be poured over the fowls until the moment of serving. Should a very large Mayonnaise be required, use 2 fowls instead of one, with an equal proportion of the remaining ingredients. *Average cost*, with one fowl, 3*s*. 6*d*. *Sufficient* for a moderate-sized dish. *Seasonable* from April to September.

FOWL, Minced (an Entrée).

[COLD MEAT COOKERY.] *Ingredients.* —The remains of cold roast fowl, 2 hard-boiled eggs, salt, cayenne, and pounded mace, 1 onion, 1 faggot of savoury herbs, 6 tablespoonfuls of cream, 1 oz. of butter, two teaspoonfuls of flour, ½ teaspoonful of finely-minced lemon-peel, 1 tablespoonful of lemon-juice. *Mode.*—Cut out from the fowl all the white meat, and mince it finely without any skin or bone; put the bones, skin, and trimmings into a stewpan with an onion, a bunch of savoury herbs, a blade of mace, and nearly a pint of water; let this stew for an hour, then strain the liquor. Chop the eggs small; mix them with the fowl; add salt, cayenne, and pounded mace, put in the gravy and remaining ingredients; let the whole just boil, and serve with sippets of toasted bread. *Time.*— Rather more than 1 hour. *Average cost,* exclusive of the fowl, 8*d*. *Seasonable* at any time.

Note.—Another way to make this is to mince the fowl, and warm it in white sauce or Béchamel. When dressed like this, 3 or 4 poached eggs may be placed on the top: oysters, or chopped mushrooms, or balls of oyster forcemeat, may be laid round the dish.

Fowl, Minced

FOWL, Minced, à la Béchamel.

[COLD MEAT COOKERY.] *Ingredients.* —The remains of cold roast fowl, 6 tablespoonfuls of Béchamel sauce, 6 tablespoonfuls of white stock, the white of 1 egg, bread-crumbs, clarified butter. *Mode.*—Take the remains of roast fowls, mince the white meat very small, and put it into a stewpan with the Béchamel and stock ; stir it well over the fire, and just let it boil up. Pour the mince into a dish, beat up the white of egg, spread it over, and strew on it a few grated bread-crumbs ; pour a very little clarified butter on the whole, and brown either before the fire or with a salamander. This should be served in a silver dish, if at hand. *Time.*—2 or 3 minutes to simmer in the sauce. *Seasonable* at any time.

FOWL, Ragoût of.

[COLD MEAT COOKERY.] *Ingredients.* —The remains of cold roast fowls, 3 shalots, 2 blades of mace, a faggot of savoury herbs, 2 or 3 slices of lean ham, 1 pint of stock or water, pepper and salt to taste, 1 onion, 1 dessertspoonful of flour, 1 tablespoonful of lemon-juice, ½ teaspoonful of pounded sugar, 1 oz. of butter. *Mode.*—Cut the fowls up into neat pieces, the same as for a fricassee ; put the trimmings into a stewpan with the shalots, mace, herbs, ham, onion, and stock (water may be substituted for this). Boil it slowly for 1 hour, strain the liquor, and put a small piece of butter into a stewpan ; when melted, dredge in sufficient flour to dry up the butter, and stir it over the fire. Put in the strained liquor, boil for a few minutes, and strain it again over the pieces of fowl. Squeeze in the lemon-juice, add the sugar and a seasoning of pepper and salt, make it hot, but do not allow it to boil ; lay the fowl neatly on the dish, and garnish with croûtons. *Time.*—Altogether 1½ hour. *Average cost,* exclusive of the cold fowl, 9d. *Seasonable* at any time.

FOWLS, Roast.

Ingredients.—A pair of fowls, a little flour. *Mode.*—Fowls, to be tender, should be killed a couple of days before they are dressed ; when the feathers come out easily ; then let them be picked and cooked. In drawing them be careful not to break the gall-bag, as, wherever it

Fowl, Roast, to Carve

touches, it would impart a very bitter taste ; the liver and gizzard should also be preserved. Truss them in the following manner : — After having carefully picked them, cut off the head, and skewer the skin of the neck down over the back. Cut off the claws, dip the legs in boiling water, and scrape them ; turn the pinions under, run a skewer through them and the middle of the legs, which should be passed through the body to the pinion and leg on the other side, one skewer securing the limbs on both sides. The

ROAST FOWL.

liver and gizzard should be placed in the wings, the liver on one side and the gizzard on the other. Tie the legs together by passing a trussing-needle, threaded with twine, through the backbone, and secure it on the other side. If trussed like a capon, the legs are placed more apart. When firmly trussed, singe them all over ; put them down to a bright clear fire, paper the breasts with a sheet of buttered paper, and keep the fowls well basted. Roast them for ¾ hour, more or less, according to the size, and 10 minutes before serving, remove the paper, dredge the fowls with a little fine flour, put a piece of butter into the basting-ladle, and as it melts baste the fowls with it ; when nicely frothed and of a rich colour, serve with good brown gravy (a little of which should be poured over the fowls), and a tureen of well-made bread sauce. Mushroom, oyster, or egg sauce, are very suitable accompaniments to roast fowl.— Chicken is roasted in the same manner. *Time.*—A very large fowl, quite 1 hour, a medium-sized one, ¾ hour ; chicken, ½ hour, or rather longer. *Average cost,* in full season, 5s. a pair : when scarce, 7s. 6d. the pair. *Sufficient* for 6 or 7 persons. *Seasonable* all the year, but scarce in early spring.

FOWL, Roast, to Carve.

A roast fowl is carved in the same manner as a boiled fowl, viz., by cutting along the line from 1 to 2, and then round the leg between it and the wing. The markings and detached pieces, as shown in the engravings under the heading of

Fowl, Roast, Stuffed

* Boiled Fowl," supersede the necessity of our lengthily again describing the ope-

ration. It may be added, that the liver, being considered a delicacy,

ROAST FOWL.

should be divided, and one half served with each wing. In the case of a fowl being stuffed, it will be proper to give each guest a portion, unless it be not agreeable to some one of the party.

FOWL, Roast, Stuffed.

Ingredients.—A large fowl, forcemeat, a little flour. *Mode.*—Select a large plump fowl, fill the breast with force-meat, truss it firmly, the same as for a plain roast fowl, dredge it with flour, and put it down to a bright fire. Roast it for nearly or quite an hour, should it be very large; remove the skewers, and serve with a good brown gravy and a tureen of bread sauce. *Time.*—Large fowl, nearly or quite 1 hour. *Average cost*, in full season, 2s. 6d. each. *Sufficient* for 4 or 5 persons. *Seasonable* all the year, but scarce in early spring.

Note.—Sausage-meat stuffing may be substituted : this is now a very general mode of serving fowl.

FOWL SAUTE with Peas (an Entrée).

[COLD MEAT COOKERY.] *Ingredients.* —The remains of cold roast fowl, 2 oz. of butter, pepper, salt, and pounded mace to taste, 1 dessertspoonful of flour, ½ pint of weak stock, 1 pint of green peas, 1 teaspoonful of pounded sugar. *Mode.*—Cut the fowl into nice pieces ; put the butter into a stewpan ; sautez or fry the fowl a nice brown colour, previously sprinkling it with pepper, salt, and pounded mace. Dredge in the flour, shake the ingredients well round, then add the stock and peas, and stew till the latter are tender, which will be in about 20 minutes ; put in the pounded sugar, and serve, placing the chicken round, and the peas in the middle of the dish. When liked, mushrooms may be substituted for the peas. *Time.*—Altogether 40 minutes. *Average cost*, exclusive of the fowl, 7d. *Seasonable* from June to August.

French Terms

FOWL SCOLLOPS.

[COLD MEAT COOKERY.] *Ingredients.*— The remains of cold roast or boiled fowl, ½ pint of Béchamel, or white sauce. *Mode.*—Strip off the skin from the fowl ; cut the meat into thin slices, and warm them in about ½ pint, or rather more, of Béchamel, or white sauce. When quite hot, serve, and garnish the dish with rolled ham or bacon toasted. *Time.*—1 minute to simmer the slices of fowl. *Seasonable* at any time.

FRENCH TERMS used in modern Household Cookery, explained.

ASPIC.—A savoury jelly, used as an exterior moulding for cold game, poultry, fish, &c. This, being of a transparent nature, allows the article which it covers to be seen through it. This may also be used for decorating or garnishing.

ASSIETTE (plate).—*Assiettes* are the small *entrées* and *hors - d'œuvres*, the quantity of which does not exceed what a plate will hold. At dessert, fruits, cheese, chestnuts, biscuits, &c., if served upon a plate, are termed *assiettes.*— ASSIETTE VOLANTE is a dish which a ser-vant hands round to the guests, but is not placed upon the table. Small cheese soufflés and different dishes, which ought to be served very hot, are frequently made *assiettes volantes.*

AU-BLEU.—Fish dressed in such a manner as to have a *bluish* appearance.

BAIN-MARIE.—An open saucepan or kettle of nearly boiling water, in which a smaller vessel can be set for cooking and warming. This is very useful for keeping articles hot, without altering their quantity or quality. If you keep sauce, broth, or soup by the fireside, the soup reduces and becomes too strong, and the sauce thickens as well as re-duces ; but this is prevented by using the *bain-marie*, in which the water should be very hot, but not boiling.

BÉCHAMEL.—French white sauce, now frequently used in English cookery.

BLANCH.—To whiten poultry, vegeta-bles, fruit, &c., by plunging them into boiling water for a short time, and after-wards plunging them into cold water, there to remain until they are cold.

BLANQUETTE.—A sort of fricassee.

BOUILLI.—Beef or other meat boiled ; but, generally speaking, boiled beef is understood by the term

French Terms

BOUILLIE.—A French dish resembling hasty-pudding.

BOUILLON.—A thin broth or soup.

BRAISE.—To stew meat with fat bacon until it is tender, it having previously been blanched.

BRAISIÈRE.—A saucepan having a lid with ledges, to put fire on the top.

BRIDER. — To pass a packthread through poultry, game, &c., to keep together their members.

CARAMEL (burnt sugar).—This is made with a piece of sugar, of the size of a nut, browned in the bottom of a saucepan; upon which a cupful of stock is gradually poured, stirring all the time, and adding the broth little by little. It may be used with the feather of a quill, to colour meats, such as the upper part of fricandeaux; and to impart colour to sauces. Caramel made with water instead of stock may be used to colour *compôtes* and other *entremets*.

CASSEROLE.—A crust of rice, which, after having been moulded into the form of a pie, is baked, and then filled with a fricassee of white meat or a purée of game.

COMPOTE.—A stew, as of fruit or pigeons.

CONSOMMÉ.—Rich stock, or gravy.

CROQUETTE. — Ball of fried rice or potatoes.

CROÛTONS.—Sippets of bread.

DAUBIÈRE.—An oval stewpan, in which *daubes* are cooked; *daubes* being meat or fowl stewed in sauce.

DÉSOSSER.—To *bone*, or take out the bones from poultry, game, or fish. This is an operation requiring considerable experience.

ENTRÉES.—Small side or corner dishes served with the first course.

ENTREMETS. — Small side or corner dishes served with the second course.

ESCALOPES.— Collops; small, round, thin pieces of tender meat, or of fish, beaten with the handle of a strong knife to make them tender.

FEUILLETAGE.—Puff-paste.

FLAMBER.—To singe fowl or game, after they have been picked.

FONCER.—To put in the bottom of a saucepan slices of ham, veal, or thin broad slices of bacon.

GALETTE.—A broad thin cake.

GÂTEAU.—A cake, correctly speaking; but used sometimes to denote a pudding and a kind of tart.

GLACER.—To glaze. or spread upon

French Terms

hot meats, or larded fowl, a thick and rich sauce or gravy, called *glaze*. This is laid on with a feather or brush, and in confectionary the term means to ice fruits and pastry with sugar, which glistens on hardening.

HORS-D'ŒUVRES. — Small dishes, or *assiettes volantes* of sardines, anchovies, and other relishes of this kind, served to the guests during the first course. (*See* ASSIETTES VOLANTES.)

LIT.—A bed or layer; articles in thin slices are placed in layers, other articles, or seasoning, being laid between them.

MAIGRE.—Broth, soup, or gravy, made without meat.

MATELOTE.—A rich fish-stew, which is generally composed of carp, eels, trout, or barbel. It is made with wine.

MAYONNAISE.—Cold sauce, or salad dressing.

MENU.—The bill of fare.

MERINGUE.—A kind of icing, made of whites of eggs and sugar, well beaten.

MIROTON.—Larger slices of meat than collops; such as slices of beef for a vinaigrette, or ragoût or stew of onions.

MOUILLER.—To add water, broth, or other liquid, during the cooking.

PANER. — To cover with very fine crumbs of bread, meats, or any other articles to be cooked on the gridiron, in the oven, or frying-pan.

PIQUER.—To lard with strips of fat bacon, poultry, game, meat, &c. This should always be done according to the vein of the meat, so that in carving you slice the bacon across as well as the meat.

POELÉE.—Stock used instead of water for boiling turkeys, sweetbreads, fowls, and vegetables, to render them less insipid. — This is rather an expensive preparation.

PURÉE.—Vegetables or meat reduced to a very smooth pulp, which is afterwards mixed with enough liquid to make it of the consistency of very thick soup.

RAGOÛT.—Stew or hash.

REMOULADE.—Salad dressing.

RISSOLES.—Pastry, made of light puff-paste, and cut into various forms, and fried. They may be filled with fish, meat, or sweets.

ROUX.— Brown and white; French thickening.

SALMI.—Ragoût of game previously roasted.

SAUCE PIQUANTE.—A sharp sauce, in which somewhat of a vinegar flavour predominates.

Fritters, Indian

SAUTER.—To dress with sauce in a saucepan, repeatedly moving it about.

TAMIS.—Tammy, a sort of open cloth or sieve through which to strain broth and sauces, so as to rid them of small bones, froth, &c.

TOURTE.—Tart. Fruit pie.

TROUSSER.—To truss a bird; to put together the body and tie the wings and thighs, in order to round it for roasting or boiling, each being tied then with pack-thread, to keep it in the required form.

VOL-AU-VENT.—A rich crust of very fine puff-paste, which may be filled with various delicate ragoûts or fricassees, of fish, flesh, or fowl. Fruit may also be inclosed in a *vol-au-vent.*

FRITTERS, Indian.

Ingredients.—3 tablespoonfuls of flour, boiling water, the yolks of 4 eggs, the whites of 2, hot lard or clarified dripping, jam. *Mode.*—Put the flour into a basin, and pour over it sufficient *boiling* water to make it into a stiff paste, taking care to stir and beat it well, to prevent it getting lumpy. Leave it a little time to cool, and then break into it (*without beating them at first*) the yolks of 4 eggs and the whites of 2, and stir and beat all well together. Have ready some boiling lard or butter; drop a dessertspoonful of batter in at a time, and fry the fritters of a light brown. They should rise so much as to be almost like balls. Serve on a dish, with a spoonful of preserve or marmalade dropped in between each fritter. This is an excellent dish for a hasty addition to dinner, if a guest unexpectedly arrives, it being so easily and quickly made, and it is always a great favourite. *Time.*—From 5 to 8 minutes to fry the fritters. *Average cost,* exclusive of the jam, 5d. *Sufficient* for **4 or 5** persons. Seasonable at any time.

FRITTERS, Plain.

Ingredients.—3 oz. of flour, 3 eggs, ½ pint of milk. *Mode.*—Mix the flour to a smooth batter with a small quantity of the milk; stir in the eggs, which should be well whisked, and then the remainder of the milk; beat the whole to a perfectly smooth batter, and should it be found not quite thin enough, add two or three tablespoonfuls more milk. Have ready a frying-pan, with plenty of boiling lard in it; drop in rather more than a tablespoonful at a time of the batter,

Fruit, to Bottle Fresh

and fry the fritters a nice brown, turning them when sufficiently cooked on one side. Drain them well from the greasy moisture by placing them upon a piece of blotting-paper before the fire; dish them on a white d'oyley, sprinkle over them sifted sugar, and send to table with them a cut lemon and plenty of pounded sugar. *Time.*—From 6 to 8 minutes. *Average cost,* 4d. *Sufficient* for 3 or 4 persons. *Seasonable* at any time.

FRUIT, to Bottle Fresh. (Very useful in Winter.)

Ingredients.—Fresh fruits, such as currants, raspberries, cherries, gooseberries, plums of all kinds, damsons, &c.; wide-mouthed glass bottles, new corks to fit them tightly. *Mode.*—Let the fruit be full grown, but not too ripe, and gathered in dry weather. Pick it off the stalks without bruising or breaking the skin, and reject any that is at all blemished: if gathered in the damp, or if the skins are cut at all, the fruit will mould. Have ready some *perfectly dry* glass bottles, and some nice *new* soft corks or bungs; burn a match in each bottle, to exhaust the air, and quickly place the fruit in to be preserved; gently cork the bottles, and put them in a very *cool* oven, where let them remain until the fruit has shrunk away a fourth part. Then take the bottles out; *do not open them,* but immediately beat the corks in tight, cut off the tops, and cover them with melted resin. If kept in a dry place, the fruit will remain good for months; and on this principally depends the success of the preparation; for if stored away in a place that is in the least damp, the fruit will soon spoil. *Time.*—**From 5 to 6 hours** in a very slow oven.

FRUIT, to Bottle Fresh.

Ingredients.—Any kind of fresh fruit, such as currants, cherries, gooseberries, all kinds of plums, &c.; wide-mouthed glass bottles, new corks to fit them tightly. *Mode.*—The fruit must be full-grown, not too ripe, and gathered on a fine day. Let it be carefully picked and put into the bottles, which must be clean and perfectly dry. Tie over the tops of the bottles pieces of bladder; stand the bottles in a large pot, copper, or boiler, with cold water to reach to their necks; kindle a fire under, let the water boil, and as the bladders begin to rise and

Fruit, to Bottle Fresh

puff, prick them. As soon as the water boils, extinguish the fire, and let the bottles remain where they are, to become cold. The next day remove the bladders, and strew over the fruit a thick layer of pounded sugar; fit the bottles with cork, and let each cork lie close at hand to its own bottle. Hold for a few moments, in the neck of the bottle, two or three lighted matches, and when they have filled the bottle neck with gas, and before they go out, remove them very quickly; instantly cork the bottle closely, and dip it in bottle-cement. *Time.*—Altogether about 8 hours.

FRUIT, to Bottle Fresh, with Sugar. (Very useful in Winter.)

Ingredients.—Any kind of fresh fruit; to each quart bottle allow ¼ lb. of pounded sugar. *Mode.*—Let the fruit be gathered in dry weather. Pick it carefully, and drop it into *clean* and *very dry* quart glass bottles, sprinkling over it the above proportion of pounded sugar to each quart. Put the corks in the bottles, and place them in a copper of cold water up to their necks, with small hay-wisps round them, to prevent the bottles from knocking together. Light the fire under, bring the water gradually to boil, and let it simmer gently until the fruit in the bottles is reduced nearly one third. Extinguish the fire, *and let the bottles remain in the water until it is perfectly cold;* then take them out, make the corks secure, and cover them with melted resin or wax. *Time.*—About ½ hour from the time the water commences to boil.

FRUIT TURNOVERS (suitable for Pic-Nics).

Ingredients.—Puff-paste, any kind of fruit, sugar to taste. *Mode.*—Make some puff-paste by recipe; roll it out to the thickness of about ¼ inch, and cut it out in pieces of a circular form; pile the fruit on half of the paste, sprinkle over some sugar, wet the edges and turn the paste over. Press the edges together, ornament them, and brush the turnovers over with the white of an egg; sprinkle over sifted sugar, and bake on tins, in a brisk oven, for about 20 minutes. Instead of putting the fruit in raw, it may be boiled down with a little sugar first, and then inclosed in the crust; or jam, of any kind, may be substituted for fresh fruit. *Time.*—20 minutes. *Sufficient.*—

Gherkins, Pickled

½ lb. of puff-paste will make a dozen turnovers. *Seasonable* at any time.

GAME, Hashed.

[COLD MEAT COOKERY.] *Ingredients.*—The remains of cold game, 1 onion stuck with 3 cloves, a few whole peppers, a strip of lemon-peel, salt to taste, thickening of butter and flour, 1 glass of port wine, 1 tablespoonful of lemon-juice, 1 tablespoonful of ketchup, 1 pint of water or weak stock. *Mode.*—Cut the remains of cold game into joints, reserve the best pieces, and the inferior ones and trimmings put into a stewpan with the onion, pepper, lemon-peel, salt, and water or weak stock; stew these for about an hour, and strain the gravy; thicken it with butter and flour; add the wine, lemon-juice, and ketchup; lay in the pieces of game, and let them gradually warm through by the side of the fire; do not allow it to boil, or the game will be hard. When on the point of simmering, serve, and garnish the dish with sippets of toasted bread. *Time.*—Altogether 1¼ hour. *Seasonable* from August to March.

Note.—Any kind of game may be hashed by the above recipe, and the flavour may be varied by adding flavoured vinegars, curry powder, &c.; but we cannot recommend these latter ingredients, as a dish of game should really have a gamy taste; and if too many sauces, essences, &c., are added to the gravy, they quite overpower and destroy the flavour the dish should possess.

GERMAN PUFFS.

Ingredients.—2 oz. of flour, 2 eggs, ½ pint of new milk, 2 oz. of melted butter, little salt and nutmeg. *Mode.*—Let the 2 eggs be well beaten, then mix all the ingredients well together, and beat them up just before they are put into little cups half full for baking. Bake for ¼ hour in a hot oven till the puffs are of a nice brown; turn out on a flat dish, rub a little butter over each puff, and dust on it powdered sugar. *Time.*—¼ hour. *Average cost,* 6d. *Seasonable* at any time.

GHERKINS, Pickled.

Ingredients.—Salt and water, 1 oz. of bruised ginger ¼ oz. of whole black pepper, ¼ oz. of whole allspice, 4 cloves,

2 blades of mace, a little horseradish. This proportion of pepper, spices, &c., for 1 quart of vinegar. *Mode.*—Let the gherkins remain in salt and water for 3 or 4 days, when take them out, wipe perfectly dry, and put them into a stone jar. Boil sufficient vinegar to cover them, with spices and pepper, &c., in the above proportion, for 10 minutes; pour it, quite boiling, over the gherkins, cover the jar with vine-leaves, and put over them a plate, setting them near the fire, where they must remain all night. Next day drain off the vinegar, boil it up again, and pour it hot over them. Cover up with fresh leaves, and let the whole remain till quite cold. Now tie down closely with bladder to exclude the air, and in a month or two they will be fit for use. *Time.*—4 days. *Seasonable* from the middle of July to the end of August.

GIBLET PIE.

Ingredients.—A set of duck or goose giblets, 1 lb. of rump-steak, 1 onion, ½ teaspoonful of whole black pepper, a bunch of savoury herbs, plain crust. *Mode.*—Clean, and put the giblets into a stewpan with an onion, whole pepper, and a bunch of savoury herbs; add rather more than a pint of water, and simmer gently for about 1½ hour. Take them out, let them cool, and cut them into pieces; line the bottom of a pie-dish with a few pieces of rump-steak; add a layer of giblets and a few more pieces of steak; season with pepper and salt, and pour in the gravy (which should be strained), that the giblets were stewed in; cover with a plain crust, and bake for rather more than 1½ hour in a brisk oven. Cover a piece of paper over the pie, to prevent the crust taking too much colour. *Time.*—1½ hour to stew the giblets, about 1 hour to bake the pie. *Average cost*, exclusive of the giblets, 1s. 4d. *Sufficient* for 5 or 6 persons.

GIBLET SOUP.

Ingredients.—3 sets of goose or duck giblets, 2 lbs. of shin of beef, a few bones, 1 ox-tail, 2 mutton-shanks, 2 large onions, 2 carrots, 1 large faggot of herbs, salt and pepper to taste, ¼ pint of cream, 1 oz. of butter mixed with a dessert-spoonful of flour, 3 quarts of water. *Mode.*—Scald the giblets, cut the gizzards in 8 pieces, and put them in a stew-

pan with the beef, bones, ox-tail, mutton-shanks, onions, herbs, pepper, and salt; add the 3 quarts of water, and simmer till the giblets are tender, taking care to skim well. When the giblets are done, take them out, put them in your tureen, strain the soup through a sieve, add the cream and butter, mixed with a dessert-spoonful of flour, boil it up for a few minutes, and pour it over the giblets. It can be flavoured with port wine and a little mushroom ketchup, instead of cream. Add salt to taste. *Time.*—3 hours. *Average cost*, 9d. per quart. *Seasonable* all the year. *Sufficient* for 10 persons.

GINGER, Apple. (A Dessert Dish.)

Ingredients.—2 lbs. of any kind of hard apples, 2 lbs. of loaf sugar, 1½ pint of water, ¼ oz. of tincture of ginger. *Mode.*—Boil the sugar and water until they form a rich syrup, adding the ginger when it boils up. Pare, core, and cut the apples into pieces; dip them in cold water to preserve the colour, and boil them in the syrup until transparent; but be careful not to let them break. Put the pieces of apple into jars, pour over the syrup, and carefully exclude the air, by well covering them. It will remain good some time, if kept in a dry place. *Time.*—From 5 to 10 minutes to boil the syrup; about ½ hour to simmer the apples. *Average cost*, 2s. *Sufficient* for 7 or 8 persons. *Seasonable.*—Make this in September, October, or November.

GINGER-BEER.

Ingredients.—2½ lbs. of loaf sugar, 1½ oz. of bruised ginger, 1 oz. of cream of tartar, the rind and juice of 2 lemons, ¼ gallons of boiling water, two large tablespoonfuls of thick and fresh brewer's yeast. *Mode.*—Peel the lemons, squeeze the juice, strain it, and put the peel and juice into a large earthen pan, with the bruised ginger, cream of tartar, and loaf sugar. Put over these ingredients 3 gallons of *boiling* water; let it stand until just warm, when add the yeast, which should be thick and perfectly fresh. Stir the contents of the pan well, and let them remain near the fire all night, covering the pan over with a cloth. The next day skim off the yeast, and pour the liquor carefully into another vessel, leaving the sediment; then bottle immediately, and tie the corks down,

Ginger Cream	Gingerbread, White

and in 3 days the ginger-beer will be fit for use. For some tastes, the above proportion of sugar may be found rather too large, when it may be diminished; but the beer will not keep so long good. *Average cost* for this quantity, 2s. ; or ½d. per bottle. *Sufficient* to fill 4 dozen ginger-beer bottles. *Seasonable.*—This should be made during the summer months.

GINGER CREAM.

Ingredients.—The yolks of 4 eggs, 1 pint of cream, 3 oz. of preserved ginger, 2 dessertspoonfuls of syrup, sifted sugar to taste, 1 oz. of isinglass. *Mode.*— Slice the ginger finely; put it into a basin with the syrup, the well-beaten yolks of eggs, and the cream ; mix these ingredients well together, and stir them over the fire for about 10 minutes, or until the mixture thickens ; then take it off the fire, whisk till nearly cold, sweeten to taste, add the isinglass, which should be melted and strained, and serve the cream in a glass dish. It may be garnished with slices of preserved ginger or candied citron. *Time.* —About 10 minutes to stir the cream over the fire. *Average cost,* with cream at 1s. per pint, 3s. 6d. *Sufficient* for a good-sized dish. *Seasonable* at any time.

GINGER, Preserved,

Comes from the West Indies. It is made by scalding the roots when they are green and full of sap, then peeling them in cold water and putting them into jars, with a rich syrup ; in which state we receive them. It should be chosen of a deep yellow colour, with a little transparency. What is dark-coloured, fibrous, and stringy, is not good. Ginger roots, fit for preserving and in size equal to West Indian, have been produced in the Royal Agricultural Garden in Edinburgh.

GINGER PUDDING.

Ingredients.—½ lb. of flour, ¼ lb. of suet, ¼ lb. of moist sugar, 2 large teaspoonfuls of grated ginger. *Mode.*— Shred the suet very fine, mix it with the flour, sugar, and ginger; stir all well together ; butter a basin, and put the mixture in *dry;* tie a cloth over, and boil for 3 hours. *Time.*—3 hours. *Average cost,* 6d. *Sufficient* for 5 or 6 persons. *Seasonable* at any time.

GINGER WINE.

Ingredients.— To 9 gallons of water allow 27 lbs. of loaf sugar, 9 lemons, 12 oz. of bruised ginger, 3 tablespoonfuls of yeast, 2 lbs. of raisins stoned and chopped, 1 pint of brandy. *Mode.* —Boil together for 1 hour in a copper (let it previously be well scoured and beautifully clean) the water, sugar, *lemon-rinds,* and bruised ginger; remove every particle of scum as it rises, and when the liquor is sufficiently boiled, put it into a large tub or pan, as it must not remain in the copper. When nearly cold, add the yeast, which must be thick and very fresh, and, the next day, put all in a dry cask with the strained lemon-juice and chopped raisins. Stir the wine every day for a fortnight ; then add the brandy, stop the cask down by degrees, and in a few weeks it will be fit to bottle. *Average cost,* 2s. per gallon. *Sufficient* to make 9 gallons of wine. *Seasonable.*— The best time for making this wine is either in March or September.

Note.—Wine made early in March will be fit to bottle in June.

GINGERBREAD, Thick.

Ingredients.—1 lb. of treacle, ¼ lb. of butter, ¼ lb. of coarse brown sugar, 1½ lb. of flour, 1 oz. of ginger, ½ oz. of ground allspice, 1 teaspoonful of carbonate of soda, ¼ pint of warm milk, 3 eggs. *Mode.*—Put the flour into a basin, with the sugar, ginger, and allspice ; mix these together ; warm the butter, and add it, with the treacle, to the other ingredients. Stir well ; make the milk just warm, dissolve the carbonate of soda in it, and mix the whole into a nice smooth dough with the eggs, which should be previously well whisked ; pour the mixture into a buttered tin, and bake it from ¾ to 1 hour, or longer, should the gingerbread be very thick. Just before it is done, brush the top over with the yolk of an egg beaten up with a little milk, and put it back in the oven to finish baking. *Time.*—¾ to 1 hour. *Average cost,* 1s. per square. *Seasonable* at any time.

GINGERBREAD, White.

Ingredients.—1 lb. of flour, ½ lb. of butter, ½ lb. of loaf sugar, the rind of 1 lemon, 1 oz. of ground ginger, 1 nutmeg grated, ½ teaspoonful of carbonate of soda, 1 gill of milk. *Mode.*—Rub the

Gingerbread-Nuts

utter into the flour; add the sugar, which should be finely pounded and sifted, and the minced lemon-rind, ginger, and nutmeg. Mix these well together; make the milk just warm, stir in the soda, and work the whole into a nice smooth paste; roll it out, cut it into cakes, and bake in a moderate oven from 15 to 20 minutes. *Time.*—15 to 20 minutes. *Average cost,* 1s. 3d. *Seasonable* at any time.

GINGERBREAD - NUTS, Rich Sweetmeats.

Ingredients.—1 lb. of treacle, ¼ lb. of clarified butter, 1 lb. of coarse brown sugar, 2 oz. of ground ginger, 1 oz. of candied orange-peel, 1 oz. of candied angelica, ½ oz. of candied lemon-peel, ½ oz. of coriander seeds, ½ oz. of caraway seeds, 1 egg; flour. *Mode.*—Put the treacle into a basin, and pour over it the butter, melted so as not to oil, the sugar, and ginger. Stir these ingredients well together, and whilst mixing, add the candied peel, which should be cut into very small pieces, but not bruised, and the caraway and coriander seeds, which should be pounded. Having mixed all thoroughly together, break in an egg, and work the whole up with as much fine flour as may be necessary to form a paste. Make this into nuts of any size, and put them on a tin plate, and bake in a slow oven from ¼ to ½ hour. *Time.* —¼ to ½ hour. *Average cost,* from 1s. to 1s. 4d. per lb. *Seasonable* at any time.

GINGERBREAD-NUTS, Sunderland. (An Excellent Recipe.)

Ingredients.—1¾ lb. of treacle, 1 lb. of moist sugar, 1 lb. of butter, 2¾ lbs. of flour, 1½ oz. of ground ginger, 1½ oz. of allspice, 1½ oz. of coriander-seeds. *Mode.*—Let the allspice, coriander-seeds, and ginger be freshly ground; put them into a basin, with the flour and sugar, and mix these ingredients well together; warm the treacle and butter together; then with a spoon work it into the flour, &c. until the whole forms a nice smooth paste. Drop the mixture from the spoon on a piece of buttered paper, and bake in rather a slow oven from 20 minutes to ½ hour. A little candied lemon-peel mixed with the above is an improvement, and a great authority in culinary matters suggests the addition of a little cayenne pepper in gingerbread. Whether it be

Glaze-Kettle

advisable to use the latter ingredient or not, we leave our readers to decide. *Time.*—20 minutes to ½ hour. *Average cost,* 1s. to 1s. 4d. per lb. *Seasonable* at any time.

GLAZE for covering Cold Hams, Tongues, &c.

Ingredients.—Stock, doubling the quantity of meat in the recipes. *Mode.*—We may remark at the outset, that unless glaze is wanted in very large quantities, it is seldom made expressly. Either of the stocks, boiled down and reduced very considerably, will be found to produce a very good glaze. Put the stock into a stewpan, over a nice clear fire; let it boil till it becomes somewhat stiff, when keep stirring, to prevent its burning. The moment it is sufficiently reduced, and come to a glaze, turn it into the glaze-pot before it gets cold. As, however, this is not to be found in every establishment, a white earthenware jar would answer the purpose; and this may be placed in a vessel of boiling water, to melt the glaze when required. It should never be warmed in a saucepan, except on the principle of the bain marie, lest it should reduce too much, and become black and bitter. If the glaze is wanted of a pale colour, more veal than beef should be used in making the stock; and it is as well to omit turnips and celery, as these impart a disagreeable bitter flavour.

GLAZE-KETTLE.

This is a kettle used for keeping the strong stock boiled down to a jelly, which is known by the name of glaze. It is composed of two tin vessels, as

GLAZE-KETTLE.

shown in the cut, one of which, the upper,—containing the glaze, is inserted into one of larger diameter, and containing boiling water.

GLAZE, to, Cold Joints, &c.

Melt the glaze by placing the vessel which contains it, into the bain marie or saucepan of boiling water; brush it over the meat with a paste-brush, and if in places it is not quite covered, repeat the operation. The glaze should not be too dark a colour.

GOLDEN PUDDING.

Ingredients.— ¼ lb. of bread-crumbs, ¼ lb. of suet, ¼ lb. of marmalade, ¼ lb. of sugar, 4 eggs. *Mode.*—Put the bread-crumbs into a basin; mix with them the suet, which should be finely minced, the marmalade, and the sugar; stir all these ingredients well together, beat the eggs to a froth, moisten the pudding with these, and when well mixed put it into a mould or buttered basin; tie down with a floured cloth, and boil for 2 hours. When turned out, strew a little fine-sifted sugar over the top, and serve. *Time.*—2 hours. *Average cost,* 11d. *Sufficient* for 5 or 6 persons. *Seasonable* at any time.

Note.—The mould may be ornamented with stoned raisins, arranged in any fanciful pattern, before the mixture is poured in, which would add very much to the appearance of the pudding. For a plainer pudding, double the quantities of the bread-crumbs; and if the eggs do not moisten it sufficiently, use a little milk.

GOOSE, Green.

Ingredients.—Goose, 3 oz. of butter, pepper and salt to taste. *Mode.*—Geese are called green till they are about four months old, and should not be stuffed. After it has been singed and trussed, put into the body a seasoning of pepper and salt, and the butter to moisten it inside. Roast before a clear fire for about ¾ hour, froth and brown it nicely, and serve with a brown gravy, and, when liked, gooseberry-sauce. This dish should be garnished with water-cresses. *Time.*—About ¾ hour. *Average cost,* 4s. 6d. each. *Sufficient* for 5 or 6 persons. *Seasonable* in June, July, and August.

GOOSE, Hashed.

[COLD MEAT COOKERY.] *Ingredients.* —The remains of cold roast goose, 2 onions, 2 oz. of butter, 1 pint of boiling water, 1 dessertspoonful of flour, pepper and salt to taste, 1 tablespoonful of port wine, 2 tablespoonfuls of mushroom

ketchup. *Mode.*—Cut up the goose into pieces of the size required; the inferior joints, trimmings, &c., put into a stew-pan to make the gravy; slice and fry the onions in the butter of a very pale brown; add these to the trimmings, and pour over about a pint of boiling water; stew these gently for ¾ hour, then skim and strain the liquor. Thicken it with flour, and flavour with port wine and ketchup in the above proportion; add a seasoning of pepper and salt, and put in the pieces of goose; let these get thoroughly hot through, but do not allow them to boil, and serve with sippets of toasted bread. *Time.*—Altogether, rather more than 1 hour. *Average cost,* exclusive of the cold goose, 4d. *Seasonable* from September to March.

GOOSE, Roast.

Ingredients. — Goose, 4 large onions, 10 sage-leaves, ¼ lb. of bread-crumbs, 1½ oz. of butter, salt and pepper to taste, 1 egg. *Choosing and Trussing.*—Select a goose with a clean white skin, plump breast, and yellow feet: if these latter are red, the bird is old. Should the weather permit, let it hang for a few days; by so doing the flavour will be very much improved. Pluck, singe, draw, and carefully wash and wipe the goose; cut off the neck close to the back, leaving the skin long enough to turn over; cut off the feet at the first joint, and separate the pinions at the first joint. Beat the breast-bone flat with a rolling-pin, put a skewer through the under part of each wing, and having drawn up the legs closely, put a skewer into the middle of

ROAST GOOSE.

each, and pass the same quite through the body. Insert another skewer into the small of the leg, bring it close down to the side-bone, run it through, and do the same to the other side. Now cut off the end of the vent, and make a hole in the skin sufficiently large for the passage of the rump, in order to keep in the seasoning. *Mode.*—Make a sage-and-onion stuffing of the above ingredients, put it into the body of the goose, and secure it

Goose, Roast, to Carve

firmly at both ends by passing the rump through the hole made in the skin, and the other end by tying the skin of the neck to the back: by this means the seasoning will not escape. Put it down to a brisk fire, keep it well basted, and roast from 1½ to 2 hours, according to the size. Remove the skewers, and serve with a tureen of good gravy, and one of well-made apple sauce. Should a very highly-flavoured seasoning be preferred, the onions should not be parboiled, but minced raw: of the two methods the mild seasoning is far superior. A ragoût, or pie, should be made of the giblets, or they may be stewed down to make gravy. Be careful to serve the goose before the breast falls, or its appearance will be spoiled by coming flattened to table. As this is rather a troublesome joint to carve, a *large* quantity of gravy should not be poured round the goose, but sent in a tureen. *Time.*—A large goose, 1¾ hour; a moderate-sized one, 1¼ to 1½ hour. *Seasonable* from September to March; but in perfection from Michaelmas to Christmas. *Average cost*, 5s. 6d. each. *Sufficient* for 8 or 9 persons. *Note.*—A teaspoonful of made mustard, a saltspoonful of salt, a few grains of cayenne, mixed with a glass of port wine, are sometimes poured into the goose by a slit made in the apron. This sauce is by many considered an improvement.

GOOSE, Roast, to Carve.

It would not be fair to say that this dish bodes a great deal of happiness to an inexperienced carver, especially if there is a large party to serve, and the slices off the breast should not suffice to satisfy the desires and cravings of many wholesome appetites, produced, may be, by the various sports in vogue at Michaelmas and Christmas. The beginning of the task, however, is not in any way difficult. Evenly-cut slices, not too thick or too thin, should be carved from the breast in the direction of the line from 2 to 3; after the first slice has been cut,

ROAST GOOSE.

a hole should be made with the knife in the part called the apron. passing it

Goose Stuffing

round the line as indicated by the figures 1, 1, 1; here the stuffing is located, and some of this should be served on each plate, unless it is discovered that it is not agreeable to the taste of some one guest. If the carver manages cleverly, he will be able to cut a very large number of fine slices off the breast, and the more so if he commences close down by the wing, and carves upwards towards the ridge of the breastbone. As many slices as can be taken from the breast being carved, the wings should be cut off, and the same process as described in carving boiled fowl is made use of in this instance, only more dexterity and greater force will most probably be required. The shape of the leg, when disengaged from the body of the goose, should be like that shown in the accompanying engraving. It will be necessary, perhaps, in taking

LEG, WING, AND NECK-BONE OF GOOSE.

off the leg, to turn the goose on its side, and then, pressing down the small end of the leg, the knife should be passed under it from the top quite down to the joint; the leg being now turned back by the fork, the knife must cut through the joint, loosening the thighbone from its socket. The merrythought, which in a goose is not so large as might be expected, is disengaged in the same way as that of a fowl—by passing the knife under it, and pressing it backwards towards the neck. The neckbones, of which we give a cut, are freed by the same process as are those of a fowl; and the same may be said of all the other parts of this bird. The breast of a goose is the part most esteemed; all parts, however, are good, and full of juicy flavour.

GOOSE STUFFING, Soyer's Recipe for.

Take 4 apples peeled and cored, 4 onions, 4 leaves of sage, and 4 leaves of lemon thyme not broken, and boil them in a stewpan with sufficient water to cover them; when done, pulp them through a

Gooseberries, Compôte of

sieve, removing the sage and thyme; then add sufficient pulp of mealy potatoes to cause it to be sufficiently dry without sticking to the hand; add pepper and salt, and stuff the bird.

GOOSEBERRIES, Compôte of.

Ingredients.—Syrup; to 1 pint of syrup allow nearly a quart of gooseberries. *Mode.*—Top and tail the gooseberries, which should not be very ripe, and pour over them some boiling water; then take them out and plunge them into cold water with which has been mixed a tablespoonful of vinegar, which will assist to keep the fruit a good colour. Make a pint of syrup, and when it boils drain the gooseberries and put them in; simmer them gently until the fruit is nicely pulped and tender without being broken; then dish the gooseberries on a glass dish, boil the syrup for 2 or 3 minutes, pour over the gooseberries, and serve cold. *Time.*—About 5 minutes to boil the gooseberries in the syrup, 3 minutes to reduce the syrup. *Average cost, 9d.* *Sufficient.*—A quart of gooseberries for 5 or 6 persons. *Seasonable* in June.

GOOSEBERRY CHIPS. (Useful for Dessert.)

Ingredients.—Gooseberries unripe and green, but quite full-grown; sifted loaf sugar. *Mode.* — Put the gooseberries, when cleaned of tops and tails, into jars, and boil them in a copper till quite soft. To every lb. of pulp add ½ lb. of loaf sugar sifted: the sugar must be stirred in very gently. Then pour out the sweetened pulp on flat dishes, about ⅛ inch thick, which must be set in the sun to dry. When sufficiently dried in the sun, the pulp may be cut into strips, and twisted into any fanciful shapes, bows, &c. *Time* for drying, according to the amount of sun. *Seasonable* at all times.

Note.—These chips may be kept for years in tin boxes, if packed quite dry, with layers of paper between the rows.

GOOSEBERRY FOOL.

Ingredients.—Green gooseberries; to every pint of pulp add 1 pint of milk, or ½ pint of cream and ½ pint of milk; sugar to taste. *Mode.*—Cut the tops and tails off the gooseberries, put them into a jar with 2 tablespoonfuls of water and a little good moist sugar; set this jar in a saucepan of boiling water, and let it boil until

Gooseberry Jam

the fruit is soft enough to mash. When done enough, beat it to a pulp, work this pulp through a colander, and stir to every pint the above proportion of milk, or equal quantities of milk and cream. Ascertain if the mixture is sweet enough, and put in plenty of sugar, or it will not be eatable; and in mixing the milk and gooseberries add the former very gradually to these: serve in a glass dish, or in small glasses. This, although a very old-fashioned and homely dish, is, when well made, very delicious, and, if properly sweetened, a very suitable preparation for children. *Time.*—From ¾ to 1 hour. *Average cost, 6d.* per pint, with milk. *Sufficient.*—A pint of milk and a pint of gooseberry pulp for 5 or 6 children. *Seasonable* in May and June.

GOOSEBERRY JAM.

Ingredients.—To every lb. of fruit allow ¾ lb. of loaf sugar; currant-juice. *Mode.*—Select red hairy gooseberries; have them gathered in dry weather, when quite ripe, without being too soft. Weigh them; with a pair of scissors cut off the tops and tails, and to every 6 lbs. of fruit have ready ½ pint of red-currant juice, drawn as for jelly. Put the gooseberries and currant-juice into a preserving-pan, let them boil tolerably quickly, keeping them well stirred; when they begin to break, add to them the sugar, and keep simmering until the jam becomes firm, carefully skimming and stirring it, that it does not burn at the bottom. It should be boiled rather a long time, or it will not keep. Put it into pots (not too large), let it get perfectly cold, then cover the pots down with oiled and egged papers. *Time.*—About 1 hour to boil the gooseberries in the currant-juice, from ½ to ¾ hour with the sugar. *Average cost,* per lb. pot, from 6d. to 8d. *Sufficient.*—Allow 1½ pint of fruit for a lb. pot. *Seasonable.*—Make this in June or July.

GOOSEBERRY JAM.

Ingredients.—To every 8 lbs. of red, rough, ripe gooseberries allow 1 quart of red-currant juice, 5 lbs. of loaf sugar. *Mode.*—Have the fruit gathered in dry weather, and cut off the tops and tails. Prepare 1 quart of red-currant juice, the same as for red-currant jelly; put it into a preserving-pan with the sugar, and keep stirring until the latter is dissolved

| Gooseberry Jam | Gooseberry Sauce |

Keep it boiling for about 5 minutes; skim well; then put in the gooseberries, and let them boil from ½ to ¾ hour; then turn the whole into an earthen pan, and let it remain for 2 days. Boil the jam up again until it looks clear; put it into pots, and when cold, cover with oiled paper, and over the jars put tissue-paper brushed over on both sides with the white of an egg, and store away in a dry place. Care must be taken, in making this, to keep the jam well stirred and well skimmed, to prevent it burning at the bottom of the pan, and to have it very clear. *Time.*—5 minutes to boil the currant-juice and sugar after the latter is dissolved; from ½ to ¾ hour to simmer the gooseberries the first time, ¼ hour the second time of boiling. *Average cost,* from 8d. to 10d. per lb. pot. *Sufficient.*—Allow 1½ pint of fruit for a lb. pot. *Seasonable.*—Make this in June or July.

GOOSEBERRY JAM, White or Green.

Ingredients.—Equal weight of fruit and sugar. *Mode.*—Select the gooseberries not very ripe, either white or green, and top and tail them. Boil the sugar with water (allowing ½ pint to every lb.) for about ¼ hour, carefully removing the scum as it rises; then put in the gooseberries, and simmer gently till clear and firm: try a little of the jam on a plate; if it jellies when cold, it is done, and should then be poured into pots. When cold, cover with oiled paper, and tissue-paper brushed over on both sides with the unbeaten white of an egg, and stow away in a dry place. *Time.*—¼ hour to boil the sugar and water, ¾ hour the jam. *Average cost,* from 6d. to 8d. per lb. pot. *Sufficient.*—Allow 1½ pint of fruit for a lb. pot. *Seasonable.*—Make this in June.

GOOSEBERRY JELLY.

Ingredients.—Gooseberries; to every pint of juice allow ¾ lb. of loaf sugar. *Mode.*—Put the gooseberries, after cutting off the tops and tails, into a preserving-pan, and stir them over the fire until they are quite soft; then strain them through a sieve, and to every pint of juice allow ¾ lb. of sugar. Boil the juice and sugar together for nearly ¾ hour, stirring and skimming all the time; and if the jelly appears firm when a little of it is poured on to a plate, it is done,

and should then be taken up and put into small pots. Cover the pots with oiled and egged papers, the same as for currant jelly, and store away in a dry place. *Time.*—¾ hour to simmer the gooseberries without the sugar; ¾ hour to boil the juice. *Average cost,* from 8d. to 10d. per ½-lb. pot. *Seasonable* in July.

GOOSEBERRY PUDDING, Baked.

Ingredients. — Gooseberries, 3 eggs, 1½ oz. of butter, ½ pint of bread-crumbs, sugar to taste. *Mode.*—Put the gooseberries into a jar, previously cutting off the tops and tails; place this jar in boiling water, and let it boil until the gooseberries are soft enough to pulp; then beat them through a coarse sieve, and to every pint of pulp add 3 well-whisked eggs, 1½ oz. of butter, ½ pint of bread-crumbs, and sugar to taste; beat the mixture well, put a border of puff-paste round the edge of a pie-dish, put in the pudding, bake for about 40 minutes, strew sifted sugar over, and serve. *Time.* —About 40 minutes. *Average cost,* 10d. *Sufficient* for 4 or 5 persons. *Seasonable* from May to July.

GOOSEBERRY PUDDING, Boiled.

Ingredients.—¾ lb. of suet crust, 1½ pint of green gooseberries, ¼ lb. of moist sugar. *Mode.*—Line a pudding-basin with suet crust rolled out to about ⅓ inch in thickness, and, with a pair of scissors, cut off the tops and tails of the gooseberries; fill the basin with the fruit, put in the sugar, and cover with crust. Pinch the edges of the pudding together, tie over it a floured cloth,

BOILED FRUIT PUDDING.

put it into boiling water, and boil from 2½ to 3 hours; turn it out of the basin, and serve with a jug of cream. *Time.*—2½ to 3 hours. *Average cost,* 10d. *Sufficient* for 6 or 7 persons. *Seasonable* from May to July.

GOOSEBERRY SAUCE for Boiled Mackerel.

Ingredients.—1 pint of green gooseberries, 3 tablespoonfuls of Béchamel

| Gooseberry Tart | Gooseberry Wine |

(veal gravy may be substituted for this), 2 oz. of fresh butter; seasoning to taste of salt, pepper, and grated nutmeg. *Mode.*—Boil the gooseberries in water until quite tender; strain them, and rub them through a sieve. Put into a saucepan the Béchamel or gravy, with the butter and seasoning; add the pulp from the gooseberries, mix all well together, and heat gradually through. A little pounded sugar added to this sauce is by many persons considered an improvement, as the saccharine matter takes off the extreme acidity of the unripe fruit. *Time.*—Boil the gooseberries from 20 minutes to ½ hour. *Sufficient.* — This quantity, for a large dish of mackerel. *Seasonable* from May to July.

GOOSEBERRY TART.

Ingredients.—1½ pint of gooseberries, ⅜ lb. of short crust, ¼ lb. of moist sugar. *Mode.*—With a pair of scissors cut off the tops and tails of the gooseberries; put them into a deep pie-dish, pile the fruit high in the centre, and put in the sugar; line the edge of the dish with short crust, put on the cover, and ornament the edges of the tart; bake in a good oven for about ¾ hour, and before being sent to table, strew over it some fine-sifted sugar. A jug of cream, or a dish of boiled or baked custards, should always accompany this dish. *Time.*— ¾ hour. *Average cost,* 9d. *Sufficient* for 5 or 6 persons. *Seasonable* from May to July.

GOOSEBERRY TRIFLE.

Ingredients.—1 quart of gooseberries, sugar to taste, 1 pint of custard, a plateful of whipped cream. *Mode.*—Put the gooseberries into a jar, with sufficient moist sugar to sweeten them, and boil them until reduced to a pulp. Put this pulp at the bottom of a trifle-dish; pour over it a pint of custard made by recipe, and, when cold, cover with whipped cream. The cream should be whipped the day before it is wanted for table, as it will then be so much firmer and more solid; but it should not be added to the fruit until a short time before it is required. The dish may be garnished as fancy dictates. *Time.*—About ¾ hour to boil the gooseberries. *Average cost,* 1s. 6d. *Sufficient* for 1 trifle. *Seasonable* in May, June, and July.

GOOSEBERRY VINEGAR. (An Excellent Recipe.)

Ingredients.—2 pecks of crystal gooseberries, 6 gallons of water, 12 lbs. of foots sugar of the coarsest brown quality. *Mode.*—Mash the gooseberries (which should be quite ripe) in a tub with a mallet; put to them the water nearly milk-warm; let this stand 24 hours; then strain it through a sieve, and put the sugar to it; mix it well, and tun it. These proportions are for a 9-gallon cask; and if it be not quite full, more water must be added. Let the mixture be stirred from the bottom of the cask two or three times daily for three or four days, to assist the melting of the sugar; then paste a piece of linen cloth over the bunghole, and set the cask in a warm place, *but not in the sun;* any corner of a warm kitchen is the best situation for it. The following spring it should be drawn off into stone bottles, and the vinegar will be fit for use twelve months after it is made. This will be found a most excellent preparation, greatly superior to much that is sold under the name of the best white wine vinegar. Many years' experience has proved that pickle made with this vinegar will keep, when bought vinegar will not preserve the ingredients. The cost per gallon is merely nominal, especially to those who reside in the country and grow their own gooseberries; the coarse sugar is then the only ingredient to be purchased. *Time.*—To remain in the cask 9 months. *Average cost,* when the gooseberries have to be purchased, 1s. per gallon; when they are grown at home, 6d. per gallon. *Seasonable.*—This should be made the end of June or the beginning of July, when gooseberries are ripe and plentiful.

GOOSEBERRY WINE, Effervescing.

Ingredients.—To every gallon of water allow 6 lbs. of green gooseberries, 3 lbs. of lump sugar. *Mode.*—This wine should be prepared from unripe gooseberries, in order to avoid the flavour which the fruit would give to the wine when in a mature state. Its briskness depends more upon the time of bottling than upon the unripe state of the fruit, for effervescing wine can be made from fruit that is ripe as well as that which is unripe. The fruit should be selected when it has near

| Gooseberry Wine | Gravy, a good Beef |

attained its full growth, and consequently before it shows any tendency to ripen. Any bruised or decayed berries, and those that are very small, should be rejected. The blossom and stalk ends should be removed, and the fruit well bruised in a tub or pan, in such quantities as to insure each berry being broken without crushing the seeds. Pour the water (which should be warm) on the fruit, squeeze and stir it with the hand until all the pulp is removed from the skin and seeds, and cover the whole closely for 24 hours ; after which, strain it through a coarse bag, and press it with as much force as can be conveniently applied, to extract the whole of the juice and liquor the fruit may contain. To every 40 or 50 lbs. of fruit one gallon more of hot water may be passed through the *marc*, or husks, in order to obtain any soluble matter that may remain, and be again pressed. The juice should be put into a tub or pan of sufficient size to contain all of it, and the sugar added to it. Let it be well stirred until the sugar is dissolved, and place the pan in a warm situation ; keep it closely covered, and let it ferment for a day or two. It must then be drawn off into clean casks, placed a little on one side for the scum that arises to be thrown out, and the casks kept filled with the remaining "must," that should be reserved for that purpose. When the active fermentation has ceased, the casks should be plugged upright, again filled, if necessary, the bungs be put in loosely, and, after a few days, when the fermentation is a little more languid (which may be known by the hissing noise ceasing), the bungs should be driven in tight, and a spile-hole made, to give vent if necessary. About November or December, on a clear fine day, the wine should be racked from its lees into clean casks, which may be rinsed with brandy. After a month, it should be examined to see if it is sufficiently clear for bottling ; if not, it must be fined with isinglass, which may be dissolved in some of the wine : 1 oz. will be sufficient for 9 gallons. In bottling the wine, it will be necessary to wire the corks down, or to tie them down with string. Old champagne bottles are the best for this wine. In March or April, or when the gooseberry bushes begin to blossom, the wine must be bottled, in order to insure its being effervescing. *Seasonable.*—Make this the end of May or beginning of June, before the berries ripen.

GRAVIES, General Stock for

By the addition of various store sauces, thickening and flavouring, good stock may be converted into good gravies. It should be borne in mind, however, that the goodness and strength of spices, wines, flavourings, &c., evaporate, and that they lose a great deal of their fragrance if added to the gravy a long time before they are wanted. If this point is attended to, a saving of one half the quantity of these ingredients will be effected, as, with long boiling, the flavour almost entirely passes away. The shank-bones of mutton, previously well soaked, will be found a great assistance in enriching gravies ; a kidney or melt, beef skirt, trimmings of meat, &c. &c., answer very well when only a small quantity is wanted, and a good gravy need not necessarily be so very expensive ; for economically-prepared dishes are oftentimes found as savoury and wholesome as dearer ones. The cook should also remember that the fragrance of gravies, should not be overpowered by too much spice, or any strong essences, and that they should always be warmed in a *bain marie*, after they are flavoured, or else in a jar or jug placed in a saucepan full of boiling water. The remains of roast-meat gravy should always be saved ; as, when no meat is at hand, a very nice gravy in haste may be made from it, and when added to hashes, ragoûts, &c., is a great improvement.

GRAVY, a Good Beef, for Poultry, Game, &c.

Ingredients.—½ lb. of lean beef, ½ pint of cold water, 1 shalot or small onion, ½ a teaspoonful of salt, a little pepper, 1 tablespoonful of Harvey's sauce or mushroom ketchup, ½ a teaspoonful of arrow-root. *Mode.*—Cut up the beef into small pieces, and put it, with the water, into a stewpan. Add the shalot and seasoning, and simmer gently for 3 hours, taking care that it does not boil fast. A short time before it is required, take the arrow root, and having mixed it with a little cold water, pour it into the gravy, which keep stirring, adding the Harvey's sauce, and just letting it boil. Strain off the gravy in a tureen, and serve very hot. *Time.*—3 hours. *Average cost,* 8d. per pint.

10

Gravy, Beef	Gravy, Cheap

GRAVY, Beef, a Quickly Made.

Ingredients.—½ lb. of shin of beef, ½ onion, ¼ carrot, 2 or 3 sprigs of parsley and savoury herbs, a piece of butter about the size of a walnut; cayenne and mace to taste, ¾ pint of water. *Mode.*— Cut up the meat into very small pieces, slice the onion and carrot, and put them into a small saucepan with the butter. Keep stirring over a sharp fire until they have taken a little colour, when add the water and the remaining ingredients. Simmer for ½ hour, skim well, strain, and flavour, when it will be ready for use. *Time.*—½ hour. *Average cost*, for this quantity, 5d.

GRAVY, Brown.

Ingredients.—2 oz. of butter, 2 large onions, 2 lbs. of shin of beef, 2 small slices of lean bacon (if at hand), salt and whole pepper to taste, 3 cloves, 2 quarts of water. For thickening, 2 oz. of butter, 3 oz. of flour. *Mode.*—Put the butter into a stewpan; set this on the fire, throw in the onions cut in rings, and fry them a light brown; then add the beef and bacon, which should be cut into small square pieces; season, and pour in a teacupful of water; let it boil for about ten minutes, or until it is of a nice brown colour, occasionally stirring the contents. Now fill up with water in the above proportion; let it boil up, when draw it to the side of the fire to simmer very gently for 1½ hour; strain, and when cold, take off all the fat. In thickening this gravy, melt 3 oz. of butter in a stewpan, add 2 oz. of flour, and stir till of a light-brown colour; when cold, add it to the strained gravy, and boil it up quickly. This thickening may be made in larger quantities, and kept in a stone jar for use when wanted. *Time.* — Altogether, 2 hours. *Average cost*, 4d. per pint.

GRAVY, Brown, without Meat.

Ingredients.—2 large onions, 1 large carrot, 2 oz. of butter, 3 pints of boiling water, 1 bunch of savoury herbs, a wineglassful of good beer; salt and pepper to taste. *Mode.*—Slice, flour, and fry the onions and carrots in the butter until of a nice light-brown colour; then add the boiling water and the remaining ingredients; let the whole stew gently for about an hour, then strain, and when cold, skim off all the fat. Thicken it, and, if thought necessary, add a few drops

of colouring. *Time.*—1 hour. *Average cost*, 2d. per pint.

Note.—The addition of a small quantity of mushroom ketchup or Harvey's sauce very much improves the flavour of this gravy.

GRAVY, Cheap, for Minced Veal.

Ingredients.—Bones and trimmings of cold roast or boiled veal, 1½ pint of water, 1 onion, ¼ teaspoonful of minced lemon-peel, ¼ teaspoonful of salt, 1 blade of pounded mace, the juice of ¼ lemon; thickening of butter and flour. *Mode.*— Put all the ingredients into a stewpan, except the thickening and lemon-juice, and let them simmer very gently for rather more than 1 hour, or until the liquor is reduced to a pint, when strain through a hair sieve. Add a thickening of butter and flour, and the lemon-juice; set it on the fire, and let it just boil up, when it will be ready for use. It may be flavoured with a little tomato sauce, and, where a rather dark-coloured gravy is not objected to, ketchup, or Harvey's sauce, may be added at pleasure. *Time.* —Rather more than 1 hour. *Average cost*, 3d.

GRAVY, Cheap, for Hashes, &c.

Ingredients.—Bones and trimmings of the cooked joint intended for hashing, ¼ teaspoonful of salt, ¼ teaspoonful of whole pepper, ¼ teaspoonful of whole allspice, a small faggot of savoury herbs, ½ head of celery, 1 onion, 1 oz. of butter, thickening, sufficient boiling water to cover the bones. *Mode.*—Chop the bones in small pieces, and put them in a stewpan, with the trimmings, salt, pepper, spice, herbs, and celery. Cover with boiling water, and let the whole simmer gently for 1½ or 2 hours. Slice and fry the onion in the butter till it is of a pale brown, and mix it gradually with the gravy made from the bones; boil for ¼ hour, and strain into a basin; now put it back into the stewpan; flavour with walnut pickle or ketchup, pickled-onion liquor, or any store sauce that may be preferred. Thicken with a little butter and flour, kneaded together on a plate, and the gravy will be ready for use. After the thickening is added, the gravy should just boil, to take off the rawness of the flour. *Time.*—2 hours, or rather more. *Average cost*, 4d., exclusive of the bones and trimmings.

| Gravy for Roast Meat | Gravy, Rich |

GRAVY for Roast Meat.

Ingredients.—Gravy, salt. *Mode.*—Put a common dish with a small quantity of salt in it under the meat, about a quarter of an hour before it is removed from the fire. When the dish is full, take it away, baste the meat, and pour the gravy into the dish on which the joint is to be served.

GRAVY for Venison.

Ingredients.—Trimmings of venison, 3 or 4 mutton shank-bones, salt to taste, 1 pint of water, 2 teaspoonfuls of walnut ketchup. *Mode.*—Brown the trimmings over a nice clear fire, and put them in a stewpan with the shank-bones and water; simmer gently for 2 hours, strain and skim, and add the walnut ketchup and a seasoning of salt. Let it just boil, when it is ready to serve. *Time.*—2 hours.

GRAVY, Jugged (Excellent).

Ingredients.—2 lbs. of shin of beef, ¼ lb. of lean ham, 1 onion or a few shalots, 2 pints of water, salt and whole pepper to taste, 1 blade of mace, a faggot of savoury herbs, ½ a large carrot, ½ a head of celery. *Mode.*—Cut up the beef and ham into small pieces, and slice the vegetables; take a jar, capable of holding two pints of water, and arrange therein, in layers, the ham, meat, vegetables, and seasoning, alternately, filling up with the above quantity of water; tie down the jar, or put a plate over the top, so that the steam may not escape; place it in the oven, and let it remain there from 6 to 8 hours; should, however, the oven be very hot, less time will be required. When sufficiently cooked, strain the gravy, and when cold, remove the fat. It may be flavoured with ketchup, wines, or any other store sauce that may be preferred. It is a good plan to put the jar in a cool oven over-night, to draw the gravy; and then it will not require so long baking the following day. *Time.*— From 6 to 8 hours, according to the oven. *Average cost, 7d. per pint.*

GRAVY-KETTLE.

This is a utensil which will not be found in every kitchen; but it is a useful one where it is necessary to keep gravies hot for the purpose of pouring over vari-

ous dishes as they are cooking. It is made of copper, and should, conse-

GRAVY-KETTLE.

quently, be heated over the hot-plate, if there be one, or a charcoal stove.

GRAVY made without Meat for Fowls.

Ingredients.—The necks, feet, livers, and gizzards of the fowls, 1 slice of toasted bread, ½ onion, 1 faggot of savoury herbs, salt and pepper to taste, ½ pint of water, thickening of butter and flour, 1 dessertspoonful of ketchup. *Mode.*—Wash the feet of the fowls thoroughly clean, and cut them and the neck into small pieces. Put these into a stewpan with the bread, onion, herbs, seasoning, livers, and gizzards; pour the water over them and simmer gently for 1 hour. Now take out the liver, pound it, and strain the liquor to it. Add a thickening of butter and flour, and a flavouring of mushroom ketchup; boil it up and serve. *Time.*—1 hour. *Average cost, 4d. per pint.*

GRAVY, Rich, for Hashes, Ragouts, &c.

Ingredients.—2 lbs. of shin of beef, 1 large onion or a few shalots, a little flour, a bunch of savoury herbs, 2 blades of mace, 2 or 3 cloves, 4 whole allspice, ¼ teaspoonful of whole pepper, 1 slice of lean ham or bacon, ½ a head of celery (when at hand), 2 pints of boiling water salt and cayenne to taste. *Mode.*—Cut the beef into thin slices, as also the onions, dredge them with flour, and fry of a pale brown, but do not allow them to get black; pour in the boiling water, let it boil up, and skim. Add the remaining ingredients, and simmer the whole very gently for 2 hours, or until all the juices are extracted from the meat; put it by to get cold, when take off all the fat. This gravy may be flavoured with ketchup, store sauces, wine, or, in fact, anything that may give additional and suitable relish to the dish it is intended for.

| Gravy Soup | Greengages, to Preserve |

Time.—Rather more than 2 hours. *Average cost,* 8*d.* per pint.

GRAVY SOUP.

Ingredients.—6 lbs. of shin of beef, a knuckle of veal weighing 5 lbs., a few pieces or trimmings, 2 slices of nicely-flavoured lean ham; ¼ lb. of butter, 4 onions, 4 carrots, 1 turnip, nearly a head of celery, 3 blades of mace, 6 cloves, a bunch of savoury herbs, seasoning of salt and pepper to taste, 3 lumps of sugar, 6 quarts of boiling soft water. It can be flavoured with ketchup, Leamington sauce, Harvey's sauce, and a little soy. *Mode.* — Slightly brown the meat and ham in the butter, but do not let them burn. When this is done, pour to it the water, and as the scum rises, take it off; when no more appears, add all the other ingredients, and let the soup simmer slowly by the fire for 6 hours without stirring it any more from the bottom; take it off, and let it settle; skim off all the fat you can, and pass it through a sieve or cloth. When perfectly cold you can remove all the fat, and leave the sediment untouched, which serves very nicely for thick gravies, hashes, &c. *Time.* —7 hours. *Average cost,* 1*s.* per quart. *Seasonable* all the year. *Sufficient* for 14 persons.

GRAVY, Veal, for White Sauces, Fricassees, &c.

Ingredients. — 2 slices of nicely-flavoured lean ham, any poultry trimmings, 3 lbs. of lean veal, a faggot of savoury herbs, including parsley, a few green onions (or 1 large onion may be substituted for these), a few mushrooms, when obtainable; 1 blade of mace, salt to taste, 3 pints of water. *Mode.*—Cut up the ham and veal into small square pieces, put these in a stewpan, moistening them with a small quantity of water; place them over the fire to draw down. When the bottom of the stewpan becomes covered with a white glaze, fill up with water in the above proportion; add the remaining ingredients, stew very slowly for 3 or 4 hours, and do not forget to skim well the moment it boils. Put it by, and when cold take off all the fat. This may be used for Béchamel, sauce tournée, and many other white sauces. *Time.*—3 or 4 hours. *Average cost,* 9*d.* per pint.

GREENGAGE JAM.

Ingredients. — To every lb. of fruit, weighed before being stoned, allow ¾ lb. of lump sugar. *Mode.*—Divide the greengages, take out the stones, and put them into a preserving-pan. Bring the fruit to a boil, then add the sugar, and keep stirring it over a gentle fire until it is melted. Remove all the scum as it rises, and, just before the jam is done, boil it rapidly for 5 minutes. To ascertain when it is sufficiently boiled, pour a little on a plate, and if the syrup thickens and appears firm, it is done. Have ready half the kernels blanched; put them into the jam, give them one boil, and pour the preserve into pots. When cold, cover down with oiled papers, and, over these, tissue paper brushed over on both sides with the white of an egg. *Time.*—¾ hour after the sugar is added. *Average cost,* from 6*d.* to 8*d.* per lb. pot. *Sufficient.*—Allow about 1½ pint of fruit for every lb. pot of jam. *Seasonable.*—Make this in August or September.

GREENGAGES, Compote of.

Ingredients.—1 pint of syrup, 1 quart of greengages. *Mode.*—Make a syrup, skim it well, and put in the greengages when the syrup is boiling, having previously removed the stalks and stones from the fruit. Boil gently for ¼ hour, or until the fruit is tender; but take care not to let it break, as the appearance of the dish would be spoiled were the fruit reduced to a pulp. Take the greengages carefully out, place them on a glass dish, boil the syrup for another 5 minutes, let it cool a little, pour over the fruit, and, when cold, it will be ready for use. *Time.* —¼ hour to simmer the fruit, 5 minutes the syrup. *Average cost,* in full season, 10*d.* *Sufficient* for 4 or 5 persons. *Seasonable* in July, August, and September.

GREENGAGES, to Preserve and Dry.

Ingredients. — To every lb. of sugar allow 1 lb. of fruit, ¼ pint of water. *Mode.*—For this purpose, the fruit must be used before it is quite ripe, and part of the stalk must be left on. Weigh the fruit, rejecting all that is in the least degree blemished, and put it into a lined saucepan with the sugar and water, which should have been previously boiled

Greengages, Preserved in Syrup

together to a rich syrup. Boil the fruit in this for 10 minutes, remove it from the fire, and drain the greengages. The next day, boil up the syrup and put in the fruit again, and let it simmer for 3 minutes, and drain the syrup away. Continue this process for 5 or 6 days, and the last time place the greengages, when drained, on a hair sieve, and put them in an oven or warm spot to dry; keep them in a box, with paper between each layer, in a place free from damp. *Time.*—10 minutes the first time of boiling. *Seasonable.*—Make this in August or September.

GREENGAGES, Preserved in Syrup.

Ingredients.—To every lb. of fruit allow 1 lb. of loaf sugar, ¼ pint of water. *Mode.* —Boil the sugar and water together for about 10 minutes; divide the green-gages, take out the stones, put the fruit into the syrup, and let it simmer gently until nearly tender. Take it off the fire, put it into a large pan, and, the next day, boil it up again for about 10 minutes with the kernels from the stones, which should be blanched. Put the fruit carefully into jars, pour over it the syrup, and, when cold, cover down, so that the air is quite excluded. Let the syrup be well skimmed both the first and second day of boiling, otherwise it will not be clear. *Time.*—10 minutes to boil the syrup; ¼ hour to simmer the fruit the first day, 10 minutes the second day. *Average cost,* from 6d. to 8d. per lb. pot. *Sufficient.*—Allow about 1 pint of fruit to fill a 1-lb. pot. *Seasonable.*—Make this in August or September.

GREENS, Boiled Turnip.

Ingredients.—To each ½ gallon of water allow 1 heaped tablespoonful of salt; turnip-greens. *Mode.*— Wash the greens well in two or three waters, and pick off all the decayed and dead leaves; tie them in small bunches, and put them into plenty of boiling water, salted in the above proportion. Keep them boiling quickly, with the lid of the saucepan uncovered, and when tender, pour them into a colander; let them drain, arrange them in a vegetable-dish, remove the string that the greens were tied with, and serve. *Time.*—15 to 20 minutes. *Average cost,* 4d. for a dish for 3 persons. *Seasonable* in March, April, and May.

Grouse, to Carve

GROUSE PIE.

Ingredients.—Grouse; cayenne, salt, and pepper to taste; 1 lb. of rump-steak, ½ pint of well-seasoned broth, puff-paste. *Mode.*—Line the bottom of a pie-dish with the rump-steak cut into neat pieces, and, should the grouse be large, cut them into joints; but, if small, they may be laid in the pie whole; season highly with salt, cayenne, and black pepper; pour in the broth, and cover with a puff-paste; brush the crust over with the yolk of an egg, and bake from ¾ to 1 hour. If the grouse is cut into joints, the backbones and trimmings will make the gravy, by stewing them with an onion, a little sherry, a bunch of herbs, and a blade of mace: this should be poured in after the pie is baked. *Time.*—¾ to 1 hour. *Average cost,* exclusive of the grouse, which are seldom bought, 1s. 9d. *Seasonable* from the 12th of August to the beginning of December.

GROUSE, Roast.

Ingredients.—Grouse, butter, a thick slice of toasted bread. *Mode.*—Let the birds hang as long as possible; pluck and draw them; wipe, but do not wash them, inside and out, and truss them without the head, the same as for a roast fowl. Many persons still continue to truss them

ROAST GROUSE.

with the head under the wing, but the former is now considered the most approved method. Put them down to a sharp clear fire; keep them well basted the whole of the time they are cooking, and serve them on a buttered toast, soaked in the dripping-pan, with a little melted butter poured over them, or with bread-sauce and gravy. *Time.* — ½ hour; if liked very thoroughly done, 35 minutes. *Average cost,* 2s. to 2s. 6d. the brace; but seldom bought. *Sufficient.*—2 for a dish. *Seasonable* from the 12th of August to the beginning of December.

GROUSE, to Carve.

Grouse may be carved in the way first

Grouse Salad

described in carving partridge. The

BOAST GROUSE.

backbone of the grouse is highly esteemed by many, and this part of many game birds is considered the finest-flavoured.

GROUSE SALAD (Soyer's Recipe improved.)

Ingredients.—8 eggs, butter, fresh salad, 2 or 3 grouse; for the sauce, 1 tablespoonful of minced shalot, 2 tablespoonfuls of pounded sugar, the yolks of 2 eggs, 1 teaspoonful of minced parsley, 1 oz. of salt, 12 tablespoonfuls of oil, 4 tablespoonfuls of Chili vinegar, 1 gill of cream, 2 tablespoonfuls of chopped tarragon and chervil. *Mode.*—Boil the eggs hard, shell them, throw them into cold water, cut a thin slice off the bottom to facilitate the proper placing of them in the dish, cut each one into four engthwise, and make a very thin flat border of butter, about one inch from the edge of the dish the salad is to be served on ; fix the pieces of egg upright close to each other, the yolk outside, or the yolk and white alternately ; lay in the centre a fresh salad of whatever is in season, and, having previously roasted the grouse rather underdone, cut it into eight or ten pieces, and prepare the sauce as follows:—Put the shalots into a basin, with the sugar, the yolk of an egg, the parsley, and salt, and mix in by degrees the oil and vinegar ; when all the ingredients are well mixed, put the sauce on ice or in a cool place. When ready to serve, whip the cream rather thick, which lightly mix with it ; then lay the inferior parts of the grouse on the salad, sauce over so as to cover each piece, then lay over the salad and the remainder of the grouse, pour the rest of the sauce over, and serve. The eggs may be ornamented with a little dot of radishes or beetroot on the point. Anchovy and gherkin, cut into small diamonds, may be placed between, or cut gherkins in slices, and a border of them laid round. Tarragon or chervil-leaves are also a pretty addition. The remains of cold black-game, pheasant, or partridge may be used in the above manner, and will make a very delicate dish. *Average cost*, 2s. 6d. *Seasonable* from the 12th of August to the beginning of December.

Gurnet

GRUEL, to make.

Ingredients.—1 tablespoonful of Robinson's patent groats, 2 tablespoonfuls of cold water, 1 pint of boiling water. *Mode.*—Mix the prepared groats smoothly with the cold water in a basin ; pour over them the boiling water, stirring it all the time. Put it into a very clean saucepan ; boil the gruel for 10 minutes, keeping it well stirred ; sweeten to taste, and serve. It may be flavoured with a small piece of lemon-peel, by boiling it in the gruel, or a little grated nutmeg may be put in ; but in these matters the taste of the patient should be consulted. Pour the gruel in a tumbler, and serve. When wine is allowed to the invalid, 2 tablespoonfuls of sherry or port make this preparation very nice. In cases of colds, the same quantity of spirits is sometimes added instead of wine. *Time.* —10 minutes. *Sufficient* to make a pint of gruel.

GUDGEONS.

Ingredients. — Egg and bread-crumbs sufficient for the quantity of fish ; hot lard. *Mode.* — Do not scrape off the scales, but take out the gills and inside, and cleanse thoroughly ; wipe them dry, flour and dip them into egg, and sprinkle over with bread-crumbs. Fry of a nice brown. *Time.*—3 or 4 minutes. *Average cost.* — Seldom bought. *Seasonable* from March to July. *Sufficient.*—3 for each person.

GUINEA-FOWL, Roast, Larded.

Ingredients.—A guinea-fowl, lardoons, flour, and salt. *Mode.*—When this bird is larded, it should be trussed the same as a pheasant ; if plainly roasted, truss it like a turkey. After larding and trussing it, put it down to roast at a brisk fire ; keep it well basted, and a short time before serving, dredge it with a little flour, and let it froth nicely. Serve with a little gravy in the dish, and a tureen of the same, and one of well-made bread-sauce. *Time.* — Guinea-fowl, larded, 1¼ hour ; plainly roasted, about 1 hour. *Sufficient* for 6 persons. *Seasonable* in winter.

Note.—The breast, if larded, should be covered with a piece of paper, and removed about 10 minutes before serving.

GURNET, or GURNARD.

Ingredients.—1 gurnet, 6 oz. of salt to

each gallon of water. *Mode.*—Cleanse
the fish thoroughly, and cut off the fins;
have ready some boiling water, with salt
in the above proportion; put the fish in,
and simmer very gently for ½ hour.
Parsley and butter, or anchovy sauce,
should be served with it. *Time.*—¼ hour.
Average cost.—Seldom bought. *Seasonable*
from October to March, but in perfection
in October. *Sufficient.*—A middling-sized
one for two persons.
Note.—This fish is frequently stuffed
with forcemeat, and baked.

HADDOCK, Baked.

Ingredients.—A nice forcemeat, butter
to taste, egg and bread-crumbs. *Mode.*—
Scale and clean the fish, without cutting
it open much; put in a nice delicate
forcemeat, and sew up the slit. Brush it
over with egg, sprinkle over bread-
crumbs, and baste frequently with butter. Garnish with parsley and cut
lemon, and serve with a nice brown
gravy, plain melted butter, or anchovy
sauce. The egg and bread-crumbs can
be omitted, and pieces of butter placed
over the fish. *Time.*—Large haddock, ¾
hour; moderate size, ¼ hour. *Seasonable*
from August to February. *Average cost,*
from 9d. upwards.
Note.—Haddocks may be filleted, rubbed over with egg and bread-crumbs,
and fried a nice brown; garnish with
crisped parsley.

HADDOCK, Boiled.

Ingredients.—Sufficient water to cover
the fish; ¼ lb. of salt to each gallon of
water. *Mode.*—Scrape the fish, take out
the inside, wash it thoroughly, and lay it
in a kettle, with enough water to cover it,
and salt in the above proportion. Simmer
gently from 15 to 20 minutes, or rather
more, should the fish be very large. For
small haddocks, fasten the tails in their
mouths, and put them into boiling water.
10 to 15 minutes will cook them. Serve
with plain melted butter, or anchovy sauce.
Time.—Large haddock, ½ hour; small, ¼
hour, or rather less. *Average cost,* from
9d. upwards. *Seasonable* from August to
February.

HADDOCK, Dried.

Dried haddock should be gradually
warmed through, either before or over a
nice clear fire. Rub a little piece of butter over, just before sending it to table.

HADDOCK, Dried.

Ingredients.—1 large thick haddock, 2
bay-leaves, 1 small bunch of savoury
herbs, not forgetting parsley, a little
butter and pepper; boiling water. *Mode.*
—Cut up the haddock into square pieces,
make a basin hot by means of hot water,
which pour out. Lay in the fish, with
the bay-leaves and herbs; cover with
boiling water; put a plate over to keep
in the steam, and let it remain for 10
minutes. Take out the slices, put them
in a hot dish, rub over with butter and
pepper, and serve. *Time.*—10 minutes,
Seasonable at any time, but best in
winter.

HAM OMELET (a delicious Break-fast Dish).

Ingredients.—6 eggs, 4 oz. of butter, ½
saltspoonful of pepper, 2 tablespoonfuls
of minced ham. *Mode.*—Mince the ham
very finely, without any fat, and fry it
for 2 minutes in a little butter; then
make the batter for the omelet, stir in
the ham, and proceed as in the case of a
plain omelet. Do not add any salt to
the batter, as the ham is usually sufficiently salt to impart a flavour to the
omelet. Good lean bacon, or tongue,
answers equally well for this dish; but
they must also be slightly cooked previously to mixing them with the batter.
Serve very hot and quickly, without
gravy. *Time.*—From 4 to 6 minutes.
Average cost, 1s. *Sufficient* for 4 persons.
Seasonable at any time.

HAM, FRIED, AND EGGS (a Breakfast Dish).

Ingredients.—Ham; eggs. *Mode.*—
Cut the ham into slices, and take care
that they are of the same thickness in
every part. Cut off the rind, and if the
ham should be particularly hard and
salt, it will be found an improvement to
soak it for about 10 minutes in hot water,
and then dry it in a cloth. Put it into a
cold frying-pan, set it over the fire, and
turn the slices 3 or 4 times whilst they
are cooking. When done, place them on
a dish, which should be kept hot in front
of the fire during the time the eggs are
being poached. Poach the eggs, slip
them on to the slices of ham, and serve
quickly. *Time.*—7 or 8 minutes to broil
the ham. *Average cost,* 8d. to 1s. per lb.
by the whole ham. *Sufficient.*—Allow 8

Ham, Potted

eggs and a slice of ham to each person. *Seasonable* at any time.

Note.—Ham may also be toasted or broiled ; but, with the latter method, to insure its being well cooked, the fire must be beautifully clear, or it will have a smoky flavour far from agreeable.

HAM, Potted, that will keep Good for some time.

Ingredients.—To 4 lbs. of lean ham allow 1 lb. of fat, 2 teaspoonfuls of pounded mace, ½ nutmeg grated, rather more than ½ teaspoonful of cayenne, clarified lard. *Mode.*—Mince the ham, fat and lean together in the above proportion, and pound it well in a mortar, seasoning it with cayenne pepper, pounded mace, and nutmeg ; put the mixture into a deep baking-dish, and bake for ½ hour ; then press it well into a stone jar, fill up the jar with clarified lard, cover it closely, and paste over it a piece of thick paper. If well seasoned, it will keep a long time in winter, and will be found very convenient for sandwiches, &c. *Time.*—½ hour. *Seasonable* at any time.

HAM, Potted (a nice addition to the Breakfast or Luncheon table).

Ingredients.—To 2 lbs. of lean ham allow ½ lb. of fat, 1 teaspoonful of pounded mace, ½ teaspoonful of pounded allspice, ½ nutmeg, pepper to taste, clarified butter. *Mode.*—Cut some slices from the remains of a cold ham, mince them small, and to every 2 lbs. of lean allow the above proportion of fat. Pound the ham in a mortar to a fine paste, with the fat, gradually add the seasonings and spices, and be very particular that all the ingredients are well mixed and the spices well pounded. Press the mixture into potting-pots, pour over clarified butter, and keep it in a cool place. *Average cost* for this quantity, 2s. 6d. *Seasonable* at any time.

HAM, to Bake.

Ingredients.—Ham ; a common crust. *Mode.*—As a ham for baking should be well soaked, let it remain in water for at least 12 hours. Wipe it dry, trim away any rusty places underneath, and cover it with a common crust, taking care that this is of sufficient thickness all over to keep the gravy in. Place it in a

Ham, to Boil

moderately-heated oven, and bake for nearly 4 hours. Take off the crust and skin, and cover with raspings, the same as for boiled ham, and garnish the knuckle with a paper frill. This method of cooking a ham is, by many persons, considered far superior to boiling it, as it cuts fuller of gravy and has a finer flavour, besides keeping a much longer time good. *Time.* — A medium-sized ham, 4 hours. *Average cost*, from 8d. to 1s. per lb. by the whole ham. *Seasonable* all the year.

HAM, to Boil.

Ingredients.—Ham, water, glaze, or raspings. *Mode.* — In choosing a ham, ascertain that it is perfectly sweet, by running a sharp knife into it, close to the bone ; and if, when the knife is withdrawn, it has an agreeable smell, the ham is good ; if, on the contrary, the blade has a greasy appearance and offensive smell, the ham is bad. If it has been

BOILED HAM

long hung, and is very dry and salt, let it remain in soak for 24 hours, changing the water frequently. This length of time is only necessary in the case of its being very hard ; from 8 to 12 hours would be sufficient for a Yorkshire or Westmoreland ham. Wash it thoroughly clean, and trim away from the under-side all the rusty and smoked parts, which would spoil the appearance. Put it into a boiling-pot, with sufficient cold water to cover it ; bring it gradually to boil, and as the scum rises, carefully remove it. Keep it simmering very gently until tender, and be careful that it does not stop boiling, nor boil too quickly. When done, take it out of the pot, strip off the skin, and sprinkle over it a few fine bread-raspings, put a frill of cut paper round the knuckle, and serve. If to be eaten cold, let the ham remain in the water until nearly cold : by this method the juices are kept in, and it will be found infinitely superior to one taken out of the water hot; it should, however, be borne in mind that the ham must *not* remain in the saucepan *all* night. When the skin is removed,

Ham, to Boil

sprinkle over bread-raspings, or, if wanted particularly nice, glaze it. Place a paper frill round the knuckle, and garnish with parsley or cut vegetable flowers. *Time.* —A ham weighing 10 lbs., 4 hours to *simmer gently ;* 15 lbs., 5 hours ; a very large one, about 6 hours. *Average cost,* from 8*d.* to 1*s.* per lb. by the whole ham. *Seasonable* all the year.

HAM, how to Boil to give it an excellent flavour.

Ingredients. — Vinegar and water, 2 heads of celery, 2 turnips, 3 onions, a large bunch of savoury herbs. *Mode.*— Prepare the ham as in the preceding recipe, and let it soak for a few hours in vinegar and water. Put it on in cold water, and when it boils, add the vegetables and herbs. Simmer very gently until tender, take it out, strip off the skin, cover with bread-raspings, and put a paper ruche or frill round the knuckle. *Time.*—A ham weighing 10 lbs., 4 hours. *Average cost,* 8*d.* to 1*s.* per lb. by the whole ham. *Seasonable* at any time.

HAM, to Carve.

In cutting a ham, the carver must be guided according as he desires to practise economy, or have, at once, fine slices out of the prime part. Under the first supposition, he will commence at the knuckle end, and cut off thin slices towards the thick part of the ham. To reach the choicer portion, the knife, which must be very sharp and thin, should be carried quite down to the bone, in the direction of the line 1 to 2. The slices

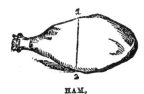

HAM.

should be thin and even, and always cut down to the bone. There are some who like to carve a ham by cutting a hole at the top, and then slicing pieces off inside the hole, gradually enlarging the circle ; but we think this is a plan not to be recommended. A ham, when hot, is usually sent to table with a paper ruffle round the knuckle.

Hams, to Pickle

HAMS, for Curing (Mons. Ude's Recipe).

Ingredients. — For 2 hams weighing about 16 or 18 lbs. each, allow 1 lb. of moist sugar, 1 lb. of common salt, 2 oz. of saltpetre, 1 quart of good vinegar. *Mode.*—As soon as the pig is cold enough to be cut up, take the 2 hams and rub them well with common salt, and leave them in a large pan for 3 days. When the salt has drawn out all the blood, drain the hams, and throw the brine away. Mix sugar, salt, and saltpetre together in the above proportion, rub the hams well with these, and put them into a vessel large enough to hold them, always keeping the salt over them. Let them remain for 3 days, then pour over them a quart of good vinegar. Turn them in the brine every day for a month, then drain them well, and rub them with bran. Have them smoked over a wood fire, and be particular that the hams are hung as high up as possible from the fire ; otherwise the fat will melt, and they will become dry and hard. *Time.*—To be pickled 1 month ; to be smoked 1 month. *Sufficient* for 2 hams of 18 lbs. each. *Seasonable* from October to March.

HAMS, to Cure Sweet, in the Westmoreland way.

Ingredients.—3 lbs. of common salt, 3 lbs. of coarse sugar, 1 lb. of bay-salt, 3 quarts of strong beer. *Mode.*—Before the hams are put into pickle, rub them the preceding day well with salt, and drain the brine well from them. Put the above ingredients into a saucepan, and boil for ¼ hour ; pour over the hams, and let them remain a month in the pickle. Rub and turn them every day, but do not take them out of the pickling-pan ; and have them smoked for a month. *Time.*— To be pickled 1 month ; to be smoked 1 month. *Seasonable* from October to March.

HAMS, to Pickle (Suffolk Recipe).

Ingredients.—To a ham from 10 to 12 lbs., allow 1 lb. of coarse sugar, ¾ lb. of salt, 1 oz. of saltpetre, ½ a teacupful of vinegar. *Mode.*—Rub the hams well with common salt, and leave them for a day or two to drain ; then rub well in the above proportion of sugar, salt, saltpetre, and vinegar, and turn them every

Hams, to Salt

other day. Keep them in the pickle 1 month, drain them, and send them to be smoked over a wood fire for 3 weeks or a month. *Time.*—To remain in the pickle 1 month ; to be smoked 3 weeks or 1 month. *Sufficient.*—The above proportion of pickle is sufficient for 1 ham. *Seasonable.* — Hams should be pickled from October to March.

HAMS, to Salt Two, about 12 or 15 lbs. each.

Ingredients.—2 lbs. of treacle, ½ lb. of saltpetre, 1 lb. of bay-salt, 2 pounds of common salt. *Mode.*—Two days before they are put into pickle, rub the hams well with salt, to draw away all slime and blood. Throw what comes from them away, and then rub them with treacle, saltpetre, and salt. Lay them in a deep pan, and let them remain one day ; boil the above proportion of treacle, saltpetre, bay-salt, and common salt for ¼ hour, and pour this pickle boiling hot over the hams : there should be sufficient of it to cover them. For a day or two rub them well with it ; afterwards they will only require turning. They ought to remain in this pickle for 3 weeks or a month, and then be sent to be smoked, which will take nearly or quite a month to do. An ox-tongue pickled in this way is most excellent, to be eaten either green or smoked. *Time.*—To remain in the pickle 3 weeks or a month ; to be smoked about a month. *Seasonable* from October to March.

HAMS, to Smoke, at Home.

Take an old hogshead, stop up all the crevices, and fix a place to put a cross-stick near the bottom, to hang the articles to be smoked on. Next, in the side, cut a hole near the top, to introduce an iron pan filled with sawdust and small pieces of green wood. Having turned the tub upside down, hang the articles upon the cross-stick, introduce the iron pan in the opening, and place a piece of red-hot iron in the pan, cover it with sawdust, and all will be complete. Let a large ham remain 40 hours, and keep up a good smoke. Fish may be smoked in the same manner.

HARE, Broiled (a Supper or Luncheon Dish).

Ingredients.—The legs and shoulders of a roast hare, cayenne and salt to taste,

Hare, Jugged

a little butter. *Mode.*—Cut the legs and shoulders from a roast hare, season them highly with salt and cayenne, and broil them over a very clear fire for 5 minutes. Dish them on a hot dish, rub over them a little cold butter, and send to table very quickly. *Time.*—5 minutes. *Seasonable* from September to the end of February.

HARE, Hashed.

[COLD MEAT COOKERY.] *Ingredients.*—The remains of cold roast hare, 1 blade of pounded mace, 2 or 3 allspice, pepper and salt to taste, 1 onion, a bunch of savoury herbs, 3 tablespoonfuls of port wine, thickening of butter and flour, 2 tablespoonfuls of mushroom ketchup. *Mode.*—Cut the cold hare into neat slices, and put the head, bones, and trimmings into a stewpan, with ¾ pint of water ; add the mace, allspice, seasoning, onion, and herbs, and stew for nearly an hour, and strain the gravy ; thicken it with butter and flour, and add the wine and ketchup, and lay in the pieces of hare, with any stuffing that may be left. Let the whole gradually heat by the side of the fire, and, when it has simmered for about 5 minutes, serve, and garnish the dish with sippets of toasted bread. Send red-currant jelly to table with it. *Time.*—Rather more than 1 hour. *Average cost*, exclusive of the cold hare, 6*d*. *Seasonable* from September to the end of February.

HARE, Jugged (very good).

Ingredients.—1 hare, 1½ lb. of gravy beef, ½ lb. of butter, 1 onion, 1 lemon, 6 cloves ; pepper, cayenne, and salt to taste ; ½ pint of port wine. *Mode.*—Skin, paunch, and wash the hare, cut it into pieces, dredge them with flour, and fry in boiling butter. Have ready 1½ pint of gravy, made from the above proportion of beef, and thickened with a little flour. Put this into a jar ; add the pieces of fried hare, an onion stuck with six cloves, a lemon peeled and cut in half, and a good seasoning of pepper, cayenne, and salt ; cover the jar down tightly, put it up to the neck into a stewpan of boiling water, and let it stew until the hare is quite tender, taking care to keep the water boiling. When nearly done, pour in the wine, and add a few forcemeat balls : these must be fried or baked in the oven for a few minutes before they are put to the gravy. Serve with red-currant jelly. *Time.*—3½ to 4 hours. If the hare is very

Hare, Jugged

old, allow 4½ hours. *Average cost, 7s. Sufficient* for 7 or 8 persons. *Seasonable* from September to the end of February.

HARE, Jugged (a Quicker and more Economical Way).

Ingredients.—1 hare, a bunch of sweet herbs, 2 onions, each stuck with 3 cloves, 6 whole allspice, ½ teaspoonful of black pepper, a strip of lemon-peel, thickening of butter and flour, 2 tablespoonfuls of mushroom ketchup, ¼ pint of port wine. *Mode.*—Wash the hare nicely, cut it up into joints (not too large), and flour and brown them as in the preceding recipe; then put them into a stewpan with the herbs, onions, cloves, allspice, pepper, and lemon-peel; cover with hot water, and when it boils, carefully remove all the scum, and let it simmer gently till tender, which will be in about 1¾ hour, or longer, should the hare be very old. Take out the pieces of hare, thicken the gravy with flour and butter, add the ketchup and port wine, let it boil for about 10 minutes, strain it through a sieve over the hare, and serve. A few fried forcemeat balls should be added at the moment of serving, or, instead of frying them, they may be stewed in the gravy, about 10 minutes before the hare is wanted for table. Do not omit to serve red-currant jelly with it. *Time.*—Altogether 2 hours. *Average cost, 5s. 6d. Sufficient* for 7 or 8 persons. *Seasonable* from September to the end of February.

Note.—Should there be any left, re-warm it the next day by putting the hare, &c., into a covered jar, and placing this jar in a saucepan of boiling water; this method prevents a great deal of waste.

HARE, Potted (a Luncheon or Breakfast Dish).

Ingredients.—1 hare, a few slices of bacon, a large bunch of savoury herbs, 4 cloves, ½ teaspoonful of whole allspice, 2 carrots, 2 onions, salt and pepper to taste, 1 pint of water, 2 glasses of sherry. *Mode.*—Skin, empty, and wash the hare; cut it down the middle, and put it into a stewpan, with a few slices of bacon under and over it; add the remaining ingredients, and stew very gently until the hare is tender, and the flesh will separate easily from the bones. When done enough, take it up, remove the bones, and pound the meat *with the bacon,* in a

Hare, Roast

mortar, until reduced to a perfectly smooth paste. Should it not be sufficiently seasoned, add a little cayenne, salt, and pounded mace, but be careful that these are well mixed with the other ingredients. Press the meat into potting-pots, pour over clarified butter, and keep in a dry place. The liquor that the hare was stewed in, should be saved for hashes, soups, &c. &c. *Time.*—About 2½ hours to stew the hare. *Seasonable* from September to the end of February.

HARE, Roast.

Ingredients.—Hare, forcemeat, a little milk, butter. *Choosing and Trussing.*—Choose a young hare; which may be known by its smooth and sharp claws, and by the cleft in the lip not being much spread. To be eaten in perfection, it must hang for some time; and, if properly taken care of, it may be kept for several days. It is better to hang without being paunched; but should it be previously emptied, wipe the inside every day, and sprinkle over it a little pepper and ginger, to prevent the musty taste which long keeping in the damp occasions, and also which affects the stuffing. After it is skinned, wash it well, and soak for an hour in warm water to draw out the blood; if old, let it lie in vinegar for a short time, but wash it well afterwards in several waters. Make a forcemeat, wipe the hare dry, fill the belly with it, and sew it up. Bring the

ROAST HARE.

hind and fore legs close to the body towards the head, run a skewer through each, fix the head between the shoulders by means of another skewer, and be careful to leave the ears on. Put a string round the body from skewer to skewer, and tie it above the back. *Mode.*—The hare should be kept at a distance from the fire when it is first laid down, or the outside will become dry and hard before the inside is done. Baste it well with milk for a short time, and afterwards with butter; and particular attention must be paid to the basting, so as to preserve the meat on the back juicy and nutritive. When it

| Hare, Roast, to Carve | Herb Powder |

is almost roasted enough, flour the hare, and baste well with butter. When nicely frothed, dish it, remove the skewers, and send it to table with a little gravy in the dish, and a tureen of the same. Red-currant jelly must also not be forgotten, as this is an indispensable accompaniment to roast hare. For economy, good beef dripping may be substituted for the milk and butter to baste with ; but the basting, as we have before stated, must be continued without intermission. If the liver is good, it may be parboiled, minced, and mixed with the stuffing ; but it should not be used unless quite fresh. *Time.*—A middling-sized hare, 1¼ hour ; a large hare, 1½ to 2 hours. *Average cost,* from 4s. to 6s. *Sufficient* for 5 or 6 persons. *Seasonable* from September to the end of February.

HARE, Roast, to Carve.

The "Grand Carver" of olden times, a functionary of no ordinary dignity, was pleased when he had a hare to manipulate, for his skill and grace had an opportunity of display. *Diners à la Russe* may possibly, erewhile, save modern gentlemen the necessity of learning the art which was in auld lang syne one of the necessary accomplishments of the youthful squire ; but, until side-tables become universal, or till we see the office of "grand carver" once more instituted, it will be well for all to learn how to assist at the carving of this dish, which, if not the most elegant in appearance, is a very general favourite. The hare, having its head to the left, as shown in the woodcut, should be first served by cutting slices from each side of the backbone, in the direction of the lines from 3 to 4. After these prime parts are disposed of, the leg should next be disengaged by cutting round the line indicated by the figures 5 to 6. The shoulders will then be taken off by passing the knife round from 7 to 8. The back of the hare should now be divided by cutting quite through its spine, as shown by the line 1 to 2, taking care to feel with the point of the knife for a joint where the back may be readily

ROAST HARE.

penetrated. It is the usual plan not to serve any bone in helping hare; and thus the flesh should be sliced from the legs and placed alone on the plate. In large establishments, and where mencooks are kept, it is often the case that the backbone of the hare, especially in old animals, is taken out, and then the process of carving is, of course, considerably facilitated. A great point to be remembered in connection with carving hare is, that plenty of gravy should accompany each helping, otherwise this dish, which is naturally dry, will lose half its flavour, and so become a failure. Stuffing is also served with it; and the ears, which should be nicely crisp, and the brains of the hare, are esteemed as delicacies by many connoisseurs.

HARE SOUP.

Ingredients.—A hare fresh-killed, 1 lb. of lean gravy-beef, a slice of ham, 1 carrot, 2 onions, a faggot of savoury herbs, ¼ oz. of whole black pepper, a little browned flour, ¼ pint of port wine, the crumb of two French rolls, salt and cayenne to taste, 3 quarts of water. *Mode.*—Skin and paunch the hare, saving the liver and as much blood as possible. Cut it in pieces, and put it in a stewpan with all the ingredients, and simmer gently for 6 hours. This soup should be made the day before it is wanted. Strain through a sieve, put the best parts of the hare in the soup, and serve.

HARE SOUP.

Proceed as above ; but, instead of putting the joints of the hare in the soup, pick the meat from the bones, pound it in a mortar, and add it, with the crumb of two French rolls, to the soup. Rub all through a sieve ; heat slowly, but do not let it boil. Send it to table immediately. *Time.*—8 hours. *Average cost,* 1s. 9d. per quart. *Seasonable* from September to February. *Sufficient* for 10 persons.

HERB POWDER, for Flavouring when Fresh Herbs are not obtainable.

Ingredients. — 1 oz, of dried lemonthyme, 1 oz. of dried winter savory, 1 oz. of dried sweet marjoram and basil, 2 oz. of dried parsley, 1 oz. of dried

Herbs, to Dry

lemon-peel. *Mode.*—Prepare and dry the herbs, pick the leaves from the stalks, pound them, and sift them through a hair sieve; mix in the above proportions, and keep in glass bottles, carefully excluding the air. This we think a far better method of keeping herbs, as the flavour and fragrance do not evaporate so much as when they are merely put in paper bags. Preparing them in this way, you have them ready for use at a moment's notice. Mint, sage, parsley, &c., dried, pounded, and each put into separate bottles, will be found very useful in winter.

HERBS, to Dry, for Winter Use.

On a very dry day, gather the herbs, just before they begin to flower. If this is done when the weather is damp, the herbs will not be so good a colour. (It is very necessary to be particular in little matters like this, for trifles constitute perfection, and herbs nicely dried will be found very acceptable when frost and snow are on the ground. It is hardly necessary, however, to state that the flavour and fragrance of fresh herbs are incomparably finer.) They should be perfectly freed from dirt and dust, and be divided into small bunches, with their roots cut off. Dry them quickly in a very hot oven, or before the fire, as by this means most of their flavour will be preserved, and be careful not to burn them; tie them up in paper bags, and keep in a dry place. This is a very general way of preserving dried herbs; but we would recommend the plan described in a former recipe. *Seasonable.* —From the month of July to the end of September is the proper time for storing herbs for winter use.

HERRINGS, White, Baked.

Ingredients.—12 herrings, 4 bay-leaves, 12 cloves, 12 allspice, 2 small blades of mace, cayenne pepper and salt to taste, sufficient vinegar to fill up the dish. *Mode.*—Take herrings, cut off the heads, and gut them. Put them in a pie-dish, heads and tails alternately, and, between each layer, sprinkle over the above ingredients. Cover the fish with the vinegar, and bake for ½ hour, but do not use it till quite cold. The herrings may be cut down the front, the backbone taken out, and closed again. Sprats done in

Hodge-Podge

this way are very delicious. *Time.*—½ an hour. *Average cost,* 1d. each.

To Choose the Herring.—The more scales this fish has, the surer the sign of its freshness. It should also have a bright and silvery look; but if red about the head, it is a sign that it has been dead for some time.

HERRINGS, Red, or YARMOUTH BLOATERS.

The best way to cook these is to make incisions in the skin across the fish, because they do not then require to be so long on the fire, and will be far better than when cut open. The hard roe makes a nice relish by pounding it in a mortar, with a little anchovy, and spreading it on toast. If very dry, soak in warm water 1 hour before dressing.

HIDDEN MOUNTAIN, The (a pretty Supper Dish).

Ingredients.—6 eggs, a few slices of citron, sugar to taste, ¼ pint of cream, a layer of any kind of jam. *Mode.*—Beat the whites and yolks of the eggs separately; then mix them and beat well again, adding a few thin slices of citron, the cream, and sufficient pounded sugar to sweeten it nicely. When the mixture is well beaten, put it into a buttered pan, and fry the same as a pancake; but it should be three times the thickness of an ordinary pancake. Cover it with jam, and garnish with slices of citron and holly-leaves. This dish is served cold. *Time.*—About 10 minutes to fry the mixture. *Average cost,* with the jam, 1s. 4d. *Sufficient* for 3 or 4 persons. *Seasonable* at any time.

HODGE-PODGE.

Ingredients.—2 lbs. of shin of beef, 3 quarts of water, 1 pint of table-beer, 2 onions, 2 carrots, 2 turnips, 1 head of celery; pepper and salt to taste; thickening of butter and flour. *Mode.*—Put the meat, beer, and water in a stewpan; simmer for a few minutes, and skim carefully. Add the vegetables and seasoning; stew gently till the meat is tender. Thicken with the butter and flour, and serve with turnips and carrots, or spinach and celery. *Time.*—3 hours, or rather more. *Average cost,* 3d. per quart. *Seasonable* at any time. *Sufficient* for 12 persons.

Hodge-Podge

HODGE-PODGE.

[COLD MEAT COOKERY.] *Ingredients.* —About 1 lb. of underdone cold mutton, 2 lettuces, 1 pint of green peas, 5 or 6 green onions, 2 oz. of butter, pepper and salt to taste, ½ teacupful of water. *Mode.*—Mince the mutton, and cut up the lettuces and onions in slices. Put these in a stewpan, with all the ingredients except the peas, and let these simmer very gently for ¾ hour, keeping them well stirred. Boil the peas separately, mix these with the mutton, and serve very hot. *Time.*—¾ hour. *Sufficient* for 3 or 4 persons. *Seasonable* from the end of May to August.

HOLLY-LEAVES, to Frost, for Garnishing and Decorating Dessert and Supper Dishes.

Ingredients. —Sprigs of holly, oiled butter, coarsely-powdered sugar. *Mode.* —Procure some nice sprigs of holly; pick the leaves from the stalks, and wipe them with a clean cloth free from all moisture; then place them on a dish near the fire, to get thoroughly dry, but not too near to shrivel the leaves; dip them into oiled butter, sprinkle over them some coarsely-powdered sugar, and dry them before the fire. They should be kept in a dry place, as the least damp would spoil their appearance. *Time.*— About 10 minutes to dry before the fire. *Seasonable.*—These may be made at any time; but are more suitable for winter garnishes, when fresh flowers are not easily obtained.

HONEY CAKE.

Ingredients. — ½ breakfast-cupful of sugar, 1 breakfast-cupful of rich sour cream, 2 breakfast-cupfuls of flour, ½ teaspoonful of carbonate of soda, honey to taste. *Mode.*—Mix the sugar and cream together; dredge in the flour, with as much honey as will flavour the mixture nicely; stir it well that all the ingredients may be thoroughly mixed; add the carbonate of soda, and beat the cake well for another 5 minutes; put it into a buttered tin, bake it from ½ to ¾ hour, and let it be eaten warm. *Time.*—½ to ¾ hour. *Average cost*, 8d. *Sufficient* for 3 or 4 persons. *Seasonable* at any time.

HORSERADISH.

This root, scraped, is always served

Hot Spice

with hot roast beef, and is used for garnishing many kinds of boiled fish. Let the horseradish remain in cold water for an hour; wash it well, and with a sharp knife scrape it into very thin shreds, commencing from the thick end of the root. Arrange some of it lightly in a small glass dish, and the remainder use for garnishing the joint; it should be placed in tufts round the border of the dish, with 1 or 2 bunches on the meat. *Average cost*, 2d. per stick. *Seasonable* from October to June.

HORSERADISH SAUCE, to serve with Roast Beef.

Ingredients.—4 tablespoonfuls of grated horseradish, 1 teaspoonful of pounded sugar, 1 teaspoonful of salt, ½ tea-spoonful of pepper, 2 teaspoonfuls of made mustard; vinegar. *Mode.*—Grate the horseradish, and mix it well with the sugar, salt, pepper, and mustard; moisten it with sufficient vinegar to give it the consistency of cream, and serve in a tureen; 3 or 4 tablespoonfuls of cream added to the above very much improve the appearance and flavour of this sauce. To heat it to serve with hot roast beef, put it in a *bain marie* or a jar, which place in a saucepan of boiling water; make it hot, but do not allow it to boil, or it will curdle.

Note.—This sauce is a great improvement on the old-fashioned way of serving cold-scraped horseradish with hot roast beef. The mixing of the cold vinegar with the warm gravy cools and spoils everything on the plate. Of course, with cold meat, the sauce should be served cold.

HORSERADISH VINEGAR.

Ingredients.—¼ lb. of scraped horseradish, 1 oz. of minced shalot, 1 drachm of cayenne, 1 quart of vinegar. *Mode.*— Put all the ingredients into a bottle, which shake well every day for a fortnight. When it is thoroughly steeped, strain and bottle, and it will be fit for use immediately. This will be found an agreeable relish to cold beef, &c. *Seasonable.*—This vinegar should be made either in October or November, as horseradish is then in its highest perfection.

HOT SPICE (a Delicious Adjunct to Chops, Steaks, Gravies, &c.)

Ingredients. —3 drachms each of gin-

Ice-Creams, Fruit

ger, black pepper, and cinnamon, 7 cloves, ½ oz. mace, ¼ oz. of cayenne, 1 oz. grated nutmeg, 1½ oz. white pepper. *Mode.*—Pound the ingredients, and mix them thoroughly together, taking care that everything is well blended. Put the spice in a very dry glass bottle for use. The quantity of cayenne may be increased, should the above not be enough to suit the palate.

ICE-CREAMS, Fruit.

Ingredients.—To every pint of fruit-juice allow 1 pint of cream; sugar to taste. *Mode.* — Let the fruit be well ripened; pick it off the stalks, and put it into a large earthen pan. Stir it about with a wooden spoon, breaking it until it is well mashed; then, with the back of the spoon, rub it through a hair sieve. Sweeten it nicely with pounded sugar; whip the cream for a few minutes, add it to the fruit, and whisk the whole again for another 5 minutes. Put the mixture into the freezing-pot, and freeze, taking care to stir the cream, &c., two or three times, and to remove it from the sides of the vessel, that the mixture may be equally frozen and smooth. Ices are usually served in glasses, but if moulded, as they sometimes are for dessert, must have a small quantity of melted isinglass added to them, to enable them to keep their shape. Raspberry, strawberry, currant, and all fruit ice-creams, are made in the same manner. A little pounded sugar sprinkled over the fruit before it is mashed assists to extract the juice. In winter, when fresh fruit is not obtainable, a little jam may be substituted for it: it should be melted and worked through a sieve before being added to the whipped cream; and if the colour should not be good, a little prepared cochineal or beet-root may be put in to improve its appearance. *Time.*—½ hour to freeze the mixture. *Average cost*, with cream at 1s. per pint, 4d. each ice. *Seasonable*, with fresh fruit, in June, July, and August.

ICE, Lemon-water.

Ingredients.—To every pint of syrup, allow ½ pint of lemon-juice; the rind of 4 lemons. *Mode.*—Rub the sugar on the rinds of the lemons, and with it make the syrup. Strain the lemon-juice, add it to the other ingredients, stir well, and put the mixture into a freezing-pot. Freeze as

Ices

directed for Ice Pudding, and when the mixture is thoroughly and equally frozen, put it into ice-glasses. *Time.*—½ hour to freeze the mixture. *Average cost*, 3d. to 4d. each. *Seasonable* at any time.

ICED-PUDDING (Parisian Recipe).

Ingredients.—½ lb. of sweet almonds, 2 oz. of bitter ones, ¾ lb. of sugar, 8 eggs, 1½ pint of milk. *Mode.*—Blanch and dry the almonds thoroughly, then pound them in a mortar until reduced to a smooth paste; add to these the well-beaten eggs, the sugar, and milk; stir these ingredients over the fire until they thicken, but do not allow them to boil; then strain and put the mixture into the freezing-pot; surround it with ice, and freeze it. When quite frozen, fill an iced-pudding mould, put on the lid, and keep the pudding in ice until required for table; then turn it out on the dish, and garnish it with a *compôte* or

ICED-PUDDING MOULD.

any fruit that may be preferred, pouring a little over the top of the pudding. This pudding may be flavoured with vanilla, Curaçoa, or Maraschino. *Time.*—½ hour to freeze the mixture. *Seasonable.* —Served all the year round.

ICES.

Ices are composed, it is scarcely necessary to say, of congealed cream or water, combined sometimes with liqueurs or other flavouring ingredients, or more generally with the juices of fruits. At desserts, or at some evening parties, ices are scarcely to be dispensed with. The principal utensils required for making ice-creams are ice-tubs, freezing-pots,

Ices, to make Fruit-water

spaddles, and a cellaret. The tub must be large enough to contain about a bushel of ice, pounded small, when brought out of the ice-house, and mixed very carefully with either *salt, nitre,* or *soda.* The freezing-pot is best made of pewter. If it be of tin, as is sometimes the case, the congelation goes on too rapidly in it for the thorough intermingling of its contents, on which the excellence of the ice greatly depends. The spaddle is generally made of copper, kept bright and clean. The cellaret is a tin vessel, in which ices are kept for a short time from dissolving. The method to be pursued in the freezing process must be attended to. When the ice-tub is prepared with fresh-pounded ice and salt, the freezing-pot is put into it up to its cover. The articles to be congealed are then poured into it and covered over ; but to prevent the ingredients from separating and the heaviest of them from falling to the bottom of the mould, it is requisite to turn the freezing-pot round and round by the handle, so as to keep its contents moving until the congelation commences. As soon as this is perceived (the cover of the pot being occasionally taken off for the purpose of noticing when freezing takes place), the cover is immediately closed over it, ice is put upon it, and it is left in this state till it is served. The use of the spaddle is to stir up and remove from the sides of the freezing-pot the cream, which in the shaking may have washed against it, and by stirring it in with the rest, to prevent waste of it occurring. Any negligence in stirring the contents of the freezing-pot before congelation takes place, will destroy the whole : either the sugar sinks to the bottom and leaves the ice insufficiently sweetened, or lumps are formed, which disfigure and discolour it.

ICES, to make Fruit-water.

Ingredients.—To every pint of fruit-juice allow 1 pint of syrup. *Mode.*— Select nice ripe fruit ; pick off the stalks and put it into a large earthen pan, with a little pounded sugar strewed over ; stir it about with a wooden spoon until it is well broken, then rub it through a hair sieve. Make a syrup, without white of egg ; let it cool, add the fruit-juice, mix well together, and put the mixture into the freezing-pot. Proceed as directed for Ice Puddings, and when the

Icing, Sugar, for Cakes

mixture is equally frozen, put it into small glasses. Raspberry, strawberry, cur-

DISH OF ICES.

rant, and other fresh-fruit-water ices, are made in the same manner. *Time.*— ½ hour to freeze the mixture. *Average cost,* 3*d.* to 4*d.* each. *Seasonable,* with fresh fruit, in June, July, and August.

ICING, Almond, for Cakes.

Ingredients.—To every lb. of finely-pounded loaf sugar, allow 1 lb. of sweet almonds, the whites of 4 eggs, a little rosewater. *Mode.*—Blanch the almonds, and pound them (a few at a time) in a mortar to a paste, adding a little rosewater to facilitate the operation. Whisk the whites of the eggs to a strong froth ; mix them with the pounded almonds, stir in the sugar, and beat altogether. When the cake is sufficiently baked, lay on the almond icing, and put it into the oven to dry. Before laying this preparation on the cake, great care must be taken that it is nice and smooth, which is easily accomplished by well beating the mixture.

ICING, Sugar, for Cakes.

Ingredients. — To every lb. of loaf sugar allow the whites of 4 eggs, 1 oz. of fine starch. *Mode.*—Beat the eggs to a strong froth, and gradually sift in the sugar, which should be reduced to the finest possible powder, and gradually add the starch, also finely powdered. Beat the mixture well until the sugar is smooth ; then with a spoon or broad knife lay the ice equally over the cakes. These should then be placed in a very cool oven, and the icing allowed to dry and harden, but not to colour. The icing may be coloured with strawberry or currant juice, or with prepared cochineal. If it be put on the cakes as soon as they are withdrawn from the oven, it will become firm and hard by the time the cakes are cold. On very rich cakes, such as wedding, christening cakes, &c., a layer of almond icing is usually spread over the top, and over that the white icing as described. All iced cakes should be kept in a very dry place.

INVALID COOKERY.

A few Rules to be observed in Cooking for Invalids.

Let all the kitchen utensils used in the preparation of invalids' cookery be delicately and *scrupulously clean ;* if this is not the case, a disagreeable flavour may be imparted to the preparation, which flavour may disgust, and prevent the patient from partaking of the refreshment when brought to him or her.

For invalids, never make a large quantity *of one thing,* as they seldom require much at a time ; and it is desirable that variety be provided for them.

Always have something in readiness ; a little beef tea, nicely made and nicely skimmed, a few spoonfuls of jelly, &c., &c., that it may be administered as soon almost as the invalid wishes for it. If obliged to wait a long time, the patient loses the desire to eat, and often turns against the food when brought to him or her.

In sending dishes or preparations up to invalids, let everything look as tempting as possible. Have a clean tray-cloth laid smoothly over the tray ; let the spoons, tumblers, cups and saucers, &c., be very clean and bright. Gruel served in a tumbler is more appetizing than when served in a basin or cup and saucer.

As milk is an important article of food for the sick, in warm weather let it be kept on ice, to prevent its turning sour. Many other delicacies may also be preserved good in the same manner for some little time.

If the patient be allowed to eat vegetables, never send them up undercooked, or half raw ; and let a small quantity only be temptingly arranged on a dish. This rule will apply to every preparation, as an invalid is much more likely to enjoy his food if small delicate pieces are served to him.

Never leave food about a sick-room ; if the patient cannot eat it when brought to him, take it away, and bring it to him in an hour or two's time. Miss Nightingale says, " To leave the patient's untasted food by his side from meal to meal, in hopes that he will eat it in the interval, is simply to prevent him from taking any food at all." She says, " I have known patients literally incapacitated from taking one article of food after another by this piece of ignorance. Let

the food come at the right time, and be taken away, eaten or uneaten, at the right time, but never let a patient have 'something always standing' by him, if you don't wish to disgust him of everything."

Never serve beef tea or broth with the *smallest particle* of fat or grease on the surface. It is better, after making either of these, to allow them to get perfectly cold, when *all the fat* may be easily removed ; then warm up as much as may be required. Two or three pieces of clean whity-brown paper laid on the broth will absorb any greasy particles that may be floating at the top, as the grease will cling to the paper.

Roast mutton, chickens, rabbits, calves' feet or head, game, fish (simply dressed), and simple puddings, are all light food, and easily digested. Of course, these things are only partaken of supposing the patient is recovering.

A mutton chop, nicely cut, trimmed, and broiled to a turn, is a dish to be recommended for invalids ; but it must not be served *with all the fat* at the end, nor must it be too thickly cut. Let it be cooked over a fire free from smoke, and sent up with the gravy in it, between two very hot plates. Nothing is more disagreeable to an invalid than *smoked* food.

In making toast-and-water, never blacken the bread, but toast it only a nice brown. Never leave toast-and-water to make until the moment it is required, as it cannot then be properly prepared,—at least the patient will be obliged to drink it warm, which is anything but agreeable.

In boiling eggs for invalids, let the white be just set ; if boiled hard, they will be likely to disagree with the patient.

In Miss Nightingale's admirable " Notes on Nursing," a book that no mother or nurse should be without, she says,—" You cannot be too careful as to quality in sick diet. A nurse should never put before a patient milk that is sour, meat or soup that is turned, an egg that is bad, or vegetables underdone." Yet often, she says, she has seen these things brought in to the sick, in a state perfectly perceptible to every nose or eye except the nurse's. It is here that the clever nurse appears,—she will not bring in the peccant article; but, not to disappoint the patient, she will whip up something else in a few minutes. Remember, that sick cookery should half do the

Invalid's Cutlet

work of your poor patient's weak digestion.

She goes on to caution nurses, by saying,—"Take care not to spill into your patient's saucer; in other words, take care that the outside bottom rim of his cup shall be quite dry and clean. If, every time he lifts his cup to his lips, he has to carry the saucer with it, or else to drop the liquid upon and to soil his sheet, or bedgown, or pillow, or, if he is sitting up, his dress, you have no idea what a difference this minute want of care on your part makes to his comfort, and even to his willingness for food."

INVALID'S CUTLET.

Ingredients.—1 nice cutlet from a loin or neck of mutton; 2 teacupfuls of water; 1 very small stick of celery; pepper and salt to taste. *Mode.*—Have the cutlet cut from a very nice loin or neck of mutton, take off all the fat, put it into a stewpan with the other ingredients; stew very gently indeed for nearly 2 hours, and skim off every particle of fat that may rise to the surface from time to time. The celery should be cut into thin slices before it is added to the meat, and care must be taken not to put in too much of this, or the dish will not be good. If the water is allowed to boil fast, the cutlet will be hard. *Time.*—2 hours very gentle stewing. *Average cost,* 6*d.* *Sufficient* for one person. *Seasonable.*— Whenever celery may be had.

INVALID'S JELLY.

Ingredients.—12 shanks of mutton, 3 quarts of water, a bunch of sweet herbs, pepper and salt to taste, 3 blades of mace, 1 onion, 1 lb. of lean beef, a crust of bread toasted brown. *Mode.*—Soak the shanks in plenty of water for some hours, and scrub them well; put them, with the beef and other ingredients, into a saucepan with the water, and let them simmer very gently for 5 hours. Strain the broth, and, when cold, take off all the fat. It may be eaten either warmed up or cold as a jelly. *Time.*—5 hours. *Average cost,* 1*s.* *Sufficient* to make from 1½ to 2 pints of jelly. *Seasonable* at any time.

INVALIDS, Lemonade for.

Ingredients.—½ lemon, lump sugar to taste, 1 pint of boiling water. *Mode.*— Pare off the rind of the lemon thinly;

January· Bills of Fare

cut the lemon into 2 or 3 thick slices, and remove as much as possible of the white outside pith, and all the pips. Put the slices of lemon, the peel, and lump sugar into a jug; pour over the boiling water; cover it closely, and in 2 hours it will be fit to drink. It should either be strained or poured off from the sediment. *Time.*—2 hours. *Average cost,* 2*d.* *Sufficient* to make 1 pint of lemonade. *Seasonable* at any time.

JAM ROLY-POLY PUDDING.

Ingredients.—¾ lb. of suet-crust, ¾ lb. of any kind of jam. *Mode.*—Make a nice light suet-crust, and roll it out to the thickness of about ½ inch. Spread the jam equally over it, leaving a small margin of paste without any, where the pudding joins. Roll it up, fasten the ends securely, and tie it in a floured cloth; put the pudding into boiling water, and boil for 2 hours. Mincemeat or marmalade may be substituted for the jam, and makes excellent puddings. *Time.*—2 hours. *Average cost,* 9*d.* *Sufficient* for 5 or 6 persons. *Seasonable.*—Suitable for winter puddings, when fresh fruit is not obtainable.

JANUARY—BILLS OF FARE.
Dinner for 18 persons.
First Course.

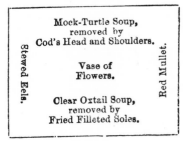

Mock-Turtle Soup,
removed by
Cod's Head and Shoulders.

Stewed Eels.

Vase of Flowers.

Red Mullet.

Clear Oxtail Soup,
removed by
Fried Filleted Soles.

Entrées.

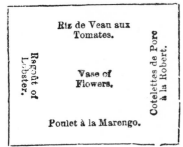

Ris de Veau aux Tomates.

Ragoût of Lobster.

Vase of Flowers.

Cotelettes de Porc à la Robert.

Poulet à la Marengo.

January—Bills of Fare

Second Course.

Roast Turkey.

Boiled Turkey and Celery Sauce.

Pigeon Pie.

Vase of Flowers.

Tongue, garnished.

Saddle of Mutton.

Boiled Ham.

Third Course.

Charlotte à la Parisienne.

Cream.

Mince Pies.

Pheasants, removed by Plum-Pudding.

Jelly.

Vase of Flowers.

Jelly.

Snipes, removed by Pommes à la Condé.

Apricot-Jam Tartlets.

Cream.

Maids of Honour.

Dinner for 12 persons.

First Course.—Carrot soup à la Crécy; ox-tail soup; turbot and lobster sauce; fried smelts, with Dutch sauce. *Entrées.* Mutton cutlets, with Soubise sauce; sweetbreads; oyster patties; fillets of rabbits. *Second Course.*—Roast turkey; stewed rump of beef à la jardinière; boiled ham, garnished with Brussels sprouts; boiled chickens and celery sauce. *Third Course.*—Roast hare; teal; eggs à la neige; vol-au-vent of preserved fruit; 1 jelly; 1 cream; potatoes à la maître d'hôtel; grilled mushrooms; dessert and ices.

Dinner for 10 persons.

First Course.—Soup à la Reine; whitings au gratin; crimped cod and oyster sauce. *Entrées.*— Tendrons de veau; curried fowl and boiled rice. *Second Course.*—Turkey, stuffed with chestnuts, and chestnut sauce; boiled leg of mutton, English fashion, with caper sauce and mashed turnips. *Third Course.*— Woodcocks or partridges; widgeo⌐⌐

January—Bills of Fare

Charlotte à la vanille; cabinet pudding; orange jelly; blancmange; artichoke bottoms; macaroni, with Parmesan cheese; dessert and ices.

Dinner for 8 persons.

First Course. — Mulligatawny soup; brill and shrimp sauce; fried whitings. *Entrées.*—Fricasseed chicken; pork cutlets, with tomato sauce. *Second Course.*— Haunch of mutton; boiled turkey and celery sauce; boiled tongue, garnished with Brussels sprouts. *Third Course.*— Roast pheasants; meringues à la crème; compôte of apples; orange jelly; cheesecakes; soufflé of rice; dessert and ices.

Dinners for 6 persons.

First Course.—Julienne soup; soles à la Normandie. *Entrées.*—Sweetbreads, with sauce piquante; mutton cutlets, with mashed potatoes. *Second Course.*— Haunch of venison; boiled fowls and bacon, garnished with Brussels sprouts. *Third Course.*—Plum-pudding; custards in glasses; apple tart; fondue à la Brillat Savarin; dessert.

First Course.—Vermicelli soup; fried slices of codfish and anchovy sauce; John Dory. *Entrées.* — Stewed rumpsteak à la jardinière; rissoles; oyster patties. *Second Course.*—Leg of mutton; curried rabbit and boiled rice. *Third Course.*—Partridges; apple fritters; tartlets of greengage jam; orange jelly; plum-pudding; dessert.

First Course.—Pea-soup; baked haddock; soles à la crème. *Entrées.*—Mutton cutlets and tomato sauce; fricasseed rabbit. *Second Course.*— Roast pork and apple sauce; breast of veal, rolled and stuffed; vegetables. *Third Course.* — Jugged hare; whipped cream; blancmange; mince pies; cabinet pudding.

First Course. —Palestine soup; fried smelts; stewed eels. *Entrées.*—Ragoût of lobster; broiled mushrooms; vol-au-vent of chicken. *Second Course.*—Sirloin of beef; boiled fowls and celery sauce; tongue, garnished with Brussels sprouts. *Third Course.*—Wild ducks; Charlotte aux pommes; cheesecakes transparent jelly, inlaid with brandy cherries, blancmange; Nesselrode pudding.

JANUARY, Plain Family Dinners for.

Sunday.—1. Boiled turbot and oyster sauce, potatoes. 2. Roast leg or griskin of pork, apple sauce, brocoli, potatoes. 3. Cabinet pudding, and damson tart made with preserved damsons.

Monday.—1. The remains of turbot warmed in oyster sauce, potatoes. 2. Cold pork, stewed steak. 3. Open jam tart, which should have been made with the pieces of paste left from the damson tart; baked arrowroot pudding.

Tuesday.—1. Boiled neck of mutton, carrots, mashed turnips, suet dumplings, and caper sauce: the broth should be served first, and a little rice or pearl barley should be boiled in it along with the meat. 2. Rolled jam pudding.

Wednesday.—1. Roast rolled ribs of beef, greens, potatoes, and horseradish sauce. 2. Bread-and-butter pudding, cheesecakes.

Thursday. — 1. Vegetable soup (the bones from the ribs of beef should be boiled down with this soup), cold beef, mashed potatoes. 2. Pheasants, gravy, bread sauce. 3. Macaroni.

Friday.—1. Fried whitings or soles. 2. Boiled rabbit and onion sauce, minced beef, potatoes. 3. Currant dumplings.

Saturday.—1. Rump-steak pudding or pie, greens, and potatoes. 2. Baked custard pudding and stewed apples.

Sunday.—1. Codfish and oyster sauce, potatoes. 2. Joint of roast mutton, either leg, haunch, or saddle; brocoli and potatoes, red-currant jelly. 3. Apple tart and custards, cheese.

Monday.—1. The remains of codfish picked from the bone, and warmed through in the oyster sauce; if there is no sauce left, order a few oysters and make a little fresh; and do not let the fish boil, or it will be watery. 2. Curried rabbit, with boiled rice served separately, cold mutton, mashed potatoes. 3. Somersetshire dumplings with wine sauce.

Tuesday.—1. Boiled fowls, parsley-and-butter; bacon garnished with Brussels sprouts; minced or hashed mutton. 2. Baroness pudding.

Wednesday.—1. The remains of the fowls cut up into joints and fricasseed; joint of roast pork and apple sauce, and, if liked, sage-and-onion, served on a dish by itself; turnips and potatoes. 2. Lemon pudding, either baked or boiled.

Thursday.—1. Cold pork and jugged hare, red-currant jelly, mashed potatoes. 2. Apple pudding.

Friday.—1. Boiled beef, either the aitchbone or the silver side of the round; carrots, turnips, suet dumplings, and potatoes: if there is a marrow-bone, serve the marrow on toast at the same time. 2. Rice snowballs.

Saturday. — 1. Pea-soup made from liquor in which beef was boiled; cold beef, mashed potatoes. 2. Baked batter fruit pudding.

JANUARY, Things in Season.

Fish.—Barbel, brill, carp, cod, crabs, crayfish, dace, eels, flounders, haddocks, herrings, lampreys, lobsters, mussels, oysters, perch, pike, plaice, prawns, shrimps, skate, smelts, soles, sprats, sturgeon, tench, thornback, turbot, whitings.

Meat. — Beef, house lamb, mutton, pork, veal, venison.

Poultry.—Capons, fowls, tame pigeons, pullets, rabbits, turkeys.

Game. — Grouse, hares, partridges, pheasants, snipe, wild-fowl, woodcock.

Vegetables. — Beetroot, brocoli, cabbages, carrots, celery, chervil, cresses, cucumbers (forced), endive, lettuces, parsnips, potatoes, savoys, spinach, turnips, various herbs.

Fruit.—Apples, grapes, medlars, nuts, oranges, pears, walnuts, crystallized preserves (foreign), dried fruits, such as almonds and raisins; French and Spanish plums; prunes, figs, dates.

JAUNEMANGE.

Ingredients.—1 oz. of isinglass, 1 pint of water, ½ pint of white wine, the rind and juice of 1 large lemon, sugar to taste, the yolks of 6 eggs. *Mode.*—Put the isinglass, water, and lemon-rind into a saucepan, and boil gently until the former is dissolved; then add the strained lemon-juice, the wine, and sufficient white sugar to sweeten the whole nicely. Boil for 2 or 3 minutes, strain the mixture into a jug, and add the yolks of the eggs, which should be well beaten; place the jug in a saucepan of boiling water; keep stirring the mixture *one way* until it thickens, but *do not allow it to boil;* then take it off the fire, and keep stirring until nearly cold. Pour it into a mould, omitting the sediment at the bottom of the jug, and let it re-

Jellies	Jelly-bag, how to make a

main until quite firm. *Time.*—¼ hour to boil the isinglass and water; about 10 minutes to stir the mixture in the jug. *Average cost,* with the best isinglass, 2s. 9d. *Sufficient* to fill a quart mould. *Seasonable* at any time.

JELLIES

Are not the nourishing food they were at one time considered to be, and many eminent physicians are of opinion that they are less digestible than the flesh, or muscular part of animals; still, when acidulated with lemon-juice and flavoured with wine, they are very suitable for some convalescents. Vegetable jelly is a distinct principle, existing in fruits, which possesses the property of gelatinizing when boiled and cooled; but it is a principle entirely different from the gelatine of animal bodies, although the name of jelly, common to both, sometimes leads to an erroneous idea on that subject. Animal jelly, or gelatine, is glue, whereas vegetable jelly is rather analogous to gum. Liebig places gelatine very low indeed in the scale of usefulness. He says, "Gelatine, which by itself is tasteless, and when eaten, excites nausea, possesses no nutritive value; that, even when accompanied by the savoury constituents of flesh, it is not capable of supporting the vital process, and when added to the usual diet as a substitute for plastic matter, does not increase, but on the contrary, diminishes the nutritive value of the food, which it renders insufficient in quantity and inferior in quality." It is this substance which is most frequently employed in the manufacture of the jellies supplied by the confectioner; but those prepared at home from calves' feet do possess some nutrition, and are the only sort that should be given to invalids. Isinglass is the purest variety of gelatine, and is prepared from the sounds or swimming-bladders of certain fish, chiefly the sturgeon. From its whiteness it is mostly used for making blancmange and similar dishes.

JELLIES, Bottled, How to Mould.

Uncork the bottle; place it in a saucepan of hot water until the jelly is reduced to a liquid state; taste it, to ascertain whether it is sufficiently flavoured, and if not, add a little wine. Pour the jelly into moulds which have been soaked in water; let it set, and turn it out by placing the mould in hot water for a minute; then wipe the outside, put a dish on the top, and turn it over quickly. The jelly should then slip easily away from the mould, and be quite firm. It may be garnished as taste dictates.

JELLY, Isinglass, or Gelatine. (Substitutes for Calf's Feet.)

Ingredients.—3 oz. of Swinborne's isinglass or gelatine, 2 quarts of water. *Mode.*—Put the isinglass or gelatine into a saucepan with the above proportion of cold water; bring it quickly to boil, and let it boil very fast, until the liquor is reduced one-half. Remove the scum as it rises, then strain it through a jelly-bag, and it will be ready for use. If not required very clear, it may be merely strained through a fine sieve, instead of being run through a bag. Rather more than ¼ oz. of isinglass is about the proper quantity to use for a quart of strong calf's-feet stock, and rather more than 2 oz. for the same quantity of fruit juice. As isinglass varies so much in quality and strength, it is difficult to give the exact proportions. The larger the mould, the stiffer should be the jelly; and where there is no ice, more isinglass must be used than if the mixture were frozen. This forms a stock for all kinds of jellies, which may be flavoured in many ways. *Time.*—1½ hour. *Sufficient,* with wine, syrup, fruit, &c., to fill two moderate-sized moulds. *Seasonable* at any time.

Note.—The above, when boiled, should be perfectly clear, and may be mixed warm with wine, flavourings, fruits, &c., and then run through the bag.

JELLY-BAG, How to make a.

The very stout flannel called double-mill, used for ironing-blankets, is the best material for a jelly-bag: those of home manufacture are the only ones to be relied on for thoroughly clearing the jelly. Care should be taken that the seam of the bag be stitched twice, to secure it against unequal filtration. The most convenient mode of using the bag

JELLY-BAG.

Jelly, Moulded with fresh Fruit

is to tie it upon a hoop the exact size of the outside of its mouth; and, to do this, strings should be sewn round it at equal distances. The jelly-bag may, of course, be made any size; but one of twelve or fourteen inches deep, and seven or eight across the mouth, will be sufficient for ordinary use. The form of a jelly-bag is the fool's-cap.

JELLY Moulded with fresh Fruit, or Macedoine de Fruits.

Ingredients.—Rather more than 1½ pint of jelly, a few nice strawberries, or red or white currants, or raspberries, or any fresh fruit that may be in season. *Mode.* —Have ready the above proportion of jelly, which must be very clear and rather sweet, the raw fruit requiring an additional quantity of sugar. Select ripe, nice-looking fruit; pick off the stalks, unless currants are used, when they are laid in the jelly as they come from the tree. Begin by putting a little jelly at the bottom of the mould, which must harden; then arrange the fruit

JELLY MOULDED WITH CHERRIES.

round the sides of the mould, recollecting that *it will be reversed when turned out;* then pour in some more jelly to make the fruit adhere, and, when that layer is set, put another row of fruit and jelly until the mould is full. If convenient, put it in ice until required for table, then wring a cloth in boiling water, wrap it round the mould for a minute, and turn the jelly carefully out. Peaches, apricots, plums, apples, &c., are better for being boiled in a little clear syrup before they are laid in the jelly; strawberries, raspberries, grapes, cherries, and currants are put in raw. In winter, when fresh fruits are not obtainable, a very pretty jelly may be made with preserved fruits or brandy cherries: these, in a bright and clear jelly, have a very pretty effect; of course, unless the jelly he very clear, the beauty of the dish will be spoiled. It may be garnished with the same fruit as is laid in the jelly; for instance, an open jelly with strawberries might have, piled

Jelly of two Colours

in the centre, a few of the same fruit prettily arranged, or a little whipped cream might be substituted for the fruit. *Time.*—One layer of jelly should remain 2 hours in a very cool place, before another layer is added. *Average cost, 2s. 6d. Sufficient,* with fruit, to fill a quart mould. *Seasonable,* with fresh fruit, from June to October; with dried, at any time.

JELLY, ORANGE, Moulded with slices of Orange.

Ingredients.—1½ pint of orange jelly, 4 oranges, ½ pint of clarified syrup. *Mode.*—Boil ½ lb. of loaf sugar with ½ pint of water until there is no scum left (which must be carefully removed as fast as it rises), and carefully peel the oranges; divide them into thin slices, without breaking the thin skin, and put these pieces of orange into the syrup, where let them remain for about 5 minutes; then take them out, and use the syrup for the jelly. When the oranges are well drained, and the jelly is nearly cold, pour a little of the latter into the bottom of the mould; then lay in a few pieces of orange; over these pour a little jelly, and when this is set, place another layer of oranges, proceeding in this manner until the mould is full. Put it in ice, or in a cool place, and, before turning it out, wrap a cloth round the mould for a minute or two, which has been wrung out in boiling water. *Time.*—5 minutes to simmer the oranges. *Average cost, 3s. 6d. Sufficient,* with the slices of orange, to fill a quart mould. *Seasonable* from November to May.

JELLY of Two Colours.

Ingredients.—1½ pint of calf's-feet jelly, a few drops of prepared cochineal. *Mode.*—Make 1½ pint of calf's-feet jelly, or, if wished more economical, of clarified syrup and gelatine, flavouring it in

JELLY OF TWO COLOURS.

any way that may be preferred. Colour one-half of the jelly with a few drops of

Jelly, Open, with whipped Cream	Jelly, to make the Stock' for

prepared cochineal, and the other half leave as pale as possible. Have ready a mould well wetted in every part; pour in a small quantity of the red jelly, and let this set; when quite firm, pour on it the same quantity of the pale jelly, and let this set; then proceed in this manner until the mould is full, always taking care to let one jelly set before the other is poured in, or the colours would run one into the other. When turned out, the jelly should have a striped appearance. For variety, half the mould may be filled at once with one of the jellies, and, when firm, filled up with the other: this, also, has a very pretty effect, and is more expeditiously prepared than when the jelly is poured in small quantities into the mould. Blancmange and red jelly, or blancmange and raspberry cream, moulded in the above manner, look very well. The layers of blancmange and jelly should be about an inch in depth, and each layer should be perfectly hardened before another is added. Half a mould of blancmange and half a mould of jelly are frequently served in the same manner. A few pretty dishes may be made, in this way, of jellies or blancmanges left from the preceding day, by melting them separately in a jug placed in a saucepan of boiling water, and then moulding them by the foregoing directions. *Time.*—¾ hour to make the jelly. *Average cost*, with calf's-feet jelly, 2s.; with gelatine and syrup, more economical. *Sufficient* to fill 1½-pint mould. *Seasonable* at any time.

Note.—In making the jelly, use for flavouring a very pale sherry, or the colour will be too dark to contrast nicely with the red jelly.

JELLY, Open, with whipped Cream (a very pretty dish).

Ingredients.—1½ pint of jelly, ½ pint of cream, 1 glass of sherry, sugar to taste. *Mode.*—Make the above proportion of calf's-feet or isinglass jelly, colouring and flavouring it in any way that may be perferred; soak a mould, open in the centre, for about ½ hour in cold water; fill it with the jelly, and let it remain in a cool place until perfectly set; then turn it out on a dish; fill the centre with whipped cream, flavoured with sherry and sweetened with pounded sugar; pile this cream high in the centre, and serve. The jelly should be

made of rather a dark colour, to contrast nicely with the cream. *Time.*—¾ hour.

OPEN JELLY WITH WHIPPED CREAM.

Average cost, 3s. 6d. *Sufficient* to fill 1½-pint mould. *Seasonable* at any time.

JELLY, Savoury, for Meat Pies.

Ingredients. −3 lbs. of shin of beef, 1 calf's-foot, 3 lbs. of knuckle of veal, poultry trimmings (if for game pies, any game trimmings), 2 onions stuck with cloves, 2 carrots, 4 shalots, a bunch of savoury herbs, 2 bay-leaves; when liked, 2 blades of mace and a little spice; 2 slices of lean ham; rather more than 2 quarts of water. *Mode.*—Cut up the meat and put it into a stewpan with all the ingredients except the water; set it over a slow fire to draw down, and, when the gravy ceases to flow from the meat, pour in the water. Let it boil up, then carefully take away all scum from the top. Cover the stewpan closely, and let the stock simmer very gently for 4 hours: if rapidly boiled, the jelly will not be clear. When done, strain it through a fine sieve or flannel bag; and when cold, the jelly should be quite transparent. If this is not the case, clarify it with the whites of eggs. *Time.*—4 hours. *Average cost*, for this quantity, 5s.

JELLY, to make the Stock for, and to Clarify it.

Ingredients.—2 calf's feet, 6 pints of water. *Mode.*—The stock for jellies should always be made the day before it is required for use, as the liquor has time to cool, and the fat can be so much more easily and effectually removed when thoroughly set. Procure 2 nice calf's feet; scald them, to take off the hair; slit them in two, remove the fat from between the claws, and wash the feet well in warm water; put them into a stewpan, with the above proportion of cold water, bring it gradually to boil,

| Jelly, to make the Stock for | June—Bills o' Fare |

and remove every particle of scum as it rises. When it is well skimmed, boil it very gently for 6 or 7 hours, or until the liquor is reduced rather more than half;

JELLY-MOULD.

then strain it through a sieve into a basin, and put it in a cool place to set. As the liquor is strained, measure it, to ascertain the proportion for the jelly, allowing something for the sediment and fat at the top. To clarify it, carefully remove all the fat from the top, pour over a little warm water, to wash away any that may remain, and wipe the jelly with a clean cloth; remove the jelly from the sediment, put it into a saucepan, and, supposing the quantity to be a quart, add to it 6 oz. of loaf sugar, the shells and well-whisked whites of 5 eggs, and stir these ingredients together cold; set the saucepan on the fire, but *do not stir the jelly after it begins to warm.* Let it boil about 10 minutes after it rises to a head, then throw in a teacupful of cold water; let it boil 5 minutes longer, then take the saucepan off, cover it closely, and let it remain ½ hour near the fire. Dip the jelly-bag into hot water, wring it out quite dry, and fasten it on to a stand or the back of a chair, which must be placed near the fire, to prevent the jelly from setting before it has run through the bag. Place a basin underneath to receive the jelly; then pour it into the bag, and should it not be clear the first time, run it through the bag again. This stock is the foundation of all *really good* jellies, which may be varied in innumerable ways, by colouring and flavouring with liqueurs, and by moulding it with fresh and preserved fruits. To insure the jelly being firm when turned out, ½ oz. of isinglass clarified might be added to the above proportion of stock. Substitutes for calf's feet are now frequently used in making jellies, which lessen the expense and trouble in preparing this favourite

dish, isinglass and gelatine being two of the principal materials employed; but although they may *look* as nicely as jellies made from good stock, they are never so delicate, having very often an unpleasant flavour, somewhat resembling glue, particularly when made with gelatine. *Time.* —About 6 hours to boil the feet for the stock; to clarify it,—¼ hour to boil, ½ hour to stand in the saucepan covered. *Average cost.*—Calf's feet may be purchased for 6d. each when veal is in full season, but more expensive when it is scarce. *Sufficient.*—2 calf's feet should make 1 quart of stock. *Seasonable* from March to October, but may be had all the year.

JOHN DORY.

Ingredients.—¼ lb. of salt to each gallon of water. *Mode.*—This fish, which is esteemed by most people a great delicacy, is dressed in the same way as a turbot, which it resembles in firmness, but not in richness. Cleanse it thoroughly and cut off the fins; lay it in a fish-kettle, cover with cold water, and add salt in the above proportion. Bring it gradually to a boil, and simmer gently for ¼ hour, or rather longer, should the fish be very large. Serve on a hot napkin, and garnish with cut lemon and parsley. Lobster, anchovy, or shrimp sauce, and plain melted butter, should be sent to table with it. *Time.*—After the water boils, ¼ to ½ hour, according to size. *Average cost, 3s.* to 5s. *Seasonable* all the year, but best from September to January.

Note.—Small John Dory are very good baked.

JUNE—BILLS OF FARE.

Dinner for 18 persons.

First Course.

Fillets of Gurnets.	Asparagus Soup, removed by Crimped Salmon.	Soles aux fines herbes.
	Vase of Flowers.	
	Vermicelli Soup, removed by Whitebait.	

June—Bills of Fare

Entrées.

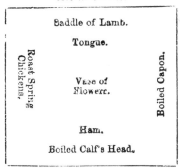

Lobster Patties.

Lamb Cutlets and Peas.

Vase of Flowers.

Larded Sweetbreads.

Tendrons de Veau à la Jardinière.

Second Course.

Roast Spring Chickens.

Saddle of Lamb.

Tongue.

Vase of Flowers.

Ham.

Boiled Calf's Head.

Boiled Capon.

Third Course.

Prawns.

Vol-au-Vent of Strawberries and Cream. Cheesecakes.

Leveret, removed by Iced Pudding.

Wine Jelly.

Vase of Flowers.

Blancmange.

Goslings, removed by Fondues, in cases.

Custards, in glasses. Plovers' Eggs.

Tartlets.

Dessert and Ices.

Dinner for 12 persons.

First Course.—Green-pea soup; rice soup; salmon and lobster sauce; trout à la Genévése; whitebait. *Entrées.*—Lamb cutlets and cucumbers; fricasseed chicken; stewed veal and peas; lobster rissoles. *Second Course.*—Roast quarter of lamb and spinach; filet de bœuf à la Jardinière; boiled fowls; braised shoulder of lamb; tongue; vegetables. *Third Course.*—Goslings; ducklings; Nesselrode pudding; Charlotte à la Parisienne; gooseberry tartlets; strawberry cream;

June—Bills of Fare

raspberry-and-currant tart; custards; dessert and ices.

Dinner for 10 persons.

First Course.—Julienne soup; salmon trout and parsley-and-butter; red mullet. *Entrées.*—Stewed breast of veal and peas; mutton cutlets à la Maintenon. *Second Course.*—Roast fillet of veal; boiled leg of lamb, garnished with young carrots; boiled bacon-cheek; vegetables. *Third Course.*—Roast ducks; leveret; gooseberry tart; strawberry cream; strawberry tartlets; meringues; cabinet pudding; iced pudding; dessert and ices.

Dinner for 8 persons.

First Course.—Vermicelli soup; trout à la Genévése; salmon cutlets. *Entrées.*—Lamb cutlets and peas; fricasseed chicken. *Second Course.*—Roast ribs of beef; half calf's head, tongue, and brains; boiled ham; vegetables. *Third Course.*—Roast ducks; compôte of gooseberries; strawberry jelly; pastry; iced pudding; cauliflower with cream sauce; dessert and ices.

Dinner for 6 persons.

First Course.—Spring soup; boiled salmon and lobster sauce. *Entrées.*—Veal cutlets and endive; ragoût of duck and green peas. *Second Course.*—Roast loin of veal; boiled leg of lamb and white sauce; tongue, garnished; vegetables. *Third Course.* — Strawberry cream; gooseberry tartlets; almond pudding; lobster salad; dessert.

First Course.—Calf's head soup; mackerel à la maître d'hôtel; whitebait. *Entrées.*—Chicken cutlets; curried lobster. *Second Course.*—Fore-quarter of lamb and salad; stewed beef à la Jardinière; vegetables. *Third Course.*—Goslings; green-currant tart; custards, in glasses; strawberry blancmange; soufflé of rice; dessert.

First Course.—Green-pea soup; baked soles aux fines herbes; stewed trout. *Entrées.*—Calf's liver and bacon; rissoles. *Second Course.*—Roast saddle of lamb and salad; calf's head à la tortue; vegetables. *Third Course.*—Roast ducks; vol-au-vent of strawberries and cream;

June, Plain Family Dinners for

strawberry tartlets ; lemon blancmange ; baked gooseberry pudding ; dessert.

First Course.—Spinach soup ; soles à la crême ; red mullet. *Entrées.*—Roast fillet of veal ; braised ham and spinach. *Second Course.*—Boiled fowls and white sauce ; vegetables. *Third Course.*—Leveret ; strawberry jelly ; Swiss cream ; cheesecakes ; iced pudding ; dessert.

JUNE, Plain Family Dinners for.

Sunday.—1. Salmon trout and parsley-and-butter, new potatoes. 2. Roast fillet of veal, boiled bacon-cheek and spinach, vegetables. 3. Gooseberry tart, custard.

Monday.—1. Light gravy soup. 2. Small meat pie, minced veal, garnished with rolled bacon, spinach, and potatoes. 3. Raspberry-and-currant tart.

Tuesday.—1. Baked mackerel, potatoes. 2. Boiled leg of lamb, garnished with young carrots. 3. Lemon pudding.

Wednesday.—1. Vegetable soup. 2. Calf's liver and bacon, peas, hashed lamb from remains of cold joint. 3. Baked gooseberry pudding.

Thursday.—1. Roast ribs of beef, Yorkshire pudding, peas, potatoes. 2. Stewed rhubarb and boiled rice.

Friday.—1. Cold beef and salad, lamb cutlets and peas. 2. Boiled gooseberry pudding and baked custard pudding.

Saturday.—1. Rump-steak pudding, broiled beef-bones and cucumber, vegetables. 2. Bread pudding.

Sunday.—1. Roast fore-quarter of lamb, mint sauce, peas, and new potatoes. 2. Gooseberry pudding, strawberry tartlets. Fondue.

Monday. —1. Cold lamb and salad, stewed neck of veal and peas, young carrots, and new potatoes. 2. Almond pudding.

Tuesday. — 1. Green-pea soup. 2. Roast ducks stuffed, gravy, peas, and new potatoes. 3. Baked ratafia pudding.

Wednesday.—1. Roast leg of mutton, summer cabbage, potatoes. 2. Gooseberry and rice pudding.

Thursday.—1. Fried soles, melted butter, potatoes. 2. Sweetbreads, hashed mutton, vegetables. 3. Bread-and-butter pudding.

Friday.—1. Asparagus soup. 2. Boiled beef, young carrots, and new potatoes, suet dumplings. 3. College puddings.

July—Bills of Fare

Saturday.—1. Cold boiled beef and salad, lamb cutlets, and green peas. 2. Boiled gooseberry pudding and plain cream.

JUNE, Things in Season.

Fish.—Carp, crayfish, herrings, lobsters, mackerel, mullet, pike, prawns, salmon, soles, tench, trout, turbot.

Meat.—Beef, lamb, mutton, veal, buck venison.

Poultry.—Chickens, ducklings, fowls, green geese, leverets, plovers, pullets, rabbits, turkey poults, wheatears.

Vegetables. — Artichokes, asparagus, beans, cabbages, carrots, cucumbers, lettuces, onions, parsnips, peas, potatoes, radishes, small salads, sea-kale, spinach,—various herbs.

Fruit.—Apricots, cherries, currants, gooseberries, melons, nectarines, peaches, pears, pineapples, raspberries, rhubarb, strawberries.

JULY—BILLS OF FARE.

Dinner for 18 persons.

First Course.

Whitebait.	Green-Pea Soup, removed by Salmon and dressed Cucumber. Vase of Flowers. Soup à la Reine, removed by Mackerel à la Maître d'Hotel.	Stewed Trout.

Entrées.

Lobster Curry en Casserole.	Lamb Cutlets and Peas. Vase of Flowers. Chicken Patties.	Scollops of Chickens.

Second Course.

```
┌─────────────────────────────────────────┐
│          Haunch of Venison.              │
│                                          │
│  B           Pigeon Pie.              S  │
│  o                                    p  │
│  i           Vase of                  r  │
│  l           Flowers.                 i  │
│  e                                    n  │
│  d           Braised Ham.             g  │
│                                          │
│  C                                    C  │
│  a           Saddle of Lamb.          h  │
│  p                                    i  │
│  o                                    c  │
│  n                                    k  │
│  s                                    e  │
│                                       n  │
│                                       s  │
│                                       .  │
└─────────────────────────────────────────┘
```

Third Course.

```
┌─────────────────────────────────────────┐
│ P         Roast Ducks,               C   │
│ r         removed by                 u   │
│ a         Vanilla Soufflé.           s   │
│ w    C                       R  T    t   │
│ n    h    Raspberry Cream.   a  a    a   │
│ s    e                       s  r    r   │
│ .    r    Vase of            p  t    d   │
│      r    Flowers.           b  .    s   │
│      y                       e       .   │
│ C    T    Strawberry Cream.  r  T        │
│ r    a                       r  a        │
│ e    r    Green Goose,       y  r        │
│ a    t    removed by         a  t        │
│ m    .    Iced Pudding.      n  l        │
│ s                            d  e        │
│                              -  t        │
│                              .  s        │
│                                 .        │
└─────────────────────────────────────────┘
```

Dessert and Ices.

Dinner for 12 persons.

First Course.—Soup à la Jardinière; chicken soup; crimped salmon and parsley-and-butter; trout aux fines herbes. in cases. *Entrées.*—Tendrons de veau and peas; lamb cutlets and cucumbers. *Second Course.*—Loin of veal à la Béchamel; roast fore-quarter of lamb; salad; braised ham, garnished with broad beans; vegetables. *Third Course.*—Roast ducks; turkey poult; stewed peas à la Francaise; lobster salad; cherry tart; raspberry-and-currant tart; custards, in glasses; lemon creams; Nesselrode pudding; marrow pudding. Dessert and ices.

Dinner for 8 persons.

First Course.—Green-pea soup; salmon and lobster sauce; crimped perch and Dutch sauce. *Entrées.*—Stewed veal and peas; lamb cutlets and cucumbers. *Second Course.*—Haunch of venison; boiled fowls à la Béchamel; braised

ham; vegetables. *Third Course.*—Roast ducks; peas à la Francaise; lobster salad; strawberry cream; blancmange; cherry tart; cheesecakes; iced pudding. Dessert and ices.

Dinner for 6 persons.

First Course.—Soup à la Jardinière; salmon trout and parsley-and-butter; fillets of mackerel à la maître d'hôtel. *Entrées.*—Lobster cutlets; beef palates, à la Italienne. *Second Course.*—Roast lamb; boiled capon and white sauce; boiled tongue, garnished with small vegetable marrows; bacon and beans. *Third Course.*—Goslings; whipped strawberry cream; raspberry-and-currant tart; meringues; cherry tartlets; iced pudding. Dessert and ices.

First Course.—Julienne soup; crimped salmon and caper sauce; whitebait. *Entrées.*—Croquettes à la Reine; curried lobster. *Second Course.*—Roast lamb; rump of beef à la Jardinière. *Third Course.*—Larded turkey poult; raspberry cream; cherry tart; custards, in glasses; Gâteaux à la Genévése; Nesselrode pudding. Dessert.

JULY, Plain Family Dinners for.

Sunday.—1. Salmon trout and parsley-and-butter. 2. Roast fillet of veal, boiled bacon-cheek, peas, potatoes. 3. Raspberry-and-currant tart, baked custard pudding.

Monday.—1. Green-pea soup. 2. Roast fowls garnished with watercresses; gravy, bread sauce; cold veal and salad. 3. Cherry tart.

Tuesday.—1. John dory and lobster sauce. 2. Curried fowl with remains of cold fowls, dish of rice, veal rolls with remains of cold fillet. 3. Strawberry cream.

Wednesday.—1. Roast leg of mutton, vegetable marrow and potatoes, melted butter. 2. Black-currant pudding.

Thursday.—1. Fried soles, anchovy sauce. 2. Mutton cutlets and tomato sauce, hashed mutton, peas, potatoes. 3. Lemon dumplings.

Friday.—1. Boiled brisket of beef, carrots, turnips, suet dumplings, peas, potatoes. 2. Baked semolina pudding.

Saturday.—1. Cold beef and salad, lamb cutlets and peas. 2. Rolled jam pudding.

|

Sunday.—1. Julienne soup. 2. Roast lamb, half calf's head, tongue and brains, boiled ham, peas and potatoes. 3. Cherry tart, custards.

Monday.—1. Hashed calf's head, cold lamb and salad. 2. Vegetable marrow and white sauce, instead of pudding.

Tuesday.—1. Stewed veal, with peas, young carrots, and potatoes. Small meat pie. 2. Raspberry-and-currant pudding.

Wednesday.—1. Roast ducks stuffed, gravy, peas, and potatoes ; the remains of stewed veal rechauffé. 2. Macaroni served as a sweet pudding.

Thursday.—1. Slices of salmon and caper sauce. 2. Boiled knuckle of veal, parsley-and-butter, vegetable marrow and potatoes. 3. Black-currant pudding.

Friday.—1. Roast shoulder of mutton, onion sauce, peas and potatoes. 2. Cherry tart, baked custard pudding.

Saturday.—1. Minced mutton, rump-steak-and-kidney pudding. 2. Baked lemon pudding.

JULY, Things in Season.

Fish.—Carp, crayfish, dory, flounders, haddocks, herrings, lobsters, mackerel, mullet, pike, plaice, prawns, salmon, shrimps, soles, sturgeon, tench, thornback.

Meat.—Beef, lamb, mutton, veal, buck venison.

Poultry.—Chickens, ducklings, fowls, green geese, leverets, plovers, pullets, rabbits, turkey poults, wheatears, wild ducks (called flappers).

Vegetables. — Artichokes, asparagus, beans, cabbages, carrots, cauliflowers, celery, cresses, endive, lettuces, mushrooms, onions, peas, radishes, small salading, sea-kale, sprouts, turnips, vegetable marrow,—various herbs.

Fruit.—Apricots, cherries, currants, figs, gooseberries, melons, nectarines, pears, pineapples, plums, raspberries, strawberries, walnuts in high season, for pickling.

JULIENNE, Soup à la.

Ingredients.—½ pint of carrots, ½ pint of turnips, ¼ pint of onions, 2 or 3 leeks, ½ head of celery, 1 lettuce, a little sorrel and chervil, if liked, 2 oz. of butter, 2 quarts of stock. *Mode.*—Cut the vegetables into strips of about 1¼ inch long, and be particular they are all the same size, or some will be hard whilst the others will be done to a pulp. Cut the

lettuce, sorrel, and chervil into larger pieces ; fry the carrots in the butter, and pour the stock boiling to them. When this is done, add all the other vegetables and herbs, and stew gently for at least an hour. Skim off all the fat, pour the soup over thin slices of bread, cut round about the size of a shilling, and serve.

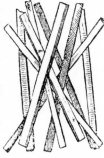

STRIPS OF VEGETABLE.

Time. — 1½ hour. *Average cost.*—1s. 3d. per quart. *Seasonable* all the year. *Sufficient* for 8 persons.

Note.—In summer, green peas, asparagus-tops, French beans, &c., can be added. When the vegetables are very strong, instead of frying them in butter at first, they should be blanched, and afterwards simmered in the stock.

KALE BROSE (a Scotch Recipe).

Ingredients.—Half an ox-head or cow-heel, a teacupful of toasted oatmeal, salt to taste, 2 handfuls of greens, 3 quarts of water. *Mode.*—Make a broth of the ox-head or cow-heel, and boil it till oil floats on the top of the liquor, then boil the greens, shred, in it. Put the oatmeal, with a little salt, into a basin, and mix with it quickly a teacupful of the fat broth : it should not run into one doughy mass, but form knots. Stir it into the whole, give one boil, and serve very hot. *Time.*—4 hours. *Average cost,* 8d. per quart. *Seasonable* all the year, but more suitable in winter. *Sufficient* for 10 persons.

KEGEREE.

Ingredients.—Any cold fish, 1 teacupful of boiled rice, 1 oz. of butter, 1 teaspoonful of mustard, 2 soft-boiled eggs, salt and cayenne to taste. *Mode.*—Pick the fish carefully from the bones, mix with the other ingredients, and serve very hot. The quantities may be varied according to the amount of fish used. *Time.*—¼ hour after the rice is boiled. *Average cost,* 5d. exclusive of the fish.

KIDNEYS, Broiled (a Breakfast or Supper Dish).

Ingredients.—Sheep kidneys, pepper and salt to taste. *Mode.*—Ascertain

Kidneys, Fried	Lamb

that the kidneys are fresh, and cut them open, very evenly, lengthwise, down to the root, for should one half be thicker than the other, one would be underdone

KIDNEYS.

whilst the other would be dried, but do not separate them; skin them, and pass a skewer under the white part of each half to keep them flat, and broil over a nice clear fire, placing the inside downwards; turn them when done enough on one side, and cook them on the other. Remove the skewers, place the kidneys on a very hot dish, season with pepper and salt, and put a tiny piece of butter in the middle of each; serve very hot and quickly, and send very hot plates to table. *Time.*—6 to 8 minutes. *Average cost*, 1½d. each. *Sufficient.*—Allow 1 for each person. *Seasonable* at any time.

Note.—A prettier dish than the above may be made by serving the kidneys each on a piece of buttered toast cut in any fanciful shape. In this case a little lemon-juice will be found an improvement.

KIDNEYS, Fried.

Ingredients.—Kidneys, butter, pepper, and salt to taste. *Mode.*—Cut the kidneys open without quite dividing them, remove the skin, and put a small piece of butter in the frying-pan. When the butter is melted, lay in the kidneys the flat side downwards, and fry them for 7 or 8 minutes, turning them when they are half done. Serve on a piece of dry toast, season with pepper and salt, and put a small piece of butter in each kidney; pour the gravy from the pan over them, and serve very hot. *Time.*— 7 or 8 minutes. *Average cost*, 1½d. each. *Sufficient.*—Allow 1 kidney to each person. *Seasonable* at any time.

KIDNEY OMELET (a favourite French Dish).

Ingredients.—6 eggs, 1 saltspoonful of salt, ⅓ saltspoonful of pepper, 2 sheep's kidneys, or 2 tablespoonfuls of minced veal kidney, 5 oz. of butter. *Mode.*— Skin the kidneys, cut them into small dice, and toss them in a frying-pan, in

1 oz. of butter, over the fire for 2 or 3 minutes. Mix the ingredients for the omelet, and when the eggs are well whisked, stir in the pieces of kidney. Make the butter hot in the frying-pan,

OMELET PAN.

and when it bubbles, pour in the omelet, and fry it over a gentle fire from 4 to 6 minutes. When the eggs are set, fold the edges over, so that the omelet assumes an oval form, and be careful that it is not too much done: to brown the top, hold the pan before the fire for a minute or two, or use a salamander until the desired colour is obtained, but never turn an omelet in the pan. Slip it carefully on to a *very hot* dish, or, what is a much safer method, put a dish on the omelet, and turn the pan quickly over. It should be served the instant it comes from the fire. *Time.*—4 to 6 minutes. *Average cost*, 1s. *Sufficient* for 4 persons. *Seasonable* at any time.

KIDNEYS, Stewed.

Ingredients.—About 8 kidneys, a large dessertspoonful of chopped herbs, 2 oz. butter, 1 dessertspoonful of flour, a little gravy, juice of half a lemon, a teaspoonful of Harvey sauce and mushroom ketchup, cayenne, and salt to taste. *Mode.*—Strew the herbs, with cayenne and salt, over the kidneys, melt the butter in the frying-pan, put in the kidneys, and brown them nicely all round; when nearly done, stir in the flour, and shake them well; now add the gravy and sauce, and stew them for a few minutes, then turn them out into a dish garnished with fried sippets. *Time.*—10 or 12 minutes. *Seasonable* at any time.

LAMB.

The most delicious sorts of lamb are those of the South-Down breed, known by their black feet; and of these, those which have been exclusively suckled on the milk of the parent ewe, are considered the finest. Next to these in estimation are those fed on the milk of several dams; and last of all, though

| Lamb, Breast of | Lamb, Fore-quarter of |

the fattest, the grass-fed lamb : this, however, implies an age much greater than either of the others.

LAMB, in the early part of the season, however reared, is in London, and indeed generally, sold in quarters, divided with eleven ribs to the fore-quarter ; but, as the season advances, these are subdivided into two, and the hind-quarter in the same manner ; the first consisting of the shoulder, and the neck and breast ; the latter, of the leg and the loin.— As lamb, from the juicy nature of its flesh, is especially liable to spoil in unfavourable weather, it should be frequently wiped, so as to remove any moisture that may form on it.

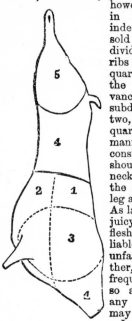

SIDE OF LAMB.

IN THE PUR-CHASING OF LAMB FOR THE TABLE, there are certain signs by which the experienced judgment is able to form an accurate opinion whether the animal has been lately slaughtered, and whether the joints possess that condition of fibre indicative of good and wholesome meat. The first of these doubts may be solved satisfactorily by the bright and dilated appearance of the eye ; the quality of the fore-quarter can always be guaranteed by the blue or healthy ruddiness of the jugular, or vein of the neck ; while the rigidity of the knuckle, and the firm, compact feel of the kidney, will answer in an equally positive manner for the integrity of the hind-quarter.

MODE OF CUTTING UP A SIDE OF LAMB IN LONDON.—1. Ribs ; 2. Breast ; 3. Shoulder ; 4. Loin ; 5. Leg ; 1, 2, 3. Fore Quarter.

LAMB, Breast of, and Green Peas.

Ingredients.—1 breast of lamb, a few slices of bacon, ½ pint of stock, 1 lemon, 1 onion, 1 bunch of savoury herbs, green-peas. *Mode.*—Remove the skin from a breast of lamb, put it into a saucepan of boiling water, and let it simmer for 5 minutes. Take it out and lay it in cold water. Line the bottom of a stewpan with a few thin slices of bacon ; lay the lamb on these ; peel the lemon, cut it into slices, and put these on the meat, to keep it white and make it tender ; cover with 1 or 2 more slices of bacon ; add the stock, onion, and herbs, and set it on a slow fire to simmer very gently until tender. Have ready some green peas, put these on a dish, and place the lamb on the top of them. The appearance of this dish may be much improved by glazing the lamb, and spinach may be substituted for the peas when variety is desired. *Time.*—1½ hour. *Average cost,* 10d. per lb. *Sufficient* for 3 persons. *Seasonable.*—Grass lamb, from Easter to Michaelmas.

LAMB, Stewed Breast of.

Ingredients.—1 breast of lamb, pepper and salt to taste, sufficient stock to cover it, 1 glass of sherry, thickening of butter and flour. *Mode.*—Skin the lamb, cut it into pieces, and season them with pepper and salt ; lay these in a stewpan, pour in sufficient stock or gravy to cover them, and stew very gently until tender, which will be in about 1½ hour. Just before serving, thicken the sauce with a little butter and flour ; add the sherry, give one boil, and pour it over the meat. Green peas, or stewed mushrooms, may be strewed over the meat, and will be found a very great improvement. *Time.*—1½ hour. *Average cost,* 10d. per lb. *Sufficient* for 3 persons. *Seasonable.*—Grass lamb, from Easter to Michaelmas.

LAMB, TO CARVE.—Leg, loin, saddle, shoulder, are carved as mutton.

LAMB, Fore-quarter of, to Carve.

We always think that a good and practised carver delights in the manipulation of this joint, for there is a little field for his judgment and dexterity which does not always occur. The separation of the shoulder from the breast is the first point to be attended to ; this is done by passing the knife round the dotted line, as shown by the figures 1, 2, 3, 4, and 5, so as to cut through the skin, and then, by raising with a little force the shoulder, into which the fork should be firmly

Lamb Cutlets

fixed, it will come away with just a little more exercise of the knife. In dividing the shoulder and breast, the carver should take care not to cut away too much of the meat from the latter, as

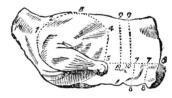

FORE-QUARTER OF LAMB.

that would rather spoil its appearance when the shoulder is removed. The breast and shoulder being separated, it is usual to lay a small piece of butter, and sprinkle a little cayenne, lemon-juice, and salt between them ; and when this is melted and incorporated with the meat and gravy, the shoulder may, as more convenient, be removed into another dish. The next operation is to separate the ribs from the brisket, by cutting through the meat on the line 5 to 6. The joint is then ready to be served to the guests ; the ribs being carved in the direction of the lines from 9 to 10, and the brisket from 7 to 8. The carver should ask those at the table what parts they prefer—ribs, brisket, or a piece of the shoulder.

LAMB CUTLETS.

Ingredients.—Loin of lamb, pepper and salt to taste. *Mode.*—Trim off the flap from a fine loin of lamb, and cut it into cutlets about ¾ inch in thickness. Have ready a bright clear fire ; lay the cutlets on a gridiron, and broil them of a nice pale brown, turning them when required. Season them with pepper and salt ; serve very hot and quickly, and garnish with crisped parsley, or place them on mashed potatoes. Asparagus, spinach, or peas are the favourite accompaniments to lamb chops. *Time.* — About 8 or 10 minutes. *Average cost*, 1s. per lb. *Sufficient.*—Allow 2 cutlets to each person. *Seasonable* from Easter to Michaelmas.

LAMB, Cutlets and Spinach (an Entrée).

Ingredients.—8 cutlets, egg and bread crumbs, salt and pepper to taste, a little clarified butter. *Mode.*—Cut the cutlets

Lamb, Roast Fore-quarter of

from a neck of lamb, and shape them by cutting off the thick part of the chine-bone. Trim off most of the fat and all the skin, and scrape the top part of the bones quite clean. Brush the cutlets over with egg, sprinkle them with bread crumbs, and season with pepper and salt. Now dip them into clarified butter, sprinkle over a few more bread crumbs, and fry them over a sharp fire, turning them when required. Lay them before the fire to drain, and arrange them on a dish with spinach in the centre, which should be previously well boiled, drained, chopped, and seasoned. *Time.*—About 7 or 8 minutes. *Average cost*, 10d. per lb. *Sufficient* for 4 persons. *Seasonable* from Easter to Michaelmas.

Note. — Peas, asparagus, or French beans, may be substituted for the spinach ; or lamb cutlets may be served with stewed cucumbers, Soubise sauce, &c., &c.

LAMB, Roast Fore-quarter of.

Ingredients. — Lamb, a little salt. *Mode.*—To obtain the flavour of lamb in perfection, it should not be long kept ; time to cool is all that it requires ; and though the meat may be somewhat thready, the juices and flavour will be infinitely superior to that of lamb that has been killed 2 or 3 days. Make up

FORE-QUARTER OF LAMB.

the fire in good time, that it may be clear and brisk when the joint is put down. Place it at a sufficient distance to prevent the fat from burning, and baste it constantly till the moment of serving. Lamb should be very *thoroughly* done without being dried up, and not the slightest appearance of red gravy should be visible, as in roast mutton : this rule is applicable to all young white meats. Serve with a little gravy made in the dripping-pan, the same as for other roasts, and send to table with it a tureen of mint sauce, and a fresh salad. A cut lemon, a small piece of fresh butter, and a little cayenne, should also be placed on the table so that when the carver separates the shoulder from the ribs, they may be ready for his use ; if, however, he should not be very expert, we would recommend that the cook should divide these joints nicely before coming to table. *Time.*—Fore-quarter of lamb weighing 10 lbs., 1¾ to 2 hours. *Average cost*, 10*d.* to 1*s.* per lb. *Sufficient* for 7 or 8 persons. *Seasonable.*—Grass lamb, from Easter to Michaelmas.

LAMB'S FRY

Ingredients.—1 lb. of lamb's fry, 3 pints of water, egg and bread crumbs, 1 teaspoonful of chopped parsley, salt and pepper to taste. *Mode.*—Boil the fry for ¼ hour in the above proportion of water, take it out and dry it in a cloth ; grate some bread down finely, mix with it a teaspoonful of chopped parsley and a high seasoning of pepper and salt. Brush the fry lightly over with the yolk of an egg, sprinkle over the bread crumbs, and fry for 5 minutes. Serve very hot on a napkin in a dish, and garnish with plenty of crisped parsley. *Time.*—¼ hour to simmer the fry, 5 minutes to fry it. *Average cost*, 10*d.* per lb. *Sufficient* for 2 or 3 persons. *Seasonable* from Easter to Michaelmas.

LAMB, Hashed, and Broiled Blade-Bone.

[COLD MEAT COOKERY.] *Ingredients.*—The remains of a cold shoulder of lamb, pepper and salt to taste, 2 oz. of butter, about ½ pint of stock or gravy, 1 tablespoonful of shalot vinegar, 3 or 4 pickled gherkins. *Mode.*—Take the blade-bone from the shoulder, and cut the meat into collops as neatly as possible. Season the bone with pepper and salt, pour a little oiled butter over it, and place it in the oven to warm through. Put the stock into a stewpan, add the ketchup and shalot vinegar, and lay in the pieces of lamb. Let these heat gradually through, but do not allow them to boil. Take the blade-bone out of the oven, and place it on a gridiron over a sharp fire to brown. Slice the gherkins, put them into the hash, and dish it with the blade-bone in the centre. It may be garnished with croûtons or sippets of toasted bread. *Time.*—Altogether ½ hour. *Average cost*, exclusive of the meat, 4*d.* *Seasonable.*—House lamb, from Christmas to March ; grass lamb, from Easter to Michaelmas.

LAMB, Boiled Leg of, à la Béchamel.

Ingredients.—Leg of lamb, Béchamel sauce. *Mode.*—Do not choose a very large joint, but one weighing about 5 lbs. Have ready a saucepan of boiling water, into which plunge the lamb, and when it boils up again, draw it to the side of the fire, and let the water cool a little. Then stew very gently for about 1¼ hour, reckoning from the time that the water begins to simmer. Make some Béchamel, dish the lamb, pour the sauce over it, and garnish with tufts of boiled cauliflower or carrots. When liked, melted butter may be substituted for the Béchamel : this is a more simple method, but not nearly so nice. Send to table with it some of the sauce in a tureen, and boiled cauliflowers or spinach, with whichever vegetable the dish is garnished. *Time.*—1¼ hour after the water simmers. *Average cost*, 10*d.* to 1*s.* per lb. *Sufficient* for 4 or 5 persons. *Seasonable* from Easter to Michaelmas.

LAMB, Roast Leg of.

Ingredients.—Lamb, a little salt. *Mode.*—Place the joint at a good distance from the fire at first, and baste well the whole time it is cooking. When nearly done, draw it nearer the fire to acquire a nice brown colour. Sprinkle a little fine salt

LEG OF LAMB.

over the meat, empty the dripping-pan of its contents ; pour in a little boiling water, and strain this over the meat. Serve with mint sauce and a fresh salad, and for vegetables send peas, spinach, or cauliflowers to table with it. *Time.*—A leg of lamb weighing 5 lbs., 1½ hour. *Average cost*, 10*d.* to 1*s.* a pound. *Sufficient* for 4 or 5 persons. *Seasonable* from Easter to Michaelmas.

LAMB, Braised Loin of.

Ingredients.—1 loin of lamb, a few slices of bacon, 1 bunch of green onions, 5 or 6 young carrots, a bunch of savoury herbs, 2 blades of pounded mace, 1 pint of stock, salt to taste. *Mode.*—Bone s

Lamb, Roast Saddle of	Landrail, Roast

loin of lamb, and line the bottom of a stewpan just capable of holding it, with a few thin slices of fat bacon ; add the remaining ingrédients, cover the meat with a few more slices of bacon,

LOIN OF LAMB.

pour in the stock, and simmer very *gently* for 2 hours ; take it up, dry it, strain and reduce the gravy to a glaze, with which glaze the meat, and serve it either on stewed peas, spinach, or stewed cucumbers. *Time.*—2 hours. *Average cost,* 11*d.* per lb. *Sufficient* for 4 or 5 persons. *Seasonable* from Easter to Michaelmas.

LAMB, Roast Saddle of.

Ingredients. — Lamb ; a little salt. *Mode.*—This joint is now very much in vogue, and is generally considered a nice

SADDLE OF LAMB.

one for a small party. Have ready a clear brisk fire ; put down the joint at a little distance, to prevent the fat from scorching, and keep it well basted all

RIBS OF LAMB.

the time it is cooking. Serve with mint sauce and a fresh salad, and send to table with it either peas, cauliflowers, or spinach. *Time.*—A small saddle, 1½ hour ; a large one, 2 hours. *Average cost,* 10*d.* to 1*s.* per lb. *Sufficient* for 5 or 6 persons. *Seasonable* from Easter to Michaelmas.

Note.—Loin and ribs of lamb are roasted in the same manner, and served with the same sauces as the above. A loin will take about 1¼ hour ; ribs, from 1 to 1½ hour.

LAMB, Roast Shoulder of.

Ingredients. — Lamb ; a little salt. *Mode.*—Have ready a clear brisk fire, and put down the joint at a sufficient distance from it, that the fat may not burn. Keep constantly basting until done, and serve with a little gravy made in the dripping-pan, and send mint sauce to table with it. Peas, spinach, or cauliflowers are the usual vegetables served with lamb, and also a fresh salad. *Time.*—A shoulder of lamb rather more than 1 hour. *Average cost,* 10*d.* to 1*s.* per lb. *Sufficient* for 4 or 5 persons. *Seasonable* from Easter to Michaelmas.

LAMB, Shoulder of, Stuffed.

Ingredients.—Shoulder of lamb, forcemeat, trimmings of veal or beef, 2 onions, ½ head of celery, 1 faggot of savoury herbs, a few slices of fat bacon, 1 quart of stock. *Mode.*—Take the blade-bone out of a shoulder of lamb, fill up its place with forcemeat, and sew it up with coarse thread. Put it into a stewpan with a few slices of bacon under and over the lamb, and add the remaining ingredients. Stew very gently for rather more than 2 hours. Reduce the gravy, with which glaze the meat, and serve with peas, stewed cucumbers, or sorrel sauce. *Time.*—Rather more than 2 hours. *Average cost,* 10*d.* to 1*s.* per lb. *Sufficient* for 4 or 5 persons. *Seasonable* from Easter to Michaelmas.

LANDRAIL, Roast, or Corn-Crake.

Ingredients.—3 or 4 birds, butter, fried bread crumbs. *Mode.*—Pluck and draw the birds, wipe them inside and out with damp cloths, and truss them in the following manner : Bring the head round

LANDRAILS.

under the wing, and the thighs close to the sides ; pass a skewer through them and the body, and keep the legs straight. Roast them before a clear fire, keep them well basted, and serve on fried bread crumbs, with a tureen of brown gravy. When liked, bread-sauce may also be sent to table with them. *Time.*— 12 to 20 minutes. *Average cost.*—Seldom

Landrail, to Carve

bought. *Sufficient.*—Allow 4 for a dish. *Seasonable* from August 12th to the middle of September.

LANDRAIL, to Carve.

Landrail, being trussed like Snipe, with the exception of its being drawn, may be carved in the same manner.

LARD, to Melt.

Melt the inner fat of the pig, by putting it in a stone jar, and placing this in a saucepan of boiling water, previously stripping off the skin. Let it simmer gently over a bright fire, and, as it melts, pour it carefully from the sediment. Put it into small jars or bladders for use, and keep it in a cool place. The flead or inside fat of the pig, before it is melted, makes exceedingly light crust, and is particularly wholesome. It may be preserved a length of time by salting it well, and occasionally changing the brine. When wanted for use, wash and wipe it, and it will answer for making into paste as well as fresh lard. *Average cost*, 10d. per lb.

LARDING.

Ingredients.—Bacon and larding-needle. *Mode.*—Bacon for larding should be firm and fat, and ought to be cured without any saltpetre, as this reddens white meats. Lay it on a table, the

BACON FOR LARDING, AND LARDING-NEEDLE.

rinds downwards; trim off any rusty part, and cut it into slices of an equal thickness. Place the slices one on the top of another, and cut them evenly into narrow strips, so arranging it that every piece of bacon is of the same size. Bacon for fricandeaux, poultry, and game, should be about 2 inches in length, and rather more than one-eighth of an inch in width. If for larding fillets of beef or loin of veal, the pieces of bacon must be thicker. The following recipe of Soyer is, we think, very explicit; and any cook, by following the directions here given, may be able to lard, if not well, sufficiently for general use :—

Larks, Roast

" Have the fricandeau trimmed; lay it, lengthwise, upon a clean napkin across your hand, forming a kind of bridge with your thumb at the part where you are about to commence ; then with the point of the larding-needle make three distinct lines across, ½ inch apart; run the needle into the third line, at the farther side of the fricandeau, and bring it out at the first, placing one of the lardoons in it ; draw the needle through, leaving out ¼ inch of the bacon at each line ; proceed thus to the end of the row; then make another line, ½ inch distant, stick in another row of lardoons, bringing them out at the second line, leaving the ends of the bacon out all the same length; make the next row again at the same distance, bringing the ends out between the lardoons of the first row, proceeding in this manner until the whole surface is larded in chequered rows. Everything else is larded in a similar way ; and, in the case of poultry, hold the breast over a charcoal fire for one minute, or dip it into boiling water, in order to make the flesh firm."

LARK PIE (an Entrée).

Ingredients.—A few thin slices of beef, the same of bacon, 9 larks, flour ; for stuffing, 1 teacupful of bread crumbs, ½ teaspoonful of minced lemon-peel, 1 teaspoonful of minced parsley, 1 egg, salt and pepper to taste, 1 teaspoonful of chopped shalot, ½ pint of weak stock or water, puff-paste. *Mode.*—Make a stuffing of bread crumbs, minced lemon-peel, parsley, and the yolk of an egg, all of which should be well mixed together ; roll the larks in flour, and stuff them. Line the bottom of a pie-dish with a few slices of beef and bacon ; over these place the larks, and season with salt, pepper, minced parsley, and chopped shalot, in the above proportion. Pour in the stock or water, cover with crust, and bake for an hour in a moderate oven. During the time the pie is baking, shake it 2 or 3 times, to assist in thickening the gravy, and serve very hot. *Time.*—1 hour. *Average cost*, 1s. 6d. per dozen. *Sufficient* for 5 or 6 persons. *Seasonable.*—In full season in November.

LARKS, Roast.

Ingredients. — Larks, egg and bread crumbs, fresh butter. *Mode.* — These

Leek Soup

birds are by many persons esteemed a great delicacy, and may be either roasted or broiled. Pick, gut, and clean them; when they are trussed, brush them over with the yolk of an egg; sprinkle with bread crumbs, and roast them before a quick fire; baste them continually with fresh butter, and keep sprinkling with the bread crumbs until the birds are well covered. Dish them on bread crumbs fried in clarified butter, and garnish the dish with slices of lemon. Broiled larks are also very excellent: they should be cooked over a clear fire, and would take about 10 minutes or ¼ hour. *Time.*—¼ hour to roast; 10 minutes to broil. *Seasonable.*—In full season in November.

Note. — Larks may also be plainly roasted, without covering them with egg and bread crumbs; they should be dished on fried crumbs.

LEEK SOUP.

Ingredients.—A sheep's head, 3 quarts of water, 12 leeks cut small, pepper and salt to taste, oatmeal to thicken. *Mode.* Prepare the head, either by skinning or cleaning the skin very nicely; split it in two; take out the brains, and put it into boiling water; add the leeks and seasoning, and simmer very gently for 4 hours. Mix smoothly, with cold water, as much oatmeal as will make the soup tolerably thick; pour it into the soup; continue stirring till the whole is blended and well done, and serve. *Time.*—4½ hours. *Average cost,* 4d. per quart. *Seasonable* in winter. Sufficient for 10 persons.

LEMON BISCUITS.

Ingredients.—1¼ lb. of flour, ¾ lb. of loaf sugar, 6 oz. of fresh butter, 4 eggs, 1 oz. of lemon-peel, 2 dessert-spoonfuls of lemon-juice. *Mode.*—Rub the flour into the butter; stir in the pounded sugar and very finely-minced lemon-peel, and when these ingredients are thoroughly mixed, add the eggs, which should be previously well whisked, and the lemon-juice. Beat the mixture well for a minute or two, then drop it from a spoon on to a buttered tin, about 2 inches apart, as the cakes will spread when they get warm; place the tin in the oven, and bake the cakes of a pale brown from 15 to 20 minutes. *Time.*—15 to 20 minutes. *Average cost,* 1s. 6d. *Seasonable* at any time.

Lemon Cake

LEMON BLANCMANGE.

Ingredients.—1 quart of milk, the yolks of 4 eggs, 3 oz. of ground rice, 6 oz. of pounded sugar, 1½ oz. of fresh butter, the rind of 1 lemon, the juice of 2, ½ oz. of gelatine. *Mode.*—Make a custard with the yolks of the eggs and ½ pint of the milk, and when done, put it into a basin; put half the remainder of the milk into a saucepan with the ground rice, fresh butter, lemon-rind, and 3 oz. of the sugar,

BLANCMANGE MOULD.

and let these ingredients boil until the mixture is stiff, stirring them continually; when done, pour it into the bowl where the custard is, mixing both well together. Put the gelatine with the rest of the milk into a saucepan, and let it stand by the side of the fire to dissolve; boil for a minute or two, stir carefully into the basin, adding 3 oz. more of pounded sugar. When cold, stir in the lemon-juice, which should be carefully strained, and pour the mixture into a well-oiled mould, leaving out the lemon-peel, and set the mould in a pan of cold water until wanted for table. Use eggs that have rich-looking yolks; and, should the weather be very warm, rather a larger proportion of gelatine must be allowed. *Time.*—Altogether, ½ hour. *Average cost,* 1s. 6d. *Sufficient* to fill 2 small moulds. *Seasonable* at any time.

LEMON CAKE.

Ingredients.—10 eggs, 3 tablespoonfuls of orange-flower water, ¾ lb. of pounded loaf sugar, 1 lemon, ¾ lb. of flour. *Mode.* —Separate the whites from the yolks of the eggs; whisk the former to a stiff froth; add the orange-flower water, the sugar, grated lemon-rind, and mix these ingredients well together. Then beat the yolks of the eggs, and add them, with the lemon-juice, to the whites, &c.; dredge in the flour gradually; keep beating the mixture well; put it into a buttered

CAKE-MOULD.

Lemon Cheesecakes	Lemon Creams

mould, and bake the cake about an hour, or rather longer. The addition of a little butter, beaten to a cream, we think, would improve this cake. *Time.* —About 1 hour. *Average cost,* 1s. 4d. *Seasonable* at any time.

LEMON CHEESECAKES.

Ingredients. —¼ lb. of butter, 1 lb. of loaf sugar, 6 eggs, the rind of 2 lemons and the juice of 3. *Mode.* —Put all the ingredients into a stewpan, carefully grating the lemo—-rind and straining the juice. Keep ~ ing the mixture over the fire until i.... sugar is dissolved, and it begins to thicken: when of the consistency of honey, it is done; then put it into small jars, and keep in a dry place. This mixture will remain good 3 or 4 months. When made into cheesecakes, add a few pounded almonds, or candied peel, or grated sweet biscuit; line some patty-pans with good puff-paste, rather more than half fill them with the mixture, and bake for about ¼ hour in a good brisk oven. *Time.* —¼ hour. *Average cost,* 1s. 4d. *Sufficient* for 24 cheesecakes. *Seasonable* at any time.

LEMON CREAM.

Ingredients. —1 pint of cream, the yolks of two eggs, ¼ lb. of white sugar, 1 large lemon, 1 oz. of isinglass. *Mode.* —Put the cream into a *lined* saucepan with the sugar, lemon-peel, and isinglass, and sim-

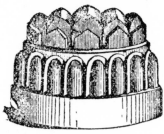

LEMON-CREAM MOULD.

mer these over a gentle fire for about 10 minutes, stirring them all the time. Strain the cream into a jug, add the yolks of eggs, which should be well beaten, and put the jug into a saucepan of boiling water; stir the mixture one way until it thickens, *but do not allow it to boil;* take it off the fire, and keep stirring it until nearly cold. Strain the lemon-juice into a basin, gradually pour

on it the cream, and *stir it well* until the juice is well mixed with it. Have ready a well-oiled mould, pour the cream into it, and let it remain until perfectly set. When required for table, loosen the edges with a small blunt knife, put a dish on the top of the mould, turn it over quickly, and the cream should easily slip away. *Time.* —10 minutes to boil the cream; about 10 minutes to stir it over the fire in the jug. *Average cost,* with cream at 1s. per pint, and the best isinglass, 3s. 6d. *Sufficient* to fill 1½-pint mould. *Seasonable* at any time.

LEMON CREAM, Economical.

Ingredients. —1 quart of milk, 8 bitter almonds, 2 oz. of gelatine, 2 large lemons, ¾ lb. of lump sugar, the yolks of 6 eggs. *Mode.* —Put the milk into a lined saucepan with the almonds, which should be well pounded in a mortar, the gelatine, lemon-rind, and lump sugar, and boil these ingredients for about 5 minutes. Beat up the yolks of the eggs, strain the milk into a jug, add the eggs, and pour the mixture backwards and forwards a few times, until nearly cold; then stir briskly to it the lemon-juice, which should be strained, and keep stirring until the cream is almost cold; put it into an oiled mould, and let it remain until perfectly set. The lemon-juice must not be added to the cream when it is warm, and should be well stirred after it is put in. *Time.* —5 minutes to boil the milk. *Average cost,* 2s. 5d. *Sufficient* to fill two 1½ pint moulds. *Seasonable* at any time.

LEMON CREAMS, Very Good.

Ingredients. —1 pint of cream, 2 dozen sweet almonds, 3 glasses of sherry, the rind and juice of 2 lemons, sugar to taste. *Mode.* —Blanch and chop the almonds, and put them into a jug with the cream: in another jug put the sherry, lemon-rind, strained juice, and sufficient pounded sugar to sweeten the whole nicely. Pour rapidly from one jug to the other till the mixture is well frothed; then pour it into jelly-glasses, omitting the lemon-rind. This is a very cool and delicious sweet for summer, and may be made less rich by omitting the almonds and substituting orange or raisin wine for the sherry. *Time.* —Altogether, ½ hour. *Average cost,* with cream at 1s. per pint, 3s. *Sufficient*

Lemon Creams, or Custards	Lemon-peel

to fill 12 glasses. *Seasonable* at any time.

LEMON CREAMS, or Custards.

Ingredients.—5 oz. of loaf sugar, 2 pints of boiling water, the rind of 1 lemon and the juice of 3, the yolks of 8 eggs. *Mode.* Make a quart of lemonade in the following manner:—Dissolve the sugar in the boiling water, having previously, with part of the sugar, rubbed off the lemon-rind, and add the strained juice. Strain the lemonade into a saucepan, and add the yolks of the eggs, which should be well beaten ; stir this *one way* over the fire until the mixture thickens, but do not allow it to boil, and serve in custard glasses, or on a glass dish. After the boiling water is poured on the sugar and lemon, it should stand covered for about ½ hour before the eggs are added to it, that the flavour of the rind may be extracted. *Time.*—½ hour to make the lemonade; about 10 minutes to stir the custard over the fire. *Average cost,* 1s. *Sufficient* to fill 12 to 14 custard glasses. *Seasonable* at any time.

LEMON DUMPLINGS.

Ingredients.—½ lb. of grated bread, ¼ lb. of chopped suet, ¼ lb. of moist sugar, 2 eggs, 1 large lemon. *Mode.*—Mix the bread, suet, and moist sugar well together, adding the lemon-peel, which should be very finely minced. Moisten with the eggs and strained lemon - juice ;

LEMON DUMPLINGS.

stir well, and put the mixture into small buttered cups. Tie them down and boil for ¾ hour. Turn them out on a dish, strew sifted sugar over them, and serve with wine sauce. *Time.* —¾ hour. *Average cost,* 7d. *Sufficient* for 6 dumplings. *Seasonable* at any time.

LEMON JELLY.

Ingredients.—6 lemons, ¾ lb. of lump sugar, 1 pint of water, 1½ oz. of isinglass, ¼ pint of sherry. *Mode.*—Peel ? of the lemons, pour ½ pint ?? boiling water on the rind, and let it infuse for ½ hour; put the sugar, isinglass, and

½ pint of water into a lined saucepan, and boil these ingredients for 20 minutes ; then put ?? the strained lemon-juice, the strained infusion of the rind, and bring the whole to the point of boiling ; skim well, add the wine, and run the jelly through a bag ; pour it into a mould that has been wetted or soaked in water ; put it in ice, if convenient, where let it remain until required for table. Previously to adding the lemon-juice to the other ingredients, ascertain that it is very nicely strained, as, if this is not properly attended to, it is liable to make the jelly thick and muddy. As this jelly is very pale, and almost colourless, it answers very well for moulding with a jelly of any bright hue ; for instance, half a jelly bright red, and the other half made of the above, would have a very good effect. Lemon jelly may also be made with calf's-feet stock, allowing the juice of 3 lemons to every pint of stock. *Time.*—Altogether, 1 hour. *Average cost,* with the best isinglass, 3s. 6d. *Sufficient* to fill 1½ pint mould. *Seasonable* at any time.

LEMON MINCEMEAT.

Ingredients.—2 large lemons, 6 large apples, ½ lb. of suet, 1 lb. of currants, ½ lb. of sugar, 2 oz. of candied lemon peel, 1 oz. of citron, mixed spice to taste. *Mode.*—Pare the lemons, squeeze them, and boil the peel until tender enough to mash. Add to the mashed lemon-peel the apples, which should be pared, cored, and minced; the chopped suet, currants, sugar, sliced peel, and spice. Strain the lemon-juice to these ingredients, stir the mixture well, and put it in a jar with a closely-fitting lid. Stir occasionally, and in a week or 10 days the mincemeat will be ready for use. *Average cost,* 2s. *Sufficient* for 18 large or 24 small pies. *Seasonable.*—Make this about the beginning of December.

LEMON-PEEL.

This contains an essential oil of a very high flavour and fragrance, and is consequently esteemed both a wholesome and agreeable stomachic. It is used, as will be seen by many recipes in this book, as an ingredient for flavouring a number of various dishes. Under the name of candied lemon-peel, it is cleared of the pulp and preserved in sugar, when it becomes an excellent sweetmeat.

LEMON PUDDING, Baked.

Ingredients.—The yolks of 4 eggs, 4 oz. of pounded sugar, 1 lemon, ¼ lb. of butter, puff-crust. *Mode.* — Beat the eggs to a froth; mix with them the sugar and warmed butter; stir these ingredients well together, putting in the grated rind and strained juice of the lemon-peel. Line a shallow dish with puff-paste; put in the mixture, and bake in a moderate oven for 40 minutes; turn the pudding out of the dish, strew over it sifted sugar, and serve. *Time.*—40 minutes. *Average cost,* 10d. *Sufficient* for 5 or 6 persons. *Seasonable* at any time.

LEMON PUDDING, Baked.

Ingredients.—10 oz. of bread crumbs, 2 pints of milk, 2 oz. of butter, 1 lemon, ¼ lb. of pounded sugar, 4 eggs, 1 table-spoonful of brandy. *Mode.*—Bring the milk to the boiling point, stir in the butter, and pour these hot over the bread crumbs; add the sugar and very finely-minced lemon-peel; beat the eggs, and stir these in with the brandy to the other ingredients; put a paste round the dish, and bake for ¾ hour. *Time.*—¾ hour. *Average cost,* 1s. 2d. *Sufficient* for 6 or 7 persons. *Seasonable* at any time.

LEMON PUDDING, Baked (Very Rich).

Ingredients.—The rind and juice of 2 large lemons, ½ lb. of loaf sugar, ¼ pint of cream, the yolks of 8 eggs, 2 oz. of almonds, ½ lb. of butter, melted. *Mode.* —Mix the pounded sugar with the cream and add the yolks of eggs and the butter, which should be previously warmed. Blanch and pound the almonds, and put these, with the grated rind and strained juice of the lemons, to the other ingredients. Stir all well together; line a dish with puff-paste, put in the mixture, and bake for 1 hour. *Time.*—1 hour. *Average cost,* 2s. *Sufficient* for 6 or 7 persons. *Seasonable* at any time.

LEMON PUDDING, Boiled.

Ingredients.—½ lb. of chopped suet, ¾ lb. of bread crumbs, 2 small lemons, 6 oz. of moist sugar, ¼ lb. of flour, 2 eggs, milk. *Mode.*—Mix the suet, bread crumbs, sugar, and flour well together, adding the lemon-peel, which should be

very finely minced, and the juice, which should be strained. When these ingredients are well mixed, moisten with the eggs and sufficient milk to make the pudding of the consistency of thick batter; put it into a well-buttered mould, and boil for 3½ hours; turn it out, strew sifted sugar over, and serve with wine sauce, or not, at pleasure. *Time.*—3½ hours. *Average cost,* 1s. *Sufficient* for 7 or 8 persons. *Seasonable* at any time.

Note.—This pudding may also be baked, and will be found very good. It will take about 2 hours.

LEMON PUDDING, Plain.

Ingredients.—¾ lb. of flour, 6 oz. of lard or dripping, the juice of 1 large lemon, 1 teaspoonful of flour, sugar. *Mode.*— Make the above proportions of flour and lard into a smooth paste, and roll it out to the thickness of about ½ an inch. Squeeze the lemon-juice, strain it into a cup, stir the flour into it, and as much moist sugar as will make it into a stiff and thick paste; spread this mixture over the paste, roll it up, secure the ends, and tie the pudding in a floured cloth. Boil for 2 hours. *Time.*—2 hours. *Average cost,* 7d. *Sufficient* for 5 or 6 persons. *Seasonable* at any time.

LEMON SAUCE, for Boiled Fowl.

Ingredients.—1 small lemon, ¾ pint of melted butter. *Mode.*—Cut the lemon into very thin slices, and these again into very small dice. Have ready ¾ pint of melted butter, put in the lemon; let it just simmer, but not boil, and pour it over the fowls. *Time.*—1 minute to simmer. *Average cost,* 6d. *Sufficient* for a pair of large fowls.

LEMON WHITE SAUCE, for Fowls, Fricassees, &c.

Ingredients.—¾ pint of cream, the rind and juice of 1 lemon, ½ teaspoonful of whole white pepper, 1 sprig of lemon thyme, 3 oz. of butter, 1 dessertspoonful of flour, 1 teacupful of white stock; salt to taste. *Mode.*—Put the cream into a very clean saucepan (a lined one is best), with the lemon-peel, pepper, and thyme, and let these infuse for ½ hour, when simmer gently for a few minutes, or until there is a nice flavour of lemon. Strain it, and add a thickening of butter and

Lemon Sauce, for Sweet Puddings	Lemons, to Pickle

flour in the above proportions; stir this well in, and put in the lemon-juice at the moment of serving; mix the stock with the cream, and add a little salt. This sauce should not boil after the cream and stock are mixed together. *Time.*—Altogether, ¾ hour. *Average cost,* 1s. 6d. *Sufficient,* this quantity, for a pair of large boiled fowls.

Note.—Where the expense of the cream is objected to, milk may be substituted for it. In this case, an additional desertspoonful, or rather more, of flour must be added.

LEMON SAUCE, for Sweet Puddings.

Ingredients.—The rind and juice of 1 lemon, 1 tablespoonful of flour, 1 oz. of butter, 1 large wineglassful of sherry, 1 wineglassful of water, sugar to taste, the yolks of 4 eggs. *Mode.*—Rub the rind of the lemon on to some lumps of sugar; squeeze out the juice, and strain it; put the butter and flour into a saucepan, stir them over the fire, and when of a pale brown, add the wine, water, and strained lemon-juice. Crush the lumps of sugar that were rubbed on the lemon; stir these into the sauce, which should be very sweet. When these ingredients are well mixed, and the sugar is melted, put in the beaten yolks of 4 eggs; keep stirring the sauce until it thickens, when serve. Do not, on any account, allow it to boil, or it will curdle, and be entirely spoiled. *Time.*—Altogether, 15 minutes. *Average cost,* 1s. 2d. *Sufficient* for 7 or 8 persons.

LEMON SPONGE.

Ingredients.—2 oz. of isinglass, 1¾ pint of water, ¾ lb. of pounded sugar, the juice of 5 lemons, the rind of 1, the whites of 3 eggs. *Mode.*—Dissolve the isinglass in the water, strain it into a saucepan, and add the sugar, lemon-rind, and juice. Boil the whole from 10 to 15 minutes; strain it again, and let it stand till it is cold and begins to stiffen. Beat the whites of the eggs, put them to it, and whisk the mixture till it is quite white; put it into a mould which has been previously wetted, and let it remain until perfectly set; then turn it out, and garnish it according to taste. *Time.*—10 to 15 minutes. *Average cost,* with the best isinglass, 4s. *Sufficient* to fill a quart mould. *Seasonabe* at any time.

LEMON SYRUP.

Ingredients.—2 lbs. of loaf sugar, 2 pints of water, 1 oz. of citric acid, ½ drachm of essence of lemon. *Mode.*—Boil the sugar and water together for ¼ hour, and put it into a basin, where let it remain till cold. Beat the citric acid to a powder, mix the essence of lemon with it, then add these two ingredients to the syrup; mix well, and bottle for use. Two tablespoonfuls of the syrup are sufficient for a tumbler of cold water, and will be found a very refreshing summer drink. *Sufficient.*—2 tablespoonfuls of syrup to a tumblerful of cold water.

LEMONS, to Pickle, with the Peel on.

Ingredients. — 6 lemons, 2 quarts of boiling water; to each quart of vinegar allow ½ oz. of cloves, ½ oz. of white pepper, 1 oz. of bruised ginger, ¼ oz. of mace and chilies, 1 oz. of mustard-seed, ½ stick of sliced horseradish, a few cloves of garlic. *Mode.*—Put the lemons into a brine that will bear an egg; let them remain in it 6 days, stirring them every day; have ready 2 quarts of boiling water, put in the lemons, and allow them to boil for ¼ hour; take them out, and let them lie in a cloth until perfectly dry and cold. Boil up sufficient vinegar to cover the lemons, with all the above ingredients, allowing the same proportion as stated to each quart of vinegar. Pack the lemons in a jar, pour over the vinegar, &c. boiling hot, and tie down with a bladder. They will be fit for use in about 12 months, or rather sooner. *Seasonable.*—This should be made from November to April.

LEMONS, to Pickle, without the Peel.

Ingredients.—6 lemons, 1 lb. of fine salt; to each quart of vinegar, the same ingredients as in the last recipe. *Mode.*—Peel the lemons, slit each one down 3 times, so as not to divide them, and rub the salt well into the divisions; place them in a pan, where they must remain for a week, turning them every other day; then put them in a Dutch oven before a clear fire until the salt has become perfectly dry; then arrange them in a jar. Pour over sufficient boiling vinegar to cover them, to which have been added the ingredients mentioned in

Lemon Wine

the foregoing recipe ; tie down closely, and in about 9 months they will be fit for use. *Seasonable.*—The best time to make this is from November to April.

Note.—After this pickle has been made from 4 to 5 months, the liquor may be strained and bottled, and will be found an excellent lemon ketchup.

LEMON WINE.

Ingredients.—To 4½ gallons of water allow the pulp of 50 lemons, the rind of 25, 16 lbs. of loaf sugar, ½ oz. of isinglass, 1 bottle of brandy. *Mode.*—Peel and slice the lemons, but use only the rind of 25 of them, and put them into the cold water. Let it stand 8 or 9 days, squeezing the lemons well every day; then strain the water off and put it into a cask with the sugar. Let it work some time, and when it has ceased working, put in the isinglass. Stop the cask down ; in about six months put in the brandy and bottle the wine off. *Seasonable.*—The best time to make this is in January or February, when lemons are best and cheapest.

LEMONADE.

Ingredients.—The rind of two lemons, the juice of 3 large or 4 small ones, ½ lb. of loaf sugar, 1 quart of boiling water. *Mode.*—Rub some of the sugar, in lumps, on 2 of the lemons until they have imbibed all the oil from them, and put it with the remainder of the sugar into a jug ; add the lemon-juice (but no pips), and pour over the whole a quart of boiling water. When the sugar is dissolved, strain the lemonade through a fine sieve or piece of muslin, and, when cool, it will be ready for use. The lemonade will be much improved by having the white of an egg beaten up in it ; a little sherry mixed with it, also, makes this beverage much nicer. *Average cost, 6d. per quart.*

LEMONADE, Nourishing.

Ingredients.—1½ pint of boiling water, the juice of 4 lemons, the rinds of 2, ¼ pint of sherry, 4 eggs, 6 oz. of loaf sugar. *Mode.*—Pare off the lemon-rind thinly, put it into a jug with the sugar, and pour over the boiling water. Let it cool, then strain it ; add the wine, lemon-juice, and eggs, previously well beaten, and also strained, and the beverage will be ready for use. If thought desirable,

Liaison of Eggs

the quantity of sherry and water could be lessened, and milk substituted for them. To obtain the flavour of the lemon-rind properly, a few lumps of the sugar should be rubbed over it, until some of the yellow is absorbed. *Time.* —Altogether 1 hour to make it. *Average cost, 1s. 8d. Sufficient* to make 2½ pints of lemonade. *Seasonable* at any time.

LETTUCES.

These form one of the principal ingredients to summer salads ; they should be blanched, and be eaten young. They are seldom served in any other way, but may be stewed and sent to table in a good brown gravy flavoured with lemon-juice. In preparing them for a salad, carefully wash them free from dirt, pick off all the decayed and outer leaves, and dry them thoroughly by shaking them in a cloth. Cut off the stalks, and either halve or cut the lettuces into small pieces. The manner of cutting them up entirely depends on the salad for which they are intended. In France, the lettuces are sometimes merely wiped with a cloth and not washed, the cooks there declaring that the act of washing them injuriously affects the pleasant crispness of the plant : in this case scrupulous attention must be paid to each leaf, and the grit thoroughly wiped away. *Average cost,* when cheapest, 1d. each. *Sufficient.*— Allow 2 lettuces for 4 or 5 persons. *Seasonable* from March to the end of August, but may be had all the year.

LEVERET, to Dress a.

Ingredients.—2 leverets, butter, flour. *Mode.*—Leverets should be trussed in the same manner as a hare, but they do not require stuffing. Roast them before a clear fire, and keep them well basted all the time they are· cooking. A few minutes before serving, dredge them lightly with flour, and froth them nicely. Serve with plain gravy in the dish, and send to table red-currant jelly with them. *Time.*—½ to ¾ hour. *Average cost,* in full season, 4s. each. *Sufficient* for 5 or 6 persons. *Seasonable* from May to August, but cheapest in July and August.

LIAISON OF EGGS, for Thickening Sauces.

Ingredients.—The yolks of 3 eggs, 8 tablespoonfuls of milk or cream.

Liqueur Jelly

Mode.—Beat up the yolks of the eggs, to which add the milk, and strain the whole through a hair-sieve. When the liaison is being added to the sauce it is intended to thicken, care must be exercised to keep stirring it during the whole time, or, otherwise, the eggs will curdle. It should only just simmer, but not boil.

LIQUEUR JELLY.

Ingredients.—1 lb. of lump sugar, 2 oz. of isinglass, 1½ pint of water, the juice of 2 lemons, ¼ pint of liqueur. *Mode.*— Put the sugar, with 1 pint of the water, into a stewpan, and boil them gently by the side of the fire until there is no scum remaining, which must be carefully removed as fast as it rises. Boil the isinglass with the other ½ pint of water, and

OVAL JELLY MOULD.

skim it carefully in the same manner. Strain the lemon-juice, and add it, with the clarified isinglass, to the syrup ; put in the liqueur, and bring the whole to the boiling-point. Let the saucepan remain covered by the side of the fire for a few minutes ; then pour the jelly through a bag, put it into a mould, and set the mould in ice until required for table. Dip the mould in hot water, wipe the outside, loosen the jelly by passing a knife round the edges, and turn it out carefully on a dish. Noyeau, Maraschino, Curaçoa, brandy, or any kind of liqueur, answers for this jelly ; and, when made with isinglass, liqueur jellies are usually prepared as directed above. *Time.*— 10 minutes to boil the sugar and water. *Average cost,* with the best isinglass, 3s. 6d. *Sufficient* to fill a quart mould. *Seasonable* at any time.

LIVER AND LEMON SAUCE, for Poultry.

Ingredients.—The liver of a fowl, one lemon, salt to taste, ½ pint of melted

Lobsters, to boil

butter. *Mode.*—Wash the liver, and let it boil for a few minutes ; peel the lemon very thin, remove the white part and pips, and cut it into very small dice ; mince the liver and a small quantity of the lemon-rind very fine ; add these ingredients to ½ pint of smoothly-made melted butter ; season with a little salt, put in the cut lemon, heat it gradually, but do not allow it to boil, lest the butter should oil. *Time.*—1 minute to simmer. *Sufficient* to serve with a pair of small fowls.

LIVER AND PARSLEY SAUCE, for Poultry.

Ingredients.—The liver of a fowl, one tablespoonful of minced parsley, ½ pint of melted butter. *Mode.*—Wash and score the liver, boil it for a few minutes, and mince it very fine ; blanch or scald a small bunch of parsley, of which there should be sufficient when chopped to fill a tablespoon ; add this with the minced liver, to ½ pint of smoothly-made melted butter ; let it just boil ; when serve. *Time.*—1 minute to simmer. *Sufficient* for a pair of small fowls.

LOBSTERS, to Boil.

Ingredients.—¼ lb. of salt to each gallon of water. *Mode.*—Buy the lobsters alive, and choose those that are heavy and full of motion, which is an indication of their freshness. When the shell is incrusted, it is a sign they are old : medium-sized lobsters are the best. Have ready a stewpan of boiling water, salted in the above proportion ; put in the lobster, and keep it boiling quickly from 20 minutes to ¾ hour, according to its size, and do not forget to skim well. If it boils too long, the meat becomes thready, and if not done enough, the spawn is not red : this must be obviated by great attention. Rub the shell over with a little butter or sweet oil, which wipe off again. *Time.*— Small lobster, 20 minutes to ½ hour ; large ditto, ½ to ¾ hour. *Average cost,* medium size, 1s. 6d. to 2s. 6d. *Seasonable* all the year, but best from March to October.

To Choose Lobsters. — This shellfish, if it has been cooked alive, as it ought to have been, will have a stiffness in the tail, which, if gently raised, will return with a spring. Care, however, must be taken in thus proving it ; for if the tail is pulled straight out, it will not

Lobster Curry

return ; when the fish might be pronounced inferior, which, in reality, may not be the case. In order to be good, lobsters should be weighty for their bulk ; if light, they will be watery ; and those of the medium size, are always the best. Small-sized lobsters are cheapest, and answer very well for sauce. In boiling lobsters, the appearance of the shell will be much improved by rubbing over it a little butter or salad-oil on being immediately taken from the pot.

LOBSTER CURRY (an Entrée).

Ingredients.—1 lobster, 2 onions, 1 oz. butter, 1 tablespoonful of curry-powder, ½ pint of medium stock, the juice of ½ lemon. *Mode.*—Pick the meat from the shell, and cut into nice square pieces; fry the onions of a pale brown in the butter, stir in the curry-powder and stock, and simmer till it thickens, when put in the lobster : stew the whole slowly for ¾ hour, stirring occasionally ; and just before sending to table, put in the lemon-juice. Serve boiled rice with it, the same as for other curries. *Time.*—Altogether, ¾ hour. *Average cost, 3s.* *Seasonable* at any time.

LOBSTER CUTLETS (an Entrée).

Ingredients.—1 large hen lobster, 1 oz. fresh butter, ½ saltspoonful of salt, pounded mace, grated nutmeg, cayenne and white pepper to taste, egg, and bread crumbs. *Mode.*—Pick the meat from the shell, and pound it in a mortar with the butter, and gradually add the mace and seasoning, well mixing the ingredients ; beat all to a smooth paste, and add a little of the spawn ; divide the mixture into pieces of an equal size, and shape them like cutlets. They should not be very thick. Brush them over with egg, and sprinkle with bread crumbs, and stick a short piece of the small claw in the top of each ; fry them of a nice brown in boiling lard, and drain them before the fire, on a sieve reversed; arrange them nicely on a dish, and pour béchamel in the middle, but not over the cutlets. *Time.*—About 8 minutes after the cutlets are made. *Average cost* for this dish, 2s. 9d. *Seasonable* all the year. *Sufficient* for 5 or 6 persons.

LOBSTERS, to Dress.

When the lobster is boiled, rub it over with a little salad-oil, which wipe off

Lobster, Potted

again ; separate the body from the tail, break off the great claws, and crack them at the joints, without injuring the meat, split the tail in halves, and arrange all neatly in a dish, with the body uprigh' in the middle, and garnish with parsley

LOBSTER, Hot.

Ingredients.—1 lobster, 2 oz. of butter, grated nutmeg ; salt, pepper, and pounded mace, to taste ; bread crumbs, 2 eggs. *Mode.*—Pound the meat of the lobster to a smooth paste with the butter and seasoning, and add a few bread crumbs. Beat the eggs, and make the whole mixture into the form of a lobster ; pound the spawn, and sprinkle over it. Bake ¼ hour, and just before serving, lay over it the tail and body shell, with the small claws underneath, to resemble a lobster. *Time.*—¼ hour. *Average cost, 2s. 6d.* *Seasonable* at any time. *Sufficient* for 4 or 5 persons.

LOBSTER PATTIES (an Entrée).

Ingredients.—Minced lobster, 4 tablespoonfuls of béchamel, 6 drops of anchovy sauce, lemon-juice, cayenne to taste. *Mode.*—Line the patty-pans with puff-paste, and put into each a small piece of bread ; cover with paste, brush over with egg, and bake of a light colour. Take as much lobster as is required, mince the meat very fine, and add the above ingredients ; stir it over the fire for 5 minutes ; remove the lids of the patty-cases, take out the bread, fill with the mixture, and replace the covers. *Seasonable* at any time.

LOBSTER, Potted.

Ingredients.—2 lobsters ; seasoning to taste, of nutmeg, pounded mace, white pepper, and salt ; ¼ lb. of butter, 3 or 4 bay-leaves. *Mode.*—Take out the meat carefully from the shell, but do not cut it up. Put some butter at the bottom of a dish, lay in the lobster as evenly as possible, with the bay-leaves and seasoning between. Cover with butter, and bake for ¾ hour in a gentle oven. When done, drain the whole on a sieve, and lay the pieces in potting-jars, with the seasoning about them. When cold, pou' over it clarified butter, and, if very highly seasoned, it will keep some time. *Time.*—¾ hour. *Average cost* for this quantity, 4s. 4d. *Seasonable* at any time.

| Lobster (à la Mode Francaise) | Lobster Soup |

Note.—Potted lobster may be used cold, or as a *fricassee* with cream sauce.

LOBSTER (à la Mode Francaise).

Ingredients.—1 lobster, 4 tablespoonfuls of white stock, 2 tablespoonfuls of cream, pounded mace, and cayenne to taste ; bread crumbs. *Mode.*—Pick the meat from the shell, and cut it up into small square pieces ; put the stock, cream, and seasoning into a stewpan, add the lobster, and let it simmer gently for 6 minutes. Serve it in the shell, which must be nicely cleaned, and have border of puff-paste ; cover it with bread crumbs, place small pieces of butter over, and brown before the fire, or with a salamander. *Time.*—¼ hour. *Average cost,* 2s. 6d. *Seasonable* at any time.

LOBSTER SALAD.

Ingredients.—1 hen lobster, lettuces, endive, small salad (whatever is in season), a little chopped beetroot, 2 hard-boiled eggs, a few slices of cucumber. For dressing, 4 tablespoonfuls of oil, 2 do. of vinegar, 1 teaspoonful of made mustard, the yolks of 2 eggs ; cayenne and salt to taste ; ¼ teaspoonful of anchovy sauce. These ingredients should be mixed perfectly smooth, and form a creamy-looking sauce. *Mode.* — Wash the salad, and thoroughly dry it by shaking it in a cloth. Cut up the lettuces and endive, pour the dressing on them, and lightly throw in the small salad. Mix all well together with the pickings from the body of the lobster ; pick the meat from the shell, cut it up into nice square pieces, put half in the salad, the other half reserve for garnishing. Separate the yolks from the whites of 2 hard-boiled eggs ; chop the whites very fine, and rub the yolks through a sieve, and afterwards the coral from the inside. Arrange the salad lightly on a glass dish, and garnish, first with a row of sliced cucumber, then with the pieces of lobster, the yolks and whites of the eggs, coral, and beetroot placed alternately, and arranged in small separate bunches, so that the colours contrast nicely. *Average cost,* 3s. 6d. *Sufficient* for 4 or 5 persons. *Seasonable* from April to October ; may be had all the year, but salad is scarce and expensive in winter.

Note.—A few crayfish make a pretty garnishing to lobster salad.

LOBSTER SAUCE, to serve with Turbot, Salmon, Brill, &c. (very Good.)

Ingredients. —1 middling-sized hen lobster, ¾ pint of melted butter, 1 tablespoonful of anchovy sauce, ½ oz. of butter, salt and cayenne to taste, a litt'4 pounded mace when liked, 2 or 3 tablespoonfuls of cream. *Mode.*—Choose a hen lobster, as this is indispensable, in order to render this sauce as good as it ought to be. Pick the meat from the shells, and cut it into small square pieces ; put the spawn, which will be found under the tail of the lobster, into a mortar with ½ oz. of butter, and pound it quite smooth ; rub it through a hair-sieve, and cover up till wanted. Make ¾ pint of melted butter ; put in all the ingredients except the lobster-meat, and well mix the sauce before the lobster is added to it, as it should retain its square form, and not come to table shredded and ragged. Put in the meat, let it get thoroughly hot, but do not allow it to boil, as the colour would immediately be spoiled ; for it must be remembered that this sauce should always have a bright red appearance. If it is intended to be served with turbot or brill, a little of the spawn (dried and rubbed through a sieve without butter) should be saved to garnish with ; but as the goodness, flavour, and appearance of the sauce so much depend on having a proper quantity of spawn, the less used for garnishing the better. *Time.*—1 minute to simmer. *Average cost,* for this quantity, 2s. *Seasonable* at any time. *Sufficient* to serve with a small turbot, a brill, or salmon for 6 persons.

Note.—Melted butter made with milk, will be found to answer very well for lobster sauce, as by employing it a nice white colour will be obtained. Less quantity than the above may be made by using a very small lobster, to which add only ½ pint of melted butter, and season as above. Where economy is desired, the cream may be dispensed with, and the remains of a cold lobster left from table, may, with a little care, be converted into a very good sauce.

LOBSTER SOUP.

Ingredients.—3 large lobsters, or 6 small ones ; the crumb of a French roll, 2 anchovies, 1 onion, 1 small bunch of

Luncheons

sweet herbs, 1 strip of lemon-peel, 2 oz. of butter, a little nutmeg, 1 teaspoonful of flour, 1 pint of cream, 1 pint of milk; forcemeat balls, mace, salt, and pepper to taste, bread crumbs, 1 egg, 2 quarts of water. *Mode.*—Pick the meat from the lobsters, and beat the fins, chine, and small claws in a mortar, previously taking away the brown fin and the bag in the head. Put it in a stewpan, with the crumb of the roll, anchovies, onions, herbs, lemon-peel, and the water; simmer gently till all the goodness is extracted, and strain it off. Pound the spawn in a mortar, with the butter, nutmeg, and flour, and mix with it the cream and milk. Give one boil up, at the same time adding the tails cut in pieces. Make the forcemeat balls with the remainder of the lobster, seasoned with mace, pepper, and salt, adding a little flour, and a few bread crumbs; moisten them with the egg, heat them in the soup, and serve. *Time.*—2 hours, or rather more. *Average cost, 3s. 6d.* per quart. *Seasonable* from April to October. *Sufficient* for 8 persons.

LUNCHEONS.

The remains of cold joints, nicely garnished, a few sweets, or a little hashed meat, poultry or game, are the usual articles placed on the table for luncheon, with bread and cheese, biscuits, butter, &c. If a substantial meal is desired, rump-steaks or mutton chops may be served, as also veal cutlets, kidneys, or any dish of that kind. In families where there is a nursery, the mistress of the house often partakes of the meal with the children, and makes it her luncheon. In the summer, a few dishes of fresh fruit should be added to the luncheon, or, instead of this, a compôte of fruit or fruit tart, or pudding.

MACARONI, as usually served with the CHEESE COURSE.

I.

Ingredients.—½ lb. of pipe macaroni, ¼ lb. of butter, 6 oz. of Parmesan or Cheshire cheese, pepper and salt to taste, 1 pint of milk, 2 pints of water, bread crumbs. *Mode.*—Put the milk and water into a saucepan with sufficient salt to flavour it; place it on the fire, and, when it boils quickly, drop in the macaroni. Keep the water boiling until it is quite

Macaroni

tender; drain the macaroni, and put it into a deep dish. Have ready the grated cheese, either Parmesan or Cheshire; sprinkle it amongst the macaroni and some of the butter cut into small pieces, reserving some of the cheese for the top layer. Season with a little pepper, and cover the top layer of cheese with some very fine bread crumbs. Warm, without oiling, the remainder of the butter, and pour it gently over the bread crumbs. Place the dish before a bright fire to brown the crumbs; turn it once or twice, that it may be equally coloured, and serve very hot. The top of the macaroni may be browned with a salamander, which is even better than placing it before the fire, as the process is more expeditious; but it should never be browned in the oven, as the butter would oil, and so impart a very disagreeable flavour to the dish. In boiling the macaroni, let it be perfectly tender but firm, no part beginning to melt, and the form entirely preserved. It may be boiled in plain water, with a little salt instead of using milk, but should then have a small piece of butter mixed with it. *Time.*—1 to 1½ hour to boil the macaroni, 5 minutes to brown it before the fire. *Average cost, 1s. 6d. Sufficient* for 6 or 7 persons. *Seasonable* at any time.

Note.—Riband macaroni may be dressed in the same manner, but does not require boiling so long a time.

II.

Ingredients.—¼ lb. of pipe or riband macaroni, ½ pint of milk, ½ pint of veal or beef gravy, the yolks of 2 eggs, 4 tablespoonfuls of cream, 3 oz. of grated Parmesan or Cheshire cheese, 1 oz. of butter. *Mode.*—Wash the macaroni, and boil it in the gravy and milk until quite tender, without being broken. Drain it, and put it into rather a deep dish. Beat the yolks of the eggs with the cream and 2 tablespoonfuls of the liquor the macaroni was boiled in; make this sufficiently hot to thicken, but do not allow it to boil; pour it over the macaroni, over which sprinkle the grated cheese and the butter broken into small pieces; brown with a salamander, or before the fire, and serve. *Time.*—1 to 1½ hour to boil the macaroni, 5 minutes to thicken the eggs and cream, 5 minutes to brown. *Average cost, 1s. 2d. Sufficient* for 3 or 4 persons. *Seasonable* at any time.

| Macaroni Pudding, Sweet | Mackerel |

III.

Ingredients.—¼ lb. of pipe macaroni, ½ pint of brown gravy No. 436, 6 oz. of grated Parmesan cheese. *Mode.*—Wash the macaroni, and boil it in salt and water until quite tender; drain it, and put it into rather a deep dish. Have ready a pint of good brown gravy, pour it hot over the macaroni, and send it to table with grated Parmesan served on a separate dish. When the flavour is liked, a little pounded mace may be added to the water in which the macaroni is boiled; but this must always be sparingly added, as it will impart a very strong flavour. *Time.*—1 to 1½ hour to boil the macaroni. *Average cost*, with the gravy and cheese, 1s. 3d. *Sufficient* for 3 or 4 persons. *Seasonable* at any time.

MACARONI, Sweet Pudding.

Ingredients.—2½ oz. of macaroni, 2 pints of milk, the rind of ½ lemon, 3 eggs, sugar and grated nutmeg to taste, 2 tablespoonfuls of brandy. *Mode.*—Put the macaroni, with a pint of the milk, into a saucepan with the lemon-peel, and let it simmer gently until the macaroni is tender: then put it into a pie-dish without the peel; mix the other pint of milk with the eggs; stir these well together, adding the sugar and brandy, and pour the mixture over the macaroni. Grate a little nutmeg over the top, and bake in a moderate oven ½ hour. To make this pudding look nice, a paste should be laid round the edges of the dish, and, for variety, a layer of preserve or marmalade may be placed on the macaroni: in this case, omit the brandy. *Time.*—1 hour to simmer the macaroni; ½ hour to bake the pudding. *Average cost*, 11d. *Sufficient* for 5 or 6 persons. *Seasonable* at any time.

MACARONI SOUP.

Ingredients.—3 oz. of macaroni, a piece of butter the size of a walnut, salt to taste, 2 quarts of clear stock. *Mode.*—Throw the macaroni and butter into boiling water, with a pinch of salt, and simmer for ½ an hour. When it is tender, drain and cut it into thin rings or lengths, and drop it into the boiling stock. Stew gently for 15 minutes, and serve grated Parmesan cheese with it. *Time.*—¾ to 1 hour. *Average cost*, 1s. per quart. *Seasonable* all the year. *Sufficient* for 8 persons.

MACARONI, a Sweet Dish of.

Ingredients.—¼ lb. of macaroni, 1½ pint of milk, the rind of ½ lemon, 3 oz. of lump sugar, ¾ pint of custard. *Mode.*—Put the milk into a saucepan, with the lemon-peel and sugar; bring it to the boiling point, drop in the macaroni, and let it gradually swell over a gentle fire, but do not allow the pipes to break. The form should be entirely preserved; and, though tender, should be firm, and not soft, with no part beginning to melt. Should the milk dry away before the macaroni is sufficiently swelled, add a little more. Make a custard, place the macaroni on a dish, and pour the custard over the hot macaroni; grate over it a little nutmeg, and, when cold, garnish the dish with slices of candied citron. *Time.*—From 40 to 50 minutes to swell the macaroni. *Average cost*, with the custard, 1s. *Sufficient* for 4 or 5 persons. *Seasonable* at any time.

MACAROONS.

Ingredients.—½ lb. of sweet almonds, ½ lb. of sifted loaf sugar, the whites of three eggs, wafer paper. *Mode.*—Blanch, skin and dry the almonds, and pound them well with a little orange flower or plain water, then add the sifted sugar and the whites of the eggs, which should be beaten to a stiff froth, and mix all the ingredients well together. When the paste looks soft, drop it at equal distances from a biscuit syringe on to sheets of wafer paper: put a strip of almond on the top of each; strew some syrup over, and bake the macaroons in rather a slow oven, of a light brown colour. When hard and set, they are done. They must not be allowed to get very brown, as that would spoil their appearance. If the cakes when baked, appear heavy, add a little more white of egg, which should be well whisked up before it is added to the other ingredients. *Time.*—From 15 to 20 minutes. *Average cost*, 1s. 8d. per lb.

MACKEREL.

In choosing this fish, purchasers should, to a great extent, be regulated by the brightness of its appearance. If it have a transparent, silvery hue, the flesh is good; but if it be red about the head, it is stale.

| Mackerel, Baked | Maigre Soup |

MACKEREL, Baked.

Ingredients.—4 middling-sized mackerel, a nice delicate forcemeat, 3 oz. of butter ; pepper and salt to taste. *Mode.* —Clean the fish, take out the roes, and fill up with forcemeat, and sew up the slit. Flour, and put them in a dish, heads and tails alternately, with the roes ; and, between each layer, put some little pieces of butter, and pepper and salt. Bake for ½ an hour, and either serve with plain melted butter or a *maître d'hôtel* sauce. *Time.*—½ hour. *Average cost* for this quantity, 1s. 10d. *Seasonable* from April to July. *Sufficient* for 6 per-·sons.

Note.—Baked mackerel may be dressed in the same way as baked herrings, and may also be stewed in wine.

MACKEREL, Boiled.

Ingredients.—¼ lb. of salt to each gallon of water. *Mode.*—Cleanse the inside of the fish thoroughly, and lay it in the kettle with sufficient water to cover it with salt as above ; bring it gradually to boil, skim well, and simmer gently till done ; dish them on a hot napkin, heads and tails alternately, and garnish with fennel. Fennel sauce and plain melted butter are the usual accompaniments to boiled mackerel ; but caper or anchovy sauce is sometimes served with it. *Time.* —After the water boils, 10 minutes ; for large mackerel, allow more time. *Average cost*, from 4d. *Seasonable* from April to July.

Note.—When variety is desired, fillet the mackerel, boil it, and pour over parsley and butter ; send some of this, besides, in a tureen.

MACKEREL, Broiled.

Ingredients.—Pepper and salt to taste, a small quantity of oil. *Mode.*—Mackerel should never be washed when intended to be broiled, but merely wiped very clean and dry, after taking out the gills and insides. Open the back, and put in ₹ little pepper, salt, and oil ; broil it over a clear fire, turn it over on both sides, and also on the back. When sufficiently cooked, the flesh can be detached from the bone, which will be in about 10 minutes for a small mackerel. Chop a little parsley, work it up in the butter, with pepper and salt to taste, and a squeeze of lemon-juice and put it in

the back. Serve before the butter is quite melted, with a *maître d'hôtel* sauce in a tureen. *Time.*—Small mackerel 10 minutes. *Average cost*, from 4d. *Seasonable* from April to July.

MACKEREL, Fillets of.

Ingredients.—2 large mackerel, 1 oz. butter, 1 small bunch of chopped herbs, 3 tablespoonfuls of medium stock, 3 tablespoonfuls of béchamel ; salt, cayenne, and lemon-juice to taste. *Mode.*—Clean the fish, and fillet it ; scald the herbs, chop them fine, and put them with the butter and stock into a stewpan. Lay in the mackerel, and simmer very gently for 10 minutes ; take them out, and put them on a hot dish. Dredge in a little flour, add the other ingredients, give one boil, and pour it over the mackerel. *Time.* — 20 minutes. *Average cost* for this quantity, 1s. 6d. *Seasonable* from April to July. *Sufficient* for 4 persons.

Note.—Fillets of mackerel may be covered with egg and bread crumbs, and fried of a nice brown. Serve with *maître d'hôtel* sauce and plain melted butter.

MACKEREL, Pickled.

Ingredients.—12 peppercorns, 2 bay-leaves, ¼ pint of vinegar, 4 mackerel. *Mode.*—Boil the mackerel, and lay them in a dish ; take half the liquor they were boiled in ; add as much vinegar, peppercorns, and bay-leaves ; boil for 10 minutes, and when cold, pour over the fish. *Time.* —½ hour. *Average cost*, 1s. 6d.

MACKEREL, Potted.

Ingredients. — Mackerel, a blade of mace, cayenne, salt, and 2 oz. or more butter, according to the quantity of mackerel. *Mode.*—Any remains of cooked mackerel may be potted as follows ; pick it well from the bones, break it into very small pieces, and put into a stewpan with the butter, pounded mace, and other ingredients ; warm it thoroughly, but do not let it boil ; press it into potting pots and pour clarified butter over it.

MAIGRE SOUP (i.e., Soup without Meat).

Ingredients.—6 oz. butter, 6 onions sliced, 4 heads of celery, 2 lettuces, small bunch of parsley, 2 handfuls of spinach, 3 pieces of bread-crust, 2 blades of mace, salt and pepper to taste, the

Maize, Boiled

yolks of 2 eggs, 3 teaspoonfuls of vinegar, 2 quarts of water. *Mode.*—Melt the butter in a stewpan, and put in the onions to stew gently for 3 or 4 minutes; then add the celery, spinach, lettuces, and parsley, cut small. Stir the ingredients well for 10 minutes. Now put in the water, bread, seasoning, and mace. Boil gently for 1½ hour, and, at the moment of serving, beat in the yolks of the eggs and the vinegar, but do not let it boil, or the eggs will curdle. *Time.*—2 hours. *Average cost,* 6d. per quart. *Seasonable* all the year. *Sufficient* for 8 persons.

MAIZE, Boiled.

Ingredients.—The ears of young and green Indian wheat; to every ½ gallon of water allow 1 heaped tablespoonful of salt. *Mode.*—This vegetable, which makes one of the most delicious dishes brought to table, is unfortunately very rarely seen in Britain; and we wonder that, in the gardens of the wealthy, it is not invariably cultivated. Our sun, it is true, possesses hardly power sufficient to ripen maize; but, with well-prepared ground, and in a favourable position, it might be sufficiently advanced by the beginning of autumn to serve as a vegetable. The outside sheath being taken off and the waving fibres removed, let the ears be placed in boiling water, where they should remain for about 25 minutes (a longer time may be necessary for larger ears than ordinary); and, when sufficiently boiled and well drained, they may be sent to table whole, and with a piece of toast underneath them. Melted butter should be served with them. *Time.*—25 to 35 minutes. *Average cost.*—Seldom bought. *Sufficient* 1 ear for each person. *Seasonable* in autumn.

MALT WINE.

Ingredients.—5 gallons of water, 28 lbs. of sugar, 6 quarts of sweet-wort, 6 quarts of tun, 3 lbs. of raisins, ½ lb. of candy, 1 pint of brandy. *Mode.*—Boil the sugar and water together for 10 minutes; skim it well, and put the liquor into a convenient-sized pan or tub. Allow it to cool; then mix it with the sweet-wort and tun. Let it stand for 3 days, then put it into a barrel; here it will work or ferment for another three days or more; then bung up the cask, and keep it undisturbed for 2 or 3 months. After this, add the raisins (whole), the candy, and brandy,

March—Bills of Fare

and, in 6 months' time, bottle the wine off. Those who do not brew, may procure the sweet-wort and tun from any brewer. Sweet-wort is the liquor that leaves the mash of malt before it is boiled with the hops; tun is the new beer after the whole of the brewing operation has been completed. *Time.*—To be boiled 10 minutes; to stand 3 days after mixing; to ferment 3 days; to remain in the cask 2 months before the raisins are added; bottle 6 months after. *Seasonable.*—Make this in March or October.

MANNA KROUP PUDDING.

Ingredients. — 3 tablespoonfuls of manna kroup, 12 bitter almonds, 1 pint of milk, sugar to taste, 3 eggs. *Mode.*—Blanch and pound the almonds in a mortar; mix them with the manna kroup; pour over these a pint of boiling milk, and let them steep for about ¼ hour. When nearly cold, add sugar and the well-beaten eggs; mix all well together; put the pudding into a buttered dish, and bake for ½ hour. *Time.*—½ hour. *Average cost,* 8d. *Sufficient* for 4 or 5 persons. *Seasonable* at any time.

MARCH—BILLS OF FARE.

Dinner for 18 persons.

First Course.

Red Mullet.	Turtle or Mock Turtle Soup, removed by Salmon and dressed Cucumber. Vase of Flowers. Spring Soup, removed by Boiled Turbot and Lobster Sauce.	Fillets of Whitings.

Entrées.

Vol-au-Vent.	Fricasseed Chicken. Vase of Flowers. Larded Sweetbreads.	Compôte of Pigeons.

Second Course.

| Boiled Tongue, garnished. | Fore-quarter of Lamb.

Braised Capon.

Vase of
Flowers.

Roast Fowls.

Rump of Beef à la Jardinière. | Ham. |

Third Course.

Apricot Tartlets.	Guinea-Fowls, larded, removed by Cabinet Pudding. Wine Jelly.	Rhubarb Tart.
Custards.	Vase of Flowers.	Jelly, in glasses.
Damson Tart.	Italian Cream. Ducklings, removed by Nesselrode Pudding.	Cheese-cakes.

Dessert and Ices.

Dinner for 12 persons.

First Course. — White soup; clear gravy soup; boiled salmon, shrimp sauce, and dressed cucumber; baked mullets in paper cases. *Entrées.*—Filet de bœuf and Spanish sauce; larded sweetbreads; rissoles; chicken patties. *Second Course.* —Roast fillet of veal and Béchamel sauce; boiled leg of lamb; roast fowls, garnished with water-cresses; boiled ham, garnished with carrots and mashed turnips; vegetables—sea-kale, spinach, or brocoli. *Third Course.*—Two duck-lings; guinea-fowl, larded; orange jelly; Charlotte Russe; coffee cream; ice pudding; macaroni with Parmesan cheese; spinach, garnished with croû-tons; dessert and ices.

Dinner for 10 persons.

First Course.—Macaroni soup; boiled turbot and lobster sauce; salmon cutlets. *Entrées.*—Compôte of pigeons; mutton cutlets and tomato sauce. *Second Course.* —Roast lamb; boiled half calf's head, tongue, and brains; boiled bacon-cheek, garnished with spoonsfuls of spinach; vegetables. *Third Course.*—Ducklings;

plum-pudding; ginger cream; trifle; rhubarb tart; cheesecakes; fondues, in cases; dessert and ices.

Dinner for 8 persons.

First Course.—Calf's-head soup; brill and shrimp sauce; broiled mackerel à la Maître d'Hôtel. *Entrées.*—Lobster cut-lets; calf's liver and bacon, aux fines herbes. *Second Course.*—Roast loin of veal; two boiled fowls à la Bécharnel; boiled knuckle of ham; vegetables—spinach or brocoli. *Third Course.*—Wild ducks; apple custards; blancmange; lemon jelly; jam sandwiches; ice pud-ding; potatoes à la Maître d'Hôtel; des-sert and ices.

Dinner for 6 persons.

First Course.—Vermicelli soup; soles à la Crême. *Entrées.*—Veal cutlets; small vols-au-vent. *Second Course.*— Small saddle of mutton; half calf's head; boiled bacon-cheek, garnished with Brus-sels sprouts. *Third Course.* — Cabinet pudding; orange jelly; custards, in glasses; rhubarb tart; lobster salad; dessert.

First Course.—Julienne soup; baked mullets. *Entrées.* — Chicken cutlets; oyster patties. *Second Course.*— Roast lamb and mint sauce; boiled leg of pork; pease pudding; vegetables. *Third Course.*—Ducklings; Swiss cream; lemon jelly; cheesecakes; rhubarb tart; maca-roni; dessert.

First Course. — Oyster soup; boiled salmon and dressed cucumber. *Entrées.* —Rissoles; fricasseed chicken. *Second Course.* — Boiled leg of mutton, caper sauce; roast fowls, garnished with water-cresses; vegetables. *Third Course.*— Charlotte aux pommes; orange jelly; lemon cream; soufflé of arrowroot; sea-kale; dessert.

First Course. — Ox-tail soup; boiled mackerel. *Entrées.* — Stewed mutton kidneys; minced veal and oysters. *Second Course.*—Stewed shoulder of veal; roast ribs of beef and horseradish sauce; vegetables. *Third Course.*—Ducklings; tartlets of strawberry jam; cheesecakes; Gâteau de Riz; carrot pudding; sea-kale; dessert.

March, Plain Family Dinners for | Marmalade and Vermicelli Pudding

MARCH, Plain Family Dinners for.

Sunday.—1. Boiled ½ calf's head, pickled pork, the tongue on a small dish with the brains round it; mutton cutlets and mashed potatoes. 2. Plum tart made with bottled fruit, baked custard pudding, Baroness pudding.

Monday.—1. Roast shoulder of mutton and onion sauce, brocoli, baked potatoes. 2. Slices of Baroness pudding warmed, and served with sugar sprinkled over. Cheesecakes.

Tuesday.—1. Mock turtle soup, made with liquor that calf's head was boiled in, and the pieces of head. 2. Hashed mutton, rump-steaks and oyster sauce. 3. Boiled plum-pudding.

Wednesday.—1. Fried whitings, melted butter, potatoes. 2. Boiled beef, suet dumplings, carrots, potatoes, marrow-bones. 3. Arrowroot blancmange, and stewed rhubarb.

Thursday.—1. Pea-soup made from liquor that beef was boiled in. 2. Stewed rump-steak, cold beef, mashed potatoes. 3. Rolled jam pudding.

Friday.—1. Fried soles, melted butter, potatoes. 2. Roast loin of mutton, brocoli, potatoes, bubble-and-squeak. 3. Rice pudding.

Saturday.—1. Rump-steak pie, haricot mutton made with remains of cold loin. 2. Pancakes, ratafia pudding.

Sunday.—1. Roast fillet of veal, boiled ham, spinach and potatoes. 2. Rhubarb tart, custards in glasses, bread-and-butter pudding.

Monday.—1. Baked soles, potatoes. 2. Minced veal and rump-steak pie. 3. Somersetshire dumplings with the remains of custards poured round them; marmalade tartlets.

Tuesday.—1. Gravy soup. 2. Boiled leg of mutton, mashed turnips, suet dumplings, caper sauce, potatoes, veal rissoles made with remains of fillet of veal. 3. Cheese.

Wednesday.—1. Stewed mullet. 2. Roast fowls, bacon, gravy, and bread sauce, mutton pudding, made with a few slices of the cold meat and the addition of two kidneys. 3. Baked lemon pudding.

Thursday.—1. Vegetable soup made with liquor that the mutton was boiled in, and mixed with the remains of gravy

soup. 2. Roast ribs of beef, Yorkshire pudding, horseradish sauce, brocoli and potatoes. 3. Apple pudding or macaroni.

Friday.—1. Stewed eels, pork cutlets, and tomato sauce. 2. Cold beef, mashed potatoes. 3. Plum tart made with bottled fruit.

Saturday.—1. Rumpsteak-and-kidney pudding, broiled beef-bones, greens and potatoes. 2. Jam tartlets made with pieces of paste from plum tart, baked custard pudding.

MARCH, Things in Season.

Fish.—Barbel, brill, carp, crabs, crayfish, dace, eels, flounders, haddocks, herrings, lampreys, lobsters, mussels, oysters, perch, pike, plaice, prawns, shrimps, skate, smelts, soles, sprats, sturgeon, tench, thornback, turbot, whiting.

Meat.—Beef, house lamb, mutton, pork, veal.

Poultry.—Capons, chickens, ducklings, tame and wild pigeons, pullets with eggs, turkeys, wild-fowl, though now not in full season.

Game.—Grouse, hares, partridges, pheasants, snipes, woodcock.

Vegetables.—Beetroot, brocoli (purple and white), Brussels sprouts, cabbages, carrots, celery, chervil, cresses, cucumbers (forced), endive, kidney-beans, lettuces, parsnips, potatoes, savoys, seakale, spinach, turnips,—various herbs.

Fruit. — Apples (golden and Dutch pippins), grapes, medlars, nuts, oranges, pears (Bon Chrétien), walnuts, dried fruits (foreign), such as almonds and raisins; French and Spanish plums; prunes, figs, dates, crystallized preserves.

MARMALADE AND VERMICELLI PUDDING.

Ingredients.—1 breakfastcupful of vermicelli, 2 tablespoonfuls of marmalade, ¼ lb. of raisins, sugar to taste, 3 eggs, milk. *Mode.*—Pour some boiling milk on the vermicelli, and let it remain covered for 10 minutes; then mix with it the marmalade, stoned raisins, sugar, and beaten eggs. Stir all well together, put the mixture into a buttered mould, boil for 1½ hour, and serve with custard sauce. *Time.*—1½ hour. *Average cost,* 1s. *Sufficient* for 5 or 6 persons. *Seasonable* at any time.

MARROW-BONES, Boiled.

Ingredients.—Bones, a small piece of common paste, a floured cloth. *Mode.*—Have the bones neatly sawed into convenient sizes, and cover the ends with a small piece of common crust, made with flour and water. Over this tie a floured cloth, and place the bones upright in a saucepan of boiling water, taking care there is sufficient to cover them. Boil them for 2 hours, remove the cloth and paste, and serve them upright on a napkin with dry toast. Many persons clear the marrow from the bones after they are cooked, spread it over a slice of toast and add a seasoning of pepper: when served in this manner, it must be very expeditiously sent to table, as it so soon gets cold. *Time.*—2 hours. *Seasonable* at any time.

Note.—Marrow-bones may be baked after preparing them as in the preceding recipe; they should be laid in a deep dish, and baked for 2 hours.

MARROW DUMPLINGS, to serve with Roast Meat, in Soup, with Salad, &c.

(*German Recipe.*)

Ingredients.—1 oz. of beef marrow, 1 oz. of butter, 2 eggs, 2 penny rolls, 1 teaspoonful of minced onion, 1 teaspoonful of minced parsley, salt and grated nutmeg to taste. *Mode.*—Beat the marrow and butter together to a cream; well whisk the eggs, and add these to the other ingredients. When they are well stirred, put in the rolls, which should previously be well soaked in boiling milk, strained, and beaten up with a fork. Add the remaining ingredients, omitting the minced onion where the flavour is very much disliked, and form the mixture into small round dumplings. Drop these into boiling broth, and let them simmer for about 20 minutes or ½ hour. They may be served in soup, with roast meat, or with salad, as in Germany, where they are more frequently sent to table than in this country. They are very good. *Time.*—20 minutes to ½ hour. *Average cost,* 6d. *Sufficient* for 7 or 8 dumplings. *Seasonable* at any time.

MARROW PUDDING, Baked or Boiled.

Ingredients.—½ pint of bread crumbs, 1½ pint of milk, 6 oz. of marrow, 4 eggs,

¼ lb. of raisins or currants, or 2 oz. of each; sugar and grated nutmeg to taste. *Mode.*—Make the milk boiling, pour it hot on to the bread crumbs, and let these remain covered for about ¼ hour; shred the marrow, beat up the eggs, and mix these with the bread crumbs; add the remaining ingredients, beat the mixture well, and either put it into a buttered mould and boil it for 2½ hours, or put it into a pie-dish edged with puff-paste, and bake for rather more than ¾ hour. Before sending it to table, sift a little pounded sugar over, after being turned out of the mould or basin. *Time.*—2½ hours to boil, ¾ hour to bake. *Average cost,* 1s. 2d. *Sufficient* for 5 or 6 persons. *Seasonable* at any time.

MAY—BILLS OF FARE.

Dinner for 18 persons.

First Course.

Fried Filleted Soles.	Asparagus Soup, removed by Salmon and Lobster Sauce. Vase of Flowers. Ox-tail Soup, removed by Brill & Shrimp Sauce.	Fillets of Mackerel, à la Maître d'Hôtel.

Entrées.

Lobster Pudding.	Lamb Cutlets and Cucumbers. Vase of Flowers. Veal Ragoût.	Curried Fowl.

Second Course.

Roast Fowls.	Saddle of Lamb. Raised Pie. Vase of Flowers. Braised Ham. Roast Veal.	Boiled Capon and White Sauce.

May—Bills of Fare

Third Course.

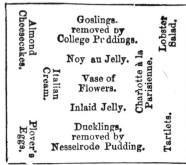

Almond Cheesecakes.

Italian Cream.

Plover's Eggs.

Goslings. removed by College Puddings.

Noy au Jelly.

Vase of Flowers.

Inlaid Jelly.

Ducklings, removed by Nesselrode Pudding.

Charlotte à la Parisienne.

Lobster Salad.

Tartlets.

Dessert and Ices.

Dinner for 12 persons.

First Course.—White soup ; asparagus soup ; salmon cutlets ; boiled turbot and lobster sauce. *Entrées.*—Chicken vol-au-vent ; lamb cutlets and cucumbers ; 'ricandeau of veal ; stewed mushrooms. *Second Course.*—Roast lamb ; haunch of mutton ; boiled and roast fowls ; vegetables. *Third Course.*—Ducklings ; goslings ; Charlotte Russe ; Vanilla cream ; gooseberry tart ; custards ; cheesecakes ; cabinet pudding and iced pudding ; dessert and ices.

Dinner for 10 persons.

First Course.—Spring soup ; salmon à la Genévése ; red mullet. *Entrées.*—Chicken vol-au-vent ; calf's liver and bacon aux fines herbes. *Second Course.*—Saddle of mutton ; half calf's head, tongue, and brains ; braised ham : asparagus. *Third Course.*—Roast pigeons ; ducklings ; sponge-cake pudding ; Charlotte à la vanille ; gooseberry tart ; cream ; cheesecakes ; apricot-jam tart ; dessert and ices.

Dinner for 8 persons.

First Course.—Julienne soup ; brill and lobster sauce ; fried fillets of mackerel. *Entrées.*—Lamb cutlets and cucumbers ; lobster patties. *Second Course.*—Roast fillet of veal ; boiled leg of lamb ; asparagus. *Third Course.*—Ducklings ; gooseberry tart ; custards ; fancy pastry ; soufflé ; dessert and ices.

Dinner for 6 persons.

First Course.—Vermicelli soup ; boiled salmon and anchovy sauce. *Entrées.*—Fillets of beef and tomato sauce ; sweet-

May, Plain Family Dinners for

breads. *Second Course.*—Roast lamb , boiled capon ; asparagus. *Third Course.*—Ducklings ; cabinet pudding ; compôte of gooseberries ; custards in glasses ; blancmange ; lemon tartlets ; fondue ; dessert.

First Course.—Macaroni soup ; boiled mackerel à la maître d'hôtel ; fried smelts. *Entrées.* — Scollops of fowl ; lobster pudding. *Second Course.*—Boiled leg of lamb and spinach ; roast sirloin of beef and horseradish sauce ; vegetables. *Third Course.*—Roast leveret ; salad ; soufflé of rice ; ramakins ; strawberry-jam tartlets ; orange jelly ; dessert.

First Course.—Julienne soup ; trout with Dutch sauce ; salmon cutlets. *Entrées.* —Lamb cutlets and mushrooms ; vol-au-vent of chicken. *Second Course.*—Roast lamb ; calf's head à la tortue ; vegetables. *Third Course.* — Spring chickens ; iced pudding ; Vanilla cream ; clear jelly ; tartlets ; cheesecakes ; dessert.

First Course.—Soup à la reine ; crimped trout and lobster sauce ; baked whitings aux fines herbes. *Entrées.* — Braised mutton cutlets and cucumbers ; stewed pigeons. *Second Course.*—Roast fille. of veal ; bacon-cheek and greens ; fillet of beef à la jardinière. *Third Course.*—Ducklings ; soufflé à la vanille ; compôte of oranges ; meringues ; gooseberry tart ; fondue ; dessert.

MAY, Plain Family Dinners for.

Sunday.—1. Vegetable soup. 2. Saddle of mutton, asparagus and potatoes. 3. Gooseberry tart, custards.

Monday.—1. Fried whitings, anchovy sauce. 2. Cold mutton, mashed potatoes, stewed veal. 3. Fig pudding.

Tuesday.—1. Haricot mutton, made from remains of cold mutton, rump-steak pie. 2. Macaroni.

Wednesday.—1. Roast loin of veal and spinach, boiled bacon, mutton cutlets and tomato sauce. 2. Gooseberry pudding and cream.

Thursday.—1. Spring soup. 2. Roast leg of lamb, mint sauce, spinach, curried veal and rice. 3. Lemon pudding.

Friday.—1. Boiled mackerel and parsley-and-butter. 2. Stewed rump-steak, cold lamb and salad. 3. Baked gooseberry pudding.

| May, Things in Season | Meringues |

Saturday.—1. Vermicelli. 2. Rump-steak pudding, lamb cutlets, and cucumbers. 3. Macaroni.

Sunday.—1. Boiled salmon and lobster or caper sauce. 2. Roast lamb, mint sauce, asparagus, potatoes. 3. Plum-pudding, gooseberry tart.

Monday.—1. Salmon warmed in remains of lobster sauce and garnished with croûtons. 2. Stewed knuckle of veal and rice, cold lamb and dressed cucumber. 3. Slices of pudding warmed, and served with sugar sprinkled over. Baked rice pudding.

Tuesday.—1. Roast ribs of beef, horse-radish sauce, Yorkshire pudding, spinach and potatoes. 2. Boiled lemon pudding.

Wednesday.—1. Fried soles, melted butter. 2. Cold beef and dressed cucumber or salad, veal cutlets and bacon. 3. Baked plum-pudding.

Thursday.—1. Spring soup. 2. Calf's liver and bacon, broiled beef-bones, spinach and potatoes. 3. Gooseberry tart.

Friday.—1. Roast shoulder of mutton, baked potatoes, onion sauce, spinach. 2. Currant dumplings.

Saturday.—1. Broiled mackerel, fennel sauce or plain melted butter. 2. Rump-steak pie, hashed mutton, vegetables. 3. Baked arrowroot pudding.

MAY, Things in Season.

Fish.—Carp, chub, crabs, crayfish, dory, herrings, lobsters, mackerel, red and gray mullet, prawns, salmon, shad, smelts, soles, trout, turbot.

Meat.—Beef, lamb, mutton, veal.

Poultry.—Chickens, ducklings, fowls, green geese, leverets, pullets, rabbits.

Vegetables.—Asparagus, beans, early cabbages, carrots, cauliflowers, cresses, cucumbers, lettuces, pease, early potatoes, salads, sea-kale,—various herbs.

Fruit.—Apples, green apricots, cherries, currants for tarts, gooseberries, melons, pears, rhubarb, strawberries.

MAYONNAISE, a Sauce or Salad-Dressing for cold Chicken, Meat, and other cold Dishes.

Ingredients.—The yolks of 2 eggs, 6 tablespoonfuls of salad oil, 4 table-spoonfuls of vinegar, salt and white pepper to taste, 1 tablespoonful of white stock, 2 tablespoonfuls of cream. *Mode.*

—Put the yolks of the eggs into a basin, with a seasoning of pepper and salt; have ready the above quantities of oil and vinegar, in separate vessels; add them *very gradually* to the eggs; continue stirring and rubbing the mixture with a wooden spoon, as herein consists the secret of having a nice smooth sauce. It cannot be stirred too frequently, and it should be made in a very cool place, or, if ice is at hand, it should be mixed over it. When the vinegar and oil are well incorporated with the eggs, add the stock and cream, stirring all the time, and it will then be ready for use.

For a fish Mayonnaise, this sauce may be coloured with lobster-spawn, pounded; and for poultry or meat, where variety is desired, a little parsley-juice may be used to add to its appearance. Cucumber, tarragon, or any other flavoured vinegar, may be substituted for plain, where they are liked. *Average cost,* for this quantity, 7d. *Sufficient* for a small salad.

Note.—In mixing the oil and vinegar with the eggs, put in first a few drops of oil, and then a few drops of vinegar, never adding a large quantity of either at one time. By this means, you can be more certain of the sauce not curdling. Patience and practice, let us add, are two essentials for making this sauce good.

MELONS.

This fruit is rarely preserved or cooked in any way, but is sent whole to table on a dish garnished with leaves or flowers, as fancy dictates. A border of any other kind of small fruit, arranged round the melon, has a pretty effect, the colour of the former contrasting nicely with the melon. Plenty of pounded sugar should be served with it; and the fruit should be cut lengthwise, in moderate-sized slices. In America, it is frequently eaten with pepper and salt. *Average cost.*— English, in full season, 3s. 6d. to 5s. each; when scarce, 10s. to 15s.; *seasonable,* June to August. French, 2s. to 3s. 6d. each; *seasonable,* June and July. Dutch, 9d. to 2s. each; *seasonable,* July and August.

MERINGUES.

Ingredients.—½ lb. of pounded sugar, the whites of 4 eggs. *Mode.*— Whisk the whites of the eggs to a stiff froth,

Meringues

and, with a wooden spoon, stir in *quickly* the pounded sugar; and have some boards thick enough to put in the oven to prevent the bottom of the meringues from acquiring too much colour. Cut some strips of paper about 2 inches wide; place this paper on the board, and drop a tablespoonful at a time of the mixture on the paper, taking care to let all the meringues be the same size. In dropping it from the spoon, give the mixture the form of an egg, and keep the meringues about 2 inches apart from each other on the paper. Strew over them some sifted sugar, and bake in a moderate oven for ½ hour. As soon as they begin to colour, remove them from the oven; take each slip of paper by the two ends, and turn it gently on the table, and, with a small spoon, take out the soft part of each meringue. Spread some clean paper on the board, turn the meringues upside

MERINGUES.

down, and put them into the oven to harden and brown on the other side. When required for table, fill them with whipped cream, flavoured with liqueur or vanilla, and sweetened with pounded sugar. Join two of the meringues together, and pile them high in the dish, as shown in the annexed drawing. To vary their appearance, finely-chopped almonds or currants may be strewn over them before the sugar is sprinkled over; and they may be garnished with any bright-coloured preserve. Great expedition is necessary in making this sweet dish; as, if the meringues are not put into the oven as soon as the sugar and eggs are mixed, the former melts, and the mixture would run on the paper, instead of keeping its egg-shape. The sweeter the meringues are made, the crisper will they be; but, if there is not sufficient sugar mixed with them, they will most likely be tough. They are sometimes coloured

Milk and Cream, to keep

with cochineal; and, if kept well covered in a dry place, will remain good for a month or six weeks. *Time.*—Altogether, about ½ hour. *Average cost*, with the cream and flavouring, 1s. *Sufficient* to make 2 dozen meringues. *Seasonable* at any time.

MILK.

Milk, when of good quality, is of an opaque white colour: the cream always comes to the top; the well-known milky odour is strong; it will boil without altering its appearance in these respects the little bladders which arise on the surface will renew themselves if broken by the spoon. To boil milk is, in fact, the simplest way of testing its quality. The commonest adulterations of milk are not of a hurtful character. It is a good deal thinned with water, and sometimes thickened with a little starch, or coloured with yolk of egg, or even saffron; but these processes have nothing murderous in them.

MILK AND CREAM, to keep, in hot Weather.

When the weather is very warm, and it is very difficult to prevent milk from turning sour and spoiling the cream, it should be scalded, and it will then remain good for a few hours. It must on no account be allowed to boil, or there will be a skin instead of a cream upon the milk; and the slower the process the safer will it be. A very good plan to scald milk, is to put the pan that contains it into a saucepan or wide kettle of boiling water. When the surface looks thick, the milk is sufficiently scalded, and it should then be put away in a cool place in the same vessel that it was scalded in. Cream may be kept for 24 hours, if scalded without sugar; and by the addition of the latter ingredient, it will remain good double the time, if kept in a cool place. All pans, jugs, and vessels intended for milk, should be kept beautifully clean, and well scalded before the milk is put in, as any negligence in this respect may cause large quantities of it to be spoiled; and milk should never be kept in vessels of zinc or copper. Milk may be preserved good in hot weather, for a few hours, by placing the jug which contains it in ice, or very cold water; or a pinch of bicarbonate of soda may be introduced into the liquid.

MILK AND CREAM, Separation of.

If it be desired that the milk should be freed entirely from cream, it should be poured into a very shallow broad pan or dish, not more than 1½ inch deep, as cream cannot rise through a great depth of milk. In cold and wet weather, milk is not so rich as it is in summer and warm weather, and the morning's milk is always richer than the evening's. The last-drawn milk of each milking, at all times and seasons, is richer than the first-drawn, and on that account should be set apart for cream. Milk should be shaken as little as possible when carried from the cow to the dairy, and should be poured into the pans very gently. Persons not keeping cows, may always have a little cream, provided the milk they purchase be pure and unadulterated. As soon as it comes in, it should be poured into very shallow open pie-dishes, and set by in a very cool place, and in 7 or 8 hours a nice cream should have risen to the surface.

MILK AND CREAM, Substitute for, in Tea and Coffee.

Ingredients.—1 new laid egg to every large breakfastcupful of tea or coffee. *Mode.*—Beat up the whole of the egg in a basin, put it into a cup, and pour over it the tea or coffee quite hot, stirring all the time to prevent the egg from curdling. In point of nourishment, both tea and coffee are much improved by this addition. *Sufficient.*—1 egg to every large breakfastcupful of tea or coffee.

MILK SOUP (a nice Dish for Children).

Ingredients.—2 quarts of milk, 1 saltspoonful of salt, 1 teaspoonful of powdered cinnamon, 3 teaspoonfuls of pounded sugar, or more if liked, 4 thin slices of bread, the yolks of 6 eggs. *Mode.*—Boil the milk with the salt, cinnamon, and sugar; lay the bread in a deep dish, pour over it a little of the milk, and keep it hot over a stove, without burning. Beat up the yolks of the eggs, add them to the milk, and stir it over the fire till it thickens. Do not let it curdle. Pour it upon the bread, and serve. *Time.*—¾ of an hour. *Average cost,* 8d. per quart. *Seasonable* all the year. *Sufficient* for 10 children.

MINCE PIES.

Ingredients.—Good puff-paste, mincemeat. *Mode.*—Make some good puff-paste by recipe; roll it out to the thickness of about ¼ inch, and line some good-sized pattypans with it; fill them with mincemeat,

MINCE PIES.

cover with the paste, and cut it off all round close to the edge of the tin. Put the pies into a brisk oven, to draw the paste up, and bake for 25 minutes, or longer, should the pies be very large; brush them over with the white of an egg, beaten with the blade of a knife to a stiff froth; sprinkle over pounded sugar, and put them into the oven for a minute or two, to dry the egg; dish the pies on a white d'oyley, and serve hot. They may be merely sprinkled with pounded sugar instead of being glazed, when that mode is preferred. To re-warm them, put the pies on the pattypans, and let them remain in the oven for 10 minutes or ¼ hour, and they will be almost as good as if freshly made. *Time.*—25 to 30 minutes; 10 minutes to re-warm them. *Average cost,* 4d. each. *Sufficient*—½ lb. of paste for 4 pies. *Seasonable* at Christmas time.

MINCEMEAT.

Ingredients.—2 lbs. of raisins, 3 lbs. of currants, 1½ lb. of lean beef, 3 lbs. of beef suet, 2 lbs. of moist sugar, 2 oz. of citron, 2 oz. of candied lemon-peel, 2 oz. of candied orange-peel, 1 large nutmeg, 1 pottle of apples, the rind of 2 lemons, the juice of 1, ½ pint of brandy. *Mode.*—Stone and *cut* the raisins once or twice across, but do not chop them; wash, dry, and pick the currants free from stalks and grit, and mince the beef and suet, taking care that the latter is chopped very fine; slice the citron and candied peel, grate the nutmeg, and pare, core, and mince the apples; mince the lemon-peel, strain the juice, and when all the ingredients are thus prepared, mix them well together, adding the brandy when the other things are well blended; press the whole into a jar, carefully exclude the air, and the mincemeat will be ready for use in a fortnight.

Mincemeat, Excellent

If an additional quantity of spice be preferred, add ½ teaspoonful of pounded mace, and the same of pounded allspice. We, however, prefer the mincemeat without the latter ingredients, and can vouch for its excellence. *Average cost for this quantity, 8s. Seasonable.*—Make this about the beginning of December.

MINCEMEAT, Excellent.

Ingredients.—3 large lemons, 3 large apples, 1 lb. of stoned raisins, 1 lb. of currants, 1 lb. of suet, 2 lbs. of moist sugar, 1 oz. of sliced candied citron, 1 oz. of sliced candied orange-peel, and the same quantity of lemon-peel, 1 teacupful of brandy, 2 tablespoonfuls of orange marmalade. *Mode.*—Grate the rinds of the lemons ; squeeze out the juice, strain it, and boil the remainder of the lemons until tender enough to pulp or chop very finely. Then add to this pulp the apples, which should be baked, and their skins and cores removed ; put in the remaining ingredients one by one, and, as they are added, mix everything very thoroughly together. Put the mincemeat into a stone jar with a closely-fitting lid, and in a fortnight it will be ready for use. *Seasonable.*—This should be made the first or second week in December.

MINT SAUCE, to serve with Roast Lamb.

Ingredients. — 4 dessertspoonfuls of chopped mint, 2 dessertspoonfuls of pounded white sugar, ¼ pint of vinegar. *Mode.*—Wash the mint, which should be young and fresh-gathered, free from grit ; pick the leaves from the stalks, mince them very fine, and put them into a tureen ; add the sugar and vinegar, and stir till the former is dissolved. This sauce is better by being made 2 or 3 hours before wanted for table, as the vinegar then becomes impregnated with the flavour of the mint. By many persons, the above proportion of sugar would not be considered sufficient ; but as tastes vary, we have given the quantity which we have found to suit the general palate. *Average cost, 3d. Sufficient* to serve with a middling-size joint of lamb.

Note.—Where green mint is scarce and not obtainable, mint vinegar may be substituted for it, and will be found very acceptable in early spring.

Mock Turtle Soup

MINT VINEGAR.

Ingredients.—Vinegar, mint. *Mode.* —Procure some nice fresh mint, pick the leaves from the stalks, and fill a bottle or jar with them. Add vinegar to them until the bottle is full ; *cover closely* to exclude the air, and let it infuse for a fortnight. Then strain the liquor, and put it into small bottles for use, of which the corks should be sealed. *Seasonable.* —This should be made in June, July, or August.

MOCK TURTLE SOUP.

I.

Ingredients.—½ a calf's head, ¼ lb. of butter, ¼ lb. of lean ham, 2 tablespoonfuls of minced parsley, a little minced lemon thyme, sweet marjoram, basil, 2 onions, a few chopped mushrooms (when obtainable), 2 shalots, 2 tablespoonfuls of flour, ¼ bottle of Madeira or sherry, force-meat balls, cayenne, salt and mace to taste, the juice of 1 lemon and 1 Seville orange, 1 dessertspoonful of pounded sugar, 3 quarts of best stock. *Mode.*—Scald the head with the skin on, remove the brain, tie the head up in a cloth, and let it boil for 1 hour. Then take the meat from the bones, cut it into small square pieces, and throw them into cold water. Now take the meat, put it into a stewpan, and cover with stock ; let it boil gently for an hour, or rather more, if not quite tender, and set it on one side. Melt the butter in another stewpan, and add the ham, cut small, with the herbs, parsley, onions, shalots, mushrooms, and nearly a pint of stock ; let these simmer slowly for 2 hours, and then dredge in as much flour as will dry up the butter. Fill up with the remainder of the stock, add the wine, let it stew gently for 10 minutes, rub it through a tammy, and put it to the calf's head ; season with cayenne, and, if required, a little salt ; add the juice of the orange and lemon ; and when liked, ¼ teaspoonful of pounded mace, and the sugar. Put in the force-meat balls, simmer 5 minutes, and serve very hot. *Time.*— 4½ hours. *Average cost, 3s. 6d.* per quart, or 2s. 6d. without wine or force-meat balls. *Seasonable* in winter. *Sufficient* for 10 persons.

Note.—The bones of the head should be well stewed in the liquor it was first

Muffins

boiled in, and will make good white stock, flavoured with vegetables, &c.

II.

(More Economical.)

Ingredients.—A knuckle of veal weighing 5 or 6 lbs., 2 cowheels, 2 large onions stuck with cloves, 1 bunch of sweet herbs, 3 blades of mace, salt to taste, 12 peppercorns, 1 glass of sherry, 24 force-meat balls, a little lemon-juice, 4 quarts of water. *Mode.*—Put all the ingredients, except the force-meat balls and lemon-juice, in an earthen jar, and stew for 6 hours. Do not open it till cold. When wanted for use, skim off all the fat, and strain carefully; place it on the fire, cut up the meat into inch-and-a-half squares, put it, with the force-meat balls and lemon-juice, into the soup, and serve. It can be flavoured with a tablespoonful of anchovy, or Harvey's sauce. *Time.*—6 hours. *Average cost*, 1s. 4d. per quart. *Seasonable* in winter. *Sufficient* for 10 persons.

MUFFINS.

Ingredients.—To every quart of milk allow 1½ oz. of German yeast, a little salt; flour. *Mode.*—Warm the milk, add to it the yeast, and mix these well together; put them into a pan, and stir in sufficient flour to make the whole into a dough of rather a soft consistence;

MUFFINS.

cover it over with a cloth, and place it in a warm place to rise, and, when light and nicely risen, divide the dough into pieces, and round them to the proper shape with the hands; place them in a layer of flour about two inches thick, on wooden trays, and let them rise again: when this is effected, they each will exhibit a semi-globular shape. Then place them carefully on a hot plate or stove, and bake them until they are slightly browned, turning them when they are done on one side. Muffins are not easily made, and are more generally purchased than manufactured at home. *To toast them*, divide the edge of the muffin all round, by pulling it open to the depth of about an inch, with the fingers. Put it on a toasting-fork, and hold it before a very clear fire until one side is nicely browned, but not burnt:

Mullagatawny Soup

turn, and toast it on the other. Do not toast them too quickly, as, if this be done, the middle of the muffin will not be warmed through. When done, divide them by pulling them open; butter them slightly on both sides, put them together again, and cut them into halves: when sufficient are toasted and buttered, pile them on a very hot dish, and send them very quickly to table. *Time.*—From 20 minutes to ½ hour to bake them. *Sufficient.*—Allow 1 muffin to each person.

MULBERRIES, Preserved.

Ingredients.—To 2 lbs. of fruit and 1 pint of juice allow 2½ lbs. of loaf sugar. *Mode.*—Put some of the fruit into a preserving pan, and simmer it gently until the juice is well drawn. Strain it through a bag, measure it, and to every pint allow the above proportion of sugar and fruit. Put the sugar into the preserving-pan, moisten it with the juice, boil it up, skim well, and then add the mulberries, which should be ripe, but not soft enough to break to a pulp. Let them stand in the syrup till warm through, then set them on the fire to boil gently; when half done, turn them carefully into an earthen pan, and let them remain till the next day; then boil them as before, and when the syrup is thick, and becomes firm when cold, put the preserve into pots. In making this, care should be taken not to break the mulberries: this may be avoided by very gentle stirring, and by simmering the fruit very slowly. *Time.*—¾ hour to extract the juice; ¼ hour to boil the mulberries the first time, ¼ hour the second time. *Seasonable* in August and September.

MULLAGATAWNY SOUP.

Ingredients.—2 tablespoonfuls of curry powder, 6 onions, 1 clove of garlic, 1 oz. of pounded almonds, a little lemon-pickle, or mango-juice, to taste; 1 fowl or rabbit; 4 slices of lean bacon; 2 quarts of medium stock, or, if wanted very good, best stock. *Mode.*—Slice and fry the onions of a nice colour; line the stewpan with the bacon; cut up the rabbit or fowl into small joints, and slightly brown them; put in the fried onions, the garlic, and stock·and simmer gently till the meat is tender, ι skim very carefully, and when the meat is done, rub the curry powder to a smooth batter;

Mullet, Grey	Mushroom Ketchup

add it to the soup with the almonds, which must be first pounded with a little of the stock. Put in seasoning and lemon-pickle or mango-juice to taste, and serve boiled rice with it. *Time.*—2 hours. *Average cost,* 1*s.* 6*d.* per quart. *Seasonable* in winter. *Sufficient* for 8 persons.

Note.—This soup can also be made with breast of veal, or calf's head. Vegetable mullagatawny is made with veal stock, by boiling and pulping chopped vegetable marrow, cucumbers, onions, and tomatoes, and seasoning with curry powder and cayenne. Nice pieces of meat, good curry powder, and strong stock, are necessary to make this soup good.

MULLET, Grey.

Ingredients.—¼ lb. of salt to each gallon of water. *Mode.*—If the fish be very large, it should be laid in cold water, and gradually brought to a boil; if small, put it in boiling water, salted in the above proportion. Serve with anchovy sauce and plain melted butter. *Time.*—According to size, ¼ to ¾ hour. *Average cost,* 8*d.* per lb. *Seasonable* from July to October.

MULLET, Red.

Ingredients.—Oiled paper, thickening of butter and flour, ½ teaspoonful of anchovy sauce, 1 glass of sherry; cayenne and salt to taste. *Mode.*—Clean the fish, take out the gills, but leave the inside, fold in oiled paper, and bake them gently. When done, take the liquor that flows from the fish, add a thickening of butter kneaded with flour; put in the other ingredients, and let it boil for 2 minutes. Serve the sauce in a tureen, and the fish, either with or without the paper cases. *Time.*—About 25 minutes. *Average cost,* 1*s.* each. *Seasonable* at any time, but more plentiful in summer.

Note.—Red mullet may be broiled, and should be folded in oiled paper, the same as in the preceding recipe, and seasoned with pepper and salt. They may be served without sauce; but if any is required, use melted butter, Italian or anchovy sauce. They should never be plain boiled.

MUSHROOM KETCHUP.

Ingredients.—To each peck of mushrooms ¼ lb. of salt; to each quart of

mushroom-liquor ¼ oz. of cayenne, ½ oz. of allspice, ½ oz. of ginger, 2 blades of pounded mace. *Mode.*—Choose full-grown mushroom flaps, and take care they are perfectly *fresh gathered* when the weather is tolerably dry; for, if they are picked during very heavy rain, the ketchup from which they are made is liable to get musty, and will not keep long. Put a layer of them in a deep pan, sprinkle salt over them, and then another layer of mushrooms, and so on alternately. Let them remain for a few hours, when break them up with the hand; put them in a nice cool place for 3 days, occasionally stirring and mashing them well, to extract from them as much juice as possible. Now measure the quantity of liquor without straining, and to each quart allow the above proportion of spices, &c. Put all into a stone jar, cover it up very closely, put it in a saucepan of boiling water, set it over the fire, and let it boil for 3 hours. Have ready a nice clean stewpan; turn into it the contents of the jar, and let the whole simmer very gently for ½ hour; pour it into a jug, where it should stand in a cool place till the next day; then pour it off into another jug, and strain it into very dry clean bottles, and do not squeeze the mushrooms. To each pint of ketchup add a few drops of brandy. Be careful not to shake the contents, but leave all the sediment behind in the jug; cork well, and either seal or rosin the cork, so as perfectly to exclude the air. When a very clear bright ketchup is wanted, the liquor must be strained through a very fine hair-sieve, or flannel bag, *after* it has been very gently poured off; if the operation is not successful, it must be repeated until you have quite a clear liquor. It should be examined occasionally, and if it is spoiling, should be reboiled with a few peppercorns. *Seasonable* from the beginning of September to the middle of October, when this ketchup should be made.

Note.—This flavouring ingredient, if genuine and well prepared, is one of the most useful store sauces to the experienced cook, and no trouble should be spared in its preparation. Double ketchup is made by reducing the liquor to half the quantity; for example, 1 quart must be boiled down to 1 pint. This goes farther than ordinary ketchup, as so little is required to flavour a good quantity of gravy.

The sediment may also be bottled for immediate use, and will be found to answer for flavouring *thick* soups or gravies.

MUSHROOM POWDER (a valuable addition to Sauces and Gravies, when fresh Mushrooms are not obtainable).

Ingredients.—½ peck of large mushrooms, 2 onions, 12 cloves, ¼ oz. of pounded mace, 2 teaspoonfuls of white pepper. *Mode.*—Peel the mushrooms, wipe them perfectly free from grit and dirt, remove the black fur, and reject all those that are at all worm-eaten ; put them into a stewpan with the above ingredients, but without water; shake them over a clear fire, till all the liquor is dried up, and be careful not to let them burn ; arrange them on tins, and dry them in a slow oven ; pound them to a fine powder, which put into small *dry* bottles ; cork well, seal the corks, and keep it in a dry place. In using this powder, add it to the gravy just before serving, when it will merely require one boil-up. The flavour imparted by this means to the gravy, ought to be exceedingly good. *Seasonable.*—This should be made in September, or at the beginning of October.

Note.—If the bottles in which it is stored away are not perfectly dry, as, also, the mushroom powder, it will keep good but a very short time.

MUSHROOM SAUCE, very rich and good, to serve with Fowls or Rabbits.

Ingredients. — 1 pint of mushroom-buttons, salt to taste, a little grated nutmeg, 1 blade of pounded mace, 1 pint of cream, 2 oz. of butter, flour to thicken. *Mode.*—Rub the buttons with a piece of flannel and salt, to take off the skin ; cut off the stalks, and put them in a stewpan with the above ingredients, previously kneading together the butter and flour ; boil the whole for about ten minutes, stirring all the time. Pour some of the sauce over the fowls, and the remainder serve in a tureen. *Time.* —10 minutes. *Average cost,* 2s. *Sufficient* to serve with a pair of fowls. *Seasonable* from August to October.

MUSHROOM SAUCE, Brown, to serve with Roast Meat, &c.

Ingredients.—½ pint of button mushrooms, ½ pint of good beef gravy, 1 tablespoonful of mushroom ketchup (if at hand), thickening of butter and flour. *Mode.*—Put the gravy into a saucepan, thicken it, and stir over the fire until it boils. Prepare the mushrooms by cutting off the stalks, and wiping them free from grit and dirt ; the large flap mushrooms cut into small pieces will answer for a brown sauce, when the buttons are not obtainable ; put them into the gravy, and let them simmer very gently for about 10 minutes ; then add the ketchup, and serve. *Time.*—Rather more than 10 minutes. *Seasonable* from August to October.

Note.—When fresh mushrooms are not obtainable, the powder may be used as a substitute for brown sauce.

MUSHROOM SAUCE, White, to serve with Boiled Fowls, Cutlets, &c.

Ingredients.—Rather more than ½ pint of button mushrooms, lemon-juice, and water, 1 oz. of butter, ½ pint of Béchamel, ¼ teaspoonful of pounded sugar. *Mode.* —Turn the mushrooms white by putting them into lemon-juice and water, having previously cut off the stalks and wiped them perfectly free from grit. Chop them, and put them in a stewpan with the butter. When the mushrooms are softened, add the Béchamel, and simmer for about 5 minutes ; should they, however, not be done enough, allow rather more time. They should not boil longer than necessary, as they would then lose their colour and flavour. Rub the whole through a tammy, and serve very hot. After this, it should be warmed in a bain marie. *Time.* — Altogether ¼ hour. *Average cost,* 1s. *Seasonable* from August to October.

MUSHROOM SAUCE, White, to serve with Boiled Fowls, Cutlets, &c. (a more simple Method).

Ingredients.—½ pint of melted butter, made with milk, ½ pint of button mushrooms, 1 dessertspoonful of mushroom ketchup, if at hand ; cayenne and salt to taste. *Mode.*—Make the melted butter with milk, and add to it the mushrooms,

/

Mushrooms, Baked

which must be nicely cleaned, and free from grit, and the stalks cut off. Let them simmer gently for about 10 minutes, or until they are quite tender. Put in the seasoning and ketchup ; let it just boil, when serve. *Time.*—Rather more than 10 minutes. *Average cost, 8d. Seasonable* from August to October.

MUSHROOMS, Baked (a Breakfast, Luncheon, or Supper Dish).

Ingredients. — 16 to 20 mushroom-flaps, butter, pepper to taste. *Mode.*— For this mode of cooking, the mushroom-flaps are better than the buttons, and should not be too large. Cut off a portion of the stalk, peel the top, and wipe the mushrooms carefully with a piece of flannel and a little fine salt. Put them into a tin baking-dish, with a very small piece of butter placed on each mushroom ; sprinkle over a little pepper, and let them bake for about 20 minutes, or longer should the mushrooms be very large. Have ready a *very hot* dish, pile the mushrooms high in the centre, pour the gravy round, and send them to table quickly, with very *hot* plates. *Time.*— 20 minutes ; large mushrooms, ½ hour. *Average cost,* 1d. each for large mushroom-flaps. *Sufficient* for 5 or 6 persons. *Seasonable.* — Meadow mushrooms in September and October ; cultivated mushrooms may be had at any time.

MUSHROOMS, Broiled (a Breakfast, Luncheon, or Supper Dish).

Ingredients.—Mushroom-flaps, pepper and salt to taste, butter, lemon-juice. *Mode.* — Cleanse the mushrooms by wiping them with a piece of flannel and a little salt; cut off a portion of the stalk, and peel the tops ;

BROILED MUSHROOMS.

broil them over a clear fire, turning them once, and arrange them on a very hot dish. Put a small piece of butter on each mushroom, season with pepper and salt, and squeeze over them a few drops of lemon-juice. Place the dish before the fire, and when the butter is melted, serve very hot and quickly. Moderate-sized flaps are better suited to this mode of cooking than the buttons : the latter are better in stews. *Time.*— 10 minutes for medium-sized mushrooms.

Mushrooms, to Preserve.

Average cost, 1d. each for large mushrooms. *Sufficient.*—Allow 3 or 4 mushrooms to each person. *Seasonable.*— Meadow mushrooms in September and October ; cultivated mushrooms may be had at any time.

MUSHROOMS, Dried.

Mode.—Wipe them clean, take away the brown part, and peel off the skin ; lay them on sheets of paper to dry, in a cool oven, when they will shrivel considerably. Keep them in paper bags, which hang in a dry place. When wanted for use, put them into cold gravy, bring them gradually to simmer, and it will be found that they will regain nearly their usual size.

MUSHROOMS, Pickled.

Ingredients. — Sufficient vinegar to cover the mushrooms ; to each quart of mushrooms, 2 blades of pounded mace, 1 oz. of ground pepper, salt to taste. *Mode.*—Choose some nice young button mushrooms for pickling, and rub off the skin with a piece of flannel and salt, and cut off the stalks ; if very large, take out the red inside, and reject the black ones, as they are too old. Put them into a stew-pan, sprinkle salt over them, with pounded mace and pepper in the above proportion ; shake them well over a clear fire until the liquor flows, and keep them there until they are all dried up again ; then add as much vinegar as will cover them ; just let it simmer for 1 minute, and store it away in stone jars for use. When cold, tie down with bladder and keep in a dry place : they will remain good for a length of time, and are generally considered delicious. *Seasonable.*— Make this the same time as ketchup, from the beginning of September to the middle of October.

MUSHROOMS, to Preserve.

Ingredients.—To each quart of mushrooms, allow 3 oz. butter, pepper and salt to taste, the juice of 1 lemon, clarified butter. *Mode.*—Peel the mushrooms, put them into cold water, with a little lemon-juice ; take them out and *dry* them very carefully in a cloth. Put the butter into a stewpan capable of holding the mushrooms ; when it is melted, add the mushrooms, lemon-juice, and a seasoning of pepper and salt ; draw them down over a slow fire, and let them remain until their liquor is

Mushrooms, Stewed

boiled away, and they have become quite dry, but be careful in not allowing them to stick to the bottom of the stewpan. When done, put them into pots, and pour over the top clarified butter. If wanted for immediate use, they will keep good a few days without being covered over. To re-warm them, put the mushrooms into a stewpan, strain the butter from them, and they will be ready for use. *Average cost, 1d.* each. *Seasonable.*—Meadow mushrooms in September and October; cultivated mushrooms may be had at any time.

MUSHROOMS, Stewed.

Ingredients.—1 pint mushroom-buttons, 3 oz. of fresh butter, white pepper and salt to taste, lemon-juice, 1 teaspoonful of flour, cream or milk, ¼ teaspoonful of grated nutmeg. *Mode.*—Cut off the ends of the stalks, and pare neatly a pint of mushroom-buttons; put them into a basin of water, with a little lemon juice, as they are done. When all are prepared, take them from the water with the hands, to avoid the sediment, and put them into a stewpan with the fresh butter, white pepper, salt, and the juice of ½ lemon; cover the pan closely, and let the mushrooms stew gently from 20 to 25 minutes; then thicken the butter with the above proportion of flour, add gradually sufficient cream, or cream and milk, to make the sauce of a proper consistency, and put in the grated nutmeg. If the mushrooms are not perfectly tender, stew them for 5 minutes longer, remove every particle of butter which may be floating on the top, and serve. *Time.*—½ hour. *Average cost*, from 9d. to 2s. per pint. *Sufficient* for 5 or 6 persons. *Seasonable.*—Meadow mushrooms in September and October.

MUSHROOMS, Stewed in Gravy.

Ingredients.—1 pint of mushroom-buttons, 1 pint of brown gravy, ¼ teaspoonful of grated nutmeg, cayenne and salt to taste. *Mode.*—Make a pint of brown gravy, cut nearly all the stalks away from the mushrooms and peel the tops; put them into a stewpan, with the gravy, and simmer them gently from 20 minutes to ½ hour. Add the nutmeg and a seasoning of cayenne and salt, and serve very hot. *Time.*—20 minutes to ½ hour. *Average cost*, 9d. to 2s. per pint. *Sufficient* for 5

Mustard, Tartar

or 6 persons. *Seasonable.*—Meadow mushrooms in September and October.

MUSTARD, How to Mix.

Ingredients.—Mustard, salt and water. *Mode.*—Mustard should be mixed with water that has been boiled and allowed to cool; hot water destroys its essential properties, and raw cold water might cause it to ferment. Put the mustard into a cup, with a small pinch of salt, and mix with it very gradually sufficient boiled water to make it drop from the spoon without being watery. Stir and mix well, and rub the lumps well down with the back of a spoon, as well-mixed mustard should be perfectly free from these. The mustard-pot should not be more than half-full, or rather less if it will not be used for a day or two, as it is so much better when it is freshly mixed.

MUSTARD, Indian, an excellent Relish to Bread and Butter, or any cold Meat.

Ingredients.—¼ lb. of the best mustard, ¼ lb. of flour, ½ oz. of salt, 4 shalots, 4 tablespoonfuls of vinegar, 4 tablespoonfuls of ketchup, ¼ bottle of anchovy sauce. *Mode.*—Put the mustard, flour, and salt into a basin, and make them into a stiff paste with boiling water. Boil the shalots with the vinegar, ketchup, and anchovy sauce, for 10 minutes, and pour the whole, *boiling*, over the mixture in the basin; stir well, and reduce it to a proper thickness; put it into a bottle, with a bruised shalot at the bottom, and store away for use. This makes an excellent relish, and if properly prepared will keep for years.

MUSTARD, Tartar.

Ingredients.—Horseradish vinegar, cayenne, ½ a teacupful of mustard. *Mode.*—Have ready sufficient horseradish vinegar to mix with the above proportion of mustard; put the mustard into a cup, with a slight seasoning of cayenne; mix it perfectly smooth with the vinegar, adding this a little at a time; rub down with the back of a spoon any lumps that may appear, and do not let it be too thin. Mustard may be flavoured in various ways, with Tarragon, shalot, celery, and many other vinegars, herbs, spices, &c.

| Mutton | Mutton, to cook a Breast of |

MUTTON.

Almost every large city has a particular manner of cutting up, or, as it is called, dressing the carcase. In London this process is very simple, and as our butchers have found that much skewering back, doubling one part over another, or scoring the inner cuticle or fell, tends to spoil the meat and shorten the time it would otherwise keep, they avoid all such treatment entirely. The carcase when flayed (which operation is performed while yet warm), the sheep when

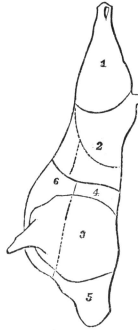

hung up and the head removed, presents the profile shown in our cut; the small numerals indicating the parts or joints into which one-half of the animal is cut. After separating the hind from the fore quarters, with eleven ribs to the latter, the quarters are usually subdivided in the manner shown in the sketch, in which the several joints are defined by the intervening lines and figures. *Hind quarter:* No. 1, the leg; 2, the loin—the two, when cut in one piece, being called the saddle. *Fore quarter:* No. 3, the shoulder; 4 and 5 the neck; No. 5 being called, for distinction, the scrag, which is generally afterwards separated from 4, the lower and better joint; No. 6, the breast. The haunch of mutton, so often served at public dinners and special entertainments, comprises all the leg and so much of the loin, short of the

SIDE OF MUTTON, SHOWING THE SEVERAL JOINTS.

ribs or lap, as is indicated on the upper part of the carcase by a dotted line.

MUTTON, Baked Minced.

[COLD MEAT COOKERY.] *Ingredients.*—The remains of any joint of cold roast mutton, 1 or 2 onions, 1 bunch of savoury herbs, pepper and salt to taste, 2 blades of pounded mace or nutmeg, 1 teacupful of gravy, mashed potatoes. *Mode.*—Mince an onion rather fine, and fry it a light-brown colour; add the herbs and mutton, both of which should be also finely minced and well mixed; season with pepper and salt, and a little pounded mace or nutmeg, and moisten with the above proportion of gravy. Put a layer of mashed potatoes at the bottom of a dish, then the mutton, and then another layer of potatoes, and bake for about ½ hour. *Time.*—½ hour. *Average cost,* exclusive of the meat, 4d. *Seasonable* at any time.

Note.—If there should be a large quantity of meat, use 2 onions instead of 1.

MUTTON, Boiled Breast of, and Caper Sauce.

Ingredients.—Breast of mutton, bread crumbs, 2 tablespoonfuls of minced savoury herbs (put a large proportion of parsley), pepper and salt to taste. *Mode.*—Cut off the superfluous fat; bone the meat; sprinkle over a layer of bread crumbs, minced herbs, and seasoning; roll, and bind it up firmly. Boil *gently* for 2 hours, remove the tape, and serve with caper sauce, a little of which should be poured over the meat. *Time.*—2 hours. *Average cost,* 6d. per lb. *Sufficient* for 4 or 5 persons. *Seasonable* all the year.

MUTTON, an excellent way to cook a Breast of.

Ingredients. — Breast of mutton, 2 onions, salt and pepper to taste, flour, a bunch of savoury herbs, green peas. *Mode.*—Cut the mutton into pieces about 2 inches square, and let it be tolerably lean; put it into a stewpan, with a little fat or butter, and fry it of a nice brown; then dredge in a little flour, slice the onions, and put it with the herbs in the stewpan; pour in sufficient water *just* to cover the meat, and simmer the whole gently until the mutton is tender. Take out the meat, strain, and skim off all the fat from the gravy, and

Mutton, Broiled, and Tomato Sauce

put both the meat and gravy back into the stewpan ; add about a quart of young green peas, and let them boil gently until done. 2 or 3 slices of bacon added and stewed with the mutton give additional flavour ; and, to insure the peas being a beautiful green colour, they may be boiled in water separately, and added to the stew at the moment of serving. *Time.*—2½ hours. *Average cost,* 6*d.* per lb. *Sufficient* for 4 or 5 persons. *Seasonable* from June to August.

MUTTON, Broiled, and Tomato Sauce.

[COLD MEAT COOKERY.] *Ingredients.*— A few slices of cold mutton, tomato sauce. *Mode.* — Cut some nice slices from a cold leg or shoulder of mutton; season them with pepper and salt, and broil over a clear fire. Make some tomato sauce, pour it over the mutton, and serve. This makes an excellent dish, and must be served very hot. *Time.*—About 5 minutes to broil the mutton. *Seasonable* in September and October, when tomatoes are plentiful and seasonable.

MUTTON BROTH, to Make.

Ingredients.—1 lb. of the scrag end of the neck of mutton, 1 onion, a bunch of sweet herbs, ½ turnip, 3 pints of water, pepper and salt to taste. *Mode.*—Put the mutton into a stewpan ; pour over the water cold, and add the other ingredients. When it boils, skim it very carefully, cover the pan closely, and let it simmer very gently for an hour ; strain it, let it cool, take off all the fat from the surface, and warm up as much as may be required, adding, if the patient be allowed to take it, a teaspoonful of minced parsley which has been previously scalded. Pearl barley or rice are very nice additions to mutton broth, and should be boiled as long as the other ingredients. When either of these is added, the broth must not be strained, but merely thoroughly skimmed. Plain mutton broth without seasoning is made by merely boiling the mutton, water, and salt together, straining it, letting the broth cool, skimming all the fat off, and warming up as much as is required. This preparation would be very tasteless and insipid, but likely to agree with very delicate stomachs, whereas the least addition of other ingredients would have

Mutton, Leg of, to Carve

the contrary effect. *Time.*—1 hour. *Average cost,* 7*d.* *Sufficient* to make from 1½ to 2 pints of broth. *Seasonable* at any time.

Note.—Veal broth may be made in the same manner ; the knuckle of a leg or shoulder is the part usually used for this purpose. It is very good with the addition of the inferior joints of a fowl, or a few shank-bones.

MUTTON BROTH, to Make Quickly.

Ingredients.—1 or 2 chops from a neck of mutton, 1 pint of water, a small bunch of sweet herbs, ¼ of an onion, pepper and salt to taste. *Mode.*—Cut the meat into small pieces ; put it into a saucepan with the bones, but no skin or fat ; add the other ingredients ; cover the saucepan, and bring the water quickly to boil. Take the lid off, and continue the rapid boiling for 20 minutes, skimming it well during the process ; strain the broth into a basin ; if there should be any fat left on the surface, remove it by laying a piece of thin paper on the top ; the greasy particles will adhere to the paper, and so free the preparation from them. To an invalid nothing is more disagreeable than broth served with a quantity of fat floating on the top ; to avoid this, it is always better to allow it to get thoroughly cool, the fat can then be so easily removed. *Time.*—20 minutes after the water boils. *Average cost,* 5*d.* *Sufficient* to make ½ pint of broth. *Seasonable* at any time.

MUTTON, Haunch of, to Carve.

A deep cut should, in the first place, be made quite down to the bone, across the knuckle-end of the joint, along the line 1 to 2. This will let the gravy escape ; and then it should be carved, in not too thick slices, along the whole

HAUNCH OF MUTTON.

length of the haunch, in the direction of the line from 4 to 3.

MUTTON, Leg of, to Carve.

This homely, but capital English joint, is almost invariably served at table as

Mutton, Loin of, to Carve

shown in the engraving. The carving of it is not very difficult: the knife should e carried sharply down in the direction of the line from 1 to 2, and slices taken from either side, as the guests may desire, some liking the knuckle-end, as well done, and others preferring the more underdone part. The

LEG OF MUTTON.

fat should be sought near the line 3 to 4. Some connoisseurs are fond of having this joint dished with the under-side uppermost, so as to get at the finely-grained meat lying under that part of the joint, known as the Pope's eye; but this is an extravagant fashion, and one that will hardly find favour in the eyes of many economical British housewives and housekeepers.

MUTTON, Loin of, to Carve.

There is one point in connection with carving a loin of mutton which includes every other; that is, that the joint should be thoroughly well jointed by the butcher before it is cooked. This knack of jointing requires practice and the proper tools; and no one but the butcher is supposed to have these. If the bones are not well jointed, the carving of a loin of mutton is not a gracious business; whereas, if that has been attended to, it is an easy and untroublesome task. The knife should be inserted at fig. 1, and after feeling your way between the bones, it should be carried sharply in the direction of the line 1 to 2. As there are some people who prefer the outside cut, while others do not like it, the question as to their choice of this should be asked.

LOIN OF MUTTON.

MUTTON, Saddle of, to Carve.

Although we have heard, at various intervals, growlings expressed at the inevitable "saddle of mutton" at the dinner-parties of our middle classes, yet we doubt whether any other joint is better liked, when it has been well hung

Mutton Chops, Broiled

and artistically cooked. There is a diversity of opinion respecting the mode of sending this joint to table; but it has only reference to whether or no there shall be any portion of the tail, or, if so, how many joints of the tail. Some trim the tail

SADDLE OF MUTTON.

with a paper frill. The carving is not difficult: it is usually cut in the direction of the line from 2 to 1, quite down to the bones, in evenly-sliced pieces. A fashion, however, patronized by some, is to carve it obliquely, in the direction of the line from 4 to 3; in which case the joint would be turned round the other way, having the tail end on the right of the carver.

MUTTON, Shoulder of, to Carve.

This is a joint not difficult to carve. The knife should be drawn from the outer edge of the shoulder in the direction of the line from 1 to 2, until the bone of the shoulder is reached. As many slices as can be carved in this manner should be taken, and afterwards the

SHOULDER OF MUTTON.

meat lying on each side of the blade-bone should be served, by carving in the direction of 3 to 4 and 3 to 4. The uppermost side of the shoulder being now finished, the joint should be turned, and slices taken off along its whole length. There are some who prefer this under-side of the shoulder for its juicy flesh, although the grain of the meat is not so fine as that on the other side.

MUTTON CHOPS, Broiled.

Ingredients.—Loin of mutton, pepper and salt, a small piece of butter. *Mode.* —Cut the chops from a well-hung tender loin of mutton, remove a portion of the fat, and trim them into a nice shape; slightly beat and level them; place the gridiron over a bright clear fire, rub the bars with a little fat, and lay on the chops. Whilst broiling, frequently turn

| Mutton-Collops | Mutton, Haricot |

them, and in about 8 minutes they will be done. Season with pepper and salt, dish them on a very hot dish, rub a small piece of butter on each chop, and serve very hot and expeditiously. *Time.—* About 8 minutes. *Average cost,* 10*d.* per lb. *Sufficient.*—Allow 1 chop to each person. *Seasonable* at any time.

MUTTON-COLLOPS.

Ingredients.—A few slices of a cold leg or loin of mutton, salt and pepper to taste, 1 blade of pounded mace, 1 small bunch of savoury herbs minced very fine, 2 or 3 shalots, 2 or 3 oz. of butter, 1 dessertspoonful of flour, ½ pint of gravy, 1 tablespoonful of lemon-juice. *Mode.*—Cut some very thin slices from a leg or the chump end of a loin of mutton; sprinkle them with pepper, salt, pounded mace, minced savoury herbs, and minced shalot; fry them in butter, stir in a dessertspoonful of flour, add the gravy and lemon-juice, simmer very gently about 5 or 7 minutes, and serve immediately. *Time.*—5 to 7 minutes. *Average cost,* exclusive of the meat, 6*d.* *Seasonable* at any time.

MUTTON. Curried.

[COLD MEAT COOKERY.] *Ingredients.* —The remains of any joint of cold mutton, 2 onions, ¼ lb. of butter, 1 dessertspoonful of curry-powder, 1 dessertspoonful of flour, salt to taste, ¼ pint of stock or water. *Mode.*—Slice the onions in thin rings, and put them into a stewpan with the butter, and fry of a light brown; stir in the curry-powder, flour, and salt, and mix all together. Cut the meat into nice thin slices (if there is not sufficient to do this, it may be minced), and add it to the other ingredients; when well browned, add the stock or gravy, and stew gently for about ½ hour. Serve in a dish with a border of boiled rice, the same as for other curries. *Time.* —½ hour. *Average cost,* exclusive of the meat, 6*d.* *Seasonable* in winter.

MUTTON CUTLETS, with Mashed Potatoes.

Ingredients.—About 3 lbs. of the best end of the neck of mutton, salt and pepper to taste, mashed potatoes. *Mode.*—Procure a well-hung neck of mutton, saw off about 3 inches of the top of the bones, and cut the cutlets of a moderate thick-

ness. Shape them by chopping off the thick part of the chine-bone; beat them flat with a cutlet-chopper, and scrape quite clean, a portion of the top of the

MUTTON CUTLETS.

bone. Broil them over a nice clear fire for about 7 or 8 minutes, and turn them frequently. Have ready some smoothly-mashed white potatoes; place these in the middle of the dish; when the cutlets are done, season with pepper and salt; arrange them round the potatoes, with the thick end of the cutlets downwards, and serve very hot and quickly. *Time.*—7 or 8 minutes. *Average cost,* for this quantity, 2*s.* 4*d.* *Sufficient* for 5 or 6 persons. *Seasonable* at any time.

Note.—Cutlets may be served in various ways: with peas, tomatoes, onions, sauce piquant, &c.

MUTTON, Braised Fillet of, with French Beans.

Ingredients.—The chump end of a loin of mutton, buttered paper, French beans, a little glaze, 1 pint of gravy. *Mode.*—Roll up the mutton in a piece of buttered paper, roast it for 2 hours, and do not allow it to acquire the least colour. Have ready some French beans, boiled, and drained on a sieve; remove the paper from the mutton, glaze it; just heat up the beans in the gravy, and lay them on the dish with the meat over them. The remainder of the gravy may be strained, and sent to table in a tureen. *Time.*— 2 hours. *Average cost,* 8½*d.* per lb. *Sufficient* for 4 or 5 persons. *Seasonable* at any time.

MUTTON, Haricot.

Ingredients.—4 lbs. of the middle or best end of the neck of mutton, 3 carrots, 3 turnips, 3 onions, pepper and salt to taste, 1 tablespoonful of ketchup or Harvey's sauce. *Mode.*—Trim off some of the fat, cut the mutton into rather thin chops, and put them into a frying-pan with the fat trimmings. Fry of a pale brown, but do not cook them enough for eating. Cut the carrots and

Mutton, Haricot

turnips into dice, and the onions into slices, and slightly fry them in the same fat that the mutton was browned in, but do not allow them to take any colour. Now lay the mutton at the bottom of a stewpan, then the vegetables, and pour over them just sufficient boiling water to cover the whole. Give the boil, skim well, and then set the pan on the side of the fire to simmer gently until the meat is tender. Skim off every particle of fat, add a seasoning of pepper and salt, and a little ketchup, and serve. This dish is very much better if made the day before it is wanted for table, as the fat can be so much more easily removed when the gravy is cold. This should be particularly attended to, as it is apt to be rich and greasy if eaten the same day it is made. It should be served in rather a deep dish. *Time.*—2½ hours to simmer gently. *Average cost,* for this quantity, 3s. *Sufficient* for 6 or 7 persons. *Seasonable* at any time.

MUTTON, Haricot.

Ingredients.—Breast or scrag of mutton, flour, pepper, and salt to taste, 1 large onion, 3 cloves, a bunch of savoury herbs, 1 blade of mace, carrots and turnips, sugar. *Mode.*—Cut the mutton into square pieces, and fry them a nice colour; then dredge over them a little flour and a seasoning of pepper and salt. Put all into a stewpan, and moisten with boiling water, adding the onion, stuck with 3 cloves, the mace, and herbs. Simmer gently till the meat is done, skim off all the fat, and then add the carrots and turnips, which should be previously cut in dice and fried in a little sugar to colour them. Let the whole simmer again for 10 minutes ; take out the onion and bunch of herbs, and serve. *Time.*— About 3 hours to simmer. *Average cost,* 6d. per lb. *Sufficient* for 4 or 5 persons. *Seasonable* at any time.

MUTTON, Haricot.

[COLD MEAT COOKERY.] *Ingredients.* —The remains of cold neck or loin of mutton, 2 oz. of butter, 3 onions, 1 dessertspoonful of flour, ½ pint of good gravy, pepper and salt to taste, 2 tablespoonfuls of port wine, 1 tablespoonful of mushroom ketchup, 2 carrots, 2 turnips, 1 head of celery. *Mode.*—Cut the cold mutton into moderate-sized chops, and

Mutton, Roast Haunch o.

take off the fat; slice the onions, and fry them with the chops, in a little butter, of a nice brown colour ; stir in the flour, add the gravy, and let it stew gently nearly an hour. In the mean time boil the vegetables until *nearly* tender, slice them, and add them to the mutton about ¼ hour before it is to be served. Season with pepper and salt, add the ketchup and port wine, give one boil, and serve. *Time.*—1 hour. *Average cost,* exclusive of the cold meat, 6d. *Seasonable* at any time.

MUTTON, Hashed.

Ingredients.—The remains of cold roast shoulder or leg of mutton, 6 whole peppers, 6 whole allspice, a faggot of savoury herbs, ½ head of celery, 1 onion, 2 oz. of butter, flour. *Mode.*—Cut the meat in nice even slices from the bones, trimming off all superfluous fat and gristle; chop the bones and fragments of the joints, put them into a stewpan with the pepper, spice, herbs, and celery ; cover with water, and simmer for 1 hour. Slice and fry the onion of a nice pale-brown colour, dredge in a little flour to make it thick, and add this to the bones, &c. Stew for ¼ hour, strain the gravy, and let it cool ; then skim off every particle of fat, and put it, with the meat, into a stewpan. Flavour with ketchup, Harvey's sauce, tomato sauce, or any flavouring that may be preferred, and let the meat gradually warm through, but not boil, or it will harden. To hash meat properly, it should be laid in cold gravy, and only left on the fire just long enough to warm through. *Time.*—1½ hour to simmer the gravy. *Average cost,* exclusive of the meat, 4d. *Seasonable* at any time.

MUTTON, Roast Haunch of.

Ingredients. — Haunch of mutton, a little salt, flour. *Mode.*—Let this joint hang as long as possible without becom-

HAUNCH OF MUTTON.

ing tainted, and while hanging dust flour over it, which keeps off the flies, and prevents the air from getting to it. If

Mutton, Boiled Leg of

not well hung, the joint, when it comes to table, will do credit neither to the butcher nor the cook, as it will not be tender. Wash the outside well, lest it should have a bad flavour from keeping; then flour it and put it down to a nice brisk fire, at some distance, so that it may gradually warm through. Keep continually basting, and about ½ hour before it is served, draw it nearer to the fire to get nicely brown. Sprinkle a little fine salt over the meat, pour off the dripping, add a little boiling water slightly salted, and strain this over the joint. Place a paper ruche on the bone, and send red-currant jelly and gravy in a tureen to table with it. *Time.*—About 4 hours. *Average cost*, 10d. per lb. *Sufficient* for 8 to 10 persons. *Seasonable.*—In best season from September to March.

MUTTON, Boiled Leg of.

Ingredients. — Mutton, water, salt. *Mode.*—A leg of mutton for boiling should not hang too long, as it will not look a good colour when dressed. Cut off the shank-bone, trim the knuckle, and wash and wipe it very clean; plunge it into sufficient boiling water to cover it; let it boil up, then draw the saucepan to the side of the fire, where it should remain till the finger can be borne in the water. Then place it sufficiently near the fire, that the water may gently simmer, and be very careful that it does not boil fast, or the meat will be hard. Skim well, add a little salt, and in about 2¼ hours after the water begins to simmer, a moderate-sized leg of mutton will be done. Serve with carrots and mashed turnips, which may be boiled with the meat, and send caper sauce to table with it in a tureen. *Time.*—A moderate-sized leg of mutton of 9 lbs., 2½ hours after the water boils; one of 12 lbs., 3 hours. *Average cost*, 8½d. per lb. *Sufficient.*—A moderate-sized leg of mutton for 6 or 8 persons. *Seasonable* nearly all the year, but not so good in June, July, and August.

Note.—When meat is liked very *thoroughly* cooked, allow more time than stated above. The liquor this joint was boiled in should be converted into soup.

MUTTON. Boned Leg of, Stuffed.

Ingredients. — A small leg of mutton, weighing 6 or 7 lbs., forcemeat, 2 shalots

Mutton, Roast Leg of

finely minced. *Mode.*—Make a forcemeat, to which add 2 finely-minced shalots. Bone the leg of mutton, without spoiling the skin, and cut off a great deal of the fat. Fill the hole up whence the bone was taken with the forcemeat, and sew it up underneath, to prevent it falling out. Bind and tie it up compactly, and roast it before a nice clear fire for about 2½ hours or rather longer, remove the tape and send it to table with a good gravy. It may be glazed or not, as preferred. *Time.*—2½ hours, or rather longer. *Average cost*, 4s. 8d. *Sufficient* for 6 or 7 persons. *Seasonable* at any time.

MUTTON, Braised Leg of.

Ingredients.—1 small leg of mutton, carrots, 3 onions, 1 faggot of savory herbs, a bunch of parsley, seasoning to taste of pepper and salt, a few slices of bacon, a few veal trimmings, ½ pint of gravy or water. *Mode.*—Line the bottom of a braising-pan with a few slices of bacon, put in the carrots, onions, herbs, parsley, and seasoning, and on these place the mutton. Cover the whole with a few more slices of bacon and the veal trimmings, pour in the gravy or water, and stew very *gently* 4 hours. Strain the gravy, reduce it to a glaze over a sharp fire, glaze the mutton with it, and send it to table, placed on a dish of white haricot beans boiled tender, or garnished with glazed onions. *Time.*—4 hours. *Average cost*, 5s. *Sufficient* for 6 or 7 persons. *Seasonable* any time.

MUTTON, Roast Leg of.

Ingredients.—Leg of mutton, a little salt. *Mode.*—As mutton, when fresh killed, is never tender, hang it almost

LEG OF MUTTON.

long as it will keep; flour it, and put in a cool airy place for a few days, if weather will permit. Wash off flour, wipe it very dry, and cut off

Mutton, Roast Loin of

shank-bone ; put it down to a brisk clear fire, dredge with flour, and keep continually basting the whole time it is cooking. About 20 minutes before serving, draw it near the fire to get nicely brown ; sprinkle over it a little salt, dish the meat, pour off the dripping, add some boiling water slightly salted, strain it over the joint, and serve. *Time.* —A leg of mutton weighing 10 lbs., about 2¼ or 2½ hours ; one of 7 lbs., about 2 hours, or rather less. *Average cost*, 8½d. per lb. *Sufficient.*—A moderate-sized leg of mutton sufficient for 6 or 8 persons. *Seasonable* at any time, but not so good in June, July, and August.

MUTTON, Roast Loin of.

Ingredients.—Loin of mutton, a little salt. *Mode.*—Cut and trim off the superfluous fat, and see that the butcher joints

LOIN OF MUTTON.

the meat properly, as thereby much annoyance is saved to the carver, when it comes to table. Have ready a nice clear fire (it need not be a very wide large one), put down the meat, dredge with flour, and baste well until it is done. Make the gravy as for roast leg of mutton, and serve very hot. *Time.*—A loin of mutton weighing 6 lbs., 1½ hour, or rather longer. *Average cost*, 8½d. per lb. *Sufficient* for 4 or 5 persons. *Seasonable* at any time.

MUTTON, Rolled Loin of (very Excellent).

Ingredients.—About 6 lbs. of a loin of mutton, ½ teaspoonful of pepper, ¼ teaspoonful of pounded allspice, ¼ teaspoonful of mace, ¼ teaspoonful of nutmeg, 6 cloves, forcemeat, 1 glass of port wine, 2 tablespoonfuls of mushroom ketchup. *Mode.*—Hang the mutton till tender, bone it, and sprinkle over it pepper, mace, cloves, allspice, and nutmeg in the above proportion, all of which must be pounded very fine. Let it remain for a day, then make a forcemeat, cover the

Mutton, Ragout of cold Neck of

meat with it, and roll and bind it up firmly. Half bake it in a slow oven, let it grow cold, take off the fat, and put the gravy into a stewpan ; flour the meat, put it in the gravy, and stew it till perfectly tender. Now take out the meat, unbind it, add to the gravy wine and ketchup as above, give one boil, and pour over the meat. Serve with red-currant jelly ; and, if obtainable, a few mushrooms stewed for a few minutes in the gravy, will be found a great improvement. *Time.*—1½ hour to bake the meat, 1½ hour to stew gently. *Average cost*, 4s. 9d. *Sufficient* for 5 or 6 persons. *Seasonable* at any time.

Note.—This joint will be found very nice if rolled and stuffed, as here directed, and plainly roasted. It should be well basted, and served with a good gravy and currant jelly.

MUTTON, Boiled Neck of.

Ingredients.—4 lbs. of the middle, or best end of the neck of mutton ; a little salt. *Mode.*—Trim off a portion of the fat, should there be too much, and if it is to look particularly nice, the chine-bone should be sawn down, the ribs stripped half-way down, and the ends of the bones chopped off ; this is, however, not necessary. Put the meat into sufficient *boiling* water to cover it ; when it boils, add a little salt and remove all the scum. Draw the saucepan to the side of the fire, and let the water get so cool that the finger may be borne in it ; then simmer very *slowly* and gently until the meat is done, which will be in about 1½ hour, or rather more, reckoning from the time that it begins to simmer. Serve with turnips and caper sauce, and pour a little of it over the meat. The turnips should be boiled with the mutton ; and when at hand, a few carrots will also be found an improvement. These, however, if very large and thick, must be cut into long thinnish pieces, or they will not be sufficiently done by the time the mutton is ready. Garnish the dish with carrots and turnips, placed alternately round the mutton. *Time.*—4 lbs. of the neck of mutton, about 1½ hour. *Average cost*, 8½d. per lb. *Sufficient* for 6 or 7 persons. *Seasonable* at any time.

MUTTON, Ragout of Cold Neck of.

[COLD MEAT COOKERY.] *Ingredients.* —The remains of a cold neck or loin of

Mutton, Roast Neck of

mutton, 2 oz. of butter, a little flour, 2 onions sliced, ½ pint of water, 2 small carrots, 2 turnips, pepper and salt to taste. *Mode.*—Cut the mutton into small chops, and trim off the greater portion of the fat; put the butter into a stewpan, dredge in a little flour, add the sliced onions, and keep stirring till brown; then put in the meat. When this is quite brown, add the water, and the carrots and turnips, which should be cut into very thin slices; season with pepper and salt, and stew till quite tender, which will be in about ¾ hour. When in season, green peas may be substituted for the carrots and turnips: they should be piled in the centre of the dish, and the chops laid round. *Time.*—¾ hour. *Average cost,* exclusive of the meat, 4*d.* *Seasonable,* with peas, from June to August.

MUTTON, Roast Neck of.

Ingredients.—Neck of mutton; a little salt. *Mode.*—For roasting, choose the middle, or the best end, of the neck of mutton, and if there is a very large proportion of fat, trim off some of it, and

NECK OF MUTTON.
1—2. *Best end.*   2—3. *Scrag.*

save it for making into suet puddings, which will be found exceedingly good. Let the bones be cut short, and see that it is properly jointed before it is laid down to the fire, as they will be more easily separated when they come to table. Place the joint at a nice brisk fire, dredge it with flour, and keep continually basting until done. A few minutes before serving, draw it nearer the fire to acquire a nice colour, sprinkle over it a little salt, pour off the dripping, add a little boiling water slightly salted; strain this over the meat and serve. Red-currant jelly may be sent to table with it. *Time.* —4 lbs. of the neck of mutton, rather more than 1 hour. *Average cost,* 8½*d.* per lb. *Sufficient* for 4 or 5 persons. *Seasonable* at any time.

Mutton Pudding

MUTTON PIE.

[COLD MEAT COOKERY.] *Ingredients.* —The remains of a cold leg, loin, or neck of mutton, pepper and salt to taste 2 blades of pounded mace, 1 dessertspoonful of chopped parsley, 1 teaspoonful of minced savoury herbs; when liked, a little minced onion or shalot; 3 or 4 potatoes, 1 teacupful of gravy; crust. *Mode.*—Cold mutton may be made into very good pies if well seasoned and mixed with a few herbs; if the leg is used, cut it into very thin slices; if the loin or neck, into thin cutlets. Place some at the bottom of the dish; season well with pepper, salt, mace, parsley, and herbs; then put a layer of potatoes sliced, then more mutton, and so on till the dish is full; add the gravy, cover with a crust, and bake for 1 hour. *Time.*—1 hour. *Seasonable* at any time.

Note.—The remains of an underdone leg of mutton may be converted into a very good family pudding, by cutting the meat into slices, and putting them into a basin lined with a suet crust. It should be seasoned well with pepper, salt, and minced shalot, covered with a crust, and boiled for about three hours.

MUTTON PIE.

Ingredients.—2 lbs. of the neck or loin of mutton, weighed after being boned; 2 kidneys, pepper and salt to taste, 2 teacupfuls of gravy or water, 2 tablespoonfuls of minced parsley; when liked, a little minced onion or shalot; puff crust. *Mode.*—Bone the mutton, and cut the meat into steaks all of the same thickness, and leave but very little fat. Cut up the kidneys, and arrange these with the meat neatly in a pie-dish; sprinkle over them the minced parsley and a seasoning of pepper and salt; pour in the gravy, and cover with a tolerably good puff crust. Bake for 1½ hour, or rather longer, should the pie be very large, and let the oven be rather brisk. A well-made suet crust may be used instead of puff crust, and will be found exceedingly good. *Time.*—1½ hour, or rather longer. *Average cost,* 2*s.* *Sufficient* for 5 or 6 persons. *Seasonable* at any time.

MUTTON PUDDING.

Ingredients.—About 2 lbs. of the chump end of the loin of mutton, weighed after being boned ; pepper and salt to taste, suet crust made with milk, in the proportion of 6 oz. of suet to each pound of flour ; a very small quantity of minced onion (this may be omitted when the flavour is not liked). *Mode.*—Cut the meat into rather thin slices, and season them with pepper and salt ; line the pudding-dish with crust ; lay in the meat, and nearly, but do not quite, fill it up with water ; when the flavour is liked, add a small quantity of minced onion ; cover with crust, and proceed in the same manner as directed in recipe for rump steak and kidney pudding. *Time.* —About 3 hours. *Average cost*, 1s. 9d. *Sufficient* for 6 persons. *Seasonable* all the year, but more suitable in winter.

MUTTON, Roast Saddle of.

Ingredients.—Saddle of mutton ; a little salt. *Mode.*—To insure this joint being tender, let it hang for ten days or a fortnight, if the weather permits. Cut off the tail and flaps, and trim away every

SADDLE OF MUTTON.

part that has not indisputable pretensions to be eaten, and have the skin taken off and skewered on again. Put it down to a bright, clear fire, and, when the joint has been cooking for an hour, remove the skin and dredge it with flour. It should not be placed too near the fire, as the fat should not be in the slightest degree burnt, but kept constantly basted, both before and after the skin is removed. Sprinkle some salt over the joint ; make a little gravy in the dripping-pan ; pour it over the meat, which send to table with a tureen of made gravy and red-currant jelly. *Time.* —A saddle of mutton weighing 10 lbs., 2½ hours ; 14 lbs., 3¼ hours. When liked underdone, allow rather less time. *Average cost*, 10d. per lb. *Sufficient.* — A moderate-sized saddle of 10 lbs. for 7 or 8 persons. *Seasonable* all the year ; not so good when lamb is in full season.

MUTTON, Roast Shoulder of.

Ingredients.—Shoulder of mutton ; little salt. *Mode.*—Put the joint down to a bright, clear fire ; flour it well, and keep continually basting. About ¼ hour before serving, draw it near the fire, that

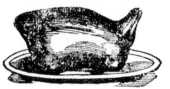

SHOULDER OF MUTTON.

the outside may acquire a nice brown colour, but not sufficiently near to blacken the fat. Sprinkle a little fine salt over the meat, empty the dripping-pan of its contents, pour in a little boiling water slightly salted, and strain this over the joint. Onion sauce, or stewed Spanish onions, are usually sent to table with this dish, and sometimes baked potatoes. *Time.*—A shoulder of mutton weighing 6 or 7 lbs., 1½ hour. *Average cost*, 8d. per lb. *Sufficient* for 5 or 6 persons. *Seasonable* at any time.

Note.—Shoulder of mutton may be dressed in a variety of ways ; boiled, and served with onion sauce ; boned, and stuffed with a good veal forcemeat ; or baked, with sliced potatoes in the dripping-pan.

MUTTON SOUP, Good.

Ingredients.—A neck of mutton about 5 or 6 lbs., 3 carrots, 3 turnips, 2 onions, a large bunch of sweet herbs, including parsley ; salt and pepper to taste ; a little sherry, if liked ; 3 quarts of water. *Mode.*—Lay the ingredients in a covered pan before the fire, and let them remain there the whole day, stirring occasionally. The next day put the whole into a stewpan, and place it on a brisk fire. When it commences to boil, take the pan off the fire, and put it on one side to simmer until the meat is done. When ready for use, take out the meat, dish it up with carrots and turnips, and send it to table ; strain the soup, let it cool, skim off all the fat, season and thicken it with a tablespoonful, or rather more, of arrowroot ; flavour with a little sherry, simmer for 5 minutes, and serve. *Time.* — 15 hours. *Average cost*, including the

Nasturtiums, Pickled

meat, 1s. 3d. per quart. *Seasonable* at any time. *Sufficient* for 8 persons.

NASTURTIUMS, Pickled (a very good Substitute for Capers).

Ingredients.—To each pint of vinegar, 1 oz. of salt, 6 peppercorns, nasturtiums. *Mode.*—Gather the nasturtium pods on a dry day, and wipe them clean with a cloth; put them in a dry glass bottle, with vinegar, salt, and pepper, in the above proportion. If you cannot find enough ripe to fill a bottle, cork up what you have got until you have some more fit; they may be added from day to day. Bung up the bottles, and seal or rosin the tops. They will be fit for use in 10 or 12 months; and the best way is to make them one season for the next. *Seasonable.*—Look for nasturtium-pods from the end of July to the end of August.

NECTARINES, Preserved.

Ingredients.— To every lb. of sugar allow ¼ pint of water; nectarines. *Mode.*—Divide the nectarines in two, take out the stones, and make a strong syrup with sugar and water in the above proportion. Put in the nectarines, and boil them until they have thoroughly imbibed the sugar. Keep the fruit as whole as possible, and turn it carefully into a pan. The next day boil it again for a few minutes, take out the nectarines, put them into jars, boil the syrup quickly for five minutes, pour it over the fruit, and, when cold, cover the preserve down. The syrup and preserve must be carefully skimmed, or it will not be clear. *Time.*—10 minutes to boil the sugar and water; 20 minutes to boil the fruit the first time, 10 minutes the second time; 5 minutes to boil the syrup. *Seasonable* in August and September, but cheapest in September.

NECTAR, Welsh.

Ingredients.—1 lb. of raisins, 3 lemons, 2 lbs. of loaf sugar, 2 gallons of boiling water. *Mode.* — Cut the peel of the lemons very thin, pour upon it the boiling water, and, when cool, add the strained juice of the lemons, the sugar, and the raisins, stoned and chopped very fine. Let it stand 4 or 5 days, stirring it every day, then strain it through a

November—Bills of Fare

jelly-bag, and bottle it for present use. *Time.*—4 or 5 days. *Average cost,* 1s. 9d. Sufficient to make 2 gallons.

NEGUS, to make.

Ingredients. — To every pint of port wine allow 1 quart of boiling water, ¼ lb. of sugar, 1 lemon, grated nutmeg to taste. *Mode.*—As this beverage is more usually drunk at children's parties than at any other, the wine need not be very old or expensive for the purpose, a new fruity wine answering very well for it. Put the wine into a jug, rub some lumps of sugar (equal to ¼ lb.) on the lemon-rind until all the yellow part of the skin is absorbed, then squeeze the juice, and strain it. Add the sugar and lemon-juice to the port-wine, with the grated nutmeg; pour over it the boiling water, cover the jug, and, when the beverage has cooled a little, it will be fit for use. Negus may also be made of sherry, or any other sweet white wine, but is more usually made of port than of any other beverage. *Sufficient.*—Allow 1 pint of wine, with the other ingredients in proportion, for a party of 9 or 10 children.

NOVEMBER—BILLS OF FARE.

Dinner for 18 persons.

First Course.

Baked Whitings.	Thick Grouse Soup, removed by Crimped Cod and Oyster Sauce. Vase of Flowers. Clear Ox-tail Soup, removed by Fillets of Turbot à la Crême.	Fried Smelts.

Entrées.

Fillets of Leveret.	Poulet à la Marengo. Vase of Flowers. Mushrooms sautés.	Ragoût of Lobster.

November—Bills of Fare

Second Course.

Haunch of Mutton.

Cold Game Pie.

Lark Pudding. | Vase of Flowers. | Roast Fowls.

Boiled Ham.

Boiled Turkey and Celery Sauce.

Third Course.

Apple Tart. | Pommes à la Condé. | Prawns. | Partridges, removed by Plum-pudding. | Wine Jelly. | Vase of Flowers. | Blancmange. | Snipes, removed by Charlotte glacée. | Vol-au-Vent of Pears. | Apricot Tartlets. | Shell-Fish.

Dessert and Ices.

Dinner for 12 persons.

First Course. — Hare soup; Julienne soup ; baked cod ; soles à la Normandie. *Entrées.*—Riz de veau aux tomates ; lobster patties ; mutton cutlets and Soubise sauce ; croûtades of marrow aux fines herbes. *Second Course.*—Roast sirloin of beef; braised goose ; boiled fowls and celery sauce ; bacon-cheek, garnished with sprouts. *Third Course.*—Wild ducks; partridges ; apples à la Portugaise ; Bavarian cream ; apricot-jam sandwiches ; cheesecakes ; Charlotte à la vanille ; plum-pudding ; dessert and ices.

Dinner for 8 persons.

First Course. — Mulligatawny soup ; fried slices of codfish and oyster sauce ; eels en matelote. *Entrées.* — Broiled pork cutlets and tomato sauce ; tendrons de veau à la jardinière. *Second Course.*

November, Plain Family Dinners

—Boiled leg of mutton and vegetables ; roast goose ; cold game pie. *Third Course.*—Snipes ; teal ; apple soufflé ; iced Charlotte ; tartlets ; champagne jelly ; coffee cream ; mince pies ; dessert and ices.

Dinners for 6 persons.

First Course.—Oyster soup ; crimped cod and oyster sauce ; fried perch and Dutch sauce. *Entrées.*—Pigs' feet à la Béchamel ; curried rabbit. *Second Course.* —Roast sucking-pig ; boiled fowls and oyster sauce ; vegetables. *Third Course.* —Jugged hare ; meringues à la crème ; apple custard ; vol-au-vent of pears ; whipped cream ; cabinet pudding ; dessert.

First Course.—Game soup ; slices of codfish and Dutch sauce ; fried eels. *Entrées.*—Kidneys à la Maître d'Hôtel ; oyster patties. *Second Course.*—Saddle of mutton ; boiled capon and rice ; small ham ; lark pudding. *Third Course.*— Roast hare ; apple tart ; pineapple cream ; clear jelly ; cheesecakes ; marrow pudding ; Nesselrode pudding ; dessert.

NOVEMBER, Plain Family Dinners for.

Sunday.—1. White soup. 2. Roast haunch of mutton, haricot beans, potatoes. 3. Apple tart, ginger pudding.

Monday.—1. Stewed eels. 2. Veal cutlets garnished with rolled bacon : cold mutton and winter salad. 3. Baked rice pudding.

Tuesday.— 1. Roast fowls, garnished with water-cresses ; boiled bacon-cheek ; hashed mutton from remains of haunch. 2. Apple pudding.

Wednesday.—1. Boiled leg of pork, carrots, parsnips, and pease-pudding ; fowl croquettes made with remainder of cold fowl. 2. Baroness pudding.

Thursday. — 1. Cold pork and mashed potatoes ; roast partridges, bread sauce and gravy. 2. The remainder of the pudding cut into neat slices, and warmed through, and served with sifted sugar sprinkled over ; apple fritters.

November—Things in Season

Friday.—1. Roast hare, gravy, and currant jelly; rump-steak and oyster-sauce; vegetables. 2. Macaroni.

Saturday.—1. Jugged hare; small mutton pudding. 2. Fig pudding.

Sunday.—1. Crimped cod and oyster sauce. 2. Roast fowls, small boiled ham, vegetables; rump-steak pie. 3. Baked apple pudding, open jam tart.

Monday.—1. The remainder of cod warmed in maître l'hôtel sauce. 2. Boiled aitchbone of beef, carrots, parsnips, suet dumplings. 3. Baked bread-and-butter pudding

Tuesday.—1. Pea-soup made from liquor in which beef was boiled. 2. Cold beef, mashed potatoes; mutton cutlets and tomato sauce. 3. Carrot pudding.

Wednesday.—1. Fried soles, melted butter. 2. Roast leg of pork, apple sauce, vegetables. 3. Macaroni with Parmesan cheese.

Thursday.—1. Bubble-and-squeak from remains of cold beef; curried pork. 2. Baked Semolina pudding.

Friday.—1. Roast leg of mutton, stewed Spanish onions, potatoes. 2. Apple tart.

Saturday.—1. Hashed mutton; boiled rabbit and onion sauce; vegetables. 2. Damson pudding made with bottled fruit.

NOVEMBER, Things in Season.

Fish.—Brill, carp, cod, crabs, eels, gudgeons, haddocks, oysters, pike, soles, tench, turbot, whiting.

Meat. — Beef, mutton, veal, doe venison.

Poultry.—Chickens, fowls, geese, larks, pigeons, pullets, rabbits, teal, turkeys, widgeons, wild-duck.

Game.—Hares, partridges, pheasants, snipes, woodcocks.

Vegetables.— Beetroot, cabbages, carrots, celery, lettuces, late cucumbers, onions, potatoes, salading, spinach, sprouts—various herbs.

Fruit. — Apples, bullaces, chestnuts, filberts, grapes, pears, walnuts

November—Bills of Fare

NOVEMBER—BILLS OF FARE FOR A GAME DINNER.

Dinner for 30 persons.

First Course.

Purée of Grouse.	Hare Soup.	Pheasant Soup.
	Vase of Flowers.	
	Soup à la Reine.	

Entrées.

Salmi of Widgeon.	Lark Pudding.	Salmi of Woodcock.	Fillets of Hare en Chevreuil.	Game Patties.	Salmi of Woodcock.	Salmi of Widgeon.
			Perdrix au Choux.			
			Vase of Flowers.			
			Curried Rabbits.			
			Fillet of Pheasant and Truffles.			

Second Course.

Cold Pheasant Pie à la Périgord.	Larded Pheasants.	Hot raised Pie of mixed Game.
	Leveret, larded and stuffed.	
	Vase of Flowers.	
	Grouse.	
	Larded Partridges.	

Third Course.

Snipes.	Golden Plovers.	Wild Duck.	Pintails.	Snipes. Widgeon. Ortolans.
			Quails.	
			Vase of Flowers.	
			Teal.	
			Woodcocks.	

| Noyeau Cream | October—Bills of Fare |

Noyeau Cream

Entremets and Removes.

```
Apricot Tart.        Boudin à la Nesselrode.    Maids of Honour.
Vol-au-Vent of Pears.   Dantzic Jelly.
                        Vase of Flowers.         Gâteau Génoise Glacé.
                        Charlotte Russe.          Compôte of Apples.
Maids of Honour.        Plum-pudding.
```

Dessert.

```
Olives.      Strawberry-Ice Cream.       Dried Fruit.     Figs.
Preserved Cherries.   Pineapples.
Ginger-Ice Cream.     Grapes.            Walnuts. Biscuits.   Orange-Water Ice.
Filberts. Wafers.     Pears.
                      Vase of Flowers.
                      Apples.            Preserved Cherries.   Olives.
Dried Fruit. Figs.    Grapes.
                      Pears.
             Lemon-Water Ice.
```

NOYEAU CREAM.

Ingredients.—1½ oz. of isinglass, the juice of 2 lemons, noyeau and pounded sugar to taste, 1½ pint of cream. *Mode.* —Dissolve the isinglass in a little boiling water, add the lemon-juice, and strain this to the cream, putting in sufficient noyeau and sugar to flavour and sweeten the mixture nicely; whisk the cream well, put it into an oiled mould, and set the mould in ice or in a cool place; turn it out, and garnish the dish to taste. *Time.* — Altogether, ½ hour. *Average cost,* with cream at 1s. per pint and the best isinglass, 4s. *Sufficient* to fill a quart mould. *Seasonable* at any time

NOYEAU, Home-made.

Ingredients.—2 oz. of bitter almonds, 1 oz. of sweet ditto, 1 lb. of loaf sugar, the rinds of 3 lemons, 1 quart of Irish whiskey or gin, 1 tablespoonful of clarified honey, ½ pint of new milk. *Mode* —Blanch and pound the almonds, and mix with them the sugar, which should also be pounded. Boil the milk; let it stand till quite cold; then mix all the ingredients together, and let them remain for 10 days, shaking them every day. Filter the mixture through blotting-paper, bottle off for use in small bottles, and seal the corks down. This will be found useful for flavouring many sweet dishes. A tablespoonful of the above noyeau, added to a pint of boiled custard instead of brandy as given in our recipe for custard, makes an exceedingly agreeable and delicate flavour. *Average cost,* 2s. 9d. *Sufficient* to make about 2½ pints of noyeau. *Seasonable.*— May be made at any time.

OCTOBER—BILLS OF FARE.

Dinner for 18 persons.

First Course.

```
Soles à la Normandie.   Mock-Turtle Soup, removed by Crimped Cod and Oyster Sauce.   Red Mullet.
                        Vase of Flowers.
                        Julienne Soup, removed by John Dory and Dutch Sauce.
```

Entrées.

```
Oyster Patties.   Sweetbreads and Tomato Sauce.   Stewed Mushrooms.
                  Vase of Flowers.
                  Fricandeau de Veau and Celery Sauce.
```

October—Bills of Fare

Second Course.

```
Roast Saddle of
    Mutton.

  Grouse Pie.

   Vase of
   Flowers.

    Ham.

 Larded Turkey.
```

Roast Goose.   Boiled Fowls and Oyster Sauce.

Third Course.

```
   Pheasants,
   removed by
Cabinet Pudding.

 Italian Cream.

   Vase of
   Flowers.

  Peach Jelly.

  Roast Hare,
  removed by
 Iced Pudding.
```

Custards. Lobster Salad.   Gâteau de Pommes.   Compôte of Plums.   Apple Tart.   Prawns.

Dessert and Ices.

Dinner for 12 persons.

First Course.—Carrot soup à la Créci ; soup à la Reine ; baked cod ; stewed eels. *Entrées.* — Riz de Veau and tomato sauce ; vol-au-vent of chicken ; pork cutlets and sauce Robert ; grilled mushrooms. *Second Course.*—Rump of beef à la jardinière ; roast goose ; boiled fowls and celery sauce ; tongue, garnished ; vegetables. *Third Course.* — Grouse ; pheasants ; quince jelly ; lemon cream ; apple tart ; compôte of peaches ; Nesselrode pudding ; cabinet pudding ; scalloped oysters ; dessert and ices.

Dinner for 8 persons.

First Course. — Calf's - head soup ; crimped cod and oyster sauce ; stewed eels. *Entrées.*—Stewed mutton kidneys ; curried sweetbreads. *Second Course.*— Boiled leg of mutton, garnished with carrots and turnips ; roast goose. *Third Course.*—Partridges ; fruit jelly ; Italian cream ; vol-au-vent of pears ; apple tart ; cabinet pudding ; dessert and ices.

October—Bills of Fare

Dinners for 6 persons.

First Course. — Hare soup ; broiled cod à la Maître d'Hôtel. Haddocks and egg sauce. *Entrées.*—Veal cutlets, garnished with French beans ; haricot mutton. *Second Course.*—Roast haunch of mutton ; boiled capon and rice ; vegetables. *Third Course.* — Pheasants ; punch jelly ; blancmange ; apples à la Portugaise ; Charlotte à la Vanille ; marrow pudding ; dessert.

First Course.—Mock-turtle soup ; brill and lobster sauce ; fried whitings. *Entrées.*—Fowl à la Béchamel ; oyster patties. *Second Course.*—Roast sucking-pig ; stewed rump of beef à la jardinière ; vegetables. *Third Course.* — Grouse ; Charlotte aux pommes ; coffee cream ; cheesecakes ; apricot tart ; iced pudding ; dessert.

OCTOBER, Plain Family Dinners for.

Sunday.—1. Roast sucking-pig, tomato sauce and brain sauce ; small boiled leg of mutton, caper sauce, turnips, and carrots. 2. Damson tart, boiled batter pudding.

Monday.—1. Vegetable soup, made from liquor that mutton was boiled in. 2. Sucking-pig en blanquette, small meat pie, French beans, and potatoes. 3. Pudding, pies.

Tuesday. — 1. Roast partridges, bread sauce, and gravy ; slices of mutton warmed in caper sauce ; vegetables. 2. Baked plum-pudding.

Wednesday. — 1. Roast ribs of beef, Yorkshire pudding, vegetable marrow, and potatoes. 2. Damson pudding.

Thursday. — 1. Fried soles, melted butter. 2. Cold beef and salad ; mutton cutlets and tomato sauce. 3. Macaroni.

Friday.—1. Carrot soup. 2. Boiled fowls and celery sauce ; bacon-cheek, garnished with greens ; beef rissoles, from remains of cold beef. 3. Baroness pudding.

Saturday.—1. Curried fowl, from remains of cold ditto ; dish of rice, rumpsteak-and-kidney pudding, vegetables. 2. Stewed pears and sponge cakes.

Sunday.—1. Crimped cod and oyster sauce. 2. Roast haunch of mutton, brown onion sauce, and vegetables. 3. Bullace pudding, baked custards in cups.

October, Things in Season.

Monday.—1. The remains of codfish, flaked, and warmed in a maître d'hôtel sauce. 2. Cold mutton and salad, veal cutlets and rolled bacon, French beans and potatoes. 3. Arrowroot blancmange and stewed damsons.

Tuesday.—1. Roast hare, gravy, and red-currant jelly ; hashed mutton, vegetables. 2. Currant dumplings.

Wednesday. — 1. Jugged hare, from remains of roast ditto ; boiled knuckle of veal and rice ; boiled bacon cheek. 2. Apple pudding.

Thursday.—1. Roast leg of pork, apple sauce, greens, and potatoes. 2. Rice snowballs.

Friday.—1. Slices of pork, broiled, and tomato sauce, mashed potatoes ; roast pheasants, bread sauce, and gravy. 2. Baked apple pudding.

Saturday.—1. Rump-steak pie, sweetbreads. 2. Ginger pudding.

OCTOBER, Things in Season.

Fish.—Barbel, brill, cod, crabs, eels, flounders, gudgeons, haddocks, lobsters, mullet, oysters, plaice, prawns, skate, soles, tench, turbot, whiting.

Meat. — Beef, mutton, pork, veal, venison.

Poultry.—Chickens, fowls, geese, larks, pigeons, pullets, rabbits, teal, turkeys, widgeons, wild ducks.

Game. — Blackcock, grouse, hares, partridges, pheasants, snipes, woodcocks, doe venison.

Vegetables. — Artichokes, beets, cabbages, cauliflowers, carrots, celery, lettuces, mushrooms, onions, potatoes, sprouts, tomatoes, turnips, vegetable marrows,—various herbs.

Fruit.—Apples, black and white bullaces, damsons, figs, filberts, grapes, pears, quinces, walnuts.

OMELET.

Ingredients.—6 eggs, 1 saltspoonful of salt, ½ saltspoonful of pepper, ¼ lb. of butter. *Mode.*—Break the eggs into a basin, omitting the whites of 3, and beat

OMELET.

them up with the salt and pepper until extremely light ; then add 2 oz. of the butter broken into small pieces, and stir this into the mixture. Put the other

Omelet, the Cure's

2 oz. of butter into a frying-pan, make it quite hot, and, as soon as it begins to bubble, whisk the eggs, &c., very briskly for a minute or two, and pour them into the pan ; stir the omelet with a spoon one way until the mixture thickens and becomes firm, and when the whole is set, fold the edges over, so that the omelet assumes an oval form ; and when it is nicely brown on one side, and quite firm, it is done. To take off the rawness on the upper side, hold the pan before the fire for a minute or two, and brown it with a salamander or hot shovel. Serve very expeditiously on a very hot dish, and never cook until it is just wanted. The flavour of this omelet may be very much enhanced by adding minced parsley, minced onion or eschalot, or grated cheese, allowing 1 tablespoonful of the former, and half the quantity of the latter, to the above proportion of eggs. Shrimps or oysters may also be added : the latter should be scalded in their liquor, and then bearded and cut into small pieces. In making an omelet, be particularly careful that it is not too thin, and, to avoid this, do not make it in too large a frying-pan, as the mixture would then spread too much, and taste of the outside. It should also not be greasy, burnt, or too much done, and should be cooked over a gentle fire, that the whole of the substance may be heated without drying up the outside. Omelets are sometimes served with gravy ; but *this should never be poured over them,* but served in a tureen, as the liquid causes the omelet to become heavy and flat, instead of eating light and soft. In making the gravy, the flavour should not overpower that of the omelet, and should be thickened with arrowroot or rice flour. *Time.*—With 6 eggs, in a frying-pan 18 or 20 inches round, 4 to 6 minutes. *Average cost, 9d. Sufficient* for 4 persons. *Seasonable* at any time.

OMELET, The Cure's, or Omelette au Thon.

Ingredients.—Take for 6 persons, the roes of 2 carp ;* bleach them, by putting them, for 5 minutes, in boiling water

* An American writer says he has followed this recipe, substituting pike, shad, &c., in the place of carp, and can recommend all these also, with a quiet conscience. Any fish, indeed, may be used with success.

Omelette aux Confitures

s ightly salted; a piece of fresh tunny the size of a hen's egg, to which add a small shalot already chopped; hash up together the roe and the tunny, so as to mix them well, and throw the whole into a saucepan, with a sufficient quantity of very good butter: whip it up until the butter is melted! This constitutes the specialty of the omelet. Take a second piece of butter, à discrétion, mix it with parsley and herbs, place it in a long-shaped dish destined to receive the omelet; squeeze the juice of a lemon over it, and place it on hot embers. Beat up 12 eggs (the fresher the better); throw up the sauté of roe and tunny, stirring it so as to mix all well together; then make your omelet in the usual manner, endeavouring. to turn it out long, thick, and soft. Spread it carefully on the dish prepared for it, and serve at once. This dish ought to be reserved for recherché déjeûners, or for assemblies where amateurs meet who know how to eat well: washed down with a good old wine, it will work wonders.

Note.—The roe and the tunny must be beaten up (sauté) without allowing them to boil, to prevent their hardening, which would prevent them mixing well with the eggs. Your dish should be hollowed towards the centre, to allow the gravy to concentrate, that it may be helped with a spoon. The dish ought to be slightly heated, otherwise the cold china will extract all the heat from the omelet.

OMELETTE AUX CONFITURES, or Jam Omelet.

Ingredients.—6 eggs, 4 oz. of butter, 3 tablespoonfuls of apricot, strawberry, or any jam that may be preferred. *Mode.*—Make an omelet, only instead of doubling it over, leave it flat in the pan. When quite firm, and nicely brown on one side, turn it carefully on to a hot dish, spread over the middle of it the jam, and fold the omelet over on each side; sprinkle sifted sugar over, and serve very quickly. A pretty dish of small omelets may be made by dividing the batter into 3 or 4 portions, and frying them separately; they should then be spread each one with a different kind of preserve, and the omelets rolled over. Always sprinkle sweet omelets with sifted sugar before being sent to table. *Time.*—4 to 6 minutes. *Average cost,*

Omelette Soufflé

1s. 2d.   *Sufficient* for 4 persons,   *Seasonable* at any time.

OMELET, Bachelor's.

Ingredients.—2 or 3 eggs, 2 oz. of butter, 1 teaspoonful of flour, ½ teacupful of milk. *Mode.*—Make a thin cream of the flour and milk; then beat up the eggs, mix all together, and add a pinch of salt and a few grains of cayenne. Melt the butter in a small frying-pan, and, when very hot, pour in the batter. Let the pan remain for a few minutes over a clear fire; then sprinkle upon the omelet some chopped herbs and a few shreds of onion; double the omelet dexterously, and shake it out of the pan on to a hot dish. A simple sweet omelet can be made by the same process, substituting sugar or preserve for the chopped herbs.   *Time.* — 2 minutes. *Average cost, 6d.   Sufficient* for 2 persons.   *Seasonable* at any time.

OMELET, Plain Sweet.

Ingredients.—6 eggs, 4 oz. of butter, 2 oz. of sifted sugar. *Mode.*—Break the eggs into a basin, omitting the whites of 3; whisk them well, adding the sugar and 2 oz. of the butter, which should be broken into small pieces, and stir all these ingredients well together. Make the remainder of the butter quite hot in a small frying-pan, and when it commences to bubble, pour in the eggs, &c. Keep stirring them until they begin to set; then turn the edges of the omelet over, to make it an oval shape, and finish cooking it. To brown the top, hold the pan before the fire, or use a salamander, and turn it carefully on to a *very hot* dish; sprinkle sifted sugar over, and serve.   *Time.*—From 4 to 6 minutes. *Average cost, 10d.   Sufficient* for 4 persons.   *Seasonable* at any time.

OMELETTE SOUFFLE.

Ingredients.—6 eggs, 5 oz. of pounded sugar, flavouring of vanilla, orange-flour water, or lemon-rind, 3 oz. of butter, 1 dessertspoonful of rice-flour. *Mode.* —Separate the yolks from the whites of the eggs, add to the former the sugar, the rice-flour, and either of the above flavourings that may be preferred, and stir these ingredients well together. Whip the whites of the eggs, mix them

Onion Sauce, Brown

ghtly with the batter, and put the utter into a small frying-pan. As soon as it begins to bubble, pour the batter into it, and set the pan over a bright but gentle fire ; and when the omelet is set, turn the edges over to make it an oval shape, and slip it on to a silver dish, which has been previously well buttered. Put it in the oven, and bake from 12 to 15 minutes ; sprinkle finely-powdered sugar over the soufflé, and *serve it immediately.* *Time.*—About 4 minutes in the pan ; to bake, from 12 to 15 minutes. *Average cost,* 1s. *Sufficient* for **3 or 4** persons. *Seasonable* at any time.

ONION SAUCE, Brown.

Ingredients.—6 large onions, rather more than ½ pint of good gravy, 2 oz. of butter, salt and pepper to taste. *Mode.* —Slice and fry the onions of a pale brown in a stewpan, with the above quantity of butter, keeping them well stirred, that they do not get black. When a nice colour, pour over the gravy, and let them simmer gently until tender. Now skim off every particle of fat, add the seasoning, and rub the whole through a tammy or sieve ; put it back into the saucepan to warm, and when it boils, serve. *Time.*—Altogether 1 hour. *Seasonable* from August to March.

Note.—Where a high flavouring is liked, add 1 tablespoonful of mushroom ketchup, **or** a small quantity of port wine.

ONION SAUCE, French, or Soubise.

Ingredients. — ½ pint of Béchamel, 1 bay-leaf, seasoning to taste of pounded mace and cayenne, 6 onions, a small piece of ham. *Mode.*—Peel the onions and cut them in halves ; put them into a stewpan, with just sufficient water to cover them, and add the bayleaf, ham, cayenne, and mace ; be careful to keep the lid closely shut, and simmer them until tender. Take them out and drain thoroughly ; rub them through a tammy or sieve (an old one does for the purpose) with a wooden spoon, and put them to ½ pint of Béchamel ; keep stirring over the fire until it boils, when serve. If it should require any more seasoning, add it to taste. *Time.*—¾ hour to boil the onions. *Average cost,* 10d. for this

Onion Soup

quantity. *Sufficient* for a moderate-sized dish.

ONION SAUCE, White, for Boiled Rabbits, Roast Shoulder of Mutton, &c.

Ingredients. — 9 large onions, or 12 middling-sized ones, 1 pint of melted butter made with milk, ½ teaspoonful of salt, or rather more. *Mode.*—Peel the onions and put them into water to which a little salt has been added, to preserve their whiteness, and let them remain for ¼ hour. Then put them into a stewpan, cover them with **water,** and let them boil until tender, and, if the onions should be very strong, change the water after they have been boiling for ¼ hour. Drain them thoroughly, chop them, and rub them through a tammy or sieve. Make 1 pint of melted butter with milk, and when that boils, put in the onions, with a seasoning of salt ; stir it till it simmers, when it will be ready to serve. If these directions are carefully attended to, this onion sauce will be delicious. *Time.*— From ¾ to 1 hour, to boil the onions. *Average cost,* 9d. per pint. *Sufficient* to serve with a roast shoulder of mutton, or boiled rabbit. *Seasonable* 'rom August to March.

Note.—To make this sauce very mild and delicate, use Spanish onions, which can be procured from the beginning of September to Christmas. 2 or 3 tablespoonfuls of cream added just before serving, will be found to improve its appearance very much. Small onions, when very young, may be cooked whole, and served in melted butter. A sieve or tammy should be kept expressly for onions : an old one answers the purpose, as it is liable to retain the flavour and smell, which of course would be excessively disagreeable in delicate preparations.

ONION SOUP.

Ingredients.—6 large onions, 2 oz. of butter, salt and pepper to taste, ½ pint of cream, 1 quart of stock. *Mode.*— Chop the onions, put them in the butter, stir them occasionally, but do not let them brown. When tender, put the stock to them, and season ; strain the soup, and add the boiling cream. *Time.*—½ hour. *Average cost,* 1s. per quart. *Seasonable* in winter. *Sufficient* for 4 persons.

ONION SOUP, Cheap.

Ingredients.—8 middling-sized onions, 3 oz. of butter, a tablespoonful of rice-flour, salt and pepper to taste, 1 teaspoonful of powdered sugar, thickening of butter and flour, 2 quarts of water. *Mode.*—Cut the onions small, put them into the stewpan with the butter, and fry them well ; mix the rice-flour smoothly with the water, add the onions, seasoning, and sugar, and simmer till tender. Thicken with butter and flour, and serve. *Time.*—2 hours. *Average cost,* 4*d.* per quart. *Seasonable* in winter. *Sufficient* for 8 persons.

ONIONS, Burnt, for Gravies.

Ingredients.—½ lb. of onions, ½ pint of water, ½ lb. of moist sugar, ⅓ pint of vinegar. *Mode.*—Peel and chop the onions fine, and put them into a stewpan (not tinned), with the water ; let them boil for 5 minutes, then add the sugar, and simmer gently until the mixture becomes nearly black and throws out bubbles of smoke. Have ready the above proportion of boiling vinegar, strain the liquor gradually to it, and keep stirring with a wooden spoon until it is well incorporated. When cold, bottle for use. *Time.*—Altogether, 1 hour.

ONIONS, Pickled (a very simple Method, and exceedingly Good).

Ingredients.—Pickling onions ; to each quart of vinegar, 2 teaspoonfuls of allspice, 2 teaspoonfuls of whole black pepper. *Mode.* — Have the onions gathered when quite dry and ripe, and, with the fingers, take off the thin outside skin ; then, with a silver knife (steel should not be used, as it spoils the colour of the onions), remove one more skin, when the onion will look quite clear. Have ready some very dry bottles or jars, and as fast as they are peeled, put them in. Pour over sufficient cold vinegar to cover them, with pepper and allspice in the above proportions, taking care that each jar has its share of the latter ingredients. Tie down with bladder, and put them in a dry place, and in a fortnight they will be fit for use. This is a most simple recipe and very delicious, the onions being nice and crisp. They should be eaten within 6 or 8 months after being done, as the onions are liable to become soft. *Seasonable*

from the middle of July to the end of August.

ONIONS, Pickled.

Ingredients.— 1 gallon of pickling onions, salt and water, milk ; to each ½ gallon of vinegar, 1 oz. of bruised ginger, ¼ tablespoonful of cayenne, 1 oz. of allspice, 1 oz. of whole black pepper, ¼ oz. of whole nutmeg bruised, 8 cloves, ¼ oz. of mace. *Mode.*—Gather the onions, which should not be too small, when they are quite dry and ripe ; wipe off the dirt, but do not pare them ; make a strong solution of salt and water, into which put the onions, and change this, morning and night, for 3 days, and save the *last* brine they were put in. Then take the outside skin off, and put them into a tin saucepan capable of holding them all, as they are always better done together. Now take equal quantities of milk and the last salt and water the onions were in, and pour this to them ; to this add 2 large spoonfuls of salt, put them over the fire, and watch them very attentively. Keep constantly turning the onions about with a wooden skimmer, those at the bottom to the top, and *vice versâ ;* and let the milk and water run through the holes of the skimmer. Remember, the onions must never boil, or, if they do, they will be good for nothing ; and they should be quite transparent. Keep the onions stirred for a few minutes, and, in stirring them, be particular not to break them. Then have ready a pan with a colander, into which turn the onions to drain, covering them with a cloth to keep in the steam. Place on a table an old cloth, 2 or 3 times double ; put the onions on it when quite hot, and over them an old piece of blanket ; cover this closely over them, to keep in the steam. Let them remain till the next day, when they will be quite cold, and look yellow and shrivelled ; take off the shrivelled skins, when they should be as white as snow. Put them into a pan, make a pickle of vinegar and the remaining ingredients, boil all these up, and pour hot over the onions in the pan. Cover very closely to keep in all the steam, and let them stand till the following day, when they will be quite cold. Put them into jars or bottles well bunged, and a tablespoonful of the best olive-oil on the top of each jar or bottle. Tie them down with bladder, and let them stand in a cool place for a month or six

| Onions, Spanish, Baked | Orange Cream |

weeks, when they will be fit for use. They should be beautifully white, and eat crisp, without the least softness, and will keep good many months. *Seasonable* from the middle of July to the end of August.

ONIONS, Spanish, Baked.

Ingredients.—4 or 5 Spanish onions, salt, and water. *Mode.*—Put the onions, with their skins on, into a saucepan of boiling water slightly salted, and let them boil quickly for an hour. Then take them out, wipe them thoroughly, wrap each one in a piece of paper separately, and bake them in a moderate oven for 2 hours, or longer, should the onions be very large. They may be served in their skins, and eaten with a piece of cold butter and a seasoning of pepper and salt ; or they may be peeled, and a good brown gravy poured over them. *Time.*—1 hour to boil, 2 hours to bake. *Average cost,* medium-sized, 2*d.* each. *Sufficient* for 5 or 6 persons. *Seasonable* from September to January.

ONIONS, Spanish, Pickled.

Ingredients.— Onions, vinegar ; salt and cayenne to taste. *Mode.*—Cut the onions in thin slices ; put a layer of them in the bottom of a jar ; sprinkle with salt and cayenne ; then add another layer of onions, and season as before. Proceeding in this manner till the jar is full, pour in sufficient vinegar to cover the whole, and the pickle will be fit for use in a month. *Seasonable.*—May be had in England from September to February.

ONIONS, Spanish, Stewed.

Ingredients.—5 or 6 Spanish onions, 1 pint of good broth or gravy. *Mode.*— Peel the onions, taking care not to cut away too much of the tops or tails, or they would then fall to pieces ; put them into a stewpan capable of holding them at the bottom without piling them one on the top of another ; add the broth or gravy, and simmer *very gently* until the onions are perfectly tender. Dish them, pour the gravy round and serve. Instead of using broth, Spanish onions may be stewed with a large piece of butter : they must be done very gradually over a slow fire or hot-plate, and will produce plenty of gravy. *Time* —To stew in gravy, 2 hours, or longer if very large. *Average*

cost, medium-sized, 2*d.* each. *Sufficient* for 6 or 7 persons. *Seasonable* from September to January.

Note.—Stewed Spanish onions are a favourite accompaniment to roast shoulder of mutton.

ORANGE BRANDY. (Excellent.)

Ingredients.—To every ½ gallon of brandy allow ¾ pint of Seville orange-juice, 1¼ lb. of loaf sugar. *Mode.*—To bring out the full flavour of the orange-peel, rub a few lumps of the sugar on 2 or 3 unpared oranges, and put these lumps to the rest. Mix the brandy with the orange-juice, strained, the rinds of 6 of the oranges pared very thin, and the sugar. Let all stand in a closely-covered jar for about 3 days, stirring it 3 or 4 times a day. When clear, it should be bottled and closely corked for a year ; it will then be ready for use, but will keep any length of time. This is a most excellent stomachic when taken pure in small quantities ; or, as the strength of the brandy is very little deteriorated by the other ingredients, it may be diluted with water. *Time.*—To be stirred every day for 3 days. *Average cost, 7s. Sufficient* to make 2 quarts. *Seasonable.*—Make this in March.

ORANGE CREAM.

Ingredients.—1 oz. of isinglass, 6 large oranges, 1 lemon, sugar to taste, water, ½ pint of good cream. *Mode.*—Squeeze the juice from the oranges and lemon ; strain it, and put it into a saucepan with the isinglass, and sufficient water to make it in all 1½ pint. Rub the sugar on the orange and lemon-rind, add it to the other ingredients, and boil all together for about 10 minutes. Strain

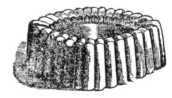

OPEN MOULD.

through a muslin bag, and, when cold, beat up with it ½ pint of thick cream. Wet a mould, or soak it in cold water ; pour in the cream, and put it in a cool place to set. If the weather is very cold,

Orange Creams

1 oz. of isinglass will be found sufficient for the above proportion of ingredients. *Time.*—10 minutes to boil the juice and water. *Average cost*, with the best isinglass, 3s. *Sufficient* to fill a quart mould. *Seasonable* from November to May.

ORANGE CREAMS.

Ingredients.—1 Seville orange, 1 tablespoonful of brandy, ¼ lb. of loaf sugar, the yolks of 4 eggs, 1 pint of cream. *Mode.*—Boil the rind of the Seville orange until tender, and beat it in a mortar to a pulp; add to it the brandy, the strained juice of the orange, and the sugar, and beat all together for about 10 minutes, adding the well-beaten yolks of eggs. Bring the cream to the boiling-point, and pour it very gradually to the other ingredients, and beat the mixture till nearly cold; put it into custard-cups, place the cups in a deep dish of boiling water, where let them remain till quite cold. Take the cups out of the water, wipe them, and garnish the tops of the creams with candied orange-peel or preserved chips. *Time.* — Altogether, ¾ hour. *Average cost*, with cream at 1s. per pint, 1s. 7d. *Sufficient* to make 7 or 8 creams. *Seasonable* from November to May.

Note.—To render this dish more economical, substitute milk for the cream, but add a small pinch of isinglass to make the creams firm.

ORANGE FRITTERS.

Ingredients.—For the batter, ½ lb. of flour, ½ oz. of butter, ½ saltspoonful of salt, 2 eggs, milk, oranges, hot lard or clarified dripping. *Mode.*—Make a nice light batter with the above proportion of flour, butter, salt, eggs, and sufficient milk to make it the proper consistency; peel the oranges, remove as much of the white skin as possible, and divide each orange into eight pieces, without breaking the thin skin, unless it be to remove the pips; dip each piece of orange in the batter. Have ready a pan of boiling lard or clarified dripping; drop in the oranges, and fry them a delicate brown from 8 to 10 minutes. When done, lay them on a piece of blotting-paper before the fire, to drain away the greasy moisture, and dish them on a white d'oyley; sprinkle over them plenty of pounded sugar, and serve quickly. *Time.*—8 to 10 minutes to fry the fritters: 5 minutes

Orange Jelly

to drain them. *Average cost*, 9d. *Sufficient* for 4 or 5 persons. *Seasonable* from November to May.

ORANGE GRAVY, for Wildfowl, Widgeon, Teal, &c.

Ingredients.—½ pint of white stock, 1 small onion, 3 or 4 strips of lemon or orange peel, a few leaves of basil, if at hand, the juice of a Seville orange or lemon, salt and pepper to taste, 1 glass of port wine. *Mode.*—Put the onion, cut in slices, into a stewpan with the stock, orange-peel, and basil, and let them simmer very gently for ¼ hour or rather longer, should the gravy not taste sufficiently of the peel. Strain it off, and add to the gravy the remaining ingredients; let the whole heat through, and, when on the point of boiling, serve very hot in a tureen which should have a cover to it. *Time.*—Altogether ½ hour. *Sufficient* for a small tureen.

ORANGE JELLY.

Ingredients.—1 pint of water, 1½ to 2 oz. of isinglass, ½ lb. of loaf sugar, 1 Seville orange, 1 lemon, about 9 China oranges. *Mode.*—Put the water into a saucepan, with the isinglass, sugar, and the rind of 1 orange, and the same of ½ lemon, and stir these over the fire until

OPEN MOULD.

the isinglass is dissolved, and remove the scum; then add to this the juice of the Seville orange, the juice of the lemon, and sufficient juice of China oranges to make in all 1 pint: from 8 to 10 oranges will yield the desired quantity. Stir all together over the fire until it is just on the point of boiling: skim well; then strain the jelly through a very fine sieve or jelly-bag, and when nearly cold, put it into a mould previously wetted, and, when quite cold turn it out on a dish, and garnish to taste. To insure this jelly being clear

Orange Marmalade

the orange- and lemon-juice should be well strained, and the isinglass clarified, before they are added to the other ingredients, and, to heighten the colour, a few drops of prepared cochineal may be added. *Time.*—5 minutes to boil without the juice; 1 minute after it is added. *Average cost*, with the best isinglass, 3s. 6d. *Sufficient* to fill a quart mould. *Seasonable* from November to May.

ORANGE MARMALADE.

Ingredients.—Equal weight of fine loaf sugar and Seville oranges; to 12 oranges allow 1 pint of water. *Mode.*—Let there be an equal weight of loaf sugar and Seville oranges, and allow the above proportion of water to every dozen oranges. Peel them carefully, remove a little of the white pith, and boil the rinds in water 2 hours, changing the water three times to take off a little of the bitter taste. Break the pulp into small pieces, take out all the pips, and cut the boiled rind into chips. Make a syrup with the sugar and water; boil this well, skim it, and, when clear, put in the pulp and chips. Boil all together from 20 minutes to ½ hour; pour it into pots, and, when cold, cover down with bladders or tissue-paper brushed over on both sides with the white of an egg. The juice and grated rind of 2 lemons to every dozen of oranges, added with the pulp and chips to the syrup, are a very great improvement to this marmalade. *Time.*—2 hours to boil the orange-rinds; 10 minutes to boil the syrup; 20 minutes to ½ hour to boil the marmalade. *Average cost*, from 6d. to 8d. per lb. pot. *Seasonable.*—This should be made in March or April, as Seville oranges are then in perfection.

ORANGE MARMALADE.

Ingredients.—Equal weight of Seville oranges and sugar; to every lb. of sugar allow ½ pint of water. *Mode.*—Weigh the sugar and oranges, score the skin across, and take it off in quarters. Boil these quarters in a muslin bag in water until they are quite soft, and they can be pierced easily with the head of a pin; then cut them into chips about 1 inch long, and as thin as possible. Should there be a great deal of white stringy pulp, remove it before cutting the rind into chips. Split open the oranges,

Orange Marmalade

scrape out the best part of the pulp, with the juice, rejecting the white pith and pips. Make a syrup with the sugar and water; boil it until clear; then put in the chips, pulp, and juice, and boil the marmalade from 20 minutes to ½ hour, removing all the scum as it rises. In boiling the syrup, clear it carefully from scum before the oranges are added to it. *Time.*—2 hours to boil the rinds, 10 minutes the syrup, 20 minutes to ½ hour the marmalade. *Average cost*, 6d. to 8d. per lb. pot. *Seasonable.*—Make this in March or April, when Seville oranges are in perfection.

ORANGE MARMALADE, an easy way of Making.

Ingredients.—To every lb. of pulp allow 1½ lb. of loaf sugar. *Mode.*—Choose some fine Seville oranges; put them whole into a stewpan with sufficient water to cover them, and stew them until they become perfectly tender, changing the water 2 or 3 times; drain them, take off the rind, remove the pips from the pulp, weigh it, and to every lb. allow 1½ of loaf sugar and ½ pint of the water the oranges were last boiled in. Boil the sugar and water together for 10 minutes; put in the pulp, boil for another 10 minutes; then add the peel cut into strips, and boil the marmalade for another 10 minutes, which completes the process. Pour it into jars; let it cool; then cover down with bladders, or tissue-paper brushed over on both sides with the white of an egg. *Time.*—2 hours to boil the oranges; altogether ½ hour to boil the marmalade. *Average cost*, from 6d. to 8d. per lb. pot. *Seasonable.*—Make this in March or April.

ORANGE MARMALADE, made with Honey.

Ingredients.—To 1 quart of the juice and pulp of Seville oranges allow 1 lb. of the rind, 2 lbs. of honey. *Mode.*—Peel the oranges, and boil the rind in water until tender, and cut it into strips. Take away the pips from the juice and pulp, and put it with the honey and chips into a preserving-pan; boil all together for about ½ hour, or until the marmalade is of the proper consistency: put it into pots, and, when cold, cover down with bladders. *Time.*—2 hours to boil the rind, ½ hour the marmalade.

15

Orange Marmalade, Pounded | Orange Wine

Average cost, from 7*d.* to 9*d.* per lb. pot. *Seasonable.* — Make this in March or April.

ORANGE MARMALADE, Pounded.

Ingredients.—Weight and ½ in sugar to every lb. of oranges. *Mode.*—Cut some clear Seville oranges in 4 pieces, put all the juice and pulp into a basin, and take out the seeds and skins; boil the rinds in hard water till tender, changing the water 2 or 3 times while boiling; drain them well, and pound them in a mortar; then put them into a preserving-pan with the juice and pulp, and their weight and ½ of sugar; boil rather more than ½ an hour. *Time.*—About 2 hours to boil the rinds, ½ an hour the marmalade.

ORANGE PUDDING, Baked.

Ingredients. — 6 oz. of stale sponge cake or bruised ratafias, 6 oranges, 1 pint of milk, 6 eggs, ½ lb. of sugar. *Mode.*— Bruise the sponge cake or ratafias into fine crumbs, and pour upon them the milk, which should be boiling. Rub the rinds of 2 of the oranges on sugar, and add this, with the juice of the remainder, to the other ingredients. Beat up the eggs, stir them in, sweeten to taste, and put the mixture into a pie-dish previously lined with puff-paste. Bake for rather more than ½ hour; turn it out of the dish, strew sifted sugar over, and serve. *Time.*—Rather more than ½ hour. *Average cost,* 1*s.* 6*d.* *Sufficient* for 3 or 4 persons. *Seasonable* from November to May.

ORANGE PUDDING, Seville.

Ingredients. —4 Seville oranges, 6 oz. of fresh butter, 12 almonds, ½ lb. of sifted sugar, the juice of 1 lemon, 8 eggs. *Mode.* —Boil the oranges and chop them finely, taking out all the pips. Put the butter, the almonds, blanched and chopped, and the sugar, into a saucepan, to which add the orange pulp and the lemon-juice. Put it on a hot plate to warm, mixing all together until the butter is thoroughly melted. Turn the mixture out, let it get cold, then add the eggs, which should be well whipped. Put all into a baking-dish, bordered with puff paste, and bake from ½ hour to 40 minutes, according to the heat of the

oven. *Time.*—½ hour to 40 minut *Seasonable* from November to May.

ORANGE SALAD.

Ingredients.—6 oranges, ¼ lb. of m catel raisins, 2 oz. of pounded sugar, tablespoonfuls of brandy. *Mode.*—Pe 5 of the oranges; divide them into slic without breaking the pulp, and arran them on a glass dish. Stone the raisin mix them with the sugar and brandy, an mingle them with the oranges. Squee the juice of the other orange over t whole, and the dish is ready for tabl A little pounded spice may be put when the flavour is liked; but this ingr dient must be added very springl *Average cost,* 1*s.* *Sufficient* for 5 or persons. *Seasonable* from November May.

ORANGE WINE, a very Simpl and Easy Method of Making very Superior.

Ingredients. —90 Seville oranges, 8 lbs. of lump sugar, water. *Mode.* - Break up the sugar into small pieces, an put it into a dry, sweet, 9-gallon cask placed in a cellar or other storehous where it is intended to be kept. Hav ready close to the cask two large pans o wooden keelers, into one of which pu the peel of the oranges pared quite thi and into the other the pulp after th juice has been squeezed from it. Strai the juice through a piece of double mu lin, and put into the cask with the suga Then pour about 1½ gallon of col spring water on both the peels and th pulp; let it stand for 24 hours, and the strain it into the cask; add more wate to the peels and pulp when this is don and repeat the same process every da for a week: it should take about a wee to fill up the cask. Be careful to appor tion the quantity as nearly as possibl to the seven days, and to stir the conten of the cask each day. On the *third* da after the cask is full—that is, the *tent* day after the commencement of making— the cask may be securely bunged dow This is a very simple and easy metho and the wine made according to it wi be pronounced to be most excellen There is no troublesome boiling, and a fermentation takes place in the cask When the above directions are attende to, the wine cannot fail to be good. should be bottled in 8 or 9 months, an

Oranges, Compôte of

will be fit for use in a twelvemonth after the time of making. Ginger wine may be made in precisely the same manner, only, with the 9-gallon cask for ginger wine, 2 lbs. of the best whole ginger, *bruised*, must be put with the sugar. It will be found convenient to tie the ginger loosely in a muslin bag. *Time.*— Altogether, 10 days to make it. *Average cost*, 2s. 6d. per gallon. *Sufficient* for 9 gallons. *Seasonable.*—Make this in March, and bottle it in the following January.

ORANGES, Compôte of.

Ingredients.—1 pint of syrup, 6 oranges. *Mode.*—Peel the oranges, remove as much of the white pith as possible, and divide them into small pieces without breaking the thin skin with which they are surrounded. Make the syrup by recipe, adding the rind of the orange cut into thin narrow strips. When the syrup has been well skimmed, and is quite clear, put in the pieces of orange, and simmer them for 5 minutes. Take them out carefully with a spoon without

COMPÔTE OF ORANGES.

breaking them, and arrange them on a glass dish. Reduce the syrup by boiling it quickly until thick; let it cool a little, pour it over the oranges, and, when cold, they will be ready for table. *Time.* —10 minutes to boil the syrup; 5 minutes to simmer the oranges; 5 minutes to reduce the syrup. *Average cost*, 9d. *Sufficient* for 5 or 6 persons. *Seasonable* from November to May.

ORANGES, a Pretty Dish of.

Ingredients.—6 large oranges, ½ lb. of loaf sugar, ¼ pint of water, ½ pint of cream, 2 tablespoonfuls of any kind of liquor, sugar to taste. *Mode.*— Put the sugar and water into a saucepan, and boil them until the sugar becomes brittle, which may be ascertained by taking up a small quantity in a spoon, and dipping it in cold water; if the sugar is sufficiently boiled, it will easily snap. Peel the oranges, remove as much of the white pith as possible, and divide them into nice-sized slices, without breaking the thin white skin which surrounds

Oranges, Preserved

the juicy pulp. Place the pieces of orange on small skewers, dip them into the hot sugar, and arrange them in layers round a plain mould, which should be well oiled with the purest salad-oil. The sides of the mould only should be lined with the oranges, and the centre left open for the cream. Let the sugar become firm by cooling; turn the oranges carefully out on a dish, and fill the centre with whipped cream, flavoured with any kind of liqueur, and sweetened with pounded sugar. This is an exceedingly ornamental and nice dish for the supper-table. *Time.*—10 minutes to boil the sugar. *Average cost*, 1s. 8d. —*Sufficient* for 1 mould. *Seasonable* from November to May.

ORANGES, Iced.

Ingredients.—Oranges; to every lb. of pounded loaf sugar allow the whites of 2 eggs. *Mode.*—Whisk the whites of the eggs well, stir in the sugar, and beat this mixture for ¼ hour. Skin the oranges, remove as much of the white pith as possible without injuring the pulp of the fruit; pass a thread through the centre of each orange, dip them into the sugar, and tie them to a stick. Place this stick across the oven, and let the oranges remain until dry, when they will have the appearance of balls of ice. They make a pretty dessert or supper dish. Care must be taken not to have the oven too fierce, or the oranges would scorch and acquire a brown colour, which would entirely spoil their appearance. *Time.*—From ½ to 1 hour to dry in a moderate oven. *Average cost*, 1½d. each. *Sufficient.*—½ lb. of sugar to ice 12 oranges. *Seasonable* from November to May.

ORANGES, Preserved.

Ingredients.—Oranges; to every lb. of juice and pulp allow 2 lbs. of loaf sugar · to every pint of water ½ lb. of loaf sugar. *Mode.*—Wholly grate or peel the oranges, taking off only the thin outside portion of the rind. Make a small incision where the stalk is taken out, squeeze out as much of the juice as can be obtained, and preserve it in a basin with the pulp that accompanies it. Put the oranges into cold water; let them stand for 3 days, changing the water twice; then boil them in fresh water till they are very tender, and put them to drain.

Ox, the

Make a syrup with the above proportion of sugar and water, sufficient to cover the oranges; let them stand in it for 2 or 3 days; then drain them well. Weigh the juice and pulp, allow double their weight of sugar, and boil them together until the scum ceases to rise, which must all be carefully removed; put in the oranges, boil them for 10 minutes, place them in jars, pour over them the syrup, and, when cold, cover down. They will be fit for use in a week. *Time.*—3 days for the oranges to remain in water, 3 days in the syrup; ½ hour to boil the pulp, 10 minutes the oranges. *Seasonable.*—This preserve should be made in February or March, when oranges are plentiful.

OX, The.

The manner in which a side of beef is cut up in London is shown in the engraving on this page. In the metropolis, on account of the large number of its population possessing the means to indulge in the "best of everything," the demand for the most delicate joints of meat is great, the price, at the same time, being much higher for these than for the other parts. The consequence is, that in London the carcass is there divided so as to obtain the greatest quantity of meat on the most esteemed joints. In many places, however, where, from a greater equality in the social condition and habits of the inhabitants, the demand and prices for the different parts of the carcasses are more equalized, there is not the same reason for the butcher to cut the best joints so large.

The meat on those parts of the animal in which the muscles are least called into action is most tender and succulent; as, for instance, along the back, from the rump to the hinder part of the shoulder; whilst the limbs, shoulder, and neck are the toughest, driest, and least-esteemed.

The names of the several joints in the hind and fore quarters of a side of beef, and the purposes for which they are used, are as follows:—

Hind Quarter:—

1. Sirloin,—the two sirloins, cut together in one joint, form a baron; this, when roasted, is the famous national dish of Englishmen, at entertainments, on occasion of rejoicing.

Ox, the

2. Rump,—the finest part for steaks.
3. Aitch-bone,—boiling piece.
4. Buttock,—prime boiling piece.
5. Mouse-round,—boiling or stewing.
6. Hock,—stewing.

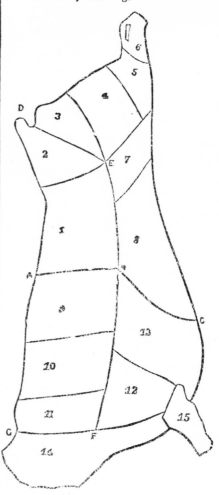

SIDE OF BEEF, SHOWING THE SEVERAL JOINTS.

7. Thick flank, cut with the udder fat,—primest boiling piece.
8. Thin flank,—boiling.

Fore Quarter:—

9. Five ribs, called the fore-rib.— This is considered the primest roasting piece.

Ox-Cheek Soup

10. Four ribs, called the middle-rib, —greatly esteemed by house-keepers as the most economical joint for roasting.
11. Two ribs, called the chuck-rib, —used for second quality of steaks.
12. Leg-of-mutton piece,—the muscles of the shoulder dissected from the breast.
13. Brisket, or breast,—used for boiling, after being salted.
14. Neck, clod, and sticking-piece, —used for soups, gravies, stocks, pies, and mincing for sausages.
15. Shin,—stewing.

The following is a classification of the qualities of meat, according to the several joints of beef, when cut up in the London manner.

First class—includes the sirloin, with the kidney suet (1), the rump-steak piece (2), the fore-rib (9).

Second class—The buttock (4), the thick flank (7), the middle-rib (10).

Third class—The aitch-bone (3), the mouse-round (5), the thin flank (8), the chuck (11), the leg-of-mutton piece (12), the brisket (13).

Fourth class—The neck, clod, and sticking-piece (14).

Fifth class—The hock (6), the shin (15).

OX-CHEEK SOUP.

Ingredients.—An ox-cheek, 2 oz. of butter, 3 or 4 slices of lean ham or bacon, 1 parsnip, 3 carrots, 2 onions, 3 heads of celery, 3 blades of mace, 4 cloves, a faggot of savoury herbs, 1 bay leaf, a teaspoonful of salt, half that of pepper, 1 head of celery, browning, the crust of a French roll, 5 quarts of water. *Mode.*—Lay the ham in the bottom of the stewpan, with the butter; break the bones of the cheek, wash it clean, and put it on the ham. Cut the vegetables small, add them to the other ingredients, and set the whole over a slow fire for ¼ of an hour. Now put in the water, and simmer gently till it is reduced to 4 quarts; take out the fleshy part of the cheek, and strain the soup into a clean stewpan; thicken with flour, put in a head of sliced celery, and simmer till the celery is tender. If not a good colour, use a little browning. Cut the meat into small square pieces, pour the soup over, and serve with the crust of a French roll in the tureen. A glass of sherry much im-

Ox-Tail, Broiled

proves this soup. *Time.*—3 to 4 hours. *Average cost,* 8d. per quart. *Seasonable* in winter. *Sufficient* for 12 persons.

OX-CHEEK, Stewed.

Ingredients.—1 cheek, salt and water, 4 or 5 onions, butter and flour, 6 cloves, 3 turnips, 2 carrots, 1 bay-leaf, 1 head of celery, 1 bunch of savoury herbs, cayenne, black pepper, and salt to taste, 1 oz. of butter, 2 dessertspoonfuls of flour, 2 tablespoonfuls of Chili vinegar, 2 tablespoonfuls of mushroom ketchup, 2 tablespoonfuls of port wine, 2 tablespoonfuls of Harvey's sauce. *Mode.*—Have the cheek boned, and prepare it the day before it is to be eaten, by cleaning and putting it to soak all night in salt and water. The next day, wipe it dry and clean, and put it into a stewpan. Just cover it with water, skim well when it boils, and let it gently simmer till the meat is quite tender. Slice and fry 3 onions in a little butter and flour, and put them into the gravy; add 2 whole onions, each stuck with 3 cloves, 3 turnips quartered, 2 carrots sliced, a bay-leaf, 1 head of celery, a bunch of herbs, and seasoning to taste of cayenne, black pepper, and salt. Let these stew till perfectly tender; then take out the cheek, divide into pieces fit to help at table, skim and strain the gravy, and thicken 1½ pint of it with butter and flour in the above proportions. Add the vinegar, ketchup, and port wine; put in the pieces of cheek; let the whole boil up, and serve quite hot. Send it to table in a ragoût-dish. If the colour of the gravy should not be very good, add a tablespoonful of the browning. *Time.* —4 hours. *Average cost,* 3d. per lb. *Sufficient* for 8 persons. *Seasonable* at any time.

OX-TAIL, Broiled (an Entrée).

Ingredients.—2 tails, 1½ pint of stock, salt and cayenne to taste, bread crumbs, 1 egg. *Mode.*—Joint and cut up the tails into convenient-sized pieces, and put them into a stewpan, with the stock, cayenne, and salt, and, if liked very savoury, a bunch of sweet herbs. Let them simmer gently for about 2½ hours, then take them out, drain them, and let them cool. Beat an egg upon a plate, dip in each piece of tail, and, afterwards, sprinkle them well with fine bread crumbs; broil them over a clear fire-

Ox-Tail Soup

until of a brownish colour on both sides, and serve with a good gravy, or any sauce that may be preferred. *Time.*—About 2½ hours. *Average cost*, from 9*d*. to 1*s*. 6*d*., according to the season. *Sufficient* for 6 persons. *Seasonable* at any time.

Note. — These may be more easily prepared by putting the tails in a brisk oven, after they have been dipped in egg and bread-crumb ; and, when brown, they are done. They must be boiled the same time as for broiling.

OX-TAIL SOUP.

Ingredients.—2 ox-tails, 2 slices of ham, 1 oz. of butter, 2 carrots, 2 turnips, 3 onions, 1 leek, 1 head of celery, 1 bunch of savoury herbs, 1 bay-leaf, 12 whole peppercorns, 4 cloves, a table-spoonful of salt, 2 tablespoonfuls of ketchup, ½ glass of port wine, 3 quarts of water. *Mode.* — Cut up the tails, separating them at the joints ; wash them, and put them in a stewpan, with the butter. Cut the vegetables in slices, and add them, with the peppercorns and herbs. Put in ½ pint of water, and stir it over a sharp fire till the juices are drawn. Fill up the stewpan with the water, and, when boiling, add the salt. Skim well, and simmer very gently for 4 hours, or until the tails are tender. Take them out, skim and strain the soup, thicken with flour, and flavour with the ketchup and port wine. Put back the tails, simmer for 5 minutes, and serve. *Time.*—4½ hours. *Average cost*, 1*s*. 3*d*. per quart. *Seasonable* in winter. *Sufficient* for 10 persons.

OX-TAILS, Stewed.

Ingredients.—2 ox-tails, 1 onion, 3 cloves, 1 blade of mace, ¼ teaspoonful of whole black pepper, ¼ teaspoonful of allspice, ½ a teaspoonful of salt, a small bunch of savoury herbs, thickening of butter and flour, 1 tablespoonful of lemon-juice, 1 tablespoonful of mushroom ketchup. *Mode.*—Divide the tails at the joints, wash, and put them into a stewpan with sufficient water to cover them, and set them on the fire ; when the water boils, remove the scum, and add the onion cut into rings, the spice, seasoning, and herbs. Cover the stewpan closely, and let the tails simmer very gently until tender, which will be in about 2½ hours. Take them out, make a thickening of butter and flour, add it

Oyster Patties

to the gravy, and let it boil for ¼ hour. Strain it through a sieve into a saucepan, put back the tails, add the lemon-juice and ketchup ; let the whole just boil up, and serve. Garnish with croûtons or sippets of toasted bread. *Time.*—2½ hours to stew the tails. *Average cost*, 9*d*. to 1*s*. 6*d*., according to the season. *Sufficien* for 8 persons. *Seasonable* all the year.

OYSTER, Forcemeat for Roast or Boiled Turkey.

Ingredients.—½ pint of bread crumbs, 1½ oz. of chopped suet or butter, 1 faggot of savoury herbs, ¼ saltspoonful of grated nutmeg, salt and pepper to taste, 2 eggs, 18 oysters. *Mode.*—Grate the bread very fine, and be careful that no large lumps remain ; put it into a basin with the suet, which must be very finely minced, or, when butter is used, that must be cut up into small pieces. Add the herbs, also chopped as small as possible, and seasoning ; mix all these well together, until the ingredients are thoroughly mingled. Open and beard the oysters, chop them, but not too small, and add them to the other ingredients. Beat up the eggs, and, with the hand, work altogether, until it is smoothly mixed. The turkey should not be stuffed too full : if there should be too much forcemeat, roll it into balls, fry them, and use them as a garnish. *Sufficient* for 1 turkey.

OYSTER KETCHUP.

Ingredients.—Sufficient oysters to fill a pint measure, 1 pint of sherry, 3 oz. of salt, 1 drachm of cayenne, 2 drachms of pounded mace. *Mode.*—Procure the oysters very fresh, and open sufficient to fill a pint measure ; save the liquor, and scald the oysters in it with the sherry ; strain the oysters, and put them in a mortar with the salt, cayenne, and mace ; pound the whole until reduced to a pulp, then add it to the liquor in which they were scalded ; boil it again five minutes, and skim well ; rub the whole through a sieve, and, when cold, bottle and cork closely. The corks should be sealed. *Seasonable* from September to April.

Note.—Cider may be substituted for the sherry.

OYSTER PATTIES (an Entrée).

Ingredients —2 dozen oysters, 2 oz. of butter, 3 tablespoonfuls of cream, a

| Oyster Sauce | Oysters Fried in Batter |

little lemon-juice, 1 blade of pounded mace ; cayenne to taste. *Mode.*—Scald the oysters in their own liquor, beard them, and cut each one into 3 pieces. Put the butter into a stewpan, dredge in sufficient flour to dry it up ; add the strained oyster-liquor with the other ingredients ; put in the oysters, and let them heat gradually, but not boil fast. Make the patty-cases as directed for lobster patties, fill with the oyster mixture, and replace the covers. *Time.*—2 minutes for the oysters to simmer in the mixture. *Average cost,* exclusive of the patty-cases, 1*s.* 4*d.* *Seasonable* from September to April.

OYSTER SAUCE, to serve with Fish, Boiled Poultry, &c.

Ingredients.—3 dozen oysters, ½ pint of melted butter, made with milk. *Mode.* —Open the oysters carefully, and save their liquor ; strain it into a clean saucepan (a lined one is best), put in the oysters, and let them just come to the boiling-point, when they should look plump. Take them off the fire immediately, and put the whole into a basin. Strain the liquor from them, mix with it sufficient melted butter made with milk to make ½ pint altogether. When this is ready and very smooth, put in the oysters, which should be previously bearded, if you wish the sauce to be really nice. Set it by the side of the fire to get thoroughly hot, *but do not allow it to boil,* or the oysters will immediately harden. Using cream instead of milk makes this sauce extremely delicious. When liked, add a seasoning of cayenne or anchovy sauce ; but, as we have before stated, a plain sauce *should* be plain, and not be overpowered by highly-flavoured essences ; therefore we recommend that the above directions be implicitly followed, and no seasoning added. *Average cost* for this quantity, 2*s.* *Sufficient* for 6 persons. Never allow fewer than 6 oysters to 1 person, unless the party is very large. *Seasonable* from September to April.

A more economical sauce may be made by using a smaller quantity of oysters, and not bearding them before they are added to the sauce : this may answer the purpose, but we cannot undertake to recommend it as a mode for making this delicious adjunct to fish, &c.

OYSTER SOUP.

Ingredients.—6 dozen of oysters, 2 quarts of white stock, ½ pint of cream, 2 oz. of butter, 1½ oz. of flour ; salt, cayenne, and mace to taste. *Mode.*— Scald the oysters in their own liquor, take them out, beard them, and put them in a tureen. Take a pint of the stock, put in the beards and the liquor, which must be carefully strained, and simmer for ½ an hour. Take it off the fire, strain it again, and add the remainder of the stock, with the seasoning and mace. Bring it to a boil, add the thickening of butter and flour, simmer for 5 minutes, stir in the boiling cream, pour it over the oysters, and serve. *Time.*— 1 hour. *Average cost,* 2*s.* 8*d.* per quart. *Seasonable* from September to April. *Sufficient* for 8 persons.

Note.—This soup can be made less rich by using milk instead of cream, and thickening with arrowroot instead of butter and flour.

OYSTER SOUP.

Ingredients.—2 quarts of good mutton broth, 6 dozen oysters, 2 oz. butter, 1 oz. of flour. *Mode.*—Beard the oysters, and scald them in their own liquor : then add it, well strained, to the broth ; thicken with the butter and flour, and simmer for ¼ of an hour. Put in the oysters, stir well. but do not let it boil, and serve very hot. *Time.*—¾ hour. *Average cost,* 2*s.* per quart. *Seasonable* from September to April. *Sufficient* for 8 persons.

OYSTERS, Fried.

Ingredients.—3 dozen oysters, 2 oz. butter, 1 tablespoonful of ketchup, a little chopped lemon-peel, ½ teaspoonful of chopped parsley. *Mode.*—Boil the oysters for 1 minute in their own liquor, and drain them ; fry them with the butter, ketchup, lemon-peel, and parsley ; lay them on a dish, and garnish with fried potatoes, toasted sippets, and parsley. This is a delicious delicacy, and is a favourite Italian dish. *Time.*—5 minutes. *Average cost* for this quantity, 1*s.* 9*d.* *Seasonable* from September to April. *Sufficient* for 4 persons.

OYSTERS Fried in Batter.

Ingredients. — ½ pint of oysters, 2 eggs. ½ pint of milk, sufficient flour to make the batter ; pepper and salt to taste :

Oysters, to Keep

when liked, a little nutmeg; hot lard. *Mode.*—Scald the oysters in their own liquor, beard them, and lay them on a cloth to drain thoroughly. Break the eggs into a basin, mix the flour with them, add the milk gradually, with nutmeg and seasoning, and put the oysters in the batter. Make some lard hot in a deep frying-pan, put in the oysters, one at a time; when done, take them up with a sharp-pointed skewer, and dish them on a napkin. Fried oysters are frequently used for garnishing boiled fish, and then a few bread crumbs should be added to the flour. *Time.*—5 or 6 minutes. *Average cost* for this quantity, 1s. 10d. *Seasonable* from September to April. *Sufficient* for 3 persons.

OYSTERS, to Keep.

Put them in a tub, and cover them with salt and water. Let them remain for 12 hours, when they are to be taken out, and allowed to stand for another 12 hours without water. If left without water every alternate 12 hours, they will be much better than if constantly kept in it. Never put the same water twice to them.

OYSTERS, Pickled.

Ingredients.—100 oysters; to each ½ pint of vinegar, 1 blade of pounded mace, 1 strip of lemon-peel, 12 black peppercorns. *Mode.*—Get the oysters in good condition, open them, place them in a saucepan, and let them simmer in their own liquor for about 10 minutes very gently; then take them out one by one, and place them in a jar, and cover them, when cold, with a pickle made as follows:—Measure the oyster-liquor; add to it the same quantity of vinegar, with mace, lemon-peel, and pepper in the above proportion, and boil it for 5 minutes; when cold, pour over the oysters, and tie them down very closely, as contact with the air spoils them. *Seasonable* from September to April.

Note.—Put this pickle away in small jars; because, directly one is opened, its contents should immediately be eaten, as they soon spoil. The pickle should not be kept more than 2 or 3 months.

OYSTERS, Scalloped.

Ingredients.—Oysters, say 1 pint, 1 oz. butter, flour, 2 tablespoonfuls of white

Oysters, Stewed

stock, 2 tablespoonfuls of cream; pepper and salt to taste; bread crumbs, oiled butter. *Mode.*—Scald the oysters in their own liquor, take them out, beard them, and strain the liquor free from grit. Put 1 oz. of butter into a stewpan; when melted, dredge in sufficient flour to dry it up; add the stock, cream, and strained liquor, and give one boil. Put in the oysters and seasoning; let them gradually heat through, but not boil. Have ready the scallop-shells buttered; lay in the oysters, and as much of the liquid as they will hold; cover them over with bread crumbs, over which drop a little oiled butter. Brown them in the oven, or before the fire, and serve quickly, and very hot. *Time.*—Altogether, ¼ hour. *Average cost,* for this quantity, 3s. 6d. *Sufficient* for 5 or 6 persons.

OYSTERS, Scalloped.

Prepare the oysters as in the preceding recipe, and put them in a scallop-shell or saucer, and between each layer sprinkle over a few bread crumbs, pepper, salt, and grated nutmeg; place small pieces of butter over, and bake before the fire in a Dutch oven. Put sufficient bread crumbs on the top to make a smooth surface, as the oysters should not be seen. *Time.*—About ¼ hour. *Average cost,* 3s. 2d. *Seasonable* from September to April.

OYSTERS, Stewed.

Ingredients.—1 pint of oysters, 1 oz. of butter, flour, ⅓ pint cream; cayenne and salt to taste; 1 blade of pounded mace. *Mode.*—Scald the oysters in their own liquor, take them out, beard them, and strain the liquor; put the butter into a stewpan, dredge in sufficient flour to dry it up, add the oyster-liquor and mace, and stir it over a sharp fire with a wooden spoon; when it comes to a boil, add the cream, oysters, and seasoning. Let all simmer for 1 or 2 minutes, but not longer, or the oysters would harden. Serve on a hot dish, and garnish with croûtons, or toasted sippets of bread. A small piece of lemon-peel boiled with the oyster-liquor, and taken out before the cream is added, will be found an improvement. *Time.* — Altogether 15 minutes. *Average cost* for this quantity, 3s. 6d. *Seasonable* from September to April. *Sufficient* for 6 persons.

PANCAKES.

Ingredients.—Eggs, flour, milk; to every egg allow 1 oz. of flour, about 1 gill of milk, ⅓ saltspoonful of salt. *Mode.*—Ascertain that the eggs are fresh; break each one separately in a cup; whisk them well, put them into a basin, with the flour, salt, and a few drops of milk, and beat the whole to a perfectly *smooth* batter; then add by degrees the remainder of the milk. The proportion of this latter ingredient must be regulated by the size of the eggs, &c. &c.; but the batter, when ready for frying, should be of the consistency of thick **cream.** Place a small frying-pan on the

PANCAKES.

fire to get hot; let it be delicately clean, or the pancakes will stick, and, when quite hot, put into it a small piece of butter, allowing about ½ oz. to each pancake. When it is melted, pour in the batter, about ⅓ teacupful to a pan 5 inches in diameter, and fry it for about 4 minutes, or until it is nicely brown on one side. By only pouring in a small quantity of batter, and so making the pancakes thin, the necessity of turning them (an operation rather difficult to unskilful cooks) is obviated. When the pancake is done, sprinkle over it some pounded sugar, roll it up in the pan, and take it out with a large slice, and place it on a dish before the fire. Proceed in this manner until sufficient are cooked for a dish; then send them quickly to table, and continue to send in a further quantity, as pancakes are never good unless eaten almost immediately they come from the frying-pan. The batter may be flavoured with a little grated lemon-rind, or the pancakes may have preserve rolled in them instead of sugar. Send sifted sugar and a cut lemon to table with them. To render the pancakes very light, the yolks and whites of the eggs should be beaten separately, and the whites added the last thing to the batter before frying. *Time.*—From 4 to 5 minutes for a pancake that does not require turning; from 6 to 8 minutes for a thicker one. *Average cost* for 3 persons, 6d. *Sufficient.*—Allow 3 eggs, with the other ingredients in proportion, for 3 persons. *Seasonable* at any time, but specially served on Shrove Tuesday.

PANCAKES.

Ingredients.—6 eggs, 1 pint of cream, ¼ lb. of loaf sugar, 1 glass of sherry, ½ teaspoonful of grated nutmeg, flour, *Mode.*—Ascertain that the eggs are extremely fresh, beat them well, strain and mix with them the cream, pounded sugar, wine, nutmeg, and as much flour as will make the batter nearly as thick as that for ordinary pancakes. Make the frying-pan hot, wipe it with a clean cloth, pour in sufficient batter to make a thin pancake, and fry it for about 5 minutes. Dish the pancakes piled one above the other, strew sifted sugar between each, and serve. *Time.*—About 5 minutes. *Average cost*, with cream at 1s. per pint, 2s. 3d. *Sufficient* to make 8 pancakes. *Seasonable* at any time, but specially served on Shrove Tuesday.

PANCAKES, French.

Ingredients.—2 eggs, 2 oz. of butter, 2 oz. of sifted sugar, 2 oz. of flour, ½ pint of new milk. *Mode.*—Beat the eggs thoroughly, and put them into a basin with the butter, which should be beaten to a cream; stir in the sugar and flour, and when these ingredients are well mixed, add the milk; keep stirring and beating the mixture for a few minutes; put it on buttered plates, and bake in a quick oven for 20 minutes. Serve with a cut lemon and sifted sugar, or pile the pancakes high on a dish, with a layer of preserve or marmalade between each. *Time.*—20 minutes. *Average cost, 7d. Sufficient* for 3 or 4 persons. *Seasonable* at any time.

PANCAKES, Snow.

Ingredients.—3 tablespoonfuls of flour, 1 egg, 3 tablespoonfuls of snow, about ½ pint of new milk. *Mode.*—Mix the flour with the milk by degrees, add the egg well beaten, and just before frying, the snow, it should then be all beaten up together quickly, and put into the frying-pan immediately. *Sufficient* for 8 pancakes.

PAN KAIL.

Ingredients.—2 lbs. of cabbage, or Savoy greens; ¼ lb. of butter or dripping, salt and pepper to taste, oatmeal for thickening, 2 quarts of water. *Mode.*—Chop the cabbage very fine, thicken the water with oatmeal, put in the cabbage

Parsley and Butter

and butter, or dripping; season and simmer for 1½ hour. It can be made sweeter by blanching and mashing the greens, adding any good liquor that a joint has been boiled in, and then further thicken with bread or pounded biscuit. *Time.*—1½ hour. *Average cost,* 1½*d.* per quart. *Seasonable* all the year, but more suitable in winter. *Sufficient* for 8 persons.

PARSLEY AND BUTTER, to serve with Calf's Head, Boiled Fowls, &c.

Ingredients. — 2 tablespoonfuls of minced parsley, ½ pint of melted butter. *Mode.*—Put into a saucepan a small quantity of water, slightly salted, and when it boils, throw in a good bunch of parsley which has been previously washed and tied together in a bunch; let it boil for 5 minutes, drain it, mince the leaves *very fine,* and put the above quantity in a tureen; pour over it ½ pint of smoothly-made melted butter; stir once, that the ingredients may be thoroughly mixed, and serve. *Time.*— 5 minutes to boil the parsley. *Average cost,* 4*d.* *Sufficient* for 1 large fowl; allow rather more for a pair. *Seasonable* at any time.

PARSLEY, Fried, for Garnishing.

Ingredients.—Parsley, hot lard or clarified dripping. *Mode.* —Gather some young parsley; wash, pick, and dry it thoroughly in a cloth; put it into the wire basket of which we have given an engraving, and hold it in boiling lard or dripping for a minute or two. Directly it is done, lift out the basket, and let it stand before the fire, that the parsley may become thoroughly crisp; and the quicker it is fried the better. Should the kitchen not be furnished with the

WIRE BASKET.

above article, throw the parsley into the frying-pan, and when crisp, lift it out with a slice, dry it before the fire, and when thoroughly crisp it will be ready for use.

Parsnip Soup

WIRE BASKET.—For this recipe a wire basket, as shown in the annexed engraving, will be found very useful. It is very light and handy, and may be used for other similar purposes besides that just described.

PARSLEY JUICE, for Colouring various Dishes.

Procure some nice young parsley; wash it and dry it thoroughly in a cloth; pound the leaves in a mortar till all the juice is extracted, and put the juice in a teacup or small jar; place this in a saucepan of boiling water, and warm it on the *bain-marie* principle just long enough to take off its rawness; let it drain, and it will be ready for colouring. *Substitute for.* — Sometimes in the middle of winter parsley-leaves are not to be had, when the following will be found an excellent substitute:—Tie up a little parsley-seed in a small piece of muslin, and boil it for 10 minutes in a small quantity of water; use this water to make the melted butter with, and throw into it a little boiled spinach, minced rather fine, which will have an appearance similar to that of parsley.

PARSLEY, to Preserve through the Winter.

Use freshly-gathered parsley for keeping, and wash it perfectly free from grit and dirt; put it into boiling water which has been slightly salted and well skimmed, and then let it boil for 2 or 3 minutes; take it out, let it drain, and lay it on a sieve in front of the fire, when it should be dried as expeditiously as possible. Store it away in a very dry place in bottles, and when wanted for use pour over it a little warm water, and let it stand for about 5 minutes. *Seasonable.* —This may be done at any time between June and October.

PARSNIP SOUP.

Ingredients.—1 lb. of sliced parsnips, 2 oz. of butter, salt and cayenne to taste, 1 quart of stock. *Mode.*—Put the parsnips into the stewpan with the butter, which has been previously melted, and simmer them till quite tender. Then add nearly a pint of stock, and boil together for half an hour. Pass all through a fine strainer, and put to it the remainder of the stock. Season, boil, and serve

| Parsnips, Boiled | Partridge, Roast |

immediately. *Time.*—2 hours. *Average cost*, 6d. per quart. *Seasonable* from October to April. *Sufficient* for 4 persons.

PARSNIPS, Boiled.

Ingredients.—Parsnips ; to each ½ gallon of water allow 1 heaped tablespoonful of salt. *Mode.*—Wash the parsnips, scrape them thoroughly, and with the point of the knife remove any black specks about them, and, should they be very large, cut the thick part into quarters. Put them into a saucepan of boiling water salted in the above proportion, boil them rapidly until tender, which may be ascertained by thrusting a fork in them; take them up, drain them, and serve in a vegetable-dish. This vegetable is usually served with salt fish, boiled pork, or boiled beef : when sent to table with the latter, a few should be placed alternately with carrots round the dish as a garnish. *Time.*—Large parsnips, 1 to 1½ hour ; small ones, ⅓ to 1 hour. *Average cost*, 1d. each. *Sufficient.*—Allow 1 for each person. *Seasonable* from October to May.

PARTRIDGE, Broiled (a Luncheon, Breakfast, or Supper Dish).

Ingredients.—3 partridges, salt and cayenne to taste, a small piece of butter, brown gravy or mushroom sauce. *Mode.*—Pluck, draw, and cut the partridges in half, and wipe the inside thoroughly with a damp cloth. Season them with salt and cayenne, broil them over a very clear fire, and dish them on a hot dish ; rub a small piece of butter over each half, and send them to table with brown gravy or mushroom sauce. *Time.*—About ½ hour. *Average cost*, 1s. 6d. to 2s. a brace. *Sufficient* for 3 or four persons. *Seasonable* from the 1st of September to the beginning of February.

PARTRIDGE PIE.

Ingredients.—3 partridges, pepper and salt to taste, 1 teaspoonful of minced parsley (when obtainable, a few mushrooms), ¾ lb. of veal cutlet, a slice of ham, ½ pint of stock, puff paste. *Mode.*—Line a pie-dish with a veal cutlet ; over that place a slice of ham and a seasoning of pepper and salt. Pluck, draw, and wipe the partridges ; cut off the legs at the first joint, and season them inside

with pepper, salt, minced parsley, and a small piece of butter ; place them in the dish, and pour over the stock ; line the edges of the dish with puff paste, cover with the same, brush it over with the yolk of an egg, and bake for ¾ to 1 hour. *Time.*—¾ to 1 hour. *Average cost*, 1s. 6d. to 2s. a brace. *Sufficient* for 4 or 5 persons. *Seasonable* from the 1st of September to the beginning of February.

Note.—Should the partridges be very large, split them in half, they will then lie in the dish more compactly. When at hand, a few mushrooms should always be added.

PARTRIDGE, Potted.

Ingredients.—Partridges ; seasoning to taste of mace, allspice, white pepper, and salt ; butter, coarse paste. *Mode.*—Pluck and draw the birds, and wipe them inside with a damp cloth. Pound well some mace, allspice, white pepper, and salt ; mix together, and rub every part of the partridges with this. Pack the birds as closely as possible in a baking-pan, with plenty of butter over them, and cover with a coarse flour and water crust. Tie a paper over this, and bake for rather more than 1½ hour ; let the birds get cold, then cut them into pieces for keeping, pack them closely into a large potting-pot, and cover with clarified butter. This should be kept in a cool dry place. The butter used for potted things will answer for basting, or for paste for meat pies. *Time.*—1½ hour. *Seasonable* from the 1st of September to the beginning of February.

PARTRIDGE, Roast.

Ingredients.—Partridge ; butter. *Choosing and Trussing.*—Choose young birds, with dark-coloured bills and yellowish legs, and let them hang a few days, or there will be no flavour to the

ROAST PARTRIDGE.

flesh, nor will it be tender. The time they should be kept entirely depends on the taste of those for whom they are intended, as what some persons would consider delicious would be to others

Partridge Soup

disgusting and offensive. They may be trussed with or without the head, the latter mode being now considered the most fashionable. Pluck, draw, and wipe the partridge carefully inside and out ; cut off the head, leaving sufficient skin on the neck to skewer back ; bring the legs close to the breast, between it and the side-bones, and pass a skewer through the pinions and the thick part of the thighs. When the head is left on, it should be brought round and fixed on to the point of the skewer. *Mode.*—When the bird is firmly and plumply trussed, roast it before a nice bright fire ; keep it well basted, and a few minutes before serving, flour and froth it well. Dish it, and serve with gravy and bread sauce, and send to table hot and quickly. A little of the gravy should be poured over the bird. *Time.*— 25 to 35 minutes. *Average cost,* 1s. 6d. to 2s. a brace. *Sufficient.*—2 for a dish. *Seasonable* from the 1st of September to the beginning of February.

PARTRIDGE SOUP.

Ingredients.—2 partridges, 3 slices of lean ham, 2 shred onions, 1 head of celery, 1 large carrot, and 1 turnip cut into any fanciful shapes, 1 small lump of sugar, 2 oz. of butter, salt and pepper to taste, 2 quarts of medium stock. *Mode.* —Cut the partridges into pieces, and braise them in the butter and ham until quite tender ; then take out the legs, wings, and breast, and set them by. Keep the backs and other trimmings in the braise, and add the onions and celery ; any remains of cold game can be put in, and 3 pints of stock. Simmer slowly for 1 hour, strain it, and skim the fat off as clean as possible ; put in the pieces that were taken out, give it one boil, and skim again to have it quite clear, and add the sugar and seasoning. Now simmer the cut carrot and turnip in 1 pint of stock ; when quite tender, put them to the partridges, and serve. *Time.*—2 hours. *Average cost,* 2s. or 1s. 6d. per quart. *Seasonable* from September to February. *Sufficient* for 8 persons.

Note.—The meat of the partridges may be pounded with a crumb of a French roll, and worked with the soup through a sieve. Serve with stewed celery cut in slices, and put in the tureen.

Partridges, Hashed

PARTRIDGES, to Carve.

There are several ways of carving this most familiar game bird. The more usual and summary mode is to carry the knife sharply along the top of the breast-bone of the bird, and cut it quite through, thus dividing it into two precisely equal and similar parts, in the same manner

ROAST PARTRIDGE.

as carving a pigeon. Another plan is to cut it into three pieces ; viz., by severing a small wing and leg on either side from the body, by following the line 1 to 2 in the upper woodcut ; thus making 2 helpings, when the breast will remain for a third plate. The most elegant manner is that of thrusting back the body from the legs, and then cutting through the breast in the direction shown by the line 1 to 2 : this plan will give 4 or more small helpings. A little bread-sauce should be served to each guest.

PARTRIDGES, Hashed, or Salmi de Perdrix.

Ingredients.—3 young partridges, 3 shallots, a slice of lean ham, 1 carrot, 3 or 4 mushrooms, a bunch of savoury herbs, 2 cloves, 6 whole peppers, ¾ pint of stock, 1 glass of sherry or Madeira, a small lump of sugar. *Mode.*—After the partridges are plucked and drawn, roast them rather underdone, and cover them with paper, as they should not be browned ; cut them into joints, take off the skin from the wings, legs, and breasts ; put these into a stewpan, cover them up, and set by until the gravy is ready. Cut a slice of ham into small pieces, and put them, with the carrots sliced, the shallots, mushrooms, herbs, cloves, and pepper, into a stewpan ; fry them lightly in a little butter, pour in the stock, add the bones and trimming from the partridges, and simmer for ¼ hour. Strain the gravy, let it cool, and skim off every particle of fat ; put it to the legs, wings, and breasts, add a glass of sherry or Madeira and a small lump of sugar, let all gradually warm through by the side of the fire, and when on the

Paste, Common, for Family Pies

point of boiling, serve, and garnish the dish with croûtons. The remains of roast partridge answer very well dressed ¦n this way, although not so good as when the birds are in the first instance only half-roasted. This recipe is equally suitable for pheasants, moorgame, &c.; but care must be taken always to skin the joints. *Time.*—Altogether 1 hour. *Sufficient.*—2 or 3 partridges for an entrée. *Seasonable* from the 1st of September to the beginning of February.

PASTE, Common, for Family Pies.

Ingredients.—1¼ lb. of flour, ½ lb. of butter, rather more than ½ pint of water. *Mode.*—Rub the butter lightly into the flour, and mix it to a smooth paste with the water; roll it out 2 or 3 times, and it will be ready for use. This paste may be converted into an excellent short crust for sweet tart by adding to the flour, after the butter is rubbed in, 2 tablespoonfuls of fine-sifted sugar. *Average cost*, 8*d.* per lb.

PASTE, Puff, French, or Feuilletage (Founded on M. Ude's Recipe).

Ingredients.—Equal quantities of flour and butter—say 1 lb. of each; ⅓ saltspoonful of salt, the yolks of 2 eggs, rather more than ¼ pint of water. *Mode.* —Weigh the flour; ascertain that it is perfectly *dry*, and sift it; squeeze all the water from the butter, and wring it in a clean cloth till there is no moisture remaining. Put the flour on the pasteboard, work lightly into it 2 oz. of the butter, and then make a hole in the centre; into this well put the yolks of 2 eggs, the salt, and about ¼ pint of water (the quantity of this latter ingredient must be regulated by the cook, as it is impossible to give the exact proportion of it); knead up the paste quickly and lightly, and, when quite smooth, roll it out square to the thickness of about ½ inch. Presuming that the butter is perfectly free from moisture, and *as cool as possible*, roll it into a ball, and place this ball of butter on the paste; fold the paste over the butter all round, and secure it by wrapping it well all over. Flatten the paste by rolling it lightly with the rolling-pin until it is quite thin, but not thin enough to allow the butter to break through, and keep the board

Paste, Puff, very Good

and paste dredged lightly with flour during the process of making it. This rolling gives it the *first* turn. Now fold the paste in three, and roll out again, and, should the weather be very warm, put it in a cold place on the ground to cool between the several turns; for, unless this is particularly attended to, the paste will be spoiled. Roll out the paste again *twice*, put it by to cool, then roll it out *twice* more, which will make 6 *turnings* in all. Now fold the paste in two, and it will be ready for use. If properly baked and well made, this crust will be delicious, and should rise in the oven about 5 or 6 inches. The paste should be made rather firm in the first instance, as the ball of butter is liable to break through. Great attention must also be paid to keeping the butter very cool, as, if this is in a liquid and soft state, the paste will not answer at all. Should the cook be dexterous enough to succeed in making this, the paste will have a much better appearance than that made by the process of dividing the butter into 4 parts, and placing it over the rolled-out paste; but until experience has been acquired, we recommend puff-paste made by recipe. The above paste is used for vols-au-vent, small articles of pastry, and, in fact, everything that requires very light crust. *Average cost*, 1*s.* 6*d.* per lb.

PASTE, Puff, very Good.

Ingredients.—To every lb. of flour allow 1 lb. of butter, and not quite ½ pint of water. *Mode.*—Carefully weigh the flour and butter, and have the exact proportion; squeeze the butter well, to extract the water from it, and afterwards wring it in a clean cloth, that no moisture may remain. Sift the flour; see that it is perfectly dry, and proceed in the following manner to make the paste, using a very *clean* paste-board and rolling-pin:—Supposing the quantity to be 1 lb. of flour, work the whole into a smooth paste with not quite ½ pint of water, using a knife to mix it with: the proportion of this latter ingredient must be regulated by the discretion of the cook; if too much be added, the paste, when baked, will be tough. Roll it out until it is of an equal thickness of about an inch; break 4 oz. of the butter into small pieces; place these on the paste, sift over it a little flour, fold it over, roll out again,

Paste, Puff, Medium

and put another 4 oz. of butter. Repeat the rolling and buttering until the paste has been rolled out 4 times, or equal quantities of flour and butter have been used. Do not omit, every time the paste is rolled out, to dredge a little flour over that and the rolling-pin, to prevent both from sticking. Handle the paste as lightly as possible, and do not press heavily upon it with the rolling-pin. The next thing to be considered is the oven, as the baking of pastry requires particular attention. Do not put it into the oven until it is sufficiently hot to raise the paste; for the best-prepared paste, if not properly baked, will be good for nothing. Brushing the paste as often as rolled out, and the pieces of butter placed thereon, with the white of an egg, assists it to rise in *leaves* or *flakes*. As this is the great beauty of puff-paste, it is as well to try this method. *Average cost*, 1s. 4d. per lb.

PASTE, Puff, Medium.

Ingredients.—To every lb. of flour allow 8 oz. of butter, 4 oz. of lard, not quite ½ pint of water. *Mode.*—This paste may be made by the directions in the preceding recipe, only using less butter, and substituting lard for a portion of it. Mix the flour to a smooth paste with not quite ½ pint of water; then roll it out 3 times, the first time covering the paste with butter, the second with lard, and the third with butter. Keep the rolling-pin and paste slightly dredged with flour, to prevent them from sticking, and it will be ready for use. *Average cost*, 1s. per lb.

PASTE, Puff (Soyer's Recipe).

Ingredients.—To every lb. of flour allow the yolk of 1 egg, the juice of 1 lemon, ½ saltspoonful of salt, cold water, 1 lb. of fresh butter. *Mode.*—Put the flour on to the paste-board; make a hole in the centre, into which put the yolk of the egg, the lemon-juice, and salt; mix the whole with cold water (this should be iced in summer, if convenient) into a soft flexible paste, with the right hand, and handle it as little as possible; then squeeze all the buttermilk from the butter, wring it in a cloth, and roll out the paste; place the butter on this, and fold the edges of the paste over, so as to hide it: roll it out again to the thickness of ¼ inch; fold over one third, over which again pass the rolling-pin; then

Pastry and Puddings

fold over the other third, thus forming square; place it with the ends, top, bottom before you, shaking a little both under and over, and repeat the and turns twice again, as before. F a baking-sheet, put the paste on and let it remain on ice or in some place for ½ hour; then roll twice m turning it as before; place it again u the ice for ¼ hour, give it 2 more r making 7 in all, and it is ready for when required. *Average cost*, 1s. per lb.

PASTRY AND PUDDINGS, Directions in connection w the making of.

A few general remarks respecting various ingredients of which pudd and pastry are composed may be acc able, in addition to the recipes in department of Household Manageme *Flour* should be of the best qua and perfectly dry, and sifted be being used; if in the least damp, paste made from it will certainly heavy.

Butter, unless fresh is used, shoul washed from the salt, and well sque and wrung in a cloth, to get out all water and buttermilk, which, if lef assist to make the paste heavy.

Lard should be perfectly sweet, w may be ascertained by cutting bladder through, and, if the knife sn sweet, the lard is good.

Suet should be finely chopped, perfe free from skin, and quite sweet; du the process of chopping, it should lightly dredged with flour, which prev the pieces from sticking together. suet is considered the best; but suet, or the outside fat of a loin or of mutton, makes good crusts; as the skimmings in which a joint of mu has been boiled, but *without* vegetab

Clarified Beef Dripping answers well for kitchen pies, puddings, cake for family use. A very good short c may be made by mixing with it a s quantity of moist sugar; but care n be taken to use the dripping sparin or a very disagreeable flavour wil imparted to the paste.

Strict cleanliness must be observe pastry-making; all the utensils should be perfectly free from dust dirt, and the things required for pa kept entirely for that purpose.

Pastry and Puddings

In mixing paste, add the water very gradually, work the whole together with the knife-blade, and knead it until perfectly smooth. Those who are inexperienced in pastry-making should work

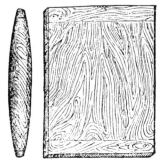

PASTE-BOARD AND ROLLING-PIN.

the butter in by breaking it in small pieces, and covering the paste rolled out. It should then be dredged with flour, and the ends folded over and rolled out very thin again: this process must be repeated until all the butter is used.

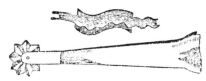

PASTE-PINCERS AND JAGGER, FOR ORNAMENTING THE EDGES OF PIE-CRUSTS.

The art of making paste requires much practice, dexterity, and skill: it should be touched as lightly as possible, made with cool hands and in a cool place (a marble slab is better than a board for the purpose), and the coolest part of the house should be selected for the process during warm weather.

PASTE-CUTTER AND CORNER-CUTTER.

To insure rich paste being light, great expedition must be used in the making and baking; for if it stand long before

Pastry and Puddings

it is put in the oven, it becomes flat and heavy.

ORNAMENTAL-PASTE CUTTER.

Puff-paste requires a brisk oven, b not too hot, or it would blacken the crust, on the other hand, if the oven be too slack, the paste will be soddened, and will not rise, nor will it have any colour.

PATTY-PANS, PLAIN AND FLUTED.

Tart-tins, cake-moulds, dishes for baked puddings, patty-pans, &c., should all be buttered before the article intended to

PIE-DISH.

be baked is put in them. Things to be baked on sheets should be placed on buttered paper. Raised-pie paste should have a soaking heat, and paste glazed

RAISED-PIE MOULD.

must have rather a slack oven, that the icing be not scorched. It is

RAISED-PIE MOULD, OPEN.

better to ice tarts, &c., when they are three-parts baked.

Pastry and Puddings

To ascertain when the oven is heated to the proper degree for puff-paste, put a small piece of the paste in previous to baking the whole, and then the heat can thus be judged of.

The freshness of all pudding ingredients is of much importance, as one bad article will taint the whole mixture.

When the *freshness* of eggs is *doubtful*, break each one separately in a cup, before mixing them altogether. Should there be a bad one amongst them, it can be thrown away ; whereas, if mixed with the good ones, the entire quantity would be spoiled. The yolks and whites beaten separately make the articles they are put into much lighter.

Raisins and dried fruits for puddings should be carefully picked, and in many cases stoned. Currants should be well washed, pressed in a cloth, and placed on a dish before the fire to get thoroughly dry : they should then be picked carefully over, and *every piece of grit or stone* removed from amongst them. To plump them, some cooks pour boiling water over them, and then dry them before the fire.

Batter pudding should be smoothly mixed and free from lumps. To insure this, first mix the flour with a very small proportion of milk, and add the remainder by degrees. Should the pudding be very lumpy, it may be strained through a hair sieve.

All boiled puddings should be put on in *boiling water*, which must not be allowed to stop simmering, and the pudding must always be covered with the water; if requisite, the saucepan should be kept filled up.

BOILED-PUDDING MOULD.

To prevent a pudding boiled in a cloth from sticking to the bottom of the saucepan, place a small plate or saucer underneath it, and set the pan *on a trivet* over the fire. If a mould is used, this precaution is not necessary ; but care must be taken to keep the pudding well covered with water.

For dishing a boiled pudding as soon as it comes out of the pot, dip it into a basin of cold water, and the cloth will

Pastry and Puddings

then not adhere to it. Great expedition is necessary in sending puddings to table, as by standing they quickly become heavy, batter puddings particularly.

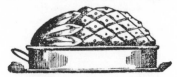

BOILED PUDDING MOULD.

For baked or boiled puddings, the moulds, cups, or basins should be always buttered before the mixture is put in them, and they should be put into the saucepan directly they are filled.

Scrupulous attention should be paid to the cleanliness of pudding-cloths, as from neglect in this particular the out-

PUDDING-BASIN.

sides of boiled puddings frequently taste very disagreeably. As soon as possible after it is taken off the pudding, it should be soaked in water, and then well washed, without soap, unless it be very greasy. It should be dried out of doors, then folded up and kept in a dry place. When wanted for use, dip it in boiling water, and dredge it slightly with flour.

The dry ingredients for puddings are better for being mixed some time before they are wanted ; the liquid portion should only be added just before the pudding is put into the saucepan.

A pinch of salt is an improvement to the generality of puddings ; but this ingredient should be added very sparingly, as the flavour should not be detected.

When baked puddings are sufficiently solid, turn them out of the dish they were baked in, bottom uppermost, and strew over them fine-sifted sugar.

When pastry or baked puddings are not done through, and yet the outside is sufficiently brown, cover them over with a piece of white paper until thoroughly cooked : this prevents them from getting burnt.

| Pastry, Iced or Glazed | Pea Soup, Inexpensive |

PASTRY, to Ice or Glaze.

To glaze pastry, which is the usual method adopted for meat or raised pies, break an egg, separate the yolk from the white, and beat the former for a short time. Then, when the pastry is nearly baked, take it out of the oven, brush it over with this beaten yolk of egg, and put it back in the oven to set the glaze.

To ice pastry, which is the usual method adopted for fruit tarts and sweet dishes of pastry, put the white of an egg on a plate, and with the blade of a knife beat it to a stiff froth. When the pastry is nearly baked, brush it over with this, and sift over some pounded sugar ; put it back into the oven to set the glaze, and, in a few minutes, it will be done. Great care should be taken that the paste does not catch or burn in the oven, which it is very liable to do after the icing is laid on. *Sufficient.*—Allow 1 egg and 1½ oz. of sugar to glaze 3 tarts.

PASTRY SANDWICHES.

Ingredients.—Puff-paste, jam of any kind, the white of an egg, sifted sugar. *Mode.*—Roll the paste out thin ; put half of it on a baking-sheet or tin, and spread equally over it apricot, greengage, or any preserve that may be preferred. Lay over this preserve another thin paste ; press the edges together all round ; and mark the paste in lines with a knife on the surface, to show where to cut it when baked. Bake from 20 minutes to ½ hour ; and, a short time before being done, take the pastry out of the oven, brush it over with the white of an egg, sift over pounded sugar, and put it back in the oven to colour. When cold, cut it into strips ; pile these on a dish pyramidically, and serve. These strips, cut about 2 inches long, piled in circular rows, and a plateful of flavoured whipped cream poured in the middle, make a very pretty dish. *Time.*—20 minutes to ½ hour. *Average cost*, with ½ lb. of paste, 1s. *Sufficient.*—½ lb. of paste will make 2 dishes of sandwiches. *Seasonable at any time.*

PATE BRISEE, Crust French, for Raised Pies.

Ingredients.—To every lb. of flour allow ½ saltspoonful of salt, 2 eggs, ⅓ pint of water, 6 oz. of butter. *Mode.*—Spread the flour, which should be sifted and

thoroughly dry, on the paste-board ; make a hole in the centre, into which put the butter ; work it lightly into the flour, and when quite fine, add the salt ; work the whole into a smooth paste with the eggs (yolks and whites) and water, and make it very firm. Knead the paste well, and let it be rather stiff, that the sides of the pie may be easily raised, and that they do not afterwards tumble or shrink. *Average cost*, 1s. per lb.

Note.—This paste may be very much enriched by making it with equal quantities of flour and butter ; but then it is not so easily raised as when made plainer.

PATTIES, Fried.

[COLD MEAT COOKERY.] *Ingredients.*— Cold roast veal, a few slices of cold ham, 1 egg boiled hard, pounded mace, pepper and salt to taste, gravy, cream, 1 teaspoonful of minced lemon-peel, good puff-paste. *Mode.*—Mince a little cold veal and ham, allowing one-third ham to two-thirds veal ; add an egg boiled hard and chopped, and a seasoning of pounded mace, salt, pepper, and lemon-peel ; moisten with a little gravy and cream. Make a good puff-paste ; roll rather thin, and cut it into round or square pieces ; put the mince between two of them, pinch the edges to keep in the gravy, and fry a light brown. They may also be baked in patty-pans ; in that case, they should be brushed over with the yolk of an egg before they are put in the oven. To make a variety, oysters may be substituted for the ham. *Time.*—15 minutes to fry the patties. *Seasonable* from March to October.

PEA SOUP (Inexpensive).

Ingredients.—¼ lb. of onions, ¼ lb. of carrots, 2 oz. of celery, ¾ lb. of split peas, a little mint, shred fine ; 1 tablespoonful of coarse brown sugar, salt and pepper to taste, 4 quarts of water, or liquor in which a joint of meat has been boiled. *Mode.*—Fry the vegetables for 10 minutes in a little butter or dripping, previously cutting them up into small pieces ; pour the water on them, and when boiling add the peas. Let them simmer for nearly 3 hours, or until the peas are thoroughly done. Add the sugar, seasoning, and mint ; boil for ¼ of an hour, and serve. *Time.*—3½ hours. *Average cost*, 1½d. p

Pea Soup, Green

quart. *Seasonable* in winter. *Sufficient* for 12 persons.

PEA SOUP (Green).

Ingredients.—3 pints of green peas, ¼ lb. of butter, 2 or 3 thin slices of ham, 3 onions sliced, 4 shredded lettuces, the crumb of 2 French rolls, 2 handfuls of spinach, 1 lump of sugar, 2 quarts of medium stock. *Mode.*—Put the butter, ½am, 1 quart of peas, onions, and lettuces, to a pint of stock, and simmer for an hour; then add the remainder of the stock, with the crumb of the French rolls, and boil for another hour. Now boil the spinach, and squeeze it very dry. Rub the soup through a sieve, and the spinach with it, to colour it. Have ready a pint of *young* peas boiled; add them to the soup, put in the sugar, give one boil, and serve. If necessary, add salt. *Time.*—2½ hours. *Average cost*, 1s. 9d. per quart. *Seasonable* from June to the end of August. *Sufficient* for 10 persons.

Note.—It will be well to add, if the peas are not quite young, a little more sugar. Where economy is essential, water may be used instead of stock for this soup, boiling in it likewise the pea-shells; but using a double quantity of vegetables.

PEA SOUP, Winter (Yellow).

Ingredients.—1 quart of split peas, 2 lbs. of shin beef, trimmings of meat or poultry, a slice of bacon, 2 large carrots, 2 turnips, 5 large onions, 1 head of celery, seasoning to taste, 2 quarts of soft water, any bones left from roast meat, 2 quarts of common stock, or liquor in which a joint of meat has been boiled. *Mode.*—Put the peas to soak over-night in soft water and float off such as rise to the top. Boil them in the water till tender enoug to pulp; then add the ingredients mentioned above, and simmer for 2 hours, stirring it occasionally. Pass the whole through a sieve, skim well, season, and serve with toasted bread cut in dice. *Time.*—4 hours. *Average cost*, 6d. per quart. *Seasonable* all the year round, but more suitable for cold weather. *Sufficient* for 12 persons.

PEACHES, Compote of.

Ingredients.—1 pint of syrup, about 15 small peaches. *Mode.*—Peaches that

Peaches Preserved in Brandy

are not very large, and that would not look well for dessert, answer very nicely for a compote. Divide the peaches, take out the stones, and pare the fruit; make a syrup by recipe, put in the peaches, and stew them gently for about 10 minutes. Take them out without breaking, arrange them on a glass dish, boil the syrup for 2 or 3 minutes, let it cool, pour it over the fruit, and, when cold, it will be ready for table. *Time.*—10 minutes. *Average cost*, 1s. 2d. *Sufficient* for 5 or 6 persons. *Seasonable* in August and September.

PEACH FRITTERS.

Ingredients.—For the batter, ½ lb. of flour, ½ oz. of butter, ½ saltspoonful of salt, 2 eggs, milk, peaches, hot lard or clarified dripping. *Mode.*—Make a nice smooth batter; skin, halve, and stone the peaches, which should be quite ripe; dip them in the batter, and fry the pieces in hot lard or clarified dripping, which should be boiling before the peaches are put in. From 8 to 10 minutes will be required to fry them; when done, drain them before the fire. Dish them on a white d'oyley. Strew over plenty of pounded sugar and serve. *Time.*—From 8 to 10 minutes to fry the fritters, 5 minutes to drain them. *Average cost*, 1s. *Sufficient* for 4 or 5 persons. *Seasonable* in July, August, and September.

PEACHES PRESERVED IN BRANDY.

Ingredients.—To every lb. of fruit weighed before being stoned, allow ¼ lb. of finely-pounded loaf sugar; brandy. *Mode.*—Let the fruit be gathered in dry weather; wipe and weigh it, and remove the stones as carefully as possible, without injuring the peaches much. Put them into a jar, sprinkle amongst them pounded loaf sugar in the above proportion, and pour brandy over the fruit. Cover the jar down closely, place it in a saucepan of boiling water over the fire, and bring the brandy to the simmering-point, but do not allow it to boil. Take the fruit out carefully, without breaking it; put it into small jars, pour over it the brandy, and, when cold, exclude the air by covering the jars with bladders, or tissue-paper brushed over on both sides with the white of an egg. Apricots

Pears, Baked

may be done in the same manner, and, if properly prepared, will be found delicious. *Time.*—From 10 to 20 minutes to bring the brandy to the simmering-point. *Seasonable* in August and September.

PEARS, Baked.

Ingredients.—12 pears, the rind of 1 lemon, 6 cloves, 10 whole allspice; to every pint of water allow ½ lb. of loaf sugar. *Mode.*—Pare and cut the pears into halves, and, should they be very large, into quarters; leave the stalks on, and carefully remove the cores. Place them in a clean baking-jar, with a closely-fitting lid;· add to them the lemon-rind cut in strips, the juice of ½ lemon, the cloves, pounded allspice, and sufficient water just to cover the whole, with sugar in the above proportion. Cover the jar down closely, put it into a very cool oven, and bake the pears from 5 to 6 hours, but be very careful that the oven is not too hot. To improve the colour of the fruit, a few drops of prepared cochineal may be added; but this will not be found necessary, if the pears are very gently baked. *Time.*—Large pears, 5 to 6 hours, in a very slow oven. *Average cost, 1d.* to *2d.* each. *Sufficient* for 7 or 8 persons. *Seasonable* from September to January.

PEARS à L'ALLEMANDE.

Ingredients.—6 to 8 pears, water, sugar, 2 oz. of butter, the yolk of an egg, ½ oz. of gelatine. *Mode.*—Peel and cut the pears into any form that may be preferred, and steep them in cold water to prevent them turning black; put them into a saucepan with sufficient cold water to cover them, and boil them with the butter and enough sugar to sweeten them nicely, until tender; then brush the pears over with the yolk of an egg, sprinkle them with sifted sugar, and arrange them on a dish. Add the gelatine to the syrup, boil it up quickly for about 5 minutes, strain it over the pears, and let it remain until set. The syrup may be coloured with a little prepared cochineal, which would very much improve the appearance of the dish. *Time.* —From 20 minutes to ½ hour to stew the pears; 5 minutes to boil the syrup. *Average cost, 1s. 3d.* *Sufficient* for a large dish. *Seasonable from* August to February.

Pears, Stewed

PEARS, Moulded.

Ingredients.—4 large pears or 6 small ones, 8 cloves, sugar to taste, water, a small piece of cinnamon, ¼ pint of raisin wine, a strip of lemon-peel, the juice of ½ lemon, ½ oz. of gelatine. *Mode.*—Peel and cut the pears into quarters; put them into a jar with ¾ pint of water, cloves, cinnamon, and sufficient sugar to sweeten the whole nicely; cover down the top of the jar, and bake the pears in a gentle oven until perfectly tender, but do not allow them to break. When done, lay the pears in a plain mould, which should be well wetted, and boil ½ pint of the liquor the pears were baked in with the wine, lemon-peel, strained juice, and gelatine. Let these ingredients boil quickly for 5 minutes, then strain the liquid warm over the pears; put the mould in a cool place, and when the jelly is firm, turn it out on a glass dish. *Time.*—2 hours to bake the pears in a cool oven. *Average cost, 1s. 3d.* *Sufficient* for a quart mould. *Seasonable* from August to February.

PEARS, Preserved.

Ingredients. — Jargonelle pears; to every lb. of sugar allow ½ pint of water. *Mode.*—Procure some Jargonelle pears, not too ripe; put them into a stewpan with sufficient water to cover them, and simmer them till rather tender, but do not allow them to break; then put them into cold water. Boil the sugar and water together for 5 minutes, skim well, put in the pears, and simmer them gently for 5 minutes. Repeat the simmering for 3 successive days, taking care not to let the fruit break. The last time of boiling, the syrup should be made rather richer, and the fruit boiled for 10 minutes. When the pears are done, drain them from the syrup, and dry them in the sun, or in a cool oven; or they may be kept in the syrup, and dried as they were wanted. *Time.*—½ hour to simmer the pears in water, 20 minutes in the syrup. *Average cost, 1d.* to *2d.* each. *Seasonable.*—Most plentiful in September and October.

PEARS, Stewed.

Ingredients. — 8 large pears, 5 oz. of loaf sugar, 6 cloves, 6 whole allspice, ½ pint of water, ¼ pint of port wine, a few drops of prepared cochineal. *Mode.* —

Peas, Boiled Green

Pare the pears, halve them, remove the cores, and leave the stalks on ; put them into a *lined* saucepan with the above ingredients, and let them simmer very gently until tender, which will be in from 3 to 4 hours, according to the quality of the pears. They should be watched, and, when done, carefully lifted

STEWED PEARS.

out on to a glass dish without breaking them. Boil up the syrup quickly for 2 or 3 minutes ; allow it to cool a little, pour it over the pears, and let them get perfectly cold. To improve the colour of the fruit, a few drops of prepared cochineal may be added, which rather enhances the beauty of this dish. The fruit must not be boiled fast, but only simmered, and watched that it be not too much done. *Time.*—3 to 4 hours. *Average cost*, 1s. 6d. *Sufficient* for 5 or 6 persons. *Seasonable* from September to January.

PEAS, Boiled Green.

Ingredients.—Green peas ; to each ½ gallon of water allow 1 *small* teaspoonful of moist sugar, 1 heaped tablespoonful of salt. *Mode.*—This delicious vegetable, to be eaten in perfection, should be young, and not *gathered* or *shelled* long before it is dressed. Shell the peas, wash them well in cold water, and drain them ; then put them into a saucepan with plenty of *fast-boiling* water, to which salt and *moist sugar* have been added in the above proportion ; let them boil quickly over a brisk fire, with the lid of the saucepan uncovered, and be careful that the smoke does not draw in. When tender, pour them into a colander ; put them into a *not* vegetable-dish, and quite in the centre of the peas place a piece of butter, the size of a walnut. Many cooks boil a small bunch of mint *with* the *peas*, or garnish them with it, by boiling a few sprigs in a saucepan by themselves. Should the peas be very old, and difficult to boil a good colour, a very tiny piece of soda may be thrown in the water previous to putting them in ; but this must be very sparingly used, as it causes the peas, when boiled, to have a smashed and broken appear-

Peas, Stewed Green

ance. With young peas, there is not the slightest occasion to use it. *Time.*—Young peas, 10 to 15 minutes ; the large sorts, such as marrowfats, &c., 18 to 24 minutes ; old peas, ½ hour. *Average cost*, when cheapest, 6d. per peck ; when first in season, 1s. to 1s. 6d. per peck. *Sufficient.*—Allow 1 peck of unshelled peas for 4 or 5 persons. *Seasonable* from June to the end of August.

PEAS, Green, à la Francaise.

Ingredients.—2 quarts of green peas, 3 oz. of fresh butter, a bunch of parsley, 6 green onions, flour, a small lump of sugar, ½ teaspoonful of salt, a teaspoonful of flour. *Mode.*—Shell sufficient fresh-gathered peas to fill 2 quarts ; put them into cold water, with the above proportion of butter, and stir them about until they are well covered with the butter ; drain them in a colander, and put them in a stewpan, with the parsley and onions ; dredge over them a little flour, stir the peas well, and moisten them with boiling water ; boil them quickly over a large fire for 20 minutes, or until there is no liquor remaining. Dip a small lump of sugar into some water, that it may soon melt ; put it with the peas, to which add ½ teaspoonful of salt. Take a piece of butter the size of a walnut, work it together with a teaspoonful of flour, and add this to the peas, which should be boiling when it is put in. Keep shaking the stewpan, and, when the peas are nicely thickened, dress them high in the dish, and serve. *Time.* — Altogether, ¾ hour. *Average cost*, 6d. per peck. *Sufficient* for 4 or 5 persons. *Seasonable* from June to the end of August.

PEAS, Stewed Green

Ingredients.—1 quart of peas, 1 lettuce, 1 onion, 2 oz. of butter, pepper and salt to taste, 1 egg, ½ teaspoonful of powdered sugar. *Mode.*—Shell the peas, and cut the onion and lettuce into slices ; put these into a stewpan, with the butter, pepper, and salt, but with no more water than that which hangs around the lettuce from washing. Stew the whole very gently for rather more than 1 hour ; then stir in a well-beaten egg, and about ½ teaspoonful of powdered sugar. When the peas, &c., are nicely thickened, serve ; but, after the egg is added, do not allow them to boil. *Time.*—1½ hour.

Perch, Boiled

Average cost, 6*d*. per peck. *Sufficient* for 3 or 4 persons. *Seasonable* from June to the end of August.

PERCH, Boiled.

Ingredients.—¼ lb. of salt to each gallon of water. *Mode.*—Scale the fish, take out the gills and clean it thoroughly ; lay it in boiling water, salted as above, and simmer gently for 10 minutes. If the fish is very large, longer time must be allowed. Garnish with parsley, and serve with plain melted butter, or Dutch sauce. Perch do not preserve so good a flavour when stewed as when dressed in any other way. *Time.*—Middling-sized perch, ¼ hour. *Seasonable* from September to November.

Note.—Tench may be boiled the same way, and served with the same sauces.

PERCH, Fried.

Ingredients.—Egg and bread crumbs, hot lard. *Mode.*—Scale and clean the fish, brush it over with egg, and cover with bread crumbs. Have ready some boiling lard ; put the fish in, and fry a nice brown. Serve with plain melted butter or anchovy sauce. *Time.*—10 minutes. *Seasonable* from September to November.

Note.—Fry tench in the same way.

PERCH, Stewed with Wine.

Ingredients.—Equal quantities of stock and sherry, 1 bay-leaf, 1 clove of garlic, a small bunch of parsley, 2 cloves, salt to taste ; thickening of butter and flour, pepper, grated nutmeg, ½ teaspoonful of anchovy sauce. *Mode.*—Scale the fish and take out the gills, and clean them thoroughly ; lay them in a stewpan with sufficient stock and sherry just to cover them. Put in the bay-leaf, garlic, parsley, cloves, and salt, and simmer till tender. When done, take out the fish, strain the liquor, add a thickening of butter and flour, the pepper, nutmeg, and the anchovy sauce, and stir it over the fire until somewhat reduced, when pour over the fish, and serve. *Time.*— About 20 minutes. *Seasonable* from September to November.

PETITES BOUCHÉES.

Ingredients.—6 oz. of sweet almonds, ¼ lb. of sifted sugar, the rind of ½ lemon, the white of 1 egg, puff-paste. *Mode.*—

Pheasant, to Carve

Blanch the almonds, and chop them fine ; rub the sugar on the lemon-rind, and pound it in a mortar ; mix this with the almonds and the white of the egg. Roll some puff-paste out ; cut it in any shape that may be preferred, such as diamonds, rings, ovals, &c., and spread the above mixture over the paste. Bake the bouchées in an oven, not too hot, and serve cold. *Time.*—¼ hour, or rather more. *Average cost*, 1*s*. *Sufficient* for ½ lb of puff-paste. *Seasonable* at any time.

PHEASANT.

If this bird be eaten three days after it has been killed, it then has no peculiarity of flavour ; a pullet would be more relished, and a quail would surpass it in aroma. Kept, however, a proper length of time,—and this can be ascertained by a slight smell and change of colour,— then it becomes a highly-flavoured dish, occupying, so to speak, the middle distance between chicken and venison. It is difficult to define any exact time to "hang" a pheasant ; but any one possessed of the instincts of gastronomical science, can at once detect the right moment when a pheasant should be taken down, in the same way as a good cook knows whether a bird should be removed from the spit, or have a turn or two more.

PHEASANT, Broiled (a Breakfast or Luncheon Dish).

Ingredients.—1 pheasant, a little lard, egg and bread crumbs, salt and cayenne to taste. *Mode.*—Cut the legs off at the first joint, and the remainder of the bird into neat pieces ; put them into a frying-pan with a little lard, and when browned on both sides, and about half done, take them out and drain them ; brush the pieces over with egg, and sprinkle with bread crumbs with which has been mixed a good seasoning of cayenne and salt. Broil them over a moderate fire for about 10 minutes, or rather longer, and serve with mushroom-sauce, sauce piquante, or brown gravy, in which a few game bones and trimmings have been stewed. *Time.*—Altogether ½ hour. *Sufficient* for 4 or 5 persons. *Seasonable* from the 1st of October to the beginning of February.

PHEASANT, to Carve.

Fixing the fork in the breast, let the carver cut slices from it in the direction

Pheasant Cutlets	Pheasant Soup

of the lines from 2 to 1: these are the prime pieces. If there be more guests to satisfy than these slices will serve, then let the legs and wings be disengaged in the same manner as described

ROAST PHEASANT.

in carving boiled fowl, the point where the wing joins the neckbone being carefully found. The merrythought will come off in the same way as that of a fowl. The most valued parts are the same as those which are most considered in a fowl.

PHEASANT CUTLETS.

Ingredients.—2 or 3 pheasants, egg and bread crumbs, cayenne and salt to taste, brown gravy. *Mode.*—Procure 3 young pheasants that have been hung a few days; pluck, draw, and wipe them inside; cut them into joints; remove the bones from the best of these; and the backbones, trimmings, &c., put into a stewpan, with a little stock, herbs, vegetables, seasoning, &c., to make the gravy. Flatten and trim the cutlets of a good shape, egg and bread - crumb them, broil them over a clear fire, pile them high in the dish, and pour under them the gravy made from the bones, which should be strained, flavoured, and thickened. One of the small bones should be stuck on the point of each cutlet. *Time.*—10 minutes. *Average cost,* 2s. 6d. to 3s. each. *Sufficient* for 2 entrées. *Seasonable* from the 1st of October to the beginning of February.

PHEASANT, Roast.

Ingredients.—Pheasant, flour, butter. *Choosing and trussing.*—Old pheasants may be known by the length and sharp-

ROAST PHEASANT.

ness of their spurs; in young ones they are short and blunt. The cock bird is generally reckoned the best, except

when the hen is with egg. They should hang some time before they are dressed, as, if they are cooked fresh, the flesh will be exceedingly dry and tasteless. After the bird is plucked and drawn, wipe the inside with a damp cloth, and truss it in the same manner as partridge. If the head is left on, as shown in the engraving, bring it round under the wing, and fix it on to the point of the skewer. *Mode.*—Roast it before a brisk fire, keep it well basted, and flour and froth it nicely. Serve with brown gravy, a little of which should be poured round the bird, and a tureen of bread sauce. 2 or 3 of the pheasant's best tail-feathers are sometimes stuck in the tail as an ornament; but the fashion is not much to be commended. *Time.*—½ to 1 hour, according to the size. *Average cost,* 2s. 6d. to 3s. each. *Sufficient,*—1 for a dish. *Seasonable* from the 1st of October to the beginning of February.

PHEASANT, Roast, Brillat Savarin's Recipe (à la Sainte Alliance).

When the pheasant is in good condition to be cooked, it should be plucked, and not before. The bird should then be stuffed in the following manner :— Take two snipes, and draw them, putting the bodies on one plate, and the livers, &c., on another. Take off the flesh, and mince it finely with a little beef, lard, a few truffles, pepper and salt to taste, and stuff the pheasant carefully with this. Cut a slice of bread, larger considerably than the bird, and cover it with the liver, &c., and a few truffles: an anchovy and a little fresh butter added to these will do no harm. Put the bread, &c., into the dripping-pan, and, when the bird is roasted, place it on the preparation, and surround it with Florida oranges.

Do not be uneasy, Savarin adds, about your dinner; for a pheasant served in this way is fit for beings better than men. The pheasant itself is a very good bird; and, imbibing the dressing and the flavour of the truffle and snipe, it becomes thrice better.

PHEASANT SOUP.

Ingredients.—2 pheasants, ¼ lb. of butter, 2 slices of ham, 2 large onions sliced, ½ head of celery, the crumb of two French rolls, the yolks of 2 eggs boiled hard, salt and cayenne to taste, a little

Pickle, an Excellent

pounded mace, if liked; 3 quarts of stock medium. *Mode.*—Cut up the pheasants, flour and braise them in the butter and ham till they are of a nice brown, but not burnt. Put them in a stewpan, with the onions, celery, stock, and seasoning, and simmer for 2 hours. Strain the soup; pound the breasts with the crumb of the roll previously soaked, and the yolks of the eggs; put it to the soup, give one boil, and serve. *Time.*—2½ hours. *Average cost,* 2s. 10d. per quart, or, if made with fragments of cold game, 1s. *Seasonable* from October to February. *Sufficient* for 10 persons.

Note.—Fragments, pieces and bones of cold game, may be used to great advantage in this soup, and then 1 pheasant will suffice.

PICKLE, an Excellent.

Ingredients.—Equal quantities of medium-sized onions, cucumbers, and sauce-apples; 1½ teaspoonful of salt, ¾ teaspoonful of cayenne, 1 wineglassful of soy, 1 wineglassful of sherry; vinegar. *Mode.* —Slice sufficient cucumbers, onions, and apples to fill a pint stone jar, taking care to cut the slices very thin; arrange them in alternate layers, adding at the same time salt and cayenne in the above proportion; pour in the soy and wine, and fill up with vinegar. It will be fit for use the day it is made. *Seasonable* in August and September.

PICKLE, Indian (very Superior).

Ingredients.—To each gallon of vinegar allow 6 cloves of garlic, 12 shalots, 2 sticks of sliced horseradish, ¼ lb. of bruised ginger, 2 oz. of whole black pepper, 1 oz. of long pepper, 1 oz. of allspice, 12 cloves, ¼ oz. of cayenne, 2 oz. of mustard-seed, ¼ lb. of mustard, 1 oz. of turmeric; a white cabbage, cauliflowers, radishpods, French beans, gherkins, small round pickling-onions, nasturtiums, capsicums, chilies, &c. *Mode.*—Cut the cabbage, which must be hard and white, into slices, and the cauliflowers into small branches; sprinkle salt over them in a large dish, and let them remain two days; then dry them, and put them into a very large jar, with garlic, shalots, horseradish, ginger, pepper, allspice, and cloves, in the above proportions. Boil sufficient vinegar to cover them, which pour over, and, when

Pickle, Mixed

cold, cover up to keep them free from dust. As the other things for the pickle ripen at different times, they may be added as they are ready: these will be radish-pods, French beans, gherkins, small onions, nasturtiums, capsicums, chilies, &c., &c. As these are procured, they must, first of all, be washed in a little cold vinegar, wiped, and then simply added to the other ingredients in the large jar, only taking care that they are *covered* by the vinegar. If more vinegar should be wanted to add to the pickle, do not omit first to boil it before adding it to the rest. When you have collected all the things you require, turn all out in a large pan, and thoroughly mix them. Now put the mixed vegetables into smaller jars, without any of the vinegar; then boil the vinegar again, adding as much more as will be required to fill the different jars, and also cayenne, mustard-seed, turmeric, and mustard, which must be well mixed with a little cold vinegar, allowing the quantities named above to each gallon of vinegar. Pour the vinegar, boiling hot, over the pickle, and when cold, tie down with a bladder. If the pickle is wanted for immediate use, the vinegar should be boiled twice more, but the better way is to make it during one season for use during the next. It will keep for years, if care is taken that the vegetables are quite covered by the vinegar.

This recipe was taken from the directions of a lady whose pickle was always pronounced excellent by all who tasted it, and who has, for many years, exactly followed the recipe given above.

Note.—For small families, perhaps the above quantity of pickle will be considered too large; but this may be decreased at pleasure, taking care to properly proportion the various ingredients.

PICKLE, Mixed (very good).

Ingredients.—To each gallon of vinegar allow ¼ lb. of bruised ginger, ¼ lb. of mustard, ¼ lb. of salt, 2 oz. of mustard-seed, 1½ oz. of turmeric, 1 oz. of ground black pepper, ¼ oz. of cayenne, cauliflowers, onions, celery, sliced cucumbers, gherkins, French beans, nasturtiums, capsicums. *Mode.*—Have a large jar, with a tightly-fitting lid, in which put as much vinegar as required, reserving a little to mix the various powders to a smooth paste. Put into a basin

Pickle for Tongues or Beef

mustard, turmeric, pepper, and cayenne; mix them with vinegar, and stir well until no lumps remain; add all the ingredients to the vinegar, and mix well. Keep this liquor in a warm place, and thoroughly stir every morning for a month with a wooden spoon, when it will be ready for the different vegetables to be added to it. As these come into season, have them gathered on a dry day, and, after merely wiping them with a cloth, to free them from moisture, put them into the pickle. The cauliflowers, it may be said, must be divided into small bunches. Put all these into the pickle raw, and at the end of the season, when there have been added as many of the vegetables as could be procured, store it away in jars, and tie over with bladder. As none of the ingredients are boiled, this pickle will not be fit to eat till 12 months have elapsed. Whilst the pickle is being made, keep a wooden spoon tied to the jar; and its contents, it may be repeated, must be stirred every morning. *Seasonable.*— Make the pickle-liquor in May or June, as the season arrives for the various vegetables to be picked.

PICKLE for Tongues or Beef (Newmarket Recipe).

Ingredients.—1 gallon of soft water, 3 lbs. of coarse salt, 6 oz. of coarse brown sugar, ½ oz. of saltpetre. *Mode.*—Put all the ingredients into a saucepan, and let them boil for ½ an hour, clear off the scum as it rises, and when done pour the pickle into a pickling-pan. Let it get cold, then put in the meat, and allow it to remain in pickle from 8 to 14 days, according to the size. It will keep good for 6 months if well boiled once a fortnight. Tongues will take 1 month or 6 weeks to be properly cured; and, in salting meat, beef and tongues should always be put in separate vessels. *Time.*— A moderate-sized tongue should remain in the pickle about a month, and be turned every day.

PICKLE, Universal.

Ingredients.—To 6 quarts of vinegar allow 1 lb. of salt, ¼ lb. of ginger, 1 oz. of mace, ½ lb. of shalots, 1 tablespoonful of cayenne, 2 oz. of mustard-seed, 1½ oz. of turmeric. *Mode.*—Boil all the ingredients together for about 20 minutes; when cold put them into a jar with

Picnic, Bill of Fare for

whatever vegetables you choose, such as radish-pods, French beans, cauliflowers, gherkins, &c. &c., as these come into season; put them in fresh as you gather them, having previously wiped them perfectly free from moisture and grit. This pickle will be fit for use in about 8 or 9 months. *Time.*—20 minutes. *Seasonable.*—Make the pickle in May or June, to be ready for the various vegetables.

Note.—As this pickle takes 2 or 3 months to make,—that is to say, nearly that time will elapse before all the different vegetables are added,—care must be taken to keep the jar which contains the pickle well covered, either with a closely-fitting lid, or a piece of bladder securely tied over, so as perfectly to exclude the air.

PICKLES.

Although pickles may be purchased at shops at as low a rate as they can usually be made for at home, or perhaps even for less, yet we would advise all housewives, who have sufficient time and convenience, to prepare their own. The only general rules, perhaps, worth stating here,—as in the recipes all necessary details will be explained—are, that the vegetables and fruits used should be sound, and not over-ripe, and that the very best vinegar should be employed.

PICNIC FOR 40 PERSONS, Bill of Fare for.

A joint of cold roast beef, a joint of cold boiled beef, 2 ribs of lamb, 2 shoulders of lamb, 4 roast fowls, 2 roast ducks, 1 ham, 1 tongue, 2 veal-and-ham pies, 2 pigeon pies, 6 medium-sized lobsters, 1 piece of collared calf's head, 18 lettuces, 6 baskets of salad, 6 cucumbers.

Stewed fruit well sweetened, and put into glass bottles well corked; 3 or 4 dozen plain pastry biscuits to eat with the stewed fruit, 2 dozen fruit turnovers, 4 dozen cheesecakes, 2 cold cabinet puddings in moulds, 2 blancmanges in moulds, a few jam puffs, 1 large cold plum-pudding (this must be good), a few baskets of fresh fruit, 3 dozen plain biscuits, a piece of cheese, 6 lbs. of butter (this, of course, includes the butter for tea), 4 quartern loaves of household bread, 3 dozen rolls, 6 loaves of tin bread (for tea), 2 plain plum cakes, 2 pound cakes,

Picnic, Things not to be forgotten

2 sponge-cakes, a tin of mixed biscuits, ½ lb. of tea. Coffee is not suitable for a picnic, being difficult to make.

PICNIC, Things not to be forgotten at.

A stick of horseradish, a bottle of mint-sauce well corked, a bottle of salad dressing, a bottle of vinegar, made mustard, pepper, salt, good oil, and pounded sugar. If it can be managed, take a little ice. It is scarcely necessary to say that plates, tumblers, wine-glasses, knives, forks, and spoons, must not be forgotten; as also teacups and saucers, 3 or 4 teapots, some lump sugar, and milk, if this last-named article cannot be obtained in the neighbourhood. Take 3 corkscrews.
Beverages.— 3 dozen quart bottles of ale, packed in hampers; ginger-beer, soda-water, and lemonade, of each 2 dozen bottles; 6 bottles of sherry, 6 bottles of claret, champagne à discrétion, and any other light wine that may be preferred, and 2 bottles of brandy. Water can usually be obtained, so it is useless to take it.

PIG, Sucking, to Carve.

A sucking-pig seems, at first sight, rather an elaborate dish, or rather animal, to carve; but by carefully mastering the details of the business, every difficulty will vanish; and if a partial failure be at first made, yet all embarrassment will quickly disappear on a second trial. A sucking-pig is usually sent to table in the manner shown in the engraving, and the first point to be

SUCKING-PIG.

attended to is to separate the shoulder from the carcase, by carrying the knife quickly and neatly round the circular line, as shown by the figures 1, 2, 3;— the shoulder will then easily come away. The next step is to take off the leg; and this is done in the same way, by cutting round this joint in the direction shown by the figures 1, 2, 3, in the same way

Pig, Sucking, Roast

as the shoulder. The ribs then stand fairly open to the knife, which should be carried down in the direction of the line 4 to 5; and two or three helpings will dispose of these. The other half of the pig is served, of course, in the same manner. Different parts of the pig are variously esteemed; some preferring the flesh of the neck; others, the ribs; and others, again, the shoulders. The truth is, the whole of a sucking-pig is delicious, delicate eating; but, in carving it, the host should consult the various tastes and fancies of his guests, keeping the larger joints, generally, for the gentlemen of the party.

PIG, Sucking, Roast.

Ingredients. — Pig, 6 oz. of bread crumbs, 16 sage-leaves, pepper and salt to taste, a piece of butter the size of an egg, salad oil or butter to baste with, about ½ pint of gravy, 1 tablespoonful of lemon-juice. *Mode.*—A sucking-pig, to be eaten in perfection, should not be more than three weeks old, and should be dressed the same day that it is killed. After preparing the pig for cooking, as in the following recipe, stuff it with

ROAST SUCKING-PIG.

finely-grated bread crumbs, minced sage, pepper, salt, and a piece of butter the size of an egg, all of which should be well mixed together, and put into the body of the pig. Sew up the slit neatly, and truss the legs back, to allow the inside to be roasted, and the under part to be crisp. Put the pig down to a bright clear fire, not too near, and let it lay till thoroughly dry; then have ready some butter tied up in a piece of thin cloth, and rub the pig with this in every part. Keep it well rubbed with the butter the whole of the time it is roasting, and do not allow the crackling to become blistered or burnt. When half done, hang a pig-iron before the middle part (if this is not obtainable, use a flat iron). to prevent its being scorched and

Pig, Sucking, to Scald a

dried up before the ends are done. Before it is taken from the fire, cut off the head, and part that and the body down the middle. Chop the brains and mix them with the stuffing; add ½ pint of good gravy, a tablespoonful of lemon-juice, and the gravy that flowed from the pig; put a little of this on the dish with the pig, and the remainder send to table in a tureen. Place the pig back to back in the dish, with one half of the head on each side, and one of the ears at each end, and send it to table as hot as possible. Instead of butter, many cooks take salad oil for basting, which makes the crackling *crisp*; and as this is one of the principal things to be considered, perhaps it is desirable to use it; but be particular that it is very pure, or it will impart an unpleasant flavour to the meat. The brains and stuffing may be stirred into a tureen of melted butter instead of gravy, when the latter is not liked. Apple sauce and the old-fashioned currant sauce are not yet quite obsolete as an accompaniment to roast pig. *Time.—* 1½ to 2 hours for a small pig. *Average cost,* 5s. to 6s. *Sufficient* for 9 or 10 persons. *Seasonable* from September to February.

PIG, Sucking, to Scald a.

Put the pig into cold water directly it is killed; let it remain for a few minutes, then immerse it in a large pan of boiling water for 2 minutes. Take it out, lay it on a table, and pull off the hair as quickly as possible. When the skin looks clean, make a slit down the belly, take out the entrails, well clean the nostrils and ears, wash the pig in cold water, and wipe it thoroughly dry. Take off the feet at the first joint, and loosen and leave sufficient skin to turn neatly over. If not to be dressed immediately, fold it in a wet cloth to keep it from the air.

PIGS' CHEEKS, to Dry.

Ingredients.—Salt, ½ oz. of saltpetre, 2 oz. of bay-salt, 4 oz. of coarse sugar. *Mode.*—Cut out the snout, remove the brains, and split the head, taking off the upper bone to make the jowl a good shape; rub it well with salt; next day take away the brine, and salt it again the following day; cover the head with ltpetre, bay-salt, and coarse sugar, in

Pig's Face, Collared

the above proportion, adding a lit common salt. Let the head be off turned, and when it has been in t pickle for 10 days, smoke it for a we or rather longer. *Time.*—To remain the pickle 10 days; to be smoked week. *Seasonable.* — Should be ma from September to March.

Note.—A pig's cheek, or Bath ch will require two hours' cooking after t water boils.

PIG'S FACE, Collared (a Breakf or Luncheon Dish).

Ingredients.—1 pig's face; salt. brine, 1 gallon of spring water, 1 of common salt, ½ handful of chopp juniper-berries, 6 bruised cloves, 2 b leaves, a few sprigs of thyme, ba sage, ¼ oz. of saltpetre. For forceme ½ lb. of ham, ½ lb. bacon, 1 teaspoon of mixed spices, pepper to taste, ¼ lb. lard, 1 tablespoonful of minced parsl 6 young onions. *Mode.*—Singe the ne carefully, bone it without breaking skin, and rub it well with salt. Ma the brine by boiling the above ing

PIG'S FACE.

lients ¼ hour, a letting stand cool. Wh cold, po it over t head, a let it ste in this for 10 days, turning and rubbi it often. Then wipe, drain, and dry For the forcemeat, pound the ham a bacon very finely, and mix with the the remaining ingredients, taking ca that the whole is thoroughly incorp rated. Spread this equally over t head, roll it tightly in a cloth, and bi it securely with broad tape. Put it i a saucepan with a few meat trimming and cover it with stock; let it simm gently for 4 hours, and be particular th it does not stop boiling the whole tim When quite tender, take it up, p it between 2 dishes with a heavy weig on the top, and when cold, remove t cloth and tape. It should be sent table on a napkin, or garnished wi a piece of deep white paper with a ruc at the top. *Time.*—4 hours. *Avera cost,* from 2s. to 2s. 6d. *Seasonable* fro October to March.

PIG'S FRY, to Dress.

Ingredients.—1½ lb. of pig's fry, 2 onions, a few sage leaves, 3 lbs. of potatoes, pepper and salt to taste. *Mode.*—Put the lean fry at the bottom of a pie dish, sprinkle over it some minced sage and onion, and a seasoning of pepper and salt ; slice the potatoes ; put a layer of these on the seasonings, then the fat-fry, then more seasoning, and a layer of potatoes at the top. Fill the dish with boiling water, and bake for 2 hours, or rather longer. *Time.*—Rather more than 2 hours. *Average cost*, 6*d.* per lb. *Sufficient* for 3 or 4 persons. *Seasonable* from September to March.

PIG'S LIVER (a Savoury and Economical Dish).

Ingredients.—The liver and lights of a pig, 6 or 7 slices of bacon, potatoes, 1 large bunch of parsley, 2 onions, 2 sage leaves, pepper and salt to taste, a little broth or water. *Mode.*—Slice the liver and lights, and wash these perfectly clean, and parboil the potatoes ; mince the parsley and sage, and chop the onion rather small. Put the meat, potatoes, and bacon into a deep tin dish, in alternate layers, with a sprinkling of the herbs, and a seasoning of pepper and salt between each ; pour on a little water or broth, and bake in a moderately-heated oven for 2 hours. *Time.*—2 hours. *Average cost*, 1*s.* 6*d.* *Sufficient* for 6 or 7 persons. *Seasonable* from September to March.

PIG'S PETTITOES.

Ingredients.—A thin slice of bacon, 1 onion, 1 blade of mace, 6 peppercorns, 3 or 4 sprigs of thyme, 1 pint of gravy, pepper and salt to taste, thickening of butter and flour. *Mode.*—Put the liver, heart, and pettitoes into a stewpan with the bacon, mace, peppercorns, thyme, onion, and gravy, and simmer these gently for ¼ hour ; then take out the heart and liver, and mince them very fine. Keep stewing the feet until quite tender, which will be in from 20 minutes to ½ hour, reckoning from the time that they boiled up first ; then put back the minced liver, thicken the gravy with a little butter and flour, season with pepper and salt, and simmer over a gentle

fire for 5 minutes, occasionally stirring the contents. Dish the mince, split the feet, and arrange them round alternately with sippets of toasted bread, and pour the gravy in the middle. *Time.*—Altogether 40 minutes. *Sufficient* for 3 or 4 persons. *Seasonable* from September to March.

PIGEON, to Carve.

A very straightforward plan is adopted in carving a pigeon : the knife is carried sharply in the direction of the line as shown from 1 to 2, entirely through the bird, cutting it into two precisely equal and similar parts. If it is necessary to make three pieces of it, a small wing should be cut off with the leg on either side, thus serving two guests ; and, by this means, there will be sufficient meat left on the breast to send to the third guest.

PIGEON.

PIGEON PIE (Epsom Grand-Stand Recipe).

Ingredients.—1½ lb. of rump-steak, 2 or 3 pigeons, 3 slices of ham, pepper and salt to taste, 2 oz. of butter, 4 eggs, puff crust. *Mode.*—Cut the steak into pieces about 3 inches square, and with it line the bottom of a pie-dish, seasoning it well with pepper and salt. Clean the pigeons, rub them with pepper and salt inside and out, and put into the body of each rather more than ½ oz. of butter ; lay them on the steak, and a piece of ham on each pigeon. Add the yolks of four eggs, and half fill the dish with stock ; place a border of puff paste round the edge of the dish, put on the cover, and ornament it in any way that may be preferred. Clean three of the feet, and place them in a hole made in the crust at the top : this shows what kind of pie it is. Glaze the crust,—that is to say, brush it over with the yolk of an egg,—and bake it in a well-heated oven for about 1¼ hour. When liked, a seasoning of pounded mace may be added. *Time.*—1¼ hour, or rather less. *Average cost*, 5*s.* 3*d.* *Sufficient* for 5 or 6 persons. *Seasonable* at any time.

PIGEONS, Broiled.

Ingredients.—Pigeons, 3 oz. of butter, pepper and salt to taste. *Mode.*—Take care that the pigeons are quite fresh, and carefully pluck, draw, and wash them; split the backs, rub the birds over with butter, season them with pepper and salt, and broil them over a moderate fire for ¼ hour or 20 minutes. Serve very hot, with either mushroom-sauce or a good gravy. Pigeons may also be plainly boiled, and served with parsley and butter; they should be trussed like boiled fowls, and take from ¼ hour to 20 minutes to boil. *Time.*—To broil a pigeon, from ¼ hour to 20 minutes; to boil one, the same time. *Average cost,* from 6d. to 9d. each. *Seasonable* from April to September, but in the greatest perfection from Midsummer to Michaelmas.

PIGEONS, Roast.

Ingredients.—Pigeons, 3 oz. of butter, pepper and salt to taste. *Trussing.*—Pigeons, to be good, should be eaten fresh (if kept a little, the flavour goes off), and they should be drawn as soon as killed. Cut off the heads and necks, truss the wings over the backs, and cut off the toes at the first joint: previous to trussing, they should be carefully cleaned, as no bird requires so much washing.

ROAST PIGEON.

Mode.—Wipe the birds very dry, season them inside with pepper and salt, and put about ¾ oz. of butter into the body of each: this makes them moist. Place them at a bright fire, and baste them well the whole of the time they are cooking (they will be done enough in from 20 to 30 minutes); garnish with fried parsley, and serve with a tureen of parsley and butter. Bread sauce and gravy, the same as for roast fowl, are exceedingly nice accompaniments to roast pigeons, as also egg-sauce. *Time.*—From 20 minutes to ½ hour. *Average cost,* 6d. to 9d. each. *Seasonable* from April to September; but in the greatest perfection from Midsummer to Michaelmas.

PIGEONS, Stewed.

Ingredients.—6 pigeons, a few slices of bacon, 3 oz. of butter, 2 tablespoonfuls of minced parsley, sufficient stock to cover the pigeons, thickening of butter and flour, 1 tablespoonful of mushroom ketchup, 1 tablespoonful of port wine. *Mode.*—Empty and clean the pigeons thoroughly, mince the livers, add to these the parsley and butter, and put it into the insides of the birds. Truss them with the legs inward, and put them into a stewpan, with a few slices of bacon placed under and over them; add the stock, and stew gently for rather more than ½ hour. Dish the pigeons, strain the gravy, thicken it with butter and flour, add the ketchup and port wine, give one boil, pour over the pigeons, and serve. *Time.*—Rather more than ½ hour. *Average cost,* 6d. to 9d. each. *Sufficient* for 4 or 5 persons. *Seasonable* from April to September.

PIKE, Baked.

Ingredients.—1 or 2 pike, a nice delicate stuffing (*see* Forcemeats), 1 egg, bread crumbs, ¼ lb. butter. *Mode.*—Scale the fish, take out the gills, wash, and wipe it thoroughly dry; stuff it with forcemeat, sew it up, and fasten the tail in the mouth by means of a skewer; brush it over with egg, sprinkle with bread crumbs, and baste with butter, before putting it in the oven, which must be well heated. When the pike is of a nice brown colour, cover it with buttered paper, as the outside would become too dry. If 2 are dressed, a little variety may be made by making one of them green with a little chopped parsley mixed with the bread crumbs. Serve anchovy or Dutch sauce, and plain melted butter with it. *Time.*—According to size, 1 hour, more or less. *Average cost.*—Seldom bought. *Seasonable* from September to March.

Note.—Pike à la génévese may be stewed in the same manner as salmon à la génévese.

PIKE, Boiled.

Ingredients.—¼ lb. of salt to each gallon of water; a little vinegar. *Mode.*—Scale and clean the pike, and fasten the tail in its mouth by means of a skewer. Lay it in cold water, and when it boils, throw in the salt and vinegar.

Pillau Fowl

The time for boiling depends, of course, on the size of the fish; but a middling-sized pike will take about ½ an hour. Serve with Dutch or anchovy sauce, and plain melted butter. *Time.*—According to size, ¾ to 1 hour. *Average cost.*—Seldom bought. *Seasonable* from September to March.

PILLAU FOWL, based on M. Soyer's Recipe (an Indian Dish).

Ingredients.—1 lb. of rice, 2 oz. of butter, a fowl, 2 quarts of stock or good broth, 40 cardamum-seeds, ½ oz. of coriander-seed, ¼ oz. of cloves, ¼ oz. of allspice, ¼ oz. of mace, ¼ oz. of cinnamon, ½ oz. of peppercorns, 4 onions, 6 thin slices of bacon, 2 hard-boiled eggs. *Mode.*—Well wash 1 lb. of the best Patna rice, put it into a fryingpan with the butter, which keep moving over a slow fire until the rice is lightly browned. Truss the fowl as for boiling, put it into a stewpan with the stock or broth; pound the spices and seeds thoroughly in a mortar, tie them in a piece of muslin, and put them in with the fowl. Let it boil slowly until it is nearly done; then add the rice, which should stew until quite tender and almost dry; cut the onions into slices, sprinkle them with flour, and fry, without breaking them, of a nice brown colour. Have ready the slices of bacon curled and grilled, and the eggs boiled hard. Lay the fowl in the form of a pyramid upon a dish, smother with the rice, garnish with the bacon, fried onions, and the hard-boiled eggs cut into quarters, and serve very hot. Before taking the rice out, remove the spices. *Time.*—½ hour to stew the fowl without the rice; ½ hour with it. *Average cost*, 4s. 3d. *Sufficient* for 4 or 5 persons. *Seasonable* at any time.

PINEAPPLE CHIPS.

Ingredients. — Pineapples; sugar to taste. *Mode.*—Pare and slice the fruit thinly, put it on dishes, and strew over it plenty of pounded sugar. Keep it in a hot closet, or very slow oven, 8 or 10 days, and turn the fruit every day until dry; then put the pieces of pine on tins, and place them in a quick oven for 10 minutes. Let them cool, and store them away in dry boxes, with paper between each layer. *Time.*—8 to 10 days. *Sea-*

Pineapple, Preserved

sonable.—Foreign pines, in July and August.

PINEAPPLE FRITTERS (an elegant dish).

Ingredients. — A small pineapple, a small wineglassful of brandy or liqueur, 2 oz. of sifted sugar; batter as for apple fritters, which see. *Mode.*—This elegant dish, although it may appear extravagant, is really not so if made when pineapples are plentiful. We receive them now in such large quantities from the West Indies, that at times they may be purchased at an exceedingly low rate; it would not, of course, be economical to use the pines which are grown in our English pineries for the purposes of fritters. Pare the pine with as little waste as possible, cut it into rather thin slices, and soak these slices in the above proportion of brandy or liqueur and pounded sugar for 4 hours; then make a batter the same as for apple fritters, substituting cream for the milk, and using a smaller quantity of flour; when this is ready, dip in the pieces of pine, and fry them in boiling lard from 5 to 8 minutes; turn them when sufficiently brown on one side, and, when done, drain them from the lard before the fire, dish them on a white d'oyley, strew over them sifted sugar, and serve quickly. *Time.*—5 to 8 minutes. *Average cost*, when cheap and plentiful, 1s. 6d. for the pine. *Sufficient* for 3 or 4 persons. *Seasonable* in July and August.

PINEAPPLE, Preserved.

Ingredients. — To every lb. of fruit, weighed after being pared, allow 1 lb. of loaf sugar; ¼ pint of water. *Mode.*—The pines for making this preserve should be perfectly sound but ripe. Cut them into rather thick slices, as the fruit shrinks very much in the boiling. Pare off the rind carefully, that none of the pine be wasted; and, in doing so, notch it in and out, as the edge cannot be smoothly cut without great waste. Dissolve a portion of the sugar in a preserving-pan with ¼ pint of water; when this is melted, gradually add the remainder of the sugar, and boil it until it forms a clear syrup, skimming well. As soon as this is the case, put in the pieces of pine, and boil well for at least ½ hour, or until it looks nearly transparent. Put it into pots, cover down when cold, and store

Pineapple, Preserved

away in a dry place. *Time.*—½ hour to boil the fruit. *Average cost*, 10*d.* to 1*s.* per lb. pot. *Seasonable.*—Foreign pines, in July and August.

PINEAPPLE, Preserved, for present use.

Ingredients.—Pineapple, sugar, water. *Mode.*—Cut the pine into slices ¼ inch in thickness; peel them, and remove the hard part from the middle. Put the parings and hard pieces into a stewpan, with sufficient water to cover them, and boil for ¼ hour. Strain the liquor, and put in the slices of pine. Stew them for 10 minutes, add sufficient sugar to sweeten the whole nicely, and boil again for another ¼ hour; skim well, and the preserve will be ready for use. It must be eaten soon, as it will keep but a very short time. *Time.*—¼ hour to boil the parings in water; 10 minutes to boil the pine without sugar, ¼ hour with sugar. *Average cost.*—Foreign pines, 1*s.* to 3*s.* each; English, from 2*s.* to 12*s.* per lb. *Seasonable.*—Foreign, in July and August; English, all the year.

PIPPINS, Normandy, Stewed.

Ingredients.—1 lb. of Normandy pippins, 1 quart of water, ½ teaspoonful of powdered cinnamon, ½ teaspoonful of ground ginger, 1 lb. of moist sugar, 1 lemon. *Mode.*—Well wash the pippins, and put them into 1 quart of water with the above proportion of cinnamon and ginger, and let them stand 12 hours; then put these all together into a stewpan, with the lemon sliced thinly, and half the moist sugar. Let them boil slowly until the pippins are half done; then add the remainder of the sugar, and simmer until they are quite tender. Serve on glass dishes for dessert. *Time.* —2 to 3 hours. *Average cost*, 1*s.* 6*d.* *Seasonable.*—Suitable for a winter dish.

PLAICE, Fried.

Ingredients. — Hot lard, or clarified dripping; egg and bread crumbs. *Mode.*—This fish is fried in the same manner as soles. Wash and wipe them thoroughly dry, and let them remain in a cloth until it is time to dress them. Brush them over with egg, and cover with bread crumbs mixed with a little flour. Fry of a nice brown in hot dripping or lard, and garnish with fried par-

Plovers, to Dress

sley and cut lemon. Send them to table with shrimp-sauce and plain melted butter. *Time.*—About 5 minutes. *Average cost*, 3*d.* each. *Seasonable* from May to November. *Sufficient*, 4 plaice for 4 persons.

Note.—Plaice may be boiled plain, and served with melted butter. Garnish with parsley and cut lemon.

PLAICE, Stewed.

Ingredients.—4 or 5 plaice, 2 onions, ½ oz. ground ginger, 1 pint of lemon-juice, ¼ pint water, 6 eggs; cayenne to taste. *Mode.*—Cut the fish into pieces about 2 inches wide, salt them, and let them remain ¼ hour. Slice and fry the onions a light brown; put them in a stewpan, on the top of which put the fish without washing, and add the ginger, lemon-juice, and water. Cook slowly for ½ hour, and do not let the fish boil, or it will break. Take it out, and when the liquor is cool, add 6 well-beaten eggs; simmer till it thickens, when pour over the fish, and serve. *Time.*—¾ hour. *Average cost* for this quantity, 1*s.* 9*d.* *Seasonable* from May to November. *Sufficient* for 4 or 5 persons; according to the size of the fish.

PLOVERS, to Carve.

Plovers may be carved like quails or woodcock, being trussed and served in the same way as those birds.

PLOVERS, to Dress.

Ingredients.—3 plovers, butter, flour, toasted bread. *Choosing and Trussing.* —Choose those that feel hard at the vent, as that shows their fatness. There are three sorts,—the grey, green, and bastard plover, or lapwing. They will keep good for some time, but if very stale, the feet will be very dry. Plovers are scarcely fit for anything but roasting; they are, however, sometimes stewed, or made into a ragoût, but this mode of cooking is not to be recommended. *Mode.*—Pluck off the feathers, wipe the outside of the birds with a damp cloth, and do not draw them; truss with the head under the wing, put them down to a clear fire, and lay slices of moistened toast in the dripping-pan, to catch the trail. Keep them *well basted*, dredge them lightly with flour a few minutes before they are done, and let them be

| Plum Cake, Common | Plum Pudding, Excellent |

nicely frothed. Dish them on the toasts, over which the *traill* should be equally spread. Pour round the toast a little good gravy, and send some to table in a tureen. *Time.*—10 minutes to ¼ hour. *Average cost*, 1*s*. 6*d*. the brace, if plentiful. *Sufficient* for 2 persons. *Seasonable.*—In perfection from the beginning of September to the end of January.

PLUM CAKE, Common.

Ingredients.—3 lbs. of flour, 6 oz. of butter or good dripping, 6 oz. of moist sugar, 6 oz. of currants, ½ oz. of pounded allspice, 2 tablespoonfuls of fresh yeast, 1 pint of new milk. *Mode.*—Rub the butter into the flour; add the sugar, currants, and allspice; warm the milk, stir to it the yeast, and mix the whole into a dough; knead it well, and put it into 6 buttered tins; place them near the fire for nearly an hour for the dough to rise, then bake the cakes in a good oven from 1 to 1¼ hour. To ascertain when they are done, plunge a clean knife into the middle, and if on withdrawal it comes out clean, the cakes are done. *Time.*— 1 to 1¼ hour. *Average cost*, 1*s*. 8*d*. *Sufficient* to make 6 small cakes.

PLUM CAKE, a Nice.

Ingredients.—1 lb. of flour, ¼ lb. of butter, ½ lb. of sugar, ½ lb. of currants, 2 oz. of candied lemon-peel, ½ pint of milk, 1 teaspoonful of ammonia or carbonate of soda. *Mode.*—Put the flour into a basin with the sugar, currants, and sliced candied peel; beat the butter to a cream, and mix all these ingredients together with the milk. Stir the ammonia into 2 tablespoonfuls of milk; add it to the dough, and beat the whole well, until everything is thoroughly mixed. Put the dough into a buttered tin, and bake the cake from 1½ to 2 hours. *Time.* 1½ to 2 hours. *Average cost*, 1*s*. 3*d*. *Seasonable* at any time.

PLUM JAM.

Ingredients.—To every lb. of plums, weighed before being stoned, allow ¾ lb. of loaf sugar. *Mode.*—In making plum jam, the quantity of sugar for each lb. of fruit must be regulated by the quality and size of the fruit, some plums requiring much more sugar than others. Divide the plums, take out the stones, and put them on to large dishes, with roughly-pounded sugar sprinkled over them in

the above proportion, and let them remain for one day; then put them into a preserving-pan, stand them by the side of the fire to simmer gently for about ½ hour, and then boil them rapidly for another 15 minutes. The scum must be carefully removed as it rises, and the jam must be well stirred all the time, or it will burn at the bottom of the pan, and so spoil the colour and flavour of the preserve. Some of the stones may be cracked, and a few kernels added to the jam just before it is done: these impart a very delicious flavour to the plums. The above proportion of sugar would answer for Orleans plums; the Impératrice, Magnum-bonum, and Winesour would not require quite so much. *Time.* ½ hour to simmer gently, ¼ hour to boil rapidly. *Best plums for preserving.*— Violets, Mussels, Orleans, Impératrice, Magnum-bonum, and Winesour. *Seasonable* from the end of July to the beginning of October.

PLUM PUDDING, Baked.

Ingredients.—2 lbs. of flour, 1 lb. of currants, 1 lb. of raisins, 1 lb. of suet, 2 eggs, 1 pint of milk, a few slices of candied peel. *Mode.*—Chop the suet finely; mix it with the flour, currants, stoned raisins, and candied peel: moisten with the well-beaten eggs, and add sufficient milk to make the pudding of the consistency of very thick batter. Put it into a buttered dish, and bake in a good oven from 2¼ to 2½ hours; turn it out, strew sifted sugar over, and serve. For a very plain pudding, use only half the quantity of fruit, omit the eggs, and substitute milk or water for them. The above ingredients make a large family pudding; for a small one, half the quantity will be found ample; but it must be baked quite 1½ hour. *Time.*—Large pudding, 2¼ to 2½ hours; half the size, 1½ hour. *Average cost*, 2*s*. 6*d*. *Sufficient* for 9 or 10 persons. *Seasonable* in winter.

PLUM PUDDING, Excellent, made without Eggs.

Ingredients.—½ lb. of flour, 6 oz. of raisins, 6 oz. of currants, ¼ lb. of chopped suet, ¼ lb. of brown sugar, ¼ lb. of mashed carrot, ¼ lb. of mashed potatoes, 1 tablespoonful of treacle, 1 oz. of candied lemon-peel, 1 oz. of candied citron. *Mode.*—Mix the flour, currants, suet as

Plum Pudding, Unrivalled

sugar well together; have ready the above proportions of mashed carrot and potato, which stir into the other ingredients; add the treacle and lemon-peel; but put no liquid in the mixture, or it will be spoiled. Tie it loosely in a cloth, or, if put in a basin, do not quite fill it, as the pudding should have room to swell, and boil it for 4 hours. Serve with brandy-sauce. This pudding is better for being mixed over-night. *Time.*—4 hours. *Average cost*, 1*s.* 6*d.* *Sufficient* for 6 or 7 persons. *Seasonable* in winter.

PLUM PUDDING, Unrivalled.

Ingredients. — 1½ lb. of muscatel raisins, 1¾ lb. of currants, 1 lb. of sultana raisins, 2 lbs. of the finest moist sugar, 2 lbs. of bread crumbs, 16 eggs, 2 lbs. of finely-chopped suet, 6 oz. of mixed candied peel, the rind of 2 lemons, 1 oz. of ground nutmeg, 1 oz. of ground cinnamon, ½ oz. of pounded bitter almonds, ¼ pint of brandy. *Mode.*—Stone and cut up the raisins, but do not chop them; wash and dry the currants, and cut the candied peel into thin slices. Mix all the dry ingredients well together, and moisten with the eggs, which should be well beaten and strained, to the pudding; stir in the brandy, and, when all is thoroughly mixed, well butter and flour a stout new pudding-cloth; put in the pudding, tie it down very tightly and closely, boil from 6 to 8 hours, and serve with brandy-sauce. A few sweet almonds, blanched and cut in strips, and stuck on the pudding, ornament it prettily. This quantity may be divided and boiled in buttered moulds. For small families this is the most desirable way, as the above will be found to make a pudding of rather large dimensions. *Time.*—6 to 8 hours. *Average cost*, 7*s.* 6*d.* *Seasonable* in winter. *Sufficient* for 12 or 14 persons.

Note.—The muscatel raisins can be purchased at a cheap rate loose (not in bunches) : they are then scarcely higher in price than the ordinary raisins, and impart a much richer flavour to the pudding.

PLUM PUDDING, a Plain Christmas, for Children.

Ingredients.—1 lb. of flour, 1 lb. of bread crumbs, ¾ lb. of stoned raisins, ¾ lb. of currants, ¼ lb. of suet, 3 or 4 eggs,

Plum Pudding, Christmas

milk, 2 oz. of candied peel, 1 teaspoonful of powdered allspice, ½ saltspoonful of salt. *Mode.*—Let the suet be finely chopped, the raisins stoned, and the currants well washed, picked and dried. Mix these with the other dry ingredients, and stir all well together; beat and strain the eggs to the pudding, stir these in, and add just sufficient milk to make it mix properly. Tie it up in a well floured cloth, put it into boiling water, and boil for at least 5 hours. Serve with a sprig of holly placed in the middle of the pudding, and a little pounded sugar sprinkled over it. *Time.*—5 hours. *Average cost*, 1*s.* 9*d.* *Sufficient* for 9 or 10 children. *Seasonable* at Christmas.

PLUM PUDDING, Christmas (very good).

Ingredients.—1½ lb. of raisins, ½ lb. of currants, ½ lb. of mixed peel, ¾ lb. of bread-crumbs, ¾ lb. of suet, 8 eggs, 1 wineglassful of brandy. *Mode.*—Stone and cut the raisins in halves, but do not chop them; wash, pick, and dry the currants, and mince the suet finely; cut the candied peel into thin slices, and grate down the bread into fine crumbs. When all these dry ingredients are prepared, mix them well together; then moisten the mixture with the eggs, which should be well beaten,

CHRISTMAS PLUM PUDDING IN MOULD.

and the brandy; stir well, that everything may be very thoroughly blended, and *press* the pudding into a buttered mould; tie it down tightly with a floured cloth, and boil for 5 or 6 hours. It may be boiled in a cloth without a mould, and will require the same time allowed for cooking. As Christmas puddings are usually made a few days before they are required for table, when the pudding is taken out of the pot, hang it up immediately, and put a plate or saucer underneath to catch the water that may drain

Plum Pudding (a Pound)	Plum Tart

from it. The day it is to be eaten, plunge it into boiling water, and keep it boiling for at least 2 hours; then turn it out of the mould, and serve with brandy-sauce. On Christmas-day a sprig of holly is usually placed in the middle of the pudding, and about a wine-glassful of brandy poured round it, which, at the moment of serving, is lighted, and the pudding thus brought to table encircled in flame. *Time.*—5 or 6 hours the first time of boiling ; 2 hours the day it is to be served. *Average cost,* 4s. *Sufficient* for a quart mould for 7 or 8 persons. *Seasonable* on the 25th of December, and on various festive occasions till March.

Note.—Five or six of these puddings should be made at one time, as they will keep good for many weeks, and in cases where unexpected guests arrive, will be found an acceptable and, as it only requires warming through, a quickly-prepared dish. Moulds of every shape and size are manufactured for these puddings, and may be purchased of Messrs. R. & J. Slack, 336, Strand.

PLUM PUDDING (a Pound).

Ingredients.—1 lb. of suet, 1 lb. of currants, 1 lb. of stoned raisins, 8 eggs, ½ grated nutmeg, 2 oz. of sliced candied peel, 1 teaspoonful of ground ginger, ½ lb. of bread crumbs, ½ lb. of flour, ½ pint of milk. *Mode.*—Chop the suet finely ; mix with it the dry ingredients ; stir

BAKED PUDDING, OR CAKE-MOULD.

these well together, and add the well-beaten eggs and milk to moisten with. Beat up the mixture well, and should the above proportion of milk not be found sufficient to make it of the proper consistency, a little more should be added. Press the pudding into a mould, tie it in a floured cloth, and boil for

five hours, or rather longer, and serve with brandy-sauce. *Time.*—5 hours, or longer. *Average cost,* 3s. *Sufficient* for 7 or 8 persons. *Seasonable* in winter.

Note.—The above pudding may be baked instead of boiled; it should be put into a buttered mould or tin, and baked for about 2 hours ; a smaller one would take about 1¼ hour.

PLUM PUDDING (Fresh Fruit).

Ingredients.—¾ lb. of suet crust, 1½ pint of Orleans or any other kind of plum, ¼ lb. of moist sugar. *Mode.*—Line a pudding-basin with suet crust rolled out to the thickness of about ½ inch ; fill the basin with the fruit, put in the sugar, and cover with crust. Fold the edges over, and pinch them together, to prevent the juice escaping. Tie over a floured cloth, put the pudding into boiling water, and boil from 2 to 2½ hours. Turn it out of the basin, and serve quickly. *Time.*—2 to 2½ hours. *Average cost,* 10d. *Sufficient* for 6 or 7 persons. *Seasonable,* with various kinds of plums, from the beginning of August to the beginning of October.

PLUM TART.

Ingredients.—½ lb. of good short crust, 1½ pint of plums, ¼ lb. of moist sugar. *Mode.*—Line the edges of a deep tart-dish with crust ; fill the dish with plums, and place a small cup or jar, upside down, in the midst of them. Put in the sugar, cover the pie with crust, ornament the edges, and bake in a good

PLUM TART.

oven from ½ to ¾ hour. When puff-crust is preferred to short crust, use that made by the given recipe, and glaze the top by brushing it over with the white of an egg beaten to a stiff froth with a knife ; sprinkle over a little sifted sugar, and put the pie in the oven to set the glaze. *Time.*—½ to ¾ hour. *Average cost,* 1s. *Sufficient* for 5 or 6 persons. *Seasonable,* with various kinds of plums, from the beginning of August to the beginning of October.

PLUMS, French, Stewed (a Dessert dish).

Ingredients.—1½ lb. of French plums, ¾ pint of syrup, 1 glass of port wine, the rind and juice of 1 lemon. *Mode.*—Stew the plums gently in water for 1 hour; strain the water, and with it make the syrup. When it is clear, put in the plums with the port wine, lemon-juice, and rind, and simmer very gently for 1½ hour. Arrange the plums on a glass dish, take out the lemon-rind, pour the syrup over the plums, and, when cold, they will be ready for table. A little allspice stewed with the fruit is by many persons considered an improvement. *Time.*—1 hour to stew the plums in water, 1½ hour in the syrup. *Average cost,* plums sufficiently good for stewing, 1s. per lb. *Sufficient* for 7 or 8 persons. *Seasonable* in winter.

PLUMS (Preserved).

Ingredients.— To every lb. of fruit allow ¾ lb. of loaf sugar; for the thin syrup, ¼ lb. of sugar to each pint of water. *Mode.*—Select large ripe plums; slightly prick them, to prevent them from bursting, and simmer them very gently in a syrup made with the above proportion of sugar and water. Put them carefully into a pan, let the syrup cool, pour it over the plums, and allow them to remain for two days. Having previously weighed the other sugar, dip the lumps quickly into water, and put them into a preserving-pan with no more water than hangs about them; and boil the sugar to a syrup, carefully skimming it. Drain the plums from the first syrup; put them into the fresh syrup, and simmer them very gently until they are clear; lift them out singly into pots, pour the syrup over, and, when cold, cover down to exclude the air. This preserve will remain good some time, if kept in a dry place, and makes a very nice addition to a dessert. The magnum-bonum plums answer for this preserve better than any other kind of plum. Greengages are also very delicious done in this manner. *Time.*— ¼ hour to 20 minutes to simmer the plums in the first syrup; 20 minutes to ½ hour very gentle simmering in the second. *Seasonable* from August to October.

PLUMS, to Preserve Dry.

Ingredients.— To every lb. of sugar allow ¼ pint of water. *Mode.*—Gather the plums when they are full grown and just turning colour; prick them, put them into a saucepan of cold water, and set them on the fire until the water is on the point of boiling. Then take them out, drain them, and boil them gently in syrup made with the above proportion of sugar and water; and if the plums shrink, and will not take the sugar, prick them as they lie in the pan; give them another boil, skim, and set them by. The next day add some more sugar, boiled almost to candy, to the fruit and syrup; put all together into a wide-mouthed jar, and place them in a cool oven for 2 nights; then drain the plums from the syrup, sprinkle a little powdered sugar over, and dry them in a cool oven. *Time.*—15 to 20 minutes to boil the plums in the syrup. *Seasonable* from August to October.

PORK.

In the country, where, for ordinary consumption, the pork killed for sale is usually both larger and fatter than that supplied to the London consumer, it is customary to remove the skin and fat down to the lean, and, salting that, roast what remains of the joint. Pork goes further, and is consequently a more economical food, than other meats, simply because the texture is closer, and there is less waste in the cooking, either in roasting or boiling.

In fresh pork, the leg is the most economical family joint, and the loin the richest.

Pork, to be preserved, is cured in several ways,—either by covering it with salt, or immersing it in ready-made brine, where it is kept till required; or it is only partially salted, and then hung up to dry, when the meat is called white bacon; or, after salting, it is hung in wood smoke till the flesh is impregnated with the aroma from the wood. The Wiltshire bacon, which is regarded as the finest in the kingdom, is prepared by laying the sides of a hog in large wooden troughs, and then rubbing into the flesh quantities of powdered bay-salt, made hot in a frying-pan. This process is repeated for four days; they are then left for three weeks, merely

Pork

turning the flitches every other day. After that time they are hung up to dry. The hogs usually killed for purposes of bacon in England average from 18 to 20 stone; on the other hand, the hogs killed in the country for farm-house purposes, seldom weigh less than 26 stone. The legs of boars, hogs, and, in Germany, those of bears, are prepared differently, and called hams. The practice in vogue formerly in this country was to cut out the hams and cure them separately; then to remove the ribs, which were roasted as "spare-ribs," and, curing the remainder of the side, call it a "gammon of bacon." Small pork to cut for table in joints, is cut up, in most places throughout the kingdom, as represented in the engraving. The side is divided with nine ribs to the fore quarter; and the following is an enumeration of the joints in the two respective quarters:—

SIDE OF A PIG, SHOWING THE SEVERAL JOINTS.

HIND QUARTER { 1. The leg.
2. The loin.
3. The spring, or belly.

FORE QUARTER { 4. The hand.
5. The fore-loin.
6. The cheek.

The weight of the several joints of a good pork pig of four stone may be as follows ; viz.:—

The leg . . . . . 8 lbs.
The loin and spring . 7 „
The hand . . . . 6 „
The chine . . . . 7 „
The cheek . from 2 to 3 „

Of a bacon pig, the legs are reserved for curing, and when cured are called hams: when the meat is separated from the shoulder-blade and bones and cured, it is called bacon. The bones, with part of the meat left on them, are divided into spare-ribs, griskins, and chines.

Pork Cutlets, or Chops

PORK CHEESE (an Excellent Breakfast Dish).

Ingredients.—2 lbs. of cold roast pork, pepper and salt to taste, 1 dessertspoonful of minced parsley, 4 leaves of sage, a very small bunch of savoury herbs, 2 blades of pounded mace, a little nutmeg, $\frac{1}{2}$ teaspoonful of minced lemon-peel; good strong gravy, sufficient to fill the mould. *Mode.*—Cut, but do not chop, the pork into fine pieces, and allow $\frac{1}{4}$ lb. of fat to each pound of lean. Season with pepper and salt; pound well the spices, and chop finely the parsley, sage, herbs, and lemon-peel, and mix the whole nicely together. Put it into a mould, fill up with good strong well-flavoured gravy, and bake rather more than one hour. When cold, turn it out of the mould. *Time.*—Rather more than 1 hour. *Seasonable* from October to March.

Note.—The remains of a pig's head, after the chops are taken off, make most excellent pork cheese.

PORK CUTLETS, or Chops.

Ingredients. — Loin of pork, pepper and salt to taste. *Mode.*—Cut the cutlets from a delicate loin of pork, bone and trim them neatly, and cut away the greater portion of the fat. Season them with pepper ; place the gridiron on the fire ; when quite hot, lay on the chops, and broil them for about $\frac{1}{4}$ hour, turning them 3 or 4 times ; and be particular that they are *thoroughly* done, but not dry. Dish them, sprinkle over a little fine salt, and serve plain, or with tomato sauce, sauce piquante, or pickled gherkins, a few of which should be laid round the dish as a garnish. *Time.*—About $\frac{1}{4}$ hour. *Average cost,* 10d. per lb. for chops. *Sufficient.*— Allow 6 for 4 persons. *Seasonable* from October to March.

PORK CUTLETS, or Chops.

Ingredients. — Loin, or fore-loin, of pork, egg and bread crumbs, salt and pepper to taste; to every tablespoonful of bread crumbs allow $\frac{1}{2}$ teaspoonful of minced sage ; clarified butter. *Mode.*— Cut the cutlets from a loin, or fore-loin, of pork ; trim them the same as mutton cutlets, and scrape the top part of the bone. Brush them over with egg, sprinkle with bread crumbs, with which have

Pork Cutlets

been mixed minced sage and a seasoning of pepper and salt ; drop a little clarified butter on them, and press the crumbs well down. Put the frying-pan on the fire, put in some lard ; when this is hot, lay in the cutlets, and fry them a light brown on both sides. Take them out, put them before the fire to dry the greasy moisture from them, and dish them on mashed potatoes. Serve with them any sauce that may be preferred ; such as tomato sauce, sauce piquante, sauce Robert, or pickled gherkins. *Time.*—From 15 to 20 minutes. *Average cost*, 10*d.* per lb. for chops. *Sufficient.*— Allow 6 cutlets for 4 persons. *Seasonable* from October to March.

Note.—The remains of roast loin of pork may be dressed in the same manner.

PORK CUTLETS.

[COLD MEAT COOKERY.] *Ingredients.* —The remains of cold roast loin of pork, 1 oz. of butter, 2 onions, 1 dessertspoonful of flour, ½ pint of gravy, pepper and salt to taste, 1 teaspoonful of vinegar and mustard. *Mode.*—Cut the pork into nice-sized cutlets, trim off most of the fat, and chop the onions. Put the butter into a stewpan, lay in the cutlets and chopped onions, and fry a light brown ; then add the remaining ingredients, simmer gently for 5 or 7 minutes, and serve. *Time.*—5 to 7 minutes. *Average cost*, exclusive of the meat, 4*d.* *Seasonable* from October to March.

PORK, Roast Griskin of.

Ingredients.—Pork ; a little powdered sage. *Mode.*—As this joint frequently comes to table hard and dry, particular care should be taken that it is well basted. Put it down to a bright fire,

SPARE-RIB OF PORK.

and flour it. About 10 minutes before taking it up, sprinkle over some powdered sage ; make a little gravy in the dripping-pan, strain it over the meat.

Pork, Boiled Leg of

and serve with a tureen of apple sauc This joint will be done in far less tin than when the skin is left on, cons quently, should have the greatest atte

GRISKIN OF PORK.

tion that it be not dried up. *Time.*- Griskin of pork weighing 6 lbs., 1½ hou *Average cost*, 7*d.* per lb. *Sufficient f* 5 or 6 persons. *Seasonable* from Se tember to March.

Note.—A spare-rib of pork is roast in the same manner as above, and wou take 1½ hour for one weighing abo 6 lbs.

PORK, Hashed.

Ingredients. — The remains of co roast pork, 2 onions, 1 teaspoonful flour, 2 blades of pounded mace, cloves, 1 tablespoonful of vinegar, ½ pi of gravy, pepper and salt to tast *Mode.*—Chop the onions and fry the of a nice brown ; cut the pork into th slices, season them with pepper and sa and add these to the remaining ingr dients. Stew gently for about ½ hou and serve garnished with sippets toasted bread. *Time.*—½ hour. *Avera cost*, exclusive of the meat, 3*d.* *Seaso able* from October to March.

PORK, Boiled Leg of.

Ingredients.—Leg of pork ; salt. *Mo* —For boiling, choose a small, compa well-filled leg, and rub it well with sa let it remain in pickle for a week ten days, turning and rubbing it eve day. An hour before dressing it, put into cold water for an hour, which i proves the colour. If the pork is pu chased ready salted, ascertain how lo the meat has been in pickle, and so it accordingly. Put it into a boiling-p with sufficient cold water to cover i let it gradually come to a boil, and move the scum as it rises. Simmer very gently until tender, and do n allow it to boil fast, or the knuckle w fall to pieces before the middle of leg is done. Carrots, turnips, or pa nips may be boiled with the pork, so of which should be laid round the di

Pork, Roast Leg of

as a garnish. A well-made pease-pudding is an indispensable accompaniment. *Time.*—A leg of pork weighing 8 lbs., 3 hours after the water boils, and to be simmered very gently. *Average cost,* 9d. per lb. *Sufficient* for 7 or 8 persons. *Seasonable* from September to March.

Note.—The liquor in which a leg of pork has been boiled makes excellent pea-soup.

PORK, Roast Leg of.

Ingredients. — Leg of pork, a little, oil, sage and onion stuffing. *Mode.*—Choose a small leg of pork, and score the skin **across** in narrow strips, about ¼ inch apart. Cut a slit in the knuckle, loosen the skin, and fill it with a sage-and-onion stuffing.

ROAST LEG OF PORK.

Brush the joint over with a little salad-oil (this makes the crackling crisper, and a better colour), and put it down to a bright, clear fire, not too near, as that would cause the skin to blister. Baste it well, and serve with a little gravy made in the dripping-pan, and do not omit to send to table with it a tureen of well-made apple sauce. *Time.*—A leg of pork weighing 8 lbs., about 3 hours. *Average cost,* 9d. per lb. *Sufficient* for 6 or 7 persons. *Seasonable* from September to March.

PORK, Leg of, to Carve.

This joint, which is such a favourite **one** with many people, is easy to carve. The knife should be carried sharply down to the bone, clean through the crackling, in the direction of the line 1 to 2. Sage and onion and apple sauce are usually sent to table with this dish,—sometimes the leg of pork is stuffed,—and the guests should be asked if they will have either or both. A frequent plan, and we think a good one, is now pursued, of

LEG OF PORK.

Pork, to Pickle

sending sage and onion to table separately from the joint, as it is not everybody to whom the flavour of this stuffing is agreeable.

Note.—The other dishes of pork do not call for any special remarks as to their carving or helping.

PORK, Roast Loin of.

Ingredients. — Pork; a little salt. *Mode.*—Score the skin in strips rather more than ¼ inch apart, and place the joint at a good distance from the fire, on

FORE LOIN OF PORK.

account of the crackling, which would harden before the meat would be heated through, were it placed too near. If very lean, it should be rubbed over with

HIND LOIN OF PORK.

a little salad oil, and kept well basted all the time it is at the fire. Pork should be very thoroughly cooked, but not dry; and be careful never to send it to table the least underdone, as nothing is more unwholesome and disagreeable than under-dressed white meats. Serve with apple sauce and a little gravy made in the dripping-pan. A stuffing of sage and onion may be made separately, and baked in a flat dish: this method is better than putting it in the meat, as many persons have so great an objection to the flavour. *Time.*—A loin of pork weighing 5 lbs., about 2 hours: allow more time should it be very fat. *Average cost,* 9d. per lb. *Sufficient* for 5 or 6 persons. *Seasonable* from September to March.

PORK, to Pickle.

Ingredients.—¼ lb. of saltpetre; salt. *Mode.*—As pork does not keep long without being salted, cut it into pieces of a suitable size as soon as the pig is cold. Rub the pieces of pork well with salt, and put them into a pan with a sprinkling of it between each piece: as

Pork, Pickled, to Boil	Potato Fritters

it melts on the top, strew on more. Lay a coarse cloth over the pan, a board over that, and a weight on the board, to keep the pork down in the brine. If excluded from the air, it will continue good for nearly 2 years. *Average cost,* 10*d.* per lb. for the prime parts. *Seasonable.*—The best time for pickling meat is late in the autumn.

PORK, Pickled, to Boil.

Ingredients.—Pork; water. *Mode.*— Should the pork be very salt, let it remain in water about 2 hours before it is dressed; put it into a saucepan with sufficient cold water to cover it, let it gradually come to a boil, then gently simmer until quite tender. Allow ample time for it to cook, as nothing is more disagreeable than underdone pork, and when boiled fast, the meat becomes hard. This is sometimes served with boiled poultry and roast veal, instead of bacon: when tender, and not over salt, it will be found equally good. *Time.*— A piece of pickled pork weighing 2 lbs., 1¼ hour; 4 lbs., rather more than 2 hours. *Average cost,* 10*d.* per lb. for the primest parts. *Seasonable* at any time.

PORK PIES (Warwickshire Recipe).

Ingredients.—For the crust, 5 lbs. of lard to 14 lbs. of flour; milk, and water. For filling the pies, to every 3 lbs. of meat allow 1 oz. of salt, 2¼ oz. of pepper, a small quantity of cayenne, 1 pint of water. *Mode.*—Rub into the flour a portion of the lard; the remainder put with sufficient milk and water to mix the crust, and boil this gently for ¼ hour. Pour it boiling on the flour, and knead and beat it till perfectly smooth. Now raise the crust in either a round or oval form, cut up the pork into pieces the size of a nut, season it in the above proportion, and press it compactly into the pie, in alternate layers of fat and lean, and pour in a small quantity of water; lay on the lid, cut the edges smoothly round, and pinch them together. Bake in a brick oven, which should be slow, as the meat is very solid. Very frequently, an inexperienced cook finds much difficulty in raising the crust. She should bear in mind that it must not be allowed to get cold, or it will fall immediately: to prevent this, the operation should be performed as

near the fire as possible. As considerable dexterity and expertness are necessary to raise the crust with the hand only, a glass bottle or small jar may be placed in the middle of the paste, and the crust moulded on this; but be particular that it is kept warm the whole time. *Sufficient.*—The proportions for 1 pie are 1 lb. of flour and 3 lbs. of meat. *Seasonable* from September to March.

PORK PIES, Little Raised.

Ingredients.—2 lbs. of flour, ½ lb. of butter, ½ lb. of mutton suet, salt and white pepper to taste, 4 lbs. of the neck of pork, 1 dessertspoonful of powdered sage. *Mode.*—Well dry the flour, mince the suet, and put these with the butter into a saucepan, to be made hot, and add a little salt. When melted, mix it up into a stiff paste, and put it before the fire with a cloth over it until ready to make up; chop the pork into small pieces, season it with white pepper, salt, and powdered sage; divide the paste into rather small pieces, raise it in a round or oval form, fill with the meat, and bake in a brick oven. These pies will require a fiercer oven than those in the preceding recipe, as they are made so much smaller, and consequently do not require so soaking a heat. *Time.*— If made small, about 1½ hour. *Seasonable* from September to March.

POTATO FRITTERS.

Ingredients.—2 large potatoes, 4 eggs, 2 tablespoonfuls of cream, 2 ditto of raisin or sweet wine, 1 dessertspoonful of lemon-juice, ½ teaspoonful of grated nutmeg, hot lard. *Mode.*—Boil the potatoes, and beat them up lightly with a fork, but do not use a spoon, as that would make them heavy. Beat the eggs well, leaving out one of the whites; add the other ingredients, and beat all together for at least 20 minutes, or until the batter is extremely light. Put plenty of good lard into a frying-pan, and drop a tablespoonful of the batter at a time into it, and fry the fritters a nice brown. Serve them with the following sauce :— A glass of sherry mixed with the strained juice of a lemon, and sufficient white sugar to sweeten the whole nicely. Warm these ingredients, and serve the sauce separately in a tureen. The fritters should be neatly dished on a white d'oyley, and pounded sugar sprinkled

Potato Pasty

over them. They should be well drained on a piece of blotting-paper before the fire previously to being dished. *Time.*—From 6 to 8 minutes. *Average cost, 9d. Sufficient* for 3 or 4 persons. *Seasonable* at any time.

POTATO PASTY.

Ingredients.—1½ lb. of rump-steak or mutton cutlets, pepper and salt to taste, ¼ pint of weak broth or gravy, 1 oz. of butter, mashed potatoes. *Mode.*—Place the meat, cut in small pieces, at the bottom of the pan ; season it with pepper and salt, and add the gravy and

POTATO-PASTY PAN.

butter broken into small pieces. Put on the perforated plate, with its valve-pipe screwed on, and fill up the whole space to the top of the tube with nicely-mashed potatoes mixed with a little milk, and finish the surface of them in any ornamental manner. If carefully baked, the potatoes will be covered with a delicate brown crust, retaining all the savoury steam rising from the meat. Send it to table as it comes from the oven, with a napkin folded round it. *Time.*—40 to 60 minutes. *Average cost,* 2s. *Sufficient* for 4 or 5 persons. *Seasonable* at any time.

POTATO PUDDING.

Ingredients.—½ lb. of mashed potatoes, 2 oz. of butter, 2 eggs, ¼ pint of milk, 8 tablespoonfuls of sherry, ¼ saltspoonful of salt, the juice and rind of 1 small lemon, 2 oz. of sugar. *Mode.*—Boil sufficient potatoes to make ½ lb. when mashed ; add to these the butter, eggs, milk, sherry, lemon-juice, and sugar ; mince the lemon-peel very finely, and beat all the ingredients well together. Put the pudding into a buttered pie-dish, and bake for rather more than ½ hour. To enrich it, add a few pounded almonds, and increase the quantity of eggs and butter. *Time.*—½ hour, or rather longer. *Average cost, 8d. Suf-*

Potato Snow

ficient for 5 or 6 persons. *Seasonable* at any time.

POTATO RISSOLES.

Ingredients.—Mashed potatoes, salt and pepper to taste ; when liked, a very little minced parsley, egg, and bread crumbs. *Mode.*—Boil and mash the

POTATO RISSOLES.

potatoes ; add a seasoning of pepper and salt, and, when liked, a little minced parsley. Roll the potatoes into small balls, cover them with egg and bread crumbs, and fry in hot lard for about 10 minutes ; let them drain before the fire, dish them on a napkin, and serve. *Time.* —10 minutes to fry the rissoles. *Seasonable* at any time.

Note.—The flavour of these rissoles may be very much increased by adding finely-minced tongue or ham, or even chopped onions, when these are liked.

POTATO SALAD.

Ingredients.—10 or 12 cold boiled potatoes, 4 tablespoonfuls of tarragon or plain vinegar, 6 tablespoonfuls of salad-oil, pepper and salt to taste, 1 teaspoonful of minced parsley. *Mode.*—Cut the potatoes into slices about ½ inch in thickness ; put these into a salad-bowl with oil and vinegar in the above proportion ; season with pepper, salt, and a teaspoonful of minced parsley ; stir the salad well, that all the ingredients may be thoroughly incorporated, and it is ready to serve. This should be made two or three hours before it is wanted for table. . Anchovies, olives, or pickles may be added to this salad, as also slices of cold beef, fowl, or turkey. *Seasonable* at any time.

POTATO SNOW.

Ingredients.—Potatoes, salt, and water. *Mode.*—Choose large white potatoes, as free from spots as possible ; boil them in their skins in salt and water until perfectly tender ; drain and *dry them thoroughly* by the side of the fire, and peel them. Put a hot dish before the fire, rub the potatoes through a coarse sieve on to this dish ; do not touch them after-

Potato Soup

wards, or the flakes will fall, and serve as hot as possible. *Time.*—½ to ¾ hour to boil the potatoes. *Average cost*, 4s. per bushel. *Sufficient,*—6 potatoes for 3 persons. *Seasonable* at any time.

POTATO SOUP.

Ingredients.—4 lbs. of mealy potatoes, boiled or steamed very dry, pepper and salt to taste, 2 quarts of stock. *Mode.*—When the potatoes are boiled, mash them smoothly, that no lumps remain, and gradually put them to the boiling stock; pass it through a sieve, season, and simmer for 5 minutes. Skim well, and serve with fried bread. *Time.*—½ hour. *Average cost*, 10d. per quart. *Seasonable* from September to March. *Sufficient* for 8 persons.

POTATO SOUP.

Ingredients.—1 lb. of shin of beef, 1 lb. of potatoes, 1 onion, ½ a pint of peas, 2 oz. of rice, 2 heads of celery, pepper and salt to taste, 3 quarts of water. *Mode.*—Cut the beef into thin slices, chop the potatoes and onion, and put them into a stewpan with the water, peas, and rice. Stew gently till the gravy is drawn from the meat; strain it off, take out the beef, and pulp the other ingredients through a coarse sieve. Put the pulp back into the soup, cut up the celery in it, and simmer till this is tender. Season, and serve with fried bread cut into it. *Time.*—3 hours. *Average cost*, 4d. per quart. *Seasonable* from September to March. *Sufficient* for 12 persons.

POTATO SOUP (very Economical).

Ingredients.—4 middle-sized potatoes well pared, a thick slice of bread, 6 leeks peeled and cut into thin slices as far as the white extends upwards from the roots, a teacupful of rice, a teaspoonful of salt, and half that of pepper, and 2 quarts of water. *Mode.*—The water must be completely boiling before anything is put into it; then add the whole of the ingredients at once, with the exception of the rice, the salt, and the pepper. Cover, and let these come to a brisk boil; put in the others, and let the whole boil slowly for an hour, or till all the ingredients are thoroughly done, and their several juices extracted and mixed. *Time.*—2½ hours. *Average cost,*

Potatoes, to Boil

3d. per quart. *Sufficient* for 8 persons. *Seasonable* in winter.

POTATOES, Baked.

Ingredients. — Potatoes. *Mode.* — Choose large potatoes, as much of a size as possible; wash them in lukewarm water, and scrub them well, for the browned skin of a baked potato is by many persons considered the better part of it. Put them into a moderate oven, and bake them for about two hours, turning them three or four times whilst they are cooking. Serve them in a napkin immediately they are done, as, if kept a long time in the oven, they have a shrivelled appearance. Potatoes may also be roasted before the fire, in an American oven; but when thus cooked, they must be done very slowly. Do not forget to send to table with them a piece of cold butter. *Time.*—Large potatoes, in a hot oven, 1½ hour to 2 hours; in a cool oven, 2 to 2½ hours. *Average cost*, 4s. per bushel. *Sufficient.*—Allow 2 to each person. *Seasonable* all the year, but not good just before and whilst new potatoes are in season.

BAKED POTATOES SERVED IN NAPKIN.

POTATOES, to Boil.

Ingredients.—10 or 12 potatoes; to each ½ gallon of water allow 1 heaped tablespoonful of salt. *Mode.*—Choose potatoes of an equal size, pare them, take out all the eyes and specks, and as they are peeled, throw them into cold water. Put them into a saucepan, with sufficient *cold* water to cover them, with salt in the above proportion, and let them *boil gently* until tender. Ascertain when they are done by thrusting a fork in them, and take them up the moment they feel soft through; for if they are left in the water afterwards, they become waxy or watery. Drain away the water, put the saucepan by the side of the fire, with the lid partially uncovered, to allow the steam to escape, and let the potatoes get thoroughly dry, and do not allow them to get burnt. Their superfluous moisture will evaporate, and the potatoes, if a good sort, should be perfectly mealy and dry. Potatoes vary so much in quality and size, that it is difficult to give the exact time for boiling; they should be

Potatoes, to Boil in their Jackets

attentively watched, and probed with a fork, to ascertain when they are cooked. Send them to table quickly, and very hot, and with an opening in the cover of the dish, that a portion of the steam may evaporate, and not fall back on the potatoes. *Time.*—Moderate-sized old potatoes, 15 to 20 minutes, after the water boils ; large ones, ½ hour to 35 minutes. *Average cost, 4s.* per bushel. *Sufficient* for 6 persons. *Seasonable* all the year, but not good just before and whilst new potatoes are in season.

Note.—To keep potatoes hot, after draining the water from them, put a folded cloth or flannel (kept for the purpose) on the top of them, keeping the saucepan-lid partially uncovered. This will absorb the moisture, and keep them hot some time without spoiling.

POTATOES, to Boil in their Jackets.

Ingredients.—10 or 12 potatoes ; to each ½ gallon of water, allow 1 heaped tablespoonful of salt. *Mode.*—To obtain this wholesome and delicious vegetable cooked in perfection, it should be boiled and sent to table with the skin on. In Ireland, where, perhaps, the cooking of potatoes is better understood than in any country, they are always served so. Wash the potatoes well, and if necessary, use a clean scrubbing-brush to remove the dirt from them ; and, if possible, choose the potatoes so that they may all be as nearly the same size as possible. When thoroughly cleansed, fill the saucepan half full with them, and just cover the potatoes with cold water salted in the above proportion: they are more quickly boiled with a small quantity of water, and, besides, are more savoury than when drowned in it. Bring them to boil, then draw the pan to the side of the fire, and let them simmer gently until tender. Ascertain when they are done by probing them with a fork ; then pour off the water, uncover the saucepan, and let the potatoes dry by the side of the fire, taking care not to let them burn. Peel them quickly, put them in a very hot vegetable-dish, either with or without a napkin, and serve very quickly. After potatoes are cooked, they should never be entirely covered up, as the steam, instead of escaping, falls down on them, and makes them watery and insipid.

Potatoes, Fried

In Ireland they are usually served up with the skins on, and a small plate is placed by the side of each guest. *Time.*—Moderate-sized potatoes, with their skins on, 20 to 25 minutes after the water boils ; large potatoes, 25 minutes to ¾ hour, or longer ; 5 minutes to dry them. *Average cost, 4s.* per bushel. *Sufficient* for 6 persons. *Seasonable* all the year, but not good just before and whilst new potatoes are in season.

POTATOES, New, to Boil.

Ingredients.—Potatoes ; to each ½ gallon of water allow 1 heaped tablespoonful of salt. *Mode.*—Do not have the potatoes dug long before they are dressed, as they are never good when they have been out of the ground some time. Well wash them, rub off the skins with a coarse cloth, and put them into *boiling* water salted in the above proportion. Let them boil until tender ; try them with a fork, and when done, pour the water away from them ; let them stand by the side of the fire with the lid of the saucepan partially uncovered, and when the potatoes are thoroughly dry, put them into a hot vegetable-dish, with a piece of butter the size of a walnut ; pile the potatoes over this, and serve. If the potatoes are too old to have the skin rubbed off, boil them in their jackets ; drain, peel, and serve them as above, with a piece of butter placed in the midst of them *Time.*—¼ to ½ hour, according to the size. *Average cost,* in full season, 1*d.* per lb. *Sufficient.*—Allow 3 lbs. for 5 or 6 persons. *Seasonable* in May and June, but may be had, forced, in March.

POTATOES, Fried (French Fashion).

Ingredients.—Potatoes, hot butter or clarified dripping, salt. *Mode.*—Peel and cut the potatoes into thin slices, as nearly the same size as possible ; make some butter or dripping *hot* in a frying-pan ; put in the potatoes, and fry them on both sides until *nearly* cooked. Now take the potatoes out of the fat, make the fat *quite boiling,* then throw in the potatoes for a minute or two until sufficiently done. The immersion of the vegetable in the grease a second time after it is partially cooked, causes it to puff or "gonfler," as the French say, which is the desired appearance for properly-dressed fried potatoes to pos-

|

scss. When they are crisp and done, take them up, place them on a cloth before the fire to drain the grease from them, and serve very hot, after sprinkling them with salt. These are delicious with rump-steak, and, in France, are frequently served thus as a breakfast dish. The remains of cold potatoes may also be sliced and fried by the above recipe, but the slices must be cut a little thicker. *Time.*—Sliced raw potatoes, 5 minutes; cooked potatoes, 5 minutes. *Average cost,* 4s. per bushel. *Sufficient,*— 6 sliced potatoes for 3 persons. *Seasonable* at any time.

POTATOES, a German Method of Cooking.

Ingredients.—8 to 10 middling-sized potatoes, 3 oz. of butter, 2 tablespoonfuls of flour, ½ pint of broth, 2 tablespoonfuls of vinegar. *Mode.*—Put the butter and flour into a stewpan; stir over the fire until the butter is of a nice brown colour, and add the broth and vinegar; peel and cut the potatoes into long thin slices, lay them in the gravy, and let them simmer gently until tender, which will be in from 10 to 15 minutes, and serve very hot. A laurel-leaf simmered with the potatoes is an improvement. *Time.*—10 to 15 minutes. *Seasonable* at any time.

POTATOES, à la Maître d'Hôtel.

Ingredients.—Potatoes, salt and water; to every 6 potatoes allow 1 tablespoonful of minced parsley, 2 oz. of butter, pepper and salt to taste, 4 tablespoonfuls of gravy, 2 tablespoonfuls of lemon-juice. *Mode.*—Wash the potatoes clean, and boil them in salt and water; when they are done, drain them, let them cool; then peel and cut the potatoes into thick slices: if these are too thin, they would break in the sauce. Put the butter into a stewpan with the pepper, salt, gravy, and parsley; mix these ingredients well together, put in the potatoes, shake them two or three times, that they may be well covered with the sauce, and, when quite hot through, squeeze in the lemon-juice, and serve. *Time.*—½ to ¾ hour to boil the potatoes; 10 minutes for them to heat in the sauce. *Average cost,* 4s. per bushel. *Sufficient* for 3 persons. *Seasonable* all the year.

POTATOES, Mashed.

Ingredients.—Potatoes; to every lb. of mashed potatoes allow 1 oz. of butter, 2 tablespoonfuls of milk, salt to taste. *Mode.*—Boil the potatoes in their skins; when done, drain them, and let them get thoroughly dry by the side of the fire; then peel them, and, as they are peeled, put them into a clean saucepan, and with a *large fork* beat them to a light paste; add butter, milk, and salt in the above proportion, and stir all the ingredients well over the fire. When thoroughly hot, dish them lightly, and draw the fork backwards over the potatoes to make the surface rough, and serve. When dressed in this manner, they may be browned at the top with a salamander, or before the fire. Some cooks press the potatoes into moulds, then turn them out, and brown them in the oven: this is a pretty mode of serving, but it makes them heavy. In whatever way they are sent to table, care must be taken to have them quite free from lumps. *Time.*— From ½ to ¾ hour to boil the potatoes. *Average cost,* 4s. per bushel. *Sufficient,* —1 lb. of mashed potatoes for 3 persons. *Seasonable* at any time.

POTATOES, Very Thin-mashed, or, Purée de Pommes de Terre.

Ingredients.—To every lb. of mashed potatoes allow ¼ pint of good broth or stock, 2 oz. of butter. *Mode.*—Boil the potatoes, well drain them, and pound them smoothly in a mortar, or beat them up with a fork; add the stock or broth, and rub the potatoes through a sieve. Put the purée into a very clean saucepan with the butter; stir it well over the fire until thoroughly hot, and it will then be ready to serve. A purée should be rather thinner than mashed potatoes, and is a delicious accompaniment to delicately broiled mutton cutlets. Cream or milk may be substituted for the broth when the latter is not at hand. A casserole of potatoes, which is often used for ragoûts instead of rice, is made by mashing potatoes rather thickly, placing them on a dish, and making an opening in the centre. After having browned the potatoes in the oven, the dish should be wiped clean, and the ragoût or fricassée poured in. *Time.*—About ½ hour to boil the potatoes; 6 or 7 minutes to warm the purée. *Average cost,* 4s. per bushel.

| Potatoes, how to use Cold | Pound Cake |

Sufficient.—Allow 1 lb. of cooked potatoes for 3 persons. *Seasonable* at any time.

POTATOES, how to use Cold.

Ingredients.—The remains of cold potatoes ; to every lb. allow 2 tablespoonfuls of flour, 2 ditto of minced onions, 1 oz. of butter-milk. *Mode.*—Mash the potatoes with a fork until perfectly free from lumps ; stir in the other ingredients, and add sufficient milk to moisten them well ; press the potatoes into a mould, and bake in a moderate oven until nicely brown, which will be in from 20 minutes to ½ hour. Turn them out of the mould, and serve. *Time.*—20 minutes to ½ hour. *Seasonable* at any time.

POTATOES, to Steam.

Ingredients.—Potatoes ; boiling water. *Mode.*—This mode of cooking potatoes is now much in vogue, particularly where they are wanted on a large scale, it being so very convenient. Pare the potatoes, throw them into cold water as they are peeled, then put them into a steamer. Place the steamer over a saucepan of boiling water, and steam the potatoes from 20 to 40 minutes, according to the size and sort. When a fork goes easily through them, they are done ; then take them up, dish, and serve very quickly. *Time.*—20 to 40 minutes. *Average cost,* 4s. per bushel. *Sufficient.*— Allow 2 large potatoes to each person. *Seasonable* all the year, but not so good whilst new potatoes are in season.

POULET AUX CRESSONS.

Ingredients.—A fowl, a large bunch of water-cresses, 3 tablespoonfuls of vinegar, ¼ pint of gravy. *Mode.*—Truss and roast a fowl by recipe, taking care that it is nicely frothed and brown. Wash and dry the water-cresses, pick them nicely, and arrange them in a flat layer on a dish. Sprinkle over a little salt and the above proportion of vinegar ; place over these the fowl, and pour over it the gravy. A little gravy should be served in a tureen. When not liked, the vinegar may be omitted. *Time.*— From ½ to 1 hour, according to size. *Average cost,* in full season, 2s. 6d. each. *Sufficient* for 3 or 4 persons *Seasonable* at any time.

POULET À LA MARENGO.

Ingredients. — 1 large fowl, 4 tablespoonfuls of salad oil, 1 tablespoonful of flour, 1 pint of stock or water, about 28 mushroom-buttons, salt and pepper to the taste, 1 teaspoonful of powdered sugar, a very small piece of garlic. *Mode.*—Cut the fowl into 8 or 10 pieces, put them with the oil into a stewpan, and brown them over a moderate fire ; dredge in the above proportion of flour, when that is brown, pour in the stock or water, let it simmer very slowly for rather more than ½ an hour, and skim off the fat as it rises to the top ; add the mushrooms, season with pepper, salt, garlic, and sugar ; take out the fowl, which arrange pyramidically on a dish, with the inferior joints at the bottom. Reduce the sauce by boiling it quickly over the fire, keeping it stirred until sufficiently thick to adhere to the back of the spoon ; pour over the fowl, and serve. *Time.*—Altogether 50 minutes. *Average cost,* 3s. 6d. *Sufficient* for 3 or 4 persons. *Seasonable* at any time.

POUND CAKE.

Ingredients.—1 lb. of butter, 1¼ lb. of flour, 1 lb. of pounded loaf sugar, 1 lb. of currants, 9 eggs, 2 oz. of candied peel, ½ oz. of citron, ½ oz. of sweet almonds ; when liked, a little pounded mace. *Mode.*— Work the butter to a cream ; dredge in the flour ; add the sugar, currants, candied peel, which should be cut into neat slices, and the almonds, which should be blanched and chopped, and mix all these well together ; whisk the eggs, and let them be thoroughly blended with the dry ingredients.

POUND CAKE.

Beat the cake well for 20 minutes, and put it into a round tin, lined at the bottom and sides with a strip of white buttered paper. Bake it from 1½ to 2 hours, and let the oven be well heated when the cake is first put in, as, if this is not the case, the currants will all sink to the bottom of it. To make this preparation light, the yolks and whites of the eggs should be beaten separately, and added separately to the other ingredients. A glass of wine is sometimes added to the mixture ; but this is scarcely necessary, as the cake will be found quite rich enough without it. *Time.*—1½ to 2 hours. *Ave-*

Prawn Soup

rage cost, 3s. 6d. Sufficient.—The above quantity divided in two will make two nice-sized cakes. *Seasonable* at any time.

PRAWN SOUP.

Ingredients.—Two quarts of fish stock, two pints of prawns, the crumb of a French roll, anchovy sauce or mushroom ketchup to taste, one blade of mace, one-fourth pint of vinegar, a little lemon-juice. *Mode.*—Pick out the tails of the prawns, put the bodies in a stewpan with 1 blade of mace, ¼ pint of vinegar, and the same quantity of water; stew them for ¼ hour, and strain off the liquor. Put the fish stock into a stewpan; add the strained liquor, pound the prawns with the crumb of a roll moistened with a little of the soup, rub them through a tammy, and mix them by degrees with the soup; add ketchup or anchovy sauce to taste with a little lemon-juice. When it is well cooked, put in a few picked prawns; let them get thoroughly hot, and serve. If not thick enough, put in a little butter and flour. *Time.*—Hour. *Average cost, 2s.* per quart. *Seasonable* at any time. *Sufficient* for 8 persons.

Note.—This can be thickened with tomatoes, and vermicelli served in it, which makes it a very tasteful soup.

PRAWNS, to Dress.

Cover a dish with a large cup reversed, and over that lay a small white napkin. Arrange the prawns on it in the form of a pyramid, and garnish with plenty of parsley. Sometimes prawns are stuck into a lemon cut in half the long way, and garnished with parsley.

PRESERVES

From the nature of vegetable substances, and chiefly from their not passing so rapidly into the putrescent state as animal bodies, the mode of preserving them is somewhat different, although the general principles are the same. All the means of preservation are put in practice occasionally for fruits and the various parts of vegetables, according to the nature of the species, the climate, the uses to which they are applied, &c. Some are dried, as nuts, raisins, sweet herbs, &c.; others are preserved by means of sugar, such as many fruits whose delicate juices would be lost by drying; some are preserved by means of vinegar, and chiefly used as condi-

Preserves

ments or pickles; a few also by salting, as French beans; while others are preserved in spirits. We have, however, in this place to treat of the best methods of preserving fruits. Fruit is a most important item in the economy of health; the epicurean can scarcely be said to have any luxuries without it; therefore, as it is so invaluable, when we cannot have it fresh, we must have it preserved. It has long been a desideratum to preserve fruits by some cheap method, yet by such as would keep them fit for the various culinary purposes, as making tarts and other similar dishes. The expense of preserving them with sugar is a serious objection; for, except the sugar be used in considerable quantities, the success is very uncertain. Sugar also overpowers and destroys the sub-acid taste so desirable in many fruits : those which are preserved in this manner are chiefly intended for the dessert. Fruits intended for preservation should be gathered in the morning, in dry weather, with the morning sun upon them, if possible; they will then have their fullest flavour, and keep in good condition longer than when gathered at any other time. Until fruit can be used, it should be placed in the dairy, an ice-house, or a refrigerator. In an ice-house it will remain fresh and plump for several days. Fruit gathered in wet or foggy weather will soon be mildewed, and be of no service for preserves.

Having secured the first and most important contribution to the manufacture of preserves—the fruit, the next consideration is the preparation of the syrup in which the fruit is to be suspended; and this requires much care. In the confectioner's art there is a great nicety in proportioning the degree of concentration of the syrup very exactly to each particular case; and he knows this by signs, and expresses it by certain technical terms. But to distinguish these properly requires very great attention and considerable experience. The principal thing to be acquainted with is the fact, that, in proportion as the syrup is longer boiled, its water will become evaporated, and its consistency will be thicker. Great care must be taken in the management of the fire, that the syrup does not boil over, and that the boiling is not carried to such an extent as to burn the sugar.

The first degree or consistency is called *the thread*, which is subdivided into the

Preserves

little and great thread. If you dip the finger into the syrup and apply it to the thumb, the tenacity of the syrup will, on separating the finger and thumb, afford a thread, which shortly breaks : this is the little thread. If the thread, from the greater tenacity, and, consequently, greater strength of the syrup, admits of a greater extension of the finger and thumb, it is called the great thread. There are half-a-dozen other terms and experiments for testing the various thickness of the boiling sugar towards the consistency called *caramel ;* but that degree of sugar-boiling belongs to the confectioner. A solution of sugar prepared by dissolving two parts of double-refined sugar (the best sugar is the most economical for preserves) in one of water, and boiling this a little, affords a syrup of the right degree of strength, and which neither ferments nor crystallizes. This appears to be the degree called *smooth* by the confectioners, and is proper to be used for the purposes of preserves. The syrup employed should sometimes be clarified, which is done in the following manner :—Dissolve 2 lbs. of loaf sugar in a pint of water ; add to this solution the white of an egg, and beat it well. Put the preserving-pan upon the fire with the solution ; stir it with a wooden spatula, and when it begins to swell and boil up, throw in some cold water or a little oil to damp the boiling ; for, as it rises suddenly, if it should boil over, it would take fire, being of a very inflammable nature. Let it boil up again ; then take it off, and remove carefully the scum that has risen. Boil the solution again, throw in a little more cold water, remove the scum, and so on for three or four times successively ; then strain it. It is considered to be sufficiently boiled when some taken up in a spoon pours out like oil.

Although sugar passes so easily into the state of fermentation, and is, in fact, the only substance capable of undergoing the vinous stage of that process, yet it will not ferment at all if the quantity be sufficient to constitute a very strong syrup : hence, syrups are used to preserve fruits and other vegetable substances from the changes they would undergo if left to themselves. Before sugar was in use, honey was employed to preserve many vegetable productions, though this substance has now given way to the juice of the sugar-cane.

Preserves

The fruits that are the most fit for preservation in syrup are apricots, peaches, nectarines, apples, greengages, plums of all kinds, and pears. As an example, take some apricots not too ripe, make a small slit at the stem end, and push out the stone ; simmer them in water till they are softened and about half done, and afterwards throw them into cold water. When they have cooled, take them out and drain them. Put the apricots into the preserving-pan with sufficient syrup to cover them ; let them boil up three or four times, and then skim them ; remove them from the fire, pour them into an earthen pan, and let them cool till next day. Boil them up three days successively, skimming each time, and they will then be finished and in a fit state to be put into pots for use. After each boiling, it is proper to examine into the state of the syrup when cold ; if too thin, it will bear additional boiling ; if too thick, it may be lowered with more syrup of the usual standard. The reason why the fruit is emptied out of the preserving-pan into an earthen pan is, that the acid of the fruit acts upon the copper, of which the preserving-pans are usually made. From this example the process of preserving fruits by syrup will be easily comprehended. The first object is to soften the fruit by blanching or boiling it in water, in order that the syrup by which it is preserved may penetrate through its substance.

Many fruits, when preserved by boiling, lose much of their peculiar and delicate flavour, as, for instance, pine-apples ; and this inconvenience may, in some instances, be remedied by preserving them without heat. Cut the fruit in slices about one-fifth of an inch thick, strew powdered loaf sugar an eighth of an inch thick on the bottom of a jar, and put the slices on it. Put more sugar on this, and then another layer of the slices, and so on till the jar is full. Place the jar with the fruit up to the neck in boiling water, and keep it there till the sugar is completely dissolved, which may take half-an-hour, removing the scum as it rises. Lastly, tie a wet bladder over the mouth of the jar, or cork and wax it.

Any of the fruits that have been preserved in syrup may be converted into dry preserves, by first draining them from the syrup, and then drying them in a stove or very moderate oven, adding

Preserves

to them a quantity of powdered loaf-sugar, which will gradually penetrate the fruit, while the fluid parts of the fruit gently evaporate. They should be dried in the stove or oven on a sieve, and turned every six or eight hours, fresh powdered sugar being sifted over them every time they are turned. Afterwards, they are to be kept in a dry situation, in drawers or boxes. Currants and cherries preserved whole in this manner, in bunches, are extremely elegant, and have a fine flavour. In this way it is, also, that orange and lemon chips are preserved.

Marmalades, jams, and fruit pastes are of the same nature, and are now in very general request. They are prepared without difficulty, by attending to a very few directions; they are somewhat expensive, but may be kept without spoiling for a considerable time. Marmalades and jams differ little from each other: they are preserves of a half-liquid consistency, made by boiling the pulp of fruits, and sometimes part of the rinds, with sugar. The appellation of marmalade is applied to those confitures which are composed of the firmer fruits, as pineapples or the rinds of oranges; whereas jams are made of the more juicy berries, such as strawberries, raspberries, currants, mulberries, &c. Fruit pastes are a kind of marmalades, consisting of the pulp of fruits, first evaporated to a proper consistency, and afterwards boiled with sugar. The mixture is then poured into a mould, or spread on sheets of tin, and subsequently dried in the oven or stove till it has acquired the state of a paste. From a sheet of this paste, strips may be cut and formed into any shape that may be desired, as knots, rings, &c. Jams require the same care and attention in the boiling as marmalade; the slightest degree of burning communicates a disagreeable empyreumatic taste, and if they are not boiled sufficiently, they will not keep. That they may keep, it is necessary not to be sparing of sugar.

In all the operations for preserve-making, when the preserving-pan is used, it should not be placed on the fire, but on a trivet, unless the jam be made on a hot plate, when this is not necessary. If the pan be placed close on to the fire, the preserve is very liable to burn, and the colour and flavour be consequently spoiled.

The Ptarmigan

Fruit jellies are compounds of the juices of fruits combined with sugar, concentrated, by boiling, to such a consistency that the liquid, upon cooling, assumes the form of a tremulous jelly.

Before fruits are candied, they must first be boiled in syrup, after which they are taken out and dried on a stove, or before the fire; the syrup is then to be concentrated, or boiled to a candy height, and the fruit dipped in it, and again laid on the stove to dry and candy; they are then to be put into boxes, and kept dry.

Conserves consist of fresh vegetable matters beat into a uniform mass with refined sugar, and they are intended to preserve the virtues and properties of recent flowers, leaves, roots, peels, or fruits, unaltered, and as near as possible to what they were when fresh gathered, and to give them an agreeable taste.

The last to be mentioned, but not the least important preparation of fruit, is the compôte, which can be made at the moment of need, and with much less sugar than would be ordinarily put to preserves. Compôtes are very wholesome things, suitable to most stomachs which cannot accommodate themselves to raw fruit or a large portion of sugar. They are the happy medium—far better than ordinary stewed fruit.

PTARMIGAN, the, or White Grouse.

This bird is nearly the same size as red grouse, and is fond of lofty situations, where it braves the severest weather, and is found in most parts of Europe, as well as in Greenland. At

THE PTARMIGAN.

Hudson's Bay they appear in such multitudes that so many as sixty or seventy are frequently taken at once in a net.

Ptarmigan, to Dress

As they are as tame as chickens, this is done without difficulty. Buffon says that the ptarmigan avoids the solar heat, and prefers the frosts of the summits of the mountains; for, as the snow melts on the sides of the mountains, it ascends till it gains the top, where it makes a hole, and burrows in the snow. In winter, it flies in flocks, and feeds on the wild vegetation of the hills, which imparts to its flesh a bitter, but not altogether an unpalatable taste. It is dark-coloured, has something of the flavour of the hare, and is greatly relished and much sought after by some sportsmen.

PTARMIGAN, to Dress the.

Ingredients.—2 or 3 birds; butter, flour, fried bread crumbs. *Mode.*—The ptarmigan, or white grouse, when young and tender, are exceedingly fine eating, and should be kept as long as possible, to be good. Pluck, draw, and truss them in the same manner as grouse, and roast them before a brisk fire. Flour and froth them nicely, and serve on buttered toast, with a tureen of brown gravy. Bread sauce, when liked, may be sent to table with them, and fried bread crumbs substituted for the toasted bread. *Time.*—About ½ hour. *Sufficient,* —2 for a dish. *Seasonable* from the beginning of February to the end of April.

PTARMIGAN, to Carve.

Ptarmigan, being much of the same size, and trussed in the same manner, as the red bird, may be carved in the manner described, in Partridge and Grouse carving.

PUDDING, Alma.

Ingredients.—½ lb. of fresh butter, ½ lb. of powdered sugar, ½ lb. of flour, ¼ lb. of currants, 4 eggs. *Mode.*—Beat the butter to a thick cream, strew in, by degrees, the sugar, and mix both these well together; then dredge the flour in gradually, add the currants, and moisten with the eggs, which should be well beaten. When all the ingredients are well stirred and mixed, butter a mould that will hold the mixture exactly, tie it down with a cloth, put the pudding into boiling water, and boil for 5 hours; when turne   strew some powdered sugar over   and serve. *Time.*—6 hours.

Pudding, Bakewell

Average cost, 1s. 6d. Sufficient for 5 or 6 persons. *Seasonable* at any time.

PUDDING, Aunt Nelly's.

Ingredients.—½ lb. of flour, ½ lb. of treacle, ½ lb. of suet, the rind and juice of 1 lemon, a few strips of candied lemon-peel, 3 tablespoonfuls of cream, 2 eggs. *Mode.*—Chop the suet finely; mix it with the flour, treacle, lemon-peel minced, and candied lemon-peel; add the cream, lemon-juice, and 2 well-beaten eggs; beat the pudding well, put it into a buttered basin, tie it down with a cloth, and boil from 3½ to 4 hours. *Time.*—3½ to 4 hours. *Average cost, 1s. 2d. Sufficient* for 5 or 6 persons. *Seasonable* at any time, but more suitable for a winter pudding.

PUDDING, a Bachelor's.

Ingredients.—4 oz. of grated bread, 4 oz. of currants, 4 oz. of apples, 2 oz. of sugar, 3 eggs, a few drops of essence of lemon, a little grated nutmeg. *Mode.* —Pare, core, and mince the apples very finely, sufficient, when minced, to make 4 oz.; add to these the currants, which should be well washed, the grated bread, and sugar; whisk the eggs, beat these up with the remaining ingredients, and, when all is thoroughly mixed, put the pudding into a buttered basin, tie it down with a cloth, and boil for 3 hours. *Time.*—3 hours. *Average cost, 9d. Sufficient* for 4 or 5 persons. *Seasonable* from August to March.

PUDDING, Bakewell (very Rich).

Ingredients.—¼ lb. of puff-paste, 5 eggs, 6 oz. of sugar, ¼ lb. of butter, 1 oz. of almonds, jam. *Mode.*—Cover a dish with thin paste, and put over this a layer of any kind of jam, ½ inch thick; put the yolks of 5 eggs into a basin with the white of 1, and beat these well; add the sifted sugar, the butter, which should be melted, and the almonds, which should be well pounded; beat all together until well mixed, then pour it into the dish over the jam, and bake for an hour in a moderate oven. *Time.*—1 hour. *Average cost, 1s. 6d. Sufficient* for 4 or 5 persons. *Seasonable* at any time.

PUDDING, Bakewell.

Ingredients.—¾ pint of bread crumbs, 1 pint of milk, 4 eggs, 2 oz. of sugar,

Pudding, Baroness

3 oz. of butter, 1 oz. of pounded almonds, jam. *Mode.*—Put the bread crumbs at the bottom of a pie-dish, then over them a layer of jam of any kind that may be preferred ; mix the milk and eggs together ; add the sugar, butter, and pounded almonds ; beat all well together ; pour it into the dish, and bake in a moderate oven for 1 hour. *Time.*—1 hour. *Average cost,* 1s. 3d. to 1s. 6d. *Sufficient* for 4 or 5 persons. *Seasonable* at any time.

PUDDING, Baroness (Author's Recipe).

Ingredients.—¾ lb. of suet, ¾ lb. of raisins weighed after being stoned, ¾ lb. of flour, ½ pint of milk, ¼ saltspoonful of salt. *Mode.*—Prepare the suet, by carefully freeing it from skin, and chop it finely ; stone the raisins, and cut them in halves, and mix both these ingredients with the salt and flour ; moisten the whole with the above proportion of milk, stir the mixture well, and tie the pudding in a floured cloth, which has been previously wrung out in boiling water. Put the pudding into a saucepan of boiling water, and let it boil, without ceasing, 4½ hours. Serve with plain sifted sugar only, a little of which may be sprinkled over the pudding. *Time.*—4½ hours. *Average cost,* 1s. 4d. *Sufficient* for 7 or 8 persons. *Seasonable* in winter, when fresh fruit is not obtainable.

Note.—This pudding the editress cannot too highly recommend. The recipe was kindly given to her family by a lady who bore the title here prefixed to it ; and with all who have partaken of it, it is an especial favourite. Nothing is of greater consequence, in the above directions, than attention to the time of boiling, which should never be *less* than that mentioned.

PUDDING, Royal Coburg.

Ingredients.—1 pint of new milk, 6 oz. of flour, 6 oz. of sugar, 6 oz. of butter, 6 oz. of currants, 6 eggs, brandy and grated nutmeg to taste. *Mode.*—Mix the flour to a smooth batter with the milk, add the remaining ingredients *gradually,* and when well mixed, put it into four basins or moulds half full ; bake for ¾ hour, turn the puddings out on a dish, and serve with wine sauce. *Time.*—¾ hour. *Average cost,* 1s. 9d.

Pudding, Comarques

Sufficient for 7 or 8 persons. *Seasonable* at any time.

PUDDING, Cold.

Ingredients.—4 eggs, 1 pint of milk, sugar to taste, a little grated lemon-rind, 2 oz. of raisins, 4 tablespoonfuls of marmalade, a few slices of sponge cake. *Mode.*—Sweeten the milk with lump sugar, add a little grated lemon-rind, and stir to this the eggs, which should be well whisked ; line a buttered mould with the raisins, stoned and cut in half ; spread the slices of cake with the marmalade, and place them in the mould ; then pour in the custard, tie the pudding down with paper and a cloth, and boil gently for 1 hour : when cold, turn it out, and serve. *Time.*—1 hour. *Average cost,* 1s. 2d. *Sufficient* for 5 or 6 persons. *Seasonable* at any time.

PUDDING, College.

Ingredients.—1 pint of bread crumbs, 6 oz. of finely-chopped suet, ¼ lb. of currants, a few thin slices of candied peel, 3 oz. of sugar, ¼ nutmeg, 3 eggs, 4 tablespoonfuls of brandy. *Mode.*—Put the bread crumbs into a basin ; add the suet, currants, candied peel, sugar, and nutmeg, grated, and stir these ingredients until they are thoroughly mixed. Beat up the eggs, moisten the pudding with these, and put in the brandy ; beat well for a few minutes, then form the mixture into round balls or egg-shaped pieces ; fry these in hot butter or lard, letting them stew in it until thoroughly done, and turn them two or three times, till of a fine light brown ; drain them on a piece of blotting-paper before the fire ; dish, and serve with wine sauce. *Time.*—15 to 20 minutes. *Average cost,* 1s. *Sufficient* for 7 or 8 puddings. *Seasonable* at any time.

PUDDING, Comarques (Excellent).

Ingredients.—5 eggs, 3 tablespoonfuls of flour, 2 tablespoonfuls of powdered sugar, rind of 1 lemon, ½ pint of cream, different kinds of preserve. *Mode.*—Beat the whites and yolks of the eggs separately, and put them into different basins ; stir the flour, sugar, and lemon-peel into the yolks ; whip the cream very thick and put it on a sieve to harden, then add it, with the whites of

Pudding, Delhi

the eggs, to the other ingredients, and pour the mixture into little deep saucers just before putting into the oven. Bake about ½ an hour. When they are taken out, a very thin layer of different kinds of preserve should be put upon each, and they should be piled one above another. A little whipped cream placed here and there on the pudding as a garnish would be found to improve the appearance of this dish. *Time.*—About ½ an hour. *Average cost,* 1s. 9d. *Sufficient* for 4 or 5 persons. *Seasonable* at any time.

PUDDING, Delhi.

Ingredients.—4 large apples, a little grated nutmeg, 1 teaspoonful of minced lemon-peel, 2 large tablespoonfuls of sugar, 6 oz. of currants, ¾ lb. of suet crust. *Mode.*—Pare, core, and cut the apples into slices; put them into a saucepan with the nutmeg, lemon-peel, and sugar, stew them over the fire till soft; then have ready the above quantity of crust, roll it out thin, spread the apples over the paste, sprinkle over the currants, roll the pudding up, closing the ends properly, tie it in a floured cloth, and boil for 2 hours. *Time.*—2 hours. *Average cost,* 1s. *Sufficient* for 5 or 6 persons. *Seasonable.*—August to March.

PUDDING, Empress.

Ingredients.—¼ lb. of rice, 2 oz. of butter, 3 eggs, jam, sufficient milk to soften the rice. *Mode.*—Boil the rice in the milk until very soft; then add the butter, boil it for a few minutes after the latter ingredient is put in, and set it by to cool. Well beat the eggs, stir these in, and line a dish with puff-paste; put over this a layer of rice, then a thin layer of any kind of jam, then another layer of rice, and proceed in this manner until the dish is full; and bake in a moderate oven for ¾ hour. This pudding may be eaten hot or cold; if the latter, it will be much improved by having a boiled custard poured over it. *Time.*—¾ hour. *Average cost,* 1s. *Sufficient* for 6 or 7 persons. *Seasonable* at any time.

PUDDING, Exeter (Very Rich).

Ingredients.—10 oz. of bread-crumbs, 4 oz. of sago, 7 oz. of finely-chopped suet, 6 oz. of moist sugar, the rind of

Pudding, German

½ lemon, ¼ pint of rum, 7 eggs, 4 tablespoonfuls of cream, 4 small sponge-cakes, 2 oz. of ratafias, ½ lb. of jam. *Mode.*—Put the bread-crumbs into a basin with the sago, suet, sugar, minced lemon-peel, rum, and 4 eggs; stir these ingredients well together, then add 3 more eggs and the cream, and let the mixture be well beaten. Then butter a mould, strew in a few bread-crumbs, and cover the bottom with a layer of ratafias; then put in a layer of the mixture, then a layer of sliced sponge-cake spread thickly with any kind of jam; then add some ratafias, then some of the mixture and sponge-cake, and so on until the mould is full, taking care that a layer of the mixture is on the top of the pudding. Bake in a good oven from ¾ to 1 hour, and serve with the following sauce:—Put 3 tablespoonfuls of black-currant jelly into a stewpan, add 2 glasses of sherry, and when warm, turn the pudding out of the mould, pour the sauce over it and serve hot. *Time.*—From 1 to 1¼ hour. *Average cost,* 2s. 6d. *Sufficient* for 7 or 8 persons. *Seasonable* at any time.

PUDDING-PIES, Folkestone.

Ingredients.—1 pint of milk, 3 oz. of ground rice, 3 oz. of butter, ¼ lb. of sugar, flavouring of lemon-peel or bay-leaf, 6 eggs, puff-paste, currants. *Mode.*—Infuse 2 laurel or bay leaves, or the rind of ½ lemon in the milk, and when it is well flavoured, strain it, and add the rice; boil these for ¼ hour, stirring all the time; then take them off the fire, stir in the butter, sugar, and eggs, and let these latter be well beaten before they are added to the other ingredients; when nearly cold, line some patty-pans with puff-paste, fill with the custard, strew over each a few currants and bake from 20 to 25 minutes in a moderate oven. *Time.*—20 to 25 minutes. *Average cost,* 1s. 1d. *Sufficient* to fill a dozen patty-pans. *Seasonable* at any time.

PUDDING, German.

Ingredients.— 2 teaspoonfuls of flour, 1 teaspoonful of arrowroot, 1 pint of milk, 2 oz. of butter, sugar to taste, the rind of ½ lemon, 4 eggs, 3 tablespoonfuls of brandy. *Mode.*—Boil the milk with the lemon-rind until well flavoured; then strain it, and mix with it the flour, ar-

Pudding, Half-pay

rowroot, butter, and sugar. Boil these ingredients for a few minutes, keeping them well stirred; then take them off the fire and mix with them the eggs, yolks and whites, beaten separately and added separately. Boil some sugar to candy; line a mould with this, put in the brandy, then the mixture; tie down with a cloth, and boil for rather more than 1 hour. When turned out, the brandy and sugar make a nice sauce. *Time.*—Rather more than 1 hour. *Average cost*, 1s. *Sufficient* for 4 or 5 persons. *Seasonable* at any time.

PUDDING, Half-Pay.

Ingredients.—¼ lb. of suet, ¼ lb. of currants, ¼ lb. of raisins, ¼ lb. of flour, ¼ lb. of bread-crumbs, 2 tablespoonfuls of treacle, ½ pint of milk. *Mode.*—Chop the suet finely; mix with it the currants, which should be nicely washed and dried, the raisins, which should be stoned, the flour, bread-crumbs, and treacle; moisten with the milk, beat up the ingredients until all are thoroughly mixed, put them into a buttered basin, and boil the pudding for 3½ hours. *Time.*—3½ hours. *Average cost*, 8d. *Sufficient* for 5 or 6 persons. *Seasonable* at any time.

PUDDING, Herodotus.

Ingredients.—½ lb. of bread-crumbs, ½ lb. of good figs, 6 oz. of suet, 6 oz. of moist sugar, ½ saltspoonful of salt, 3 eggs, nutmeg to taste. *Mode.*—Mince the suet and figs very finely; add the remaining ingredients, taking care that the eggs are well whisked; beat the mixture for a few minutes, put it into a buttered mould, tie it down with a floured cloth, and boil the pudding for 5 hours. Serve with wine sauce. *Time.*—5 hours. *Average cost*, 10d. *Sufficient* for 5 or 6 persons. *Seasonable* at any time.

PUDDING, Hunter's.

Ingredients.—1 lb. of raisins, 1 lb. of currants, 1 lb. of suet, 1 lb. of bread-crumbs, ½ lb. of moist sugar, 8 eggs, 1 tablespoonful of flour, ¼ lb. of mixed candied peel, 1 glass of brandy, 10 drops of essence of lemon, 10 drops of essence of almonds, ½ nutmeg, 2 blades of mace, 6 cloves. *Mode.*—Stone and shred the raisins rather small, chop the suet finely, and rub the bread until all lumps are well broken; pound the spice

Pudding, Mansfield

to powder, cut the candied peel into thin shreds, and mix all these ingredients well together, adding the sugar Beat the eggs to a strong froth, and as they are beaten, drop into them the essence of lemon and essence of almonds; stir these to the dry ingredients, mix well, and add the brandy. Tie the pudding firmly in a cloth, and boil it for 6 hours at the least · 7 or 8 hours would be still better for it. Serve with boiled custard, melted red-currant jelly, or brandy sauce. *Time.*—6 to 8 hours. *Average cost*, 3s. 6d. *Sufficient* for 9 or 10 persons. *Seasonable* in winter.

PUDDING, Manchester (to eat Cold).

Ingredients.—3 oz. of grated bread, ½ pint of milk, a strip of lemon-peel, 4 eggs, 2 oz. of butter, sugar to taste, puff-paste, jam, 3 tablespoonfuls of brandy. *Mode.*—Flavour the milk with lemon-peel, by infusing it in the milk for ½ hour; then strain it on to the bread-crumbs, and boil it for 2 or 3 minutes; add the eggs, leaving out the whites of 2, the butter, sugar, and brandy; stir all these ingredients well together; cover a pie-dish with puff-paste, and at the bottom put a thick layer of any kind of jam; pour the above mixture, cold, on the jam, and bake the pudding for an hour. Serve cold, with a little sifted sugar sprinkled over. *Time.*—1 hour. *Average cost*, 1s. *Sufficient* for 5 or 6 persons. *Seasonable* at any time.

PUDDING, Mansfield.

Ingredients.—The crumb of 2 rolls, 1 pint of milk, sugar to taste, 4 eggs, 2 tablespoonfuls of brandy, 6 oz. of chopped suet, 2 tablespoonfuls of flour, ½ lb. of currants, ½ teaspoonful of grated nutmeg, 2 tablespoonfuls of cream. *Mode.*—Slice the roll very then, and pour upon it a pint of boiling milk; let it remain closely covered for ¼ hour, then beat it up with a fork, and sweeten with moist sugar; stir in the chopped suet, flour, currants, and nutmeg. Mix these ingredients well together, moisten with the eggs, brandy, and cream; beat the mixture for 2 or 3 minutes, put it into a buttered dish or mould, and bake in a moderate oven for 1¼ hour. Turn it out, strew sifted sugar over, and serve. *Time.*—1¼ hour. *Average cost*, 1s. 3d. *Sufficient* for 6 or 7 persons. *Seasonable* at any time.

PUDDING, Marlborough.

Ingredients.—¼ lb. of butter, ¼ lb. of powdered lump sugar, 4 eggs, puff-paste, a layer of any kind of jam. *Mode.*—Beat the butter to a cream, stir in the powdered sugar, whisk the eggs, and add these to the other ingredients. When these are well mixed, line a dish with puff-paste, spread over a layer of any kind of jam that may be preferred, pour in the mixture, and bake the pudding for rather more than ½ hour. *Time.*—Rather more than ½ hour. *Average cost,* 1s. *Sufficient* for 5 or 6 persons. *Seasonable* at any time.

PUDDING, Military.

Ingredients.—½ lb. of suet, ½ lb. of bread-crumbs, ½ lb. of moist sugar, the rind and juice of 1 large lemon. *Mode.*—Chop the suet finely, mix it with the bread-crumbs and sugar, and mince the lemon-rind and strain the juice; stir these into the other ingredients, mix well, and put the mixture into small buttered cups, and bake for rather more than ¼ hour; turn them out on the dish, and serve with lemon-sauce. The above ingredients may be made into small balls, and boiled for about ½ hour; they should then be served with the same sauce as when baked. *Time.*—Rather more than ¼ hour *Average cost, 9d. Sufficient* to fill 6 or 7 moderate-sized cups. *Seasonable* at any time.

PUDDING, Monday's.

Ingredients. — The remains of cold plum-pudding, brandy, custard made with 5 eggs to every pint of milk. *Mode.*—Cut the remains of a *good* cold plum-pudding into finger-pieces, soak them in a little brandy, and lay them cross-barred in a mould until full. Make a custard with the above proportion of milk and eggs, flavouring it with nutmeg or lemon-rind; fill up the mould with it; tie it down with a cloth, and boil or steam it for an hour. Serve with a little of the custard poured over, to which has been added a tablespoonful of brandy. *Time.*—1 hour. *Average cost,* exclusive of the pudding, 6d. *Sufficient* for 5 or 6 persons. *Seasonable* at any time.

PUDDING, Nesselrode (a fashionable Iced Pudding—Carême's Recipe).

Ingredients.— 40 chestnuts, 1 lb. of sugar, flavouring of vanilla, 1 pint of cream, the yolks of 12 eggs, 1 glass of Maraschino, 1 oz. of candied citron, 2 oz. of currants, 2 oz. of stoned raisins, ½ pint of whipped cream, 3 eggs. *Mode.*—Blanch the chestnuts in the boiling water, remove the husks, and pound them in a mortar until perfectly smooth, adding a few spoonfuls of syrup. Then rub them through a fine sieve, and mix them in a basin with a pint of syrup made from 1 lb. of sugar, clarified, and flavoured with vanilla, 1 pint of cream, and the yolks of 12 eggs. Set this mixture over a slow fire, stirring it *without ceasing*, and just as it begins to boil, take it off and pass it through a tammy. When it is cold, put it into a freezing-pot, adding the Maraschino, and make the mixture set; then add the sliced citron, the currants, and stoned raisins (these two latter should be soaked the day previously in Maraschino and sugar pounded with vanilla); the whole thus mingled, add a plateful of whipped cream mixed with the whites of 3 eggs, beaten to a froth with a little syrup. When the pudding is perfectly frozen, put it into a pine-apple-shaped mould; close the lid, place it again in the freezing-pan, covered over with pounded ice and saltpetre, and let it remain until required for table; then turn the pudding out, and serve. *Time.*—½ hour to freeze the mixture. *Seasonable* from October to February.

PUDDING, Paradise.

Ingredients.—3 eggs, 3 apples, ¼ lb. of bread-crumbs, 3 oz. of sugar, 3 oz. of currants, salt and grated nutmeg to taste, the rind of ½ lemon, ½ wineglassful of brandy. *Mode.*—Pare, core, and mince the apples into small pieces, and mix them with the other dry ingredients; beat up the eggs, moisten the mixture with these, and beat it well; stir in the brandy, and put the pudding into a buttered mould; tie it down with a cloth, boil for 1½ hour, and serve with sweet sauce. *Time.*—1½ hour. *Average cost,* 1s. *Sufficient* for 4 or 5 persons.

PUDDING, Pease.

Ingredients.—1½ pint of split peas, 2 oz. of butter, 2 eggs, pepper and salt

Pudding, Quickly-made

to taste. *Mode.*—Put the peas to soak over night, in rain-water, and float off any that are worm-eaten or discoloured. Tie them loosely in a clean cloth, leaving a little room for them to swell, and put them on to boil in cold rain-water, allowing 2½ hours after the water has simmered up. When the peas are tender, take them up and drain ; rub them through a colander with a wooden spoon ; add the butter, eggs, pepper, and salt ; beat all well together for a few minutes, until the ingredients are well incorporated ; then tie them tightly in a floured cloth ; boil the pudding for another hour, turn it on to the dish, and serve very hot. This pudding should always be sent to table with boiled leg of pork, and is an exceedingly nice accompaniment to boiled beef. *Time.*—2½ hours to boil the peas, tied loosely in the cloth ; 1 hour for the pudding. *Average cost,* 6*d.* *Sufficient* for 7 or 8 persons. *Seasonable* from September to March.

PUDDING, Quickly-Made.

Ingredients.—¼ lb. of butter, ½ lb. of sifted sugar, ¼ lb. of flour, 1 pint of milk, 5 eggs, a little grated lemon-rind. *Mode.* —Make the milk hot ; stir in the butter, and let it cool before the other ingredients are added to it ; then stir in the sugar, flour, and eggs, which should be well whisked, and omit the whites of 2 ; flavour with a little grated lemon-rind, and beat the mixture well. Butter some small cups, rather more than half fill them ; bake from 20 minutes to ½ hour, according to the size of the puddings, and serve with fruit, custard or wine-sauce, a little of which may be poured over them. *Time.*—20 minutes to ½ hour. *Average cost,* 1*s.* 2*d.* *Sufficient* for 6 puddings. *Seasonable* at any time.

PUDDING, Somersetshire.

Ingredients.—3 eggs, their weight in flour, pounded sugar and butter, flavouring of grated lemon-rind, bitter almonds, or essence of vanilla. *Mode.*—Carefully weigh the various ingredients, by placing on one side of the scales the eggs, and on the other the flour ; then the sugar, and then the butter. Warm the butter, and with the hands beat it to a cream ; gradually dredge in the flour and pounded sugar, and keep stirring and beating the mixture without ceasing until it is perfectly smooth. Then add the eggs, which should be well whisked, and either

Pudding, West Indian

of the above flavourings that may be preferred ; butter some small cups, rather more than half fill them, and bake in a brisk oven for about ½ hour. Turn them out, dish them on a napkin, and serve custard or wine-sauce with them. A pretty little supper-dish may be made of these puddings cold, by cutting out a portion of the inside with the point of a knife, and putting into the cavity a little whipped cream or delicate preserve, such as apricot, greengage, or very bright marmalade. The paste for these puddings requires a great deal of mixing, as the more it is beaten, the better will the puddings be. When served cold, they are usually called *gâteaux à la Madeleine.* *Time.*—½ hour. *Average cost,* 10*d.* *Sufficient* for 6 or 7 puddings. *Seasonable* at any time.

PUDDING, Vicarage.

Ingredients.—¼ lb. of flour, ¼ lb. of chopped suet, ¼ lb. of currants, ¼ lb. of raisins, 1 tablespoonful of moist sugar, ½ teaspoonful of ground ginger, ⅓ saltspoonful of salt. *Mode.*—Put all the ingredients into a basin, having previously stoned the raisins, and washed, picked, and dried the currants ; mix well with a clean knife ; dip the pudding-cloth into boiling water, wring it out, and put in the mixture. Have ready a saucepan of boiling water, plunge in the pudding, and boil for 3 hours. Turn it out on the dish, and serve with sifted sugar. *Time.*—3 hours. *Average cost,* 8*d.* *Sufficient* for 5 or 6 persons. *Seasonable.*—Suitable for a winter pudding.

PUDDING, West-Indian.

Ingredients.—1 pint of cream, ¼ lb. of loaf-sugar, ½ lb. of Savoy or sponge-cakes, 8 eggs, 3 oz. of preserved green ginger. *Mode.*—Crumble down the cakes, put them into a basin, and pour over them the cream, which should be previously sweetened and brought to the boiling-point ; cover the basin, well beat the eggs, and when the cream is soaked up, stir them in. Butter a mould, arrange the ginger round it, pour in the pudding carefully, and tie it down with a cloth ; steam or boil it slowly for 1½ hour, and serve with the syrup from the ginger, which should be warmed, and poured over the pudding. *Time.*—1½ hour. *Average cost,* with cream at 1*s.* per pint, 2*s.* 8*d.* *Sufficient* for 5 or 6 persons. *Seasonable* at any time.

PUDDING, Yorkshire, ⁀ serve with hot Roast Beef.

Ingredients.—1½ pint of milk, 6 *large* tablespoonfuls of flour, 3 eggs, 1 salt-spoonful of salt. *Mode.*—Put the flour into a basin with the salt, and stir gradually to this enough milk to make it into a stiff batter. When this is perfectly smooth, and all the lumps are well

YORKSHIRE PUDDING.

rubbed down, add the remainder of the milk and the eggs, which should be well beaten. Beat the mixture for a few minutes, and pour it into a shallow tin, which has been previously well rubbed with beef dripping. Put the pudding into the oven, and bake it for an hour; then, for another ½ hour, place it under the meat, to catch a little of the gravy that flows from it. Cut the pudding into small square pieces, put them on a hot dish, and serve. If the meat is baked, the pudding may at once be placed under it, resting the meat on a small three-cornered stand. *Time.*—1½ hour. *Average cost, 7d. Sufficient* for 5 or 6 persons. *Seasonable* at any time.

PUFF-PASTE RINGS, or Puits d'Amour.

Ingredients.—Puff-paste (*see* Paste), the white of an egg, sifted loaf sugar. *Mode.*—Make some good puff-paste by recipe; roll it out to the thickness of about ¼ inch, and, with a round fluted paste-cutter, stamp out as many pieces as may be required; then work the paste up again, and roll it out to the same thickness, and with a *smaller* cutter, stamp out sufficient pieces to correspond with the larger ones. Again stamp out the centre of these smaller rings; brush over the others with the white of an egg, place a small ring on the top of every large circular piece of paste, egg over the tops, and bake from 15 to 20 minutes. Sift over sugar, put them back in the oven to colour them; then fill the rings with preserve of any bright colour. Dish them high on a napkin, and serve. So many pretty dishes of pastry may be made by stamping puff-paste out with fancy cutters, and filling the pieces, when baked, with jelly or preserve, that our space will not allow us to give a separate recipe for each of them; but as they are all made from one paste, and only the shape and garnishing varied, perhaps it is not necessary, and by exercising a little ingenuity, variety may always be obtained. Half-moons, leaves, diamonds, stars, shamrocks, rings, &c., are the most appropriate shapes for fancy pastry. *Time.*—15 to 25 minutes. *Average cost,* with ½ lb. of paste, 1s. *Sufficient* for 2 dishes of pastry. *Seasonable* at any time.

PUMPKIN, Preserved.

Ingredients.—To each lb. of pumpkin allow 1 lb. of roughly pounded loaf sugar, 1 gill of lemon-juice. *Mode.*—Obtain a good sweet pumpkin; halve it, take out the seeds, and pare off the rind; cut it into neat slices, or into pieces about the size of a five-shilling piece. Weigh the pumpkin, put the slices in a pan or deep dish in layers, with the sugar sprinkled between them; pour the lemon-juice over the top, and let the whole remain for 2 or 3 days. Boil altogether, adding ½ pint of water to every 3 lbs. of sugar used, until the pumpkin becomes tender; then turn the whole into a pan, where let it remain for a week; then drain off the syrup, boil it until it is quite thick; skim, and pour it, boiling, over the pumpkin. A little bruised ginger and lemon-rind, thinly pared, may be boiled in the syrup to flavour the pumpkin. *Time.*—From ½ to ¾ hour to boil the pumpkin tender. *Average cost, 5d.* to 7d. per lb. pot. *Seasonable* in September and October; but better when made in the latter month, as the pumpkin is then quite ripe.

Note.—Vegetable marrows are very good prepared in the same manner, but are not quite so rich.

PUNCH, to make Hot.

Ingredients.—½ pint of rum, ½ pint of brandy, ¼ lb. of sugar, 1 large lemon, ½ teaspoonful of nutmeg, 1 pint of boiling water. *Mode.*—Rub the sugar over the lemon until it has absorbed all the yellow part of the skin, then put the sugar into a punch bowl; add the lemon-juice (free from pips), and mix these

Quails, to Dress	Rabbit, Boiled

two ingredients well together. Pour over them the boiling water, stir well together, add the rum, brandy, and nutmeg; mix thoroughly, and the punch will be ready to serve. It is very important in making good punch that all the ingredients are thoroughly incorporated; and to insure success, the processes of mixing must be diligently attended to. *Sufficient.*—Allow a quart for 4 persons; but this information must be taken *cum grano salis;* for the capacities of persons for this kind of beverage are generally supposed to vary considerably.

QUAILS, to Dress.

Ingredients. — Quails, butter, toast. *Mode.*—These birds keep good several days, and should be roasted without drawing. Truss them in the same manner as woodcocks; roast them before a clear fire, keep them well basted, and serve on toast. *Time.*—About 20 minutes. *Average cost.*—Seldom bought. *Sufficient,* 2 for a dish. *Seasonable* from October to December.

QUAILS.

Quails, being trussed and served like Woodcock, may be similarly carved.

QUINCE JELLY.

Ingredients.—To every pint of juice allow 1 lb. of loaf sugar. *Mode.*—Pare and slice the quinces, and put them into a preserving-pan with sufficient water to float them. Boil them until tender, and the fruit is reduced to a pulp; strain off the clear juice, and to each pint allow the above proportion of loaf sugar. Boil the juice and sugar together for about ¾ hour; remove all the scum as it rises, and if the jelly appears firm when a little is poured on a plate, it is done. The residue left on the sieve will answer to make a common marmalade, for immediate use, by boiling it with ½ lb. of common sugar to every lb. of pulp. *Time.*—3 hours to boil the quinces in water; ¾ hour to boil the jelly. *Average cost,* from 8d. to 10d. per lb. pot. *Seasonable* from August to October.

QUINCE MARMALADE.

Ingredients.—To every lb. of quince pulp allow ¾ lb. of loaf sugar. *Mode.*—

Slice the quinces into a preserving-pan, adding sufficient water for them to float; place them on the fire to stew, until reduced to a pulp, keeping them stirred occasionally from the bottom, to prevent their burning; then pass the pulp through a hair sieve, to keep back the skin and seeds. Weigh the pulp, and to each lb. add lump sugar in the above proportion, broken very small. Place the whole on the fire, and keep it well stirred from the bottom of the pan with a wooden spoon, until reduced to a marmalade which may be known by dropping a little on a cold plate, when, if it jellies, it is done. Put it into jars whilst hot; let it cool, and cover with pieces of oiled paper cut to the size of the mouths of the jars. The tops of them may be afterwards covered with pieces of bladder, or tissue-paper brushed over on both sides with the white of an egg. *Time.*—3 hours to boil the quinces without the sugar; ¾ hour to boil the pulp with the sugar. *Average cost,* from 8d. to 9d. per lb. pot. *Sufficient.* — Allow 1 pint of sliced quinces for a lb. pot. *Seasonable* in August, September, and October.

RABBIT, Boiled.

Ingredients.—Rabbit; water. *Mode.* —For boiling, choose rabbits with smooth and sharp claws, as that denotes they are young: should these be blunt and rugged, the ears dry and tough, the animal is old. After emptying and skinning it, wash it well in cold water, and let it soak for about ¼ hour in warm

BOILED RABBIT.

water, to draw out the blood. Bring the head round to the side, and fasten it there by means of a skewer run through that and the body. Put the rabbit into sufficient hot water to cover it, let it boil very gently until tender, which will be in from ½ to ¾ hour, according to its size and age. Dish it, and smother it either with onion, mushroom, or liver-sauce, or parsley-and-butter; the former is, however, generally preferred to any of the last-named sauces. When liver-sauce is preferred, the liver should be

Rabbit, Curried

boiled for a few minutes, and minced very finely, or rubbed through a sieve before it is added to the sauce. *Time.*— A very young rabbit, ½ hour; a large one, ¾ hour; an old one, 1 hour or longer. *Average cost*, from 1s. to 1s. 6d. each. *Sufficient* for 4 persons. *Seasonable* from September to February.

RABBIT, Curried.

Ingredients.—1 rabbit, 2 oz. of butter, 3 onions, 1 pint of stock, 1 tablespoonful of curry powder, 1 tablespoonful of flour, 1 tablespoonful of mushroom powder, the juice of ½ lemon, ½ lb. of rice. *Mode.* —Empty, skin, and wash the rabbit thoroughly, and cut it neatly into joints. Put it into a stewpan with the butter and sliced onions, and let them acquire a nice brown colour, but do not allow them to blacken. Pour in the stock, which should be boiling; mix the curry powder and flour smoothly with a little water, add it to the stock, with the mushroom powder, and simmer gently for rather more than ½ hour; squeeze in the lemon-juice, and serve in the centre of a dish, with an edging of boiled rice all round. Where economy is studied, water may be substituted for the stock; in this case, the meat and onions must be very nicely browned. A little sour apple and rasped cocoa-nut stewed with the curry will be found a great improvement. *Time.*—Altogether ¾ hour. *Average cost*, from 1s. to 1s. 6d each. *Sufficient* for 4 persons. *Seasonable* in winter.

RABBIT, Fried.

Ingredients.—1 rabbit, flour, dripping, 1 oz. of butter, 1 teaspoonful of minced shalot, 2 tablespoonfuls of mushroom ketchup. *Mode.*—Cut the rabbit into neat joints, and flour them well; make the dripping boil in a fryingpan, put in the rabbit, and fry it a nice brown. Have ready a very hot dish, put in the butter, shalot, and ketchup; arrange the rabbit pyramidically on this, and serve as quickly as possible. *Time.*—10 minutes. *Average cost*, from 1s. to 1s. 6d. each. *Sufficient* for 4 or 5 persons. *Seasonable* from September to February.

Note.—The rabbit may be brushed over with egg, and sprinkled with breadcrumbs, and fried as above. When cooked in this manner, make a gravy in the pan, and pour it round, but not over the pieces of rabbit.

Rabbit or Hare, Ragoût of

RABBIT, à la Minute.

Ingredients.—1 rabbit, ¼ lb. of butter, salt and pepper to taste, 2 blades of pounded mace, 8 dried mushrooms, 2 tablespoonfuls of minced parsley, 2 teaspoonfuls of flour, 2 glasses of sherry, 1 pint of water. *Mode.*—Empty, skin, and wash the rabbit thoroughly, and cut it into joints. Put the butter into a stewpan with the pieces of rabbit; add salt, pepper, and pounded mace, and let it cook until three parts done; then put in the remaining ingredients, and boil for about 10 minutes; it will then be ready to serve. Fowls or hare may be dressed in the same manner. *Time.*—Altogether, 35 minutes. *Average cost*, from 1s. to 1s. 6d. each. *Sufficient* for 4 or 5 persons. *Seasonable* from September to February.

RABBIT PIE.

Ingredients.—1 rabbit, a few slices of ham, salt and white pepper to taste, 2 blades of pounded mace, ½ teaspoonful of grated nutmeg, a few forcemeat balls, 3 hard-boiled eggs, ½ pint of gravy, puff crust. *Mode.*—Cut up the rabbit (which should be young), remove the breastbone, and bone the legs. Put the rabbit, slices of ham, forcemeat balls, and hard eggs, by turns, in layers, and season each layer with pepper, salt, pounded mace, and grated nutmeg. Pour in about ½ pint of water, cover with crust, and bake in a well-heated oven for about 1½ hour. Should the crust acquire too much colour, place a piece of paper over it to prevent it from burning. When done, pour in at the top, by means of the hole in the middle of the crust, a little good gravy, which may be made of the breast- and leg-bones of the rabbit, and 2 or 3 shank-bones of the rabbit, flavoured with onion, herbs, and spices. *Time.*—1½ hour. *Average cost*, from 1s. to 1s. 6d. each. *Sufficient* for 4 or 5 persons. *Seasonable* from September to February.

Note.—The liver of the rabbit may be boiled, minced, and mixed with the forcemeat balls, when the flavour is liked.

RABBIT OR HARE, Ragoût of.

Ingredients.—1 rabbit, 3 teaspoonfuls of flour, 3 sliced onions, 2 oz. of butter, a few thin slices of bacon, pepper and salt to taste, 2 slices of lemon, 1 bay-leaf,

Rabbit, Roast or Baked

1 glass of port wine. *Mode.*—Slice the onions, and put them into a stewpan with the flour and butter ; place the pan near the fire, stir well as the butter melts, till the onions become a rich brown colour, and add, by degrees, a little water or gravy till the mixture is of the consistency of cream. Cut some thin slices of bacon; lay in these with the rabbit, cut into neat joints ; add a seasoning of pepper and salt, the lemon and bay-leaf, and let the whole simmer until tender. Pour in the port wine, give one boil, and serve. *Time.*—About ½ hour to simmer the rabbit. *Average cost*, from 1s. to 1s. 6d. each. *Sufficient* for 4 or 5 persons. *Seasonable* from September to February.

RABBIT, Roast or Baked.

Ingredients. — 1 rabbit, forcemeat, buttered paper, sausage-meat. *Mode.*—Empty, skin, and thoroughly wash the rabbit ; wipe it dry, line the inside with sausage-meat and forcemeat, and to which has been added the minced liver. Sew the stuffing inside, skewer back the head between the shoulders, cut off the fore-joints of the shoulders and legs, bring them close to the body, and secure them by means of a skewer. Wrap the rabbit in buttered paper, and put it

ROAST RABBIT.

down to a bright clear fire ; keep it well basted and a few minutes before it is done remove the paper, flour and froth it, and let it acquire a nice brown colour. Take out the skewers, and serve with brown gravy and red-currant jelly. To bake the rabbit, proceed in the same manner as above ; in a good oven, it will take about the same time as roasting. *Time.*—A young rabbit, 35 minutes ; a large one about ¾ hour. *Average cost*, from 1s. to 1s. 6d. each. *Sufficient* for 4 persons. *Seasonable* from September to February.

RABBIT SOUP.

Ingredients.—2 large rabbits, or 3 small ones; a faggot of savoury herbs, ½ head of celery, 2 carrots, 1 onion, 1 blade of mace, salt and white pepper to taste, a little pounded mace, ½ pint of

Rabbit Stewed, Larded

cream, the yolks of 2 eggs boiled hard, the crumb of a French roll, nearly 3 quarts of water. *Mode.*—Make the soup with the legs and shoulders of the rabbit, and keep the nice pieces for a dish or *entrée.* Put them into warm water, and draw the blood ; when quite clean, put them into a stewpan, with a faggot of herbs, and a teacupful, or rather more, of veal stock or water. Simmer slowly till done through, add the three quarts of water, and boil for an hour. Take out the rabbit, pick the meat from the bones, covering it up to keep it white ; put the bones back in the liquor, add the vegetables, and simmer for two hours ; skim and strain, and let it cool. Now pound the meat in a mortar, with the yolks of the eggs, and the crumb of the roll previously soaked ; rub it through a tammy, and gradually add it to the strained liquor, and simmer for 15 minutes. Mix arrowroot or rice-flour with the cream (say 2 dessert-spoonfuls), and stir in the soup ; bring it to a boil, and serve. This soup must be very white, and instead of thickening it with arrowroot or rice-flour, vermicelli or pearl barley can be boiled in a little stock, and put in five minutes before serving. *Time.*—Nearly 4 hours. *Average cost*, 1s. per quart. *Seasonable* from September to March. *Sufficient* for 10 persons.

RABBIT, Stewed.

Ingredients.—1 rabbit, 2 large onions, 6 cloves, 1 small teaspoonful of chopped lemon-peel, a few forcemeat balls, thickening of butter and flour, 1 large tablespoonful of mushroom ketchup. *Mode.*—Cut the rabbit into small joints ; put them into a stewpan, add the onions sliced, the cloves, and minced lemon-peel. Pour in sufficient water to cover the meat, and, when the rabbit is nearly done, drop in a few forcemeat balls, to which has been added the liver, finely chopped. Thicken the gravy with flour and butter, put in the ketchup, give one boil, and serve. *Time.*—Rather more than ½ hour. *Average cost*, 1s. to 1s. 6d. each. *Sufficient* for 4 or 5 persons. *Seasonable* from September to February.

RABBIT STEWED, Larded.

Ingredients.—1 rabbit, a few strips of bacon, rather more than 1 pint of good broth or stock, a bunch of savoury herbs, salt and pepper to taste, thicken-

Rabbits, Stewed in Milk

ing of butter and flour, 1 glass of sherry. *Mode.*—Well wash the rabbit, cut it into quarters, lard them with slips of bacon, and fry them; then put them into a stewpan with the broth, herbs, and a seasoning of pepper and salt; simmer gently until the rabbit is tender, then strain the gravy, thicken it with butter and flour, add the sherry, let it boil, pour it over the rabbit, and serve. Garnish with slices of cut lemon. *Time.* —Rather more than ½ hour. *Average cost,* 1s. to 1s. 6d. each. *Sufficient* for 4 or 5 persons. *Seasonable* from September to February.

RABBITS, Stewed in Milk.

Ingredients.—2 very young rabbits, not nearly half grown; 1½ pint of milk, 1 blade of mace, 1 dessertspoonful of flour, a little salt and cayenne. *Mode.*— Mix the flour very smoothly with 4 tablespoonfuls of the milk, and when this is well mixed, add the remainder. Cut up the rabbits into joints, put them into a stewpan, with the milk and other ingredients, and simmer them *very gently* until quite tender. Stir the contents from time to time, to keep the milk smooth and prevent it from burning. ½ hour will be sufficient for the cooking of this dish. *Time.*—½ hour. *Average cost,* from 1s. to 1s. 6d. each. *Sufficient* for 5 or 6 persons. *Seasonable* from September to February.

RABBITS, to carve.

In carving a boiled rabbit, let the knife be drawn on each side of the backbone, the whole length of the rabbit, as shown by the dotted line 3 to 4 : thus the rabbit will be in three parts. Now

BOILED RABBIT.

let the back be divided into two equal parts in the direction of the line from 1 to 2 ; then let the leg be taken off, as shown by the line 5 to 6, and the shoulder, as shown by the line 7 to 8. This, in our opinion, is the best plan to carve a rabbit, although there are other modes which are preferred by some.

Raised Pie, of Poultry or Game

A roast rabbit is rather differently trussed from one that is meant to be boiled; but the carving is nearly similar

ROAST RABBIT.

as will be seen by the cut. The back should be divided into as many pieces as it will give, and the legs and shoulders can then be disengaged in the same manner as those of the boiled animal.

RAISED PIE, of Poultry or Game.

Ingredients.—To every lb. of flour allow ½ lb of butter, ½ pint of water, the yolks of 2 eggs, ½ teaspoonful of salt (these are for the crust); 1 large fowl or pheasant, a few slices of veal cutlet, a few slices of dressed ham, forcemeat, seasoning of nutmeg, allspice, pepper and salt, gravy. *Mode.*—Make a stiff short crust with the above proportion of butter, flour, water, and eggs, and work it up very smoothly: butter a raised-pie mould, and line it with paste. Previously to making the crust, bone the fowl, or whatever bird is intended to be used, lay it, breast downwards, upon a cloth, and season the inside well with pounded mace, allspice, pepper, and salt; then spread over it a layer of forcemeat, then a layer of seasoned veal, and then one of ham, and then another layer of forcemeat, and roll the fowl over, making the skin meet at the back. Line the pie with forcemeat, put in the fowl, and fill up the cavities with slices of seasoned veal, and ham, and forcemeat; wet the edges of the pie, put on the cover, pinch the edges together with the paste-pincers, and decorate it with leaves; brush it over with beaten yolk of egg, and bake in a moderate oven for 4 hours. In the mean time, make a good strong gravy from the bones, pour it through a funnel into the hole at the top; cover this hole with a small leaf, and the pie, when cold, will be ready for use. Let it be remembered that the gravy must be considerably reduced before it is poured into the pie, as, when cold, it should form a firm jelly, and not be the least degree in a liquid state. This recipe is suitable for all kinds of poultry or game, using one or more birds, according to the size of the pie intended to be made;

Raised Pie, of Veal and Ham	Raisin Pudding, Boiled

but the birds must always be boned. Truffles, mushrooms, &c., added to this pie, make it much nicer; and, to enrich it, lard the fleshy parts of the poultry or game with thin strips of bacon. This method of forming raised pies in a mould is generally called a *timbale*, and has the advantage of being more easily made than one where the paste is raised by the hands; the crust, besides, being eatable. *Time.*—Large pie, 4 hours. *Average cost*, 6s. 6d. *Seasonable*, with poultry, all the year; with game, from September to March.

RAISED PIE, of Veal and Ham.

Ingredients.—3 or 4 lbs. of veal cutlets, a few slices of bacon or ham, seasoning of pepper, salt, nutmeg, and allspice, forcemeat, 2 lbs. of hot-water paste, ½ pint of good strong gravy. *Mode.*—To raise the crust for a pie with the hands is a very difficult task, and can only be accomplished by skilled and experienced cooks. The process should be seen to be satisfactorily learnt, and plenty of practice given to the making of raised pies, as by that means only will success be insured. Make a hot-water paste by

RAISED PIE.

recipe, and from the mass raise the pie with the hands; if this cannot be accomplished, cut out pieces for the top and bottom, and a long piece for the sides; fasten the bottom and side-piece together by means of egg, and pinch the edges well together; then line the pie with forcemeat, put in a layer of veal, and a plentiful seasoning of salt, pepper, nutmeg, and allspice; for, let it be remembered, these pies taste very insipid unless highly seasoned. Over the seasoning place a layer of sliced bacon or cooked ham, and then a layer of forcemeat, veal seasoning, and bacon, and so on until the meat rises to about an inch above the paste; taking care to finish with a layer of forcemeat, to fill all the cavities of the pie, and to lay in the meat

firmly and compactly. Brush the to edge of the pie with beaten egg, put the cover, press the edges, and pin them round with paste-pincers. Make hole in the middle of the lid, and orn ment the pie with leaves, which shou be stuck on with the white of an egg; th brush it all over with the beaten yolk an egg, and bake the pie in an ov with a soaking heat from 3 to 4 hour To ascertain when it is done, run a shar pointed knife or skewer through the ho at the top into the middle of the pi and if the meat feels tender, it is suf ciently baked. Have ready about ½ pi of very strong gravy, pour it through funnel into the hole at the top, stop the hole with a small leaf of bak paste, and put the pie away until want for use. Should it acquire too mu colour in the baking, cover it with whi paper, as the crust should not in t least degree be burnt. Mushroom truffles, and many other ingredien may be added to enrich the flavour these pies, and the very fleshy parts the meat may be larded. These pies a more frequently served cold than ho and form excellent dishes for co suppers or breakfasts. The cover of t pie is sometimes carefully remove leaving the perfect edges, and the t decorated with square pieces of ve bright aspic jelly: this has an excee ingly pretty effect. *Time.*—About hours. *Average cost*, 6s. 6d. *Sufficie* for a very large pie. *Seasonable* fro March to October.

RAISIN CHEESE.

Ingredients.—To every lb. of raisi allow ½ lb. of loaf sugar; pound cinnamon and cloves to taste. *Mode.* Stone the raisins; put them into stewpan with the sugar, cinnamon, a cloves, and let them boil for 1½ hou stirring all the time. Let the prep ration cool a little, pour it into a gla dish, and garnish with strips of cand lemon-peel and citron. This will rema good some time, if kept in a dry plac *Time.*—1½ hour. *Average cost*, 9d. *Su cient.*—1 lb. for 4 or 5 persons. *Seaso able* at any time.

RAISIN PUDDING, Boiled. (Pla and Economical).

Ingredients.—1 lb. of flour, ½ ℔. stoned raisins, ½ lb. of chopped suet,

Raisin Pudding, Baked

saltspoonful of salt, milk. *Mode.*—After having stoned the raisins and chopped the suet finely, mix them with the flour, add the salt, and when these dry ingredients are thoroughly mixed, moisten the pudding with sufficient milk to make it into a rather stiff paste. Tie it up in a floured cloth, put it into boiling water, and boil for 4 hours: serve with sifted sugar. This pudding may also be made in a long shape, the same as a rolled jam-pudding, and will not require quite so long boiling ;—2½ hours would then be quite sufficient. *Time.*—Made round, 4 hours ; in a long shape, 2½ hours. *Average cost, 9d. Sufficient* for 8 or 9 persons. *Seasonable* in winter.

RAISIN PUDDING, Baked. (Plain and Economical.)

Ingredients.—1 lb. of flour, ¾ lb. of stoned raisins, ½ lb. of suet, a pinch of salt, 1 oz. of sugar, a little grated nutmeg, milk. *Mode.*—Chop the suet finely ; stone the raisins and cut them in halves ; mix these with the suet, add the salt, sugar, and grated nutmeg, and moisten the whole with sufficient milk to make it of the consistency of thick batter. Put the pudding into a pie-dish, and bake for 1½ hour, or rather longer. Turn it out of the dish, strew sifted sugar over, and serve. This is a very plain recipe, and suitable where there is a family of children. It, of course, can be much improved by the addition of candied peel, currants, and rather a larger proportion of suet : a few eggs would also make the pudding richer. *Time.*—1½ hour. *Average cost, 9d. Sufficient* for 7 or 8 persons. *Seasonable* in winter.

RAMAKINS, to serve with the Cheese Course.

Ingredients.—¼ lb. of Cheshire cheese, ¼ lb. of Parmesan cheese, ¼ lb. of fresh butter, 4 eggs, the crumb of a small roll ; pepper, salt, and pounded mace to taste. *Mode.*—Boil the crumb of the roll in milk for 5 minutes ; strain, and put it into a mortar ; add the cheese, which should be finely scraped, the butter, the yolks of the eggs, and seasoning, and pound these ingredients well together. Whisk the whites of the eggs, mix them with the paste, and put it into small pans or saucers, which should not be more than half filled. Bake them from 10 to 12 minutes, and serve them

very hot and very quickly. This batter answers equally well for macaroni after it is boiled tender. *Time.*—10 or 12 minutes. *Average cost, 1s. 4d. Sufficient* for 7 or 8 persons. *Seasonable* at any time.

RAMAKINS PASTRY, to serve with the Cheese Course.

Ingredients.—Any pieces of very good light puff-paste, Cheshire, Parmesan, or Stilton cheese. *Mode.*—The remains or odd pieces of paste left from large tarts, &c., answer for making these little dishes. Gather up the pieces of paste, roll it out evenly, and sprinkle it with grated cheese of a nice flavour. Fold the paste in three, roll it out again, and sprinkle more cheese over ; fold the paste, roll it out, and with a paste-cutter shape it in any way that may be desired. Bake the ramakins in a brisk oven from 10 to 15 minutes, dish them on a hot napkin, and serve quickly. The appearance of this dish may be very much improved by brushing the ramakins over with the yolk of egg before they are placed in the oven. Where expense is not objected to, Parmesan is the best kind of cheese to use for making this dish. *Time.*—10 to 15 minutes. *Average cost,* with ½ lb. of paste, 10d. *Sufficient* for 6 or 7 persons. *Seasonable* at any time.

RASPBERRY CREAM.

Ingredients.—¾ pint of milk, ¾ pint of cream, 1½ oz. of isinglass, raspberry jelly, sugar to taste, 2 tablespoonfuls of brandy. *Mode.*—Boil the milk, cream, and isinglass together for ¼ hour, or until the latter is melted, and strain it through a hair sieve into a basin. Let it cool a little ; then add to it sufficient

RASPBERRY-CREAM MOULD.

raspberry jelly, which, when melted, would make ¼ pint, and stir well till the ingredients are thoroughly mixed. If not sufficiently sweet, add a little pounded

Raspberry Jam	Rataflas

sugar with the brandy; whisk the mixture well until nearly cold, put it into a well-oiled mould, and set it in a cool place till perfectly set. Raspberry jam may be substituted for the jelly; but must be melted, and rubbed through a sieve, to free it from seeds: in summer, the juice of the fresh fruit may be used, by slightly mashing it with a wooden spoon, and sprinkling sugar over it; the juice that flows from the fruit should then be used for mixing with the cream. If the colour should not be very good, a few drops of prepared cochineal may be added to improve its appearance. *Time.* —¼ hour to boil the cream and isinglass. *Average cost*, with cream at 1*s.* per pint, and the best isinglass, 3*s.* *Sufficient* to fill a quart mould with fresh fruit in July. *Seasonable*, with jelly, at any time.

Note.—Strawberry cream may be made in precisely the same manner, substituting strawberry jam or jelly for the raspberry.

RASPBERRY JAM.

Ingredients.—To every lb. of raspberries allow 1 lb. of sugar, ¼ pint of red-currant juice. *Mode.*—Let the fruit for this preserve be gathered in fine weather, and used as soon after it is picked as possible. Take off the stalks, put the raspberries into a preserving-pan, break them well with a wooden spoon, and let them boil for ¼ hour, keeping them well stirred. Then add the currant-juice and sugar, and boil again for ¼ hour. Skim the jam well after the sugar is added, or the preserve will not be clear. The addition of the currant-juice is a very great improvement to this preserve, as it gives it a piquant taste, which the flavour of the raspberries seems to require. *Time.*—¼ hour to simmer the fruit without the sugar; ½ hour after it is added. *Average cost*, from 6*d.* to 8*d.* per lb. pot. *Sufficient.*—Allow about 1 pint of fruit to fill a 1 lb. pot. *Seasonable* in July and August.

RASPBERRY JELLY.

Ingredients.—To each pint of juice allow ¾ lb. of loaf sugar. *Mode.*—Let the raspberries be freshly gathered, quite ripe, and picked from the stalks; put them into a large jar, after breaking the fruit a little with a wooden spoon, and place this jar, covered, in a saucepan of boiling water. When the juice is well

drawn, which will be in from ¾ to 1 hour, strain the fruit through a fine hair sieve or cloth; measure the juice, and to every pint allow the above proportion of loaf sugar. Put the juice and sugar into a preserving-pan, place it over the fire, and boil gently until the jelly thickens when a little is poured on a plate; carefully remove all the scum as it rises, pour the jelly into small pots, cover down, and keep in a dry place. This jelly answers for making raspberry cream, and for flavouring various sweet dishes, when, in winter, the fresh fruit is not obtainable. *Time.*—¾ to 1 hour to draw the juice. *Average cost*, from 9*d.* to 1*s.* per lb. pot. *Sufficient.*—From 3 pints to 2 quarts of fruit should yield 1 pint of juice. *Seasonable.*—This should be made in July or August.

RASPBERRY VINEGAR.

Ingredients.—To every 3 pints of the best vinegar allow 4½ pints of freshly-gathered raspberries; to each pint of liquor allow 1 lb. of pounded loaf sugar, 1 wineglassful of brandy. *Mode.*—Let the raspberries be freshly gathered, pick them from the stalks, and put 1½ pint of them into a stone jar; pour 3 pints of the best vinegar over them, and let them remain for 24 hours; then strain the liquor over another 1½ pint of fresh raspberries. Let them remain another 24 hours, and the following day repeat the process for the third time; then drain off the liquor without pressing, and pass it through a jelly-bag (previously wetted with plain vinegar) into a stone jar. Add to every pint of the liquor 1 lb. of pounded loaf sugar; stir them together, and, when the sugar is dissolved, cover the jar, set it upon the fire in a saucepan of boiling water, and let it boil for an hour, removing the scum as fast as it rises; add to each pint a glass of brandy, bottle it, and seal the corks. This is an excellent drink in cases of fevers and colds: it should be diluted with cold water, according to the taste or requirement of the patient. *Time.*—To be boiled 1 hour. *Average cost*, 1*s.* per pint. *Sufficient* to make 2 quarts. *Seasonable.*—Make this in July or August, when raspberries are most plentiful.

RATAFIAS.

Ingredients.—½ lb. of sweet almonds, ½ lb. of bitter ones, ¾ lb. of sifted loaf

Ravigotte, a French Salad Sauce	Rhubarb and Orange Jam

sugar, the white of 4 eggs. *Mode.*—Blanch, skin, and dry the almonds, and pound them in a mortar with the white of an egg; stir in the sugar, and gradually add the remaining whites of eggs, taking care that they are very thoroughly whisked. Drop the mixture, through a small biscuit syringe, on to cartridge-paper, and bake the cakes from 10 to 12 minutes in rather a quick oven. A very small quantity should be dropped on the paper to form one cake, as the mixture spreads; when baked, the ratifias should be about the size of a large button. *Time.*—10 to 12 minutes.—*Average cost*, 1s. 8d. per lb.

RAVIGOTTE, a French Salad Sauce (Mons. Ude's Recipe).

Ingredients.—1 teaspoonful of mushroom ketchup, 1 teaspoonful of cavice, 1 teaspoonful of Chili vinegar, 1 teaspoonful of Reading sauce, a piece of butter the size of an egg, 3 tablespoonfuls of thick Béchamel, 1 tablespoonful of minced parsley, 3 tablespoonfuls of cream; salt and pepper to taste. *Mode.*—Scald the parsley, mince the leaves very fine, and add to it all the other ingredients; after mixing the whole together thoroughly, the sauce will be ready for use. *Average cost*, for this quantity, 10d. *Seasonable* at any time.

REMOULADE, or French Salad-Dressing.

Ingredients.—4 eggs, ½ tablespoonful of made mustard, salt and cayenne to taste, 3 tablespoonfuls of olive-oil, 1 tablespoonful of tarragon or plain vinegar. *Mode.*—Boil 3 eggs quite hard for about ¼ hour, put them into cold water, and let them remain in it for a few minutes; strip off the shells, put the yolks in a mortar, and pound them very smoothly; add to them, very gradually, the mustard, seasoning, and vinegar, keeping all well stirred and rubbed down with the back of a wooden spoon. Put in the oil drop by drop, and when this is thoroughly mixed with the other ingredients, add the yolk of a raw egg, and stir well, when it will be ready for use. This sauce should not be curdled; and to prevent this, the only way is to mix a little of everything at a time, and not to cease stirring. The quantities of oil and vinegar may be increased or diminished according to taste, as many

persons would prefer a smaller proportion of the former ingredient.

GREEN REMOULADE is made by using tarragon vinegar instead of plain, and colouring with a little parsley-juice. Harvey's sauce, or Chili vinegar, may be added at pleasure. *Time.*—¼ hour to boil the eggs. *Average cost*, for this quantity, 7d. *Sufficient* for a salad made for 4 or 6 persons.

RHUBARB JAM.

Ingredients.—To every lb. of rhubarb allow 1 lb. of loaf sugar, the rind of ½ lemon. *Mode.*—Wipe the rhubarb perfectly dry, take off the string or peel, and weigh it; put it into a preserving-pan, with sugar in the above proportion; mince the lemon-rind very finely, add it to the other ingredients, and place the preserving-pan by the side of the fire; keep stirring to prevent the rhubarb from burning, and when the sugar is well dissolved, put the pan more over the fire, and let the jam boil until it is done, taking care to keep it well skimmed and stirred with a wooden or silver spoon. Pour it into pots, and cover down with oiled and egged papers. *Time.*—If the rhubarb is young and tender, ¾ hour, reckoning from the time it simmers equally; old rhubarb, 1¼ to 1½ hour. *Average cost*, 5d. to 7d. per lb. pot. *Sufficient.*—About 1 pint of sliced rhubarb to fill a lb. pot. *Seasonable* from February to May.

RHUBARB AND ORANGE JAM, to resemble Scotch Marmalade.

Ingredients.—1 quart of finely-cut rhubarb, 6 oranges, 1½ lb. of loaf sugar. *Mode.*—Peel the oranges; remove as much of the white pith as possible, divide them, and take out the pips; slice the pulp into a preserving-pan, add the rind of half the oranges cut into thin strips, and the loaf sugar, which should be broken small. Peel the rhubarb, cut it into thin pieces, put it to the oranges, and stir altogether over a gentle fire until the jam is done. Remove all the scum as it rises, put the preserve into pots, and, when cold, cover down. Should the rhubarb be very old, stew it alone for ¼ hour before the other ingredients are added. *Time.*—¾ to 1 hour. *Average cost*, from 6d. to 8d. per lb. pot. *Seasonable* from February to May.

Rhubarb Pudding, Boiled	Rice Blancmange

RHUBARB PUDDING, Boiled.

Ingredients.—4 or 5 sticks of fine rhubarb, ¼ lb. of moist sugar, ¾ lb. of suet-crust. *Mode.*—Make a suet-crust with ¾ lb. of flour, and line a buttered basin with it. Wash and wipe the rhubarb, and, if old, string it—that is so say, pare off the outside skin. Cut it into inch lengths, fill the basin with it, put in the sugar, and cover with crust. Pinch the edges of the pudding together, tie over it a floured cloth, put it into boiling water, and boil from 2 to 2½ hours. Turn it out of the basin, and serve with a jug of cream and sifted sugar. *Time.*—2 to 2½ hours. *Average cost, 7d. Sufficient* for 6 or 7 persons. *Seasonable* from February to May.

RHUBARB TART.

Ingredients.—½ lb. of puff-paste, about 5 sticks of large rhubarb, ¼ lb. of moist sugar. *Mode.*—Make a puff-crust; line the edges of a deep pie-dish with it, and wash, wipe, and cut the rhubarb into pieces about 1 inch long. Should it be old and tough, string it—that is to say, pare off the outside skin. Pile the fruit high in the dish, as it shrinks very much in the cooking; put in the sugar, cover with crust, ornament the edges, and bake the tart in a well-heated oven from ½ to ¾ hour. If wanted very nice, brush it over with the white of an egg beaten to a stiff froth, then sprinkle on it some sifted sugar, and put it in the oven just to set the glaze: this should be done when the tart is nearly baked. A small quantity of lemon-juice, and a little of the peel minced, are by many persons considered an improvement to the flavour of rhubarb tart. *Time.*—½ to ¾ hour. *Average cost, 9d. Sufficient* for 5 persons. *Seasonable* from February to May.

RHUBARB WINE.

Ingredients.—To every 5 lbs. of rhubarb pulp allow 1 gallon of cold spring water; to every gallon of liquor allow 3 lbs. of loaf sugar, ½ oz. of isinglass, the rind of 1 lemon. *Mode.*—Gather the rhubarb about the middle of May; wipe it with a wet cloth, and, with a mallet, bruise it in a large wooden tub or other convenient means. When reduced to a pulp, weigh it, and to every 5 lbs. add 1 gallon of cold spring water; let these remain for 3 days, stirring 3 or 4 times a

day; and on the fourth day, press the pulp through a hair sieve; put the liquor into a tub, and to every gallon put 3 lbs. of loaf sugar; stir in the sugar until it is quite dissolved, and add the lemon-rind; let the liquor remain, and, in 4, 5, or 6 days, the fermentation will begin to subside, and a crust or head will be formed, which should be skimmed off, or the liquor drawn from it, when the crust begins to crack or separate. Put the wine into a cask, and if, after that, it ferments, rack it off into another cask, and in a fortnight stop it down. If the wine should have lost any of its original sweetness, add a little more loaf sugar, taking care that the cask is full. Bottle it off in February or March, and in the summer it should be fit to drink. It will improve greatly by keeping; and, should a very brilliant colour be desired, add a little currant-juice. *Seasonable.* Make this about the middle of May.

RICE BISCUITS, or Cakes.

Ingredients.—To every ½ lb. of rice-flour, allow ¼ lb. of pounded lump sugar, ¼ lb. of butter, 2 eggs. *Mode.*—Beat the butter to a cream, stir in the rice-flour and pounded sugar, and moisten the whole with the eggs, which should be previously well beaten. Roll out the paste, shape it with a round paste-cutter into small cakes, and bake them from 12 to 18 minutes in a very slow oven. *Time.* —12 to 18 minutes. *Average cost, 9d. Sufficient* to make about 18 cakes. *Seasonable* at any time.

RICE BLANCMANGE.

Ingredients.—¼ lb. of ground rice, 3 oz. of loaf sugar, 1 oz. of fresh butter, 1 quart of milk, flavouring of lemon-peel, essence of almonds or vanilla, or laurel-leaves. *Mode.*—Mix the rice to a smooth batter with about ½ pint of the milk, and the remainder put into a saucepan, with the sugar, butter, and whichever of the above flavourings may be preferred; bring the milk to the boiling-point, quickly stir in the rice, and let it boil for about 10 minutes, or until it comes easily away from the saucepan, keeping it well stirred the whole time. Grease a mould with pure salad-oil, pour in the rice, and let it get perfectly set, when it should turn out quite easily, garnish it with jam, or pour round a compôte of any kind of fruit, just before

Rice Bread

it is sent to table. This blancmange is better for being made the day before it is wanted, as it then has time to become firm. If laurel-leaves are used for flavouring, steep 3 of them in the milk, and take them out before the rice is added : about 8 drops of essence of almonds, or from 12 to 16 drops of essence of vanilla, would be required to flavour the above proportion of milk. *Time.*—From 10 to 15 minutes to boil the rice. *Average cost, 9d. Sufficient* to fill a quart mould. *Seasonable* at any time.

RICE BREAD.

Ingredients.—To every lb. of rice allow 4 lbs. of wheat flour, nearly 3 tablespoonfuls of yeast, ¼ oz. of salt. *Mode.*—Boil the rice in water until it is quite tender ; pour off the water, and put the rice, before it is cold, to the flour. Mix these well together with the yeast, salt, and sufficient warm water to make the whole into a smooth dough ; let it rise by the side of the fire, then form it into loaves, and bake them from 1½ to 2 hours, according to their size. If the rice is boiled in milk instead of water, it makes very delicious bread or cakes. When boiled in this manner, it may be mixed with the flour without straining the liquid from it. *Time.*—1½ to 2 hours.

RICE, Buttered.

Ingredients.—¼ lb. of rice, 1½ pint of milk, 2 oz. of butter, sugar to taste, grated nutmeg or pounded cinnamon. *Mode.*—Wash and pick the rice, drain, and put it into a saucepan with the milk ; let it swell gradually, and, when tender, pour off the milk ; stir in the butter, sugar, and nutmeg or cinnamon, and, when the butter is thoroughly melted, and the whole is quite hot, serve. After the milk is poured off, be particular that the rice does not burn : to prevent this, do not cease stirring it. *Time.*—About ¾ hour to swell the rice. *Average cost, 7d. Sufficient* for 4 or 5 persons. *Seasonable* at any time.

RICE CAKE.

Ingredients.—½ lb. of ground rice, ½ lb. of flour, ½ lb. of loaf sugar, 9 eggs, 20 drops of essence of lemon, or the rind of one lemon, ¼ lb. of butter. *Mode.* —Separate the whites from the yolks of the eggs ; whisk them both well, and

Rice, Savoury Casserole of

add to the latter the butter beaten to a cream. Stir in the flour, rice, and lemon (if the rind is used it must be very finely minced), and beat the mixture well ; then add the whites of the eggs, beat the cake again for some time, put it into a buttered mould or tin, and bake it for nearly 1½ hour. It may be flavoured with essence of almonds, when this is preferred. *Time.*—Nearly 1½ hour. *Average cost,* 1s. 6d. *Seasonable* at any time.

CAKE-MOULD.

RICE, SAVOURY CASSEROLE OF ; or Rice Border, for Ragoûts, Fricassées, &c. (An Entrée.)

Ingredients.—1½ lb. of rice, 3 pints of weak stock or broth, 2 slices of fat ham, 1 teaspoonful of salt. *Mode.*—A casserole of rice, when made in a mould, is not such a difficult operation as when it is moulded by the hand. It is an elegant and inexpensive entrée, as the remains of cold fish, flesh, or fowl, may be served as ragoûts, fricassées, &c., inclosed in the casserole. It requires great nicety in its preparation, the principal thing to attend to being the boiling of the rice, as, if this is not sufficiently cooked, the casserole, when moulded, will have a rough appearance, which would entirely spoil it. After having washed the rice in two or three waters, drain it well, and put it into a stewpan with the stock, ham, and salt ; cover the pan closely, and let the rice gradually swell over a slow fire, occasionally stirring, to prevent its sticking. When it is quite soft, strain it, pick out the pieces of ham, and, with the back of a large wooden spoon, mash the rice to a perfectly smooth paste. Then well grease a mould (moulds are made purposely for rice borders), and turn it upside down for a minute or two, to drain away the fat, should there be too much ; put some rice all round the bottom and sides of it ; place a piece of soft bread in the middle, and cover it with rice ; press it in equally with the spoon,

CASSEROLE OF RICE.

Rice, Sweet Casserole of

and let it cool. Then dip the mould into hot water, turn the casserole carefully on to a dish, mark where the lid is to be formed on the top, by making an incision with the point of a knife about an inch from the edge all round, and put it into a *very hot* oven. Brush it over with a little clarified butter, and bake about ½ hour, or rather longer; then carefully remove the lid, which will be formed by the incision having been made all round, and remove the bread, in small pieces, with the point of a penknife, being careful not to injure the casserole. Fill the centre with the ragoût or fricassée, which should be made thick; put on the cover, glaze it, place it in the oven to set the glaze, and serve as hot as possible. The casserole should not be emptied too much as it is liable to crack from the weight of whatever is put in; and, in baking it, let the oven be very hot, or the casserole will probably break. *Time.* —About ¾ hour to swell the rice. *Sufficient* for 2 moderate-sized casseroles. *Seasonable* at any time.

RICE, SWEET CASSEROLE OF (an Entremets).

Ingredients. —1½ lb. of rice, 3 pints of milk, sugar to taste, flavouring of bitter almonds, 3 oz. of butter, the yolks of 3 eggs. *Mode.* —This is made in precisely the same manner as a savoury casserole, only substituting the milk and sugar for the stock and salt. Put the milk into a stewpan, with sufficient essence of bitter almonds to flavour it well; then add the rice, which should be washed, picked, and drained, and let it swell gradually in the milk over a slow fire. When it is tender, stir in the sugar, butter, and yolks of eggs; butter a mould, press in the rice, and proceed in exactly the same manner as in preceding recipe. When the casserole is ready, fill it with a compôte of any fruit that may be preferred, or with melted apricot-jam, and serve. *Time.* —From ¾ to 1 hour to swell the rice, ½ to ¾ hour to bake the casserole. *Average cost,* exclusive of the compôte or jam, 1s. 9d. *Sufficient* for two casseroles. *Seasonable* at any time.

RICE CROQUETTES.

Ingredients. —½ lb. of rice, 1 quart of milk, 6 oz. of pounded sugar, flavouring of vanilla, lemon-peel, or bitter almonds,

Rice-Milk.

egg and bread-crumbs, hot lard. *Mode.* —Put the rice, milk, and sugar into a saucepan, and let the former gradually swell over a gentle fire until all the milk is dried up; and just before the rice is done, stir in a few drops of essence of any of the above flavourings. Let the rice get cold; then form it into small round balls, dip them into yolk of egg, sprinkle them with bread-crumbs, and fry them in boiling lard for about 10 minutes, turning them about, that they may get equally browned. Drain the greasy moisture from them, by placing them on a cloth in front of the fire for a minute or two; pile them on a white d'oyley, and send them quickly to table. A small piece of jam is sometimes introduced into the middle of each croquette, which adds very much to the flavour of this favourite dish. *Time.* —From ¾ to 1 hour to swell the rice; about 10 minutes to fry the croquettes. *Average cost,* 10d. *Sufficient* to make 7 or 8 croquettes. *Seasonable* at any time.

RICE FRITTERS.

Ingredients. —6 oz. of rice, 1 quart of milk, 3 oz. of sugar, 1 oz. of fresh butter, 6 oz. of orange marmalade, 4 eggs. *Mode.* —Swell the rice in the milk, with the sugar and butter, over a slow fire until it is perfectly tender, which will be in about ¾ hour. When the rice is done, strain away the milk, should there be any left, and mix with it the marmalade and well-beaten eggs; stir the whole over the fire until the eggs are set; then spread the mixture on a dish to the thickness of about ½ inch, or rather thicker. When it is perfectly cold, cut it into long strips, dip them in a batter the same as for apple fritters, and fry them a nice brown. Dish them on a white d'oyley, strew sifted sugar over, and serve quickly. *Time.* —About ¾ hour to swell the rice; from 7 to 10 minutes to fry the fritters. *Average cost,* 1s. 6d. *Sufficient* to make 7 or 8 fritters. *Seasonable* at any time.

RICE-MILK.

Ingredients. —3 tablespoonfuls of rice, 1 quart of milk, sugar to taste; when liked, a little grated nutmeg. *Mode.* —Well wash the rice, put it into a saucepan with the milk, and simmer gently until the rice is tender, stirring it from time to time to prevent the milk from

Rice Pudding, Baked

burning; sweeten it, add a little grated nutmeg, and serve. This dish is also very suitable and wholesome for children; it may be flavoured with a little lemon-peel, and a little finely-minced suet may be boiled with it, which renders it more strengthening and more wholesome. Tapioca, semolina, vermicelli, and macaroni, may all be dressed in the same manner. *Time.*—From ¾ to 1 hour. *Seasonable* at any time.

RICE PUDDING, Baked.

Ingredients.—1 small teacupful of rice, 4 eggs, 1 pint of milk, 2 oz. of fresh butter, 2 oz. of beef marrow, ¼ lb. of currants, 2 tablespoonfuls of brandy, nutmeg, ¼ lb. of sugar, the rind of ½ lemon. *Mode.*—Put the lemon-rind and milk into a stewpan, and let it infuse till the milk is well flavoured with the lemon; in the mean time, boil the rice until tender in water, with a very small quantity of salt, and, when done, let it be thoroughly drained. Beat the eggs, stir to them the milk, which should be strained, the butter, marrow, currants, and remaining ingredients; add the rice, and mix all well together; Line the edges of the dish with puff-paste, put in the pudding, and bake for about ¾ hour in a slow oven. Slices of candied-peel may be added at pleasure, or Sultana raisins may be substituted for the currants. *Time.*—¾ hour. *Average cost*, 1s. 3d. *Sufficient* for 5 or 6 persons. *Seasonable* for a winter pudding, when fresh fruits are not obtainable.

RICE PUDDING, Baked (Plain and Economical; a nice Pudding for Children).

Ingredients.—1 teacupful of rice, 2 tablespoonfuls of moist sugar, 1 quart of milk, ½ oz. of butter or two small tablespoonfuls of chopped suet, ½ teaspoonful of grated nutmeg. *Mode.*—Wash the rice, put it into a pie-dish with the sugar, pour in the milk, and stir these ingredients well together; then add the butter cut up into very small pieces, or, instead of this, the above proportion of finely-minced suet; grate a little nutmeg over the top, and bake the pudding, in a *moderate* oven, from 1½ to 2 hours. As the rice is not previously cooked, care must be taken that the pudding be very slowly baked, to give plenty of time for the rice to swell, and for it to be very

Rice Pudding, Boiled

thoroughly done. *Time.*—1½ to 2 hours. *Average cost, 7d. Sufficient* for 5 or 6 children. *Seasonable* at any time.

RICE PUDDING, Plain Boiled.

Ingredients.—½ lb. of rice. *Mode.*— Wash the rice, tie it in a pudding-cloth, allowing room for the rice to swell, and put it into a saucepan of cold water; boil it gently for two hours, and if, after a time, the cloth seems tied too loosely, take the rice up and tighten the cloth. Serve with sweet melted butter, or cold butter and sugar, or stewed fruit, jam, or marmalade, any of which accompaniments are suitable for plain boiled rice. *Time.*—2 hours after the water boils. *Average cost, 2d. Sufficient* for 4 or 5 persons. *Seasonable* at any time.

RICE PUDDING, Boiled.

Ingredients.—½ lb. of rice, 1½ pint of new milk, 2 oz. of butter, 4 eggs, ½ saltspoonful of salt, 4 large tablespoonfuls of moist sugar, flavouring to taste. *Mode.*—Stew the rice very gently in the above proportion of new milk, and, when it is tender, pour it into a basin; stir in the butter, and let it stand to cool; then beat the eggs, add these to the rice with the sugar, salt, and any flavouring that may be approved, such as nutmeg, powdered cinnamon, grated lemon-peel, essence of bitter-almonds, or vanilla. When all is well stirred, put the pudding into a buttered basin, tie it down with a cloth, plunge it into boiling water, and boil for 1¼ hour. *Time.*— 1¼ hour. *Average cost, 1s. Sufficient for* 5 or 6 persons. *Seasonable* at any time.

RICE PUDDING, Boiled (with Dried or Fresh Fruit; a nice Dish for the Nursery).

Ingredients.—½ lb. of rice, 1 pint of any kind of fresh fruit that may be preferred, or ½ lb of raisins or currants. *Mode.*—Wash the rice, tie it in a cloth, allowing room for it to swell, and put it into a saucepan of cold water; let it boil for an hour, then take it up, untie the cloth, stir in the fruit, and tie it up again tolerably tight, and put it into the water for the remainder of the time. Boil for another hour, or rather longer, and serve with sweet sauce if made with dried fruit, and with plain sifted sugar if made with

19

| Rice Pudding, French | Rice Puddings, Miniature |

fresh fruit. *Time.*—1 hour to boil the rice without the fruit ; 1 hour, or longer, afterwards. *Average cost, 6d. Sufficient* for 6 or 7 children. *Seasonable* at any time.

Note.—This pudding is very good made with apples ; they should be pared, cored, and cut into thin slices.

RICE PUDDING, French, or Gateau de Riz.

Ingredients.—To every ¼ lb. of rice allow 1 quart of milk, the rind of 1 lemon, ½ teaspoonful of salt, sugar to taste, 4 oz. of butter, 6 eggs, bread crumbs. *Mode.*—Put the milk into a stewpan with the lemon-rind, and let it infuse for ½ hour, or until the former is well flavoured ; then take out the peel, have ready the rice washed, picked, and drained ; put it into the milk, and let it gradually swell over a very slow fire. Stir in the butter, salt, and sugar, and, when properly sweetened, add the yolks of the eggs, and then the whites, both of which should be well beaten, and added separately to the rice. Butter a mould, strew in some fine bread crumbs, and let them be spread equally over it ; then carefully pour in the rice, and bake the pudding in a *slow* oven for 1 hour. Turn it out of the mould, and garnish the dish with preserved cherries, or any bright-coloured jelly or jam. This pudding would be exceedingly nice flavoured with essence of vanilla. *Time.*—¾ to 1 hour for the rice to swell ; to be baked 1 hour in a slow oven. *Average cost, 1s. 8d. Sufficient* for 5 or 6 persons. *Seasonable* at any time.

RICE PUDDING, Baked or Boiled Ground.

Ingredients.—2 pints of milk, 6 table-spoonfuls of ground rice, sugar to taste, 4 eggs, flavouring of lemon-rind, nutmeg, bitter-almonds or bay-leaf. *Mode.*—Put 1½ pint of the milk into a stewpan with any of the above flavourings, and bring it to the boiling point, and, with the other ½ pint of milk, mix the ground rice to a smooth batter ; strain the boiling milk to this, and stir over the fire until the mixture is tolerably thick ; then pour it into a basin, leave it uncovered, and when nearly or quite cold sweeten it to taste, and add the eggs, which should be previously well beaten, with a little salt. Put the pudding into

a well-buttered basin, tie it down with a cloth, plunge it into boiling water, and boil for 1½ hour. For a baked pudding, proceed in precisely the same manner, only using half the above proportion of ground rice, with the same quantity of all the other ingredients : an hour will bake the pudding in a moderate oven. Stewed fruit, or preserves, or marmalade, may be served with either the boiled or baked pudding, and will be found an improvement. *Time.*—1½ hour to boil, 1 hour to bake. *Average cost, 10d. Sufficient* for 5 or 6 persons. *Seasonable* at any time.

RICE PUDDING, Iced.

Ingredients.—6 oz. of rice, 1 quart of milk, ½ lb. of sugar, the yolks of 6 eggs, 1 small teaspoonful of essence of vanilla. *Mode.*—Put the rice into a stewpan, with the milk and sugar, and let these simmer over a gentle fire until the rice is sufficiently soft to break up into a smooth mass, and should the milk dry away too much, a little more may be added. Stir the rice occasionally, to prevent its burning, then beat it to a smooth mixture ; add the yolks of the eggs, which should be well whisked, and the vanilla (should this flavouring not be liked, essence of bitter almonds may be substituted for it) ; put this rice custard into the freezing-pot, and proceed as directed in the recipe for Iced Pudding. When wanted for table, turn the pudding out of the mould, and pour over the top and round it a compôte of oranges, or any other fruit that may be preferred, taking care that the flavouring in the pudding harmonizes well with the fruit that is served with it. *Time.*—½ hour to freeze the mixture. *Average cost, 1s. 6d.* ; exclusive of the compôte, 1s. 4d. *Seasonable.*—Served all the year round.

RICE PUDDINGS, Miniature.

Ingredients.—¼ lb. of rice, 1½ pint of milk, 2 oz. of fresh butter, 4 eggs, sugar to taste, flavouring of lemon-peel, bitter almonds, or vanilla ; a few strips of candied peel. *Mode.*—Let the rice swell in 1 pint of the milk over a slow fire, putting with it a strip of lemon-peel ; stir to it the butter and the other ½ pint of milk, and let the mixture cool. Then add the well-beaten eggs, and a few drops of essence of almonds or essence of vanilla, whichever may be preferred ·

Rice Snowballs	Rice for Curries, &c., Boiled

ter well some small cups or moulds, line them with a few pieces of candied peel sliced very thin, fill them three parts full, and bake for about 40 minutes ; turn them out of the cups on to a white d'oyley, and serve with sweet sauce. The flavouring and candied peel might be omitted, and stewed fruit or preserve served instead, with these puddings. *Time.*—40 minutes. *Average cost*, 1s. *Sufficient* for 6 puddings. *Seasonable* at any time.

RICE SNOWBALLS (A Pretty Dish for Juvenile Suppers).

Ingredients.—6 oz. of rice, 1 quart of milk, flavouring of essence of almonds, sugar to taste, 1 pint of custard. *Mode.* —Boil the rice in the milk, with sugar and a flavouring of essence of almonds, until the former is tender, adding, if necessary, a little more milk, should it dry away too much. When the rice is quite soft, put it into teacups, or *small* round jars, and let it remain until cold ; then turn the rice out on a deep glass dish, pour over a custard, and on the top of each ball place a small piece of bright-coloured preserve or jelly. Lemon-peel or vanilla may be boiled with the rice instead of the essence of almonds, when either of these is preferred ; but the flavouring of the custard must correspond with that of the rice. *Time.*— About ¾ hour to swell the rice in the milk. *Average cost*, with the custard, 1s. 6d. *Sufficient* for 5 or 6 children. *Seasonable* at any time.

RICE SOUFFLE.

Ingredients. — 3 tablespoonfuls of ground rice, 1 pint of milk, 5 eggs, pounded sugar to taste, flavouring of lemon-rind, vanilla, coffee, chocolate, or anything that may be preferred, a piece of butter the size of a walnut. *Mode.*— Mix the ground rice with 6 tablespoonfuls of the milk quite smoothly, and put it into a saucepan with the remainder of the milk and butter, and keep stirring it over the fire for about ¼ hour, or until the mixture thickens. Separate the yolks from the whites of the eggs, beat the former in a basin, and stir to them the rice and sufficient pounded sugar to sweeten the soufflé ; but add this latter ingredient as sparingly as possible, as the less sugar there is used the lighter will be the soufflé. Now whisk the

whites of the eggs to a stiff froth or snow ; mix them with the other preparation, and pour the whole into a soufflé-dish, and put it instantly into the oven ; bake it about ½ hour in a moderate oven, take it out, hold a salamander or hot shovel over the top, sprinkle sifted sugar over it, and send the soufflé to table in the dish it was baked in, either with a napkin pinned round, or inclosed in a more ornamental dish. The excellence of this fashionable dish entirely depends on the proper whisking of the whites of the eggs, the manner of baking, and the expedition with which it is sent to table. Soufflés should be served *instantly* from the oven, or they will sink, and be nothing more than an ordinary pudding. *Time.*—About ½ hour. *Average cost*, 1s. *Sufficient* for 3 or 4 persons. *Seasonable* at any time.

RICE SOUP.

Ingredients.—4 oz. of Patna rice, salt, cayenne, and mace, 2 quarts of white stock. *Mode.*—Throw the rice into boiling water, and let it boil until tender ; then pour it into a sieve, and allow it to drain well. Now add it to the stock boiling, and allow it to simmer a few minutes ; season to taste. Serve quickly. *Time.*—1½ hour. *Average cost*, 1s. 3d. per quart. *Sufficient* for 8 persons. *Seasonable* all the year.

RICE SOUP.

Ingredients.--6 oz. of rice, the yolks of 4 eggs, ½ a pint of cream, rather more than two quarts of stock. *Mode.* —Boil the rice in the stock, and rub half of it through a tammy ; put the stock in the stewpan, add all the rice, and simmer gently for 5 minutes. Beat the yolks of the eggs, mix them with the cream (previously boiled), and strain through a hair sieve ; take the soup off the fire, add the eggs and cream, stirring frequently. Heat it gradually, stirring all the time ; but do not let it boil, or the eggs will curdle. *Time.*—2 hours. *Average cost*, 1s. 4d. per quart. *Sufficient* for 8 persons. *Seasonable* all the year.

RICE for Curries, &c., Boiled.

Ingredients.—¾ lb. of rice, water, salt. *Mode.*—Pick, wash, and soak the rice in plenty of cold water ; then have ready a saucepan of boiling water. drop the rice

Rice, to Boil, for Curries

into it, and keep it boiling quickly, with the lid uncovered, until it is tender, but not soft. Take it up, drain it, and put it on a dish before the fire to dry; do not handle it much with a spoon, but shake it about a little with two forks, that it may all be equally dried, and strew over it a little salt. It is now ready to serve, and may be heaped lightly on a dish by itself, or be laid round the dish as a border, with a curry or fricassee in the centre. Some cooks smooth the rice with the back of a spoon, and then brush it over with the yolk of an egg, and set it in the oven to colour; but the rice, well boiled, white, dry, and with every grain distinct, is by far the more preferable mode of dressing it. During the process of boiling, the rice should be attentively watched, that it be not overdone, as, if this is the case, it will have a mashed and soft appearance. *Time.*—15 to 25 minutes, according to the quality of the rice. *Average cost*, 3d. *Sufficient* for a large dish of curry. *Seasonable* at any time.

RICE, To Boil, for Curries, &c. (Soyer's Recipe.)

Ingredients.—1 lb. of the best Carolina rice, 2 quarts of water, 1½ oz. of butter, a little salt. *Mode.*—Wash the rice well in two waters; make 2 quarts of water boiling, and throw the rice into it; boil it until three-parts done, then drain it on a sieve. Butter the bottom and sides of a stewpan, put in the rice, place the lid on tightly, and set it by the side of the fire, until the rice is perfectly tender, occasionally shaking the pan to prevent its sticking. Prepared thus, every grain should be separate and white. Either dish it separately, or place it round the curry as a border. *Time.*—15 to 25 minutes. *Average cost*, 7d. *Sufficient* for 2 moderate-sized curries. *Seasonable* at any time.

ROASTING, Memoranda in.

The management of the fire is a point of primary importance in roasting. A radiant fire throughout the operation is absolutely necessary to insure a good result. When the article to be dressed is thin and delicate, the fire may be small; but when the joint is large the fire must fill the grate. Meat must never be put down before a hollow or exhausted fire, which may soon want recruiting;

Rolls, Hot

on the other hand, if the heat of the fire become too fierce, the meat must be removed to a considerable distance till it has somewhat abated. Some cooks always fail in roasting, though they succeed in nearly everything else. A French writer on the culinary art says that anybody can learn how to cook, but one must be born a roaster. According to Liebig, beef or mutton cannot be said to be sufficiently roasted, until it has acquired throughout the whole mass a temperature of 158°. But poultry may be well cooked when the inner parts have attained a temperature of 130° to 140°. This depends on the greater amount of blood which beef and mutton contain, the colouring matter of blood not being coagulable under 158°.

ROLLS, Excellent.

Ingredients.—To every lb. of flour allow 1 oz. of butter, ¼ pint of milk, a large teaspoonful of yeast, a little salt. *Mode.*—Warm the butter in the milk, add to it the yeast and salt, and mix these ingredients well together. Put the flour into a pan, stir in the above ingre-

ROLLS.

dients, and let the dough rise, covered in a warm place. Knead it well, make it into rolls, let them rise again for a few minutes, and bake in a quick oven. Richer rolls may be made by adding 1 or 2 eggs and a larger proportion of butter, and their appearance improved by brushing the tops over with yolk of egg or a little milk. *Time.*—1 lb. of flour, divided into 6 rolls, from 15 to 20 minutes.

ROLLS, Hot.

This dish, although very unwholesome and indigestible, is nevertheless a great favourite, and eaten by many persons. As soon as the rolls come from the baker's, they should be put into the oven, which, in the early part of the morning, is sure not to be very hot; and the rolls must not be buttered until wanted. When they are quite hot, divide them lengthwise into three; put some thin flakes of good butter between

Rolls, Fluted	Rump-steak and Kidney Pudding

the slices, press the rolls together, and put them in the oven for a minute or two, but not longer, or the butter would oil ; take them out of the oven, spread the butter equally over, divide the rolls in half, and put them on to a very hot clean dish, and send them instantly to table.

ROLLS, Fluted.

Ingredients.—Puff-paste, the white of an egg, sifted sugar, jelly or preserve. *Mode.*—Make some good puff-paste (trimmings answer very well for little dishes of this sort) ; roll it out to the thickness of ¼ inch, and with a round fluted paste-cutter stamp out as many round pieces as may be required ; brush over the upper side with the white of an egg ; roll up the pieces, pressing the paste lightly together where it joins ; place the rolls on a baking-sheet, and bake for about ¼ hour. A few minutes before they are done, brush them over with the white of an egg ; strew over sifted sugar, put them back in the oven ; and when the icing is firm and of a pale brown colour, they are done. Place a strip of jelly or preserve across each roll, dish them high on a napkin, and serve cold. *Time.*—¼ hour before being iced ; 5 to 10 minutes after. *Average cost,* 1s. 3d. *Sufficient.*—½ lb. of puff-paste for 2 dishes. *Seasonable* at any time.

ROUX, Brown, a French Thickening for Gravies and Sauces.

Ingredients.—6 oz. of butter, 9 oz. of flour. *Mode.*—Melt the butter in a stewpan over a slow fire, and dredge in, very gradually, the flour ; stir it till of a light-brown colour—to obtain this do it very slowly, otherwise the flour will burn and impart a bitter taste to the sauce it is mixed with. Pour it in a jar, and keep it for use : it will remain good some time. *Time.*—About ½ hour. *Average cost,* 7d.

ROUX, White, for thickening White Sauces.

Allow the same proportions of butter and flour as in the preceding recipe, and proceed in the same manner as for brown roux, but do not keep it on the fire too long, and take care not to let it colour. This is used for thickening white sauce. Pour it into a jar to use when wanted. *Time.*—¼ hour. *Average cost,* 7d.

Sufficient.—A dessertspoonful will thicken a pint of gravy.

Note.—Besides the above, sauces may be thickened with potato flour, ground rice, baked flour, arrowroot, &c. : the latter will be found far preferable to the ordinary flour for white sauces. A slice of bread, toasted and added to gravies, answers the two purposes of thickening and colouring them.

RUMP-STEAK, Fried.

Ingredients.—Steaks, butter or clarified dripping.—*Mode.*—Although broiling is a far superior method of cooking steaks to frying them, yet, when the cook is not very expert, the latter mode may be adopted ; and, when properly done, the dish may really look very inviting, and the flavour be good. The steaks should be cut rather thinner than for broiling, and with a small quantity of fat to each. Put some butter or clarified dripping into a frying-pan ; let it get quite hot, then lay in the steaks. Turn them frequently until done, which will be in about 8 minutes, or rather more, should the steaks be very thick. Serve on a very hot dish, in which put a small piece of butter and a tablespoonful of ketchup, and season with pepper and salt. They should be sent to table quickly, as when cold the steaks are entirely spoiled. *Time.*—8 minutes for a medium-sized steak, rather longer for a very thick one. *Average cost,* 1s. per lb. *Seasonable* all the year, but not good in summer, as the meat cannot hang to get tender.

Note.—Where much gravy is liked, make it in the following manner :—As soon as the steaks are done, dish them, pour a little boiling water into the frying-pan, add a seasoning of pepper and salt, a small piece of butter, and a tablespoonful of Harvey's sauce or mushroom ketchup. Hold the pan over the fire for a minute or two, just let the gravy simmer, then pour on the steak, and serve.

RUMP-STEAK AND KIDNEY PUDDING.

Ingredients.—2 lbs. of rump-steak, 2 kidneys, seasoning to taste of salt and black pepper, suet crust made with milk (*see* Pastry), in the proportion of 6 oz. of suet to each 1 lb. of flour. *Mode.*—Procure some tender rump-steak (that which has been hung a little time), and divide it into pieces about an inch square, and

Rump-steak and Oyster Sauce

cut each kidney into 8 pieces. Line the dish with crust made with suet and flour in the above proportion, leaving a small piece of crust to overlap the edge. Then cover the bottom with a portion of the steak and a few pieces of kidney; season with salt and pepper (some add a little flour to thicken the gravy, but it is not necessary), and then add another layer of steak, kidney, and seasoning. Proceed in this manner till the dish is full, when pour in sufficient water to come within 2 inches of the top of the basin. Moisten the edges of the crust, cover the pudding over, press the two crusts together, that the gravy may not escape, and turn up the overhanging paste. Wring out a cloth in hot water, flour it, and tie up the pudding; put it into boiling water, and let it boil for at least 4 hours. If the water diminishes, always replenish with some hot in a jug, as the pudding should be kept covered all the time, and not allowed to stop boiling. When the cloth is removed, cut out a round piece in the top of the crust, to prevent the pudding bursting, and send it to table in the basin, either in an ornamental dish, or with a napkin pinned round it. Serve quickly. *Time.*—For a pudding with 2 lbs. of steak and 2 kidneys allow 4 hours. *Average cost*, 2s. 8d. *Sufficient* for 6 persons. *Seasonable* all the year, but more suitable in winter.

Note.—Rump-steak pudding may be very much enriched by adding a few oysters or mushrooms. In Sussex, the inhabitants are noted for their savoury puddings, which are usually made in the manner just described. It differs from the general way of making them, as the meat is cut up into very small pieces and the basin is differently shaped, resembling a very large saucer: on trial, this pudding will be found far nicer, and more full of gravy, than when laid in large pieces in the dish.

RUMP-STEAK AND OYSTER SAUCE.

Ingredients.—3 dozen oysters, ingredients for oyster sauce, 2 lb. of rump-steak, seasoning to taste of pepper and salt. *Mode.*—Make the oyster sauce, and when that is ready, put it by the side of the fire, but do not let it keep boiling. Have the steaks cut of an equal thickness, broil them over a

Rump-steak or Beef-steak, Broiled

very clear fire, turning them often, that the gravy may not escape. In about 8 minutes they will be done, when put them on a very hot dish; smother with the oyster sauce, and the remainder send to table in a tureen. Serve quickly. *Time.*—About 8 to 10 minutes, according to the thickness of the steak. *Average cost*, 1s. per lb. *Sufficient* for 4 persons. *Seasonable* from September to April.

RUMP-STEAK or BEEF-STEAK, Broiled.

Ingredients.—Steaks, a piece of butter the size of a walnut, salt to taste, 1 tablespoonful of good mushroom ketchup or Harvey's sauce. *Mode.*—As the success of a good broil so much depends on the state of the fire, see that it is bright and clear, and perfectly free from smoke, and do not add any fresh fuel just before you require to use the gridiron. Sprinkle a little salt over the fire, put on the gridiron for a few minutes, to get thoroughly hot through; rub it with a piece of fresh suet, to prevent the meat from sticking, and lay on the steaks, which should be cut of an equal thickness, about ¾ of an inch, or rather thinner, and level them by beating them as *little* as possible with a rolling pin. Turn them frequently with steak-tongs (if these are not at hand, stick a fork in the edge of the fat, that no gravy escapes), and in from 8 to 10 minutes they will be done. Have ready a very hot dish, into which put the ketchup, and, when liked, a little minced shalot; dish up the steaks, rub them over with butter, and season with pepper and salt. The exact time for broiling steaks must be determined by taste, whether they are liked underdone or well done; more than from 1 to 10 minutes for a steak ¾ inch in thickness, we think, would spoil and dry up the juices of the meat. Great expedition is necessary in sending broiled steaks to table; and, to have them in perfection, they should not be cooked till everything else prepared for dinner has been dished up, as their excellence entirely depends on their being served very hot. Garnish with scraped horseradish, or slices of cucumber. Oyster, tomato, onion, and many other sauces, are frequent accompaniments to rump-steak, but true lovers of this English dish generally reject all additions but pepper and salt. *Time.*—8 to 10

Rump-steak Pie

minutes. *Average cost,* 1*s.* per lb. *Sufficient.*—Allow ½ lb. to each person ; if the party consist entirely of gentleman, ¾ lb. will not be too much. *Seasonable* all the year, but not good in the height of summer, as the meat cannot hang long enough to be tender.

RUMP-STEAK PIE.

Ingredients.—3 lbs. of rump-steak, seasoning to taste of salt, cayenne, and black pepper, crust, water, the yolk of an egg. *Mode.*—Have the steaks cut from a rump that has hung a few days, that they may be tender, and be particular that every portion is perfectly sweet. Cut the steaks into pieces about 3 inches long and 2 wide, allowing a *small* piece of fat to each piece of lean, and arrange the meat in layers in a pie-dish. Between each layer sprinkle a seasoning of salt, pepper, and, when liked, a few grains of cayenne. Fill the dish sufficiently with meat to support the crust, and to give it a nice raised appearance when baked, and not to look flat and hollow. Pour in sufficient water to half fill the dish, and border it with paste (*see* Pastry) ; brush it over with a little water, and put cn the cover ; slightly press down the edges with the thumb, and trim off close to the dish. Ornament the pie with leaves, or pieces of paste cut in any shape that fancy may direct, brush it over with the beaten yolk of an egg ; make a hole in the top of the crust, and bake in a hot oven for about 1½ hour. *Time.*—In a hot oven, 1½ hour. *Average cost,* for this size, 3*s.* 6*d.* *Sufficient* for 6 or 8 persons. *Seasonable* at any time.

RUMP-STEAK PUDDING, Baked.

Ingredients.—6 oz. of flour, 2 eggs, not quite 1 pint of milk, salt to taste, 1½ lb. of rump-steaks, 1 kidney, pepper and salt. *Mode.*—Cut the steaks into nice square pieces, with a small quantity of fat, and the kidney divide into small pieces. Make a batter of flour, eggs, and milk in the above proportion ; lay a little of it at the bottom of a pie-dish ; then put in the steaks and kidney, which should be well seasoned with pepper and salt, and pour over the remainder of the batter, and bake for 1½ hour in a brisk but not fierce oven.—*Time.*—1½ hour.

Rump-steak with Fried Potatoes

Average cost, 2*s.* *Sufficient* for 4 or 5 persons. *Seasonable* at any time.

RUMP-STEAK, Rolled, Roasted, and Stuffed.

Ingredients.—2 lbs. of rump-steak, forcemeat, pepper and salt to taste, clarified butter. *Mode.*—Have the steaks cut rather thick from a well-hung rump of beef, and sprinkle over them a seasoning of pepper and salt. Make a forcemeat ; spread it over *half* of the steak ; roll it up, bind and skewer it firmly, that the forcemeat may not escape, and roast it before a nice clear fire for about 1½ hour, or rather longer, should the roll be very large and thick. Keep it constantly basted with butter, and serve with brown gravy, some of which must be poured round the steak, and the remainder sent to table in a tureen. *Time.*—1½ hour. *Average cost,* 1*s.* per lb. *Sufficient* for 4 persons. *Seasonable* all the year, but best in winter.

RUMP-STEAK WITH FRIED POTATOES, or BIFTEK AUX POMMES-DE-TERRE (à la Mode Française).

Ingredients.—2 lb. of steak, 8 potatoes, ¼ lb. of butter, salt and pepper to taste, 1 teaspoonful of minced herbs. *Mode.*—Put the butter into a frying or *sauté* pan, set it over the fire, and let it get very hot ; peel, and cut the potatoes into long thin slices ; put them into the hot butter, and fry them till of a nice brown colour. Now broil the steaks over a bright clear fire, turning them frequently, that every part may be equally done : as they should not be thick, 5 minutes will broil them. Put the herbs and seasoning in the butter the potatoes were fried in, pour it under the steak, and place the fried potatoes round, as a garnish. To have this dish in perfection, a portion of the fillet of the sirloin should be used, as the meat is generally so much more tender than that of the rump, and the steaks should be cut about ⅓ of an inch in thickness. *Time.*—5 minutes to broil the steaks, and about the same time to fry the potatoes. *Average cost,* 1*s.* per lb. *Sufficient* for 4 persons. *Seasonable* all the year ; but not so good in warm weather, as the meat cannot hang to get tender

RUMP- or BEEF-STEAK, Stewed (an Entrée).

Ingredients.—About 2 lbs. of beef or rump steak, 3 onions, 2 turnips, 3 carrots, 2 or 3 oz. of butter, ½ pint of water, 1 teaspoonful of salt, ¼ do. of pepper, 1 tablespoonful of ketchup, 1 tablespoonful of flour. *Mode.*—Have the steaks cut tolerably thick and rather lean; divide them into convenient-sized pieces, and fry them in the butter a nice brown on both sides. Cleanse and pare the vegetables, cut the onions and carrots into thin slices, and the turnips into dice, and fry these in the same fat that the steaks were done in. Put all into a saucepan, add ½ pint of water, or rather more should it be necessary, and simmer very gently for 2½ or 3 hours; when nearly done, skim well, add salt, pepper, and ketchup in the above proportions, and thicken with a tablespoonful of flour mixed with 2 of cold water. Let it boil up for a minute or two after the thickening is added, and serve. When a vegetable-scoop is at hand, use it to cut the vegetables in fanciful shapes; and tomato, Harvey's sauce, or walnut-liquor may be used to flavour the gravy. It is less rich if stewed the previous day, so that the fat may be taken off when cold; when wanted for table, it will merely require warming through. *Time.*—3 hours. *Average cost*, 1s. per lb. *Sufficient* for 4 or 5 persons. *Seasonable* at any time.

RUSKS, to make (Suffolk Recipe).

Ingredients.—To every lb. of flour allow 2 oz. of butter, ¼ pint of milk, 2 oz. of loaf sugar, 3 eggs, 1 tablespoonful of yeast. *Mode.*—Put the milk and butter into a saucepan, and keep shaking it round until the latter is melted. Put the flour into a basin with the sugar, mix these well together, and beat the eggs. Stir them with the yeast to the milk and butter,

RUSKS.

and with this liquid work the flour into a smooth dough. Cover a cloth over the basin, and leave the dough to rise by the side of the fire; then knead it, and divide it into 12 pieces; place them in a brisk oven, and bake for about 20 minutes. Take the rusks out, break them in half, and then set them in the oven to get crisp on the other side. When cold, they should be put into tin canisters to keep them dry; and if intended for the cheese course, the sifted sugar should be omitted. *Time.*—20 minutes to bake the rusks; 5 minutes to render them crisp after being divided. *Average cost*, 8d. *Sufficient* to make 2 dozen rusks. *Seasonable* at any time.

RUSKS, Italian.

A stale Savoy or lemon cake may be converted into very good rusks in the following manner. Cut the cake into slices, divide each slice in two; put them on a baking-sheet, in a slow oven, and when they are of a nice brown and quite hard, they are done. They should be kept in a closed tin canister in a dry place, to preserve their crispness.

SAGE-AND-ONION STUFFING, for Geese, Ducks, and Pork.

Ingredients.—4 large onions, 10 sage-leaves, ¼ lb. of bread crumbs, 1½ oz. of butter, salt and pepper to taste, 1 egg. *Mode.*—Peel the onions, put them into boiling water, let them simmer for 5 minutes or rather longer, and just before they are taken out, put in the sage-leaves for a minute or two to take off their rawness. Chop both these very fine, add the bread, seasoning, and butter, and work the whole together with the yolk of an egg, when the stuffing will be ready for use. It should be rather highly seasoned, and the sage-leaves should be very finely chopped. Many cooks do not parboil the onions in the manner just stated, but merely use them raw. The stuffing then, however, is not nearly so mild, and, to many tastes, its strong flavour would be very objectionable. When made for goose, a portion of the liver of the bird, simmered for a few minutes and very finely minced, is frequently added to this stuffing; and where economy is studied, the egg may be dispensed with. *Time.*—Rather more than 5 minutes to simmer the onions. *Average cost*, for this quantity, 4d. *Sufficient* for 1 goose, or a pair of ducks.

SAGO PUDDING.

Ingredients.—1½ pint of milk, 3 tablespoonfuls of sago, the rind of ¼ lemon,

Sago Sauce for Sweet Puddings

3 oz. of sugar, 4 eggs, 1½ oz. of butter, grated nutmeg, puff-paste. *Mode.*— Put the milk and lemon-rind into a stewpan, place it by the side of the fire, and let it remain until the milk is well flavoured with the lemon ; then strain it, mix with it the sago and sugar, and simmer gently for about 15 minutes. Let the mixture cool a little, and stir to it the eggs, which should be well beaten, and the butter. Line the edges of a pie-dish with puff-paste, pour in the pudding, grate a little nutmeg over the top, and bake from ¾ to 1 hour. *Time.*—¾ to 1 hour, or longer if the oven is very slow. *Average cost*, 1s. Sufficient for 5 or 6 persons. *Seasonable* at any time.

Note.—The above pudding may be boiled instead of baked ; but then allow 2 extra tablespoonfuls of sago, and boil the pudding in a buttered basin from 1¼ to 1¾ hour.

SAGO SAUCE FOR SWEET PUDDINGS.

Ingredients.—1 tablespoonful of sago, ½ pint of water, ¼ pint of port or sherry, the rind and juice of 1 small lemon, sugar to taste ; when the flavour is liked, a little pounded cinnamon. *Mode.*— Wash the sago in two or three waters ; then put it into a saucepan, with the water and lemon-peel ; let it simmer gently by the side of the fire for 10 minutes, then take out the lemon-peel, add the remaining ingredients, give one boil, and serve. Be particular to strain the lemon-juice before adding it to the sauce. This, on trial, will be found a delicious accompaniment to various boiled puddings, such as those made of bread, raisins, rice, &c. *Time.*—10 minutes. *Average cost*, 9d. *Sufficient* for 7 or 8 persons.

SAGO SOUP.

Ingredients.—5 oz. of sago, 2 quarts of stock. *Mode.*—Wash the sago in boiling water, add it, by degrees, to the boiling stock, and simmer till the sago is entirely dissolved, and forms a sort of jelly. *Time.*—Nearly an hour. *Average cost*, 10d. per quart. *Sufficient* for 8 persons. *Seasonable* all the year.

Note.—The yolks of 2 eggs, beaten up with a little cream, previously boiled, and added at the moment of serving, much improves this soup.

SALAD, Boiled.

Ingredients.—2 heads of celery, 1 pint of French beans, lettuce, and endive.

Salad Dressing.

Mode.—Boil the celery and beans separately until tender, and cut the celery into pieces about 2 inches long. Put these into a salad-bowl or dish ; pour over either of the salad dressings, and garnish the dish with a little lettuce finely chopped, blanched endive, or a few tufts of boiled cauliflower. This composition, if less agreeable than vegetables in their raw state, is more wholesome ; for salads, however they may be compounded, when eaten uncooked, prove to some people indigestible. Tarragon, chervil, burnet, and boiled onion, may be added to the above salad with advantage, as also slices of cold meat, poultry, or fish. *Seasonable.*—From July to October.

SALAD DRESSING (Excellent).

Ingredients.—1 teaspoonful of mixed mustard, 1 teaspoonful of pounded sugar, 2 tablespoonfuls of salad oil, 4 tablespoonfuls of milk, 2 tablespoonfuls of vinegar, cayenne and salt to taste *Mode.*—Put the mixed mustard into a salad-bowl with the sugar, and add the oil drop by drop, carefully stirring and mixing all these ingredients well together. Proceed in this manner with the milk and vinegar, which must be added very *gradually*, or the sauce will curdle. Put in the seasoning, when the mixture will be ready for use. If this dressing is properly made, it will have a soft creamy appearance, and will be found very delicious with crab, or cold fried fish (the latter cut into dice), as well as with salads. In mixing salad dressings, the ingredients cannot be added *too gradually*, or *stirred too much*. *Average cost*, for this quantity, 3d. *Sufficient* for a small salad.

This recipe can be confidently recommended by the editress, to whom it was given by an intimate friend noted for her salads.

SALAD DRESSING (Excellent).

Ingredients.—4 eggs, 1 teaspoonful of mixed mustard, ¼ teaspoonful of white pepper, half that quantity of cayenne, salt to taste, 4 tablespoonfuls of cream, vinegar. *Mode.*—Boil the eggs until hard, which will be in about ¼ hour or 20 minutes ; put them into cold water, take off the shells, and pound the yolks in a mortar to a smooth paste. Then add all the other ingredients, except the vinegar, and stir them well until

Salad Dressing

the whole are thoroughly incorporated one with the other. Pour in sufficient vinegar to make it of the consistency of cream, taking care to add but little at a time. The mixture will then be ready for use. *Average cost*, for this quantity, *7d. Sufficient* for a moderate-sized salad.

Note.—The whites of the eggs, cut into rings, will serve very well as a garnishing to the salad.

SALAD DRESSING (Excellent).

Ingredients.—1 egg, 1 teaspoonful of salad oil, 1 teaspoonful of mixed mustard, ¼ teaspoonful of salt, ½ teaspoonful of pounded sugar, 2 tablespoonfuls of vinegar, 6 tablespoonfuls of cream. *Mode.*—Prepare and mix the ingredients by the preceding recipe, and be very particular that the whole is well stirred.

Note.—In making salads, the vegetables, &c., should never be added to the sauce very long before they are wanted for table; the dressing, however, may always be prepared some hours before required. Where salads are much in request, it is a good plan to bottle off sufficient dressing for a few days' consumption, as, thereby, much time and trouble are saved. If kept in a cool place, it will remain good for 4 or 5 days.

Poetic Recipe for Salad.—The Rev. Sydney Smith's recipe.

"Two large potatoes, pass'd through kitchen sieve,
Smoothness and softness to the salad give:
Of mordent mustard add a single spoon,
Distrust the condiment that bites too soon;
But deem it not, thou man of herbs, a fault,
To add a double quantity of salt:
Four times the spoon with oil of Lucca crown,
And twice with vinegar procured from 'town;'
True flavour needs it, and your poet begs,
The pounded yellow of two well-boil'd eggs.
Let onion's atoms lurk within the bowl,
And, scarce suspected, animate the whole;
And, lastly, in the flavour'd compound toss
A magic spoonful of anchovy sauce.
Oh! great and glorious, and herbaceous treat,
'Twould tempt the dying anchorite to eat.
Back to the world he'd turn his weary soul,
And plunge his fingers in the salad-bowl."

SALAD, French.

Ingredients.—Lettuces; a little chopped burnet. To every 4 tablespoonfuls of oil allow 1½ of either Tarragon or plain *French vinegar;* 1 saltspoonful of salt, ¼ saltspoonful of pepper. *Mode.*—Wash the lettuces, shake them in a cloth, and

Salad, Red Cabbage

cut them into inch lengths. Put the lettuce into a salad-bowl, sprinkle over the chopped burnet, and mix these well together. Put the salt and pepper into the salad-spoon, moisten with the vinegar, disperse this amongst the salad, pour the oil over, and mix the whole well together for at least five minutes, when the preparation will be ready for table. This is the very simple and expeditious mode of preparing a salad generally adopted by our French neighbours, who are so noted for the delicious manner in which they dress their bowl. Success will not be obtained if the right vinegar is not procured, therefore we advise our friends who wish to excel in making a French salad to procure a bottle of the best French vinegar, flavoured with Tarragon or not as the taste may dictate. Those persons living in or near London, can purchase the vinegar of Messrs. Crosse & Blackwell, Soho Square, at whose establishment the quality of this important ingredient in a salad can be relied on. *Time.*—To be stirred at least 5 minutes after all the ingredients are put in. *Sufficient.* Allow 2 moderate-sized lettuces for 4 persons. *Seasonable.* Plentiful in summer, but scarce and dear during the winter season.

SALAD, Fresh Fruit (A Dessert Dish).

Mode.—Fruit salads are made by stripping the fruit from the stalks, piling it on a dish, and sprinkling over it finely pounded sugar. They may be made of strawberries, raspberries, currants, or any of these fruits mixed; peaches also make a very good salad. After the sugar is sprinkled over, about 6 large tablespoonfuls of wine or brandy, or 3 tablespoonfuls of liqueur, should be poured in the middle of the fruit; and, when the flavour is liked, a little pounded cinnamon may be added. In helping the fruit, it should be lightly stirred, that the wine and sugar may be equally distributed. *Sufficient.*—1½ pint of fruit, with 3 oz. of pounded sugar, for 4 or 5 persons. *Seasonable* in summer.

SALAD, Red Cabbage.

Ingredients.—A small red cabbage, 2 teaspoonfuls of salt, ½ pint of vinegar, 3 teaspoonfuls of oil, a small quantity of cayenne pepper. *Mode.*—Take off the outside leaves of a fresh red cabbage,

Salad, Summer

and cut the remainder very finely into small thin slices. Mix with the cabbage the above salad ingredients, and let it remain for two days, when it will be fit for use. This salad will keep very well for a few days. The quantity of the ingredients may of course be a little varied, according to taste. *Time.*—2 days. *Average cost*, from 2*d.* to 3*d.* each. *Seasonable* in July and Augus\.

SALAD, Summer.

Ingredients.—3 lettuces, 2 handfuls of mustard-and-cress, 10 young radishes, a few slices of cucumber. *Mode.*—Let the herbs be as fresh as possible for a salad, and, if at all stale or dead-looking, let them lie in water for an hour or two, which will very much refresh them.

Wash and carefully pick them over, remove any decayed or worm-eaten leaves, and drain them thoroughly by swinging

SALAD IN BOWL.

them gently in a clean cloth. With a silver knife, cut the lettuces into small pieces, and the radishes and cucumbers into thin slices; arrange all these ingredients lightly on a dish, with the mustard-and-cress, and pour under, but not over the salad, either of the salad dressings, and do not stir it up until it is to be eaten. It may be garnished with hard-boiled eggs, cut in slices, sliced cucumbers, nasturtiums, cut vegetable-flowers, and many other things that taste will always suggest to make a pretty and elegant dish. In making a good salad, care must be taken to have the herbs freshly gathered, and *thoroughly drained* before the sauce is added to them, or it will be watery and thin. Young spring onions, cut small, are by many persons considered an improvement to salads; but, before these are added, the cook should always consult the taste of her employer. Slices of cold meat or poultry added to a salad make a convenient and quickly-made summer luncheon-dish; or cold fish, flaked, will also be found exceedingly nice, mixed with it. *Average cost*, 9*d.* for a salad for 5 or 6 persons; but more expensive when the herbs are forced.

Salmon (à la Genevese)

Sufficient for 5 or 6 persons. *Seasonable* from May to September.

SALAD, Winter.

Ingredients. — Endive, mustard-and-cress, boiled beetroot, 3 or 4 hard-boiled eggs, celery. *Mode.*—The above ingredients form the principal constituents of a winter salad, and may be converted into a very pretty dish, by nicely contrasting the various colours, and by tastefully garnishing it. Shred the celery into thin pieces, after having carefully washed and cut away all worm-eaten pieces; cleanse the endive and mustard-and-cress free from grit, and arrange these high in the centre of a salad-bowl or dish; garnish with the hard-boiled eggs and beetroot, both of which should be cut in slices; and pour into the dish, but not over the salad, either of the salad dressings. Never dress a salad long before it is required for table, as, by standing, it loses its freshness and pretty crisp and light appearance; the sauce, however, may always be prepared a few hours beforehand, and when required to use, the herbs laid lightly over it. *Average cost*, 9*d.* for a salad for 5 or 6 persons. *Sufficient* for 5 or 6 persons. *Seasonable* from the end of September to March.

SALMON (à la Genevese).

Ingredients.—2 slices of salmon, 2 chopped shalots, a little parsley, a small bunch of herbs, 2 bay-leaves, 2 carrots, pounded mace, pepper and salt to taste, 4 tablespoonfuls of Madeira, ½ pint of white stock, thickening of butter and flour, 1 teaspoonful of essence of anchovies, the juice of 1 lemon, cayenne and salt to taste. *Mode.*—Rub the bottom of a stewpan over with butter, and put in the shalots, herbs, bay-leaves, carrots, mace, and seasoning; stir them for 10 minutes over a clear fire, and add the Madeira or sherry; simmer gently for ½ hour, and strain through a sieve over the fish, which stew in this gravy. As soon as the fish is sufficiently cooked, take away all the liquor, except a little to keep the salmon moist, and put it into another stewpan; add the stock, thicken with butter and flour, and put in the anchovies, lemon-juice, cayenne, and salt; lay the salmon on a hot dish, pour over it part of the sauce, and serve the remainder in a tureen. *Time.*—1¼ hour. *Average cost*

Salmon, Boiled

for this quantity, 3s. 6d. *Sufficient* for 4 or 5 persons.

SALMON, Boiled.

Ingredients.—6 oz. of salt to each gallon of water,—sufficient water to cover the fish. *Mode.*—Scale and clean the fish, and be particular that no blood is left inside ; lay it in the fish-kettle with sufficient cold water to cover it, adding salt in the above proportion. Bring it quickly to a boil, take off all the scum, and let it simmer gently till the fish is done, which will be when the meat separates easily from the bone. Experience alone can teach the cook to fix the time for boiling fish ; but it is especially to be remembered, that it should never be under-dressed, as then nothing is more unwholesome. Neither let it remain in the kettle after it is sufficiently cooked, as that would render it insipid, watery, and colourless. Drain it, and if not wanted for a few minutes, keep it warm by means of warm cloths laid over it. Serve on a hot napkin, garnish with cut lemon and parsley, and send lobster or shrimp sauce, and plain melted butter to table with it. A dish of dressed cucumber usually accompanies this fish. *Time* —8 minutes to each lb. for large thick salmon ; 6 minutes for thin fish. *Average cost*, in full season, 1s. 3d. per lb. *Sufficient*, ¼ lb, or rather less, for each person. *Seasonable* from April to August.

Note.—Cut lemon should be put on the table with this fish ; and a little of the juice squeezed over it is regarded by many persons as a most agreeable addition. Boiled peas are also, by some connoisseurs, considered especially adapted to be served with salmon.

To CHOOSE SALMON.—To be good, the belly should be firm and thick, which may readily be ascertained by feeling it with the thumb and finger The circumstance of this fish having red gills, though given as a standing rule in most cookery-books, as a sign of its goodness, is not at all to be relied on, as this quality can be easily given them by art.

SALMON AND CAPER SAUCE.

Ingredients.—2 slices of salmon, ¼ lb. butter, ½ teaspoonful of chopped parsley, 1 shalot ; salt, pepper, and grated nutmeg to taste. *Mode.*—Lay the salmon

Salmon, Curried

in a baking-dish, place pieces of butter over it, and add the other ingredients, rubbing a little of the seasoning into the fish ; baste it frequently ; when done, take it out and drain for a minute or two ; lay it in a dish, pour caper sauce over it, and serve. Salmon dressed in this way, with tomato sauce, is very delicious. *Time.*—About ¾ hour. *Average cost*, 1s. 3d. per lb. *Sufficient* for 4 or 5 persons. *Seasonable* from April to August.

SALMON, Collared.

Ingredients.—A piece of salmon, say 3 lb., a high seasoning of salt, pounded mace, and pepper ; water and vinegar, 3 bay-leaves. *Mode.*—Split the fish ; scale, bone, and wash it thoroughly clean ; wipe it, and rub in the seasoning inside and out ; roll it up, and bind firmly ; lay it in a kettle, cover it with vinegar and water (⅓ vinegar, in proportion to the water) ; add the bay-leaves and a good seasoning of salt and whole pepper, and simmer till done. Do not remove the lid. Serve with melted butter or anchovy sauce. For preserving the collared fish, boil up the liquor in which it was cooked, and add a little more vinegar. Pour over when cold. *Time.*—¾ hour, or rather more.

SALMON, Crimped.

Salmon is frequently dressed in this way at many fashionable tables, but must be very fresh, and cut into slices 2 or 3 inches thick. Lay these in cold salt and water for 1 hour ; have ready some boiling water, salted, and well skimmed ; put in the fish, and simmer gently for ¼ hour, or rather more ; should it be very thick, garnish the same as boiled salmon, and serve with the same sauces. *Time.*—¼ hour, more or less, according to size.

Note.—Never use vinegar with salmon, as it spoils the taste and colour of the fish.

SALMON, Curried.

Ingredients.—Any remains of boiled salmon, ¾ pint of strong or medium stock, 1 onion, 1 tablespoonful of curry-powder, 1 teaspoonful of Harvey's sauce, 1 teaspoonful of anchovy sauce, 1 oz. of butter, the juice of ½ lemon, cayenne and salt to taste. *Mode.*—Cut up the

Salmon Cutlets

onions into small pieces, and fry them of a pale brown in the butter ; add all the ingredients but the salmon, and simmer gently till the onion is tender, occasionally stirring the contents ; cut the salmon into small square pieces, carefully take away all skin and bone, lay it in the stewpan, and let it gradually heat through ; but do not allow it to boil long. *Time.*— ¾ hour. *Average cost,* exclusive of the cold fish, 9d.

SALMON CUTLETS.

Cut the slices 1 inch thick, and season them with pepper and salt ; butter a sheet of white paper, lay each slice on a separate piece, with their ends twisted ; broil gently over a clear fire, and serve with anchovy or caper sauce. When higher seasoning is required, add a few chopped herbs and a little spice. *Time.* —5 to 10 minutes.

SALMON, Pickled.

Ingredients.—Salmon, ½ oz. of whole pepper, ½ oz. of whole allspice, 1 teaspoonful of salt, 2 bay-leaves, equal quantities of vinegar and the liquor in which the fish was boiled. *Mode.*—After the fish comes from table, lay it in a nice dish with a cover to it, as it should be excluded from the air, and take away the bone ; boil the liquor and vinegar with the other ingredients for 10 minutes, and let it stand to get cold ; pour it over the salmon, and in 12 hours this will be fit for the table. *Time.*—10 minutes.

SALMON, Potted.

Ingredients.—Salmon, pounded mace, cloves, and pepper to taste ; 3 bay-leaves, ¼ lb. butter. *Mode.*—Skin the salmon, and clean it thoroughly by wiping with a cloth (water would spoil it) ; cut it into square pieces, which rub with salt ; let them remain till thoroughly drained, then lay them in a dish with the other ingredients, and bake. When quite done, drain them from the gravy, press into pots for use, and, when cold, pour over it clarified butter. *Time.*—½ hour.

SALMON, to Cure.

This process consists in splitting the fish, rubbing it with salt, and then putting it into pickle in tubs provided for the purpose. Here it is kept for about

Salsify, to Dress

six weeks, when it is taken out, pressed and packed in casks, with layers of salt.

SALMON, to Help.

First run the knife quite down to the bone, along the side of the fish, from *a* to *b*, and also from *c* to *d*. Then help the thick part lengthwise, that is, in the direction of the lines from *a* to *b* ; and the thin part breadthwise, that is, in the direction of the lines from *e* to *f*, as shown in the engraving. A slice of the thick part should always be accompanied by a smaller piece of the thin from the belly, where lies the fat of the fish.

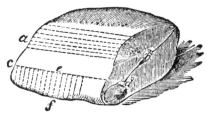

Note. — Many persons, in carving salmon, make the mistake of slicing the thick part of this fish in the opposite direction to that we have stated ; and thus, by the breaking of the flakes, the beauty of its appearance is destroyed.

SALSIFY, to Dress.

Ingredients.—Salsify ; to each ½ gallon of water allow 1 heaped tablespoonful of salt, 1 oz. of butter, 2 tablespoonfuls of lemon-juice. *Mode.*—Scrape the roots gently, so as to strip them only of their outside peel ; cut them into pieces about 4 inches long, and, as they are peeled, throw them into water with which has been mixed a little lemon-juice, to prevent their discolouring. Put them into boiling water, with salt, butter, and lemon-juice in the above proportion, and let them boil rapidly until tender ; try them with a fork ; and, when it penetrates easily, they are done. Drain the salsify, and serve with a good white sauce or French melted butter. *Time.*—30 to 50 minutes. *Seasonable* in winter.

Note.—This vegetable may be also boiled, sliced, and fried in batter of a nice brown. When crisp and a good colour, they should be served with fried parsley in the centre of the dish, and a little fine salt sprinkled over the salsify.

SANDWICHES, Victoria.

Ingredients.—4 eggs; their weight in pounded sugar, butter, and flour; ¼ saltspoonful of salt, a layer of any kind of jam or marmalade. *Mode.*—Beat the butter to a cream; dredge in the flour and pounded sugar; stir these ingredients well togther, and add the eggs, which should be previously thoroughly whisked. When the mixture has been well beaten for about 10 minutes, butter a Yorkshire-pudding tin, pour in the batter, and bake it in a moderate oven for 20 minutes. Let it cool, spread one half of the cake with a layer of nice preserve, place over it the other half of the cake, press the pieces slightly together, and then cut it into long finger-pieces; pile them in crossbars, on a glass dish, and serve. *Time.*—20 minutes. *Average cost*, 1s. 3d. *Sufficient* for 5 or 6 persons. *Seasonable* at any time.

SAUCES, General Remarks upon.

The preparation and appearance of sauces and gravies are of the highest consequence, and in nothing does the talent and taste of the cook more display itself. Their special adaptability to the various viands they are to accompany cannot be too much studied, in order that they may harmonize and blend with them as perfectly, so to speak, as does a pianoforte accompaniment with the voice of the singer.

The general basis of most gravies and some sauces is the same stock as that used for soups; and, by the employment of these, with, perhaps, an additional slice of ham, a little spice, a few herbs, and a slight flavouring from some cold sauce or ketchup, very nice gravies may be made for a very small expenditure. A milt (either of a bullock or sheep), the shank-end of mutton that has already been dressed, and the necks and feet of poultry may all be advantageously used for gravy, where much is not required. It may, then, be established as a rule, that there exists no necessity for good gravies to be expensive, and that there is no occasion, as many would have the world believe, to buy ever so many pounds of fresh meat, in order to furnish an ever so little quantity of gravy.

Brown sauces, generally speaking, should scarcely be so thick as white sauces; and it is well to bear in mind, that all those which are intended to mask the various dishes of poultry or meat, should be of a sufficient consistency to slightly adhere to the fowls or joints over which they are poured. For browning and thickening sauces, &c., browned flour may be properly employed.

Sauces should possess a decided character; and whether sharp or sweet, savoury or plain, they should carry out their names in a distinct manner, although, of course, not so much flavoured as to make them too piquant on the one hand, or too mawkish on the other.

Gravies and sauces should be sent to table very hot; and there is all the more necessity for the cook to see to this point, as, from their being usually served in small quantities, they are more liable to cool quickly than if they were in a larger body. Those sauces, of which cream or eggs form a component part, should be well stirred, as soon as these ingredients are added to them, and must never be allowed to boil; as, in that case, they would instantly curdle.

SAUCE à L'AURORE, for Trout, Soles, &c.

Ingredients.—The spawn of 1 lobster, 1 oz. of butter, ½ pint of Béchamel, the juice of ½ lemon, a high seasoning of salt and cayenne. *Mode.*—Take the spawn and pound it in a mortar with the butter, until quite smooth, and work it through a hair sieve. Put the Béchamel into a stewpan, add the pounded spawn, the lemon-juice, which must be strained, and a plentiful seasoning of cayenne and salt; let it just simmer, but do not allow it to boil, or the beautiful red colour of the sauce will be spoiled. A small spoonful of anchovy essence may be added at pleasure. *Time.*—1 minute to simmer. *Average cost*, for this quantity, 1s. *Sufficient* for a pair of large soles. *Seasonable* at any time.

SAUCE à la MATELOTE, for Fish.

Ingredients.—½ pint of Espagnole, 3 onions, 2 tablespoonfuls of mushroom ketchup, ½ glass of port wine, a bunch of sweet herbs, ½ bay-leaf, salt and pepper to taste, 1 clove, 2 berries of allspice, a little liquor in which the fish has been boiled, lemon-juice, and anchovy sauce. *Mode.*—Slice and fry the onions of a nice brown colour, and put them into a stewpan with the Espagnole, ketchup, wine, and a little liquor in

Sauce Allemande

which the fish has been boiled. Add the seasoning, herbs, and spices, and simmer gently for 10 minutes, stirring well the whole time; strain it through a fine hair sieve, put in the lemon-juice and anchovy sauce, and pour it over the fish. This sauce may be very much enriched by putting in a few small quenelles, or force-meat balls made of fish, and also glazed onions or mushrooms. These, however, should not be added to the matelote till it is dished. *Time.*—10 minutes. *Average cost,* 1s 6d. *Seasonable* at any time.

Note.—This sauce originally took its name as being similar to that which the French sailor (*matelot*) employed as a relish to the fish he caught and ate. In some cases cider and perry were substituted for the wine. The Norman *matelotes* were very celebrated.

SAUCE ALLEMANDE, or German Sauce.

Ingredients.—½ pint of sauce tournée, the yolks of 2 eggs. *Mode.*—Put the sauce into a stewpan, heat it, and stir to it the beaten yolks of 2 eggs, which have been previously strained. Let it just simmer, but not boil, or the eggs will curdle; and after they are added to the sauce, it must be stirred without ceasing. This sauce is a general favourite, and is used for many made dishes. *Time.*—1 minute to simmer. *Average cost,* 6d.

SAUCE ARISTOCRATIQUE (a Store Sauce).

Ingredients.—Green walnuts. To every pint of juice, 1 lb. of anchovies, 1 drachm of cloves, 1 drachm of mace, 1 drachm of Jamaica ginger bruised, 8 shalots. To every pint of the boiled liquor, ¼ pint of vinegar, ¼ pint of port wine, 2 table-spoonfuls of soy. *Mode.*—Pound the walnuts in a mortar, squeeze out the juice through a strainer, and let it stand to settle. Pour off the clear juice, and to every pint of it, add anchovies, spices, and cloves in the above proportion. Boil all these together till the anchovies are dissolved, then strain the juice again, put in the shalots (8 to every pint), and boil again. To every pint of the boiled liquor add vinegar, wine, and soy, in the above quantities, and bottle off for use. Cork well and seal the corks. *Seasonable.*—Make this sauce from the beginning to

Sauce, Bread

the middle of July, when walnuts are in perfection for sauces and pickling. *Average cost,* 3s. 6d. for a quart.

SAUCE, Benton (to serve with Hot or Cold Roast Beef).

Ingredients. — 1 tablespoonful of scraped horseradish, 1 teaspoonful of made mustard, 1 teaspoonful of pounded sugar, 4 tablespoonfuls of vinegar. *Mode.*—Grate or scrape the horseradish very fine, and mix it with the other ingredients, which must be all well blended together; serve in a tureen. With cold meat, this sauce is a very good substitute for pickles. *Average cost* for this quantity, 2d.

SAUCE, Mango Chetney, Bengal Recipe for Making.

Ingredients. — 1½ lb. of moist sugar, ¾ lb. of salt, ¼ lb. of garlic, ¼ lb. of onions, ¾ lb. of powdered ginger, ¼ lb. of dried chilies, ¾ lb. of mustard-seed, ¾ lb. of stoned raisins, 2 bottles of best vinegar, 30 large unripe sour apples. *Mode.*—The sugar must be made into syrup; the garlic, onions, and ginger be finely pounded in a mortar; the mustard-seed be washed in cold vinegar, and dried in the sun; the apples be peeled, cored, and sliced, and boiled in a bottle and a half of the vinegar. When all this is done, and the apples are quite cold, put them into a large pan, and gradually mix the whole of the rest of the ingredients, including the remaining half-bottle of vinegar. It must be well stirred until the whole is thoroughly blended, and then put into bottles for use. Tie a piece of wet bladder over the mouths of the bottles, after they are well corked. This chetney is very superior to any which can be bought, and one trial will prove it to be delicious.

Note.—This recipe was given by a native to an English lady, who had long been a resident in India, and who, since her return to her native country, has become quite celebrated amongst her friends for the excellence of this Eastern relish.

SAUCE, Bread (to serve with Roast Turkey, Fowl, Game, &c).

Ingredients.—1 pint of milk, ¾ lb. of the crumb of a stale loaf, 1 onion; pounded mace, cayenne, and salt to

Sauce, Bread

taste ; 1 oz. of butter. *Mode.*—Peel and quarter the onion, and simmer it in the milk till perfectly tender. Break the bread, which should be stale, into small pieces, carefully picking out any hard or side pieces ; put it in a very clean saucepan, strain the milk over it, cover it up, and let it remain for an hour to soak. Now beat it up with a fork very smoothly, add a seasoning of pounded mace, cayenne, and salt, with 1 oz. of butter; give the whole one boil, and serve. To enrich this sauce, a small quantity of cream may be added just before sending it to table. *Time.*—Altogether, 1¾ hour. *Average cost* for this quantity, 4*d.* *Sufficient* to serve with a turkey, pair of fowls, or brace of partridges.

SAUCE, Bread (to serve with Roast Turkey, Fowl, Game, &c).

Ingredients.—Giblets of poultry, ¾ lb. of the crumb of a stale loaf, 1 onion, 12 whole peppers, 1 blade of mace, salt to taste, 2 tablespoonfuls of cream or melted butter, 1 pint of water. *Mode.*—Put the giblets, with the head, neck, legs, &c., into a stewpan ; add the onion, pepper, mace, salt, and rather more than 1 pint of water. Let this simmer for an hour, when strain the liquor over the bread, which should be previously grated or broken into small pieces. Cover up the saucepan, and leave it for an hour by the side of the fire ; then beat the sauce up with a fork until no lumps remain, and the whole is nice and smooth. Let it boil for 3 or 4 minutes ; keep stirring it until it is rather thick ; when add 3 tablespoonfuls of good melted butter or cream, and serve very hot. *Time.*—2¼ hours. *Average cost, 6d.*

SAUCE, Christopher North's, for Meat or Game.

Ingredients.—1 glass of port wine, 2 tablespoonfuls of Harvey's sauce, 1 dessertspoonful of mushroom ketchup, ditto of pounded white sugar, 1 tablespoonful of lemon juice, ½ teaspoonful of cayenne pepper, ditto of salt. *Mode.*—Mix all the ingredients thoroughly together, and beat the sauce gradually, by placing the vessel in which it is made in a saucepan of boiling water. Do not allow it to boil, and serve directly it is ready. This sauce, if bottled immediately, will keep good for a fortnight, and will be found excellent.

Sauce, Epicurean

SAUCE, Dutch, for Fish.

Ingredients. — ½ teaspoonful of flour, 2 oz. of butter, 2 tablespoonfuls of vinegar, 4 tablespoonfuls of water, the yolks of 2 eggs, the juice of ½ lemon ; salt to taste. *Mode.*—Put all the ingredients, except the lemon-juice, into a stewpan ; set it over the fire, and keep continually stirring. When it is sufficiently thick, take it off, as it should not boil. If, however, it happens to curdle, strain the sauce through a tammy, add the lemon-juice, and serve. Tarragon vinegar may be used instead of plain, and, by many, is considered far preferable. *Average cost, 6d.*

Note.—This sauce may be poured hot over salad, and left to get quite cold, when it should be thick, smooth, and somewhat stiff. Excellent salads may be made of hard eggs, or the remains of salt fish flaked nicely from the bone, by pouring over a little of the above mixture when hot, and allowing it to cool.

SAUCE, Green Dutch, or Hollandaise Verte.

Ingredients. — 6 tablespoonfuls of Béchamel, seasoning to taste of salt and cayenne, a little parsley-green to colour, the juice of ½ a lemon. *Mode.*—Put the Béchamel into a saucepan with the seasoning, and bring it to a boil. Make a green colouring by pounding some parsley in a mortar, and squeezing all the juice from it. Let this just simmer, when add it to the sauce. A moment before serving, put in the lemon-juice, but not before ; for otherwise the sauce would turn yellow, and its appearance be thus spoiled. *Average cost, 4d.*

SAUCE, Epicurean, for Steaks, Chops, Gravies, or Fish.

Ingredients.—¼ pint of walnut ketchup, ¼ pint of mushroom ditto, 2 tablespoonfuls of Indian soy, 2 tablespoonfuls of port wine ; ¼ oz. of white pepper, 2 oz. of shalots, ¼ oz. of cayenne, ¼ oz. of cloves, ¾ pint of vinegar. *Mode.*—Put the whole of the ingredients into a bottle, and let it remain for a fortnight in a warm place, occasionally shaking up the contents. Strain, and bottle off for use. This sauce will be found an agreeable addition to gravies, hashes, stews, &c. *Average cost, for this quantity, 1s. 6d.*

Sauce, Genevese	Sauce, Leamington

SAUCE, Genevese, for Salmon, Trout, &c.

Ingredients.—1 small carrot, a small faggot of sweet herbs, including parsley, 1 onion, 5 or 6 mushrooms (when obtainable), 1 bay-leaf, 6 cloves, 1 blade of mace, 2 oz. of butter, 1 glass of sherry, 1½ pint of white stock, thickening of butter and flour, the juice of half a lemon. *Mode.*—Cut up the onion and carrot into small rings, and put them into a stewpan with the herbs, mushrooms, bay-leaf, cloves, and mace; add the butter, and simmer the whole very gently over a slow fire until the onion is quite tender. Pour in the stock and sherry, and stew slowly for 1 hour, when strain it off into a clean saucepan. Now make a thickening of butter and flour, put it to the sauce, stir it over the fire until perfectly smooth and mellow, add the lemon-juice, give one boil, when it will be ready for table. *Time.*—Altogether 2 hours. *Average cost,* 1s. 3d. per pint. *Sufficient,* half this quantity for two slices of salmon.

SAUCE, Green, for Green Geese or Ducklings.

Ingredients.—¼ pint of sorrel-juice, 1 glass of sherry, ½ pint of green gooseberries, 1 teaspoonful of pounded sugar, 1 oz. of fresh butter. *Mode.*—Boil the gooseberries in water until they are quite tender; mash them and press them through a sieve; put the pulp into a saucepan with the above ingredients; simmer for 3 or 4 minutes, and serve very hot. *Time.*—3 or 4 minutes.

Note.—We have given this recipe as a sauce for green geese, thinking that some of our readers might sometimes require it; but, at the generality of fashionable tables, it is now seldom or never served.

SAUCE, Indian Chetney.

Ingredients. — 8 oz. of sharp, sour apples, pared and cored; 8 oz. of tomatoes, 8 oz. of salt, 8 oz. of brown sugar, 8 oz. of stoned raisins, 4 oz. of cayenne, 4 oz. of powdered ginger, 2 oz. of garlic, 2 oz. of shalots, 3 quarts of vinegar, 1 quart of lemon juice. *Mode.*—Chop the apples in small square pieces, and add to them the other ingredients. Mix the whole well together, and put in a well-covered jar. Keep this in a warm place, and stir every day for a month,

taking care to put on the lid after this operation; strain, but do not squeeze it dry; store it away in clean jars or bottles for use, and the liquor will serve as an excellent sauce for meat or fish. *Seasonable.*—Make this sauce when tomatoes are in full season, that is, from the beginning of September to the end of October.

SAUCE, Italian (Brown).

Ingredients.—A few chopped mushrooms and shalots, ½ pint of stock, ½ glass of Madeira, the juice of ½ lemon, ½ teaspoonful of pounded sugar, 1 teaspoonful of chopped parsley. *Mode.*—Put the stock into a stewpan with the mushrooms, shalots, and Madeira, and stew gently for ¼ hour, then add the remaining ingredients, and let them just boil. When the sauce is done enough, put it in another stewpan, and warm it in a *bain marie.* The mushrooms should not be chopped long before they are wanted as they will then become black. *Time.*—¼ hour. *Average cost,* for this quantity, 7d. *Sufficient* for a small dish.

SAUCE, Italian (White).

Ingredients.—½ pint of white stock, 2 tablespoonfuls of chopped mushrooms, 1 dessertspoonful of chopped shalots, 1 slice of ham, minced very fine; ¼ pint of Béchamel; salt to taste, a few drops of garlic vinegar, ½ teaspoonful of pounded sugar, a squeeze of lemon-juice. *Mode.*—Put the shalots and mushrooms into a stewpan with the stock and ham, and simmer very gently for ½ hour, when add the Béchamel. Let it just boil up, and then strain it through a tammy; season with the above ingredients, and serve very hot. If this sauce should not have retained a nice white colour, a little cream may be added. *Time.*—½ hour. *Average cost,* for this quantity, 10d. *Sufficient* for a moderate-sized dish.

Note.—To preserve the colour of the mushrooms after pickling, throw them into water to which a little lemon-juice has been added.

SAUCE, Leamington (an Excellent Sauce for Flavouring Gravies, Hashes, Soups, &c.—Author's Recipe).

Ingredients.—Walnuts. To each quart of walnut-juice allow 2 quarts of vinegar,

Sauce, Maître d'Hotel	Sauce, a Good

1 pint of Indian soy, 1 oz. of cayenne, 2 oz. of shalots, ¾ oz. of garlic, ½ pint of port wine. *Mode.*—Be very particular in choosing the walnuts as soon as they appear in the market; for they are more easily bruised before they become hard and shelled. Pound them in a mortar to a pulp, strew some salt over them, and let them remain thus for two or three days, occasionally stirring and moving them about. Press out the juice, and to *each quart* of walnut-liquor allow the above proportion of vinegar, soy, cayenne, shalots, garlic, and port wine. Pound each ingredient separately in a mortar, then mix them well together, and store away for use in small bottles. The corks should be well sealed. *Seasonable.*—This sauce should be made as soon as walnuts are obtainable, from the beginning to the middle of July.

SAUCE, Maître d'Hotel (Hot), to serve with Calf's Head, Boiled Eels, and different Fish.

Ingredients.—1 slice of minced ham, a few poultry-trimmings, 2 shalots, 1 clove of garlic, 1 bay-leaf, ¾ pint of water, 2 oz. of butter, 1 dessertspoonful of flour, 1 heaped tablespoonful of chopped parsley; salt, pepper, and cayenne, to taste; the juice of ½ large lemon, ¼ teaspoonful of pounded sugar. *Mode.*—Put at the bottom of a stewpan the minced ham, and over it the poultry-trimmings (if these are not at hand, veal should be substituted), with the shalots, garlic, and bay-leaf. Pour in the water, and let the whole simmer gently for 1 hour, or until the liquor is reduced to a full ½ pint. Then strain this gravy, put it in another saucepan, make a thickening of butter and flower in the above proportions, and stir it to the gravy over a nice clear fire, until it is perfectly smooth and rather thick, care being taken that the butter does not float on the surface. Skim well, add the remaining ingredients, let the sauce gradually heat, but do not allow it to boil. If this sauce is intended for an entrée, it is necessary to make it of a sufficient thickness, so that it may adhere to what it is meant to cover. *Time.*—1½ hour. *Average cost,* 1s. 2d. per pint. *Sufficient* for rewarming the remains of ½ calf's head, or a small dish of cold flaked turbot, cod, &c.

SAUCE, Maigre Maître d'Hotel (Hot.—Made without Meat).

Ingredients.—½ pint of melted butter, 1 heaped tablespoonful of chopped parsley, salt and pepper to taste, the juice of ½ large lemon; when liked, 2 minced shalots. *Mode.*—Make ½ pint of melted butter, stir in the above ingredients, and let them just boil; when it is ready to serve. *Time.*—1 minute to simmer. *Average cost,* 9d. per pint.

SAUCE PIQUANTE, for Cutlets, Roast Meat, &c.

Ingredients.—2 oz. of butter, 1 small carrot, 6 shalots, 1 small bunch of savoury herbs, including parsley, ½ a bay-leaf, 2 slices of lean ham, 2 cloves, 6 peppercorns, 1 blade of mace, 3 whole allspice, 4 tablespoonfuls of vinegar, ½ pint of stock, 1 small lump of sugar, ¼ saltspoonful of cayenne, salt to taste. *Mode.*—Put into a stewpan the butter, with the carrots and shalots, both of which must be cut into small slices; add the herbs, bay-leaf, spices, and ham (which must be minced rather finely), and let these ingredients simmer over a slow fire, until the bottom of the stewpan is covered with a brown glaze. Keep stirring with a wooden spoon, and put in the remaining ingredients. Simmer very gently for ¼ hour, skim off every particle of fat, strain the sauce through a sieve, and serve very hot. Care must be taken that this sauce be not made too acid, although it should possess a sharpness indicated by its name. Of course the above quantity of vinegar may be increased or diminished at pleasure, according to taste. *Time.*—Altogether ½ hour. *Average cost,* 10d. *Sufficient* for a medium-sized dish of cutlets. *Seasonable* at any time.

SAUCE, a Good, for Various Boiled Puddings.

Ingredients.—¼ lb. of butter, ¼ lb. of pounded sugar, a wineglassful of brandy or rum. *Mode.*—Beat the butter to a cream, until no lumps remain; add the pounded sugar, and brandy or rum; stir once or twice until the whole is thoroughly mixed, and serve. This sauce may either be poured round the pudding or served in a tureen, according to the taste or fancy of the cook or mistress. *Average*

Sauce, Plum-Pudding	Sauce, a Good, for Steaks

cost, 8*d.* for this quantity. *Sufficient* for a pudding.

SAUCE, Plum-Pudding.

Ingredients.—1 wineglassful of brandy, 2 oz. of very fresh butter, 1 glass of Madeira, pounded sugar to taste. *Mode.*—Put the pounded sugar in a basin, with part of the brandy and the butter; let it stand by the side of the fire until it is warm and the sugar and butter are dissolved; then add the rest of the brandy, with the Madeira. Either pour it over the pudding, or serve in a tureen. This is a very rich and excellent sauce. *Average cost,* 1*s.* 3*d.* for this quantity. *Sufficient* for a pudding made for 6 persons.

SAUCE, Quin's, an Excellent Fish Sauce.

Ingredients.—½ pint of walnut pickle, ½ pint of port wine, 1 pint of mushroom ketchup, 1 dozen anchovies, 1 dozen shalots, ¼ pint of soy, ½ teaspoonful of cayenne. *Mode.*—Put all the ingredients into a saucepan, having previously chopped the shalots and anchovies very small; simmer for 15 minutes, strain, and, when cold, bottle off for use; the corks should be well sealed to exclude the air. *Time.*—¼ hour. *Seasonable* at any time.

SAUCE, Reading

Ingredients.—2½ pints of walnut pickle, 1½ oz. of shalots, 1 quart of spring water, ¾ pint of Indian soy, ½ oz. of bruised ginger, ½ oz. of long pepper, 1 oz. of mustard-seed, 1 anchovy, ½ oz. of cayenne, ¼ oz. of dried sweet bay-leaves. *Mode.*—Bruise the shalots in a mortar, and put them in a stone jar with the walnut-liquor; place it before the fire, and let it boil until reduced to 2 pints. Then, into another jar, put all the ingredients except the bay-leaves, taking care that they are well bruised, so that the flavour may be thoroughly extracted; put this also before the fire, and let it boil for 1 hour, or rather more. When the contents of both jars are sufficiently cooked, mix them together, stirring them well as you mix them, and submit them to a slow boiling for ½ hour; cover closely, and let them stand 24 hours in a cool place; then open the jar and add the bay-leaves; let it stand a week longer closed down when strain through a

flannel bag, and it will be ready for use. The above quantities will make ⅛ gallon. *Time.*—Altogether, 3 hours. *Seasonable.*—This sauce may be made at any time.

SAUCE, Robert, for Steaks, &c.

Ingredients.—2 oz. of butter, 3 onions, 1 teaspoonful of flour, 4 tablespoonfuls of gravy or stock, salt and pepper to taste, 1 teaspoonful of made mustard, 1 teaspoonful of vinegar, the juice of ½ lemon. *Mode.*—Put the butter into a stewpan, set it on the fire, and, when browning, throw in the onions, which must be cut into small slices. Fry them brown, but do not burn them; add the flour, shake the onions in it, and give the whole another fry. Put in the gravy and seasoning, and boil it gently for 10 minutes; skim off the fat, add the mustard, vinegar, and lemon-juice; give it one boil, and pour round the steaks, or whatever dish the sauce has been prepared for. *Time.*—Altogether, ½ hour. *Average cost,* for this quantity, 6*d.* *Sufficient* for about 2 lbs. of steak. *Seasonable* at any time.

Note.—This sauce will be found an excellent accompaniment to roast goose, pork, mutton cutlets, and various other dishes.

SAUCE, Soyer's, for Plum-Pudding.

Ingredients.—The yolks of 3 eggs, 1 tablespoonful of powdered sugar, 1 gill of milk, a very little grated lemon-rind, 2 small wineglassfuls of brandy. *Mode.*—Separate the yolks from the whites of 3 eggs, and put the former into a stewpan; add the sugar, milk, and grated lemon-rind, and stir over the fire until the mixture thickens; but do *not* allow it to *boil*. Put in the brandy; let the sauce stand by the side of the fire, to get quite hot; keep stirring it, and serve in a boat or tureen separately, or pour it over the pudding. *Time.*—Altogether, 10 minutes. *Average cost,* 1*s.* *Sufficient* for 6 or 7 persons.

SAUCE, a Good, for Steaks.

Ingredients.—1 oz. of whole black pepper, ½ oz. of allspice, 1 oz. of salt, ½ oz. grated horseradish, ½ oz. of pickled shalots, 1 pint of mushroom ketchup or walnut pickle. *Mode.*—Pound all the ingredients finely in a mortar, and pu

|

them into the ketchup or walnut-liquor. Let them stand for a fortnight, when strain off the liquor and bottle for use. Either pour a little of the sauce over the steaks, or mix it in the gravy. *Seasonable.*—This can be made at any time.

Note.—In using a jar of pickled walnuts, there is frequently left a large quantity of liquor. This should be converted into a sauce like the above, and will be found a very useful relish.

SAUCE, Sweet, for Puddings.

Ingredients.—½ pint of melted butter made with milk, 3 teaspoonfuls of pounded sugar, flavouring of grated lemon-rind or cinnamon. *Mode.*—Make ½ pint of melted butter, omitting any salt; stir in the sugar, add a little grated lemon-rind, nutmeg, or powdered cinnamon, and serve. Previously to making the melted butter, the milk can be flavoured with bitter almonds, by infusing about half a dozen of them in it for about ½ hour; the milk should then be strained before it is added to the other ingredients. This simple sauce may be served for children with rice, batter, or bread pudding. *Time.*—Altogether, 15 minutes. *Average cost,* 4d. *Sufficient* for 6 or 7 persons.

SAUCE, Sweet, for Venison.

Ingredients.—A small jar of red-currant jelly, 1 glass of port wine. *Mode.*—Put the above ingredients into a stewpan, set them over the fire, and, when melted, pour in a tureen and serve. It should not be allowed to boil. *Time.*—5 minutes to melt the jelly. *Average cost,* for this quantity, 1s.

SAUCE, Tournée.

Ingredients.—1 pint of white stock, thickening of flour and butter, or white roux, a faggot of savoury herbs, including parsley, 6 chopped mushrooms, 6 green onions. *Mode.*—Put the stock into a stewpan with the herbs, onions, and mushrooms, and let it simmer very gently for about ½ hour; stir in sufficient thickening to make it of a proper consistency; let it boil for a few minutes, then skim off all the fat, strain and serve. This sauce, with the addition of a little cream, is now frequently called velouté. *Time.*—½ hour. *Average cost,* for this quantity, 6d.

Note.—If poultry trimmings are a hand, the stock should be made of these The above sauce should not be mad too thick, as it does not then admit the fat being nicely removed.

SAUCE FOR WILDFOWL.

Ingredients.—1 glass of port win 1 tablespoonful of Leamington sauc 1 tablespoonful of mushroom ketchu 1 tablespoonful of lemon-juice, 1 slice lemon-peel, 1 large shalot cut in slice 1 blade of mace, cayenne to taste. *Mod* —Put all the ingredients into a stewpa set it over the fire, and let it simmer f about 5 minutes; then strain and ser the sauce in a tureen. *Time.*—5 minute *Average cost,* for this quantity, 8d.

SAUSAGE-MEAT, Fried.

Ingredients.—To every 1 lb. of lea pork, add ¾ lb. of fat bacon, ½ oz. of sal 1 saltspoonful of pepper, ¼ teaspoonful grated nutmeg, 1 teaspoonful of mince parsley. *Mode.*—Remove from the por all skin, gristle, and bone, and chop finely with the bacon; add the remainin ingredients, and carefully mix altogethe Pound it well in a mortar, make it int convenient-sized cakes, flour these, an fry them a nice brown for about 1 minutes. This is a very simple metho of making sausage-meat, and on tri will prove very good, its great recom mendation being, that it is so easil made. *Time.*—10 minutes. *Seasonab* from September to March.

SAUSAGE - MEAT STUFFIN FOR TURKEYS.

Ingredients.—6 oz. of lean pork, 6 o of fat pork, both weighed after bein chopped (beef-suet may be substitute for the latter), 2 oz. of bread-crumbs 1 small tablespoonful of minced sage, blade of pounded mace, salt and peppe to taste, 1 egg. *Mode.*—Chop the mea and fat very finely, mix with them th other ingredients, taking care that th whole is thoroughly incorporated. Mois ten with the egg, and the stuffing will b ready for use. Equal quantities of thi stuffing and forcemeat will be found t answer very well, as the herbs, lemon peel, &c., in the latter, impart a ver delicious flavour to the sausage-meat As preparations, however, like stuffing and forcemeats, are matters to be de

Sausage or Meat Rolls

cided by individual palates, they must be left, to a great extent, to the discrimination of the cook, who should study her employer's taste in this as in every other respect. *Average cost, 9d. Sufficient* for a small turkey.

SAUSAGE OR MEAT ROLLS.

Ingredients.—1 lb. of puff-paste, sausage-meat, the yolk of 1 egg. *Mode.*—Make 1 lb. of puff-paste; roll it out to the thickness of about ½ inch, or rather less, and divide it into 8, 10, or 12 squares, according to the size the rolls are intended to be. Place some sausage-meat on one-half of each square, wet the edges of the paste, and fold it over the meat; slightly press the edges together, and trim them neatly with a knife. Brush the rolls over with the yolk of an egg, and bake them in a well-heated oven for about ½ hour, or longer should they be very large. The remains of cold chicken and ham, minced and seasoned, as also cold veal or beef, make very good rolls. *Time.*—½ hour, or longer if the rolls are large. *Average cost, 1s. 6d. Sufficient.*—1 lb. of paste for 10 or 12 rolls. *Seasonable,* with sausage-meat, from September to March or April.

SAUSAGES, Beef.

Ingredients.—To every lb. of suet allow 2 lbs. of lean beef, seasoning to taste of salt, pepper, and mixed spices. *Mode.*—Clear the suet from skin, and chop that and the beef as finely as possible; season with pepper, salt, and spices, and mix the whole well together. Make it into flat cakes, and fry of a nice brown. Many persons pound the meat in a mortar after it is chopped; but this is not necessary when the meat is minced finely. *Time.*—10 minutes. *Average cost,* for this quantity, 1s. 6d. *Seasonable* at any time.

SAUSAGES, Fried.

Ingredients.—Sausages: a small piece of butter. *Mode.*—Prick the sausages with a fork (this prevents them from bursting), and put them into a frying-

FRIED SAUSAGES.

pan with a small piece of butter. Keep moving the pan about, and turn the

Sausages, Veal

sausages 3 or 4 times. In from 10 to 12 minutes they will be sufficiently cooked, unless they are *very large,* when a little more time should be allowed for them. Dish them with or without a piece of toast under them, and serve very hot. In some counties, sausages are boiled and served on toast. They should be plunged into boiling water, and simmered for about 10 or 12 minutes. *Time.*—10 to 12 minutes. *Average cost,* 10d. per lb. *Seasonable.*—Good from September to March.

Note.—Sometimes, in close warm weather, sausages very soon turn sour; to prevent this, put them in the oven for a few minutes with a small piece of butter to keep them moist. When wanted for table, they will not require so long frying as uncooked sausages.

SAUSAGES, Pork (Author's Oxford Recipe).

Ingredients.—1 lb. of pork, fat and lean, without skin or gristle; 1 lb. of lean veal, 1 lb. of beef suet, ½ lb. of bread-crumbs, the rind of ½ lemon, 1 small nutmeg, 6 sage-leaves, 1 teaspoonful of pepper, 2 teaspoonfuls of salt, ½ teaspoonful of savory, ¼ teaspoonful of marjoram. *Mode.*—Chop the pork, veal, and suet finely together, add the bread-crumbs, lemon-peel (which should be well minced), and a small nutmeg grated. Wash and chop the sage-leaves very finely; add these with the remaining ingredients to the sausage-meat, and when thoroughly mixed, either put the meat into skins, or, when wanted for table, form it into little cakes, which should be floured and fried. *Average cost,* for this quantity, 2s. 6d. *Sufficient* for about 30 moderate-sized sausages. *Seasonable* from October to March.

SAUSAGES, Veal.

Ingredients.—Equal quantities of fat bacon and lean veal; to every lb. of meat, allow 1 teaspoonful of minced-sage, salt and pepper to taste. *Mode.*—Chop the meat and bacon finely, and to every lb. allow the above proportion of very finely-minced sage; add a seasoning of pepper and salt, mix the whole well together, make it into flat cakes, and fry a nice brown. *Seasonable.* from March to October.

Savoy Cake

SAVOY CAKE.

Ingredients.—The weight of 4 eggs in pounded loaf sugar, the weight of 7 in flour, a little grated lemon-rind, or essence of almonds, or orange-flower water. *Mode.*—Break the 7 eggs, putting the yolks into one basin and the whites into another. Whisk the former, and mix with them the sugar, the grated lemon-rind, or any other flavouring to taste; beat them well together, and add the whites of the eggs, whisked to a froth. Put in the flour by degrees, continuing to beat the mixture for ¼ hour, butter a mould, pour in the cake, and bake it from 1¼ to 1½ hour. This is a very nice cake for desert, and may be iced for a supper table, or cut into slices and spread with jam, which converts it into sandwiches. *Time.*—1¼ to 1½ hour. *Average cost,* 1s. *Sufficient* for 1 cake. *Seasonable* at any time.

SEA-BREAM, Baked.

Ingredients.—1 bream. Seasoning to taste of salt, pepper, and cayenne; ¼ lb. of butter. *Mode.*—Well wash the bream, but do not remove the scales, and wipe away all moisture with a nice dry cloth. Season it inside and out with salt, pepper, and cayenne, and lay it in a baking-dish. Place the butter, in small pieces, upon the fish, and bake for rather more than ½ an hour. To stuff this fish before baking, will be found a great improvement. *Time.*—Rather more than ½ an hour. *Seasonable* in summer.

Note.—This fish may be broiled over a nice clear fire, and served with a good brown gravy or white sauce, or it may be stewed in wine.

SEA-KALE, Boiled.

Ingredients.—To each ½ gallon of water allow one heaped tablespoonful of salt. *Mode.*—Well wash the kale, cut away any worm-eaten pieces, and tie it into small bunches; put it into *boiling* water, salted in the above proportion, and let it boil quickly until tender. Take it out, drain, untie the bunches, and serve with plain melted butter or

BOILED SEA-KALE.

white sauce, a little of which may be

Seed-Cake, a Very Good

poured over the kale. Sea-kale may also be parboiled and stewed in good brown gravy: it will then take about ½ hour altogether. *Time.*—15 minutes; when liked very thoroughly done, allow an extra 5 minutes. *Average cost,* in full season, 9d. per basket. *Sufficient.*—Allow 12 heads for 4 or 5 persons. *Seasonable* from February to June.

SEED BISCUITS.

Ingredients.—1 lb. of flour, ¼ lb. of sifted sugar, ¼ lb. of butter, ½ oz. of caraway seeds, 3 eggs. *Mode.*—Beat the butter to a cream; stir in the flour, sugar, and caraway seeds; and when these ingredients are well mixed, add the eggs, which should be well whisked. Roll out the paste, with a round cutter shape out the biscuits, and bake them in a moderate oven from 10 to 15 minutes. The tops of the biscuits may be brushed over with a little milk or the white of an egg, and then a little sugar strewn over. *Time.*—10 or 15 minutes. *Average cost,* 1s. *Sufficient* to make 3 dozen biscuits. *Seasonable* at any time.

SEED-CAKE, Common.

Ingredients.—½ quartern of dough, ¼ lb. of good dripping, 6 oz. of moist sugar, ½ oz. of caraway seeds, 1 egg. *Mode.*—If the dough is sent in from the bakers, put it in a basin covered with a cloth, and set it in a warm place to rise. Then with a wooden spoon beat the dripping to a liquid; add it, with the other ingredients, to the dough, and beat it until everything is very thoroughly mixed. Put it into a buttered tin, and bake the cake for rather more than 2 hours. *Time.*—Rather more than 2 hours. *Average cost,* 8d. *Seasonable* at any time.

SEED-CAKE, a Very Good.

Ingredients.—1 lb. of butter, 6 eggs, ¾ lb. of sifted sugar, pounded mace and grated nutmeg to taste, 1 lb. of flour, ¾ oz. of caraway seeds, 1 wineglassful of brandy. *Mode.*—Beat the butter to a cream; dredge in the flour; add the sugar, mace, nutmeg, and caraway seeds, and mix these ingredients well together. Whisk the eggs, stir to them the brandy, and beat the cake again for 10 minutes. Put it into a tin lined with buttered

Semolina Pudding, Baked.

paper, and bake it from 1½ to 2 hours. This cake would be equally nice made with currants, and omitting the caraway seeds. *Time.*—1½ to 2 hours. *Average cost,* 2*s.* 6*d.* *Seasonable* at any time.

SEMOLINA PUDDING, Baked.

Ingredients.—3 oz. of semolina, 1½ pint of milk, ¼ lb. of sugar, 12 bitter almonds, 3 oz. of butter, 4 eggs. *Mode.*—Flavour the milk with the bitter almonds, by infusing them in it by the side of the fire for about ½ hour; then strain it, and mix with it the semolina, sugar, and butter. Stir these ingredients over the fire for a few minutes; then take them off, and gradually mix in the eggs, which should be well beaten. Butter a pie-dish, line the edges with puff-paste, put in the pudding, and bake in rather a slow oven from 40 to 50 minutes. Serve with custard sauce or stewed fruit, a little of which may be poured over the pudding. *Time.*—40 to 50 minutes. *Average cost,* 1*s.* 2*d.* *Sufficient* for 5 or 6 persons. *Seasonable* at any time.

SEMOLINA SOUP.

Ingredients.—5 oz. of semolina, 2 quarts of boiling stock. *Mode.*—Drop the semolina into the boiling stock, and keep stirring, to prevent its burning. Simmer gently for half an hour, and serve. *Time.* ½ an hour. *Average cost,* 10*d.* per quart, or 4*d.* *Sufficient* for 8 persons. *Seasonable* all the year.

SEPTEMBER—BILLS OF FARE.

Dinner for 18 Persons.

First Course.

Red Mullet & Italian Sauce.	Julienne Soup, removed by Brill & Shrimp Sauce.	
	Vase of Flowers.	Fried Eels.
	Giblet Soup, removed by Salmon and Lobster Sauce.	

September—Bills of Fare

Entrées.

Fillets of Chicken and Truffles.	Lamb Cutlets and French Beans.	
	Vase of Flowers.	Oysters au gratin.
	Sweetbreads and Tomato Sauce.	

Second Course.

Chickens à la Béchamel.	Saddle of Mutton.	
	Veal-and-Ham Pie.	Braised Goose.
	Vase of Flowers.	
	Broiled Ham, garnished with Cauliflowers.	
	Fillet of Veal.	

Third Course.

Custards.	Noyeau Jelly. Plum Tart.	Partridges, removed by Plum-pudding.	Lemon Cream.	Apple Tart.
		Compôte of Greengages.		
		Vase of Flowers.		
		Pastry Sandwiches.	Custards.	
		Grouse & Bread Sauce, removed by Nesselrode Pudding.		

Dessert and Ices.

Dinner for 12 persons.

First Course.—Mock-turtle soup; soup à la Jardinière; salmon and lobster sauce; fried whitings; stewed eels. *Entrées*—Veal cutlets; scalloped oysters; curried fowl; grilled mushrooms. *Second Course.*—Haunch of mutton; boiled calf's head à la Béchamel; braised ham roast fowls aux Cressons. *Third Course*—Leveret; grouse; cabinet pudding. iced pudding; compôte of plums: dam

September, Plain Family Dinners

son tart; cream; fruit jelly; prawns; lobster salad. Dessert and ices.

Dinner for 8 persons.

First Course.—Flemish soup; turbot, garnished with fried smelts; red mullet and Italian sauce. *Entrées.*—Tendrons de veau and truffles; lamb cutlets and sauce piquante. *Second Course.*—Loin of veal à la Béchamel; roast haunch of venison; braised ham; grouse pie; vegetables. *Third Course.* — Roast hare; plum tart; whipped cream; punch jelly; compôte of damsons; marrow pudding; dessert.

Dinner for 6 persons.

First Course.—Game soup; crimp skate; slices of salmon à la genévèse. *Entrées.* — Fricasseed sweetbreads; savoury rissoles. *Second Course.*—Sirloin of beef and horseradish sauce; boiled leg of mutton and caper sauce; vegetables. *Third Course.*—Roast partridges; charlotte Russe; apricots and rice; fruit jelly; cabinet pudding; dessert.

First Course. — Thick gravy soup; fillets of turbot à la crême; stewed eels. *Entrées.*—Vol-au-vent of lobster; salmi of grouse. *Second Course.*—Haunch of venison; rump of beef à la Jardinière; hare, boned and larded, with mushrooms. *Third Course.*—Roast grouse; apricot blancmange; compôte of peaches; plum-tart; custards; plum-pudding; dessert.

SEPTEMBER, Plain Family Dinners for.

Sunday.—1. Julienne soup. 2. Roast ribs of beef, Yorkshire pudding, horseradish sauce, French beans, and potatoes. 3. Greengage pudding, vanilla cream.

Monday.—1. Crimped skate and crab sauce. 2. Cold beef and salad, small veal-and-ham pie. 3. Vegetable marrow and white sauce.

Tuesday. — 1. Fried soles, melted butter. 2. Bowled fowls, parsley-and-butter; bacon-cheek, garnished with French beans; beef rissoles, made from remains of cold beef. 3. Plum tart and cream.

Wednesday.—1. Boiled round of beef, carrots, turnips, and suet dumplings; marrow on toast. 2. Baked damsons and rice.

Thursday.—1. Vegetable soup, made from liquor that beef was boiled in. 2.

September, Things in Season

Lamb cutlets and cucumbers, cold beef and salad. 3. Apple pudding.

Friday.—1. Baked soles. 2. Bubble-and-squeak, made from cold beef; veal cutlets and rolled bacon. 3. Damson tart.

Saturday.—1. Irish stew, rump-steaks and oyster-sauce. 2. Somersetshire dumplings.

Sunday. — 1. Fried filleted soles and anchovy sauce. 2. Roast leg of mutton, brown onion sauce, French beans, and potatoes; half calf's head, tongue, and brains. 3. Plum-tart; custards, in glasses.

Monday.—1. Vegetable-marrow soup. 2. Calf's head à la maître d'hôtel, from remains of cold head; boiled brisket of beef and vegetables. 3. Stewed fruit and baked rice pudding.

Tuesday.—1. Roast fowls and watercresses; boiled bacon, garnished with tufts of cauliflower; hashed mutton, from remains of mutton of Sunday. 2. Baked plum-pudding.

Wednesday.—1. Boiled knuckle of veal and rice, turnips, potatoes; small ham, garnished with French beans. 2. Baked apple pudding.

Thursday.—1. Brill and shrimp sauce. 2. Roast hare, gravy, and red-currant jelly; mutton cutlets and mashed potatoes. 3. Scalloped oysters, instead of pudding.

Friday. — 1. Small roast loin of mutton; the remains of hare, jugged; vegetable marrow and potatoes. 2. Damson pudding.

Saturday.—1. Rump-steaks, broiled, and oyster-sauce, mashed potatoes; veal-and-ham pie,—the ham may be cut from that boiled on Wednesday, if not all eaten cold for breakfast. 2. Lemon pudding.

SEPTEMBER, Things in Season.

Fish.—Brill, carp, cod, eels, flounders, lobsters, mullet, oysters, plaice, prawns, skate, soles, turbot, whiting, whitebait.

Meat.—Beef, lamb, mutton, pork, veal.

Poultry. — Chickens, ducks, fowls, geese, larks, pigeons, pullets, rabbits, teal, turkeys.

Game. — Blackcock, buck venison, grouse, hares, partridges, pheasants.

Vegetables. — Artichokes, asparagus, beans, cabbage sprouts, carrots, celery, lettuces, mushrooms, onions, pease, potatoes, salads, sea-kale, sprouts, tomatoes, turnips, vegetable marrows, various herbs.

Shad, to Dress

Fruit.—Bullaces, damsons, figs, filberts, grapes, melons, morella cherries, mulberries, nectarines, peaches, pears, plums, quinces, walnuts.

SHAD, to Dress.

Ingredients.—1 shad, oil, pepper, and salt. *Mode.*—Scale, empty and wash the fish carefully, and make two or three incisions across the back. Season it with pepper and salt, and let it remain in oil for ½ hour. Broil it on both sides over a clear fire, and serve with caper sauce. This fish is much esteemed by the French, and by them is considered excellent. *Time.*—Nearly 1 hour. *Average cost.* —Seldom bought. *Seasonable* from April to June.

SHEEP'S BRAINS, en Matelote (an Entrée).

Ingredients.—6 sheep's brains, vinegar, salt, a few slices of bacon, 1 small onion, 2 cloves, a small bunch of parsley, sufficient stock or weak broth to cover the brains, 1 tablespoonful of lemon-juice, matelote sauce. *Mode.*—Detach the brains from the head without breaking them, and put them into a pan of warm water; remove the skin, and let them remain for two hours. Have ready a saucepan of boiling water, add a little vinegar and salt, and put in the brains. When they are quite firm, take them out and put them into very cold water. Place 2 or 3 slices of bacon in a stewpan, put in the brains, the onion stuck with 2 cloves, the parsley, and a good seasoning of pepper and salt; cover with stock, or weak broth, and boil them gently for about 25 minutes. Have ready some croûtons; arrange these in the dish alternately with the brains, and cover with a matelote sauce, to which has been added the above proportion of lemon-juice. *Time.*—25 minutes. *Average cost,* 1s. 6d. *Sufficient* for 6 persons. *Seasonable* at any time.

SHEEP'S FEET or TROTTERS (Soyer's Recipe).

Ingredients.—12 feet, ¼ lb. of beef or mutton suet, 2 onions, 1 carrot, 2 bay-leaves, 2 sprigs of thyme, 1 oz. of salt, ¼ oz. of pepper, 2 tablespoonfuls of flour, 2½ quarts of water, ¼ lb. of fresh butter, 1 teaspoonful of salt, 1 teaspoonful of flour, ¼ teaspoonful of pepper, a

Shortbread, Scotch

little grated nutmeg, the juice of 1 lemon, 1 gill of milk, the yolks of 2 eggs. *Mode.*—Have the feet cleaned, and the long bone extracted from them. Put the suet into a stewpan, with the onions and carrot sliced, the bay-leaves, thyme, salt, and pepper, and let these simmer for 5 minutes. Add 2 tablespoonfuls of flour and the water, and keep stirring till it boils; then put in the feet. Let these simmer for 3 hours, or until perfectly tender, and take them and lay them on a sieve. Mix together, on a plate, with the back of a spoon, butter, salt, flour (1 teaspoonful), pepper, nutmeg, and lemon-juice as above, and put the feet, with a gill of milk, into a stewpan. When very hot, add the butter, &c., and stir continually till melted. Now mix the yolks of 2 eggs with 5 tablespoonfuls of milk; stir this to the other ingredients, keep moving the pan over the fire continually for a minute or two, but do not allow it to boil after the eggs are added. Serve in a very hot dish, and garnish with croûtons, or sippets of toasted bread. *Time.* —3 hours. *Average cost,* 1s. 6d. *Sufficient* for 4 persons. *Seasonable* at any time.

SHEEP'S HEAD.

Ingredients.—1 sheep's head, sufficient water to cover it, 3 carrots, 3 turnips, 2 or 3 parsnips, 3 onions, a small bunch of parsley, 1 teaspoonful of pepper, 3 teaspoonfuls of salt, ¼ lb. of Scotch oatmeal. *Mode.*—Clean the head well, and let it soak in warm water for 2 hours, to get rid of the blood; put it into a saucepan, with sufficient cold water to cover it, and when it boils, add the vegetables, peeled and sliced, and the remaining ingredients; before adding the oatmeal, mix it to a smooth batter with a little of the liquor. Keep stirring till it boils up; then shut the saucepan closely, and let it stew gently for 1½ or 2 hours. It may be thickened with rice or barley, but oatmeal is preferable. *Time.*—1½ to 2 hours. *Average cost,* 8d. each. *Sufficient* for 3 persons. *Seasonable* at any time.

SHORTBREAD, Scotch.

Ingredients.—2 lbs. of flour, 1 lb. of butter, ¼ lb. of pounded loaf sugar, ½ oz. of caraway seeds, 1 oz. of sweet almonds, a few strips of candied orange-peel.

Shrimp Sauce

Mode.—Beat the butter to a cream, gradually dredge in the flour, and add the sugar, caraway seeds, and sweet almonds, which should be blanched and cut into small pieces. Work the paste until it is quite smooth, and divide it into six pieces. Put each cake on a separate piece of paper, roll the paste out square to the thickness of about an

SHORTBREAD.

inch, and pinch it upon all sides. Prick it well, and ornament with one or two strips of candied orange-peel. Put the cakes into a good oven, and bake them from 25 to 30 minutes. *Time.*—25 to 30 minutes. *Average cost,* for this quantity, 2s. *Sufficient* to make 6 cakes. *Seasonable* at any time.

Note.—Where the flavour of the caraway seeds is disliked, omit them, and add rather a larger proportion of candied peel.

SHRIMP SAUCE, for Various Kinds of Fish.

Ingredients.—½ pint of melted butter, ¼ pint of picked shrimps, cayenne to taste. *Mode.*—Make the melted butter very smoothly, shell the shrimps (sufficient to make ¼ pint when picked), and put them into the butter; season with cayenne, and let the sauce just simmer, but do not allow it to boil. When liked, a teaspoonful of anchovy sauce may be added. *Time.*—1 minute to simmer. *Average cost,* 6d. *Sufficient* for 3 or 4 persons.

SHRIMPS OR PRAWNS, to Boil.

Ingredients.—¼ lb. salt to each gallon of water. *Mode.*—Prawns should be very red, and have no spawn under the tail; much depends on their freshness and the way in which they are cooked. Throw them into boiling water, salted as above, and keep them boiling for about 7 or 8 minutes. Shrimps should be done in the same way; but less time must be allowed. It may easily be known when they are done by their changing colour. Care should be taken that they are not over-boiled, as they then become tasteless and indigestible. *Time.*—Prawns,

Skate, Boiled

about 8 minutes; shrimps, about 5 minutes. *Average cost,* prawns, 2s. per lb.; shrimps, 6d. per pint. *Seasonable* all the year.

SHRIMPS OR PRAWNS, Buttered.

Ingredients.—1 pint of picked prawns or shrimps, ¾ pint of stock, thickening of butter and flour; salt, cayenne, and nutmeg to taste. *Mode.*—Pick the prawns or shrimps, and put them in a stewpan with the stock; add a thickening of butter and flour; season, and simmer gently for 3 minutes. Serve on a dish garnished with fried bread or toasted sippets. Cream sauce may be substituted for the gravy. *Time.*—3 minutes. *Average cost* for this quantity, 1s. 4d.

SHRIMPS, Potted.

Ingredients.—1 pint of shelled shrimps, ¼ lb. of fresh butter, 1 blade of pounded mace, cayenne to taste; when liked, a little nutmeg. *Mode.*—Have ready a pint of picked shrimps, and put them, with the other ingredients, into a stewpan; let them heat gradually in the butter, but do not let it boil. Pour into small pots, and when cold, cover with melted butter, and carefully exclude the air. *Time.*—¼ hour to soak in the butter. *Average cost* for this quantity, 1s. 3d.

SKATE, to choose.

This fish should be chosen for its firmness, breadth, and thickness, and should have a creamy appearance. When crimped, it should not be kept longer than a day or two, as all kinds of crimped fish soon become sour. Thornback is often substituted for skate, but is very inferior in quality to the true skate.

SKATE, Boiled.

Ingredients.—¼ lb. of salt to each gallon of water. *Mode.*—Cleanse and skin the skate, lay it in a fish-kettle, with sufficient water to cover it, salted in the above proportion. Let it simmer very gently till done; then dish it on a hot napkin, and serve with shrimp, lobster, or caper sauce. *Time.*—According to size, from ½ to 1 hour. *Average cost,* 4d. per lb. *Seasonable* from August to April.

Skate, Crimped

SKATE, Crimped.

Ingredients—½ lb. of salt to each gallon of water. *Mode.*—Clean, skin, and cut the fish into slices, which roll and tie round with string. Have ready some water highly salted, put in the fish, and boil till it is done. Drain well, remove the string, dish on a hot napkin, and serve with the same sauces as above. Skate should never be eaten out of season, as it is liable to produce diarrhœa and other diseases. It may be dished without a napkin, and the sauce poured over. *Time.*—About 20 minutes. *Average cost,* 4*d.* per lb. *Seasonable* from August to April.

SKATE, With Caper Sauce (à la Française).

Ingredients.—2 or 3 slices of skate, ½ pint of vinegar, 2 oz. of salt, ½ teaspoonful of pepper, 1 sliced onion, a small bunch of parsley, 2 bay-leaves, 2 or 3 sprigs of thyme, sufficient water to cover the fish. *Mode.*—Put in a fish-kettle all the above ingredients, and simmer the skate in them till tender. When it is done, skin it neatly, and pour over it some of the liquor in which it has been boiling. Drain it, put it on a hot dish, pour over it caper sauce, and send some of the latter to table in a tureen. *Time.*—½ hour. *Average cost,* 4*d.* per lb. *Seasonable* from August to April.

Note.—Skate may also be served with onion sauce, or parsley and butter.

SKATE, Small, Fried.

Ingredients.—Skate, sufficient vinegar to cover them, salt and pepper to taste, 1 sliced onion, a small bunch of parsley, the juice of ½ lemon, hot dripping. *Mode.*—Cleanse the skate, lay them in a dish, with sufficient vinegar to cover them; add the salt, pepper, onion, parsley, and lemon-juice, and let the fish remain in this pickle for ½ hour. Then drain them well, flour them, and fry of a nice brown, in hot dripping. They may be served either with or without sauce. Skate is not good if dressed too fresh, unless it is crimped; it should, therefore, be kept for a day, but not long enough to produce a disagreeable smell. *Time.*—10 minutes. *Average cost,* 4*d.* per lb. *Seasonable* from August to April.

Snipes, to Dress

SMELTS.

When good, this fish is of a fine silvery appearance, and when alive, their backs are of a dark brown shade, which, after death, fades to a light fawn. They ought to have a refreshing fragrance, resembling that of a cucumber.

SMELTS, to Bake.

Ingredients.—12 smelts, bread-crumbs, ¼ lb. of fresh butter, 2 blades of pounded mace ; salt and cayenne to taste. *Mode.*—Wash, and dry the fish thoroughly in a cloth, and arrange them nicely in a flat baking-dish. Cover them with fine bread-crumbs, and place little pieces of butter all over them. Season and bake for 15 minutes. Just before serving, add a squeeze of lemon-juice, and garnish with fried parsley and cut lemon. *Time.*—¼ hour. *Average cost,* 2*s.* per dozen. *Seasonable* from October to May. *Sufficient* for 6 persons.

SMELTS, to Fry.

Ingredients.—Egg and bread-crumbs, a little flour ; boiling lard. *Mode.*—Smelts should be very fresh, and not washed more than is necessary to clean them. Dry them in a cloth, lightly flour, dip them in egg, and sprinkle over with very fine bread-crumbs, and put them into boiling lard. Fry of a nice pale brown, and be careful not to take off the light roughness of the crumbs, or their beauty will be spoiled. Dry them before the fire on a drainer, and serve with plain melted butter. This fish is often used as a garnishing. *Time.*—5 minutes. *Average cost,* 2*s.* per dozen. *Seasonable* from October to May.

SNIPES, to Dress.

Ingredients. — Snipes, butter, flour, toast. *Mode.*—These, like woodcocks, should be dressed without being drawn. Pluck, and wipe them outside, and truss them with the head under the wing, having previously skinned that and the neck. Twist the legs at the first joint, press the feet upon the thighs, and pass a skewer through these and the body. Place four on a

ROAST SNIPE.

skewer, tie them on to the jack or spit, and roast before a clear fire for about

Snipes, to Carve

¼ hour. Put some pieces of buttered toast into the dripping-pan to catch the trails; flour and froth the birds nicely, dish the pieces of toast with the snipes on them, and pour round, but not over them, a little good brown gravy. They should be sent to table very hot and expeditiously, or they will not be worth eating. *Time.*—About ¼ hour. *Average cost,* 1s. 6d. to 2s. the brace. *Sufficient.*— 4 for a dish. *Seasonable* from November to February.

Note.—Ortolans are trussed and dressed in the same manner.

SNIPES, to Carve.

One of these small but delicious birds may be given, whole, to a gentleman; but, in helping a lady, it will be better to cut them quite through the centre, from 1 to 2, completely dividing them into equal and like portions, and put only one half on the plate.

SNIPE.

SNOW-CAKE.

Ingredients.—½ lb. of *tous-les-mois,* ¼ lb. of white pounded sugar, ¼ lb. of fresh or washed salt butter, 1 egg, the juice of 1 lemon. *Mode.*—Beat the butter to a cream; then add the egg, previously well beaten, and then the other ingredients; if the mixture is not light, add another egg, and beat for ¼ hour, until it turns white and light. Line a flat tin, with raised edges, with a sheet of buttered paper; pour in the cake, and put it into the oven. It must be rather slow, and the cake not allowed to brown at all. If the oven is properly heated, 1 to 1¼ hour will be found long enough to bake it. Let it cool a few minutes, then with a clean sharp knife cut it into small square pieces, which should be gently removed to a large flat dish to cool before putting away. This will keep for several weeks. *Time.* —1 to 1¼ hour. *Average cost,* 1s. 3d. *Seasonable* at any time.

SNOW-CAKE (a genuine Scotch Recipe).

Ingredients.—1 lb. of arrowroot, ½ lb. of pounded white sugar, ½ lb. of butter, the whites of 6 eggs; flavouring to taste, of essence of almonds, or vanilla, or lemon. *Mode.*—Beat the butter to a cream; stir in the sugar and arrowroot gradually, at the same time beating the

Soda-Cake

mixture. Whisk the whites of the eggs to a stiff froth, add them to the other ingredients, and beat well for 20 minutes. Put in whichever of the above flavourings may be preferred; pour the cake into a buttered mould or tin, and bake it in a moderate oven from 1 to 1½ hour. *Time.*—1 to 1½ hour. *Average cost,* with the best Bermuda arrowroot, 4s. 6d.; with St. Vincent ditto, 2s. 9d. *Sufficient* to make a moderate-sized cake. *Seasonable* at any time.

SODA-BISCUITS.

Ingredients.—1 lb. of flour, ½ lb. of pounded loaf sugar, ¼ lb. of fresh butter, 2 eggs, 1 small teaspoonful of carbonate of soda. *Mode.*—Put the flour (which should be perfectly dry) into a basin, rub in the butter, add the sugar, and mix these ingredients well together. Whisk the eggs, stir them into the mixture, and beat it well, until everything is well incorporated. Quickly stir in the soda, roll the paste out until it is about ½ inch thick, cut it into small round cakes with a tin cutter, and bake them from 12 to 18 minutes in rather a brisk oven. After the soda is added, great expedition is necessary in rolling and cutting out the paste, and in putting the biscuits *immediately* into the oven, or they will be heavy. *Time.*—12 to 18 minutes. *Average cost,* 1s. *Sufficient* to make about 3 dozen cakes. *Seasonable* at any time.

SODA-BREAD.

Ingredients.—To every 2 lbs. of flour allow 1 teaspoonful of tartaric acid, 1 teaspoonful of salt, 1 teaspoonful of carbonate of soda, 2 breakfast-cupfuls of cold milk. *Mode.*—Let the tartaric acid and salt be reduced to the finest possible powder; then mix them well with the flour. Dissolve the soda in the milk, and pour it several times from one basin to another, before adding it to the flour. Work the whole quickly into a light dough, divide it into 2 loaves, and put them into a well-heated oven immediately, and bake for an hour. Sour milk or buttermilk may be used, but then a little less acid will be needed. *Time.*—1 hour.

SODA-CAKE.

Ingredients.—¼ lb. of butter, 1 lb. of flour, ½ lb. of currants, ½ lb. of moist

Sole or Cod Pie

sugar, 1 teacupful of milk, 3 eggs, 1 tea-spoonful of carbonate of soda. *Mode.*—Rub the butter into the flour, add the currants and sugar, and mix these ingredients well together. Whisk the eggs well, stir them to the flour, &c., with the milk, in which the soda should be previously dissolved, and beat the whole up together with a wooden spoon or beater. Divide the dough into two pieces, put them into buttered moulds or cake-tins, and bake in a moderate oven for nearly an hour. The mixture must be extremely well beaten up, and not allowed to stand after the soda is added to it, but must be placed in the oven immediately. Great care must also be taken that the cakes are quite done through, which may be ascertained by thrusting a knife into the middle of them : if the blade looks bright when withdrawn, they are done. If the tops acquire too much colour before the inside is sufficiently baked, cover them over with a piece of clean white paper, to prevent them from burning. *Time.*—1 hour. *Average cost*, 1s. 6d. *Sufficient* to make 2 small cakes. *Seasonable* at any time.

SOLE OR COD PIE.

Ingredients.—The remains of cold boiled sole or cod, seasoning to taste of pepper, salt, and pounded mace, 1 dozen oysters to each lb. of fish, 3 tablespoonfuls of white stock, 1 teacupful of cream thickened with flour, puff paste. *Mode.*—Clear the fish from the bones, lay it in a pie-dish, and between each layer put a few oysters and a little seasoning ; add the stock, and, when liked, a small quantity of butter ; cover with puff paste, and bake for ½ hour. Boil the cream with sufficient flour to thicken it ; pour in the pie, and serve. *Time.*—½ hour. *Average cost* for this quantity, 10d. *Sufficient* for 4 persons. *Seasonable* at any time.

SOLES, to Choose.

This fish should be both thick and firm. If the skin is difficult to be taken off, and the flesh looks grey, it is good.

SOLES, Baked.

Ingredients.—2 soles, ¼ lb. of butter, egg, and bread-crumbs, minced parsley, 1 glass of sherry, lemon-juice ; cayenne and salt to taste. *Mode.*—Clean, skin, and well wash the fish, and dry them

Soles, Filleted, à l'Italienne

thoroughly in a cloth. Brush them over with egg, sprinkle with bread-crumbs mixed with a little minced parsley, lay them in a large flat baking-dish, white side uppermost ; or if it will not hold the two soles, they may each be laid on a dish by itself ; but they must not be put one on the top of the other. Melt the butter, and pour it over the whole, and bake for 20 minutes. Take a portion of the gravy that flows from the fish, add the wine, lemon-juice, and seasoning, give it one boil, skim, pour it *under* the fish, and serve. *Time.*—20 minutes. *Average cost*, 1s. to 2s. per pair. *Sufficient* for 4 or 5 persons. *Seasonable* at any time.

SOLES, Boiled.

Ingredients.—¼ lb. salt to each gallon of water. *Mode.*—Cleanse and wash the fish carefully, cut off the fins, but do not skin it. Lay it in a fish-kettle, with sufficient cold water to cover it, salted in the above proportion. Let it gradually come to a boil, and keep it simmering for a few minutes, according to the size of the fish. Dish it on a hot napkin after well draining it, and garnish with parsley and cut lemon. Shrimp, or lobster sauce, and plain melted butter, are usually sent to table with this dish. *Time.*—After the water boils, 7 minutes for a middling-sized sole. *Average cost*, 1s. to 2s. per pair. *Sufficient.*—1 middling-sized sole for two persons. *Seasonable* at any time.

SOLES, Boiled or Fried, to Help.

The usual way of helping this fish is to cut it right through, bone and all, distributing it in nice and not too large pieces. A moderately-sized sole will be sufficient for three slices ; namely, the head, middle, and tail. The guests should be asked which of these they prefer. A small one will only give two slices. If the sole is very large, the upper side may be raised from the bone, and then divided into pieces ; and the under side afterwards served in the same way.

In helping Filleted Soles, one fillet is given to each person.

SOLES, Filleted, à l'Italienne.

Ingredients. — 2 soles ; salt, pepper, and grated nutmeg to taste ; egg and

Soles, Fricasseed

bread-crumbs, butter, the juice of 1 lemon. *Mode.*—Skin, and carefully wash the soles, separate the meat from the bone, and divide each fillet in two pieces. Brush them over with white of egg, sprinkle with bread-crumbs and seasoning, and put them in a baking-dish. Place small pieces of butter over the whole, and bake for ½ hour. When they are nearly done, squeeze the juice of a lemon over them, and serve on a dish, with Italian sauce (*see* Sauces) poured over. *Time.*—½ hour. *Average cost,* from 1s. to 2s. per pair. *Sufficient* for 4 or 5 persons. *Seasonable* at any time.

Whiting may be dressed in the same manner, and will be found very delicious.

SOLES, Fricasseed.

Ingredients.—2 middling-sized soles, 1 small one, ½ teaspoonful of chopped lemon-peel, 1 teaspoonful of chopped parsley, a little grated bread ; salt, pepper, and nutmeg to taste ; 1 egg, 2 oz. butter, ½ pint of good gravy, 2 tablespoonfuls of port wine, cayenne and lemon-juice to taste. *Mode.*—Fry the soles of a nice brown, and drain them well from fat. Take all the meat from the small sole, chop it fine, and mix with it the lemon-peel, parsley, bread, and seasoning ; work altogether, with the yolk of an egg and the butter ; make this into small balls, and fry them. Thicken the gravy with a dessertspoonful of flour, add the port wine, cayenne, and lemon-juice ; lay in the 2 soles and balls ; let them simmer gently for 5 minutes ; serve hot, and garnish with cut lemon. *Time.*—10 minutes to fry the soles. *Average cost* for this quantity, 3s. *Sufficient* for 4 or 5 persons. *Seasonable* at any time.]

SOLES, Fried Filleted.

Soles for filleting should be large, as the flesh can be more easily separated from the bones, and there is less waste. Skin and wash the fish, and raise the meat carefully from the bones, and divide it into nice handsome pieces. The more usual way is to roll the fillets, after dividing each one in two pieces, and either bind them round with twine, or run a small skewer through them. Brush over with egg, and cover with bread-crumbs ; fry them as directed in the

Soles, with Mushrooms

foregoing recipe, and garnish with fried parsley and cut lemon. When a pretty dish is desired, this is by far the most elegant mode of dressing soles, as they look much better than when fried whole. Instead of rolling the fillets, they may be cut into square pieces, and arranged in the shape of a pyramid on the dish. *Time.*—About 10 minutes. *Average cost,* from 1s. to 2s. per pair. *Sufficient,* 2 large soles for 6 persons. *Seasonable* at any time.

SOLES, Fried.

Ingredients.—2 middling-sized soles, hot lard or clarified dripping, egg, and bread-crumbs. *Mode.*—Skin and carefully wash the soles, and cut off the fins, wipe them very dry, and let them remain in the cloth until it is time to dress them. Have ready some fine bread-crumbs and beaten egg ; dredge the soles with a little flour, brush them over with egg, and cover with bread-crumbs. Put them in a deep pan, with plenty of clarified dripping or lard (when the expense is not objected to, oil is still better) heated, so that it may neither scorch the fish nor make them sodden. When they are sufficiently cooked on one side, turn them carefully, and brown them on the other : they may be considered ready when a thick smoke rises. Lift them out carefully, and lay them before the fire on a reversed sieve and soft paper, to absorb the fat. Particular attention should be paid to this, as nothing is more disagreeable than greasy fish : this may be always avoided by dressing them in good time, and allowing a few minutes for them to get thoroughly crisp, and free from greasy moisture. Dish them on a hot napkin, garnish with cut lemon and fried parsley, and send them to table with shrimp sauce and plain melted butter. *Time.*—10 minutes for large soles ; less time for small ones. *Average cost,* from 1s. to 2s. per pair. *Sufficient* for 4 or 5 persons. *Seasonable* at any time.

SOLES, with Mushrooms.

Ingredients.—1 pint of milk, 1 pint of water, 1 oz. butter, 1 oz. salt, a little lemon - juice, 2 middling - sized soles. *Mode.*—Cleanse the soles, but do not skin them, and lay them in a fish-kettle, with the milk, water, butter, salt, and lemon-juice. Bring them gradually to boil, and let them simmer very gently till done, which will be in about 7 minutes. Take them up, drain them well on a cloth, put them on a hot dish, and pour over them a good mushroom sauce. (*See* Sauces.) *Time.*—After the water boils, 7 minutes. *Sufficient* for 4 persons. *Seasonable* at any time.

SOLES, with Cream Sauce.

Ingredients. — 2 soles; salt, cayenne, and pounded mace to taste; the juice of ½ lemon, salt and water, ½ pint of cream. *Mode.*—Skin, wash, and fillet the soles, and divide each fillet in 2 pieces; lay them in cold salt and water, which bring gradually to a boil. When the water boils, take out the fish, lay it in a delicately clean stewpan, and cover with the cream. Add the seasoning, simmer very gently for ten minutes, and, just before serving, put in the lemon-juice. The fillets may be rolled, and secured by means of a skewer; but this is not so economical a way of dressing them, as double the quantity of cream is required. *Time.*—10 minutes in the cream. *Average cost*, from 1s. to 2s. per pair. *Sufficient* for 4 or 5 persons. *Seasonable* at any time.

This will be found a most delicate and delicious dish.

SOUFFLE, to make.

Ingredients.—3 heaped tablespoonfuls of potato-flour, rice-flour, arrowroot, or tapioca, 1 pint of milk, 5 eggs, a piece of butter the size of a walnut, sifted sugar to taste, ¼ saltspoonful of salt flavouring. *Mode.*—Mix the potato-flour, or whichever one of the above ingredients is used, with a little of the milk; put it into a saucepan, with the remainder of the milk, the butter, salt, and sufficient pounded sugar to sweeten the whole nicely. Stir these ingredients over the fire until the mixture thickens; then take it off the fire, and let it cool a little. Separate the whites from the yolks of

 the eggs, beat the latter, and stir them into the soufflé batter. Now whisk the whites of the eggs to the firmest possible

SOUFFLÉ-PAN.

froth, for on this depends the excellence of the dish; stir them to the other ingredients, and add a few drops of essence of any flavouring that may be preferred ·

such as vanilla, lemon, orange, ginger, &c. &c. Pour the batter into a soufflé-dish, put it immediately into the oven, and bake for about ½ hour; then take it out, put the dish into another more ornamental one, such as is made for the purpose; hold a salamander or hot shovel over the soufflé, strew it with sifted sugar, and send it instantly to table. The secret of making a soufflé well, is to have the eggs well whisked, but particularly the whites, the oven not too hot, and to send it to table the moment it comes from the oven. If the soufflé be ever so well made, and it is allowed to stand before being sent to table, its appearance and goodness will be entirely spoiled. Soufflés may be flavoured in various ways, but must be named accordingly. Vanilla is one of the most delicate and recherché flavourings that can be used for this very fashionable dish. *Time.*—About ½ hour in the oven; 2 or 3 minutes to hold the salamander over. *Average cost*, 1s. *Sufficient* for 3 or 4 persons. *Seasonable* at any time.

SOUPS, General Directions for Making.

LEAN, JUICY BEEF, MUTTON, AND VEAL form the basis of all good soups; therefore it is advisable to procure those pieces which afford the richest succulence, and such as are fresh-killed. Stale meat renders soups bad, and fat is not well adapted for making them. The principal art in composing good rich soup is so to proportion the several ingredients that the flavour of one shall not predominate over another, and that all the articles of which it is composed shall form an agreeable whole. Care must be taken that the roots and herbs are perfectly well cleaned, and that the water is proportioned to the quantity of meat and other ingredients, allowing a quart of water to a pound of meat for soups, and half that quantity for gravies. In making soups or gravies, gentle stewing or simmering is absolutely necessary. It may be remarked, moreover, that a really good soup can never be made but in a well-closed vessel, although, perhaps, greater wholesomeness is obtained by an occasional exposure to the air. Soups will, in general, take from four to six hours doing, and *are much better prepared the day before they are wanted.* When the soup is cold, the fat may be easily

Soups, General Directions for

and completely removed ; and in pouring it off, care must be taken not to disturb the settlings at the bottom of the vessel, which are so fine that they will escape through a sieve. A very fine hair-sieve or cloth is the best strainer ; and if the soup is strained while it is hot, let the tamis or cloth be previously soaked in cold water. Clear soups must be perfectly transparent, and thickened soups about the consistency of cream. To obtain a really clear and transparent soup, it is requisite to continue skimming the liquor until there is not a particle of scum remaining, this being commenced immediately after the water is added to the meat. To thicken and give body to soups and gravies, potato-mucilage, arrowroot, bread-raspings, isinglass, flour and butter, barley, rice, or oatmeal are used. A piece of boiled beef pounded to a pulp, with a bit of butter and flour, and rubbed through a sieve, and gradually incorporated with the soup, will be found an excellent addition. When soups and gravies are kept from day to day in hot weather, they should be warmed up every day, put into fresh-scalded pans or tureens, and placed in a cool larder. In temperate weather, every other day may be sufficient. Stock made from meat only keeps good longer than that boiled with vegetables, the latter being liable to turn the mixture sour, particularly in very warm weather.

VARIOUS HERBS AND VEGETABLES are required for the purpose of making soups and gravies. Of these the principal are,— Scotch barley, pearl barley, wheat flour, oatmeal, bread-raspings, pease, beans, rice, vermicelli, macaroni, isinglass, potato-mucilage, mushroom or mushroom-ketchup, champignons, parsnips, carrots, beetroot, turnips, garlic, shalots, and onions. Sliced onions, fried with butter and flour till they are browned, and then rubbed through a sieve, are excellent to heighten the colour and flavour of brown soups and sauces, and form the basis of many of the fine relishes furnished by the cook. The older and drier the onion, the stronger will be its flavour. Leeks, cucumber, or burnet vinegar ; celery or celery seed pounded. The latter, though equally strong, does not impart the delicate sweetness of the fresh vegetable ; and when used as a substitute, its flavour should be corrected by the addition of a bit of sugar. Cress-seed, parsley, common thyme, lemon thyme, orange

Soup-making, the Chemistry &c of

thyme, knotted marjoram, sage mint, winter savoury, and basil. As fresh green basil is seldom to be procured, and its fine flavour is soon lost, the best way of preserving the extract is by pouring wine on the fresh leaves.

FOR THE SEASONING OF SOUPS, bay-leaves, tomato, tarragon, chervil, burnet, allspice, cinnamon, ginger, nutmeg, clove, mace, black and white pepper, essence of anchovy, lemon peel and juice, and Seville orange juice, are all taken. The latter imparts a finer flavour than the lemon, and the acid is much milder. These materials, with wine, mushroom ketchup, Harvey's sauce, tomato sauce, combined in various proportions, are, with other ingredients, manipulated into an almost endless variety of excellent soups and gravies. Soups, which are intended to constitute the principal part of a meal, certainly ought not to be flavoured like sauces, which are only designed to give a relish to some particular dish.

SOUP-MAKING, the Chemistry and Economy of.

Stock being the basis of all meat soups, and, also, of all the principal sauces, it is essential to the success of these culinary operations, to know the most complete and economical method of extracting, from a certain quantity of meat, the best possible stock, or broth. The theory and philosophy of this process we will, therefore, explain, and then proceed to show the practical course to be adopted.

As all meat is principally composed of fibres, fat, gelatine, osmazome, and albumen, it is requisite to know that the fibres are inseparable, constituting almost all that remains of the meat after it has undergone a long boiling.

FAT is dissolved by boiling ; but as it is contained in cells covered by a very fine membrane, which never dissolves a portion of it always adheres to the fibres. The other portion rises to the surface of the stock, and is that which has escaped from the cells which were not whole, or which have burst by boiling.

GELATINE is soluble ; it is the basis and the nutritious portion of the stock. When there is an abundance of it, it causes the stock, when cold, to become a jelly.

OSMAZOME is soluble even

Soup-making, the Chemistry, &c. of

and is that part of the meat which gives flavour and perfume to the stock. The flesh of old animals contains more *osmazome* than that of young ones. Brown meats contain more than white, and the former make the stock more fragrant. By roasting meat, the osmazome appears to acquire higher properties; so, by putting the remains of roast meats into your stock-pot, you obtain a better flavour.

ALBUMEN is of the nature of the white of eggs; it can be dissolved in cold or tepid water, but coagulates when it is put into water not quite at the boiling-point. From this property in albumen, it is evident that if the meat is put into the stock-pot when the water boils, or after this is made to boil up quickly, the albumen, in both cases, hardens. In the first it rises to the surface, in the second it remains in the meat, but in both it prevents the gelatine and osmazome from dissolving; and hence a thin and tasteless stock will be obtained. It ought to be known too that the coagulation of the albumen in the meat always takes place, more or less, according to the size of the piece, as the parts farthest from the surface always acquire *that degree* of heat which congeals it before entirely dissolving it.

BONES ought always to form a component part of the stock-pot. They are composed of an earthy substance,—to which they owe their solidity,—of gelatine, and a fatty fluid, something like marrow. *Two ounces* of them contain as much gelatine as *one pound* of meat; but in them, this is so incased in the earthy substance, that boiling-water can dissolve only the surface of whole bones. By breaking them, however, you can dissolve more, because you multiply their surfaces; and by reducing them to powder or paste, you can dissolve them entirely; but you must not grind them dry. We have said that gelatine forms the basis of stock; but this, though very nourishing, is entirely without taste; and to make the stock savoury, it must contain *osmazome* Of this, bones do not contain a particle; and that is the reason why stock made entirely of them is not liked; but when you add meat to the broken or pulverized bones, the osmazome contained in it makes the stock sufficiently savoury.

In concluding this part of our subject, the following condensed hints and direc-

Soup-making, the Chemistry, &c. of

tions should be attended to in the economy of soup-making:—

BEEF MAKES THE BEST STOCK; veal stock has less colour and taste; whilst mutton sometimes gives it a tallowy smell, far from agreeable, unless the meat has been previously roasted or broiled. Fowls add very little to the flavour of stock, unless they be old and fat. Pigeons, when they are old, add the most flavour to it; and a rabbit or partridge is also a great improvement. From the freshest meat the best stock is obtained.

IF THE MEAT BE BOILED solely to make stock, it must be cut up into the smallest possible pieces; but, generally speaking, if it is desired to have good stock and a piece of savoury meat as well, it is necessary to put a rather large piece into the stock-pot, say sufficient for two or three days, during which time the stock will keep well in all weathers. Choose the freshest meat, and have it cut as thick as possible; for if it is a thin flat piece, it will not look well, and will be very soon spoiled by the boiling.

NEVER WASH MEAT, as it deprives its surface of all its juices; separate it from the bones, and tie it round with tape, so that its shape may be preserved, then put it into the stock-pot, and for each pound of meat, let there be one pint of water; press it down with the hand, to allow the air, which it contains, to escape, and which often raises it to the top of the water.

PUT THE STOCK-POT ON A GENTLE FIRE, so that it may heat gradually. The albumen will first dissolve, afterwards coagulate; and as it is in this state lighter than the liquid, it will rise to the surface, bringing with it all its impurities. It is this which makes *the scum*. The rising of the hardened albumen has the same effect in clarifying stock as the white of eggs; and, as a rule, it may be said that the more scum there is, the clearer will be the stock. Always take care that the fire is very regular.

REMOVE THE SCUM when it rises thickly, and do not let the stock boil, because then one portion of the scum will be dissolved, and the other go to the bottom of the pot; thus rendering it very difficult to obtain a clear broth. If the fire is regular, it will not be necessary to add cold water in order to make the scum rise; but if the fire is too large at first, it will then be necessary to do so.

WHEN THE STOCK IS WELL SKIMMED, and begins to boil, put in salt and vegetables, which to every 3 lbs. of meat should consist of three carrots, two turnips, one parsnip, a few leeks, and a little celery. You can add, according to taste, a piece of cabbage, two or three cloves stuck in an onion, and a tomato. The latter gives a very agreeable flavour to the stock. If burnt onion be added, it ought, according to the advice of a famous French *chef*, to be tied in a little bag : without this precaution, the colour of the stock is liable to be clouded.

BY THIS TIME we will now suppose that you have chopped the bones which were separated from the meat, and those which were left from the roast meat of the day before. Remember, as was before pointed out, that the more these are broken, the more gelatine you will have. The best way to break them up is to pound them roughly in an iron mortar, adding, from time to time, a little water, to prevent them getting heated. It is a great saving thus to make use of the bones of meat, which, in too many English families, we fear, are entirely wasted ; for it is certain, as previously stated, that two ounces of bone contain as much gelatine (which is the nutritive portion of stock) as one pound of meat. In their broken state tie them up in a bag, and put them in the stock-pot ; adding the gristly parts of cold meat, and trimmings, which can be used for no other purpose. If, to make up the weight, you have received from the butcher a piece of mutton or veal, broil it slightly over a clear fire before putting it in the stock-pot, and be very careful that it does not contract the least taste of being smoked or burnt.

ADD NOW THE VEGETABLES, which, to a certain extent, will stop the boiling of the stock. Wait, therefore, till it simmers well up again, then draw it to the side of the fire, and keep it gently simmering till it is served, preserving, as before said, your fire always the same. Cover the stock-pot well, to prevent evaporation ; do not fill it up, even if you take out a little stock, unless the meat is exposed ; in which case a little boiling-water may be added, but only enough to cover it. After six hours' slow and gentle simmering, the stock is done ; and it should not be continued on the

fire longer than is necessary, or it will tend to insipidity.

Note.—It is on a good stock, a first good broth and sauce, that excellence in cookery depends. If the preparation of this basis of the culinary art is intrusted to negligent or ignorant persons, and the stock is not well skimmed, but indifferent results will be obtained The stock will never be clear ; and when it is obliged to be clarified, it is deteriorated both in quality and flavour. In the proper management of the stock-pot an immense deal of trouble is saved, inasmuch as one stock, in a small dinner, serves for all purposes. Above all things, the greatest economy, consistent with excellence, should be practised, and the price of everything which enters the kitchen correctly ascertained. The *theory* of this part of Household Management may appear trifling, but its practice is extensive, and therefore it requires the best attention.

SOUP, Baked.

Ingredients.—1 lb. of any kind of meat, any trimmings or odd pieces ; 2 onions, 2 carrots, 2 oz. of rice, 1 pint of split peas, pepper and salt to taste, 4 quarts of water. *Mode.*—Cut the meat and vegetables in slices, add to them the rice and peas, season with pepper and salt. Put the whole in a jar, fill up with the water, cover very closely, and bake for 4 hours. *Time.*—4 hours. *Average cost,* 2½d. per quart. *Seasonable* at any time. *Sufficient* for 10 or 12 persons.

Note.—This will be found a very cheap and wholesome soup, and will be convenient in those cases where baking is more easily performed than boiling.

SOUP, Brilla.

Ingredients.—4 lbs. of shin of beef, 3 carrots, 2 turnips, a large sprig of thyme, 2 onions, 1 head of celery, salt and pepper to taste, 4 quarts water. *Mode.*—Take the beef, cut off all the meat from the bone, in nice square pieces, and boil the bone for 4 hours. Strain the liquor, let it cool, and take off the fat ; then put the pieces of meat in the cold liquor ; cut small the carrots, turnips, and celery ; chop the onions add them with the thyme and seasoning, and simmer till the meat is tender. If not brown enough, colour it with browning. *Time.*—6 hours. *Average cost.*

Soup, Chantilly

5d. per quart. *Seasonable* all the year. *Sufficient* for 10 persons.

SOUP, Chantilly.

Ingredients.—1 quart of young green peas, a small bunch of parsley, 2 young onions, 2 quarts of medium stock. *Mode.*—Boil the peas till quite tender, with the parsley and onions ; then rub them through a sieve, and pour the stock to them. Do not let it boil after the peas are added, or you will spoil the colour. Serve very hot. *Time.*—½ hour. *Average cost*, 1s. 6d. per quart. *Seasonable* from June to the end of August. *Sufficient* for 8 persons.

Note.—Cold peas pounded in a mortar, with a little stock added to them, make a very good soup in haste.

SOUP, Calf's-head.

Ingredients.—½ of calf's head, 1 onion stuck with cloves, a very small bunch of sweet herbs, 2 blades of mace, salt and white pepper to taste, 6 oz. of rice-flour, 3 tablespoonfuls of ketchup, 3 quarts of white stock, or pot-liquor, or water. *Mode.*—Rub the head with salt, soak it for 6 hours, and clean it thoroughly, put it in the stewpan, and cover it with the stock, or pot-liquor, or water, adding the onion and sweet herbs. When well skimmed and boiled for 1½ hour, take out the head, and skim and strain the soup. Mix the rice-flour with the ketchup, thicken the soup with it, and simmer for 5 minutes. Now cut up the head into pieces about two inches long, and simmer them in the soup till the meat and fat are quite tender. Season with white pepper and mace finely pounded, and serve very hot. When the calf's head is taken out of the soup, cover it up or it will discolour. *Time.*—2½ hours. *Average cost*, 1s. 9d. per quart, with stock. *Seasonable* from May to October. *Sufficient* for 10 persons.

Note.—Force-meat balls can be added, and the soup may be flavoured with a little lemon-juice, or a glass of sherry or Madeira. The bones from the head may be stewed down again, with a few fresh vegetables, and it will make a very good common stock.

SOUP, à la Cantatrice. (An Excellent Soup, very Beneficial for the Voice.)

Ingredients.—3 oz. of sago, ½ pint of cream, the yolks of 3 eggs, 1 lump of

Soup, à la Flamande

sugar, and seasoning to taste, 1 bay-leaf (if liked), 2 quarts of medium stock.—*Mode.*—Having washed the sago in boiling water, let it be gradually added to the nearly boiling stock. Simmer for ½ hour, when it should be well dissolved. Beat up the yolks of the eggs, add to them the boiling cream ; stir these quickly in the soup, and serve immediately. Do not let the soup boil, or the eggs will curdle. *Time.*—40 minutes. *Average cost*, 1s. 6d. per quart. *Seasonable* all the year. *Sufficient* for 8 persons.

Note.—This is a soup, the principal ingredients of which, sago and eggs, have always been deemed very beneficial to the chest and throat. In various quantities, and in different preparations, these have been partaken of by the principal singers of the day, including the celebrated Swedish Nightingale, Jenny Lind, and, as they have always avowed, with considerable advantage to the voice, in singing.

SOUP, à la Crecy.

Ingredients.—4 carrots, 2 sliced onions, 1 cut lettuce, and chervil ; 2 oz. butter, 1 pint of lentils, the crumbs of 2 French rolls, half a teacupful of rice, 2 quarts of medium stock. *Mode.*—Put the vegetables with the butter in the stewpan, and let them simmer 5 minutes ; then add the lentils and 1 pint of the stock, and stew gently for half an hour. Now fill it up with the remainder of the stock, let it boil another hour, and put in the crumb of the rolls. When well soaked, rub all through a tammy. Have ready the rice boiled ; pour the soup over this, and serve. *Time.*—1¾ hour. *Average cost*, 1s. 2d. per quart. *Seasonable* all the year. *Sufficient* for 8 persons.

SOUP, à la Flamande (Flemish).

Ingredients.—1 turnip, 1 small carrot, ½ head of celery, 6 green onions shred very fine, 1 lettuce cut small, chervil, ¼ pint of asparagus cut small, ¼ pint of peas, 2 oz. butter, the yolks of 4 eggs, ½ pint of cream, salt to taste, 1 lump of sugar, 2 quarts of stock. *Mode.*—Put the vegetables in the butter to stew gently for an hour with a teacupful of stock ; then add the remainder of the stock, and simmer for another hour. Now beat the yolks of the eggs well, mix with the cream (previously boiled), and strain through a hair sieve. Take the

Soup, à la Flamande

soup off the fire, put the eggs, &c., to it and keep stirring it well. Bring it almost to boiling point, but do not leave off stirring, or the eggs will curdle. Season with salt, and add the sugar. *Time.—* 2½ hours. *Average cost,* 1s. 9d. per quart. *Seasonable* from May to August. *Sufficient* for 8 persons.

SOUP, à la Flamande (Flemish).

Ingredients. — 5 onions, 5 heads of celery, 10 moderate-sized potatoes, 3 oz. butter, ½ pint of water, ½ pint of cream, 2 quarts of stock. *Mode.* — Slice the onions, celery, and potatoes, and put them with the butter and water into a stewpan, and simmer for an hour. Then fill up the stewpan with stock, and boil gently till the potatoes are done, which will be in about an hour. Rub all through a tammy, and add the cream (previously boiled). Do not let it boil after the cream is put in. *Time.—* 2½ hours. *Average cost,* 1s. 4d. per quart. *Seasonable* from September to May. *Sufficient* for 8 persons. *Note.*—This soup can be made with water instead of stock.

SOUP, a Good Family.

Ingredients.—Remains of a cold tongue, 2 lbs. of shin of beef, any cold pieces of meat or beef-bones, 2 turnips, 2 carrots, 2 onions, 1 parsnip, 1 head of celery, 4 quarts of water, ½ teacupful of rice ; salt and pepper to taste. *Mode.*—Put all the ingredients in a stewpan, and simmer gently for 4 hours, or until all the goodness is drawn from the meat. Strain off the soup, and let it stand to get cold. The kernels and soft parts of the tongue must be saved. When the soup is wanted for use, skim off all the fat, put in the kernels and soft parts of the tongue, slice in a small quantity of fresh carrot, turnip, and onion ; stew till the vegetables are tender, and serve with toasted bread. *Time.—*5 hours. *Average cost,* 3d. per quart. *Seasonable* at any time. *Sufficient* for 12 persons.

SOUP, Hessian.

Ingredients.—Half an ox's head, 1 pint of split peas, 8 carrots, 6 turnips, 6 potatoes, 6 onions, 1 head of celery, 1 bunch of savoury herbs, pepper and salt to taste, 2 blades of mace, a little allspice, 4 cloves, the crumb of a French roll, 6 quarts of water. *Mode.*—Clear

Soup, Prince of Wales's

the head, rub it with salt and water, and soak it for 5 hours in warm water. Simmer it in the water till tender, put it into a pan and let it cool ; skim off all the fat ; take out the head, and add the vegetables cut up small, and the peas which have been previously soaked ; simmer them without the meat, till they are done enough to pulp through a sieve. Put in the seasoning, with the pieces of meat cut up ; give one boil, and serve. *Time.—*4 hours. *Average cost,* 6d. per quart. *Seasonable* in winter. *Sufficient* for 16 persons. *Note.*—An excellent hash or ragoût can be made by cutting up the nicest parts of the head, thickening and seasoning more highly a little of the soup, and adding a glass of port wine and 2 tablespoonfuls of ketchup.

SOUP, Portable.

Ingredients. — 2 knuckles of veal, 3 shins of beef, 1 large faggot of herbs, 2 bay-leaves, 2 heads of celery, 3 onions, 3 carrots, 2 blades of mace, 6 cloves, a teaspoonful of salt, sufficient water to cover all the ingredients. *Mode.*—Take the marrow from the bones ; put all the ingredients in a stock-pot, and simmer slowly for 12 hours, or more, if the meat be not done to rags ; strain it off, and put it in a very cool place ; take off all the fat, reduce the liquor in a shallow pan, by setting it over a sharp fire, but be particular that it does not burn ; boil it fast and uncovered for 8 hours, and keep it stirred. Put it into a deep dish, and set it by for a day. Have ready a stewpan of boiling water, place the dish in it, and keep it boiling ; stir occasionally, and when the soup is thick and ropy, it is done. Form it into little cakes by pouring a small quantity on to the bottom of cups or basins ; when cold, turn them out on a flannel to dry. Keep them from the air in tin canisters. *Average cost* of this quantity, 16s. *Note.*—Soup can be made in 5 minutes with this, by dissolving a small piece, about the size of a walnut, in a pint of warm water, and simmering for 2 minutes. Vermicelli, macaroni, or other Italian pastes, may be added.

SOUP, Prince of Wales's.

Ingredients. — 12 turnips, 1 lump of sugar, 2 spoonfuls of strong veal stock, salt and white pepper to taste, 2 quarts

Soup, Regency

of very bright stock. *Mode.*—Peel the turnips, and with a cutter cut them in balls as round as possible, but very small. Put them in the stock, which must be very bright, and simmer till tender. Add the veal stock and seasoning. Have little pieces of bread cut round, about the size of a shilling; moisten them with stock; put them into a tureen and pour the soup over without shaking, for fear of crumbling the bread, which would spoil the appearance of the soup, and make it look thick. *Time.*—2 hours. *Seasonable* in the winter. *Sufficient* for 8 persons.

SOUP, Regency.

Ingredients.—The bones and remains of any cold game such as of pheasants, partridges, &c.; 2 carrots, 2 small onions, 1 head of celery, 1 turnip, ¼ lb. of pearl barley, the yolks of 3 eggs boiled hard, ¼ pint of cream, salt to taste, 2 quarts of medium or common stock. *Mode.*— Place the bones or remains of game in the stewpan, with the vegetables sliced; pour over the stock, and simmer for 2 hours; skim off all the fat, and strain it. Wash the barley, and boil it in 2 or 3 waters before putting it to the soup; finish simmering in the soup, and when the barley is done, take out half, and pound the other half with the yolks of the eggs. When you have finished pounding, rub it through a clean tammy, add the cream, and salt if necessary; give one boil, and serve very hot, putting in the barley that was taken out first. *Time.*—2½ hours. *Average cost,* 1s. per quart, if made with medium stock, or 6d. per quart, with common stock. *Seasonable* from September to March. *Sufficient* for 8 persons.

SOUP, à la Reine.

Ingredients.—1 large fowl, 1 oz. of sweet almonds, the crumb of 1½ French roll, ½ pint of cream, salt to taste, 1 small lump of sugar, 2 quarts of good white veal stock. *Mode.*—Boil the fowl gently in the stock till quite tender, which will be in about an hour, or rather more; take out the fowl, pull the meat from the bones, and put it into a mortar with the almonds, and pound very fine. When beaten enough, put the meat back in the stock, with the crumb of the rolls, and let it simmer for an hour; rub it through a tammy, add the sugar, ½ pint of cream that has boiled, and, if you

Soup à la Solferino

prefer, cut the crust of the roll into small round pieces, and pour the soup over it, when you serve. *Time.*—2 hours, or rather more. *Average cost,* 2s. 7d. per quart. *Seasonable* all the year. *Sufficient* for 8 persons.

Note. — All white soups should be warmed in a vessel placed in another of boiling water.

SOUP, à la Reine (Economical).

Ingredients. — Any remains of roast chickens, ½ teacupful of rice, salt and pepper to taste, 1 quart of stock. *Mode.* —Take all the white meat and pound it with the rice, which has been slightly cooked, but not too much. When it is all well pounded, dilute with the stock, and pass through a sieve. This soup should neither be too clear nor too thick. *Time.* —1 hour. *Average cost,* 4d. per quart. *Seasonable* all the year. *Sufficient* for 4 persons.

Note.—If stock is not at hand, put the chicken-bones in water, with an onion, carrot, a few sweet herbs, a blade of mace, pepper and salt, and stew for 3 hours.

SOUP, à la Solferino (Sardinian Recipe).

Ingredients.—4 eggs, ½ pint of cream, 2 oz. of fresh butter, salt and pepper to taste, a little flour to thicken, 2 quarts of bouillon. *Mode.*—Beat the eggs, put them into a stewpan, and add the cream, butter, and seasoning; stir in as much flour as will bring it to the consistency of dough; make it into balls, either round or egg-shaped, and fry them in butter; put them in the tureen, and pour the boiling bouillon over them. *Time.*— 1 hour. *Average cost,* 1s. 3d. per quart. *Seasonable* all the year. *Sufficient* for 8 persons.

Note.—This recipe was communicated to the Editress by an English gentleman, who was present at the battle of Solferino, on June 24, 1859, and who was requested by some of Victor Emmanuel's troops, on the day before the batttle, to partake of a portion of their *potage.* He willingly enough consented, and found that these clever campaigners had made a palatable dish from very easily-procured materials. In sending the recipe for insertion in this work, he has, however, Anglicised, and somewhat, he thinks, improved it.

SOUP, Spring, or Potage Printanier.

Ingredients.—½ a pint of green peas, if in season, a little chervil, 2 shredded lettuces, 2 onions, a very small bunch of parsley, 2 oz. of butter, the yolks of 3 eggs, 1 pint of water, seasoning to taste, 2 quarts of stock. Put in a clean stewpan the chervil, lettuces, onions, parsley, and butter, to 1 pint of water, and let them simmer till tender. Season with salt and pepper; when done, strain off the vegetables, and put two-thirds of the liquor they were boiled in to the stock. Beat up the yolks of the eggs with the other third, give it a toss over the fire, and at the moment of serving, add this, with the vegetables which you strained off, to the soup. *Time.*—¾ of an hour. *Average cost*, 1s. per quart. *Seasonable* from May to October. *Sufficient* for 8 persons.

SOUP, Stew.

Ingredients.—2 lbs. of beef, 5 onions, 5 turnips, ¾ lb. of rice, a large bunch of parsley, a few sweet herbs, pepper and salt, 2 quarts of water. *Mode.*—Cut the beef up in small pieces, add the other ingredients, and boil gently for 2½ hours. Oatmeal or potatoes would be a great improvement. *Time.*—2½ hours. *Average cost*, 6d. per quart. *Seasonable* in winter. *Sufficient* for 6 persons.

SOUP, Stew.

Ingredients.—½ lb. of beef, mutton, or pork; ½ pint of split peas, 4 turnips, 8 potatoes, 2 onions, 2 oz. of oatmeal or 3 oz. of rice, 2 quarts of water. *Mode.*—Cut the meat in small pieces, as also the vegetables, and add them, with the peas, to the water. Boil gently for 3 hours; thicken with the oatmeal, boil for another ¼ hour, stirring all the time, and season with pepper and salt. *Time.*—3½ hours. *Average cost*, 4d. per quart. *Seasonable* in winter. *Sufficient* for 8 persons.

Note.—This soup may be made of the liquor in which tripe has been boiled, by adding vegetables, seasoning, rice, &c.

SOUP, Stew, of Salt Meat.

Ingredients.—Any pieces of salt beef or pork, say 2 lbs.; 4 carrots, 4 parsnips, 4 turnips, 4 potatoes, 1 cabbage, 2 oz. of oatmeal or ground rice, seasoning of salt and pepper. 2 quarts of water. *Mode.*—

Cut up the meat small, add the water, and let it simmer for 2¾ hours. Now add the vegetables, cut in thin small slices; season, and boil for 1 hour. Thicken with the oatmeal, and serve. *Time.*—2 hours. *Average cost*, 3d. per quart without the meat. *Seasonable* in winter. *Sufficient* for 6 persons.

Note.—If rice is used instead of oatmeal, put it in with the vegetables.

SOUP, Useful for Benevolent Purposes.

Ingredients.—An ox-cheek, any pieces of trimmings of beef, which may be bought very cheaply (say 4 lbs.), a few bones, any pot-liquor the larder may furnish, ¼ peck of onions, 6 leeks, a large bunch of herbs, ½ lb. of celery (the outside pieces, or green tops, do very well); ½ lb. of carrots, ½ lb. of turnips, ½ lb. of coarse brown sugar, ½ a pint of beer, 4 lbs. of common rice, or pearl barley; ½ lb. of salt, 1 oz. of black pepper, a few raspings, 10 gallons of water. *Mode.*—Divide the meat in small pieces, break the bones, put them in a copper, with the 10 gallons of water, and stew for half an hour. Cut up the vegetables, put them in with the sugar and beer, and boil for 4 hours. Two hours before the soup is wanted, add the rice and raspings, and keep stirring till they are well mixed in the soup, which simmer gently. If the liquor boils away a little, fill up with water. *Time.*—6½ hours. *Average cost*, 1½d. per quart.

SOUP, White.

Ingredients.—¼ lb. of sweet almonds, ¼ lb. of cold veal or poultry, a thick slice of stale bread, a piece of fresh lemon-peel, 1 blade of mace, pounded, ¾ pint of cream, the yolks of 2 hard-boiled eggs, 2 quarts of white stock. *Mode.*—Reduce the almonds in a mortar to a paste, with a spoonful of water, and add to them the meat, which should be previously pounded with the bread. Beat all together, and add the lemon-peel, very finely chopped, and the mace. Pour the boiling stock on the whole, and simmer for an hour. Rub the eggs in the cream, put in the soup, bring it to a boil, and serve immediately. *Time.*—1½ hour. *Average cost*, 1s. 6d. per quart. *Seasonable* all the year. *Sufficient* for 8 persons.

Note.—A more economical white soup may be made by using common veal

Spinach, to Boil

stock, and thickening with rice, flour, and milk. Vermicelli should be served with it. *Average cost, 5d.* per quart.

SPINACH, to Boil (English Mode).

Ingredients.—2 pailfuls of spinach, 2 heaped tablespoonfuls of salt, 1 oz. of of butter, pepper to taste. *Mode.*—Pick the spinach carefully, and see that no stalks or weeds are left amongst it; wash it in several waters, and, to prevent it being gritty, act in the following manner:—Have ready two large pans or tubs filled with water; put the spinach into one of these, and thoroughly wash it; then, *with the hands*, take out the spinach, and put it into the *other tub* of water (by this means all the grit will be left at the bottom of the tub); wash it again, and should it not be perfectly free from dirt, repeat the process. Put it

SPINACH GARNISHED WITH CROÛTONS.

into a very large saucepan, with about ½ pint of water, just sufficient to keep the spinach from burning, and the above proportion of salt. Press it down frequently with a wooden spoon, that it may be done equally; and when it has boiled for rather more than 10 minutes, or until it is perfectly tender, drain it in a colander, squeeze it quite dry, and chop it finely. Put the spinach into a clean stewpan, with the butter and a seasoning of pepper; stir the whole over the fire until quite hot; then put it on a hot dish, and garnish with sippets of toasted bread. *Time.*—10 to 15 minutes to boil the spinach, 5 minutes to warm with the butter. *Average cost* for the above quantity, *8d. Sufficient* for 5 or 6 persons. *Seasonable.* —Spring spinach from March to July; winter spinach from November to March.

Note.—Grated nutmeg, pounded mace, or lemon-juice may also be added to enrich the flavour; and poached eggs are also frequently served with spinach: they should be placed on the top of it, and it should be garnished with sippets of toasted bread.

SPINACH dressed with Cream, à la Française.

Ingredients.—2 pailfuls of spinach, 2 tablespoonfuls of salt, 2 oz. of butter, 8 tablespoonfuls of cream, 1 small teaspoonful of pounded sugar, a very little

Spinach-Green

grated nutmeg. *Mode.*—Boil and drain the spinach; chop it fine, and put it into a stewpan with the butter; stir it over a gentle fire, and, when the butter has dried away, add the remaining ingredients, and simmer for about 5 minutes. Previously to pouring in the cream, boil it first, in case it should curdle. Serve on a hot dish, and garnish either with sippets of toasted bread or leaves of puff-paste. *Time.*—10 to 15 minutes to boil the spinach; 10 minutes to stew with the cream. *Average cost* for the above quantity, *8d. Sufficient* for 5 or 6 persons. *Seasonable.*—Spring spinach from March to July; winter spinach from November to March.

SPINACH, French Mode of Dressing.

Ingredients.—2 pailfuls of spinach, 2 tablespoonfuls of salt, 2 oz. of butter, 1 teaspoonful of flour, 8 tablespoonfuls of good gravy; when liked, a very little grated nutmeg. *Mode.*—Pick, wash, and boil the spinach, and when tender, drain and squeeze it perfectly dry from the water that hangs about it. Chop it very fine, put the butter into a stewpan, and lay the spinach over that; stir it over a gentle fire, and dredge in the flour. Add the gravy, and let it boil *quickly* for a few minutes, that it may not discolour. When the flavour of nutmeg is liked, grate some to the spinach, and when thoroughly hot, and the gravy has dried away a little, serve. Garnish the dish with sippets of toasted bread. *Time.*—10 to 15 minutes to boil the spinach; 10 minutes to simmer in the gravy. *Average cost* for the above quantity, *8d. Sufficient* for 5 or 6 persons. *Seasonable.*—Spring spinach from March to July; winter spinach from October to February.

Note.—For an *entremets* or second-course dish, spinach dressed by the above recipe may be pressed into a hot mould; it should then be turned out quickly, and served immediately.

SPINACH-GREEN, for Colouring various Dishes.

Ingredients.—2 handfuls of spinach. *Mode.*—Pick and wash the spinach free from dirt, and pound the leaves in a mortar to extract the juice; then press it through a hair sieve, and put the juice into a small stewpan or jar. Place this

Spinach Soup	Sprats

in a bain marie, or saucepan of boiling water, and let it set. Watch it closely, as it should not boil; and, as soon as it is done, lay it in a sieve, so that all the water may drain from it, and the green will then be ready for colouring. If made according to this recipe, the spinach-green will be found far superior to that boiled in the ordinary way.

SPINACH SOUP (French Recipe).

Ingredients. — As much spinach as, when boiled, will half fill a vegetable-dish, 2 quarts of very clear medium stock. *Mode.*—Make the cooked spinach into balls the size of an egg, and slip them into the soup-tureen. This is a very elegant soup, the green of the spinach forming a pretty contrast to the brown gravy. *Time.*—1 hour. *Average cost,* 1s. per quart. *Seasonable* from October to June.

SPONGE-CAKE.

Ingredients.—The weight of 8 eggs in pounded loaf sugar, the weight of 5 in flour, the rind of 1 lemon, 1 tablespoonful of brandy. *Mode.*—Put the eggs into one side of the scale, and take the weight of 8 in pounded loaf sugar, and the weight of 5 in good *dry* flour. Separate the yolks from the whites of the eggs; beat the former, put them into a saucepan with the sugar, and let them remain over the fire until *milk-warm*, keeping them well stirred. Then put them into a basin, add the grated lemon-rind mixed with the brandy, and stir these well together, dredging in the flour very gradually. Whisk the whites of the eggs to a very stiff froth, stir them to the flour, &c., and beat the cake well for ¼ hour.

SPONGE-CAKE.

Put it into a buttered mould strewn with a little fine-sifted sugar, and bake the cake in a quick oven for 1½ hour. Care must be taken that it is put into the oven immediately, or it will not be light. The flavouring of this cake may be varied by adding a few drops of essence of almonds instead of the grated lemon-rind. *Time.*—1½ hour. *Average cost,* 1s. 3d. *Sufficient* for 1 cake. *Seasonable* at any time.

SPONGE-CAKE.

Ingredients.—½ lb. of loaf sugar, not quite ¼ pint of water, 5 eggs, 1 lemon, ¼ lb. of flour, ¼ teaspoonful of carbonate of soda. *Mode.*—Boil the sugar and water together until they form a thick syrup; let it cool a little, then pour it to the eggs, which should be previously well whisked; and after the eggs and syrup are mixed together, continue beating them for a few minutes. Grate the lemon-rind, mix the carbonate of soda with the flour, and stir these lightly to the other ingredients; then add the lemon-juice, and, when the whole thoroughly mixed, pour it into a buttered mould, and bake in rather a quick oven for rather more than 1 hour. The remains of sponge or Savoy cakes answer very well for trifles, light puddings, &c.; and a very stale one (if not mouldy) makes an excellent tipsy cake. *Time.*—Rather more than 1 hour. *Average cost,* 10d. *Sufficient* to make 1 cake. *Seasonable* at any time.

SPONGE-CAKES, Small.

Ingredients.—The weight of 5 eggs in flour, the weight of 8 in pounded loaf sugar; flavouring to taste. *Mode.*—Let the flour be perfectly dry, and the sugar well pounded and sifted. Separate the whites from the yolks of the eggs, and beat the latter up with the sugar; then whisk the whites until they become rather stiff, and mix them with the yolks, but do not stir them more than is just necessary to mingle the ingredients well together. Dredge in the flour by degrees, add the flavouring; butter the tins well, pour in the batter, sift a little sugar over the cakes, and bake them in rather a quick oven, but do not allow them to take too much colour, as they should be rather pale. Remove them from the tins before they get cold, and turn them on their faces, where let them remain until quite cold, when store them away in a closed tin canister or wide-mouthed glass bottle. *Time.*—10 to 15 minutes in a quick oven. *Average cost,* 1d. each. *Seasonable* at any time.

SPRATS.

Sprats should be cooked very fresh, which can be ascertained by their bright and sparkling eyes. Wipe them dry; fasten them in rows by a skewer run

Sprats, Dried

through the eyes; dredge with flour, and broil them on a gridiron over a nice clear fire. The gridiron should be rubbed with suet. Serve very hot. *Time.*— 3 or 4 minutes. *Average cost*, 1d. per lb. *Seasonable* from November to March.

To CHOOSE SPRATS. — Choóse these from their silvery appearance, as the brighter they are, so are they the fresher.

SPRATS, Dried.

Dried sprats should be put into a basin, and boiling water poured over them; they may then be skinned and served, and this will be found a much better way than boiling them.

SPRATS, Fried in Batter.

Ingredients. — 2 eggs, flour, bread-crumbs; seasoning of salt and pepper to taste. *Mode.*—Wipe the sprats, and dip them in a batter made of the above ingredients. Fry of a nice brown, serve very hot, and garnish with fried parsley. Sprats may be baked like herrings.

SPROUTS, to Boil Young.

Ingredients.—To each ½ gallon of water allow 1 heaped tablespoonful of salt; a *very small* piece of soda. *Mode.*— Pick away all the dead leaves, and wash the greens well in cold water; drain them in a colander, and put them into fast-boiling water, with salt and soda in the above proportion. Keep them boiling quickly, with the lid uncovered, until tender; and the moment they are done, take them up, or their colour will be spoiled; when well drained, serve. The great art in cooking greens properly, and to have them a good colour, is to put them into *plenty of fast-boiling* water, to let them boil very quickly, and to take them up the moment they become tender. *Time.* —Brocoli sprouts, 10 to 12 minutes; young greens, 10 to 12 minutes; sprouts, 12 minutes, after the water boils. *Seasonable.*—Sprouts of various kinds may be had all the year.

STEW, Irish.

Ingredients.—3 lbs. of the loin or neck of mutton, 5 lbs. of potatoes, 5 large onions, pepper and salt to taste, rather more than 1 pint of water. *Mode.*— Trim off some of the fat of the above quantity of loin or neck of mutton, and cut it into chops of a moderate thickness.

Stilton Cheese

Pare and halve the potatoes, and cut the onions into thick slices. Put a layer of potatoes at the bottom of a stewpan, then a layer of mutton and onions, and season with pepper and salt; proceed in this manner until the stewpan is full, taking care to have plenty of vegetables at the top. Pour in the water, and let it stew very gently for 2½ hours, keeping the lid of the stewpan closely shut the *whole* time, and occasionally shaking the preparation to prevent its burning. *Time.* —2½ hours. *Average cost*, for this quantity, 2s. 8d. *Sufficient* for 5 or 6 persons. *Seasonable.*—Suitable for a winter dish.

STEW, Irish.

Ingredients.—2 or 3 lbs. of the breast of mutton, 1½ pint of water, salt and pepper to taste, 4 lbs. of potatoes, 4 large onions. *Mode.*—Put the mutton into a stewpan with the water and a little salt, and let it stew gently for an hour; cut the meat into small pieces, skim the fat from the gravy, and pare and slice the potatoes and onions. Put all the ingredients into the stewpan, in layers, first a layer of vegetables, then one of meat, and sprinkle seasoning of pepper and salt between each layer; cover closely, and let the whole stew very gently for 1 hour, or rather more, shaking it frequently to prevent its burning. *Time.* —Rather more than 2 hours. *Average cost*, 1s. 6d. *Sufficient* for 5 or 6 persons. *Seasonable.*—Suitable for a winter dish.

Note.—Irish stew may be prepared in the same manner as above, but baked in a jar instead of boiled. About 2 hours or rather more in a moderate oven will be sufficient time to bake it.

STILTON CHEESE.

Stilton cheese, or British Parmesan, as it is sometimes called, is generally preferred to all other cheeses by those whose authority few will dispute. Those made in May or June are usually served at Christmas; or, to be in prime order, should be kept from

STILTON CHEESE.

10 to 12 months, or even longer. An artificial ripeness in Stilton cheese is

Stocks for all kinds of Soups

sometimes produced by inserting a small piece of decayed Cheshire into an aperture at the top. From 3 weeks to a month is sufficient time to ripen the cheese. An additional flavour may also be obtained by scooping out a piece from the top, and pouring therein port, sherry, Madeira, or old ale, and letting the cheese absorb these for two or three weeks. But that cheese is the finest which is ripened without any artificial aid, is the opinion of those who are judges in these matters. In serving a Stilton cheese, the top of it should be cut off to form a lid, and a napkin or piece of white paper, with a frill at the top, pinned round. When the cheese goes from table, the lid should be replaced.

STOCKS for all kinds of Soups (Rich Strong Stock).

Ingredients.—4 lbs. of shin of beef, 4 lbs. of knuckle of veal, ¼ lb. of good lean ham ; any poultry trimmings ; 2 oz. of butter ; 3 onions, 3 carrots, 2 turnips (the latter should be omitted in summer, lest they ferment), 1 head of celery, a few chopped mushrooms, when obtainable ; 1 tomato, a bunch of savoury herbs, not forgetting parsley ; 1½ oz. of salt, 3 lumps of sugar, 12 white peppercorns, 6 cloves, 3 small blades of mace, 4 quarts of water. *Mode.*—Line a delicately clean stewpan with the ham cut in thin broad slices, carefully trimming off all its rusty fat ; cut up the beef and veal in pieces about 3 inches square, and lay them on the ham ; set it on the stove, and draw it down, and stir frequently. When the meat is equally browned, put in the beef and veal bones, the poultry trimmings, and pour in the cold water. Skim well, and occasionally add a little cold water, to stop its boiling, until it becomes quite clear ; then put in all the other ingredients, and simmer very slowly for 5 hours. Do not let it come to a brisk boil, that the stock be not wasted, and that its colour may be preserved. Strain through a very fine hair sieve, or cloth, and the stock will be fit for use. *Time.* — 5 hours. *Average cost, 1s. 3d. per quart.*

STOCK, Economical.

Ingredients.—The liquor in which a joint of meat has been boiled, say 4 quarts ; trimmings of fresh meat or poultry, shank-bones, &c., roast-beef bones, any pieces the larder may fur-

Stock, to Clarify

nish ; vegetables, spices, and the same seasoning as in the foregoing recipe. *Mode.*—Let all the ingredients simmer gently for 6 hours, taking care to skim carefully at first. Strain it off, and put by for use. *Time.*—6 hours. *Average cost, 3d. per quart.*

STOCK, Medium.

Ingredients.—4 lbs. of shin of beef, or 4 lbs. of knuckle of veal, or 2 lbs. of each ; any bones, trimmings of poultry, or fresh meat, ¼ lb. of lean bacon or ham, 2 oz. of butter, 2 large onions, each stuck with 3 cloves ; 1 turnip, 3 carrots, 1 head of celery, 3 lumps of sugar, 2 oz. of salt, ½ a teaspoonful of whole pepper, 1 large blade of mace, 1 bunch of savoury herbs, 4 quarts and ½ pint of cold water. *Mode.*—Cut up the meat and bacon or ham into pieces of about 3 inches square ; rub the butter on the bottom of the stewpan ; put in ½ a pint of water, the meat, and all the other ingredients. Cover the stewpan, and place it on a sharp fire, occasionally stirring its contents. When the bottom of the pan becomes covered with a pale, jelly-like substance, add the 4 quarts of cold water, and simmer very gently for 5 hours. As we have said before, do not let it boil quickly. Remove every particle of scum whilst it is doing, and strain it through a fine hair sieve. This stock is the basis of most of the soups mentioned in this dictionary, and will be found quite strong enough for ordinary purposes. *Time.*—5½ hours. *Average cost, 9d. per quart.*

STOCK, To Clarify.

Ingredients.—The whites of 2 eggs, ½ pint of water, 2 quarts of stock. *Mode.*—Supposing that by some accident the soup is not quite clear, and that its quantity is 2 quarts, take the whites of 2 eggs, carefully separated from their yolks, whisk them well together with the water, and add gradually the 2 quarts of boiling stock, still whisking. Place the soup on the fire, and when boiling and well skimmed, whisk the eggs with it till nearly boiling again ; then draw it from the fire, and let it settle, until the whites of the eggs become separated. Pass through a fine cloth, and the soup should be clear.

Note.—The rule is, that all clear soups should be of a light straw-colour, and should not savour too strongly of the

Stock, White

meat; and that all white or brown thick soups should have no more consistency than will enable them to adhere slightly to the spoon when hot. All *purées* should be somewhat thicker.

STOCK, White (to be used in the preparation of White Soups).

Ingredients.—4 lbs. of knuckle of veal, any poultry trimmings, 4 slices of lean ham, 3 carrots, 2 onions, 1 head of celery, 12 white peppercorns, 2 oz. of salt, 1 blade of mace, a bunch of herbs, 1 oz. butter, 4 quarts of water. *Mode.*—Cut up the veal, and put it with the bones and trimmings of poultry, and the ham, into the stewpan, which has been rubbed with the butter. Moisten with ½ a pint of water, and simmer till the gravy begins to flow. Then add the 4 quarts of water and the remainder of the ingredients; simmer for 5 hours. After skimming and straining it carefully through a very fine hair sieve. it will be ready for use. *Time.*—5½ hours. *Average cost,* 9d. per quart.

Note.—When stronger stock is desired, double the quantity of veal, or put in an old fowl. The liquor in which a young turkey has been boiled, is an excellent addition to all white stock or soups.

STOCK, Consommé or White, for many Sauces.

Consommé is made precisely in the same manner as white stock, and, for ordinary purposes, will be found quite good enough. When, however, a stronger stock is desired, either put in half the quantity of water, or double that of the meat. This is a very good foundation for all white sauces.

STRAWBERRY JAM.

Ingredients.—To every 1b. of fruit allow ½ pint of red-currant juice, 1¼ lb. of loaf sugar. *Mode.*—Strip the currants from the stalks, put them into a jar; place this jar in a saucepan of boiling water, and simmer until the juice is well drawn from the fruit; strain the currants, measure the juice, put it into a preserving pan, and add the sugar. Select well-ripened but sound strawberries; pick them from the stalks, and when the sugar is dissolved in the cur-

Strawberries and Cream

rant-juice, put in the fruit. Simmer the whole over a moderate fire, from ½ to ¾ hour, carefully removing the scum as it rises. Stir the jam only enough to prevent it from burning at the bottom of the pan, as the fruit should be preserved as whole as possible. Put the jam into jars, and when cold, cover down. *Time.*—½ to ¾ hour, reckoning from the time the jam simmers all over. *Average cost,* from 7d. to 8d. per lb. pot. *Sufficient.*—12 pints of strawberries will make 12 lbs. of jam. *Seasonable* in June and July.

STRAWBERRY JELLY.

Ingredients.—Strawberries, pounded sugar; to every pint of juice allow 1¼ oz. of isinglass. *Mode.*—Pick the strawberries, put them into a pan, squeeze them well with a wooden spoon, add sufficient pounded sugar to sweeten them nicely, and let them remain for 1 hour, that the juice may be extracted; then add ½ pint of water to every pint of juice. Strain the strawberry-juice and water through a bag; measure it, and to every pint allow 1¼ oz. of isinglass, melted and clarified in ¼ pint of water. Mix this with the juice; put the jelly into a mould. and set the mould in ice. A little lemon-juice added to the strawberry-juice improves the flavour of the jelly, if the fruit is very ripe; but it must be well strained before it is put to the other ingredients, or it will make the jelly muddy. *Time.*—1 hour to draw the juice. *Average cost,* with the best isinglass, 3s. *Sufficient.*—Allow 1½ pint of jelly for 5 or 6 persons. *Seasonable* in June, July, and August.

STRAWBERRIES and CREAM.

Ingredients.—To every pint of picked strawberries allow ½ pint of cream, 2 oz of finely-pounded sugar. *Mode.*—Pick the stalks from the fruit, place it on a glass dish, sprinkle over it pounded sugar, and slightly stir the strawberries, that they may all be equally sweetened; pour the cream over the top, and serve. Devonshire cream, when it can be obtained, is exceedingly delicious for this dish; and, if very thick indeed, may be diluted with a little thin cream or milk. *Average cost* for this quantity, with cream at 1s. per pint, 1s. *Sufficient* for 2 persons. *Seasonable* in June and July.

| Strawberries, Preserved in Wine | Sturgeon, Roast |

STRAWBERRIES, Preserved in Wine.

Ingredients. — To every quart bottle allow ¼ lb. of finely-pounded loaf sugar ; sherry or Madeira. *Mode.*—Let the fruit be gathered in fine weather, and used as soon as picked. Have ready some perfectly dry glass bottles, and some nice soft corks or bungs. Pick the stalks from the strawberries, drop them into the bottles, sprinkling amongst them pounded sugar in the above proportion, and when the fruit reaches to the neck of the bottle, fill up with sherry or Madeira. Cork the bottles down with new corks, and dip them into melted resin. *Seasonable.*—Make this in June or July.

STRAWBERRIES, to Preserve Whole.

Ingredients. — To every lb. of fruit allow 1½ lb. of good loaf sugar, 1 pint of red-currant juice. *Mode.*—Choose the strawberries not too ripe, of a fine large sort and of a good colour. Pick off the stalks, lay the strawberries in a dish, and sprinkle over them half the quantity of sugar, which must be finely pounded. Shake the dish gently, that the sugar may be equally distributed and touch the under-side of the fruit, and let it remain for 1 day. Then have ready the currant-juice, drawn as for red-currant jelly ; boil it with the remainder of the sugar until it forms a thin syrup, and in this simmer the strawberries and sugar, until the whole is sufficiently jellied. Great care must be taken not to stir the fruit roughly, as it should be preserved as whole as possible. Strawberries prepared in this manner are very good served in glasses and mixed with thin cream. *Time.*—¼ hour to 20 minutes to simmer the strawberries in the syrup. *Seasonable* in June and July.

STRAWBERRY, Open Tart of, or any other Kind of Preserve.

Ingredients.—Trimmings of puff-paste, any kind of jam. *Mode.*—Butter a tart-pan of the shape shown in the engraving, roll out the paste to the thickness of ⅜ an inch, and line the pan with it ; prick a few holes at the bottom with a fork, and bake the tart in a brisk oven from 10 to 15 minutes. Let the paste cool a little ; then fill it with preserve, place a

few stars or leaves on it, which have been previously cut out of the paste and baked, and the tart is ready for table.

OPEN TART.

By making it in this manner, both the flavour and colour of the jam are preserved, which would otherwise be lost,

OPEN-TART MOULD.

were it baked in the oven on the paste ; and, besides, so much jam is not required. *Time.*—10 to 15 min. *Average cost,* 8d. *Sufficient.*—1 tart for 3 persons. *Seasonable* at any time.

STURGEON, Baked.

Ingredients.—1 small sturgeon, salt and pepper to taste, 1 small bunch of herbs, the juice of ½ lemon, ¼ lb. of butter, 1 pint of white wine. *Mode.*— Cleanse the fish thoroughly, skin it, and split it along the belly without separating it ; have ready a large baking-dish, in which lay the fish, sprinkle over the seasoning and herbs very finely minced, and moisten it with the lemon-juice and wine. Place the butter in small pieces over the whole of the fish, put it in the oven, and baste frequently ; brown it nicely, and serve with its own gravy. *Time.*—Nearly 1 hour. *Average cost,* 1s. to 1s. 6d. per lb. *Seasonable* from August to March.

STURGEON, Roast.

Ingredients.—Veal stuffing, buttered paper, the tail-end of a sturgeon. *Mode.* — Cleanse the fish bone and skin it ; make a nice veal stuffing (*see* Forcemeats), and fill it with the part where the bones came from ; roll it in buttered paper, bind it up firmly with tape, like a fillet of veal, and roast it in a Dutch oven before a clear fire. Serve with good brown gravy, or plain melted butter. *Time.* — About 1 hour. *Average costs,* 1s. to 1s. 6d. per lb. *Seasonable* from August to March.

Note.—Sturgeon may be plainly boiled, and served with Dutch sauce. The fish is very firm, and requires long boiling.

SUET PUDDING, to serve with Roast Meat.

Ingredients.—1 lb. of flour, 6 oz. of finely-chopped suet, ½ saltspoonful of salt, ½ saltspoonful of pepper, ½ pint of milk or water. *Mode.*—Chop the suet very finely, after freeing it from skin, and mix it well with the flour; add the salt and pepper (this latter ingredient may be omitted if the flavour is not liked), and make the whole into a smooth paste with the above proportion of milk or water. Tie the pudding in a floured cloth, or put it into a buttered basin, and boil from 2½ to 3 hours. To enrich it, substitute 3 beaten eggs for some of the milk or water, and increase the proportion of suet. *Time.*—2½ to 3 hours. *Average cost,* 6d. *Sufficient* for 5 or 6 persons. *Seasonable* at any time.

Note.—When there is a joint roasting or baking, this pudding may be boiled in a long shape, and then cut into slices a few minutes before dinner is served; these slices should be laid in the dripping-pan for a minute or two, and then browned before the fire. Most children like this accompaniment to roast-meat.

SUGAR, to Boil, to Caramel.

Ingredients. — To every lb. of lump sugar allow 1 gill of spring water. *Mode.* — Boil the sugar and water together very quickly over a clear fire, skimming it very carefully as soon as it boils. Keep it boiling until the sugar snaps when a little of it is dropped in a pan of cold water. If it remains hard, the sugar has attained the right degree; then squeeze in a little lemon-juice, and let it remain an instant on the fire. Set the pan into another of cold water, and the caramel is then ready for use. The insides of well-oiled moulds are often ornamented with this sugar, which with a fork should be spread over them in fine threads or network. A dish of light pastry, tastefully arranged, looks very pretty with this sugar spun lightly over it.

SUPPERS.

Much may be done in the arrangement of a supper-table, at a very small expense, provided *taste* and *ingenuity* are exercised. The colours and flavours of the various dishes should contrast nicely; there should be plenty of fruit and flowers on the table, and the room should be well lighted. We have endeavoured to show how the various dishes may be placed; but of course these little matters entirely depend on the length and width of the table used, on individual taste, whether the tables are arranged round the room, whether down the centre, with a cross one at the top, or whether the supper is laid in two separate rooms, &c., &c. The garnishing of the dishes has also much to do with the appearance of a supper-table. Hams and tongues should be ornamented with cut vegetable flowers, raised pies with aspic jelly cut in dice, and all the dishes garnished sufficiently to be in good taste without looking absurd. The eye, in fact, should be as much gratified as the palate. Hot soup is now often served at suppers, but is not placed on the table. The servants fill the plates from a tureen on the buffet, and then hand them to the guests: when these plates are removed, the business of supper commences.

Where small rooms and large parties necessitate having a standing supper, many things enumerated in the following bill of fare may be placed on the buffet. Dishes for these suppers should be selected which may be eaten standing without any trouble. The following list may, perhaps, assist our readers in the arrangement of a buffet for a standing supper.

Beef, ham, **and tongue-sandwiches,** lobster and oyster-patties, sausage-rolls, meat-rolls, lobster-salad, dishes of fowls, the latter *all cut up;* dishes of sliced ham, sliced tongue, sliced beef, and galantine of veal; various jellies, blancmanges, and creams; custards in glasses, compôtes of fruit, tartlets of jam, and several dishes of small fancy pastry; dishes of fresh fruit, bonbons, sweetmeats, two or three sponge-cakes, a few plates of biscuits, and the buffet ornamented with vases of fresh or artificial flowers. The above dishes are quite sufficient for a standing supper; where more are desired, a supper must then be laid and arranged in the usual manner.

SUPPER, BILL OF FARE FOR A BALL, FOR 60 PERSONS
(for Winter).

BOAR'S HEAD,
garnished with Aspic Jelly.

Lobster Salad.	Two Roast Fowls, cut up.	Lobster Salad.	Two Roast Fowls, cut up.	Lobster Salad.					Lobster Salad.	Two Roast Fowls, cut up.	Lobster Salad.	Two Roast Fowls, cut up.	Lobster Salad.

Fruited Jelly.　　　Mayonnaise of Fowl.　　　Charlotte Russe.

Small Pastry.　　　Small Ham, garnished.　　　Biscuits.

　　　　　　　　Iced Savoy Cake.

Vanilla Cream.　　| Epergne, with Fruit. |　　Fruited Jelly.

Prawns.　　Two Boiled Fowls, with Béchamel　　Prawns.
　　　　　　　　Sauce.
Biscuits.　　　　　　　　　　　　Small Pastry.
　　　　　Tongue, ornamented.

Custards,　　| Trifle, ornamented. |　　Custards,
in glasses.　　　　　　　　　　in glasses.

　　　　　Raised Chicken Pie.

Fruited Jelly.　　　Tipsy Cake.　　　Swiss Cream.

　　　　　Roast Pheasant.

Meringues.　　| Epergne, with Fruit. |　　Meringues.

　　　　Galantine of Veal.
Raspberry Cream.　　Tipsy Cake.　　　Fruited Jelly.

Small Pastry.　　Raised Game Pie.　　Biscuits.

Custards,　　| Trifle, ornamented. |　　Custards,
in glasses.　　　　　　　　　　in glasses.

　　　　Tongue, ornamented.
Prawns　　Two Boiled Fowls, with Béchamel　　Prawns.
　　　　　　　　Sauce.
Biscuits.　　　　　　　　　　　　Small Pastry.

　　　　EPERGNE, WITH FRUIT.

Fruited Jelly.　　　Iced Savoy Cake.　　　Blancmange.

　　　　Small Ham, garnished.

　　　　Mayonnaise of Fowl.

Charlotte Russe.　　Larded Capon.　　Fruited Jelly.

Note.—When soup is served from the buffet, Mock Turtle and Julienne may be
selected. Besides the articles enumerated above, Ices, Wafers, Biscuits, Tea, Coffee,
Wines, and Liqueurs will be required. Punch à la Romaine may also be added to the
list of beverages.

SUPPER, BILL OF FARE FOR A BALL,

Or a Cold Collation for a Summer Entertainment, or Wedding or Christening Breakfast for 70 or 80 Persons (July),

3 Compôtes of Fruit. 3 Blancmanges, to be placed down the table.

4 Blancmanges, to be placed down the table. 3 Dishes of Small Pastry. 3 English Pines. 3 Fruit Tarts.

4 Jellies, to be placed down the table. 3 Cheesecakes. 20 Small Dishes of various Summer Fruits.

Dish of Lobster, cut up.

Tongue.
Ribs of Lamb.
Two Roast Fowls.
Mayonnaise of Salmon.

Veal-and-Ham Pie.

Charlotte Russe à la Vanille.

Lobster Salad.

Epergne, with Flowers.

Lobster Salad.

Savoy Cake.

4 Blancmanges, to be placed down the table. 3 Fruit Tarts. 3 Cheesecakes. 20 Small Dishes of various Summer Fruits.

Pigeon Pie.

Mayonnaise of Trout.
Tongue, garnished.
Boiled Fowls and Béchamel Sauce.
Collared Eel.
Ham.
Raised Pie.
Two Roast Fowls.
Shoulder of Lamb, stuffed.
Mayonnaise of Salmon.

Dish of Lobster, cut up.

Lobster Salad.

Dish of Lobster, cut up.

Larded Capon.

Epergne, with Flowers.

Boar's Head.

Lobster Salad.

Pigeon Pie.

Mayonnaise of Trout.
Tongue.
Boiled Fowls and Béchamel Sauce.
Raised Pie.
Ham, decorated.
Shoulder of Lamb, stuffed.
Two Roast Fowls.
Mayonnaise of Salmon.

Lobster Salad.

Lobster Salad.

4 Jellies, to be placed down the table. 3 Dishes of Small Pastry. 3 English Pines. 3 Compôtes of Fruit.

Pigeon Pie.

Dish of Lobster, cut up.

Dish of Lobster, cut up.

Savoy Cake.

Lobster Salad.

Epergne, with Flowers.

Lobster Salad.

Char-lotte Russe à la Vanille.

Veal and Ham Pie.

Mayonnaise of Trout.
Tongue, garnished.
Boiled Fowls and Béchamel Sauce.
Collared Eel.

Dish of Lobster, cut up.

Note—The length of the page will not admit of our giving the dishes as they should be placed on the table; they should be arranged with the large and high dishes down the centre, and the spaces filled up with the smaller dishes, fruit, and flowers, taking care that the flavours and colours contrast nicely, and that no two dishes of a sort come together. This bill of fare may be made to answer three or four purposes, placing a wedding cake or christening cake in the centre on a high stand, if required for either of these occasions. A few dishes of fowls, lobster salads, &c. &c., should be kept in reserve to replenish those that are most likely to be eaten first. A joint of cold roast and boiled beef should be placed on the buffet, as being something substantial for the gentlemen of the party to partake of. Besides the articles enumerated in the bill of fare, biscuits and wafers will be required, cream-and-water ices, tea, coffee wines, liqueurs, soda-water, ginger-beer, and lemonade.

Sweetbreads, Baked

SWEETBREADS, Baked (an Entrée).

Ingredients.—3 sweetbreads, egg and bread-crumbs, oiled butter, 3 slices of toast, brown gravy. *Mode.* — Choose large white sweetbreads; put them into warm water to draw out the blood, and to improve their colour ; let them remain for rather more than 1 hour; then put them into boiling water, and allow them to simmer for about 10 minutes, which

SWEETBREADS.

renders them firm. Take them up, drain them, brush over with egg, sprinkle with bread-crumbs; dip them in egg again, and then in more bread-crumbs. Drop on them a little oiled butter, and put the sweetbreads into a moderately-heated oven, and let them bake for nearly ¾ hour. Make 3 pieces of toast; place the sweetbreads on the toast, and pour round, but not over them, a good brown gravy. *Time.*—To soak 1 hour, to be boiled 10 minutes, baked 40 minutes. *Average cost,* 1s. to 5s. *Sufficient* for an entrée. *Seasonable.*—In full season from May to August.

SWEETBREADS, Fried (à la Maître d'Hôtel), an Entrée.

Ingredients.—3 sweetbreads, egg and bread-crumbs, ¼ lb. of butter, salt and pepper to taste, rather more than ⅓ pint of maître-d'hôtel sauce. *Mode.*—Soak the sweetbreads in warm water for an hour ; then boil them for 10 minutes ; cut them in slices, egg and bread-crumb them, season with pepper and salt, and put them into a frying-pan, with the above proportion of butter. Keep turning them until done, which will be in about 10 minutes; dish them, and pour over them a maître-d'hôtel sauce. The dish may be garnished with slices of cut lemon. *Time.*—To soak 1 hour, to be broiled 10 minutes, to be fried about 10 minutes. *Average cost,* 1s. to 5s., according to the season. *Sufficient for an* entrée. *Seasonable.*—In full season from May to August.

Note.—The egg and bread-crumb may be omitted, and the slices of sweetbread dredged with a little flour instead, and a

Sweetbreads, Lambs'

good gravy may be substituted for the maître-d'hôtel sauce. This is a very simple method of dressing them.

SWEETBREADS, Stewed (an Entrée).

Ingredients.—3 sweetbreads, 1 pint white stock, thickening of butter and flour, 6 tablespoonfuls of cream, 1 tablespoonful of lemon-juice, 1 blade pounded mace, white pepper and salt to taste. *Mode.*—Soak the sweetbreads in warm water for 1 hour, and boil them for 10 minutes ; take them out, put them into cold water for a few minutes ; put them in a stewpan with the stock, and simmer them gently for rather more than ½ hour. Dish them ; thicken the gravy with a little butter and flour ; let it boil up, add the remaining ingredients, allow the sauce to get quite *hot,* but *not boil,* and pour it over the sweetbreads. *Time.* —To soak 1 hour, to be boiled 10 minutes, stewed rather more than ½ hour. *Average cost,* from 1s. to 5s., according to the season. *Sufficient* for an entrée. *Seasonable.*—In full season from May to August.

Note.—A few mushrooms added to this dish, and stewed with the sweetbread, will be found an improvement.

SWEETBREADS, Lambs', larded and Asparagus (an Entrée).

Ingredients. — 2 or 3 sweetbreads, pint of veal stock, white pepper and salt to taste, a small bunch of green onions, 1 blade of pounded mace, thickening of butter and flour, 2 eggs, nearly ½ pint cream, 1 teaspoonful of minced parsley, a very little grated nutmeg. *Mode.*—Soak the sweetbreads in lukewarm water and put them into a saucepan with sufficient boiling water to cover them, and let them simmer for 10 minutes ; then take them out and put them into cold water. Now lard them, lay them in a stewpan, add the stock, seasoning, onions, mace, and a thickening of butter and flour, and stew gently for ¼ hour or 2 minutes. Beat up the egg with the cream, to which add the minced parsley and a very little grated nutmeg. Put this to the other ingredients; stir it well till quite hot, but do not let it boil after the cream is added, or it will curdle. Have ready some asparagus-tops, boiled; add these to the sweetbreads, and serve. *Time.*—Altogether ½ hour. *Average co*

Sweetbreads, another way to Dress

2s. 6d. to 3s. 6d. each. *Sufficient.*—3 sweetbreads for 1 entrée. *Seasonable* from Easter to Michaelmas.

SWEETBREADS, another Way to Dress (an Entrée).

Ingredients. — Sweetbreads, egg and bread-crumbs, ½ pint of gravy, ¼ glass of sherry. *Mode.*—Soak the sweetbreads in water for an hour, and throw them into boiling water to render them firm. Let them stew gently for about ¼ hour, take them out and put them into a cloth to drain all the water from them. Brush them over with egg, sprinkle them with bread-crumbs, and either brown them in the oven or before the fire. Have ready the above quantity of gravy, to which add ½ glass of sherry; dish the sweetbreads, pour the gravy under them, and garnish with water-cresses. *Time.* — Rather more than ½ hour. *Average cost,* 2s. 6d. to 3s. 6d. each. *Sufficient*—3 sweetbreads for 1 entrée. *Seasonable,* from Easter to Michaelmas.

SYLLABUB.

Ingredients.—1 pint of sherry or white wine, ½ grated nutmeg, sugar to taste, 1½ pint of milk. *Mode.*—Put the wine into a bowl, with the grated nutmeg and plenty of pounded sugar, and milk into it the above proportion of milk from the cow. Clouted cream may be laid on the top, with pounded cinnamon or nutmeg and sugar; and a little brandy may be added to the wine before the milk is put in. In some counties, cider is substituted for the wine: when this is used, brandy must always be added. Warm milk may be poured on from a spouted jug or teapot; but it must be held very high. *Average cost,* 2s. *Sufficient* for 5 or 6 persons. *Seasonable* at any time.

SYLLABUBS, Whipped.

Ingredients. — ½ pint of cream, ¼ pint of sherry, half that quantity of brandy, the juice of ½ lemon, a little grated nutmeg, 3 oz. of pounded sugar, whipped cream the same as for trifle. *Mode.*—Mix all the ingredients together, put the syllabub into glasses, and over the top of them heap a little whipped cream, made in the same manner as for trifle. Solid syllabub is made by whisking or milling the mixture to a stiff froth, and putting it in the glasses, with-

out the whipped cream at the top. *Average cost,* 1s. 8d. *Sufficient* to fill 8 or 9 glasses. *Seasonable* at any time.

SYRUP for Jellies, to Clarify.

Ingredients.—To every quart of water allow 2 lbs. of loaf sugar; the white of 1 egg. *Mode.*—Put the sugar and water into a stewpan; set it on the fire, and, when the sugar is dissolved, add the white of the egg, whipped up with a little water. Whisk the whole well together, and simmer very gently until it has thrown up all the scum. Take this off as it rises, strain the syrup through a fine sieve or cloth into a basin, and keep it for use.

TAPIOCA PUDDING.

Ingredients.—3 oz. of tapioca, 1 quart of milk, 2 oz. of butter, ¼ lb. of sugar, 4 eggs, flavouring of vanilla, grated lemon-rind, or bitter almonds. *Mode.* —Wash the tapioca, and let it stew gently in the milk by the side of the fire for ¼ hour, occasionally stirring it; then let it cool a little; mix with it the butter, sugar, and eggs, which should be well beaten, and flavour with either of the above ingredients, putting in about 12 drops of the essence of almonds or vanilla, whichever is preferred. Butter a pie-dish, and line the edges with puff-paste; put in the pudding, and bake in a moderate oven for an hour. If the pudding is boiled, add a little more tapioca, and boil it in a buttered basin 1½ hour. *Time.*—1 hour to bake, 1½ hour to boil. *Average cost,* 1s. 2d. *Sufficient* for 5 or 6 persons. *Seasonable* at any time.

TAPIOCA SOUP.

Ingredients.—5 oz. of tapioca, 2 quarts of stock. *Mode.*—Put the tapioca into cold stock, and bring it gradually to a boil. Simmer gently till tender, and serve. *Time.*—Rather more than 1 hour. *Average cost,* 1s. 6d. per quart. *Seasonable* all the year. *Sufficient* for 8 persons.

TARTLETS.

Ingredients.—Trimmings of puff-paste, any jam or marmalade that may be preferred. *Mode.*—Roll out the paste to the thickness of about ½ inch; butter some small round patty-pans, line them with it, and cut off the superfluous paste

Tartlets, Polish   Tea-Cakes

close to the edge of the pan. Put a small piece of bread into each tartlet (this is to keep them in shape), and bake in a brisk oven for about 10 minutes, or rather longer. When they are done, and are of a nice colour, take the pieces of bread out carefully, and replace them by a spoonful of jam or marmalade. Dish them high on a white d'oyley, piled high in the centre, and serve. *Time.*—10 to 15 minutes. *Average cost,* 1*d.* each. *Sufficient.*—1 lb. of paste will make 2 dishes of tartlets. *Seasonable* at any time.

DISH OF TARTLETS.

TARTLETS, Polish.

Ingredients.—Puff-paste, the white of an egg, pounded sugar. *Mode.*—Roll some good puff-paste out thin, and cut it into 2½-inch squares; brush each square over with the white of an egg, then fold down the corners, so that they all meet in the middle of each piece of paste; slightly press the two pieces together, brush them over with the egg, sift over sugar, and bake in a nice quick oven for about ¼ hour. When they are done, make a little hole in the middle of the paste, and fill it up with apricot jam, marmalade, or red-currant jelly. Pile them high in the centre of a dish, on a napkin, and garnish with the same preserve the tartlets are filled with. *Time.*—¼ hour or 20 minutes. *Average cost,* with ½ lb. of puff-paste, 1*s. Sufficient* for 2 dishes of pastry. *Seasonable* at any time. *Note.*—It should be borne in mind, that, for all dishes of small pastry, such as the preceding, trimmings of puff-paste, left from larger tarts, answer as well as making the paste expressly.

TEA, to make.

There is very little art in making good tea; if the water is boiling, and there is no sparing of the fragrant leaf, the beverage will almost invariably be good. The old-fashioned plan of allowing a teaspoonful to each person, and one over, is still practised. Warm the teapot with boiling water; let it remain for two or three minutes for the vessel to become thoroughly hot, then pour it away. Put in the tea, pour in from ½

to ¾ pint of *boiling* water, close the lid, and let it stand for the tea to draw from 5 to 10 minutes; then fill up the pot with water. The tea will be quite spoiled unless made with water that is actually *boiling,* as the leaves will not open, and the flavour not be extracted from them; the beverage will consequently be colourless and tasteless,—in fact, nothing but tepid water. Where there is a very large party to make tea for, it is a good plan to have two teapots, instead of putting a large quantity of tea into one pot; the tea, besides, will go farther. When the infusion has been once completed, the addition of fresh tea adds very little to the strength; so, when more is required, have the pot emptied of the old leaves, scalded, and fresh tea made in the usual manner. Economists say that a few grains of carbonate of soda, added before the boiling water is poured on the tea, assist to draw out the goodness; if the water is very hard, perhaps it is a good plan, as the soda softens it; but care must be taken to use this ingredient sparingly, as it is liable to give the tea a soapy taste if added in too large a quantity. For mixed tea, the usual proportion is four spoonfuls of black to one of green; more of the latter when the flavour is very much liked; but strong green tea is highly pernicious, and should never be partaken of too freely. *Time.*—2 minutes to warm the teapot, 5 to 10 minutes to draw the strength from the tea. *Sufficient.*—Allow 1 teaspoonful to each person.

TEA-CAKES.

Ingredients.—2 lbs. of flour, ½ teaspoonful of salt, ¼ lb. of butter or lard, 1 egg, a piece of German yeast the size of a walnut, warm milk. *Mode.*—Put the flour (which should be perfectly dry) into a basin; mix with it the salt, and rub in the butter or lard; then beat the egg well, stir to it the yeast, and add these to the flour with as much warm milk as will make the whole into a smooth paste, and knead it well. Let it rise near the fire, and, when well risen, form it into cakes; place them on tins, let them rise again for a few minutes before putting them into the oven, and bake from ¼ to ½ hour in a moderate oven. These are very nice with a few currants and a little sugar added to the other ingredients.

Tea-Cakes, to toast

they should be put in after the butter is rubbed in. These cakes should be buttered, and eaten hot as soon as baked; but, when stale, they are very nice split and toasted; or, if dipped in milk, or even water, and covered with a basin in the oven till hot, they will be almost equal to new. *Time.*—¼ to ½ hour. *Average cost,* 10*d.* *Sufficient* to make 8 tea-cakes. *Seasonable* at any time.

TEA-CAKES, to toast.

Cut each tea-cake into three or four slices, according to its thickness; toast them on both sides before a nice clear fire, and as each slice is done, spread it with butter on both sides. When a cake is toasted, pile the slices one on the

TEA-CAKES.

top of the other, cut them into quarters, put them on a very hot plate, and send the cakes immediately to table. As they are wanted, send them in hot, one or two at a time, as, if allowed to stand, they spoil, unless kept in a muffin-plate over a basin of boiling water.

TEAL, Roast.

Ingredients.—Teal, butter, a little flour. *Mode.*—Choose fat, plump birds, after the frost has set in, as they are generally better flavoured; truss them in the same manner as wild duck; roast them before a brisk fire, and keep them well basted. Serve with brown or orange gravy, water-cresses, and a cut lemon. The remains of teal make excellent hash. *Time.*—From 9 to 15 minutes. *Average cost,* 1*s.* each; but seldom bought. *Sufficient.*—2 for a dish. *Seasonable* from October to February.

TEAL.

TEAL, being of the same character as widgeon and wild duck, may be treated, in carving, in the same style.

TENCH, Matelot of.

Ingredients.—½ pint of stock, ½ pint of port wine, 1 dozen button onions, a few mushrooms, a faggot of herbs, 2 blades of mace, 1 oz. of butter, 1 teaspoonful of minced parsley, thyme, 1 shalot, 2 anchovies, 1 teacupful of stock, flour, 1 dozen oysters, the juice of ½ lemon; the number of tench, according to size. *Mode.*—

Tendrons de Veau, Stewed

Scale and clean the tench, cut them into pieces, and lay them in a stewpan; add the stock, wine, onions, mushrooms, herbs, and mace, and simmer gently for ½ hour. Put into another stewpan all the remaining ingredients but the oysters and lemon-juice, and boil slowly for 10 minutes, when add the strained liquor from the tench, and keep stirring it over the fire until somewhat reduced. Rub it through a sieve, pour it over the tench with the oysters, which must be previously scalded in their own liquor, squeeze in the lemon-juice, and serve. Garnish with croûtons. *Time.*—¾ hour. *Seasonable* from October to June.

TENCH, Stewed with Wine.

Ingredients.—½ pint of stock, ½ pint of Madeira or sherry, salt and pepper to taste, 1 bay-leaf, thickening of butter and flour. *Mode.*—Clean and crimp the tench, carefully lay it in a stewpan with the stock, wine, salt and pepper, and bay-leaf, let it stew gently for ½ hour; then take it out, put it on a dish, and keep hot. Strain the liquor, and thicken it with butter and flour kneaded together, and stew for 5 minutes. If not perfectly smooth, squeeze it through a tammy, add a very little cayenne, and pour over the fish. Garnish with balls of veal forcemeat. *Time.*—Rather more than ½ hour. *Seasonable* from October to June.

TENDRONS DE VEAU, Stewed (an Entrée).

Ingredients. —The gristles from 2 breasts of veal, white stock, 1 faggot of savoury herbs, 2 blades of pounded mace, 4 cloves, 2 carrots, 2 onions, a strip of lemon-peel. *Mode.*—The *tendrons* or gristles, which are found round the front of a breast of veal, are now very frequently served as an entrée, and when well dressed, make a nice and favourite dish. Detach the gristles from the bone, and cut them neatly out, so as not to spoil the joint for roasting or stewing. Put them into a stewpan, with sufficient stock to cover them; add the herbs, mace, cloves, carrots, onions, and lemon, and simmer for nearly, or quite, 4 hours. They should be stewed until a fork will enter the meat easily. Take them up, drain them, strain the gravy, boil it down to a glaze, with which glaze the meat. Dish the *tendrons* in a circle

Tendrons de Veau

with croûtons fried of a nice colour placed between each; and put mushroom sauce, or a purée of green peas or tomatoes, in the middle. *Time.*—4 hours. *Sufficient* for 1 entrée. *Seasonable.*—With peas, from June to August.

TENDRONS DE VEAU (an Entrée).

Ingredients. — The gristles from 2 breasts of veal, white stock, 1 faggot of savoury herbs, 1 blade of pounded mace, 4 cloves, 2 carrots, 2 onions, a strip of lemon-peel, egg and bread-crumbs, 2 tablespoonfuls of chopped mushrooms, salt and pepper to taste, 2 tablespoonfuls of sherry, the yolk of 1 egg, 3 tablespoonfuls of cream. *Mode.*—After removing the gristles from a breast of veal, stew them for 4 hours, as in the preceding recipe, with stock, herbs, mace, cloves, carrots, onions, and lemon-peel. When perfectly tender, lift them out and remove any bones or hard parts remaining. Put them between two dishes, with a weight on the top, and when cold, cut them into slices. Brush these over with egg, sprinkle with bread-crumbs, and fry a pale brown. Take ½ pint of the gravy they were boiled in, add 2 tablespoonfuls of chopped mushrooms, a seasoning of salt and pepper, the sherry, and the yolk of an egg beaten with 3 tablespoonfuls of cream. Stir the sauce over the fire until it thickens; when it is on the *point of boiling*, dish the tendrons in a circle, and pour the sauce in the middle. Tendrons are dressed in a variety of ways,—with sauce à l'Espagnole, vegetables of all kinds: when they are served with a purée, they should always be glazed. *Time.*—4½ hours. *Average cost.*—Usually bought with breast of veal. *Sufficient* for an entrée. *Seasonable* from March to October.

TETE DE VEAU EN TORTUE (an Entrée).

Ingredients.—Half a calf's head, or the remains of a cold boiled one; rather more than 1 pint of good white stock, 1 glass of sherry or Madeira, cayenne and salt to taste, about 12 mushroom-buttons (when obtainable), 6 hard-boiled eggs, 4 gherkins, 8 quenelles, or forcemeat balls, 12 crayfish, 12 croûtons. *Mode.*—Half a calf's head is sufficient to make a good entrée, and if there are any remains of a cold one left from the preceding day, it

Tipsy Cake

will answer very well for this dish. After boiling the head until tender, remove the bones, and cut the meat into neat pieces; put the stock into a stewpan, add the wine, and a seasoning of salt and cayenne; fry the mushrooms in butter for 2 or 3 minutes, and add these to the gravy. Boil this quickly until somewhat reduced; then put in the yolks of the hard-boiled eggs *whole*, and the whites cut in small pieces, and the gherkins chopped. Have ready a few veal quenelles, add these, with the slices of head, to the other ingredients, and let the whole get thoroughly hot, *without boiling.* Arrange the pieces of head as high in the centre of the dish as possible; pour over them the ragoût, and garnish with the crayfish and croûtons placed alternately. A little of the gravy should also be served in a tureen. *Time.*—About ½ hour to reduce the stock. *Sufficient* for 6 or 7 persons. *Average cost,* exclusive of the calf's head, 2s. 9d. *Seasonable* from March to October.

TIPSY CAKE.

Ingredients.—1 moulded sponge or Savoy cake, sufficient sweet wine or sherry to soak it, 6 tablespoonfuls of brandy, 2 oz. of sweet almonds, 1 pint of rich custard. *Mode.*—Procure a cake that is three or four days old, — either sponge, Savoy, or rice answering for the purpose of a tipsy cake. Cut the bottom of the cake level, to make it stand firm in the dish; make a small hole in the centre, and pour in and over the cake sufficient sweet wine or sherry, mixed with the above proportion of brandy, to soak it nicely. When the cake is well soaked, blanch and cut the almonds into strips, stick them all over the cake, and pour round it

TIPSY CAKE.

a good custard, made by our recipe, allowing 8 eggs instead of 5 to the pint of milk. The cakes are sometimes crumbled and soaked, and a whipped cream heaped over them, the same as for trifles. *Time.*—About 2 hours to soak the cake. *Average cost,* 4s. 6d. *Sufficient* for 1 dish. *Seasonable* at any time.

TIPSY CAKE, an easy way of making.

Ingredients.—12 stale small sponge-cakes, raisin wine, ½ lb. of jam, 1 pint of custard (see Custard). *Mode.*—Soak the sponge-cakes, which should be stale (on this account they should be cheaper), in a little raisin wine; arrange them on a deep glass dish in four layers, putting a layer of jam between each, and pour round them a pint of custard, made by recipe, decorating the top with cut preserved-fruit. *Time.*—2 hours to soak the cakes. *Average cost,* 2s. 6d. *Sufficient* for 1 dish. *Seasonable* at any time.

TOAD-IN-THE-HOLE (Cold Meat Cookery).

Ingredients.—6 oz. of flour, 1 pint of milk, 3 eggs, butter, a few slices of cold mutton, pepper and salt to taste, 2 kidneys. *Mode.*—Make a smooth batter of flour, milk, and eggs in the above proportion; butter a baking-dish, and pour in the batter. Into this place a few slices of cold mutton, previously well seasoned, and the kidneys, which should be cut into rather small pieces; bake about 1 hour, or rather longer, and send it to table in the dish it was baked in. Oysters or mushrooms may be substituted for the kidneys, and will be found exceedingly good. *Time.*—Rather more than 1 hour. *Average cost,* exclusive of the cold meat, 8d. *Seasonable* at any time.

TOAD-IN-THE-HOLE (a Homely but Savoury Dish).

Ingredients.—1½ lb. of rump-steak, 1 sheep's kidney, pepper and salt to taste. For the batter, 3 eggs, 1 pint of milk, 4 tablespoonfuls of flour, ½ saltspoonful of salt. *Mode.*—Cut up the steak and kidney into convenient-sized pieces, and put them into a pie-dish, with a good seasoning of salt and pepper; mix the flour with a small quantity of milk at first, to prevent its being lumpy; add the remainder, and the 3 eggs, which should be well beaten; put in the salt, stir the batter for about 5 minutes, and pour it over the steak. Place it in a tolerably brisk oven immediately, and bake for 1½ hour. *Time.*—1½ hour. *Average cost,* 1s. 9d. *Sufficient* for 4 or 5 persons. *Seasonable* at any time.

Note.—The remains of cold beef, rather

underdone, may be substituted for the steak, and, when liked, the smallest possible quantity of minced onion or shalot may be added.

TOAST, to make Dry.

To make dry toast properly, a great deal of attention is required; much more, indeed, than people generally suppose. Never use new bread for making any kind of toast, as it eats heavy, and, besides, is very extravagant. Procure a loaf of household bread about two days old; cut off as many slices as may be required, not quite ¼ inch in thickness; trim off the crusts and ragged edges, put the bread on a toasting-fork, and hold it before a very clear fire. Move it backwards and forwards until the bread is nicely coloured; then turn it and toast the other side, and do not place it so near the fire that it blackens. Dry toast should be more gradually made than buttered toast, as its great beauty consists in its crispness, and this cannot be attained unless the process is slow and the bread is allowed gradually to colour. It should never be made long before it is wanted, as it soon becomes tough, unless placed on the fender in front of the fire. As soon as each piece is ready, it should be put into a rack, or stood upon its edges, and sent quickly to table.

TOAST, to make Hot Buttered.

A loaf of household bread about two days old answers for making toast better than cottage bread, the latter not being a good shape, and too crusty for the purpose. Cut as many nice even slices as may be required, rather more than ¼ inch in thickness, and toast them before a very bright fire, without allowing the bread to blacken, which spoils the appearance and flavour of all toast. When of a nice colour on both sides, put it on a hot plate; divide some good butter into small pieces, place them on the toast, set this before the fire, and when the butter is just beginning to melt, spread it lightly over the toast. Trim off the crust and ragged edges, divide each round into 4 pieces, and send the toast quickly to table. Some persons cut the slices of toast across from corner to corner, so making the pieces of a three-cornered shape. Soyer recommends that each slice should be cut into pieces as soon as it is buttered, and when all are ready, that they should be piled lightly on the dish they are intended to be served on. He says that by cutting through 4 or 5 slices at a time, all the butter is squeezed out of the upper ones, while the bottom one is swimming in fat liquid. It is highly essential to use good butter for making this dish.

TOAST-AND-WATER.

Ingredients.—A slice of bread, 1 quart of boiling water. *Mode.*—Cut a slice from a stale loaf (a piece of hard crust is better than anything else for the purpose), toast it of a nice brown on every side, but *do not allow it to burn or blacken.* Put it into a jug, pour the boiling water over it, cover it closely, and let it remain until cold. When strained, it will be ready for use. Toast-and-water should always be made a short time before it is required, to enable it to get cold: if drunk in a tepid or lukewarm state, it is an exceedingly disagreeable beverage. If, as is sometimes the case, this drink is wanted in a hurry, put the toasted bread into a jug, and only just cover it with the boiling water; when this is cool, cold water may be added in the proportion required, the toast-and-water strained; it will then be ready for use, and is more expeditiously prepared than by the above method.

TOAST SANDWICHES.

Ingredients. — Thin cold toast, thin slices of bread-and-butter, pepper and salt to taste. *Mode.* — Place a very thin piece of cold toast between 2 slices of thin bread-and-butter in the form of a sandwich, adding a seasoning of pepper and salt. This sandwich may be varied by adding a little pulled meat, or very fine slices of cold meat, to the toast, and in any of these forms will be found very tempting to the appetite of an invalid.

TOFFEE, Everton.

Ingredients.—1 lb. of powdered loaf sugar, 1 teacupful of water, ¼ lb. of butter, 6 drops of essence of lemon. *Mode.*—Put the water and sugar into a brass pan, and beat the butter to a cream. When the sugar is dissolved, add the butter, and keep stirring the mixture over the fire until it sets, when a little is poured on to a buttered dish; and just before the toffee is done, add the essence of lemon. Butter a dish or tin, pour on it the mixture, and when cool, it will

easily separate from the dish. Butter-Scotch, an excellent thing for coughs, is made with brown, instead of white sugar, omitting the water, and flavoured with ½ oz. of powdered ginger. It is made in the same manner as toffee. *Time.*—18 to 35 minutes. *Average cost,* 10d. *Sufficient* to make a lb. of toffee.

TOMATO SAUCE for Keeping (Excellent).

Ingredients.—To every quart of tomato-pulp allow 1 pint of cayenne vinegar, ¾ oz. of shalots, ¾ oz. of garlic, peeled and cut in slices; salt to taste. To every six quarts of liquor, 1 pint of soy, 1 pint of anchovy-sauce. *Mode.*—Gather the tomatoes quite ripe; bake them in a slow oven till tender; rub them through a sieve, and to every quart of pulp add cayenne vinegar, shalots, garlic, and salt, in the above proportion; boil the whole together till the garlic and shalots are quite soft; then rub it through a sieve, put it again into a saucepan, and, to every six quarts of the liquor, add 1 pint of soy and the same quantity of anchovy-sauce, and boil altogether for about 20 minutes; bottle off for use, and carefully seal or resin the corks. This will keep good for 2 or 3 years, but will be fit for use in a week. A useful and less expensive sauce may be made by omitting the anchovy and soy. *Time.*—Altogether 1 hour. *Seasonable.*—Make this from the middle of September to the end of October.

TOMATO SAUCE for Keeping (Excellent).

Ingredients.—1 dozen tomatoes, 2 teaspoonfuls of the best powdered ginger, 1 dessertspoonful of salt, 1 head of garlic chopped fine, 2 tablespoonfuls of vinegar, 1 dessertspoonful of Chili vinegar (a small quantity of cayenne may be substituted for this). *Mode.*—Choose ripe tomatoes, put them into a stone jar, and stand them in a cool oven until quite tender; when cold, take the skins and stalks from them, mix the pulp with the liquor which is in the jar, but do not strain it; add all the other ingredients, mix well together, and put it into well-sealed bottles. Stored away in a cool, dry place, it will keep good for years. It is ready for use as soon as made, but the flavour is better after a week or two. Should it not appear to keep, turn it out, and boil it up with a little additional

Tomato Sauce for Keeping	Tomatoes, Stewed

ginger and cayenne. For immediate use, the skins should be put into a wide-mouthed bottle with a little of the different ingredients, and they will be found very nice for hashes or stews. *Time.*— 4 or 5 hours in a *cool* oven. *Seasonable* from the middle of September to the end of October.

TOMATO SAUCE for Keeping (Excellent).

Ingredients. — 3 dozen tomatoes; to every pound of tomato-pulp allow 1 pint of Chili vinegar, 1 oz. of garlic, 1 oz. of shalot, 2 oz. of salt, 1 large green capsicum, ¼ teaspoonful of cayenne, 2 pickled gherkins, 6 pickled onions, 1 pint of common vinegar, and the juice of 6 lemons. *Mode.* — Choose the tomatoes when quite ripe and red; put them in a jar with a cover to it, and bake them till tender. The better way is to put them in the oven overnight, when it will not be too hot, and examine them in the morning to see if they are tender. Do not allow them to remain in the oven long enough to break them; but they should be sufficiently soft to skin nicely and rub through the sieve. Measure the pulp, and to each pound of pulp add the above proportion of vinegar and other ingredients, taking care to chop very fine the garlic, shalot, capsicum, onion, and gherkins. Boil the whole together till everything is tender; then again rub it through a sieve, and add the lemon-juice. Now boil the whole again till it becomes as thick as cream, and keep continually stirring; bottle it when quite cold, cork well, and seal the corks. If the flavour of garlic and shalot is very much disliked, diminish the quantities. *Time.*— Bake the tomatoes in a *cool* oven all night. *Seasonable* from the middle of September to the end of October.

Note. — A quantity of liquor will flow from the tomatoes, which must be put through the sieve with the rest. Keep it well stirred whilst on the fire, and use a wooden spoon.

TOMATO SAUCE, Hot, to serve with Cutlets, Roast Meats, &c.

Ingredients. — 6 tomatoes, 2 shalots, 1 clove, 1 blade of mace, salt and cayenne to taste, ¼ pint of gravy or stock. *Mode.*— Cut the tomatoes in two, and squeeze the juice and seeds out; put them in a stewpan with all the ingredients, and let them

simmer *gently* until the tomatoes are tender enough to pulp; rub the whole through a sieve, boil it for a few minutes, and serve. The shalots and spices may be omitted when their flavour is objected to. *Time.*—1 hour, or rather more, to simmer the tomatoes. *Average cost,* for this quantity, 1s. *In full season* in September and October.

TOMATOES, Baked (Excellent).

Ingredients.—8 or 10 tomatoes, pepper and salt to taste, 2 oz. of butter, bread-crumbs. *Mode.* — Take off the stalks from the tomatoes; cut them into thick slices, and put them into a deep baking-dish; add a plentiful seasoning of pepper and salt, and butter in the above proportion; cover the whole with bread-crumbs; drop over these a little clarified butter; bake in a moderate oven from 20 minutes to ½ hour, and serve very hot. This vegetable, dressed as above, is an exceedingly nice accompaniment to all kinds of roast meat. The tomatoes, instead of being cut in slices, may be baked whole; but they will take rather longer time to cook. *Time.*—20 minutes to ½ hour. *Average cost,* in full season, 9d. per basket. *Sufficient* for 5 or 6 persons. *Seasonable* in August, September, and October; but may be had, forced, much earlier.

TOMATOES, Baked (another Mode).

Ingredients.—Some bread-crumbs, a little butter, onion, cayenne, and salt. *Mode.*—Bake the tomatoes whole, then scoop out a small hole at the top; fry the bread crumbs, onion, &c., and fill the holes with this as high up as possible; then brown the tomatoes with a salamander, or in an oven, and take care that the skin does not break.

TOMATOES, Stewed.

Ingredients.—8 tomatoes, pepper and salt to taste, 2 oz. of butter, 2 table-spoonfuls of vinegar. *Mode.*—Slice the tomatoes into a *lined* saucepan; season them with pepper and salt, and place small pieces of butter on them. Cover the lid down closely, and stew from 20 to 25 minutes, or until the tomatoes are perfectly tender; add the vinegar, stir two or three times, and serve with any kind of roast meat, with which they will

Tomatoes, Stewed

be found a delicious accompaniment. *Time.*—20 to 25 minutes. *Average cost,*

STEWED TOMATOES.

in full season, 9*d.* per basket. *Sufficient* for 4 or 5 persons. *Seasonable* from August to October; but may be had, forced, much earlier.

TOMATOES, Stewed.

Ingredients.—8 tomatoes, about ½ pint of good gravy, thickening of butter and flour, cayenne and salt to taste. *Mode.* —Take out the stalks of the tomatoes; put them into a wide stewpan, pour over them the above proportion of good brown gravy, and stew gently until they are tender, occasionally *carefully* turning them, that they may be equally done. Thicken the gravy with a little butter and flour worked together on a plate; let it just boil up after the thickening is added, and serve. If it be at hand, these should be served on a silver or plated vegetable-dish. *Time.*—20 to 25 minutes, very gentle stewing. *Average cost,* in full season, 9*d.* per basket. *Sufficient* for 4 or 5 persons. *Seasonable* in August, September, and October; but may be had, forced, much earlier.

TONGUE, Boiled.

Ingredients.—1 tongue, a bunch of savoury herbs, water. *Mode.*—In choosing a tongue, ascertain how long it has been dried or pickled, and select one with a smooth skin, which denotes its being young and tender. If a dried one, and rather hard, soak it at least for 12 hours previous to cooking it; if, however, it is fresh from the pickle, 2 or 3 hours will be sufficient for it to remain in soak. Put the tongue into a stewpan with plenty of cold water and a bunch of savoury herbs; let it gradually come to a boil, skim well, and simmer very gently until tender. Peel off the skin, garnish with tufts of cauliflowers or Brussels sprouts, and serve. Boiled tongue is frequently sent to table with boiled poultry, instead of ham, and is, by many persons, preferred. If to serve cold, peel it, fasten it down to a piece of board by sticking a fork through the root, and another through the top, to straighten it. When cold, glaze it, and

Tongue, to Pickle and Dress a

put a paper ruche round the root, and garnish with tufts of parsley. *Time.*— A large smoked tongue, 4 to 4½ hours; a small one, 2½ to 3 hours. A large unsmoked tongue, 3 to 3½ hours; a small one, 2 to 2½ hours. *Average cost,* for a moderate-sized tongue, 3*s.* 6*d.* *Seasonable* at any time.

TONGUES, to Cure.

Ingredients.—For a tongue of 7 lbs., 1 oz. of saltpetre, ½ oz. of black pepper, 4 oz. of sugar, 3 oz. of juniper berries, 6 oz. of salt. *Mode.*—Rub the above ingredients well into the tongue, and let it remain in the pickle for 10 days or a fortnight; then drain it, tie it up in brown paper, and have it smoked for about 20 days over a wood fire; or it may be boiled out of this pickle. *Time.* —From 10 to 14 days to remain in the pickle; to be smoked 24 days. *Average cost,* for a medium-sized uncured tongue, 2*s.* 6*d.* *Seasonable* at any time.
Note.—If not wanted immediately, the tongue will keep 3 or 4 weeks without being too salt; then it must not be rubbed, but only turned in the pickle.

TONGUES, to Cure.

Ingredients.—9 lbs. of salt, 8 oz. of sugar, 9 oz. of powdered saltpetre. *Mode.* —Rub the above ingredients well into the tongues, and keep them in this curing mixture for 2 months, turning them every day. Drain them from the pickle, cover with brown paper, and have them smoked for about 3 weeks. *Time.* —The tongues to remain in pickle 2 months; to be smoked 3 weeks. *Sufficient.*—The above quantity of brine sufficient for 12 tongues, of 5 lbs. each. *Seasonable* at any time.

TONGUE, to Pickle and Dress a, to Eat Cold.

Ingredients.—6 oz. of salt, 2 oz. of bay-salt, 1 oz. of saltpetre, 3 oz. of coarse sugar; cloves, mace, and allspice to taste; butter, common crust of flour and water. *Mode.*—Lay the tongue for a fortnight in the above pickle, turn it every day, and be particular that the spices are well pounded; put it into a small pan just large enough to hold it, place some pieces of butter on it, and cover with a common crust. Bake in a slow oven until so tender that a straw would penetrate it,

| Treacle Pudding, Rolled | Trifle, Indian |

take off the skin, fasten it down to a piece of board by running a fork through the root, and another through the tip, at the same time straightening it and putting it into shape. When cold, glaze it, put a paper ruche round the root, which is generally very unsightly, and garnish with tufts of parsley. *Time.*—From 3 to 4 hours in a slow oven, according to size. *Average cost*, for a medium-sized uncured tongue, 2s. 6d. *Seasonable* at any time.

TREACLE PUDDING, Rolled.

Ingredients.—1 lb. of suet crust, ¼ lb. of treacle, ½ teaspoonful of grated ginger. *Mode.*—Make, with 1 lb. of flour, a suet crust by our given recipe, roll it out to the thickness of ½ inch, and spread the treacle equally over it, leaving a small margin where the paste joins ; close the ends securely, tie the pudding in a floured cloth, plunge it into boiling water, and boil for 2 hours. We have inserted this pudding, being economical, and a favourite one with children ; it is, of course, only suitable for a nursery, or very plain family dinner. Made with a lard instead of a suet crust, it would be very nice baked, and would be sufficiently done in from 1½ to 2 hours. *Time.*—Boiled pudding, 2 hours ; baked pudding, 1½ to 2 hours. *Average cost,* 7d. *Sufficient* for 5 or 6 persons. *Seasonable* at any time.

TRIFLE, to make a.

Ingredients.—For the whip, 1 pint of cream, 3 oz. of pounded sugar, the white of 2 eggs, a small glass of sherry or raisin wine. For the trifle, 1 pint of custard, made with 8 eggs to a pint of milk ; 6 small sponge cakes, or 6 slices of sponge-cake ; 12 macaroons, 2 dozen ratafias, 2 oz. of sweet almonds, the grated rind of 1 lemon, a layer of raspberry or strawberry jam, ½ pint of sherry or sweet wine, 6 tablespoonfuls of brandy. *Mode.*—The whip to lay over the top of the trifle should be made the day before it is required for table, as the flavour is better, and it is much more solid than when prepared the same day. Put into a large bowl the pounded sugar, the whites of the eggs, which should be beaten to a stiff froth, a glass of sherry or sweet wine, and the cream. Whisk these ingredients well in a cool place,

and take off the froth with a skimmer as fast as it rises, and put it on a sieve to drain ; continue the whisking till there is sufficient of the whip, which must be put away in a cool place to drain. The next day, place the sponge-cakes, macaroons, and ratafias at the bottom of a trifle-dish ; pour over them ½ pint of sherry or sweet wine, mixed with 6 tablespoonfuls of brandy, and, should this pro-

TRIFLE.

portion of wine not be found quite sufficient, add a little more, as the cakes should be well soaked. Over the cakes put the grated lemon-rind, the sweet almonds, blanched and cut into strips, and a layer of raspberry or strawberry jam. Make a good custard, by recipe, using 8 instead of 5 eggs to the pint of milk, and let this cool a little ; then pour it over the cakes, &c. The whip being made the day previously, and the trifle prepared, there remains nothing to do now but heap the whip lightly over the top : this should stand as high as possible, and it may be garnished with strips of bright currant jelly (see illustration), crystallized sweetmeats, or flowers ; the small coloured comfits are sometimes used for the purpose of garnishing a trifle, but they are now considered rather old-fashioned. *Average cost*, with cream at 1s. per pint, 5s. 6d. *Sufficient* for 1 trifle. *Seasonable* at any time.

TRIFLE, Indian.

Ingredients.—1 quart of milk, the rind of ½ large lemon, sugar to taste, 5 heaped tablespoonfuls of rice-flour, 1 oz. of sweet almonds, ½ pint of custard. *Mode.*—Boil the milk and lemon-rind together until the former is well flavoured; take out the lemon-rin and stir in the rice-flour, which should first be moistened with cold milk, and add sufficient loaf sugar to sweeten it nicely. Boil gently for about 5 minutes, and keep the mixture stirred; take it off the fire, let it cool *a little*, and pour it into a glass dish. When cold, cut the rice out in the form of a star, or any other shape that may be preferred; take out the spare rice, and fill the space with boiled custard. Blanch and cut the almonds into strips; stick them over the trifle, and garnish it with pieces of bright-coloured jelly, or preserved fruits, or candied citron. *Time.*—¼ hour to simmer the milk, 5 minutes after the rice is added. *Average cost,* 1s. *Sufficient* for 1 trifle. *Seasonable* at any time.

TRIPE, to Dress.

Ingredients.—Tripe, onion sauce, milk and water. *Mode.*—Ascertain that the tripe is quite fresh, and have it cleaned and dressed. Cut away the coarsest fat, and boil it in equal proportions of milk and water for ¾ hour. Should the tripe be entirely undressed, more than double that time should be allowed for it. Have ready some onion sauce, made by our given recipe, dish the tripe, smother it with the sauce, and the remainder send to table in a tureen. *Time.*—¾ hour; for undressed tripe, from 2½ to three hours. *Average cost,* 7d. per lb. *Seasonable* at any time.

Note.—Tripe may be dressed in a variety of ways: it may be cut in pieces and fried in batter, stewed in gravy with mushrooms, or cut into collops, sprinkled with minced onion and savoury herbs, and fried a nice brown in clarified butter.

TROUT, Stewed.

Ingredients.—2 middling-sized trout, ½ onion cut in thin slices, a little parsley, 2 cloves, 1 blade of mace, 2 bay-leaves, a little thyme, salt and pepper to taste, 1 pint of medium stock, 1 glass of port wine, thickening of butter and flour. *Mode.*—Wash the fish very clean, and wipe it quite dry. Lay it in a stewpan, with all the ingredients but the butter and flour, and simmer gently for ½ hour, or rather more, should not the fish be quite done. Take it out, strain the gravy, add the thickening, and stir it over a sharp fire for 5 minutes; pour it over the trout, and serve. *Time.*—According to size, ½ hour or more. *Average cost.*—Seldom bought. *Seasonable* from May to September, and fatter from the middle to the end of August than at any other time. *Sufficient* for 4 persons. Trout may be served with anchovy or caper sauce, baked in buttered paper, or fried whole like smelts. Trout dressed à

la Génévese is extremely delicate; for this proceed the same as with salmon.

TRUFFLES, to Dress, with Champagne.

Ingredients.—12 fine black truffles, a few slices of fat bacon, 1 carrot, 1 turnip, 2 onions, a bunch of savoury herbs, including parsley, 1 bay-leaf, 2 cloves, 1 blade of pounded mace, 2 glasses of champagne, ½ pint of stock. *Mode.*—Carefully select the truffles, reject those that have a musty smell, and wash them well with a brush, in cold water only, until perfectly clean. Put the bacon into a stewpan, with the truffles and the remaining ingredients; simmer these gently for an hour, and let the whole cool in the stewpan. When to be served, rewarm them, and drain them on a clean cloth; then arrange them on a delicately white napkin, that it may contrast as strongly as possible with the truffles, and serve. The trimmings of truffles are used to flavour gravies, stock, sauces, &c. and are an excellent addition to ragouts, made dishes of fowl, &c. *Time.*—1 hour *Average cost.*—Not often bought in this country. *Seasonable* from November to March.

TRUFFLES A L'ITALIENNE.

Ingredients.—10 truffles, 1 tablespoonful of minced parsley, 1 minced shalot, salt and pepper to taste, 2 oz. of butter, 2 tablespoonfuls of good brown gravy, the juice of ½ lemon, cayenne to taste. *Mode.*—Wash the truffles and cut them into slices about the size of a pennypiece; put them into a frying-pan, with the parsley, shalot, salt, pepper, and 1 oz. of butter; stir them over the fire, that they may all be equally done, which will be in about 10 minutes, and drain off some of the butter; then add a little more fresh butter, 2 tablespoonfuls of good gravy, the juice of ½ lemon, and a little cayenne; stir over the fire until the whole is on the point of boiling, when serve. *Time.*—Altogether, 20 minutes. *Average cost.*—Not often bought in this country. *Seasonable* from November to March.

TRUFFLES, Italian Mode of Dressing.

Ingredients.—10 truffles, ¼ pint of salad-oil, pepper and salt to taste, 1

Truffles au Naturel

tablespoonful of minced parsley, a very little finely minced garlic, 2 blades of pounded mace, 1 tablespoonful of lemon-juice. *Mode.*—After cleansing and brushing the truffles, cut them into thin slices, and put them in a baking-dish, on a seasoning of oil, pepper, salt, parsley, garlic, and mace in the above proportion. Bake them for nearly an hour, and, just before serving, add the lemon-juice, and send them to table very hot. *Time.*—Nearly 1 hour. *Average cost.*—Not often bought in this country. *Seasonable* from November to March.

TRUFFLES AU NATUREL.

Ingredients.—Truffles, buttered paper. *Mode.*—Select some fine truffles ; cleanse them, by washing them in several waters with a brush, until not a particle of sand or grit remains on them ; wrap each truffle in buttered paper, and bake in a hot oven for quite an hour ; take off the paper, wipe the truffles, and serve them in a hot napkin. *Time.*—1 hour. *Average cost.*—Not often bought in this country. *Seasonable* from November to March.

TURBOT.

In choosing turbot see that it is thick, and of a yellowish white ; for if of a bluish tint, it is not good. The turbot-kettle, as will be seen by our cut, is made

TURBOT-KETTLE.

differently from ordinary fish kettles, it being less deep, whilst it is wider, and more pointed at the sides ; thus exactly answering to the shape of the fish which it is intended should be boiled in it.

TURBOT, Boiled.

Ingredients.—6 oz. of salt to each gallon of water. *Mode.*—Choose a middling-sized turbot ; for they are invariably the most valuable : if very large, the meat will be tough and thready. Three or four hours before dressing, soak the fish in salt and water to take off the slime ; then thoroughly cleanse it, and with a knife make an incision down the middle

Turbot à la Creme

of the back, to prevent the skin of the belly from cracking. Rub it over with lemon, and be particular not to cut off the fins. Lay the fish in a very clean turbot-kettle, with sufficient cold water to cover it, and salt in the above proportion. Let it gradually come to a boil, and skim very carefully ; keep it gently simmering, and on no account let it boil fast, as the fish would have a very unsightly appearance. When the meat separates easily from the bone, it is done ; then take it out, let it drain well, and dish it on a hot napkin. Rub a little lobster spawn through a sieve, sprinkle it over the fish, and garnish with tufts of parsley and cut lemon. Lobster or shrimp sauce, and plain melted butter, should be sent to table with it. *Time.* — After the water boils, about ½ hour for a large turbot ; middling size, about 20 minutes. *Average cost,*—large turbot, from 10s. to 12s. ; middling size, from 12s. to. 15s. *Seasonable* at any time. *Sufficient,* 1 middling-sized turbot for 8 persons.

TURBOT, to Help.

First run the fish-slice down the thickest part of the fish lengthwise, quite through to the bone, and then cut handsome and regular slices across the fish until all the meat on the upper side is helped. When the carver has removed all the meat from the upper side of the fish, the backbone should be raised, put on one side of the dish, and the under side helped as the upper.

TURBOT A LA CREME.

Ingredients. — The remains of cold turbot. For sauce, 2 oz. of butter, 4 tablespoonfuls of cream ; salt, cayenne, and pounded mace to taste. *Mode.*—Clear away all skin and bone from the flesh of the turbot, which should be done when it comes from table, as it causes less waste when trimmed hot. Cut the flesh into nice square pieces, as equally as possible ; put into a stewpan the butter, let it melt, and add the cream and seasoning ; let it just simmer for one minute, but not boil. Lay in the fish to warm, and serve it garnished with croûtons or a paste border. *Time.*—10 minutes. *Seasonable* at any time.

Note.—The remains of cold salmon may be dressed in this way, and the above mixture may be served in a *vol-au vent*

Turbot, Baked Fillets of

Turkey, Boiled

TURBOT, Baked Fillets of.

Ingredients. — The remains of cold turbot, lobster sauce left from the preceding day, egg, and bread-crumbs; cayenne and salt to taste; minced parsley, nutmeg, lemon-juice. *Mode.*—After having cleared the fish from all skin and bone, divide it into square pieces of an equal size; brush them over with egg, sprinkle with bread-crumbs mixed with a little minced parsley and seasoning. Lay the fillets in a baking-dish, with sufficient butter to baste with. Bake for ¼ hour, and do not forget to keep them well moistened with the butter. Put a little lemon-juice and grated nutmeg to the cold lobster sauce; make it hot, and pour over the fish, which must be well drained from the butter. Garnish with parsley and cut lemon. *Time.* —Altogether, ½ hour. *Seasonable* at any time.

Note.—Cold turbot thus warmed in the remains of lobster sauce will be found much nicer than putting the fish again in water.

TURBOT A L'ITALIENNE, Fillets of.

Ingredients. — The remains of cold turbot, Italian sauce. *Mode.* — Clear the fish carefully from the bone, and take away all skin, which gives an unpleasant flavour to the sauce. Make the sauce hot, lay in the fish to warm through, but do not let it boil. Garnish with croûtons. *Time.*—5 minutes. *Seasonable* all the year.

TURBOT, or other Large Fish, Garnish for.

Take the crumb of a stale loaf, cut it into small pyramids with flat tops, and on the top of each pyramid put rather more than a tablespoonful of white of egg beaten to a stiff froth. Over this, sprinkle finely-chopped parsley and fine raspings of a dark colour. Arrange these on the napkin round the fish, one green and one brown alternately.

TURBOT AU GRATIN.

Ingredients.—Remains of cold turbot, béchamel (*see* Sauces), bread-crumbs, butter. *Mode.* — Cut the fish of the turbot into small dice, carefully freeing it from all skin and bone. Put them

into a stewpan, and moisten with 4 or 5 tablespoonfuls of béchamel. Let it get thoroughly hot, but do not allow it to boil. Spread the mixture on a dish, cover with finely-grated bread-crumbs, and place small pieces of butter over the top. Brown it in the oven, or with a salamander. *Time.*—Altogether, ½ hour. *Seasonable* at any time.

TURKEY, Boiled.

Ingredients. — Turkey; forcemeat. *Choosing and Trussing.*—Hen turkeys are preferable for boiling, on account of their whiteness and tenderness, and one of moderate size should be selected, as a large one is not suitable for this mode of cooking. They should not be dressed until they have been killed 3 or 4 days, as they will neither look white, nor will they be tender. Pluck the bird, carefully draw, and singe it with a piece of white paper; wash it inside and out, and wipe it thoroughly dry with a cloth. Cut off the head and neck, draw the strings or sinews of the thighs, and cut off the legs at the first joint; draw the legs into the body, fill the breast with forcemeat; run a skewer through the

BOILED TURKEY.

wing and the middle joint of the leg, quite into the leg and wing on the opposite side; break the breastbone, and make the bird look as round and as compact as possible. *Mode.*—Put the turkey into sufficient *hot* water to cover it; let it come to a boil, then carefully remove all the scum: if this is attended to, there is no occasion to boil the bird in a floured cloth; but it should be well covered with the water. Let it simmer very gently for about 1½ hour to 1¾ hour, according to the size, and serve with either white, celery, oyster, or mushroom sauce, or parsley-and-butter, a little of which should be poured over the turkey. Boiled ham, bacon, tongue, or pickled pork, should always accompany this dish; and when oyster sauce is served, the turkey should be stuffed with oyster forcemeat. *Time.*—A small turkey, 1½ hour; a large one, 1¾ hour.

Turkey, Croquettes of

Average cost, 5s. 6d. to 7s. 6d. each, but more expensive at Christmas, on account of the great demand. Sufficient for 7 or 8 persons. Seasonable from December to February.

TURKEY, Croquettes of (Cold Meat Cookery).

Ingredients. — The remains of cold turkey ; to every ½ lb. of meat allow 2 oz. of ham or bacon, 2 shalots, 1 oz. of butter, 1 tablespoonful of flour, the yolks of 2 eggs, egg and bread-crumbs. Mode.— The smaller pieces, that will not do for a fricassée or hash, answer very well for this dish. Mince the meat finely with ham or bacon in the above proportion ; make a gravy of the bones and trimmings, well seasoning it : mince the shalots, put them into a stewpan with the butter, add the flour ; mix well, then put in the mince, and about ½ pint of the gravy made from the bones. (The proportion of the butter must be increased or diminished according to the quantity of mince.) When just boiled, add the yolks of 2 eggs ; put the mixture out to cool, and then shape it in a wineglass. Cover the croquettes with egg and bread-crumbs, and fry them a delicate brown. Put small pieces of parsley-stems for stalks, and serve with rolled bacon cut very thin. Time.—8 minutes to fry the croquettes. Seasonable from December to February.

TURKEY, Fricasseed (Cold Meat Cookery).

Ingredients.—The remains of cold roast or boiled turkey ; a strip of lemon-peel, a bunch of savoury herbs, 1 onion, pepper and salt to taste, 1 pint of water, 4 tablespoonfuls of cream, the yolk of an egg. Mode.—Cut some nice slices from the remains of a cold turkey, and put the bones and trimmings into a stewpan, with the lemon-peel, herbs, onion, pepper, salt, and the water ; stew for an hour, strain the gravy, and lay in the pieces of turkey. When warm through, add the cream and the yolk of an egg ; stir it well round, and, when getting thick, take out the pieces, lay them on a hot dish, and pour the sauce over. Garnish the fricassée with sippets of toasted bread. Celery or cucumbers, cut into small pieces, may be put into the sauce ; if the former, it must be

Turkey, Roast

boiled first. Time.—1 hour to make the gravy. Average cost, exclusive of the cold turkey, 4d. Seasonable from December to February.

TURKEY, Hashed.

Ingredients.—The remains of cold roast turkey, 1 onion, pepper and salt to taste, rather more than 1 pint of water, 1 carrot, 1 turnip, 1 blade of mace, a bunch of savoury herbs, 1 tablespoonful of mushroom ketchup, 1 tablespoonful of port wine, thickening of butter and flour. Mode.—Cut the turkey into neat joints ; the best pieces reserve for the hash, the inferior joints and trimmings put into a stewpan with an onion cut in slices, pepper and salt, a carrot, turnip, mace, herbs, and water in the above proportion ; simmer these for an hour, then strain the gravy, thicken it with butter and flour, flavour with ketchup and port wine, and lay in the pieces of turkey to warm through ; if there is any stuffing left, put that in also, as it so much improves the flavour of the gravy. When it boils, serve, and garnish the dish with sippets of toasted bread. Time.—1 hour to make the gravy. Seasonable from December to February.

TURKEY, Roast.

Ingredients. — Turkey ; forcemeat. Choosing and Trussing.—Choose cock turkeys by their short spurs and black legs, in which case they are young ; if the spurs are long, and the legs pale and rough, they are old. If the bird has been long killed, the eyes will appear sunk and the feet very dry ; but, if fresh, the contrary will be the case. Middling-sized fleshy turkeys are by many persons considered superior to those of an immense growth, as they are, generally speaking, much more tender. They should never be dressed the same day they are killed ; but, in cold weather, should hang at least 8 days ; if the weather is mild, 4 or 5 days will be found sufficient. Carefully pluck the bird, singe it with white paper, and wipe it thoroughly with a cloth ; draw it, preserve the liver and gizzard, and be particular not to break the gall-bag, as no washing will remove the bitter taste it imparts where it once touches. Wash it inside well, and wipe it thoroughly dry with a cloth ; the outside merely requires

Turkey, Roast

nicely wiping, as we have just stated. Cut off the neck close to the back, but leave enough of the crop-skin to turn over; break the leg-bone close below the knee, draw out the strings from the thighs, and flatten the breastbone to make it look plump. Have ready a forcemeat; fill the breast with this, and, if a trussing-needle is used, sew the neck over to the back; if a needle is not at hand, a skewer will answer the purpose. Run a skewer through the pinion and thigh into the body to the pinion and thigh on the other side, and press the

ROAST TURKEY.

legs as much as possible between the breast and the side-bones, and put the liver under one pinion and the gizzard under the other. Pass a string across the back of the bird, catch it over the points of the skewer, tie it in the centre of the back, and be particular that the turkey is very firmly trussed. This may be more easily accomplished with a needle and twine than with skewers. *Mode.*—Fasten a sheet of buttered paper on to the breast of the bird, put it down to a bright fire, at some little distance *at first* (afterwards draw it nearer), and keep it well basted the whole of the time it is cooking. About ¼ hour before serving, remove the paper, dredge the turkey lightly with flour, and put a piece of butter into the basting-ladle; as the butter melts, baste the bird with it. When of a nice brown and well frothed, serve with a tureen of good brown gravy and one of bread sauce. Fried sausages are a favourite addition to roast turkey; they make a pretty garnish, besides adding very much to the flavour. When these are not at hand, a few forcemeat balls should be placed round the dish as a garnish. Turkey may also be stuffed with sausage-meat, and a chestnut forcemeat with the chestnut sauce is, by many persons, very much esteemed as an accompaniment to this favourite dish. *Time.*—Small turkey, 1½ hour; moderate-sized one, about 10 lbs., 2 hours; large turkey, 2½ hours, or longer. *Average cost,* from 10s. to 12s., but ex-

Turkey Poults, Roast

pensive at Christmas, on account of the great demand. *Sufficient.*—A moderate-sized turkey for 7 or 8 persons. *Seasonable* from December to February.

TURKEY, Roast.

A noble dish is a turkey, roast or boiled. A Christmas dinner, with the middle-classes of this empire, would scarcely be a Christmas dinner without its turkey; and we can hardly imag an object of greater envy than is p sented by a respected portly pate familias carving, at the season devoted to good cheer and genial charity, his own fat turkey, and carving it well. The only art consists, as in the carving of a goose, in getting from the breast as many fine slices as possible; and all must have remarked the very great difference in the large number of people whom a good carver will find slices for, and the comparatively few that a bad carver will succeed in serving. As we have stated

ROAST TURKEY.

in both the carving of a duck and goose, the carver should commence cutting slices to the wing, from 2 to 3, and then proceed upwards towards the ridge of the breastbone: this is not the usual plan, but, in practice, will be found the best. The breast is the only part which is looked on as fine in a turkey, the legs being very seldom cut off and eaten at table: they are usually removed to the kitchen, where they are taken off, as here marked, to appear only in a form which seems to have a special attraction at a bachelor's supper-table,—we mean devilled: served in this way, they are especially liked and relished. A boiled turkey is carved in the same manner as when roasted.

TURKEY POULTS, Roast.

Ingredients. — Turkey poult; butter. *Choosing and Trussing.*—Choose a plump bird, and truss it in the following manner:—After it has been carefully plucked, drawn, and singed, skin the neck, and fasten the head under the wing; turn the

Turkey Soup	Turnips, Mashed

legs at the first joint, and bring the feet close to the thighs, as a woodcock should be trussed, *and do not stuff it. Mode.*— Put it down to a bright fire, keep it well basted, and at first place a piece of paper on the breast to prevent its taking too much colour. About 10 minutes before serving, dredge it lightly with flour, and baste well; when nicely frothed, send it to table immediately, with a little gravy in the dish, and some in a tureen. If at hand, a few water-cresses may be placed round the turkey as a garnish, or it may be larded. *Time.*—About 1 hour. *Average cost, 7s.* to 8s. each. *Sufficient* for 6 or 7 persons. *Seasonable.*—In full season from June to October.

TURKEY SOUP (a Seasonable Dish at Christmas).

Ingredients.—2 quarts of medium stock, the remains of a cold roast turkey, 2 oz. of rice-flour or arrowroot, salt and pepper to taste, 1 tablespoonful of Harvey's sauce or mushroom ketchup. *Mode.*— Cut up the turkey in small pieces, and put it in the stock; let it simmer slowly until the bones are quite clean. Take the bones out, and work the soup through a sieve; when cool, skim well. Mix the rice-flour or arrowroot to a batter with a little of the soup; add it with the seasoning and sauce, or ketchup. Give one boil, and serve. *Time.*—4 hours. *Average cost,* 10d. per quart. *Seasonable* at Christmas. *Sufficient* for 8 persons.

Note.—Instead of thickening this soup, vermicelli o. macaroni may be served in it.

TURNIP SOUP

Ingredients.—3 oz. of butter, 9 good-sized turnips, 4 onions, 2 quarts of stock, seasoning to taste. *Mode.* — Melt the butter in the stewpan, but do not let it boil; wash, drain, and slice the turnips and onions very thin; put them in the butter, with a teacupful of stock, and stew very gently for an hour. Then add the remainder of the stock, and simmer another hour. Rub it through a tammy, put it back into the stewpan, but do not let it boil. Serve very hot. *Time.*—2½ hours. *Average cost,* 8d. per quart. *Seasonable* from October to March. *Sufficient* for 8 persons.

Note.—By adding a little cream, this soup will be much improved.

TURNIPS, Boiled.

Ingredients. — Turnips; to each ⅓ gallon of water allow 1 heaped tablespoonful of salt. *Mode.* — Pare the turnips, and, should they be very large, divide them into quarters; but, unless this is the case, let them be cooked whole. Put them into a saucepan of boiling water, salted in the above proportion, and let them boil gently until tender. Try them with a fork, and, when done, take them up in a colander; let them thoroughly drain, and serve. Boiled turnips are usually sent to table with boiled mutton, but are infinitely nicer when mashed than served whole: unless nice and young, they are scarcely worth the trouble of dressing plainly as above. *Time.*—Old turnips, ¾ to 1¼ hour; young ones, about 18 to 20 minutes. *Average cost,* 4d. per bunch. *Sufficient.*—Allow a bunch of 12 turnips for 5 or 6 persons. *Seasonable.*—May be had all the year; but in spring only useful for flavouring gravies, &c.

TURNIPS, German Mode of Cooking.

Ingredients.—8 large turnips, 3 oz. of butter, pepper and salt to taste, rather more than ⅓ pint of weak stock or broth, 1 tablespoonful of flour. *Mode.*—Make the butter hot in a stewpan, lay in the turnips, after having pared and cut them into dice, and season them with pepper and salt. Toss them over the fire for a few minutes, then add the broth, and simmer the whole gently till the turnips are tender. Brown the above proportion of flour with a little butter; add this to the turnips, let them simmer another 5 minutes, and serve. Boiled mutton is usually sent to table with this vegetable, and may be cooked with the turnips by placing it in the midst of them: the meat would then be very delicious, as, there being so little liquid with the turnips, it would almost be steamed, and, consequently, very tender. *Time.*—20 minutes. *Average cost,* 4d. per bunch. *Sufficient* for 4 persons. *Seasonable.*— May be had all the year.

TURNIPS, Mashed.

Ingredients.—10 or 12 large turnips; to each ½ gallon of water allow 1 heaped tablespoonful of salt, 2 oz. of butter, cayenne or white pepper to taste. *Mode.*—

Turnips in White Sauce.

Pare the turnips, quarter them, and put them into boiling water, salted in the above proportion ; boil them until tender ; then drain them in a colander, and squeeze them as dry as possible by pressing them with the back of a large plate. When quite free from water, rub the turnips with a wooden spoon through the colander, and put them into a very clean saucepan ; add the butter, white pepper, or cayenne, and, if necessary, a little salt. Keep stirring them over the fire until the butter is well mixed with them, and the turnips are thoroughly hot ; dish, and serve. A little cream or milk added after the turnips are pressed through the colander, is an improvement to both the colour and flavour of this vegetable. *Time.*—From ½ to ¾ hour to boil the turnips ; 10 minutes to warm them through. *Average cost*, 4d. per bunch. *Sufficient* for 4 or 5 persons. *Seasonable.*—May be had all the year ; but in early spring only good for flavouring gravies.

TURNIPS IN WHITE SAUCE. (An Entremets, or to be served with the Second Course as a Side-dish.)

Ingredients.—7 or 8 turnips, 1 oz. of butter, ⅓ pint of white sauce. *Mode.*—Peel and cut the turnips in the shape of pears or marbles ; boil them in salt and water, to which has been added a little butter, until tender ; then take them out, drain, arrange them on a dish, and pour over the white sauce made by either of the recipes, and to which has been added a small lump of sugar. In winter, when other vegetables are scarce, this will be found a very good and pretty-looking dish : when approved, a little mustard may be added to the sauce. *Time.*—About ¾ hour to boil the turnips. *Average cost*, 4d. per bunch. *Sufficient* for 1 side dish. *Seasonable* in winter.

VANILLA CUSTARD SAUCE, to serve with Puddings.

Ingredients.—½ pint of milk, 2 eggs, 2 oz. of sugar, 10 drops of essence of vanilla. *Mode.*—Beat the eggs, sweeten the milk ; stir these ingredients well together, and flavour them with essence of vanilla, regulating the proportion of this latter ingredient by the strength of the essence, the size of the eggs, &c. Put the mixture

Veal, Breast of, to Carve.

into a small jug, place this jug in a saucepan of boiling water, and stir the sauce *one way* until it thickens ; but do not allow it to boil, or it will instantly curdle. Serve in a boat or tureen separately, with plum, bread, or any kind of dry pudding. Essence of bitter almonds or lemon-rind may be substituted for the vanilla, when they are more in accordance with the flavouring of the pudding with which the sauce is intended to be served. *Time.*—To be stirred in the jug from 8 to 10 minutes. *Average cost*, 4d. *Sufficient* for 4 or 5 persons.

VEAL, Baked (Cold Meat Cookery).

Ingredients.—½ lb. of cold roast veal, a few slices of bacon. 1 pint of bread-crumbs, ½ pint of good veal gravy, ½ teaspoonful of minced lemon-peel, 1 blade of pounded mace, cayenne and salt to taste, 4 eggs. *Mode.*—Mince finely the veal and bacon ; add the bread-crumbs, gravy, and seasoning, and stir these ingredients well together. Beat up the eggs thoroughly ; add these, mix the whole well together, put into a dish, and bake from ¾ to 1 hour. When liked, a little good gravy may be served in a tureen as an accompaniment. *Time.*—from ¾ to 1 hour. *Average cost*, exclusive of the cold meat, 6d. *Sufficient* for 3 or 4 persons. *Seasonable* from March to October.

VEAL, Roast Breast of.

Ingredients. — Veal ; a little flour. *Mode.*—Wash the veal, well wipe it, and dredge it with flour ; put it down to a bright fire, not too near, as it should not be scorched. Baste it plentifully until done ; dish it, pour over the meat some good melted butter, and send to table with it a piece of boiled bacon and a cut lemon. *Time.*—From 1½ to 2 hours. *Average cost*, 8½d. per lb. *Sufficient* for 5 or 6 persons. *Seasonable* from March to October.

VEAL, Breast of, to Carve.

The carving of a breast of veal is not dissimilar to that of a fore-quarter of lamb, when the shoulder has been taken off. The breast of veal consists of two parts, — the rib-bones and the gristly brisket. These two parts should first be separated by sharply passing the knife in the direction of the lines 1, 2 ; when

Veal, Stewed Breast of, and Peas

they are entirely divided, the rib-bones should be carved in the direction of the lines 5 to 6; and the brisket can be helped by cutting pieces in the direction

BREAST OF VEAL.

8 to 4. The carver should ask the guests whether they have a preference for the brisket or ribs; and if there be a sweetbread served with the dish, as it often is with roast breast of veal, each person should receive a piece.

VEAL, Stewed Breast of, and Peas.

Ingredients.—Breast of veal, 2 oz. of butter, a bunch of savoury herbs, including parsley; 2 blades of pounded mace, 2 cloves, 5 or 6 young onions, 1 strip of lemon-peel, 6 allspice, ¼ teaspoonful of pepper, 1 teaspoonful of salt, thickening of butter and flour, 2 tablespoonfuls of sherry, 2 tablespoonfuls of tomato sauce, 1 tablespoonful of lemon-juice, 2 tablespoonfuls of mushroom ketchup, green peas. *Mode.*—Cut the breast in half, after removing the bone underneath, and divide the meat into convenient-sized pieces. Put the butter into a frying-pan, lay in the pieces of veal, and fry until of a nice brown colour. Now place these in a stewpan with the herbs, mace, cloves, onions, lemon-peel, allspice, and seasoning; pour over them just sufficient boiling water to cover the meat; well close the lid, and let the whole simmer very gently for about 2 hours. Strain off as much gravy as is required, thicken it with butter and flour, add the remaining ingredients, skim well, let it simmer for about 10 minutes, then pour it over the meat. Have ready some green peas, boiled separately; sprinkle these over the veal, and serve. It may be garnished with forcemeat balls, or rashers of bacon curled and fried. Instead of cutting up the meat, many persons prefer it dressed whole; — in that case it should be half-roasted before the water, &c. are put to it. *Time.*—2¼ hours. *Average cost,* 8½d. *Sufficient* for 5 or 6 persons. *Seasonable* from March to October.

Veal, Curried

VEAL, à la Bourgeoise (Excellent).

Ingredients.—2 to 3 lbs. of the loin or neck of veal, 10 or 12 young carrots, a bunch of green onions, 2 slices of lean bacon, 2 blades of pounded mace, 1 bunch of savoury herbs, pepper and salt to taste, a few new potatoes, 1 pint of green peas. *Mode.*—Cut the veal into cutlets, trim them, and put the trimmings into a stewpan with a little butter; lay in the cutlets and fry them a nice brown colour on both sides. Add the bacon, carrots, onions, spice, herbs, and seasoning; pour in about a pint of boiling water, and stew gently for 2 hours on a very slow fire. When done, skim off the fat, take out the herbs, and flavour the gravy with a little tomato sauce and ketchup. Have ready the peas and potatoes, boiled *separately;* put them with the veal, and serve. *Time.*— 2 hours. *Average cost,* 2s. 9d. *Sufficient* for 5 or 6 persons. *Seasonable* from June to August with peas; — rather earlier when these are omitted.

VEAL CAKE (a Convenient Dish for a Picnic).

Ingredients.—A few slices of cold roast veal, a few slices of cold ham, 2 hard-boiled eggs, 2 tablespoonfuls of minced parsley, a little pepper, good gravy. *Mode.*—Cut off all the brown outside from the veal, and cut the eggs into slices. Procure a pretty mould; lay veal, ham, eggs, and parsley in layers, with a little pepper between each, and when the mould is full, get some *strong* stock, and fill up the shape. Bake for ½ hour, and when cold, turn it out. *Time.*—½ hour. *Seasonable* at any time.

VEAL, Curried (Cold Meat Cookery).

Ingredients.—The remains of cold roast veal, 4 onions, 2 apples sliced, 1 tablespoonful of curry-powder, 1 dessertspoonful of flour, ½ pint of broth or water, 1 tablespoonful of lemon-juice. *Mode.*—Slice the onions and apples, and fry them in a little butter; then take them out, cut the meat into neat cutlets, and fry these of a pale brown; add the curry powder and flour, put in the onion, apples, and a little broth or water, and stew gently till quite tender; add the lemon-juice, and serve with an edging of

23

Veal Cutlets (an Entrée)

boiled rice. The curry may be ornamented with pickles, capsicums, and gherkins, arranged prettily on the top. *Time.*—¾ hour. *Average cost*, exclusive of the meat, 4d. *Seasonable* from March to October.

VEAL CUTLETS (an Entrée).

Ingredients.—About 3 lbs. of the prime part of the leg of veal, egg and breadcrumbs, 3 tablespoonfuls of minced savoury herbs, salt and pepper to taste, a small piece of butter. *Mode.*—Have the veal cut into slices about ¾ of an inch in thickness, and, if not cut perfectly even, level the meat with a cutlet-bat or rolling-pin. Shape and trim the cutlets, and brush them over with egg. Sprinkle with bread-crumbs, with which have been mixed minced herbs and a seasoning of pepper and salt, and press the crumbs

VEAL CUTLETS.

down. Fry them of a delicate brown in fresh lard or butter, and be careful not to burn them. They should be very thoroughly done, but not dry. If the cutlets be thick, keep the pan covered for a few minutes at a good distance from the fire, after they have acquired a good colour: by this means, the meat will be done through. Lay the cutlets in a dish, keep them hot, and make a gravy in the pan as follows:—Dredge in a little flour, add a piece of butter the size of a walnut, brown it, then pour as much boiling water as is required over it, season with pepper and salt, add a little lemon-juice, give one boil, and pour it over the cutlets. They should be garnished with slices of broiled bacon, and a few forcemeat balls will be found a very excellent addition to this dish. *Time.*—For cutlets of a moderate thickness, about 12 minutes; if very thick, allow more time. *Average cost*, 10d. per lb. *Sufficient* for 6 persons. *Seasonable* from March to October.

Note.—Veal cutlets may be merely floured and fried of a nice brown: the gravy and garnishing should be the same as in the preceding recipe. They may also be cut from the loin or neck, as shown in the engraving.

Veal, Fillet of, au Béchamel

VEAL CUTLETS, Broiled, à la Italienne (an Entrée).

Ingredients.—Neck of veal, salt and pepper to taste, the yolk of 1 egg, breadcrumbs, ½ pint of Italian sauce. *Mode.*—Cut the veal into cutlets, flatten and trim them nicely; powder over them a little salt and pepper; brush them over with the yolk of an egg, dip them into bread-crumbs, then into clarified butter, and, afterwards, in the bread-crumbs again; boil or fry them over a clear fire, that they may acquire a good brown colour. Arrange them in the dish alternately with rashers of broiled ham, and pour the sauce (made by recipe for Italian sauce, p. 305) in the middle. *Time.*—10 to 15 minutes, according to the thickness of the cutlets. *Average cost*, 10d. per lb. *Seasonable* from March to October.

VEAL CUTLETS, à la Maintenon (an Entrée).

Ingredients.—2 or 3 lbs. of veal cutlets, egg and bread-crumbs, 2 tablespoonfuls of minced savoury herbs, salt and pepper to taste, a little grated nutmeg. *Mode.*—Cut the cutlets about ¾ inch in thickness, flatten them, and brush them over with the yolk of an egg; dip them into bread-crumbs and minced herbs, season with pepper and salt and grated nutmeg, and fold each cutlet in a piece of buttered paper. Broil them, and send them to table with melted butter or a good gravy. *Time.*—From 15 to 18 minutes. *Average cost*, 10d. per lb. *Sufficient* for 5 or 6 persons. *Seasonable* from March to October.

VEAL, Fillet of, au Béchamel (Cold Meat Cookery).

Ingredients.—A small fillet of veal, 1 pint of béchamel sauce, a few breadcrumbs, clarified butter. *Mode.*—A fillet of veal that has been roasted the preceding day will answer very well for this dish. Cut the middle out rather deep, leaving a good margin round, from which to cut nice slices, and if there should be any cracks in the veal, fill them up with forcemeat. Mince finely the meat that was taken out, mixing with it a little of the forcemeat to flavour, and stir to it sufficient béchamel to make it of a proper consistency. Warm the veal in the oven for about an hour, taking care to baste it well, that it may not be dry;

Veal, Roast Fillet of

put the mince in the place where the meat was taken out, sprinkle a few bread-crumbs over it, and drop a little clarified butter on the bread-crumbs; put it into the oven for ¼ hour to brown, and pour béchamel round the sides of the dish. *Time.*—Altogether 1½ hour. *Seasonable* from March to October.

VEAL, Roast Fillet of.

Ingredients.—Veal, forcemeat, melted butter. *Mode.*—Have the fillet cut according to the size required; take out the bone, and after raising the skin from the meat, put under the flap a nice forcemeat. Prepare sufficient of this, as there should be some left to eat cold, and to season and flavour a mince if required. Skewer and bind the veal up in a

FILLET OF VEAL.

round form; dredge well with flour, put it down at some distance from the fire at first, and baste continually. About ½ hour before serving, draw it nearer the fire, that it may acquire more colour, as the outside should be of a rich brown, but not burnt. Dish it, remove the skewers, which replace by a silver one; pour over the joint some good melted butter, and serve with either boiled ham, bacon, or pickled pork. Never omit to send a cut lemon to table with roast veal. *Time.*—A fillet of veal weighing 12 lbs., about 4 hours. *Average cost*, 9d. per lb. *Sufficient* for 9 or 10 persons. *Seasonable* from March to October.

VEAL, Fillet of.

The carving of this joint is similar to that of a round of beef. Slices, not too

FILLET OF VEAL.

thick, in the direction of the line 1 to 2 are cut; and the only point to be careful about is, that the veal be *evenly* carved. Between the flap and the meat the stuffing is inserted, and

Veal, Fricandeau of

a small portion of this should be served to every guest. The persons whom the host wishes most to honour should be asked if they like the delicious brown outside slice, as this, by many, is exceedingly relished.

VEAL, Stewed Fillet of.

Ingredients.—A small fillet of veal, forcemeat, thickening of butter and flour, a few mushrooms, white pepper to taste, 2 tablespoonfuls of lemon-juice, 2 blades of pounded mace, ½ glass of sherry *Mode.*—If the whole of the leg is purchased, take off the knuckle to stew, and also the square end, which will serve for cutlets or pies. Remove the bone, and fill the space with a forcemeat. Roll and skewer it up firmly; place a few skewers at the bottom of a stewpan to prevent the meat from sticking, and cover the veal with a little weak stock. Let it simmer very *gently* until tender, as the more slowly veal is stewed, the better. Strain and thicken the sauce, flavour it with lemon-juice, mace, sherry, and white pepper; give one boil, and pour it over the meat. The skewers should be removed, and replaced by a silver one, and the dish garnished with slices of cut lemon. *Time.*—A fillet of veal weighing 6 lbs., 3 hours' very gentle stewing. *Average cost*, 9d. per lb. *Sufficient* for 5 or 6 persons. *Seasonable* from March to October.

VEAL, Fricandeau of (an Entrée).

Ingredients.—A piece of the fat side of a leg of veal (about 3 lbs.), lardoons, 2 carrots, 2 large onions, a faggot of savoury herbs, 2 blades of pounded mace, 6 whole allspice, 2 bay-leaves, pepper to taste, a few slices of fat bacon, 1 pint of stock. *Mode.*—The veal for a

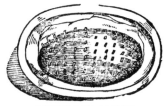

FRICANDEAU OF VEAL.

fricandeau should be of the best quality, or it will not be good. It may be known by the meat being white and not thready. Take off the skin, flatten the veal on the

Veal, Fricandeau of

table, then at one stroke of the knife, cut off as much as is required, for a fricandeau with an uneven surface never looks well. Trim it, and with a sharp knife make two or three slits in the middle, that it may taste more of the seasoning. Now lard it thickly with fat bacon, as lean gives a red colour to the fricandeau. Slice the vegetables, and put these, with the herbs and spices, in the *middle* of a stewpan, with a few slices of bacon at the top: these should form a sort of mound in the centre for the veal to rest upon. Lay the fricandeau over the bacon, sprinkle over it a little salt, and pour in just sufficient stock to cover the bacon, &c., without touching the veal. Let it gradually come to a boil; then put it over a slow and equal fire, and let it *simmer very* gently for about 2½ hours, or longer should it be very large. Baste it frequently with the liquor, and a short time before serving, put it into a brisk oven, to make the bacon firm, which otherwise would break when it was glazed. Dish the fricandeau, keep it hot, skim off the fat from the liquor, and reduce it quickly to a glaze, with which glaze the fricandeau, and serve with a purée of whatever vegetable happens to be in season—spinach, sorrel, asparagus, cucumbers, peas, &c. *Time.* —2½ hours. If very large, allow more time. *Average cost*, 3s. 6d. *Sufficient* for an entrée. *Seasonable* from March to October.

VEAL, Fricandeau of (more economical).

Ingredients.—The best end of a neck of veal (about 2½ lbs.), lardoons, 2 carrots, 2 onions, a faggot of savoury herbs, 2 blades of mace, 2 bay-leaves, a little whole white pepper, a few slices of fat bacon. *Mode.*—Cut away the lean part of the best end of a neck of veal with a sharp knife, scooping it from the bones. Put the bones in with a little water, which will serve to moisten the fricandeau: they should stew about 1½ hour. Lard the veal, proceed in the same way as in the preceding recipe, and be careful that the gravy does not touch the fricandeau. Stew very gently for 3 hours; glaze, and serve it on sorrel, spinach, or with a little gravy in the dish. *Time.*—3 hours. *Average cost*, 2s. 6d. *Sufficient* for an entrée. *Seasonable* from March to October.

Veal, Stewed Knuckle of, and Rice.

Note.—When the prime part of the leg is cut off, it spoils the whole; consequently, to use this for a fricandeau is rather extravagant. The best end of the neck answers the purpose nearly or quite as well.

VEAL, to Carve a Knuckle of.

The engraving, showing the dotted line from 1 to 2, sufficiently indicates the direction which should be given to the knife in carving this dish. The best slices are those from the thickest part of the knuckle, that is, outside the line 1 to 2.

KNUCKLE OF VEAL.

VEAL, to Ragout a Knuckle of.

Ingredients.—Knuckle of veal, pepper and salt to taste, flour, 1 onion, 1 head of celery, or a little celery-seed, a faggot of savoury herbs, 2 blades of pounded mace, thickening of butter and flour, a few young carrots, 1 tablespoonful of tomato sauce, 3 tablespoonfuls of sherry, the juice of ½ lemon. *Mode.*—Cut the meat from a knuckle of veal into neat slices, season with pepper and salt, and dredge them with flour. Fry them in a little butter of a pale brown, and put them into a stewpan with the bone (which should be chopped in several places); add the celery, herbs, mace, and carrots; pour over all about 1 pint of hot water, and let it simmer very gently for 2 hours over a slow but clear fire. Take out the slices of meat and carrots, strain and thicken the gravy with a little butter rolled in flour; add the remaining ingredients, give one boil, put back the meat and carrots, let these get hot through, and serve. When in season, a few green peas, *boiled separately*, and added to this dish at the moment of serving, would be found a very agreeable addition. *Time.* —2 hours. *Average cost*, 5d. to 6d. per lb. *Sufficient* for 4 or 5 persons.

VEAL, Stewed Knuckle of, and Rice.

Ingredients.—Knuckle of veal, 1 onion, 2 blades of mace, 1 teaspoonful of salt ½ lb. of rice. *Mode.*—Have the knuckle

Veal, Roast Loin of

cut small, or cut some cutlets from it, that it may be just large enough to be eaten the same day it is dressed, as cold boiled veal is not a particularly tempting dish. Break the shank-bone, wash it clean, and put the meat into a stewpan with sufficient water to cover it. Let it gradually come to a boil, put in the salt, and remove the scum as fast as it rises. When it has simmered gently for

KNUCKLE OF VEAL.

about ¾ hour, add the remaining ingredients, and stew the whole gently for 2¼ hours. Put the meat into a deep dish, pour over it the rice, &c., and send boiled bacon, and a tureen of parsley and butter to table with it. *Time.*—A knuckle of veal weighing 6 lbs., 3 hours' gentle stewing. *Average cost,* 5d. to 6d. per lb. *Sufficient* for 5 or 6 persons. *Seasonable* from March to October.

Note. — Macaroni, instead of rice, boiled with the veal, will be found good; or the rice and macaroni may be omitted, and the veal sent to table smothered in parsley and butter.

VEAL, Roast Loin of.

Ingredients. — Veal; melted butter. *Mode.*—Paper the kidney fat; roll in and skewer the flap, which makes the joint a good shape; dredge it well with flour, and put it down to a bright fire. Should the loin be very large, skewer the kidney back for a time to roast

LOIN OF VEAL.

thoroughly. Keep it well basted, and a short time before serving, remove the paper from the kidney, and allow it to acquire a nice brown colour, but it should not be burnt. Have ready some melted butter, put it into the dripping-pan after it is emptied of its contents, pour it over

Veal, to Carve Loin of

the veal, and serve. Garnish the dish with slices of lemon and forcemeat balls, and send to table with it boiled bacon, ham, pickled pork, or pig's cheek. *Time.* —A large loin, 3 hours. *Average cost,* 9½d. per lb. *Sufficient* for 7 or 8 persons. *Seasonable* from March to October.

Note.—A piece of toast should be placed under the kidneys when the veal is dished.

VEAL, Loin of, au Béchamel (Cold Meat Cookery).

Ingredients.—Loin of veal, ½ teaspoonful of minced lemon-peel, rather more than ½ pint of béchamel or white sauce. *Mode.*—A loin of veal which has come from table with very little taken off, answers well for this dish. Cut off the meat from the inside, mince it, and mix with it some minced lemon-peel; put it into sufficient béchamel to warm it through. In the mean time, wrap the joint in buttered paper, and place it in the oven to warm. When thoroughly hot, dish the mince, place the loin above it, and pour over the remainder of the béchamel. *Time.*—1½ hour to warm the meat in the oven. *Seasonable* from March to October.

VEAL, Loin of, à la Daube.

Ingredients.—The chump end of a loin of veal, forcemeat, a few slices of bacon, a bunch of savoury herbs, 2 blades of mace, ½ teaspoonful of whole white pepper, 1 pint of veal stock or water, 5 or 6 green onions. *Mode.*—Cut off the chump from a loin of veal, and take out the bone; fill the cavity with forcemeat, tie it up tightly, and lay it in a stewpan with the bones and trimmings, and cover the veal with a few slices of bacon. Add the herbs, mace, pepper, and onions, and stock or water; cover the pan with a closely-fitting lid, and simmer for 2 hours, shaking the stewpan occasionally. Take out the bacon, herbs, and onions; reduce the gravy, if not already thick enough, to a glaze, with which glaze the meat, and serve with tomato, mushroom, or sorrel sauce. *Time.*—2 hours. *Average cost,* 9d. per lb. *Sufficient* for 4 or 5 persons. *Seasonable* from March to October.

VEAL, to Carve Loin of.

As is the case with a loin of mutton, the careful jointing of a loin of veal is

Veal, Minced, with Béchamel Sauce

more than half the battle in carving it. If the butcher be negligent in this matter, he should be admonished;

LOIN OF VEAL.

for there is nothing more annoying or irritating to an inexperienced carver than to be obliged to turn his knife in all directions to find the exact place where it should be inserted in order to divide the bones. When the jointing is properly performed, there is little difficulty in carrying the knife down in the direction of the line 1 to 2. To each guest should be given a piece of the kidney and kidney fat, which lie underneath, and are considered great delicacies.

VEAL, Minced, with Béchamel Sauce (Cold Meat Cookery, very good).

Ingredients.—The remains of a fillet of veal, 1 pint of béchamel sauce, ½ teaspoonful of minced lemon-peel, forcemeat balls. *Mode.* — Cut — but do not *chop*—a few slices of cold roast veal as finely as possible, sufficient to make rather more than 1 lb., weighed after being minced. Make the above proportion of béchamel, by recipe ; add the lemon-peel, put in the veal, and let the whole gradually warm through. When it is at the point of simmering, dish it, and garnish with forcemeat balls and fried sippets of bread. *Time.* —To simmer 1 minute. *Average cost,* exclusive of the cold meat, 1s. 4d. *Sufficient* for 5 or 6 persons. *Seasonable* from March to October.

VEAL, Minced (more economical).

Ingredients. — The remains of cold roast fillet or loin of veal, rather more than 1 pint of water, 1 onion, ½ teaspoonful of minced lemon-peel, salt and white pepper to taste, 1 blade of pounded mace, 2 or 3 young carrots, a faggot of sweet herbs, thickening of butter and flour, 1 tablespoonful of lemon-juice, 3 tablespoonfuls of cream or milk. *Mode.* —Take about 1 lb. of veal, and should there be any bones, dredge them with flour, and put them into a stewpan with the brown outside, and a few meat trim-

Veal, Minced, and Macaroni

mings ; add rather more than a pint of water, the onion cut in slices, lemon-peel, seasoning, mace, carrots, and herbs ; simmer these well for rather more than 1 hour, and strain the liquor. Rub a little flour into some butter ; add this to the gravy, set it on the fire, and, when it boils, skim well. Mince the veal finely by *cutting,* and not chopping it ; put it in the gravy ; let it get warmed through gradually ; add the lemon-juice and cream, and, when it is on the point of boiling, serve. Garnish the dish with sippets of toasted bread and slices of bacon rolled and toasted. Forcemeat balls may also be added. If more lemon-peel is liked than is stated above, put a little very finely minced to the veal, after it is warmed in the gravy. *Time.* —1 hour to make the gravy. *Average cost,* exclusive of the cold meat, 6d. *Seasonable* from March to October.

VEAL, Minced, and Macaroni (a pretty side or corner dish).

Ingredients.—¾ lb. of minced cold roast veal, 3 oz. of ham, 1 tablespoonful of gravy, pepper and salt to taste, ¼ teaspoonful of grated nutmeg, ¼ lb. of bread-crumbs, ¼ lb. of macaroni, 1 or 2 eggs to bind, a small piece of butter. *Mode.*—Cut some nice slices from a cold fillet of veal, trim off the brown outside, and mince the meat finely with the above proportion of ham : should the meat be very dry, add a spoonful of good gravy. Season highly with pepper and salt, add the grated nutmeg and bread-crumbs, and mix these ingredients with 1 or 2 eggs well beaten, which should bind the mixture and make it like forcemeat. In the mean time, boil the macaroni in salt and water, and drain it ; butter a mould, put some of the macaroni at the bottom and sides of it, in whatever form is liked ; mix the remainder with the forcemeat, fill the mould up to the top, put a plate or small dish on it, and steam for ½ hour. Turn it out carefully, and serve with good gravy poured round, but not over, the meat. *Time.*—½ hour. *Average cost,* exclusive of the cold meat, 10d. *Seasonable* from March to October.

Note.—To make a variety, boil some carrots and turnips separately in a little salt and water ; when done, cut them into pieces about ½ inch in thickness ; butter an oval mould, and place these in it, in white and red stripes alternately at the bottom and sides. Proceed as in the foregoing recipe, and be very careful in turning it out of the mould.

VEAL, Moulded Minced (Cold Meat Cookery).

Ingredients.—¾ lb. of cold roast veal, a small slice of bacon, ½ teaspoonful of minced lemon-peel, ⅓ onion chopped fine, salt, pepper, and pounded mace to taste, a slice of toast soaked in milk, 1 egg. *Mode.*—Mince the meat very fine, after removing from it all skin and outside pieces, and chop the bacon; mix these well together, adding the lemon-peel, onion, seasoning, mace, and toast. When all the ingredients are thoroughly incorporated, beat up an egg, with which bind the mixture. Butter a shape, put in the meat, and bake for ¾ hour; turn it out of the mould carefully, and pour round it a good brown gravy. A sheep's head dressed in this manner is an economical and savoury dish. *Time.* ¾ hour. *Average cost,* exclusive of the meat, 6d. *Seasonable* from March to October.

VEAL, Braised Neck of.

Ingredients.—The best end of the neck of veal (from 3 to 4 lbs.), bacon, 1 tablespoonful of minced parsley, salt, pepper, and grated nutmeg to taste; 1 onion, 2 carrots, a little celery (when this is not obtainable, use the seed), ½ glass of sherry, thickening of butter and flour, lemon-juice, 1 blade of pounded mace. *Mode.*—Prepare the bacon for larding, and roll it in minced parsley, salt, pepper, and grated nutmeg; lard the veal, put it into a stewpan with a few slices of lean bacon or ham, an onion, carrots, and celery; and do not quite cover it with water. Stew it gently for 2 hours, or until it is quite tender; strain off the liquor; stir together over the fire, in a stewpan, a little flour and butter until brown; lay the veal in this, the upper side to the bottom of the pan, and let it remain till it is a nice brown colour. Place it in the dish; pour into the stewpan as much gravy as is required, boil it up, skim well, add the wine, pounded mace, and lemon-juice; simmer for 3 minutes, pour it over the meat, and serve. *Time.* — Rather more than 2 hours. *Average cost,* 8d. per lb. *Sufficient* for 5 or 6 persons. *Seasonable* from March to October.

VEAL, Roast Neck of.

Ingredients. — Veal, melted butter, forcemeat balls. *Mode.*—Have the veal cut from the best end of the neck; dredge it with flour, and put it down to a bright clear fire; keep it well basted; dish it, pour over it some melted butter, and garnish the dish with fried forcemeat balls; send to table with a cut lemon. The scrag may be boiled or stewed in various ways, with rice, onion-sauce, or parsley and butter. *Time.*—About 2 hours. *Average cost,* 8d. per lb. *Sufficient.*—4 or 5 lbs. for 5 or 6 persons. *Seasonable* from March to October.

VEAL OLIVE PIE (Cold Meat Cookery).

Ingredients.—A few thin slices of cold fillet of veal, a few thin slices of bacon, forcemeat, a cupful of gravy, 4 tablespoonfuls of cream, puff-crust. *Mode.* —Cut thin slices from a fillet of veal, place on them thin slices of bacon, and over them a layer of forcemeat, made by recipe, with an additional seasoning of shalot and cayenne; roll them tightly, and fill up a pie-dish with them; add the gravy and cream, cover with a puff-crust, and bake for 1 to 1½ hour: should the pie be very large, allow 2 hours. The pieces of rolled veal should be about 3 inches in length, and about 3 inches round. *Time.*—Moderate-sized pie, 1 to 1½ hour. *Seasonable* from March to October.

VEAL PIE.

Ingredients.—2 lbs. of veal cutlets, 1 or 2 slices of lean bacon or ham, pepper and salt to taste, 2 tablespoonfuls of minced savoury herbs, 2 blades of pounded mace, crust, 1 teacupful of gravy. *Mode.* — Cut the cutlets into square pieces, and season them with pepper, salt, and pounded mace; put them in a pie-dish with the savoury herbs sprinkled over, and 1 or 2 slices of lean bacon or ham placed at the top: if possible, this should be previously cooked, as undressed bacon makes the veal red, and spoils its appearance. Pour in a little water, cover with crust, ornament it in any way that is approved; brush it over with the yolk of an egg, and bake in a well-heated oven for about 1½ hour. Pour in a good gravy after baking, which is done by removing the

Veal and Ham Pie	Veal Rolls

top ornament, and replacing it after the gravy is added. *Time.*—About 1½ hour. *Average cost,* 2s. 6d. *Sufficient* for 5 or 6 persons. *Seasonable* from March to October.

VEAL AND HAM PIE.

Ingredients.—2 lbs. of veal cutlets, ½ lb. of boiled ham, 2 tablespoonfuls of minced savoury herbs, ¼ teaspoonful of grated nutmeg, 2 blades of pounded mace, pepper and salt to taste, a strip of lemon-peel finely minced, the yolks of 2 hard-boiled eggs, ½ pint of water, nearly ½ pint of good strong gravy, puff-crust. *Mode.*—Cut the veal into nice square pieces, and put a layer of them at the bottom of a pie-dish; sprinkle over these a portion of the herbs, spices, seasoning, lemon-peel, and the yolks of the eggs cut in slices; cut the ham very thin, and put a layer of this in. Proceed in this manner until the dish is full, so arranging it that the ham comes at the top. Lay a puff-paste on the edge of the dish, and pour in about ½ pint of water; cover with crust, ornament it with leaves, brush it over with the yolk of an egg, and bake in a well-heated oven for 1 to 1½ hour, or longer, should the pie be very large. When it is taken out of the oven, pour in at the top, through a funnel, nearly ½ pint of strong gravy: this should be made sufficiently good that, when cold, it may cut in a firm jelly. This pie may be very much enriched by adding a few mushrooms, oysters, or sweetbreads; but it will be found very good without any of the last-named additions. *Time.*— 1½ hour, or longer, should the pie be very large. *Average cost,* 3s. *Sufficient* for 5 or 6 persons. *Seasonable* from March to October.

VEAL, Potted (for Breakfast).

Ingredients. — To every lb. of veal allow ¼ lb. of ham, cayenne and pounded mace to taste, 6 oz. of fresh butter; clarified butter. *Mode.*—Mince the veal and ham together as finely as possible, and pound well in a mortar, with cayenne, pounded mace, and fresh butter in the above proportion. When reduced to a perfectly smooth paste, press it into potting-pots, and cover with clarified butter. If kept in a cool place, it will remain good some days. *Seasonable* from March to October.

VEAL, Ragout of Cold (Cold Meat Cookery).

Ingredients.—The remains of cold veal, 1 oz. of butter, ½ pint of gravy, thickening of butter and flour, pepper and salt to taste, 1 blade of pounded mace, 1 tablespoonful of mushroom ketchup, 1 tablespoonful of sherry, 1 dessertspoonful of lemon-juice, forcemeat balls. *Mode.*—Any part of veal will make this dish. Cut the meat into nice-looking pieces, put them in a stewpan with 1 oz. of butter, and fry a light brown; add the gravy (hot water may be substituted for this), thicken with a little butter and flour, and stew gently about ¼ hour; season with pepper, salt, and pounded mace; add the ketchup, sherry, and lemon-juice; give one boil, and serve. Garnish the dish with forcemeat balls and fried rashers of bacon. *Time.*— Altogether ½ hour. *Average cost,* exclusive of cold meat, 6d. *Seasonable* from March to October.

Note.—The above recipe may be varied, by adding vegetables, such as peas, cucumbers, lettuces, green onions cut in slices, a dozen or two of green gooseberries (not seedy), all of which should be fried a little with the meat, and then stewed in the gravy.

VEAL RISSOLES (Cold Meat Cookery).

Ingredients.—A few slices of cold roast veal, a few slices of ham or bacon, 1 tablespoonful of minced parsley, 1 tablespoonful of minced savoury herbs, 1 blade of pounded mace, a very little grated nutmeg, cayenne and salt to taste, 2 eggs well beaten, bread-crumbs. *Mode.* —Mince the veal very finely with a little ham or bacon; add the parsley, herbs, spices, and seasoning; mix into a paste with an egg; form into balls or cones; brush these over with egg, sprinkle with bread-crumbs, and fry a rich brown. Serve with brown gravy, and garnish the dish with fried parsley. *Time.*—About 10 minutes to fry the rissoles. *Seasonable* from March to October.

VEAL ROLLS (Cold Meat Cookery).

Ingredients.—The remains of a cold fillet of veal, egg and bread-crumbs, a few slices of fat bacon, forcemeat. *Mode.* —Cut a few slices from a cold fillet of veal

Veal, Shoulder of

½ inch thick ; rub them over with egg ; lay a thin slice of fat bacon over each piece of veal ; brush these with the egg, and over this spread the forcemeat thinly ; roll up each piece tightly, egg and bread-crumb them, and fry them a rich brown. Serve with mushroom sauce or brown gravy. *Time.*—10 to 15 minutes to fry the rolls. *Seasonable* from March to October.

V E A L, Stuffed and Stewed Shoulder of.

Ingredients. — A shoulder of veal, a few slices of ham or bacon, forcemeat, 3 carrots, 2 onions, salt and pepper to taste, a faggot of savoury herbs, 3 blades of pounded mace, water, thickening of butter and flour. *Mode.*—Bone the joint by carefully detaching the meat from the blade-bone on one side, and then on the other, being particular not to pierce the skin ; then cut the bone from the knuckle, and take it out. Fill the cavity whence the bone was taken with a forcemeat. Roll and bind the veal up tightly ; put it into a stewpan with the carrots, onions, seasoning, herbs, and mace ; pour in just sufficient water to cover it, and let it stew *very gently* for about 5 hours. Before taking it up, try if it is properly done by thrusting a larding-needle in it : if it penetrates easily, it is sufficiently cooked. Strain and skim the gravy, thicken with butter and flour, give one boil, and pour it round the meat. A few young carrots may be boiled and placed round the dish as a garnish, and, when in season, green peas should always be served with this dish. *Time.*—5 hours *Average cost, 7d.* per lb. *Sufficient* for 8 or 9 persons. *Seasonable* from March to October.

VEAL, Stewed with Peas, Young Carrots, and New Potatoes.

Ingredients.—3 or 4 lbs. of the loin or neck of veal, 15 young carrots, a few green onions, 1 pint of green peas, 12 new potatoes, a bunch of savoury herbs, pepper and salt to taste, 1 tablespoonful of lemon-juice, 2 tablespoonfuls of tomato sauce, 2 tablespoonfuls of mushroom ketchup. *Mode.* — Dredge the meat with flour, and roast or bake it for about ¾ hour: it should acquire a nice brown colour. Put the meat into a stewpan with the carrots, onions, pota-

Vegetable Marrow, Boiled

toes, herbs, pepper, and salt ; pour over it sufficient boiling water to cover it, and stew gently for 2 hours. Take out the meat and herbs, put it in a deep dish, skim off all the fat from the gravy, and flavour it with lemon-juice, tomato sauce, and mushroom ketchup, in the above proportion. Have ready a pint of green peas boiled *separately;* put these with the meat, pour over it the gravy, and serve. The dish may be garnished with a few forcemeat balls. The meat, when preferred, may be cut into chops, and floured and fried instead of being roasted ; and any part of veal dressed in this way will be found extremely savoury and good. *Time.* — 3 hours. *Average cost, 9d.* per lb. *Sufficient* for 6 or 7 persons. *Seasonable,* with peas, from June to August.

VEGETABLE MARROW, Boiled.

Ingredients. — To each ½ gallon of water, allow 1 heaped tablespoonful of salt; vegetable marrows. *Mode.*—Have ready a saucepan of boiling water, salted in the above proportion ; put in the marrows after peeling them, and boil them until quite tender. Take them up with a slice, halve, and, should they be very large, quarter them. Dish them on toast, and send to

VEGETABLE MARROW ON TOAST.

table with them a tureen of melted butter, or, in lieu of this, a small pat of salt butter. Large vegetable marrows may be preserved throughout the winter by storing them in a dry place ; when wanted for use, a few slices should be cut and boiled in the same manner as above ; but, when once begun, the marrow must be eaten quickly, as it keeps but a short time after it is cut. Vegetable marrows are also very delicious mashed : they should be boiled, then drained, and mashed smoothly with a wooden spoon. Heat them in a saucepan, add a seasoning of salt and pepper, and a small piece of butter, and dish with a few sippets of toasted bread placed round as a garnish. *Time.*— Young vegetable marrows, 10 to 20 minutes ; old ones, ½ to ¾ hour. *Average cost,* in full season, 1s. per dozen. *Sufficient.*—Allow 1 moderate-sized marrow for each person. *Seasonable* in July,

August, and September; but may be preserved all the winter.

VEGETABLE MARROW, Fried.

Ingredients. — 3 medium-sized vegetable marrows, egg and bread-crumbs, hot lard. *Mode.*—Peel, and boil the marrows until tender in salt and water; then drain them and cut them in quarters, and take out the seeds. When thoroughly drained, brush the marrows over with egg, and sprinkle with bread-crumbs; have ready some hot lard, fry the marrow in this, and, when of a nice brown, dish; sprinkle over a little salt and pepper, and serve. *Time.*—About ¼ hour to boil the marrow, 7 minutes to fry it. *Average cost*, in full season, 1s. per dozen. *Sufficient* for 4 persons. *Seasonable* in July, August, and September.

VEGETABLE MARROWS IN WHITE SAUCE.

Ingredients. — 4 or 5 moderate-sized marrows, ½ pint of white sauce. *Mode.* —Pare the marrows; cut them in halves, and shape each half at the top in a point, leaving the bottom end flat for it to stand upright in the dish. Boil the marrows in salt and

VEGETABLE MARROW IN WHITE SAUCE.

water until tender; take them up very carefully, and arrange them on a hot dish. Have ready ½ pint of white sauce; pour this over the marrows, and serve. *Time.*—From 15 to 20 minutes to boil the marrows. *Average cost*, in full season, 1s. per dozen. *Sufficient* for 5 or 6 persons. *Seasonable* in July, August, and September.

VEGETABLE MARROW SOUP.

Ingredients.—4 young vegetable marrows, or more, if very small, ½ pint of cream, salt and white pepper to taste, 2 quarts of white stock. *Mode.*—Pare and slice the marrows, and put them in the stock boiling. When done almost to a mash, press them through a sieve, and at the moment of serving, add the boiling cream and seasoning. *Time.*— 1 hour. *Average cost*, 1s. 2d. per quart. *Seasonable* in summer. *Sufficient* for 8 persons.

VEGETABLE SOUP.

Ingredients.—7 oz. of carrot, 10 oz. of parsnip, 10 oz. of potato, cut into thin slices; 1¼ oz. of butter, 5 teaspoonfuls of flour, a teaspoonful of made mustard, salt and pepper to taste, the yolks of 2 eggs, rather more than 2 quarts of water. *Mode.*—Boil the vegetables in the water 2½ hours; stir them often, and if the water boils away too quickly, add more, as there should be 2 quarts of soup when done. Mix up in a basin the butter and flour, mustard, salt, and pepper, with a teacupful of cold water; stir in the soup, and boil 10 minutes. Have ready the yolks of the eggs in the tureen; pour on, stir well, and serve. *Time.*—3 hours. *Average cost*, 4d. per quart. *Seasonable* in winter. *Sufficient* for 8 persons.

VEGETABLE SOUP.

Ingredients. — Equal quantities of onions, carrots, turnips; ¼ lb. of butter, a crust of toasted bread, 1 head of celery, a faggot of herbs, salt and pepper to taste, 1 teaspoonful of powdered sugar, 2 quarts of common stock or boiling water. Allow ¾ lb. of vegetables to 2 quarts of stock. *Mode.*—Cut up the onions, carrots, and turnips; wash and drain them well, and put them in the stewpan with the butter and powdered sugar. Toss the whole over a sharp fire for 10 minutes, but do not let them brown, or you will spoil the flavour of the soup. When done, pour the stock or boiling water on them; add the bread, celery, herbs, and seasoning; stew for 3 hours; skim well and strain it off. When ready to serve, add a little sliced carrot, celery, and turnip, and flavour with a spoonful of Harvey's sauce, or a little ketchup. *Time.*— 3½ hours. *Average cost*, 6d. per quart. *Seasonable* all the year. *Sufficient* for 8 persons.

VEGETABLE SOUP.

(*Good and Cheap, made without Meat.*)

Ingredients.—6 potatoes, 4 turnips, or 2 if very large; 2 carrots, 2 onions; if obtainable, 2 mushrooms; 1 head of celery, 1 large slice of bread, 1 small saltspoonful of salt, ¼ saltspoonful of ground black pepper, 2 teaspoonfuls of Harvey's sauce, 6 quarts of water. *Mode.*—Peel the vegetables, and cut

Vegetables, Cut for Soups, &c.

them up into small pieces; toast the bread rather brown, and put all into a stewpan with the water and seasoning. Simmer gently for 3 hours, or until all is reduced to a pulp, and pass it through a sieve in the same way as pea-soup, which it should resemble in consistence; but it should be a dark brown colour. Warm it up again when required; put in the Harvey's sauce, and, if necessary, add to the flavouring. *Time.*—3 hours, or rather more. *Average cost, 1d.* per quart. *Seasonable* at any time. *Sufficient* for 16 persons.

Note.—This recipe was forwarded to the Editress by a lady in the county of Durham, by whom it was strongly recommended.

VEGETABLES, Cut for Soups, &c.

The annexed engraving represents a cutter for shaping vegetables for soups, ragoûts, stews, &c.; carrots and turnips being the usual vegetables for which this utensil is used. Cut the vegetables into slices about ¼ inch in thickness, stamp them out with the cutter, and boil them for a few minutes in salt and water, until tender. Turnips should be cut in rather thicker slices than carrots, on account of the former boiling more quickly to a pulp than the latter.

VEGETABLE-CUTTER.

VENISON, Hashed.

Ingredients. — The remains of roast venison, its own or mutton gravy, thickening of butter and flour. *Mode.* —Cut the meat from the bones in neat slices, and, if there is sufficient of its own gravy left, put the meat into this, as it is preferable to any other. Should there not be enough, put the bones and trimmings into a stewpan, with about a pint of mutton gravy; let them stew gently for an hour, and strain the gravy. Put a little flour and butter into the stewpan, keep stirring until brown, then add the strained gravy, and give it a boil up; skim and strain again, and, when a little cool, put in the slices of venison. Place the stewpan oy the side

Venison, Roast Haunch of

of the fire, and, when on the point of simmering, serve: do not allow it to boil, or the meat will be hard. Send red-currant jelly to table with it. *Time.* —Altogether, 1½ hour. *Seasonable.*— Buck venison, from June to Michaelmas; doe venison, from November to the end of January.

Note.—A small quantity of Harvey's sauce, ketchup, or port wine, may be added to enrich the gravy: these ingredients must, however, be used very sparingly, or they will overpower the flavour of the venison.

VENISON, Roast Haunch of.

Ingredients. — Venison, coarse flour-and-water paste, a little flour. *Mode.*— Choose a haunch with clear, bright, and thick fat, and the cleft of the hoof smooth and close; the greater quantity of fat there is, the better quality will the meat be. As many people object to venison when it has too much *haut goût*, ascertain how long it has been kept, by running a sharp skewer into the meat close to the bone: when this is withdrawn, its sweetness can be judged of. With care and attention, it will keep good a fortnight, unless the weather is very mild. Keep it perfectly dry by wiping it with clean cloths till not the least damp remains, and sprinkle over powdered ginger or pepper, as a preventive against the fly. When required for use,

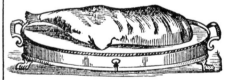

ROAST HAUNCH OF VENISON.

wash it in warm water, and *dry* it well with a cloth; butter a sheet of white paper, put it over the fat, lay a coarse paste, about ½ inch in thickness, over this, and then a sheet or two of strong paper. Tie the whole firmly on to the haunch with twine, and put the joint down to a strong close fire; baste the venison immediately, to prevent the paper and string from burning, and continue this operation, without intermission, the whole of the time it is cooking. About 20 minutes before it is done, carefully remove the paste and paper, dredge the joint with flour, and baste well with *butter* until it is nicely frothed, and of a nice pale-brown colour; garnish the knuckle-bone with a frill of white paper, and serve with a good, strong, but un-flavoured gravy, in a tureen, and currant jelly; or melt the jelly with a little port wine, and serve that also in a tureen. As the principal object in roasting veni-son is to preserve the fat, the above is the best mode of doing so where expense is not objected to; but, in ordinary cases, the paste may be dispensed with, and a double paper placed over the roast instead: it will not require so long cooking without the paste. Do not omit to send very hot plates to table, as the venison fat so soon freezes: to be thoroughly enjoyed by epicures, it should be eaten on hot-water plates. The neck and shoulder may be roasted in the same manner. *Time.*—A large haunch of buck venison, with the paste, 4 to 5 hours; haunch of doe venison, 3¼ to 3¾ hours. Allow less time without the paste. *Average cost, 1s. 4d. to 1s. 6d. per lb. Sufficient* for 18 persons. *Seasonable.*—Buck venison in greatest per-fection from June to Michaelmas; doe venison from November to the end of January.

VENISON, to Carve Haunch of.

Here is a grand dish for a knight of the carving-knife to exercise his skill upon, and, what will be pleasant for many to know, there is but little diffi-culty in the performance. An incision being made completely down to the bone, in the direction of the line 1 to 2, the gravy will then be able easily to flow; when slices, not too thick, should be cut

HAUNCH OF VENISON.

along the haunch, as indicated by the line 4 to 3; that end of the joint marked 3 having been turned towards the carver, so that he may have a more complete command over the joint. Although some epicures affect to believe that some parts of the haunch are superior to others, yet we doubt if there is any difference between the slices cut above and below the line. It should be borne

in mind to serve each guest with a por-tion of fat; and the most expeditious carver will be the best carver, as, like mutton, venison soon begins to chill, when it loses much of its charm.

VENISON, Stewed.

Ingredients.—A shoulder of venison, a few slices of mutton fat, 2 glasses of port wine, pepper and allspice to taste, 1½ pint of weak stock or gravy, ½ tea-spoonful of whole pepper, ½ teaspoonful of whole allspice. *Mode.*—Hang the venison till tender; take out the bone, flatten the meat with a rolling-pin, and place over it a few slices of mutton fat, which have been previously soaked for 2 or 3 hours in port wine; sprinkle these with a little fine allspice and pepper, roll the meat up, and bind and tie it securely. Put it into a stewpan with the bone and the above proportion of weak stock or gravy, whole allspice, black pepper, and port wine; cover the lid down closely, and simmer, very gently, from 3½ to 4 hours. When quite tender, take off the tape, and dish the meat; strain the gravy over it, and send it to table with red currant jelly. Un-less the joint is very fat, the above is the best mode of cooking it. *Time.*—3½ to 4 hours. *Average cost, 1s. 4d. to 1s. 6d. per lb. Sufficient* for 10 or 12 persons. *Seasonable.* — Buck venison, from June to Michaelmas; doe venison, from November to the end of January.

VERMICELLI PUDDING.

Ingredients.—4 oz. of vermicelli, 1½ pint of milk, ½ pint of cream, 3 oz. of butter, 3 oz. of sugar, 4 eggs. *Mode.*—Boil the vermicelli in the milk until it is tender; then stir in the remaining ingre-dients, omitting the cream, if not obtain-able. Flavour the mixture with grated lemon-rind, essence of bitter almonds, or vanilla; butter a pie-dish; line the edges with puff-paste, put in the pud-ding, and bake in a moderate oven for about ¾ hour. *Time.* — ¾ hour. *Ave-rage cost, 1s. 2d.* without cream. *Suffi-cient* for 5 or 6 persons. *Seasonable* at any time.

VERMICELLI SOUP.

Ingredients.—1½ lb. of bacon, stuck with cloves; ½ oz. of butter, worked up in flour; 1 small fowl, trussed for boil-

Vermicelli Soup

ing: 2 oz. of vermicelli, 2 quarts of white stock. *Mode.* — Put the stock, bacon, butter, and fowl, into the stewpan, and stew for ¾ of an hour. Take the vermicelli, add it to a little of the stock, and set it on the fire, till it is quite tender. When the soup is ready, take out the fowl and bacon, and put the bacon on a dish. Skim the soup as clean as possible; pour it, with the vermicelli, over the fowl. Cut some bread thin, put in the soup, and serve. *Time.* —2 hours. *Average cost,* exclusive of the fowl and bacon, 10d. per quart. *Seasonable* in winter. *Sufficient* for 4 persons.

VERMICELLI SOUP.

Ingredients. — ¼ lb. of vermicelli, 2 quarts of clear gravy stock. *Mode.*— Put the vermicelli in the soup, boiling; simmer very gently for ½ an hour, and stir frequently. *Time.* — ½ an hour. *Average cost,* 1s. 3d. per quart. *Seasonable* all the year. *Sufficient* for 8 persons.

VOL-AU-VENT (an Entrée).

Ingredients.—¾ to 1 lb. of puff-paste, fricasseed chickens, rabbits, ragoûts, or the remains of cold fish, flaked and warmed in thick white sauce. *Mode.*— Make from ¾ to 1 lb. of puff-paste, taking care that it is very evenly rolled out each time, to ensure its rising properly; and if the paste is not extremely light, and put into a good hot oven, this cannot be accomplished, and the *vol-au-vent* will look very badly. Roll out the paste to the thickness of about 1½ inch,

VOL-AU-VENT.

and, with a fluted cutter, stamp it out to the desired shape, either round or oval, and, with the point of a small knife, make a slight incision in the paste all round the top, about an inch from the edge, which, when baked, forms the lid. Put the *vol-au-vent* into a good brisk oven, and keep the door shut for a few minutes after it is put in. Particular attention should be paid to the heating of the oven, for the paste *cannot* rise without a tolerable degree of heat. When of a

Vol-au-Vent of Fresh Strawberries

nice colour, without being scorched, withdraw it from the oven, instantly remove the cover where it was marked, and detach all the soft crumb from the centre: in doing this, be careful not to break the edges of the *vol-au-vent;* but should they look thin in places, stop them with small flakes of the inside paste, stuck on with the white of an egg. This precaution is necessary to prevent the fricassee or ragoût from bursting the case, and so spoiling the appearance of the dish. Fill the *vol-au-vent* with a rich mince, or fricassee, or ragoût, or the remains of cold fish flaked and warmed in a good white sauce, and do not make them very liquid, for fear of the gravy bursting the crust: replace the lid, and serve. To improve the appearance of the crust, brush it over with the yolk of an egg *after* it has risen properly. *Time.*—¾ hour to bake the *vol-au-vent.* *Average cost,* exclusive of the interior, 1s. 6d. *Seasonable* at any time.

Note.—Small *vol-au-vents* may be made like those shown in the engraving, and filled with minced veal, chicken, &c. They should be made of

SMALL VOL-AU-VENTS.

the same paste as the larger ones, and stamped out with a small fluted cutter.

VOL-AU-VENT OF FRESH STRAWBERRIES, WITH WHIPPED CREAM.

Ingredients. — ¾ lb. of puff-paste, 1 pint of freshly-gathered strawberries, sugar to taste, a plateful of whipped cream. *Mode.*—Make a *vol-au-vent* case, only not quite so large nor so high as for a savoury one. When nearly done, brush the paste over with the white of an egg, then sprinkle on it some pounded sugar, and put it back in the oven to set the glaze. Remove the interior, or soft crumb, and, at the moment of serving, fill it with the strawberries, which should be picked, and broken up with sufficient sugar to sweeten them nicely. Place a few spoonfuls of whipped cream on the top and serve. *Time.*—½ hour to 40 minutes to bake the *vol-au-vent.* *Average cost,* 2s. 3d. *Sufficient* for 1 *vol-au-vent.* *Seasonable* in June and July.

Vol-au-Vent, Sweet

Walnuts, to have Fresh

VOL-AU-VENT, Sweet, of Plums, Apples, or any other Fresh Fruit.

Ingredients.—¾ lb. of puff-paste, about 1 pint of fruit compôte. *Mode.*—Make ½ lb. of puff-paste, taking care to bake it in a good brisk oven, to draw it up nicely and make it look light. Have ready sufficient stewed fruit, the syrup of which must be boiled down until very thick ; fill the *vol-au-vent* with this, and pile it high in the centre ; powder a little sugar over it, and put it back in the oven to glaze, or use a salamander for the purpose : the *vol-au-vent* is then ready to serve. It may be made with any fruit that is in season, such as rhubarb, oranges, gooseberries, currants, cherries, apples, &c. ; but care must be taken not to have the syrup too thin, for fear of its breaking through the crust. *Time.*—½ hour to 40 minutes to bake the *vol-au-vent. Average cost,* exclusive of the compôte, 1s. 1d. *Sufficient* for 1 entremets.

WAFERS, Geneva.

Ingredients.—2 eggs, 3 oz. butter, 3 oz. flour, 3 oz. pounded sugar. *Mode.*—Well whisk the eggs ; put them into a basin, and stir to them the butter, which should be beaten to a cream ; add the flour and sifted sugar gradually, and then mix all well together. Butter a baking-sheet, and drop on it a teaspoonful of the mixture at a time, leaving a space between each. Bake in a cool oven ; watch the pieces of paste, and, when half done, roll them up like wafers, and put in a small wedge of bread or piece of wood, to keep them in shape. Return them to the oven until crisp. Before serving, remove the bread, put a spoonful of preserve in the widest end, and fill up with whipped cream. This is a very pretty and ornamental dish for the supper-table, and is very nice and easily made. *Time.*—Altogether from 20 to 25 minutes. *Average cost,* exclusive of the preserve and cream, 7d. *Sufficient* for a nice-sized dish. *Seasonable* at any time.

WALNUT KETCHUP.

Ingredients.—100 walnuts, 1 handful of salt, 1 quart of vinegar, ¼ oz. of mace, ¼ oz. of nutmeg, ¼ oz. of cloves, ¼ oz. of ginger, ¼ oz. of whole black pepper, a

small piece of horseradish, 20 shalots, ¼ lb. of anchovies, 1 pint of port wine. *Mode.*—Procure the walnuts at the time you can run a pin through them, slightly bruise, and put them into a jar with the salt and vinegar ; let them stand 8 days, stirring every day ; then drain the liquor from them, and boil it, with the above ingredients, for about ½ hour. It may be strained or not, as preferred, and, if required, a little more vinegar or wine can be added, according to taste. When bottled well, seal the corks. *Time.*—½ hour. *Seasonable.*—Make this from the beginning to the middle of July, when walnuts are in perfection for pickling purposes.

WALNUT KETCHUP.

Ingredients.—½ sieve of walnut-shells, 2 quarts of water, salt, ½ lb. of shalots, 1 oz. of cloves, 1 oz. of mace, 1 oz. of whole pepper, 1 oz. of garlic. *Mode.*—Put the walnut-shells into a pan, with the water, and a large quantity of salt ; let them stand for 10 days, then break the shells up in the water, and let it drain through a sieve, putting a heavy weight on the top to express the juice ; place it on the fire, and remove all scum that may arise. Now boil the liquor with the shalots, cloves, mace, pepper, and garlic, and let all simmer till the shalots sink ; then put the liquor into a pan, and, when cold, bottle, and cork closely. It should stand 6 months before using : should it ferment during that time, it must be again boiled and skimmed. *Time.* — About ¾ hour. *Seasonable* in September, when the walnut-shells are obtainable.

WALNUTS, to have Fresh throughout the Season.

Ingredients.—To every pint of water allow 1 teaspoonful of salt. *Mode.*—Place the walnuts in the salt and water for 24 hours at least ; then take them out, and rub them dry. Old nuts may be freshened in this manner ; or walnuts, when first picked, may be put into an earthen pan with salt sprinkled amongst them, and with damped hay placed on the top of them, and then covered down with a lid. They must be well wiped before they are put on table. *Seasonable.*—Should be stored away in September or October.

| Walnuts, Pickled | White Sauce, Good |

WALNUTS, Pickled (very Good).

Ingredients. — 100 walnuts, salt and water. To each quart of vinegar allow 2 oz. of whole black pepper, 1 oz. of allspice, 1 oz. of bruised ginger. *Mode.* — Procure the walnuts while young; be careful they are not woody, and prick them well with a fork; prepare a strong brine of salt and water (4 lbs. of salt to each gallon of water), into which put the walnuts, letting them remain 9 days, and changing the brine every third day; drain them off, put them on a dish, place it in the sun until they become perfectly black, which will be in 2 or 3 days; have ready dry jars, into which place the walnuts, and do not quite fill the jars. Boil sufficient vinegar to cover them, for 10 minutes, with spices in the above proportion, and pour it hot over the walnuts, which must be quite covered with the pickle; tie down with bladder, and keep in a dry place. They will be fit for use in a month, and will keep good 2 or 3 years. *Time.* — 10 minutes. *Seasonable.* — Make this from the beginning to the middle of July, before the walnuts harden.

Note. — When liked, a few shalots may be added to the vinegar, and boiled with it.

WATER SOUCHY.

Perch, tench, soles, eels, and flounders are considered the best fish for this dish. For the souchy, put some water into a stewpan with a bunch of chopped parsley, some roots, and sufficient salt to make it brackish. Let these simmer for 1 hour, and then stew the fish in this water. When they are done, take them out to drain, have ready some finely-chopped parsley, and a few roots cut into slices of about one inch thick and an inch in length. Put the fish in a tureen or deep dish, strain the liquor over them, and add the minced parsley and roots. Serve with brown bread and butter.

WHEATEARS, to Dress.

Ingredients. — Wheatears; fresh butter. *Mode.* — After the birds are picked, gutted, and cleaned, truss them like larks, put them down to a quick fire, and baste them well with fresh butter. When done, which will be in about 20 minutes, dish them on fried bread-crumbs, and garnish the dish with slices of lemon

Time. — 20 minutes. *Seasonable* from July to October.

WHISKEY CORDIAL.

Ingredients. — 1 lb. of ripe white currants, the rind of 2 lemons, ¼ oz. of grated ginger, 1 quart of whiskey, 1 lb. of lump sugar. *Mode.* — Strip the currants from the stalks; put them into a large jug; add the lemon-rind, ginger, and whiskey; cover the jug closely, and let it remain covered for 24 hours. Strain through a hair-sieve, add the lump sugar, and let it stand 12 hours longer; then bottle, and cork well. *Time.* — To stand 24 hours before being strained; 12 hours after the sugar is added. *Seasonable.* — Make this in July.

WHITEBAIT, to Dress.

Ingredients. — A little flour, hot lard, seasoning of salt. *Mode.* — This fish should be put into iced water as soon as bought, unless they are cooked immediately. Drain them from the water in a colander, and have ready a nice clean dry cloth, over which put 2 good handfuls of flour. Toss in the whitebait, shake them lightly in the cloth, and put them in a wicker-sieve to take away the superfluous flour. Throw them into a pan of boiling lard, very few at a time, and let them fry till of a whitey-brown colour. Directly they are done, they must be taken out, and laid before the fire for a minute or two on a sieve reversed, covered with blotting-paper to absorb the fat. Dish them on a hot napkin, arrange the fish very high in the centre, and sprinkle a little salt over the whole. *Time.* — 3 minutes. *Seasonable* from April to August.

WHITE SAUCE, Good.

Ingredients. — ½ pint of white stock, ¼ pint of cream, 1 dessertspoonful of flour, salt to taste. *Mode.* — Have ready a delicately-clean saucepan, into which put the stock, which should be well flavoured with vegetables, and rather savoury; mix the flour smoothly with the cream, add it to the stock, season with a little salt, and boil all these ingredients very gently for about 10 minutes, keeping them well stirred the whole time, as this sauce is very liable to burn. *Time.* — 10 minutes. *Average cost, 1s. Sufficient* for a pair of fowls. *Seasonable* at any time.

WHITE SAUCE, Made without Meat.

Ingredients.—2 oz. of butter, 2 small onions, 1 carrot, ½ a small teacupful of flour, 1 pint of new milk, salt and cayenne to taste. *Mode.*—Cut up the onions and carrot very small, and put them into a stewpan with the butter; simmer them till the butter is nearly dried up; then stir in the flour, and add the milk; boil the whole gently until it thickens, strain it, season with salt and cayenne, and it will be ready to serve. *Time.*—¼ hour. *Average cost,* 5d. *Sufficient* for a pair of fowls. *Seasonable* at any time.

WHITE SAUCE (a very Simple and Inexpensive Method).

Ingredients.—1½ pint of milk, 1½ oz. of rice, 1 strip of lemon-peel, 1 small blade of pounded mace, salt and cayenne to taste. *Mode.*—Boil the milk with the lemon-peel and rice until the latter is perfectly tender, then take out the lemon-peel and pound the milk and rice together; put it back into the stewpan to warm, add the mace and seasoning, give it one boil, and serve. This sauce should be of the consistency of thick cream. *Time.*—About 1½ hour to boil the rice. *Average cost,* 4d. *Sufficient* for a pair of fowls. *Seasonable* at any time.

WHITING, Boiled.

Ingredients. — ¼ lb. of salt to each gallon of water. *Mode.*—Cleanse the fish, but do not skin them; lay them in a fish-kettle, with sufficient cold water to cover them, and salt in the above proportion. Bring them gradually to a boil, and simmer gently for about 5 minutes, or rather more should the fish be very large. Dish them on a hot napkin, and garnish with tufts of parsley. Serve with anchovy or caper sauce, and plain melted butter. *Time.*—After the water boils, 5 minutes. *Average cost* for small whitings, 4d. each. *Seasonable* all the year, but best from October to March. *Sufficient.*—1 small whiting for each person.

To Choose Whiting.—Choose for the firmness of its flesh, and the silvery hue of its appearance.

WHITING, Broiled.

Ingredients.—Salt and water; flour. *Mode.*—Wash the whiting in salt and water, wipe them thoroughly, and let them remain in the cloth to absorb all moisture. Flour them well, and broil over a very clear fire. Serve with *maître d'hôtel* sauce, or plain melted butter (*see* Sauces). Be careful to preserve the liver, as by some it is considered very delicate. *Time.*—5 minutes for a small whiting. *Average cost,* 4d. each. *Seasonable* all the year, but best from October to March. *Sufficient.*—1 small whiting for each person.

WHITING, &c.

Whiting, pike, haddock, and other fish, when of a sufficiently large size, may be carved in the same manner as salmon. When small, they may be cut through, bone and all, and helped in nice pieces, a middling-sized whiting serving for two slices.

WHITING, Fried.

Ingredients.—Egg and bread-crumbs, a little flour, hot lard, or clarified dripping. *Mode.*—Take off the skin, clean, and thoroughly wipe the fish free from all moisture, as this is most essential, in order that the egg and bread-crumbs may properly adhere. Fasten the tail in the mouth by means of a small skewer, brush the fish over with egg, dredge with a little flour, and cover with bread-crumbs. Fry them in hot lard or clarified dripping of a nice colour, and serve them on a napkin, garnished with fried parsley. Send them to table with shrimp sauce and plain melted butter. *Time.*—About 6 minutes. *Average cost,* 4d. each. *Seasonable* all the year, but best from October to March. *Sufficient.*—1 small whiting for each person.

Note.—Large whitings may be filleted, rolled, and served as fried filleted soles. Small fried whitings are frequently used for garnishing large boiled fish, such as turbot, cod, &c.

WHITING AU GRATIN, BAKED WHITING.

Ingredients. — 4 whiting, butter, 1 tablespoonful of minced parsley, a few chopped mushrooms when obtainable; pepper, salt, and grated nutmeg to taste, butter, 2 glasses of sherry or Madeira, bread-crumbs. *Mode.*—Grease the bottom of a baking-dish with butter, and

Whiting aux Fines Herbes	Wine Sauce for Puddings

over it strew some minced parsley and mushrooms. Scale, empty, and wash the whitings, and wipe them thoroughly dry, carefully preserving the livers. Lay them in the dish, sprinkle them with bread-crumbs and seasoning, adding a little grated nutmeg, and also a little more minced parsley and mushrooms. Place small pieces of butter over the whiting, moisten with the wine, and bake for 20 minutes in a hot oven. If there should be too much sauce, reduce it by boiling over a sharp fire for a few minutes, and pour under the fish. Serve with a cut lemon, and no other sauce. *Time.*— 20 minutes. *Average cost, 4d.* each. *Seasonable* all the year, but best from October to March. *Sufficient.* — This quantity for 4 or 5 persons.

WHITING AUX FINES HERBES.

Ingredients.—1 bunch of sweet herbs chopped very fine ; butter. *Mode.*— Clean and skin the fish, fasten the tails in the mouths, and lay them in a baking-dish. Mince the herbs very fine, strew them over the fish, and place small pieces of butter over ; cover with another dish, and let them simmer in a Dutch oven for ¼ hour or 20 minutes. Turn the fish once or twice, and serve with the sauce poured over. *Time.*—¼ hour or 20 minutes. *Average cost, 4d.* each. *Seasonable* all the year, but best from October to March. *Sufficient.*—1 small whiting for each person.

WIDGEON, Roast.

Ingredients.—Widgeons, a little flour, butter. *Mode.* — These are trussed in the same manner as wild duck, but must not be kept so long before they are dressed. Put them down to a brisk fire ; flour, and baste them continually with butter, and, when brown d and nicely frothed, send them to table hot and quickly. Serve with brown gravy, or orange gravy, and a cut lemon. *Time.*— ¼ hour ; if liked well done, 20 minutes. *Average cost, 1s.* each : but seldom bought. *Sufficient.*—2 for a dish. *Seasonable* from October to February.

WIDGEON.

Widgeon may be carve l in the same way as described in regard to wild duck.

WINE OR BRANDY SAUCE FOR PUDDINGS.

Ingredients.—1 pint of melted butter, 3 heaped teaspoonfuls of pounded sugar, 1 *large* wineglassful of port or sherry, or ¾ of a *small* glassful of brandy. *Mode.*— Make ¼ pint of melted butter, omitting the salt ; then stir in the sugar and wine or spirit in the above proportion, and bring the sauce to the point of boiling. Serve in a boat or tureen separately, and, if liked, pour a little of it over the pudding. To convert this into punch sauce, add to the sherry and brandy a small wineglassful of rum and the juice and grated rind of ½ lemon. Liqueurs, such as Maraschino or Curaçoa, substituted for the brandy. make excellent sauces. *Time.*—Altogether, 15 minutes. *Average cost, 8d. Sufficient* for 6 or 7 persons.

WINE SAUCE FOR PUDDINGS.

Ingredients.—½ pint of sherry, ¼ pint of water, the yolks of 5 eggs, 2 ozs. of pounded sugar, ½ teaspoonful of minced lemon-peel, a few pieces of candied citron cut thin. *Mode.*—Separate the yolks from the whites of 5 eggs ; beat them, and put them into a very clean saucepan (if at hand, a lined one is best) ; add all the other ingredients, place them over a sharp fire, and keep stirring until the sauce begins to thicken ; then take it off and serve. If it is allowed to boil, it will be spoiled, as it will immediately curdle. *Time.*—To be stirred over the fire 3 or 4 minutes ; but it must not boil. *Average cost, 2s. Sufficient* for a large pudding ; allow half this quantity for a moderate-sized one. *Seasonable* at a time.

WINE SAUCE FOR PUDDINGS. Excellent.

Ingredients.—The yolks of 4 eggs, 1 teaspoonful of flour, 2 oz. of poun ed sugar, 2 oz. of fresh butter, ¼ saltspo n-ful of salt, ½ pint of sherry or Madeir *Mode.*—Put the butter and flour into a saucepan, and stir them over the fire until the former thickens ; then add the sugar, salt, and wine, and mix these ingredients well together. Separate the yolks from the whites of 4 eggs ; beat up the former, and stir them briskly to the sauce ; let it remain over the fire until "

24⅛

is on the point of simmering ; but do not allow it to boil, or it will instantly curdle. This sauce is delicious with plum, marrow, or bread puddings ; but should be served separately, and not poured over the pudding. *Time.*—From 5 to 7 minutes to thicken the butter ; about 5 minutes to stir the sauce over the fire. *Average cost*, 1s. 10d. *Sufficient* for 7 or 8 persons.

WINE, to Mull.

Ingredients.—To every pint of wine allow 1 large cupful of water, sugar, and spice to taste. *Mode.*—In making preparations like the above, it is very difficult to give the exact proportions of ingredients like sugar and spice, as what quantity might suit one person would be to another quite distasteful. Boil the spice in the water until the flavour is extracted, then add the wine and sugar, and bring the whole to the boiling-point, when serve with strips of crisp dry toast, or with biscuits. The spices usually used for mulled wine are cloves, grated nutmeg, and cinnamon or mace. Any kind of wine may be mulled, but port and claret are those usually selected for the purpose ; and the latter requires a very large proportion of sugar. The vessel that the wine is boiled in must be delicately clean, and should be kept exclusively for the purpose. Small tin warmers may be purchased for a trifle, which are more suitable than saucepans, as, if the latter are not scrupulously clean, they will spoil the wine, by imparting to it a very disagreeable flavour. These warmers should be used for no other purposes.

WOODCOCK, Roast.

Ingredients. — Woodcocks ; butter, flour, toast. *Mode.*—Woodcocks should not be drawn, as the trails are, by epicures, considered a great delicacy. Pluck, and wipe them well outside ; truss them

ROAST WOODCOCK.

with the legs close to the body, and the feet pressing upon the thighs ; skin the neck and head, and bring the beak

round under the wing. Place some slices of toast in the dripping-pan to catch the trails, allowing a piece of toast for each bird. Roast before a clear fire from 15 to 25 minutes ; keep them well basted, and flour and froth them nicely. When done, dish the pieces of toast with the birds upon them, and pour round a very little gravy ; send some more to table in a tureen. These are most delicious birds when well cooked ; but they should not be kept too long : when the feathers drop, or easily come out, they are fit for for table. *Time.*—When liked underdone, 15 to 20 minutes ; if liked well done, allow an extra 5 minutes. *Average cost.*—Seldom bought. *Sufficient.*—2 for a dish. *Seasonable* from November to February.

WOODCOCK.

This bird, like a partridge, may be carved by cutting it exactly into two like portions, or made into three helpings, as described in carving partridge. The backbone is considered the tit-bit of a woodcock, and by many the thigh is

WOODCOCK.

also thought a great delicacy. This bird is served in the manner advised by Brillat Savarin, in connection with the pheasant, viz., on toast which has received its drippings whilst roasting ; and a piece of this toast should invariably accompany each plate.

WOODCOCK, SCOTCH.

Ingredients. — A few slices of hot buttered toast ; allow 1 anchovy to each slice. For the sauce,—¼ pint of cream, the yolks of 3 eggs. *Mode.*—Separate the yolks from the whites of the eggs ; beat the former, stir to them the cream, and bring the sauce to the boiling-point, but do not allow it to boil, or it will curdle. Have ready some hot buttered toast, spread with anchovies pounded to a paste ; pour a little of the hot sauce on the top, and serve very hot and very quickly. *Time.*—5 minutes to make the sauce hot. *Sufficient.*—Allow ½ slice to each person. *Seasonable* at any time.

YEAST-CAKE.

Ingredients.—1½ lb. of flour, ½ lb. of butter, ½ pint of milk, 1½ tablespoonful of good yeast, 3 eggs, ¾ lb. of currants, ⅛ lb. of white moist sugar, 2 oz. of candied peel. *Mode.*—Put the milk and butter into a saucepan, and shake it round over a fire until the butter is melted, but do not allow the milk to get very hot. Put the flour into a basin, stir to it the milk and butter, the yeast and eggs, which should be well beaten, and form the whole into a smooth dough. Let it stand in a warm place, covered with a cloth, to rise, and, when sufficiently risen, add the currants, sugar, and candied peel cut into thin slices. When all the ingredients are thoroughly mixed, line 2 moderate-sized cake-tins with buttered paper, which should be about six inches higher than the tin ; pour in the mixture, let it stand to rise again for another ½ hour, and then bake the cakes in a brisk oven for about 1½ hour. If the tops of them become too brown, cover them with paper until they are done through. A few drops of essence of lemon, or a little grated nutmeg, may be added when the flavour is liked. *Time.*—From 1¼ to 1½ hour. *Average cost*, 2s. *Sufficient* to make 2 moderate-sized cakes. *Seasonable* at any time.

YEAST-DUMPLINGS.

Ingredients. — ½ quartern of dough, boiling water. *Mode.*—Make a very light dough as for bread, using to mix it, milk, instead of water; divide it into 7 or 8 dumplings ; plunge them into boiling water, and boil them for 20 minutes. Serve the instant they are taken up, as they spoil directly, by falling and becoming heavy ; and in eating them do not touch them with a knife, but tear them apart with two forks. They may be eaten with meat gravy, or cold butter and sugar ; and if not convenient to make the dough at home, a little from the baker's answers as well, only it must be placed for a few minutes near the fire, in a basin with a cloth over it, to let it rise again before it is made into dumplings. *Time.*—20 minutes. *Average cost*, 4d. *Sufficient* for 5 or 7 persons. *Seasonable* at any time.

YEAST, to Make, for Bread.

Ingredients.—1½ oz. of hops, 3 quarts of water, 1 lb. of bruised malt, ½ pint of yeast. *Mode.* — Boil the hops in the water for 20 minutes ; let it stand for about 5 minutes, then add it to 1 lb. of bruised malt prepared as for brewing. Let the mixture stand covered till about lukewarm ; then put in not quite ¼ pint of yeast ; keep it warm, and let it work 3 or 4 hours ; then put it into small ½-pint bottles (ginger-beer bottles are the best for the purpose), cork them well, and tie them down. The yeast is now ready for use ; it will keep good for a few weeks, and 1 bottle will be found sufficient for 18 lbs. of flour. When required for use, boil 3 lbs. of potatoes without salt, mash them in the same water in which they were boiled, and rub them through a colander. Stir in about ½ lb. of flour ; then put in the yeast, pour it in the middle of the flour, and let it stand warm on the hearth all night, and in the morning let it be quite warm when it is kneaded. The bottles of yeast require very careful opening, as it is generally exceedingly ripe. *Time.*— 20 minutes to boil the hops and water, the yeast to work 3 or 4 hours. *Sufficient.*—½ pint sufficient for 18 lbs. of flour.

YEAST, Kirkleatham.

Ingredients.—2 oz. of hops, 4 quarts of water, ¼ lb. of flour, ½ pint of yeast. *Mode.*—Boil the hops and water for 20 minutes ; strain, and mix with the liquid ½ lb. of flour and not quite ½ pint of yeast. Bottle it up, and tie the corks down. When wanted for use, boil potatoes according to the quantity of bread to be made (about 3 lbs. are sufficient for about a peck of flour) ; mash them, add to them ½ lb. of flour, and mix about ½ pint of the yeast with them ; let this mixture stand all day, and lay the bread to rise the night before it is wanted. *Time.*—20 minutes to boil the hops and water. *Sufficient.*—½ pint of this yeast sufficient for a peck of flour, or rather more.

COLOURED PLATES:

A BRIEF DESCRIPTION OF THOSE INSERTED THROUGHOUT THIS WORK.

In the eight coloured Plates in this volume the various figures are authentic representations of the present fashion of serving the several dishes comprised in either a family or an ordinary party dinner. The following descriptive matter will, we hope, be found thoroughly practical, and, to the veriest novice in the culinary art, as " plain as a pikestaff."

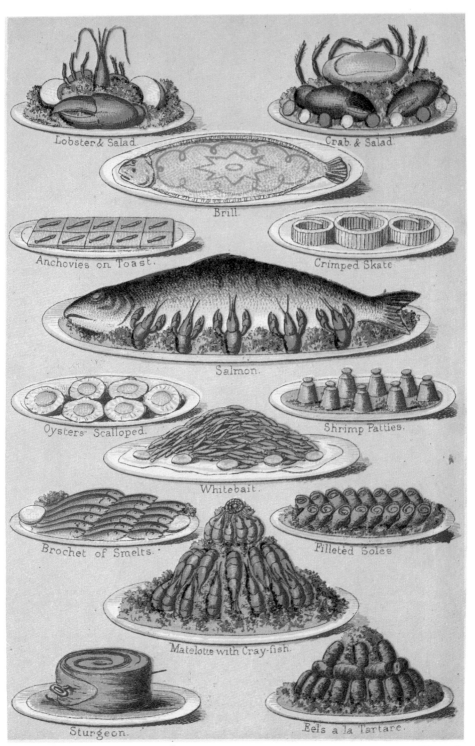

Lobster & Salad.

Crab. & Salad.

Brill.

Anchovies on Toast.

Crimped Skate.

Salmon.

Oysters Scalloped.

Shrimp Patties.

Whitebait.

Brochet of Smelts.

Filleted Soles.

Matelotte with Cray-fish.

Sturgeon.

Eels a la Tartare.

Plate I.

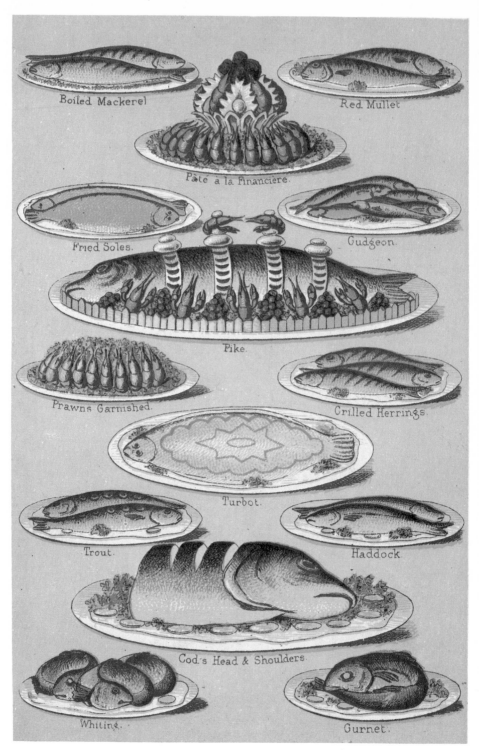

Boiled Mackerel

Red Mullet

Pâte a la Financiere.

Fried Soles.

Gudgeon.

Pike.

Prawns Garnished.

Grilled Herrings.

Turbot.

Trout.

Haddock.

Cod's Head & Shoulders.

Whiting.

Gurnet.

Plate II

Pig's Feet & Truffles.

Puree of Game & Rice.

Lyons Sausage.

Pigeon Pie.

Calf's Heart.

Brawn.

Larks & Potatoes.

Calf's Tongue.

Lamb Chops & Potatoes.

Scotch Eggs & Forcemeat.

Stuffed Tomatoes.

Chaud-froid of Fowl & Jelly.

Veal Cutlets & Olives.

Veal Cutlets en Papillotte.

Fillet of Beef à la Jardinière.

Fillets of Beef.

Lamb Cutlets & Green Peas.

Ham Garnished.

Partridges aux Choux.

Tongue Garnished.

Croquettes of Fowl.

Fricassee of Fowl Garnished.

Fricandeau of Veal.

Chartreuse of Partridges.

Half Calf's Head.

Timbale Milanaise (Macaroni).

Plate III

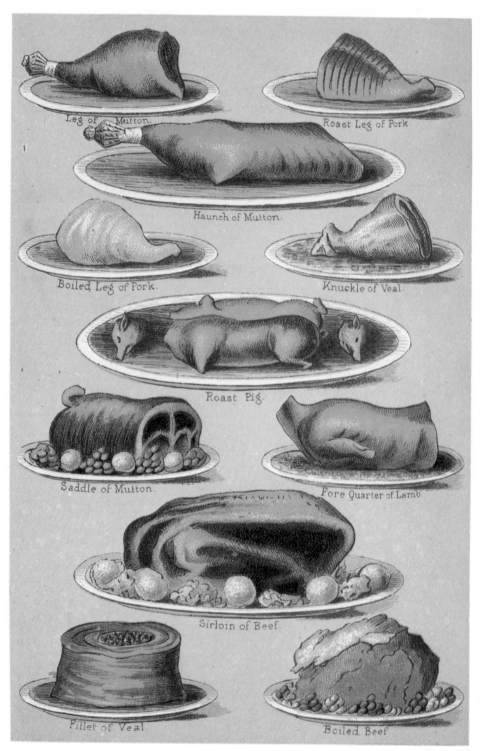

Leg of Mutton.

Roast Leg of Pork

Haunch of Mutton.

Boiled Leg of Pork.

Knuckle of Veal.

Roast Pig.

Saddle of Mutton.

Fore Quarter of Lamb.

Sirloin of Beef.

Fillet of Veal.

Boiled Beef.

Plate IV

Grouse.

Woodcock.

Hare.

Snipe.

Plovers.

Pheasant.

Partridges.

Wild Duck.

Capon.

Wheat-ears.

Land-rails.

Goose.

Pigeon.

Duck.

Guinea Fowl.

Roast Fowl.

Boiled Fowl.

Turkey.

Boiled Rabbit.

Roast Rabbit.

Plate V.

Olives.

Potatoes.

Parsnips.

Tomatoes.

Brussels Sprouts.

Cabbage

Vegetable Marrow.

Spanish Onions.

Broad Beans.

Salad.

Carrots.

Radishes.

Cauliflowers.

Green Peas.

Kidney Beans.

Mixed Pickles.

Asparagus.

Artichokes.

Plate VI.

Nougat Almond Cake.

Trifle.

Blanc Mange.

Apple Marmalade Tart.

Cherry Tart.

Galette.

Peach Tartlet.

Dessert Biscuits.

Iced Oranges.

Christmas Plum Pudding.

Compote of Pears.

Mince Pies.

Roly-Poly Jam Pudding.

Apples with Rice.

Cold Apple Pudding.

Coffee Custard à la Religieuse.

Baked Apple & Pear Dumplings.

Meringues & Preserves.

Apricot Tartlet.

Apple Tart.

Pancakes & Jam.

Apples à la Parisienne.

Fruit Macedoine & Jelly.

Charlotte of Pears.

Plate VII.

Almonds and Raisins.

Raspberries and Strawberries.

Filberts and Cobs.

Gooseberries.

Peaches and Apricots.

Apples and Pears.

Walnuts and Brazil Nuts.

Figs and Dates.

Plums and Greengages.

Oranges.

Mulberries.

Blackberries.

Currants.

Epergne.

Cherries.

Plate VIII.

PLATE I.

LOBSTER AND SALAD.

Arrange the lobster as in the Plate. Make a good salad of lettuce, endive, any small green stuff that happens to be in season, chopped beetroot, and 2 hard-boiled eggs, Get this dry by lightly squeezing in a cloth after being washed. The dressing should be of oil, 3 or 4 tablespoonfuls, 2 of vinegar, 1 teaspoonful of made mustard, the yolks of 2 hard-boiled eggs. Sometimes a very small quantity of anchovy sauce is added. These ingredients must be mixed with the pieces of meat from the body of the lobster. Toss all together thoroughly and lightly with a wooden fork. Arrange it around the lobster and garnish with beetroot sliced, cucumber sliced, and the yolks and whites of eggs also divided. Take care to exercise taste in the blending of the colours.

CRAB AND SALAD.

Prepare a fish salad, and the crab as usual for eating. Garnish with egg and beetroot as in Plate.

BRILL.

The brill will of course first be well washed and cleaned: then dry it on a cloth rub it all over with the juice of a lemon and a little salt, and put it into its kettle, just covering it with water. Put in a handful of salt, and so soon as the water begins to boil let it be removed, so that it can simmer only for about half an hour, but the time will depend upon the size of the brill. Now skim the water, take out the fish gently upon the drainer, slide it with the utmost care upon a dish covered with a folded serviette, and garnish as in Plate.

ANCHOVIES ON TOAST.

Make thin dry toast, and divide it into either oblong or square portions, about 2 inches long. Put these into the oven to get crisp, but not hard and dry; spread anchovy butter all over, and lay the anchovies upon them as shown in Plate.

CRIMPED SKATE.

The skate must be as fresh as it is possible to obtain it, if alive all the better skin it and wash it quite clean; cut slips the whole length of the fish about an inch wide, roll it over one or two of your fingers and instantly drop it into cold water. The other part of the fish must also be put with the liver into water. This done, boil the skate thus rolled (a piece of the liver being put in the centre) in vinegar, salt and water, for from 15 to 20 minutes; let them drain by holding them just above the stewpan Pour brown butter sauce all over them and serve. When putting the rolled pieces of fish in to boil, tie them lightly with fine string that they may not uncurl. A pretty corner dish.

SALMON À LA CHAMBORD.

Boil a fine salmon in the usual manner. Drain it thoroughly and serve on a napkin with garnishings of parsley and crayfish, as in Plate. A splendid second (or first) course dish.

OYSTERS, SCALLOPED.

Take oysters according to the number of guests, strain their liquor into a stewpan, adding to it 2 oz. each of flour and butter, well kneaded together with a small quantity of cream, anchovy, cayenne, and nutmeg. Boil this over the fire for 10 minutes till reduced. Then put in the yolks of two eggs beaten and some chopped parsley. Cut the oysters in halves and add to the rest; stir all over the fire for 6 or 7 minutes and fill scallop shells with the mixture. Cover with bread crumbs fried, and put them in the oven in a baking tin for 5 minutes. Serve hot, garnish with tufts of parsley. They may be served in the oyster shells if these have been washed quite clean. An always acceptable side or supper dish.

SHRIMP PATTIES.

The paste must be puff, and half an inch thick. Cut with a 2½ or 3 inch cutter (round) as many pieces as are wanted for the dish. Next take an inch cutter, dip it for a second in hot water and press it in the centre of the paste about half through. Brush the pieces cut with yolk of egg, bake in a quick oven, remove the piece marked with the inch cutter, also the soft parts from the middle, and fill them with the shrimps prepared as follows:—Pick a quart of shrimps that are not very salt, flavour them with mace and a clove or so; mince three anchovies and mix them with the spice. Add a glass of wine (not sweet). These are an elegant side dish or supper dish.

WHITEBAIT.

Drain your whitebait on a sieve. Sprinkle a cloth with flour thickly, and let the fish get lightly covered with it by dropping them gently upon it and moving them about deftly with your fingers. This operation requires a little skill. Put them into a wire frying-basket, shake it to dust away all extra flour and dip the basket into some very hot lard (this must be particularly clean and nice). A few minutes is enough to fry them perfectly, when they should look rather silvery in colour and be very crisp. Serve as in Plate.

BROCHET OF SMELTS.

Spread melted butter (butter that has been melted before the fire) on a dish, and dredge raspings of bread upon it. Season with pepper, salt, chopped parsley, and shalots. Over the fish pour one glass of wine, and a little Harvey and anchovy sauces. Put also on the top of the smelts exactly the same as you put at the bottom of the dish; put them in the oven for 15 minutes. Serve quite hot on a napkin, and garnish the dish with pieces of lemon and fried parsley. Arrange the smelts upon small skewers as shown in Plate.

FILLETED SOLES.

Take 2 or 3 soles, remove the head, fins, and tail, and divide them from the back bone. Sprinkle a small quantity of salt on the inside, cut them into pieces, dip these into egg and then into bread crumbs, and again into egg with more crumbs. Fry them in boiling lard; arrange them round a centre of parsley and garnish with slices of lemon. Or they may be rolled; but the former way is that shown in the Plate. This forms a pretty side dish.

MATELOTTE, WITH CRAYFISH.

Procure a large lemon, and cut a small portion off one end so that it stands firmly upon a folded serviette. If the lemon is not large enough, or you require a larger dish than usual, use two lemons, fastening them together with a bone or wooden skewer. They must stand firm, however. Arrange as in Plate, filling up all the gaps with fresh-picked parsley. This is a remarkably pretty dish, and may be served at breakfast, luncheon, dinner, or supper, as part of a second course.

STURGEON.

About 2 lbs. of fish are required for this dish; cut away their skin with a sharp knife, but do it carefully. Tie the fish round with string as in the Plate, and put it in to boil with some parsley, thyme, a bay-leaf, a wineglass of vinegar, 4 or 5 cloves, salt, a slip of mace, and a sliced carrot and onion. Let this boil gently. The time cannot be definitely given, as it depends on the age and size of the sturgeon it was cut from. It may be served with sauce in a tureen (allemande or other), on a plain dish as in our illustration; or it may be garnished with a border of quenelles, whiting and crayfish placed round it. There are numerous ways of preparing and cooking this delicious fish, thus—obtain, say 5lbs. from the thick part of the sturgeon, boil it in a good quantity of water with half a tea-cupful of salt. Simmer, not boil, for two hours (it may want a few minutes more), as slowly as possible, or it will crack. Find out that it is done by running a straw through the flesh; if this can be managed easily, take out the fish, put it to drain. Now put it into a soup-tureen or a large stone jar, make it very hot with Cayenne pepper, add salt, 10 cloves, 4 blades of mace. In another vessel make a kind of pickle by putting 2 parts of vinegar, to 1 of water, put the Sturgeon in this, completely covering it, mix a small tea-cupful of pounded loaf-sugar in water, let it dissolve, add it to the vinegar and water, gently stirring the whole. Put the whole aside for 24 hours, well covered over. After this it is ready for use. To serve it, cut enough for your purpose, lay it in a shallow dish, in a little of the pickle.

EELS A LA TARTARE.

Prepare a fish salad and pile it in the centre of the dish. Cut the eels into pieces about 3 inches long, trim them nicely, dip them in flour, paste them over with yolk of egg, bread crumb them all over, fry in hot lard as you would soles, and arrange as in Plate. A side or supper dish.

FISH IN GENERAL.

Fish as a nutritive article of food comes between meat and vegetables, being not so good, however, in this respect as the former. High authorities upon the subject say that where a fish diet is the rule and not the exception, the human frame loses much of its natural power.

PLATE II.

———◆———

BOILED MACKEREL.

These are boiled in the same manner as the haddock, are garnished with parsley and sent to table with gooseberry sauce, or with fennel or parsley ditto. The same remarks apply to this fish as to haddocks.

RED MULLET.

Put the fish in a sauté pan with a glass of wine, an ounce of butter, and a few drops each of anchovy and Harvey sauces; either put them in the oven, or covered up, over a gentle fire. When done, and they will take from 25 to 30 minutes, put the mullet on to their dish without a napkin; add to some of their liquor some chopped mushrooms, shalot, a little parsley, a sprinkling of nutmeg, a truffle if possible, the juice of a lemon, and a little flour. Stir all these over the fire for 4 or 5 minutes, pour the sauce over the mullet, and garnish the edge of the dish with tufts of parsley and cut lemon.

PÂTÉ À LA FINANCIÈRE.

Make some good pâté paste, about 1½ lb., mould it into the form of an orange, roll it out to the size of an ordinary dinner plate ; with the knuckles or fist make a deep indentation in the centre of this; it should be about 4 or 5 inches in diameter. Raise the paste up on all sides, basin shape, pressing the sides to give them firmness, to about 8 inches in height. This is called a shell ; place it upon a buttered paper upon a greased baking tin, press out the edge so as to form a slanting border, fill the inside with bran or flour to keep it in shape. Decorate by pinching, etc. with proper pastry pinches, egg it over and bake for about 45 minutes till it is of a pretty light brown colour. It should have a lid on to help to keep it in form When done, remove the lid by passing a knife along the edge of the upper part and pour out the bran or flour. Fill with financière ragôut as follows :—Get a few button mushrooms, truffles, quenelles, cock's-combs, and scallops of sweetbread (these must be already cooked), and add to them ½ pint of good dark sauce, flavoured with game is a desideratum, a glass of sherry, and a dash of cayenne. Boil these ingredients together for 3 minutes. Garnish with crayfish, &c., as in Plate. N.B.—The bottom of the pâté case is to be made with paste in the same way as the case itself.

FRIED SOLES.

Trim a pair of soles by removing their fins after they have been properly prepared for cooking. Wipe them quite dry, run the point of a knife straight along the back part of the spinal bone, rub the fish over with flour, and afterwards with beaten eggs put on with a brush on both sides. Cover completely with fine bread crumbs. Fry the soles in enough *very* hot lard to swim them. When done through, drain them on a cloth to absorb the grease. They should be of a beautiful amber colour. Dish on a serviette with tufts of fried parsley. Serve with lobster, anchovy, or shrimp sauce. A most popular and favourite first or second course, or supper dish, and a good breakfast relish.

GUDGEON.

Cut off the gills of two dozen live gudgeon (fresh-water fish, to eat to perfection, should be cooked as nearly alive as possible). Take the inside away very carefully, making a small aperture in the side of the fish. Clean thoroughly, wipe on a cloth, soak for a few minutes in milk; dredge them all over with flour. Fry in hot fat, crisp, and of a pretty tempting brown. Serve on a dish on a folded serviette garnished with fried parsley.

PIKE À LA GODARD.

The inside of a fine pike must be removed through the gills and the fish put into scalding water in order that the skin may be stripped off easily. Also tie the head with fine twine. Wrap the fish in buttered paper, put it in a fish kettle and cover it entirely with ellirepoix and French wine (white). When the pike is cooked, which can be told by touching it gently, drain it; cross it with four double rows of nailed-shaped pieces of truffle (this is called "to clouter it"), and with some pike forcemeat, put a fillet of sole between each row, and put the fish in the oven in order to cook the fillets. Now make a ragoût of truffles, mushrooms, and quenelles of pike forcemeat. Glaze the pike, garnish with quenelles and crayfish, and stick on silver skewers, mushrooms and truffles at the top of the fish. Serve with financière fish sauce. There is little difference between this and pike à la chambord.

The term "à la Godard" is a moot point amongst many cooks. Each has his own especial way of preparing meats and other edibles *à la Godard,* making it thus a little difficult for the mere housewifely cook to know what ground she is treading upon. They are in point of fact a kind of grand remove, dressed with a large supply of garnishes that we may call "big," such as mushrooms, truffles, quenelles and cock's-combs.

PRAWNS GARNISHED.

This is a very pretty dish as a salad, a breakfast relish, or in the menu of a light supper. Let the lemon be the foundation, cutting the end off that it may stand firmly. Arrange parsley on the top and sides, and the prawns all around as in Plate.

GRILLED HERRINGS.

Scale and wash the herrings, rub them dry and put them on a gridiron. Whilst they are grilling, make the following sauce:—Put into a saucepan 2 oz. of butter 1 teaspoonful of flour, 2 of vinegar, 4 of French mustard, $\frac{1}{2}$ gill of water, and some ordinary mustard, pepper, and salt, smooth these and thicken on the fire. Boil five minutes and pour it over the fish. Garnish with parsley.

TURBOT.

Turbot, which very much resembles brill, may be dressed in exactly the same manner as the latter fish. But it is preferable to have a little saltpetre in the boiling water. The turbot in the Plate is supposed to weigh 10 pounds A small clean cut should be made with the point of a knife in the skin of the back reaching almost to the bone to avoid any splitting of the meat. It is sometimes served with the white side uppermost (the old-fashioned way) even now, but the popular way is to have the dark side in view. Garnish as in Plate.

TROUT.

Put the trout in salt and water and boil it. When cooked, put it in a dish on a serviette folded, garnish with picked parsley and small pieces of lemon. Serve with parsley, butter, shrimp, ravigotte or anchovy sauce, &c.

HADDOCK.

The fish shown in our illustration are merely boiled. Haddocks should be boiled from 15 to 25 minutes, in just enough water to cover them and salt. Garnish with lemon and parsley and serve with melted butter or anchovy sauce. A nice breakfast dish, as well as a side or corner one in the first course. Fried haddock, as under, are very good. Divide the fish into suitable portions for serving; wash these very clean, wipe them quite dry upon a cloth, sprinkle a dessert-spoonful of indian meal upon the table, and roll the haddock in this. Cut some nice slices of *salt* pork and fry them in a very little lard. When done, remove the pork, taking care to keep it hot. Put a little more lard in the pan, let it get to boiling heat when put in the fish, which must be fried of a light brown. Arrange the slices of pork and fish in a dish together, and serve with melted butter. This is a capital impromptu, little supper dish, the arrangement being to merely lay the slices of meat, etc., as temptingly as possible together.

COD'S HEAD AND SHOULDERS.

If large, this is a fine dish for the fish course. After having rubbed salt upon the fish, tie folds of tape round and round it moderately tight to avoid any breakage. Put it in its kettle with cold water to cover it nicely, with a large handful of salt, a dessert-spoonful of vinegar and a little horseradish. Let the water approach boiling point, then let it simmer only. Put it, sliding it gently, on to the dish with a napkin folded upon it. Garnish with slices of lemon, double parsley, and the roe and liver of the cod.

FRIED WHITING.

The whiting must be skinned and then the tails turned round and affixed by means of a tiny wooden skewer between the jaws. Flour well and dip in beaten egg. Roll in bread-crumbs and fry in a good quantity of boiling fat. Dish up with fried parsley, garnish with sliced lemon, and serve with anchovy or lemon sauce. Also a nice entrée.

GURNET.

Make some nice veal stuffing and stuff the inside of the gurnets, securing the flaps with a fine sewing. Boil in salt and water. Put it on a dish with a folded napkin; garnish with picked parsley and lemon, and serve with white or brown caper sauce or with any good piquant fish sauce.

PLATE III.

PIGS' FEET AND TRUFFLES.

Boil 3 or 4 pigs' feet till done; drain them in a cloth, and cut them into small dicelike portions. Get truffles that have been cooked in Madeira and cut them in thin slices. Make forcemeat of some veal, fat bacon, and spiced salt. Put a pig's caul in cold water, drain it on a cloth, dry it and spread some of the forcemeat on it about a ¼ inch thick. The layer of this should be about 3 inches long and 1½ inches wide. Put a layer of the cut truffles on the forcemeat, and upon this spread some of the bits of pigs' feet, then one more spreading of the forcemeat. Wrap all round with the caul. These are called *crépinettes*. When a sufficiency of them is done dip them first into melted butter, then into bread-crumb, and boil them *slowly* for a quarter of an hour. They should be nicely coloured. Serve on a hot dish with parsley as a slight garnish.

LYONS SAUSAGE.

This belongs to that class of dishes styled " hors d'œuvre," literally " by dishes." Lyons, as well as German, sometimes called Bologna sausages, are dished up in various forms as to the simple arrangements of them and their garnishes upon a dish. In each and every case they are sent to table with parsley. Our illustration shows the sausage cut into slices not quite ¼ of an inch thick; the pieces skinned and laid overlapping each other around a mound of parsley. This is a salad, and comes in with the cheese course, or as an " appetiser," just after the soup and fish courses.

PIGEON PIE.

Pies of this kind are usually called "raised" or "standing" pies, and are so composed that they can remain a reasonable time perfectly good before being eaten. Make a wall of paste; bone the pigeons, taking as many as you think will be required for your pie; lay them down upon a cloth back upwards, and season inside with pepper, salt, and chopped onions. Put some forcemeat in a layer ½ an inch thick, cut pieces of veal ¼ inch thick, and the length of the pigeons, and some pieces of fat bacon of the same size; lay these pieces alternately upon the birds and cover with another layer of forcemeat. Line your pie mould with paste, then with forcemeat about ½ an inch in thickness, put in the meat and the forcemeat raised domelike in the centre. Put 2 bay leaves on the top of this and a little pat of butter. Cover and bake. The legs should be stuck into the pie. See Plate.

BRAWN.

An appetising breakfast, luncheon, and supper dish. Cut the head (pickled) of young pig in halves, and let it lie a night in water, covering it with salt; boil gently for about 6 hours. When it is quite cold remove the bones. Get the feet and tongue and ears, together with an extra tongue and pair of ears; boil for an hour and a half the gristle and bones having been removed. This done, cut all the meat into little pieces, and add to it a nice well-mixed seasoning of salt, pepper, and sage. Cut 4 dried sausages into slices, together with slices of red ox tongue, and press these into an ornamental mould. Put in the other prepared meat, press it firmly down, and stand a heavy weight on the top. Sometimes the tongues are not cut to pieces, but are put in whole in the middle of the mould.

LARKS AND POTATOES.

Roast the birds carefully, having previously prepared them for this operation. Melt some butter, add to it the yolk of an egg, and paste them all over with the mixture. Bread-crumb them; baste them very frequently whilst roasting, also flour them, and before they are quite ready to be taken up flour and salt them slightly. Prepare a dish of nicely-browned (light golden colour) potatoes mashed, and place the larks round it, as in Plate. This is a delicate and elegant remove.

LAMB CHOPS AND POTATOES.

This is also a dish where a pyramid of gold-brown mashed potatoes is used, and makes a pretty entrée. Choose as many lamb chops as are required, according to the number to be catered for; pare them of fat, leaving just a thin border of it, and trim them well before cooking. Let the fat in which they are to be fried be quite boiling when the chops are put in, turn them frequently, and when nicely coloured they will be done. Arrange them round the potato centre.

SCOTCH EGGS AND FORCEMEAT.

Boil as many new-laid eggs as will serve for your dish for ten minutes. Cut them in two, and a small portion off the ends, so that they will stand. Take out the yolks and beat them, after having passed them through a sieve, in a mortar with an equal quantity of butter, a little salt, pepper, nutmeg, and two eggs; also a large tablespoonful of chopped parsley. Mix these ingredients very thoroughly and put the preparation in a dish. Fill the eggs with this mixture. Make some good forcemeat; almost any kind will do, but veal is generally preferred. Smooth a layer of it in a nice dish (this should be of silver or electro), place the filled eggs round it, put a second layer of the forcemeats in the centre, and arrange the other eggs upon it, baste gently with butter, and set the dish for a few minutes in the oven just to colour them. Instead of forcemeat, the stuffing may be used for the layers. Serve with tomato sauce. A dish that will do either as an entrée, or for breakfast, luncheon, or supper.

STUFFED TOMATOES.

Take fine tomatoes, and scoop the inside out very carefully, so as not to break the rinds. Mince finely some fresh underdone meat, mix with a little salt, pepper and sweet herbs or a forcemeat can be made, and mixed with the scoopings of the tomatoes. Make into a good consistence, and stuff the tomatoes with it. Put the vegetables so done into a dish with a little lard in a slow oven, and bake until tender. Pile them as in Plate, and serve with the liquor that comes from the tomatoes whilst cooking. They should be of a pretty brown colour. A good rich gravy may, or may not be, poured over them.

VEAL CUTLETS AND OLIVES.

A very pretty and simple little entrée, appropriate either as a dinner or luncheon or supper dish. Prepare veal cutlets about the size of a crown piece, and half an inch thick; brush them over with egg, and dip them in bread-crumbs and chopped herbs (a bunch of sweet herbs). Fry the cutlets slightly in butter, turn them gently when required, and remove when done. Now with 1 oz. sweet butter put a sprinkling each of nutmeg and flour, the grated peel of half a small lemon and a little water into a fry-pan. Let the cutlets get hot in this. Serve as in illustration, and garnish with olives as in Plate VI.

VEAL CUTLETS EN PAPILLOTTE.

Prepare some nice cutlets and semi-fry them. Put them in a dish and pour white sauce over them. Let them stand till quite cold. Now cut out so many heart-shaped pieces of foolscap, or other stiff white paper, as you have cutlets, dip them a moment in some good fresh oil, lay the cutlets in them, with a little of the sauce on one half the paper. To encase them turn the paper over and crimp or plait the two edges of the paper together, beginning at the top of the heart and finishing with a strong twist at the bottom, so that the sauce within cannot escape. Broil slowly on a gridiron over a very slow fire for 20 minutes, or place them in the oven for that time. Forms a nice entrée.

FILLETS OF BEEF.

Cut good fillets from the under part of the rump or sirloin. Pare off all sinew and some fat if there be too much. Cut them about half an inch thick and trim them neatly. Season them with a little oil, pepper, and salt, broil on both sides and glaze them. Garnish with fried potatoes or merely with *maître d'hôtel* butter.

LAMB CUTLETS AND GREEN PEAS.

Trim lamb cutlets nicely and fry them carefully in the usual way. When almost cold, dip them separately up to the bone in stiff Allemande sauce well flavoured with mushrooms. After being dipped, set each cutlet flat on a baking tin or a dish upon rough ice, so that the sauce shall become set as firmly as possible upon them. Brush them with yolk of egg, bread-crumb them, fry them slightly again in boiling lard, lay them round a pyramid of green peas; pour white sauce round the base. A pretty entrée.

HAM GARNISHED.

Well soak a ham in a good deal of water for 24 hours, then scrape it quite clean and put it into a stewpan with more than enough water to cover it. Put in a blade of mace, a sprig of thyme, a few cloves, and a couple of bay leaves. Boil it, estimating its weight, for 4 or 5 hours, let it get cold in the liquor it has been boiled in. Remove the rind by lifting it up at the thick end of the ham without injuring the fat. With a cloth absorb as much grease as you can from it. Shake raspings over it, cut devices upon it with a short sharp knife, ornament the knuckle with a paper frill and vegetable flowers, and serve with a garnishing of aspic jelly.

TONGUE GARNISHED.

Boil a tongue very slowly for two hours and a half. When done, place it in cold water, which will admit of your being able easily to remove the rough coating and skin. Place it then with the root end against the back of the dresser, and put a strong fork in the top of the tongue. This will make it assume an erect and nice appearance. Let it get quite cold, glaze it then, ornament it with a paper ruff and a vegetable flower, and garnish with aspic jelly.

CROQUETTES OF FOWL.

Cold roast chicken will come into requisition here. Cut fillets of these, freeing them perfectly from all skin, bone, gristle, &c., and cut them again into tiny square portions. Weigh these, and have exactly the same proportion of truffles cut into small slice. This done, mix all into some very stiff Allemande sauce. Put on a dish. Prepare bread-crumbs, and put some on your table or board. Now part the chicken and truffles thus mixed into pieces of an equal size, rolling them as in Plate (sometimes they are rolled into ball shapes), dip them in a mixture of beaten eggs, oil, salt, and pepper, and into the bread-crumbs. Fry the rolls (now croquettes) in hot fat till nice and crisp and of a gold brown colour; drain on a cloth (this frees them of superfluous grease), and put a sprinkling of salt over them. Arrange them on a napkin in a dish with garnishings of fried parsley.

FRICANDEAU OF VEAL.

Get about 2 lbs. of the meatiest part of a fillet of veal, trim it neatly, and lard the outside with thin strips of bacon. Now put in a glazing-pan with the trimmings of the meat, 2 oz. each of sliced carrot and sliced onion, a quarter of a teaspoonful of pepper and the same of salt. Put the veal on the top (the fricandeau) with ½ pint of broth. Boil till the broth is lessened and has turned thick and yellowish in colour, and at this stage add 1½ pint more broth. Simmer this for 75 minutes, only half covering the stewpan. Now quite close the stewpan and put some hot coals from the fire on the cover. Baste the fricandeau with the gravy about once in 4 minutes, when it will glaze. When this is done sufficiently, take the fricandeau out and place it on its dish. Pour gravy round it, and garnish with mushrooms and sorrel round the edge of the dish, and white cock's-combs and decorated quenelles upon the top of the fricandeau. (See Index for sorrel garnish.) It is also admissible to garnish with spinach and endive.

CHARTREUSE OF PARTRIDGES.

Prepare and roast 3 partridges, and also prepare some cabbage as in the direction for "*Partridges aux Choux.*" Add a little essence of partridge, and stir both lightly over fire till the cabbage is free from any moisture. With a long vegetable cutter, ½ an inch in diameter, cut some pieces of carrot and turnip about 2 inches long and cook them separately. Line a plain entrée mould slightly with butter, and cut a circular piece of paper to put upon the bottom: garnish this with the bits of vegetable named. Next put a layer of cabbage into the mould. Divide the birds and place four fillets on the cabbage, and over these put another layer of cabbage. Do this alternately till the mould is filled. Warm the mould and its contents in a *bain-marie* pan, and then turn the contents of the mould (the *chartreuse*) into its proper entrée dish. Garnish round the bottom with alternate rounds of carrots and turnips with a French bean between each. On the top put rings of turnip and a Brussels sprout in each. Make a cup out of carrot, fix it in the centre of the chartreuse, and fill it with French beans. Serve with a tureen of *Espagnole* sauce, made thinner with essence of partridge.

TIMBALE MILANAISE (MACARONI).

This is an elegant dish, and belongs to "high-class cooking." It makes an effective entrée. Line an entrée mould thinly with butter. Make paste as follows:—Mix into ¼ lb. of flour, 1 oz. of butter, the yolks of 2 eggs, and about a quarter of a teaspoonful of fine loaf sugar. Knead this thoroughly but lightly, and roll it out very thin indeed. Cut it into fancy and ornamental shapes with some proper cutters. Place these according to your fancy in a pretty design inside the buttered mould all round. Stand it in ice, and when set and quite cold paste the patterns over with a wet brush. Line the mould with fine puff paste. Boil some macaroni in stock or broth, drain it, season it with grated Parmesan cheese, nutmeg, salt and pepper. Put the macaroni, when cold, in the *timbale*, put a paste lid on and bake in a moderate oven. When baked turn the *timbale* out on the dish. Cut out the top about an inch from the side, take away half the macaroni it is filled with, putting in its place some *Milanaise ragoût*. This is made of fillets of tongue, chicken, and truffles cut into scollops, some cock's-combs and mushrooms sliced, all mixed in *Allemande* sauce and piled up quite 1½ inch above the height of the *timbale* itself. Place a dozen small larded and glazed fillets in a circle all round the edge of the crust, as in the illustration, and finish with one fine cock's-comb in the middle of the ragout.

PUREE OF GAME AND RICE.

This is a pretty and economical dish coming under the head of secondary cookery. Take the remains of any kind of roast or boiled game from yesterday's dinner, and put them into a stewpan with ¼ of a pint of water, a stick of celery, a little faggot of thyme, and a shalot. Gently boil these together. Mince the meat and pound it in a mortar with a small knob of butter, and a spoonful of gravy from the bones. This should now be in a state of pulp; rub it through a hair sieve, and put it in the stewpan with the stock from the bones, which ought to be reduced to less than a gill in quantity. Add a gill of cream, a mere sprinkling of pepper, salt, and nutmeg, and a teaspoonful of flour. Dish with rice, potato croquettes, poached eggs, and thin narrow strips of bacon as a garnishing, or with merely the rice and tufts of parsley.

CALF'S HEART.

The heart should be a nice sized one, and should be put into water for an hour. Wipe it with a cloth quite dry, and stuff it with either veal stuffing or forcemeat, but whichever of these is used it must be very highly seasoned. Cover the heart with buttered paper, and let it roast at a good fire. Serve with good gravy and as hot as possible. This is a capital luncheon dish, as well as a plain entrée for the dinner-table.

CALF'S TONGUE.

Trim a calf's tongue, blanch it, and boil it slowly, it will take about an hour, but this according to size. Plunge it for a moment into cold water to enable you to peel off the thick fur or skin, press it into shape as given in directions for "tongue garnished," trim it and glaze it. Dress it with a frill, and garnish with aspic jelly round the tongue in the dish. A delicate little entrée.

CHAUD FROID OF FOWL.

Boil a nice sized tender chicken in some white veal stock, using some of this afterwards to make the *Allemande* sauce required with this remove. When cooked, neatly cut up the chicken in trim looking joints. Cover them all over with the sauce and set them aside in a dish to become cold and firm. Garnish and ornament with aspic jelly. This is a superior kind of entrée.

FILLET OF BEEF A LA JARDINIÈRE.

Get a piece of fillet of beef off the sirloin, which latter would do afterwards for roasting. Cut or pare away with a sharp knife the sinewy outside portion of the fillet, and lard the plain surface thus obtained with small pieces of fat bacon $1\frac{1}{4}$ inch long and $\frac{1}{4}$ inch broad. These must be arranged in straight rows across the fillet in such a way that each row dovetails the other and represents as a whole a kind of basket work. Put the fillet in a braising pan upon its drainer together with the trimmings, carrot, celery, a couple of onions stuck with 6 cloves in all, 2 teaspoonfuls of salt, a blade of mace, and about enough stock to reach up to the commencement of the larding (no further), and set to braise either in a rather quick oven, or over a slow fire with live coals on the top of the pan. Cook it for about 2 hours, when it ought to be quite tender. Place it now in a dish, and set it in the oven to dry the larding. Glaze it over, and put in the dish it is to be served in. The liquor must be strained and can be used as sauce for the fillet, if clarified and reduced. Garnish the fillet with potatoes cut into shapes and fried in butter, and placed alternately with small groups or bunches of green peas, French beans and cauliflower. Pour the sauce round and serve.

PARTRIDGES AUX CHOUX.

This is an elegant entreé. The partridges must not be old. Prepare two for boiling, and in the breast insert 3 or 4 strips of fat bacon cutting off the protruding ends. Get a good Savoy cabbage, cut it in quarters, pick it thoroughly well over and let it lie in cold water for an hour. Remove the stalk, let no water remain in it, put the quarters into a $\frac{1}{2}$ gallon stewpan, let the partridges be beneath them and put in also 6 oz. of carrot, 6 oz. of onion, with a clove stuck in one (these must not be *cut*), a faggot of sweet herbs, $\frac{1}{4}$ of a teaspoonful of pepper, $\frac{1}{4}$ lb. of Bologna sausage (not cooked), and $\frac{1}{2}$ lb. of streaky bacon blanched. Put in broth to cover the cabbage and 2 gills of good dripping that has been melted and strained. Put a circular piece of *thick* white paper over all before the lid of the saucepan is put on. Put this in closely. Boil and simmer for $1\frac{1}{2}$ hours. Take out the meat and set it in the oven that it may not get cool. Next drain the cabbage and put it in a stewpan with a sprinkling of pepper and salt. Keep stirring till it is free from all moisture. Put a layer of the vegetable rather thickly in a dish, undo the birds, arrange them as in the Plate. Put more cabbage in the centre, and cut the sausage and the bacon into slices. Cut the carrots into cork-like pieces, and garnish with bacon, sausage, and carrots. Serve with the following sauce:—Into a stewpan put an ounce each of flour and butter, and mix over the fire for 3 minutes. Put in a pint of some good gravy and let it boil for 10 minutes. Strain and send to table in a tureen.

FRICASSEE OF FOWL.

Housekeepers who do not already know it should pay a little attention to the preparation of a *Fricassee of Fowl*. For this reason: it is a dish of high repute both for the family and the party dinner. It is at once simple, and yet may be considered an elaborate dish and to belong in part to high class cookery. It is always welcome, and always an elegant dish. The chicken for a fricassee should weigh nearly or quite 3 pounds, and thus is sufficient for, say 4, persons. The proper method of cutting it up is this:—Make an opening from the point of the breast bone to both wing joints. Then reverse the chicken and make two incisions, separating the legs from the fowl. The neck and the pinions must be cut off at the *second* joint, the feet at the *first*. Cut away the wings and legs, and divide the breast from the back, cutting each of these across in two pieces. Trim evenly and neatly, but leaving the skin on. Soak the portions thus divided in cold water for an hour, drain on a cloth, and put them in a stewpan that will contain them amply with a large onion with a clove stuck in it, 2 pints of water, ¼ of a teaspoonful of pepper, the same of salt, and a small bundle of sweet herbs. Boil up and skim, and let it simmer merely for 30 minutes afterwards. Do not close the lid of the stewpan during the simmering. The chicken being fully cooked put it into a colander to drain, and put it into *cold* water for 4 or 5 minutes (not longer) to cool. Now put 3 oz. each of butter and flour into a ½ gallon stewpan, and put them on the fire for 5 minutes, not allowing them to get brown, however. Put in the broth that the chicken was boiled in, and ½ a pint of mushroom liquor. Boil up and simmer again for 30 minutes, place the portions of fowl into a *sauté* pan. Put over them ½ a pint of the sauce strained, and warm gently over the fire. Put the yolks of 4 eggs and an ounce of butter with the remainder of the sauce to thicken it, smoothing it gradually to avoid all lumpiness in the usual way. Strain and add some ready cooked mushrooms, and dish as in our illustration. Pour the sauce over and garnish with mushrooms, croûtons, and button onions or artichoke bottoms (cooked). Often crayfish are placed one at each corner of the dish, and this improves the appearance considerably.

HALF CALF'S HEAD.

Boil ½ a calf's head until tender, bone it when cool and replace the brain; lay the head in a stewpan and simmer for an hour in good rich gravy. About ½ an hour before it is served add ½ pint of button mushrooms, thickening the gravy with rice flour or with flour and butter; a few herbs will improve the flavour or the rind of a fresh lemon. Serve with a garnish of forcemeat balls and mushrooms. A plain entrée, but always acceptable. Calf's head fricasseed as an ordinary fricassee, with a sauce of cream, butter, and the liquor poured over it is a tempting dish.

PLATE IV.

ROAST LEG OF MUTTON.

This is a leg of mutton plainly roasted, decorated with a frill, and served with gravy in the dish. Wash the leg, wipe it dry, and put it in the dripping pan. Season it with salt and pepper, and dredge with flour. Pour about a tea-cupful of water in the pan, and roast, or bake it (if the latter the oven must be really hot) for rather more than 2 hours. When done, remove the joint, have good gravy in readiness, pour a table-spoonful of it over the meat, and send the remainder to table in a sauce-tureen. Serve with currant jelly.

ROAST LEG OF PORK.

Just below the knuckle of a leg of pork, between the skin and the flesh, make a wide incision with not too sharp a knife, and fill this cavity with sage and onion stuffing. Sew up this securely with fine twine or coarse whitey-brown thread. Score the pork all over, which means cutting the rind through in narrow bands of about ½ an inch in width. After this hang up the leg before a good roasting fire, roasting it about two hours; it must be basted often. Dish it up with brown gravy or tomato sauce, and also serve apple sauce and sage and onion gravy in tureens. A substantial second course dish; and, when cold, an excellent supper dish.

HAUNCH OF MUTTON.

Irish, Welsh, and Devonshire mutton are all in their several good qualities worthy of note to the chooser of a good haunch. This meat should hang for a few days—say 10—in a very cool larder. There is a thin skin upon it which must be removed before cooking, and the shank-bone must be sawed off. Cover the haunch with a large sheet of well-greased paper, and hang it ½ a yard away from a good clear roasting fire. It will take about 2½ hours. Baste it with perfectly good dripping at least every 5 or 6 minutes. Ten minutes before the joint is cooked take off the paper surrounding it, sprinkle salt and flour lightly over it, and put a basting of butter that has been melted over it; it must look brown and frothy. Serve with gravy poured over it, and red currant jelly sauce, or red currant jelly. A plain, good, old English second course dish.

BOILED LEG OF PORK.

The leg should be a trim neat-looking one. It should have remained a week in pickle. Put it for ¾ of an hour in *cold* water before it is cooked (this will give it a good colour). Put it into a saucepan and well cover it with water. Boil gradually, and serve plain on a dish (as in our illustration) or garnish with turnips or parsnips. Boiled in a floured cloth, a leg of pork presents a very appetising appearance.

KNUCKLE OF VEAL.

Put it into a sufficiently large pan to allow of its being nicely covered with water. Boil quite gently, and when upon the point of boiling put into the liquor 2 teaspoonfuls of salt. Skim the surface thoroughly, boil till tender, garnish with parsley, and serve with parsley and butter.

ROAST PIG.

As in our illustration, there must be two pigs. Fill their paunches with the usual stuffing, or one made as follows: Chop together very finely 12 or 14 sage leaves and 4 onions, and having melted two ounces of butter, simmer these all together over a slow fire for 5 or 6 minutes, adding afterwards ½ a pound of bread crumbs, the yolks of 2 eggs, and some pepper and salt. Sew the paunches up safely and neatly, roast the pigs before a brisk fire for about two hours. Baste very often, and the best way to do this is to use a flat ordinary paste brush, dipped in fresh salad oil. When the pigs are cooked, cut off the heads, and split the bodies in halves by sawing perfectly straight down the spine. Put brown gravy round the pigs, and make a sauce of the brains and a little of the stuffing, with 4 or 5 spoonfuls of melted butter. Serve the butter in a tureen. A grand old English dish.

SADDLE OF MUTTON.

Remove all bones from a saddle of young mutton with the greatest care, so that no injury accrue to the skin on the upper side. Fill this with appropriate forcemeat, and fasten this stuffing in securely and neatly by rolling up the joint in a cloth, spread with butter, and afterwards tying the ends with fine string. Braize the saddle in white stock for 1½ hour, using the usual amount of stock vegetables. Then take it out of the braize, putting it in a cloth and leaving it till cold between two dishes, with a heavy weight on the top dish. Make it hot in a little of the stock (do not boil it), place it on a dish, garnish with button mushrooms, truffles, cock's-combs, &c., and pour *allemande* sauce in the dish. A handsome entrée.

FORE-QUARTER OF LAMB.

This is esteemed as the best joint in the lamb. Let it be fresh, and take care that it is done so that there be no red gravy in it as in mutton. This is a rule applying to young white meat. Put it at first at a considerable distance from the fire, and when it is commencing to cook baste it well. The fire must be a good one, but not fierce. If the joint weigh from 10 to 11 pounds it will take 2 hours. Remove the shoulder from the ribs, but before quite lifting this off lay beneath it a lump of butter, a little lemon-juice, and some pepper and salt. The shoulder must go upon another dish. Garnish with any kind of small dressed vegetables or with merely good brown gravy.

SIRLOIN OF BEEF.

This joint ought to be and look a *noble* one, and, therefore, one under the weight of 16 pounds would hardly attain to this. It can be stuffed or not ; if stuffed, proceed as follows: Gently lift up the fat from the inside of the sirloin with a sharp knife, and remove all the meat close to the bone, mincing it small. Chop fine ½ pound of suet, and mix it with a little thyme, eschalot, and lemon-peel, all minced very small indeed, a few grated bread-crumbs, and one wineglassful of port wine. Put this mixture into the cavity the removed meat has made. Cover it neatly with the skin and fat, and skewer it thus with tiny wooden skewers. The sirloin will take about 2½ hours to cook before a good roasting fire. Keep it half a yard from the fire, basting very often with plenty of fat. A quarter of an

t

hour before it is to be taken up sprinkle salt and flour over it. When put on its dish ready to serve, pour good gravy over it, or simply a cupful of hot water in which you have placed a few drops of colouring. Garnish with horseradish, potato croquets in balls, and Bordelaise sauce.

Yorkshire pudding is often eaten with this, but it is not so much in vogue as formerly. A smaller sirloin, however, of from 6 to 8 pounds weight will make, and look, a very fair dish of roast beef for a small party of diners. Take out the bone, but if you cannot do this neatly, let your butcher do it. Shape the meat into a fillet, sprinkle it well with flour, season with salt and black pepper, roast it, basting very often. In carving this joint, slice it horizontally.

FILLET OF VEAL.

The bone must be taken out of the joint, and a deep aperture made with a sharp knife between the fillet and the udder. Fill this aperture with veal stuffing ; bind the veal up as in our illustration, and keep it together with wooden skewers and twine. Put the spit as nearly in the centre as possible, and cover the joint with well greased paper. Do not put the meat very close to the fire at first, but let it go there gradually. Baste continuously, and when almost done sprinkle a little flour about it, basting it with butter. Draw out the wooden skewers and put in silver or electro ones. The surface of the fillet should now have a frothy appearance. Pour round it some melted butter coloured with a little browning and flavoured with lemon juice; lay a tuft of parsley on the top. A fine looking remove.

BOILED BEEF.

This is an ever popular dish, and comes next to the " roast beef of old England" in English tastes. Garnish with carrots and parsnips well boiled, and of a good shape. Serve with its own liquor very slightly browned, or tomato catsup as a sauce in a tureen. The beef must be put into cold water, let it come to a boil, put it aside that it may simmer only till done ; boiled beef is frequently ruined both in look and taste by being allowed to *boil*, and very often boil unmercifully. To serve this dish cold, it should be allowed to remain in the liquor it was cooked in until quite cold, when it must be well drained, and set aside.

PLATE V.

GROUSE.

These are trussed in the same manner as pheasants. Roast them before a good brisk fire, and a few minutes before they are to be taken up sprinkle flour upon them and butter that has been melted, to give them a frothy appearance. Put them on the dish on a layer of fried bread-crumbs, and serve with fried bread-crumbs and bread sauce in separate tureens.

HARE.

Stuff the paunch of the hare with veal or hare stuffing, and sew it up with fine twine, or secure it with a skewer. Get it ready for the spit by tying the body of the hare in the usual way with string. Roast for 45 minutes or thereabouts, basting it very often with fresh butter. This should froth up, and give a tempting look to the hare. About 4 or 5 minutes before removing it from the spit shake a little flour over it, and baste by sprinkling dissolved butter upon it. Garnish with watercresses and lemon. Pour brown gravy in the dish, and serve with red currant jelly.

WOODCOCK.

These are trussed, roasted, and sent to table in precisely the same manner as snipe, and are served with the same sauce.

SNIPE.

A pretty second course dish. Roast them for about 25 minutes, often basting them with butter or good fresh beef dripping. Place toasted bread beneath the birds to catch the droppings from the trail. Dish them on this toast, a piece to each, garnish with watercresses or not, serve melted butter in a separate tureen.

PHEASANT.

Prepare the pheasant as customary for roasting. Put it before a brisk fire for 30 minutes, basting it constantly. Send to table with good brown gravy in the dish, and with bread sauce separately in a tureen.

PLOVERS.

Roast plovers in the same manner as woodcock, without drawing. Arrange as in Plate on toast, with gravy and butter over them. Serve as hot as possible. This is a very effective little dish as part of the second course.

PARTRIDGES.

Roast the birds before a brisk fire, according to the directions for hare. Pour a little good brown gravy over them, serve with bread sauce and gravy in separate tureens.

CAPON À LA MILANAISE.

This is a first class remove, and a very elegant and delicate dish. Stuff a capon, and after dressing it in the usual manner with truffles roast it, putting it not too near at first to a brisk roasting fire. Place a layer of rice on the dish, lay the capon on it. Dish up, and pour tomato sauce over. Garnish as in Plate.

WILD DUCK.

This is an entrée of the first class. (The chief fault in cooking these is usually cooking them too much. Some great cook has observed, it is said, that wild fowl should only look at the kitchen.) Roast the fowl underdone before a clear roasting fire, and baste it very often with butter. Send it to table with rich brown gravy, and garnish with slices of lemon. Wild duck *à la chasseur*, a splendid dish for epicures, is sent to table and prepared in exactly the same way, but when on the table there should be placed near the carver a deep silver dish, or a spirit of wine or other burner. This dish should contain a mixture of 2 glasses of port wine 1 of cavice sauce, the juice of a lemon, a pinch each of salt and cayenne, with the gravy. The carver cuts up the fowl, and puts all the joints and slices into this dish, which is then handed round for the guests to take from.

ROAST WHEATEARS.

Spit them on a small bird spit, dredge them well with flour, and baste them with butter. Toast a slice of bread without crust, and let it gather dripping from under the birds as they cook. They will take 15 minutes to get done. Then lay them on the toast, which is placed upon a dish, pour good dark gravy over them, and serve plain as in our Plate, or garnish with pieces of lemon.

ROAST GOOSE.

This dish, one of our old standard dishes, needs little description. Serve with good brown gravy in the dish, and, separately, apple sauce.

LANDRAILS.

These are a nice side dish. After they have been drawn they should be wiped very clean with a damp cloth. They must be continuously basted with butter, and will take about 15 minutes to cook. Put them on a layer of fried bread crumbs, on an exceedingly hot dish. Send to table with a tureen of bread sauce, and one of good gravy.

PIGEONS.

Pigeons should be cooked as soon as possible after they are killed, otherwise they lose their flavour. Season with pepper and salt sprinkled inside; roast before a very clear brisk fire. When of a nice gold-brown colour serve plain, or with a good brown gravy.

GUINEA FOWL.

Roast before a good fire, with layers of fat bacon over the bird, for from 20 to 25 minutes. Take up, glaze and garnish with watercresses. Put good brown gravy the dish, and serve with bread sauce apart in a tureen.

DUCK.

Prepare a duck for roasting, stuff it and roast for 20 minutes, then put it into a stewpan with an onion cut in slices, a few chopped herbs, a sprig each of sage and mint, a pint of good beef gravy nicely seasoned with pepper and salt, and stew it gently for 20 minutes. Lift out the bird, keep it hot, strain the gravy into a clean stewpan, and when hot, but not boiling, put the duck and a quart of young green peas in it. Let it simmer for half an hour. A little flour, butter, and a glass of good old port may be added with advantage. Dish with the peas round the duck. (This is sometimes called stewed duck). It forms an elegant remove.

ROAST FOWL.

Our illustration represents a roast fowl stuffed, although it serves equally well for one that is not stuffed. Let it be trussed nicely, and make a good stuffing of sausage-meat, truffles, if procurable, or of chestnuts if not. Roast according to size from 20 minutes to three-quarters of an hour. Serve with bread sauce, parsley and butter, or egg sauce (separate). (A piece of good salt butter, the size of a small walnut, dipped in black pepper and placed inside the bird before roasting, will be found to remove very much of the dryness often met with in the back and side bones.) Fowls are always an addition to the courses of a dinner.

TURKEY.

Prepare the bird for roasting as usual, and put it before a good but not fierce roasting fire, basting it very often, for this will keep the gravy in. Turkeys sometimes disappoint the eaters because of their dryness, and this, it should be borne in mind, is chiefly through the want of a really constant and thorough basting Serve with fried sausage and forcemeat balls, pour good brown gravy over, and send to table with a tureen of bread sauce.

BOILED FOWL.

This also represents a plain boiled fowl, although our directions for it will be as stuffed. The appearance, as in the foregoing roast fowl, will be exactly similar.

Get a young fowl, dress it for boiling as usual, and fill the interior with oysters. Put it into a jar or vessel that will hold it comfortably, and stand this in a saucepan of water. Boil it for an hour and a half. Much gravy will come from the fowl and its oyster stuffing; make it with an egg into a nice white sauce, adding also some cream, or failing this a little flour and butter beaten up. Serve this in a tureen, with or without oysters. The fowl will be very white and tender, two most essential requisites in such meat, and loses nothing of its mildness. Garnish with parsley.

BOILED RABBIT.

Soak the rabbit in milk and water for 2 hours, truss as usual, and take care not to destroy the shape. Boil it in water sufficient to cover it, and no more. Season with a bunch of parsley, a carrot, an onion, a blade of mace, 3 or 4 peppercorns, and a salt-spoonful of salt. Cook for three-quarters of an hour, dish up, and serve with celery sauce round it, and a garnishing of small strips of fried bacon and parsley.

ROAST RABBIT.

Our rabbit, done as follows, will taste like hare. Select a young one, but of good size (fully grown). Let it be skinned and prepared, and *without* washing it lay it in this mixture:—A wineglass each of vinegar and port wine, and a teaspoonful of black pepper and powdered allspice. Baste this often during 2 days, and afterwards stuff and roast it as ordinarily. Pour sauce round it, made thus:— After boiling the liver tender, chop it finely with some parsley, an ounce of butter, a teaspoonful each of gravy and sauce, some grated lemon peel and nutmeg. Boil this slightly and pour under the rabbit, and garnish with a few forcemeat balls.

PLATE VI.

—————

OLIVES.

These are opened very carefully, the stones removed, and the cavities thus made are filled in with pounded anchovy. They are "appetisers," and are eaten with a little oil or with the cheese. [They are served occasionally when quite sweet and as imported with a little of the liquor in which they have been preserved, at dessert. They are also often sent to table with the stones in.]

POTATOES

Our Plate shows a dish of plain boiled potatoes. No better second course dish is there than this when really well cooked. There are, it is well known, various methods of cooking potatoes; two very good ones are as follows—Wash moderately young potatoes well, boil them, in their skins, in just enough water to cover them nicely. They should be put to cook about 1 hour before they are required. When almost done, peel them very carefully (they must go to table as whole as possible), put them in the dripping pan, and set them in the oven for 30 minutes. No. 2. Peel some good potatoes, let them be as near one size as possible, if this cannot be, put the larger ones at the bottom of the saucepan. Let them boil until the fork can go easily into them, but they must not be at all in a state of "breakage." Drain the water away, stuff a cloth into the saucepan, put the lid on, and stand it aside on a *hot* part of the hob for 5 to 8 minutes. Take them out carefully with a vegetable spoon, and they ought to appear mealy and white,

PARSNIPS.

These are arranged in the same manner as carrots. They require long boiling, and should be of a yellowish-white colour. Scrape them well, and as evenly as possible or their appearance will be spoilt. Wash them, cut them quite through, lengthwise, down the centre, if large they must be cut in quarters, boil them in water slightly salted, when soft drain them, and send to table either plain, or with melted butter poured over them in the dish.

TOMATOES.

The Plate illustrates a plain dish of tomatoes. These are pretty and tasteful, and look best in a quiet dish, the colour being vivid.

BRUSSELS SPROUTS.

In boiling these the great thing is to preserve their greenness. Boil sufficient for your dish, and when done put them into a stewpan, with a taste merely of lemon-juice, pepper (that called mignonette pepper, if procurable), two ounces of fresh butter, and a spoonful of white sauce. Toss all these ingredients about till the butter is dissolved and incorporated with the rest. Dish as in our Plate, or with a border of sippets of toasted bread round the dish.

CABBAGE.

" Am I going to tell you how to cook a simple cabbage, and after all these years too ? " No, I hope everybody, save a few obliged-to-be-left-out people know all this well enough without any interference from me.

Take off the outer leaves, and remove the stalk from as nice and large a cabbage as you can obtain. Scald it in scalding water for 10 minutes. Make a cavity in the centre by the stalk, and fill it and between every leaf with forcemeat. Bind it so that it does not let this stuffing drop out, and put it in a pan with some gravy, a slice of bacon, a stick of thyme, a bay leaf, and a couple of carrots. Stew all gently together, and when done untie the string, and serve with the strained gravy round it.

VEGETABLE MARROW.

The marrows must be cut into pieces according to their size, and according to the size and capacity of the dish they are to be put in. Trim them very neatly after peeling them thinly. Put them in a *sauté* pan (deep) that is spread with butter, and add sprinklings only of nutmeg, pepper, salt, and about 1 teaspoonful of pounded sugar, and make them moist by the addition of ½ pint of white broth. Boil very gently for 10 minutes, boil them down in their glaze, add 2 ounces of butter, stirring it in, and the juice of ½ a lemon. Pour this sauce over the marrow and se e.

SPANISH ONIONS.

Peel as usual, and force out the cores or hearts with an ordinary long vegetable cutter. Boil them in water for 10 minutes, and lay them on a cloth to drain. Spread butter over the bottom of a *sauté* pan as in the directions for the vegetable marrow, and put in the onions. Now pour in enough gravy to cover them and boil them on a slow fire, turning them now and then. When nearly done, add 2 teaspoonfuls of pounded sugar, boil them quite quickly to a glaze, put a little tomato sauce with them, and put them in a dish close together. [These are not a dish to be strongly recommended as part of a second course. They form an excellent garnish for braized beef, &c.]

BROAD BEANS.

This is a much-liked dish. Get young beans, boil them with a bunch of parsley and a teaspoonful of salt. Drain them when cooked, put them in a stewpan, with a sprinkling of pepper, nutmeg, and salt, a small bunch of chopped parsley, 2 ounces of butter, and as much winter savory as will lie on a sixpence. Shake the beans over the fire for a few minutes, and mix them with a mixture of the yolks of 4 eggs and the juice of ½ a lemon.

SALAD.

If your salad is to be an excellent one—that is to say, an eatable one, for salads are *not* eatable unless they are excellent—the vegetables used in the preparation must be young and fresh, and they should be prepared only just before they are to be used. These may seem little unimportant matters, but if they are neglected your salad will be a failure, however careful you may be upon all other points. Endive (blanched) and cos lettuce are almost *the* best vegetables that can be used as a salad. Strip off the green leaves leaving nothing but the crisp white hearts,

Wash these and put them in cold water for quite 1½ hour. Wipe them quite dry Add to these hearts a couple of heads of celery, and 2 anchovies (these are better for your purpose than essence of anchovies), and a few chives or young onions all cut small. Make the dressing of the yolks of 2 hard-boiled eggs, with a tea-spoonful of salt and 2 of mustard mixed (a drop of assafœtida will give to the mustard a slight flavour of garlic). To every tablespoonful of vinegar add one of oil, one spoonful being impregnated with chilies. The finest oil should be used, and a little tarragon and walnut ketchup may be added if liked. Mix the dressing lightly with the salad. Put the whole preparation into your bowl, and ornament with hard-boiled egg and boiled beet cut in slices.

CARROTS.

The plate represents a dish of plain-boiled carrots : each split into four quarters.

RADISHES.

These hardly require detailing. Choose the best possible radishes, both long and round, and also red and white. Pile them prettily, as in the Plate, on a foundation of parsley or endive. These form a pretty dish, and can hardly be left out of one's list of " green stuff," but they contain much water, and are not con-sidered very nutritious therefore ; but they form a pleasant accompaniment with other things, and are also somewhat of a stimulating nature.

CAULIFLOWERS.

To dress these well cut the green part as in our illustration, and cut the stalk quite close up to the flower. Let them soak for at least an hour in cold water, and lay them in boiling milk and water (or water alone). It is done when the stalk is tender. Drain and serve with plain butter sauce separately. This is a hand-some and deservedly popular dish.

GREEN PEAS.

Peas should never be sent to table unless they are really and truly of a tempting autumnal green hue, nor unless they are young. Boil them as soon after shelling them as possible. Put them into a colander and let clean cold water run upon them from a tap. Salt the water slightly that they are to be placed in ; let it boil and pour in the peas. Keep the pan uncovered and boiling rapidly till they are tender. At the end of 20 minutes drain them. Pour them into their dish, put a knob of fresh butter in the centre, and add a sprinkling of pepper and salt. Stir the peas gently, not breaking them, with a wooden spoon, and serve quickly. [For a dinner party it is *not* advisable to boil a sprig of mint with the peas, as many persons dislike the flavour. There might, however, be two dishes served.]

FRENCH BEANS.

Boil as ordinarily. Put ¼lb. of butter into a saucepan with a sprinkling of nutmeg, pepper, and salt, the juice of a lemon, a tablespoonfu of chopped and parboiled parsley, and two chopped shalots. Put these on the fire to melt (not boil) the butter, put the beans in, shake to and fro, and dish either with or without croûtons round the dish. [For dinner parties these ways of cooking such popular vegetables are to be recommended, as they form tasteful as well as tasty dishes.]

MIXED PICKLES.

This is a dish easily arranged with a pretty dish to hold the pickles, and a selection of pickles that will blend together in colour and taste. Gherkins, French beans, radish pods, tomatoes, &c.

ASPARAGUS.

The asparagus must be washed and cleansed very carefully. Cut away all the superfluous hard part at the bottom, leaving enough only to take it up comfortably between the fingers. Scrape this thoroughly, cut and trim them of equal lengths and tie them in parcels. Now lay them in boiling water with a teaspoonful of salt. Boil them rather quickly, and when tender lift them out. Toast bread the shape of the dish the vegetable is to occupy, dip it in the liquor the latter was boiled in, and put it for the asparagus to lie upon it as in the Plate. Serve with melted butter in a sauce tureen.

ARTICHOKES.

These must be trimmed neatly round the bottom, and the tips of the leaves cut off. Boil them for about 45 minutes. Drain them on a sieve for a few minutes. With a tablespoon handle loosen and take away the inner stringy portion of the vegetable, pour a little butter sauce inside the holes thus made, and send to table arranged on a napkin with melted butter in a tureen. Artichokes are a delicious as well as a most nutritious food. The bottom part is often called, but vulgarly so, the " choke." The part cooked as an edible is the head of the flower not yet come to perfection.

PLATE VII.

NOUGAT ALMOND CAKE.

Our "Nougat" is in the form of a high cake and is made in a mould, but they can be made in almost any shape, and are small as well as large. Proceed in this way :— Cut into dice 1 lb. sweet almonds bleached, and 6 bitter ones; dry them in the oven, but preserve their white appearance. Get 4 tablespoonfuls of white pounded sugar and put it over a gentle fire in a preserving pan. Use no water with the sugar. When this is melted throw in the almonds, which must be perfectly dry, oil your mould, and lay in almonds, pressing them in with an oiled lemon. When cold turn it out of the mould and serve.

TRIFLE.

This dish has rather an ironical title, for, made as a trifle should be made for a "company" dinner, its expense is no trifle. Always make your trifle early in the day on which it will be required. I give an excellent and not too expensive a recipe that will do for a "little dinner" or for "home dinner." Take a stale sponge cake and cut in slices about an inch thick, and lay it at the bottom of your trifle dish. On this put a thin layer of almost any kind of jam or preserve, such as raspberry, &c., and on these place some ratafia cakes and macaroons. Cover all with some sponge cakes, and mix together 3 glasses of sherry, 1 of brandy, 1 of rum, and 1 of *noyeau*. Pour this over the cake preparation and let it stand till well soaked through. When this has been accomplished satisfactorily, pour over all rich custard, thick, and about one inch thick on top. Into a basin put one pint of cream, with some fine, sifted white sugar, $\frac{1}{2}$ a teaspoonful of lemon juice, and 2 tablespoonfuls of sherry and spirits mixed (such as were poured over the cake layers). Beat this mixture thoroughly but as lightly and deftly as possible with a whisk, and place it high upon the custard. This cream is coloured pink occasionally. Blanch and cut into shreds some almonds, and decorate the trifle with them. If your dish is small use a part only of the ingredients here mentioned. (This is one of the old standard dessert dishes, and will never go out of fashion ; it is far too elegant and too "nice.")

BLANCMANGE.

All blancmanges are pretty dishes, and are a valuable aid to the ornamentation of the table. To make these is now easy with Nelson's gelatine. Boil the gelatine in milk with a vanilla bean or a few drops of vanilla essence. When dissolved, strain through a flannel straining bag, and when cool pour it into your mould. The mould should be as highly ornamental as possible, and if liked, the blancmange may be of two colours by simply filling the mould partly with white and partly with coloured mixture.

APPLE MARMALADE TART.

Make a tart as in the "apple tart" direction, omitting the quince if preferred. Fill with apple marmalade and cover with mosaic work in paste. Paste over the top and sides as usual with egg and bake of a light colour. To make this mosaic work recourse must be had to the turner who supplies the requisite article to form it in all shapes and sizes. They are, in case any reader does not know it, boards with designs upon them representing various ornamental matters. The paste is pressed into the board by the aid of the rolling pin, the superfluous paste must be cut neatly away, and the design will fall out of the board.

GALETTE.

A very pretty dish, and a great favourite with our friends the French people Get 1 lb. of butter and 1 lb. of flour, a pinch of salt and 2 eggs. Mix well together. Knead to a paste lightly and roll it out to an inch thick, the size of a dessert plate. Bake for 15 minutes. Remove it ; beat up 2 eggs, with a pinch of salt and enough cream for your purpose. Pour it over the cake and ornament with strips of candied lemon and orange-peel.

CHERRY TART.

A favourite side or corner dish for the pastry course. It is open, with bars of paste laid cross-wise on the top of the preserve or upon the top of fresh-stewed cherries.

PEACH TARTLET.

This is rather a large size tartlet intended for a corner dish, and is filled with peach preserve or fresh peaches in season.

DESSERT BISCUITS.

Any nice dessert biscuits will do to form this dish, provided they are of a suitable shape. Arrange them as in Plate. A good biscuit can be made as follows :—Put the white of 6 eggs into a basin, and the yolks into another basin. Add to the yolks $\frac{1}{2}$ pound sifted sugar, stirring continuously for 5 minutes. Whip the whites as stiff as possible and put them to the yolks, with 5 oz. of dry and sifted flour. Mix all well together. Shape a stiff piece of white paper into the form of a funnel, fastening it thus with a little ordinary paste. Wait till it gets dry, when fill it up with the biscuit preparation. Fold the paper over like a lid at the top and cut off the end of the funnel, leaving an opening $\frac{3}{4}$ inch in diameter. Force some of the biscuits out at the opening in the shape of a finger 1 inch wide and 3 inches long on to a stiff sheet of white paper and leave ample space between the biscuits. Sift pounded sugar over them and put on a baking tin and bake in a moderately hot oven for 10 minutes. When cool, remove and arrange. These can be flavoured with any flavouring preferred, as vanilla, &c.

ICED ORANGES.

Peel a few oranges carefully and divide them, pulling them apart into thin portions. Whip together on a plate the white of an egg and a wineglassful of water, with the blade of a knife now add a dessertspoonful of icing sugar. Mix all thoroughly together and strain through a sieve into another plate or flat vessel. Dip the fruit, with the white pith removed, into this mixture, shake to throw off clinging drops of water, and roll carefully in hot sifted white sugar, and then place in rows to dry. Arrange as in Plate.

CHRISTMAS PLUM PUDDING.

This is made in a mould, garnished with sprigs of holly and leaves round the dish and on the top. (Stone ½ lb. raisins and well wash ½ lb. currants. Chop to powder ½ lb. good beef suet, and add 1 oz. blanched and chopped almonds and ½ oz. of butter. Mix all these thoroughly with ½ lb. sifted flour and ½ lb. bread crumbs steeped in milk and squeezed dry and mashed with a wooden spoon before being added to the flour. Cut small 1 oz. each of citron, lemon, and orange peel, add 2 teaspoonfuls of mixed spice and 2 oz. moist sugar. Well whisk 8 eggs and stir in, and make it like stiff batter by pouring in milk by degrees. It should be a good stiff batter, for if thin the fruit will all go to the bottom. Pour in 2 wine-glassfuls of brandy. Let the mixture stand 2 hours, and then put into the mould or moulds to boil.) Serve with cream or other sauce over the pudding, or in a tureen and brandy in a small silver boat.

COMPOTE OF PEARS.

Pick out 7 medium-sized cooking pears, peel carefully, and put them whole into a ½ gallon stewpan. Cover with syrup and colour with cochineal, adding a flavouring of vanilla by putting a stick of vanilla into the mixture. Simmer the fruit for 1½ hours and let it cool in the syrup. Drain and reduce the syrup considerably over the fire. Arrange 6 pears round a compote dish and put the other one in the centre. Pour the *cold* syrup over *just before* sending them to table.

MINCE PIES.

These need no description, but I append a splendid recipe for the mincemeat. Peel 6 oranges and 6 lemons and rub the rinds well on sugar. Add 1 oz. of ground ginger, 1 oz. of powdered bitter almonds, 1 oz. coriander seeds, 2 oz. cloves 2 oz. cinnamon, and 1 oz. nutmeg. Pound the spices thoroughly and sift them. Mix with the scrapings of the rinds that were rubbed with sugar and put away in a closely-stoppered jar. Get 2 lbs. each of raisins and currants, 1 lb. of the best figs, 1 lb. preserved ginger, 2 lbs. mixed peel, 2 lbs. boiled salt beef, 2 lbs. tripe, 3¼ lbs. chopped suet, 3 lbs. peeled apples, 3 lbs. moist sugar. Chop all together and mix with the spices in readiness. Put into stone vessels. Let it stand 2 days, and then pour upon them, giving each jar its full share, 1 bottle of brandy and 1 of port wine.

ROLY POLY JAM PUDDING.

The paste should be rich for a "company roly poly." I say "company," because of these puddings being so popular for the nursery dinner. Make the paste, then, with flour and butter, or excellent beef dripping, roll out as lightly as possible and *thin*. Cut it to the breadth of 8 or 10 inches, making it as long as you like. Spread upon it a liberal layer of raspberry, currant, or other suitable jam, leaving an inch at the edges bare. Roll it over and over, wrap in a well-floured cloth, and boil for 2 or 3 hours according to size. Cut as in the illustration.

APPLES AND RICE.

Cut as many nice apples as you require to arrange in a dish, as in Plate. Boil them in a light syrup (the cores must be stamped out). Boil ¼ lb. of rice in milk with a spoonful of sugar and a pinch of salt. Put some of the rice in the bottom of the dish, arrange the apples in a pyramid, with rice between, and ornament with real or artificial leaves.

COLD APPLE PUDDING.

Peel and pare 10 or 12 good baking apples, cut in small portions, and put them together with an ounce of butter, a sprinkling of nutmeg, grated lemon peel, and a ¼ lb. of sugar, into a sauté pan. When the fruit is softened, set it by to cool. Line a mould with good pudding paste ; fill in the apples, cover with paste, tie in a cloth and boil 1¼ hour. Turn it out and ornament with a flower on top. Or it can be baked in a mould, pie-crust being used instead of pudding paste.

COFFEE CUSTARD A LA RELIGIEUSE.

Put a quart of new milk into a saucepan with about 6 ounces of white sugar. Beat separately from these the yolks of 10 eggs, and pour the milk slowly over them. Roast 3 or 4 oz. of coffee to a good light brown colour, crush it slightly in a mortar, and add it still hot to the hot custard. Strain through a jelly bag into two basins, one larger than the other. When set, turn one out upon the other, and decorate with almost anything that will assimilate with the custard as in Plate.

APPLE AND PEAR DUMPLINGS.

These are very pretty. They are made with paste formed to the shape of the fruit, and are baked. The ornamentations are made with cutters. The fruit should be pared neatly, leaving the stalks on of the pears, cut in half, the cores removed, and deftly put together again. The paste must be worked with the fingers lightly. (See directions for Pâté à la Financière, Plate II.)

APPLE TART.

This is in a circular dish. Peel and core some apples, and cut them in slices. Cut up one small quince in slices, and stew it in water with sugar and a little piece of butter over a very gentle fire. Put the apples in the dish and the layer of quince between them, with sufficient sugar to sweeten, and some grated lemon peel. Put a band of puff paste on the edge of your dish, and a cover of same on the whole; decorate by means of the usual cutters, paste it over with egg, bake it, and at the last dredge it over with sugar. An apple tart nicely made will never be old-fashioned.

MERINGUES AND PRESERVE.

A very pretty pastry course dish for sides or corners. Pound and sift 1 pound of loaf sugar, beat the whites of a dozen eggs as stiff as it is possible to beat them, throw the sugar gently and lightly upon them, and stir with a wooden spoon, mixing these two ingredients perfectly. Take a table-spoon and lay some of the mixture upon stiff white paper in the form of eggs, sift pounded sugar thickly over them, and let them rest 10 minutes. Snake off any odd pieces of sugar or powder, place the meringues upon boards or tins, and put them in a slow oven, just hot enough to let them get tinged with colour. When quite crisp, turn them over and take off the papers. Put your spoon for a minute into *hot* water and with it clear out a great part of the middle portion, putting them aside now to dry. Fill with preserve when wanted (whipped cream will do as well). These meringues may be made several days before they are wanted, a great advantage to a mistress of a house sometimes.

APRICOT TARTLET.

See peach tartlet.

FRUIT MACEDOINE AND JELLY.

This is a handsome dish for the sweet course and looks a very elaborate one, but it is exceedingly easy to prepare. Any description of bright-coloured jelly flavoured nicely—preferably with noyeau or maraschino—will do for the purpose, and these are speedily prepared by means of the patent gelatine now so justly patronised and so extensively used by most of our best cooks. First put your mould upon ice, and proceed to fill it with jelly and different kinds of fruit. Large fruit can be cut in portions; when firm turn it out and surmount the whole with mixed fruit. Whole fruits can be done in a like way, and a pretty arrangement may be effected, showing through the jelly with but a little ordinary taste and judgment.

PANCAKES AND JAM.

This is a most effective and delicious though plain side or corner dish for the pastry course. The pancakes are plain ones, thus: Put a pint of milk (cream if to be very good) into a vessel with ¼ lb. flour, a pinch of salt, 3 or 4 ratafias 4 eggs, and some grated lemon peel. Mix these ingredients well together, and fry in spoonfuls. Fry on both sides, and place on a drainer to let superfluous grease run from them. Dredge sugar inside them, and send to table, not doubled as in Plate, with jam spread between the cakes.

APPLES À LA PARISIENNE.

Get some good apple marmalade. Cut open 12 apples into halves, pare and remove the cores. Put them into a rather deep *sauté* pan that has a thick layer of butter upon it. Sprinkle some sugar and grated lemon peel over them. Next bake them. Make some pastry custard (see Index), a small quantity only and a decorated case (see Index). Fill the case nearly to the top with the marmalade, and pile the pieces of apple upon it, leaving a kind of well in the middle, which fill with the custard, and cover all over with some good orange marmalade. Beat the whites of 4 eggs to a stiff consistence, mix in 4 oz. of sifted sugar, and spread this entirely over the domelike top of your filled case. Mark out a design on the top with a paper cornet, shake sugar over it, and put to bake of a light gold colour in the oven. When ready to send it to table, fill up the stripes you have made with layers of red or other coloured preserves arranging them tastefully as regards hues. Serve this *entremet* hot.

CHARLOTTE OF PEARS.

Procure a charlotte mould, butter it inside, and line it with thin slices of bread dipped in clarified butter. Take care to join the bread nicely, or the preserve will slip through and spoil the look of the charlotte. Fill the mould with pear marmalade and any other kind of jam suitable. Cover all with slices of bread dipped in butter as before, and put a weight upon the top of the mould. Put the mould in a quick oven for nearly or quite an hour according to size. Turn it out gently and sift loaf sugar over it Serve hot.

PLATE VIII.

ALMONDS AND RAISINS.

These are merely almonds and raisins, the latter being of a kind sold expressly for dessert purposes, intermixed. The almonds must be blanched and thrown in amongst the other fruit.

RASPBERRIES AND STRAWBERRIES.

This is a very pretty dish, the green layer of leaves between each arrangement of fruit taking away the " unkind " contrast of the two reds, and yet giving to each of these beautiful hues its due meed of merit. Take care that the fruit is really red and ripe, but not too ripe, or they will be too soft to pile up without crushing one into the other.

FILBERTS AND COBS.

These require no leaves, and are merely a mixed pyramid of the two sorts of nuts named.

APRICOTS AND PEACHES.

These are a perfectly lovely dish, the velvet cheeks of the two fruits nestling almost lovingly against each other. Here again the green must be used to part them. Remember too, that though you must make your dish look full, it must not be too full.

GOOSEBERRIES.

Three sorts of gooseberries are here, the " yellow rough," the red, and the pale yellow. See remarks concerning " Cherries" in this Plate as to blending colours.

APPLES AND PEARS.

This is an easily arranged dish. The apples must be rosy and good, and placed in rather prim order at the base, while the pears, stalks upwards, are laid upon them in a little pleasant confusion. A leaf here and there relieves the monotony of the red and yellow.

WALNUTS AND BRAZIL NUTS.

Pile opened and peeled walnuts upon a row of Brazil nuts in the form of a pyramid.

FIGS AND DATES.

These two colours give themselves a distinct character. Arrange with a few leaves in tufts.

PLUMS AND GREENGAGES.

These two fruits show off each other admirably Use green leaves merely as an enhancement to the vivid purple red of the plums.

ORANGES.

This dish requires little or no description at my hands. Do net put too many in your dish, and let the order of their arrangement take some definite form.

MULBERRIES.

Pile these on an arrangement of leaves. Their superb, dark crimson tint looks very beautiful upon emerald green.

BLACKBERRIES.

These are arranged in the same manner as the mulberries in the corresponding dish, their red-black colour showing up equally well as the green leaves.

CURRANTS.

These are the three kinds of currants grown in almost every kitchen garden, the white, the red, and the black. There should be a foundation of the fruit first, and the rest piled in alternate rows of red and white as in the Plate, the black crowning the whole.

CHERRIES.

Here we have several sorts of our national—almost—fruit, and of different colours, the red heart, the black heart, and the white and red varieties. Arrange as in our illustration. Try putting a few of all kinds of cherries into a dish piled pell-mell upon each other, and then see the wonderful difference in their appearance when put *tastefully* in order.

EPERGNE.

This is a remarkably handsome centre-piece, light and elegant, yet useful withal, the style far surpassing the heavy, gaunt, sometimes positively uncouth, middle ornaments that the souls of our ancestors delighted in. Perhaps—who knows—somebody in the ages yet to come will lay hands on our never-to-be-put-aside "Mrs. Beeton's Every-Day Cookery," and call this centre-piece of ours a spindle-legged affair. But in the present age of, fortunately, refined taste nobody can justly say anything else of it than "how exceedingly pretty." It will be seen that the bouquet at the top is of a light and feathery order, with but one large blossom; and this is right, as it would not do to have even a slightly "heavy" group of flowers here. The bouquet is moderately high, and while branching out a little, still does not hide the vase-like vessel it is in, in the least. The remainder of the Plate sufficiently explains itself.

**

HIGH-CLASS BOOKS OF REFERENCE.

Price	
30/-	**A COMPLETE ENCYCLOPÆDIA FOR THIRTY SHILLINGS.** In Four Vols., royal 8vo, cloth, *30s.*; strongly bound, half-Persian, *42s.*; half-russia, *60s.*; half-calf, *63s.*; in Six Vols., cloth, *36s.*; half-Persian, *54s.*
36/- 42/-	**BEETON'S ILLUSTRATED ENCYCLOPÆDIA OF UNIVERSAL INFORMATION.** Comprising GEOGRAPHY, HISTORY, BIOGRAPHY, CHRONOLOGY, ART, SCIENCE, LITERATURE, RELIGION AND PHILOSOPHY, and containing 4,000 Pages, 50,000 Articles, and Hundreds of Engravings and Coloured Maps. *"We know of no book* which in such small compass gives *so much information."*—THE SCOTSMAN. *"A perfect mine of information."*—LEEDS MERCURY.
18/-	**HAYDN'S DICTIONARY OF DATES.** Relating to all Ages and Nations; for Universal Reference. Containing about 10,000 distinct Articles, and 90,000 Dates and Facts. EIGHTEENTH EDITION, Enlarged, Corrected and Revised by BENJAMIN VINCENT, Librarian of the Royal Institution of Great Britain. In One Vol., medium 8vo, cloth, price *18s.*; half-calf, *24s.*; full or tree-calf, *31s. 6d.* *THE TIMES* on the New Edition :—"We see no reason to reverse or qualify the judgment we expressed upon a former edition, that the 'Dictionary of Dates' is *the most Universal Book of Reference in a moderate compass that we know of in the English Language."*
7/6	**VINCENT'S DICTIONARY OF BIOGRAPHY,** Past and Present. Containing the Chief Events in the Lives of Eminent Persons of all Ages and Nations. By BENJAMIN VINCENT, Librarian of the Royal Institution of Great Britain, and Editor of "Haydn's Dictionary of Dates." In One Vol., medium 8vo, cloth, *7s. 6d.*; half-calf, *12s.*; full or tree-calf, *18s.* "It has the merit of condensing into the smallest possible compass *the leading events in the career of every man and woman of eminence.* . . . It is very carefully edited, and must evidently be the result of constant industry, combined with good judgment and taste."—THE TIMES.
7/6	**HAYDN'S DOMESTIC MEDICINE.** By the late EDWIN LANKESTER, M.D., F.R.S., assisted by Distinguished Physicians and Surgeons. New Edition, including an Appendix on Sick Nursing and Mothers' Management. With full pages of Engravings. In One Vol., medium 8vo, cloth gilt, *7s. 6d.*; half-calf, *12s.* *"The best work of its kind."*—MEDICAL PRESS AND CIRCULAR. *"The fullest and most reliable work of its kind."*—LIVERPOOL ALBION.
7/6	**HAYDN'S BIBLE DICTIONARY.** For the use of all Readers and Students of the Old and New Testaments, and of the Apocrypha. Edited by the late Rev. CHARLES BOUTELL, M.A. New and Revised Edition. With many pages of Engravings, separately printed on tinted paper. In One Vol., medium 8vo, cloth gilt, *7s. 6d.*; half-calf, *12s.* *"Marked by great care and accuracy, clearness combined with brevity, and a vast amount of information which will delight and benefit readers."*—THE WATCHMAN.

WARD, LOCK & CO., London, Melbourne, and New York.

HIGH-CLASS BOOKS OF REFERENCE.

HELP FOR THOSE WHO HELP THEMSELVES.

NEW AND STANDARD REFERENCE BOOKS.

Price	
	IMPORTANT WORK ON THE VIOLIN.—SECOND EDITION. *Dedicated by Special Permission to H.R.H. the Duke of Edinburgh.*
10/6	**VIOLIN-MAKING: As it Was and as it Is.** A Historical, Theoretical, and Practical Treatise on the Art, for the Use of all Violin Makers and Players, Amateur and Professional. Preceded by an Essay on the Violin and its Position as a Musical Instrument. By EDWARD HERON-ALLEN. With **Photographs, Folding Supplements** and 200 **Engravings.** Demy 8vo, cloth gilt, price *10s. 6d.* "A book which all who love to hear or play the instrument will receive with acclamation."—YORKSHIRE POST.
7/6	**EVERYBODY'S LAWYER (Beeton's Law Book).** Revised by a BARRISTER. Entirely New Edition, brought down to date, including the Results of the Legislation of 1887. A Practical Compendium of the General Principles of English Jurisprudence: comprising upwards of 15,000 Statements of the Law. With a full Index, 27,000 References. Crown 8vo, 1,720 pp., cloth gilt, *7s. 6d.*
7/6	**BEETON'S DICTIONARY OF GEOGRAPHY:** A Universal Gazetteer. Illustrated by **Maps**—Ancient, Modern, and Biblical, and several Hundred **Engravings.** Containing upwards of 12,000 distinct and complete Articles. Post 8vo, cloth gilt, *7s. 6d.*; half-calf, *10s. 6d.*
7/6	**BEETON'S DICTIONARY OF BIOGRAPHY.** Containing upwards of 10,000 Articles, profusely **Illustrated by Portraits.** Post 8vo, cloth gilt, *7s. 6d.*; half-calf, *10s. 6d.*
7/6	**BEETON'S DICTIONARY OF NATURAL HISTORY.** Containing upwards of 2,000 Articles and 400 **Engravings.** Crown 8vo, cloth gilt, *7s. 6d.*; half-calf, *10s. 6d.*
7/6	**BEETON'S BOOK OF HOME PETS:** How to Rear and Manage in Sickness and in Health. With many **Coloured Plates,** and upwards of 200 **Woodcuts** from designs principally by HARRISON WEIR. Post 8vo, half-bound, *7s. 6d.*; half-calf, *10s. 6d.*
7/6	**THE TREASURY OF SCIENCE,** Natural and Physical. By F. SCHOEDLER, Ph.D. Translated and Edited by HENRY MEDLOCK, Ph.D., &c. With more than 500 **Illustrations.** Crown 8vo, cloth gilt, *7s. 6d.*; half-calf, *10s. 6d.*
7/6	**A MILLION OF FACTS** of Correct Data and Elementary Information concerning the entire Circle of the Sciences, and on all subjects of Speculation and Practice. By Sir RICHARD PHILLIPS. Crown 8vo, cloth gilt, *7s. 6d.*; half-calf, *10s. 6d.*
10/6	**THE SELF-AID CYCLOPÆDIA,** for Self-Taught Students. Comprising General Drawing; Architectural, Mechanical, and Engineering Drawing; Ornamental Drawing and Design; Mechanics and Mechanism; the Steam Engine. By ROBERT SCOTT BURN, F.S.A.E., &c. With upwards of 1,000 **Engravings.** Demy 8vo, half-bound, price *10s. 6d.*
12/–	**LAVATER'S ESSAYS ON PHYSIOGNOMY.** With Memoir of the Author. Illustrated with 400 **Profiles.** Royal 8vo, cloth, *12s.*
12/–	**BROOKES' (R.) GENERAL GAZETTEER;** or, Geographical Dictionary. Medium 8vo, cloth, price *12s.*
7/–	**BROWN'S (Rev. J.) DICTIONARY OF THE BIBLE.** Medium 8vo, cloth, price *7s.*

WARD, LOCK & CO., London, Melbourne, and New York.

GARDENING BOOKS.

Price

THE
STANDARD GARDENING BOOKS.

NEW, ENLARGED AND REVISED EDITION.

10/6 — **BEETON'S NEW BOOK OF GARDEN MANAGEMENT.** A New and Greatly Enlarged Edition, entirely Remodelled and thoroughly Revised; forming a Compendium of the Theory and Practice of Horticulture, and a Complete Guide to Gardening in all its Branches. Profusely Illustrated with Coloured Plates and 600 Engravings. Royal 8vo, very handsomely bound, cloth gilt, bevelled boards, *10s. 6d.*

BEETON'S NEW BOOK OF GARDEN MANAGEMENT is a complete and exhaustive work on the THEORY and PRACTICE OF GARDENING in all its Branches, embodying Full and Detailed Information on every subject that is directly or indirectly connected with the Art, leading up from the preparation of any description of Ground, to render it fit and suitable for Horticultural purposes, to the Culture of every kind of Flower, Fruit, Vegetable, Herb and Tree that is or can be grown in it.

"The work is exceedingly comprehensive . . . . *appears to leave no detail of the subject without adequate treatment.*"— THE DAILY TELEGRAPH.

6/— — **BEETON'S BOOK OF GARDEN MANAGEMENT.** The Original Crown 8vo Edition. Embracing all kinds of information connected with Fruit, Flower, and Kitchen Garden Cultivation, Orchid Houses, &c. &c. Illustrated with a large number of **Engravings.** Crown 8vo, cloth gilt, price *6s. ;* or in half-calf, *10s. 6d.*

3/6 — **BEETON'S DICTIONARY OF EVERY-DAY GARDENING.** Constituting a Popular Cyclopædia of the Theory and Practice of Horticulture. Illustrated with Coloured Plates, made after Original Water Colour Drawings, and Woodcuts in the Text. Crown 8vo, cloth gilt, price *3s. 6d.*

2/6 — **ALL ABOUT GARDENING.** Being a Popular Dictionary of Gardening, containing full and practical Instructions in the different Branches of Horticultural Science. With Illustrations. Crown 8vo, cloth gilt, price *2s. 6d.*

1/— **1/6** — **BEETON'S GARDENING BOOK.** Containing full and practical Instructions concerning general Gardening Operations, the Flower Garden, the Fruit Garden, the Kitchen Garden, Pests of the Garden, with a Monthly Calendar of Work to be done in the Garden throughout the Year. With Illustrations. Post 8vo, cloth, price *1s. ;* or cloth gilt, with Coloured Plates, price *1s. 6d.*

1/— — **KITCHEN AND FLOWER GARDENING FOR PLEASURE AND PROFIT.** A Practical Guide to the Cultivation of Vegetables, Fruits, and Flowers. With upwards of 100 Engravings. Crown 8vo, boards, *1s.*

1/— — **GLENNY'S ILLUSTRATED GARDEN ALMANAC AND FLORISTS' DIRECTORY.** Published Annually, with Engravings of the Year's New Fruits, Flowers, and Vegetables, List of Novelties, Special Tables for Gardeners, Wrinkles for Gardeners, Alphabetical Lists of Florists, &c. &c. Demy 8vo, price *1s.*

1d. — **BEETON'S PENNY GARDENING BOOK.** Price *1d. ;* post free, 1½d.

WARD, LOCK & CO., London, Melbourne, and New York.

14

POPULAR SHILLING MANUALS.

WARD, LOCK & CO., London, Melbourne, and New York.

Price | THE FAMILY GIFT SERIES—*continued.*

2/6

35 Wonders and Beauties of the Year. H. G. ADAMS.

36 Modern Society. By CATHERINE SINCLAIR.

37 Beatrice. By CATHERINE SINCLAIR.

38 Looking Heavenward: A Series of Tales and Sketches for the Young. With numerous Illustrations.

39 Life's Contrasts; or, The Four Homes. Illustrated.

40 Nature's Gifts, and How we Use Them. Illust.

41 Pilgrims Heavenward: Counsel and Encouragement.

42 Children's Hymns and Rhymes. Illustrated.

43 Preachers and Preaching, in Ancient and Modern Times. By Rev. HENRY CHRISTMAS. With Portraits.

44 Character and Culture. By the BISHOP OF DURHAM.

45 Popular Preachers: Their Lives and their Works.

46 Boy's Handy Book of Games and Sports. Illust.

47 Boy's Handy Book of Natural History. Illust.

48 A Knight of the Nineteenth Century. E. P. ROE.

49 Near to Nature's Heart. By E. P. ROE.

50 A Day of Fate. By E. P. ROE.

51 Odd or Even? By Mrs. WHITNEY.

52 Gutenburg, and the Art of Printing. Illustrated.

53 Uncle Mark's Money; or, More Ways than One.

54 Without a Home. By E. P. ROE.

55 The Arabian Nights' Entertainments. Illustrated.

56 Andersen's Popular Tales. Illustrated.

57 Andersen's Popular Stories. Illustrated.

58 Lion Hunting. By GERARD. Illust. by DORÉ and others.

59 The Backwoodsman. Ed. by Sir C. F. L. WRAXALL.

60 The Young Marooners. By F. R. GOULDING. Illust.

61 The Crusades and Crusaders. By J. G. EDGAR. Do.

62 Hunting Adventures in Forest and Field. Illust.

63 The Boy's Book of Modern Travel and Adventure.

64 Famous People and Famous Places. Illustrated.

65 Cheerful Homes; How to Get and Keep them. Author of "Buy your Own Cherries," &c. (Also Cheap Edition, *2s.*)

66 Helen. By MARIA EDGEWORTH.

67 Our Helen. By SOPHIE MAY.

68 The Little Ragamuffins of Outcast London. By the Author of "A Night in a Workhouse," &c. Illustrated.

69 Heaven's Messengers: A Series of Stirring Addresses.

70 From Log Cabin to White House: The Life of General GARFIELD. Illustrated.

WARD, LOCK & CO., London, Melbourne, and New York.

GIFT BOOKS AT EIGHTEENPENCE EACH.

Price	
1/– 1/6 and 2/–	

THE LILY SERIES—*continued.*

13 **Aunt Jane's Hero.**   Author of "Stepping Heavenward."
The object of "Aunt Jane's Hero" is to depict a Christian Home, whose happiness flows from the living rock, Christ Jesus.

14 **The Wide, Wide World.**   By Miss WETHERELL.
Dear to every girl who has read it.

15 **Queechy.**   By the Author of "The Wide, Wide World."
A fascinating story, fresh and true to life.

16 **Looking Round.** By the Author of "I've been Thinking."
His books are just the sort to put into the hands of youth.

17 **Fabrics:** A Story of To-Day.
Full of interest, and cannot fail to secure a wide popularity.

18 **Our Village:** Tales. By MISS MITFORD.
An engaging little volume, full of feeling, spirit, and variety.

19 **The Winter Fire.** By ROSE PORTER.
Cannot fail to make its way in domestic circles, especially where religion is held to be of the first moment.

20 **The Flower of the Family.**   By Mrs. E. PRENTISS.
The "Flower of the Family" abounds with admirable moral lessons.

21 **Mercy Gliddon's Work.**   By the Author of "The Gates Ajar."
Earnest in tone and interesting in style.

22 **Patience Strong's Outings.**   By Mrs. WHITNEY.
A more wholesome or readable book it would be difficult to find.

23 **Something to Do.** By the Author of "Little Women," &c.
Miss Alcott's writings are as charming in style as they are pure in tone.

24 **Gertrude's Trial.**   By MARY JEFFERIS.
This book has given comfort to many a sorrowing heart and counsel to many an erring soul.

25 **The Hidden Path.**   By the Author of "Alone."
An extremely interesting story.

26 **Uncle Tom's Cabin.**   By Mrs. H. B. STOWE.
No work of fiction has ever approached the popularity of "Uncle Tom's Cabin."

27 **Fireside and Camp Stories.**   By the Author of "Little Women."
These are tales, some of a stirring and some of a domestic character, suited to all tastes.

28 **The Shady Side.** By a Pastor's Wife.
A true and interesting record of a young parson's life and troubles.

29 **The Sunny Side.** By H. TRUSTA.
A worthy companion in all respects to the popular volume, "The Shady Side."

30 **What Katy Did.** By SUSAN COOLIDGE.
A pleasant and naturally written tale.

31 **Fern Leaves from Fanny's Portfolio.** By FANNY FERN.
Fanny Fern's inspiration comes from nature.

WARD, LOCK & CO., London, **Melbourne, and New York.**

GIFT BOOKS AT EIGHTEENPENCE EACH.

Price	THE LILY SERIES—*continued.*
1/–	**54 Dunallan.** By GRACE KENNEDY.
	Her writings possess irresistible charms to multitudes of readers.
1/6	**55 From Jest to Earnest.** By Rev. E. P. ROE.
and	*While Mr. Roe tells a story admirably well, and paints with the*
2/–	*skill of a master, he carefully eschews sensationalism.*

56 Jessamine. By MARION HARLAND.
A sweet and interesting story.

57 Miss Gilbert's Career. By J. G. HOLLAND.
Remarkable for moral purpose and sympathetic touches.

58 The Old Helmet. Author of "The Wide, Wide World."
The story is admirably told, and its lessons are many and valuable.

59 Forging their Own Chains. By C. M. CORNWALL.
Admirably written; conveys some valuable lessons.

60 Daisy. Sequel to "Melbourne House." By E. WETHERELL.
Leaves nothing to be desired save a re-perusal.

61 Our Helen. By SOPHIE MAY.
As free from the sensational and impossible as could be desired.

62 That Lass o' Lowrie's. By Mrs. F. H. BURNETT.
One of the sweetest tales ever written.

63 The Years that are Told. By the Author of "The Winter Fire."
Unexceptionable as to moral principle and refinement of tone.

64 Near to Nature's Heart. By Rev. E. P. ROE.
The high and wholesome lesson of each of this author's works is not for a moment left in doubt or obscurity.

65 Esther Douglas. By MARY BASKIN.
A story by a new author, worthy of acceptance by all readers.

66 A Knight of the Nineteenth Century. By E. P. ROE.
Contains the elements of perfect work, clearness and brilliancy of style, beauty of expression, and a most excellent moral.

67 Released. By the Author of "Esther Douglas."
A most interesting story, with a high moral tone.

68 Quinnebasset Girls. By ROSE PORTER.
A most delightful story for girlhood.

69 Helen. By MARIA EDGEWORTH.
The most popular of Miss Edgeworth's brilliant novels.

70 The Fairchild Family. By Mrs. SHERWOOD.
Shows the importance and effects of a religious education.

71 Freston Tower. By the Author of "Margaret Catchpole."
An interesting story of the times of Cardinal Wolsey.

72 Godwyn's Ordeal. By Mrs. J. KENT SPENDER.
A tender and graceful story, thoroughly pure in tone.

73 Madeleine: A Story of French Love.
A singularly pure and interesting story.

74 Onward to the Heights of Life.
A story of a struggle and a victory over temptation.

75 Perry Harrison's Mistake. By "PANSY" and F. HUNTINGDON.
A story which has already gained a reputation.

WARD, LOCK & CO., London, Melbourne, and New York.

GIFT BOOKS AT EIGHTEENPENCE EACH.

Price
1/—
1/6
and
2/—

THE LILY SERIES—*continued.*

76 **Carl Krinken.** By ELIZABETH WETHERELL.
Another welcome work by this celebrated author.

77 **Without a Home.** By E. P. ROE.
An interesting story of the time of the American Civil War.

78 **Her Wedding Day.** By MARION HARLAND.
Will be heartily welcomed by all who have read "Alone."

79 **His Sombre Rivals.** By E. P. ROE.
The author's rush of incident, clear, vigorous style, and other qualities, are present in full strength.

80 **Odd or Even.** By Mrs. WHITNEY.
Healthful and stimulating, as well as extremely interesting.

81 **Julamerk.** By Mrs. WEBB.
A remarkable instance of the saving power of Faith.

82 **Martyrs of Carthage.** By Mrs. WEBB.
An interesting narrative of the times of the early Christian converts.

83 **The Nun.** By Mrs. SHERWOOD.
A valuable narrative, exposing the dangers of false doctrine.

84 **The Basket of Flowers.**
Long one of the most popular of children's stories.

85 **Autobiography of a £5 Note.** By Mrs. WEBB.
Sermons may be found in stones, and lessons in a £5 note.

86 **Pilgrims of New England.** By Mrs. WEBB.
A sympathetic account of the trials of the early Puritan settlers.

87 **Only a Dandelion.** By Mrs. PRENTISS.
A collection of stories from the pen of a charming writer.

88 **Follow Me.** By Mrs. PRENTISS.
Another collection by this ever-welcome authoress.

89 **Nidworth.** By Mrs. PRENTISS.
This story of the "Three Magic Wands" may be read by all with advantage.

90 **Nellie of Truro.** A Tale from Life.
A stirring and remarkably interesting story of courage and adventure.

91 **An Original Belle.** By E. P. ROE.
This story by Mr. Roe bids fair to attain greater popularity than any of its predecessors.

That the love of good literature has developed is practically shown by the unparalleled success of the series of pure, healthy, and improving books entitled the LILY SERIES.

ABOUT THREE MILLION VOLUMES

have been printed; and on the very moderate assumption that each copy has been perused by six persons, the LILY SERIES may claim EIGHTEEN MILLIONS OF READERS. The statistics of such an undertaking generally possess a certain interest for the public, and it may be stated, accordingly, that above TWENTY-FOUR THOUSAND REAMS OF PAPER, representing a weight of FOUR HUNDRED AND TWENTY-THREE TONS, or nine hundred and forty-eight thousand three hundred and nineteen pounds, have been worked up in the three million copies of the LILY SERIES.

WARD, LOCK & CO., London, Melbourne, and New York.

Nicola Beauman was born in London in 1944, and grew up there. She was educated at St Paul's Girls' School and won an Exhibition to Newnham College, Cambridge, where she read English. In 1965 she married for the first time and subsequently went to New York where she worked in publishing and in journalism. She returned to London in 1967 and her first child was born the next year. Since then she has worked as a freelance editor and reader for a number of publishers and has reviewed books for the *Observer* and other newspapers. She is also a qualified librarian. Nicola Beauman lives in London with her second husband and four children aged from six to fifteen.

The theme of this book has been developing in the author's mind for ten years. She has always been deeply interested in the 1920s and 30s and especially in the lives of middle-class women living at this time. When her mother arrived in this country from Germany in 1933 she announced: 'The only English family I know are the Forsytes', and Nicola Beauman was much influenced by her mother's wide reading of novelists of the period. This book is about the lives of middle-class women between the wars, lives generally ignored by social historians, but wonderfully recorded in the novels of the time. The author draws on the work of May Sinclair, Elinor Glyn, E. M. Delafield and Rosamond Lehmann and many others whose work has been unjustly forgotten – some now rediscovered, some still waiting to be so. She writes about topics such as domestic life, romantic love, sex and psychoanalysis, thus creating a fascinating portrait of people who have had little recognition – those women who live at home, members of 'a very great profession'.

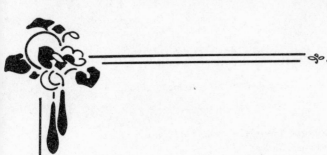

A Very Great Profession

The Woman's Novel 1914–39

NICOLA BEAUMAN

Virago

Published by VIRAGO PRESS Limited 1983
41 William IV Street, London WC2

Copyright © Nicola Beauman 1983

British Library Cataloguing in Publication Data
Beauman, Nicola
  A very great profession.
  1. English fiction—20th century—History and
  criticism   2. English fiction—Women authors—
  History and criticism
  I. Title
  823'.912'300355   PR830.S/

  ISBN 0-86068-304-4
  ISBN 0-86068-309-5

Printed in Great Britain by litho at
The Anchor Press, Tiptree, Essex

The cover illustration shows an illustration from
the film, *Brief Encounter* reproduced by courtesy
of The Rank Organisation

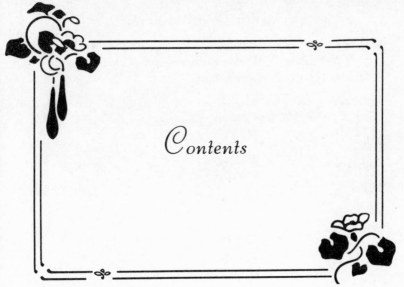

Contents

Introduction

*'Three new library books lay virginally
on the fender-stool'*

A *Very Great Profession* was conceived ten years ago when I first saw the film of *Brief Encounter* on television. In it the heroine, Laura Jesson, goes into the local town every week to do a bit of shopping, have a café lunch, go to the cinema and change her library book. This is the highlight of her week. It was the glimpse of her newly borrowed Kate O'Brien in her shopping basket that made me want to find out about the other novels the doctor's wife had been reading during her life as 'a respectable married woman with a husband and a home and three children'.[1] (This is how she describes herself in *Still Life* (1935), the Noel Coward play upon which *Brief Encounter* (1945) was based.)

I wanted, also, to learn something about Laura's life, which, because it *was* so respectable, ordinary and everyday, has been little documented. She lived uneventful days and was, like Katharine in Virginia Woolf's *Night and Day* (1919), 'a member of a very great profession which has, as yet, no title and very little recognition, although the labour of mill and factory is, perhaps, no more severe and the results of less benefit to the world. She lived at home.'[2] History in the past has been about kings and queens and revolutions, and social history explains bastardy or spinning methods; but history is also about life as it is perceived in the minds of people living in a particular period.

1

When I 'did' history and English literature at school this was not something that exercised my mind. It seemed to me utterly unsurprising to be taught these 'subjects' by elderly, rather dry women with whom I was unlikely ever to have very much in common; and that the topics of the 'lessons' should be treaties, dictators, or (in 'social history', period three on Wednesdays) sanitation, factory acts and costume. And we were never bemused by the paradox that our parents rarely envisaged more for us than a home-based existence (even if we were thought liable to 'get in' to university, that was three years of respectable pleasure rather than a stepping-stone to a career); yet at school the values thrust at us were entirely male-biased.

Naturally Virginia Woolf's *A Room of One's Own* (1929) was not on our reading-list and it was not until some years later that I came across the passage in which she discusses another paradox – that the few female names most people remember shine like beacons on the pages of literature. And, 'if woman had no existence save in the fiction written by men, one would imagine her a person of the utmost importance; very various; heroic and mean; splendid and sordid; infinitely beautiful and hideous in the extreme; as great as a man, some think even greater'.[3]

In imaginative literature woman is of the highest importance; in everyday life she is insignificant.

> What one must do to bring her to life was to think poetically and prosaically at one and the same moment, thus keeping in touch with fact – that she is Mrs Martin, aged thirty-six, dressed in blue, wearing a black hat and brown shoes; but not losing sight of fiction either – that she is a vessel in which all sorts of spirits and forces are coursing and flashing perpetually.[4]

Mrs Martin, Laura and Katharine, Mrs 'Everywoman' are, in the pages of history, found to have vanished without trace, since 'by no possible means could middle-class women with nothing but brains and character at their command have taken part in any one of the great movements which, brought together, constitute the historian's view of the past.' Indeed, except in a few pioneering works like Iris Origo's *The Merchant of Prato*, Peter Laslett's *The World We Have Lost*, Molly Hughes's *A London Child of the 1870s* or Maud Pember Reeves's *Round about a Pound a Week*, little has been documented about the kind of ordinary, unremarkable dailiness that is the norm for the great majority.

A Very Great Profession tries to correct some of this imbalance and to present a portrait through their fiction of English middle-class women during the period between two world wars. To the women writers who made their voices heard in those years 'this curious silent unrepresented life,' as Virginia Woolf called it, did begin to have its own significance; many of the novels are remarkable works of fiction – and they are all memorable because of what they tell the reader about what women did, thought and felt at the time.

The 'woman's novel' between the wars was usually written by middle-class women for middle-class women. Novelists wrote for women leading much the same kind of lives as themselves, the leisured who could perhaps still afford one or even two servants, who were beginning to enjoy the new labour-saving devices such as vacuum-cleaners and refrigerators, and who would still have been considered unusual if they tried to do anything 'for themselves'. Middle-class families were at this period generally small and boys were often sent early to boarding school, so it is hardly surprising that time hung heavy on many women's hands and that novel reading was one of life's chief pleasures.

Since writers and readers formed a homogenous group it is clear that the woman's novel at this period was permeated through and through with the certainty of like speaking to like. Elizabeth Bowen described her own and her contemporaries' work in the following terms (with presumably unconscious criticism of her own novels):

> Pre-assumptions are bad. They limit the novel to a given circle of readers. They cause the novel to act immorally *on* that given circle. (The lady asking the librarian for a 'nice' novel to take home is, virtually, asking for a novel whose

3

pre-assumptions will be identical with her own.) Outside the given circle, a novel's pre-assumptions must invalidate it for all other readers.[5]

But *within* that given circle writer and reader were linked by their mutual 'pre-assumptions'; they spoke the same language, were interested in the same kind of things, led the same kind of lives. As a modern critic observed in 1973, with reference to Elizabeth Taylor:

> Her detractors too often seem to me to be criticising her subject matter, as if to write about a part of the world where people take elevenses in the Tudor Tea Rooms, play bridge, and attend point-to-points were to be immediately discounted from making any claims to creating serious literature. But since there are human beings who *do* take elevenses, etc., it should follow that they are as worthy of being written about as anyone else.[6]

It was in the same year that I called on my former supervisor at Cambridge and told her that I was proposing to write a book about women novelists during the 1920s and 1930s. This dear, white-haired, unashamedly intellectual don, the author of a classic work on Virginia Woolf, was almost too appalled to speak; her only comfort was that I might continue some of the work pioneered by Queenie Leavis forty years earlier. From her point of view, there were no twentieth-century women writers worthy of critical attention, with the obvious exception of Virginia Woolf and the possible exceptions of Rosamond Lehmann and Elizabeth Bowen.

This was not an encouraging start. But all through the subsequent years of breeding, nurturing and nursery tea, I kept the picture in my mind of Laura Jesson taking elevenses in the refreshment room of Milford Junction and returning home with her Boots library book. It seemed so strange that an enormous body of fiction should influence and delight a whole generation and then be ignored or dismissed. Much of my reading was directed, too, towards finding out about Laura's life and preoccupations – which is why, when I came to write *A Very Great*

Profession, it seemed more revealing to construct the chapters by themes rather than by chronology, author or type of novel. And it soon became clear that those novels which school, university and critical dogma had chosen to ignore were, to me, infinitely greater and more memorable than those which had for so long and so regularly appeared on reading lists. A novel is 'good', I believe, because it moves the reader and feeds her imagination. And there are very few novels in this book to which this canon does not apply.

For me, as well, a good novel must usually be one with a distinctively 'feminine note', a novel which in some way or another illuminates female attitudes to experience, throws light on the texture of women's lives. Another modern critic once announced that he could 'gain no pleasure from serious reading . . . that lacks a strong male thrust, an almost pedantic allusiveness, and a brutal intellectual content'.[7] Sadly, or happily, I only read novels with these characteristics under duress – and have found among the novels discussed in the following pages greater enjoyment and excitement than I found in most of my reading of the previous twenty years, though they are clearly deficient in strong male thrust.

Writers and critics have frequently expressed their disgust at women novelists being restricted to a ghetto defined by sex and their reasons are perfectly understandable. But to anyone interested in the fiction written during the period between the wars it soon becomes clear that there *is* a category of fiction written for women – 'the woman's novel'. Not all of the novels under discussion in the following pages were written by women, but the majority were, and they all have an unmistakably female tone of voice. They generally have little action and less histrionics – they are about the 'drama of the undramatic', the steadfast dailiness of a life that brings its own rewards, the intensity of the emotions and, above all, the importance of human relationships.

Rebecca West once observed that 'nearly every good novel which has ever been written by a woman bears a stamp which proclaims beyond all doubt that it is the work of a woman'.[8] The hyperbole is deliberately provocative and ignores those male writers with the 'feminine note'. In this book, male novelists such as E. M. Forster, Martin Armstrong and Denis Mackail who also write mostly about the personal, the small-scale and the everyday are obviously not excluded on the grounds of sex; nor are H. G. Wells or A. S. M. Hutchinson, who write about women's themes from a masculine stance.

The years between the wars were the heyday of fiction written by women. Novel writing was, finally, a respectable occupation and no longer could people like Mrs Honeychurch in *A Room with a View* 'abandon every topic to inveigh against those women who (instead of minding their houses and their children) seek notoriety through print'.[9] Middle-class women had time, warmth, freedom from drudgery and an intelligence unsullied by the relentless and wearying monotony of housework. And, as in Jane Austen's day, when her manuscript was hidden as visitors arrived, fiction was easy to pick up and put down, as well as quietly boosting the often bruised spirit.

Many potential male writers had died in the First World War. As Ivy Compton-Burnett observed:

> They say that before the first war there were four or five men novelists to one woman, but that in the time between the two wars there were more women. Well, I expect that's because the men were dead, you see, and the women didn't marry so much because there was no one for them to marry, and so they had leisure, and, I think in a good many cases they had money, because their brothers were dead, and all that would tend to writing, wouldn't it, being single, and having some money, and having the time — having no men, you see.[10]

And as Rebecca West pointed out, conceding that male novelists still held the major positions in the literary batting order, the preponderance 'of the female on the lesser fields of glory is as likely as not one of the consequences of the war. No doubt there lie many dead in France and in the East and under the seas who desired nothing better than to live and keep certain appointments between their imaginations and pen and ink'.[11] While Madeleine Henrey speculated that 'brilliant moments mixed with bitter sorrow'[12] had produced the experience women needed for writing great works.

Yet this 'bitter sorrow' theory does not allow for the great mass of English fiction which has stemmed from personal, everyday concerns and has centred round heroines who would all have echoed Katharine in *Night and Day* when she reflected that 'the only truth which she could discover was the truth of what she herself felt'. And such heroines would, of course, have had to have the leisure for such preoccupations – which is another aspect of the extreme class bias of fiction, for, of all art forms, the novel is the one which belongs particularly to the middle classes; and it is still true today that

> there is an aspect of fiction of so delicate a nature that less has been said about it than its importance deserves. One is supposed to pass over class distinctions in silence; one person is supposed to be as well born as another; and yet English fiction is so steeped in the ups and downs of social rank that without them it would be unrecognisable.[13]

It is the 'ups and downs' within one class that have provided the English novel's most fruitful source. Women writers were ladies and they dealt with ladies, with what E. M. Forster called 'gentlefolk', part of the class to which

> most of us belong, the class which strangled the aristocracy in the nineteenth century, and has been haunted ever since by the ghost of its victim. It is a class of tradesmen and professional men and little Government officials, and it has come into power consequent on the Industrial Revolution and Reform Bills and Death Duties.[14]

It is neither the castle nor the hovel, the top drawer nor the bottom, but that large class of people in between who would prefer life to go on rather as it always has done, people of a comfortable frame of mind who cling, conservatively, on to the established moral framework.

Lucy Honeychurch in E. M. Forster's *A Room with a View* (1908) is typical of the kind of heroine who tries, usually in vain, to escape the polite, decent, discreet outlook on life with which she had grown up.

Hitherto she had accepted their ideals without questioning – their kindly affluence, their inexplosive religion, their dislike of paper bags, orange-peel and broken bottles. A͞ Radical out and out, she learned to speak with horror of Suburbia. Life, so far as she troubled to conceive it, was a circle of rich, pleasant people, with identical interests and identical foes. In this circle one thought, married and died. Outside it were poverty and vulgarity, for ever trying to enter.[15]

But travel abroad has entirely changed her vision of her suburban neighbours and among the Tuscan olive groves she learns to feel 'that there was no one whom she might not get to like'. When she returns to England she is deemed to have been purged of the suburban Honeychurch taint – the ultimate accolade is that now 'she is not always quoting servants, or asking how the pudding is made'.

The heroine of the woman's novel does frequently ask how the pudding is made. This kind of light, concerned, inoffensive yet silence-filling question was one familiar to all middle-class women at a period when the problem was which pudding rather than no pudding at all. It would have been a question familiar to Rachel in *The Voyage Out* who, after luncheon, used to go

shopping with one of my aunts. Or we went to see someone, or we took a message; or we did something that had to be done – the taps might be leaking. They visit the poor a good deal – old charwomen with bad legs, women who want tickets for hospitals. Or I used to walk in the park by myself. And after tea people sometimes called; in winter I read aloud, while they worked; after dinner I played the piano and they wrote letters. If father was at home we had friends of his to dinner, and about once a month we went up to the play. Every now and then we dined out; sometimes I went to a dance in London, but that was difficult because of getting back. The people we saw were old family friends, and relations, but we didn't see many people . . . A house takes up a lot of time if you do it properly. Our servants were always bad, and so Aunt Lucy used to do a good deal in the kitchen, and Aunt Clara, I think, spent most of the morning dusting the drawing-room and going through the linen and silver. Then there were the dogs. They had to be exercised, besides being washed and brushed.[16]

Familiar, too, to the heroine of *Diary of a Provincial Lady* (1930) by E. M. Delafield or to that of *Mrs Miniver* (1939) by Jan Struther, and familiar to countless others who, like Mrs Miniver, often passed their days something like this:

Every morning you awake to the kind of list which begins: – Sink-plug. Ruffle-tape. X-hooks. Glue . . . and ends: – Ring plumber. Get sweep. Curse laundry. Your horizon contracts, your mind's eye is focused upon a small circle of exasperating detail. Sterility sets in; the hatches of your mind are battened down. Your thoughts, once darling companions, turn into club bores, from which only sleep can bring release. When you are in this state, to be kept waiting for half an hour in somebody else's house is nothing but the purest joy. At home the footstool limps, legless, thirsting for its glue; the curtain material lies virginally unruffled; the laundry, unconscious of your displeasure, dozes peacefully at Acton: while you yourself are free.[17]

For women at home rarely had much real freedom. But undoubtedly library books brought their own kind of release, which is why Laura Jesson tried not to miss her weekly visit to Boots. At the beginning of *Still Life* she is described in the following terms:

Laura Jesson is sitting at the downstage table having tea. She is an attractive woman in the thirties. Her clothes are not particularly smart but obviously chosen with taste. She looks exactly what she is, a pleasant ordinary woman, rather pale, for she is not very strong, and with the definite charm of personality which comes from natural kindliness, humour and reasonable conscience. She is reading a Boots library book at which she occasionally smiles. On the chair

9

beside her there are several parcels as she has been shopping.[18]

John Betjeman, too, was astute enough to realise that books from Boots were once as crucial a part of middle-class existence as country life, Harrods and proper meals.

Think of what our Nation stands for,
    Books from Boots, and country lanes,
Free speech, free passes, class distinction,
    Democracy and proper drains.
Lord, put beneath Thy special care
    One-eighty-nine Cadogan Square.[19]

Boots had provided women with reading material ever since it was first founded at the turn of the century. By the mid-1930s it was the largest circulating library of its kind, with over four hundred branches and half a million subscribers. The annual subscription seemed reasonable enough if one compares it with the £60 a year it cost Vera Brittain and Winifred Holtby to rent a flat in Bloomsbury with four rooms, kitchen and bathroom in 1923. (The housekeeping bill for them and a maid was less than £3 a week.)[20] In 1926 it cost 42s a year to get books out from Boots 'on demand', 17s 6d to be able to choose from all works in circulation and 10s 6d for the 'ordinary' service. This was cheaper than the small but exclusive London lending libraries such as Day's, Mudie's or the Times Book Club, but not as cheap as W. H. Smith's library.

Class distinction dictated even the type of circulating library to which a woman belonged. Virginia Woolf did not go to Boots but to Day's or Mudie's.

Day's at 4 in the afternoon is the haunt of fashionable ladies, who want to be told what to read. A more despicable set of creatures I never saw. They come in furred like seals and scented like civets, condescend to pull a few novels about on the counter, and then demand languidly whether there is *anything* amusing?[21]

Boots, on the other hand, was a far more broadly-based library, catering more for suburban shoppers than for fashionable ladies.

Until the Second World War the circulating library was an intrinsic part of social life. In 1933 a town like Poole, whose population was then 43,000, had a library which issued 6,000 books a week. Daphne, in *The Death of the Heart* (1938) by Elizabeth Bowen, is a library assistant. She is not actually fond of reading, but it matters to the management to have

> a girl who *is* someone, if you know what I mean. A girl who – well, I don't quite know how to express it – a girl who did not come from a nice home would not do at all, *here*. You know, choosing books is such a personal thing; Seale is a small place and the people are so nice. Personality counts for so much here. The Corona Café is run by ladies, you know.[22]

Electricity, the wireless set and the motor car were part of the considerable material advancement which the average middle-class household enjoyed in the 1920s and 1930s. But the growth of the lending library must also have had an enormous impact, given that twenty-five million volumes were exchanged among the Boots branches in 1925 and thirty-five million by the time of the outbreak of the Second World War. Generally the sub-scribers came in to the library with their book list, sometimes the girl behind the desk made suggestions. The Boots Staff Training Pamphlet stressed the importance of not suggesting a book unless the customer's taste was well understood. 'You have only to imagine a person sitting down at the weekend to enjoy a time of good reading to which they have looked forward, only to dis-cover they have been given something which, to them, is utterly unreadable.' This happens all too often to Felicity in Denis Mackail's novel *Greenery Street* (1925) when she goes to her local circulating library.

> Twice, sometimes three times a week, she sets out with a bundle of books under her arm, goes up in one of Andrew Brown's lifts, presents herself at the desk which is labelled 'FAB to KYT' and smiles at the young lady who sits behind it. In Felicity's case the young lady always returns this smile and the following dialogue then takes place:

Felicity: 'I've brought two books back, and here's my new list. Have you got the first volume of *Indiscreet Reminiscences* yet?'

Attendant: 'I'm afraid they're all out still. But can I give you the second?'

Felicity: 'No, thank you. We've had that. Oh – I say – have you got *Spate*? No? Well, have you got *That The Swine Did Eat*? Oh, aren't you taking it? I see. Well, have you got *The Gutter*? Oh, but I'm *sure* it's published. I saw a long review of it in – Oh, yes; perhaps it was an advertisement. Well, have you got *The Braxingfield Mystery*? My husband is *always* asking for it. Oh; I see. Well, have you got anything on my list? And nothing on the old list, either? Well, what *have* you got, then?'

(The Attendant, who has been waiting for this moment, dives under the desk and fetches up about half a dozen novels, which she offers for Felicity's inspection.)

Attendant: 'Here are some of the latest, Mrs Foster.'
(Felicity looks at the backs of these works, and fails to recognise either their titles or their authors.)

Felicity (politely, but disparagingly): 'I don't think I – '

Attendant (briskly): '*Prendergast's Property* – that's a very pretty story.'

Felicity (doubtfully): 'Oh . . . I never seem to like books where the people are called Prendergast.'

Attendant: 'Well, what about *The Transept*? It's going very well, you know.'

Felicity (suspiciously): 'Is it religious?'

Attendant (surprisingly): 'Oh, no. It's about Rhodesia.'

Felicity (with conviction): 'I always hate that.'

(By this time, however, a small queue has formed behind her, which has the effect of weakening her critical judgement. The attendant realises this, and goes quickly ahead.)

Attendant: 'I think you'd like this, Mrs Foster. *Illumination*.'

(Felicity picks up *Illumination* and opens it. Nice

short paragraphs, anyhow; and quite large print.)

Felicity: 'All right. That'll do for one.' (The queue shows fresh signs of impatience.) 'And – oh, very well. I'll take *The Transept* for the other. Perhaps my husband will like it.'

Attendant (more briskly than ever): 'Oh, he's sure to, Mrs Foster.'

Felicity: 'Well, thank you very much. Good morning.'

Exit[23]

The Boots First Literary Course for librarians divided literature into categories, presumably so that the harassed attendant could at least decide which type of book her customer would find acceptable. One of the most popular (along with the detective and the love story) was 'Light Romance'. The course lecturer said: 'We often hear [women] say they like a "pretty book". I am sure that your own taste in reading has developed far above this level, but to a librarian books are but tools and it our duty to supply them to our subscribers without questioning their taste.' He lent rather more of his approval to Family Stories, defined as being 'for those tired of romance' who are often seeking something with some reality in it; the subscriber may define these as a 'well-written book'.[24]

It would be safe to conclude that it was either a Light Romance or a Family Story that Laura had in her basket, and that Mrs Miniver was looking forward to reading when, one day in 1938, she arrived home for tea.

Tea was already laid: there were honey sandwiches, Brandy-snaps, and small ratafia biscuits; and there would, she knew, be crumpets. Three new library books lay virginally on the fender-stool, their bright paper wrappers unsullied by subscriber's hand. The clock on the mantelpiece chimed, very softly and precisely, five times . . .[25]

CHAPTER ONE

War

'But for me — a war is poor fun'

War is an essentially masculine occupation, part of E. M. Forster's 'great outer life . . . in which telegrams and anger count'.[1]

Along with the City, clubs, smoking rooms, shooting, sport and other middle-class male concerns it is by tradition alien to women's preoccupations. Yet war influences both the most important and the most minute details of women's lives, shaping them significantly enough to justify the sub-title of this book, 1914–39.

Women's writing is conventionally assigned to the department marked personal relations and emotional response – opposite the department marked masculine, anger and telegrams. R. Brimley Johnson, in his 1920 volume called *Some Contemporary Novelists (Women)*, suggested that women novelists did not mention the war very much because 'the truth about human nature is to be found in individual experience'[2] rather than in the broader sweep of the battlefield. This too is the common explanation for Jane Austen's disregard for the war across the channel, and is echoed by the editor of Virginia Woolf's letters who observes that there were signs of war everywhere: 'Yet so little did all this mean to her that her letters contain almost no reflection on it . . . She thought the war an inevitable outcome of male chauvinism.'³

Certainly the prevalent assumption during the Great War was that it was nothing to do with women. Not for them the sense of a new life starting, a great adventure towards which their whole previous existence had unconsciously turned. They could not cry out with an almost religious ecstacy:

> Now, God be thanked Who has matched us with His hour,
> And caught our youth, and wakened us from sleeping . . .⁴

Indeed, women had not been bred for the ritual of war. It is this point that echoes, clarion-like, from the biographies of the young men who went to war in 1914, for example from Nicholas Mosley's *Julian Grenfell* (1976):

> The pattern for men was not to ask questions, not to think, but to make jokes and to do one's duty: if this was not too difficult, it was perhaps because it was part of men's duty to fight and kill. It was like this in law, in politics, in business; with thought disencouraged, furious instincts were satisfied by ritual.⁵

And Julian Grenfell himself found no purpose in life until 1914 and then wrote to his mother: 'Isn't it luck for me to have been born so as to be just the right age and just in the right place – not too high up to be worried – to enjoy it the most?'⁶

Women could knit socks, nurse the wounded, even work in factories or on the land; but questioning the wisdom of their male superiors was quite out of order. There was little room for a woman to assume any sort of control, as Mr Britling's son points out in H. G. Wells's *Mr Britling Sees It Through* (1916):

> all this business could be done far better and far cheaper if it wasn't left to these absolutely inexperienced and extremely exclusive military gentlemen. They think they are leading England and showing us all how; instead of which they are just keeping us back. Why in thunder are they doing everything? Not one of them, when he is at home, is allowed to order the dinner or poke his nose into his own kitchen or check the household books . . . The

ordinary British colonel is a helpless old gentleman; he
ought to have a nurse . . . This is not merely the trivial
grievance of my insulted stomach, it is a serious matter for
the country.[7]

Eventually women were allowed to make positive contribu-
tions to the war effort. Many were already used to working
outside the home – in 1914 nearly six million out of the 19
million women over ten in Great Britain and Ireland were
employed, mainly in industry, domestic service and commerce;
and over the next four years this figure rose to 7.3 million, an
increase in industry from 2.4 to 3.9 million.[8]

But now many middle- and upper-class women were anxious
to be useful. At first there was little for them to do – as Vera
Brittain wrote: 'Women get all the dreariness of war, and none
of its exhilaration.'[9] *The Lady* (a journal for gentlewomen)
offered its readers some consolation when it suggested:

> The fact that one cannot bear arms does not excuse any one
> from helping their country's cause by fighting such foes as
> misery, pain and poverty . . . If we cannot in our inner-
> most hearts feel really hopeful, we can at least pretend we
> do, and talk hopefully to those about us, write hopeful
> letters to distant, anxious friends, and do our very best to
> inspire a calm, courageous view of the situation among all
> with whom we come in contact . . . We can visit the
> smaller houses about us, and talk hopefully to those poor
> wives and mothers whose anxiety equals our own.[10]

Any efforts more positive than this were firmly squashed.
When Elsie Inglis, a well-known woman doctor, offered a
ready-made Medical Unit staffed by qualified women to the
Royal Army Medical Corps she found her efforts unappreciated
('My good lady, go home and sit still,' the War Office told her)
and was instead paid by the French government to take her unit
to Serbia.[11] And when May Wedderburn Cannan carried out the
orders of the War Office and upon mobilisation set up a hospital
of sixty beds, she was told by the Red Cross Headquarters that
they did not want it. (She offered it to a family connection at the

Military Base at Oxford and it was gratefully received.)[12] As Cicely Hamilton commented in 1935: 'It was because British authorities showed little enthusiasm for the idea of war hospitals run by women that all our units were placed at the service of our Allies – two or three in France, two or three in the Balkans, one in pre-Bolshevik Russia.'[13]

Knitting was not always occupation enough, as Rose Macaulay found:

> Was there a scrap or ploy in which you, the boy,
>   Could better me? You could not climb higher,
> Ride straighter, run as quick (and to smoke made you sick)
>   . . . But I sit here, and you're under fire.
> Oh, it's you that have the luck, out there in blood and muck:
>   You were born beneath a kindly star;
> All we dreamt, I and you, you can really go and do,
>   And I can't, the way things are.
> In a trench you are sitting, while I am knitting
>   A hopeless sock that never gets done.
> Well, here's luck, my dear; – and you got it, no fear;
>   But for me . . . a war is poor fun.[14]

(Later she was to write more heartfelt poems about the horrors of the Great War.)

Even the Suffragettes, who had abandoned the Cause upon the declaration of war, at first found little for their energies; and despite the stories in the newspapers, initially women were not employed in large numbers – for example, by March 1916 there were still only a hundred women bus conductresses in London. The setting up of the Ministry of Munitions in 1915 gave some boost to the employment of women; things began to change properly with the introduction of universal military conscription in May 1916, upon which the Government launched its first concerted national drive to fill the places about to be vacated by men.[15] Increasing numbers of women were soon to be found working in industry (including munitions factories), transport and commerce, while middle-class women turned to organising, to driving motor vehicles and to nursing. By 1918 there were over one and a quarter million more women working than there had been in 1914, and for many middle-class women the First World War brought with it their first opportunity for employment outside the confines of their home. As Cicely Hamilton observed just at the beginning of the Second World War:

> Long before the conflict had dragged to its end, the munition factories of the country were staffed to a great extent by women's labour; while with the need to increase the supply of home-grown food – a pressing need by 1917 – there came into being a body of volunteers for agricultural work; a body many thousand strong and known as the Women's Land Army. And in addition to the girls who laboured on the land and who worked in factories; in addition to the various corps attached to the Army, the Navy, and the Air Force, and the host of women employed in hospitals and convalescent homes, there was another host that worked in canteens and drove ambulances, cars and lorries. The old line of division between men's work and women's was broken down during the war.[16]

In E. M. Delafield's *The War-Workers* (1918) a group of women help run the Midland Supply Depot. They are all mesmerised by Miss Vivian, the Director, a woman who in normal life would have nothing to occupy her energies except petty social machinations but in wartime is in her element being queen bee. It is clear that the war is bringing her enormous personal satisfaction, allowing her scope to dominate, coerce, win adulation and yet assume an air of cheerful martyrdom. Her devotion to duty is absurd and the reader is left with the impression that the soldiers could have been billeted and the canteens supplied without so many pieces of paper being pushed about and so many women working to the limit of their endurance. The same point was made by Amber Reeves in her documentary novel *Give and Take* written in 1918 and published in 1923. Her setting is the fictional Ministry of Reconciliation and her purpose is to describe the petty and obsessive preoccupations of many of the characters.

Neither novel focuses at all clearly on the war, and because their main concern is character dissection they might just as well have been set in a girl's school. (Indeed both have some affinities with Clemence Dane's *Regiment of Women* (1917) which *is* set in a girl's school.) For, surprisingly, war work may have expanded middle-class women's horizons, but it provided relatively few themes for novelists. Although wartime experiences were described in those novels women wrote about nursing or ambulance driving, nevertheless, except in the autobiographies (such as *Testament of Youth*), the job remains incidental to the main theme, usually the heroine's intense and personal emotions about what is happening to her. Charlotte Redhead in May Sinclair's *The Romantic* (1920) goes out to Belgium as a volunteer field ambulance driver. She goes as part of a small group with the man she loves, John Conway. Under the stress of the work they do – braving shell bombardment to go out and bring in the wounded – it transpires that John 'funks'. As soon as she has fully realised his cowardice, this destroys her love. When he dies a coward's death no one has much sympathy and later, going back to England, Charlotte declares that she is not even sorry that he is dead. (Naturally, she is herself fearless and carelessly risks shells and bullets in order to get the men through.)

The war, although described as a backcloth to Charlotte's dawning realisation about John (a view of cowardice much ingrained in men and women at that time), is not at all important. Its causes or its wider implications are not even hinted at, the fact that she is a competent ambulance driver matters only in so far as it gives her a chance to compete on the same level with her lover. Similarly, in Enid Bagnold's *The Happy Foreigner* (1920) an English girl goes to France after the Armistice and drives a car for the French Army. Fanny is fearless, practical and optimistic. While driving through rain and snow, living with mud and rats and few creature comforts, she retains to the last a detached good cheer. As Katharine Mansfield observed: 'nothing can overwhelm her or cast her down, because it is her nature, and unchangeable, to find in all things a grain of living beauty. We have the feeling that she is, above all, unbroken.'[17]

There is very little detachment in Dorothy Canfield's *Home Fires in France* (1919). The eleven short stories that make up the volume give the reader a picture of civilian life in France during the war which is deadly and unforgettable, including a very moving short story called 'La Pharmacienne'. The first few pages describe the idyllic life of Madeleine who, awaiting the birth of her third child, is cosseted and cherished and idle. In the first days of August, Jules, 'in his wrinkled uniform, smelling of moth-balls', marches away and of course '*no* one had the faintest idea that his peaceful home town would see anything of the war'.[18] But after a brief period of terror and rumours, the village is horribly looted and its inhabitants are left with all their certainties destroyed virtually overnight; and Dorothy Canfield makes it clear that the plight of the civilians in France was often as ghastly as that of their menfolk in the trenches.

Though some grasped the full horror of the war, for many across the Channel it was viewed as nothing more profound than casualty lists, relevant to everyday life only if their tragedies became personal ones. What mattered to most middle-class people in England were 'the universal topics of maids and ration-cards', as Vera Brittain found in 1918:

From a world in which life or death, victory or defeat, national survival or national extinction, had been the sole issues, I returned to a society where no one discussed anything but the price of butter and the incompetence of the latest 'temporary' – matters which, in the eyes of Kensington and of various acquaintances who dropped in to tea, seemingly far out-weighted in importance the operations at Zeebrugge, or even such topical controversies as those which raged round Major-General Maurice's letter to *The Times*, and the Pemberton-Billing case.

Keyed up as I had been by the month-long strain of daily rushing to and fro in attendance on the dying, and nightly waiting for the death which hovered darkly in the sky over-head, I found it excruciating to maintain even an appear-ance of interest and sympathy. Probably I did not succeed, for the triviality of everything drove me to despair.[19]

The contrast between the life-and-death problems of wartime and the trivia of civilian life was a recurring theme. Soldiers on leave found that their friends and relations viewed the Front as something ghastly 'over there' that was nothing to do with them. People didn't really want to know, and this was so even in the parts of France that happened to have escaped the first-hand effects of war. A foretaste of the insularity that was to be a part of the 1914–18 war is given in May Sinclair's *The Tree of Heaven* (1917). To Frances and Anthony Harrison, the Boer War 'wasn't real'. When Frances's brother Maurice comes back from South Africa he tries to make them realise what he has been through; he evokes some lurid detail:

> Frances looked at him. He thought: 'At last she's turned; at last I've touched her; she can realise that.'
>
> 'Morrie dear, it must have been awful,' she said. 'It's *too* awful. I don't mind your telling me and Anthony about it; but I'd rather you did it when the children aren't in the room.'[20]

But this novel has a firm moral, and Frances and Anthony do finally learn to be touched by the reality of war and so do all their children. Dorothea, their daughter, is told by her lover as he departs for Mons in 1914 that 'it's *your* War, too – it's the biggest fight for freedom' and when he is killed, one of her chief regrets is all the time they wasted – 'All those years – like a fool – over that silly suffrage.' Her brother Nicky finds that it is 'absolute happiness' to go over the top. 'And the charge is – well, it's simply heaven. It's as if you'd never really lived till then; I certainly hadn't, not up to the top-notch'. Even Michael, who had originally funked the idea of enlisting, finally understands that this is the greatest War of Independence that has ever been.

> Now that he could look at it by himself he saw how the War might take hold of you like a religion. It was the Great War of Redemption. And redemption meant simply thousands and millions of men in troop-ships and troop-trains coming from the ends of the world to buy the freedom of the world with their bodies . . . He wondered how at this moment any sane man could be a pacifist.[21]

And the couple in May Sinclair's *Tasker Jevons* (1916) find that the war brings them happiness, for before the war Jimmy had been used to nothing more than exercising his genius. When he finds hidden reserves of courage in himself, he and his wife are brought close together. But this theme is very unusual, for most novelists depict their characters as being embroiled finally in terrible unhappiness because of the effects of the war. The fiancé killed at the Front was often and poignantly described, and then there was the frequent concomitant moral dilemma: 'I could bear it if I'd given myself to him that night — even for one night' (Dorothea in *The Tree of Heaven*).

May Sinclair's novels about war are among the very few propaganda books to have been written by a woman. (And *The Romantic* is quite unambivalent in its attitudes to cowardice in a soldier.) But their message is in fact two-pronged. For the author is at pains to point out that the miseries of peace can be as profound as those of war, and that peace definitely lacks the glory of war. The peaceful house in Hampstead, with its garden dominated by a tree of Heaven, has its tranquillity destroyed by the war but there is to be no ecstasy as a substitute. And this is the other moral, namely that without sacrifice there is no heroism, that only by loving and giving can we crush our self-absorption and selfishness, can we attain glory.

Clearly war is a natural theme for women because of the chance it provides for self-sacrifice; and, since women have been glorying in this for centuries, it is perhaps odd that more novelists did not avail themselves of the theme of war as an opportunity for women's sacrifice.

In the novels about nursing, the opportunities for self-abnegation are mingled with an awareness of the horror of war. Nursing was such hard work that no girl would volunteer to do it if she was uninterested in the joy of sacrifice; the emotional pleasure in serving heroes was restrained by the almost saintly devotion needed for the daily handling of men's wounds. And a degree of religious detachment was probably vital if a girl was to retain the necessary calm to make her a good nurse, as Enid Bagnold wrote in *A Diary without Dates* (1918): 'In all honesty the hospital is a convent, and the men in it my brothers.' But there were no war memorials for women who nursed their wounded brothers.

In *A Diary without Dates*, a series of autobiographical sketches, the reader is briefly immersed in the world of the Royal Hospital at Woolwich. Enid Bagnold was a Voluntary Aid Detachment nurse (VAD for short) and her book poignantly describes the back-breaking work, the tyranny of routine and the remorseless drudgery. The tone is resigned rather than grumbling, for the mood is one of self-sacrifice and more than once the author compares herself to a nun. The Sister in charge might be a Mother Superior and the hard work an act of piety to God. In the following passage, the young Enid Bagnold might as well be feeling her rosary beads and standing in the dim timelessness of a church:

> I lay my spoons and forks. Sixty five trays. It takes an hour to do. Thirteen pieces on each tray. Thirteen times sixty-five . . . eight hundred and forty-five things to collect, lay, square up symmetrically. I make little absurd reflections and arrangements – taking a dislike to the knives because they will not lie still on the polished metal of the tray, but pivot on their shafts, and swing out at angles after my fingers have left them.
>
> I love the long, the dim and lonely, corridors; the light centred in the gleam of the trays, salt-cellars, yellow butters, cylinders of glass.[22]

Yet the war itself does not really intrude, it is something remote. Certainly the men are in pain and their agony is greatly to be deplored. But what matters is the delight of nursing them back to health – when the ward is emptied and the ambulances hurry out of the yard there is no sigh of relief – on the contrary, 'the attack has begun . . . we shall get that convoy for which I longed'. Without the fighting there could be no nursing and

> when the ward is empty and there is, as now, so little work to do, how we, the women, watch each other over the heads of the men! And because we do not care to watch, nor are much satisfied with what we see, we want more work. At what a price we shall get it.[23]

There is a clear-sighted awareness of the opportunities for martyrdom and perhaps too little thought about the wider effects of the battle – yet within its limits *A Diary without Dates* is a great literary achievement.

The same disclaimer applies to another diary, that written by Lady Cynthia Asquith between 1915 and 1918. Although written entirely from the vantage point of the upper classes, the *Diaries* give an evocative portrait of this society as it limped into the post-war world. Life 'for the duration' was a question of keeping going in the face of grim odds; grief had to be dealt with as speedily and sensibly as possible and, because the pleasures of civilian life continued virtually unabated, Cynthia Asquith fell ill only *after* the Armistice – when she had to accept that the dead would not clamber to their feet off the schoolroom carpet and continue with their games. She wrote in October 1918:

> I am beginning to rub my eyes at the prospect of peace. I think it will require more courage than anything that has gone before. It isn't until one leaves off spinning round that one realises how giddy one is. One will have to look at long vistas again, instead of short ones, and one will at last fully recognise that the dead are not only dead for the duration of the war.[24]

While normal life went on, it was punctuated rather than dominated by grief. When her brother was reported killed in 1916 and the news had to be broken to her sister-in-law she wrote that 'the poignancy of what followed was so inconceivably beyond anything in my experience that I don't feel as if I could ever be unhaunted by it for a minute'.[25] But most days passed relatively phantom-free, not because she was callous but because far-off fighting seems so unreal to those at home. When, for an ecstatic moment, she thinks her brother might after all be alive she writes:

> *Oh*, that was *my cruellest moment*! I really believed and my heart had bounded with joy for a second. That one can so hope shows how little one has really taken it in. His being so far away, unseen for so long, and the way the news has trickled in makes it quite impossible to realise.[26]

So life goes on:

Saturday, 6th January 1917
Swam before breakfast. Went a-shopping – bought a
blouse. Beb [her husband] returned and we went to the
Metropole to lunch. The course restrictions involve a great
deal of mental arithmetic at meals. One is only allowed
two courses, but some things count as half a course . . .

Beb was on duty, so I had one of my little Creamery
dinners and went straight to bed. I am in best looks. Marie
Bashkirtseff is always apologetic when she makes a similar
entry in her diary, but why should one be? Today I could
really pass a great deal of time very happily just looking at
myself in the glass. It's extraordinary how one's whole
outline seems to alter, as well as complexion and eyes.[27]

And even when she takes a hand at nursing, the serious side of the
war is deftly brushed aside.

Thursday, 29th March 1917
I was caught in a heavy hail storm on my way to Fortnum
and Mason to order some fun-foods for Beb, and only got
back just in time to change into my uniform and go out to
lunch at Bruton Street. I have blossomed out into the out-
door uniform – dark blue *crêpe-de-Chine* veil and the
orthodox cloak. It is very becoming, but I feel self-
conscious in it and walk in terror of being called on for a
street accident. What could I say, but 'Give him air'?[28]

The joy of Cynthia Asquith's *Diaries* consists in entering into a
real world and into the mind of someone humane, unabashed,
tender but realistic. The reader is aware that during the war
years she never really 'faces up' to the cataclysm around her, but
admires her for having the energy and the spirit to keep going.
And the ending is almost more moving than what has gone
before because, with the breaking off of the diaries, comes the
acceptance of truth and of this we are given only a small glimpse.
Clearly, however, the innocent child of the Edwardian era has
been forced to face up to the scale of the tragedy around her.

Full acceptance came eighteen years later when she published her novel *The Spring House* (1936). Presumably Cynthia Asquith, reading her diaries some years after the war, had seen herself in a not altogether favourable light and wrote a novel in order to exorcise her inevitable feelings of self-loathing. As her diaries were not published until after her death she did not have a reading public to correct her negative impressions, to tell her that although the diaries reveal some extremely feminine, self-centred and perhaps 'silly' aspects of her character, she is revealed as someone quite exceptional. Yet her attempts at atonement in *The Spring House* do not succeed. The plot is blatantly autobiographical but the heroine, Miranda, is denied a happy ending. She discovers that she is in fact illegitimate and that her moral principles are the product of a vague sense of loyalty to her mother's deeply felt sense of virtue and propriety – now seen as merely an 'outward seemliness' that have cheated her of the chance of a few days of happiness with her now dead lover. She sails for Canada, determined to make a fresh start with her husband, only to find a letter announcing that he is no longer heart-whole. So Miranda is left with nothing except a last beautiful letter from her lover and a vague determination to face the future bravely.

Very little of the writing rings true and the war is a mere backcloth to the trivial machinations of the heroine. This was now less forgivable, since the late 1920s and early 1930s had seen a revival in novels about the First World War, in most of which war is the fundamental, inescapable fact and the characters its victims. But at the time of the war most writers lacked the necessary detachment to see it as anything other than a background to individual behaviour. Some of them were unable to settle to anything concentrated once hostilities broke out, or were firmly discouraged by publishers from mentioning anything political or military. The shining exception to this generalisation was H. G. Wells. He believed with great sincerity that it was no use blaming others for the folly of war, for we all were to blame for the antics of our fellow men: and forgiveness is all.

Mr Britling sees the truth of this in the climax of *Mr Britling Sees It Through*, one of the greatest of all the books to emerge from the First World War. When fighting began in

1914 he took much the same line as his fellow Englishmen which was

> to treat it as a monstrous joke. It is a disposition traceable in a vast proportion of the British literature of the time. In spite of violence, cruelty, injustice, and the vast destruction and still vaster dangers of the struggles, that disposition held. The English mind refused flatly to see anything magnificent or terrible in the German attack, or to regard the German Emperor or the Crown Prince as anything more than figures of fun.[29]

But by the time the war was six months old, Mr Britling has run the entire gamut of emotion from rage to despair to, finally, compassion.

> This thing was done neither by devils nor fools, but by a conspiracy of foolish motives, by the weak acquiescences of the clever, by a crime that was no man's crime but the natural necessary outcome of the ineffectiveness, the blind motives and muddleheadedness of all mankind . . . These Germans were an unsubtle people, a people in the worst and best sense of the words, plain and honest; they were prone to moral indignation; and moral indignation is the mother of most of the cruelty in the world . . . Is there not, he now asked himself plainly, a creative and corrective impulse behind all hate? . . . He was no longer thinking of the Germans as diabolical. They were human; they had a case. It was a stupid case. How stupid were all our cases! . . . He whispered the words. No unfamiliar words could have had the same effect of comfort and conviction . . . 'Father, forgive them, for they know not what they do.'[30]

Mr Britling learns forgiveness, Cynthia Asquith has to accept reality, the boys in *The Tree of Heaven* come to reject pacifism. But these are all 'quick reactions' and it was to be a decade before writers began to formulate their considered reactions. The public were alleged to be sick to death of war as a topic and hardly anything was allowed through the publishers' net. The exceptions were usually jingoistic, for example F. Tennyson

Jesse's *The Sword of Deborah* (1919) which was written at the request of the Ministry of Information and is about VAD and WAAC (Women's Army Auxiliary Corps) life in France. It ends thus:

> Not a woman I met, English or American, working in France, but said something like this, and meant it: 'What, after all, is anything we can do except inasmuch as it may help the men a little? How could we bear to do nothing when the men are doing the most wonderful thing that has ever been done in the world?'

Many fiercely resented the ostrich-like attitude demanded by publishers and provided by writers. Katharine Mansfield, for example, was shocked by Virginia Woolf's *Night and Day* (1919). She wrote a fairly kind review of it ('we had never thought to look upon its like again!')[32] but wrote to John Middleton Murry:

> My private opinion is that it is a lie in the soul. The war never has been: that is what its message is. I don't want (G. forbid!) mobilization and the violation of Belgium, but the novel can't just leave the war out. There *must* have been a change of heart. It is really fearful to see the 'settling down' of human beings. I feel in the *profoundest* sense that nothing can ever be the same – that, as artists, we are traitors if we feel otherwise: we have to take it into account and find new expressions, new moulds for our new thoughts and feelings . . . We have to face our war.[33]

But such feelings were exceptional immediately after the war. Only one novel – the wonderful, incomparable *William–An Englishman* which Cicely Hamilton published in 1919 and which won the Femina Prize in that year – expresses some of this immediacy. This masterpiece is understated and low key but is nevertheless a deeply profound comment on the impact of war on two 'ordinary' people.

William is a clerk in the City who inherits a small private income upon the death of his mother. 'His mind was blank and virgin for the sowing of any seed' and by chance it is Socialism that is sown there. He 'devoted himself to what he termed public life – a ferment of protestation and grievance' and becomes by turns a steward, a heckler and a full-blown speaker. 'As a matter of course he was a supporter of votes for women' and so he meets Griselda, 'his exact counterpart in petticoats; a piece of blank-minded, suburban young womanhood caught into the militant suffrage movement and enjoying herself therein'. 'Like William, she had found peace of mind and perennial interest in the hearty denunciation of those who did not agree with her.'

They marry, these two like-minded souls, 'cocksure, contemptuous, intolerant, self-sacrificing after the manner of their kind'. As pacifists, they are little interested in the assassination of Franz Ferdinand and set off serenely for four weeks' honeymoon in a remote woodman's cottage in the Belgian Ardennes. The days pass idyllically until eventually their distance from the 'daily whirl' begins to pall. They start to regret the lack of letters and newspapers in their remote hideaway.

> William pined unconsciously for the din and dust of the platform and Griselda missed the weekly temper into which she worked herself in sympathy with her weekly *Suffragette*. She missed it so much that at last she was moved to utterance – late on a still, heavy evening in August when once or twice there had come up the valley a distant mutter as of thunder.[34]

There are only the vaguest forebodings of the future: the farmer's family seems to have gone in a hurry and a newly made mound by the gooseberry bushes looks very much like a grave. They set off, baggage in hand, eagerly anticipating their return to civilised life. At first they think the three German soldiers they meet are merely impertinent. 'Neither William nor Griselda had ever entertained the idea of a European War; it was not entertained by any of their friends or their pamphlets.' But soon, in a scene that is written with unusual verbal power, the reality of the war is brought home to them. They are forced to watch the local mayor and the village schoolmaster being shot. We see the scene through William's eyes:

Never before, in all his twenty-eight years, had he seen a

man come to his end; so far death had touched him only once, and but slightly, by the unseen passing of a mother he had not loved; thus the spectacle of violent and bloody dying would of itself have sufficed to unnerve and unman him. To the natural shrinking from that spectacle, to his natural horror at the slaying of helpless men, to his pity and physical nausea was added the impotent, gasping confusion of the man whose faith has been uprooted, who is face to face with the incredible. Before his eyes had been enacted the impossible – the ugly and brutal impossible – and beneath his feet the foundations of the earth were reeling.[35]

Now the tone of the novel changes to one of dark, nightmarish sombreness. Cicely Hamilton was too subtle a writer to spell out her moral – that, for all their participation in big issues and real life, William and Griselda are in fact completely naive and horribly unprepared for what confronts them. After the shooting, William endures the horrors of forced labour, eventually escaping to go and search for Griselda. He finds her finally; and she who had been so open, so laughing, so supremely confident, cannot tell him what has happened – 'but his own eyes had seen that she turned from him as if there was a barrier between them, as if there was something to hide that yet she wished him to know'. It is the shock of the rape which kills her: all through their flight into the countryside it is apparent that her body and soul have been irreparably wounded. She never speaks to William again (at one point, very humanly, he feels 'a sort of irritation at her long and persistent silence'); but she is past words and 'died very quietly in the straw at the bottom of the cart'.

The feelings of the new husband are poignantly described and what is particularly well evoked is the deep love this insignificant London clerk has for his rather unmemorable wife. And at the same time there is the larger awareness, that even though Griselda had been proud to wear 'a badge denoting that she had suffered for the Cause in Holloway' she had no conception of real suffering, which killed her when she met it. William, who is left desolate and alive, is changed in a way that Griselda would probably have been had she lived. His hatred for the German soldiers turns him into staunch patriot and he intends henceforward to devote his life to his country. Glory is not to be his: first he is rejected by the army and then he is only allowed to push pieces of paper about. He dies, albeit in a bombing raid, not in a trench, and his death is not heroic. But in his small way, the reader feels, he has made his contribution.

William—An Englishman was certainly not written as a patriotic novel. But it has a moral which almost transcends patriotism which is that everyone matters in his own way, that integrity is the important quality and that the little, secondhand clerk has his grandeur as much as the swash-buckling soldier. Cicely Hamilton shows the effect of the enormous, uncontrollable might of war upon the lives of the petty, the unimportant and the ordinary. She also makes the point that was made by Sheila Kaye-Smith a year earlier – that soldiers die not for an abstract concept of patriotism but for their own corner of their country: 'They had not died for England – what did they know of England and the British Empire? They had died for a little corner of ground which was England to them, and the sprinkling of poor common folk who lived in it.'[36]

The grandeur of the ordinary is a concept that is central to most women's lives, a concept that the later, more detached writing about the war was to display to the full. A 'second wave' of war fiction started in 1928-9 with Siegfried Sassoon's *Memoirs of a Fox-Hunting Man* and Robert Graves's *Goodbye to All That*. By this time the reading public was able to accept fiction about the ten-years distant war and writers wanted to publish it; in 1928 the reader could start to view those years with some historical perspective. In *The Hounds of Spring*, a bestselling novel by Sylvia Thompson published in 1926, the real story concerns a heroine who thinks her lover is dead and marries someone else and her subsequent moral dilemma when he reappears. But the author (who was one of that bright Oxford generation that included Vera Brittain, Winifred Holtby and Margaret Kennedy) manages to give her novel some more resonance than that of plot. She suggests that women are entirely altered by grief while men fit it in to their lives.

There was no anger, not even amazement, any more in her grief – that had come at first, like a storm – [but] horror and misery and resentment, shaking the foundations of her happiness and beliefs, destroying all the rare complex beauty of her outlook and changing, by what seemed sheer devastation, the very confirmation of her character. Edgar himself had taken John's death as one more and most intimate tragedy in the prolonged horrors of the war, but it hadn't, he knew, 'changed' him, altered his whole *tempo*, as it had Cynthia's; hadn't taken so much from him. Yet . . . whatever had gone, in youth and gaiety and pride, she had gained 'something' – the knowledge didn't explain itself verbally in [her] mind – which made her, not only to him but absolutely, greater, finer and more sensitive than she had been . . . He kissed her hand – thought with an ache of love and pity which held him speechless, 'It *is* worst of all for *her* . . . for women; they are most at the mercy of the fate of those they love.[37]

Sylvia Thompson also expressed the view that women in particular need safety and order unless they are to disintegrate, that lacking their own resources they will instinctively clutch at any passing straw to avoid drowning:

[Zina had] been brought up, we all had (madly, considering the condition of the world) to an accepted security, social, financial, moral: to postulate safety. And when the whole fabric thundered to atoms like that, she instinctively played for safety, to get back even a kind of skeleton of her native security. It was only too grimly natural.[38]

But neither of these two theories about women are anything to do with war except in its most personal aspects – the war caused the crisis in Zina's life, but of its wider effect we learn very little. On the other hand, we *do* gain a good deal of insight into the way women behave faced with tragedy and it was this personal aspect which lent the novel its wide appeal.

A more depersonalised approach to tragedy was that of the American Mary Borden, who did not try to publish her work about nursing until 1929 – or perhaps she wished to but had to keep it in a bottom drawer for ten years. Her book *The Forbidden Zone* consists of some poems and sketches which she produced between 1914 and 1918 during four years of hospital work with the French Army, and five stories that she wrote after the war. Of the title the author writes in the short preface:

> I have called the collection of fragments 'The Forbidden Zone' because the strip of land immediately behind the zone of fire where I was stationed went by that name in the French Army. We were moved up and down inside it; our hospital unit was shifted from Flanders to the Somme, then to Champagne, and then back again to Belgium, but we never left 'La Zone Interdite'.[39]

The title refers to the forbidden zone on the battlefield, to the boundaries of common sense and understanding which in wartime are pushed impossibly back and thus mark off forbidden territory, and to the areas in life which are to a woman forbidden, which are a masculine preserve. It is of the women watching the men slaughtering each other that one might say 'theirs not to reason why' and certainly Mary Borden does not ask questions, she merely describes exactly as it was to her stoical but appalled gaze.

Her experiences as a nurse were quite different from Enid Bagnold's because at a hospital just behind the front line the nurses have to endure infinitely more, and Mary Borden describes what she saw in a succinct prose style which has affinities with Ernest Hemingway's in *A Farewell to Arms* (1929).

> I had received by post that same morning a dozen beautiful new platinum needles. I was very pleased with them. I said to one of the dressers as I fixed a needle on my syringe and held it up, squirting the liquid through it: 'Look. I've some lovely new needles.' He said: 'Come and help me a moment. Just cut this bandage, please.' I went over to his dressing-table. He darted off to a voice that was shrieking somewhere. There was a man stretched on the table. His brain came off in my hands when I lifted the bandage from his head.

When the dresser came back I said: 'His brain came off on the bandage.'

'Where have you put it?'

'I put it in the pail under the table.'

'It's only one half of his brain,' he said, looking into the man's skull. 'The rest is here.'

I left him to finish the dressing and went about my own business. I had much to do.

It was my business to sort out the wounded as they were brought in from the ambulances and to keep them from dying before they got to the operating rooms: it was my business to sort out the nearly dying from the dying. I was there to sort them out and tell how fast life was ebbing in them. Life was leaking away from all of them; but with some there was no hurry, with others it was a case of minutes. It was my business to create a counter-wave of life, to create the flow against the ebb. It was like a tug of war with the tide.[40]

One of the purposes of this grim detail is to make it plain that in wartime women can be as staunch and as heroic as any man. And then war work could also mean 'freedom, exhilarating activity and romance', as it did for the heroine of Mary Borden's 1931 novel *Sarah Gay*. Working in France

she had been happy, surrounded by sights, sounds and smells that made the colonels of infantry, who came back from the front line to the hospital to pin military medals on the breasts of their dying men, turn pale with horror.

She made a good nurse, strong, serious, quick and not squeamish. She didn't seem to mind what she had to do; would scrub big, yellow feet, empty bedpans or hold a dying man in her arms, unaffected, apparently, by the smells of dirt, sweat, blood or gangrene. Sometimes she would go out behind the wooden hut where the men lay in their iron beds and be sick. Sometimes, alone in the cubicle where she slept, she would sob, stifling her face in her rough pillow, but no one knew this; and the surgeons realized that they could count on her to fight stubbornly and efficiently for the flickering lives of the broken battered men they sent her from the operating room. They marvelled at her British phlegm and gave up, quite soon, any attempt at the badinage that relieved their grim intercourse with the other nurses. She remained aloof from them, but with her helpless men she was different. She had learned the Poilu's argot and talked to them as if she were one of them, exchanging childish jokes with them while she dressed their hideous wounds, a friendly smile on her lips, her eyes grave, intent and professional.[41]

Women did not give their lives in the 1914–18 war, but this was the last war in which this was to be so, for modern air warfare kills men and women indiscriminately. When Vera Brittain wrote *Testament of Youth* (1933) she was remembering a war whose impact was uneven both between class and sex. The major impact was of course against the 'tommy', although popular myth would have us believe that the 'officer' class was the one which suffered the huge losses. But, as Robert Wohl has pointed out, out of 700,000 British combatants killed in the war only 37,000 were officers; the literate have kept their memory fiercely alive while the tommies have not had the good fortune to be similarly enshrined in myth.[42]

The impact on women was more enduring: often their lives were irrevocably warped. No one can read *Testament of Youth* without tears and it is a great tribute to Vera Brittain's prose style that she holds the reader enthralled through nearly seven hundred pages. She describes her childhood in provincial Buxton, her brief spell at Oxford, her growing love for Roland Leighton and her four years of nursing. Yet the relentless dramas of the war years leave her emotionally numbed, and although she finally finds a new love she makes no pretence that it will be anything but a very good second-best to the dead Roland, who embodies so much tragedy and so much heroism. For this is one of the most haunting themes of the few novels written by women whose lovers were killed in the war: they may find someone else but they will never replace what they have lost.

May Wedderburn Cannan, for example, describes in her

autobiography how her fiancé Bevil Quiller-Couch dies of pneumonia just after the Armistice: in 1924 she meets a new love who 'wore loose brown tweeds and had a bull-nosed Morris two-seater and was nice to my dog'. These affectionate but unpassionate phrases are echoes of the words written by May Wedderburn Cannan in her one novel *The Lonely Generation* (1934). In it, Delphine loses her lover Bobby, and five years later is wooed by Hugh, 'the perfect friend'. When she seeks the advice of an old family friend she describes him in phrases which are friendly, resigned, tender, but not lover-like: 'So she told him, quietly, soberly, as befitted a tale not of bright morning, but of evening; a tale of a new riding on an adventure, lovely, but sad for an earlier hour.'[43]

The dead can easily retain their romance, that is their prerogative. And at least the heroines of these books, by making it plain that they would never forget, revealed a strength and a compassion that many others in fact curiously lacked. They revealed, also, an idealism to which subsequent generations had to adjust themselves. This consisted partly in a moral and religious repulsion to war and also, more importantly, in an almost mystical reverence for the dead heroes. For many women who came to maturity during and after the First World War no living man could ever have the golden qualities of the dead, an attitude which has had far-reaching effects on the cultural and social life of England in the present century. There were too the 'surplus' women who never married, those with dead fiancés and those who never found a husband after so many millions had been killed – and whose lives were spent working or caring for elderly relatives. The past, and the dead that were part of it, became for many of far greater interest and glory than the unspectacular tawdriness of the present.

> I like to think of you as brown and tall,
> As strong and living as you used to be,
> In khaki tunic, Sam Browne belt and all,
> And standing there and laughing down at me.[44]

CHAPTER TWO

Surplus Women

*'Lord Lord! how many daughters have been
murdered by women like this!'*

'Members of the professional and business classes marrying within the nineteenth century had normally been brought up in large families, seven or eight being usual numbers, and only higher ones attracting attention.'[1] Thus Ensor in his classic account of late Victorian England published in 1936. The theme of Eleanor Mordaunt's novel *The Family* (1915) explored the effects of this *largesse*, being about the destructive effect of the large Victorian family when the parents proved ineffectual. They went on 'having child after child, content with trimming up the cradle afresh, in pink and blue ribbons and muslin. As though human beings were always babies, could live in the cradle!'[2]

And it was the girls who suffered most, for all they could do was stay at home waiting to marry; if hope finally died, they occupied themselves with domestic duties, social engagements, extended visits to relatives and other feminine pursuits. Without a husband to give them a home of their own, the unmarried daughter was forced to stay at home, dwindling into Aunt Laetitia or Great-Aunt Cecily, passing her days observing the joys of others. Very few complained, but filled their lives with notions of duty, respectability, kindliness and of course Godliness. By the time they were middle-aged they had become a familiar and indeed indispensable part of the domestic land-scape, a figure well known in fiction and memoirs.

Florence Nightingale's frustration was unusual. ' "What is my business in this world and what have I done this fortnight?" she wrote on July 7th, 1846. "I have read the 'Daughter at Home' to Father and two chapters of Macintosh; a volume of *Sybil* to Mamma. Learnt seven tunes by heart. Written various letters. Ridden with Papa. Paid eight visits. Done Company. And that is all." ' And in the same year she jotted down: ' "Oh if one has but a toothache . . . what remedies are invented! What carriages, horses, ponies, journeys, doctors, chaperones, are urged on one; but if it is something the matter with the *mind* . . . it is neither believed nor understood." '3

She wrote her tract *Cassandra* in 1852 and it was privately circulated seven years later and not openly published for another seventy-five years, when Ray Strachey printed it as an appendix to *The Cause* in 1928. It is a rousing castigation of the lot of unmarried middle-class women who had neither the need, the means or the chance to fend for themselves.

> The family uses people, *not* for what they are, nor for what they are intended to be, but for what it wants them for – its own uses. It thinks of them not as what God has made, but as the something which it has arranged that they shall be. If it wants someone to sit in the drawing-room, *that* someone is supplied by the family, though that member may be destined for science, or for education, or for active superintendence by God, i.e. by the gifts within.
>
> This system dooms some minds to incurable infancy, others to silent misery.4

Although most middle-class women were less rebellious than this, the circumstances of the unmarried daughter of the house were very similar. Her opportunities were drastically limited by the demands of propriety and the restricted possibilities for education and paid work. But few grumbled, taking it for granted that they, the unlucky, should stay meekly at home and, whether they were still waiting for a husband, or, once they were over thirty, had gently given up hope, their occupations were much the same, probably very like Jane Osborne's in *Vanity Fair* (1848):

It was an awful existence. She had to get up of black winter's mornings to make breakfast for her scowling old father, who would have turned the whole house out of doors if his tea had not been ready at half-past eight. She remained silent opposite to him, listening to the urn hissing, and sitting in tremor while the parent read his paper, and consumed his accustomed portion of muffins and tea. At half-past nine he rose and went to the City, and she was almost free till dinner-time, to make visitations in the kitchen, and to scold the servants; to drive abroad and descend upon the tradesmen, who were prodigiously respectful; to leave her cards and her papa's at the great, glum, respectable houses of their City friends; or to sit alone in the large drawing-room, expecting visitors, and working at a huge piece of worsted by the fire, on the sofa hard by the great Iphigenia clock, which ticked and tolled with mournful loudness in the dreary room.[5]

Little had changed outwardly over seventy years later for Katharine Hilbery who, as *Night and Day* (1919) opens, is to be found 'in common with many other young ladies of her class . . . pouring out tea'.

She had the reputation, which nothing in her manner contradicted, of being the most practical of people. Ordering meals, directing servants, paying bills, and so contriving that every clock ticked more or less accurately in time, and a number of vases were always full of fresh flowers was supposed to be a natural endowment of hers.[6]

She is beset by the same paraphernalia of clocks, servants and tea as was Jane Osborne and, like Florence Nightingale, is forced to read her mathematics books secretly in her bedroom since it was only at night 'that she felt secure enough from surprise to concentrate her mind to the utmost'. Yet, given that the domestic trappings had remained the same over the years, it is obvious that for Katharine everything else has changed a great deal.

She is free to make choices. Not as free as her daughters will be in the England of the 1920s (the novel is set pre-1914), but far freer than her immediate predecessors. For one of the most memorable qualities of *Night and Day* is its historical awareness; in contrast to the timelessness of, for example, *The Waves*, this earlier novel by Virginia Woolf is an elegy on time – or rather, tradition – past when the conventions of society held sway. The climax comes when Katharine rejects what tradition has handed down to her and realises that

> the only truth which she could discover was the truth of what she herself felt – a frail beam when compared with the broad illumination shed by the eyes of all the people who are in agreement to see together; but having rejected the visionary voices, she had no choice but to make this her guide through the dark masses which confronted her.[7]

Previously she had accepted that 'the rules which should govern the behaviour of unmarried women are written in red ink, graved upon marble, if, by some freak of nature, it should fall out that the unmarried woman has not the same writing scored upon her heart'. But now, for Katharine and other women like her, the red ink was fading and the tradition was relaxing its hold. To what had they owed this change in circumstances?

From about the mid-nineteenth century, middle-class women had been forced into the role of 'angel in the house', increasingly debarred from any form of occupation; 'they became custodians of the moral conscience, the repository of all virtue, and as such were obliged to live apart from the sordid everyday cares of material life'.[8] But as the century drew to a close, economic retrenchment had become an increasing necessity among the middle classes, and as a result family size decreased. There were now fewer unmarried daughters at home, but home itself was smaller and the way of life less lavish. And with fewer siblings and smaller households, the daughter of the house became less of an essential prop, and one which it was increasingly difficult to maintain.

At the same time the chances of finding a husband were diminishing since that constant proportion of surplus women ever present in the population had dramatically increased because of the demands of the Empire. The colonies offered steady employment and attracted three hundred thousand young males every year in the thirty years or so leading up to 1914. Not all of them could come home on leave in search of a bride, nor were they all lucky enough to find one among the young women who came out to the Colonies on a visit in order to husband-hunt. Yet many women were eager to abandon the comfort of the drawing room for the rigours of the tropics – they were grateful to find a husband and if a life in India was the price they had to pay, then they would pay it gladly.

The 1911 census demonstrates the difficulty of getting married: out of an average one thousand women 579 were married, 119 were widowed and 302 were unmarried.[9] Overall there was a female majority of 1.3 million, of whom some were too young for marriage and some were widowed; a 'surplus' that the First World War and the ravages of the 'Spanish' flu pushed up to 1.7 million by the 1921 census.

Thus growing numbers of unsupported middle-class women had begun to work as teachers and governesses and, by the beginning of the twentieth century, as 'typewriters', nurses and clerical workers; others began to enjoy the increasing opportunities for higher education. (Prior to inheriting her five hundred a year, the imaginary narrator of Virginia Woolf's *A Room of One's Own* 'had earned a few pounds by addressing envelopes, reading to old ladies, making artificial flowers, teaching the alphabet to small children in a kindergarten. Such were the chief occupations that were open to women before 1918.')

In a handful of late Victorian novels there appeared a type of woman who became known as the 'New Woman'. Olive Schreiner's *The Story of an African Farm* (1883), George Egerton's *Keynotes* (1893), Sarah Grand's *The Heavenly Twins* (1893), Grant Allen's *The Woman Who Did* (1895) and George Meredith's *Diana of the Crossways* (1895) have heroines who in various ways exemplify women who were struggling to throw off the stereotyped image of the middle-class woman and to grow into autonomous free spirits. By far the finest of this group of novels is George Gissing's *The Odd Women* (1893) which movingly constrasts the lives of four women who are 'odd' because, for various reasons, they are unmarried but not living at home.

Rhoda Nunn is a feminist who devotes her life to helping women to lead useful, independent lives; Alice and Virginia spend their days eking out their minuscule income rather than become companion helps to those better off than themselves, and their sister Monica rejects Rhoda's offer of help and quickly 'vanishes into matrimony' with a man who restricts her every impulse and tells her:

> Woman's sphere is the home, Monica. Unfortunately girls are often obliged to go out and earn their living, but this is unnatural, a necessity which advanced civilization will altogether abolish . . . If a woman can neither have a home of her own, nor find occupation in any one else's she is deeply to be pitied; her life is bound to be unhappy.[10]

But the Rhoda Nunns or Miss Minivers (*Ann Veronica*) or Mary Datchets (*Night and Day*) were in a minority; not many women could be described as is Mary in the following passage:

> She was some twenty-five years of age, but looked older because she earned, or intended to earn, her own living and had already lost the look of the irresponsible spectator, and taken on that of the private in the army of workers. Her gestures seemed to have a certain purpose; the muscles round eyes and lips were set rather firmly, as though the senses had undergone some discipline and were held ready for a call on them.[11]

For most middle-class women continued to be reared in the expectation that they stayed at home until marriage claimed them. And even though the high employment rate among the working class meant that by 1914 women made up one-third of the total labour force, novelists continued to ignore this vast proportion (some five million women) as a subject for fiction. The 146,000 female clerks who declared themselves in the 1911 census remained unlikely material for novels, which were still dominated by the love interest, by the subject of women's lives as, how and when they were rearranged by men.

Novels, being largely a middle-class art form, tend to reflect middle-class expectations, and at this time the chief of these was that a woman should conform to the way of life so deplored by Ann Veronica when she realised that the world 'had no particular place for her at all, nothing for her to do, except a functionless existence varied by calls, tennis, selected novels, walks, and dusting in her father's house'.[12] Interestingly, by the time H. G. Wells wrote *Ann Veronica* in 1909 the heroine's rebellion was no longer as striking as it would have been two or three decades previously. But because he was the most popular middlebrow novelist of his time and was alert to a groundswell that already existed, his novel outshone in popularity all the other 'New Woman' novels from which it derived so much. For it is indeed a truism of literary history that the 'modern' is in fact only an echo of what is already there; novels that are too far before their time do not sell.

Thus it was only when the tide was beginning to turn, when women were beginning to nurture expectations wider than the confines of their parents' home, that novelists began to write about their plight. Before the second decade of the new century no one had chosen as heroine the type of woman living at home in the mid-nineteenth century, described by Edward Carpenter as having

> absolutely nothing to do except dabble in paints and music
> . . . and wander aimlessly from room to room to see if by
> chance 'anything was going on'. Dusting, cooking, sewing,
> darning – all light household duties were already fore-
> stalled; there was no private garden, and if there had been
> it would have been 'unladylike' to do anything in it . . .
> every aspiration and outlet, except in the direction of dress
> and dancing, was blocked; and marriage, with the grow-
> ing scarcity of men, was becoming every day less likely, or
> easy to compass.[13]

Multiply this picture by thousands and here, among Carpenter's six sisters, one might assume there was material for a novel. But it would be a novel without a climax, with a beginning, certainly, and a middle, but no end. For what end can there be for the woman at home with no marriage prospects, no possibility of occupation more taxing than endlessly spinning out her days and with no chance in a servanted, affluent home to use up the little energy remaining to her after boredom, depression and psychosomatic illness have claimed their share?

The inactive woman can only be the heroine of a novel when the options are there; because then, even if she chooses to ignore these options, there is the dramatic tension which inevitably accompanies her longings, indecision or even decisiveness. So it was only when the possibility of of choice became a real one that fiction began to exploit this particular theme, to describe a fate familiar to so many but hitherto ignored in literature. Ignored, that is, as a figure of crucial interest, for obviously from Jane Austen onward the unmarried daughter at home was a familiar walk-on part.

The New Woman of the 1890s was a forerunner of the heroines of the 1920s. But both were unrepresentative. Thousands and thousands of women accepted the convention that they did not feel sexual desire, must not assert themselves, must not think of any occupation except living at home or vanishing into matrimony; in short they were unrebellious. Looking back, it seems remarkable that the agitation for the vote was not carried much further inside the middle classes. But before the 1914–18 war offered middle-class women the chance to work outside the home, most would have accepted their imprisonment and would have agreed with Frederick Harrison's article on 'The Emancipation of Women' in which he said that:

> The true function of women is to educate not children only, but men, to train to a higher civilization not the rising generation but the actual society. And to do this by diffusing the spirit of affection, of self-restraint, self-sacrifice, fidelity and purity . . . as mother, as wife, as sister, as daugher, as friend, as nurse, as teacher, as servant, as counsellor, as purifier, as example, in a word – as woman.[14]

And he declared that 'to keep the family true, refined, affectionate, faithful, is a grander task than to govern the state'.

But for the woman without children, and with servants to run the home, it was a life wherein nothing much happened, not much was expected and time was endlessly and depressingly spun out. *The Rector's Daughter* (1924) is a novel by F. M. Mayor about a heroine in exactly this mould. We are told early on about Mary that

> as time passed on her contemporaries married, or settled into spinsters with objects in life. The neighbourhood arranged its friendships. At the tea-parties she had neither the charm of novelty nor familiarity. She was rather a fish out of water with the married. She played games with their children better than they did, for she kept something of a child in her; but the Rectory never had to search for servants, so that the topic of registries was closed. She could not hunt; she cared for no sport; she was useless at committees; she did not like gardening. This cut her off. She longed for friends, but friend-making needs practice and beginning early in life, and her best friend-making years slipped by unused.[15]

Nothing ever changes for her, yet Mary keeps our involvement, despite the centre of interest shifting at times to her might-have-been lover's wife. At the end of the book all three meet for a matinée.

> 'Well, old thing, it *is* jolly seeing you again, and not changed one bit, except that you're so awfully fit. You haven't told me a thing about yourself. What do you do with yourself all day, without me to see that you don't get into mischief?'
>
> Mary thought of her busy, happy life. She compared it to Kathy's fullness; it seemed starvation.
>
> 'I don't think there's much to tell,' she said. 'I only –' She stopped; she felt herself near tears.
>
> 'I *say*!' cried Kathy. 'It's nearly the half-hour. We must fly. I loathe being late.'[16]

Mary's devotion to her father is a mixture of habit, inertia, gratitude and deference to the accepted, conventional way of life which for years had been good enough for thousands of women like her. It was not going to be an overnight event, women's growing dislike of their domestic chains and their new yearning for self-fulfilment. Mary is described as being unexceptional and perfectly conformist. Not for her any ideas of supporting herself and putting her mind to some use. Her one attempt at writing is smartly crushed by her father and her one hope of marriage is snatched from her through her own lack of assertiveness and her 'niceness'.

Yet her life is not entirely empty, and some see *The Rector's Daughter* as an optimistic novel, describing an empty, useless life which, nevertheless, *matters*. For Mary loves and is loved by all around her in her enclosed world, and even though fulfilment eludes her she has known compassion, tenderness and deep feeling.

And, of course, she has never done anything of which people might disapprove – for it was so important to be nice. 'No nice girl . . .' was a phrase often on parents' lips and to behave badly was a far, far greater crime than to leave one's brain quietly to wither or to spin out an existence in which nothing marked the passing of the years except the passing seasons. The amount of sacrifice that took place upon the altar of convention was greater than we can ever imagine, since of course it is impossible to assess how much might have happened if the gods of manners, status and what-people-might-think had not exerted their influence. And we, the generations that have grown up since those days, should never forget that one of our most hard-won freedoms is our ability to do things, to exist, without so continually and obsessively caring about how others see us.

The novelist who would most have delighted in this freedom and who wrote so often on the theme of the devouring of the individual's needs and emotions by society was E. M. Delafield. Specifically, in two of her novels she wrote about the daughter at home whose only chance of self-fulfilment was ruthlessly sacrificed to the demands of convention and its mouthpiece, the mother. Alex, the heroine of *Consequences* (1919), has an unhappy childhood, annoying Nurse because she is unable to charm and dissemble. The Convent at Liège to which she is sent continues the process of subduing all that within her is spontaneous and heartfelt. She longs to be good and clever but is too transparent to manage pretence and too ashamed to be herself. She emerges ill-equipped to cope with the contrast between the moral and physical rigours of Liège and the ruthless hedonism involved in 'coming out'.

She had hated the physical discomfort of the conventual system, the insufficient hours of sleep, the bitter cold of the Belgian winters and the streaming rain that defiled the summers . . .

It seemed to Alex that when she joined the mysterious ranks of grown-up people everything would be different. She never doubted that with long dresses and piled-up hair, her whole personality would change, and the meaningless chaos of life reduce itself to some comprehensible solution. Everything all her life had been tending towards the business of 'growing up'. Everything that she was taught at home impressed the theory that her 'coming out' would usher in the realities of life . . . but she was also rather bewildered. The contrast between all this preoccupation with her clothes and her appearance, and the austere mental striving after spiritual or moral results which had permeated the convent atmosphere, was too violent.[17]

Alex is swiftly thrust into what Virginia Woolf called 'the crowded dance of modern life' and for her it literally is a dance. She is completely and touchingly naïve which is hardly surprising given that the previous boundaries of her world had been defined by the nursery and the convent. Exhortations like ' "Never more than three dances with the same man, Alex, at the very *outside*. It's such bad form to make yourself conspicuous with any one – your father would dislike it very much" ' leave her bewildered and are impossible to reconcile with the success of her convent friend Queenie. When *she* appears 'every man in the little waiting group was pressing round her, claiming first possession of her attention . . . she dispensed her favours right and left, always with the same chilly, composed sweetness.'

But, although observed with interest by Alex's father, Queenie is pronounced 'not – altogether'. And Alex flounders in a world organised on lines understood by most people but which prove a confusion to her; she is never taught how to negotiate the tight-rope between friendly flirtation and being '– altogether', that line at which social relationships with men come to grief unless clearly defined. She wants to be friendly but feels awkward, she wants to be part of a group but feels different. Unless chance in the form of a knight on a white charger is to play its part, the novel can only end tragically. For of course there is no possibility of Alex finding a job as an outlet for her energies and emotions, even if 'so many girls take up slummin' and good works now-a-days'.

She dutifully agrees to marry a man who abhors sentimental-ity and has to remove his pince-nez before gingerly touching the middle of her cheek with his lips. Then he polishes the glass before replacing it – 'It was the apotheosis of their anti-climax.' And, although E. M. Delafield's perceptions are sometimes not very subtle, she is always acute when she points out that depth of feeling is usually irreconcilable with convention.

> On making up her mind that she must break off her engagement, Alex, unaware, took the bravest decision of her life.
>
> She was being true to an instinctive standard, in which she herself only believed with part of her mind, and which was absolutely unknown to any of those who made up her surroundings.[18]

So now there is no future for the 'weakly impulsive' Alex. Her reputation is sullied, her chances ruined and, in any other house-hold, she would adopt the role of stay-at-home daughter. But Lady Isabel has never been one for affection and views the idea of an unmarried daughter as not only a social stigma but a slur upon her own charms. She makes it plain that Alex cannot expect to stay at home indefinitely and that, unmarried, there is no future for her. There is nothing for Alex to do except return to the convent life which has so far, apart from life in the nursery, been her only reality. But her passionate if repressed feelings render her unsuitable for the rigorous, self-disciplined life of a nun. Released from her vows, she returns to her widowed sister in Hampstead; but her sister does not want her, no one wants her and she has no money. After a misunderstanding with her brother Cedric over money, she drowns herself in one of the ponds on Hampstead Heath. And the reader is left shaken and depressed. Why for so long and until so recently were female offspring reared to have no purpose in life other than to be kept by someone else? Why, with her tremendous and stifled potential for love, was Alex deprived of the chance to tend others, teach others or be of service to others?

E. M. Delafield does not have an answer but she places a large part of the blame upon mothers. *Thank Heaven Fasting*, written in 1932, is again about a girl whose mother has only reared her in order to marry her off, preferably as rapidly and suitably as possible. From her earliest days Monica is groomed for the future and she is far luckier than Alex in that she does have some idea of how her particular world works; for example, she understands what Mrs Ingram means when she, at frequent intervals, exhorts her never to 'fall in love with a man who isn't quite, *quite* –'.

She could never, looking backwards, remember a time when she had not known that a woman's failure or success in life depended entirely upon whether or not she succeeded in getting a husband. It was not, even, a question of marrying well, although mothers with pretty and attractive daughters naturally hoped for that. But any husband at all was better than none. If a girl was neither married nor engaged by the end of her third season it was usually said, discreetly, amongst her mother's acquaintances, that no one had asked her.[19]

Monica flirts with a cad, makes friends with a man in love with a married woman, and generally, despite her anxiety to please, fails to pull it off. Then her father dies and she becomes her mother's only solace.

She said that Monica was her only child – all that she had

left in the world. Sometimes she thought that Monica might want to leave her, and she couldn't bear it.

'Not that I'd ever grudge you your happiness, my precious one, but just for a few years more – I don't suppose it'll be for very long.'

Monica, sick with pity, understood.

Her mother wanted to save her face.

She wanted both of them to be able to say that Monica had deliberately chosen not to marry, so that she might devote herself to her mother.[20]

But finally, happily, from an old family friend whose ramblings tend to send Monica into a brown study and whose eyes are earnest and prawn-like, finally she receives a proposal. In church Monica is 'conscious of nothing, save that the moment towards which the whole of life had been tending had come at last'.

She was to have a life of her own, after all.

A home, a husband, a recognised position as a married woman – an occupation. At last, she would have justified her existence.

Up to the very last moment she had been afraid, and had known that her mother was afraid, lest something should happen to prevent her marriage.

Nothing had happened: she was safe for ever.

There was no further need to be afraid, or ashamed, or anxious, any more.

She prayed that she might be a good wife to Herbert, and that if ever they had a child it might be a son.[21]

Monica's mother displays her generosity by longing for her only child to marry. Many mothers who had never been taught to have any inner resources, to manage for themselves rather than battening on others, clung to their daughters like limpets. The mother in *The Heel of Achilles*, E. M. Delafield's 1921 novel, deludes herself into thinking she is doing the best for her daughter, when really she is overpossessive and does not want her to be independent. Her sister-in-law is provoked into telling her that she is a 'monstrous egotist' – 'Nothing matters to you so much as having the *beau rôle* . . . you care for nothing and nobody on earth, except as it affects your self.' And the vicar says, more gently, that 'one knows very well . . . that it is less painful to endure bodily anguish than to watch it endured by one's beloved . . . Beyond that there is a greater immolation. That of relinquishing the privilege of suffering to another, and accepting the pain of watching that suffering.'

Some women, having themselves been deprived of independence by society, have chosen, consciously or unconsciously, to pass this deprivation on to their daughters (see, for example, *Mary Olivier*); some have battened on to their children for pleasure and self-aggrandisement; while others have clung to their daughters out of selfishness and fear, usually disguised as invalidism, loneliness or general helplessness. The deformities imposed by society on women's lives have too often been passed from mother to daughter.

But once the Great War had widened women's horizons, the restrictions of domestic ties became doubly irksome to the daughter left at home. Joan in Radclyffe Hall's *The Unlit Lamp* (1924) is in this position. She wishes to be a doctor and because of this and her unacknowledged affection for her governess she refuses a proposal. Her mother's response is unusual: ' "Oh, Joan, I am so glad! . . . It's the thought of losing you . . . I can't face the thought of that – and other things; you know what I mean, the thought of your being maltreated by a man, the thought that it might happen to you as it happened to me." '23

From early on Joan doubts whether her mother really loves her but the thought of her 'so small and so inadequate' prevents her from escaping to London, to a flat, independence and medical school. When her father dies and it transpires that he had 'borrowed' her small inheritance she realises that she will never get away. She is not harsh enough to resist the explicit blackmail in her mother's outburst:

'I see,' she said; 'you and Milly wish to leave home, to leave me now that I have no one else to care for me. You want to hide me away in a tenement house, while you two lead the life that seems amusing to you. This home is to be broken up and I am to go to London – my health doesn't matter. Well, I suppose I'd be better dead and then you'd be rid of the trouble of me.'[24]

This scene comes about half-way through the novel and the momentum lapses after that. To the reader it is obvious that Joan will never get away, but Radclyffe Hall gives us many potential but rejected false-starts before she finally brings the novel to its sad conclusion. One reason for the meandering construction may be that she, the author, was evidently unclear in her mind whether her theme was devouring mothers or the girl afraid of men because of the petty tyrannies she has, throughout childhood, watched her father inflict on her mother. In the final scene, Richard asks Joan yet again to marry him:

'How long is it to go on,' he cried, 'this preying of the weak on the strong, the old on the young; this hideous, unnatural injustice that one sees all around one, this incredibly wicked thing that tradition sanctifies? . . . I tell you, Joan, the sin of it lies at the door of that old woman up there in Lynton; that mild, always ailing, cruelly gentle creature who's taken everything and given nothing and battened on you year by year. She's like an octopus who's drained you dry. You struggled to get free, you nearly succeeded, but as quickly as you cut through one tentacle, another shot out and fixed on you.'[25]

But Joan, replying, is thinking more of her own nature than of her mother: ' "I shall never marry anyone. I am not a woman who could ever have married. I've never been what you call in love with a man in my life".' It is clear that Radclyffe Hall is implying that some unmarried daughters used their mothers as shields, almost welcoming the insidious grasp of the maternal tentacles if it protected them from recognising sides of their natures they would rather ignore. Yet whether Joan is rejecting men or revelling in the pleasures of martyrdom is not quite clear. She is certainly more complex than Rachel in Lorna Rea's *Rachel Moon* (1931), whose spirit of self-sacrifice is so highly developed that she barely regrets her lover who has told her sharply but truthfully, 'you're deliberately immolating yourself on a cheap altar; an altar of martyrdom and victimisation and pathetic frustration and all that'. Even her sister declares, 'you love yourself – the noble daughter, the self-sacrificing one'. Yet in her own way Rachel is perfectly happy, even if it is probable that the main inspiration for *The Unlit Lamp* and *Rachel Moon* did come from the frequent occurrence of the unmarried daughter chained unwillingly to the parental home by the claims of the elderly. At times these 'claims' were scorned. Even before the Great War, *The Times* of 19 April 1914 came out with a vigorous statement on this theme:

> Every day a host of human vampires drain the life-blood of those who are their nearest and should be their dearest . . . the most usual species is the widowed mother with a daughter of any age from 20 to 50. The other children have gone out into the world to marry and to work, and incidentally to live their own lives in homes of their own. Clearly it is the duty of the one who is left to look after the little mother. That is the universal verdict of the world and the family. If she submits, if she sacrifices her youth and individuality on the altar of the Fifth Commandment, her doom is sealed. The longer she stays on with her mother the more impossible it is for her to break away. Day and night she is at her beck and call. Her opinions, her gifts, her ambitions she must keep in the background till they atrophy from want of use. She must come when she is called, go where she is sent, walk or drive cheek by jowl with the vampire who saps her vitality, write her letters, pay calls, 'do' the flowers, exercise the dog, order the dinner, pay the wages, engage and dismiss her servants, count the linen, keep the books, and, to speak generally, run the house for the vampire's convenience from the vampire's point of view . . . The vampire ('Such a devoted mother, my dear!') has them by the throat, and slowly but surely squeezes the life out of them and drains them of youth and joy and hope. In all the long catalogue of woman's real and fancied woes there is hardly one more infuriating and none more depressing to contemplate

than the commonplace tragedies of these spoilt and wasted lives.

Mothers in fiction do not often get sympathetic treatment, unless they are the reincarnation of the loving maternal instinct like Mrs Ramsay in Virginia Woolf's *To the Lighthouse* (1927) or of aloof graciousness like Lady Spencer in Rosamond Lehmann's *The Weather in the Streets* (1936); or unless they are shown wanting nothing better than to get away from their ever-pressing daughter like Lady Slane in *All Passion Spent* (1931) by Vita Sackville-West. But it is rare for a woman novelist to portray a mother of the kind imagined by Joan in *The Unlit Lamp*. Her ideal kind of motherly love

> ought to be a patient, waiting, unchanging love; the kind that went with making up the fire and sitting behind the tea-tray awaiting your return. The love that wrote and told you that you were expected home for Christmas, and that when you arrived your favourite pudding would be there to greet you. Yes, that was the ideal mother-love; it never wanted but it never exacted. It was a beautiful thing, all of one restful colour.[26]

In *The Crowded Street* (1924) (originally called *The Wallflower*) Winifred Holtby wrote about a theme which E. M. Delafield often explored: that of a mother meaning well but having no idea how to introduce her children to the complexities of life (boys of course were meant to have this done for them at their public school). Muriel, like Alex in *Consequences*, is sent away to school and then finds it hard to reconcile its values with those of home. She too finds the rules and regulations of dancing particularly confusing (although she is lucky enough to confront them early on, when she is only eleven).

> Muriel's orderly mind registered a new item of information. The unforgivable sin at a party was to have no partners. To sit quietly in the drawing-room at home was a virtue. The same conduct in the Kingsport Assembly Rooms was an undesirable combination of naughtiness and misfortune. In order to realize the Party in its full magnifi-

cence, one must have a full programme. All else was failure. Enjoyment of the music, the people, the prettiness – all this counted for nothing. It was not the Party.[27]

Like so many young girls before and since, Muriel reflects rue-fully on grown-up conventions.

Being grown-up was puzzling. It seemed to make no differ-ence at all in most things, and then to matter frightfully in quite unexpected ways. It meant, for instance, not so much the assumption of new duties as the acceptance of new values.

Was she more stupid than other people, or did everyone feel like this at first? She was travelling in a land of which she only imperfectly understood the language.[28]

She too has a friend from school days (Alex has Queenie) whose purpose in the novel is to import sexuality. Clare is bohemian rather than 'not altogether', but the contrast with her friend is equally telling. Muriel's mother realises that Clare's visit must come to an end when Clare has too many dances with the only available eligible man: in any way she can, she is determined to thrust her own daughters in front of him.

But her world crumbles when her other daughter, Connie, announces that she is expecting a baby and derides her mother's two-faced attitude to men. On the one hand, she has kept her daughters at home in order not to spoil their chances of a good marriage, on the other hand, she is deeply upset when one of them has used her sexuality to lure her lover to her. (There is the same irony in May Sinclair's wonderful novel *The Allinghams* (1927) where Margaret is pronounced mad for wanting to show her naked body to her lover but her sister Angie is forgiven because she has succeeded in seducing her lover, and her illegiti-mate son reconciles her parents to her – see page 130.)

Connie is forced by her family to get married and to live a farming life, the descriptions of which anticipate Stella Gibbons's satirical *Cold Comfort Farm* (1932). But she dies in childbirth, Muriel rejects a proposal and Mrs Hammond has failed to marry off either of her daughters suitably. But she does not have one to keep at home with her because Muriel has found work in London. It is unclear whether we are meant to see this as a triumph or ignominy for Mrs Hammond. Certainly most mothers in fiction between the wars would have preferred to keep their daughters at home because their upbringing had so ill-equipped them to face life without a prop.

Mrs Powell in Lettice Cooper's novel *The New House* (1936) is of this type, but her attitude is described as both intolerably selfish and completely out of date. She has two daughters, Delia who has 'escaped' to a laboratory in London and the prospect of a harmonious, carefully considered marriage to a fellow-scientist, and Rhoda, who has stayed at home. Rhoda is clearly following in the footsteps of her Aunt Ellen: they both had had one chance of marriage and escape from home, but both had been incapable of showing their love. And like Mary in *The Rector's Daughter* and Muriel in *The Crowded Street* Rhoda is ignorant of the very meaning of the word seduction, let alone of its practice. She remembers:

> How often had she heard her mother and other people say critically, 'Molly (or Betty, or Peggy) is running after that young man' with an implication of intolerable condemnation? How often had she been told not to show off, not to look at herself in the glass, not to attract people's attention? Spoken and unspoken, her upbringing had forbidden her to invite love; had been based, she now saw, on her mother's unexpressed conviction that love was wrong.[29]

Rhoda's aunt had rejected a proposal because, for her, love for a parent had to take precedence over love for anyone else.

> Aunt Ellen was practised in resignation. She had been brought up to think it a virtue not to expect much. The virtue had been instilled into her by parents who had not envisaged the inevitable result, that she wouldn't get much; or, if they had, they had perhaps concluded that for their daughter virtue should be its own reward. It never occurred to Ellen, recalling those god-like parents out of the past, that they themselves had pursued and enjoyed a

lot of other rewards besides virtue. She had accepted their serene conviction that they were always right, just as she had accepted their view that it was a pity when 'the lower classes' became discontented or tried to do or have things 'above their station'. Ellen's father and mother had laid great stress on the duty of being satisfied, one which they were well able to perform themselves, and which suited them in their children, dependants and employees. I'm sure, Ellen thought, I ought to be very thankful. Such a happy home with Mamma for so many years![30]

And at the beginning of the novel Rhoda's thoughts are much the same, that it would be cruel to leave her mother for 'it was better to forego your own wishes, and enjoy the more rarefied happiness that came from being on the side of the angels'. Throughout the day on which she helps her mother to move from the decaying family mansion into a 'new house' she continually comes back to this question. We watch her 'terrible notions of duty' gradually being swayed by other considerations, her mother's petty demands, the tedium of the life mapped out for her and, in particular, her aunt's entrenched and rather annoying 'ways'. For example, there is an unselfishness so extreme that it only makes the recipients of any generosity feel guilty, 'which made you impatient with Aunt Ellen, when she would sit in the draughty chair and eat the burnt piece of toast, thrusting selfishness upon you against your will'.

Rhoda reaches a crisis in her life when the bareness of the family home and her own prospects force her to reassess both the past and the future. Aunt Ellen is there helping them to move house, anxious to help, trying to cheer up her sister, implacably resentful at the thought of change. 'Her tone had the automatic brightness and encouragement of someone who had lived with an elderly invalid for very many years, of someone who for very many years had begun two-thirds of her remarks with, "Never mind!" ' Suddenly Rhoda hears herself saying, 'Never mind!' 'She heard in her own voice the shallow, bright tone that she had heard so often in her grandmother's drawing-room when Aunt Ellen poked the fire, or picked up a dropped stitch, or closed the window.'

And she admits to herself what she had half come to realise:

> It was safe to stay at home and be a good daughter, to be unselfish. When you give up your life to other people you think you do it for their sake. I'm beginning to wonder whether you don't often do it to reduce your own risks. When you are like Aunt Ellen, old and alone with nothing to do, and no one needing you, people despise you or pity you, kindly, perhaps, but they do. I've always thought less of them for doing it, but perhaps there's something right at the bottom of it. When the small children at Tatty's dancing class cry and won't try to dance, their mothers are ashamed of them. You must join in or not count.[31]

Rhoda tremulously decides to reject duty.

> I want to get away! For the first time the wish was definite and clear in her mind. It was Aunt Ellen she wanted to get away from, from being like her, so unselfish and good and devoted, thinking of people's latter ends. You ought to be selfish! Being selfish kept you alive! But Grandmamma had been selfish, using up Aunt Ellen, absorbing her life, sitting there, the stately old lady in her handsome gowns, sipping the gruel Aunt Ellen had made, and saying, if there were lumps in it, 'I may not be here next Christmas.'[32]

Even by the 1930s it was not so easy for the daughter of the house to get away. Lallie in E. Arnot Robertson's *Ordinary Families* (1933) rapidly finds 'the kindly tyranny of family interest' a crushing burden. Because her parents are so concerned and caring she can find no convincing reason for wanting to leave home.

> In very few of the thousands of good homes, from which the children struggle to escape, can the truth ever be told, I suppose, even in the heat of a family row – the unfortunate truth that devotion easily grows unbearable when it is given to the young by those whose own lives are no longer, for some reason, of self-absorbing interest . . .
>
> We had no open disagreements. Using her incongruously adroit social manner, mother always managed to get

the subject of a job for me safely shelved again almost as soon as I had re-introduced it, in some roundabout way.

What decent argument had I on my side, with the labour market for women so low? If I earned two pounds ten a week in Ipswich, which was all that I could hope for after learning shorthand and typing, almost a third of my salary would go in lunches and fares. The remainder, even if I handed over every penny, would obviously be negligible compared with mother's satisfaction in having all her daughters with her again . . . London was out of the question financially as well as spiritually: it would cost the family at least a pound a week more than my salary for me to live there. London, indeed, could not be mentioned: the realization that I wanted to get away as badly as that would have been deeply wounding.[33]

For what had changed for Rhoda and others like her is that the stigma attached to the unmarried girl was not as powerful as it had been. As Ruth Adam has observed, 'this [the 1920s] was the era of the spinster. At last, after so many years of being grudged the right to exist at all, she came into her own.'[34] There were many reasons for this change, which became gradually apparent during the 1920s and, by Rhoda's time, were more firmly established. Firstly, the ravages of the war years meant that a woman of marriageable age might easily have lost her potential husband on the battlefield – and this was rather more glamorous than merely having failed to find one. Secondly, greater opportunities for education, new opportunities for work, wider availability of birth control and a little more sexual freedom gave middle-class women a new measure of equality and the unmarried woman more opportunity to support herself.

The women who pursued their careers with the most conspicuous success were the schoolteachers (of whom the heroine of Winifred Holtby's *South Riding* (1935) is the most outstanding fictional example). In fact their numbers did not increase greatly over twenty years, the 180,000 of the 1911 census barely reaching the million mark by 1931, but their status had risen during the 1920s and their salaries allowed them to live reasonably comfortably. Muriel Spark, a novelist who began writing in the 1950s, described the surplus woman's successor in the following terms:

> There were legions of her kind during the nineteen-thirties, women from the age of thirty and upward, who crowded their war-bereaved spinsterhood with voyages of discovery into new ideas and energetic practices in art or social welfare, education or religion . . . They went to lectures, tried living on honey and nuts, took lessons in German and then went walking in Germany; they bought caravans and went off with them into the hills among the lochs; they played the guitar, they supported all the new little theatre companies; they took lodgings in the slums and, distributing pots of paint, taught their neighbours the arts of simple interior decoration; they preached the inventions of Marie Stopes; they attended the meetings of the Oxford Group and put Spiritualism to their hawk-eyed test.[35]

The unmarried girl no longer had to stay shyly at home. The Victorian emphasis on obedience to the demands of the family was gradually replaced by a slightly more permissive individualism, and blame was now sometimes attached to the mother who tried to keep her daughter at her side. In Rachel Ferguson's *Alas, Poor Lady* (1937), the real culprit is Mrs Scrimgeour who is selfish, thoughtless, evasive and lacking in any real concern for her children beyond that of trying to make sure they fulfil society's expectations of them. Given that she has far too many unmarriageable daughters, it is rather hard for her to ensure that they do what is required – which is to marry suitably. Yet she trains them neither to be attractive to men nor to find a way of occupying themselves. One daughter becomes a nun. Another expects a proposal and receives instead the news that the young man in question loves someone else. And a family inheritance is so badly invested and badly managed that the youngest daughter, Grace, is forced to become a companion help. She eventually ends up friendless in one room, courtesy of the Distressed Gentlefolk Protective Association – a victim of a way of life which anticipated nothing more than a round of leaving cards, waiting for people to call, directing servants and keeping up appearances – and which, when it failed, envisaged no substitute.

But at least unmarried women had during the 1920s ceased to have the humiliating status so familiar to their unmarried aunts; nor had the demanding mothers remained immune to the kind of criticism voiced by *The Times* in 1914. Even Virginia Woolf grumbled in her diary about her mother-in-law 'who is so "painfully sensitive" – so fond of cakes, so incapable of amusing herself, so entirely without any interest in my feelings or friends; so vampire-like & vast in her demand for my entire attention & sympathy . . . Lord Lord! how many daughters have been murdered by women like this!'[36] And it is made quite plain by Margaret Kennedy in her novel *Together and Apart* (1936) that the absolutely futile divorce would never have happened if the mothers-in-law had left their children alone. Only their 'well-meaning' interference stopped the couple from patching over a trivial quarrel, and so a normally harmonious family was needlessly destroyed.

As the shadow of the nineteenth century receded, the concept of the 'matriarch' became ever more obsolete. And there is during the 1920s very little deference to duty and a large amount of sympathy for those who have been ensnared in its name. Olivia, in *Invitation to the Waltz* (1932) by Rosamond Lehmann, feels terribly sorry for Miss Robinson who makes her dresses:

> she wouldn't get a husband: she hadn't a chance now. She was thirty. Letting I dare not wait upon I would, youth had gone by; and now the candour of her desires was muddied, her spark of spirit spent. Never would she do now what once she had almost done: walked out of the house and left them all whining and gone to London to earn her living . . . That was after the death of Mr Robinson . . . and Mother said I need all my dear daughters round me now, God willing we shall never part in this life, I feel it won't be long before I too Go Home.[37]

By the 1930s, then, women's lives were less constricted. On the one hand, their chances of marrying had greatly increased, for the men who had been schoolboys at the end of the Great War were now of a marrying age, while in addition some half a million men who had emigrated overseas in the difficult days after the war had now begun to return.[38] On the other hand, if they chose not to marry, the attitude of society was kinder than it had been before the Great War. Countless middle-class women lived independent lives in comfortable circumstances, supporting themselves through their own efforts and being able to choose whether to marry or to have a career. Cicely Hamilton commented in 1940 with justifiable pride:

> If a woman is destined to go through life unwed, my country of England has many advantages as a domicile; there are, I imagine, few parts of the world where the once traditional contempt for the spinster is more thoroughly a thing of the past. Time was – and not so very long ago – when the middle-aged Englishwoman who had not found a husband was considered fair game for the jester; by the humorists of the Victorian age she was always depicted as a figure of fun – an unattractive creature who, in spite of all her efforts, had failed to induce a man to marry her. That was the old maid as a past generation saw her – and as we do not see her today; we have too many unmarried women successful in business or professional life, distinguished in literature, science, and art, to be able to keep up that joke.[39]

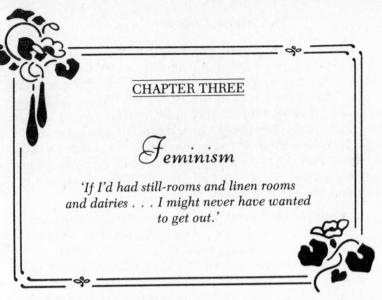

CHAPTER THREE

Feminism

*'If I'd had still-rooms and linen rooms
and dairies . . . I might never have wanted
to get out.'*

'My personal revolt was feminist rather than suffragist; what I rebelled at chiefly was the dependence implied in the idea of "destined" marriage, "destined" motherhood – the identification of success with marriage, of failure with spinsterhood, the artificial concentration of the hopes of girlhood on sexual attraction and maternity.'[1] Cicely Hamilton, who throughout her autobiography displays an unusually modest insight into the pleasures and difficulties of the unmarried woman, was always wary of 'the Cause', believing that its 'fanatical' aspects were inherently dangerous. Indeed, she went so far as to suggest that the militant suffrage movement was the beginning of the dictatorship movements 'which are by way of thrusting democracy out of the European continent' and that Mrs Pankhurst was the first of the European dictators because of her imperiousness and fanaticism. So, to her, the cause of Birth Control was of far greater interest because there could be no permanent advance in the position of women except 'under a system of voluntary motherhood'.

For most middle-class women, however, feminism, until the end of the First World War, was synonymous with the fight for the vote. The heroine of Elizabeth Robins's *The Convert* (1905) finds an object in life in the Cause and gives up 'managing things' (charity concerts) because she finds that 'there is work to do'. Ellen in Rebecca West's *The Judge* (1922) had, before she met her lover, displayed her independence of spirit because 'every Saturday afternoon [she] sold Votes for Women in Princes Street'. And Dorothy in May Sinclair's *The Tree of Heaven* (1917) displays hers not only by taking a first-class in Economics at Newnham but by attending meetings of the Committee of the North Hampstead Branch of the Women's Franchise Union. Here a vehement lady named Miss Blackadder harangues her minuscule crowd with some passion:

> 'Until you're enfranchised you are not going to own any *man* as father, or brother, or husband' (her voice rang with a deeper and stronger vibration) 'or lover, or friend. And the man who does not agree with you, the man who refuses you the vote, the man who opposes your efforts to get the vote, the man who, whether he agrees with you or not, *will not help you to get it*, you count as your enemy.'[2]

But Dorothy, too, opposes vehemence. She

> was afraid of the Feminist Vortex as her brother Michael had been afraid of the little vortex of school. She was afraid of the herded women. She disliked the excited faces, and the high voices skirling their battle-cries, and the silly business of committees, and the platform slang. She was sick and shy before the tremor and the surge of collective feeling; she loathed the gestures and the movements of the collective soul, the swaying and heaving and rushing forward of the many as one. She would not be carried away by it; she would keep the clearness of her soul . . . She would fight for freedom, but not in their way and not at their bidding.[3]

Dorothy retains the clearness of her soul, for, like Cicely Hamilton, her real revolt is feminist rather than suffragist. This is partly in her nature, and partly an inevitable consequence of the passing of time. By the second decade of the twentieth century, Dorothy has realised that the 'work to do' encompasses more than the question of votes, and leads her life accordingly;

yet when her lover, whom she had refused to marry because of her commitment to personal freedom, is killed in the retreat from Mons, her former cry of 'I think love isn't love and can't last unless it's free' has become meaningless to her.

This less than optimistic attitude to a woman's 'personal revolt' was often to be repeated in women's writing between the wars. The search for freedom and independence would either be brought to a halt by marriage; or the loss of the loved one would bring bitter regrets; or the determined would be shown to have given up, painfully, something to which their less singleminded sisters had capitulated. There are only a few equivalents in fiction to Cicely Hamilton's cheerful renunciation of marriage in favour of the rich and varied life that she created for herself.

Many of the 'New Woman' novels of the 1880s and 1890s already had plots where the search for freedom and sexual independence by the heroine is either cut short by marriage or later regretted. *Marcella* (1894) by Mrs Humphry Ward is only one of these. And novels written just before the First World War often portray heroines who struggle at first but soon defer gratefully to their lovers.

Lucy in E. M. Forster's *A Room with a View* (1908) tries to escape suburban ideals and towards the end of the novel she summons up the courage to tell her mother, amidst the hush of Mudie's circulating library, that she is thinking of sharing a flat for a little with some other girls.

'And mess with typewriters and latchkeys,' exploded Mrs Honeychurch. 'And agitate and scream, and be carried off kicking by the police. And call it a Mission – when no one wants you! And call it Duty – when it means that you can't stand your own home! And call it Work – when thousands of men are starving with the competition as it is!'

'I want more independence,' said Lucy lamely; she knew that she wanted something, and independence is a useful cry; we can always say that we have not got it. She tried to remember her emotions in Florence: those had been sincere and passionate, and had suggested beauty rather than short skirts and latchkeys. But independence was certainly her cue.

'Very well. Take your independence and be gone. Rush up and down and round the world, and come back as thin as a lath with the bad food. Despise the house that your father built and the garden that he planted, and our dear view – and then share a flat with another girl.'[4]

But no sooner have Lucy and her mother caught the train back to Dorking than she becomes engaged to be married and her brief clawing at freedom is rapidly ended.

In the same way Mrs Havelock Ellis shows her heroine deferring to received ideas of womanhood. In *Attainment* (1909) she describes Rachel deciding to use her private income to come to London, live with her maid in a flat and work for the poor. When she finally decides to give this up, a radical poet informs her that

you know in your heart that this game of puss-in-the-corner, called philanthropy, is no use to you. You are too sane and healthy for it. It's all right for love-sick girls and dyspeptic widows. It fills gaps. It will even do as a general introduction to realities for a girl of your make, but you'd rot if you stayed in it.'[5]

After some time attempting to form a commune called the Brotherhood of the Perfect Life, Rachel goes home and retreats into marriage. But at least her money has allowed her to have a taste of independence.

H.G. Wells was equally conventional, for he portrays the heroine of *Ann Veronica* (1909) as losing her assertiveness once she is in love. Some have criticised him for belittling Ann Veronica's aspirations. Most will conclude that he was a realistic middle-class novelist who was well aware of the boundaries of propriety and one who, while admiring the intelligent, free-spirited and free-loving woman, liked her, finally, to subdue her liveliness in deference to the male. The taming was for him as exciting as the wooing, which is why so many of his mistresses were writers whose minds he could respect. (They included

Violet Hunt, Dorothy Richardson, Rosalind Bland, Amber Reeves, Rebecca West and Elizabeth von Arnim.)

When Ann Veronica has finally realised that the world 'had no particular place for her at all', she runs away from home to study biology. Her father, in true Victorian fashion, divided women into either Angels in the House or prostitutes. 'His ideas about girls and women were of a sentimental and modest quality; they were creatures, he thought, either too bad for a modern vocabulary, and then frequently most undesirably desirable, or too pure and good for life.' But he could not visualise a woman living regardless of the approval of a man and it was vain for Ann Veronica to declare: ' "I want to be a human being; I want to learn about things and know about things, and not to be protected as something too precious for life, cooped up in one narrow little corner." '[6] In her father's eyes she is misguided and muddle-headed and he puts it down to the influence of fiction. ' "There was a time when girls didn't get these extravagant ideas . . . It's these damned novels. All this torrent of misleading spurious stuff that pours from the press. These sham ideals and advanced notions".'[7]

To Ann Veronica, Morningside Park, where she lives ('a suburb that had not altogether, as people say, come off') is impossibly stuffy, a place where her free spirit would of necessity wither. She anticipates the rebellion of Vera Brittain who, weary of passing her days 'in all those conventional pursuits with which the leisured young woman of every generation has endeavoured to fill the time that she is not qualified to use',[8] wrote in *Testament of Friendship*:

> I had read Olive Schreiner and followed the militant campaigns with the excitement of a sympathetic spectator, but my growing consciousness that women suffered from remediable injustices was due less to the movement for the vote than to my early environment with its complacent acceptance of female subordination.[9]

Being of an earlier generation, Ann Veronica's rebellion against female subordination *was* crystallised by the fight for the vote and she accepts that 'the Vote is the symbol of everything'.

The result of her joining the struggle for the Vote is imprisonment and a period of contemplation.

> As the long solitary days wore on Ann Veronica found a
> number of definite attitudes and conclusions in her mind.
> One of these was a classification of women into women
> who are and women who are not hostile to men. 'The real
> reason why I am out of place here,' she said, 'is because I
> like men. I can talk with them. I've never found them
> hostile. I've got no feminine class feeling. I don't want any
> laws or freedoms to protect me from a man like Mr Capes. I
> know that in my heart I would take whatever he gave . . .'
> 'A woman wants a proper alliance with a man, a man
> who is better stuff than herself. She wants that and needs it
> more than anything else in the world. It may not be just, it
> may not be fair, but things are so. It isn't law, nor custom,
> nor masculine violence settled that. It is just how things
> happen to be. She wants to be free – she wants to be legally
> and economically free, so as not to be subject to the wrong
> man; but only God, who made the world, can alter things
> to prevent her being slave to the right one.'[10]

She concludes that previously she had been driven by stark
egotism and that only now does she 'begin to understand Jane
Austen and chintz covers and decency and refinement and all the
rest of it'. And so the novel retires into romance, with Ann
Veronica open-eyed to the virtues of love and humility and her
gesture of defiance taking the form of living with a married man.
Wells was thereby fulfilling his own fantasies, which involved
subduing a spirited girl to the will of a good man while keeping
bourgeois morals at bay. The defiance of the first part of the
novel and the immorality of the second ensured that *Ann
Veronica* became a *cause célèbre*; for those middle-class parents,
and they were the majority, who assumed decency and
refinement to be unquestionably a part of life it was potentially
explosive and many forbade their daughters to read it.

Its danger was by far the greater because Wells was a respected middle-class writer. He could not be dismissed as a mere
oddity like the earlier feminist writers such as Olive Schreiner,

'George Egerton', Grant Allen or Sarah Grand. And he was additionally dangerous since he did not only show a young girl rebelling against the constrictions of suburbia: he also showed a girl who, once she has admitted to herself that she loves, declares her feelings and gets away with it. He wrote in 1934:

> The particular offence was that Ann Veronica was a virgin who fell in love and showed it, instead of waiting as all popular heroines had hitherto done, for someone to make love to her. It was held to be an unspeakable offence that an adolescent female should be sex-conscious before the thing was forced upon her attention. But Ann Veronica wanted a particular man who excited her and she pursued him and got him. With gusto . . . if I had been a D. H. Lawrence, with every fig leaf pinned aside, I could not have been considered more improper than I was.[11]

By the 1920s, feminism for some middle-class women became more a question of personal integrity, of women fulfilling themselves for themselves. To do this, they felt that they must fight for equality for women. As Winifred Holtby wrote:

> I am a feminist because I dislike everything that feminism implies. I desire an end of the whole business, the demands for equality, the suggestions of sex warfare, the very name of feminism. I want to be about the work in which my real interests lie, the study of inter-race relationships, the writing of novels and so forth. But while the inequality exists, while injustice is done and opportunity denied to the great majority of women, I shall have to be a feminist with the motto Equality First. And I shan't be happy till I get . . . a society in which sex-differentiation concerns those things alone which by the physical laws of nature it must govern, a society in which men and women work together for the good of all mankind, a society in which there is no respect of persons, either male or female, but a supreme regard for the importance of the human being.[13]

Winifred Holtby was following in the tradition of the 'Old Feminism' in her desire to see 'an end of the whole business'. She was unsympathetic to the 'New Feminism' which was far more politically orientated than the 'Old'. The doctrine of the 'New' feminists was defined by Eleanor Rathbone. In direct contradiction to the 'Old', they argued that the time had come to stop concentrating on equality, defined as demands for those things that men had and women were without, and to work for those things women needed 'not because it is what men have got but because it is what women need to fulfil the potentialities of their own natures and to adjust themselves to the circumstances of their own lives'.[14] The 'Old' feminists fought for equal pay, equal opportunities, equal rights, while the 'New' feminists were anxious to emphasise the differences between men and women and to use the basic fact of this difference as a starting-point for their efforts on women's behalf. Fifty years later these different approaches are still with us. The feminist movement in fact includes many 'feminisms' and indeed this has been a strength. Dora Russell is one example of a feminist who expresses both the 'Old' and the 'New' – declaring the need for equal rights, for laws which offer justice to women as well as men, but who believes in the necessity for women's own values and concerns to be developed and to be represented in our male-dominated society. If anyone asks me 'are you a feminist?' I say 'no, not if it means having aggressive, "anti-men" feelings.' But when pressed, I admit to being a passionate feminist in the sense that I want an end to the whole business as quickly as possible, even though I begin to think it will not be in my lifetime.

The feminist novels that were written between the wars tend to be in the tradition of the 'Old' feminism, being concerned less with the stark realities of either male or political oppression than with women's chances for self-fulfilment in a still unequal society. They were about the importance of the human being when that being happens to be female. Yet the solutions were far from clear-cut and many of the novels which try to show a female soul winging its way to the heights of self-development still end with the same old sop to convention, namely the heroine deferring gratefully to the protection of her male lover. In this respect the Ann Veronica theme set a pattern which was to be frequently imitated. There is for example *The Rebel Generation*

(1925) by Jo van Ammers-Küller, a Dutch novel which achieved some popular success in England when it was translated in 1928.

The novel is divided into three parts, set in 1840, 1872 and 1923. The first part describes a tyrannical father presiding undisputed over his cowering family. The women pass their lives in a round of ironing, sewing, cooking and petty economising, and the idea of a girl even thinking for herself is abhorrent. Thirty years later we see that even the ones who did marry suitably have led futile, unhappy lives, thinking only about their status in the eyes of others. They continue to bring up their daughters to believe that 'God's will is that a daughter should obey her parents and help her mother at home until she fulfils her proper destiny by marriage'. The one girl who escaped is now a writer, active on behalf of women's causes, unmarried and eager to bring freedom to the daughters of those with whom she shared her life thirty years previously. But the moral is that even emancipation does not bring happiness at least in the long run:

> They were so blissfully certain, all these ardent young things, that they possessed the one secret of true happiness and had found a complete solution for all the ills and grievances of womankind . . . although the lords of creation held 'blue stockings' in the most undisguised contempt, this did not in the least deter the women from their folly but seemed rather to egg them on to fiercer efforts.[15]

One of 'these ardent young things' escapes: she becomes a doctor and we see her in the 1920s when she goes back to Leyden to live with her nephew and his wife. Yet even she is surprised when the wife 'made out an irrefutable case against housekeeping, averring that it was a mere abstract idea. Only teachers of domestic economy and a handful of old frumps would dream of attaching any importance to it. Housekeeping to a modern woman is just ordering the meals, keeping the accounts and arranging the servants' work'. Freedom from drudgery there may be but clearly emancipation does not mean happiness for everyone. The daughter of this 'modern woman' declares angrily: ' "Hasn't Mother's precious *work* always been placed far before any 'old-fashioned domesticity' as you call it?" ' The author comments:

> The women of fifty years ago in despair at the barren aimlessness of their lives had sought happiness in intellectual development and the equality of the sexes. And now the younger generation were already proposing to reject the privileges their elders had so hardly won and to go back to the days of thraldom.[16]

So a young 'career woman' falls into her lover's arms.

> He was so different from the rest. *He* didn't care in the least whether she were clever. To him she was weak and dependent, just a little girl he longed to hold tight in his arms while she whispered that she loved him and would be his for ever and ever.
>
> And all at once she knew that it was just this kind of girl that she wanted to be; that all the things with which she had tried to fill her life were not such as brought lasting happiness to any woman.[17]

It is the same moral as Rose Macaulay was so fond of making. Each generation thinks it is unique but they are just treading a well-worn path. As Rome declares in *Told by an Idiot* (1923) ' "there's one thing about freedom . . . each generation of people begin by thinking they've got it for the first time in history, and end by being sure the generation younger than themselves have too much of it" '.[18] And her mother remembers

> in her own youth the older people talking about the New Girl, the New Woman. Were girls and women really always newer than boys and men, or was it only that people noticed it more, and said more about it? . . . The New Young Woman. Bold, fast, blue-stockinged, reading and talking about things of which their mothers had never, before marriage, heard – in brief, NEW.[19]

And G. B. Stern wrote on the same theme in *Tents of Israel* (1924) (published in America the following year under the title of *The Matriarch*). The novel is a family chronicle, complete with family tree, about the Rakonitz family. Traits of character are handed down from generation to generation and however hard members of the family try to escape it is impossible for them to do so. One of them tries. She

> would not be absurdly chaperoned, nor drilled into marriage; she was modern; she would not be ruled by the *jeune-fille* traditions of etiquette; she would make her own arrangements; she would make no arrangements at all; live as she liked; live free; snap her fingers at the out-of-date solemnities of dowry, and parents who 'approached' each other.[20]

But those around her react in the way that Ann Veronica's father had reacted – they assume she gets her foolish notions from books: ' "Modern girl, indeed! . . . all this idiocy of free love and light love and love for an hour – pagans up-to-date – isn't her own inspiration. She's been reading too much, silly goose." ' Both novelists were making the same point, one which Cicely Hamilton echoed:

> One of Nature's devices to save the world from stagnation is to implant in the breast of each generation a certain amount of contempt for the old-fashioned manners and outlook of its immediate predecessors; a contempt which youth, grown older in its turn, will receive from its own sons and daughters.[21]

The main theme of A. S. M. Hutchinson's *This Freedom* (1922) is whether the post-1918 world had changed for the better or worse. The novel's style is facile and its tone of voice sentimental, but it had a wide popular appeal. Yet, in the manner of bestselling fiction, the author flits from one moral stance to another, declaring roundly against one and then another, caring nothing for consistency but concerned only with airing all the arguments. For example, when Rosalie, the heroine, is a child the author sympathises with her for the servile position she holds in relation to the men in her family. But when she is adult and tries to fulfil her own aspirations, then she is condemned for not ministering to her husband and children. It may be a necessary ingredient of bestsellers that they do not offend anyone, paying lip service first to one, then to another; but the end result always appears unprovocative.

The opening of *This Freedom* is similar in some ways to that of *The Crowded Street*, which was to appear two years later, although Winifred Holtby can evoke the father's brutish selfishness while Hutchinson has to spell it out; he tells one what to think where a more subtle novelist works on the reader's perceptions indirectly. But the following passage from *This Freedom* must none the less be representative of something that happened daily throughout middle-class England:

Her mother – her mother and her sisters and the servants and the entire female establishment of the universe – seemed to Rosalie always to be waiting for something from her father or for her father himself, or waiting for or upon some male other than her father. That was another of the leading principles that Rosalie first came to know in her world. Not only were the males, paramountly her father, able to do what they liked and always doing wonderful and mysterious things, but everything that the females did either had some relation to a male or was directly for, about or on behalf of a male.

Getting Robert off to school in the morning for instance. That was another early picture.

There would be Robert eating; and there was the entire female population of the rectory feverishly attending upon Robert while he ate. Six females, intensely and as if their lives depended upon it, occupied with one male. Three girls – Anna about sixteen, Flora fourteen, Hilda twelve – and three grown women, all exhaustingly occupied in pushing out of the house one heavy and obstinate male aged about ten! Rosalie used to stand and watch entranced. How wonderful he was! Where did he go to when at last he was pushed off? What happened to him? What did he do?[22]

When Rosalie grows up she works in a bank and lives in a lodging house. She is determined not to marry. But Cupid shoots his arrow and despite her good intentions she is smitten.

> And she told Harry: marriage should be a partnership – not an absorption by the greater of the less; not one part active and the other passive; one giving, the other receiving; one maintaining, the other maintained; none of these, but instead a perfect partnering, a perfect equality that should be equality of place, equality of privilege, equality of duty, equality of freedom. 'Harry, each with work and with a career. Harry, each living an own life as every man, away from home, shutting his front door upon that home and off to work, leads an own and separate life. Harry –.'[23]

Hutchinson comments, in his sickly, pompous way: 'Do try to imagine her, tremulous in this her vital enterprise, tremulous in this wonder that her armies found.'

At first 'it all worked splendidly':

> In those early years, when two were in the nursery and as yet no third, there wasn't a sign that Harry, who had married for a home, ever could say 'I have a right to a home.' He had, and he was often saying so, the most perfect home. He came not home of a night to a wife peevish with domestic frets and solitary confinement and avid he should hear the tale of them, nor yet to one that butterflied the day long between idleness and pleasures and gave him what was left. He came nightly to a home that his wife sought as eagerly as he sought, a place of rest well-earned and peace well-earned.[24]

But as time goes on, life is not so easy. Outwardly all is contentment, Harry a successful barrister and Rosalie a successful banker, their children nurtured by devoted nannies and governesses, summers by the sea at Cromer with their parents' undivided attention, good nature and cheerfulness perpetually since 'children, she held, ought not to see their parents bad-tempered or distressed or in any way out of sorts or out of control'.[25] So Rosalie is 'able to come to her children only when all her undivided attention and wholehearted love could be given to them'. Yet something jars. The children seem too self-contained, they are not spontaneous in their affection. Harry never admitted to his wife that he felt this until the day when she announces that she wishes to go to the East for a year on business and he is finally driven to saying that, yes, he *does* think that men are different from women and that she *should* shoulder the greater burden of domesticity.

Rosalie looks at her children properly for the first time and, noticing that her eldest child claims not to believe in Bible stories, decides to leave the office. But it is too late. She cannot reclaim her children's love and she cannot be happy at home. So, much against Harry's will, she returns to work. To have rejected your maternal duty *twice* is going too far, and retribution strikes hard. Of her children Hugo is imprisoned for felony and goes out to the colonies; Doda dies after a backstreet abortion; and Benjie kills himself. At the end Harry and Rosalie are left with their granddaughter and the moral is clear: 'She has all her meals with them. There's no nurse . . . She trumpets in her tiny voice, "Lessons, lessons. On mother's knee! On mother's knee!" '

This Freedom was written at a time when middle-class women were beginning to take for granted that they could accept paid employment should they so wish. Many working-class women had always worked. Yet after the First World War, women of all classes in paid employment were seen no longer as patriots serving their country but as selfish 'limpets' who would not give up their jobs to the men in need of work. Most middle-class women escaped being thus stigmatised by working only as a way of filling in time between school and marriage. And those who continued once they were married often found the same problems as Rosalie or as Laurence, the heroine of Storm Jameson's *Three Kingdoms* (1926).

The theme of this novel is stated in the first chapter when Laurence fights against her sister-in-law's calm belief that 'I have a life. You just try being the wife of a rising young publisher and the mother of a publisher's three daughters and see whether it's a whole time job or not . . . There can't be more than one centre to a marriage. And if the man isn't the centre, it's an unhappy marriage.' Laurence leaves her son to be cared for by

someone else, goes to work in an advertising agency and discovers, as did Rosalie,

> the difficulty of doing decently three jobs of work. She saw
> that neither her son nor her husband got the best out of her,
> and the Napier Advertising Service had just been taught
> that there were times when it ran neither first, second,
> nor third, but was left out of the running
> altogether – scratched at the post . . .
>
> If she could do eight or nine or ten hours' work in seven at
> the office, she could, beginning at nine, get away at five
> every day. That meant two hours for Sandy, not counting
> Saturday afternoon and Sunday, and every evening for
> Dysart, if he wanted her.
>
> 'It's all a question of getting down to it,' she said.
>
> She got down to it with methodical ardour and a fair
> measure of success.[26]

But after many vicissitudes she too accepts that she cannot
cope. ' "A woman like me . . . can't do three things . . . a
woman ought not to be a mother at all if she isn't prepared to do
it properly." '[27] And Laurence realises that her sense of
frustration is an outcome of modern life – in the past women
had played a crucial role in running their homes, but since the
Industrial Revolution the housewife's traditional skills had
become redundant, with a consequent lessening of her sense of
worth: ' "If I'd had still-rooms and linen rooms and dairies . . . I
might never have wanted to get out." ' So Laurence returns
north to the family home and concludes that the best life has to
offer is the ability to cherish another. Of course, as she recognises, 'the ideal itself is a little out of fashion' but that is to be her
main commitment: to cherish, to get away to the country as
often as possible, and to keep her brain ticking over with a part-
time job ('Come in one day a week. Take stuff home to read . . .
do some editing for me', a kindly publisher tells her).

Laurence's perceptive recognition of the waning role of
women and her desire to do useful work clearly owes something
to Olive Schreiner's *Woman and Labour* (1911), which is a plea
for women to emerge from the parasitic role that has been thrust

upon them by modern life. Schreiner points out that in our society women's work has contracted and, with the division of labour, many women have been forced into parasitic dependence on men:

> Exactly as in the earlier conditions of society an excessive and almost crushing amount of the most important physical labour generally devolved upon the female, so under modern civilised conditions among the wealthier and fully civilised classes, an unduly excessive share of labour tends to devolve upon the male.[28]

The male can certainly have no grounds for complaining that modern life has deprived him of an active role or 'reduced him to a condition of morbid inactivity'. But women have been robbed almost wholly 'of the more valuable of her ancient domain of productive and social labour'.

> Our spinning-wheels are all broken . . . Our hoes and our grindstones passed from us long ago . . . The history of our household drinks we know no longer . . . Day by day machine-prepared and factory-produced viands take a larger and larger place in the dietary of rich and poor, till the working man's wife places before her household little that is of her preparation . . . The army of rosy milkmaids has passed away for ever, to give place to the cream-separator and the, largely, male-and-machinery manipulated butter pat.
>
> Year by year, day by day, there is a silently working but determined tendency for the sphere of woman's domestic labours to contract itself; and the contraction is marked exactly in proportion as that complex condition which we term 'modern civilisation' is advanced.[29]

Olive Schreiner would not allow for compromise. Her book ends with this famous and rousing homage to idealism:

> Always in our dreams we hear the turn of the key that shall close the door of the last brothel; the clink of the last coin that pays for the body and soul of a woman; the falling of

the last wall that encloses artificially the activity of woman
and divides her from man; always we picture the love of
the sexes, as, once a dull, slow, creeping worm; then a
torpid, earthy chrysalis; at last the full-winged insect,
glorious in the sunshine of the future.[30]

Laurence had once had these kind of ideals but is forced into the
kind of compromise that has been the lot of all married women
since they emerged from the linen room. (The theme recurs in
several of Storm Jameson's novels, for instance in *Company
Parade* (1934): the conflict between domestic life and work
remains, but the heroine in the later novels often abandons husband and child for her work, however guiltily.) E. M. Delafield
wrote a novel which treats the dilemma in a humorous way, in
which she shows a woman who has, for purely selfish motives,
cherished her career too much and her family too little. *Faster,
Faster* (1936) could not have been written before the 1930s since
at the heart of the novel is the assumption that the career woman
is here to stay. But given that women want to work, to what
extent should their families be sacrificed? (It was the question
asked by the daughter in the Dutch novel *The Rebel Generation*,
although the children never ask *directly* why Mother's precious
work should always come first.)

Claudia, the heroine, has qualities similar to those of Alice in
Rebecca West's short story 'The Salt of the Earth' which had
been published the year before (see page 168.) She puts herself
second continually, stretching herself in all directions and never
complaining, taking all burdens on her shoulders both at home
and in the office of the agency she runs. She, like Alice, will not
accept that she adores martyrdom, abhors the role of second
fiddle and actually runs her life only to suit herself and not, as she
always pretends, because she is devotedly serving others. As in
the Rebecca West story, her relations try and disillusion her but
she will not listen. Her sister tells her that 'you like seeing yourself
as Atlas supporting the world' and tries to make her see that she's
'posing' – ' "Aren't you, all day and every day, acting as the
perfect, selfless mother, the sole support of them all, the woman
who's gallantly working herself to death?" '

Claudia, again like Alice, dies. And the last chapter shows her family completely happy, free of her stranglehold, able to live unencumbered by the guilt caused by another's martyrdom. And yet Claudia had played out her role on the assumption that she was indispensable and that without her the whole edifice would crumble. She is a classic example of the woman who insists on doing everything, refusing to delegate to anyone, being self-deprecating and 'honest' while forcing those around her into roles of dependence when they would be much happier thinking for themselves. She also epitomises the woman who prefers to have a paid job but continues her domestic role as an excuse for martyrdom.

Dorothy Canfield's brilliant novel *The Home-Maker* (1924) dissects another aspect of this theme. The novel, set in America, is about a deeply unhappy marriage in which the husband is inefficient at his job and has lost all respect for himself and the wife is so frustrated by having to stay ineffectually at home watching his incompetence that she has become a martinet. But the husband, Lester, has a crippling accident and his wife, Evangeline, gets a job as a sales assistant. And so life takes a wonderful turn for them both, with Lester able, from his sick-bed, to cherish and understand his children and his wife able to excel in the way she had always longed for and escape the family's dependence on her.

There are memorable descriptions of father and children together, for example an eight-page scene in which Lester allows his son to learn how to use an egg-beater. It is perfectly clear that Evangeline is happy and fulfilled earning more money than her husband had ever dreamed of and he is equally happy bringing up the children with tenderness and love. But then one night Evangeline sees her husband turning over in his sleep, for the first time since his accident.

> She was a wicked woman. God be merciful to me, a sinner. She had no heart. She did not want her husband to get well. She did not want to go home and live with her children.
>
> But she must. She must! There was no other way . . . If Lester got well, of course he could not stay at home and keep house and take care of the children . . . no able-

bodied man ever did that. What would people say? It was out of the question. People would laugh at Lester. They would laugh at her. They would not admire her any more. What would people say if she did not go back at once to the children? She who had always been so devoted to them, she whom people pitied now because she was forced to be separated from them.[31]

When Lester realises he can walk again, his reaction is the same. He is sick at heart at the thought of going back to his loathed job and seeing his children shrivelling into the timid souls they had been before his accident; for now he has learnt to understand his wife's faults and virtues as well as his own.

Eva had passionate love and devotion to give them, but neither patience nor understanding. There was no sacrifice in the world which she would not joyfully make for her children except to live with them. They had tried that for fourteen dreadful years and knew what it brought them. That complacent unquestioned generalization, 'The mother is the natural home-maker'; what a juggernaut it had been in their case! How poor Eva, drugged by the cries of its devotees, had cast herself down under its grinding wheels — and had dragged the children in under with her. It wasn't because Eva had not tried her best. She had nearly killed herself trying. But she had been like a gifted mathematician set to paint a picture.[32]

Lester wonders whether he and his wife could exchange roles but he knows this is impossible. Tradition decreed 'that men are of worth in so far as they achieve . . . material success, and worthless if they do not'.

Why, the fanatic feminists were right, after all. Under its greasy camouflage of chivalry, society is really based on a contempt for women's work in the home. The only women who were paid, either in human respect or in money, were women who gave up their traditional job of creating harmony out of human relationships and did something really useful, bought or sold or created material objects. As

81

for any *man's* giving his personality for the woman's work of trying to draw out of children the best there might be in them . . . fiddling foolishness! Leave it to the squaws! He was sure that he was the only man who had ever conceived even the possibility of such a lapse from virile self-respect as to do what all women are supposed to do. He knew well enough that other men would feel for such a conception on his part a stupefaction only equalled by their red-blooded scorn.[33]

After a night of agonised mental torment Lester makes up his mind to sham and persuades the doctor into the conspiracy. He has accepted that society would not condone his role of home-maker if it was voluntary but if he continued to be forced by illness to be the wife then it would admire him for his pluck.

Ironically, had Lester wanted to stay at home in order to paint or write, society would accept this – as long as he did not also bring up his children himself. For Cyril Connolly's classic observation that 'there is no more sombre enemy of good art than the pram in the hall' is universally accepted as a truism – no self-respecting male could hope to do creative work within earshot of tiny feet. Whether women can is another question, which makes the theme of creativity and women crucially important in any discussion about feminism.

Very few novels by women in the period 1914–39 described a woman finally giving up love and marriage for her career. The moral was almost always that in order to be happy, to fulfil herself as a woman, it was important for her to sacrifice, to dote and – eventually – to self-abnegate. After all, the staple readership of the circulating libraries was largely women who had done just this, or, if they were unmarried, they were presumed to be longing not to be. But there were a few exceptions, apart from the novels of Storm Jameson already mentioned. One of these, *Mainspring* (1922) by V. H. Friedlaender, was described by Winifred Holtby in a 'Letter to a Friend':

> The theme is to some extent similar to that of *This Freedom*, but differently worked out. The heroine is an artist who eventually renounces the man she loves for the

sake of her art. It is a hard thing to do well, but the author somehow has made it convincing both that the girl would act so and that her pictures would be worth it.[34]

The heroine, Bridget, decides that to marry her lover would be to sacrifice her genius. Bolstered by the unstinting praise of a world-famous art-critic she gives her lover up.

It was done; it could never be undone. And all for what – for what? *That she might paint!*

In that moment it seemed to her that she had surely touched the limits of human folly, so insignificant did she feel, so void of all power or inspiration, so impiously pre-sumptuous . . . Now she understood what it would mean to fail. It would mean becoming one of that great, tragic army of women without a mainspring; mateless women drifting despairingly away from their youth, clutching at straws of memory and hope as they passed, finding them break, ending on the pitiless rocks. It would mean the sense of loss and frustration, the fading face, the body weakening beneath the starvation of the mind; insomnia, nerves, disease; death before life, death without life.[35]

So she goes off to her garret, knowing what she will miss but determined to be a painter. We have to assume that she has 'a room of her own and five hundred a year'[36] for any woman at this period who wanted to be creative and was not married had to have a private income; women could not at this time think in terms of the part-time teaching job. They had either to make money by their art, or give it up to support themselves, or live off someone else's money. It is this latter assumption that permeated Virginia Woolf's discussions of women and fiction in *A Room of One's Own* (1928) and her related essays: the male literary tradition would continue to retain its grip as long as women remained financially dependent on men and as long as male-dominated conventions continued to hold sway.

The case against male self-importance is memorably put by Terence Hewet in Virginia Woolf's first novel *The Voyage Out* (1915). He is prompted by Rachel's frank admission that she found Gibbon boring to wonder aloud at the stranglehold exerted by men over women.

'The respect that women, even well-educated, very able women, have for men,' he went on. 'I believe we must have the sort of power over you that we're said to have over horses. They see us three times as big as we are or they'd never obey us. For that very reason, I'm inclined to doubt that you'll ever do anything even when you have the vote.' He looked at her reflectively. She appeared very smooth and sensitive and young. 'It'll take at least six generations before you're sufficiently thick-skinned to go into law courts and business offices. Consider what a bully the ordinary man is,' he continued, 'the ordinary hard-working, rather ambitious solicitor or man of business with a family to bring up and a certain position to maintain. And then, of course, the daughters have to give way to the sons; the sons have to be educated; they have to bully and shove for their wives and families, and so it all comes over again. And meanwhile there are the women in the background . . . Do you really think that the vote will do you any good?'[37]

In this key passage it is clear that Virginia Woolf is describing an ideal man who has no respect for the world of 'telegrams and anger', one who can see things from the point of view of a woman, who actually likes women. When Rachel describes to him her particular 'accumulation of unrecorded life'[38] she is confused when Hewet tells her that he is interested in her description because she is a woman. All the men in Rachel's sphere up till now have provided for women, tolerated women, but have not been interested in them. And here is one who can actually laugh at the way men have organised society.

'There's no doubt it helps to make up for the drudgery of a profession if a man's taken very, very seriously by everyone – if he gets appointments, and has offices and a title, and lots of letters after his name, and bits of ribbons and degrees. I don't grudge it 'em, though sometimes it comes over me – what an amazing concoction! What a miracle the masculine conception of life is – judges, civil servants, army, navy, Houses of Parliament, lord mayors – what a world we've made of it! Look at Hirst now. I assure you,' he said, 'not a day's passed since we came here without a discussion as to whether he's to stay on at Cambridge or to go to the Bar. It's his career – his sacred career. And if I've heard it twenty times, I'm sure his mother and sister have heard it five hundred times. Can't you imagine the family conclaves, and the sister told to run out and feed the rabbit because St John must have the schoolroom to himself – "St John's working", "St John wants his tea brought to him". Don't you know the kind of thing? No wonder that St John thinks it a matter of considerable importance. It is too. He has to earn his living. But St John's sister – ' Hewet puffed in silence. 'No one takes her seriously, poor dear. She feeds the rabbits.'[39]

These lines have been engraved on my heart ever since I first read them in my teens and I believe they constitute one of the most important statements in feminist writing this century. They are also a clue as to why Virginia Woolf has been criticised by some for her failure to carry her feminism through into her novels. Early on in her writing life she had created a man who liked women, who was in an intellectual sense androgynous because he empathised so deeply with women. After that she turned to her primary interest, which was women. She was bored by the idea of anti-male carping or by creating more 'sympathetic' men; so she confined her attention to portraying the woman's perspective. When she tried, as in *Jacob's Room* (1922), to create a male point of view she endowed her hero with so much feminine perception that as a man he is unconvincing. In her other novels she describes the world through female eyes and men are very much the minor focus of interest. Only occasionally in her fiction does she lampoon male egoism, as in the following passage from *The Years* (1937) where Peggy is talking to a spare-time poet:

My people, he was saying . . . hunted. Her attention

wandered. She had heard it all before. I,I,I – he went on. It was like a vulture's beak pecking, or a vacuum-cleaner sucking, or a telephone bell ringing. I,I,I. But he couldn't help it, not with that nerve-drawn egotist's face, she thought, glancing at him. He could not free himself, could not detach himself. He was bound on the wheel with tight iron hoops. He had to expose, had to exhibit. But why let him? she thought, as he went on talking. For what do I care about his 'I,I,I'? Or his poetry? Let me shake him off then, she said to herself, feeling like a person whose blood has been sucked, leaving all the nerve-centres pale. She paused. He noted her lack of sympathy. He thought her stupid, she supposed.

'I'm tired,' she apologized. 'I've been up all night,' she explained. 'I'm a doctor –'

The fire went out of his face when she said 'I'. That's done it – now he'll go, she thought. He can't be 'you' – he must be 'I'. She smiled. For up he got and off he went.[40]

Peggy is here ridding herself of temporary male domination. But, as Virginia Woolf made explicit, the creative woman will only ever be able to find her own style when she is free, independent and untrammelled by the burdens of domesticity; and when she is unhampered by male traditions and impositions. Until this day comes she has to charm, conciliate and tell lies, she has to defer to 'the extreme conventionality of the other sex'[41] and she even has to use an unwieldy male sentence unsuited for a woman's use. But 'give her another hundred years . . . let her speak her mind and leave out half that she now puts in'[42] and she will write a masterpiece.

May Sinclair had written a novel in 1910 about a group of writers struggling to do this without changing the accustomed social patterns and conventions. *The Creators* is about the problem of reconciling marriage and writing. Three varying marriages are described but the most interesting is Jinny's, since she becomes a well-known middlebrow novelist who is shown as a warm, very human personality; whereas her fellow-writer Tanqueray writes more 'difficult' fiction and has a moody, egotistical character. ('He doesn't see anything except his genius.')

Jinny's problems begin when she has children and domestic life inevitably encroaches; the crisis comes when her adorable baby is six months and she tells the nurse to 'take him down to the bottom of the garden, where I can't see him'. Her husband, who has always admired her 'genius', finds his ideas have changed. He now regards genius

> as a malady, a thing abnormal, disastrous, not of nature; or if normal and natural – for Jinny – a thing altogether subordinate to Jinny's functions as a wife and mother. There was no sane man who would not take that view, who would not feel that nature was supreme. And Jinny had proved that left to nature, her womanhood, she was sound and perfect. Jinny's genius had had, as he put it, pretty well its fling. It was nature's turn.[43]

A compromise is reached in the form of a housekeeper and Jinny 'gave her mornings to her work, a portion of the afternoon to her son, and the evenings to her husband'. At first 'she was a fine juggler on her tight-rope' but then tension develops. Breakfast in bed helps, even if the relations deem it rather sad; eventually, however, her health breaks down and it is decided that her genius is a crime, 'a power in the highest degree destructive and malign, a power utterly disintegrating to its possessor and yet a power entirely within her own control'. Jinny is submissive but cannot escape retribution and her third child, a girl, is born dead.

So she goes away to Devon, but even there cannot find peace since it is there that she recognises that she loves Tanqueray. When she returns home on learning of her child's illness, rumours are rife that she has left her husband. But May Sinclair allows us no pulp novel reconciliation. The ending is inconclusive; marriage and creativity are irreconcilable unless one partner abnegates her entire being to the other's genius. And it is not in the nature of genius nor of men to be self-abnegating; so that when the creative partner is a woman the problem will be insuperable. And the only one of Jinny's friends who goes on writing is Nina, who lives true to her belief that 'virginity was the law, the indispensable condition'.

Cicely Hamilton must have approved of Nina, for her revo
against 'destined' marriage echoes Nina's belief. In *Marriage as
Trade* (1909), written the year before *The Creators* wa
published, she wrote:

> It is not, of course, actual sexual intercourse, legalised or
> the reverse, which renders a woman incapable of great
> creative art; it is the servile attitude of mind and soul
> induced in her by the influences brought to bear on her in
> order to fit her for the compulsory trade of marriage . . .
> their aim [is] to induce the girl who would eventually
> become a woman to conform to one particular and
> uniform type . . . Hence the crushing out of individuality,
> the elimination of the characteristics that make for variety
> and the development of the imitative at the expense of the
> creative qualities . . . The deliberate stunting and repres-
> sion of her intellectual faculties, the setting up for her
> admiration and imitation of the ideal of the 'silly angel',
> have all contributed to make of her not only a domestic
> animal, more or less sleek and ornamental, but Philistine as
> well.[44]

A woman can, in short, only be successful in literature by di
carding the 'conventional ideals of dependence' and cultivatir
an individual cast of mind – and marriage cannot align wit
these ideals.

Again and again women writers ask themselves whether the
can juggle their work, their husband, their children and the
friends, still have some time left for themselves *and* retain the
sanity. As Anne Morrow Lindbergh observed in 1937:

> Isn't it possible for a woman to be a woman and yet
> produce something tangible besides children, something
> that stands up in a man's world? In other words, is it
> possible to live up to women's standards and men's
> standards at the same time? Is it possible to make them the
> same? (As the feminists do.)
> I have finally, through many stages, come round to the
> conclusion that for me, it isn't . . . I am not prepared to

sacrifice . . . those advantages and qualities that are truly feminine.[45]

For her the important aspect of a woman is that she should be 'rounded and receptive and sensitive in all directions'. And she feels optimistic:

Oddly enough, you know, I feel that out of this new rounded life one is going to get 'tangible' results from women, too, but only as by-products and in *quantity*. But I feel that out of a truly feminine life some very great art might spring: something far more startling than anything we have seen from women yet – not much, but pure gold. A little of it has come already: Virginia Woolf writing about Mrs Ramsay in *To the Lighthouse*; Vita Sackville-West in *All Passion Spent*; the thread about marriage that runs through Rebecca West's *Thinking Reed*; some of Rosamond Lehmann's writing. There must be more, but I haven't read much lately. And in the other worlds of art and accomplishments. But never 'professional' in the sense that men's accomplishments are professional.[46]

Apart from the novels Anne Morrow Lindbergh mentions, which are indeed about 'truly feminine' lives, other writers worried at the problem of reconciling domesticity and writing. In *Far End* (1926), May Sinclair describes a novelist who is driven, by the pram in the hall and his baby's crying, to rent a room away from home. He has two affairs, one sensual and one intellectual, but before he and his wife have come to a parting of the ways his baby luckily passes the four-year-old milestone and stops crying, life gets back to normal and his wife can do his typing once more because she is not constantly alert for the baby's wails. And the Provincial Lady in E. M. Delafield's *Diary of a Provincial Lady* (1930) tries to 'find time for herself' – to manage her household and write short stories. Neither occupation ever quite succeeds in shaking off the other:

June 3rd – Astounding and enchanting change in the weather, which becomes warm. I carry chair, writing materials, rug, and cushion into the garden, but am called in to have a look at the Pantry Sink, please, as it seems to have blocked itself up. Attempted return to garden frustrated by arrival of note from the village concerning Garden Fête arrangements, which requires immediate answer, necessity for speaking to the butcher on the telephone, and sudden realisation that Laundry List hasn't yet been made out, and the Van will be here at eleven.[47]

As Virginia Woolf wrote: 'How any woman with a family ever put pen to paper I cannot fathom. Always the bell rings and the baker calls.'[48] E. M. Delafield was unusual in continuing, through financial necessity, to keep up the struggle both to write and to run her household. Sadly, she never wrote a novel in which the heroine is forced to earn a living by her diminished circumstances. Selina in Edna Ferber's novel *So Big* (1924) turns herself, after a tremendous struggle, into a businesswoman, as does the heroine of *Joanna Godden* (1921) by Sheila Kaye-Smith. Others take an interest in the world of money merely because they can no longer be content with the shrinking-violet role. In Amber Reeves's *A Lady and Her Husband* (1914), Mary is introduced to radical ideas by her daughter. When she learns the truth about the way her husband has been running his chain of teashops she feels it is hypocritical to continue with her former easy-going life – she realises that its comfort and luxury were entirely dependent on the exploitation of hundreds of over-worked and under-paid waitresses. She determines to live a new, better existence, one which is not supported by the degradation of others. How passionate is her concern is not quite clear, but it is deep enough to make her leave her comfortable home and take lodgings while she works out her feelings. She is wonderfully contrasted to her husband, who is ordinary, uncorrupt, but all too human and comfortable to want to change.

Some women writers produced fiction with semi-autobiographical portraits of women who try hard to be creative and maternal simultaneously. The heroine of *Hostages to Fortune* (1933) by Elizabeth Cambridge soon gives up the unequal struggle to write a novel. 'By the time she had provided for their bodily needs she had little energy left for their affections. She didn't want to love anybody or to be loved. She wanted to sit down, and not even think.'[49] The heroine of Enid Bagnold's *The Squire* (1938) finds that maternity *is* creativity in a deeply satisfying way. And the heroine of Dorothy Canfield's *The Brimming Cup* (1921) finally decides that it is possible to be receptive and sensitive while continuing to cherish her brood. All the women in these novels see life as it is, accept their femininity and their role ungrudgingly and reconcile themselves to their loss of freedom. Ultimately it is true that 'if there was chicken, she took the leg; if there was a draught she sat in it'.[50]

It is not only the spirit of renunciation and self-sacrifice that debars women from being creative, nor their gentleness which forbids them the necessary ruthlessness to be creative. They are hampered also by their vitality, a quality remarked on by Rebecca West: she would have expected that

> women, with their greater faculty of being pleased by little things and imponderables, would write more and better poetry. The explanation [why not] lies perhaps in the unfortunate identity of the source of genius and the source of sexual attractiveness; vitality is the secret of both. This means that the women who are most fitted for the arts are the first to be called away to follow an occupation than which is none more continuously prohibitive of the listening attitude of mind which is the necessary prelude to the creative process.[51]

'The listening attitude of mind' is the faculty most women with children long to have back again – mostly they are merely listening for a cry from the nursery rather than for the faint breath of the muse. Even women without children find that the womanly role is not exactly conducive to creativity. Katharine Mansfield wrote to John Middleton Murry that

> the house seems to take up so much time if it isn't looked after with some sort of method. I mean . . . when I have to clean up twice over or wash up extra unnecessary things I get frightfully impatient and want to be working. So often this week, I've heard you and Gordon talking while I washed dishes. Well, someone's got to wash dishes and get

food. Otherwise − 'There's nothing in the house but eggs to eat.' [After] you . . . have gone I walk about with a mind full of ghosts of saucepans and primus stoves and 'Will there be enough to go round?' . . . and you calling (whatever I am doing) '*Tig*, isn't there going to be tea? It's five o'clock' as though I were a dilatory housemaid.[52]

Katharine Mansfield had no children and was also forced by her illness to be a good deal apart from her demanding husband. Others, such as Vita Sackville-West and Virginia Woolf, were married to men who revered their wives and were perfectly prepared to defer to their needs for peace and quiet. Even the unmarried, such as May Sinclair, organised devoted housekeepers and remote writing 'huts'. Margaret Kennedy always had nannies for her children, while Stella Benson, who had no children and an amenable husband, wrote to him firmly:

The only thing I cling to in the last resort [is that] I *must* put my writing first . . . I insist on being a writer first and a wife second . . . I wasn't *born* to be a wife to anyone, but to be a writer − however I am your wife, and I'm very glad I am; and if only you would realize that I can only be the kind of wife I am − only secondarily domestic − it would be much better.[53]

On the other hand, 'George Egerton', who *did* have a child, wrote towards the end of her life that 'until woman makes as deliberate a choice as a nun who never bungles her job because she accepts the sacrifice her vocation demands, she will never meet man, at his best, on equal terms as a writer − and perhaps not then.'[54]

Perhaps the last word should be Lady Slane's in *All Passion Spent* (1931) by Vita Sackville-West. She is the newly widowed wife of an extraordinarily distinguished man whose life has been heaped with honours. Upon his death she, at the age of eighty-eight, is firm in her resolve to do what she wants, which is to live peacefully in Hampstead and do whatever she feels like for the first time in her life. She thinks back over her life and remembers Henry's reaction when she asked where in the scheme of things there was going to be a studio for her? He had smiled again, more fondly and indulgently than ever, and had said there would be plenty of time to see about that, but for his own part, he fancied that after marriage she would find plenty of other occupations to help her pass the days.

Then, indeed, she felt trapped and wild . . . [yet] he had only taken for granted the things he was entitled to take for granted, thereby ranging himself with the women and entering into the general conspiracy to defraud her of her chosen life . . . She had her answer. She never referred to it again.

Yet she was no feminist. She was too wise a woman to indulge in such luxuries as an imagined martyrdom. The rift between herself and life was not the rift between the worker and the dreamer.[55]

And accordingly she subdued all her ambition to her love for her husband.

She was, after all, a woman. Thwarted as an artist, was it perhaps possible to find fulfilment in other ways? Was there, after all, some foundation for the prevalent belief that woman should minister to man? Had the generations been right, the personal struggle wrong? Was there something beautiful, something active, something creative even, in her apparent submission to Henry? Could she not balance herself upon the tight-rope of her relationship with him, as dangerously and precariously as in the act of creating a picture? Was it not possible to see the tones and half-tones of her life with him as she might have seen the blue and violet shadows of a landscape; and so set them in relation and ordain their values, that she thereby forced them into beauty? Was not this also an achievement of the sort peculiarly suited to women? of the sort, indeed, which women alone could compass; a privilege, a prerogative, not to be despised? All the woman in her answered, yes! All the artist in her countered, no![56]

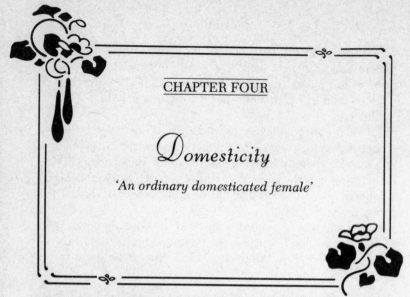

CHAPTER FOUR

Domesticity

'*An ordinary domesticated female*'

The marriage ceremony is the novel's conventional happy ending. But the ensuing domestic bliss is an unfruitful topic for fiction, presumably because it is even-tempered, everyday and therefore dull. In the first work of fiction she ever wrote, George Eliot apologised to her readers for writing about someone commonplace:

> 'An utterly uninteresting character!' I think I hear a lady reader exclaim – Mrs Farthingale, for example, who prefers the ideal in fiction; to whom tragedy means ermine tippets, adultery, and murder; and comedy, the adventures of some personage who is quite a 'character'.[1]

But she believes it would be to the reader's gain to be able to see into 'a human soul that looks out through dull grey eyes, and that speaks in a voice of quite ordinary tones'.

Yet, once Dorothea (in *Middlemarch*) is in turmoil no longer and has found her life's companion, the novel ends, with only a brief note to tell the reader what happened afterwards. And once Natasha has dwindled contentedly into a wife, Tolstoy tells us almost nothing about the texture of her life except that her upper lip is faintly and maternally shadowed with hair and that her main preoccupation is the colour of her babies' napkins.

Generations of female readers have regretted these omissions, believing that their 'quite ordinary tones' were as interesting a topic for fiction as the extremes preferred by Mrs Farthingale.

Male writers tended to ignore domesticity and female ones generally followed suit. As Cicely Hamilton pointed out:

> Women who have treated of maternity in books or pictures have usually handled it in exactly the same spirit in which it is commonly handled by men – from what may be termed the conventional or Raphaelesque point of view. That is to say, they treat it from the superficial point of view of the outsider, the person who has no actual experience of the subject.[2]

But, during the 1920s, women writers gradually began to write about basic, everyday middle-class female preoccupations such as married love, the bringing up of children, the finding and keeping of domestic help, the choosing and enduring of schools – describing the pleasures and pains of a generally rather steadfast daily life. A new kind of female writer was for the first time addressing herself to a new kind of female reader, asking questions such as Norah's in *A Note in Music* (1930) by Rosamond Lehmann.

> Why should this vampire family so prey on her and pin her down that even one afternoon's freedom became a matter of importance, to be regretted afterwards? Why should she let him for ever drain her to sustain himself? . . . Only, to-night she hated the active life, wanted to have a rest from this perpetual crumbling of the edges, this shredding out of one's personality upon minute obligations and responsibilities. She wanted, even for a few moments, to feel her own identity peacefully floating apart from them all, confined and dissolved within a shell upon which other people's sensibilities made no impression. But this was not possible, never for a second, in one's own home.
>
> What it is, she thought, ceasing with a jerk to indulge in self-pitying reflections, to be an ordinary domesticated female![3]

At first, few defied the convention that once a woman was married her life was of no interest unless she was, or was tempted to be, unfaithful to her husband. But E. M. Delafield broke new ground in this respect. She, of all her contemporaries, excelled at describing the everyday life of the upper middle-class women of England and in one of her best novels, *The Way Things Are* (1927), the 'love interest' is clearly a sop to convention rather than the main theme.

Laura, its heroine, married for the same reason as so many others (but is honest enough to admit this to herself).

> She had been rather anxious to be married, just when she first met Alfred.
>
> The war was over, and there had been a question of her returning home, which she did not want to do, and so many other people seemed to be getting married . . . She wanted the experience of marriage, and she was just beginning to be rather afraid of missing it altogether, because so many of the men belonging to her own generation had gone.[4]

Her life is perfectly happy in a rather uneventful way.

> Alfred had sometimes said, and frequently implied, that Laura was ruled by her servants.
>
> Laura, in return, said and implied that Alfred did not know anything at all about the domestic problem from the inside.
>
> She often felt that Alfred did not understand her, and that he still less understood what a difficult and fatiguing affair life was for her, and it also vexed her to know that their ideas differed widely on the important subject of Edward's and Johnnie's upbringing, but nevertheless, Laura knew that she and Alfred were what is called 'happily married' . . . they lived at Applecourt, which had belonged to the Temples for three generations, and the house had nine bedrooms, two bath-rooms and three sitting-rooms, and two kitchens and a pantry, and a good deal of passage-way, and a staircase with two landings, and no lighting whatever.

And there was – or, very frequently, there were not – a cook-general, a house-parlourmaid, and a children's nurse. A gardener received thirty-five shillings a week and a cottage and helped Alfred with the cleaning of the car, and worked in the garden and in the kitchen-garden.

Laura had been brought up in a house that entirely resembled Applecourt, except that it had been more comfortable, because everything had been much less expensive and difficult, in the time before the war.[5]

At the beginning of the novel, Laura is feeling, as usual, that life should have more to offer than daily confrontations with cook.

Gladys was twenty-six and Laura thirty-four. Gladys was the servant of Laura, paid to work for her. She had been at Applecourt only six months, and it was highly improbable that she would remain for another six. Nevertheless, it was Gladys who, in their daily interviews, was entirely at her ease, and Laura who was nervous.

'I'll just see what we've got in the larder.'

The attentuated remainder of the Sunday joint was in the larder, with half of a cold rhubarb tart and a fragment of jelly.

'Better make the beef into cottage pie,' said Laura. 'And what about a pudding for mid-day?'

As though these words possessed a magic, her mind, as she uttered them, became impervious to any idea whatever. Just as though the word 'pudding' had the power to stultify intelligence.

Laura looked at the cook, and the cook looked out of the little barred window of the larder, entirely detached.

'It's so difficult to think of a *new* pudding, isn't it?' said Laura pleadingly.

Gladys smiled, as though at a small jest.[6]

Laura's existence is beset with difficulties with her husband, children, neighbours, nanny or cook – but E. M. Delafield makes it quite plain by the satirical tones in which she describes these that as far as fiction is concerned their interest-value is second best. So her heroines face up to domestic trivia but they also devalue them: the reader may smile at and sympathise with their predicament, but it is ephemeral, what Virginia Woolf called 'the froth of the moment'.

> To know the outside of one's age, its dresses and its dances and its catchwords, has an interest and even a value which the spiritual adventures of a curate, or the aspiration of a high-minded schoolmistress, solemn as they are, for the most part lack. It might well be claimed, too, that to deal with the crowded dance of modern life so as to produce the illusion of reality needs far higher literary skill than to write a serious essay upon the poetry of John Donne or the novels of M. Proust. The novelist, then, who is a slave to life and concocts his books out of the froth of the moment is doing something difficult, something which pleases, something which, if you have a mind that way, may even instruct. But his work passes as the year 1921 passes, as fox-trots pass, and in three years' time looks as dowdy and dull as any other fashion which has served its turn and gone its way.[7]

But women readers, whose lives are of necessity filled with the minutiae of the material world, have always wanted to know about 'the outside of one's age' and there is no real reason, except that the conventions of criticism had so decreed, why fiction that describes it should lack staying power.

Why are Laura's troubles with cook more dowdy and dull than her troubles with her lover? The answer lies buried in the traditions of fiction in a culture which is class-bound and male-dominated. Yet the effect on the female reader, sixty years later, is to leave her with a desperate and almost perverted yearning for a mere crumb of everyday reality. We would be enchanted to find a novel written in the 1920s or 1930s which actually told us how a woman organised contraception. How did Mrs Dalloway hold up her stockings? What did the breast-feeding mother do about milk leaking on to her dress? Yet when an already well-established writer like Naomi Mitchison tried to be straightforward about matters such as contraception in *We*

Have Been Warned (1935), she encountered great difficulty in having the novel published.

There are many critics who would retort that this kind of domestic detail is of interest to no one, and there are some who would say that this is the trouble with women writers, anyway, that they avoid the large issues and concentrate on the trivial. It is only when women are certain of an overall female audience that they are free to explore one of the most basic of female preoccupations – the reconciliation and connections of the everyday with the issues which society defines as broader and more important. Virginia Woolf left the everyday out of her novels and confined it instead to her diaries and letters, to astonishing effect: there is no other diary of the twentieth century which conveys a woman's daily life in such absorbing detail. But it is literature's loss that this detail is excluded from the fiction, and there must be many readers who are now reading the novels with new delight because their imagination has been fed by the diaries with the everyday texture often so disastrously absent from the fiction.

So the true subject of *The Way Things Are* had to be Laura's love for Another Man and her resigned realisation that passion must not be allowed to destroy a home. To many female readers, however, the key issue is the heroine's role as the hub of a household, the focus without whom her dependents could not function, but who is forbidden a personality other than that of administrator and cherisher.

> She would never give herself to Duke, but hers was not the Great Refusal that ennobles the refuser and remains a beautiful memory for ever.
>
> The children, her marriage vows, the house, the ordering of the meals, the servants, the making of a laundry list every Monday – in a word, the things of respectability – kept one respectable. In a flash of unavoidable clear-sightedness, that Laura would never repeat if she could avoid it, she admitted to herself that the average attributes only, of the average woman, were hers.
>
> Imagination, emotionalism, sentimentalism . . . what

woman is not the victim of these insidious and fatally unpractical qualities?

But how difficult, Laura reflected, to see oneself as an average woman and not, rather, as one entirely unique, in unique circumstances . . .

It dawned upon her dimly that only by envisaging and accepting her own limitations could she endure the limitations of her surroundings.[8]

Many novelists describe their heroines at home to show them in context, but they are scene-setting rather than touching the heart of things. Virginia Woolf avoided the 'accumulation of unrecorded life'[9] almost completely after her first two novels and there must be many readers who would feel more empathy with Clarissa Dalloway if her domestic trappings had been evoked with a little more enthusiasm and her sensitive psychological antennae with a little less. The following passage is an unforgettable description of Mrs Dalloway in her role as domestic centre – but it is sadly brief:

The hall of the house was cool as a vault. Mrs Dalloway raised her hand to her eyes, and, as the maid shut the door to, and she heard the swish of Lucy's skirts, she felt like a nun who has left the world and feels fold round her the familiar veils and the response to old devotions. The cook whistled in the kitchen. She heard the click of the typewriter. It was her life, and bending her head over the hall table, she bowed beneath the influence, felt blessed and purified, saying to herself, as she took the pad with the telephone message on it, how moments like this are buds on the tree of life.[10]

And why did no one portray, in fiction, the kind of lives described by Margery Spring Rice in *Working-Class Wives, Their Health and Conditions* (1939)? Might not *Round About a Pound A Week* (1913) by Maud Pember Reeves have had more impact if presented to the public as a novel? The answers are clear: for fiction to be believable it demands first-hand knowledge and involvement from the writer – write about what you know is a familiar exhortation to the aspiring novelist. It would have been quite impossible for any of the poor, struggling, coping women described in either of these two books to have won the time or quiet to put pen to paper; or for 'Mrs Britain' in Leonora Eyles's documentary book *The Woman in the Little House* (1922) to do the same:

> She makes an effort to do the bedrooms, and manages to make the children's bed; she cleans the front; she talks to the passing coalman about his child in hospital; she goes to the shop for onions and hears all about Mrs Wilson's lodger; she peels the potatoes and hushes the baby; she slaps Tommy again because he has fetched the breakfast tea-spoons off the sink and poked them down the drain; looking through the window to see if she can see a neighbour's child who would come and play with Tommy, she sees Mrs Allen, and has a quarrel with her because Johnny Allen hit her Peroy last evening – and then the children come home from school. She washes the breakfast plates and doles out the greyish-looking stew that smells violently of onions, carefully reserving the most meaty portions on a big plate for Mr Britain's tea.
>
> The children eat rapidly; they have noticed that, when the doling out was done there was about a teacupful left in the saucepan, and the first to finish will probably get it.
>
> Mrs Britain, with a sigh, sits down to her plateful, but just as she does so the baby cries again, and, pushing the comforter in his mouth, she takes him on her knee. Her body, which feels tired and needs to relax, gets no rest; it has to remain taut to hold the child and enable her to eat at the same time.[11]

Leonora Eyles was trying to make people sit up and take notice. She attempted the same thing in her fiction, but because *The Woman in the Little House* is so straightforward and commonsensical it undoubtedly had more effect. In her fiction she is overwhelmingly emotional; in her non-fiction she can come straight out with remarks like 'looking round Number 9 Taraline Street [Peckham], one is struck by its supreme incon-

venience. *It was designed by men architects, and men don't live
and move and have their being in their houses.'*[12]

Twenty years later than Leonora Eyles, Edith Sitwell wrote,
at the height of the 'people's war',

> I would like to have written of those unrecorded women
> . . . who have never found fame, but whose daily example
> has helped to civilise our race: the ordinary women in their
> hundreds of thousands, beings whose warmth of heart and
> love of country and family, whose unswerving loyalty and
> gallantry, and gay, not dour, sense of duty, are among the
> glories of Britain.[13]

One can only regret that she did not write about them. For the
lives of the upper middle-class women who were described in
fiction were not the same as those of these 'unrecorded women';
compared with working-class women their lives were cushioned
and the reader needs to extend a different kind of sympathy to
the woman who complained that 'life would be perfectly
bearable if it were not for teeth and cooks' from that she bestows
upon 'Mrs Britain'. It is an inescapable fact that while a small
segment of British society was being articulately resentful about
registry offices and the housemaids who 'used to give me notice
as I tried to climb the stairs to my writing room',[14] the larger
proportion of the population was living from day to day enduring appalling hardship.

In her autobiography, Naomi Mitchison describes being the
hub of a large household, managing to entertain her friends and
write novels only because of the attentions of servants and
delivery-boys.

> So there we were and rooms were clean and tidy, the meals
> were cooked and served, orders to shops were delivered on
> time and there were at least three posts a day, all based on
> our being at the top end of the class structure. We could
> presumably have sat back and enjoyed it but we filled up
> all that lovely spare time which nobody seems to have
> today with our friends and children, ours and our friends'
> love affairs, our good causes and committees, Dick's bar
> work, my writing, interest in the other arts, letters, trips

abroad and as time went on the growth of social conscience.[15]

She expected her domestic life to run smoothly, was grateful when it did, but could not imagine life otherwise. It would not have been quite the thing for a woman of her social position to give up love affairs or a social conscience in order to do the housework herself, and in any case why should she have done so? The question might be asked with more relevance about the heroines of E. M. Delafield's novels, who often live in the country, do not entertain very much and have fewer children than the real-life Naomi Mitchison. I often think that Laura or the Provincial Lady would have been far happier giving up endless tussles with maids, cooks and nannies and doing the housework for themselves – but it occurred to very few to do this until they had to do so through necessity.

Sometimes the 'leisured' classes did not have it so easy. In an excellent explanation of 'the servant problem' Quentin Bell tries to make the modern reader have some imaginative understanding of what domestic life was like, even for the affluent.

Now, when Virginia Woolf went to Asham she found none of these [modern] commodities. To get there at all she had to walk or to bicycle for several miles or to go to the expense of a taxi or a fly. To make a light she had candles which dropped grease on the carpet, or lamps which smoked and had to be refilled with oil and trimmed every morning; heat was supplied by wood or coal – and coal was in short supply from 1916 to 1919; the coal had to be carried about in scuttles, grates had to be cleaned, fires laid, and if they were not competently managed they would fill the room with smoke or die miserably. In the country you got hot water by boiling it over a stove. Cold water had to be pumped up into a tank every day and Asham was furnished only with an earth closet. There were no refrigerators or frozen foods, a tin-opener was a kind of heavy dagger with which you attacked the tin hoping to win a jagged victory. All the processes of cooking and cleaning were incredibly laborious, messy and slow. There are still plenty of people who live in conditions of this kind or worse – far worse – but obviously in these circumstances someone must be perpetually at work if any kind of comfort or cleanliness is to be maintained.[16]

It was fortunate that, just as servants were becoming a rare luxury, houses were becoming somewhat easier to run. For example, by the end of the twenties there were 30,000 vacuum cleaners in Britain, by 1935 400,000 and by 1939 nearer a million. For some at least, a car made shopping easier and refrigerators meant that food did not have to be bought every day. But economic changes could not alter social expectations overnight – which accounts for the 'Nelly saga' running as an unbroken thread throughout Virginia Woolf's life. She could not manage entirely on her own but was weary of being dependent and having someone else dependent on her.

> In Bloomsbury the domestic servants were not offered the servile status of the Victorian age, but neither had they the businesslike employer/employee relationship which can be established today between the 'daily' woman who 'helps' and the woman who is 'helped'. They were part of the household, in a sense a part of the family, but they were also independent human beings, equals with feelings to be respected. Ideally, hopefully, they were friends. But how many of one's friends are there whom one can see daily, who are dependent on one for a livelihood, who hold one's comforts in their hands, and with whom one is never bored or cross?[18]

E. M. Delafield, Enid Bagnold and others, who were not as 'advanced' as Bloomsbury, still tried to maintain the old patriarchal relationship with their servants, lacking the courage and the *savoir-faire* to turn it into something more in keeping with the post-war world. Many women felt that their social status necessitated servants, but could not tolerate their friendship. Others openly hated living a life with strangers perpetually watching them but, again, lacked the initiative to organise their domestic arrangements on different lines. Over and over again in novels of this period one finds scenes of a couple lying in their twin beds as the light comes through the curtains. Gladys the maid either brings the tea late, or she forgets to run the bath, or she has quarrelled with cook and so there is an 'atmosphere'. Whether husband and wife are feeling argumentative or loving, the intrusion of someone whom they pay but who resents their payment can never have been a good start to the day.

In Martin Armstrong's *St Christopher's Day* (1928), the reader cannot but conclude that Christopher and Rosamund would have been happier together if only they had ever been alone and if she had had something to do all day. As it is, he is perpetually tense and can only relax on the bus journey to Lincoln's Inn Fields, while she neurotically builds up petty resentments and grudges with her mind empty of any real challenges. The novel covers the events of one day, which is Christopher's birthday.

> She was often angry with him for no reason, a blind, unreasoning resentment which she had long ceased to be able to control. But this morning she had a reason for her anger, though she was not aware of it as such. She was angry with him because it was his birthday and she knew she ought to wish him many happy returns. She ought to and she wanted to, but a sulky devil in her would not allow her, made it utterly impossible for her to speak pleasantly and kindly to him. And because she could not do so she felt resentful towards him.[19]

Because it is his special day Christopher makes a great effort. He leans across the table: ' "Rosamund . . . why do we go on like this? It's enough to break a man's heart." ' She replies in a 'cold, hard voice that chilled and wounded even herself: "My dear Christopher, what *are* you talking about?" '

Throughout the day they both brood: Rosamund because she has nothing else to do and Christopher because he is neglecting his legal practice.

> She had by now laid the dinner-table and arranged the fruit and flowers on it; the last details had been settled with the cook; the drawing-room was ready. There were still

four hours before the dinner-party, and the only matter that remained still unsettled was that of the wine.

She was sitting now in the little morning-room on the ground-floor, with her tea on a tray at her elbow. The preparations for the evening and this gnawing anxiety about Christopher had exhausted her, and she lay, with limbs and body relaxed, in a deep armchair, gazing into the fire.[20]

Rosamund, true to her middle-class background, uses her domestic circumstances to keep her husband at a distance, for the constant presence of servants often made it hard for members of the same family to be informal with each other. The quite unsurprising distance that could grow up between parent and child is illustrated by the following anecdote from the *Diaries* of Cynthia Asquith.

Eddie told a very good child story, about a dog called Paddy run over by motor and killed. Mother hardly dared break news to child. Did so during pudding. To her intense relief, after a second's pause, the child calmly continued pudding. Later mother heard crying, and found child with absolutely tear-congealed face. 'Oh Mummie, Paddy's killed.'

Mother: 'Yes, but I told you that at lunch, darling.'

Child: 'Oh, I thought you said it was Daddy!'[21]

For the child, his father was probably someone less loved and admired than the cook or butler, a state of affairs it would have occurred to few upper middle-class parents to change. Many preferred to keep their children at an emotional distance but became jealous if they became too fond of anyone else. The short-lived nanny in *Miss Linsey and Pa* (1936) by Stella Gibbons is told by her employer not to tell Tabiatha fairy stories. She should 'just leave her alone as much as possible to day-dream and make her own games . . . It's much better for the child than overheating her imagination with stories and complicated toys.' But after a weekend away

Perdita pushed open the door, which was ajar, and walked

in. The air of enchanted intimacy in the room struck her at
once with a shock of jealousy. Tabiatha, her hair ragged-
robin from sleep and her eyes reflecting the soft glow of a
bedside lamp, sat on Miss Linsey's knee, looking up into her
face, while Miss Linsey, gently stroking her little hand,
gazed down at her with smiling love.[22]

So Miss Linsey goes, because though a child's mother may not
love the child herself, she will not allow another to substitute for
her. They are all victims of the prevailing argument that a
middle-class woman must have help to be free to bring up her
children properly.

'The servant problem' runs like a thread throughout the
women's novels of this period. It is in a sense a parable of the
changes taking place in England between 1914 and 1939. In the
early part of the period it was to most middle-class women
merely an unavoidable annoyance (as Vera Brittain had found
on her fortnight's leave, 'the universal topics of maids and ration-
cards now completely dominated the conversation') but one they
were unsuited to deal with — Mrs Brittain demanded that her
daughter Vera return from her nursing at the Front to help her
because of the inefficiency of the domestic help then available.
As time went on the shortage of domestic help became an
accepted fact of life, although most middle-class women never
really understood why young girls preferred to work in a factory.
Many solutions were put forward: some even considered that the
servant problem might be solved if middle-class homes swapped
unmarried daughters amongst each other. A reviewer of *The
Psychology of the Servant Problem* (1925) by Violet Firth
suggested that 'Mary Ann' should go 'and the superfluous
daughter of one middle-class home must supplement the labour
of another middle-class home, thus solving the problem of
assistance for one woman and maintenance for another'.[23]

In Lettice Cooper's *The New House* (1936), Mrs Powell has
rather the same unthinking attitude to others as Mrs Brittain
appeared to have. Her daughter Rhoda is, however, able to see
the other point of view.

Rhoda came into the kitchen and stood just inside the

doorway, looking shy. She always felt shy when she penetrated to that downstairs world. The life lived so near to them and so far apart from them was a dark continent, full of unexplored mystery. It had distressed her lately to think that cook and Ivy were managing somehow to do the work of a house that had once been run by five maids. It had not really distressed her mother. Mrs Powell would be very kind to a servant who was ill or in trouble, but she could never feel that they were independent human beings. It astonished her that they should be unwilling to sacrifice an afternoon out for her convenience. When they had birthdays and were given presents of bath salts, powder-puffs, and coloured beads, she commented on it to Rhoda with surprise. What did they want with things like that? Regarding them at the bottom of her heart as automata, she handled them with assurance and precision, while Rhoda was secretly afraid of asking too much, and got a far more unwilling and inefficient service.[24]

To a less 'literary' writer there might have been material for a novel in these two entries from Virginia Woolf's diaries.

I am sordidly debating within myself the question of Nelly; the perennial question. It is an absurdity, how much time L & I have wasted in talking about servants. And it can never be done with because the fault lies in the system . . . Here is a fine rubbish heap left by our parents to be swept[25] . . . it is the freedom from servants that is the groundwork & bedrock of all this expansion. After lunch we are alone till Breakfast. I say, as I walk the downs, never again never again. Cost what it may, I will never put my head into that noose again.

I walk; I read; I write, without terrors and constrictions. I make bread. I cook mushrooms. I wander in & out of the kitchen. I have a resource besides reading.[26]

For the same reasons that 'Mrs Britain' could not have described her life in a novel, so England's great army of servants could not have described their lives. (Only in the 1970s have we had books, written long after the event, like Margaret Powell's *Below Stairs* to evoke servants' lives from their own point of view, and to leave us marvelling at a way of life in which other people were employed to iron boot laces and pages of *The Times*.) But the servant problem was fast becoming the province of the women's magazines. Before the war the 'society' journals such as *The Lady* and *The Queen* would have written about domestic matters only incidentally. But during the twenties there was a great expansion in magazines aimed at the middle classes. These ranged from the shilling ones such as *Homes and Gardens* and *Ideal Home* which then, as now, described affluent surroundings for middle-class couples, to the sixpenny ones for the rather more penny-pinching woman such as *Modern Woman*, *Wife and Home* or *Mother*. They all carried the same message – a woman's place is in the home and any normal woman should find cooking, shopping, sewing and mothering of all-absorbing interest. It was economic forces that dictated the tone of the magazines – once so many women had been forced out of their jobs after the return of the men in 1918 it was important that they should stay contentedly at home and they therefore had to accept domestic responsibility as an entirely worthwhile occupation. The new 'women's pages' in the national newspapers and the magazines were all used to impress upon women that it would have been morally reprehensible for them to emerge from the confines of their home. (Some novels were also written on this theme, notably *This Freedom*, see page 73.)

Fashions became more 'feminine' again and there was much discussion of the best way to remain alluring to a husband. One magazine wrote:

> The tide of progress which leaves woman with the vote in her hand and scarcely any clothes upon her back is ebbing, and the sex is returning to the deep, very deep sea of femininity from which her newly-acquired power can be more effectively wielded.[27]

During the Depression, women's magazines of all types concentrated on budgeting hints and by the late thirties *The Lady* commented:

> It looks as though a good deal of suburban elegance will have to be abandoned, and simple household ways adopted. The luxury of an attendant almost constantly on duty will have to go the way of candlelight, open fires and other amenities now only possible to the rich.[28]

After the First World War, when housework should have been increasingly less of a burden because of better mechanical aids, women were encouraged to strive for such ridiculously high standards that they could have had little time to wonder whether their lives might have been better spent than in this endless round of domestic ritual. Here is part of a prize-winning entry to a competition run by *Our Homes and Gardens* in 1920. The brief ran: 'What we want readers to do is send us an account of how they run, or would run, a servantless house for a middle-class family.' The winner modestly admits her good fortune in living in a house built in 1912 'when already the domestic service problem was looming large, so there is no hearth-stoning to be done at the front entrance'. She owns a vacuum cleaner, cinder sifter and other appliances. She uses the patent mop daily and dusts pictures and skirtings, electric light and cupboard tops thoroughly once a week.

> After breakfast, while beds are airing, any root vegetables are prepared. These are put to boil while the washing-up is in progress, afterwards cooking themselves in the hay-box cooker without supervision . . . The meal-table crockery is washed and lifted from the sink to the rack. Here it stays to dry and polish itself while other tasks are done. Knives, forks and spoons must be dried at once. I find rubbing the forks and spoons with a damp cloth on which a cleaning powder is sprinkled removes the stains, and saves much plate polishing . . . After dinner the gas stove should be wiped with a hot dish cloth. A thin coating of oil on the outside obviates the use of black-lead.[29]

But the owner of the servantless house had a harder life than the other prizewinner, the owner of 'the daily-help house'. Every room is turned out once a week and this is the daily's typical Monday:

The daily-help arrives and washes up the breakfast dishes and the supper dishes from the evening before, then cleans the front door step, brasses and taps.

Then, on Monday, she washes the flannels, handker-chiefs, small white articles, blouses, towels and kitchen towels, while the mistress brushes and dusts the sitting-rooms. Then she rubs over the bedrooms with an O-Cedar mop (the rooms are covered with cork carpet), and brushes the stairs and hall, afterwards dusting them. The other member of the family, who is elderly, peels potatoes and makes a pudding. The 'help' cleans up the small scullery and kitchen. The mistress lays the table, and has dinner ready by 1 o'clock. The 'help' washes up, cleans saucepans, fills coal boxes and cleans knives. By then it is 3 o'clock.[30]

Yet all this seems effortless compared with the lot of the poor housewife who bought *How to Run Your Home without Help* published just after the Second World War. Although middle-class housewives had by this time adjusted to lower standards, yet the manuals and magazines obviously lagged behind. Merely to read the chapter on 'adapting the routine when baby comes' induces exhaustion and most modern readers would not know whether to laugh or cry when they read the end of the section on 'how to plan your day':

After the meal, given some willing help with the clearing away, you should be free of the kitchen between 8 and 8.30 pm.

And is the rest of the day yours? Well, don't forget the ironing, and mending or knitting. But you can sit down for these, and with a companion to talk to, or a good programme on the radio, that last hour or so won't seem too much like work.[31]

By the time this little book was published in 1949 it must already have seemed like a relic from a bygone age. But in the

inter-war period, high standards still mattered to almost all
middle-class women: very few women novelists mocked the conventions that held such a tight grip, even if some like E. M.
Delafield railed at their tyranny. Rose Macaulay was an exception: in *Crewe Train* (1926) she describes a heroine who tries to
flout convention but is, after a struggle, firmly crushed. After
growing up abroad, Denham arrives in London, untamed and
unconformist, believing 'that the thing was to be happy and
comfortable in a nice place'. She dreams that 'one would be
alone; one would have no standards' – but in vain, for she is
gradually subdued and has to thrust aside her dreams of 'a very
low-class, lazy, common life; it was better not to think about it
while one was trying to be civilised and high-class'.

Denham tries hard to conform and her final submission after a
fierce struggle is described by Rose Macaulay as a minor tragedy.
The ending is far from any 'so they lived happily ever after' story;
in order to appease society Denham has had to stifle her inner
nature. The last scene of the book is particularly poignant, with
Denham's mother-in-law proposing to arrange her life for her:

> 'Well, first, then, you should really make out a time-table
> for the maid's week's work. It's the only way of getting
> everything done in order. Monday morning, clean the
> silver, Tuesday the knives, Wednesday, the paint,
> Thursday, the taps – and so on through the week. No day
> without something cleaned. And one room thoroughly
> turned out each day, too – that's most important.'
>
> 'Turned out . . .' Denham repeated it vaguely.
>
> 'Yes, turned out. The things all taken out of the room
> and put back again, you know . . .
>
> 'And,' continued her mother-in-law kindly, 'it needn't
> only be the maids who have a time-table either. I'm quite
> sure it's a great help in one's life to have some kind of
> scheme mapped out for the day, to which one tries to keep.
> It's wonderful what a help it is to see it written down. One
> should begin it right after breakfast – 9.30–9.45: see the
> servants; 9.45–10: do the flowers; 10–11: read the papers
> and write one's letters; 11–1: serious reading; 1–1.30:

lunch (an early lunch is nice in winter, I think, it leaves a longer afternoon); 1.30–2.30: lie down; 2.30–4: exercise or gardening, either alone or with friends; 4–5: tea and see friends . . . And so on, do you see? It regularises the day so, and prevents one drifting and idling the time away, as one's often inclined to do . . .

'There needn't really be *any* empty moments in one's day, if it's properly schemed out. Think of that! Not one empty idle, useless, minute.'

Denham thought of it . . .[32]

And thus the novel ends, a depressing tribute to the triumph of domestic convention over free will.

Authors like Rose Macaulay and E. M. Delafield made their readers reassess the nature of their everyday lives. By laughing at domesticity, they made its iron laws less sacred and encouraged their readers to view their households with a wry if daring detachment. The heroine of *Diary of a Provincial Lady* by E. M. Delafield embodied a certain attitude: married women, like it or not, were the focus of their households but gaiety and good humour were the appropriate qualities, not stuffiness or an unseeing passion for convention. When, inevitably and continually, Robert grunts and retires behind *The Times*, the reader too smiles ruefully with only a hint of edginess, knowing that the Provincial Lady is calmly picking up her darning and planning tomorrow's lunch rather than casting herself in the role of a second Madame Bovary. Society was never overturned by women like these, nor, for them, did knights charge up the drive on a white horse: nowadays we tend to describe the provincial ladies of England as the kind of women who won the war, paying homage to their activites in the WVS, behind tea urns, cherishing evacuees or, cheerily, digging up the lawn for victory.

The reason for the *Diary*'s unique qualities is the tone in which the Provincial Lady writes in it. It is inimitable: wry, witty, observant, yet hinting at a more profound awareness. Without castigating her heroine's daily round, E. M. Delafield yet makes the reader horribly aware of the empty complacency of provincial life – but her *alter ego* is too generous and self-deprecating to do more than laugh at it. Much of the comedy of the wonderful diaries (commissioned as a serial in *Time and Tide*) lies in the heroine's continual and irrepressible fight for life and vigour, a fight which is always lost to superior forces.

> November 12th – Home yesterday and am struck, as so often before, by immense accumulation of domestic disasters that always await one after any absence. Trouble with kitchen range has resulted in no hot water, also Cook says the mutton has *gone*, and will I speak to the butcher, there being no excuse in weather like this. Vicky's cold, unlike the mutton, hasn't gone. Mademoiselle says, '*Ah, cette petite! Elle ne sera peut-être pas longtemps pour ce bas monde, madame.*' Hope that this is only her Latin way of dramatising the situation.
>
> Robert reads *The Times* after dinner, and goes to sleep.[33]

It is of course not coincidental that the other novel which captures a middle-class woman's everyday life to brilliant effect was also presented in an unconventional form, but in weekly articles rather than a diary. In 1938, Peter Fleming, an editor on *The Times*, commissioned a series of articles from Jan Struther about her family life. Her brief for her fifteen-hundred-word weekly episodes was to write 'about an ordinary woman – someone rather like yourself'. The atmosphere and activities described in what was to be the book *Mrs Miniver* (1939) are very similar to the Struther family life 'observed with tenderness, humour and astuteness, yet imbued with witticisms, family jokes and a deep knowledge of natural history'.[34] The chapters breathe the atmosphere of 1938–9 as lived by a middle-class Englishwoman not a stone's throw from Harrods whose greatest problems are domestic. The film *Mrs Miniver* (1942) displayed the same down-to-earth, sensible, liberal (and liberated) values as the book. Its effect on American audiences was to make them more pro-British – indeed Roosevelt said he was certain it inspired the Americans to help the British war effort, and Churchill said in the House of Commons that 'the film was more use to the war effort than a flotilla of destroyers'.

Some readers today may find books like *Mrs Miniver* impossibly dated and therefore uninteresting: others may dub it a period piece and find it absorbing. But the original readers of these articles would have been loyal to family, country and friends, in that order, and would have agreed with Mrs Miniver's musings as she lies in bed on Christmas morning listening to the children opening their stockings.

> This was one of the moments, thought Mrs Miniver, which paid off at a single stroke all the accumulations on the debit side of parenthood: the morning sickness and the quite astonishing pain; the pram in the passage, the cold mulish glint in the cook's eye; the holiday nurse who had been in the best families; the pungent white mice, the shrivelled caterpillars; the plasticine on the door-handles, the face-flannels in the bathroom . . . the shortened step, the tempered pace, the emotional compromises, the divided loyalties, the adventures continually foresworn.[35]

Like all the other home-centred heroines of the period, she is continually juggling private pleasures with family duties:

> As a rule she managed to keep household matters in what she considered their proper place. They should be no more, she felt, than a low unobtrusive humming in the background of consciousness; the mechanics of life should never be allowed to interfere with living. But every now and then some impish poltergeist seemed to throw a spanner into the works. Everything went wrong at once; chimneys smoked, pipes burst, vacuum-cleaners fused, china and glass fell to pieces, net curtains disintegrated in the wash. Nannie sprained her ankle, the cook got tonsilitis, the house-parlourmaid left to be married, and the butterfly nut off the mincing machine was nowhere to be found.[36]

The tone is rueful but uncomplaining. The unspoken moral is that in order 'to keep household matters in . . . their proper place' the mother who provides the bulwark between nursery and outside world must sacrifice thoughts of self – but the rewards are worthwhile and ultimately greater than those of money, fame or achievement. Elizabeth Cambridge took the title of her 1933 *Hostages to Fortune* from Francis Bacon: 'He that hath wife and children hath given hostages to fortune; for they are impediments to great enterprises, either of virtue or mischief'. For the heroine the rewards are a long time revealing themselves; most of the time, life with small children seems a harsh routine of meals, mending and fading boilers:

> Other women had managed to write novels and bring up families. Catherine wondered if they had all washed behind their children's ears and pushed them about in perambulators and swept under their beds and weeded the garden and picked the fruit and made their children's clothes and done the hundred and one odd jobs that fell to her share because William was always out and odd labour was ruinously dear. Perhaps they were so successful that they managed to pay for decorators and carpenters and sewing-maids and expensive reliable nannies.[37]

The children become people, Catherine is less consumed with weariness, the house becomes less bitterly cold. The novel's ending is optimistic. Catherine and a friend admit to themselves that they are thoroughly worn out by their years of domestic toil and they resolve to approach their lives with a new honesty:

> 'I'd be happier if everybody gave up pretending,' Catherine said. 'We've had such a lot of that . . . cheerful idiots yapping encouragement whilst we got on with the work. "Business as usual" in the War, the "good time" afterwards . . . wasn't it fantastic and wasn't it stale? . . . And this sickening constant cant about "personal freedom". Freedom! There isn't room in this world to get your elbows away from your sides.'[38]

The pessimism is muted by the verdict of the children – 'You see, you all expected such a lot.' But Catherine has no regrets, she would do it all over again.

> We've had hard times, we've been hungry, we've been starved for amusement and interest and friends. We've

been desperately tired. I've sat down again and again and howled with disappointment. I've made mistakes. I've been angry. I haven't often understood what I was doing for the children. But I've loved them. I've had a wonderful time.

Those who haven't had them can't understand. Fancy expecting your children to be grateful to you! I'm grateful to them. I used to think it would never be over . . . the bringing them up, the endless work . . . But all the time I was enjoying it.[39]

And she is sensible enough to realise that the time has come for her to sit back, out of the way, to stop caring about her children's happiness and to accept them in their own right. 'And with the loss of that, the last of her ambitions, she lay still, and was content.'

Elizabeth Cambridge's approach to motherhood might be called the realistic one. In Enid Bagnold's *The Squire* (1938) we are, however, shown a different kind of heroine. She is quite remote from the 'outside' world, living snugly rather like a knight's lady in her castle, impinged upon by very few practical details. With all domesticity off-stage, so to speak, 'the squire' (whose husband is away) is free to explore the emotional complexities both of her fifth pregnancy and of her four existing children. The novel is one of the few written by a woman which sets aside swollen ankles, heartburn or the question of 'to layette or not to layette' and preoccupies itself almost exclusively with the more philosophical aspects of motherhood.

Admittedly cook gives notice and the last hours of the squire's pregnancy are spent telephoning registry offices. But otherwise the novel is birth-centred: the whole household is in suspended animation. For a very short time, the squire manages to escape her role of queen bee and to concentrate on the baby who is about to be born. And by so doing, she is closer to death than at any other time in her life, as indeed she had anticipated in pregnancy, with her thoughts of 'walking in undergrowth, walking in a wood, sitting in a wood, sinking in a wood, buried in a wood, *gone* . . .' During labour,

117

she would have seemed tortured, tossing, crying, muttering, grunting. She was not unconscious but she had left external life. She was blind and deaf to world surface. Every sense she had was down in Earth to which she belonged, fighting to maintain a hold on the pain, to keep pace with it, not to take an ounce of will from her assent to its passage.[40]

The squire, too, like so many other mothers in fiction, has surrendered what once she yearned for. Her gaze is fixed now on her family and her thoughts of self have evaporated.

How her ambitions had changed! How nature, almost without her consent, had set her horizon on the next generation! How short a time ago was it that she had cried, '*My* life! *My* life!' stretching her arms and her young body, fierce, alone, adventurous, – and now a mother five times![41]

All too soon, the already-grown children begin to devour her, she is rapidly 'tired and testy' and the midwife tries hard to protect her from the iniquity of the temporary, disastrous cook. 'Gentle life, with the little untroublesome companion. Any trouble was the midwife's; all the heaven was the squire's.' And so the days of lying-in, punctuated as they are by scenes of wonderfully tender and satisfying breast-feeding, draw to a close. The midwife would extend them, but for her patient 'the instrument of her household had so many keys; she longed to be back at her playing'.

The overall effect of this unique book is of unashamed, passionate devotion to the pleasures of the nursery. It is a panegyric to motherhood. Of course, the cynic might observe, who would not enjoy maternity with all domestic worries coped with by others and the mother granted so much harmony and contemplation that she has time to brood not on tomorrow's puddings but on the idyll of birth? And it is true, the squire lives in a world removed from the ordinary realities. To visit the house where it was set, Enid Bagnold's home at Rottingdean in Sussex, is to be aware that she did lead a charmed life and the pressures and the worries of most of her contemporaries were unknown to her.

Nevertheless 'the attempt to get servants at the last ditch of servanthood pierced my happiness and filtered through my sleep. They were a dying class. Mine too. Treacherous courtiers round a paper queen on a paper throne. (With exceptions.)'[42] Yet in *The Squire* Enid Bagnold achieved a work of art of outstanding quality. It is a memorable and original statement about the cutting of the umbilical cord; even though the squire knows that in Europe 'the tempest howled', she ignores it, immersed in her children and her responsibility for them.

The heroine of *The Brimming Cup* (1921) is less accepting. Dorothy Canfield's novel, set in America but widely read in England, was reviewed by Rebecca West; in her review she singled out Chapter XV, 'Home Life', as encapsulating all that is worst and best about the true daily round of a mother. Marise has three children and has suffered some soul-searching because the 'baby' has gone to school for the first time. She flirts with a neighbour and, eventually, is drawn closer to her husband when his trusting patience becomes apparent to her. In 'Home Life' she is finding it hard to cope with her household because her antennae are so unusually sensitive. Her children demand all her attention and she is exhausted.

Oh, her very soul felt crumpled with all this pressure from the outside, never-ending!

The worst was not the always recurring physical demands, the dressing and undressing the children, preparing their food and keeping them clean. The crushing part was the moral strain: to carry their lives always with you, incalculably different from each other and from your own. And not only their present lives, but the insoluble question of how their present lives were affecting their future. Never for a moment from the time they were born, to be free from them though, 'Where are they? What are they doing? Is that the best thing for them?' till every individual thought of your own was shattered, till your intelligence was atrophied, till your sensibilities to finer things were dulled and blunted.[43]

By the end of this severely moral book Marise has accepted

where her true affections have always been. But she still dreads her lover's presence: 'Would he come back to haunt her in those inevitable moments of flat ebb-tide in life, when what should be moist and living withered and crisped in the merciless drought of drudgery and routine?' Quite soon, however, he holds no more fears for her and her spirit returns with renewed affection to her husband. With an uncomfortable sugariness, Dorothy Canfield writes: 'The ineffable memory of all the priceless past, the ineffable certainty of the priceless future was in their kiss.' And once more they are a united family, cherishing their children, protecting them from the blows of the world, finding time among the domestic chores to listen and respond to them. The reader can take comfort in the knowledge that by being domestic, ordinary and maternal Marise is being both creative and life-giving; she embodies the lines Frances Cornford was to write a decade later:

> They must go free
> Like fishes in the sea
> Or starlings in the skies
> Whilst you remain
> The shore where casually they come again.[44]

CHAPTER FIVE

Sex

'A pagan body
and a Chislehurst mind'

'She had thought of something, something about the body, about the passions which it was unfitting for her as a woman to say. Men, her reason told her, would be shocked. The consciousness of what men will say of a woman who speaks the truth about her passions had roused her from her artist's state of unconsciousness. She could write no more.'[1]

Virginia Woolf saw clearly that many prejudices would have to be overturned before women were free to write about those aspects of their existence which had for so long been ignored. For the Victorians sex was *the* great unmentionable. Sexual impulses, particularly in women, were feared and therefore denied. Male sexuality was seen as inevitable and therefore tolerated: women, pure creatures, were claimed to be free from the sexual instinct, as Acton noted so anxiously and so memorably:

I should say that the majority of women (happily for them) are not very much troubled with sexual feeling of any kind. What men are habitually, women are only exceptionally . . . The best mothers, wives, and managers of households, know little or nothing of sexual indulgences. Love of home, children, and domestic duties, are the only passions they feel.

As a general rule, a modest woman seldom desires any sexual gratification for herself. She submits to her husband, but only to please him; and, but for the desire of maternity, would far rather be relieved from his attentions.[2]

But, by the last two decades of the nineteenth century, women were beginning to challenge this suppression of their sexuality. The publicity given to the 1877 Bradlaugh–Besant trial over their birth control pamphlet *The Fruits of Knowledge* meant that many middle-class people were at least aware that it was now possible to prevent conception. With the recognition that it was no longer necessary to have large families, a few brave women began to look for other ways of controlling their lives, and a new kind of heroine began to appear in the 'New Woman' novels as well as in those of writers, such as Mrs Humphry Ward, who were opposed to some aspects of feminism, for example votes for women. And by the 1890s writers such as Thomas Hardy in *Tess of the D'Urbervilles* (1891) and *Jude the Obscure* (1895) and George Moore in *Esther Waters* (1894) were, too, describing women 'as complete human beings with individual and sexual rights'.[3]

It was not only in fiction that a change was evident. In English society at the time women were becoming less restricted: for example, the bicycle gave them a new mobility; the Rational Dress Society campaigned for clothes which gave some freedom of movement after the fearsome constriction of Victorian petticoats. In addition, the activities of the suffragettes and suffragists and the gradual growth of educational and job opportunities meant that women were beginning to break free from the restraints that had so deeply irked Florence Nightingale.

Yet the Victorian ethic of sexual purity held a tight enough grip: and Christabel Pankhurst's particular sexual purity campaign in 1913, though criticised by many women, was a reflection of the high incidence and overwhelming fear of venereal disease. During the Great War, moral standards began to be eroded and the pieties that had prevailed for so long began to crumble a little. By the 1920s, contraception had become a reality at least for the informed middle classes, and the work of the 'sexologists' (Krafft-Ebing and Havelock Ellis for example) and of Freud in particular, with his insistence on the existence of infantile sexuality, had played a part, too, in changing middle-class sexual attitudes. Popular books began to explain to the general reading public the importance of sexuality in normal life.

As a contemporary writer said, Freud 'attributed very many of the Neuroses which exist in modern civilized societies'[4] to the sex-repression so widespread in Western Europe. And by the 1920s, in certain strata of society, the Victorian strait-jacket had been set aside, for, as Winifred Holtby remarked, a woman had to learn to 'enjoy the full cycle of sex-experience, or she would become riddled with complexes like a rotting fruit'.[5]

Whether women had as yet found the method for speaking 'the truth about her passions' was, according to Virginia Woolf, extremely doubtful. Other writers believed themselves quite free of inhibitions — much to the disgust of Katharine Mansfield, who wrote in 1920:

> I don't know whether it's I that have 'fallen behind' in this procession but truly the books I read nowadays astound me. Female writers discovering a freedom, a frankness, a license, to speak their hearts reveal themselves as . . . sex maniacs. There's not a relationship between a man and woman that isn't the one sexual relationship — at its lowest.[6]

And a year later, extolling the charms of *Emma* to Lady Ottoline Morrell, she wrote:

> It's such an exquisite comfort to escape from the modern novels I have been forcibly reading. Wretched affairs! This fascinated pursuit of the sex adventure is beyond words boring! I am so bored by sex *qua* sex, by the gay dog sniffing round the prostitute's bedroom or by the ultra modern snigger — worse still — that I could die — at least.[7]

The majority of women writers were, at this period, taking

heed of the words of Lord Riddell who advised the popular
novelist Ruby M. Ayres that writers of her type should 'take her
heroines as far as the bedroom door and then leave them'.[8] There
were two kinds of writers who tried to describe women in the
throes of sexual passion. The first group inherited the mantle of
such Edwardian novelists as Miss Braddon, Rhoda Broughton,
Ouida and Marie Corelli, and were often blatantly erotic. Elinor
Glyn and E. M. Hull (who are discussed in greater detail in
Chapter Seven) are two examples of writers who wrote quite
openly about sexuality but had various fail-safes to protect their
work from the attentions of reviewers, police or other censorious
bodies. To begin with, they often received little critical attention
and could therefore afford to be more daring than the kind of
novelist whose work was reviewed and discussed in intellectual
circles and came to the attention of those responsible for
directing good taste. In addition, they set their sexual adventures
in remote surroundings, and used a vocabulary imbued with
moral overtones.

The second kind of writer who tried to explore female
sexuality was thus in a different category from the romantic
novelist – but lacked a vocabulary and an approach to release
her from her inhibitions. She had accepted that 'the majority of
women are neither harlots nor courtesans',[9] and wanted to
describe the ordinarily sensual woman without resorting to the
methods of pulp fiction, or making publication impossible by
being obscene. Yet there was a fatal self-consciousness where the
erotic was concerned, and the undeniable association of fictional
sensuality with either the perverse or the absurdly exotic.
Ordinary love presented to these writers far greater problems
than out-of-the-ordinary eroticism.

Virginia Woolf largely avoided the issue by writing about pre-
sexual heroines (*The Voyage Out*, *Night and Day*), a firmly
maternal one (*To the Lighthouse*) or heroines who have not
achieved sexual happiness (*The Years*); while in *Orlando* she
explored the nature of sexuality as an almost philosophical
concept. Only in *Mrs Dalloway* does she tentatively explore her
heroine's sexual self, and then by making it clear that her
marriage is loveless. Clarissa Dalloway has rejected sexuality,

unable to forget the exquisite moment in her life when Sally Seton kissed her, when 'the whole world might have turned upside down!' She no longer sleeps with her husband but in a narrow bed in the attic and 'she could not dispel a virginity preserved through childbirth which clung to her like a sheet'.

> She could see what she lacked. It was not beauty; it was not mind. It was something central which permeated; something warm which broke up surfaces and rippled the cold contact of man and woman, or of woman together. For *that* she could dimly perceive. She resented it, had a scruple picked up Heaven knows where, or, as she felt, sent by Nature (who is invariably wise); yet she could not resist sometimes yielding to the charm of a woman, not a girl, of a woman confessing, as to her they often did, some scrape, some folly. And whether it was pity, or their beauty, or that she was older, or some accident − like a faint scent, or a violin next door (so strange is the power of sound at certain moments), she did undoubtedly then feel what men felt.[10]

What men feel is the norm; what women feel is 'a tinge like a blush', an illumination quickly over − Mrs Dalloway has only the standard of men's feelings by which to measure her passion for Sally Seton; her own tenuous emotions are considered unreal, insubstantial. Although the vocabulary in this part of the narrative may be the thinking woman's equivalent of purple prose, nevertheless its overtones are heavily erotic ('a tinge like a blush which one tried to check and then, as it spread, one yielded to its expansion, and rushed to the farthest verge and there quivered and felt the world come closer, swollen with some astonishing significance, some pressure of rapture, which split its thin skin and gushed and poured with an extraordinary alleviation over the cracks and sores').[11]

Mrs Dalloway's asexuality is, however, implicit in the title of the book. She is a wife. And as such she is not an object of desire to her husband. This concept held sway not only in fiction but also in upper- and middle-class life. In Freud's 1912 paper 'The Most Prevalent Form of Degradation in Erotic Life', he argued that very few cultured people can achieve an ideal fusion of tenderness and sensuality, and that this manifests itself in a lack of sexual desire for women who inspire affection – in other words the well-brought-up wife.

The question of whether one woman can be all things to one man was raised often in women's fiction between the wars (though the corollary far less often). The marrying of the opposing sides of a woman's personality is perhaps the most crucial struggle in which twentieth-century woman is engaged, welding as she tries to do her erotic, intellectual, maternal, domestic and managerial qualities in a unity of undoubted but precarious magnificence. And novelists often used the themes of a man falling carelessly out of love with someone merely because she is his wife, the 'little woman', and of a man loving and needing two women at once. In *Third Act in Venice* (1936), for example, Sylvia Thompson describes one man's battle to shrug off his Profane love in favour of his Sacred one. But he cannot do it, and continues to love Adria for her mind and Josephine for her sexuality. Unfortunately, but unsurprisingly, the novel is written from his point of view, so we never fully understand why Adria was less erotic to her lover than her rival manages to be. The implication is that she is too 'nice', while Josephine is not at all averse to some Elinor Glyn erotics:

> Soon he stopped seeing with his eyes, and began to feel her looks in his nerves and in his body, the texture of her skin choking him in his throat, and the shape of her mouth making his head hot and aching, and her neck, the shape of her thigh under her tight dress making him feel sickish, and her ugly hands making his own hands shake stupidly . . . [Later] she hadn't more than a minute's passive nonsense, and then went ahead, with an adept alternation of ferocity and languor, of silences and half choked husky talk, that word by word, and gesture by hesitant experimental gesture, maddened instinct again and again to appetite.[12]

In Rosamond Lehmann's *The Weather in the Streets* (1936), Rollo accepts if not encourages his wife's delicacy in order to exonerate his guilt for wishing to be unfaithful to her. His mistress Olivia imagines her 'under a white satin quilted bed-spread with pink and apricot satin cushions, monogrammed, propping her head, and a blue satin and lace wrap on, being visited by assiduous doctors, exuding that restrained pervasive hygienic sex-appeal that is so telling'.[13] In Rollo's case, it is clearly the 'my-wife-doesn't-understand-me' (my wife won't do what I want in bed *and* understands me all too well) syndrome with which all women are only too familiar. As Margaret Lawrence wrote in 1937: 'does the question still have to be asked whether or not the cultivation of a woman decreases in some hidden way her erotic attractiveness, or does the whole matter go back to the man's hidden need of feeling superior to a woman?'[14]

Isabelle, in Rebecca West's *The Thinking Reed* (1936), defines a male type which must be excruciatingly familiar to many women but which no novelist, either male or female, had ever portrayed in fiction.

When he was her lover he was grave and reverent but too often there was afterwards this solemn clowning about sex, this midwife chatter about the bringing to birth of pleasure. Don Juan, it seemed, was a case of split person-ality; his other half was Mr Gamp. And he did what he could to draw her with him into the madhouse, for he tried to split her personality into two. It was suggested to her that her beauty and her capacity for passion were a separate entity, a kind of queen within her, and that it was to this that his loyalty was given, and that the rest of her was a humbler being, who ought to feel grateful that this superior part had caused her to be associated with such a grand gesture of chivalry. She, Isabelle, was supposed to be possessed by *la femme* as by a devil.[15]

Then there is the over-sexed man towards whom Stella Gibbons turned her malicious wit in *Cold Comfort Farm* (1932). Mr Mybug asks Flora, the sensible and good-humoured heroine, to go for a walk with him.

Flora was now in a dreadful fix, and earnestly wished that the dog-kennel would open and Amos, like a fiery angel, come to rescue her. For if she said that she adored walking, Mr Mybug would drag her for miles in the rain while he talked about sex, and if she said that she liked it only in moderation, he would make her sit on wet stiles, while he tried to kiss her. If, again, she parried his question and said that she loathed walking, he would either suspect that she suspected that he wanted to kiss her, or else he would make her sit in some dire tea-room while he talked more about sex and asked her what she felt about it.[16]

And yet, despite the clear female loathing of some of the male approaches to sexuality, many women have no choice but to bind themselves to them. For some it is uncomplicated love and affection, and this is the main theme of 'pulp' fiction. For others, it is a response to the world they live in, a kind of socialisation process dictated by habit and convenience. Isabelle in *The Thinking Reed* is portrayed as a woman who, given the chance, would probably be far happier leading an independent life. But she cannot imagine a life unconstrained by a male presence, and in any case society applauds the couple and still disapproves of the woman alone. She dislikes her lover in many ways (for his Mr Gamp qualities, for example) but

> he had a hold on her for the simple reason that when he and she were linked by passion they formed a pattern which was not only aesthetically pleasing but was approved, and indeed almost enjoined, by everything in civilisation that was not priggish . . . She felt herself the victim of some form of public opinion, which was so firmly based on primitive physical considerations that the mind could not argue with it, and it operated powerfully even in the extremest privacy.[17]

This perceptive passage defines in a haunting way one woman's struggle to reconcile her warring emotions of conformism and independence. It is a far more subtle approach to sexuality than was usual; the more conventional novel described love with intermittent scenes of love-making, whereas Isabelle realises that society ensures that the success or failure of

'primitive, physical considerations' actually dictate life's more
sophisticated aspects. The central question in *The Thinking
Reed* is why does a sensible woman have to disrupt her life
because of physical appetite? Why, indeed, cannot the sexual
appetite be assuaged in the same way as other appetites (food,
fresh air, music and so on) without the disruption of normal
existence? Miss Clephane (see page 139) would have argued that
it could, but Isabelle had the wrong group of friends for this kind
of *insouciance*. And of course she was bound by the old morality
which declared that a sexual male was potent and manly but a
sexual woman was a nymphomaniac. As the heroine of Michael
Arlen's *The Green Hat* (1924) put it, 'it is not good to have a
pagan body and a Chislehurst mind, as I have'.[18]

The light-hearted abandon with which, in 1913, Enid
Bagnold surrendered her virginity was clearly unusual. 'The
great and terrible step was taken. What else could you expect
from a girl so expectant? "Sex," said Frank Harris, "is the
gateway to life." So I went through the gateway in an upper
room in the Café Royal.'[19] And even after the war few unmarried women can have welcomed sexual experience with the same
unabashed eagerness as Charlotte in *The Romantic* (1920) by
May Sinclair:

> That evening in the office when he came to her − she could
> remember the feeling that shot up suddenly, and ran over
> her and shook her brain, making her want him to take her
> in his arms. It was that. It had never been anything but
> that. She *had* wanted him to take her; and he knew it.[20]

The old-fashioned morality was still widely prevalent in the
homes of the great majority. A woman learnt to temper her sensuality with discretion and moderation − otherwise the fabric of
society would disintegrate. In any case the whole sex-obsession
was very much exaggerated. Beatrice Kean Seymour probably
summed it up for many readers when she wrote in *The Romantic
Tradition* (1925) of her

> own secret conviction that men and women weren't half so
> interested in sex as we novelists pretended. It wasn't even

that we recognised it as a little bit of life . . . the only little bit worth writing about! . . . but that we wrote of the part as if it were the whole. And all the time people were interested in so many other things. In horse-racing, politics and clothes, in dining and lunching out; in getting comfortable shoes and more money to spend; in taking holidays, assuaging thirsts and in seeing their friends; in doing odd jobs about the house; in fretwork, gardening and the price of food; in the interchange of ideas, in the theatre, in books, sight-seeing and in work.[21]

The American novelist Ellen Glasgow, writing in the *New York Herald Tribune* in 1928, was even harder-hitting. She puts paid to a 'favourite myth', that of woman as inspiration, seeing her instead as a hindrance to man's higher activities. 'Never, at least in fiction, has she impeded so successfully as in her latest literary aspect of nymphomaniac.' In her view a woman's search for sexual fulfilment fatally encroaches on 'man's exclusive right to the pursuit of liberty and happiness'.[22] She concludes her article by noting approvingly that May Sinclair tended to consign 'unfortunates' of this persuasion (nymphomaniac) to an asylum. Which is indeed true. In *The Allinghams* (1927), the heroine is shown as unstable from early childhood, jealous of her sister's lover and given to tantrums. Finally someone proposes to her and the engagement sees the real beginning of her 'queerness'.

As the days of her engagement went on, Margie's excitement increased. When she was with her lover she talked on with a strained intensity and emphasis; her high-pitched laughter rose on a trembling, unstable note, as if it would break into crying. And there was always a deep flush on her face . . . One day she was taking tea with him in his house . . . suddenly Margie began unhooking her bodice, which she took off and flung from her. She had slipped off her skirt and was unbuttoning her underbodice when he cried out, 'Margie, what on earth are you doing?'

She looked at him with glittering eyes, eyes of madness.

'I am going to take off all my clothes, so that you can see how beautiful I am.'

He was terrified. But he kept his head. He was calm and quiet. Margie was mad. He knew that mad people must be humoured.[23]

So poor, infinitely pathetic Margie is taken home, locked up and eventually carted off to the asylum. Her mother remarks poignantly 'the doctor told us she would be completely cured if she were married'. Yet the fashion for long, celibate engagements must have brought many women to a severe pitch of frustration or thrown them despairingly into frigidity. Ironically, Margie's sister, who has become pregnant by her lover, is welcomed back into the family fold by her family once she has had the baby. Margie had lacked the sophistication to be efficiently seductive and therefore had to be punished.

The theme of the unmarried mother was the exception to the sexual conservatism of the Victorian novel. If *The Allinghams* had been written thirty or forty years earlier, the illegitimate baby would not have been welcomed cheerfully into the bosom of the family; but then Margie, had she tried to undress for her lover, would have been portrayed to the reader as genuinely deranged rather than a victim of sexual repression. By the 1920s, it would be a relatively unsophisticated reader who was totally ignorant of Freudian theory and did not wonder whether repressed libido was perhaps an unfortunate liability.

Havelock Ellis was one of the most powerful influences on post-Victorian attitudes to sexuality. His work was banned in England when it first appeared in 1897 but a revised version was published in 1906 and the final version of *Studies in the Psychology of Sex* was published in 1910. Ellis, and Edward Carpenter, whose *Love's Coming of Age* appeared in 1906, both argued that women were not biologically condemned to be frigid but that sexual pleasure was a normal part of human existence. Their ideas gradually began to be widely read and understood. In 1914, the British Society for the Study of Sex and Psychology was formed, the works of Freud were beginning to be read in translation, and in 1918 Marie Stopes published

Married Love and then *Wise Parenthood*, which was more specific about birth control methods.

Stopes had written about Ellis's books that they had 'made me feel that *abnormalities* are for experts only, and that what the world needed was knowledge about the normal and how to handle it rightly'.[24] She was in part prompted by her own unhappy experiences. It had taken her a year to realise that her marriage was unusual in any way and, as her biographer Ruth Hall observes, 'Marie wanted children, but, incredible though it now seems, did not link their appearance with anything beyond botanical chit-chat in Liberty-printed drawing rooms and passionate, if inconclusive loveplay in her sweet-memoried bedroom.'[25] After two years of unconsummated marriage, she realised that something was wrong and 'in a very impersonal manner, she took up her own case as a piece of scientific research. She went to the British Museum and read pretty nearly every book on sex in English, French or German.'[26] As Ruth Hall points out, 'the lifelong justification for Marie Stopes in her campaign for sexual reform, her burning light on the way to Damascus, was the experience of her first marriage.'[27] On her divorce five years after her marriage, when she was thirty-six, Marie Stopes was still a virgin. Yet there was more to her zeal than personal frustration, for her interest in sexual reform began before she had any inkling of the problems that her marriage would bring.

In *Married Love*, Stopes insisted that sexual pleasure was a female as well as male prerogative. So lyrical were her descriptions of the orgasm that writers must have wondered who needed fiction when they had Marie Stopes? For example:

> The half-swooning sense of flux which overtakes the spirit in that eternal moment at the apex of rapture sweeps into its flaming tides the whole essence of the man and woman and, as it were, the heat of the contact vaporises their consciousness so that it fills the whole of cosmic space.[28]

In the book (which had sold a quarter of a million copies by the mid-1920s) she addressed herself to people like Mr LW, who in 1920 wrote to her:

Lately I have felt a sexual longing when sitting on the couch with my fiancée. I often get this feeling. It is as if, although both are fully dressed, I long to get near her. You probably understand better than I can explain.

Am I normal and natural to feel this sexual longing or am I abnormal? I suppose I should try and smother my sexual feeling?[29]

But she replied bracingly: 'From what you tell me you are quite normal. It is indeed the usual result of a long engagement.'

Thousands of others would clearly have benefited from her sensible advice – for example the young Enid Starkie who, in 1926 at the age of twenty-eight, had a shattering experience: she resisted yielding to a man but did so finally because she sensed

urgency in his voice and I thought it was pain. I was so ignorant and inexperienced that I imagined I might harm him physically by withdrawal then . . . I thought I had incurred obligations towards him. I knew nothing at all. Nothing of that scene has faded from my mind though it is many years ago now. It is burnt into me . . . Maybe you will think it is a small thing, but to me it was the most terrible thing in my life.[30]

In 1927 Jonathan Cape brought out Bernhard Bauer's *Woman*, a book published in Vienna in 1923 and translated into English by E. S. Jerdan and Norman Haire; by 1929 it was into its third edition. The book presumably escaped the attention of the law by announcing on the cover that it should 'be sold only to Members of the Medical and Learned Professions or to Adult Students of Psychology and Sociology'. Norman Haire, an eminent gynaecologist and an apostle for sexual freedom, wrote in his foreword:

The present volume, which has enjoyed enormous popular success in Austria and Germany, gives a clear presentation of the sexual anatomy and physiology of woman, deals with her psychology and love-life, and shows how sex dominates all her activities from the cradle to the grave. The appendix on prostitution is particularly valuable for the English reader, as so little is available on this subject elsewhere.[31]

Haire warns the reader that Bauer 'is diametrically opposed to the conception of the Victorian age, which invested woman with a halo'. The modern reader must agree that Bauer and his translators have indeed shrugged off all possible associations with prudery, inhibition or coyness. In the chapter on 'Touch' he describes various types of kisses:

> The fact must be frankly faced that the tongue kiss and the kiss last described play a great part in female eroticism. The woman wants her kisses to eroticise both the man and herself as highly as possible, and it is only her training which prevents her admitting this. There is no woman who does not really desire, and who would not willingly permit, these kisses. Even the woman who has been chaste all her life; even the woman who, in the very climax of passion, still pursues that phantom, modesty; even such women will easily be brought to the point where they cannot forgo the pleasure of these 'unchaste, unaesthetic' kisses, when once they have been fully and completely eroticised by means of them.[32]

In 1930 Helena Wright published *The Sex Factor in Marriage*, which was to be reprinted eleven times over the next twelve years. The first line informs the reader that 'sex is one of the most fundamentally important things in life' and the book is 'based on the knowledge that a healthy and satisfying sex-life is a beautiful and creative element, and should be in the possession of every married person'.[33] Helena Wright set out to help the reader enjoy her sex life through an understanding of herself: 'The attainment of complete sex-pleasure in a woman is the fine flowering of a healthy body.'[34] And she must have been one of the first writers in English to assert that 'the only purpose of the clitoris is to provide sensation; a full understanding of its capabilities and place in the sex-act is therefore of supreme importance'.[35]

For the middle classes, birth control had become a possibility and therefore sexual pleasure was beginning to be a practical proposition without the fear of pregnancy and with a decreasing risk of venereal disease. Yet economic causes were also an important factor in the fall in the birth rate (21 per cent between 1911 and 1931). 'The reasons for the decline in middle-class birth rates . . . include the so-called "emancipation" of women, the desire to improve the chances of life of those children who *are* born, and the desire of parents to maintain a high rate of consumption of goods and services.'[36] This section of the population was lucky enough, thanks to Marie Stopes and her followers, to be able to control their family size; but the upper middle classes did not have the same financial incentive for birth control as did the professional middle classes, and there was a strong feeling among those families who had lost male relations during the First World War that if they could afford to do so it was their duty to try and replace the flower of England's manhood with a new generation of sons.

Social historians have not written a great deal about contraceptive methods and opinions differ as to the methods actually used. A. J. P. Taylor guesses that 'in the eighteen eighties, when the decline in the birth rate appears statistically, the middle classes, who were the first to limit their families, simply abstained from sexual intercourse'. He notes the introduction of the sheath during the First World War and the invention of the diaphragm in 1919, but says that between the wars only one man in ten used a sheath regularly and that very few enlightened women in the upper middle classes used a diaphragm. (He ignores the use of the vinegar sponge, and the 'safe' period was not promoted as a method of birth control.[37]) Taylor asserts that 'interrupted intercourse was apparently the normal pattern in at least 70 per cent of marriages' and makes the rather astonishing observation that between 1880 (when limitation started) and 1940 (when the use of the sheath had become widespread) the British were 'a frustrated people': 'the restraint exercised in their private lives may well have contributed to their lack of enterprise elsewhere.'

Sadly, it seems that some middle-class women 'in the know' about birth control were secretive about it because they nurtured confused ideas that working-class women would become depraved if they too could practise it. And contraception was of course very expensive – in the early 1930s one sheath cost ten pence,[38] while a diaphragm, although cheaper because at 1s 3d it could be re-used far more often, demanded good washing facilities and privacy for its use to be tolerable. As Mrs Peel pointed out in 1933, while the middle classes 'discuss birth control with the same freedom as they discuss the latest novel . . . it is practised in all strata of Society, except, perhaps, in the one in which it is most needed, that is, amongst the poorest and most degraded of the community'.[39] And so, although middle-class women used diaphragms or their husbands used sheaths, working-class women had all too often to resort to abortion (called 'bringing on periods'), one of the degradations condemned by Leonora Eyles in her polemic novel *Margaret Protests* (1919):

> Her face was greenish white, her eyes dull and fish-like. I spoke to her, but she did not answer, and I was getting into a state of panicky indecision again, wondering whether to risk all and fetch a doctor, when there was a smothered, coughing moan, a few convulsive writhings and she clutched my hand with one of hers, tearing off the bed-clothes with the other, and throwing them on to the floor.
>
> I had to summon every shred of courage, then, to see the thing through. Not only was I disgusted and frightened but I was physically sick and faint, trying not to see what was happening, conscious that I *must* see, for her life, for a while, was in my hands. When it was all over, she lay back, white and still, her damp hair streaked over the greyish pillow, and I collapsed into the big chair . . .
>
> 'Thenk Gord it's all over safely,' she said, in heartfelt tones. 'Never no more. By Christ, I'll watch it – that I will. I shan't get out of the next as easy! Was it a girl or a boy?'
>
> 'A boy,' I whispered, looking across to the chipped enamelled basin over which I had laid a white cloth and a newspaper.
>
> 'Good job it never come to anything, then,' she said, with sudden vicious spite. 'One less man in the world to ruin some poor girl, and lead her wrong.'[40]

The lack of birth control is, by implication, at the heart of Margaret's protest throughout the novel, although her greatest hardship is due to the poverty she experiences when her husband dies. (The book, greeted with enthusiasm when it first came out and reprinted in the 1960s, is nevertheless too simply an impassioned plea for an improvement in women's circumstances for it to stand up as a work of fiction; it would have benefited from the mock-realism technique of *The Woman in the Little House*.)

For the working classes, as portrayed in the novels of the 1920s and 1930s, sexuality often had little to do with eroticism or happiness. In *Treasure in Heaven* (1937) by Rosalind Wade, the 'do-gooding' Fanny visits one of the mothers in the 'Dwellings'.

Mr Ruxton had been almost continually unemployed ever since the wedding, and there were five children to provide for. 'And that's just where the trouble comes in now,' Mrs Ruxton continued sadly; 'when the last little one was born I made up my mind that it wasn't right to bring any more into the world till Mr Ruxton finds regular work. He agrees with me in the day-time but when the evenings draw in, and we can't afford to burn the gas, all his reasoning and common sense flies out of the window and he's got one idea of passing the time, and one only. He don't care what it means to me to bear another child nor to the kid neither to grow up in a home like this. 'E'll satisfy his feelings, he says, or beat me till I give in, and, as I told you, miss, he's as good as 'is word. Lately, I've made 'im sleep in the chair or I've done so myself to keep him away from temptation: it seems 'e's nothing else to think about since he can't afford to go to the pictures, and I can't leave the kids to go out with him anywhere. But I've made up my mind, miss, to stick to what I think's right, no matter how much he knocks me about. I know I'm right, aren't I, miss?'

Fanny could not answer. Within her breast a horde of conflicting curiosities and repressions battled, while she tried to offer the wholesome, impartial advice expected of the social worker. Mrs Ruxton addressed her frankly, as one woman to another, ignoring the unsurmountable

barrier of experience and inexperience which lay like a pall
between them.[41]

Leonora Eyles, in an excellent chapter called 'The Sex
Problem' in *The Woman in the Little House* discusses the issues
evoked by Mrs Ruxton. She describes a Mrs Smith where she
lodged complaining that she 'could put up with anything but the
going to bed side of it'. And how

> when Smith came in for his tea, I looked at him
> curiously – a big, hefty sort of man, quite nice to look at,
> with horny hands and stooping back. I noticed how he
> loved his whippet, a little frail thing that sat between his
> legs as he ate, trembling with joy because she was so near to
> her beloved master; and he was infinitely kind to the girls
> when they were ill. I used to puzzle about the Smith
> problem for many years.[42]

Mrs Eyles goes on to deplore the lack of sex education and
describes how pregnancy only adds to the burden of the
working-class wife. She points out 'how disastrous for a woman
is this male idea that continence is unhealthy, self-control a
cheating of their rights; and most working-class men seem to
think that the use of preventives is bad for them; the idea that it
causes consumption is pretty general'. Finally she puts in a plea
for 'wooing' and for an end to the 'queer ill-humour and nervous
irritability' that seems to result from sexual desire. And she
describes a typical evening.

> The man's work, in many cases, has tired his muscles, and
> he comes home to rest for the evening after a good meal; his
> muscles relax pleasantly during the evening until, at bed-
> time, he feels very well, very virile. His wife, on the other
> hand, has both tired muscles and nerves. Her muscles are
> tired with lifting heavy children, carrying coal, water,
> food – cleaning, cooking, washing, ironing, and running
> about in an enclosed space practically the whole day. Her
> nerves, because she is alone practically all day with only
> the children, have become frayed before her husband
> reaches home; she has not eaten very sensibly, and drunk

much strong tea; during the evening, while she is ironing, or mending, or nursing the baby, her husband has been resting; when bed-time comes, she feels light-headed, aching in every limb, a little hysterical; she would like to sit down and cry. It would not take much to make her jump clean through the window; a doctor examining her at that moment would tell her that she was in a state of nervous exhaustion produced by too long hours, too much monotony, too little wholesome food and fresh air, too much worrying about trifles. He would put her in a cool, quiet room, and give her a sedative. Instead, she unfastens her clothes and lets them drop off; and hears some disparaging remark about her unattractiveness; she dashes away a few tears, because she knows that if she cries she will cry and cry until she loses control completely; she drops into bed, hoping devoutly that the baby won't waken; she stretches herself carefully on the bed, afraid to move for the aching of her back, now that the support of her corsets has gone − and she prays devoutly that the man will go to sleep.[43]

Clearly it was only too true that 'sexual emancipation in the twenties and thirties remained confined to a narrow, privileged section of society'.[44] But there was nevertheless a franker attitude to sex and the Victorian horror of the naked body had diminished. By the time Irene Clephane published *Towards Sex Freedom* in 1935 it was less controversial to write that

sex is one of the fundamental elements of life, and without it no life is simple or normal. Fear of sex, fear of nakedness have poisoned life too long, and every experiment that helps to exorcise these twin fears from the human mind is to be praised.[45]

And Miss Clephane even declared that

the idea that physical infidelity means the end − even the desire for the end − of an established relationship is dying fast among women . . . A new love gives new colour to life, but, if the basic relationship is sound, it will appear the more valuable in its serene familiarity by contrast with the fire of the unfamiliar.[46]

She went so far as to recommend an affair to bring new life to an ailing marriage, believing that 'the ready acceptance of new loves, new loyalties in the life of husband, wife, or lover is an essential part of a revised sex ethic'.

Yet only a few women led this kind of emancipated life. In her autobiography Naomi Mitchison describes hers so clearly that one tends to forget that she was rather exceptional. She attributes the change in attitudes to marriage at this period almost entirely to effective contraception, although makes allowance for women's newly independent feelings after the First World War. Describing her and her husband's love-making after their wartime marriage, she wrote:

> We were both virgins, but you must remember that at this period that was not unusual for a young man in his early twenties . . . I got little or no pleasure except for the touch of a loved body and the knowledge that for a time he was out of the front line. The final act left me on edge and uncomfortable. Why was it so unlike Swinburne? Where were the raptures and roses? Was it going to be like this all my life? I began to run a temperature.[47]

But by the end of 1918 she was longing to visit her husband in France.

> I was all the more anxious to come because I had just read Marie Stopes's *Married Love* which seemed to me to have the answers to some of my own troubles if Dick too would read it and put some of it into practice. This was the first serious sex-instruction book for my generation and must have made an immense difference to the happiness and well-being of thousands of couples.[48]

Although Marie Stopes helped them a great deal ('Why had none of these elementary techniques occurred to either of us before?') their marriage was already bruised and some years later they both began to have affairs, albeit with dignity and control and great concern not to endanger their marriage: it was enriching and pleasurable and, even though guilt was unavoidable, going to bed with other people was obviously an accepted gloss on life for the Mitchisons and their friends. But the essential factor was contraception, usually a Dutch cap used with an ointment or pessary, provided either by a doctor or a clinic, at which middle-class women often helped with interviews and form-filling. Money-raising was another activity; for example, in 1924 there was a birth-control ball at the Hammersmith Palais. 'To show that it was a philoprogenitive movement, rather than otherwise, a leading woman novelist [Naomi Mitchison] attended it in an advanced stage of pregnancy.'[49]

Naomi Mitchison tried to describe in her fiction some of what she experienced in life, particularly in *We Have Been Warned* (1935), one of her few novels set in contemporary England (she is best known as a historical novelist). In her autobiography she relates in some detail the reluctance of publishers to print a novel that contained sentences like 'she had brought these contraceptive things for herself and Tom', 'she found a dirty shirt and smelt it tentatively; yes, this was how he smelt', or 'her hands were now on his trouser buttons − he couldn't let a woman do that!' As published (by Constable, finally), the novel contains some scenes that are more explicit sexually than anything that had as yet been written by a woman writer (and that was with many cuts made at the publisher's request).

After her difficulties with *We Have Been Warned*, Naomi Mitchison returned to writing historical fiction and commented in 1979, 'in some of the stories in *The Delicate Fire* (1933) there is, I would have thought, far more overt sex than in *We Have Been Warned*, but apparently it's all right when people wear wolfskins and togas'[50] (the convention exploited by Elinor Glyn and other romantic writers earlier in the century). And it is true that a modern reader of *The Delicate Fire* does feel some surprise that Jonathan Cape rejected the realism of *We Have Been Warned* in the same year that they printed scenes from the former novel such as that in which a man helps her to express breast milk into a cup:

I looked down and saw my breast lying in the cupped palm of his rather dirty hand; it was white and blue-veined, the veins standing out now that it was so full, and hard like a fruit, a great fruit. And his brown fingers worked at it gently and the milk spurted in four or five little jets, and the cup filled and Drako drank it up. And then Damis's fingers did the same thing for my right breast, easing me.[51]

Two years later, Pamela Hansford Johnson was 'sick with fear lest it [her novel *This Bed Thy Centre* (1935)] should become a subject for prosecution'.[52] The local (Battersea Rise) library refused to stock it and she received many obscene postcards. She meant merely to tell the truth about a group of young people in a London suburb, though Dylan Thomas's suggestion for the title undoubtedly did give the book 'an immediate shine of lubricity' very far from her intentions. But although the reviews used words like 'outspoken', 'fearless' and 'frank', the moral sentiments were perfectly 'pure' compared with those of non-fiction works like *Towards Sex Freedom*, or even Dora Russell's *Hypatia* (1925), which proclaimed women's right to sexual pleasure and liberty. These books gained licence from abstract argument while a novel is necessarily explicit, and could shock, even with a description like the following from *This Bed Thy Centre*:

> Slipping his hands under the ribbing at the waist of her sweater, he felt for her breasts.
> 'Sweet.'
> 'Roly, darling, darling. Kiss me.'
> Her mouth was as fresh as the grass. She locked her lips over his. They lay together on the ground, lost in their love and want. At last she drew his hands away.
> 'Why?'
> 'No.'
> 'But why? Don't we love each other?'
> 'Just because.'

Most readers would surely have found this scene less 'outspoken' than the breast-milk one in Naomi Mitchison's novel; or E. Arnot Robertson's references to periods (a more or less taboo subject in fiction until even more recently) in *Ordinary Families* (1933) and in *Four Frightened People* (1931) in which the heroine, trekking through the jungle, is

> expecting the usual curse of my sex, which came to add another minor trouble to my lot the next day, and (as with most women) the turmoil in the blood beforehand and at the time inclined me to be unreasonable if I was subjected to any strain.[54]

This, I believe, is the first mention of 'the curse' in English fiction.

But no one objected to the heady atmosphere of sexuality of this novel, which makes it quite clear that Arnold and Judith fall in love with each other only after they have become lovers. 'Physical and mental impulses are too inseparable, at least sexually in women, for me to say that this love was of the flesh alone, but it was mainly physical.'[55]

> – Judith, my poor girl, I said inwardly, trying to ridicule myself out of this stupid state, you aren't becoming a nymphomaniac, are you? Surely it isn't natural to want two men so much in so short a time?
> – It is natural, in an atmosphere of death and imminent danger, answered another part of me soberly.
> – One love affair in twenty years is enough! More than enough, I think.
> – It makes no difference what I *think*. No man should have hands that look so strong and are so shapely.[56]

Clearly Arnold had been feeling something similar: ' "I touch nothing these days," he said, looking at me but not altering his normal, matter-of-fact tone, "that isn't your body, Judy." '

Yet, despite the efforts of Naomi Mitchison and E. Arnot Robertson, and the influence of Joyce, Lawrence, Freud, Ellis and so many others, the average middle-class reader in the period between the wars, going to her local library to get her weekly novel quota, would still have heartily echoed the words of Rose Macaulay's Mrs Potter when she remarked, ' "I hope I am as modern as any one . . . but I see no call to be indecent." '[57] They preferred their fiction not to threaten the *status quo* as they knew it, and still associated anything vaguely 'indecent' with 'rubber shops'. Society may have found a new freedom in the eyes of Dora Russell or Mrs Clephane, but for most women the shadow of the Victorian age still hovered. Not for them the pleasure of a lover to comfort a loveless marriage: the sacrifice of Laura and Alec in Noel Coward's play *Still Life* may have seemed quaint to some, but millions of women identified passionately with them when they agreed to part. (It was only after 1934 that the divorced mother guilty of adultery was allowed access to her children as of right.)

Laura meets Alec by chance and they fall in love. They become lovers, but two months later the furtiveness and deceit become too much for Laura, who declares that it is not only their love that matters – 'other things matter, too, self-respect matters, and decency – I can't go on any longer'. (It is interesting that in the 1935 stage version the couple become lovers but in the famous and much-loved 1945 film version, *Brief Encounter*, they never do.)

They agree to give each other up, Alec murmuring understandingly, 'The feeling of guilt – of doing wrong is a little too strong, isn't it?' When their final meeting comes (the one which is so memorably interrupted by the bustling intrusion of Dolly Messiter), Alec and Laura talk entirely in terms of renunciation and sacrifice. They agree not even to write:

> Alec: Please know this – please know that you'll be with me for ages and ages yet – far away into the future. Time will wear down the agony of not seeing you, bit by bit the pain will go – but the loving you and the memory of you won't ever go – please know that.
> Laura: I know it.
> Alec: It's easier for me than for you. I do realise that, really I do. I at least will have different shapes to look at, and new work to do – you have to go on among familiar things – my heart aches for you so.[58]

There is nothing here of the pleasurably abandoned sex recommended in textbooks and some novels. The audience was meant to weep in sympathy, not to scoff, to admire their heroism and emulate it themselves. The distasteful aspect of the play is to be found in the parallel theme of the refreshment room waitress and her cheery flirtation with the porter. They do not really 'count', with their slap-and-tickle humour and their derisory references to the Romeo and Juliet who meet over tea and bath buns: there is an uncomfortable air of class warfare in the play which disappeared to some extent in the film *Brief Encounter* – here Myrtle (the tea-lady) and Albert (the ticket inspector) may provide light relief but they are not figures of fun. The hint, evident in the 1935 version, that they are feckless and sensually over-indulgent, was, sensitively, removed by 1945. In fact, the good humour and vigour of the station staff provide a rather marked contrast to the cerebral intensity of Alec and Laura. For those who looked beyond the intended moral, there was a parallel one that perhaps if they had made love with more passion and less soul-searching, thinking of pleasure more than duty, they might not have got into this mess.

Yet it is clear that, by the late 1930s, women were finding it hard to reach an equilibrium between the prudery of their mothers and grandmothers and the uninhibited attitude of a small minority of their contemporaries. Magazines were as divided as the reading public for which they catered: in 1938, *Good Housekeeping* deplored 'the obsession with sex which had prevailed now for some years', yet *Woman's Own* claimed that 'ignorance of the obligations, privileges and marvels of married life is as widespread today as it was in the darkest ages of the history of women'.[59] And if contemporary writers disagreed about the sexual habits of a group which was after all in some ways fairly homogeneous, it is hardly surprising that we, fifty years later, find it hard to draw convincing conclusions. There can be no firm generalisations as regards the interest or disinterest, pleasure or repugnance, with which the average middle-class woman viewed the sensual side of her nature. Safest, perhaps, to accept the point of view of Linda in *The Pursuit of Love*:

'I was forced to the conclusion,' she said, when telling me about this time, 'that neither Tony nor Christian had an inkling of what we used to call the facts of life. But I suppose all Englishmen are hopeless as lovers.'

'Not all,' I said, 'the trouble with most of them is that their minds are not on it, and it happens to require a very great deal of application. Alfred,' I told her, 'is wonderful.'

'Oh, good,' she said, but she sounded unconvinced, I thought.[60]

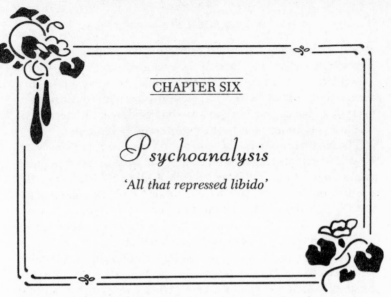

CHAPTER SIX

Psychoanalysis

'All that repressed libido'

'I fancy that there is some truth in the view that is being put forward nowadays that it is our less conscious thoughts and our less conscious actions which mainly mould our lives and the lives of those who spring from us.'[1] Samuel Butler wrote this in the early 1880s. He sensed a fresh current in the air and, had he been writing thirty years later, might have chosen to explore his characters' thoughts and feelings as they experienced them rather than as he, 'the all-wise' author, arranged them.

We have had sixty years to get used to Freud.

To us he is no more a person
Now but a whole climate of opinion[2]

wrote Auden after Freud's death – but in the 1920s he was still new and radical. Yet thoughts of the unconscious were much in the air. The reason was partly scientific – new discoveries in the field of neurophysiology – and partly philosophical and his-torical: and writers, reacting against the nineteenth century's firm repression of anything disagreeable, were becoming increasingly obsessed with the hidden side of people's natures. The individual began to be seen *as* an individual, and behaviour seen in the light of unconscious as well as conscious motives.

What is more, childhood experiences were seen to be crucial factors in adult life and this included children's sexual experiences – a radical and shocking notion to many. Previously secure ideas about behaviour were overturned, and ordinary everyday behaviour began to be analysed in terms of unconscious desires and needs, often severely repressed.

The first translation of Freud's work came out in 1909, with new works appearing almost annually after that. Soon popular books began to be published which explained his ideas to the general public; one such was Barbara Low's *Psycho-Analysis* (1920), sub-titled 'A Brief Account of the Freudian Theory', which is a succinct explanation meant for the literate reader rather than for the professional psychologist.

The author begins by explaining the relationship between the Unconscious and the Conscious. The latter is 'all the mental processes of which a person is aware', while the former is 'all that realm of mind which is unknown and cannot be spontaneously recalled by the subject, which is only made manifest (and only then in disguised form) in special states such as Dreams, Trances, Fantasies, Mania, etc.' She defines the Pleasure-Principle and the Reality-Principle and the Repressions in the Conscious Mind.

> Bit by bit a Censorship develops both from without (due to training, parental commands, education, etc.) and from within (due to its increasing 'civilization' and psychic development), and the primitive desires begin to be repressed – a prison-house is created for them – and as the forces of civilization close in around the individual, so does the barrier or Censorship between the Unconscious and the Conscious grow stronger in potency and more extended in its sphere.[3]

Barbara Low then explains that human beings have taken the path of Sublimation, 'a result of the creation of manifold moral, religious, and cultural taboos, which latter give rise to conflict with the primitive impulses pursuing the Pleasure-principle'. We are all involved in a continuous process of adjustment between the primitive and the more evolved; 'the need for Repression leads to the creation of Complexes' and it is these that cause mental illness. But 'the interpretation of dreams is the *Via Regia* to the knowledge of the Unconscious in mental life': they are of primary importance in psychoanalytic knowledge, the purpose of which 'is to set free the Unconscious with a view to the discovery and comprehension of the Patient's buried Complexes'. And the book's final chapter is a summary of the uses of psychoanalysis, particularly with reference to children.

Many writers have commented on the effect of Freudian theory upon their lives, of whom Dora Russell was one:

It is still not easy to explain fully the liberating effect of Freud's theories when they first became known. There was a good deal of amateur psychoanalysing; doctors and others went through a long and arduous analysis at great financial expense, in order to understand and/or treat patients. People would urge their friends to get 'analysed' in order to recover from traumas of their childhood; it became the fashion at least to get rid of your inhibitions and persuade others to do likewise. A searchlight was turned on family life, and sex as a pervasive element within it; sons were deemed to be in love with their mothers, daughters with their fathers . . . Parental confidence in handling their children was shaken, through fear that they might harm them by excessive dominance, or by excessive love.[4]

In this period between the wars, a small group of novelists, greatly influenced by psychoanalysis, were writing fiction in which they explored the inner workings of their characters' minds at the expense of plot, action, description and direct statement. May Sinclair was one of the most important of the 'psychological' novelists. She, indeed, explored her characters' thoughts and behaviour in preference to their actions and sociability, and was so obsessed by the twin ogres of environment and heredity, and used psychoanalytical case-histories so blatantly, that parts of her novels have been criticised for their textbook tone.

'It is very nearly medical'[5] was Frank Swinnerton's comment upon *Harriett Frean*, while Katharine Mansfield had written fifteen years earlier about *The Romantic* that 'what we do deplore is that she has allowed her love of writing to suffer the eclipse of psycho-analysis'.[6] Virginia Woolf, too, complained in these terms. Heading a review 'Freudian Fiction', she observed spikily that 'a patient who has never heard a canary sing without falling down in a fit can now walk through an avenue of cages without a twinge of emotion since he has faced the fact that his mother kissed him in his cradle. The triumphs of science are beautifully positive'.[7] But for novelists it is a different matter and when 'all the characters have become cases', fiction suffers. May Sinclair did not agree, and combined her love of psychoanalysis with her love of novel writing. In 1913 she became a founding member of the Medico-Psychological Clinic of London and in 1916 she wrote her first article on psychoanalysis called 'A Clinical Lecture on Symbolism and Sublimation'. In all her later novels the theories of psychoanalysis are clearly visible for those familiar with them: occasionally the jargon overtakes the writer of fiction.

For May Sinclair was very much ahead of her times, her interest in abstract philosophy having impelled her to study at first hand the theories of the psychoanalysts. Her novel *Far End* (1926) is about a writer who explains his methods with clarity and insight. It is quite clear that the novelist hero and May Sinclair share a voice, since his opening reference to God Almighty echoes an interview she had given five years earlier to the *Pall Mall Gazette* when she had said much the same thing:

> I'm eliminating God Almighty, the all-wise, all-seeing author . . . I don't display a superior understanding . . . There's no author running about arranging and analysing and explaining and representing. It's presentation, not representation, all the time. There's nothing but the stream of Peter's consciousness. The book *is* a stream of consciousness, going on and on; it's life itself going on and on. I don't draw Peter feeling and thinking. Peter feels and thinks and his thoughts and feelings are the actual stuff of the book. No reflected stuff. I just turn out the contents of Peter's mind . . .

I gain a unity which is a unity of form, and more than a unity of form, a unity of substance, an intense reality where no film or shadow of anything extraneous comes between. I present a world of one consciousness, undivided and undefiled, a world which is everybody's world. You can't stand outside of your own consciousness, and the nearer you get down to one consciousness the nearer you'll be to reality.[8]

The phrase 'stream of consciousness' had been used by May Sinclair in 1918, in an essay on Dorothy Richardson. She was echoing William James, who had written in 1890 that 'consciousness does not appear to itself chopped up in bits . . . It is nothing jointed; it flows . . . Let us call it the stream of thought, of consciousness, or of subjective life'.[9] May Sinclair pointed out that the basic subject matter of the thirteen-volume sequence *Pilgrimage* (1915–38) was the heroine's consciousness and she observed 'nothing happens. It is just life going on and on.'[10] And Virginia Woolf wrote a year later:

The reader is not provided with a story; he is invited to embed himself in Miriam Henderson's consciousness, to register one after another, and one on top of another, words, cries, shouts, notes of a violin, fragments of lectures, to follow these impressions as they flicker through Miriam's mind, waking incongruously other thoughts, and plaiting incessantly the many-coloured and innumerable threads of life.[11]

There are clear disadvantages involved in this paring down of the novel to the bare essential. If the reader is interested in the character whose mind is being exposed she will read on; if not, it will soon seem rather a tedious business to continue to participate in a long drawn-out exploration of Miriam's self. Frank Swinnerton wrote in 1935:

I find it excellent as impressionism – tones, looks, turns of speech all as they might, as they *must*, have been. But if I am asked whether I consider such impressionism anything more than a marvellous feat of memory, or reproduction, I

must answer there comes a moment in which one wishes
that Miriam had died young, or that she had moved
through life at a less even and ample pace.[12]

As he so wittily pointed out, Miriam does not impose herself
upon life, she suffers its effect and its humiliations; 'she does not
act; she resents and records'.

There is also the problem of the form in which psychological
novels should be written. Many critics had pointed out that this
new subject-matter of the novel demanded a bold new form and
most seemed to think that the 'stream of consciousness' technique
served this purpose rather well. Virginia Woolf made the point
most memorably:

> The writer seems constrained, not by his own free will but
> by some powerful and unscrupulous tyrant who has him in
> thrall, to provide a plot, to provide comedy, tragedy, love
> interest, and an air of probability embalming the whole
> . . . [but] life is not a series of gig-lamps symmetrically
> arranged; life is a luminous halo, a semi-transparent
> envelope surrounding us from the beginning of conscious-
> ness to the end.[13]

In other words, the traditional form of the novel would not
really do. Something more fluid, less intent on a story-line was
needed to replace the old-fashioned descriptive novel (Virginia
Woolf's 'loose, baggy monster') with a firm beginning, middle
and end. But such fiction was, by its very nature, difficult to
mark, learn and inwardly digest and this drawback created an
efficient censorship process which ensured that the proportion of
psychological novels was small. Dorothy Richardson wrote out
of a kind of obsessive *daemon* (she was distraught at the thought
of ever finishing *Pilgrimage* and after her death was found to
have been working on a fourteenth volume). Virginia Woolf sacrificed a great deal to technique and the admirers of her novels
among the general public were never great in numbers. May
Sinclair, although never so obsessed with the form of her novels,
sacrificed some elements of action and characterisation to her
interest in the scientific analysis of human nature.

Yet Dorothy Richardson in some respects set the pattern for the woman's novel in the twentieth century and her successors should not avoid paying her homage. In her use of language, she anticipated the work of Joyce and Woolf. She was the first (as she wrote years later) to 'attempt to produce a feminine equivalent of the current masculine realism'.[14] By exploring Miriam Henderson's mental processes, she was seeking the truth behind the material, male-dominated world defined by Virginia Woolf as one of 'rents and freeholds and copyholds and fines'.[15] Miriam is inward looking; her kind of feminism is a private one because she has freed herself from the male version of reality, and she is one of the first women in fiction to be shown *other* than in relation to a man.

This is the major stumbling block for most readers: in the traditional novel action is paramount, while in the psychological novel so little tends to *happen*. Indeed, it was often what did *not* happen to a character that mattered far more than what did. As so many people have pointed out, the tragedies in Dorothy Richardson, May Sinclair, Virginia Woolf or Rosamond Lehmann are all tragedies of wish-fulfilment rather than of mistakes decisively made. For the characters to be more assertive, to go out into the world and fight for themselves, the all-important unconscious perception would have to defer to conscious thrust and action, which would result in a quite different kind of fiction. Hence Miriam's lack of active feminism: she may perceive that woman consistently play second fiddle, but she is too bound up in her own self-awareness to consider righting the wrongs she sees around her. Campaigning feminism and self-absorption are impossible bedfellows since the former can only have an influence if it is articulated; if suppressed, it is futile and deteriorates into a general sense of grievance. And where relationships with men are concerned, it is impossible for Miriam's lovers to be intuitive enough, clever enough, manly enough, because if they displayed all the vital qualities, they would have to be given the key to her heart, and this her self-interest would forbid.

As a portrait, Miriam is a superb creation. At the same time it is rather heartening for the reader to be able to make her own judgements, to imagine her own settings, without God Almighty in the shape of the novelist continually stepping in and doing so for her. When Miriam decides, for example, to break from yet another would-be suitor, the author does not need to give us explanations, we can draw conclusions for ourselves by reading Miriam's thoughts:

> *He* had never for a moment shared her sense of endlessness. More sociably minded than she, but not more sociable, more quickly impatient of the cessations made by social occasions, *he* had no visions of waiting people. His personal life was centred on her completely. But the things she threw out to screen her incommunicable blissfulnesses, or to shelter her vacuous intervals from the unendurable sound of his perpetual circling round his set of ideas, no longer reached him. She could silence and awaken him only in those rare moments when she was lifted out of her growing fatigues to where she could grasp and state in all its parts any view of life that was different from his own. Since she could not hold him to these shifting visions, nor drop them and accept his world, they had no longer anything to exchange.
>
> At the best they were like long-married people, living alone, side by side; meeting only in relation to outside things.[16]

'Incommunicable blissfulnesses' are perhaps the first things that would have to go were Miriam to become generous enough to love and be loved. But Dorothy Richardson does not have to tell us this, and in this respect her fictional technique is very much warts and all, it cannot edit or hide but has to reveal the reality of a mind in all its light and shade. And when it succeeds, when the central character endears herself to the reader, then the novel can be far more moving than the 'old-fashioned' outside-in novel, for the reader has *been* the heroine, has shared her consciousness, throughout the book. *Mrs Dalloway* nearly succeeds in this respect, but there is something about her character that ensures that we are moved, tinged with some of her sadness, but remain ultimately detached, caring but not distraught.

The same could not be said of Rosamond Lehmann's *The Weather in the Streets* (1936), a superb novel which uses some of the methods of Dorothy Richardson, May Sinclair and Virginia Woolf but moulds them into the form of 'a woman's novel' in the sense in which the phrase is used as the sub-title of this book. For it is a novel which draws on established literary techniques but handles them without obscurity or evasiveness to create a whole which manages to be readable and moving without being trite or self-indulgent. The novel avoids the stodginess of *Pilgrimage* because it interweaves the thoughts of Olivia, the heroine, with dialogue. Also, although courting disaster by gravitating towards 'impossible' men, Olivia is not as serenely passive as Miriam. She endures unhappiness in the name of love rather than as by-product of a form of long-suffering hostility. Her sexuality is her undoing, whereas in Miriam's case it is her asexuality, and few readers have any doubts as to which they would rather read about.

For *The Weather in the Streets* is one of those rare novels which enters into a woman's mind fully and intimately without being obscure. Olivia appeals to anyone who has ever loved foolishly and recklessly; and, apart from Kay Boyle's *Plagued by the Nightingale* (1931), is the only novel in English describing pregnancy sickness, an agony which for some women far exceeds that of labour and delivery. How innovative both writers were can be judged by the fact that Rose Macaulay was attacked by Patrick Braybrooke for her 'extreme frankness' in writing in *Crewe Train* (1926) 'Denham felt, and often was, sick in the mornings.' He wrote the next year that the author's 'realism is tinged with an obvious pandering to the disgusting license that certain women novelists take such a pernicious delight in exhibiting'.[17]

When I am pregnant I gain some modicum of comfort from re-reading *The Weather in the Streets*. I identified with it particularly during my first pregnancy, when I wandered the streets of New York, spinning out the minutes until I could retreat yet again to 'Choc Full O' Nuts' for a creamcheese-and-walnut on toasted brown, the shiny red leather top of the stool sticking to my thighs, my stomach heaving yet imperious for food. And then the climb up the stone stairs to the eighth floor of a brownstone, my body so weak that I eventually crawled through the door towards the floor cushions. Things were not very different for Olivia:

> Sluggishly, reluctantly, the days ranged themselves one after the other into a routine. Morning: wake heavy from heavy sleep, get up, one must be sick, go back to bed; nibble a biscuit, doze, half-stupefied till midday; force oneself then to dress, each item of the toilet laborious, distasteful, the body a hateful burden. Tidy the bedroom more or less, dust a bit in the sitting-room, let in what air there was: for Mrs Banks was on holiday, there was no one to keep one up to the mark, no sharp eye and sharper tongue to brace one or contend against. Prepare to go out for lunch. Rouge, lipstick, powder . . . do what one might, it wasn't one's own face, it wasn't a face at all, it was a shoddy construction, a bad disguise. Walk down two side streets to the Bird Cage: morning coffee, light lunches, dainty teas, controlled by gentlewomen; blue tables, orange chairs.
>
> She maintained in one compartment of her handbag a supply of salted almonds and these she chewed on the way . . . She kept on at them steadily till the mob-capped lady waitress set before her the first delicacy of her two-shilling three-course ladies' lunch. At least there was no particular smell in the Bird Cage, nobody smoked much or drank anything stronger than orangeade. There was nothing to remind one of men. The china was sweet and the menus came out of *Woman's World*.[18]

It is also a novel about love, about the near-impossibility of two individuals creating a domestic, harmonious unit, and about the love that embraces more than the individual lover. Olivia says to Lady Spencer, her lover's mother, that she was more than fond of her and her family and thinks that she was 'in love with the whole lot of them'. Yet recognition of this difficult kind of love (Charles Ryder embroils himself in similar difficulties in *Brideshead Revisited*) does not allow her to exorcise it, to seek out something more lasting and comfortable. Indeed, some streak in her personality had earlier impelled her to reject her comfortable husband. When he comes temporarily to her rescue after the abortion, she has no regrets, yet appreciates his qualities:

> Off he trotted, delighted: a midnight spread! . . . He's awfully willing and domesticated. He'd be happy if he could live like this always: with some one or other for company — some one just in practical control but shelved as an exacting aggressive individual — some one being agreeable, not picking on him. He'd be a treasure to a lady invalid with cultured tastes. He'd push her chair round and round the garden, and take an interest in the bulbs, and they'd have hot scones for tea.[19]

If Rosamond Lehmann had been more interested in expounding her psychological insights as a fictional technique she would have explained what it was in Olivia's upbringing that had made her exacting and aggressive, determined to reject the ordinary domestic bliss that her sister Kate had embraced so wholeheartedly. But Olivia is such flesh-and-blood, so palpably a creature of motive, complex, libido and repression that we *need* no jargon to explain her. Nor, indeed, would the novel be what it is, for it would have needed an omniscient author to step in and explain things. Rosamond Lehmann's method was similar to that of Virginia Woolf, which was to allow Olivia's consciousness to unfold, the author responding rather than masterfully creating. Olivia *is*. She is neither case history nor pointed moral; and as such she lives.

Rosamond Lehmann was herself conscious that her role as novelist was receptive as much as manipulative. She wrote in 1946, when describing how a novel germinates:

> When the moment comes (it cannot be predicted, but it can be helped on by the right kind of passivity) these images will start to become pregnant, to illuminate one another,

to condense and form hitherto unsuspected relationships. The characters will begin to emerge, to announce their names and reveal their faces, voices, purposes, and destinies. The author does not 'invent' his characters or know about them from the outset. They reveal themselves gradually to him in and through that state of doubtful conviction which I have mentioned before. Characters must make plot or action; never the other way around.[20]

And six years later she observed in a similar vein:

Yet when I come to think harder, it seems truer to say that the creator is *acted upon*: that what one really feels at the outset of the enterprise is: 'This has started *to be done to me.*' And that what is necessary is to remain as it were actively passive, with mind and senses at full stretch, incorporating, selecting, discarding; in fact abandoned – not to sanctimonious looseness – but to every unbargained-for, yet acceptable, inevitable possibility of fertilization.[21]

From this it is clear that Rosamond Lehmann tried to allow her characters to behave and develop in a way that was true to their inner natures. She would not have 'worked out' what they were going to do next, she allowed them to behave through instinct and intuition rather than through rhyme and reason. In this she was very different from her mentor May Sinclair.

Nevertheless, Katharine Mansfield noted, at the time she was reviewing *The Romantic*:

I am amazed at the sudden 'mushroom growth' of cheap psycho-analysis everywhere. *Five* novels one after the other are based on it: it's in everything. And I want to prove it won't do – it's turning Life into a *case*. And yet, of course, I do believe one ought to be able to – not ought – one's novel if it's a good one will be capable of being *proved* scientifically correct. Here – the thing that's happening now is – *the impulse to write is a different impulse*. With an artist – one has to allow – Oh tremendously – for the sub-conscious element in his work. He writes he knows not what – he's *possessed*. I don't mean, of course, always, but when he's *inspired* – as a sort of divine flower to all his terrific hard gardening there comes this sub-conscious . . . wisdom. Now these people who are nuts on analysis seem to me to have *no* sub-conscious at all. They write to *prove* – not to tell the truth. Oh, I am so dull aren't I? I'll stop. I wish they'd stop, tho'! It's such gross impertinence.[22]

Some would disagree with Katharine Mansfield. In *Mary Olivier* (1919), May Sinclair was much more subtle than the short-story writer Ethel Colburn Mayne who, in 'Light', makes a mother explain her adolescent daughter's feelings to her.

'Daughters sometimes don't love mothers very much, Athene. It would take too long to tell you why, but there's a reason, and it's no one's fault. Daughters love their fathers so much better that sometimes they don't want their mothers there at all. You would have liked *me* to be gone away from you for ever, but you couldn't bear to feel that, so you held me tight and cried, and all the while that other part of you was trying to get on the top . . . Next time you will know what's happened, and you'll find it stops much sooner, for you'll know the way to stop it. You will say: "I love my Daddy best, but I love Mummy all I can, and Mummy knows I do." You see, you'll have control of that part of you, for it won't be shut away. It's always trying to get out, and when we don't know *what* it is that's trying to get out, we're like blind people fighting something they can't see. But if we know, and give it room in us, and let it *breathe* . . . well, then it won't torment us half so much.'[23]

In May Sinclair's novels the characters are often shown to be so completely lacking in self-knowledge or any wish for happiness that, unlike Rosamond Lehmann's characters, they become implausible. Yet one might expostulate – 'but none of May Sinclair's people *want* to be happy' and she would have answered perhaps that that was just the point – she is showing the reader what it was in their environment (their childhood in particular) that made them deny themselves pleasure and fulfilment.

For the fundamental theme running through her novels, one which her reading of psychoanalysis was to confirm, was that infantile traumas and childhood frustrations can damage a person irrevocably. This is why many of her novels start with childhood, for it is here that the seeds are sown. It also makes her novels more interesting, for the reader can have far more empathy for a character known virtually from birth. The girls in *The Three Sisters* (1914) react in different ways to the paternal domination that has been their fate since childhood. And it is her mother's shameful treatment of her as a child that makes the heroine of *Mary Olivier* come to life; if we had merely seen her as an unhappy adult we would care less. It was perhaps with justification that G. B. Stern wrote to May Sinclair that 'of course the reason why she's so infinitely more wonderful than anything Dorothy Richardson has done is that Mary herself matters, and Miriam didn't – Heavens, how Miriam bored me!'[24] While Rebecca West concluded that, in *Mary Olivier*, May Sinclair was showing Dorothy Richardson how to do what, throughout *Pilgrimage*, she was trying to achieve.

Despite the difficulties of language (how to achieve Virginia Woolf's sentence 'which we might call the psychological sentence of the feminine gender'[25]), the form of *Mary Olivier* is relatively straightforward. It combines a 'stream of consciousness' style with a brevity and nimbleness of structure which is what endears the novel to those who cannot get along with Dorothy Richardson's slow-paced volumes. Katharine Mansfield disagreed and wrote in her review:

> It is too late in the day for this new form, and Miss Sinclair's skilful handling of it serves but to make its failure the more apparent. She has divided her history of Mary Olivier into five periods, infancy, childhood, adolescence, maturity and middle-age, but these divisions are negligible. In the beginning Mary is two, but at the end she is still two – and forty-seven – and so it is throughout. At any moment, whatever her real age may be she is two – or forty-seven – either, both.[26]

But many readers point to the fluidity of the time-scale as one of the novel's great achievements, and so might Katharine Mansfield if she had read the work of Proust (which had begun to be published in France in 1913 and in English translation in 1922). When Mary Olivier is a child the seeds of adulthood are sown but when she is an adult she is still a child. It is not for nothing that she remarks ' "I shall go on growing younger and younger till it's all over" '; she is mature, but she has not managed, in adult life, to transcend her infancy, during which her mother thwarted her at every turn from developing into a self-contained, confident personality. Mary's tragedy is that she does not hate her mother. She longs for her to love her and bows to her domination. She only accepts fully that her mother's jealousy derives from her own frustration when it is much too late: by then she is middle-aged, heart-whole and clear-sighted – but too good a person to desert the mother whom, in spite of all, she still loves. She tells her brother who has got away:

'It's different for you,' she said. 'Ever since I began to grow up I felt there was something about Mamma that would kill me if I let it. I've had to fight for every single thing I've ever wanted. It's awful fighting her, when she's so sweet and gentle. But it's either that or go under . . . She doesn't *know* she hates me. She never knows that awful sort of thing. And of course she loved me when I was little. She'd love me now if I stayed little, so that she could do what she liked with me; if I'd sit in a corner and think as she thinks, and feel as she feels and do what she does . . . I *should* be lying then, the whole time. Hiding my real self and crushing it. It's your *real* self she hates – the thing she can't see and touch and get at – the thing that makes you different. Even when I was little she hated it and tried to crush it.'[27]

For Mary Olivier, self-sacrifice is ecstasy, or rather, it has a real spiritual meaning for her: it is, in its own way, its own reward. Indeed, in almost all her novels May Sinclair sounds out that 'feminine note' in literature that E. M. Forster defined in 1910 as 'a preoccupation with relative worthiness. The characters in a woman's novel try not so much to be good, to measure up to some impersonal standard, as to be worthy of one of the other

characters'.[28] This is truer of no one than of Harriett in Ma
Sinclair's *Life and Death of Harriett Frean* (1922). She has been
taught by her mother that 'it's better to go without than to take
from other people' and thus when she grows up she gives up the
only man she loves in order not to take him from her friend
Priscilla. But this novel is about far more than one girl and her
personal, pernicious self-sacrifice. It is about a whole way of life,
a whole breed of people, embodied by the word Victorian. The
renunciation, sacrifice and martyrdom which they thought so
crucial and so fulfilling is here by implication shown as sterile
and life-denying – even selfish; a whole way of life was founded
on these principles and it is one of the most far-reaching effects of
the fresh air that blew in with the twentieth century that new
ideals came with it. The novel is putting into fictional form some
of the ideas thrown out by Virginia Woolf when she wrote that

> in or about December, 1910, human character changed
> . . . In life one can see the change, if I may use a homely
> illustration, in the character of one's cook. The Victorian
> cook lived like a leviathan in the lower depths, formidable,
> silent, obscure, inscrutable; the Georgian cook is a creature
> of sunshine and fresh air; in and out of the drawing-room,
> now to borrow the *Daily Herald*, now to ask advice about a
> hat . . . All human relations have shifted – those between
> masters and servants, husbands and wives, parents and
> children.[29]

But Harriett Frean, because of her early conditioning,
represses her true needs and feelings, thereby sacrificing her
happiness. Her parents have, blindly and ineptly, failed to
nudge her into the twentieth century, because they too fail to
acknowledge that personal self-fulfilment and happiness matter
more than some 'notion of duty'. Psychoanalysis represented
more than a method of dealing with neuroses – it signified a
new and passionate concern for the individual and her personal
welfare. At the same time it symbolised a sloughing off of some of
the old ideas, customs and conventions. As Virginia Woolf said,
the modern woman was born 'in or about December 1910'
because she began to develop a sense of what it was to act freely

and for herself: Harriett Frean was already an anachronism, symbolic of something dead and gone.

I always think of my mother when I read this novel. Born in 1907, she was brought up by a nanny who was so exceptionally repressive, and presumably cruel, that she affected my mother for the rest of her life. She did all the usual things that ogre-like nannies did (do they still?). But she went even further; for example, she used to tell her two charges that if they always walked along the street with their eyes down they would eventually see enough pins for it to be unnecessary to buy any. I used to laugh at this; yet, as May Sinclair realised, if these ideas are impressed on someone from an early enough age, even an intelligent woman may never slough them off. But the nanny's more enduring legacy to my mother was her rigid denial of the pleasure-principle. 'We are in this world to do good, not to be happy,' my mother used to exhort us three children and I really believe that she meant it. (It has taken me most of my life to learn how to seek pleasure guiltlessly, but I am learning slowly; thankfully I have no trouble buying pins.)

When Harriett Frean tells a young girl about her renunciation years ago, the girl's response is firm. She unhesitatingly declares that Harriett had thought purely of herself, 'of her own moral beauty' rather than of others, that her self-sacrifice was egocentric rather than genuinely giving. And Harriett realises that 'the beauty of that unique act no longer appeared to her as it once was, uplifting, consoling, incorruptible'. (Here again one is reminded of the theme of *Still Life*, where some might conclude that there is an element of cowardice in Laura's heroic renunciation of Alec. It is one of the most important questions engendered by romantic love which fails to run smooth – is it braver to wound the discarded first love and go to the second or to renounce happiness and thereby blight one's own life?)

In all her novels May Sinclair manages, with varying degrees of success, to combine her insight into the individual consciousness with her art as a novelist. *The Romantic*, for example, is only flawed as a novel because of the way the ends are tied: a psychotherapist is brought in to explain the truth of the matter to Charlotte, the heroine. Other novelists kill people off, or find them a priest or a lover to explain their plight; but they have a private language in the same way that scientists do. The explanation given by the doctor to Charlotte is, certainly, not one that would have graced the pages of the traditional novel, but the jargon used is very much of its time (1920).

> Conway was an out and out degenerate. He couldn't help *that*. He suffered from some physical disability. It went through everything. It made him so that he couldn't live a man's life. He was afraid to enter a profession. He was afraid of women . . . The balance had to be righted somehow. His whole life must have been a struggle to right it. Unconscious, of course. Instinctive. His platonics were just a glorifying of his disability. All that romancing was a gorgeous transformation of his funk . . . So that his very lying was a sort of truth. I mean it was part of the whole desperate effort after completion. He jumped at everything that helped him to get compensation, to get power. He jumped at your feeling for him because it gave him power. He sucked manhood out of you. He sucked it out of everything – out of blood and wound.[30]

Happily, this explanation of her dead lover's impotence and cruelty is a tonic to Charlotte. The doctor has helped her to exorcise her lover, she is able to feel compassion for the dead man and is cleansed and ready should love come her way again. Had the doctor not explained the truth to her, she might have remained obsessed, either full of hatred or unable to forget, but in any case with her mind deeply troubled. It was, in Rebecca West's view, 'from a technical point of view, unfortunate' that the novel was rounded off in this way: but presumably from the heroine's it was a happy release.

And, after all, Rebecca West herself had used a device not so altogether different in her own novel published two years earlier, *The Return of the Soldier* (1918). This too is a novel which allows the central character to 'come through' because of someone's insight into the unconscious, but in this case it is a warm, intuitive woman who makes the cure while the doctor stands by approvingly. It is not primarily a novel about war, for the war is only the device which causes Chris to lose his memory because of the trauma of shell-shock. But Rebecca West had read about doctors who, in treating those suffering from shell-shock, used Freud's theories to try and discover what fears their patients were suppressing. The only direct reference to the fighting is right at the end when, in a memorable passage, Rebecca West points to the irony that only when a man is 'cured' is he considered fit enough to face death again. (It is the same ghastly paradox as the condemned man being denied the means of suicide because he must be kept alive and ready for his executioner.) At the end Chris walks back across the lawn 'with his back turned on this fading happiness'.

> He wore a dreadful decent smile; I knew how his voice would resolutely lift in greeting us. He walked not loose-limbed like a boy, as he had done that very afternoon, but with the soldier's hard tread upon the heel. It recalled to me that, bad as we were, we were yet not the worst circumstances of his return. When we had lifted the yoke of our embraces from his shoulders he would go back to that flooded trench in Flanders under that sky more full of flying death than clouds, to that No Man's Land where bullets fall like rain on the rotting faces of the dead.[31]

The central impetus to the novel is the new, twentieth-century insight into the unconscious. Chris is 'cured', or rather is forced to face up to reality again, because the sight of his dead son's jersey involuntarily jerks him into remembrance of the life of which his son had been part and which he had been obliterating from his mind. But it was not a conscious obliteration, and he could not cure himself even if his conscious self had wished to do so: the doctor is quite sure of this:

> 'A complete case of amnesia,' he was saying . . . 'His unconscious self is refusing to let him resume his relations with his normal life, and so we get this loss of memory.'
> 'I've always said,' declared Kitty, with an air of good sense, 'that if he would make an effort . . .'
> 'Effort!' He jerked his round head about. 'The mental

life that can be controlled by effort isn't the mental life that matters. You've been stuffed up when you were young with talk about a thing called self-control – a sort of barmaid of the soul that says, "Time's up, gentlemen," and "Here, you've had enough." There's no such thing. There's a deep self in one, the essential self, that has its wishes. And if those wishes are suppressed by the superficial self – the self that makes, as you say, efforts and usually makes them with the sole idea of putting up a good show before the neighbours – it takes its revenge. Into the house of conduct erected by the superficial self it sends an obsession.'[32]

Despite these wise words, the doctor is obviously something of a radical, for he declares, 'It's my profession to bring people from various outlying districts of the mind to the normal. There seems to be a general feeling it's the place where they ought to be. Sometimes I don't see the urgency myself.' He concludes that Chris has forgotten his life with his wife because he was 'discontented' with it. And the ending is doubly poignant, for not only will a 'cured' man have to be returned to the trenches but he will have to face up to reality, 'make an effort' and recognise that the tender, innocent love that he once had for Margaret has gone for ever except in his dreams. He has to face the truth, emerge from a fantasy world and face up to cold reality.

'Reality' and 'psychoanalysis' were, by the 1920s, linked words in many people's minds, and even the most middlebrow writer would have expected her readers to know something of what she was talking about when they were mentioned. Laura, in *The Way Things Are* (1927) by E. M. Delafield, is kept up to the mark by her sister.

'Well,' said Christine kindly, 'I can't say that I believe you. And any decent analyst would tell you that you're doing yourself a great deal of harm by this constant pretence. It's bound to create the most frightful repressions. What sort of dreams do you have?'

But Laura, even though she did live in the country, knew all about Herr Freud and his theories, and declined to commit herself in any way upon the subject of dreams.[33]

Indeed, by the 1930s Freudian ideas about memory and repression had become near-clichés of popular fiction and drama. They were certainly a good way of rounding things off, as May Sinclair and Rebecca West had demonstrated. In Rosalind Wade's *Treasure in Heaven* (1937), the explanations of the analyst are used to bring the novel to a calm, generally optimistic conclusion rather as if he were vicar or nanny or other *savant*. Fanny, the middle-aged heroine, is left desolate because all her attempts at helpfulness and charity in the slums of the East End have come to nothing – worse, her efforts have so misfired that she has been forbidden any more contact with her 'cases' or her fellow workers. She tells the 'very young man' about her misery and humiliation, and he reassures her. He tells her that she is suffering from a sense of failure but that if she comes to understand her true motives then she will understand herself and be at peace.

> Sometimes she winced, for he did not spare her feelings. He suggested, in no uncertain terms, that her interest in Mr Waters, her devotion to Neil and her passionate enthusiasm for the work at Maylie Street had been nothing more or less than a repression and sublimation of the sex impulse. Because life denied her husband and children she had instinctively found substitutes.
>
> 'But I haven't really regretted that,' she whispered, 'not for years, anyway. I have Janet's children, you see, and I was always so busy – there wasn't time to mope.'
>
> That was just the trouble, he explained. She had forced her natural wishes so severely into the background that the necessity for 'compensation' was redoubled . . .
>
> 'Oh, you're so cruel,' she told him, 'you leave me no pretences, no illusions, nothing. And what do you suggest? That every woman who hasn't got a husband must go about miserable and degraded because life's cheated her?'[34]

Poor Fanny has to admit that 'she had wanted love, her own home, protection and babies'. She asks herself whether it was not too late, but catching a glimpse in the mirror of 'her round face lined and tear-stained, the unpretentious felt hat pushed from her forehead, she knew, unquestionably, that it was too late . . . She had missed something that could never now be claimed on this side of death'. And the truth *is* comforting: Fanny has no illusions any longer and is grateful and, finally, optimistic.

This was understandably a rather unsuitable theme for the lending libraries. But the analyst is a useful prop to de-fuse an otherwise emotional scene. In her short story 'The Salt of the Earth', written in 1935, Rebecca West allows no such easy way out. The heroine, Alice, is unshakeable in her conviction that she is always right, sensitive to others and admired by everyone for her good sense. She cannot allow herself to go behind the screen that stands between her and reality, since to do this would be to destroy all her illusions and thus the very fabric of her life. Even when her husband finally, desperately, tries to make her see the truth, she will not even begin to accept it. Yet it is as if she cannot help her behaviour and therefore cannot control it. As she explains to her husband, in her nightmares something awful comes nearer and nearer which she knows is eventually going to destroy her. But, as she says, 'the funny thing is . . . I could perfectly well stop this awful horror coming at me. Only for some reason I can't. I have to go on doing the very thing that brings it nearer.'

Clearly, Alice's conscious self prevents her from controlling her unconscious self, even though her dreams are showing her the way out. But because there was no doctor or other perceptive person to help her to understand her 'true' self, there is no solution apart from stalemate or violence; and Rebecca West would have spoilt the shape of her story if she had sought for explanations, though she does hint that Alice has a paranoid personality by making her say plaintively, 'people have always loved being nasty to me all my life'. But deeper than this she does not go.

Her acuteness as a critic must have rendered Rebecca West's task as a novelist rather more difficult, since she was so aware of the difficulties. And she was sometimes guilty of shortcomings which she had pointed out in the work of others. For example, in an essay written in 1926 she observed very wittily that

Henry James and Mrs Wharton and Miss Sedgwick were responsible for an entire school of fiction writers who invariably ended their stories with an elliptical remark on the part of their principal figure: 'Oh, but you see,' he said humbly, 'I never really did,' and rounded them off with a brief passage ecstatically ascribing to him reduced circumstances and spiritual radiance. These are the glycerine tears of fiction.[35]

So indeed they may be, but tears that were not entirely unknown to Rebecca West herself. Nor was a rather simplistic view of Freudian theory unknown to her. In *The Judge* (1922), the reader cannot but wish that she had followed more faithfully the methods of Henry James and Edith Wharton and made the things that are *not* said count for more than the things that are. It is rather heavy-handed when the mother cries out as if with the full force of a revelation: ' "Of course! Of course! He cannot love Ellen because he loves me too much! He has nothing left to love her with!" ' And because she wants him to be happy she tries to syphon off some of his love for her towards Ellen. But the ending is melodrama and there must be many readers who would have opted for something more 'glycerine', less over-stated if they had had the choice.

Although many writers of this period must have been familiar with Freud's precepts, few would have read him at first hand. Virginia Woolf wrote in 1932 that 'I have not studied Dr Freud or any psychoanalyst – indeed I think I have never read any of their books; my knowledge is merely from superficial talk . . . any use of their methods must be instinctive.'[36] Certainly it is possible that she had never read Freud, although unlikely since the Woolfs' Hogarth Press had been publishing the translations of his work since 1924. Yet her understanding of the subconscious could plausibly have evolved without any knowledge of his work at first hand merely because simplified versions of his ideas were so much 'in the air'. And in some ways they were too much in the air for comfort, for writers like Virginia Woolf were pursuing their careers at a difficult time as far as women were concerned. Winifred Holtby pointed out with some acuteness that at the very moment when an artist might have climbed out of the traditional limitations of domestic obligation by claiming to be a human being, she was thrust back into them by the authority of the psychologist. A woman, she was told, must enjoy the full cycle of sex-experience, or she would become riddled with complexes like a rotting fruit . . . All the doubts and repudiations of those who reacted against the Edwardian tradition were hers, combined with all the tumult of the conflict surging round Mrs Fawcett and the Pankhursts. The full weight of the Freudian revelation fell upon her head.[37]

Cynics might reply that if it hadn't been the Freudian apple falling upon her head it would have been another variety and that all women, and men, consider themselves to have been born into a difficult period. This theme was a particular favourite of Rose Macaulay's. It is a pity that this writer, once so popular, perhaps because she was writing for an England more classbound than now, is now out of fashion: certainly it is hard to admire the way she dandles her characters rather like puppets, contemplates their follies and asks the reader to laugh at their dear, funny ways. There is something spiteful about the novels; one is reminded of the child's guilty delight in cutting a worm in half or impaling an insect on a pin; there is little of the tenderness of the mature writer or observer.

In *Dangerous Ages* (1921) the women all imagine that they are at a difficult stage in their lives, and the moral is, rather obviously, that no age is easy until we are so old that we have the wisdom, finally, to perceive this. Mrs Hilary embraces psycho-analysis rather as she might have welcomed a confessor. 'To pour it all out – what comfort! To feel that some one was interested, even though it might only be as in a case.' And at first the doctor comes up to her expectations. When she confesses to depression, to feeling useless, he says to her:

If you are perfectly frank, you can be cured. You can be adjusted to life. Every age in human life has had its own adjustments to make, its own relation to its environment to establish. All that repressed libido must be released and diverted . . . You have some bad complexes, which must be sublimated.

It sounded awful, the firm way he said it, like teeth or appendixes which must be extracted. But Mrs Hilary knew it wouldn't be like that really but delightful and luxurious, more like a Turkish bath.[38]

She enjoys her treatment very much, explaining her 'troubles with the maids' as well as more profound worries. Not that she exactly welcomes the truth about her dreams (she perceives 'that terrible Unconscious' rather as if it 'were a sewer, sunk beneath an inadequate grating'). Nevertheless she faces up to it and is not even wounded when her analyst tells her that her gratitude to him merely means 'that your ego is at present in what is called the state of infantile dependence or tutelage'. But it cannot, of course, last, and by the final chapter Mrs Hilary is to be found 'worse than before'.

She was like a drunkard deprived suddenly of stimulants; she had nothing to turn to, no one who took an interest in her soul. She missed Mr Cradock and that bi-weekly hour; she was like a creeper wrenched loose from its support and flung flat on the ground.[39]

Rose Macaulay wishes the reader to adopt her own brisk and breezy attitude to analysis, which is that it passes the time pleasurably enough but is no better a solution than any other time-filling device. She is not, as a novelist, especially interested in her characters and it is hardly surprising that her creations are usually cardboard cut-outs who cease to exist in the reader's imagination the moment they have put down the book. (*The Towers of Trebizond* is an exception, where she uses her wit and malice to excellent effect.) Whereas writers who managed to absorb the methods of psychoanalysis to genuine purpose used them to create characters of flesh and blood and spirit, characters whose subconscious behaviour was both *felt* and understood by the novelist.

Some writers managed on their own, in blissful ignorance of 'the full weight of the Freudian revelation'. 'George Egerton' wrote in 1932, long after she had finished writing novels:

Unless one is androgynous, one is bound to look at life through the eyes of one's sex, to toe the limitations imposed on one by its individual physiological functions. I came too soon. If I did not know the technical jargon current to-day of Freud and the psycho-analysts, I did know something of complexes and inhibitions, repressions and the subconscious impulses that determine actions and reactions. I used them in my stories. I recognised that in the main, woman was the ever-untamed, unchanging, adapting herself as far as it suited her ends to male expectations; even if repression was altering her subtly. I would use situations or conflicts as I saw them with a total disregard of man's opinions. I would unlock a closed door with a key of my own fashioning.[40]

CHAPTER SEVEN

Romance

'Came the Dawn'

The novels which Laura Jesson or Mrs Miniver or the Provincial Lady borrowed once a week from Boots were firmly middlebrow. No woman with intellectual pretensions (the 'professional' woman or the university-educated) would have read them, preferring Huxley and Virginia Woolf and, at a pinch, Rosamond Lehmann and Elizabeth Bowen. Only with detective fiction (Dorothy Sayers and Agatha Christie) would their tastes have overlapped – here middlebrow and highbrow would have presented a concerted front in opposition to romantic or 'Came the Dawn' novels. Luckily (and unsurprisingly in a class-dominated society) there were libraries especially for the lowbrows.

There is a photograph on my desk taken in about 1923, of G. Stevens, Newsagents and Lending Library, 25 Church Street, Basingstoke, Hampshire. The manager, his wife and the shop assistants are to be seen standing outside: it is they who served their daily customers with their newspapers, magazines and library books and it is the novels stocked by this 'twopenny library' that are the subject of this chapter. G. Stevens's customers would have been less well-off than the customers of his rival library, Boots or W. H. Smith in the High Street; they would have been about half male and half female, whereas at

Boots only one-quarter of the library customers were male. Stevens's shop would have stocked between two hundred and three hundred titles, divided roughly as follows: Mysteries (45 per cent), Westerns (15 per cent), Romances (30 per cent) and 'Other' (10 per cent). (Whereas at W. H. Smith about half were romance, a quarter were adventure stories and a quarter crime.) The big names in thriller and western writers were Nat Gould, Edgar Wallace, 'Sapper', Sax Rohmer, Zane Grey and William Le Queux, and then there were the detective novelists. The most popular romantic novelists were Ruby M. Ayres and Ethel M. Dell, although at least a dozen other writers of romance such as Margaret Pedlar and Denise Robins made a good showing.

It cost twopence or sometimes threepence to borrow a book from a small lending library and there was no danger of being unable to find a new book since the small shopkeeper rented his library stock from a wholesale library which generally held about 2,500 books. And since over two hundred new titles were published in Britain every week the wholesaler too had no trouble in turning over his stock. The women who came in to choose their novels off the two or three shelves at the back of Stevens's shop were part of the new leisured class who needed to while away a good deal of time and the twopenny library was a vital part of their lives.

The sugary, unreal qualities of the inter-war romance and thriller fiction would seem to some modern readers both delightfully harmless and infinitely preferable to the wares on offer at any airport bookstall. Yet there was then rather more disapproval of the 'pulp' qualities of light fiction than there is nowadays, when most people seem to take for granted the crudity of many of the novels published. Few today would write with the vehemence of Rebecca West when she said, with reference to Charles Rex, one of Ethel M. Dell's heroes:

> And in every line that is written about him one hears the thudding, thundering hooves of a certain steed at full gallop; of the true Tosh-horse. For even as one cannot walk on one's own trudging diligent feet if one desires to attain to the height of poetry, but must mount Pegasus, so one

cannot reach the goal of best selling by earnest pedestrian-ism, but must ride thither on the Tosh-horse. No one can write a best-seller by taking thought.[1]

But, then as now, it was the thoughtlessness, the predict-ability, of romance that provided its main appeal. Mr Stevens knew what he had on offer and his customers knew what they were getting. They wanted exactly what Storm Jameson wished they did not want when she wrote in 1939:

> You can see how dangerous the novelist is, because the medium in which he works is not words but it is your mind. He plays on it to make you laugh and cry . . . There are novelists who make a great deal of money by playing over and over *All That I Want is Somebody to Love Me* . . . And when we want to wear grief or joy we take down some shabby ill-made garment belonging to Miss So-and-so, the popular novelist, and muffle our foolish heads in it . . .
>
> A novelist who is merely clever or merely witty or merely, as we say of children, very noticing, may write novels which amuse or excite or soothe us, but at least he is only helping us to pass our time. At worst he is unfitting us for life by giving us weak or distorted or foolish notions about it.[2]

Storm Jameson wrote her attack on popular fiction, of which this is part, in 1932, the same year that Queenie Leavis published her full-length study, *Fiction and the Reading Public*. They were both preoccupied with lowbrow fiction as a force for good or evil and were both secure in their belief that its influence was corrupting. Mrs Leavis's oft-quoted stricture was that popular novels 'actually get in the way of genuine feeling and responsible thinking by creating cheap mechanical responses and by throwing their weight on the side of social, national and herd prejudices'.[3]

Ever since the character in Jane Austen's *Northanger Abbey* (1818) confessed to reading 'only a novel', and the French censors of the late 1850s declared that Flaubert's *Madame Bovary* was corrupting because it showed a married woman led astray by an over-rich diet of light fiction, this argument has refused to go away. Mary McCarthy even managed rather subtly to extend the corrupting influence as far as the library itself.

> Emma [Bovary] and Léon agree that membership in a circulating library is a necessity if you have to live in the provinces and they are both wholly dependent on this typical bourgeois institution. The lending library is a central metaphor of *Madame Bovary* because it is the inexhaustible source of *idées reçues* – borrowed ideas and stock sentiments which circulate tritely among the population . . . the lending library is an image of civilization itself. Ideas and feelings as well get more and more soiled and grubby, like library books, as they pass from hand to hand.[4]

At some private circulating libraries subscribers could pay extra for the privilege of borrowing new books – perhaps they did this not merely to avoid germs but also to give the sentiments they proposed to imbibe a better chance of being unspoilt by the common touch.

But light fiction had millions of supporters, as sales and borrowing figures demonstrated. The publisher Michael Joseph wrote in *The Commercial Side of Literature* (1925) that

> the demand for fiction on such a wholesale scale must be due to the artificial complexities of a civilised state. Men and women, especially women, seek in the vicarious realm of fiction the wider range of human experiences which a complex and narrowed life denies them. Having neither time nor opportunity in this crowded, hustled existence to taste the joys and sorrows, the vicissitudes and triumphs of a more elemental experience, they turn to fiction to satisfy their natural craving . . . for emotional satisfaction, civilisation-hampered people turn to fiction.[5]

He pointed out that people read fiction for entertainment, escape, instruction, enlargement of their range of experience, to enjoy observing and criticising and, fundamentally, to enjoy the illusions which real life fails to sustain. (Realists refuse to hand the reader a pair of rose-coloured spectacles and have, therefore, to cater for a more discriminating public.) And he defined the best-seller as needing sincerity, a good story, strong and sustained human interest, a happy ending *after* great troubles and tribulations, and an outstanding theme or moral. Readers were generally prejudiced against the psychological and morbid novel and the types of story that would be difficult to 'place' included historical romances, stories with a religious or spiritual bias, stories with a very strong moral flavour and 'pre-war' stories. Short stories were also disliked, the ideal length for a novel being one that could be read at a sitting (i.e. in an afternoon or evening).

The comparative excitement of 'the times in which we live' was Michael Joseph's explanation for why the historical novel was then out of favour. But by the middle of the 1920s, writers like Anya Seton and Georgette Heyer were just beginning long writing careers which were to last for fifty years. In the latter's novels, historical trappings are combined with the basic Jane Eyre plot of the socially underprivileged girl falling in love with a superior man who does not notice. A variation on the theme was the heroine proudly refusing to admit her love, as in *Regency Buck* (1935), in which Judith fights with her handsome guardian for three hundred pages before they are finally reconciled.

'Nonsensical child! I have been in love with you almost from the first moment of setting eyes on you.'

'Oh, this is dreadful!' said Miss Taberner, shaken by remorse. 'I disliked you amazingly for weeks!'

The Earl kissed her again. 'You are wholly adorable,' he said.

'No, I am not,' replied Miss Taverner, as soon as she was able. 'I am as disagreeable as you are. You would like to beat me. You said you would once, and I believe you meant it!'

'If I only said it once I am astonished at my own forbearance. I have wanted to beat you at least a dozen times, and came very near doing it once . . . But I still think you adorable. Give me your hand.'[6]

Michael Joseph's distinction between 'pulp' fiction and the rest is clear. One is escapist, the other enlarges the reader's experience, one is widely read and the other minimally, one is not reviewed in newspapers and magazines, the other is. It is a situation which persists today and only very occasionally are the barriers breached, as in the case of *Jane Eyre*, *Rebecca* and *Gone with the Wind*. (Although I can think of one or two women of my mother's generation who profess to intellectual and social awareness but still managed to ignore an outstanding work of fiction like *Rebecca*. Of couse, a small minority censors good novels on the grounds *alone* of mass appeal, being loath to associate itself in any way with Mrs Leavis's 'herd prejudices'. But it has always mystified me that someone can have political, often socialist, feelings without wanting even occasionally to share in a mass imaginative experience – people were reading *Rebecca* at the time of the 'phoney war'; any good historian of the period should read it in tandem with contemporary newspapers.)

The stock of twopenny libraries stayed firmly on one side of the barrier, avoiding any possible pretensions to literary quality and these libraries provided their customers precisely with what they asked for, a good light romantic novel which would not make them feel 'uncomfortable', preferably on the theme of 'All That I Want is Somebody to Love Me'. The basic storyline should be boy meeting girl, various seemingly insuperable difficulties coming between them and, finally, the revelation of their true and hitherto suppressed feelings. The arch-exponent of this theme was Ethel M. Dell, and she established her reputation with her first novel *The Way of an Eagle* (1912), a novel which was to set the pattern for pulp fiction for the next seventy years at least. Complaining about the lazily eulogistic reviewer who corruptly praises everything he reads, George Orwell described him

> sinking his standards to a depth at which, say, Ethel M. Dell's *Way of an Eagle* is a fairly good book. But on a scale of values which makes *The Way of an Eagle* a good book, *The Constant Nymph* is a superb book, and *The Man of*

Property is – what? A palpitating tale of passion, a terrific soul-shattering masterpiece, an unforgettable epic which will last as long as the English language and so on and so forth. (As for any *really* good book it would burst the thermometer.)[7]

The Way of an Eagle had been rejected by more than eight publishers before Fisher Unwin accepted it for their First Novel Library on condition that it was cut from 300,000 to 90,000 words. Published in January 1912, the novel was an instant success, being reprinted twenty-seven times in the next three years alone. Its author was a recluse, refusing to be photographed and knitting her own clothes rather than having to face the publicity of a department store changing room. Although she married when she was forty, she remained by temperament extremely virginal and had no direct experience either of India (where so many of her novels are set) or of the physical violence which runs as an exotic, titillating thread throughout her work.

Most modern readers will greatly enjoy *The Way of an Eagle*, for it remains the best kind of read for anyone wishing to curl up in an armchair, flu-bound and lackadaisical, and wallow unashamedly in a book that is entirely timeless, oblivious of realities and predictions – even if it is written by an author who is part of what George Orwell called that 'huge tribe of Barries and Deepings and Dells who simply don't notice what is happening'.[8] There is also something undeniably cheering in reading and enjoying a novel that has given pleasure to so many for so long; I love to imagine my mother and grandmother sobbing over books like this.

The Way of an Engle opens dramatically with the final days of a siege at a British-held North-west Frontier fort. Muriel, the Brigadier's daughter, is under great strain from the prolonged bombardment and tension and 'there came a time when Muriel Roscoe, driven to extremity, sought relief in a remedy from which in her normal senses she would have turned in disgust' (opium). As the crisis nears, her father chooses Nick Ratcliffe to look after her. Muriel does not care for him.

'Only the other day I heard him laugh at something that

was terrible – something it makes me sick to think of. Indeed, Daddy, I would far rather have Captain Grange to take care of me. Don't you think he would if you asked him? He is so much bigger and stronger, and – and kinder.'

'Ah! I know,' her father said. 'He seems so to you. But it is nerve that your protector will need, child; and Ratcliffe possesses more nerve than all the rest of the garrison put together.'[9]

This passage holds the clues to the rest of the novel. Nick is sexual yet frightening – he is not tender like Grange. But Muriel dislikes him for reasons she would rather not admit (he is unashamedly sensual and intolerant of convention). Eventually, however, the two will be lovers, but the reader settles comfortably into her chair knowing there are 350 pages of difficulties before the happy climax. Their escape from the fort is dramatic but they reach the haven of Simla unscathed. Muriel agrees to marry Nick, who is described as too careless of propriety to bother about a courtship. But she cannot shake off the frightening memory she has of Nick in the desert

bent to destroy like an eagle above his prey, merciless, full of strength, terrible – saw the man beneath him, writhing, convulsed, tortured – saw his upturned face, and starting eyes – saw the sudden downward swoop of Nick's right hand – the flash of the descending steel.[10]

She may have been bred to be the wife of a fearless soldier, but a killing in cold-blood was going too far and something that, she imagined, the scrupulous Grange would not have undertaken. So whenever Nick even takes her hand 'once more her old aversion to this man swept over her in a nauseating wave'.

A few days later Muriel overhears a conversation in which her shallow, small-minded English hostess makes it clear that the English community assume that the couple are only marrying because he has fatally compromised her on their trek through the desert. She breaks off her engagement, in a scene which places Nick firmly in the line of irresistible, incorrigible heroes stretching from Mr Rochester to Rhett Butler; and goes home. Here she becomes engaged to Grange, the smooth, polite but clearly sexually inept officer from the days at the garrison. Nick too comes home on leave and, after various dramas, Muriel has to recognise the truth.

> She knew now! She knew now! He had forced her to realize it. He had captured her, had kindled within her − by what magic she knew not − the undying flame. Against her will, in spite of her utmost resistance, he had done this thing. Above and beyond and through her fiercest hatred, he had conquered her quivering heart. He had let her go again, but not till he had blasted her happiness for ever. None other could ever dominate her as this man dominated. None other could ever kindle in her − or ever quench − the torch that this man's hand had lighted.
>
> And this was Love − this hunger that could never be satisfied, this craving which would not be stifled or ignored − Love triumphant, invincible, immortal − the thing she had striven to slay at its birth, but which had lived on in spite of her, growing, spreading, enveloping, till she was lost, till she was suffocated, in its immensity. There could never be any escape for her again. She was fettered hand and foot. It was useless any longer to strive. She stood and faced the truth.
>
> She did not ask herself how it was she had ever come to care. She only numbly realized that she had always cared. And she knew now that to no woman is it given to so hate as she had hated without the spur of Love goading her thereto. Ah, but Love was cruel! Love was merciless! For she had never known − nor ever could know now − the ecstasy of Love. Truly it conquered; but it left its prisoners to perish of starvation in the wilderness.[11]

But there is still Pride and matters remain unresolved when Muriel and Nick both, separately, go back to India.

> Life was a horrible emptiness to her in those days. She was weary beyond expression, and had no heart for the gaieties

in which she was plunged. Idle compliments had never attracted her, and flirtations were an abomination to her. She looked through and beyond them with the eyes of a sphinx. But there were very few who suspected the intolerable ache that throbbed unceasingly behind her impassivity – the loneliness of spirit that oppressed her like a crushing, physical weight.[12]

Nick has seemingly disappeared and it is rumoured he has entered a monastery in Tibet. When he reappears it transpires that he has disguised himself as a beggar in order to remain undetected near her, and is well placed from his customary begging posture at the foot of the Residency steps to foil an assassination attempt on Muriel's host. But Muriel still has to find the words to tell him of her change of heart.

The tumult of her emotions swelled to sudden uproar, thunderous, all-possessing, overwhelming, so that she gasped and gasped again for breath. And then all in a moment she knew that the conflict was over. She was as a diver, hurling with headlong velocity from dizzy height into deep waters, and she rejoiced – she exulted – in that mad rush into depth.

With a quivering laugh she moved. She loosened her convulsive clasp upon his hand, turned it upwards, and stooping low, she pressed her lips closely, passionately, lingeringly, upon his open palm. She had found a way.[13]

Nick is as masterful as Muriel or any reader could have wished.

'I warn you, Muriel, you are putting yourself irrevocably in my power, and you will never break away again. You may come to loathe me with your whole soul, but I shall never let you go. Have you realized that? If I take you now, I take you for all time.'

He spoke almost with violence, and, having spoken, drew back from her abruptly, as though he could not wholly trust himself.

But nothing could dismay her now. She had fought her last battle, had made the final surrender. Her fear was dead. She stretched out her hands to him with unfaltering confidence.

'Take me then, Nick,' she said.[14]

Ethel M. Dell was a pleasure-giver pure and simple. She seems to have felt no need for heart-searching about her merit or her role as a writer, but after her initial success, continued to write novels on the same lines, aimed at the same kind of audience and guaranteed to give the same kind of enjoyment. Contemporary critics had no trouble in pinning her down:

> Her books are unpretentious contributions to the literature of escape: that is, they enable the weary and bored and depressed to transfer themselves temporarily to another sphere of life . . . Those below a certain standard of literary culture desire, in their imaginative exercises, to move in a world as different from their own as any world can be. Girls who travel on crowded tramcars and Underground trains among hordes of plain young men, or who live in kitchens and are visited by few save plain young butchers and plain young bakers, are likely to be responsive to the emotions of a heroine carried long distances through strange romantic country by a Nick Ratcliffe; or to those of another heroine attracted by the magnetic personality of a Charles Rex in the supposed romantic atmosphere of a liner.[15]

Mr Ward then retreats into what one might call the Madame Bovary argument and speculates whether 'fiction-fed minds may become in time permanently depressed and disgruntled by the conviction that life has not allowed them a fair deal'.

Books like *The Way of an Eagle* are superbly good at telling stories of drama and intricacy in which everything turns out all right in the end. The hero and heroine endure tests of endurance which would crush ordinary mortals, but the reader has the satisfaction of knowing that they will come through with flying colours. Herein lies one of the main counter-agruments to the Madame Bovary question – no shop girl, factory girl, skivvy or housewife could see the merest glimmer of a parallel between her life and those of Dell's heroines. Nor would she probably wish her daily existence to imitate the dramas that she is reading about. The only point at which she would certainly have liked life to imitate art was with respect to male sexuality. Dell's heroes may be proud, aloof, withdrawn and in need of taming. But at the same time they are passionate, loyal, forceful and (usually) moneyed enough to find no practical hindrance should they wish to follow their women to the ends of the earth. A. P. Herbert wrote about this problem in *The Water Gipsies* (1930) and also in this song:

Jack loves me well enough, I know,
But does he ever bite his lip,
And does he chew his cheek to show
That Passion's got him in a grip?
An' does his gun go pop-pop-pop –
When fellers get familiar? No.
He just says, ' 'Op it!' and they 'op –
It may be life, but ain't it slow?[16]

There is a serious issue here that is crucial to the next chapter. If men and women are to conform to the romantic ideal which, in the twentieth century, demands that domestic harmony should partner romantic love, how are they to achieve this if their imaginations are feeding on quite different fantasies? Poor Jack in A. P. Herbert's poem had probably never read a novel by Ethel M. Dell and would not have known Nick Ratcliffe, the most famous of her heroes, had he met him. But then should his wife have been secretly resentful that he was not more Ratcliffe-like? And again one thinks of Emma Bovary, privately in despair with Charles because he was so unlike a romantic hero. Who can say whether women should read less romantic fiction and demand less of their only-too-everyday men or whether men should read their fiction and try in private at least to live up more to the Dell-ideal? – an ideal which recognises sexuality as a vital part of intimacy. But if one reads the imaginary but horribly plausible description of 'Mrs Britain's' typical bedtime routine or that of Norah in Rosamond Lehmann's *A Note in Music* it is hardly surprising that they should seek oblivion in a romantic novel.

The heroes of romantic novels behave in a romantic way. They are also far more obviously sensual than the heroes of 'well-written' novels. In 1910, Arnold Bennett wondered why Elinor Glyn's 'magnificently sexual novel' (*His Hour*) had not been banned by the Library Censorship Committee, while Rebecca West commented in her inimitable way on the absurd double standards at work when she wrote, 'how true it is that there are those who may not look at a horse over a hedge; and there are those who may lead it out through the gate'. And she referred to the serious writer's wistfulness with which 'he gazes across the esplanade of any watering-place and looks at the old ladies reading their Ethel Dells. Truly we are a strange nation.'[17]

Already in the early years of the century Elinor Glyn had made it quite clear that women experience sexual desire and that this is something both usual and admirable. Yet she sidestepped the censor by ensuring that some form of retribution invariably struck, and by using language which gave an air of purity to her work. Mrs Leavis was the first to point out that many bestselling novels 'make play with the key words of the emotional vocabulary which provoke the vague warm surges of feeling associated with religion and religion substitutes – e.g. life, death, love, good, evil, sin, home, mother, noble, gallant, purity, honour'.[18] And it is true that when an Elinor Glyn hero finally seduces or is conquered there is always a mention of heaven, worship or eternity, as if religious allusions add the necessary moral tone.

But when one looks beyond the various disguises provided by religion, Nemesis or generally exalted implications, it is quite clear that the true goal for her heroines is sexual pleasure. Yet her grandson claimed that she personally 'was not much interested in sex; she thought it unromantic, animal, earthy. She was interested in love, in the romantic disguise which enveloped more material thoughts, and feelings, and the maintenance of which was the great ideal of her life.'[19] (And Barbara Cartland has declared: 'All my heroines are virgins – I don't think sleeping together is romantic.'[20]) Elinor Glyn nevertheless invented the word 'it' as shorthand for sex appeal; and few could seriously claim that *Three Weeks* (1907), her most famous novel, which had sold five million copies by the early thirties, was popular because of its emphasis on the merely spiritual qualities of love.

In this silly but very readable novel a young Englishman on holiday in Switzerland meets a mysterious and beautiful young woman who uses his gift of a tiger skin as a bed on which to teach him all there is to know about sexual pleasure.

> At the first glow of dawn, he awoke, a strange sensation, almost of strangling and suffocation, upon him. There, bending over, framed in a mist of blue-black waves, he saw his lady's face. Its milky whiteness lit by her strange eyes – green as [a] cat's they seemed, and blazing with the fiercest passion of love – while twisted round his throat he felt a great strand of her splendid hair. The wildest thrill as yet his life had known then came to Paul, he clasped her in his arms with a frenzy of mad, passionate joy.[21]

For three weeks the idyll continues, with Paul's mistress, who naturally turns out to be a queen, instructing him in all the ways of love, which includes the stress on masochism which was such an important element in popular erotic fiction:

> You see, Paul, a man can always keep a woman loving him if he kisses her enough, and make her feel that there is no use struggling because he is too strong to resist. A woman will stand almost anything from a passionate lover. He may beat her and pain her soft flesh; he may shut her up and deprive her of all other friends – while the motive is raging love and interest in herself on his part, it only makes her love him the more.[22]

Paul loses his queen but remembers something more practical she had once told him in between her coos and flutters (they are in a gondola by now): ' "You must not just drift, my Paul, like so many of your countrymen do. You must help to stem the tide of your nation's decadence, and be a strong man." '[23] This he does, becoming an important diplomat but forever mourning his queen, unable to marry anyone else, because, after all, what would an English girl know about love? ' "The women of your country are sweet and soft, but they know not the passion I know, my Paul – the fierceness and madness of love – ." ' Erotic love was all right in Ruritania or in a gondola with its suitably honeymoon overtones, but the Library Censorship Committee could not condone it when it was associated with the kind of girls they might invite to their tennis parties. As Mr Justice Younger said in 1915 of the 'grossly immoral' *Three Weeks*, at a hearing when Elinor Glyn was suing for infringement of copyright, 'stripped of its trappings which are mere accident, it is nothing more nor less than a sensual, adulterous intrigue'.[24]

Thus sexual bliss in the fiction written in the afterglow of Victorianism had to take place somewhere far away and exotic, otherwise the circulating libraries would not be able to continue with their comfortable equation of distance equalling decency. If distance was impractical, then the surroundings had to be very unusual, as in Elinor Glyn's *Six Days* (1924), where the couple's honeymoon actually takes place in a makeshift church. David and Laline ('all that a really lovely American heiress should be') arrange to tour the battlefields together – a popular pastime in the early 1920s. A priest shows them round a dug-out, there is a landslide and the priest's dying gesture is to marry the happy couple who spend their honeymoon alternately making love and scrabbling to get out. (Once rescued, David rapidly disappears on a secret mission; Laline is about to marry his best friend for the sake of the coming child when David arrives on a horse, declaring memorably, ' "I forbid this marriage to go on." ') The sexuality is, however, rather less obvious in this novel, partly because the couple are married and partly because a dug-out had unromantic if not morbid associations for most readers.

Another fictional method of bowing to the dictates of propriety was that of treating sexuality medically, rather as if the woman was a 'case' history. The heroine of *Anna Lombard* (1901) by 'Victoria Cross' is an English girl newly arrived in India who has a reputation for seriousness. She soon becomes engaged to Gerald, the narrator, but they cannot marry because of her secret and shameful passion for a native.

In the day she never saw him or sent for him except in his capacity as servant, and he was in no way favoured in money, dress or quarters above the other servants . . . In the day Anna was entirely with me, and if slander could have touched her at all it would have connected her name with mine and none other. Yet, even so, it seemed to me as if the whole matter must rise to the light in some way, and I waited in dread for the hour of discovery.

The more I studied Anna, the more incomprehensible and terrible this strange dual passion of hers became for me. But, also, I became more and more convinced I had decided rightly in not abandoning her to herself. Neither would she have deserved my desertion. For this miserable love that had overtaken her she was no more to be held responsible than she would have been for any physical malady she might have been stricken with. She loved me with the same faithful, tender devotion she had given me from the first, and it seemed, when we were alone together, impossible to me that she could be living the life she was. But, indeed, her love for Gaida seemed to have no sort of influence upon her love for, and her relations with, me. It was a thing utterly separate and apart from that self which she gave to me. Within her the two loves, the higher and the lower, seemed to exist together without touching or disturbing the other, just as in a river sometimes one sees two streams, one muddy, the other clear, flowing side by side without mixing.[25]

Sexuality at some distance and sexuality as 'physical malady' were both acceptable, but neither of them were such best-selling ingredients as sexuality as sadism. Until the mid-1920s, sexual pleasure for women was closely linked with cruelty; writers like E. M. Hull and Ethel M. Dell took firmly to heart Elinor Glyn's observation that 'a woman will stand almost anything from a passionate lover'. The most famous personification of a male brute was 'the sheik', in the novel of that name published in 1919 by Edith Maud Hull. She was the most unlikely kind of author for a novel which is the nearest thing to pornography written by any of the inter-war female novelists. Married to a pig-farmer, she lived quietly in the country. *The Bookman* wrote:

> One of the most popular of present-day novelists is Mrs E. M. Hull who is seldom to be met with in literary circles, for she spends a good deal of her time in travelling, and, when at home, prefers a country life in Derbyshire, and is keen on all manner of games and sports. She wrote her first novel *The Sheik* with no idea of publishing it, but as a means of personal distraction during the war when she had to be very much alone. When it was finished she decided to let it try its fortune with a publisher, and its prompt and unexpected success encouraged her to write a second book, *The Shadow of the East.*[26]

The Sheik is the story of a cold, cool English girl who is kidnapped in the desert by an Arabian sheik, endures rape for months and finally realises that she loves him. The novel relies neither on veiled erotic description nor on religious imagery, but on uninhibited sado-masochism.

> The flaming light of desire burning in his eyes turned her sick and faint. Her body throbbed with the consciousness of a knowledge that appalled her. She understood his purpose with a horror that made each separate nerve in her system shrink against the understanding that had come to her under the consuming fire of his ardent gaze, and in the fierce embrace that was drawing her shaking limbs closer and closer against the man's own pulsating body.[27]

By Chapter Three she is marginally less horror-struck by it all for she is 'resisting him dumbly with tight-locked lips till he held her palpitating in her arms . . . "Oh, you brute! You brute!" she wailed, until his kisses silenced her.' By Chapter Five, halfway through the novel, brutality has won the day for 'Love had come to her at last who had scorned it so fiercely'. From now on Diana is all submission — even to an Arab whom 'Aubrey would indiscriminately class as a "damned nigger" . . . She did not care . . . Oriental though he was, might he not be capable of a deep and lasting affection?' (Luckily the sheik turns out to be a decent English chap by birth.)

Other writers too used sadism as a perfectly acceptable substitute for eroticism. Ruth, in Vita Sackville-West's *Heritage* (1919), says, 'he cringes to me, and then I bully him; or else he bullies me, and then I cringe to him. But quarrel as we may, we always come together again.' But in another of her novels, *Challenge* (1923), which was only published in America, the love-making of Eve and Julian, modelled on the author and her lover Violet Trefusis, is described as a clash of personalities rather than a harmony of souls for 'they had no tenderness for one another . . . Violence was never very far out of sight.' And Ethel M. Dell used pain to excite her readers, presumably knowing that sensuality would be deplored by them but that sadism was perfectly acceptable. Rebecca West was among those dismayed by this paradox; reviewing *Charles Rex* (1922), in which an elderly roué takes a page on board his yacht and, discovering that he has rescued a girl in disguise, continues to treat her as a page-boy, she wrote:

> For five chapters the story titillates us (us includes, one amazedly estimates, the mass of the population of Surbiton, Bournemouth, and Cheltenham) with a description of the peculiar intercourse that takes place between them in these circumstances. There is a specially pleasing incident when they are playing cards and the girl-boy cheats, and Lord Saltash beats her with a riding-switch. We afterwards learn that she had cheated on purpose that she might have this delicious revelation of the gentleman's quality.[28]

It is one of the most mysterious aspects of the barriers and restraints a society chooses to impose upon itself that, in England in the 1920s, respectable middle-class readers cheerfully devoured the 'pleasing incidents' of E. M. Hull and Ethel M. Dell while denying themselves *Lady Chatterley's Lover*, *The Well of Loneliness* or *Sleeveless Errand*, all of which were banned. Yet *Sleeveless Errand* by Norah James, which came out in 1929, was banned merely because it accepted sensuality as an integral part of life and contained remarks like ' "we're bored with people who aren't bawdy. We call them prigs and prudes if they don't want to talk about copulation at lunchtime and buggery at dinner." '[29] It also offended because its characters were unrestrained on topics where restraint was more usual (' "For Christ's sake give me a drink" ') without the author appearing to disapprove. Similarly H. G. Wells had, in *Ann Veronica*, violated the prevailing moral code by condoning his heroine's behaviour. He and Norah James were attacking prevailing pieties while the middlebrow female novelists stayed firmly on the side of good manners. Anna Lombard's lover dies, she murders her dusky baby and endures a year's exile before being pronounced cured. Paul and his queen have only three weeks together, while the sheik turns out to have been ill-treated by his English father (which excuses many faults in his character).

The British legal system also took exception to the tenderness and lesbian love displayed by the two women Stephen and Mary in *The Well of Loneliness*, of whom we are told, finally, after many emotional vicissitudes, 'and that night they were not divided'. But their love was far more distasteful to the majority of readers than any amount of flogging or brutality. The reason for this hypocrisy was well understood by Elinor Glyn. Sensuality was acceptable in a far-off country, lesbianism, like 'rudeness', would taint and threaten the ordered respectability of the middle-class home and family. But no one nice was really going to step off the Metropolitan Line from Baker Street to Pinner and have to imitate Doctor Carew in E. M. Hull's *The Desert Healer* (1923):

> A piercing shriek rang through the silent house. A shriek that was followed by others so terrible, so frenzied, that for a moment he reeled under the horror of them. And with the agonising screams was mingled the sound of a man's raving and other more pregnant sounds that drove Carew to the verge of madness . . .
>
> Laying her on the bed he stripped the blood-wet silken rags from her lacerated shoulders, wincing in agony as they

191

clung to the delicate broken flesh his trembling lips covered with passionate kisses. But he was doctor as well as lover and, forcing his shaking fingers to steadiness, he bathed the cruel wounds with tender skill.[30]

Had Carew been merely lover, Mrs Hull would not have been able to write about him kissing flesh or stripping off rags; but in the context of violence it was perfectly acceptable. Perhaps if Stephen in *The Well of Loneliness* had had a penchant for beating her fellow sex the book would not have been banned. But, of course, Radclyffe Hall overstepped another mark – she was being realistic and the reader was not to be offered the anodyne of a romantic finale. What most readers of women's novels wanted was a story that, after various vicissitudes, comes all right in the end. This point was well understood by a reviewer in *The Bookman*, who wrote in June 1923 (*The Desert Healer* having recently been published but not reviewed):

Those weary of realism – more or less real – provided so lavishly in the novels of the day, turn with relief to writers like Margaret Peterson [popular novelist, author of *The Scent of the Rose*]. The tale is full of trouble and misunderstandings, certainly, but we know from the beginning all will be all right in the end, so we regard these stoically . . . It is a pity Mrs Peterson has followed the revolting example of another popular woman novelist by introducing flogging on a grand scale. One writer with that idiosyncrasy is one too many.[31]

In his book on *Woman* (1927), Bauer argues that women are erotically stimulated by reading, far more so than men. He explained the censorship prevalent in highbrow and middlebrow novels by suggesting that their female readers kept their sensuality under better control.

Where is the flapper who has not secretly read at least one of the novels of Zola? Or the woman who has not read some chapter or other of the Decameron? Where is the woman of the lower classes who does not give up much of her free time to the reading of appalling 'love-stories'? Why are women the greatest purchasers of 'realistic' novels? Why is it that women spend all their time reading sensational novels, while their menfolk devote their studies to the more serious sorts of literature? Weininger insists in *Sex and Character* that there is something of the procuress in every woman, which finds a certain satisfaction in the union of lovers even in a novel or on the stage.[32]

What Bauer failed to point out is that male values are peculiar neither to highbrow nor to lowbrow novels, though they dominate less in the middlebrow 'woman's novel'. There is only a difference in tone and style between the forcefulness of Nick Ratcliffe and the domination of Mellors in *Lady Chatterley's Lover* (1928). Connie Chatterley, like Muriel, has a choice: she can either remain mentally aloof and self-contained or she can surrender herself body and soul to the demands of her man. To begin with she does the former:

And a woman had to yield. A man was like a child with his appetites. A woman had to yield him what he wanted, or like a child he would probably turn nasty and flounce away and spoil what was a very pleasant connexion. But a woman could yield to a man without yielding her inner free self . . . she could use this sex thing to have power over him.[33]

But once Mellors has brought her to orgasm she swiftly capitulates. Having been waiting, separate, watchful, 'now in her heart the queer wonder of him was awakened' and she concedes her sexuality, she yields. And while Mellors is shown as kind and potent and sensual, Connie's body is depersonalised, it is erotic only in so far as it arouses desire in the man.

Lawrence takes the same stance as a romantic novelist, which is to show the woman's initial repulsion ('surely the man was intensely ridiculous in this posture and this act!'[34]) swiftly removed by the orgasm her lover is kind enough to bestow. The main focus of his interest is in the life-affirming, energy-releasing qualities of Mellor's potency, but apart from the mere fact of Connie's capitulation and subsequent pleasure very little more of her character is explained to us. And it is the same with Muriel – she concedes to Nick, she is full of joy, but we still only know about her with reference to her lover: the male fights and wins, the female receives pleasure and submits.

Lawrence's novels were banned because, while sharing the attitudes of many of his contemporary writers, his language was uncomfortably explicit; whereas writers like Ethel M. Dell used a kind of shorthand vocabulary – 'tumult', 'thunderous', 'gasping', 'conflict', 'rush' and so on – to hint not at actual but at potential orgasmic fulfilment. Lawrence also offended because he did not disguise matters with religious imagery, which is often heavily in evidence in Ethel M. Dell's reconciliation scene, to take the gloss off the sexual overtones. And he chose settings for most of his novels which were rather too close to home.

Ethel M. Dell and her imitators used settings far enough away to have a romantic, intense quality but which were at the same time plausible enough to make the reader identify with them. The choice of India and the Far East was a tradition initiated by Flora Annie Steel and continued by writers like Maud Diver, 'Sydney C. Grier' and Alice Perrin; in their novels they often explored the theme of the initially doomed but ultimately triumphant love of a pure English girl for a man who often displays distressing Eastern leanings but thankfully turns out to be an Englishman after all. Sometimes it was the other way round, as in *Anna Lombard*, in which Gerald marries Anna, but full atonement is only made when the poor dusky baby is smothered by its mother who, after a long period of mourning and heart-searching, finally comes to her husband cleansed of her passion and ready to be a demure English bride. It is a different pattern from the conventional 'Indian' romance in which the trimmings were North-west Frontier but the tone definitely Cheltenham, and in which the English are usually described as cold-blooded but civilised and the Indians as torrid but socially impossible.

India was a favourite setting when a firm moral line was required. Passion exiled to India meant that the Anglo-Indian sensibility, for example, which was promoted as upright, sensible, pukka sahib, could be contrasted with that of the sensual, feckless and inscrutable Indian. Forster took the opposite stance in *A Passage to India* (1924) when he disparagingly contrasted the passionless, socialised, constrained behaviour of the English with the warmer, more loving, more life-giving and spiritual qualities of the Indian.

When romantic novels no longer had to display quite such an upright moral tone, passion could take place closer to hand; and so during the late 1920s, writers like Berta Ruck, Ruby M. Ayres and Denise Robins began to make millinery shops, advertising agencies or tennis courts almost as torrid as any hill-station or bazaar. What remained constant was the vital necessity for the heroine to be well bred ('silly novels by lady novelists rarely introduce us into any other than very lofty and fashionable society,'[35] observed George Eliot). Just as the sheik turned out to be an English aristocrat, so the heroine of a romantic novel had to be one rung up the social ladder. This was not merely for reasons of snobbery; it was part of a pattern of wish-fulfilment, the assumption being that all readers of light novels would prefer to be a little better off, a little better connected than they in fact are. Those who borrowed books from the twopenny library wanted to sure that they *were* clamping the proverbial rose-coloured spectacles on to their noses. As Berta Ruck wrote in her autobiography:

> I think it is very wrong to give Youth the impression that it is unalterably doomed to disappointment. '*C'est en croyant aux roses*', says a French proverb, '*qu'on les fait éclorer.*' It is by believing in roses that one brings them into bloom . . .
>
> It is my creed that the world was created to be merry as a marriage-bell and for the whole human race to be healthy, wealthy and wise enough to be happy on all cylinders.[36]

After the Great War this belief was still firmly held by romantic novelists, but a shade more realism was introduced into their work. The settings were more often home-based and the heroines often had some kind of job or occupation (which they would of course discontinue at Cupid's bidding). The adventure aspect of the pulp novel began to wane, the plots became more timid and the psychological machinations began

to take on a greater importance; writers began to perceive
adventures rather more in the mind than on the slopes of the
Himalayas or the desert dunes.

Partly this was due to the prevalent interest in the inner
workings of the human heart, partly because the drama of the
war years had left the reading public with a distaste for the
harrowing tragedies of which previously they had been fond.
The settings of romantic novels became, during the 1920s, those
with which the reader could identify; the hat or dress shop was a
particular favourite, as the heroine of Angela Thirkell's *High
Rising* (1933) discovers. Left a widow, realising that she had
somehow to support herself and her sons, Laura Morland

> had considered the question carefully, and decided that,
> next to racing, murder and sport, the great reading public
> of England (female section) like to read about clothes.
> With real industry she got introductions, went over big
> department stores, visited smart dressmaking friends,
> talked to girls she knew who had become buyers or high-
> brow window-dressers, and settled down to write best-
> sellers. Her prevision was justified, and she now had a
> large, steady reading public, who apparently could not
> hear too much about the mysteries of the wholesale and
> retail clothes business.[37]

And indeed there were many writers, like Laura Morland, who
turned out innumerable novels using just this formula: the poor
little shop-girl theme appears over and over again during the
next two decades – the editorial précis for a story in *My Weekly*
being typical of countless others:

> Once upon a time there was a milliner, young, beautiful
> and attractive and her name was Peggy. She sold wonder-
> ful model hats to old, plain dowagers and pretty young
> girls; but none of her wealthy customers could boast of the
> beauty and charm which Peggy possessed, though she had
> not a penny to her name. Then one sunny morning,
> Romance stepped right across Peggy's path with such
> allurement and witchery that it well-nigh turned Peggy's

head. For it led her right away from the hat-shop and the drabness which had made up her life, and introduced her to an absolutely new world, where wealth made life easy and love paved the way to happiness.[38]

Whatever the gloss given to the romantic novel by the jazz age, there was nothing to beat the old formula. When the lecturer teaching Boots First Literary Course for librarians reached the love story, he defined it in the following terms – and in a sense nothing more needs to be said. The essential was a 'strong and silent' hero, the strength applying to his physique and the silence to a rather dour temperament. He usually comes from a good family but owing to some misunderstanding has cut himself off from society to brood about it in the outposts of Empire. The heroine is very well bred, with a distant ethereal sort of beauty. Delicately nurtured, it is therefore imperative to find someone to lean on. The two opposites meet. At first she is repulsed by the brute but gradually her delicate charm brings forth a softer side to his nature – and the story ends with a fervent embrace.[39]

CHAPTER EIGHT

*L*ove

' *"Oh, dulling,"* said my mother sadly.
*"One always thinks that.
Every, every time."* '

The Pursuit of Love (1945) by Nancy Mitford is the apotheosis of the woman's novel about love. In some ways it rounds off everything that was written on this topic during the inter-war period, mingling tenderness and wit into an unsentimental but deeply emotional whole. There are few novels which explore with such insight women's real natures, and critics who condemn Nancy Mitford as catering entirely for a snob-public are sadly missing the point.

What she is saying, as she steers Linda Radlett through three marriages, is that whatever society may pretend to the contrary women are, or ought to be, moved primarily by their passions. Economic and domestic necessity, as well as the lack of a suitable lover, conspire together to ensure that we place most stress on marriage, achievement, financial rewards, the breeding of children or a large circle of friends. But in our heart of hearts most of us are no different from the readers of pulp fiction: given the chance, we would sacrifice everything else to romantic love. Other happinesses are second best: yet they come first in most lives because a sensible upbringing or the pulls of propriety or the dictates of money push themselves to the foreground.

Linda marries the first time for reasons of money and status, and the second out of misplaced idealism. When, in the classic and unforgettable scene on the Gare du Nord, she meets Fabrice, there are few women who would not long to emulate her. The following scene is the sophisticated epitome of female fantasy.

She became aware that somebody was standing beside her, not an old lady, but a short, stocky, very dark Frenchman in a black Homburg hat. He was laughing. Linda took no notice, but went on crying. The more she cried the more he laughed. Her tears were tears of rage now, no longer of self-pity.

At last she said, in a voice which was meant to be angrily impressive, but which squeaked and shook through her handkerchief:

'*Allez-vous en.*'

For answer he took her hand and pulled her to her feet.

'*Bonjour, bonjour,*' he said.

'*Voulez-vous vous en aller?*' said Linda, rather more doubtfully, here at least was a human being who showed signs of taking some interest in her. Then she thought of South America.

'*Il faut expliquer que je ne suis pas,*' she said, '*une esclave blanche. Je suis la fille d'un très important lord anglais.*'

The Frenchman gave a great bellow of laughter.

'One does not,' he said in the nearly perfect English of somebody who has spoken it from a child, 'have to be Sherlock Holmes to guess that.'[1]

Fabrice and Linda have lunch together.

So this silly conversation went on and on, but it was only froth on the surface. Linda was feeling, what she had never so far felt for any man, an overwhelming physical attraction. It made her quite giddy, it terrified her. She could see that Fabrice was perfectly certain of the outcome, so was she perfectly certain, and that was what frightened her. How could she, Linda, with the horror and contempt she had always felt for casual affairs, allow herself to be picked up by any stray foreigner and, having seen him for only an hour, long and long and long to be in

bed with him? He was not even good-looking, he was
exactly like dozens of other dark men in Homburgs that can
be seen in the streets of any French town. But there was
something about the way he looked at her which seemed to
be depriving her of all balance. She was profoundly
shocked, and at the same time, intensely excited.[2]

Fabrice is out of line with heroes from Rochester, through
Nick Ratcliffe to Rhett Butler and Max de Winter, because he is a
gossip. He is not merely sensual, and unhesitatingly so, he can
chatter and likes nothing better: which doubles his attraction for
Linda. He is described in such a way that, for two generations of
women, a small dark man in a Homburg is sex appeal
personified. And his tenderness, his insight and his sensuality are
combined with an understated heroism – Fabrice dies fighting
for the French resistance at about the same time as Linda dies in
childbirth. To Fanny, the narrator, their love was clearly
unique: but her mother (who has run off with so many men in
her life that she has become known as the Bolter) thinks
otherwise.

'But Fanny, don't you think perhaps it's just as well? The
lives of women like Linda and me are not so much fun
when one begins to grow older.'
I didn't want to hurt my mother's feelings by protesting
that Linda was not that sort of woman.
'But I think she would have been happy with Fabrice,' I
said. 'He was the great love of her life, you know.'
'Oh, dulling,' said my mother sadly. 'One always thinks
that. Every, every time.'[3]

There is no novel in English which ends on such a memorable
note. It is *the* great ending, comparable in emotional effect to the
opening of *Rebecca* (1938): 'Last night I dreamt I went to
Manderley again.' The Bolter defines the resigned acceptance
and the passionate romanticism which belong, inevitably, one to
another: it is the continual and tortuous juggling of romance and
reality which is the touchstone of most women's lives – even if,
like Fanny, they have, sensibly but not bitterly, given up on the

former. When Linda tells her about her happiness, Fanny reflects:

> Alfred and I are happy, as happy as married people can be. We are in love, we are intellectually and physically suited in every possible way, we rejoice in each other's company, we have no money troubles and three delightful children. And yet when I consider my life, day by day, hour by hour, it seems to be composed of a series of pin-pricks. Nannies, cooks, the endless drudgery of housekeeping, the nerve-racking noise and boring repetitive conversation of small children (boring in the sense that it bores into one's very brain), their absolute incapacity to amuse themselves, their sudden and terrifying illnesses, Alfred's not infrequent bouts of moodiness, his invariable complaints at meals about the pudding, the way he will always use my tooth-paste and will always squeeze the tube in the middle. These are the components of marriage, the wholemeal bread of life, rough, ordinary, but sustaining; Linda had been feeding upon honey-dew, and that is an incomparable diet.[4]

Fanny is here summing up one of the 'pre-assumptions' (as defined on page 4) crucial to the world of *A Very Great Profession*. Marriage and passion are irreconcilable – society has organised itself in such a way that the depth of emotion prompting a couple to join together for life is invariably diffused by the demands of this life. Only the very rich or the very lucky or the very calculating can continue to feast upon honey-dew when the daily round is so relentlessly wholemeal. No novelist during the inter-war period, or perhaps ever, has described the raptures of married love, and with good reason – the placid joy of marriage is so unhistrionic, so self-satisfied even, that in fiction it would appear downright dull. There is no interest in sex that always goes well or in quarrels that vanish without sulks or bitterness. Nor is there the *frisson* of the forbidden or the transient, only the smugness of the condoned and the certain. So, in life and in fiction, passion is assumed to be the prerogative of the unmarried or the adulterous. Whether this is the flattening effect of domesticity or whether it is the need to separate lover from spouse is not at all clear – but as a pre-assumption it is undeniable.

This chapter explores a few of the novels by women which go beyond the 'and so they lived happily ever after' stereotype of 'Came the Dawn' novels; and which also reject as tedious the deep, deep peace of the double bed. Rather, they are about the romantic ideal of being 'in love', and they have one crucial factor in common: they end unhappily. If the trappings of romantic love cannot adapt themselves to domestic use, then the lovers must be thwarted by fate, family circumstance or death. Pulp novelists might describe the mildly-interrupted courtship followed by the clinch but novelists writing about love have simultaneously to introduce disaster. For, true to the conventions of courtly love, marriage and passion are ill-suited companions and hence true love must either be thwarted or come to fruition only after endless and stormy tribulations. Fabrice and Linda *have* to die to keep their love on an ideal plane: they are immortalised, and neither the passing of the years nor the obligations of domesticity can overshadow their romance. In the same way Vera Brittain created a memorial in *Testament of Youth* not only to Roland Leighton but to a whole generation of potential lovers, a memorial that she recreated three years later in her novel *Honourable Estate* (1936).

The ostensible theme of this book is 'how the women's revolution – one of the greatest in all history – united with the struggle for other democratic ideals and the cataclysm of the War to alter the private destinies of individuals'.[5] But the most powerful part of the six-hundred-page novel is the eighty or so pages which describe the love affair between Ruth, a nurse in France in 1917, and an American soldier named Eugene. She is so stirred by the grief of a fellow-nurse whose fiancé has been killed in action ('if only I'd had 'im! If I'd had 'im just the once, I wouldn't tyke on so, I swear!')[6] that, on the night before Eugene has to return to the front line, they make love:

> Will he think me abandoned, disreputable, unworthy of his respect, because I offered myself to him in that way?

202

Does he understand what I really meant – that I wished him, before he goes back to face death, to have the whole and not just an incomplete knowledge of love? Does he realise how much I wanted to abandon, for him, all the cautions and calculations with which my life has been hedged, to give all I had to give and hold back nothing for lack of gallantry and generosity? . . . Suppose his love for me turns to contempt, because I let him take me so easily? Well, let him despise and humiliate me afterwards if he must! I'll accept even humiliation at his hands, rather than let him risk going to his death without all the experience of love that I can give him.[7]

An important factor helping Ruth overcome her scruples is the knowledge she has picked up about the contraceptive uses of quinine tablets. But when Eugene is killed she is bitterly regretful, knowing

with the blinding force of full understanding that in all the gigantic desolation of earth and sky there remained no breath of his life – not even in her body, where alone it might have achieved continuation.

Lying with her arms outstretched on the sand-dunes in the bitter October wind, she cried aloud.

'Oh, why was I so afraid of consequences – such a coward, such a coward! Why did I fear my family, my upbringing, my traditions! . . . Because their hold on me was so strong in spite of everything, I sacrificed the existence of Eugene's child. Whatever they did and said I could have faced it, lived it down, and at the end of it all something of him would have been left. Now there's nothing – nothing – nothing!'[8]

But there are memories – and even when Ruth marries someone else she allots a place in her heart to the sacred remembrance of her dead lover; death has immortalised her love in a splendid and final way, bestowing a romantic glory with which mere separation cannot quite compete. And if the heroine of Edith Wharton's *The Age of Innocence* (1920) had died, the hero could have cherished his memories of her for ever; but faced with a meeting years after their affair, he is forced to accept that his love has become stagnant, that he would rather not have to face the ravages of time but would prefer to keep his ideal intact.

The reading public of the 1920s and 1930s was judged to have had its fill of death, and so enforced separation was the impediment more frequently used to keep lovers apart. In addition, whereas death has an implacable finality, parting raises all kinds of everyday and shared questions. One of the most poignant themes is that of the lover who is already married to someone else. Tolstoy used it to memorable effect in *Anna Karenina* (1875) and he has had many imitators, for example Noel Coward in *Brief Encounter*.

Both writers upheld the established moral code, Tolstoy by making his heroine pay for her conduct with her life and Coward by making his sacrifice her passion and remain a staunch bastion of such middle-class values as family loyalty and self-sacrifice. James Agate wrote in a review of *Brief Encounter* that when he associated the film with the best of woman's magazine fiction he did not intend a backhanded compliment. 'For it seems to me that few writers of supposedly more serious talent ever undertake themes as simple and important any more: so that, relatively dinky and sentimental as it is – a sort of vanity-sized *Anna Karenina* – *Brief Encounter* is to be thoroughly respected.'[9]

Anna and Laura are both victims of a double standard that encourages women's romantic fantasies at the same time as it rigorously crushes them with notions of duty, deference and sacrifice. The only thing the middle-class housewife is allowed is a mild form of self-congratulation. She can hug compliments to her (while vigorously denying their truth) even if she is forbidden to hug her lover. This again is a leftover from the conventions of courtly love – the woman is expected to retain a certain mystery and aloofness, to be fickle and reserved, to receive homage. 'Hole-in-the-corner' stuff is not quite what she wants. Thus Laura is clearly doubtful when Alec explains to her:

Everything's against us – all the circumstances of our lives

– those have got to go on unaltered. We're nice people, you
and I, and we've got to go on being nice. Let's enclose this
love of ours with real strength, and let that strength be that
no one is hurt by it except ourselves.
Laura: Must we be hurt by it?
Alec: Yes – when the time comes.
Laura: Very well.
Alec: All the furtiveness and the secrecy and the hole-in-
corner cheapness can be justified if only we're strong
enough – strong enough to keep it to ourselves, clean and
untouched by anybody else's knowledge or even suspicion
– something of our own for ever – to be remembered –
Laura: Very well.[10]

Depending on their sympathies, the audience for *Brief
Encounter* may see it as a tragedy of true love, or may condemn
either Alec for disrupting a previously secure existence or Laura
for foolishly allowing herself to be placed at risk. The romantic
would rest content with the this-thing-is-bigger-than-both-of-us
theory – that the lovers were thrown together by the hand of
fate but are denied happiness by the conventions of society.
E. M. Delafield uses this convention twice, once to show her
heroine sensibly giving up her lover and counting her blessings
and once to show her deprived both of her lover and of family
happiness. In *The Way Things Are* (1927), Laura is rewarded at
the end, because of her sacrifice, with a kind of low-key
optimism. She is an 'ordinary domesticated female' who falls in
love with a man with the improbable name of Duke Ayland. He
is not actually portrayed as a rotter but the name makes the
reader doubtful and in any case he makes love to Laura on her
home ground (whereas Coward's Alec and Laura at least meet in
the anonymous surroundings of Milford Junction). He pretty
soon wants to bring things to some sort of conclusion:

'I'm not going on like this.'
'But, Duke –'
'Darling, you can see for yourself that it's impossible. I'm
madly in love with you, and I can neither marry you, nor

take you away with me. And to meet as we do at present is more than I can stand.'

'You don't mean that you'd rather we didn't see one another any more?'

'Honestly, Laura, dear, there are times when I feel that might almost be easier than – this sort of thing.' Ayland glanced round the semi-deserted picture-gallery, in the middle of which, on a long red plush seat, he sat with Laura.

'You've told me that there's no hope whatever of my having you altogether, because of your children.'

'And because of my husband, too,' Laura pointed out, with ill-judged honesty. 'I'm fond of Alfred.'

Duke winced slightly.[11]

When Laura gives Duke up she 'at last admitted to herself that she and Duke Ayland, in common with the vast majority of their fellow-beings, were incapable of the ideal, imperishable, love for which the world was said to be well lost'. She is regretful but realistic, and is in the rational if miserable frame of mind that the film-goer presumes Coward's Laura to be in when she sits down in her usual chair opposite her husband and lets the events of the previous weeks unroll in her thoughts. In a sense, neither Laura has lost that much since they have the satisfaction of knowing that they can be something other than mere wife and mother; Coward's Laura will obviously take far longer to 'get over it', but E. M. Delafield's Laura was in fact done something of a service by Duke Ayland. A 'lovely, lovely lover' may be the complete answer to the syndrome of the nearing-forty, bored housewife and, in this Laura's case, she is shown by the end of the book to have gained a new, cheerier outlook on life.

This can hardly be said for the heroine of E. M. Delafield's novella *We Meant to Be Happy* (published in *Three Marriages*, 1939). It is the story of Cathleen who marries late and unexpectedly and is so grateful to have a husband and children that 'never, never would Cathleen get used to the miracle, not only of having children of her very own, but of being able to give them all the things that she herself had never had'. But she falls in love with the doctor and after an afternoon of radiant joy she lies awake that night

> alternating between her bliss and a dreadful sense of uncertainty.
>
> What would happen?
>
> She hardly wondered at all whether she and Kavanagh would become lovers. It seemed probable that they would, but Cathleen felt, with absolute certainty, that this would make her infidelity to her husband no greater than it was already. She was, at that very minute, being completely unfaithful to him, and she told herself so without hesitation or circumlocution.
>
> The thing that really puzzled her was whether she was, as she supposed most people would undoubtedly say that she was, a very wicked woman. If so, wickedness had taken possession of her without any volition of her own. An overwhelming force had driven her towards Maurice, and Maurice towards her. Supposing, she thought, she could just go to Philip and tell him the truth and say that she was just as fond of him as she had ever been, and ask him to tell her what would hurt him least, and what they had better do?[12]

But Philip reacts with outrage, has a heart attack and uses the children and Cathleen's financial dependence to dominate her. By the last page it is clear that her life is in ruins because she has neither lover nor her husband's respect and affection. Yet the culprit is the 'overwhelming force' rather than the lovers – the moral is that the most serene, orderly existence can unexpectedly be destroyed if fate steps in unopposed. For Cathleen's marriage was not unhappy – she does not resent the unexacting companionship of her husband and is not deceiving herself when she thinks that 'she knew a lot about affection and kindness, and in her opinion they counted for most when it came to living one's life'. But because she allowed fate to take a hand, she has surrendered her happiness, doubly so because she was honest and confessed her infidelity. Only those women who can hug their love to themselves can be allowed to continue, outwardly, as they were before – those who have been found out or declared their love cannot expect the *status quo* to continue.

The clear message is that if a woman does have the good luck/misfortune to fall adulterously in love she must not let her husband know, for then she will be able to return to her marriage refreshed and renewed, indeed virtuous. Ann Bridge shows Rose in *Four-Part Setting* (1939) doing just this, although her sacrifice is even more noble because her husband Charles is unashamedly unfaithful – in fact some readers would probably condemn her behaviour as pointless martyrdom, since she considers her own virtue rather than her lover's happiness. But during a concert at the Queen's Hall, Rose has a kind of vision of the truth of civilisation, of 'something beyond love . . . beyond the agonies and passions . . . more born of effort and a sort of faithfulness'; and

> her part in it became clear . . . To go back, and then to go straight on; to give Charles his life, and to give it without grudging or counting; to relinquish the joyful thought of Antony, and join her life, all there was of it, to Charles; and to do this, not with sad eyes and a set mouth, like the resigned women with the impossible husbands, but with interest and curiousity and gaiety and zest.[13]

No such joyful self-sacrifice is allowed for the heroine of Kate O'Brien's novel *Mary Lavalle* (1936), in which a girl chooses to leave her suitable and devoted fiancé behind in Ireland and go to Spain as a governess. Here she falls in love with the married son of the house; the love scenes are written with unusual skill and tenderness and are far removed from the cliché-laden prose of a pulp novel. As Mary sits desolate in the train carrying her away from her lover, the reader accepts her emotions as a reality, for Kate O'Brien gives two deft twists to a novel otherwise straightforwardly about a love affair. She makes it clear that there is a roving side to Mary's nature which made her want to come to Spain in the first place, even though her fiancé begged her to stay submissively at home. And she leaves the reader in some doubt as to whether Mary is going to 'tell' her love or hug it to her in the years to come 'like patience on a monument'.

Some readers presumably believe in the primeval compulsiveness of Mary's passion, others, more cynically, assume that she has the fatal female penchant for the wrong man. In novels about love, it is on the whole essential that the reader believes in the this-thing-is-bigger-than-both-of-us concept, in other words that she sustains the romantic ideal; there would be no point in reading *Mary Lavalle* if one part of one's mind was grumbling that the heroine had a perfectly good man at home and should have kept her gaze off another. One must believe whole-heartedly in the overpowering Force of Love if any of these novels are to be a good read or to make their point. For example, in *The Weather in the Streets* (1936), Olivia nurtures no illusions that Rollo will give up his wife for her, she is pleased when he says reflectively, ' "I don't believe you'd ever make a scene." ' On the other hand she wants to keep their affair on the level of a *grand amour*.

> Driving back he'd say: 'Is there *nowhere* we can go?' . . .
> He suggested a hotel, and I wouldn't. Then he said couldn't
> we take a room, why didn't I let him rent a flat for me or
> something. But no, I said, no . . . In his heart of hearts I
> don't believe he wanted to either. I didn't want even the
> shadow of a situation the world recognises and tolerates as
> long as it's *sub rosa*, decent, discreet; that means a word in
> the ear, a wink, an eye at a keyhole . . . My idea being we
> were too fine for the world, our love should have no
> dealings whatsoever with its coarseness, I'd spurn the least
> foothold.[14]

Yet it is hardly surprising when Rollo admits that he is always interested in other women's 'figures', or when he is spellbound by a dancer called Thalassa (for Olivia, 'the worst feeling of my life'). She is expecting to be wounded, her masochistic streak needs to be fed, even the pain of the abortion is a kind of pleasure. Her inherently self-deprecating quality has, in fact, been anticipated in the earlier *Invitation to the Waltz* (1932) when, after Kate has been asked without her to the hunt ball, she thinks, 'I'm left behind, but I don't care.' She expects to fail and in her resigned acceptance of life's blows she is a clear successor to May Sinclair's heroines. When she is grown up, she chooses the 'hopeless' Ivor, she succumbs to the married, charming but selfish Rollo, and she has her negative expectations about life and love confirmed when things fail to work out. Similarly, the heroine of Rosamond Lehmann's first novel *Dusty Answer* (1927) luxuriates in her apartness, expecting to be disappointed. When, at the end, she realises that her friend Jennifer was not going to keep their appointment she thinks:

> Farewell to Cambridge, to whom she was less than nothing . . . She was going home again to be alone. She smiled, thinking suddenly that she might be considered an object for pity, so complete was her loneliness.
>
> One by one they had all gone from her . . . She was rid at last of the weakness, the futile obsession of dependence on other people. She had nobody now except herself; and that was best.[15]

In a brilliantly perceptive essay written in 1963, Simon Raven analysed the qualities shared by all Rosamond Lehmann's heroines and pointed out that, for them, love is vocation. Judith, Norah, Olivia and the others all embrace the ethic of romanticism without cavil, seeing their love as something sacred, unencumbered by the triviality of happiness or self-fulfilment.

> It is not, for them, a question of fun, of good value for money and effort, *because what has happened was in any case inevitable*. It was a solemn duty to obey the heart, which may not be denied. Love, indeed any personal relationship, is a matter of dedication. Given Olivia's love for Rollo, she must follow it up, live it out, take what comes for better or worse and never commit the blasphemy of counting the cost. She can do no other; and when it is all over, her only resource must be a Stoic withdrawal and the knowledge that she has submitted, with dignity and self-abnegation, to her allotted fate.[16]

Rosamond Lehmann, like Nancy Mitford, is intensely in favour of women sacrificing everything to love. A new generation of readers was moved recently to hear her bringing a radio interview to an end by declaring that she would rather have had the joy of a lastingly happy marriage than have been a writer; echoing a contemporary novelist, Denise Robins, who asserts in her autobiography that 'the only thing a woman truly needs is to love and be loved, and that nothing can be emptier than the golden bowl of success'. Yet, sadly, since there is something of every novelist in her heroines, I would conclude that Rosamond Lehmann herself loved men who could not return her love with the same intensity and that her novels are in a sense an elegy to this fatality. Yet they convey the intense, if different, feeling that comes with loss, the rediscovery of self that comes with love.

Dusty Answer, like Alain-Fournier's *Le Grand Meaulnes* and Evelyn Waugh's *Brideshead Revisited*, is best read when young because the intensity and mournfulness of their central characters can prove rather unremitting for the older reader. The over-sensitive, naked mind of the immature reader enjoys misery in a way which makes the more world-weary impatient; but *Dusty Answer*'s unhappiness probably inflicts irrevocable bruising on the spirit of the impressionable adolescent. The eighteen year-old reader is left with the conviction that life deals blows to the romantic nature – she will *expect* to be stood up in the Copper Kettle, expect her man to throw her over – it is the fate of those who love.

In this sense the nameless heroine of *Rebecca*, Daphne du Maurier's 1938 bestseller, *is* the young reader: she is professionally downtrodden, constitutionally crushed, and would never venture to do more than expect the worst of life and love. She is gratified when Max de Winter, having failed to make his intentions crystal-clear, declares rudely, 'I am asking you to marry me, you little fool', and so insecure are her feelings that when he tells her that he had murdered Rebecca her first emotion is not one of shock-horror but of delight: 'My heart was light like a feather floating in the air. He had never loved Rebecca.'

Similarly, the heroine of Elizabeth von Arnim's *Vera* (1921) resolutely ignores the truth about Vera, her husband's first wife. Lucy meets Wemyss at a vulnerable moment, on the day her father has died; but his wife had died the previous week and so the 'two stricken ones' are drawn together. He appears to her immensely kind and responsible and when he kisses her she is in turmoil.

> Death all round them, death pervading every corner of their lives, death in its blackest shape brooding over him, and – kisses. Her mind, if anything so gentle could be said to be in anything that sounded so loud, was in an uproar. She had the complete, guileless trust in him of a child for a tender and sympathetic friend . . .
>
> These kisses – and his wife just dead – and dead so terribly – how long would she have to stand there with this going on . . .[17]

But his grief succeeds in arousing her maternal instinct and so, unspokenly, they become engaged, although 'what the faces of his so-called friends would look like if he, before Vera had been dead a fortnight, should approach them with the news of his engagement even Wemyss, a person not greatly imaginative, could picture'.[18] Eventually he wins through and Lucy, brushing off rumours about Vera's death, or doubts about Wemyss himself, becomes his wife. The relationship continues deeply maternal, Lucy the assuager, Wemyss the assuaged.

> Yes, he was a baby, a dear, high-spirited baby, but a baby now at very close quarters and one that went on all the time. You couldn't put him in a cot and give him a bottle and say, 'There now,' and then sit down quietly to a little sewing; you didn't have Sundays out; you were never, day or night, an instant off duty. Lucy couldn't count the number of times a day she had to answer the question, 'Who's my own little wife?'[19]

In fact, Wemyss proves not merely an egoist, not merely a bully, but a sadistic brute who deluded the affectionate, innocent Lucy into marrying him because he has exploited her deep-rooted desire to give and to cherish and to be worthy. The clear moral is that if women like Lucy were taught as children *not* rigorously to put others first, *not* to take the leg of the chicken, *not* to sit in a draught, they would be learning how to crush their incipient masochism and therefore have some chance of happiness. It is the same with Grace in Rosamond Lehmann's *A Note in Music* (1932). She allows herself to marry Tom even though she knows it is a 'shame'; her depression contains the joy of martyrdom. When she tentatively declares her love to Hugh she replies to his muttered regrets:

> 'It's all right,' she said, smiling radiantly. 'It doesn't matter. You mustn't be sorry for me. I can't bear to be pitied.' (Really, he thought, she was extraordinarily nice.) 'I can stand *anything*. I'm very tough.'
>
> And she thought: there was something in her that was not herself; something that seemed to prevail even beyond her own resources – an inheritance of strength, of endurance, of a religion that had no faith or hope.[20]

And when he has finally run down the front steps she exults in the integrity she has held on to so firmly. 'It could not have been better, she told herself . . . feeling her agony rise . . . it could not have been a more satisfactory parting.' Here the exultant joy with which Grace renounces passionate feelings again echoes the heroines of May Sinclair, so many of whom find strength through sacrifice.

If Grace had had children, she might have sublimated her emotional frustration in them. The tragedy of Margaret Kennedy's excellent *Together and Apart* (1936) is that the heroine sacrifices her husband *and* her children to her boredom. It is the other side of the coin from *A Long Time Ago* (1932), in which Margaret Kennedy describes a happily married man's passionate affair with a summer guest; his wife never finds out about his infidelity since her family and friends conspire together to keep her ignorant of the realities of her husband's friendship. The moral is that it was far nobler for the husband to have loved and lost than never to have loved at all but that it was doubly noble not to have jeopardised his family's happiness.

But in *Together and Apart* the theme is re-cast, with a soul-destroying description of a perfectly contented couple who needlessly destroy their own marriage. The blame lies partly with the 'interfering' mothers-in-law and partly with the immature selfishness of the heroine Besty.

It's not fair, she thought.

It never had been. All her life the essential unfairness of things had oppressed her. As a child she had complained of it loudly, it had seemed so monstrous that no impartial scheme of justice, no natural law, existed which should ensure that Betsy Hewitt got her rights. She still felt it to be monstrous, though she had learnt to keep the sentiment to herself. Not Alec, not her mother, not anybody in particular, but life had betrayed her. Now she was thirty-seven and she had never known real happiness. She had been cheated. Life had left her always hungry, always craving for something and unable to put a name to it . . .

Still, she did not know what she wanted, unless it was to go out and lie in the sun instead of being so busy. Nobody else had such a burden to bear. Alec was happy, and the children, and the maids. They did not have to think and plan and order a car to meet the London train that afternoon. Only she, upon whom they all depended, must be kept so active and so restless that now she was thirty-seven, would soon be forty, would soon be dead, without ever getting her rights.[21]

A woman in this frame of mind has five options open to her: she can either move house, have another baby, get a job, acquire a lover or leave home. Betsy determines to risk her marriage merely because she imagines 'the future' might be more fun.

Very much happier was how she imagined it. And not lonely at all. Of course she would marry again some time. And the other man, whoever he was, would love her better than Alec ever had, would worship and cherish her. She was experienced now; she knew how to make herself prized. She would not throw everything away a second time, giving all she had to give with both hands, as she had done when she was a girl. The other man should never be too sure of her, never take her for granted.[22]

In reality Betsy has no intention of destroying the fabric of her life, she is merely consumed with *ennui* and a natural human longing for some excitement. When the mechanism of divorce does grind into action she goes along with it because she thinks it is what she wants, and it is only when it is too late, when Alec has dutifully married someone else, that she regrets her impetuous behaviour. Like Anna Karenina, she is a victim of society's rules, but in her case she was allowed, even encouraged, to have her own way, with disastrous results for the rest of her family. Only when it is all too late, when she and Alec catch an unexpected glimpse of each other as they pass on escalators in the underground, does the reader fully realise what has been destroyed – for Alec could have given Betsy all she craved for, if the restraints of domesticity had not destroyed their love. (As Helena Wright observed in *The Sex Factor in Marriage*: 'At the present day much thought is given to household matters – food, servants, clothes, and so on – and little or none to the far more vital question of how to preserved the ardour and freshness of the honeymoon into old age.')[23]

Betsy, after all, had experienced boredom, but emotions any deeper and longer-lasting were outside the limited range of her experience. She had not known a lover die, nor was she forced by her husband to give anyone up. In fact she had no inkling of any of the misfortunes that can overcome women when they fall in love. For example, although Alec flirted with other women, he was still faithful to her and gave her no real cause for jealousy. But one of the most poignant themes running through women's fiction of this period is that of the woman who longs for the man to love her but is thwarted of that delight: for example, Mrs Britling in *Mr Britling Sees It Through* (1916) by H. G. Wells

> went through life, outwardly serene and dignified, one of a great company of rather fastidious, rather unenterprising women who have turned for their happiness to secondary things, to those fair inanimate things of household and garden which do not turn again and rend one, to aestheticisms and delicacies, to order and seemliness. Moreover she found great satisfaction in the health and welfare, the growth and animation of her own two little boys. And no

one knew, and perhaps even she had contrived to forget, the phases of astonishment and disillusionment, of doubt and bitterness and secret tears, that spread out through the years in which she had slowly realised that this strange, fitful, animated man who had come to her, vowing himself hers, asking for her so urgently and persuasively, was ceasing, had ceased, to love her, that his heart had escaped her, that she had missed it; she never dreamt that she had hurt it, and that after its first urgent, tumultuous, incomprehensible search for her it had hidden itself bitterly away.[24]

Oddly enough, there are very few novels of the inter-war period about jealousy – indeed, overall there are far fewer novels than one might expect on this subject and, at the one time in my life when I suffered acute agonies from this emotion, I found only *Othello* and Proust to turn to for comfort. Of course, Proust did write at great length about jealousy but his long novel suggests a possible reason why other novelists have generally ignored it as a topic – an inward-looking, obsessive emotion is, ultimately, cloying and in the same unfortunate way that the depressed are depressing, there is something negative and uninteresting about jealousy which, unless it is happening to you, often has a fatal lack of vitality. But one novelist, E. B. C. Jones, managed to describe this emotion without making it seem dull, partly because the heroine of *Quiet Interior* (1920) comes so clearly to life. Katharine Mansfield summed her up with some insight:

Claire Norris is not a simple character. She is one of those who are 'precious – but not generally prized'. Her feeling for life is exquisite; she is capable of rare appreciations, rare intensities – but for some mysterious reason life with-holds its gifts from her. They go to lesser people who deserve them less and do not so greatly care. Why should this be? What has she done that she, who could cherish so beautifully, should be left empty-handed?[25]

The action of *Quiet Interior* brings these questions into sharp focus. Claire falls in love with Clement, but he prefers her sister Pauline who is livelier and prettier than she is; and Claire suffers.

> The strain of the past weeks was beginning to affect her – the continuous effort to appear normally cheerful, the perpetual dissembling of her pain and her emotion at Clement's proximity, her almost shuddering distaste at being left alone with him and Pauline, and her simultaneous unwillingness amounting to inability to leave them alone together. She had begun to wonder how long she could hold out. She spent more and more time with her father, more and more time alone; and, bitterest thought of all, she was not missed.[26]

She does not, as she could so easily have done, sink into despair; she rises above the pettiness of resentment and self-pity and takes comfort in her own strength of character, remembering that 'though simply to be herself seemed now a forlorn, small destiny, stripped of beauty and promise, it had seemed (once) a splendid responsibility'. Again, as in Rosamond Lehmann, there is the familiar feminine rejoicing in giving something up, and the determination to overcome the crushing dependence on others. Claire, by losing her lover, can anticipate the joys of independence and rely enough on her own intelligence not to become embittered. Clearly she will not allow her sorrow to take precedence in her life but will firmly and sensibly repress the emotions defined by one of the characters in Ethel Mannin's *Hunger of the Sea* (1924):

> This jealousy business . . . all the unhappiness it brought. It was the fierce unreasoning passion for possession, the property instinct. People were selfish, egotistical. Each individual was a free agent – yet all the time there was someone trying to chain up the individual, so that nobody was free to give either their bodies or their spirits where they willed . . . People weren't content to take a part; they must have a whole; nothing less would satisfy them; but why should one give the whole of oneself to one person to

the exclusion of all others? Didn't a thousand hands of life tear at one? Yet one was forbidden to respond because someone or other wanted the whole of you.[27]

E. Arnot Robertson was preoccupied in all her novels with the theme of jealousy and possessiveness. In *Cullum* (1928), she described a woman in love with a philanderer. In *Ordinary Families* (1933), a rather straightforward saga of boating and romance is given a sinister twist at the end. Lallie, the heroine who narrates the story, has a sister who is more disturbingly beautiful, more obvious than she is: but clearly the charm Margaret exerts over Lallie's new husband is almost involuntary, it is what is often called an 'animal magnetism' that she is barely aware of:

> He greeted Margaret friendlily. I was conscious of the difference between us, I, tired and dishevelled after the long drive in the shaky little car, and she radiant and with that fine, hard, new polish about her which made even her present untidiness seem too perfect to be uncalculated – but he did not appear to be. 'Lord, what a beautiful family I've married!' he said. 'Staggering when one sees it in bulk,' and fussed over getting us both some tea.
>
> I went into the bedroom to take off my things.
>
> They had not moved when I came back. Margaret was in our worn armchair, and he was bending over the gas-ring by the fire, but they were tense and still – unnaturally stilled for me by the sudden stopping of Time as I stood in the doorway – and looking at one another with the expression I knew, having seen it once before.
>
> Even this she must have, in all but face at least. Even this.[28]

And with a kind of vague obeisance to optimism, the novel ends, the reader disquieted and definitely cheated of a happy ending.

Jealousy and indifference, possession and surrender are opposed states which cannot possibly be compromised where love is concerned; they become particularly important when the love in question is of a kind frowned upon by society. Death, family ties, self-sacrifice, indifference and jealousy are some of the obstacles in the path of true love, but no less important are the incompatibility of sex and age. If a woman in fiction loves another woman the novel will inevitably end unhappily, for it is difficult for a lesbian couple to dwindle into contented domesticity or embrace on a and-so-they-lived-happily-ever-after note. In Radclyffe Hall's notorious novel *The Well of Loneliness* (1928), the reader is aware by the fifth page that Stephen is not going to grow into a conventional young woman, for her mother 'hated the way Stephen moved or stood still, hated a certain largeness about her, a certain crude lack of grace in her movements, a certain unconscious defiance'. The plot revolves around Stephen's attempt to love and be loved by another woman. When, finally, she is fulfilled (Mary cries out 'what do I care for the world's opinion? What do I care for anything but you . . .') she has three years of happiness with her lover. But when a man falls in love with Mary, Stephen finds the courage to give her up – and her future is bleak and desolate.

Some readers are moved by *The Well of Loneliness*, others cannot stifle a giggle when faced with its intense, overblown prose. Stella Gibbons was obviously in the latter category, for in *Miss Linsey and Pa* (1936) she cheerfully satirised a lesbian couple who are coming to blows over a man. As a gesture of protest Dorothy munches aspirins and threatens to do it again.

> 'I mean it. I swear before God I mean it. You're all I've got
> in the world; you're life; and I'd sooner die than let him
> have you. You know I'm not afraid to do it now, don't you?
> – as I've got so far. And it's easy to get stuff. Unless you
> swear a solemn oath, on all you hold sacred – on Beauty,
> on your Work – not to see him again, I'll do it, E. V. I
> swear I will.'[29]

But once the engagement is official, Dorothy, pausing only to burn her ex-lover's manuscript, rings up a close friend.

> 'Elizabeth, E. V.'s left me. She's gone to him.'
> 'My dear. What can I say?'
> 'There's nothing anyone can say – now. Only . . . I was
> wondering . . . it's so ghastly here alone.'
> 'I'll come at once. I'll be with you in fifteen minutes.'

'Elizabeth, what about Tim? Won't he . . .?
'He'll *have* to understand. He's working late, but I'll leave him a note.'
'It's pretty Christian of you, Elizabeth. I'm not quite sane, I think.'
'My dear . . . you know how I feel. I can't say things over the instrument. In fifteen minutes, then.'[30]

Lesbian love is frowned upon by society; so too are certain age differences. *Love* (1925) by Elizabeth von Arnim and *Family History* (1932) by Vita Sackville-West are both about women in love with men much younger than themselves. Both raise some of the same issues, though in the one the man's love is something of an adoring homage which the woman is, finally, grateful to accept, while in the other the lovers are spiritual equals but divided by their years. *Family History* also continues some of the themes of Vita Sackville-West's earlier and best novel *The Edwardians* (1930), particularly the importance of not being found out and the inadvisability of crossing the class barriers.

The Edwardians is about pre-war aristocrats who have been bred to 'take their place in a world where pleasure fell like a ripened peach for the outstretching of a hand'.[31] It is a world where unfaithfulness after marriage is condoned by all as long as the lovers do not make the cardinal error of being found out, a world where tradition reigns supreme. The true theme of the novel is class – the petty snobbishnesses revealed when the upper class comes into contact with the middle class. Sebastian (the heir to Chevron, a barely disguised Knole, the home of Vita Sackville-West's family) 'takes up' first with an exotic contemporary of his mother's and then with a doctor's wife. She visits Chevron for Christmas. Here

all her standards were revolutionised; instead of the petty economies and 'managings' of her life she contemplated his thoughtless extravagance; instead of her envious interest in the great, the notorious, or the socially eminent, she beheld his bored and casual familiarity; instead of the careful restrictions of middle-class codes and manners, she breathed the larger air of a laxer ease; instead of any rare little departure from the monotony of every day being regarded as an event, she came into contact with one to whom such diversions were no more exciting than a bit of bread.[32]

But when Sebastian tries to impress his moral code on Teresa, and casually to make love to her, she is genuinely shocked and tries stutteringly to explain how much she loves her husband and how her relations would never speak to her again if she was unfaithful to him. It is the clash of two worlds, since Sebastian genuinely cannot understand that the unfaithfulness would matter or that anyone would care as long as they were discreet about it. And Sebastian reflects angrily, 'love was one thing; middle-class virtue was another'.

Love and virtue have, in the novels described in this chapter, been accepted as two stark opposites, the soberness of marriage being assumed to be irreconcilable with the all-consuming passion felt by lovers. An additional pre-assumption is woman's unarguable dependence on her lover – there are no novels by women which chart the course of a love affair during which the female retains her previous autonomy. Women are shown, inevitably and shockingly, as subject to their lovers' demands, for example Isabelle in *The Thinking Reed* (1936) by Rebecca West:

> She had never been able to live according to her own soul, to describe her own course through life as her intellect would have been able to plan it. She had progressed erratically, dizzily, often losing sight of her goal, by repercussion after repercussion with men travelling at violent rates of speed on paths chosen for no other motive than the opportunities they gave for violence . . . In terror she thought, 'All men are my enemies, what am I doing with any of them?' But then it flashed into her mind, 'That is why making love is important, it is a reconciliation between all such enemies.'[33]

Only occasionally does one come across a portrait of a woman who accepts the differences between men and women not only cheerfully but gladly, who also rejoices in marriage's subsumptive effect on passion. One such is Una in Kate O'Brien's *Pray for the Wanderer* (1938). She sacrifices her being on the altar of maternity rather as does the heroine of *The Squire* (which was published in the same year). It is a type of love experienced by rather few women and which brings rewards unimaginable to those with their gaze on more worldly achievements – unimaginable too to men, for the saintliness of women like Una is definitely unsexual.

> She loved her husband and, deriving from him, her children, with an unheeding, unaware strength of generosity such as Matt had never before observed in an adult. He had never before met in normal worldly life someone who quite precisely lived for others. Una did that – as naturally as she drank tea. He concluded, watching her, that here was a woman who actually never stared at her own face in the mirror and said 'Oh, God, I'm tired of this effort, I'm tired, I'm tired!' Or 'I'm so good to that man – Heaven, I'm much too good to everyone!' Or 'I wish, I wish – what do I wish?' If Una was tired, she said so to Will, not to her mirror, and she rested until she felt better. She was no one's martyr and had no idea that there was need for a martyr in the cause of domestic happiness. If the children plagued her too much, she shooed them off without pious pleadings. She lost her mild temper with them sometimes, and finding it again apologised as easily as if she were one of themselves. She respected their rights of liberty and secrecy without having to think of doing so. She was completely subservient to Will without once remembering that so she had vowed to be at the altar. She was occupied in one way or another for her household all day, but her blue eyes remained unflurried and it was clear that, were self-regarding in her nature, she would regard herself as a free creature, a self-directed and normally selfish woman. And Matt would have wagered a good deal that she was without a fantasy life, without a day-dream. All of her was in the here-and-now; she was complete. Without

thinking of such a thing for a second, without self-consciousness or piety or even a breath of wonder, she was fulfilled. Will and the children used her up, and in so doing vitalised her.[34]

Una's life 'rose from the accident of perfect mating'. In other words, her love for her husband inspires her serenity – 'she was no one's martyr' – and she finds her life deeply fulfilling. She is the embodiment of married love, and although the portrait of her is rather flat-faced (since we never really see into her mind) she remains an unforgettable image, a symbol of a perfect wife and mother. She represents one ideal of love, a love which transcends passion to find itself in domestic bliss.

One of the key ideas in most novels about love is summed up by the two words 'if only' – it is the impediments to fulfilment that tug at the reader's heart-strings, turning love and disillusion into essential partners. 'Those damned romantic novels of romantically damned love'[35] is how a modern critic referred to Jean Rhys's work, but his definition could well apply to many of the novelists who were her contemporaries. Nor are the trappings of romance necessary to the subject of romantically damned love. Mary in *The Rector's Daughter* is far from the conventional ideal of a romantic heroine and in this has something in common with Charlotte Brontë's Lucy Snow and Jane Eyre. The reader is given few glimpses of the pulsating soul beneath the commonplace exterior – Mary's daily round is crushingly dull and it is hard to imagine passion burgeoning in her 'insignificant village'. But the smallest hint is enough to give the reader an idea of the depth of feeling that is being so rigorously and efficiently repressed.

'To love and be loved,' said Mary musingly. 'Did you feel it like a key, Dora, to let you out of prison and open a treasure-house to you?'

'Is that a pretty bit out of your writings?' said Dora with a kindness that would have checked the flow, but Mary was not listening. 'I have *longed* for it,' she went on.

She spoke with an intensity that startled Dora. She

turned round . . . Mary's eyes burnt . . . with a fire which made Dora uncomfortable. She turned away, and wondered when they would get back again to the dear, quiet Mary she knew.

'I have sometimes thought – ' Mary said with feeling, 'the kisses – '[36]

Epilogue

'Things she would never know again'

'Where, then, lay the truth? Henry by the compulsion of love had cheated her of her chosen life, yet had given her another life, an ample life, a life in touch with the greater world, if that took her fancy; or a life, alternatively, pressed close up against her own nursery. For a life of her own, he had substituted his life with its interests, or the lives of her children with their potentialities. He assumed that she might sink herself in either, if not in both, with equal joy. It had never occurred to him that she might prefer simply to be herself.'[1]

This is Lady Slane in Vita Sackville-West's *All Passion Spent*, looking back, after her eminent husband's death, at a long life spent servicing him; only in extreme old age does she have the chance to do what she wants, 'to be herself'. For her this chance has come almost, but not quite, too late: for her great-granddaughter it has come in her youth and the reader has no doubt that in terms of 'self-fulfilment' the younger generation will be far better off. Lady Slane is too generous a person to contemplate begrudging Deborah's freedom of choice, but dies content because she knows that some of the entrenched attitudes that bedevilled her life are being subtly sabotaged.

If I as author or you as reader were to venture to draw any overall conclusions from the eight chapters of *A Very Great*

Profession, these musings of Lady Slane would symbolise the most important. Whatever aspect of women's lives is being described – domesticity, psychoanalysis, love – it is clear that the woman of 1939 had far more autonomy than her mother had in 1914. Deliberately, throughout the book, I have avoided making comparisons with the present day, leaving the reader to mutter to herself *'plus ça change, plus c'est la même chose'*. But I cannot avoid pointing out how similar the middle-class woman of the 1930s is to her 1980s descendant. This is particularly obvious in the chapter on feminism, in which it is apparent that women had broken many of the barriers debarring them from a working life but had the identical difficulties when it came to reconciling a career with children. During the 1920s, it became less and less remarkable for a middle-class married woman to work outside the home – at the same time as it became more and more difficult for her to organise her domestic commitments. And by the 1930s, my mother's cheery grumble – that she had the misfortune to run a household after the servant era and before the invention of properly labour-saving machinery – had clearly become a reality.

But, housework apart, if they had married after the Second World War, Henry Slane would have had at least to *consider* his wife's wishes. He could not so easily have dismissed her painting as something he expected her to put aside, or assumed so automatically that her life would be spent ministering to his. Of course many, many men continued to coerce their wives – but it was not the norm in the same way as it had been. The climax of Dorothy Whipple's *Greenbanks* (1932) comes when Letty, who has been subdued and dominated by her husband all their married life, seizes her last chance of personal contentment. Ambrose announces that he proposes to use a legacy of his wife's to enable them to move.

> 'Well,' said Letty, drawing a long breath as if she were about to take a plunge. 'You must do as you like, of course, but I may as well tell you now as later, Ambrose, that I shall not go to Bournemouth.'
> Ambrose stared fixedly at her.

'I've always made it clear that I should go to Bournemouth when I retired,' he said.

'I know. And there's nothing to stop you from going; but I shan't go.'

'You won't go!' He was astounded. 'You calmly suggest that I should go and that you should not go?'

Letty nodded her head.

'What on earth do you mean?' asked Ambrose.

'Simply that I shall not go Bournemouth.'

'You mean you want to stop here?'

'No.'

'What on earth do you mean then?' asked Ambrose again, his anger growing.

'Do you realize,' said Letty, 'that I am almost fifty? For thirty years I've done what you wanted; I've hardly done one thing I wanted to do, but I'm going to do it now. I've done my duty, I've had four children, I've looked after them and you and the house . . . you must look after yourself now for a bit . . .'

This was frightful. Ambrose perspired with horror. He could only stare at her and try to believe his ears. She was going to leave him – after thirty years of married life! But it was impossible! It couldn't happen. No one ever did that kind of thing .[2]

Letty's rebellion is remarkable because she has not been portrayed as a fighter: she is perfectly ordinary, rather meek and by nature a giver. She might not have had the courage to speak out if she had lived twenty years earlier – and even by the early 1930s it takes all her courage to strive for 'something for herself' and to refuse to hand her legacy over to her husband. But she does do it – she and many of her contemporaries have begun to refuse to submerge their identity in their husband's (although those with their own money have an easier time of it). In another novel by Dorothy Whipple, *The Priory* (1939), the heroine is only too well aware of the difficulties most married women face if they wish to be married no longer. Reading the newspapers in a vain hope of offers of employment she asks herself:

What did women in her position do? What did they *do*? If there was only marriage for girls brought up in the way she and Penelope had been brought up and marriage failed, what then?

It was a question parents, in her world, did not ask themselves . . .

'People say: "Oh, it's not like that for girls *now*." But it is, and it's going to be more like it than ever, it seems to me. According to these papers it is. Women are being pushed back into homes and told to have more babies. They're being told to make themselves helpless. Men are arming like mad, but women are expected to disarm, and make themselves more vulnerable than they already are by nature . . . In this newspaper, the headlines are about the necessity of preparations for war and the leader is about the necessity for an increase in the population. "The only hope," they say. They urge women to produce babies so they can wage war more successfully with them when their mothers have brought them up.'

What a world! For herself, for everybody, what a world!

'Well, this has taught me one thing,' she thought wearily, picking up another paper and turning to the advertisement columns. 'If I've to scrub floors or eat the bread of dependence all my life, Angela shall be educated to earn her own living. She shan't find herself in the hold I'm in now if I can help it.'[3]

The preceding chapters have shown that women enjoyed a new frame of mind in the inter-war period. They also enjoyed certain benefits undreamed of by their mothers, particularly birth control, the motor car, gas, electricity and the wireless. E. M. Delafield wrote about the latter, in 1937:

If I were asked to name a symbol of modern homelife I should choose the wireless . . . All over the country, in every house, sooner or later the well-known discussions arise. Jazz or no jazz. Symphony concert or variety. Henry Hall as a background to conversation: conversation as an

interruption to Henry Hall. Absolute silence for The News,
or The News ignored until next morning's paper.[4]

And it is instructive to reflect on the following figures: in 1923
there were 200,000 early valve receivers (wirelesses); in 1925,
1,200,000; in 1927, 2,269,644 (and very accurate records); and
by 1939, 8,968,338. The number of cars shows a similar kind of
rise, increasing within the decade from 200,000 to over a
million.[5] Virginia Woolf wrote in her diary in 1927:

> We talk of nothing but cars . . . This is a great opening up
> in our lives. One may go to Bodiam, to Arundel, explore
> the Chichester downs, expand that curious thing, the map
> of the world in ones mind. It will I think demolish loneli-
> ness, & may of course imperil complete privacy . . . the
> motor is turning out the joy of our lives, an additional life,
> free & mobile & airy to live alongside our usual stationary
> industry . . . Soon we shall look back at our pre-motor days
> as we do now at our days in the caves.[6]

Any reader of her diaries will have been struck by the difficulty,
in the pre-motor car days, that the two sisters, Virginia and
Vanessa, had in seeing each other when they were in the country
– a carefully planned expedition was inevitable if the short
distance between Rodmell and Charleston was to be managed,
and sheer logistics made life as complicated as the lack of a refrigerator or as the self-imposed rule which necessitated Virginia
spending the first day of her monthly 'affaires' firmly in bed.

The reader of *A Very Great Profession*, aware of the effect of
the 1914–18 war and its aftermath, will have been alert to the
changes enjoyed by the women of the inter-war period. But for
middle-class women who lived through it, the changes were not
necessarily for the better – obviously they appreciated electric
heating or the invention of antiseptics such as DDT (until the
early 1920s most people would have endured the perpetually
itchy scalp caused by nits) – but many advances were viewed as
mere regressions. Most obviously this was so with the waning of
the servant class, and middle-class women began to miss the way
of life that had been made possible by their servants. Evelyn

Waugh captured their grievances when he described Mrs Scrope-Weld in *Unconditional Surrender* (1961) longing for a return to life as it had been before the Second World War.

> Almost all women in England at that time believed that peace would restore normality. Mrs Scrope-Weld in Staffordshire meant by 'normality' having her husband at home and the house to themselves; also certain, to her, rudimentary comforts to which she had always been used; nothing sumptuous; a full larder and cellar; a lady's maid (but one who did her bedroom and darned and sewed for the whole family), a butler, a footman (but one who chopped and carried fire-logs), a reliable, mediocre cook training a kitchen-maid to succeed her in simple skills, self-effacing house-maids to dust and tidy; one man in the stable, two in the garden; things she would never know again.[7]

While I love and admire the kind of women portrayed in *A Very Great Profession*, while I identify in so many ways with the *zeitgeist* of the inter-war period, I cannot but feel that the self-reliance of post-war women is far preferable to the helpless dependence on others which our mothers and grandmothers in the middle classes deemed to be their birthright. And indeed the majority of women adapted to the new demands made upon their energies and capabilities with complete calm and resilience, with the ironic good nature that Joyce Grenfell captured to such good effect, for example in 'The Countess of Coteley'. Her life was that of an aristocrat (in 1910 when 'she was at her zenith' she had three homes, twenty-seven servants and all the attendant trappings) but the changes in her life were not so different to those being felt, albeit on a smaller scale, by the entire middle class. After a verse describing the Countess's firmly upper-crust life, Joyce Grenfell takes us forward to 1947.

> When you see her in this flashback it is rather hard
>   to guess
> That she'll be a sort of typist in the W.V.S.
> She will learn to woo her grocer: she won't have a
>   cook to woo,

But a Czechoslovak cleaner may pop in from
    twelve to two.
Speaking worldlily she'll dwindle. She will change
    her books at Boots,
And lecture on Make-do-and-Mend to Women's
    Institutes. . . .
She will seldom dress for dinner, she will dote on
    Vera Lynn,
She will take in the *New Stateman*, but she won't
    be taken in.[8]

The implication is that the Countess, as a citizen of the Welfare State, has developed political antennae. This was probably not typical of most middle-class women, although many of them, unlike Mrs Scrope-Weld, had displayed a chameleon-like ability to adapt to new circumstances. Only very few were so attuned to the catastrophe of the Depression and the rise of fascism in the 1930s that they deliberately renounced all their former certainties – Storm Jameson was one exception who did resolve to give up her previous obsession with aesthetic, moral and philosophical comment in order to turn her undivided attention to the novel of social concern.[9] And few could have foreseen that the 'overwhelming influence of contemporary events' would have led, from about 1932 onwards, to 'a galloping consumption in the English novel'.[10]

Many women at this time were still trying to come to terms with the devastating after-effects of the First World War upon their lives. The pessimistic self-awareness that runs throughout the work of so many writers was an oblique expression of their sense of loss; and when another war loomed, many ceased to write (which is why there are fewer novels of note published at the end of the 1930s than might have been anticipated from the fertility of the previous years).

It was not until the Second World War was over that Mollie Panter-Downes wrote an elegy to the inter-war period which is so unique that the novel stands out as one of its greatest memorials. The line from *As You Like It*, 'True is it that we have seen better days' is written on the frontispiece of *One Fine Day* (1947) and runs as a *leitmotif* throughout the book – not in a mournful or complaining way, but rather in a resigned, tender, philosophical one. The world as it was has gone never to return; and for Laura, its heroine, it was a world of ease and comfort, cushioned by servants and domestic harmony. By showing how the world has changed for Laura, Mollie Panter-Downes shows how the world has changed for the middle classes: she wrote a social novel, one which went beyond the particular to change the reader's view of the world.

The plot is of a rare simplicity and, with a kind of classical unity as far as form is concerned, it is set during one day in the summer of 1946. The prologue describes a village nestling in the downs. Something had recently disturbed its placidity: 'there were signs of an occupation by something, an idea, an emotion'. War has come and gone and although the immediate danger has passed life has been disrupted: but not fatally.

> Up here, on the empty hilltop, something said I am England. I will remain. The explosions in the valley, the muffled rumbles and distant flashes far our to sea, had sounded remote as the quarrelling voices of children some-where in the high, cool rooms of an ancient house from which they would soon be gone. But the house said I will stand when you are dust.[11]

Early on we are, immediately and obviously, with a middle-class couple for whom life has, irrevocably, changed. We are shown Stephen's dismay at the state of his garden, and his gloom prompts a brief but poignant vignette of life as it had been before 1939.

> My man's good on roses, Stephen used to say to friends who motored down for lunch on Sundays before the war . . . and from the opposite deck-chair a guest would make a polite murmuring of approval. He liked that, he had to own it, but The soil suits 'em, he would say, as though they sprang up like buttercups. And they would sit there, look-

ing at the roses, talking idly, enjoying the hot sun – was it imagination that all the summer Sunday afternoons before the war had been hot? – until out from the house tripped Ethel or Violet, smart in their pretty uniforms, to take away the coffee-tray. He could see them now, making an entrance as though the lovely afternoon were a ballet, impossibly dancing across the smooth lawn, for ever lifting the tray in that perpetual remembered sunlight and bearing it away with a whisk of an apron streamer, a gleam of a neat ankle.[12]

But the garden has run riot, and the house has assumed a different character. Laura reflects over her breakfast tea, in a passage which is a faint echo of the one in which Mrs Dalloway listens to the noises of her house, how she is more intimate with her home than she ever was in the past.

Now, said the house to Laura, we are alone together. Now I am yours again. The yellow roses in the bowl shed half a rose in a sudden soft, fat slump on the polished wood, a board creaked on the stairs, distant pipes chirped. She knew all her house's little voices, as she had never done in the old days when there had been more people under her roof. Then there had been nothing but cheerful noises all day long. In the kitchen, caps and aprons shrieked with sudden merriment.[13]

But the noises have gone and the house is silent and 'here they were awkwardly saddled with a house which, all those pleasant years, had really been supported and nourished by squawks over bread-and-cheese elevenses, by the sound of Chandler's boots on the paths, by the smell of ironing and toast from the nursery'.

Stephen and Laura find it hard to capitulate. 'Wretched victims of their class, they still had dinner.' Certainly Mrs Prout comes 'to circulate the dust a little' but even she cannot stop the house looking down on its luck. For the house is a tyrant, enslaving and enthralling Laura with its demands: 'my day is a feeble, woman's day, following a domestic chalk line, bound to the tyranny of my house with its voices saying, Clean me, polish

me, save me from the spider and the butterfly.' Food, too, is
minimal and shoppers are grateful for anything, arriving early
to strip the counters bare. 'After eleven, for those in the know,
the little town had nothing much to offer. Sorry, the shaken
heads would signal to those foolish virgins who came late with
their baskets to seek the rare orange, the spotted plaice, the
yellow and unyielding bun.'

But Laura has adapted to her changed circumstances in a way
that her mother, for instance, has not. She realises that, for her
mother,

> the war had flowed past her like a dark, strong river, never
> pulling her into its currents, simply washing to her feet the
> minor debris of evacuees who broke the statue's fingers and
> spoiled a mattress, of food shortages, or worry over Laura
> who was close to bombs, and worked too hard, and had
> tragically lost her fresh looks. Now, said Mrs Heriot, thank
> God it was over, and eveything could get back to normal
> again . . . Now, darling, said Mrs Heriot, the servants will
> be coming back, they will be glad to get out of those awful
> uniforms, out of those appalling huts into a decent house
> with hot baths and a nice bed. And when they did not, she
> simply could not understand it . . . So the mahogany
> continued to reflect the silver polo cups pleasantly, the
> Heriot world held together for a little longer in its deadness
> of glacial chintz strewn with violets and side tables strewn
> with the drooping moustached faces of yesteryear. The
> war had been horrible, really ghastly – had not the
> Carruthers lost three nephews, the Whyte-Jevons two
> airmen sons and a daughter drowned in a torpedoed ship,
> Colonel Heriot's niece Betty her husband in a Jap prison
> camp? But mercifully it was over, said Mrs Heriot, and
> Laura must really pay attention to her appearance a little
> more now that Stephen was home.[14]

During her day Laura tries and fails to get someone to help in
the garden, then triumphs by finding oranges on her morning's
shopping expedition. At tea time she goes to tea up at the Manor
for the last time – it is being sold for development – and then
wanders up on to the downs in search of her lost dog. There is no

more action than this. But by the end of this marvellous novel, at the close of the day, Laura and Stephen have, almost unconsciously, perceived a new direction for themselves. They will cheerfully compromise: Stephen will stop mourning after the lost Ethels and Violets, for it has 'struck him as preposterous how dependent he and his class had been on the anonymous caps and aprons who lived out of sight and worked the strings'. And Laura, walking with the dog, stretches out on the hillside and, with a rush of happiness, gloats over her blessings and plans a carefree future: for the first time she can be truly and serenely grateful for the wonderful peace which had been bestowed upon England only a year before. Never had she felt 'quite this rush of overwhelming thankfulness, so that the land swam and misted and danced before her. She had had to lose a dog and climb a hill, a year later, to realize what it would have meant if England had lost. We are at peace, we still stand, we will stand when you are dust, sang the humming land in the summer evening.'

The tone of the novel is deeply optimistic. By the spring of 1945 much had been destroyed never to return, but a year later Stephen and Laura are able to lift their heads from their domestic round and realise that everything that mattered and lasted had survived unscarred. There are few other novels which are lyrical in quite this way, elegies to something lost, eulogies on something newly come to life. Laura is our final member of a very great profession – and she has all the qualities that have been continuously displayed throughout this book – staunchness, good humour and a deep appreciation of life.

> The long nightmare was over, the land sang its peaceful song. Thank God, thought Laura again as she had thought in the bus while the young man in the blue shirt read his map, but this time the feeling of thankfulness was so overwhelming that the view suddenly misted, gathered, and hung shining, and she rummaged in her bag for her handkerchief. Heavens knows, she thought sarcastically, the fact should have registered before, she had had occasions in plenty to get her weeping done with official sanction . . . Nothing better than this. A quiet evening, a house and a child in the valley, time to climb a hill by herself.

Introduction

1. Noel Coward, *Still Life* (1935), published in *To-night at 8.30* (Heinemann, 1936), p. 348 in *Plays: Three* (Eyre Methuen, 1979).
2. Virginia Woolf, *Night and Day* (Duckworth, 1919), p. 40 in Penguin edition, 1969.
3. Virginia Woolf, *A Room of One's Own* (The Hogarth Press, 1929), p. 44 in Penguin edition, 1963.
4. *Ibid.*, p. 45.
5. Elizabeth Bowen, 'Notes on Writing a Novel' (1945), *Collected Impressions* (Longmans, Green, 1950), p. 258.
6. Paul Bailey, *New Statesman* (London, 10 August 1973).
7. Anthony Burgess, *New York Times Book Review* (New York, 4 December 1966), quoted in Mary Ellmann, *Thinking about Women* (New York, 1968), p. 23 in Virago edition, 1979.
8. Rebecca West, *New Statesman* (London, 10 July 1920).
9. E. M. Forster, *A Room with a View* (Edward Arnold, 1908), p. 158 in Penguin edition, 1978.
10. Kay Dick, *Ivy and Stevie* (Duckworth, 1971), p. 7.
11. Rebecca West, *New Statesman* (London, 2 December 1922).
12. Vera Brittain, *Lady into Woman* (Andrew Dakers, 1953), p. 219.
13. Virginia Woolf, 'The Niece of an Earl' (1928), reprinted in *The Common Reader*, Second Series, (The Hogarth Press, 1932), p. 214.

14. E. M. Forster, 'Mrs Miniver', 1939, reprinted in *Two Cheers for Democracy* (Edward Arnold, 1951), p. 303 in Penguin edition, 1965.
15. E. M. Forster, *A Room with a View*, *op. cit.*, p. 129.
16. Virginia Woolf, *The Voyage Out* (Duckworth, 1915), p. 212 in Penguin edition, 1970.
17. Jan Struther, *Mrs Miniver* (Chatto & Windus, 1939), p. 221.
18. Noel Coward, *op. cit.*, p. 338.
19. John Betjeman, 'In Westminster Abbey', in *Old Lights for New Chancels* (1940), p. 85 in *Collected Poems* (John Murray, 1958).
20. Vera Brittain, *Thrice a Stranger* (Gollancz, 1938), p. 59.
21. Virginia Woolf, *The Diary of Virginia Woolf* Volume 1, ed. Anne Olivier Bell (The Hogarth Press, 1977), 13 January 1915, p. 17.
22. Elizabeth Bowen, *The Death of the Heart* (Gollancz, 1938); p. 157 in Penguin edition, 1962.
23. Denis Mackail, *Greenery Street* (Heinemann, 1925); p. 115 in Penguin edition, 1937.
24. Boots *First Literary Course*, pamphlet privately circulated in 1948.
25. Jan Struther, *op. cit.*, p. 6.

1 War

1. E. M. Forster, *Howards End* (Edward Arnold, 1910), p. 27 in Penguin edition, 1941.
2. R. Brimley Johnson, *Some Contemporary Novelists (Women)* (Leonard Parsons, 1920), p. x.
3. *The Question of Things Happening*, The Letters of Virginia Woolf, Volume II 1912–1922, ed. Nigel Nicolson (The Hogarth Press, 1976), p. xvii.
4. Rupert Brooke, 'Peace', 1914, *Collected Poems* (Sidgwick & Jackson, 1958), p. 146.
5. Nicholas Mosley, *Julian Grenfell* (Weidenfeld & Nicolson, 1976), p. 51.
6. *Ibid.*, p. 237.
7. H. G. Wells, *Mr Britling Sees It Through* (Cassell, 1916), p. 306.
8. Arthur Marwick, *Women at War 1914–1918* (Fontana, 1977), p. 166.

9. Vera Brittain, *Testament of Youth* (Gollancz, 1933), p. 104 in Virago edition, 1978.
10. *The Lady* (London, 13 August 1914.)
11. Lady Frances Balfour, *Dr Elsie Inglis* (Hodder & Stoughton, 1918), p. 144.
12. May Wedderburn Cannan, *Grey Ghosts and Voices* (Roundwood Press, 1976), p. 79.
13. Cicely Hamilton, *Life Errant* (J. M. Dent, 1935), p. 98.
14. Rose Macaulay, 'Many Sisters to Many Brothers', *Poems of Today* (English Association, 1915), p. 23.
15. Arthur Marwick, *op. cit.*, p. 73.
16. Cicely Hamilton, *The Englishwoman* (Longmans, 1940), p. 36.
17. Katharine Mansfield, in *The Atheneum* (London, 16 July 1920), reprinted in *Novels and Novelists* (Constable, 1930), p. 224.
18. Dorothy Canfield, *Home Fires in France* (Jonathan Cape, 1919), p. 275.
19. Vera Brittain, *Testament of Youth*, *op. cit.*, p. 429.
20. May Sinclair, *The Tree of Heaven* (Cassell, 1917), p. 71.
21. *Ibid.*, p. 330.
22. Enid Bagnold, *A Diary Without Dates* (Heinemann, 1918), p. 5 in Virago edition, 1978.
23. *Ibid.*, p. 114.
24. Lady Cynthia Asquith, *Diaries* 1915–18 (Hutchinson, 1968), p. 480.
25. *Ibid.*, p. 183.
26. *Ibid.*, p. 191.
27. *Ibid.*, p. 254.
28. *Ibid.*, p. 285.
29. H. G. Wells, *op. cit.*, p. 203.
30. *Ibid.*, p. 293.
31. F. Tennyson Jesse, *The Sword of Deborah* (Heinemann, 1919), p. 135.
32. Katharine Mansfield, in *The Atheneum*, (London, 21 November 1919), *op. cit.*, p. 111.
33. Katharine Mansfield, letter, 10 November 1919, *Letters and Journals of Katharine Mansfield: A Selection*, edited by C. K. Stead (Penguin, 1977), p. 147.
34. Cicely Hamilton, *William – An Englishman* (Skeffington & Son, 1919), p. 49.
35. *Ibid.*, p. 99.

36. Sheila Kaye-Smith, *Little England* (Nisbet, 1918), p. 293.
37. Sylvia Thompson, *The Hounds of Spring* (Heinemann, 1926), p. 124.
38. *Ibid.*, p. 326.
39. Mary Borden, *The Forbidden Zone* (Heinemann, 1929), Preface.
40. *Ibid.*, p. 142.
41. Mary Borden, *Sarah Gay* (Heinemann, 1931), p. 19.
42. Robert Wohl, *The Generation of 1914* (Weidenfeld & Nicolson, 1980), p. 121.
43. May Wedderburn Cannan, *The Lonely Generation* (Hutchinson, 1934), p. 287.
44. Marion Allen, 'The Wind on the Downs', in *The Wind on the Downs* (London, 1918), reprinted in *Scars Upon My Heart* (Virago, 1981), p. 1.

2 Surplus Women

1. R. C. K. Ensor, *England 1870–1914* (Oxford University Press, 1936), p. 272.
2. Eleanor Mordaunt, *The Family* (Methuen, 1915), p. 313.
3. Cecil Woodham-Smith, *Florence Nightingale* (Constable, 1950), pp. 60–61.
4. Ray Strachey, *The Cause* (G. Bell, 1928), p. 404 in Virago edition, 1979.
5. W. Thackeray, *Vanity Fair* (London, 1848), p. 501 in Penguin edition, 1982.
6. Virginia Woolf, *Night and Day*, *op. cit.*, p. 39.
7. *Ibid.*, p. 291.
8. Patricia Stubbs, *Women and Fiction* (Methuen, 1979), p. 6.
9. *The Edwardian Age*, ed. Alan O'Day (Macmillan, 1979), p. 135.
10. George Gissing, *The Odd Women* (Lawrence & Bullen, 1893), p. 152 in Virago edition, 1980.
11. Virginia Woolf, *Night and Day*, *op. cit.* p. 42.
12. H. G. Wells, *Ann Veronica* (Fisher Unwin, 1909), p. 5 in Virago edition, 1980.
13. E. Carpenter, *My Days and Dreams* (G. Allen & Unwin, 1916), p. 31.
14. F. Harrison, in *The Fortnightly Review* (London, October 1891), quoted Stubbs, *op. cit.*, p. 7.

15. F. M. Mayor, *The Rector's Daughter* (The Hogarth Press, 1924), p. 14 in Penguin edition, 1973.
16. *Ibid.*, p. 210.
17. E. M. Delafield, *Consequences* (Hodder & Stoughton, 1919), p. 74.
18. *Ibid.*, p. 142.
19. E. M. Delafield, *Thank Heaven Fasting* (Macmillan, 1932), p. 5.
20. *Ibid.*, p. 247.
21. *Ibid.*, p. 282.
22. E. M. Delafield, *The Heel of Achilles* (Hutchinson, 1921), p. 322.
23. Radclyffe Hall, *The Unlit Lamp* (Cassell, 1924), p. 128 in Virago edition, 1981.
24. *Ibid.*, p. 152.
25. *Ibid.*, p. 300.
26. *Ibid.*, p. 141.
27. Winifred Holtby, *The Crowded Street* (The Bodley Head, 1924), p. 16 in Virago edition, 1981.
28. *Ibid.*, p. 44.
29. Lettice Cooper, *The New House* (Gollancz, 1936), p. 75 in Penguin edition, 1946.
30. *Ibid.*, p. 116.
31. *Ibid.*, p. 129.
32. *Ibid.*, p. 163.
33. E. Arnot Robertson, *Ordinary Families* (Jonathan Cape, 1933), p. 217 in Virago edition, 1982.
34. Ruth Adam, *A Woman's Place* (Chatto & Windus, 1975), p. 100.
35. Muriel Spark, *The Prime of Miss Jean Brodie* (Macmillan, 1961), p. 42 in Penguin edition, 1965.
36. Virginia Woolf, *The Diary of Virginia Woolf* Volume 111, ed. Anne Olivier Bell (The Hogarth Press, 1980), 29 September 1930, p. 321.
37. Rosamond Lehmann, *Invitation to the Waltz* (Chatto & Windus, 1932), p. 52 in Virago edition, 1981.
38. Ruth Adam, *op. cit.*, p. 118.
39. Cicely Hamilton, *The Englishwoman, op. cit.*, p. 27.

3 Feminism

1. Cicely Hamilton, *Life Errant, op. cit.*, p. 65.

Notes

2. May Sinclair, *The Tree of Heaven, op. cit.*, p. 104.
3. *Ibid.*, p. 110.
4. E. M. Forster, *A Room with a View, op. cit.*, p. 214.
5. Mrs Havelock Ellis, *Attainment* (Alston Rivers, 1909), p. 106.
6. H. G. Wells, *Ann Veronica, op. cit.*, p. 24.
7. *Ibid.*, p. 20.
8. Vera Brittain, *Testament of Youth, op. cit.*, p. 51.
9. Vera Brittain, *Testament of Friendship* (Macmillan, 1942), p. 133 in Virago edition, 1980.
10. H. G. Wells, *Ann Veronica, op. cit.*, p. 205.
11. H. G. Wells, *An Experiment in Autobiography* Volume II (Gollancz/Cresset Press, 1934), p. 470.
12. Amy Cruse, *After the Victorians* (G. Allen & Unwin, 1938), p. 244.
13. Vera Brittain, *Testament of Friendship, op. cit.*, p. 134.
14. Mary Stocks, *Eleanor Rathbone*, (Gollancz, 1949), p. 116.
15. Jo van Ammers-Küller, *The Rebel Generation* (J. M. Dent, 1928), p. 279 in Dent edition, 1932.
16. *Ibid.*, p. 345.
17. *Ibid.*, p. 365.
18. Rose Macaulay, *Told by an Idiot* (Collins, 1923), p. 39 in Penguin edition, 1940.
19. *Ibid.*, p. 21.
20. G. B. Stern, *Tents of Israel* (Chapman & Hall, 1924), p. 206.
21. Cicely Hamilton, *Modern England* (J. M. Dent, 1938), p. 185.
22. A. S. M. Hutchinson, *This Freedom* (Hodder & Stoughton, 1922), p. 11.
23. *Ibid.*, p. 188.
24. *Ibid.*, p. 207.
25. *Ibid.*, p. 221.
26. Storm Jameson, *Three Kingdoms* (Constable, 1926), p. 336.
27. *Ibid.*, p. 396.
28. Olive Schreiner, *Woman and Labour* (Fisher Unwin, 1911), p. 49 in Virago edition, 1978.
29. *Ibid.*, p. 50.
30. *Ibid.*, p. 281.
31. Dorothy Canfield, *The Home-Maker* (Jonathan Cape, 1924), p. 257.
32. *Ibid.*, p. 276.
33. *Ibid.*, p. 280.

34. Winifred Holtby, *Letters to a Friend* (Collins, 1937), 27 September 1922, p. 128.
35. V. Friedlaender, *Mainspring* (Collins, 1922), p. 319.
36. Virginia Woolf, *A Room of One's Own, op. cit.*, p. 93.
37. Virginia Woolf, *The Voyage Out, op. cit.*, p. 210.
38. Virginia Woolf, *A Room of One's Own, op. cit.*, p. 89.
39. Virginia Woolf, *The Voyage Out, op. cit.*, p. 211.
40. Virginia Woolf, *The Years* (The Hogarth Press, 1937), p. 275 in Triad/Panther edition, 1977.
41. Virginia Woolf, 'Professions for Women', 1931, published in *The Death of the Moth* (The Hogarth Press, 1942), p. 152.
42. Virginia Woolf, *A Room of One's Own, op. cit.*, p. 93.
43. May Sinclair, *The Creators* (Constable, 1910), p. 334.
44. Cicely Hamilton, *Marriage as a Trade* (Chapman & Hall, 1909), p. 108 in The Women's Press edition, 1981.
45. Anne Morrow Lindbergh, *The Flower and the Nettle* (Harcourt Brace Jovanovich, 1976), p. 123.
46. *Ibid.*, p. 126.
47. E. M. Delafield, *Diary of a Provincial Lady* (Macmillan, 1930), p. 179.
48. *A Reflection of the Other Person*, The Letters of Virginia Woolf, Volume IV 1929–1931, ed. Nigel Nicolson (The Hogarth Press, 1978), 8 June 1930, p. 176.
49. Elizabeth Cambridge, *Hostages to Fortune* (Jonathan Cape, 1933), p. 41.
50. Virginia Woolf, 'Professions for women', 1931, in *The Death of the Moth, op. cit.*, p. 150.
51. Rebecca West, in the *Bookman* (London, May 1922).
52. Katharine Mansfield, *Letters and Journals, op. cit.*, p. 43, letter, summer 1913.
53. R. Ellis Roberts, *Portrait of Stella Benson* (Macmillan, 1939), p. 215.
54. John Gawsworth, ed. *Ten Contemporaries* (Ernest Benn, 1932), p. 59.
55. Vita Sackville-West, *All Passion Spent* (The Hogarth Press, 1931), p. 164.
56. *Ibid.*, p. 175.

4 Domesticity

1. George Eliot, *Amos Barton* in *Scenes of Clerical Life* (Edinburgh: Blackwoods, 1857), p. 80 in Penguin edition, 1980.

Notes

2. Cicely Hamilton, *Marriage as a Trade, op. cit.*, p. 113.

3. Rosamond Lehmann, *A Note in Music* (Chatto & Windus, 1930), p. 52 in Virago edition, 1982.

4. E. M. Delafield, *The Way Things Are* (Hutchinson, 1927), p. 16.

5. *Ibid.*, p. 12.

6. *Ibid.*, p. 31.

7. Virginia Woolf, 'Life and the Novelist', 1926, published in *Granite and Rainbow* (The Hogarth Press, 1958), p. 46.

8. E. M. Delafield, *The Way Things Are, op. cit.*, p. 287.

9. Virginia Woolf, *A Room of One's Own, op. cit.*, p. 89.

10. Virginia Woolf, *Mrs Dalloway* (The Hogarth Press, 1925), p. 33 in Penguin edition, 1964.

11. Leonora Eyles, *The Woman in the Little House* (Grant· Richards, 1922), p. 110.

12. *Ibid.*, p. 38.

13. Edith Sitwell, *English Women* (Collins, 1942), p. 8.

14. Enid Bagnold, quoted in the Introduction to *The Girl's Journey*, reissue of *The Happy Foreigner* and *The Squire* (Heinemann, 1954), p. xi.

15. Naomi Mitchison, *You May Well Ask* (Gollancz, 1979), p. 28.

16. Quentin Bell, *Virginia Woolf* Volume Two (The Hogarth Press, 1972), p. 55.

17. Maureen Duffy, *The Emancipation of Women* (Oxford: Basil Blackwell, 1967), p. 32.

18. Quentin Bell, *op. cit.*, p. 57.

19. Martin Armstrong, *St Christopher's Day* (Gollancz, 1928), p. 34.

20. *Ibid.*, p. 179.

21. Cynthia Asquith, *Diaries, op. cit.*, p. 150.

22. Stella Gibbons, *Miss Linsey and Pa* (Longmans, 1936), p. 217.

23. *New Statesman*, (London, 17 October 1925).

24. Lettice Cooper, *The New House, op. cit.*, p. 82

25. Virginia Woolf, *The Diary of Virginia Woolf* Volume 111, *op. cit.*, 13 April 1929, p. 220.

26. *Ibid.*, 6 August 1930, p. 311.

27. Cynthia White, *Women's Magazines 1693–1968* (Michael Joseph, 1970), p. 99, quoting *Woman's Life*, (London, 1920).

28. *Ibid.*, p. 104, quoting *The Lady*, (London, 1938).

29. *Our Homes and Gardens*, London, February 1920, reprinted in *Homes and Gardens*, London, June 1979.
30. *Ibid*.
31. Kay Smallshaw, *How to Run Your Home without Help* (John Lehmann, 1949), p. 153.
32. Rose Macaulay, *Crewe Train* (Collins, 1926), p. 305.
33. E. M. Delafield, *Diary of a Provincial Lady*, *op. cit.*, p. 6.
34. Interview with Janet Graham Rance, Jan Struther's daughter, 17 September 1980, Radio Four, 'Woman's Hour'.
35. Jan Struther, *Mrs Miniver*, *op. cit.*, p. 47.
36. *Ibid.*, p. 220.
37. Elizabeth Cambridge, *Hostages to Fortune*, *op. cit.*, p. 88.
38. *Ibid.*, p. 253.
39. *Ibid.*, p. 256.
40. Enid Bagnold, *The Squire* (Heinemann, 1938), p. 145.
41. *Ibid.*, p. 154.
42. Enid Bagnold, *Autobiography* (Heinemann, 1969), p. 179.
43. Dorothy Canfield, *The Brimming Cup* (Jonathan Cape, 1921), p. 250.
44. Frances Cornford, 'Ode on the Whole Duty of Parents' in *Mountains and Molehills* (1934), *Collected Poems* (Cresset Press, 1954), p. 59.

5 Sex

1. Virginia Woolf, 'Professions for Women', *The Death of the Moth*, *op. cit.*, p. 152.
2. Acton, *The Functions and Disorders of the Reproductive Organs* (London, 1857), quoted Steven Marcus, *The Other Victorians* (Weidenfeld & Nicolson, 1966), p. 31 in Corgi edition, 1969.
3. Patricia Stubbs, *Women and Fiction*, *op. cit.*, p. xiv.
4. Barbara Low, *Psycho-Analysis* (G. Allen & Unwin, 1920), p. 96.
5. Winifred Holtby, *Virginia Woolf* (Wishart, 1932), p. 29.
6. Katharine Mansfield, *Letters*, Vol. II, edited by J. Middleton Murry (Constable, 1928), 17 October 1920, p. 57.
7. *Ibid.*, December 1921, p. 159.
8. John Montgomery, *The Twenties* (G. Allen & Unwin, 1957), p. 216.
9. Virginia Woolf, *A Room of One's Own*, *op. cit.*, p. 88.
10. Virginia Woolf, *Mrs Dalloway*, *op. cit.*, p. 36.
11. *Ibid.*, p. 36.

12. Sylvia Thompson, *Third Act in Venice* (Heinemann, 1936), p. 103.
13. Rosamond Lehmann, *The Weather in the Streets* (Collins, 1936), p. 158 in Virago edition, 1981.
14. Margaret Lawrence, *We Write as Women* (Michael Joseph, 1937), p. 220.
15. Rebecca West, *The Thinking Reed* (Hutchinson, 1936), p. 28 in Macmillan edition, 1966.
16. Stella Gibbons, *Cold Comfort Farm* (Longmans, 1932), p. 112 in Penguin edition, 1956.
17. Rebecca West, *The Thinking Reed, op. cit.*, p. 12.
18. Michael Arlen, *The Green Hat* (Collins, 1924), p. 47.
19. Enid Bagnold, *Autobiography, op. cit.*, p. 92.
20. May Sinclair, *The Romantic* (Collins, 1920), p. 12.
21. Beatrice Kean Seymour, *The Romantic Tradition* (Chapman & Hall, 1925), p. 21.
22. Ellen Glasgow, in the *New York Herald-Tribune Books* (New York, 27 May 1928).
23. May Sinclair, *The Allinghams* (Hutchinson, 1927), p. 279.
24. Marie Stopes, *Literary Guide* (London, 1939), quoted in Vincent Brome, *Havelock Ellis* (Routledge & Kegan Paul, 1979), p. 147.
25. Ruth Hall, *Marie Stopes* (André Deutsch, 1977), p. 93 in Virago edition.
26. Aylmer Maude, *The Authorized Life of Marie Stopes* (London, 1924), quoted Ruth Hall, *Marie Stopes, op. cit.*, p. 101.
27. *Ibid.*, p. 109.
28. Marie Stopes, *Married Love* (Putnam, 1918), p. 108 in 1924 edition.
29. Ruth Hall (ed.), *Dear Dr Stopes* (André Deutsch, 1978), p. 170 in Penguin edition, 1981.
30. Enid Starkie, letter to Rosamond Lehmann, 1945, quoted Joanna Richardson, *Enid Starkie* (John Murray, 1973), p. 78.
31. Bernhard Bauer, *Woman* (Jonathan Cape, 1927), p. 7.
32. *Ibid.*, p. 227.
33. Helena Wright, *The Sex Factor in Marriage* (Noel Douglas, 1930), p. 65.
34. *Ibid.*, p. 59.
35. *Ibid.*, p. 50.
36. R. Lewis and A. Maude, *The English Middle Classes* (Phoenix House, 1949), p. 222.

37. A. J. P. Taylor, *English History 1914–45* (Oxford University Press, 1965), p. 218, in Pelican edition, 1970.
38. Letter to author from LRC.
39. Mrs C. Peel, *Life's Enchanted Cup* (John Lane, 1933), p. 262.
40. Leonora Eyles, *Margaret Protests* (Erskine Macdonald, 1919), p. 46.
41. Rosalind Wade, *Treasure in Heaven* (Collins, 1937), p. 249.
42. Leonora Eyles, *The Woman in the Little House, op. cit.*, p. 130.
43. *Ibid.*, p. 144.
44. Sheila Rowbotham, *Hidden from History* (Pluto Press, 1973), p. 142.
45. Irene Clephane, *Towards Sex Freedom* (The Bodley Head, 1935), p. 212.
46. *Ibid.*, p. 221.
47. Naomi Mitchison, *You May Well Ask, op. cit.*, p. 69.
48. Naomi Mitchison, *All Change Here* (The Bodley Head, 1975), p. 157.
49. Robert Graves and Alan Hodge, *The Long Weekend* (Faber & Faber, 1940), p. 103 in Penguin edition, 1971.
50. Naomi Mitchison, *You May Well Ask, op. cit.*, p. 179.
51. Naomi Mitchison, *The Delicate Fire* (Jonathan Cape, 1933), p. 161.
52. Pamela Hansford Johnson, *Important To Me* (Macmillan, 1974), p. 118.
53. Pamela Hansford Johnson, *This Bed Thy Centre* (Chapman & Hall, 1935), p. 249.
54. E. Arnot Robertson, *Four Frightened People* (Jonathan Cape, 1931), p. 147 in Virago edition, 1982.
55. *Ibid.*, p. 226.
56. *Ibid.*, p. 238.
57. Rose Macaulay, *Potterism* (Collins, 1920), p. 7.
58. Noel Coward, *Still Life, op. cit.*, p. 376.
59. Cynthia White, *Women's Magazines, op. cit.*, p. 108.
60. Nancy Mitford, *The Pursuit of Love* (Hamish Hamilton, 1945), p. 138 in Penguin edition, 1976.

6 Psychoanalysis

1. Samuel Butler, *The Way of all Flesh* (Grant Richards, 1903), p. 54 in Penguin edition, 1980.

2. W. H. Auden, 'In Memory of Sigmund Freud', p. 66, in *W. H. Auden*, A Selection by the Author (Penguin, 1958).

3. Barbara Low, *op. cit.*, p. 61.

4. Dora Russell, *The Tamarisk Tree 2* (Virago, 1980), p. 21.

5. Frank Swinnerton, *The Georgian Literary Scene* (Heinemann, 1935), p. 402.

6. Katharine Mansfield, in *The Atheneum* (London, 22 October 1920), *Novels and Novelists, op. cit.*, p. 274.

7. Virginia Woolf, 'Freudian Fiction', 1920, reprinted in *Contemporary Writers* (The Hogarth Press, 1965), p. 152.

8. May Sinclair, *Far End* (Hutchinson, 1926), pp. 106–110.

9. William James, *Principles of Psychology* (London, 1890), quoted in Walter Allen, *The English Novel* (Phoenix House, 1954), p. 345 in Penguin edition, 1958.

10. May Sinclair, 'The Novels of Dorothy Richardson', *The Little Review* (London, April 1918).

11. Virginia Woolf, review of *The Tunnel*, February 1919, reprinted in *Contemporary Writers, op. cit.*, p. 120.

12. Frank Swinnerton, *The Georgian Literary Scene, op. cit.*, p. 403.

13. Virginia Woolf, 'Modern Fiction', *The Common Reader* (London, 1925), p. 188.

14. Dorothy Richardson, Foreword to *Pilgrimage* 1938, quoted in R. A. Scott-James, *Fifty Years of English Literature* (Longmans, 1951), p. 137.

15. Virginia Woolf, 'Mr Bennett and Mrs Brown', May 1924, reprinted in *Collected Essays* Volume One (The Hogarth Press, 1966), p. 330.

16. Dorothy Richardson, *Revolving Lights* (Duckworth, 1923), the seventh novel in the *Pilgrimage* sequence, p. 304 of Volume Three of the Virago edition, 1979.

17. Patrick Braybrooke, *Some Goddesses of the Pen* (C. W. Daniel, 1927), p. 45.

18. Rosamond Lehmann, *The Weather in the Streets, op. cit.*, p. 263.

19. *Ibid.*, p. 303.

20. Rosamond Lehmann, 'The Future of the Novel', in *Britain Today* (London, June 1946).

21. Rosamond Lehmann, 'Rosamond Lehmann Reading', in *New World Writing* Number Two (London, 1952).

22. Katharine Mansfield, *Letters, op. cit.*, 13 October 1920, p. 53.

23. Ethel Colburn Mayne, 'Light', *Nine of Hearts* (London, 1923), p. 180.

24. Letter from G. B. Stern to May Sinclair, 15 June 1919, quoted in T. E. M. Boll, *Miss May Sinclair: Novelist* (Rutherford, New Jersey, Fairleigh Dickinson University Press, 1973), p. 122.

25. Virginia Woolf, review of *Revolving Lights*, May 1923, reprinted in *Contemporary Writers, op. cit.*, p. 124.

26. Katharine Mansfield, in *The Atheneum* (London, 20 June 1919), *Novels and Novelists, op. cit.*, p. 42.

27. May Sinclair, *Mary Olivier* (Cassell, 1919), p. 249 in Virago edition, 1980.

28. *E. M. Forster, A Life* by P. N. Furbank (Secker & Warburg, 1977), Volume One, p. 193.

29. Virginia Woolf, 'Mr Bennett and Mrs Brown', May 1924, *Collected Essays* Volume One, *op. cit.*, p. 320.

30. May Sinclair, *The Romantic, op. cit.*, p. 245.

31. Rebecca West, *The Return of the Soldier* (Nisbet, 1918); p. 187 in Virago edition, 1980.

32. *Ibid.*, p. 163.

33. E. M. Delafield, *The Way Things Are, op. cit.*, p. 100.

34. Rosalind Wade, *Treasure in Heaven, op. cit.*, p. 377.

35. Rebecca West, 'The Long Chain of Criticism', 1926, reprinted in *The Strange Necessity* (Jonathan Cape, 1928), p. 262.

36. *The Sickle Sidē of the Moon*, The Letters of Virginia Woolf Volume V 1932–1935, ed. Nigel Nicolson (The Hogarth Press, 1979), 19 March 1932, p. 36.

37. Winifred Holtby, *Virginia Woolf, op. cit.*, p. 29.

38. Rose Macaulay, *Dangerous Ages* (Collins, 1921), p. 112.

39. *Ibid.*, p. 265.

40. George Egerton, in John Gawsworth, ed., *Ten Contemporaries, op. cit.*, p. 58.

7 Romance

1. Rebecca West, review of Ethel M. Dell's *Charles Rex, New Statesman* (London, 16 September 1922), reprinted in *The Strange Necessity, op. cit.*, p. 320 as 'The Tosh Horse'.

2. Storm Jameson, 'The Craft of the Novelist', 1932, reprinted in *Civil Journey* (Cassell, 1939), pp. 58–61.

3. Q. D. Leavis, *Fiction and the Reading Public* (Chatto & Windus, 1932), p. 74.

4. Mary McCarthy, 'On Madame Bovary', 1964, in *The Writing on the Wall* (Weidenfeld & Nicolson, 1970), p. 72.

5. Michael Joseph, *The Commercial Side of Literature* (Hutchinson, 1925), p. 9.

6. Georgette Heyer, *Regency Buck* (Heinemann, 1935), p. 316 in Pan edition, 1972.

7. George Orwell, 'In Defence of the Novel', 1936, reprinted in *The Collected Essays, Journalism and Letters of George Orwell* Volume One (Secker & Warburg, 1968), p. 284 in Penguin edition, 1970.

8. George Orwell, 'Inside the Whale' 1940, reprinted, *op. cit.*, p. 570.

9. Ethel M. Dell, *The Way of an Eagle* (Fisher Unwin, 1912), p. 27.

10. *Ibid.*, p. 56.

11. *Ibid.*, p. 298.

12. *Ibid.*, p. 313.

13. *Ibid.*, p. 354.

14. *Ibid.*, p. 355.

15. A. C. Ward, *The Nineteen-Twenties* (Methuen, 1930), p. 193.

16. A. P. Herbert, *Riverside Nights* (London, 1926) quoted in A. C. Ward, *ibid.*, p. 191.

17. Rebecca West, *The Strange Necessity*, *op. cit*., p. 325.

18. Q. D. Leavis, *Fiction and the Reading Public*, *op. cit.*, p. 64.

19. Anthony Glyn, *Elinor Glyn* (Hutchinson, 1955), p. 129 in 1968 edition.

20. Radio interview, 15 January 1975.

21. Elinor Glyn, *Three Weeks* (Duckworth, 1907), p. 127.

22. *Ibid.*, p. 173.

23. *Ibid.*, p. 199.

24. Alec Craig, *The Banned Books of England* (G. Allen & Unwin, 1962), p. 73.

25. Victoria Cross, *Anna Lombard* (John Long, 1901), p. 167 in Queensway Library edition n.d.

26. The *Bookman* (London, July 1922).

27. E. M. Hull, *The Sheik* (Eveleigh Nash, 1919), p. 59.

28. Rebecca West, *The Strange Necessity*, *op. cit*., p. 323.

29. Norah James, *Sleeveless Errand* (New York: Morrow, 1929), p. 227.

30. E. M. Hull, *The Desert Healer* (Grayson & Grayson, 1923), p. 277.
31. The *Bookman* (London, June 1923).
32. Bernhard Bauer, *Women, op. cit.*, p. 260.
33. D. H. Lawrence, *Lady Chatterley's Lover* (privately printed abroad, 1928), p. 7 in Penguin edition, 1961.
34. *Ibid.*, p. 131.
35. George Eliot, 'Silly Novels by Lady Novelists', 1856, reprinted in *Collected Essays*, ed. T. Pinney (Routledge & Kegan Paul, 1963), p. 300.
36. Berta Ruck, *A Story-Teller Tells the Truth* (Hutchinson, 1935), p. 406.
37. Angela Thirkell, *High Rising* (Hamish Hamilton, 1933), p. 14 in Penguin edition, 1941.
38. *My Weekly*, January 1920, quoted in Cynthia White, *Women's Magazines, op. cit.*, p. 98.
39. Boots *First Literary Course, op. cit.*

8 Love

1. Nancy Mitford, *The Pursuit of Love, op. cit.*, p. 125.
2. *Ibid.*, p. 129.
3. *Ibid.*, p. 192.
4. *Ibid.*, p. 159.
5. Vera Brittain, *Honourable Estate* (Gollancz, 1936), p. 13.
6. *Ibid.*, p. 328.
7. *Ibid.*, p. 425.
8. *Ibid.*, p. 440.
9. Molly Haskell, *From Reverence to Rape* (New English Library, 1975), p. 158.
10. Noel Coward, *Still Life, op. cit.*, p. 363.
11. E. M. Delafield, *The Way Things Are, op. cit.*, p. 240.
12. E. M. Delafield, *Three Marriages* (Macmillan, 1939), p. 339.
13. Ann Bridge, *Four-Part Setting* (Chatto & Windus, 1939), p. 393.
14. Rosamond Lehmann, *The Weather in the Streets, op. cit.*, p. 165.
15. Rosamond Lehmann, *Dusty Answer* (Chatto & Windus, 1927), p. 302 in Penguin edition, 1981.
16. Simon Raven, in the *London Magazine* (London, April 1963), p. 62.

Notes

17. Elizabeth von Arnim, *Vera* (Macmillan, 1921), p. 58.
18. *Ibid.*, p. 63.
19. *Ibid.*, p. 147.
20. Rosamond Lehmann, *A Note in Music, op. cit.*, p. 251.
21. Margaret Kennedy, *Together and Apart* (Cassell, 1936), p. 25 in Virago edition, 1981.
22. *Ibid.*, p. 59.
23. Helena Wright, *The Sex Factor in Marriage, op. cit.*, p. 77.
24. H. G. Wells, *Mr Britling Sees It Through, op. cit.*, p. 105.
25. Katharine Mansfield, in *The Atheneum*, 19 November 1920, reprinted in *Novels and Novelists, op. cit.*, p. 296.
26. E. B. C. Jones, *Quiet Interior* (Richard Cobden-Sanderson, 1920), p. 264.
27. Ethel Mannin, *Hunger of the Sea* (Jarrolds, 1924), p. 216.
28. E. Arnot Robertson, *Ordinary Families, op. cit.*, p. 330.
29. Stella Gibbons, *Miss Linsey and Pa, op. cit.*, p. 116.
30. *Ibid.*, p. 141.
31. Vita Sackville-West, *The Edwardians* (The Hogarth Press, 1930), p. 15 in Penguin edition, 1935.
32. *Ibid.*, p. 171.
33. Rebecca West, *The Thinking Reed, op. cit.*, p. 308.
34. Kate O'Brien, *Pray for the Wanderer* (Heinemann, 1938), p. 88.
35. Bill Webb in the *Guardian* (London, 14 December 1967).
36. F. M. Mayor, *The Rector's Daughter, op. cit.*, p. 76.

Epilogue

1. Vita Sackville-West, *All Passion Spent, op. cit.*, p. 178.
2. Dorothy Whipple, *Greenbanks* (John Murray, 1932), p. 330.
3. Dorothy Whipple, *The Priory* (John Murray, 1939), p. 424.
4. E. M. Delafield, *Ladies and Gentlemen in Victorian Fiction* (The Hogarth Press, 1937), p. 12.
5. Jonathan Hill, *The Cat's Whiskers — Fifty Years of Wireless Design* (Oresko Books, 1978), p. 53 and Ruth Adam, *A Woman's Place, op. cit.*, p. 98.
6. Virginia Woolf, *The Diary of Virginia Woolf* Volume 111, *op. cit.*, 11 July and 10 August 1927, p. 146 and p. 151.
7. Evelyn Waugh, *Unconditional Surrender* (Chapman & Hall, 1961), p. 146 in Penguin edition, 1964.

8. Joyce Grenfell, 'The Countess of Coteley', reprinted in *Stately as a Galleon* (Macmillan, 1978), p. 32 in Futura edition, 1979.

9. Storm Jameson, *Journey from the North* I (Collins, 1969), p. 301.

10. Philip Toynbee, 'The Decline and Future of the English Novel', in *The Penguin New Writing* Number 23 (Penguin, 1945), p. 128.

11. Mollie Panter-Downes, *One Fine Day* (Hamish Hamilton, 1947), p. 9.

12. *Ibid.*, p. 11.

13. *Ibid.*, p. 17.

14. *Ibid.*, p. 74.

15. *Ibid.*, p. 148.

Glossary

This glossary is not comprehensive, but gives some salient facts about most of the English women novelists mentioned in *A Very Great Profession*. It omits those novelists who, because of the author's personal taste, or because they failed to 'fit in', have not been included in this book – such as Antonia White, Julia Strachey, Ivy Compton-Burnett, Jean Rhys or Edith Olivier; all of them excellent writers who, through no fault of their prose, did not seem relevant to any of the eight chapters.

There is no bibliography in the conventional sense because nearly all the books used are referred to in the notes. There are a few that have been indirectly useful and that would be essential reading for anyone interested in pursuing the subject further, such as Colin Watson's *Snobbery with Violence* (Eyre & Spottiswoode, 1971) or Rachel Anderson's *The Purple Heart Throbs* (Hodder & Stoughton, 1974). It will become rapidly evident from the notes that I have tried to use primary sources throughout – partly because there are very few secondary sources (the two examples just given are rare exceptions) and partly to convey a sense of period.

Elizabeth von Arnim, also known as Elizabeth, Countess von Arnim and Countess Russell, 1866–1941: a cousin of Katharine Mansfield, she had a great success with her first novel *Elizabeth and her German Garden* (1898) about her life with her first husband on their estate in Pomerania. Later she was briefly married to Earl Russell – Wemyss in

Vera (1921) is thought to have something of his character. *Love* (1925) is a memorable novel about an older woman and a younger man. Her daughter Leslie de Charms has written a good biography, *Elizabeth of the German Garden* (1958).

Cynthia Asquith 1887–1960: daughter of the 11th Earl of Wemyss, she married Herbert Asquith, the son of H. H. Asquith (Prime Minister 1908–16). During the First World War she kept a detailed and fascinating diary which was published in 1968. She was for a while a close friend of D. H. Lawrence and was secretary to J. M. Barrie for nearly twenty years; she herself wrote and edited many books, mostly for children and on subjects connected with royalty. Her novel *The Spring House* (1936) draws on the material in her diary.

Enid Bagnold 1889–1981: wrote *A Diary without Dates* (1918) about her nursing experiences and *The Happy Foreigner* (1920) about serving with a French transport unit. She lived with her family in London and in the beautiful house in Rottingdean in Sussex which is the setting for *The Squire* (1938). She wrote a few other novels and some successful plays; *Serena Blandish* (1925) is by 'A Lady of Quality'.

Mary Borden 1886–1968: an American who settled in England upon her marriage. She worked with a mobile hospital in France and was awarded the Croix de Guerre and made a member of the Legion of Honour. *The Forbidden Zone* (1929), about the war, is her best work, but her novels are very readable, especially *Passport for a Girl* (1939) about English attitudes to the rise of Nazism. A favourite subject was the impact of the Old World on an arrival from the New.

Elizabeth Bowen 1889–1973: born in Ireland, she lived in England with her husband and began writing in the early 1920s. She is a novelist of outstanding technique and verbal power. *The Death of the Heart* (1938) and *The Heat of the Day* (1949) are her best novels, although *Friends and Relations* (1931) is her most readable; it makes an interesting comparison with her friend Rosamond Lehmann's *The Echoing Grove* (1953).

Ann Bridge 1891–1974: pseudonym of Mary, later Lady O'Malley. Lived with relations in Italy as a child and, upon her marriage to a diplomat, lived in China, Dalmatia, Turkey etc; these countries provided the settings for her excellent novels. Like so many of her contemporaries she 'fitted in' her writing when she could, usually writing for a mere couple of hours a day before breakfast; she, too, was very shy of personal publicity. It is interesting to compare her novels of

Foreign Office life with that other excellent example of the genre, Mary McMinnies's *The Visitors* (1958), which is about the wife of a diplomat in Poland.

Vera Brittain 1896–1970: her experiences during the First World War are described in *Testament of Youth* (1933), her most famous work. After a provincial upbringing in Buxton and a career at Somerville interrupted by the war, she devoted her energies to political causes, especially pacifism, and to freelance journalism and writing novels. Her friendship with Winifred Holtby is well documented; her daughter is the politician Shirley Williams. Many of her novels are reworkings of the cataclysm of the First World War in one form or another.

Elizabeth Cambridge 1893–1949: pseudonym of Barbara Hodges. She was both the daughter and the wife of country doctors, and almost all of her novels have a medical background. *The Two Doctors* (1936) is about the petty jealousies of village life; *Hostages to Fortune* (1933) decribes the harshness of this life during the 1920s and is perceptive on the subject of child-rearing.

Dorothy Canfield, also known as Dorothy Canfield Fisher, 1879–1958: an American author with a deep interest in family life, education and the New England farming community in which she lived. *Home Fires in France* (1918) consists of stories based on her own experience of life in France during the First World War. *The Brimming Cup* (1921), *The Home-Maker* (1924) and *Her Son's Wife* (1926) are all excellent novels on domestic themes.

E. M. Delafield 1890–1943: pseudonym of Edmée Elizabeth Monica de la Pasture, daughter of Mrs Henry de la Pasture who also wrote novels. *The War-Workers* (1918) drew on her experiences as a VAD. In 1921 she settled with her husband in Devon and wrote many very witty novels, *The Way Things Are* (1927), *The Diary of a Provincial Lady* (1930) and *Thank Heaven Fasting* (1932) being her best. She often satirised the kind of life she herself lived — the JP, mother, pillar of the community role. She also wrote some plays, some non-fiction and a great deal of journalism.

Ethel M. Dell 1881–1939: an extremely popular novelist who achieved her first success with *The Way of an Eagle* (1912). Thirty-four other novels followed, all with the same salient characteristics. She led an extraordinarily retiring life, locking herself into the bathroom to write and knitting her own clothes rather than having to face the publicity of a changing room. Her life has been well described by her adopted daughter Penelope Dell in *Nettie and Sissie* (1977).

Leonora Eyles 1889–1960: the daughter of the owner of a Staffordshire pottery works, she had a deep understanding of working men and women. *Margaret Protests* (1919) is a powerful novel about the difficulties of women's lives, and *The Woman in the Little House* (1922) pursues the same theme in a documentary form. She also wrote more novels, books on women's careers and home economics, e.g. *Eat Well in Wartime* (1940) and, finally, *Commonsense About Sex* (1956).

Stella Gibbons 1902 – : worked as a journalist before publishing her highly successful *Cold Comfort Farm* (1932), a very funny novel which parodies 'rural' novelists such as Mary Webb and the Powys brothers. Although she has written thirty-four other books, none of them ever had quite the success of her first. *Here Be Dragons* (1956) should not be overlooked.

Elinor Glyn 1864–1943: her career as a novelist began in 1900 but it was *Three Weeks* (1907) that brought her fame and success, for it was an overnight sensation, eventually selling over two million copies. She continued to produce extravagantly romantic novels, writing over forty in all, and was renowned for her personal charisma and rather caustic wit. Her grandson, Anthony Glyn, wrote her biography in 1955.

Radclyffe Hall 1883–1943: began by writing poetry and then turned to novels, of which her best is *The Unlit Lamp* (1924) and her most notorious *The Well of Loneliness* (1928). This was a study of lesbianism, and although it was far less explicit than Rosamond Lehmann's *Dusty Answer*, published the year before, it attracted far more attention because of its plea for tolerance, and was banned in Britain as an obscene libel. *Miss Ogilvie Finds Herself* (1934) is a volume of short stories on the theme in which she had a lifelong interest – psychical research.

Cicely Hamilton 1872–1952: worked as a teacher, actress and journalist, was active in the suffrage movement and fought for other causes such as birth control and pacifism. *Marriage as a Trade* (1909) is as anti-romantic as its title suggests. *William – An Englishman* (1919) is an excellent novel about the First World War, while *Theodore Savage* (1922) is a grim vision of anarchy. She also wrote plays, travel books, a very good authobiography, *Life Errant* (1935), and, during the Second World War, *Lament for Democracy*.

Georgette Heyer 1902–74: like Ethel M. Dell and E. M. Hull, she had a horror of personal publicity and was virtually a recluse, although, like many very private people, was intensely loyal to her small circle of friends. Her success as a novelist began with *These Old Shades* (1926) and all her subsequent novels were either popular historical romances set largely in the Regency period, or detective novels.

Winifred Holtby 1898–1935: born in Yorkshire, she was at Somerville with, among others, Vera Brittain. She joined the staff of Lady Rhondda's *Time and Tide* and was a director from 1926. Her novel *The Crowded Street* (1924) is very fine, although her reputation rests on *South Riding* (1936).

E. M. Hull (no dates available): the shy, retiring wife of a gentleman-farmer in Derbyshire, she wrote her bestsellers to make money for her family; she started writing her most famous novel *The Sheik* (1919) to alleviate boredom while her husband was away during the First World War. All her subsequent novels had desert settings although she is alleged never to have been there (just as Ethel M. Dell never went to India).

Norah James 1901–79: was organising secretary to the Civil Service Clerical Association and worked in publishing. She wrote many novels, often one a year, and specialised in hospital romances; her most notorious was *Sleeveless Errand* (1929) because it was banned in England. Every bookshop known to have copies in stock was raided – although no one was ever quite sure why.

Storm Jameson 1891– : born in Yorkshire, she married Professor Guy Chapman and wrote many books, short stories, plays, criticism and forty-five novels. A lifelong and passionate liberal, her *In the Second Year* (1936) is a horrifying indictment of fascism.

F. Tennyson Jesse 1889–1958: was a freelance correspondent in the First World War and wrote many novels of which *The Lacquer Lady* (1929) is perhaps the best. She often wrote about murders and murder trials and, like E. M. Delafield, wrote a book about the Thompson-Bywaters murder trial, *A Pin to see the Peepshow* (1934).

E. B. C. Jones 1893–1966: was for a while married to the Cambridge don F. L. Lucas and was known as 'Topsy'. She is sometimes mentioned in rather cutting tones in Virginia Woolf's letters and diaries; Lytton Strachey was, however, fond of her. Her first novel *Quiet Interior* (1920) has great power and charm and her other novels deserve attention as well.

Sheila Kaye-Smith 1887–1956: married an Anglican clergyman, but both became Roman Catholics in 1929. Her novels are regional ones set in the Sussex she knew and loved. *Joanna Godden* (1921) is one of her best, revealing her deep affection for the countryside and its people. She is one of that group of novelists (Mary Webb and Constance Holme are others) whose work was satirised by, among others, Stella Gibbons in *Cold Comfort Farm* (1932). Her novels were once much more popular than those of most of her contemporaries.

Margaret Kennedy 1896–1967: after reading history at Oxford during the First World War she wrote the superb *The Ladies of Lyndon* (1923), but achieved overnight success with *The Constant Nymph* (1924). She wrote many other novels and had a wide following but never wrote another novel which caught the public imagination in quite the same way.

Rosamond Lehmann 1901– : a renowned beauty and Girton scholar, her first novel *Dusty Answer* (1927) was an immediate success, partly because of the delicate yet sensuous manner in which it handled the theme of lesbianism. All her novels reveal great insight into the feminine mind and are indeed wonderfully readable works of fiction; until recently she was probably one of the most underrated novelists of the interwar period.

Rose Macaulay 1881–1958: spent her childhood in Italy and after Oxford started to write the satirical novels with which she had such a great success. *Told by an Idiot* (1923) and the historical *They Were Defeated* (1932) are among her best novels; she is another novelist whose fame has been greatly eclipsed in recent years and whose novels, almost more than anyone else's, have become period pieces. Her possessions having been destroyed in the Blitz, she wrote a brilliant short story 'Miss Anstruther's Letters' based on this disaster.

Ethel Mannin 1900– : a very popular and prolific novelist whose books have stayed in demand. She joined the Independent Labour Party in 1932 and has been a lifelong campaigner for sexual freedom. Born in London of working-class origins, she worked in advertising and journalism before turning to writing her very readable novels.

Katharine Mansfield 1888–1923: a short story writer whose life, curtailed by tuberculosis, has been exhaustively documented. *Prelude* (1918) was her first story published in book form and is considered by many to be her finest achievement. Her letters, journals and reviews are outstanding literary works, the latter proving fascinating comparison with the reviews of Rebecca West and Virginia Woolf.

Glossary

Ethel Colburn Mayne 1870–1941: best known as a short story writer, she also wrote biographies. During the second decade of the century her work was very well known. *Nine of Hearts* (1923) has one or two very touching stories; her Irish background is often apparent in her writing.

F. M. Mayor 1872–1932: she came from an academic background and went up to Newnham to read history. Forced by ill-health to give up the idea of acting, she published her first novel in 1901. Her second, *The Third Miss Symons* (1913), was praised by reviewers, more so than *The Rector's Daughter* (1924), her masterpiece. Because of illness, she led a very retiring life.

Naomi Mitchison 1897– : married at the age of nineteen, she led an elaborate domestic and social life, but managed to become a well-known historical novelist, often using ancient Greece and Rome as settings. *The Corn King and the Spring Queen* (1931) is one of her best-known novels. Much of her energies were devoted to political and social causes. Her autobiographies give a fascinating picture of her own life and of the society in which she lived.

Nancy Mitford 1904–73: the daughter of Lord Redesdale, she was educated at home and grew up in the inimitable atmosphere which is familiar to readers of her most famous novel *The Pursuit of Love* (1945). She moved to Paris after the war, partly in order to be near her lover (who evidently had many similarities to Fabrice in *The Pursuit of Love*.) In later years she wrote biographies and studies in French history, and helped to edit *Noblesse Oblige* (1956) about the definition of 'U' and 'non-U'.

Elinor Mordaunt 1877–1942: her life with her first husband, a planter in Mauritius, provided the settings for some of her novels, giving them overtones not dissimilar from those found in the novels of her contemporary Jean Rhys. *The Family* (1915) and *The Park Wall* (1916) are excellent, very underrated novels on domestic themes. Her life was very varied, full of death and disaster, and all her novels are worth reading. Her work influenced that of Rosamond Lehmann.

Kate O'Brien 1897–1974: most of her novels were set either in Ireland (where she was born) or Spain, since she knew both countries intimately. She saw deeply into the psychology of the Irish middle-class, and also often wrote about religious conflict. *Without my Cloak* (1931) and *That Lady* (1946) are among her best novels. Laura Jesson appears to have one of her novels in her shopping basket in the film *Brief Encounter*.

Mollie Panter-Downes 1906– : another novelist with an Irish background, her first novel was published when she was eighteen. She seems to have written a few popular novels when young, but ignores these in her list of publications in *Who's Who*. From 1939 onwards she was the *New Yorker*'s London Correspondent. In my opinion *One Fine Day* (1947) is one of the few great novels of the 1940s.

Dorothy Richardson 1873–1957: author of one novel *Pilgrimage* which was published in thirteen parts from 1915–1938. Her detailed exploration of the life and mind of her *alter ego* Miriam Henderson can appear daunting but her technique anticipated that of James Joyce. Her life has been well documented by biographers. She was a close friend of Mrs H. G. Wells.

E. Arnot Robertson 1903–61: a novelist whose light, ironic, sometimes bitter, touch disguised a woman of fiercely independent feeling. She wrote her best novels in the five years 1928–1933; *Ordinary Families* (1933) has had a lasting success. Her descriptive powers were outstanding, particularly in *Four Frightened People* (1931) in which she brilliantly evoked the Malay jungle without ever having been there. In her later years she wrote trenchant film criticism. By some she is remembered with affection for her remark that Hampstead is not just a place but a way of life.

Berta Ruck 1878–1978: after a childhood in Wales, she married another writer, Oliver Onions, and turned to writing romantic novels. She was at the height of her popularity in the 1930s and earned enormous advances, often larger than those of her rivals Ruby M. Ayres, May Christie and Margaret Pedlar. (She is mentioned in Virginia Woolf's letters and diaries: there was an incident when the latter used her name unconsciously in one of her novels, presumably because she had, again unconsciously, noticed the name Berta Ruck on the side of an omnibus, where it often appeared advertising her latest book.)

Vita Sackville-West 1892–1962: born at Knole, she married Harold Nicolson but this is no way diminished the varied nature of her private life. Her love affair with Violet Trefusis has been described by her son Nigel Nicolson in *Portrait of a Marriage* (1973), while her relationship with Virginia Woolf is recorded in great detail in the latter's diaries and letters. Virginia Woolf's *Orlando* (1928) is a fictional portrait of her; *The Edwardians* (1930) and *All Passion Spent* (1931) are her best novels. The last twenty-five years of her life were devoted to gardening and to writing about it.

Beatrice Kean Seymour 1890–1955: married to a fellow writer William Kean Seymour, she wrote many novels which were popular at the time but are now hard to find; usually she wrote a new novel every two years. *The Romantic Tradition* (1925) and *Youth Rides Out* (1928) have charm and power but never pretend to be profound. She was one of the many women novelists (G. B. Stern, Sheila Kaye-Smith, Margaret Kennedy and Elizabeth Jenkins are among the others) who wrote a study of Jane Austen.

May Sinclair 1870–1946: one of the most important novelists of the early twentieth century, she has been largely forgotten until the last few years, although she exercised a profound influence on, for example, Rosamond Lehmann and Rebecca West. *Mary Olivier* (1919) is her outstanding achievement, but all her novels have memorable qualities, being about the life of the mind rather than a world of action and excitement. No life of her has so far been written except that by the American T. E. M. Boll (1973).

G. B. Stern 1890–1973: a novelist who gained a wide following for her 'Matriarch' novels about the Jewish Rakonitz family, of which the first was *Tents of Israel* (1924). She was a friend of May Sinclair's, and was once highly regarded as a writer, for example Somerset Maugham considered her one of the great novelists of the century.

Jan Struther 1901–53: pseudonym of Joyce Anstruther. She contributed to *Punch* for many years from 1927, and also wrote for other publications. Her outstanding success was *Mrs Miniver* (1939), originally a series for *The Times*, based on her own family life. The film on which it was based is alleged to have helped precipitate American entry into World War Two.

Angela Thirkell 1890–1961: only after two failed marriages did she begin to write her popular middlebrow novels, often set in Trollope's imaginary Barsetshire. Burne-Jones was her grandfather, Rudyard Kipling a cousin, and she used to spend childhood holidays at Rottingdean (cf. Enid Bagnold) and wrote *Three Houses* (1930) about it. Denis Mackail, author of *Greenery Street* (1925) and a close friend of J. M. Barrie, was her brother.

Sylvia Thompson 1902–68: soon after she came down from Oxford she published the very successful *The Hounds of Spring* (1926). She wrote many subsequent novels but never recaptured the bestselling magic. In 1926 she married an American artist and lived in Venice until the

Second World War. Almost all her novels are about young people between the wars.

Rosalind Wade 1909– : was the second wife of William Kean Seymour (cf. Beatrice Kean Seymour). She has written many novels and has led an active public life connected with writing. *Treasure in Heaven* (1937) deserves to be remembered, and all her novels are readable.

Rebecca West 1892– : pseudonym of Cicily Fairfield. Began her long and distinguished career as a journalist when she was nineteen and soon gained a reputation for clarity and wit. Her book reviews, especially those in the *New Statesman* in the 1920s, have for far too long remained uncollected. The short novels contained in *The Harsh Voice* (1935) are perhaps her most memorable works of fiction, although all her novels are, in their way, excellent; the post-war *The Fountain Overflows* (1957) is considered by some to be her best work of fiction.

Dorothy Whipple 1890–1966: a once popular writer who is now largely forgotten, although she has been called 'a North-Country Jane Austen.' *Greenbanks* (1932) has a great deal of period charm. She wrote her autobiography in 1936.

Virginia Woolf 1882–1941: her reputation eclipsed for many years after her death, but she has become in recent years the best-known woman writer of the twentieth century. Her novels are sometimes thought difficult, although most enjoy *The Voyage Out* (1915) and *Night and Day* (1919). Her literary criticism was of the highest quality and her letters and diaries, now nearing complete publication, are among the great documents of the century; few other women, except perhaps Anaïs Nin and Anne Morrow Lindbergh, have kept such a detailed and absorbing record of their day-to-day existence. *A Room of One's Own* (1929) has rightly had a far-reaching influence on women's perceptions of themselves.

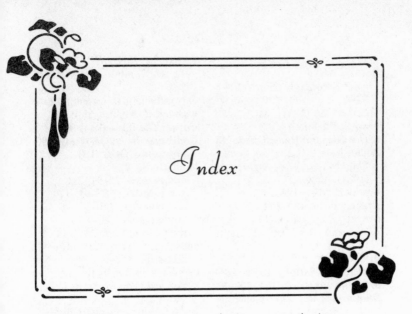

Index

Index

Index

If you would like to know more about Virago books, write to us at Ely House, 37 Dover Street, London W1X 4HS for a full catalogue.

Please send a stamped addressed envelope

Book Tokens

Give them
the pleasure of choosing
Book Tokens can be bought
and exchanged at most
bookshops